Praise for *American Ulysses*

"White delineates Grant's virtues better than any author before. . . . By the end, readers will see how fortunate the nation was that Grant went into the world—to save the Union, to lead it and, on his deathbed, to write one of the finest memoirs in all of American letters."
—T. J. STILES, *The New York Times Book Review*

"Ronald White has restored Ulysses S. Grant to his proper place in history with a biography whose breadth and tone suit the man perfectly. Like Grant himself, this book will have staying power."
—*The Wall Street Journal*

"Superb . . . illuminating, inspiring and deeply moving . . . The Grant we meet in *American Ulysses* is richly deserving of a fuller understanding and of celebration for the man he was and the legacy he left us."
—*Chicago Tribune*

"Magisterial . . . Grant's esteem in the eyes of historians has increased significantly in the last generation. . . . [*American Ulysses*] is the newest heavyweight champion in this movement."
—*The Boston Globe*

"A game-changing biography . . . of one of the most consequential figures in American history."
—*The Christian Science Monitor*

"In this sympathetic, rigorously sourced biography, White . . . conveys the essence of Grant the man and Grant the warrior. . . . [Grant] deserved better from posterity, and from White he gets it."
—*Newsday*

"A fresh interpretation of [Ulysses S. Grant] . . . [*American Ulysses*] portrays a deeply introspective man of ideals, a man of measured thought and careful action who found himself in the crosshairs of American history at its most crucial moment."
—*USA Today*

"With *American Ulysses*, White has made a bold new case for immediate reconsideration of its subject on many levels. . . . His effort more than pays off with a fresh, detailed look at a man who, in his lifetime, saw a medal cast with the images of Washington, Lincoln and himself. And that's pretty damn good company."
—*Houston Press*

"A fresh, friendly reassessment [of the] . . . military hero who became his country's leader."
—*The Dallas Morning News*

"Certain to be recognized as the classic work on Ulysses S. Grant, *American Ulysses* is a monumental examination of one of the most compelling figures in American history."   —GENERAL DAVID H. PETRAEUS (RET.)

"In this thorough and engaging new book, Ronald C. White restores Ulysses S. Grant to the pantheon of great Americans. As a soldier and a president, Grant rendered his nation invaluable service, and White's epic biography is invaluable as well."
—JON MEACHAM, Pulitzer Prize winner and
#1 *New York Times* bestselling author

"A fresh assessment of this enigmatic leader, who, like his Homeric namesake, failed at many things before he succeeded in life. . . . [White] ably [portrays] a sense of the transformation of his subject from civilian to soldier and, from there, to reluctant hero. . . . An engaging resurrection of Grant featuring excellent maps and character sketches."
—*Kirkus Reviews* (starred review)

"A remarkable biography of a remarkable life . . . [White's] style is fluid and engaging. . . . His mastery of history is clear on every page."
—*Publishers Weekly*

"This thoughtful and sympathetic portrayal will be appreciated by Civil War enthusiasts and readers of presidential history alike."
—*Library Journal*

"[A] necessary and large-scale reevaluation of one of America's greatest— and most underappreciated—presidents."   —*Brooklyn Magazine*

"Bestselling author and historian Ronald C. White combines exemplary scholarship and storytelling in this monumental and well-illustrated reevaluation of an extraordinary character, life and career. . . . [An] inspiring biography."   —*Shelf Awareness*

"Author and historian Ronald C. White has written a biography for the ages."   —*RealClearBooks*

"White at last solves the Grant Enigma—reconciling in character and ability the hero of Appomattox with the (allegedly) failed president. This is the biography that Grant deserves."
—RICHARD NORTON SMITH, former director of the Lincoln, Reagan, Eisenhower, Ford, and Hoover presidential libraries

"Ronald C. White is a master biographer, and his *American Ulysses* is the beautifully told culmination of a major revival of Grant studies; rarely has an epic life met so fruitfully with its talented author."
—DAVID W. BLIGHT, author of *Frederick Douglass: A Life*

"In the generations after his death in 1885, Grant's reputation as a general and president spiraled downward until a current generation of biographers and historians has persuasively resurrected it. *American Ulysses* represents a culmination of that process."
—JAMES MCPHERSON, Pulitzer Prize–
winning author of *Battle Cry of Freedom*

"Ronald C. White's superb new study of Ulysses S. Grant completes the vindication of one of the greatest Americans. More than biography, *American Ulysses* is a revelation."
—SEAN WILENTZ, author of *The Rise of American Democracy*

"With this sweeping, exhaustively researched biography, Ronald C. White has done justice to the remarkable life and turbulent times of Ulysses S. Grant."
—JOAN WAUGH, author of *U. S. Grant:
American Hero, American Myth*

"Ronald C. White's extensive earlier work on Lincoln prepared him to capture Lincolnian elements in Grant that many have missed: quiet charisma, measured confidence, concern for equal rights, and unusual literary skill. White's own writing talent makes this book impossible to put down."
—RICHARD WIGHTMAN FOX, author of
Lincoln's Body: A Cultural History

"This refreshingly new comprehensive study of a genuine American hero rises above overworked analyses of Ulysses S. Grant."
—FRANK J. WILLIAMS, president of the Ulysses S. Grant Association

"No one reading this marvelously researched and superbly written book will ever again be able to see U. S. Grant as other than a great person."
—JOHN F. MARSZALEK, executive director of the Ulysses S. Grant
Association's Ulysses S. Grant Presidential Library

BY RONALD C. WHITE

American Ulysses: A Life of Ulysses S. Grant

A. Lincoln: A Biography

The Eloquent President: A Portrait of Lincoln Through His Words

Lincoln's Greatest Speech: The Second Inaugural

Liberty and Justice for All: Racial Reform and the Social Gospel

An Unsettled Arena: Religion and the Bill of Rights (editor with Albright G. Zimmerman)

Partners in Peace and Education (editor with Eugene J. Fisher)

American Christianity: A Case Approach (with Garth Rosell and Louis B. Weeks)

The Social Gospel: Religion and Reform in Changing America (with C. Howard Hopkins)

AMERICAN ULYSSES

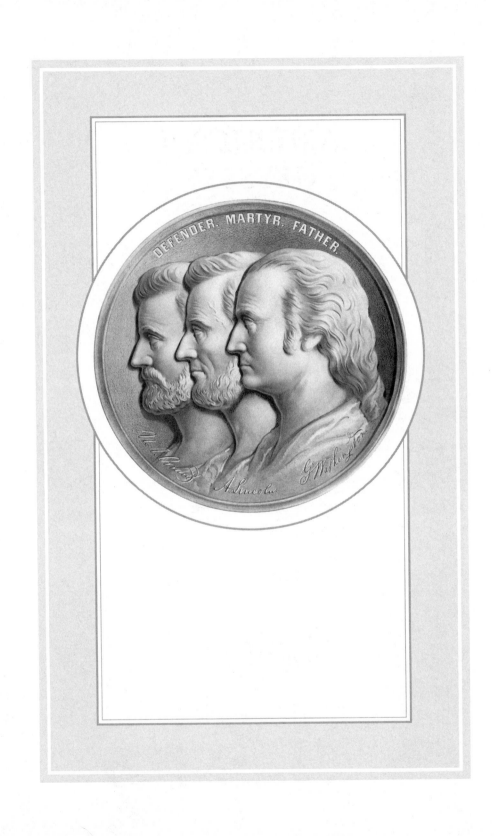

AMERICAN ULYSSES

A Life of Ulysses S. Grant

Ronald C. White

RANDOM HOUSE

NEW YORK

2017 Random House Trade Paperback Edition

Published in the United States by Random House, an imprint and division
of Penguin Random House LLC, New York.

RANDOM HOUSE and the HOUSE colophon are registered trademarks
of Penguin Random House LLC.

Originally published in hardcover in the United States by Random House,
an imprint and division of Penguin Random House LLC, in 2016.

LIBRARY OF CONGRESS CATALOGING-IN-PUBLICATION DATA
Names: White, Ronald C. (Ronald Cedric), author.
Title: American Ulysses: a life of Ulysses S. Grant / Ronald C. White.
Description: New York : Random House, 2016. | Includes bibliographical
references and index.
Identifiers: LCCN 2015044513 | ISBN 9780812981254 | ISBN 9781588369925 (ebook)
Subjects: LCSH : Grant, Ulysses S. (Ulysses Simpson), 1822–1885. | Presidents—United
States—Biography. | Generals—United States—Biography. | United States—History—Civil
War, 1861–1865—Biography. | United States—Politics and government—1869–1877.
Classification: LCC E672.W48 2016 | DDC 973.8/2092—dc23 LC record available at
http://lccn.loc.gov/2015044513

Printed in the United States of America on acid-free paper

randomhousebooks.com

2 4 6 8 9 7 5 3 1

Book design by Victoria Wong

For Cynthia Conger White

In him the negro found a protector, the Indian a friend,
a vanquished foe a brother, an imperiled nation a savior.

—Frederick Douglass

Mightiest among the mighty dead loom the three great
figures of Washington, Lincoln, and Grant.

—Theodore Roosevelt

Contents

Part Four: Reconstruction, 1865–1868

Part Five: President, 1869–1877

Part Six: World Citizen, 1879–1885

List of Maps

Author's Note

For the sake of clarity I have sometimes modernized the spelling and punctuation of Grant and his correspondents. Spelling and punctuation in the nineteenth century were far from regular or consistent. Grant's spelling was often imaginative. Any revisions were made with the goal of maintaining the original meaning for contemporary readers.

Cast of Characters

BABCOCK, ORVILLE E. (1835–1884) Young and ambitious, Babcock joined Grant's staff for the Overland Campaign in Virginia in March 1864. He served as secretary to Grant in the White House and was subsequently charged in the whiskey ring scandal.

BADEAU, ADAM (1831–1895) An essayist and theater critic, Badeau joined Grant's staff in 1864, remaining until 1869. He helped Grant with his *Personal Memoirs* and wrote two noteworthy books about Grant: *Military History of Ulysses S. Grant* (1881) and *Grant in Peace* (1887).

BUCKNER, SIMON BOLIVAR (1823–1914) A West Point classmate, Buckner commanded Confederate forces at the end of the crucial Battle of Fort Donelson, where Grant offered famous terms of surrender.

BUELL, DON CARLOS (1818–1898) Union general, often cautious and rigid, whose lateness, absence, and then participation played a controversial role in the Battle of Shiloh.

BUTLER, BENJAMIN (1818–1893) A Massachusetts congressman and "political general" who tangled with Grant during the Civil War. After the war, reelected to Congress, he became one of Grant's strongest supporters.

CHANDLER, ZACHARIAH (1813–1879) Big in size, and bluff in politics, Chandler first met Second Lieutenant Grant in a Detroit courtroom. Decades later, Senator Chandler became a staunch ally of President Grant, who appointed him secretary of the interior.

CHILDS, GEORGE W. (1829–1894) Publisher of the *Philadelphia Public Ledger,* Childs was a neighbor in Long Branch, New Jersey, who became a close friend and financial adviser.

CONKLING, ROSCOE (1829–1888) A New York senator known for his tough-minded machine politics, especially his espousal of patronage. Conkling became a leader among a group of younger Republican senators Grant courted to advance his policies as president.

DANA, CHARLES A. (1819–1897) A quixotic figure who as assistant secretary of war (1863–1865) praised General Grant but as publisher of the *New York Sun* (1868 on) criticized President Grant.

DOUGLASS, FREDERICK (1818–1895) A former slave turned abolitionist leader, editor, and social reformer, Douglass became a strong supporter of Grant during both presidential terms.

FISH, HAMILTON (1808–1893) As secretary of state during Grant's administration, Fish entered his duties skeptical of Grant's leadership abilities, but he subsequently changed his mind and became the only cabinet officer to serve the complete eight years of Grant's tenure.

HALLECK, HENRY W. (1815–1872) "Old Brains" was a military theorist with a reputation as a desk-job general. While commander over Grant, he cultivated a relationship of trust and mistrust. When Grant became general in chief, Halleck served as his chief of staff.

HANCOCK, WINFIELD SCOTT (1824–1886) "Hancock the Superb" served with Grant in the Overland Campaign in Virginia in 1864. After the war, Grant became disappointed in Hancock, a conservative Democrat who displayed a reluctance to defend the freedmen in his Military District, based in New Orleans.

JOHNSON, ANDREW (1808–1875) Vice President Johnson was sworn in as the seventeenth president of the United States after Lincoln's death. Grant, believing in military deference to civilian leadership, tried mightily to work with him.

McCLERNAND, JOHN A. (1812–1900) As a "political general" appointed by Lincoln, McClernand continually clashed with Grant and Sherman. Grant tried hard to placate the president's Illinois friend, but their conflicts came to a head in the long campaign against Vicksburg.

McPherson, James B. (1828–1864) Graduating at the top of his 1853 West Point class, McPherson served as Grant's chief engineer during the victories at Forts Henry and Donelson. After further winning Grant's confidence at Shiloh and Vicksburg, he was appointed commander of the Army of the Tennessee, ranking with Sherman and Sheridan among Grant's most trusted commanders.

Meade, George Gordon (1815–1872) Victorious at Gettysburg, Meade suffered criticism for letting Lee escape back into Virginia. As commander of the Army of the Potomac, he expected to be replaced when Grant became general in chief. The story of their evolving relationship is central in understanding the drama of the final year of the Civil War.

Porter, David Dixon (1813–1891) Descended from a distinguished line of naval heroes, Porter initially approached Grant with an ingrained distrust of West Point army generals. Their ability to work together in the Vicksburg Campaign became critical to success in the western theater of the war.

Porter, Horace (1837–1921) Graduated third in his 1860 West Point class and first joined Grant's staff at Chattanooga. Despite a multifaceted career both in the army and, after the war, in business, Porter most wanted to be remembered simply as aide-de-camp to Grant. His book *Campaigning with Grant* remains one of the best contemporary portraits of Grant.

Rawlins, John (1831–1869) A lawyer whom Grant met in Galena, Rawlins became Grant's chief of staff and trusted confidant. Rawlins was appointed secretary of war in Grant's first term as president.

Romero, Matías (1837–1898) Grant's friendship with this young Mexican diplomat is an overlooked story. Their relationship points to Grant's advocacy of the triumph of a liberal democracy in Mexico and his hopes for an economic relationship between the two nations.

Sheridan, Philip H. (1831–1888) "Little Phil," a leader in rethinking the role of the Union cavalry, became one of Grant's favorite generals. He would play a crucial role in the 1864–1865 Virginia Campaign through his cavalry attacks in the Shenandoah Valley.

SHERMAN, WILLIAM TECUMSEH (1820–1891) So different in personality from Grant, Sherman became Grant's closest military friend. They served together in the battles at Shiloh, Vicksburg, and Chattanooga and in the long Overland Campaign in Virginia. When elected president, Grant appointed Sherman general in chief.

STANTON, EDWIN M. (1814–1869) As secretary of war, Stanton served in both the Lincoln and Johnson administrations. Grant had an on-again, off-again relationship with the often caustic Stanton, as President Johnson alternately sought to displace both of them.

THOMAS, GEORGE H. (1816–1870) Grant had a complex relationship with this Virginian who fought for the Union, a quiet man who enjoyed a contradictory set of nicknames: "the Rock of Chickamauga" and "Old Slow-Trot."

TWAIN, MARK (CLEMENS, SAMUEL L.) (1835–1910) The celebrated American writer, author of *Adventures of Huckleberry Finn,* admitted to being "Grant-intoxicated." Admiring Grant, he became the publisher of his *Personal Memoirs.*

VINCENT, JOHN HEYL (1832–1920) Grant first met Vincent at the Methodist church in Galena. Fifteen years later, Vincent cofounded the Chautauqua Institution in New York. As president, Grant accepted Vincent's invitation to speak at the institution in its second summer.

WASHBURNE, ELIHU B. (1816–1887) A Republican congressman from Galena, Washburne became Grant's advocate with President Lincoln and Congress throughout the Civil War. During the Grant presidency, he served as U.S. minister to France.

YOUNG, JOHN R. (1840–1899) As a *New York Herald* correspondent, Young accompanied Grant on his world tour of 1877–1879. Young's two-volume *Around the World with General Grant* helped enhance Grant's reputation after the scandals of his second term as president.

Prologue

The man, of middle height, accompanied by a young boy, arrived at the crowded Baltimore and Ohio Railroad station in Washington on a cold, crisp morning. It was March 8, 1864. He hailed a carriage and asked the driver to take them to Willard's Hotel.

At the northwest corner of Pennsylvania Avenue and Fourteenth Street, only two blocks from the White House, the man and boy stepped from the carriage and walked directly to the front desk. The man, forty-two years old and wearing a travel-stained duster, asked for a room. The clerk sniffed brusquely; did not the visitor know that in wartime Washington few rooms were available, especially at Willards—the finest hotel in the nation's capital?

The clerk dallied, then informed the travelers he could give them a small room on the top floor. That would be fine, the man said softly. The clerk asked the guest to sign the hotel register.

When the clerk turned the register around and read the signature—"U. S. Grant and son, Galena, Illinois"—he turned pale. He gasped, "General Grant, why didn't you tell me who you were?"

Peering more closely, the clerk could now see that underneath the duster, mostly hidden, was the blue uniform of a Union officer. He had seen posters portraying "the Hero of the West" everywhere in Washington. Suddenly attentive, he blurted out that he was reassigning Grant and his son to Parlor Suite 6, the best in the hotel—indeed, the same suite Abraham and Mary Lincoln had stayed in three years earlier when they'd arrived in Washington.

Now that he knew who was standing in front of him, the clerk handed Grant a sealed envelope. The general opened it, finding an invitation to join President Lincoln at a reception that evening at the White House as the guest of honor.

Because he had not served in the eastern theater of the Civil War, curiosity about Grant punctuated conversations everywhere. Many knew the outline of his rise to fame, but still they wondered out loud: Who was he? How had he succeeded when so many Union generals had failed over the past three years? Why had the president elevated him to the position of lieutenant general, the first man since George Washington to hold that rank? Why had Lincoln tapped him to come from the western theater to lead all the Union armies?

HAVING LOST THE key to his trunk, Grant was forced to wear his untidy traveling uniform to dinner in the Willard's ornate dining room. No sooner had Grant and the boy by his side—his son Fred—sat down than people began to crane their necks to look over at the new diners. A gentleman rapped a knife on his table for silence, and everyone hushed. He rose and announced he had "the honor to inform them that General Grant was present in the room." A shout echoed: "Grant!" "Grant!" "Grant!" As cheers escalated, people pounded their tables, celebrating him.

Looking embarrassed, Grant rose and quickly sat down.

After dinner, he walked the short two blocks to the Executive Mansion. Unrecognized, he worked his way through the swarm of visitors to

This illustration portrays the historic meeting of Lincoln and Grant on March 8, 1864, at a White House reception. The next day, Lincoln commissioned Grant commander of all the Union armies.

enter the East Room. There he spotted a tall, gangling man surrounded by people at the far side.

Lincoln looked over everyone's heads and saw the small man whom he had not met before. He stopped his conversation. Smiling, he advanced toward the man he had summoned to Washington. A good nine inches taller than his guest, Lincoln thrust out his large hands to pump Grant's again and again. "Why, here is General Grant! Well, this is a great pleasure, I assure you!"

THE HERO WHOM Lincoln welcomed enthusiastically in 1864 has slipped from our American memory. Friends at the Ulysses S. Grant National Historic Site near St. Louis tell me most visitors arrive with little knowledge of Grant—but leave with deep appreciation. In my biography of Lincoln, I wrote of Grant the decorated Civil War general, but I now confess: I did not fully know the man. Grant's rise to fame has always remained something of a mystery. As I dug deeper, I discovered his intellectual journey was filled with surprises, detours, questions, and insights. His personality is a palette not unlike the rich colors he learned to paint with at West Point.

After growing up on the Ohio frontier, young Ulysses was accepted at West Point, from which he graduated in 1843. He subsequently served with honors in the Mexican War and then returned to marry Julia Dent, who accompanied him to his assignments in New York and Michigan over the next several years. Forced to leave her behind when he was posted to the Oregon Territory and California between 1852 and 1854, he grew so heartsick that he resigned his commission. And for the next seven years he struggled to make a living for himself, his wife, and his four children, mostly on his pro-slavery father-in-law's property outside St. Louis.

Then came the Civil War, and everything changed. In a story of transformation, Grant moved in the next seven years from clerk at his father's leather goods store in Galena, Illinois, to commander of all the Union armies and president of the United States. His remarkable rise constitutes one of the greatest stories of American leadership.

Although he was renowned at the time of his death in 1885, it was not long before Grant began to fall from favor. Historians writing under the influence of the Southern "Lost Cause" lifted up Robert E. Lee and the Confederacy in "the War of Northern Aggression." In their retelling, Grant became the "butcher" who supposedly countenanced the merciless slaughter of his soldiers to overwhelm by sheer numbers the courageous Southern army.

When Grant is remembered, he is too often described as a simple man of action, not of ideas. Pulitzer Prize–winning Grant biographer William S. McFeely declared, "I am convinced that Ulysses Grant had no organic, artistic, or intellectual specialness." Describing Grant's midlife crisis: "The only problem was that until he was nearly forty, no job he liked had come his way—and so he became a general and president because he could find nothing better to do."

No. I believe Grant was an exceptional person and leader. A popular 1870s medallion depicted George Washington, Abraham Lincoln, and Ulysses S. Grant as the three great leaders of the nation. Lionized as the general who saved the Union, he was celebrated in his lifetime as the "hero of Appomattox," the warrior who offered magnanimous peace terms to General Robert E. Lee. Elected president twice, he would be the only such leader of the United States to serve two consecutive terms between Lincoln and Woodrow Wilson. Even with the scandals that tainted his second term, he retained enormous popularity with the American people and probably would have been elected to a third term in 1876 if he had chosen to run. But let's not get ahead of our story.

The nature of Grant's greatness is a puzzle with many pieces. Like his namesake, the Greek hero Ulysses, his contemporaries came to know him as a tragic hero who had failed again and again before he succeeded. The frontier boy who did not like to hunt became the great soldier. His friendship with William Tecumseh Sherman seemed to outsiders like a pairing of opposites. In his transformation through the Civil War, he combined modesty and magnanimity. His quiet strength energized the soldiers who served with him. He could tell a story that often ended with self-deprecating humor. He could be decisive yet understated, strong but gentle. He possessed the trait he most admired, what he regularly called "moral courage." Although a good judge of character in the military, he sometimes failed in politics to appreciate the motives and morals of those he invited into his administration. His capacity for self-improvement and willingness to confront his mistakes won over leaders such as Hamilton Fish, his eminent secretary of state. At the end of his life, Grant wrote one of the finest memoirs in American letters, which modern presidents invariably refer to when they write their own. In this last piece of the puzzle, one question must be asked: Accomplishing such a literary feat required extraordinary gifts; did we miss something along the way?

Grant loved his wife, Julia, his four children, horses, the theater, his Missouri farm, painting, travel, Mexico, and novels. A maxim declares: "Good writers are invariably good readers." What did Grant read? The breadth of his reading, beginning with the long list of novelists he read at West Point, hints at a story of his imaginative depth yet to be told. He was not an eloquent speaker like Lincoln or a fiery personality like Theodore Roosevelt; his leadership was of a different kind.

In this biography, I bring into conversation elements of Grant overlooked or undervalued. Early on I became convinced I could not understand Ulysses's story without understanding Julia's story. Too often discounted or marginalized, she occupies a larger place in this biography. Others might describe her as plain, but to Ulysses she was beautiful in ways that counted—in her gentleness, warmth, and joy. Their young love, more than they initially understood, would be tested by families who vigorously defended opposite sides of the slavery question. All Ulysses's friends observed his "devotion" to the woman he called "my dear Julia." She became his anchor in the furor of many storms.

Grant was renowned for his ability to ride and gentle horses. But what do horse stories mean to a modern reader? In an earlier era when horses were central to everyday life, people understood that the man whom horses trust is the kind of man who can be trusted.

Another underexplored story is Grant's lifelong love affair with Mexico. His involvement in the Mexican War is well known; more obscure, but no less fascinating are his various efforts, both as general and president, to enlist American support for Mexico's aspirations to become a liberal democracy.

Biography often focuses on war and politics. I shall try to understand Grant from the inside out. That is not an easy task when engaging the figure called "the silent man." Grant was esteemed for his humility and modesty. Over the course of pondering him, I came to believe that modern psychological studies of "introversion" can offer clues to the nature of his personality.

Grant's religious odyssey has been overlooked or misunderstood. He is a son of Methodism. When the fastest-growing Protestant denomination in the nineteenth century decided to build a national church in Washington, as one of its trustees Grant took part in its dedication four days before his inauguration as president in 1869. The unrecognized person in Grant's faith story is John Heyl Vincent, his Methodist pastor in Galena who went on to found the now world-famous Chautauqua Institution in New York in 1874 and summoned President Grant to participate there the following summer.

Grant never sought pride in position. In April 1861, hoping for an opportunity in the new Union army, he wrote his father from Springfield,

Illinois, "I was perfectly sickened at the political wire-pulling for all these commissions and would not engage in it." Seven years later, as the Republican candidate for president, he allowed his name to be offered for nomination because the country, in crisis after the divisive presidency of Andrew Johnson, could not afford any "trading politicians."

What to make of Grant's two terms as president? The specter of scandals in his second term has tended to demolish the accomplishments of both terms. Yet Grant as president defended the political rights of African Americans, battled against the Ku Klux Klan and voter suppression, reimagined Indian policy, rethought the role of the federal government in a changing America, and foresaw that as the United States would now assume a larger place in world affairs, a durable peace with Great Britain would provide the nation with a major ally.

If Grant's *Personal Memoirs,* written at the end of his life, have been appreciated as a hallmark of American memoirs—never out of print since their publication—far less noted are Grant's personal letters and military orders. The pure gold of this enormous treasure are the hundreds of letters to his "dear Julia," who saved all his correspondence to her over the years. Grant, who often kept his feelings close to himself, reveals his hopes, struggles, and beliefs in these letters.

In exploring the viability of this project, I consulted Civil War historians Jim McPherson, Gary Gallagher, and Joan Waugh to ask if they believed it was time for a new biography of Grant. They were generous in their affirmation and encouragement. In recent years, several distinguished historians have provided thoughtful reappraisals of Grant. Brooks Simpson penned two groundbreaking books: *Let Us Have Peace: Ulysses S. Grant and the Politics of Reconstruction* (1991) and *Ulysses S. Grant: Triumph Over Adversity, 1822–1865* (2000). Jean Edward Smith authored the comprehensive *Grant* (2001). Joan Waugh herself, in *U. S. Grant: American Hero, American Myth* (2009), offered an adroit reappraisal within the larger story of American memory. Building on what they have done, in particular by utilizing new resources, I want both to place Grant centrally in his tumultuous historical context and to make him immediate to modern audiences.

I have benefited immensely from the completion—after forty-nine years—of *The Papers of Ulysses S. Grant.* Superbly edited by John Y. Simon, and recently by John Marszalek, these thirty-two volumes provide both a wide-angle and a zoom lens on Grant's ideas, thinking, and action. Multiple visits to the library have unearthed rich resources not included in the printed and online papers.

In these past seven years, I discovered that Grant's life story has so many surprising twists and turns, highs and lows, as to read like a suspense novel. His nineteenth-century contemporaries knew his story well. They offered him not simply admiration but affection. In their eyes he stood with Washington and Lincoln. But like an old photograph blurred from wear, his story needs to be refocused for today. My hope is that readers will discover a fresh meaning of Grant—for his time and for ours.

PART ONE

Formation

1630–1848

I read but few lives of great men because biographers do not, as a rule, tell enough about the formative period of life. What I want to know is what a man did as a boy.

—Ulysses S. Grant

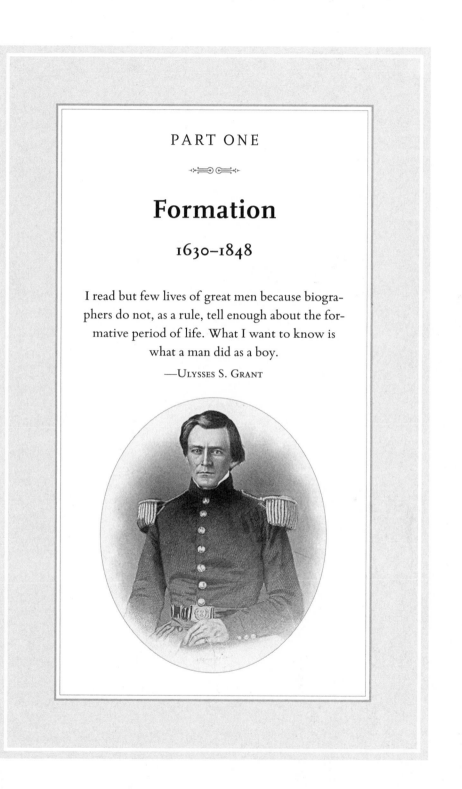

CHAPTER 1

"My Family Is American"

My family is American, and has been for generations,
in all its branches, direct and collateral.

—ULYSSES S. GRANT, *Personal Memoirs*

Although he was celebrated in his lifetime as a prime example of the mythic American self-made man, Ulysses S. Grant understood the formation of his life to be a family affair. His appreciation looked back through the prism of seven generations and two hundred years of Grants.

MATTHEW AND PRISCILLA Grant sailed from Plymouth, England, on March 20, 1630. Married for five years, the Grants were "West-country people" from Dorsetshire in southwest England. Their home that spring would be the *Mary and John,* a four-hundred-ton wooden ship very much like the *Mayflower,* which had carried the first Pilgrims to a new England only ten years earlier. The Grants sailed with 138 other passengers who traveled together as members of a congregation, complete with two ministers and lay officers.

The *Mary and John* would be one of seventeen ships sailing from England to the New World between February and August 1630. In the next eleven years, nearly three hundred ships would carry twenty thousand passengers in a huge exodus called "the Great Migration." Disdainfully dubbed "Puritans" by opponents, these immigrants hoped to purify the Church of England according to the best ideas of the Reformed or Calvinist churches of Europe, which traced their origins to John Calvin of Geneva in the previous century. The Grants joined Puritans who hoped to restart their lives in a new land where they could escape persecution by both King Charles I and Archbishop William Laud and put their religious and political ideas into practice.

After seventy perilous days sailing across the North Atlantic, the *Mary and John* made its way into the narrow entrance of the Boston harbor. Following their arrival in the Massachusetts Bay Colony, the first American Grants helped settle the new town of Dorchester (now part of Boston). Priscilla Grant died after bearing four children in as many years.

In 1635, five years after his arrival, Matthew Grant linked his dreams with the Reverend John Warham and fifty-eight members of the Dorchester parish in journeying 105 miles to begin another new town, Windsor, at the confluence of the Connecticut and Farmington rivers in the Connecticut Valley. The first English settlers traveled west, displacing Native Americans, who were already being killed off in large numbers by disease. Matthew would come to occupy a central place in the new community, serving as town clerk, county surveyor, and deacon of First Church.

Henry Reed Stiles, writing *The History of Ancient Windsor, Connecticut* in the nineteenth century, stated, "Few men indeed filled so large a place in the early history of Windsor, or filled it so well, as honest Matthew Grant! His name figures in almost every place of trust." Grant represented, for Stiles, "a type of the best settlers of New England, and left to his descendants an untarnished name and the example of an unswerving fidelity to the public trusts committed to him." In reflecting on the Puritan priority of the community over the individual, Matthew Grant declared: "I have been careful to do nothing upon one man's desire."

THE NEXT FIVE generations of Grants were Connecticut Yankees, spreading across Windsor, East Windsor, and Tolland, Connecticut. Young Ulysses knew the story of his great-grandfather Noah, Matthew Grant's great-great-grandson. Born in 1718, Noah grew to manhood as the English and French struggled for domination on the North American continent. Ulysses enjoyed recounting how Noah and his brother Solomon held commissions in the English army in the war against both French and Indians. Noah and Solomon were killed in separate battles in New York in 1756.

Noah's son, also named Noah and Ulysses's grandfather, was only nine years old when his father and uncle were killed fighting under the flag of the king of England. Born in 1748, this Noah enlisted in the Continental army after the Battles of Lexington and Concord. Ulysses would recount proudly how his grandfather was present at the Battle of Bunker Hill. He believed his grandfather served through the entire Revolutionary War, and this heritage would become central to Grant's self-identity.

As a new nation emerged after the war, Noah Grant struggled to make a living as a farmer and cobbler in the Connecticut Valley. When his wife,

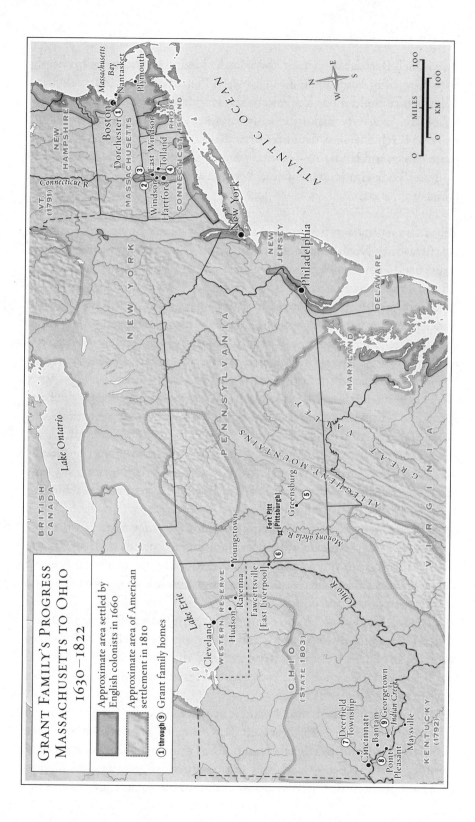

GRANT FAMILY'S PROGRESS
MASSACHUSETTS TO OHIO
1630–1822

Approximate area settled by
English colonists in 1660

Approximate area of American
settlement in 1810

① through ⑨ Grant family homes

BRITISH
CANADA

Lake Ontario

Lake Erie

NEW
HAMPSHIRE

VT.
(1791)

Connecticut R.

NEW YORK

Massachusetts
Bay
Nantasket

Boston ①
Dorchester

MASSACHUSETTS

Plymouth

Windsor ②
③ East Windsor
Hartford ④ Tolland

CONNECTICUT

RHODE
ISLAND

New York

ATLANTIC OCEAN

PENNSYLVANIA

NEW
JERSEY

Philadelphia

DELAWARE

MARYLAND

GREAT VALLEY

ALLEGHENY MOUNTAINS

Greensburg ⑤

Fort Pitt
[Pittsburgh]

Monongahela R.

⑥

Youngstown

WESTERN RESERVE

Cleveland

Hudson
Ravenna
Fawcettsville
[East Liverpool]

OHIO
(STATE 1803)

Ohio R.

VIRGINIA

Deerfield ⑦
Township
Cincinnati

Bantam
⑨ Georgetown
⑧ Indian Creek
Point
Pleasant

Maysville

KENTUCKY
(1792)

N
E
S
W

0   MILES   100

0   KM   100

Anna Buell Richardson Grant, died, he decided to join some of his neighbors in settling lands opening in western Pennsylvania. He traveled 475 miles before building a cabin along the wooded banks of the Monongahela River near Greensburg in southwestern Pennsylvania. There, Noah married Rachel Kelley, daughter of an Irish pioneer, and began acquiring more babies and lands.

Jesse Root Grant, who would become Ulysses's father, was born on January 23, 1794.

WHEN JESSE TURNED five years old, the Grant family moved yet again. At age fifty-one, Noah loaded his family on a boat, the popular means of transportation west. At the village at Fort Pitt (today's Pittsburgh), they turned southwest and floated onto a broad watercourse known as the Ohio (adopted from the Seneca *O-hi-yo,* meaning "Great River"). They stopped at the first village beyond Pennsylvania, a picturesque hamlet that fronted a serpentine bend of the majestic river. This was Fawcettstown (now East Liverpool), named after its founder, Thomas Fawcett, who had established the community just the year before.

The newly settling Ohio Country was part of lands ceded by the British to the United States at the end of the Revolutionary War. Four seaboard states, Massachusetts, Connecticut, New York, and Virginia, gave their western lands to the new federal government to form the Northwest Territory. On July 13, 1787, Congress ratified the Northwest Ordinance, establishing a system of government for this territory reaching all the way to the Mississippi River.

Even though the new federal government, in order to attract the participation of all thirteen colonies, had not taken a stand on slavery in the new Constitution, the founding Congress looked far to the future and decreed, "There shall be neither slavery nor involuntary servitude in the said territory."

By 1800, the young nation comprised five million people divided into sixteen states plus the Northwest and Mississippi territories. On February 19, 1803, President Thomas Jefferson signed the law authorizing Ohio as the first state organized in the Northwest Territory and the seventeenth state in the United States.

When Jesse turned ten, Noah moved the family forty-five miles through virgin forests to Deerfield Township in Warren County. One year later Jesse's mother, Rachel Grant, the family's stable center, died. At age fifty-seven, Noah—work-shy and too fond of alcohol—decided to break up his family. The two oldest children, Susan and Jesse, were expected to find their way with relatives or neighbors. For the next three years, Jesse would work for several farmers in the area, earning his board and room but not much more.

In 1808, Jesse went to work for the Tod family on their farm near Youngstown, Ohio. Over the next two years, a new world opened up for the fourteen-year-old. George Tod, a respected politician and jurist, was a father figure to young Jesse, introducing him to political discussion. Among Jesse's playmates was little David Tod, only three years old, who would become governor of Ohio during the Civil War.

In the evenings, with George often away serving as a judge on the Ohio Supreme Court, his wife, Sally, furthered Jesse's reading through books she provided. Encouraged by his eagerness to learn, the Tods sent Jesse to a subscription school for two winter terms—the only formal education he would receive in his life. Years later, Ulysses would recall his father saying that Sally Tod was "the most admirable woman he had ever known."

The Tods suggested to Jesse that the occupation of tanning would be more financially rewarding than farming. At this time, technological innovations were facilitating the purchase of leather goods by all classes of society, because leather products became cheaper and the process became more accessible. In 1805, Sir Humphry Davy, a British chemist and inventor, found that trees other than oak could be utilized in the tanning process. Ash, chestnut, hemlock, and mimosa trees, all plentiful in the United States, quickly expanded tanning resources. American Samuel Parker further advanced the tanning industry in 1809 by inventing a machine to split hides. With the aid of Parker's invention, one man could split up to one hundred hides in a single day. The need for leather goods grew apace with rapid population growth in the West.

Jesse had watched his own father, Noah, begin with extensive property and lose nearly all of it. During his teenage years, Jesse determined to work diligently in order to acquire the culture and possessions he had discovered in the Tod home.

JESSE SET OUT to be a tanner. In 1810, he traveled to Maysville, Kentucky, to ask his older half-brother, Peter, if he could learn the tanning business as his apprentice. Under Peter's guidance, Jesse saw that he could advance by tanning leather for everything from shoes and boots to harnesses and saddles. In addition, Peter taught Jesse how to manage his financial affairs and run a business, skills equally important to the craft of tanning and something their father, Noah, had never learned.

In 1815, having completed his commitment to Peter, Jesse returned to Ohio. He wanted to go back to the land and people he knew, but he would also say later of his move back across the Ohio River, "I would not own slaves and I would not live where there were slaves."

In Ohio young Grant, now twenty-one, went to work for Owen Brown, a burly man who operated a successful tannery in Hudson, twenty-five miles southeast of Cleveland. In his year with the outspoken Brown family, Jesse heard constant conversation about the evils of slavery. While participating in a cattle drive to an army fort, Owen's son John had seen a young black boy beaten with an iron fire shovel. John Brown returned to his family filled with an anger that would grow until it exploded decades later in Kansas and finally at Harpers Ferry in 1859. In Hudson, John Brown would assert his indictment of slavery to anybody who would listen. Jesse listened.

In 1817, Jesse was invited to become the operating partner of a tannery in Ravenna. Within two years, his hard-work ethic turned the joint venture into a success. He saved his earnings and accumulated the considerable sum of $1,500—nearly $27,000 in today's money.

In January 1820, Grant moved to Point Pleasant, a village on the Ohio River twenty-five miles southeast of Cincinnati, to work as foreman in a new tannery. Thomas Page hired Jesse in part because he wanted him to teach the craft of tanning to his own son. Jesse's new goal became acquiring enough money to start his own tannery.

AT AGE TWENTY-FIVE, Jesse had another goal: finding a wife. Page pointed his young employee thirteen miles north, near the crossroads town of Bantam, to the home of John and Sarah Simpson. Descended from Scottish Presbyterians, the Simpsons, while living in Montgomery County, Pennsylvania, had caught "Ohio fever." They headed west in the summer of 1817, gliding the final miles on a flatboat. Upon arriving in Bantam, the Simpsons purchased six hundred acres of fertile land for $6 an acre from Page and built a brick house.

Jesse appreciated the stability he encountered in the Simpson family, enjoyed the books he read in their house, and felt comfortable in their company. Of the three Simpson daughters, he felt drawn to the eldest, Hannah. Jesse described Hannah as "a plain unpretending country girl, handsome but not vain." A neighbor described her to be of "Christian character," whom everyone found "graceful in manner." Five years younger than Jesse, she attracted him with her quiet kindness and patience. Hannah seemed quite a contrast to the voluble Jesse.

Sometimes, opposites do attract. Jesse and Hannah married on June 24, 1821, in her family home.

The young couple moved into an unadorned one-story frame house Jesse had rented next to the tannery in Point Pleasant. Built in 1817 of Allegheny pine, the small house was 16 by 19½ feet, with two rooms and a large fireplace on the north side. A majestic expanse of Indian Creek flowing south into the Ohio River dominated the view from the front of the cabin; standing in their doorway, Jesse and Hannah could watch the *Daniel Boone* and the *Simon Kenton,* stern-wheel steamers named for two heroes of the Kentucky frontier, pass by on the way to St. Louis or Pittsburgh. In the back, a hill sloped up to the surrounding forests of ash, oak, and walnut.

Ten months and three days after their marriage, on April 27, 1822, Hannah gave birth to their first child, a boy weighing a hefty ten and three-quarter pounds. Jesse decided this first member of the eighth generation of American Grants would remain unnamed until a proper family convocation could be held.

A month later, the Grant and Simpson families gathered at the Simpson family home for a naming ceremony. The lusty infant, a charmer with blue eyes and reddish-brown hair, held center stage as a remarkable dialogue began. Hannah, a fierce Democrat, suggested the name "Albert," in honor of Albert Gallatin from her home state of Pennsylvania, who had served both in Congress and as secretary of the Treasury under President Thomas Jefferson. Hannah's younger sister, Anne, suggested "Theodore." John Simpson favored "Hiram," which he thought a handsome name. Sarah Simpson, caught up in reading French novelist François Fénelon's *The Adventures of Telemachus*—the romantic story about the

This simple home was the birthplace of Ulysses S. Grant on April 27, 1822.

son of mythical Greek general Ulysses, who defeated the Trojans—spoke up strongly for "Ulysses." Jesse seconded her nomination, in part because he had loaned his mother-in-law this book from his personal library and wanted to please her. In the end, someone suggested drawing lots to decide. After depositing the names in a hat, the youngest Simpson, Anne, drew out the name "Ulysses."

Wanting to honor his father-in-law, Jesse announced that the baby's name would be "Hiram Ulysses." But Jesse never called him "Hiram." Bubbling with pride, he insisted from the beginning on calling his first-born son "my Ulysses."

"Ulysses" was certainly not the name of any previous noteworthy American. It was not the biblical name—Matthew, Samuel, Noah—of the previous Grant generations. "Ulysses" would be the most unusual name of an American Grant.

The baby boy with the Greek name had much to live up to. Fénelon tells the story of the moral and political education of Telemachus, the young son of the Greek hero Ulysses. In the course of the novel, Telemachus travels to every part of the Mediterranean world. Along the way he learns, by trial and error, the virtues of courage, humility, patience, and simplicity. These were all the traits he would need if he was to succeed his heroic father, Ulysses, as a ruler.

Jesse and Hannah Grant, on naming day, were putting their family hopes on little Ulysses.

CHAPTER 2

"My Ulysses"

I never missed a quarter term from school from the time I was old
enough to attend till the time of leaving home.

—ULYSSES S. GRANT, *Personal Memoirs*

U lysses would grow up with no memory of his birthplace. In the
spring of 1823, shortly after he turned one, Jesse and Hannah Grant
decided to move. With accumulated savings of $1,100, Jesse made plans
to start his tannery in yet another Ohio town: Georgetown, a village
twenty-five miles to the east. The road from Point Pleasant to Georgetown wound through the lush forested hills of the White Oak Creek
valley. Jesse placed his bet for economic success in Georgetown because it
had recently been selected the county seat of the newly settling Brown
County.

Jesse presented himself to the county's justice of the peace, Thomas L.
Hamer, on August 23, 1823, to pay $50 and take formal possession of Lot
No. 264, one hundred yards east of the Georgetown public square. He
built a two-story brick home for Hannah and Ulysses. Over the next
sixteen years, Ulysses would grow from a child to a youth in this house.

Jesse set up his tannery one-half block south of his home. He knew
water and wood held the keys to his success. White Oak Creek, running
swiftly just to the west of Georgetown, provided water as it snaked its
way from northern Ohio to empty into the Ohio River ten miles south
of town. As for wood, Georgetown was encircled by hardwood forests of
ash, maple, walnut, and large, girdled oaks, some more than six feet in
diameter. These trees would provide limitless resources for bark.

The purpose of tanning is to strengthen the animal skin, making it
resistant to decay. This process dates back to prehistoric times. Hebrews
tanned with oak bark, Egyptians with pods from babul trees, and Romans with both bark and berries. Jesse drew tannic acid from the bark of
oaks surrounding Georgetown. He would peel the bark from the tall

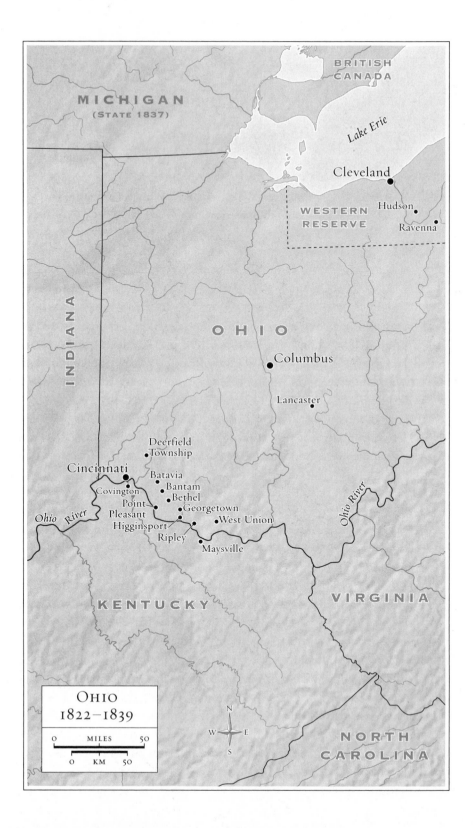

BRITISH
CANADA

MICHIGAN
(STATE 1837)

Lake Erie

Cleveland

WESTERN
RESERVE

Hudson

Ravenna

INDIANA

OHIO

Columbus

Lancaster

Deerfield
Township

Cincinnati

Batavia

Covington

Bantam

Bethel

Point
Pleasant

Georgetown

Higginsport

West Union

Ohio River

Ripley

Maysville

Ohio River

KENTUCKY

VIRGINIA

OHIO
1822–1839

0   MILES   50

0   KM   50

N
W   E
S

NORTH
CAROLINA

The Grants moved to this Georgetown home in 1823.

trees in strips about three feet long. He intended to teach Ulysses, when he was old enough, to hold the bark in his left hand, while with a hammer in his right hand he would break the bark into smaller pieces four to five inches long.

Jesse purchased cattle hides, salted them, and soaked them in lime vats, called "bates," to de-hair them. Next, he de-limed them in an acid solution, sometimes manure, then soaked them repeatedly in increasingly strong oak-bark liquor or solution.

If tanning was economically productive, it was aesthetically repugnant. Odor from hides was difficult to get off one's hands. As a young boy, Ulysses hated the strong smells that seeped into the house from his father's clothing.

Jesse worked hard by day to make his tannery a success; at night he devoted himself to reading. Largely self-educated, he had about thirty-five books in a cabinet in the sitting room, what Ulysses's friend Jimmy Sanderson called "a mighty big book collection" for Ohio at that time. And his passion for learning soon became evident to his neighbors.

He was not bashful about speaking at the local debating society on topics of the day. Embracing the northern antislavery wing of the national Whig Party while living in a Democratic town with pro-slavery sympathies only strengthened Jesse's resolve to speak and write vigorously against slavery, which he deemed a cancer on the nation's democratic virtues. Jesse took pride in never backing down from expressing his ideas, especially on slavery.

· · ·

JESSE WAS ALSO not bashful about speaking of young Ulysses. The child was the delight of his life. With light reddish-brown hair and blue eyes, Ulysses grew into a chubby little boy with a ruddy complexion. To the boy's growing discomfort, it seemed his father's favorite pastime was tooting his horn about "my Ulysses."

With business prospering, Jesse paid off their Georgetown home within one year of purchasing it. At the time of the birth of a second son, Samuel Simpson, Jesse began the first of several expansions of the house.

Ulysses and Simp, three years apart, grew up together. The two boys delighted in playing outdoor games like rolling the hoop, leapfrog, marbles, hopscotch, and hide-and-seek. Indoors, in cold winter months, the brothers would invite friends in to play for hours, checkers and the peg games Fox and Geese and Nine Men's Morris.

When Ulysses turned five, with the expectation of more children, Jesse doubled the size of the Grant home by adding a wing. In 1828, a first sister, Clara, was born. In the 1830s, three more children joined the Grant family: Virginia ("Nellie") in 1832; Orvil in 1835; and Mary Frances in 1839.

ULYSSES. SOME GEORGETOWN citizens chortled at a pretentious foreign name in a frontier town of plain-speaking people. One neighbor asked Jesse, "How did you come to saddle such a name on the poor child?"

As Ulysses grew, boys and girls began to call him "Lys" or, in the melodious drawl of some southern tongues, "Lyssus." As children learned how to be cruel to one another, some parodied his name as "Useless." He did not like the nicknames. On the blank front pages of his schoolbooks, he preferred to write "Hiram U. Grant."

Of course, in recounting Grant's early life, one risks mythologizing him—turning a boy into a larger-than-life hero based on glorified anecdotes from long ago. But even if they may not be literally true in every respect, stories from Grant's childhood, preciously guarded, told, and retold across the decades, offer real insight into Ulysses's character in formation, and, perhaps even more important, insight into the qualities he embodied that managed to live on in historical memory: patience, common sense, physical bravery, love of animals.

One of Ulysses's first close friends was Daniel Ammen. Dan's father, David Ammen, had moved his family and weekly newspaper, the *Castigator,* from Ripley, Ohio, to Georgetown in 1826. Originally from Virginia, David and Sally Ammen left the South because they wanted to raise their four children in a nonslaveholding state. Ulysses and Dan, two years apart, began a friendship that would last a lifetime.

Ulysses's friend Jimmy Sanderson remembered him having "such a quiet, sedate way that made him liked by the school teachers." He was quiet—more like his mother than his father. "He got his *sense* from his mother," said one neighbor. However, these observations did not mean he lacked self-confidence.

Ulysses inherited his patience from Hannah. While some mothers expressed their maternal instincts in protectiveness for risk-taking sons, she seemed content and supportive of Ulysses, his ways and whereabouts.

The sensible boy often found himself receiving the aftershocks of his father's sometimes bellicose behavior. Townsfolk transferred the sins of the father's negative reputation to the son. According to another neighbor, this meant that a group of boys in town "were always laying for him," but Ulysses avoided them and ran with an older, "good, clean" set.

Young Ulysses enjoyed "fishing, going to the creek a mile away to swim in summer, taking a horse and visiting [his] grandparents in the adjoining county, fifteen miles off, skating on the ice in winter, or taking a horse and sleigh when there was snow." His friends remembered him as a strong swimmer and "expert diver." Ulysses was admired for being able to swim underwater for what seemed to his pals an incredibly long time.

Girls were fond of Ulysses. In the winter he took them sleighing. An older boy, W. T. Galbreath, remembered girls were keen about Ulysses because "he was a careful driver and the girls liked to drive with him." He also didn't chew tobacco and didn't use "bad words" like the other boys.

Ulysses loved ice-skating at the same swimming hole on White Oak Creek. Once, at age nine or ten, he skated so long that when he arrived home his mother discovered his feet were frozen from fastening his bootstraps too tight. Hannah Grant applied a homemade remedy: she smoked Ulysses's frozen feet with hay, then wrapped them in bacon to thaw the frost.

One early summer afternoon, Ulysses and Dan Ammen started on a horseback ride. Upon arriving at a stream, they dismounted because, Dan would say later, "we thought that the fish would be more plentiful" in waters swollen from spring rains. Ulysses found a large poplar log for a seat and threw his line with hooks of bent pins into the stream, hoping to hook some "chubs" or "shiners." Within a few minutes he tumbled headfirst into the current. As Ammen described it, "his heels were in the air and he plunged head downward into the rapidly flowing muddy water."

Young Dan, glimpsing his friend submerged, raced ahead until he found some willows that "bent over the stream" at a point where the stream narrowed. Hanging on to them, Ammen grabbed "my young companion as he was borne down by the swift current" and "helped him to reach the bank." A narrow escape that neither would forget.

Hunting was a popular pastime for boys growing up in frontier Ohio. The woods were full of deer and wild turkey. In daylight the boys hunted rabbits, partridges, and gray squirrels. At night, with their dogs, they dashed about treeing raccoons.

Ulysses did not join in on this male rite of passage. His boyhood friend Chilton White reported, "Ulysses [was] no hunter. He never took a gun." Sanderson confirmed this, musing, "That was strange because there was scarcely a boy in all that region that did not like to hunt." Another friend recalled, "He was unusually sensitive to pain, and his aversion to taking any form of life was so great that he would not hunt." Although young Ulysses would win an award for marksmanship with a pistol at a Fourth of July picnic, he found no sport in killing animals.

JESSE DETERMINED HIS firstborn would receive a good education. In a time when many fathers believed they could not spare their sons from the farm or family business, he wanted Ulysses to gain a better education than he was afforded as a boy. Jesse had two reasons for valuing education: First, despite his own meager formal education, he was a voracious reader, an exercise that opened up a virtual landscape larger than the forests and fields of southwestern Ohio. Second, he believed education had utilitarian value, the potential to give his son the instruments to succeed in both the family business of tanning and the larger world of business just now beginning to blossom in Ohio.

Ulysses's formal schooling began when he turned five. Education in small communities in the old Northwest merged public and private spheres: public in that it was open to all boys and girls in the community; private in that parents decided which of their children would attend, then provided a "subscription" to pay the teacher. Parents who had the money gave between $1 and $2 for a typical thirteen-week session; others paid in corn, wheat, or tobacco. Class sessions were usually conducted only in winter, when it was too cold for boys to be working outside on family farms.

School met in a low brick building built in 1829 on a knoll just south of town. Quiet Ulysses cheerfully spoke up when it came time for "mental arithmetic." A schoolmate recalled that most children "hated" this exercise, "while the young Grant was anxious to have the teacher fire them at him." As the teacher sent volley after volley—4 plus 5 take away 2 times 7—at the retreating children, "Ulysses would shout an answer."

Ulysses also enjoyed art. He became skilled at drawing all kinds of different horses upon his slate.

But there was one school exercise he did not like. Every other week, the teacher would ask each student to "declaim." In a typical assignment, students would recite a selection from George Washington's Farewell Address. Sanderson remembered that Ulysses "could not bear to get up and face a whole room full of boys and girls." He so loathed the experience that after school he told Jimmy he would "never speak there again, no matter what happened."

At age seven, Ulysses read *The Life of George Washington* by Mason Locke Weems, an Episcopal minister. Weems's biography was as much an exposition of moral values as a story of Washington.

The first teacher, Mr. Barney, did not last. Totally immersed in Ulysses's education, Jesse decided Barney had "no stamina." He was forthwith succeeded by John D. White, who had moved his family from Kentucky. White was the father of Carr and Chilton White, two and four years younger than Ulysses, who would become two of his best friends. White built a house on the hill above the Grant home.

Most teachers were young and not much more schooled than their pupils. White was older and well educated. And demanding. Books White assigned included Noah Webster's *American Dictionary of the English Language,* Samuel Kirkham's *English Grammar in Familiar Lectures,* and Jesse Olney's *A Practical System of Modern Geography.*

Under White, Ulysses learned that education and discipline went hand in hand. Years later, Grant would write, "I can see John D. White—the school teacher—now, with his long beech switch always in his hand." White brought in his switches each day in bundles. "Often a whole bundle would be used up in a single day. . . . I never had any hard feelings against my teacher, either while attending the school, or in later years when reflecting upon my experience. Mr. White was a kindhearted man, and was much respected by the community in which he lived. He only followed the universal custom of the period."

Despite his appreciation of teacher White, looking back, Grant believed "the schools . . . were very indifferent." One problem: None of "the scholars were classified." This meant a single teacher would be responsible for thirty to forty students ranging from "the infant learning the ABC's up to the young lady of eighteen and the boy of twenty, studying the highest branches taught—the three R's, Reading, 'Riting, 'Rithmetic."

FOR A BOY growing up on the frontier, work began at an earlier age than school. In addition to his tannery, Jesse cultivated thirty acres of land and maintained an additional fifty acres of forest within a mile of the village— and he expected his oldest son to handle whatever tasks he could manage. By age seven, Ulysses was hauling wood used in house and tannery. "I could not load it on the wagons, of course, at that time, but I could drive."

One winter day in 1829, Jesse left early for Ripley, twelve miles away, and returned late to find a huge mound of brush piled up next to the house. How did it get there?

The next morning, Ulysses explained. The family owned a frisky three-year-old colt he had ridden with a saddle, but no one had ever attempted to put a collar on the animal. Ulysses not only put a collar and a harness on the colt but hitched him to a sled. On that day, in his father's words, he hauled "successive loads, all day, and when I came home at night, he had a pile of brush as big as a cabin."

ULYSSES BECAME KNOWN for his fast riding. He liked to ride bareback, sometimes putting a sheepskin on the horse's back so he would not slip, his arms wrapped around the horse's neck and his bare feet bearing down on its flanks. His highest joy was to circle the town square standing tall on a horse's back, balancing on just one leg.

His love of horses lingered in every memory of friends and neighbors. Chilton White recalled, "He was a splendid rider and loved horses." Jimmy Sanderson remarked, "He seemed perfectly fearless of horses." He said Ulysses delighted in riding bareback at breakneck speed through the village and "frightened nearly every female old and young."

Ulysses began to establish a reputation throughout Brown County and beyond for his love for horses—and their love for him. Farmers began to bring young or rambunctious horses to him to train. Ulysses's method, which people gathered around to watch, was not to strong-arm these fractious horses, but to gentle them.

At age eleven, Ulysses became the center of another horse story when a traveling circus came to town. A trick pony was the center of each performance. The circus clown offered $5 for anyone who could ride it, but the fat bay pony, whose mane had been completely cut off to eliminate any "handle," had been trained to throw off anybody who made the attempt.

One by one, Ulysses's friends mounted the pony but usually lasted mere seconds on his back. Ulysses watched this unfair contest for a while before stepping forward and announcing to the clown, "I believe I can ride that pony."

The pony immediately reared, bucked, and kicked, doing everything he could to throw off the young intruder. Ulysses, with no mane to hold on to, wrapped his arms tightly around the pony's neck. Rider and pony careened around and around in the tiny circus ring.

Finally, after minutes that seemed like ages, the clown stepped forward and awarded young Ulysses the $5. The crowd's earsplitting cheers were his greatest reward as they applauded him for his feat—a story Georgetown residents would talk about for years.

Around this time, Jesse developed a delivery service. Capitalizing on his young son's prowess with horses, the father became comfortable with "my Ulysses" transporting travelers in a small carriage to various destinations: the nearby river towns Ripley and Higginsport, where passengers could get an Ohio River steamer; inland to West Union; across the river twenty miles to Maysville in Kentucky; and fifty miles east to Cincinnati. Eleven-year-old Ulysses created quite a sensation when he arrived in Cincinnati and attempted to check into the Dennison House for an overnight stay. According to the story, the hotel manager was not sure what to make of the boy standing in front of him; finally, with reluctance, he let Ulysses sign the register and handed him a room key.

FOR JESSE, SCHOOL and church went hand in hand. He and Hannah helped found the Georgetown Methodist Church, which began holding services in 1827 in a meetinghouse across the street from their home. Hannah's parents, Presbyterians back in Pennsylvania, could find no Presbyterian churches on the Ohio frontier, so they had joined a Methodist meetinghouse in Bantam.

American Methodism was expanding rapidly owing to Methodist clergymen who traveled a geographic area, called a "circuit," in order to establish a church in a rural settlement or minister to existing congregations. The Methodist emphasis on experience, a democratic value open to anyone regardless of educational attainment or economic standing, highlighted a major reason the denomination grew so rapidly in the early decades of the century. The Grants invited these Methodist "circuit riders" to stay at their home.

The Grants worshipped in a thirty-by-fifty-foot brick church. Though small, it was built with two front doors to separately accommodate men and women, an arrangement lasting until 1846. The builders furnished the interior with poplar benches backed by a narrow strip, just enough to lean against but not wide enough to fall asleep on. Pews were free, unlike those available only for rent by other denominations.

Jesse became a pillar of the congregation. A Methodist leader remembered him as "a ruling spirit in church affairs," serving as a trustee and steward.

Jesse and Hannah were not drawn to the emotional aspects prevalent in many early Methodist congregations. According to Chilton White, "The Methodists shouted in those days but the Grant family never took a part in it." However, the Methodists were a musical people, and the Grants enjoyed singing the hearty hymns of Charles Wesley.

Jesse and Hannah Grant affirmed the Methodist emphasis on sanctification—the imperative to live a holy and upright life. They taught their children respect for the Sabbath. The family did not play cards. Jesse and Hannah did not dance, nor did they permit their children to dance. Ulysses was taught never to swear because this would take the Lord's name in vain.

Ulysses inherited some of his mother's Methodist piety. In Hannah Grant, known for her quiet behavior, Chilton White detected what many missed—that she was a woman of "deep feeling but not demonstrative." Hannah taught Ulysses an ethic of self-effacing Christian love. Her Methodist faith taught her to praise the Creator rather than the creature. Therefore, she was not inclined to laud Ulysses or any of her children. A relative captured the spirit of Hannah: "She thought nothing you could do would entitle you to praise . . . you ought to praise the Lord for giving you the opportunity to do it."

SEEKING A BETTER education for his firstborn son, in the autumn of 1836 Jesse sent Ulysses, now fourteen, to Maysville, Kentucky, twenty miles away, to study at the Maysville Academy. Founded in 1832, the school was led by Jacob W. Rand, from New England, and William West Richeson, a graduate of the University of Virginia. Ulysses stayed with Peter and Permelia Grant, his uncle and aunt, at their handsome brick home just above the steamboat landing.

Rand initially served as principal, with Richeson as his assistant, but it was the younger Virginian, whose great hero was Thomas Jefferson, who excelled as the teacher. Also an officer of the Presbyterian church in Maysville, he brought an ethical dimension into the classroom.

A classmate at Maysville Academy, Richard Dawson, recalled Ulysses as "a quiet matter-of-fact boy, modest and conservative." Just as he had in Georgetown, Ulysses shone in arithmetic. Despite this success, however, he yawned when he went "over the same old arithmetic which I knew every word of before." The school proved not as challenging as Jesse had hoped.

While at Maysville Academy, Ulysses joined the Philomathean Society, a debating club. "Philomathean," derived from the Greek *philomath,* means "a lover of learning." He participated in nine of the weekly debates in the winter term. Classmate A. H. Markland recalled Ulysses as "a good debater for one of his years." For reasons he never explained, Ulysses found debating different from the declamation he had loathed. At his second meeting, he took the winning affirmative side on *"Resolved:* That females wield greater influence than males." The following week, when the debate topic became *"Resolved:* That it would not be just and politic to liberate the slaves at this time," Ulysses stood again with the winning affirmative side. He also took the affirmative position at another winter debate: *Resolved:* That intemperance is a greater evil than war."

Looking back on their experience at Maysville Academy, Dawson recalled Ulysses not as one of the leading scholars, but as someone who "was always very liberal and generous in sharing anything he had with other boys." Independently, Markland confirmed this judgment, remembering Ulysses as "exceedingly kind, popular, even-tempered and generous."

During his sixteenth year, Ulysses returned to Georgetown and John White's school. It was never explained why he changed schools so frequently, but one year later, in autumn 1838, Jesse decided to send his son to John Rankin's academy in Ripley.

Standing at one of the Ohio River's narrower stretches, Ripley was

Young Lys attended an academy founded by abolitionist Presbyterian minister John Rankin in Ripley, Ohio.

becoming known as a hotbed of abolitionist sentiment. Rankin, a Presbyterian minister with intense eyes and a firm jaw, had left the South because of his unpopular views on slavery. "I consider involuntary slavery a never failing fountain of the grossest immorality . . . ," he had declared, "it hangs like the mantle of night over our republic, and shrouds its rising glories." Ultimately, the Ohio represented the river Jordan for African American slaves seeking freedom, and Ripley became a stop on the Underground Railroad.

ULYSSES BOARDED WITH R. Marion Johnson, a tanner living on Second Street, and made himself at home by teaching Betty Osborn, the Johnsons' cook, how to turn out the best buckwheat cakes, his mother's specialty.

At school, Ulysses, dressed in butternut jeans, sat at a double desk with W. B. Campbell. His seatmate remembered Ulysses as "not much of a talker but quiet and serious." Campbell watched, admiring, as Ulysses excelled once again at drawing horses on his slate. The new boy participated in the sports and games, including wrestling, but was not "quarrelsome, never saw him fight."

At first glance, Ulysses often came across with his mother's impassive exterior, but people who took time to get to know him discovered a great depth of caring. Campbell's chief memory of Ulysses at Rankin's academy was that he was respected as "a great fellow to stick to his friends."

This academy also offered a debating club, the Eromathean Society. Some of the topics included "Are men raised to eminence more by circumstances than intellect?" "Is there more pleasure in married life or in the single life?" and "Have slaveholders the right to take back their fugitive slaves after they have escaped into the state of Ohio?"

One classmate, Ben Johnson, said of Ulysses, "He was a great hand to ask questions, and I think I have heard him ask a million."

Despite his curiosity, Ulysses recalled, "I was not studious in habit." Allowing for Ulysses's lifelong self-deprecation, there appears to be some truth in his confession that he "did not make progress enough to compensate for the outlay for board and tuition."

IN THE SUMMER of 1838, as Ulysses approached his seventeenth birthday, his father announced, "I reckon you are now old enough to go to work in the beam-house" in addition to his schooling.

The most repulsive part of the tanning process took part in the beam-house. *Beamhouse* derives from an ancient practice of hanging the hide over a curved log or table known as a "beam" for the arduous process of de-hairing. In the beamhouse, workers removed flesh and hair from raw hides, wielding long knives for this tough and unpleasant task.

Ulysses responded, "Well, father, this tanning is not the kind of work I like. I'll work at it here, though, if you wish me to, until I am one-and-twenty, but you may depend upon it, I'll never work a day longer at it after that." With these words, Ulysses voiced his generation's fealty to a father's wishes for a son but at the same time declared his determination to chart his own life path.

Jesse replied, "My son, I don't want you to work at it *now,* if you don't like it, and don't mean to stick to it. I want you to work at whatever you like and intend to follow. Now, what do you think you would like?"

Ulysses responded, "I'd like to be a farmer, or a down-the-river trader, or get an education."

Acknowledging that Ulysses did not want to follow him into the family business, Jesse expanded his vision for his son's future. He did not need to look far to find an alternative possibility for "my Ulysses."

Jesse was aware that Jacob Ammen, Dan's older brother, had attended the new military academy in New York, where he had graduated with honors in 1831. Jake had returned to Georgetown in the summer of 1837, having resigned from the army in order to take a teaching job at Bacon College in Kentucky.

Jesse understood that attending West Point did not commit a boy to a life in the military. Because it was one of only two engineering schools in the nation, graduates often resigned to pursue more lucrative careers in business or in newly developing railroads. Besides, since West Point was funded by the government, Jesse knew the four years of education for Ulysses would be free.

Unbeknownst to Ulysses, his father had been working his political contacts to secure an appointment for his son. Prospects were not promising. Thomas Hamer, congressman for Brown County, had "the right of nomination" but had already given the appointment to Bart Bailey, son of George and Jane Bailey, who lived up the street from the Grants. The families, starting with the fathers, were friends but also competitors for Georgetown distinction. Even the Bailey home, still standing today with its prominent columns, seemed to compete with Grant's home. Bart had a reputation in Georgetown as a brilliant boy, outshining Ulysses in school.

Bart Bailey left for West Point in early summer 1837, ready to make his parents and Georgetown proud. But events did not go as expected. In January 1838 he resigned, and his father enrolled him in a private military school so he could prepare to retake the entrance exams. Unfortunately, young Bailey's problems were more than academic—he was charged with making "false reports and representations." His second resignation was accepted by the academy on November 13, 1838. Dr. Bailey, deeply disappointed, did not allow his son to return home to Georgetown.

When Ulysses returned from Ripley for the Christmas holidays, he met Mrs. Jane Bailey on the street and was told Bart's sad story.

Despite Bart's resignation, however, Jesse still faced an obstacle to his hopes for Ulysses. He and Hamer, once intimate friends, had earlier found themselves in an angry disagreement over Andrew Jackson, especially the president's removal of public funds from the Second Bank of the United States. In the heat of the 1832 congressional campaign, Jesse wrote in the *Castigator,* "Mr. Hamer would do well to try to remove the beam from his own eye, before he picks the mote from his neighbor's." As for the decade of friendship between the two men, Jesse challenged, "And I can assure him, he is at perfect liberty, to withdraw it from me."

So he decided to bypass Hamer as his son's sponsor to West Point and instead petitioned Thomas Morris, the senator from Ohio. In February 19, 1839, Jesse heard back from Morris: only Hamer was authorized to make such an appointment.

That day, Jesse, burying seven years of estrangement, wrote Hamer. Acknowledging that "your consent will be necessary to enable him to obtain the appointment," he conceded, "I have thought it advisable to consult you on the subject." He approached his request gingerly: "If you have no other person in view for the appointment, & feel willing to consent to the appointment of Ulysses, you will please signify that consent to the department."

Ohio congressman Thomas Hamer nominated young Ulysses for an appointment to West Point in 1839.

Congressman Hamer, there then being no other applicant, wrote Jesse informing him he would nominate Ulysses. He added, "Why didn't you apply to me sooner?" With the stroke of his pen, Hamer "healed the breach" with Jesse.

Hamer, in a hurry to meet the deadline for nominations, wrote Secretary of War Joel R. Poinsett asking for the appointment of "Ulysses Simpson Grant." (Hamer probably assumed Ulysses's middle name was Simpson, which he knew to be the maiden name of Ulysses's mother.)

Only one problem remained: Ulysses knew nothing of these events. Finally, Jesse read him Congressman Hamer's letter and then said, "I believe you are going to receive the appointment."

"What appointment?" Ulysses asked, puzzled.

"To West Point. I have applied for it."

"But I won't go."

The father replied that he thought Ulysses would go.

Ulysses remembered his reaction distinctly: "*I thought so too, if he did.*"

Ulysses made it clear he did not want the appointment, but he was willing if his father wanted him to go. His response speaks loudly to child-parent roles in the nineteenth century.

AT AGE SEVENTEEN, Ulysses, by now a rugged, freckle-faced youth, tipped the scale at 117 pounds but was barely five feet tall—the minimum height for West Point. Although he could be fast in mental arithmetic, he was slow when it came to public speaking. Ulysses was at his best as a problem solver—in mental arithmetic in school or hitching a never-before-harnessed horse to a sled.

In spring 1839, Ulysses was willing to follow his father's insistence that he attend West Point. But many in Georgetown wondered aloud whether Ulysses would have what it took to succeed.

CHAPTER 3

West Point

Much of the time, I am sorry to say, was devoted to novels.
—Ulysses S. Grant, *Personal Memoirs*

Filled with both anticipation and misgiving, Ulysses prepared to leave Georgetown for West Point in May 1839. His spirits soared as he imagined the adventure of the travel that lay ahead, but he felt weighed down at the thought of his destination.

During Ulysses's last days at home, Thomas Walker, a local craftsman, made him a handsome trunk. But when he saw it, he was dismayed. Walker had finished it by riveting the initials *H.U.G.* in brass tacks on the cover. Ulysses told his cousin Jimmy Marshall that he worried his West Point classmates would call him HUG: "The boys would plague me about it." The initials were reversed to *U.H.G.*

On May 15, he said goodbye to his parents and brothers and sisters. Neighbors gathered on the central square to bid farewell. Family and friends waved as he caught the stage to Ripley.

From there, Ulysses boarded a steamer that took him east on the broad Ohio River to Pittsburgh. With no schedule to follow, the side-wheeler would run at its own pace, picking up people or parcels at any place and at any time. He was on his way, and it was exciting.

"I always had a great desire to travel," Grant acknowledged. Now, traveling to West Point would give him the opportunity to visit two of the great cities of the continent—Philadelphia and New York City. Equally exciting, he would be journeying by means of the latest innovations wrought by the transportation revolution in the early decades of the nineteenth century.

After three days on the Ohio River, Ulysses arrived in Pittsburgh. Forty years earlier, his grandfather Noah, and his father, Jesse, then a boy of five, had passed by this same place as they traveled west to make their home in Ohio. In 1839, approaching twenty thousand residents, Pittsburgh had grown into the largest city west of the Alleghenies.

From Pittsburgh, Ulysses had a choice of taking the overland stage, speedy at eight to nine miles an hour but sure to jangle your bones, or traveling on the newer (but slower) canal boats. Familiar with jostling stages, he chose to glide to Harrisburg, Pennsylvania's capital, by canal: "This gave a better opportunity of enjoying the fine scenery of Western Pennsylvania."

The Erie Canal, built in New York between 1817 and 1825, spurred Pennsylvania to build its own canal system to remain competitive for people, farming, and industry. Ulysses traveled east from Pittsburgh on a patchwork of waterways. He may even have purchased a traveler's pocket map, which allowed the 1830s traveler to trace his route.

In Harrisburg, where the Susquehanna River waters stretched almost a mile across, he boarded a train for Philadelphia, "the first I had ever seen." What an experience! "I thought the perfection of rapid transit had been reached." The train, at top speed, could reach eighteen miles an hour. To the boy from a small Ohio town, "this seemed like annihilating space."

In Philadelphia, Ulysses stayed with the Hare family, Elizabeth, Sarah, and Silas, unmarried cousins on his mother's side. Although in Georgetown friends called him "quiet," Elizabeth found Ulysses a good talker as he entertained them with stories of his life in Ohio.

Over the next five days, Ulysses made Silas's hat store on Chestnut Street his hub as his coarse shoes took him over the streets of Philadelphia, bringing a later reprimand from his father for "dallying by the way so long." Philadelphia, home of the birth of the nation, could tantalize the curiosity of any young man. Ulysses remembered that he "saw about every street in the city." But beyond that cursory remark, did he say why he stayed for almost a week?

He "attended the theatre." Behind this succinct comment lies a larger, unexplored, story.

Although there is no way of knowing which theatre performance he attended, two dramas drawing rave reviews in Philadelphia at that time were by the English novelist Edward Bulwer (he added his mother's surname, "Lytton," later in life). Ulysses may have attended *Richelieu,* the popular Bulwer play about the cardinal who, as a statesman, foiled a conspiracy against the French throne. Fresh from Ohio, the slate-sketching schoolboy would have been impressed by the splendid backdrop of

Richelieu's room, decorated with heavy arras of gold-tissue figures. One can imagine the seventeen-year-old riveted by the magic of live theater, enthralled by a dramatic model of strong leadership as he anticipated enrolling in West Point.

Ulysses might also have seen a second popular Bulwer play, *The Lady of Lyons,* set in the early years of the French Republic and performed by a renowned cast at the Chestnut Theatre near Silas's hat shop. He could have easily afford the ticket price of 25 cents.

AFTER "DALLYING" IN Philadelphia for five days, Ulysses spent barely a day in New York City. At his hotel, he met young Frederick T. Dent from St. Louis. Dent recalled, "Being both from the west we struck up an acquaintance." Ulysses told Fred he had "an appointment at the Military Academy and I am going up to stand my examination"—which he would have to pass to be admitted.

"So have I," Fred replied, and suggested they go up together.

As much as Ulysses had enjoyed traveling on various conveyances—stage, steamer, canal, and rail—his journey had been accompanied by a sense of foreboding. "I would have been glad to have had a steamboat or railroad collision, or any other accident happen, by which I might have received a temporary injury sufficient to make me ineligible, for a time, to enter the Academy." Unfortunately, he mused, "nothing of the *kind* occurred, and I had to face the music."

Ulysses and Fred traveled by steamer fifty-five miles north up the Hudson River to West Point, which was situated on a windy, rocky plateau. After disembarking at the South Dock, they clambered up the stairs to the famous West Point Hotel, built in 1829 at the edge of the military reservation. Ulysses registered as "U. H. Grant."

THE ACADEMY THAT Grant entered in 1839 was the product of a political tug-of-war dating back to the Revolutionary War, when colonial armies found themselves dependent on foreign engineers and artillery officers. Proponents of a new military academy had argued that it would remedy that situation by producing engineers. Other voices, mindful that their struggling nation relied on an all-volunteer army to fight courageously, felt wary of formalizing a military institute that promoted the traditional European standing army model, which had been known to overthrow the very government it had been trained to protect.

Thomas Jefferson, the nation's third president, had opposed establish-

Ulysses would attend West Point, situated on a plain overlooking the Hudson River, from 1839 to 1843.

ing a military institute in the 1790s, but after being elected president in 1800, he took a fresh look. He recognized that the proposed academy would be able to offer a free military education to families who did not have the means to send their sons to college. And he overcame his government's fears concerning a standing army by assuring Congress that officers educated at the academy would serve the interests of the new democratic Republic. In the end, he signed the Military Peace Establishment Act of 1802, creating the United States Military Academy at West Point.

The academy endured an initial fifteen years of mismanagement before President James Monroe, a leader with military experience in the Revolutionary War, named Colonel Sylvanus Thayer to be its new superintendent in 1817. Thayer had graduated first in his class at Dartmouth in 1807 and earned his commission in the Corps of Engineers in 1808 after studying one year at West Point. Following the Napoleonic Wars, Thayer was sent by Secretary of War James Monroe to France to study the curriculum of the École Polytechnique. The French school would become the model for reshaping the academy under Thayer's leadership.

Thayer would earn the title "Father of the Military Academy." Destined to serve longer than any other superintendent at West Point—

seventeen years—Thayer deserves credit for raising the stature of the academy. Although he departed in 1833, his spirit and ideas hovered everywhere when Ulysses arrived six years later.

AFTER STAYING THE night at the West Point Hotel, Ulysses went the next day to register. Having decided to reverse his first two names, he reported to the adjutant, presented his deposit of $48, and signed the register "Ulysses Hiram Grant." By transposing his two names, he believed he could start afresh at West Point—no more HUG.

To his surprise, his name was challenged. After checking the official list, the adjutant told the young man standing before him the records showed clearly that a Ulysses Simpson Grant from Ohio was to be enrolled in the entering class.

Ulysses protested, unaware that Congressman Hamer had bungled his name. The adjutant informed Ulysses that any changes to his name would have to be approved by the secretary of war.

All right. If the government would accept his name only as U. S. Grant, he determined he would still sign his personal correspondence U. Hiram Grant or Ulysses. He received the *Book of Regulations* and started for the Barracks. He had not taken many steps before he heard mocking yells: "What an animal." "Who is your tailor?" His homemade western clothes marked him out for derision.

As Ulysses and other first-year cadets registered, gray-coated cadets clustered around the bulletin board to scan the list of newcomers. One fourth-year cadet, a slim young man from Ohio with red hair and blue eyes, wrote later, "I remember seeing his name on the bulletin board, where all the names of the newcomers were posted." William Tecumseh Sherman, three years ahead of Grant, recalled, "I ran my eye down the columns, and there saw 'U.S. Grant.' A lot of us began to make up names to fit the initials. One said: 'United States Grant.' Another: 'Uncle Sam Grant.' A third: 'Sam Grant.'"

Sam Grant. That name stuck. Over the next several days, catcalls followed wherever he went. Shouts descended from barrack windows—"Salute, Mister Grant"—"Send him home"—"Left, right, left, right." His name became the butt of jokes—"You're a hell of an Uncle Sam."

In June, Sam stood for his entrance examinations. Having heard tales that 30 percent of the applicants never made it past this examination, he wondered what to expect. He faced an examining board of thirteen officers, but the exam was straightforward enough—reading, writing, spelling, arithmetic. He passed.

One of his rewards for passing became the privilege of wearing a cadet uniform—purchased from his own meager funds. Sam bought an account book for 36 cents and from that day forward kept a meticulous record of his expenditures at West Point. His coat of "Cadet Gray" cost $10.88. He could not wait to wear the big, flat Morocco hats—what the cadets called "gigtops"—which cost $2.44. He bought six pairs of pantaloons but was unsure about them. As he wrote home to Ohio, the pantaloons were "as tight to my skin as the bark to tree, and if I do not walk *military*—that is, if I bend over quickly or run, they are very apt to crack with a report as loud as a pistol."

For entering students, the two-month summer encampment on the plain at West Point was a boot camp to start developing them as professional military officers. Day after day, drill after drill, in the roiling sun, sleeping in tents, all Sam's apprehensions about life at the academy seemed to come true. He quickly discovered that as an incoming first-year student, he and his classmates were the lower than low in a military hierarchy.

He wrote his cousin R. McKinstry Griffith, "First, I slept for two months upon one single pair of blankets." Probably after reading what he wrote, he added, "Now this sounds romantic and you may think it very easy. But I tell you what coz, it is *tremendous hard*." He confessed he missed his home and friends. "I wish some of the pretty girls of Bethel were here just so I might look at them." Sam Grant, a small boy from the West with a new name thrust upon him, felt lonely.

But Sam Grant survived the first summer obstacle course. He did not react resentfully, as some of his classmates did when they met abuse at every hour of the long, hot summer days. He kept his head down and his wits about him. Quiet and tough, he did not need to fight back.

After sleeping outside on the Academy Plain for eight weeks, he climbed the stairs of the North Barracks to his first-year room. The best part was the window in the eave where he could view the lovely surrounding countryside. He drew Rufus Ingalls as his roommate, two years older, a high-spirited boy from Maine.

At the beginning of the fall term, Sam shared his early impressions with his Ohio cousin: "It is decidedly the most beautiful place that I have ever seen; here are hills and dales, rocks and river; all pleasant to look upon." He told Griffith that "from the window near I can see the Hudson; that far famed, that beautiful river with its bosom studded with hundreds of snow sails." Looking from his room in another direction, Sam saw history. "I can see Fort Putnam frowning far above; a stern monument of a sterner age which seems placed there on purpose to tell us of the glorious deeds of our fathers and to bid us remember *their* sufferings—to follow their examples."

Sam punctuated his letter with humorous, self-deprecating views of himself. "If you were to see me at a distance, the first question you would ask would be, 'is that a Fish or an animal'?" He concluded, "When I come home in two years (if I live) the way I shall astonish you *natives* will be *curious*. I hope you won't take me for a Baboon." At the beginning of his four years at West Point, he had entered a strange new world.

THE WEST POINT Grant entered incarnated two objectives. First, future officers were to be shaped through an academic curriculum reflecting the technical emphasis of French military schools. A mastery of French thus became essential for aspiring officers to read the military literature. Thayer believed France to be the "sole repository of military science." He had purchased many books on military theory and practice while in France.

West Point understood itself to be primarily an engineering school. During Grant's four years at West Point, nearly 70 percent of his classes would be concentrated in engineering, mathematics, and science. In the curriculum before the Civil War, cadets studied military strategy for merely eight class periods in their final year.

The liberal arts, especially the study of English and American literature, went missing in action. The heavy technical emphasis at West Point would be challenged from time to time, but Thayer and the superintendents who followed argued that mathematics and engineering promoted reasoning power. Future officers like Grant would need this kind of mental discipline in the pressures of war.

The second objective was the creation of disciplined professional military officers. Sam found himself living a Spartan existence within an authoritarian structure of training and discipline. His role models were the teachers, nearly all of whom saw themselves first as military officers. Their purpose in an academy insulated from the outside world was to create a homogeneous corps of cadets who lived and breathed the military ethos. Regimentation took place even in the classroom, where cadets sat according to their academic rank. Ceaseless drilling became the means to create both commitment and cohesion.

IN HIS FIRST year, Sam excelled in mathematics. However, he struggled with French. The strong dose of French weighed heavily in the first- and second-year ranking system. Students were not asked to speak French but were expected to be able to translate French into English.

Because the professional military officer united academics with military training and discipline, a cadet's class rank would be a combination of both. For Sam, who had almost never been reprimanded at home, entrance into the world of "crimes," as they were called, meant a radical adjustment. Seven categories of crimes contributed to a system of demerits that could be added to a cadet's record.

From five A.M. to ten P.M., from roll call to inspection to drill to meals to class to study to evening parade, Sam quickly learned that every occasion offered the possibility of acquiring the dreaded demerits. The list was endless: there were prohibitions against drinking, tobacco, "play[ing] at cards or other games of chance," cooking or preparing food in one's room, keeping "a waiter, dog, or horse."

WHILE SAM STRUGGLED to adjust to life at West Point, a struggle was taking place in Washington among politicians who wanted to cut the ties between the national government and the thirty-seven-year-old academy and those who wished the bond to continue. Andrew Jackson, during his two terms as president from 1829 to 1837, derided what he called the elitism of the officer corps graduating at West Point. His public stance may have been influenced by earlier attempts to persuade Superintendent Thayer to disregard regulations and appoint two nephews to the engineers and the artillery. Thayer refused.

A bill presented in Congress in December 1839 sought to abolish the academy. Sam expressed mixed feelings about the bill: "I saw in this an honorable way to obtain a discharge, and read the debates with much interest, but with impatience at the delay in taking action, for I was selfish enough to favor the bill."

AN UNEXPECTED PLEASURE in Sam's second year came with a new academy course on horsemanship. In horseback riding, he could be himself. Because of the dirt and dust of riding, the cadets were excused from wearing their uniforms. Sam strode from his small dorm room, dressed in old clothes and riding spurs, suddenly free as he galloped confidently about the large West Point grounds and beyond.

The best horsemen at the academy traditionally hailed from the South, where horseback riding was a way of life, but this slight youth from the West quickly won his classmates' admiration. In an echo of his experiences at Georgetown, fractious horses began to be brought to Sam to gentle, harness, and ride. Classmate Ingalls said Sam's success with horses was "not by punishing the animal . . . but by patience and tact, and his skill in making the creature know what he wanted to have it do." The small United States Army, consisting of barely eight thousand men, had only a solitary cavalry or dragoon unit. In the early 1840s, the role of mounted horsemen was still in its adolescence in terms of battle deployment. Sam dreamed of joining the dragoons upon graduation—but it all would depend upon his grades.

AT THE END of Sam's first year, in a class reduced by attrition from seventy-three to sixty, he finished with a rank of twenty-seven. He earned a ranking of sixteen in mathematics but only forty-nine in French. In his second year, he stayed in about the same place, ranking twenty-four out of a class that had shrunk to fifty-three.

He would complete his four years ranking twenty-first in a graduating class of thirty-nine students. This has been used to measure Grant's intellectual abilities, but in fact the narrative of his intellectual evolution at West Point has been left untold. Later in life he wrote, "Much of the time, I am sorry to say, was devoted to novels, but not those of a trashy sort."

His apology may have been rooted in faculty attitudes toward novels. The West Point faculty considered popular novels to be "frivolous."

He does not say "now and then" or "occasionally." Sam Grant spent considerable time reading novels.

He tells us, "I read all of Bulwer's then published, Cooper's, Marryat's, Scott's, Washington Irving's works, Lever's, and many others that I do not now remember."

He is quite specific: "I read all of Bulwer's then published." Typical of Grant, he points in a direction, but in an understated way. With these clues, even at a distance, it may be possible to track down his reading lists and ask what he might have learned from reading these novels.

THE ACADEMIC CULTURE of West Point in the 1830s and 1840s was not conducive to book lovers. Sam quickly discovered the library was not primarily for students. The library stood as a central building on campus. Although Superintendent Thayer and those who followed him accumulated a fair-sized library, access remained mainly for faculty and staff. Library resources were placed at their disposal to help them advance in their careers. The *Book of Regulations* stated, "Cadets shall be allowed to take from the Library such books only as are calculated to assist them in their

Class studies." Furthermore, "No Cadet shall draw more than one volume at a time, nor keep any volume longer than one week." Once inside the library, "No Cadet shall enter beyond the Librarian's table, or take down any book from its place." Translation: No leisure reading.

He also discovered the library was heavily weighted toward the engineering curriculum. In 1833, the Board of Visitors submitted a report on the library's academic content, commending its "very valuable collection of works adapted to the peculiar objects of this Institution. It is rich in works on Military Science and on Civil Engineering." The report did admit that "in works of polite literature it is as yet rather deficient." It would remain "deficient" six years later.

But students, even as they were learning the military codes of conduct, were getting skilled at circumventing academy rules. Sam and his classmates pooled their meager resources to buy novels and then passed them around in their own informal lending library.

SAM BEGAN HIS list of novelists with Edward Bulwer, including the two that had been turned into plays in Philadelphia. In 1834, two years after Sir Walter Scott's death, the *American Quarterly Review* hailed Bulwer as "without doubt, the most popular writer now living." Decades later, Grant remembered he read all of Bulwer's novels, suggesting how important they were to the young cadet.

By 1839, Bulwer had published eleven novels. In his first novel, *Falkland* (1827), a hero must discover the disparity between outward appearances and inner realities, the difference between "the fair show and the good deed." In *Pelham* (1828), the hero begins a quest to discover what true individuality is in a world where most people hide their true selves. Sam was just then living in a military world where emotions were to be subdued.

In his next four novels—*The Disowned* (1828), *Devereux* (1829), *Paul Clifford* (1830), and *Eugene Aram* (1832)—Bulwer focused on the contrast that emerges between the superficialities of the prevailing culture and the depths of the human heart. Just as Sam developed a disdain for West Point's disciplinary hearings, he may have been reading Bulwer's crime thriller, *Paul Clifford,* where in a famous courtroom scene the reader is invited to see how misleading appearances can be and therefore change one's perspective.

Bulwer's reputation would decline in the twentieth century, in part because of the didactic injunctions to his readers that permeated his next four novels. In *Godolphin* (1833), *Ernest Maltravers* (1837), *Alice* (1838), and

Zanoni (1842), he invited the reader to look into himself for similarities with the characters.

These novels, read after hours in his room, suggest Bulwer's ideal audience. He wrote in *The Student* (1836), "Our imagination, kept rigidly from the world, is the Eden in which we walk with God. . . . We learn thus to make our own dreams and thoughts our companion." His addressing the reader directly may have seemed to the young cadet like listening to a virtual tutor.

SAM WAS ALSO attracted to Sir Walter Scott, pioneer of the historical novel. His heroes, like Bulwer's, are young men who reluctantly leave home and, through dramatic testing, learn to judge people more perceptively. These journeys are set in realistic historical settings where the young heroes often observe military conflicts.

Sam probably read Scott's Waverley novels, immensely popular with young people. Lonely Edward Waverley, when retreating into his uncle's library, finds himself caught up in the plots and themes of romances found in the books discovered there. Waverley would appeal to a curious young man realizing he must also move from reading to participating in the real world.

As in Bulwer, in Scott Sam found himself addressed by first-person narrators speaking directly to the reader. Scott's lessons were overt. Narrators give advice, as do characters. In *Rob Roy* (1817), Frank Osbaldistone, a newer kind of Celtic hero who is aware of his flaws, observes his own anxiety: "I suppose that all men, in situations of peculiar doubt and difficulty, when they have exercised their reason to little purpose, are apt, in a sort of despair, to abandon the reins to their imagination." Sam encountered in reading Scott young men learning to be more discerning about people's appearance and motives. Heroes, seeing complexities, vacillate in making difficult decisions. But the hero is law-abiding and steered by an internal moral compass. In the midst of conflict, the hero wants to be a peacemaker.

IN READING JAMES Fenimore Cooper, Sam turned to the first major American novelist. Cooper shared many traits with Bulwer and Scott, writing about young men on journeys, learning about themselves and the changing world around them.

Growing up in Cooperstown, New York, which his father had founded, young James roamed the virgin forests next to Otsego Lake and developed a love of nature that is reflected in his novels. The hero of

Cooper's five-volume *Leatherstocking Tales*—Natty Bumppo—is honest and perceptive. Each of Cooper's novels is a saga of a young male rite of passage. In *The Pathfinder* (1840), Natty speaks words that could have been spoken to Sam Grant: "Now, when I find a man all fair words, I look close to his deeds; for when the heart is right and rally [*sic*] intends to do good, it is generally satisfied to let the conduct speak, instead of the tongue."

Cooper's vivid military descriptions would have appealed to the young cadet. Cooper, an officer in the New York State Militia, was praised by contemporary critics for his battle scenes in *Lionel Lincoln* (1824). This fast-paced novel contains a lucid description of the Battle of Breed's Hill, where Grant's grandfather Noah may have fought at the beginning of the Revolutionary War.

BESIDES HIS DELIGHT in the extracurricular art of novels, Sam thrived in the one artistic endeavor included in the curriculum. In his second year, he studied topographical and anatomical drawing each weekday afternoon for two hours. A year later, he flourished in the class on landscape drawing. These courses took him far beyond his youthful enthusiasm for sketching horses on his slate.

How did drawing come to be included in the curriculum? The answer was utilitarian. The faculty reasoned that the cadets would one day need to sketch the battlefields where they would exercise command. Their ability to draw the terrain accurately, with full details, could mean success or failure in the ebb and flow of battle. Grant's arts skill would be tested years later on some distant battlefield.

Sam was fortunate to study with Robert Walter Weir. During his forty-two years at West Point, Weir would become one of America's most renowned painters, most famous for *Embarkation of the Pilgrims,* depicting Pilgrim families congregating around their pastor, John Robinson, in a shipboard farewell service on the *Speedwell,* before they departed from Holland for the New World. The painting can be seen today in the Rotunda of the United States Capitol in Washington, D.C.

Under Weir, Sam produced pen-and-ink drawings of Italian cityscapes, exhibiting a precision that was the object of the exercise. Next he painted with watercolors, portraying people strolling in colorful marketplaces in Europe. The young artist (not surprisingly) rendered a draft horse with its nose in a feedbag, complete with minute details of the shape of the horse.

Another sympathetic oil painting is of a Native American—Sam

While studying topographical and anatomical drawing with Robert W. Weir at West Point, Grant painted this large draft horse in 1842. Known for his remarkable riding ability, Grant brought his own intimate understanding of horses to this watercolor.

might have been reading Cooper—with his wife and dog, bartering with a trader. Sam captured the rounded shoulders of the mother breast-feeding her child. He used soft hues of orange, yellow, brown, and blue accentuated by the colored blanket held by the merchant.

While at times luminous in their shadowy style, Grant's paintings are striking not for their technique, but for his desire to enter into the humanity of his subjects—including the draft horse. We do not know how many paintings he composed at West Point, but nine from his student days exist today.

SAM WAS PARTICULARLY struck with two military leaders among the many he encountered at West Point. One highlight was the visit of General Winfield Scott, hero of the War of 1812, who reviewed the cadets. A giant of a man at six feet five inches tall, he was known everywhere as "Old Fuss and Feathers" because of his liking for colorful uniforms. "With his commanding figure, his quite colossal size and showy uniform, I thought him the finest specimen of manhood my eyes had ever beheld, and the most to be envied."

Captain Charles F. Smith, a fine-looking man with a drooping mustache, also impressed Sam. Descended from eminent forebears—college presidents and Presbyterian clergymen—he embodied the position he held through his martial bearing. Appointed to the faculty in 1831, Smith had become commandant of cadets in 1838. "I regarded General Scott and Captain C. F. Smith, the Commandant of Cadets, as the two men most to be envied in the nation." Sam, by now looking forward to a military career, was seeking military models.

ALTHOUGH SAM STUDIED alongside cadets who would become renowned two decades later on both sides of the Civil War, he made friends slowly. But if his circle of close friends at West Point remained relatively small—the academy hovered at nearly 250 cadets—he knew about most of his fellow cadets, even if he did not know them personally.

In Sam's first year, the senior class included two inseparable friends who could not have been more different. Ohioan Bill Sherman made his presence known by his impulsiveness and penchant for humor and high jinks. Sherman's friend George H. Thomas, from Virginia, well built and serious about his studies, was nicknamed "General Washington."

As cadets talked about members of other classes, they speculated about who would stay and who would leave the military after gradua-

This painting of a Native American trader, a dog, and a woman breast-feeding was one of Grant's favorites among his own work. He would keep it in his possession until the 1870s.

tion. The ultimate question was who might one day achieve the rank of general. If cadets had a vote on "Most Likely to Succeed," the winner would have been William S. "Rosy" Rosecrans in the class of 1842. Everyone knew him as a talker who backed up his talk with good grades and an excellent record of military behavior.

One of Sam's best friends was also in the class of 1842. James "Pete" Longstreet, born into a well-connected farming family, grew up as a privileged son of Georgia and Alabama. At six feet two inches tall, with brown hair and blue eyes, he towered over Sam.

Longstreet remembered Sam Grant as a "rather small boy of country manners." The two were "fast friends" from the start, brought together by a natural sense of being outsiders. Longstreet believed Sam had "a hesitancy in presenting his own claims; a taciturnity born of his modesty."

Possessed of enormous physical strength, Longstreet excelled at sports, unlike his friend. For example, the cadets played an early form of football; Longstreet reveled in the game, whereas Sam, he said, "was not heavy enough to be good in the rush." And it was true that Sam's loneliness was compounded by the fact that he was not large enough or strong enough to compete in the rough-and-tumble athletics popular at the academy. However, on a different playing field, the two friends were able to commiserate in equal measure: like Sam, Longstreet struggled with academics, finding himself more often at the foot than at the head of his class.

One year behind Sam, the class of 1844 included the handsome but taciturn Simon Bolivar Buckner, a native of Kentucky, and Winfield Scott Hancock of Pennsylvania, whose outgoing personality brought him popularity.

In Sam's final year, West Point's first-year class included one cadet hard to miss and another who could be easily overlooked. George B. McClellan, raised in an affluent Philadelphia family, was the youngest cadet, entering at age fifteen. Homespun Thomas T. Jackson, from the Virginia mountains, arrived at West Point with little formal schooling but determined to receive a West Point education that would prepare him for a military career.

Sam's friends in his own class of 1843 included Rufus Ingalls; George Deshon ("Dragon") from Connecticut, Sam's second-year roommate and an outstanding student; William B. Franklin of Pennsylvania, who would graduate first in the class; Isaac F. Quinby ("Nykins") from New Jersey, who would finish first in engineering; and Joseph J. Reynolds of Indiana, who shared Sam's dexterity in mathematics. This group included some of the best scholars in the class, and almost every one of them ranked ahead of Sam.

Sam seemed to have little interest in romance with the young women who visited West Point for special social occasions. Daniel M. Frost, one year behind Sam at West Point, recalled, "He had no facility in conversation with the ladies, a total absence of elegance."

In Sam's final year, he roomed with Fred Dent. Unlike Sam, Fred had been raised in a pro-slavery family. One afternoon, so the story goes, when they failed to remember their agreement not to talk about politics and slavery, the boys stripped off their shirts, ready to fight. Just as they began, the ridiculousness of the fight surprised Sam, who burst out laughing, thus ending their altercation.

SAM PROTESTED AGAINST yet another example of regimentation: "This is not exactly republican." The dreaded regulations stated, "Every member of the Academic Staff and Cadet shall attend divine service on Sunday." The stone chapel, built two years before Sam's arrival, was of Renaissance Revival design with a Roman Doric portico—so different from the Methodist meetinghouses he had experienced in Ohio. He wrote his cousin back in Ohio, "We are not only obliged to go to church, but must *march* there by companies." Cadets sat for two hours on backless benches, listening to what they complained were dry sermons.

The Episcopal Church functioned as the de facto established church of the academy. No one bothered to defend this role except to suggest that the Episcopal Church was the denomination of the officers in charge and therefore deemed the best Christian tradition to help shape young men into officers and gentlemen.

The Reverend Martin P. Parks, appointed chaplain in 1840, was just then navigating a journey from Low Church Methodism to High Church Episcopalianism to—some cadets gossiped—Roman Catholicism.

Protests against required chapel took the form of groaning and shuffling during services. Nonverbal protests brought a stern response: "It has been brought to the notice of the Commandant that some cadets are in the habit of spitting tobacco spittle on the floor of the church on Sunday morning to such a degree as to render part of it unfit for use in the afternoon." Sam, used to worshipping in the voluntary tradition of Methodism, resisted any form of religious coercion.

"GRANT'S MENTAL MACHINE is of the powerful low-pressure class, which condenses its own steam and consumes its own smoke; and which pushes steadily forward and drives all obstacles before it." So spoke Dennis Hart Mahan, professor of civil and military engineering and the art of war and West Point's best-known faculty member, about Sam as a student.

Son of an Irish immigrant, Mahan graduated first in his class from West Point in 1824. He lived in Europe for four years, studying at L'École d'application de l'artillerie (the School for Engineers and Artillerists) in Metz, France. Then, traveling widely, he observed the latest developments in water, roads, and the new phenomenon: the railroad. He received a permanent appointment to the faculty in 1832. Mahan, who taught at West Point for his whole career, was just beginning to stake out his place of eminence when Grant arrived in 1839.

Sam took several of Mahan's courses, including "Military and Civil Engineering and the Science of War," a capstone course in his final academic year. He appreciated the short, slender, demanding teacher with the high-pitched voice. Mahan cross-examined students who arrived unprepared, but he also praised students who did their lessons well, and he was one of the professors who believed in the humanities. He encouraged the "self-study" of history and literature in a cadet's room.

IN SAM'S FINAL months at West Point, he continued acquiring novels. When the informal student library did not have Charles Lever's *The Confessions of Harry Lorrequer* and *Charles O'Malley,* he wrote the publisher, enclosing $2 and specifying that he wanted the illustrated editions. When he did not receive them right away, he wrote one week later, "I would desire you to send me the works as soon as possible."

Four decades after West Point, Grant remembered the name of this author most people would not rank with Scott and Cooper.

Lever's *The Confessions of Harry Lorrequer* is about a reluctant military officer. In this comic novel he describes unnecessary military exercises, pokes fun at regulations, and tells stories of regimental capers. As he was ending four years of training for a military career he did not plan to begin, Sam must have enjoyed this spoof highlighting a young officer's ingenuity.

Charles O'Malley celebrates horses as characters and ends with a benediction that must have spoken to Sam in 1843, about to close an important chapter of his life: "Life is marked out in periods in which, like stages in a journey, we rest and repose ourselves, casting a look now back upon the road we have been traveling; now throwing a keener glance toward the path left us."

· · ·

ON A JUNE afternoon, as part of the final graduation exercises, the cadets gathered in the riding hall, a big barn with colorful flags and cavalry sabers displayed on the walls. James B. Fry, a candidate for admission from Illinois, described what happened next. All members of the graduating class performed their final riding exercises in front of Superintendent Richard Delafield, the academic board, and a sizable number of spectators. The collective pounding of the horses' hooves sounded like the beating of drums. Exercises finished, the cadets formed a line with their horses at the center of the hall.

Sergeant Henry Hershberger, the riding master, went to the bar and raised it nearly a foot, higher than a man's head. Then he called out, "Cadet Grant." A murmur hummed through the crowd.

With that, as Fry would write, "a clean-faced, slender young fellow, weighing about one hundred and twenty pounds, dashed from the ranks on a powerfully built chestnut-sorrel horse, and galloped down the opposite side of the hall."

All the cadets recognized the horse, York, and knew that they could not ride the powerful, long-legged animal. A classmate, Charles Hamilton, had warned Sam, "That horse will kill you some day." To which Sam had shrugged and replied, "Well, I can't die but once."

As the audience hushed in anticipation, Sam maneuvered the horse to the far end of the riding hall to begin his command performance. The crowd gasped as the small rider and the huge horse raced toward the bar. With a great leap, Sam Grant and York cleared the bar to thundering applause. To Fry it appeared "as if man and beast had been welded together."

"Very well done, sir!" barked riding master Hershberger. With Sam's spectacular jump, the graduating class was dismissed.

IN THE FOUR years since he had entered West Point, Sam had grown from five feet one inch tall to five feet seven inches. However, his more important growth had occurred in matters less measurable.

He had expanded his mental universe beyond the traditional engineering curriculum to the unaccepted world of literature. Reading novels had enlarged the intellectual and emotional scope of Sam's world. He benefited from great authors' tutorials in character development, history, moral dilemmas, and decision making. His peers recognized his literary acumen when, in his final year, the Dialectic Society, the selective West Point literary club, elected him their president. As president, he signed his name "U. H. Grant."

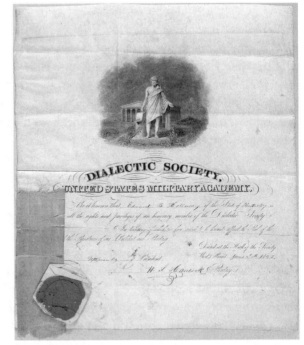

Elected president of the Dialectic Society in his final year, Sam Grant signed his name "U. H. Grant" on this society certificate.

. . .

SAM GRANT EMERGED from his four years at West Point a cadet more sure of himself, even if he was unsure about his long-term future in the military; a young man whose successes at the academy were in art and horsemanship, not in French or engineering; a prospective second lieutenant who, if sometimes still shy and reticent in male social circles and with young women, was growing in self-confidence.

Questions about Grant's intellect lurk at the edges of his graduation ranking: twenty-one in a class of thirty-nine. Was his persistent novel reading the fad of a young man seeking escape from the academy's regimented life? How would he fare in cadet speculations about who would and would not persevere and prosper in a military career? These questions and others would begin to be answered when, after graduation, Ulysses S. Grant received his first military assignment.

CHAPTER 4

"My Dear Julia"

You can have but little idea of the influence you have over me Julia,
even while so far away . . . I am more or less governed by
what I think is your will.

—Ulysses S. Grant to Julia Dent, July 11, 1845

If Sam Grant entered West Point reluctantly, Ulysses S. Grant graduated proudly. With no war on the horizon in the summer of 1843, with
prospects for promotion slow and uncertain in a small peacetime army,
he imagined returning to West Point to teach mathematics as a more attractive option than serving in some far-off frontier fort, protecting settlers traveling west. Prior to the Civil War, no service time was required
of West Point graduates; however, it was expected they would serve for
a period of time.

At graduation, Grant did not know to what unit or location he would
be assigned. When all members of his class were asked to state their choice
of arms and regiments, he put in "first choice, dragoons; second, 4th infantry." Hedging his bets, he gave the West Point tailor instructions for a
uniform for either the dragoons, the mounted regiments, or the Fourth
Infantry. When his measurements were taken, he learned that he'd grown
a full six inches since entering West Point; unfortunately, he was also
down to just 117 pounds, his freshman-year weight, the result of fighting
a terrible cough over the last six months.

Ulysses planned to make the most of his three-month leave before he
had to report for active duty. He headed home, wanting to spend time
with his parents, who had moved to Bethel, Ohio, and friends in Georgetown, not knowing when he would see them again.

While in Ohio he received his first assignment. Because of his lower
class standing, he was placed in the Fourth Infantry, stationed at Jefferson
Barracks, ten miles south of St. Louis, Missouri. Learning of his assign-

ment, "I was impatient to get on my uniform and see how it looked." He "wanted my old school-mates, particularly the girls, to see me in it."

When his uniform finally arrived, he decided to show it off in Cincinnati. Riding proudly into the city, "imagining that everyone was looking at me, with a feeling akin to mine when I first saw General Scott," he encountered a small boy, "bareheaded, barefooted, with dirty and ragged pants," who mocked him. "Soldier! Will you work? 'No, sir-ee; I'll sell my shirt first.'"

Embarrassed by this street urchin, Ulysses retreated to the Bethel family house. Opposite the home stood a stage tavern run by a man with a sense of humor he aimed at Ulysses. The man marched up and down the street dressed in "a pair of sky-blue pantaloons—just the color of my uniform trousers—with a strip of white cotton sheeting sewed down the outside seams in imitation of mine," his "joke" targeting the newly arrived West Point graduate. "I did not appreciate it so highly." Graduates of West Point did not necessarily garner admiration in the early 1840s, when questions about the need for or desirability of a standing army still lingered. Young Grant would not forget these early lessons mocking his fancy army uniform.

IN SEPTEMBER, TRAVELING with Fashion, the handsome brown horse his proud father had given him as a graduation present, Brevet Second Lieutenant Grant made his way from Cincinnati to St. Louis by steamer. In the world of military parlance, "brevet" entitled an officer to hold a rank temporarily without commensurate pay; when a position opened, the "brevet" would be dropped, allowing the officer formally to assume both rank and pay. For a government-sponsored military that lacked a retirement system, "brevet" was also a way both to honor soldiers for meritorious service and keep them in the army. At the time Grant graduated from West Point, second lieutenant positions were limited, so he would have to wait his turn patiently.

He arrived at Jefferson Barracks on September 20, 1843. Established in 1826, the post had been named in honor of President Thomas Jefferson, who died on July 4, 1826, exactly fifty years to the day after the signing of the Declaration of Independence. Situated on seventeen hundred acres next to the Mississippi River, it occupied a splendid location close to the growing city of St. Louis, offering rows of whitewashed barracks with wide verandas bounded by white fences. By 1843, it was home to the largest military force in the United States.

Jefferson Barracks was commanded by Colonel Stephen W. Kearney, a veteran of the War of 1812 who had led explorations of the West. Although he demanded punctuality for roll calls, drills, and meals, Kearney gave the men latitude for social life beyond the barracks, not requiring a written application detailing where they would be.

Grant knew some of his West Point friends had preceded him or would join him soon at Jefferson Barracks. Bob Hazlitt had been assigned to the Fourth Infantry, while Charley Jarvis was in the Third Infantry. James Longstreet, who had come west one year earlier, was also assigned to the Fourth.

Still daydreaming about becoming a teacher, Grant kept his future options open. Shortly after his arrival he wrote Albert E. Church, professor of mathematics at West Point, "requesting him to ask my designation as his assistant, when next a detail had to be made." He was pleased when "the answer from Professor Church was entirely satisfactory." With hope for such an appointment, Grant set out a regular course of study in mathematics "to be pursued in garrison, with regularity, if not persistency." He "read many valuable historical works, besides an occasional novel," continuing the habit he had developed at West Point. Fellow soldier W. W. Smith recalled while Grant "was at Jefferson Barracks he reviewed all his studies. Every day he wrote down in his Ledger, all that he had acquired during that day."

UPON LEARNING OF Ulysses's assignment, Fred Dent, his fourth-year roommate at West Point, encouraged him to call on his father and mother. They were sure to welcome him at their home, White Haven, only five miles from Jefferson Barracks. Fred told his friend that he had two brothers as well as three sisters at White Haven.

Shortly after his arrival at Jefferson Barracks, Ulysses decided to take Fred up on his offer. Dressed in his blue coat with gold buttons, he saddled Fashion and started on the path following gentle Gravois Creek toward White Haven. As he arrived at the Dent home, a little girl, ringlets overflowing her shoulders, ran from the front porch to greet him.

"How do you do, little girl," Ulysses greeted her. "Does Mr. Dent live here?"

Six-year-old Emmy, the youngest of the Dent children, recalled later how she felt embarrassed yet impressed when she first saw the handsome young lieutenant sitting so "gracefully" on his "splendid horse."

"Come, little girl. Can't you answer me? Is this Mr. Dent's house?"

"Yes, sir," tumbled from her mouth.

Ulysses, Emmy, and the little black slave children surrounding her tripped along to the large porch, heading for a tall, imposing figure Ulysses assumed was Colonel Frederick Dent. Fifty-six years old, with steel-gray hair and a beardless face, he wore the long dark coat popular with men of his generation, and in his mouth rested a long-stemmed churchwarden pipe.

He and Ulysses introduced themselves and were soon joined by Dent's wife, Ellen, a slender, pretty woman, along with her fifteen-year-old daughter, Ellen (affectionately called "Nellie"). Julia, the Dents' oldest daughter, was away for the winter in St. Louis, he was told.

No one thought the young officer's visit unusual, for soldiers often rode up from Jefferson Barracks to spend part of their afternoon on the long front porch, where in spring they could enjoy the scent of Mrs. Dent's rosebushes. James Longstreet's mother, Mary Ann Dent Long-street, was a distant relative of the Dents, and he had often enjoyed their hospitality.

Ulysses told the Dents that Fred had been his roommate in their final year at West Point. Pleased, they invited him to stay for the afternoon. Recalling that first meeting, Emmy wrote that young Grant "looked as pretty as a doll."

FREDERICK DENT GREW up in the frontier town of Cumberland in western Maryland. He had acquired the title "Colonel" not in recognition of any military service, but as a popular designation of courtesy. Ellen Bray Wrenshall Dent, born in England, grew up the child of a Methodist minister in western Pennsylvania.

The Dents married in 1814 and moved west to St. Louis in 1816, to an area then called Upper Louisiana. As their family grew, the Dents decided they wanted a summer place in the country, which they purchased in 1820. White Haven, named after an ancestral Maryland tidewater home, grew into a spacious house over time. White Haven was actually beige, not white, with dark brown trim. The banister of solid black walnut can be seen today on the stairs leading to the second floor.

The Colonel gradually acquired more surrounding land, so that when Ulysses first visited, the home sat on 850 acres. In appearance, White Haven seemed more like a western farm than a plantation: visitors found themselves greeted by an anomalous mixture of buffalo skins and Dresden china, and the Colonel often entertained guests dressed in a ruffled shirt, a white tie, and a beaver hat.

The Dents used slave labor in their home and on their farm. In 1830, Dent owned eighteen slaves, half under the age of ten. By 1840, after

White Haven, the Dent family home south of St. Louis, where young Ulysses would meet Julia Dent, would become a center of both hospitality and tension.

several difficult years following the 1837 economic depression, their slave population fell to thirteen. Throughout the 1840s, as his economic fortunes recovered, Dent acquired more slaves, and by 1850 he owned thirty, eighteen female and twelve male.

ULYSSES BEGAN TO visit White Haven once or sometimes twice a week, and Emmy recalled that it was not long before "sister Nellie and I began to wrangle as to which one of us should 'have' him." Since he had grown up with younger sisters, Ulysses enjoyed little Emmy and pretty young Nellie and felt at ease around them. He carried Emmy around on his shoulders, and when she pestered him too much, he and Nellie rode off into the woods on horseback. An uneven path led through elms, oaks, linden, and maple trees, then opened out on a meadow that offered wondrous space for riding.

Ulysses listened patiently as the Colonel, a Jacksonian Democrat, talked southern pro-slavery politics. He frequently expressed anger about the growing menace of northern abolitionists, whom he resented for criticizing the South. Ulysses, whose own father could be overbearing when arguing Whig antislavery politics, had become practiced at self-controlled listening.

JULIA RETURNED TO White Haven in February 1844. Several days after her return, Ulysses rode Fashion north along Gravois Creek to pay one of his regular calls on the Dent family. Before he really knew what happened, he had eyes for Miss Julia only.

Four years younger than Grant, at barely eighteen, Julia Boggs Dent, born January 26, 1826, the first girl after four boys, was by her own admission "necessarily something of a pet." While the Colonel could be stern with his sons, she had learned early how to wrap her father around her small fingers.

Barely five feet tall, with brown eyes, dark brown hair drawn back in a chignon, and skin burnished by her love of the outdoors, she was the plainest of the Dent girls. Young men in St. Louis and at Jefferson Barracks found her attractive because of her sparkle, wit, and fun-loving personality. She had a cast in her right eye (a condition known as "strabismus") that caused it to look up slightly, the result of an accident when an infant. The only photographs of her are from much later in life and fail to capture the radiant young Julia.

Julia grew up in a home that followed Methodist devotional practices passed down from her mother's minister father. Each day centered in a tradition of family prayers. Methodism is a musical piety, and Julia loved to sing Methodist hymns with her fine voice.

Frederick Dent liked nothing better than to read while sitting in a rocking chair on the large porch in the summer. In the winter he sat, contented, reading in an easy chair by a blazing fire for hours. Ellen Dent read aloud to her children. Like her parents, and like Ulysses, Julia was an avid reader.

As a child, Julia joined her brothers in attending a log schoolhouse nestled in the woods about a half mile from their home. She must have shown promise, for in 1837 her father sent her to St. Louis to attend a private boarding school run by P. Mauro and his daughters at Fifth and Market streets. In this school for the daughters of affluent St. Louis families, Julia could take advantage of a broader range of subjects.

There, she furthered her interest in literature. She read Edward Bulwer's *Rienzi* and *Paul Clifford* and Sir Walter Scott's *Ivanhoe* and *Peveril of the Peak*—the same novels Ulysses was reading at West Point. Her female teachers introduced her to the works of women writers, including *The Bandit's Bride* by the fine English author Louisa Sidney Stanhope and *Elizabeth; or, The Exiles of Siberia* by the not-so-fine French writer Sophie Ristaud Cottin.

Julia also improved her ability in sketching. She took delight in sketching flowers and was drawn to watercolor landscapes.

Julia graduated from the Mauros' school in June 1843, the month her brother Fred and Ulysses graduated from West Point. After a summer at White Haven, she decided to spend the winter with classmate Carrie O'Fallon, daughter of Colonel John R. O'Fallon, a widower who had recently married Caroline Ruth Sheetz. Mrs. O'Fallon loved Julia like a daughter. Julia learned to play piano on an instrument that the O'Fallons later sent to her at White Haven.

WITH JULIA AGAIN at White Haven, "Lieutenant Grant," as she called him in the company of family and friends, suddenly evolved from a weekly to an almost daily visitor.

As winter turned into spring, Julia enjoyed what she would call two "winged months." She and Ulysses would ride in the woods and on the meadow, he on Fashion and she on Psyche, a part Arabian chestnut-brown mare. For Julia, horseback riding became an instant bond between them. Sometimes the lieutenant would stay overnight, then they would ride together before breakfast: "Such rides."

Often, as they sat on the banks of Gravois Creek, he would read to her from Scott, Cooper, Washington Irving, and Frederick Marryat. On other afternoons they fished in the creek. Sister Emmy recalled "many a fine mess of perch I've seen them catch together." Emmy guessed that something more catching existed between them.

Together in almost everything, Ulysses and Julia parted company on music and dancing. Ulysses had no ear for music—military bands or Methodist hymn sings.

Whether because of music or Methodism, Ulysses would not dance. He escorted Julia to Jefferson Barracks dances but was content to watch other young officers dance with her.

NEITHER WOULD FORGET the night they traveled to a Methodist camp meeting. Longstreet, Hazlitt, and several of Julia's friends joined them in a farm wagon, sitting together on beds of hay. They stayed "until the last hymn was sung," and on their way home in the dark, a spring thunderstorm suddenly burst from the sky. No houses were nearby, and the shrieking young women did not want to take cover under trees, fearing lightning strikes. Lieutenant Grant took command. Asking tall Bob Hazlitt to stand as a tent pole, he draped a tarpaulin over his head while he held the edges; the grateful women crouched, mostly dry, in a circle at his feet.

ULYSSES GOT ON well with almost everyone at Jefferson Barracks—the exception was Captain Robert C. Buchanan. "Old Buch" arrived at Jefferson Barracks preceded by word of his brave service in the Black Hawk War in Wisconsin and the recent Seminole Wars in Florida. If Commandant Kearney offered his young officers breathing space for their social life, Buchanan swooped down on every infraction.

As Ulysses courted Julia, he was late more than once for dinner at Jefferson Barracks. Buchanan, as president of the mess, enforced the custom of fining an officer a bottle of wine for arriving late for dinner. "Grant, you're late as usual, another bottle of wine, sir."

Ulysses, believing Buchanan overbearing, replied, "Mr. President, I have been fined three bottles of wine within the last ten days and if I am to be fined again, I shall be obliged to repudiate."

Buchanan responded, "Mr. Grant, young people should be seen and not heard, sir!"

BUCHANAN WASN'T THE only older man challenging Ulysses. More than the young lieutenant understood at first, father Dent posed a challenge to his courting Julia. Ulysses eventually comprehended it was not enough to court her, he had to court her parents also, especially her father, who would have the final say as to whom his daughter would marry. Dent harbored ambitions of his oldest daughter marrying a prominent, economically stable man, not a poorly paid officer with an uncertain future.

But from the first, Ulysses found a supporter in Mrs. Dent. Emmy recalled that her mother grew fond of Lieutenant Grant "because of the simplicity of his demeanor and unconsciousness of self." She admired the way he talked politics with her husband. "His quiet, even tones, free from gestures and without affectation, especially attracted her."

Mary Robinson, a slave whom Ellen Dent entrusted with the cooking, corroborated Emmy's memory: "Old man Dent was opposed to him, when he found he was courting his daughter, and did everything he could to prevent the match." But "Mrs. Dent took a great fancy to Grant and encouraged him in his venture." On more than one occasion, Ellen Dent told Mary Robinson, "I like that young man. There is something noble in him."

THEN, POLITICS ERECTED a further barrier to Ulysses's courtship. A bugle blared on April 10, 1844, across the parade grounds, the month of his twenty-second birthday, signaling an announcement that the Third Infantry should prepare to depart on April 20 for Fort Jesup in Louisiana, near the Texas border. They were to be the leading edge of what was being called an "Army of Observation." Their public task: Observe events unfolding in Texas. Their real task: Warn Mexico not to interfere. Could orders for Ulysses's Fourth Infantry be far behind?

The American migration into Texas had started in earnest in 1821, when Moses Austin received permission from Spain to bring three hundred families into the sparsely populated area in the northern part of New Spain. In 1821, the year Mexico declared its independence, Moses's son Stephen F. Austin secured authorization from the new Mexican government to continue this migration. By 1830, with American settlers fast outpacing Mexican residents, Mexico forbade further immigration.

Under the banner of the lone star, a "Texian" military campaign culminated in a declaration of independence from Mexico on March 2, 1836. By that year, American settlers outnumbered Mexican residents ten to one, almost all of them having emigrated from southern states.

Different forces pushed for and against annexation. President John Tyler, a slaveholder from Virginia, made such a strong case for annexation that Tyler and Texas quickly became synonymous. On April 12, 1844, Secretary of State John C. Calhoun and representatives of the Republic of Texas formalized an agreement whereby the independent republic would be declared a United States territory, with the proviso that it would qualify for statehood in the future.

Ten days later, President Tyler presented the treaty to the Senate for ratification. And then came the unexpected. In a highly charged Washington, Calhoun was forced to make public a letter on the issue that he had written to Great Britain's minister to the United States, Richard Pakenham. In it, South Carolinian Calhoun had injudiciously informed the minister that the motivation for annexation was to protect American slavery from British intrusion. In extolling the virtues of slavery, Calhoun had included statistics to prove southern slaves lived better lives than northern free blacks or English white laborers. The resulting uproar was so acrimonious that Missouri senator Thomas Hart Benton labeled Calhoun's letter the "Texas bombshell."

On April 27, Henry Clay and former president Martin Van Buren, leaders of the Whig and Democratic parties, declared their opposition to annexation, fearing that in the near future Texas would become a vast slaveholding state. Clay also argued that "annexation and war with Mexico are identical." Van Buren contended that such a step would break with fundamental American values: "It has hitherto been our pride and our boast" that the "lust of power" had led other governments "to aggression and conquest," whereas "our movements in these respects have always been regulated by reason and justice."

Ulysses followed this debate at Jefferson Barracks but discovered that "generally the officers of the army were indifferent whether the annexa-

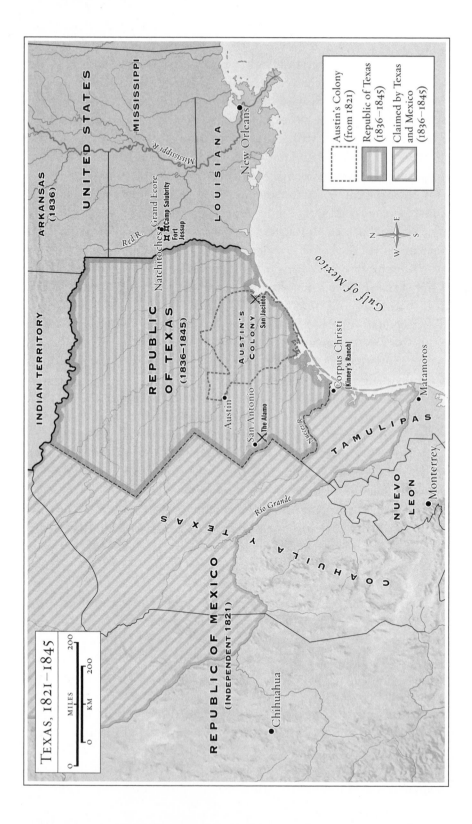

tion was consummated or not." However, he knew his own mind: "For myself, I was bitterly opposed to the measure."

He also found himself at odds in a debate in Julia's family. He listened to the Colonel's heated advocacy of annexing Texas, but this time, instead of listening quietly, he argued with the older man. As Ellen Dent eavesdropped, she marveled at the way Ulysses expressed himself. "That young man can explain politics so clearly I can understand the situation perfectly."

SUSPECTING THE FOURTH Infantry would be ordered to Fort Jesup soon, Ulysses requested a twenty-day leave to visit his parents in Ohio. First, though, he rushed to White Haven to say goodbye to Julia. Toward the end of a special day, as they sat alone on the veranda, he took his class ring from his finger and, as Julia recalled, "asked me if I would not wear it." Ulysses had told Julia previously that if he gave his class ring to a woman, he would give it as an engagement ring.

"Oh, no, mamma would not approve of my accepting a gift from a gentleman."

Ulysses, unsure of himself, did not know how to respond. Well then, would she think of him during his absence? Years later she remembered, "I, child that I was, never for a moment thought of him as a lover."

A few days after Ulysses's visit, Julia learned the Fourth Infantry was about to leave for Louisiana. With the hope of seeing Lys, as she now called him, one more time, she rode alone toward Jefferson Barracks. "I halted my horse and waited and listened, but he did not come. The beating of my own heart was all the sound I heard. So I rode slowly and sadly home."

As ULYSSES BOARDED a steamer for Cincinnati at the end of April, a messenger arrived telling him his regiment should be prepared to leave from Jefferson Barracks for Louisiana on May 7. What should he do? He decided to stick to his plans to visit Ohio. He received a second message at Bethel. Charley Jarvis, a West Point classmate, wrote he was taking all Ulysses's possessions with him to Louisiana and not to open any more orders until returning to Jefferson Barracks from his leave.

On the steamer from Missouri to Ohio, Ulysses realized why he had been so happy these past months and why the prospect of his departure from Julia made him feel so sad. "I now discovered that I was exceedingly anxious to get back to Jefferson Barracks, and I understood the reason without explanation from any one."

He was not in Ohio long before he rushed back to St. Louis. He reported to Lieutenant Richard Ewell and asked for an extension so he could take care of a personal matter.

With the request approved, Ulysses started for White Haven. It was a stormy day, with the Mississippi River flooding its banks as he approached Gravois Creek. On almost every other day, "there is not water enough in the creek at ordinary stages to run a coffee mill," but now he confronted a violent, rushing river. He "looked at it a moment to consider what to do."

Determined to see Julia, Ulysses "struck into the stream, and in an instant the horse was swimming and I being carried down by the current." Later, recalling how he had struggled with the turbulent, foam-flecked water, he acknowledged that "one of my superstitions had always been when I started to go anywhere, or to do anything, not to turn back, or stop until the thing intended was accomplished." Holding on for his life, he "headed the horse towards the other bank" and finally reached it.

Ulysses arrived at White Haven dripping wet, his clothes "flopping about him like wet rags." Everyone laughed at the sight, no one more than Julia. She took charge, telling her tall brother John to supply Ulys with some clothes. Finally he emerged, dry but wearing clothes ridiculously large for his frame.

The Dents had been preparing to leave for a wedding. Throughout her life, Julia delighted in telling the story of what happened next. Looking for an opportunity to speak with Julia alone, Ulysses asked John to ride his horse to the wedding while he drove the buggy with Julia. As they prepared to cross over a usually dry gulch, both noticed that the raging water almost reached the bridge. Julia "asked several times if he thought the water dangerous to breast, and told him I would go back rather than take any risk." As they reached the planks of the old bridge, Julia spoke: "Now, if anything happens, remember I shall cling to you, no matter what you say to the contrary."

Once they were over the bridge, Ulysses's countenance changed, his spirit warmed, and he proposed to Julia. She remembered that Ulysses, "in asking me to be his wife, used my threat as a theme."

Julia wanted to delay, aware her father would likely object. Ulysses told her he would be willing to resign from the army if that would be what it took to marry her.

Ulysses spent many days at White Haven, but the day of his departure arrived too soon. On this final visit, Julia "begged him not to say anything to papa about our engagement." He consented, but she said he did so more "on account of his shyness" in speaking to her father. Ulysses gave her his West Point class ring; this time she accepted it to wear as the seal of their secret engagement.

ULYSSES BOARDED A steamer again, this time to join his regiment in Louisiana near the Texas frontier. Always enthusiastic about travel, he savored the trip down the Mississippi and up the Red River.

Because it was deemed impractical to house all the incoming troops at Fort Jesup, the army established Camp Salubrity, twenty-five miles to the east and three miles from Natchitoches, the oldest town in the original Louisiana Purchase. The camp took its name from its pristine setting: a high, pine-forested ridge with clear springs, supposedly above the flight of mosquitoes. Although the dictionary might define "salubrity" as "well-being" and "health," Ulysses soon learned more about oppressive summer heat, ticks, and—yes—mosquitoes than he cared to know.

In his first letter to Julia, Ulysses struggled to move beyond his limited ability to express his affection. Thus, he closed it in a curious manner: "Blank _____ _____ _____ _____ _____ _____ _____ _____ _____

_____ _____ _____ _____ _____ ____ _____ _____ _____

_____ Read these blank lines just as I intend them and they will express more than words."

Two days later, he wrote Mrs. Jane Bailey in Georgetown. Sworn to secrecy by Julia, he told Mrs. Bailey that since he had seen her on his recent leave, his time had been "marked with no incident, save one, worth relating and that one is *laughable curious, important, surprising, &c, &c,* but I can't tell it now. . . . You must not guess what it is."

TO COMMAND THE First Military District at Fort Jesup, General in Chief Winfield Scott appointed Brigadier General Zachary Taylor. Taylor, at age fifty-nine, had the task of assembling their "Army of Observation."

Born in Virginia in 1784, Taylor grew up on the Kentucky frontier near Louisville. He enlisted in the army in 1806 and commanded troops in the War of 1812, the Black Hawk War in Wisconsin in 1832, and the Battle of Okeechobee during the Second Seminole War in Florida in 1837, for which he earned promotion to brevet brigadier general.

One inch taller than Ulysses at five feet eight, but big-boned and muscular, Taylor appeared more commanding mounted on his horse, Old Whitey, than in his bowlegged walk. Unlike General Scott, "Old Fuss and Feathers," Taylor earned his nickname, "Old Rough and Ready," for his dislike of military formalities, his preference for plain dress, and his readiness to share privations of army life with his troops.

On June 8, 1844, shortly after Ulysses arrived at Camp Salubrity, the United States Senate rejected the annexation of Texas by a vote of 35 to 16.

As the weeks plodded on, Ulysses began to express anxiety about not hearing from Julia. He entreated, "Be as punctual in writing to me Julia and then I will be compensated in a slight degree,—nothing could fully compensate—for your absence."

Before they parted, Ulysses and Julia had promised that no matter where he would be, they would remember each day to "think of each other at sun setting." But soon Ulysses encountered an unexpected problem: "At that time I am most always on parade and no doubt I sometimes appear very absent minded." Whatever the time of day, he had Julia on his mind.

Julia's letters to Ulysses have not survived. Throughout his life, Ulysses, often on the move, did not keep letters. Sometimes we can piece together parts of what she wrote, either when he paraphrases one of her ideas or questions or when he repeats a direct quotation. Thus, she told him she was "at a loss to ascribe a meaning to t[he] blank lines in my first letter!"

Surprised, Ulysses replied, "Nothing is easier, they were only intended to express an attachment which words would fail to express." In a "PS," he added, "I think in the course of a few days Julia, I will write to Col. Dent to obtain his consent to our correspondence."

In a second letter from Camp Salubrity, he began calling her "my dear Julia," not just in an initial greeting, but again and again within the body of the letter, savoring the endearment.

Finally, the first two letters from Julia arrived toward the end of August. Ulysses replied immediately, wanting her to know how his spirits had been lifted: "Since the arrival of your letters I have read them over and over again and will continue to do so until another comes."

While waiting for orders, Ulysses understood the Army of Observation's future might well be decided by the 1844 presidential election. The Whig candidate, Kentuckian Henry Clay, had served as Speaker of the House of Representatives and secretary of state under John Quincy

Adams. The Democratic candidate, James Polk of Tennessee, a protégé of Andrew Jackson's, finally won the Democratic nomination on the ninth ballot at the convention at Baltimore. Once nominated, Polk spoke increasingly of the "re-annexation of Texas," arguing that Texas had been part of Thomas Jefferson's initial Louisiana Purchase. The election of 1844 witnessed the rise of a third party vigorously opposed to annexation. James G. Birney, a southern plantation owner turned Christian abolitionist, was chosen as the Liberty Party candidate. Ulysses followed Birney's candidacy with interest because his vice-presidential candidate was Tom Morris of Bethel, Ohio, the senator whom Jesse had first approached about appointing Ulysses to West Point.

In the closest contest to that date in American history, Polk won 1,339,494 votes to Clay's 1,300,004 votes. Antislavery candidate James G. Birney, who had polled only 7,453 votes in the 1840 election, won 62,103 votes.

Both Polk and Tyler understood the Tennessean's victory as a vote for the annexation of Texas. The House voted yes on December 29, and the Senate, by the narrowest of margins (27 to 25), agreed on February 27, 1845. Tyler signed the bill annexing Texas as the twenty-eighth state on March 1, 1845, three days before he surrendered his office.

"HURRY UP AND wait." Life at Camp Salubrity in fall 1844 and winter 1845 carried a mixed message. "Hurry"—Ulysses wrote that rumors were filtering through the camp that very soon now they would be "hurried off" for some location on the Texas frontier, with most bets placed on Corpus Christi or San Antonio. "Wait"—regimental officers, in order to replace the leaky tents, began conscripting men to build two rows of blockhouses for a long winter ahead in camp.

"Hurry up and wait" also characterized Ulysses's relationship with Julia. He desperately wanted to hurry up and marry her but knew he had to wait until he'd completed his present deployment. When he wrote her, he felt encumbered, knowing her family's custom required Julia to read his letters aloud. "I imagined all the time that I saw your Pa & Ma reading it and when they were done, raising all kinds of objections." So in his letters he sought to anticipate and answer her parents' objections. "Assure them my dear Julia that the longest acquaintance, or a few years more experience in the world could not create a feeling deeper or more durable." Suspecting her parents were asking whether their relationship could endure such a long absence, he wrote in January 1845, "The more than ordinary attachment that I formed for *yourself* and your family during my stay at Jeff. Bks. cannot be changed to forgetfulness by a few months absence."

Symbols of their love passed back and forth by uncertain mail delivery. He thanked her for a cherished lock of her hair. For her part, "I was constantly receiving letters and books from Mr. Grant."

IN SPRING 1845, with talk of war increasing, Ulysses requested a thirty-five-day leave to return to Missouri. He was determined to see Julia and secure Colonel Dent's permission to marry her.

Emmy spied a more mature Lieutenant Grant riding up to White Haven on a dapple-gray horse. He arrived just as the family was gathering to see Colonel Dent off on a business trip to Washington.

As eager as he was to see Julia, "he scarcely touched my hand" before he aimed to speak to her father alone inside. The rest of the family leaned forward to listen through the shutters.

Ulysses summoned his courage. "Mr. Dent, I want to marry your daughter, Miss Julia."

Dent retorted that he did not think the "roving life" of the military would be good for Julia. This was not the answer Ulysses was hoping for. He offered to resign the army and secure a teaching appointment at a college. Dent, who by now had come to admire Ulysses, told him he should stick to his profession in the army.

"Mr. Grant, if it were Nellie you wanted, I would make no objection."

Ulysses was dumbfounded at what he called Colonel Dent's "Laban-like suggestion." In the Bible, Jacob wanted to marry Laban's daughter Rachel, but after working seven years to earn her, he discovered on the wedding night that Laban had exchanged Leah for Rachel. Jacob was forced to work another seven years before he could marry Rachel.

"But I don't want Nellie. I want Julia."

"Oh, you do, do you? Well, then, I s'pose it'll have to be Julia."

By his directness, Ulysses finally overcame the obstacle of Julia's father. Later, Ulysses enjoyed teasing Nellie, telling her that her papa had offered her but he'd declined. He and Julia could marry after a year's engagement and separation. But because of his military commitment, no date could be set.

WITHIN WEEKS OF securing the Colonel's permission, Ulysses began preparing to move south from Camp Salubrity. On July 3, 1845, his company in the Fourth Infantry departed with more anticipation than dread. For these young officers, prepared by West Point and then forced to spend more than a year of "hurry up and wait" in Louisiana, the prospect of serving as part of the Army of Occupation in Texas brought possibilities of glory and promotion.

While stopping in New Orleans, Ulysses wrote Julia three letters within eleven days. This exuberance was fed by his new plan to send two letters simultaneously, one directed solely to Julia, the other to be read aloud to her parents. In his private letter, he tried to express himself in more amorous language but, laughing at himself, told her, "What an oaf I make at expressing anything like love or sentiment: You know what I mean at all events." Anticipating the coming mission into Texas: "In going away now I feel as if I had someone else than myself to live and strive to do well for." Finally: "You can have but little idea of the influence you have over me Julia, even while so far away." He confessed, "If I feel tempted to do anything that I think is not right I am sure to think, 'Well now if Julia saw me would I do so.' and thus it is absent or present I am more or less governed by what I think is your will."

ULYSSES NEVER ANTICIPATED his first year as a young officer to be completely dominated by courting Julia Boggs Dent. In letter after letter, he writes of his growing emotional dependence on her. He tries, sometimes haltingly, to express his love for her in ways he had never done with anyone before.

In meeting Julia, he met an outgoing young woman who expanded his emotional universe. Brought up in a home with a mother who guarded her emotions closely, he encountered in Julia a woman with a warm personality. Ulysses, shy by nature, was enthralled.

In the summer of 1845, Ulysses and his Fourth Infantry company were about to receive new orders. In a postscript to his last letter to Julia from New Orleans, he announced, "We will start for Texas in the course of three or four days." The Army of Observation was about to become the Army of Occupation.

Second Lieutenant Grant, on the left, with his racing horse Dandy, and Alexander Hays, with his horse Sunshine, in a photo taken at Camp Salubrity in Louisiana in 1845.

CHAPTER 5

"Either by Treaty or the Sword"

We were sent to provoke a fight, but it was essential that
Mexico should commence it.

—ULYSSES S. GRANT, *Personal Memoirs*

The United States entered the 1840s with an expanding national identity. The population of the growing Republic exceeded seventeen
million, an increase of nearly one-third since 1830. John O'Sullivan, a
northern journalist, summed up the national spirit in coining the term
Manifest Destiny to justify and celebrate expansion.

The Mexican War would become a defining experience for Grant and
the young nation. If grandfathers had fought the Revolutionary War,
and fathers battled Great Britain a second time in the War of 1812, the
prospect of war with Mexico proved a unique challenge to a new generation of Americans. This war would be the first fought on foreign soil; the
first against a non-European army; and the first against a people who
spoke a different language.

Grant and his fellow soldiers knew little about the neighbor to the
south. In the early sixteenth century, Spanish explorers entered what
they called New Spain, a vast area stretching north into today's American
Southwest and south into today's Central America. Even as the area west
of the Alleghenies filled with settlers in the early nineteenth century, the
area to the far north of Mexico City remained thinly populated. Throughout Mexico, regional customs and politics, plus inadequate transportation, hindered building a national state.

Before the conflict in Texas erupted, Mexicans regarded the United
States highly. Many politicians wished to emulate American democratic
institutions. But Americans did not appreciate how much more difficult
and complex Mexico's path to becoming a nation was as it sought to shed
the bonds of imperial Spain. From the Mexican perspective, America's

determination to tear Texas from Mexico initiated generations of distrust.

IN SEPTEMBER 1845, Grant set sail from New Orleans for Texas. President James Polk instructed his representative, Louisiana congressman John Slidell, to secure an agreement from the Mexican government that the Rio Grande would be the southern boundary of Texas. But with negotiations in Mexico City at a standstill, Polk instructed General Zachary Taylor to cross into Texas.

Ulysses wrote to Julia optimistically, "In all probability this movement to the Rio Grande will hasten the settlement of the boundary question, either by treaty or the sword, and in either case we may hope for early peace and a more settled life in the army."

Taylor set up his Texas camp in disputed territory alongside the blue Gulf of Mexico at the small village of Corpus Christi by the mouth of the Nueces River. Established in 1838 by Colonel Henry L. Kinney, what locals called "Kinney's Ranch" consisted of a string of thirty weathered buildings; inhabitants used the port to smuggle tobacco into Mexico.

Grant's was an inauspicious arrival. Thanks to the shallow channel, the ships had to unload soldiers and cargo to smaller boats some distance from land. After an initial debarkation, Grant returned to his ship, the *Suviah,* days later. "By the time I was ready to leave the ship again I thought I had learned enough of the working of the double and single pulley, by which passengers were let down from the upper deck of the ship to the steamer below, and determined to let myself down without assistance." Saying nothing to anyone, he mounted the railing, grabbed the rope, and, edging one foot down, began to lower himself. Suddenly someone shouted: "Hold on!" Too late. "I tried to 'hold on' with all my might, but my heels went up, and my head went down so rapidly that my hold broke, and I plunged head foremost into the water, some twenty-five feet below, with such velocity that it seemed to me I never would stop." With all eyes riveted, "and not having lost my presence of mind, I swam around until a bucket was let down for me, and I was drawn up without a scratch or injury." Safe, but embarrassed: "I do not believe there was a man on board who sympathized with me in the least when they found me uninjured. I rather enjoyed the joke myself."

By October, reinforcements swelled Taylor's command to 3,922, the largest assemblage of American troops in one place since the War of 1812. Row after row of tents stretched more than a mile in the sand. The camp's open alignment underscored Taylor's conviction that the Mexicans, even though they were estimated to have more than eight thousand men in arms—double the U.S. force—would not be the aggressors against his superb army. Taylor's "Army of Occupation" was in truth an army of provocation.

GRANT, ALWAYS ADVENTURESOME, began investigating the wide-open Texas countryside. He rode 150 miles north and west to San Antonio and Austin and saw no American settlers in the territory he and his fellow soldiers were to occupy.

He purchased a horse from among the many that Mexicans in Texas were selling to the army for the high price of $12. Other officers were afraid of Grant's choice, a strong-willed stallion. His friend James Longstreet described what happened next. He blindfolded the horse, bridled and saddled him, and then, once in the saddle, threw off the blind, sank his spurs into the horse's flanks, and soon disappeared from sight.

For three hours, no one caught sight of him. Finally, Longstreet recounted that when "horse and rider returned to camp the horse was thoroughly tamed." Grant's friend reported that the story of Grant and the Texas stallion was told around army campfires for years.

On one trip to Austin, the soldiers stopped several times to hunt for deer and wild turkeys. "I, however, never went out, and had no occasion to fire my gun." Finally, Calvin Benjamin encouraged Grant to accompany him to the nearby creek. Grant remembered, "We had scarcely reached the edge of the timber when I heard the flutter of wings overhead, and in an instant I saw two or three turkeys flying away." These few were followed quickly by twenty to thirty more flying directly overhead. "All this time I stood watching the turkeys to see where they flew—with my gun on my shoulder, and never once thought of levelling it at the birds." Reflecting on this experience, "I came to the conclusion that as a sportsman I was a failure."

On their way back to Corpus Christi, Grant was startled by "the most unearthly howling of wolves." Because of high prairie grass, he could not see any wolves, but from the sound it seemed that they were near. Now frightened, he had the impression that there must be a pack of wolves. To Grant's surprise, Benjamin kept moving forward, toward the noise. Grant wrote later, "I followed in his trail, lacking moral courage to turn back," but admitted that if Benjamin had proposed turning back, he would have "seconded the motion." Finally, Benjamin spoke softly: "Grant, how many wolves do you think there are in that pack?" Reluctant to show his ignorance, Grant decided to answer with a low estimate: "Oh, about twenty." Benjamin smiled and the two rode on.

In a few minutes, Grant and Benjamin encountered the wolves. "There were just *two* of them. Seated upon their haunches, with their mouths close together, they had made all the noise we had been hearing for the past ten minutes."

These stories of turkeys and wolves reveal a paradoxical side of Grant. In a culture that admired male strength, Grant, writing long after he became famous as a warrior, volunteered that he avoided the sport of hunting and as a young soldier had found himself frightened by wolves. Americans do not want their heroes to reveal their vulnerabilities, but Grant freely admitted his—with humor.

GOOD NEWS CAME in December, when Grant received word that he had been promoted from brevet second lieutenant to second lieutenant. The official day of his appointment was September 30, the date the Fourth Infantry had fully assembled in Corpus Christi. He had not asked for advancement in rank—he had a strong aversion to self-promotion—nor would he let his friends recommend him.

With the onset of winter, a change in weather coupled with boredom began to sap camp morale. At this low tide, General William J. Worth, ever resourceful, asked Lieutenant John B. Magruder to build a theater. "Prince John," so named because of his courtly behavior, announced that his eight-hundred-seat theater would open on January 8. Box seats would be $1; regular seats, 50 cents.

One of the first productions would be William Shakespeare's *The Tragedy of Othello, The Moor of Venice*. Magruder conscripted soldiers to build sets, sent to New Orleans for costumes, and announced tryouts. He wanted to cast James Longstreet as Desdemona, the Venetian beauty, but fellow cast members objected that the six-foot-two-inch Longstreet was too tall. Magruder then invited the shorter Grant, known to enjoy the theater, to try out for the part. Although Longstreet said Grant "looked very like a girl dressed up" and appeared better than Longstreet in crinolines, Magruder rejected him as well, concluding that "male heroines could not support the character." Finally, Magruder sent to New Orleans for an actress to play Desdemona.

AT THE BEGINNING of 1846, with Mexico showing no enthusiasm to come north to the Nueces River to drive the "invaders" from its soil,

*President James K. Polk of Tennessee
drove the United States military
aggression against Mexico.*

Polk decided to force the government to the bargaining table by instructing Taylor to move his infantry farther south. The president consciously
courted war, but in doing so he misjudged his adversary.

The Mexican government, smarting from the loss of Texas, believed
its national honor was at stake. Nevertheless, the Rio Grande commander,
General Mariano Arista, operated under orders to remain on the defense
and steer clear of any provocation from the *yanquis*.

Grant's optimism did not dampen as Taylor posted Polk's new orders.
He wrote Julia, "It is to be hoped that our troops being so close on the
borders of Mexico will bring about a speedy settlement of the boundary
question."

In preparation for the move south, Grant was assigned the task of securing hundreds of mules for the trip. The army had 307 wagons for supplies, 84 to be pulled by oxen. This left 223 to be pulled by mules.

The Mexicans sold mules to the army, but Grant discovered they were
"all young and unbroken." He had them roped and branded with the
initials *U.S.,* but they still had to be broken in to wear a saddle and pack.
Grant quickly discovered this process to be "amusing": the "Corpus
Christi mule resisted the new use to which he was being put."

Newly arrived volunteers, most of them foreigners from the larger
cities, were assigned to help him; having agreed to accept a mere $7 a
month, they represented a cost-effective alternative to draining the regular army pool of soldiers. But officers scoffed that the army got what it
paid for—unreliable work habits by day, drinking and brawling by night.

Grant's letters contained none of this criticism, although later he acknowledged that "it is not probable that any of the men who reported
themselves as competent teamsters had ever driven a mule-team in their
lives, or indeed that many had had any previous experience in driving any

animal whatever to harness." Nevertheless, he directed them to hitch up five mules to each wagon. Once all had been assembled—no easy process—the real contest began. As the recruits pulled and pushed, the mules leapt in the air; then, one after another they sat down; finally, in a desperate struggle of wills, they lay down. In the end, however, Grant, the teamsters, and the mules learned to work together.

Grant's developing leadership did not go unnoticed. One morning, he led a squad charged with raking oyster beds and removing obstructions so boats could advance from Aransas Bay to Corpus Christi. When his words failed to communicate what he wanted, he "jumped into the water, which was up to his waist, and worked with the men." Officers standing nearby "made fun of his zeal." Zachary Taylor, taking in the whole scene, mused, "I wish I had more officers like Grant who would stand ready to set a personal example when needed."

FINALLY, THE DAY of departure arrived. By now Grant had acquired three horses he intended to take to the Rio Grande: one for himself; one for Alere, the servant he shared with Hazlitt; and an extra horse. Shortly before the day of departure, Alere rode one horse and led the other two to fresh water. Suddenly, those he was leading yanked on their ropes, unseating him. Before Alere could recover, all three horses bounded off.

When Grant learned he had lost all his horses, he did not criticize Alere. He called the incident a "sad accident" and prepared to walk to the Rio Grande.

Just as the troops prepared to depart, Captain William W. S. Bliss, Taylor's chief of staff, learned Grant had lost his horses. Bliss, who had served as assistant professor of mathematics during Grant's four years at West Point, was well aware of his love of horses. At the last moment, Grant was approached by Captain George McCall, a company commander under Bliss. "Do you intend to get another horse before the march begins?" he asked.

"No," Grant replied. "I belong to the foot regiment." McCall stepped away, then reappeared. "There, Grant, is a horse for you."

Unbeknownst to Grant, McCall had recently purchased a mustang for just $3 for his servant. But he could not abide seeing a servant ride while an officer walked. Grant recalled, "I was sorry to take him, because I really felt that, belonging to a foot regiment, it was my duty to march with the men."

The first day of the journey was the first day the mustang had ever been under a saddle. He and Grant had to negotiate: "There were frequent disagreements between us as to which way we should go, and sometimes whether we should go at all. . . . At no time during the day could I choose exactly the part of the column I would march with." But under Grant's gentle rein, "I had as tractable a horse as any with the army, and there was none that stood the trip better."

GRANT AND HIS Fourth Infantry left Corpus Christi with the Third Brigade on March 11, the last brigade to leave. Traveling mostly west, the soldiers were greeted in this early spring by a profusion of wildflowers, including blue lupine, drought-resistant verbena, and yellow and orange marigolds. After a few days, Grant suddenly saw an even more spectacular scene: "As far as the eye could reach," there were wild horses. "There was no estimating the number of animals in it; I have no idea that they could all have been corralled in the State of Rhode Island, or Delaware, at one time."

When the army turned south, marching over a desolate salt plain, their fortunes changed. The Army of Occupation met not one settlement. They encountered more and more chaparral, a shrub growing so densely that even animals—let alone humans—could not penetrate it. And if anyone tried, he would soon feel the penalty the prickly chaparral would impose on the human body. It became more difficult to proceed, eat, and rest.

On March 28, Grant arrived at a bluff overlooking the meandering Rio Grande directly opposite the town of Matamoros, named for Don Mariano Matamoros, a hero of Mexican independence. As the army approached the river, he heard bands playing patriotic music and saw Mexican regiments unfurling their colors. Grant was surprised to find the object of their march a muddy, yellow-gray river no more than one hundred yards wide and only four feet deep.

Grant began to help set up camp as curious eyes stared from the south side of the muddy river, watching his brigade's every move. Staring back, he saw the Catedral de Nuestra Señora del Refugio, a beacon across from the town square. He spied the colorful Mexican flag fluttering defiantly in the morning sun everywhere throughout the town. Red, the color of blood, was a tribute to those who died winning the Mexican War of Independence from 1810 to 1821. White symbolized the purity of the Catholic faith. Green represented hope for a better nation.

For the next three weeks, the two armies spied each other from both sides of the Rio Grande in what at times seemed more like a comic opera than the beginning of an international war.

But it was another sight that drew the most attention. Each morning, almost like clockwork, scores of young Mexican women would come to the river, lift their white chemise blouses over their heads, and begin to bathe. A Tennessee soldier wrote in his diary, "They laugh, shout, sing, wrestle with each other, and display their graceful forms in a thousand agile movements."

First scores and then hundreds of soldiers came to watch. One morning, some of the soldiers jumped headlong into the river and began to swim toward the mermaids. When the señoritas did not retreat, Mexican soldiers aimed their rifles. They fired just over the Americans' heads while the laughing women continued frolicking in the river.

TENSIONS ROSE BY the day in April 1846. On April 11, clanging bells heralded the arrival of Mexican general Pedro de Ampudia and his advance cavalry of two hundred men. They had ridden 180 miles from Monterrey in four days. Coming up behind him was an army of almost three thousand. On April 20, a still hopeful Grant wrote Julia, "Everything is very quiet here." He admitted, "Everything looks belligerent to a spectator but I believe there will be no fight."

On April 24, General Mariano Arista reached Matamoros to succeed General Ampudia in overall command. The red-haired Arista, forty-two years old, had lived in exile in Cincinnati and spoke fluent English. He commanded a force of about five thousand men. He advised Taylor that Mexico was now at war with the United States. Taylor replied he hoped it was still possible for negotiations between the two countries to avert hostilities.

Unknown to Taylor, General Arista had orders to probe across the Rio Grande. He sent General Anastasio Torrejón with sixteen hundred men to cross the river west of Matamoros and cut the road between the recently built Fort Texas and Point Isabel. At eleven that evening, scouts informed Taylor of the crossing. He immediately instructed Captain Seth Thornton to take two companies of dragoons to discover the nature and extent of the Mexican incursion.

The mounted regiment rode through the darkness and the next morning checked Rancho de Carricitos. Thornton knocked on the main house door. As he began to question an old man, bullets suddenly rained down. They had ridden into an ambush. In the next minutes, eleven Americans were killed and twenty-six captured. Thornton's guide, who was not inside the ranch grounds, galloped back to inform Taylor of the disaster.

Taylor wrote President Polk, "Hostilities may now be considered as commenced."

GRANT AWAKENED AT five on Sunday morning, May 3, 1846, to the distant boom of guns. As he lay in his tent, the artillery at the fort could be distinctly heard. "The war had begun."

Grant was suddenly aware of his anxious feelings. "What General Taylor's feelings were during this suspense I do not know; but for myself, a young second lieutenant who had never heard a hostile gun before, I felt sorry that I had enlisted." Teaching mathematics seemed a distant dream.

Grant knew the thunder he heard was guns at Fort Texas on the Rio Grande, where five hundred defenders were under attack. Taylor sent a courier from Point Isabel with instructions to the fort's commander, Major Jacob Brown, to defend Fort Texas to the last man. On May 6, Major Brown was mortally wounded, but the defenders fought on.

General Arista's strategy was to raze Fort Texas before Taylor could arrive with reinforcements. If that failed, Arista wanted to intercept and destroy Taylor's army at a place and time of his determination. That place would be Palo Alto.

On May 8 at midday, Taylor's army of twenty-three hundred men and 250 supply wagons marched along the Matamoros road and began to cross the plain at Palo Alto. Situated ten miles north of the Rio Grande, Palo Alto, "Tall Tree," took its name from the woods that encircled this coastal prairie. Grant described the shoulder-high grass on the plain as "almost as sharp as a darning-needle."

Taylor had no desire to be trapped defending a fort and hoped to meet the Mexican forces in the open. But General Arista already had his thirty-two hundred men setting up cannons to prevent Taylor's forces from advancing. The Mexican general believed that Matamoros's defenders could not turn back an attack, even though they enjoyed numerical superiority, so he positioned his troops in a place where he would have the advantage.

Grant described the substantial Mexican force as "composed largely of cavalry armed with lances," daunting as "their bayonets and spearheads glistened in the sunlight formidably." At each end of this mile-long line, General Arista placed cavalry. He intended to flank and then destroy the advancing American army.

The Mexicans opened fire, first with cannon, then with smoothbore muskets. But their firing did not reach the Americans. Taylor's men

General Zachary Taylor, under whom Grant served in the opening campaigns of the Mexican War, would become a role model of military leadership for the young lieutenant.

marched forward. The Mexicans fired solid cannonballs, but they were ineffective, striking the ground long before they reached the American troops.

Grant and the American soldiers did not panic. The Mexicans made the fatal mistake for advancing armies: they began firing too soon.

Taylor advanced, then paused so the ox-drawn cannons could catch up. Grant was impressed. "I looked down that long line of about three thousand armed men, advancing towards a larger force also armed, I thought what a fearful responsibility General Taylor must feel, commanding such a host and so far away from friends." Grant readied his 1822 musket to be charged with powder, buckshot, and ball.

Finally, Taylor, riding Old Whitey and wearing his battered palmetto hat—a visible target if there ever was one—ordered his forces to advance to seven hundred yards of the Mexican lines. He would not let his men fire until he was certain his canister could reach all the way to the Mexican forces.

Then he ordered up his artillery. He prepared to use all four of his six-pound brass guns, which fired solid shot, as well as four of his twelve-pound howitzers. These "flying artillery" could be moved swiftly to wherever they were needed and be fired more quickly than the artillery employed by the Mexicans.

His special weapons this day were a pair of eighteen-pound cannon, heretofore used only for defense because their massive weight made it so difficult to haul them into battle. Breaking convention, Taylor had each cannon pulled by six yoked oxen across seven miles of open prairie, to use them as offensive weapons. Instead of cannonballs, they employed canister, a tin can filled with up to twenty-seven lead balls stuffed in sawdust. Most important, they possessed a range of up to three hundred yards. Seeing that the shells of the light Mexican artillery were falling short, Taylor hoped his heavier cannon would traverse the battlefield. The two seven-man crews shouted: "Ram, heave, ready," and, finally, "Fire!"

Grant watched, approving. "The infantry stood at order arms as spectators, watching the effect of our shots upon the enemy." He wrote Julia, "Every moment we could see the charges from our pieces cut a way through their ranks making a perfect road."

Artillery won the day. On the American side, only 9 died, 44 were wounded, and 2 were missing, representing just 2.5 percent of the 2,288 men engaged in the hostilities, while the Mexicans lost 102 killed, 129 wounded, and 26 missing.

Grant wrote a friend after his first battle, "During that night I believe all slept as soundly on the ground at Palo Alto as if they had been in a palace." When he awoke the next morning ready to renew hostilities, a patrol discovered the Mexicans had retreated into the prickly chaparral.

BEFORE THE NEXT afternoon, Grant would find himself in a situation he could not have predicted. Taylor ordered Captains George McCall and Charles Ferguson Smith to take 150 men and scout for the retreating Mexican army. They reported that the Mexicans were waiting for them at Resaca de la Palma, a dry river channel or ravine a dozen feet deep along the Point Isabel–Matamoros road, named for the palm trees that lined its banks.

When Taylor and his men arrived shortly after three P.M., he pulled his eighteen-pound cannon once more to the front of his line. But unlike at Palo Alto, at Resaca de la Palma the Mexican troops were hidden; one advance group, unaware of the enemy, immediately suffered five killed.

In the fast-moving battle, because of the deaths, Grant suddenly found himself in charge of a company. As he sensed his own fears, he felt a rush of adrenaline. Moving forward, he discovered that in addition to dense chaparral, the Mexicans had further fortified their position by dragging dead trees and brush to the front of their line. Because of this concealment, Grant led his company to where they "got pretty close up without knowing it." Under fire, they were forced to retreat briefly, until Grant led his company in a charge to capture "a Mexican colonel and a few of his men." Grant won his first victory.

One of Taylor's skills as a military leader was his ability to change tactics quickly. Unable to see his enemy, he ordered an attack by infantry and cavalry as well as light artillery. His men charged with their bayonets into the sagebrush, yelling at the top of their lungs. Immediately they found themselves engaged in hand-to-hand combat. Within two hours, the fighting was over.

The Americans won the first two battles of the war because of the mobility of their artillery, the longer range of their cannon, the superiority of their ammunition, and the training and proficiency of soldiers led by trained officers. Thanks to the performance of the West Point officers, all previous criticism of the academy and its graduates ceased.

But as Grant looked around in the aftermath of the battle, it dawned on him that his charge had not penetrated the front line but actually covered ground already won minutes before. His captives had already been captured. Grant wrote, "This left no doubt in my mind but that the battle of Resaca de la Palma would have been won, just as it was, if I had not been there."

By now Julia was living in St. Louis. In the first months of 1846, Colonel Dent, land-rich but cash-poor, had put White Haven up for sale. When he received no acceptable offers, he decided to rent his country home and lease a brick home at Fourth and Cerre streets for his family.

After the Battles of Palo Alto and Resaca de la Palma, Ulysses became more open in sharing his emotions with Julia: "Although the balls were whizzing thick and fast about me, I did not feel a sensation of fear until nearly the close of the firing." He described what happened to the men right around him: "A ball struck close by me killing one man instantly, it knocked Capt. Page's under jaw entirely off and broke in the roof of his mouth, and knocked Lt. Wallen and one Sergeant down besides, but they were not much hurt."

One can imagine Julia's feelings as she read these terrifying lines in Ulysses's letter. But he wasn't finished. "It was a terrible sight to go over the ground the next day and see the amount of life that had been destroyed." Toward the end of the letter, he assured her, "There is no great sport in having bullets flying about one in every direction but I find they have less horror when among them than when in anticipation." Grant had been baptized into battle. His self-discovery: He could indeed be a good soldier.

ON MAY 11, President Polk sent a Declaration of War to Congress. The president's representatives worked to suffocate debate, limiting questions and discussion to just two hours. Polk's message and supporting documents took up nearly one and a half hours. The president linked the deaths of soldiers in Thornton's patrol with the subject of the boundary: "The redress of the wrongs of our citizens naturally and inseparably blended itself with the question of boundary." He placed the blame solely on the Mexican government: "Mexico has passed the boundary of the United States, has invaded our territory and shed American blood upon the American soil. She has proclaimed that hostilities have commenced, and that the two nations are at war." Polk asked for an appropriation of $10 million and the authorization to raise fifty thousand troops to repel a foreign invasion.

THE BATTLES OF Palo Alto and Resaca de la Palma were turning points in the way Grant understood himself. He faced battle bravely and discovered within himself what he would begin to call "moral courage." He now began to envision a vocation in the army.

With the Declaration of War by President Polk and Congress, and confident in the arrival of a growing number of volunteers, General Taylor decided he would cross the Rio Grande and oust the Mexican army from Matamoros. Second Lieutenant Ulysses S. Grant was about to become part of the "Army of Invasion."

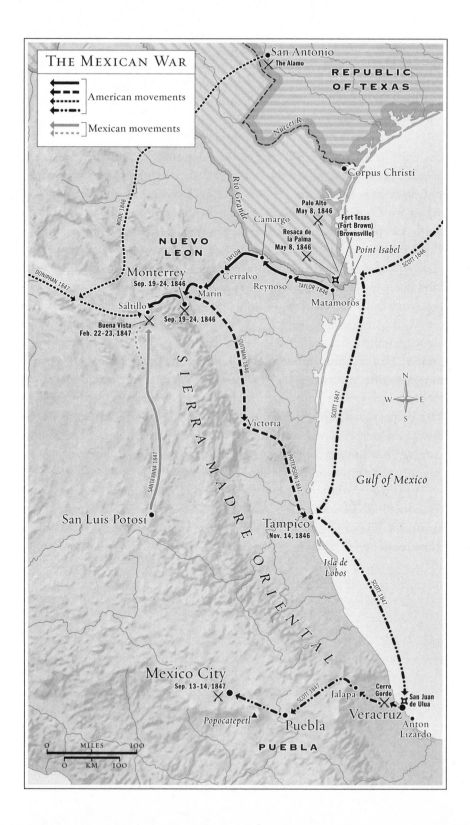

THE MEXICAN WAR

American movements

Mexican movements

San Antonio
The Alamo

REPUBLIC
OF TEXAS

Nueces R.

Corpus Christi

WOOL 1846

Rio Grande

Palo Alto
May 8, 1846

Camargo

Fort Texas
(Fort Brown)
[Brownsville]

NUEVO
LEON

Resaca de
la Palma
May 8, 1846

Point Isabel

DONIPHAN 1847

Monterrey
Sep. 19–24, 1846

Cerralvo

Reynoso

TAYLOR

SCOTT 1846

Marin

Matamoros

Saltillo

Sep. 19–24, 1846

TAYLOR 1846

Buena Vista
Feb. 22–23, 1847

QUITMAN 1846

S
I
E
R
R
A

Victoria

SANTA ANNA 1847

PATTERSON 1847

SCOTT 1847

M
A
D
R
E

Gulf of Mexico

N
W   E
S

San Luis Potosí

Tampico
Nov. 14, 1846

Isla de
Lobos

O
R
I
E
N
T
A
L

SCOTT 1847

Mexico City
Sep. 13–14, 1847

SCOTT 1847

Jalapa

Cerro
Gordo

San Juan
de Ulua

Veracruz

Popocatepetl

Puebla

Anton
Lizardo

PUEBLA

0   MILES   100

0   KM   100

CHAPTER 6

"Army of Invasion"

I have found in Lieutenant Grant a most remarkable and valuable young
soldier. I anticipate for him a brilliant future, if he should have the
opportunity to display his powers when they mature.

—Brigadier General Thomas L. Hamer, Monterrey,
Mexico, November 1846

As Grant crossed the physical boundary of the Rio Grande into Mexico, in the months ahead he would be crossing other boundaries as well. Entering Mexico, he would meet a different people, encounter a diverse culture, serve in an unusual army, and be appointed to a new military position.

The usual interest in Grant during the Mexican War has been in his growth as a military officer, but his development as a cultural observer mattered just as much. For many who find themselves in a foreign country for the first time, this kind of growth radiates in at least three directions. It starts as an attempt to appreciate a new country, then looks with fresh eyes back at one's own country, and finally may result in new self-understanding.

American soldiers marched into Mexico in the summer of 1846 with a bravado born from their victories at Palo Alto and Resaca de la Palma. Despite his troops' confidence, Zachary Taylor understood their two recent successes were merely skirmishes fought in largely open territory where American superior firepower triumphed easily. He knew the coming battle for Monterrey, the major northern Mexican city, would present a more difficult challenge.

Not so clearly understood was the challenge of crossing the boundary into a foreign country. Taylor's army, now joined by volunteers, was about to receive a crash course in the geography, history, and culture of Mexico that no books could supply. Like many visitors to foreign countries, the soldiers would make quick judgments based on first impressions: poverty existed in Mexico simply because the people were not willing to work hard; or, seen through largely Protestant eyes, a wealthy Catholic Church oppressed a poor people. In coming months, not many soldiers bothered to learn the language. Because language and culture are inseparable, only a few would be able to see beyond their first impressions.

Grant would defy the norm and strive to understand this different culture. Always an inquisitive explorer, he brought his relentless curiosity to Mexico. He picked up some Spanish.

In his first letter to Julia from within Mexico, a lighthearted Ulysses promised to pick a wildflower from the banks of the Rio Grande and send it to her. He also sent her a mental picture: he was growing a beard that was now three inches long.

Despite his tone, Julia's anxiety mounted with each week. Offering her comfort anchored his letters: "Every one of them full of sweet nothings, love and war and now and then some pressed leaves and flowers." She "prized" these letters; she would read them over and over and keep them for the rest of her life. She read the letters to her family—although younger sister Emmy suspected not all of each letter. Emmy noted that Ulysses's letters "generally had more to say about the movements of the army than of himself." He "was never a great hand to talk about himself."

TAYLOR SET SEPTEMBER 1 as the target for beginning the march on Monterrey. To meet this goal, much needed to be done in three months. The biggest challenge became integrating the thousands of volunteers who streamed through Point Isabel and into camps along the Rio Grande. Thanks to a growing patriotic fervor, more than fifty thousand men had signed up. Among the volunteer regiments was one from Mississippi led by a gray-eyed young congressman named Jefferson Davis.

Grant watched as volunteers, seemingly hell-bent on breaking every rule of civility and decency, became a mounting challenge. Almost every day young boys would run through the camps shouting, *"Fandango! Fandango! Bonita señoritas!"*—dances where soldiers could embrace pretty Mexican women. Too often the volunteers, in the aftermath of fandangos, raped the women and plundered the homes of local civilians. Grant told Julia the volunteers "seem to think it perfectly right to impose upon the people of a conquered City to any extent, and even to murder them when the act can be covered by the dark." His sympathy for civilians within war would follow him all his life.

THE PRESENCE OF volunteers became personal when Grant's old friends from Georgetown arrived. Thomas Hamer, who as an Ohio congressman had nominated him for West Point, was among the newcomers. And Grant greeted Carr and Chilton White, his schoolboy playmates, now members of Company G of the First Ohio Volunteers, led by Hamer.

The Whites told Ulysses how Hamer had taken the lead in encouraging volunteers. Hamer had become one of six civilians, all reliable Democrats, whom President Polk had appointed as brigadier generals. They were dubbed "political generals" because none of them had previous military training. The *Cincinnati Gazette* criticized Hamer's appointment: "The thing is absolutely ridiculous."

Upon his arrival, Hamer was given command of the First Brigade under General William O. Butler. Hamer impressed the regular soldiers by diligently studying his new duties.

He asked Grant, half his age, to tutor him on military strategy. One day the pair rode into the country and took positions on an elevated spot. "He explained to me many army evolutions," wrote Hamer. In one situation Grant, supposing he and Hamer to be generals commanding opposing armies, explained various maneuvers to the political general who was twice his age. Just when Hamer thought Grant's imaginary force had routed his army, "he suddenly suggested a strategic move for my forces which crowned them with triumphant victory, and himself with defeat." Grant "ended by gracefully offering to surrender his sword!"

AS TAYLOR'S COMMANDERS planned for the march to Monterrey, they knew they faced a series of challenges. First, while the victories at Palo Alto and Resaca de la Palma had been won by professional soldiers, the current army encompassed thousands of volunteers. Second, in earlier American wars the military moved by land or water, but the barren desert of northern Mexico would provide no roads and little water. Third, in both the Revolutionary War and the War of 1812 the soldiers had lived off the land, which would be impossible on this march.

By August, Polk and the press became uneasy at what they viewed as the holdup in the march to Monterrey. Taylor, hailed as a hero, was now being criticized as "General Delay."

One reason Taylor took his time was the realization that his army needed to be well supplied for an arduous march. To help meet this need, he created a new rank: regimental quartermaster. He knew he would need officers with leadership and organizational skills who were not afraid to work hard to keep troops fully supplied in the arduous march ahead. As a result, he tapped Grant to act as quartermaster for the Fourth Infantry.

Quartermaster General Thomas Sidney Jesup had held the top-ranking quartermaster post since 1818. Over the years, Jesup had improved systems for supplies and transportation, utilizing canals, the new railroads, even camels. But he was not ready for the logistic nightmare of the Mexican War. A colorful character willing to clash with generals and Congress, Jesup wrote Secretary of War William Marcy, "There has been no provident foresight exercised by any one in command." He felt "obliged to guess what might be wanted."

Under Jesup, Grant once again had to overcome a lengthy period of unpreparedness. He was handed a series of difficult tasks: provide clothing for his soldiers, find equipment (including extra rifles), and acquire more horses for the cavalry. But his primary burden would be transportation. This meant procuring carts, wagons, mules, and oxen.

Grant chafed at the new position. He wanted to be on the front lines, not ordering beans. He wrote Colonel John Garland: "I respectfully protest against being assigned to a duty which removes me from sharing in the dangers and honors of service with my company at the front." He asked to be transferred back to "my place in line."

Garland, writing from the perspective of thirty years' experience, replied, "Lt. Grant is respectfully informed that his protest cannot be considered. Lt. Grant was assigned to duty as Quartermaster and Commissary because of his observed ability, skill, and persistency in the line of duty."

Who "observed" him? The man at the top. This source was confirmed

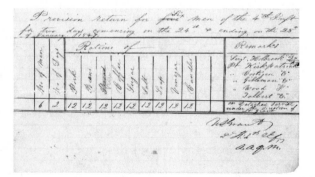

Grant's quartermaster ledger. Grant initially resisted his appointment as quartermaster, but it taught him the importance of provisioning a large, mobile army operating in hostile territory.

when Taylor's chief of staff, William Bliss (now a major), wrote Garland, "The Commanding General desires that you retain Lieut. Grant in his position of Quartermaster to the 4th Infantry." Grant, who had increasing respect for Taylor, had unknowingly been appreciated by him.

THE MOST URGENT problem: Whereas Taylor had started with more than 300 wagons at Corpus Christi, he was now reduced to 175. It fell to Grant to secure more wagons plus many more mules.

Once he had the mules, Grant recruited Mexican *arrieros,* whose job was to load the animals by lashing tents and packing cooking utensils on the mules' backs. Every morning it took several hours to get the mules to start walking.

Just as they were finally ready, the mules began to act up. Already tired of bearing heavy packs, "one would start to run, bowing his back and kicking up until he scattered his load; others would lie down and try to disarrange their loads by attempting to get on the top of them by rolling on them."

Observing this daily melee, Grant commented, "I am not aware of ever having used a profane expletive in my life; but I would have the charity to excuse those who may have done so, if they were in charge of a train of Mexican pack mules at the time."

Alexander Hays, a West Point friend, watched the new quartermaster on the road to Monterrey. "There was no road . . . so obstructed . . . but that Grant, in some mysterious way, would work his [mule] train through and have it in the camp of his brigade before the campfires were lighted." James D. Elderkin, of the Fourth Infantry, recounted that Grant "would generally go ahead of the regiment and get his supplies ready for the regiment for the night. When the regiment got there they would have nothing to do but pitch their tents." Grant may not have wanted the position of quartermaster originally, but his organizational skills and ability to work well with others brought him plaudits from observers.

MONTERREY, A CITY of fifteen thousand residents at the time, sat on the north bank of the Santa Catarina River, at the base of several spurs of the Sierra Madre. For its defense, General Ampudia was returned to command. City buildings were constructed of stone with flat roofs, so each building was easily converted into a fort. With three brigades recently arrived from Guadalajara, Ampudia had seven thousand regular troops. He also counted on three thousand rancheros, irregular troops raised from local ranches. French textbooks like the ones Grant studied at West

Point suggested that when assaulting an armed fortress, the attacking army should outnumber the defenders at least two to one, but Taylor approached Monterrey with a force of little more than six thousand men. Also, he and his staff, entering Mexico without understanding its history, did not reckon on the rancheros, guerrilla cavalry units that fought, disappeared, and then appeared again when least expected.

As the Americans approached Monterrey on September 18, they encountered a Mexican fort constructed from an unfinished cathedral. "Our army gave [it] the name of 'Black Fort,'" and on this day it bristled with guns, challenging anyone daring to approach from the north. To the west the city was defended both by the unfinished Bishop's Palace, situated on Independence Hill, and by Fort Soldado, which sat atop Federation Hill. Forts Diablo and de La Tenería protected the city on the east. On the south, the fast-flowing Santa Catarina River provided a natural barrier.

Taylor placed his confidence in fifty-two-year-old General William Worth, a handsome man who started his military career as a private in the War of 1812 and earned his way up the ranks. Even though Taylor knew Worth could be impetuous and ill-tempered, he regarded him as the best soldier in his army.

On Sunday, September 20, at two P.M., Taylor put his plan into action. He divided his army against a numerically superior foe. He believed he could make this unconventional strategy work by concealment and speed. To conceal his main objective, Taylor sent General David E. Twiggs's regulars and William O. Butler's volunteers, including Hamer's First Brigade, to threaten the city's eastern approaches. He sent Worth as his primary force to cut the Saltillo road, blocking reinforcements to Ampudia from the west.

In the evening, Taylor put the third prong of his plan in position. He moved his cannon onto the plain, just out of the Black Fort's range, in a low spot where the guns might be concealed. He dispatched Grant's Fourth Infantry to support the artillerists. Grant, as regimental quartermaster, was "ordered to remain in charge of camp and the public property."

The next morning, as the mist cleared, Grant saw "fire was opened on both sides and continued with, what seemed to me at that day, great fury." His instincts took over. "My curiosity got the better of my judgment, and I mounted a horse and rode to the front to see what was going on." Shortly after arriving, "an order to charge was given, and lacking the moral courage to return to camp—where I had been ordered to stay—I charged with the regiment."

The only officer on horseback, he charged with Garland's brigade. The horror of war happens fast. Men on foot fell all around him. "About one-third of the men engaged in the charge were killed or wounded in the space of a few minutes."

As the regiment began to retreat, thirty-two-year-old Charles Hoskins, whom Grant had known at Jefferson Barracks, "found himself very much fatigued," so "I offered him my horse." Continuing the retreat, Grant shortly came upon Hoskins again, now dead.

American losses this day were staggering—394 killed, including 34 officers. That night Calvin Benjamin returned to the plain, where men were trying to find survivors, guided by their moans. Benjamin discovered Grant cradling the head of a wounded comrade, "giving him water from a canteen and wiping his face with his moistened handkerchief."

A few hours later, as a wagon lumbered by filled with the dead, Grant found the body of Bob Hazlitt. He learned that his Camp Salubrity tent mate had been killed bringing his wounded captain to safety.

AT THREE THE next morning, Worth's troops began moving again toward the Saltillo road. They stormed the western slope of Independence Hill and fired a twelve-pound howitzer at Bishop's Palace, decimating its defenders. Worth entered the city and penned a note to Taylor: "The town is ours."

He wrote prematurely. Before the day was out, however, Twiggs's and Butler's divisions occupied the eastern portion of the city.

Early on September 23, the "Army of Invasion" began moving toward the central plaza. Mexican strategy now became clear: defend their city house by house, street by street. Residents placed sandbags on top of flat-roofed homes to protect soldiers as they fired down on Americans. They even drilled holes into walls from which they could fire.

Grant's Fourth Infantry, along with the Third Infantry, began advancing. The Mexicans fought with courage, and American loss of life was heavy. Halting two blocks from the plaza to assess their position, the two regiments discovered they were dangerously low on ammunition. Colonel Garland needed to get a message through to send either more ammunition or reinforcements.

"Men, I've got to send someone back to General Twiggs. It's a dangerous job, and I don't like to order any man to do it. Who'll volunteer?"

Grant volunteered.

He knew his ride through the streets of the center of Monterrey would be "an exposed one." After mounting a gray horse, Nellie, Grant slid down her side. "With only one foot holding to the cantle of the saddle, and an arm over the neck of the horse exposed, I started at full run."

He rode swiftly, wrapping his arm around the horse's neck just as he had done as a little boy to win the circus prize. When Mexican soldiers did catch sight of him at intersections, "I crossed at such a flying rate that generally I was past and under cover of the next block of houses before the enemy fired. I got out safely without a scratch." But before Grant could begin his return with the requested ammunition, the Third and Fourth infantry regiments were withdrawn.

In the early hours of September 25, General Taylor ordered an armistice. General Ampudia agreed to surrender the city. Taylor, believing he had won a great victory, hoped a generous peace could end this costly war. In that spirit, he allowed Ampudia to lead his army out from the city to a line south of the Rinconada Pass. Taylor agreed not to advance beyond this line for eight weeks, giving negotiators time to work out peace between the United States and Mexico.

Word did not reach Washington of the victory at Monterrey for more than two weeks. President Polk became furious when he learned Taylor's terms of armistice. He declared that Taylor "had the enemy in his power and should have taken them prisoners, deprived them of their arms." Instead, Polk believed, Taylor allowed the Mexican army to fight another day.

Grant did not see it Polk's way at all. He understood that the American army was battered at Monterrey and needed these eight weeks to rest and recuperate.

JULIA DENT'S LIFE did not stand still while Grant fought in Mexico. She frequented the French Market and attended the circuses and menageries popular in the 1840s. Accompanied by her sisters and friend Carrie O'Fallon, she listened to celebrity lecturers, including Henry Clay and Daniel Webster. N. M. Ludlow and Sol Smith, who operated theaters in New Orleans and Mobile, opened a theater in St. Louis. Encouraged by Carrie, Julia attended Shakespearean and French plays. Several plays by Edward Bulwer, including *The Lady of Lyons,* were also produced.

With returning soldiers speaking of the frequent fandangos in Mexico, young women worried about the fidelity of their young men. Perhaps Julia comforted herself with the thought that Ulysses could not dance.

Ulysses wrote Julia after the Battle of Monterrey. He did not tell her of his heroic dash under fire to secure ammunition for his beleaguered comrades. He did tell her, "I am getting very tired of this war." He was "impatient of being separated from one I love so much."

THE WELCOME ARMISTICE allowed Ulysses to write longer letters to Julia in the fall of 1846. These letters reveal his observant, artistic eye. While some soldiers wrote home disparagingly of Mexico, he marveled about Monterrey: "This is the most beautiful spot that it has been my fortune to see in this world." With feeling, he described the "beautiful city enclosed on three sides by the mountains with a pass through them to the right and to the left." Knowing her love of trees, he described this city "so full of Orange, Lime, and Pomegranate trees that the houses can scarcely be seen until you get into the town."

By November, having had time to explore the city and its immediate environs, he wrote, "The climate is excellent, the soil rich, and the scenery beautiful." He stood by his earlier compliment: "If it was an American city I have no doubt it would be considered the handsomest one in the Union." But however much he seemed to be enjoying his surroundings, the young second lieutenant remained lonely. Ulysses, even if enjoying the splendors of his days in Monterrey, wanted Julia to know: "Without you *dearest* a Paradise would become lonesome."

TO THE EXTENT Grant developed his military abilities during the Mexican War, he did so largely by observing the leadership of senior officers.

He was impressed by both Taylor's dress and his approachability. "General Taylor never made any great show or parade, either of uniform or retinue." On the road to Monterrey, he dressed in a dusty green coat and topped his head with a straw hat. Observing his outfit, an Indiana volunteer said Taylor reminded him of a farmer bound for market with eggs to sell. Grant would be permanently influenced by Taylor's accessibility. He "was known to every soldier in his army, and was respected by all."

As regimental quartermaster, Grant began to understand that army officers in the field depended upon civilian and military leaders back home for supplies and troops. Despite plenty of reasons to grumble, "General Taylor was not an officer to trouble the administration much with his demands, but was inclined to do the best he could with the means given him."

Finally, what impressed Grant most was Taylor's demeanor in the face of danger. "No soldier could face either danger or responsibility more calmly than he. These are qualities more rarely found than genius or physical courage." Taylor's leadership style became a model for the young lieutenant.

ANOTHER MODEL LEADER, Thomas Hamer, died after the Battle of Monterrey. He contracted dysentery, seemed to recover, then died suddenly on December 2, 1846. Upon hearing of Hamer's death, Taylor lamented, "I have lost the balance wheel of my volunteer army."

If Taylor had lost a general, Grant had lost his early champion and later comrade. Profoundly saddened, he wrote Hamer's wife that her husband "died within the sound of battle, and that was a pleasure to him as a brave soldier." He concluded, "Personally, his death is a loss to me which no words can express."

MORE THAN SIXTEEN hundred miles from Monterrey, President Polk, Secretary of War Marcy, and General in Chief Scott, facing a lengthening war with the public's patriotic fervor beginning to wane, resolved to stop Taylor at Monterrey. Taylor faced an eight-hundred-mile march to Mexico City; instead, Polk envisioned ending the war by landing an army at the port city of Veracruz, where it could march less than three hundred miles west to the capital city.

The president knew that whatever military strategy he chose would be fraught with political consequences. During his 1844 campaign, he had promised to be a one-term president. The Democrats won the presidency in 1828 with a military hero, Andrew Jackson, as their standard-bearer. Now they feared a Whig military hero, perhaps Taylor or Scott, might sweep the 1848 elections. After Taylor's victory at Monterrey, Whigs won both houses of Congress in the 1846 midterm elections and began boosting Taylor for president in 1848.

Polk toyed with appointing a Democratic commander but found himself boxed in. He no longer liked Taylor and did not trust Scott. In the end, reluctantly, he appointed Scott.

As 1847 DAWNED, Grant dreamed of going home. It had been two and a half years since he had last seen "dear Julia." He departed Monterrey on January 11, not sure of his ultimate destination. He knew only that he was being transferred from General David Twiggs's division to William Worth's division.

Grant soon perceived Worth to be "a different man from any I had before served directly under." On the trek from Monterrey, Grant saw no reason for haste since it would take weeks before Scott could assemble troops to land at Veracruz. Yet the general pushed his troops. On one occasion, after an all-day march, Grant was helping tired men set up their tents and prepare their food when Worth suddenly ordered tents struck with preparations for an immediate march that could just have been undertaken the next day. Grant observed, "Some commanders can move troops so as to get the maximum distance out of them without fatigue, while others can wear them out in a few days without accomplishing so much. Worth belonged in this latter class." Further, he was "nervous, impatient and restless on the march." If Grant had learned from Taylor how to be a calm, effective, and admired leader, from Worth he learned how not to be.

Grant's division traveled by steamer down the Rio Grande to a camp near the site of the Battle of Palo Alto. Here he learned he was not going home. Instead, he received orders to join Scott's army for a landing at Veracruz. He wrote Julia, "As soon as Gen. Scott took command everything was changed."

WHEN GRANT TOOK his place in Scott's army, he entered into a new form of warfare. A main port city and commercial hub, Veracruz was as critical to Mexico as Boston or Charleston was to the United States. The crowded city, shaped like an irregular hexagon, was protected by fifteen-foot-high walls. It was defended by San Juan de Ulúa, a fortress on an island a half mile opposite the city and considered unassailable. Scott planned to land near the city, force it to surrender, and defeat Mexican general Juan Esteban Morales.

Scott requested that the navy build surfboats, the first ever amphibious craft used by the American military. These flat-bottomed boats could carry seventy to eighty men.

March 9 became D-Day for the launch from Antón Lizardo, a fishing town fourteen miles south of Veracruz. Eighty transport vessels, protected by five gunboats and two steamers, readied themselves for the landing on Collado Beach, a long shoreline of gently sloping sand dunes dotted with chaparral three miles south of Veracruz and beyond the range of the guns of San Juan de Ulúa. The boats presented a panorama of white canvas as far as the eye could see. Scott unfurled his blue-and-red pennant on his wooden steamship *Massachusetts* and passed through the armada of ships to "shouts and cheers from every deck."

Grant, not in a boat, described the tense scene as blue-and-gray-clad troops entered the surfboats for the 450-yard dash to the beach. Mexican cavalry could be seen topping the sand hills just beyond the beach. "The

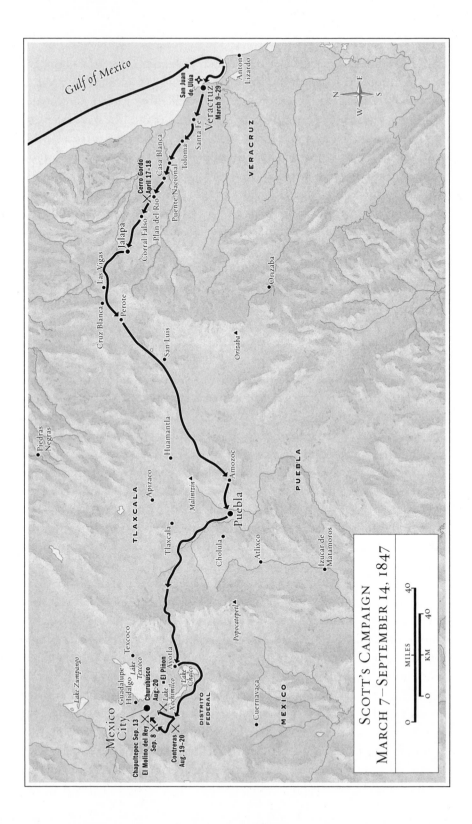

Gulf of Mexico

San Juan
de Ulúa

Antón
Lizardo

Veracruz
March 9–29

VERACRUZ

Santa Fe

Tolomé

Casa Blanca

Puente Nacional

Plan del Río

Corral Falso

Cerro Gordo
✕ **April 17–18**

Jalapa

Las Vigas

Orizaba

Cruz Blanca

Perote

San Luis

Orizaba▲

Piedras
Negras

Huamantla

Apizaco

Amozoc

PUEBLA

TLAXCALA

Malinzin▲

Puebla

Tlaxcala

Cholula

Atlixco

Izúcar de
Matamoros

Popocatepetl▲

MEXICO

Cuernavaca

Lake Zumpango

Guadalupe
Hidalgo Lake
Texcoco

Texcoco
Lake
Texcoco

Mexico
City

Xaltocan

Churubusco
Aug. 20

El Piñón

Ayotla
Lake
Xochimilco

Lake
Chalco

DISTRITO
FEDERAL

Chapultepec Sep. 13
El Molino del Rey
Sep. 8

Contreras
Aug. 19–20

N

W   E

S

SCOTT'S CAMPAIGN
MARCH 7–SEPTEMBER 14, 1847

MILES   40

KM   40

0

breakers were sometimes high, so that the landing was tedious." Each moment, he expected the crack of cannon or musket fire from beyond the small sand hills.

To his relief, except for a few poorly aimed shells, the Mexicans made no attempt to repel the landing. Worth, in a leading boat, jumped into the water and sloshed to shore, followed by more and more men, all holding their guns above their heads. Grant dashed up the sand hills, but the Mexican cavalry had disappeared. In this unprecedented landing, not one man on either side was killed in the assault. General Juan Morales decided not to oppose the landing but to make his stand behind the invincible walls of the fort and city.

To replace soldiers killed at Monterrey, new officers joined the Fourth Infantry, including Virginian Tom Jackson and South Carolinian D. H. Hill. Grant saw older officers he had been hearing about: Captain Robert E. Lee, Scott's favorite; Joe Johnston, much talked about for his leadership in the Seminole Wars in Florida; and Major Jubal Early, a Virginia lawyer. Grant was especially pleased to see Fred Dent with the Fifth Infantry. He wrote Julia, "Fred is here and well. I see him every day."

With General Morales refusing to surrender, by March 13 Scott had completed a seven-mile siege line with which to cannonade the city from all directions. The Mexicans, with 3,000 soldiers inside the city and 1,030 in the fortress, fought valiantly but finally surrendered on March 29 after twenty days of attack. As they stacked their arms and marched out, Americans marched in to the tune of "Yankee Doodle."

Since no American army had ever marched through hostile territory before, except for brief raids into Canada in the War of 1812, Scott's campaign had no American precedent. Grant admired Scott's efforts to soothe the feelings of the defeated Veracruz citizens, determined as he was not to alienate the Mexican citizens. He imposed martial law and even hung an American soldier for raping a Mexican woman. He posted sentries in front of each Catholic church. He assured merchants he would pay fair prices for goods needed to supply his army, a reproach to Polk, who had advised him to seize supplies without payment.

EAGER TO START for Mexico City, Scott marched west with barely ten thousand soldiers, leaving behind one thousand troops who helped tend another one thousand sick and wounded Americans. He started on the National Road—the same road Spaniard Hernán Cortés had traveled in 1519.

Grant foresaw problems ahead. First, he observed that Scott com-

*Grant served under Winfield Scott,
"Old Fuss and Feathers," a different kind
of military leader from Zachary Taylor,
on the U.S. advance from Veracruz to
Mexico City in 1847.*

manded "a very small army with which to penetrate two hundred and sixty miles into an enemy's country, and to besiege the capital." With an army half the size he had requested, Scott expressed his fury at "the perfidy of Mr. Polk."

Second, Quartermaster General Jesup presented Scott with impending logistic problems. He calculated that Scott's army would require 2,893,950 pounds of supplies to be transported in 9,303 wagons and carried by 17,413 mules. Included among his requirements would be 300 bottles of ink and 5,000 quills.

Third, it was important to get away from Veracruz to avoid the yellow fever, or *vómito,* which usually visited that city early in the year. The first two victims succumbed on April 9.

Scott set the first leg of the march as seventy-four miles to Jalapa. Starting out on April 13, Grant had to push and pull his supply wagons through ten miles of burning sand before he reached the paved road. As if the recalcitrant mules did not provide enough problems, he was forced to use unbroken mustangs that kicked their harnesses and wagon trees to bits. When the horses gave out, Grant fastened ropes so already worn-down infantrymen could drag the wagons through ankle-deep sand. Men fell with sunstroke. Six members of the Fourth Infantry died in the first days.

Fifteen miles east of Jalapa, advance scouts spied General Antonio López de Santa Anna's troops dug in at Cerro Gordo, a narrow passage at the foot of the eastern Cordilleras. Santa Anna, military and political leader, had first gained fame by destroying the defenders of the Alamo in 1836. At Cerro Gordo, he had placed artillery at crucial bends of the zig-zag road. Grant saw that a direct attack along the road was not possible. But a flanking movement seemed equally impossible.

On April 17, Scott dispatched Captain Robert E. Lee on a reconnaissance mission to find a way to get behind the Mexican forces. Awed, Grant watched as Lee's engineers opened roadways "over chasms to the right where the walls were so steep that men could barely climb them." Working into the evening darkness, "artillery was let down the steep slopes by hand." Remarkably, "in like manner the guns were drawn by hand up the opposite slopes."

The next day, Scott struck the rear of Santa Anna's positions. "The surprise of the enemy was complete." Within hours, the Americans won a decisive victory. They took three thousand prisoners and sent Santa Anna's battered troops backpedaling toward Puebla. In his official report, Scott wrote, "I am compelled to make special mention of . . . Captain R. E. Lee, Engineer." Grant agreed. "Perhaps there was not a battle of the Mexican War, or of any other, where orders issued before an engagement were nearer being a correct report of what afterwards took place."

Having learned of the victory at Veracruz, Polk decided to send a peace negotiator to accompany Scott. Secretary of State James Buchanan suggested they send a Democrat, Nicholas P. Trist, chief clerk in the State Department, who spoke fluent Spanish. Trist was sent to negotiate a treaty that established the Rio Grande as the northern boundary of Mexico, relinquished New Mexico and California to the United States, and secured the right of transit across the Isthmus of Tehuantepec. Polk authorized his negotiator to pay Mexico up to $30 million.

Scott misunderstood Trist's mission and refused to meet him when he arrived on May 14. The general fired off a letter to Secretary of War Marcy, bristling at yet another attempt by a Democratic White House "to degrade me, by requiring that the commander of this army should defer to . . . the chief clerk of the Department of State [on] the question of continuing or discontinuing hostilities." Marcy had failed to communicate the president's agreement that if Trist negotiated a peace settlement acceptable to Scott, the general was free to execute it without referring back to Washington.

Scott called upon Grant in Puebla, where the army spent the next three months refitting and waiting for reinforcements. Following the example of Cortés, but challenging the textbooks studied at West Point, Scott decided to cut his 175-mile supply line back to Veracruz. He was losing too many soldiers defending it against roving guerrillas and believed he needed every soldier for the seventy-five-mile march to Mexico City.

Because the army needed supplies, he sent Grant with a group of wagons on a two-day march to collect fruits and vegetables and to forage from plantations they had passed. Protected by troops, Grant noted the presence of rancheros ready to pick off army stragglers.

Back in Puebla, Grant worked to refit and reclothe the army. Time and again, new troops had been told they would receive clothing and blankets in New Orleans, only to be told they would instead receive them at Veracruz, only to be told they would surely receive them at Puebla. Grant helped oversee "one thousand Mexican men and women" to make everything from shoes to overcoats.

He wrote Julia about Puebla, the "largest city we have yet seen in Mexico, with houses large and well built. . . . I wish I could see you here for one day to see all the grand churches, the beautiful public walks &c. &c. they are far superior to anything you expect." He must have surprised her when he wrote that Puebla "surpasses St. Louis by far both in appearance and size."

Scott remained in Puebla longer than he intended while waiting for reinforcements. On July 8, Major General Gideon Pillow arrived with nearly forty-five hundred men. Another Democrat appointed as a political general, Pillow had been President Polk's law partner in Tennessee, apparently a qualification sufficient for command. Finally, on August 6, Brigadier General Franklin Pierce, a former New Hampshire congressman and senator who had turned down the position as attorney general in the Polk administration to enlist as a volunteer, arrived with twenty-four hundred men.

ON AUGUST 9, Grant left Puebla with Scott's reconstituted army of 10,638. Scott was forced to leave behind 2,500 sick in hospitals and 600 convalescing in barracks. After several days' march, from a ridge below the 17,802-foot volcano known as Popocatépetl, "Smoking Mountain," Grant could see the enormous Valley of Mexico stretching out before him. Not more than thirty miles away loomed the outline of the capital, with its population approaching two hundred thousand. At an altitude of seventy-eight hundred feet, the city sat on a high plateau in a slowly drying lake bed whose floor contained six lakes, marshes, and fields traversed by elevated roads. There, Santa Anna waited once more with an army of nearly thirty-five thousand men. These wetlands limited Scott's avenues of approach. He ordered Lee, recently promoted to major, to investigate possible attack routes.

By August 12, Scott's advance troops arrived within fifteen miles of the capital. Since Lee's reconnaissance reported the national road funneled directly into thickly defended positions, Scott decided to approach the city from the south, traveling near El Pedrégal, an ancient lava bed nearly five miles wide. While Scott formulated his final plan, Grant helped set up tents as Worth's division stopped for several days along the shores of Lake Chalco.

On August 19, Scott began his assault on the outer ring of defenses, overrunning Mexican forces at the town of Contreras. Grant, in Garland's brigade, rushed forward as Mexicans retreated in disarray across the Churubusco River. For one of the few times in the war, intelligence did not detect fifteen hundred Mexican national guardsmen stationed inside the Franciscan Convent of San Mateo directly in their path. There, General Manuel Rincón ordered his men to wait until the Americans were almost upon the convent. Then, in some of the fiercest fighting in the war, a desperate battle erupted between Mexican defenders inside the convent and Americans outside attacking under the cover of six-foot-high cornfields. The Americans prevailed, but at a heavy cost. At Contreras and Churubusco, they suffered casualties of 133 dead and 865 wounded. Mexican casualties were much heavier: Santa Anna lost nearly one-third of his 10,000 men, dead, wounded, or captured.

Now at the gates of the capital, Scott paused, hoping that Santa Anna's overwhelming defeat would produce negotiations. A truce began on August 21. Scott and Trist, who had overcome their misunderstandings, hoped that agreeing to an armistice would lead to negotiating for peace. But as day followed disappointing day, Santa Anna rearmed for yet another fight, banking on the courage of the Mexican people to defend their capital.

By September 7, Scott received reports from spies that church bells were being melted to produce cannon at a lightly defended flour mill, El Molino del Rey ("the King's Mill").

On September 8, a select group of five hundred men, including Grant, prepared to storm the cluster of buildings at dawn. As they surged forward, a pair of twenty-four-pounders fired ten shots each from inside the stone buildings. And then silence. However, the silence was only a ploy. The attackers, including Fred Dent, charged forward—into a bloodbath.

Within five minutes Worth lost ten officers. Santa Anna, alerted to Scott's intentions, had prepared a welcome.

Grant was with the first troops to enter the mill. As some Mexican soldiers began to run, he glimpsed a few close by on the roof. Quickly, he positioned a cart and used the shafts of the building as a ladder to climb to the roof; there, in hand-to-hand fighting, he helped disarm some Mexican officers.

In the fighting, Fred Dent suffered a wound to his thigh. Grant came upon Julia's brother on the ground, losing blood. He examined the wound and, believing it not serious, lifted Fred to the top of the wall, where medics would see him. Then he dashed forward once more.

With Molino del Rey overcome, on September 13 Scott set his sights on the heavily fortified Chapultepec Castle as the last assault before attacking the city center. Perched on a two-hundred-foot rocky hill with the Colegio Militar—Mexico's military academy—on its grounds, the castle bristled with guns, some manned by hired French gunners.

Grant watched as the volunteer divisions led by Gideon Pillow and John A. Quitman scaled the rocky slopes from the south and west. At the base of the castle, in order to climb the twelve- to fifteen-foot-high walls, they erected scaling ladders. Troops cheered when the American flag was raised above the ramparts.

With Chapultepec in American hands, Grant's regiment advanced down a double-track road, divided by a narrow aqueduct, toward the San Cosme *garita* ("gate") to the city. Fired upon from rooftops lining the route, he described soldiers protecting themselves "by keeping under the arches supporting the aqueduct, advancing an arch at a time."

As Grant approached the *garita,* looking for a way to silence the gate's defenders, he spotted a church belfry. He took several men and crossed a field with ditches of water to arrive at the church's back door.

"When I knocked for admission a priest came to the door, who, while extremely polite, declined to admit us." Grant, in the Spanish he had picked up, "explained to him that he might save property by opening the door, and he certainly would save himself from becoming a prisoner . . . and besides, I intended to go in whether he consented or not." The door opened.

Grant was only several hundred yards from the San Cosme gate when "shots from our little gun dropped in upon the enemy and created great confusion." He waited for the Mexicans to fire in return or come to seize him, but to his surprise, all was silent.

Worth had noticed the effect of Grant's effort and sent his aide, John

Pemberton, to the church to bring Grant to him. When Pemberton climbed the belfry, Grant replied he was too busy to come just now. Worth offered Grant a second gun, which he did not refuse, but "I could not tell the General that there was not room enough in the steeple for another gun."

ON SEPTEMBER 14 at seven A.M., the American flag was slowly raised over the Zócalo, the magnificent plaza bounded by the National Palace, the Cathedral of the Assumption of Mary, and City Hall. Santa Anna's forces had abandoned the city the night before, but not before releasing thirty thousand convicts from the city's prisons as a welcoming committee for the Americans. One hour later, Scott, "Old Fuss and Feathers," now the new Cortés, entered Mexico City in full dress uniform. He took up residence in a palace built at the site where Aztec emperors, the viceroy of New Spain, and presidents of the Republic of Mexico had all ruled.

GRANT WOULD COME to believe the Mexican War was unjust—a large nation attacking a small nation—but he had high praise for the American army. "The men engaged in the Mexican War were brave, and the officers of the regular army, from highest to lowest, were educated in their profession," he declared. "A more efficient army for its number and armament I do not believe ever fought a battle."

Grant commended the two commanders with whom he served but offered insightful comparisons. Zachary Taylor, dressed for "comfort," moved throughout the field of battle by his own timetable, without staff, trusting "his own eyes" to size up the situation. Winfield Scott "wore all the uniform prescribed" and traveled with a large staff who notified his troops of the exact hour he would arrive, so that "all the army might be under arms to salute their chief as he passed." Grant admired Taylor and Scott; "with their opposite characteristics both were great and successful soldiers." But in his praise, Grant tipped his hand as to what kind of leader he wished to be: "Both were pleasant to serve under—Taylor was pleasant to serve with."

THE MEXICAN WAR was the first time West Point graduates fought in an American conflict in substantial numbers. If at the beginning of the war many Americans had little knowledge of West Point graduates, by war's end their names and accomplishments forever turned the tide of opinion about the academy's value and the importance of a trained officer corps.

Although Grant did not realize it at the time, his duties in the Mexican War as a quartermaster, procuring much-needed supplies for American armies fighting on foreign soil, had taught him a valuable lesson that he would employ years later in a war fought on American soil: An army without adequate transportation is an army without supplies that will become an army unable to fight.

From Mexico, Grant wrote his parents, "My new post of quartermaster is considered to afford an officer an opportunity to be relieved from fighting, but I do not and cannot see it in that light." He wanted his parents to know of his debt to them: "You have always taught me that the post of danger is the post of duty."

Grant's experiences in Mexico also deepened his curiosity about other cultures. It would be ten long months after the declaration of victory before he would be able to go home to Julia. He used those months well, expanding his knowledge of a foreign country and its people. But his journey outward was also a journey inward. The young officer who crossed the boundary back into the United States would arrive with a deepened sense of awareness. The war prompted him to ask questions about himself, the army he served, and the American nation he loved.

The Mexican War of 1846–1848, largely forgotten today, was the second costliest war in American history in terms of the percentage of soldiers who died. Of the 78,718 American soldiers who served, 13,283 died, constituting a casualty rate of 16.87 percent. By comparison, the casualty rate was 2.5 percent in World War I and World War II, 0.1 percent in Korea and Vietnam, and 21 percent for the Civil War. Of the casualties, 11,562 died of illness, disease, and accidents. Thirty-nine men Grant had known at West Point died. Four members of his 1843 class lost their lives.

No one could forecast the future of Grant's military career, but Thomas Hamer had made a prescient prediction before his death: "Of course, Lieutenant Grant is too young for command, but his capacity for future military usefulness is undoubted."

PART TWO

Trial

1848–1861

Suffering produces endurance, and endurance
produces character, and character produces hope.

—Romans 5:3–4

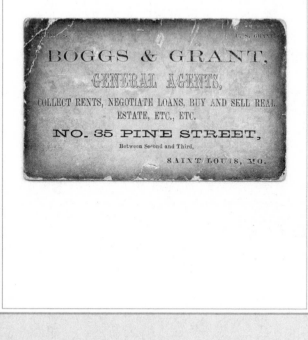

CHAPTER 7

Panama

One of the coolest men in all these trying circumstances I ever saw.
—Lieutenant Henry D. Wallen, crossing the Isthmus
of Panama, summer 1852

Grant may have finished twenty-first out of thirty-nine in his West Point class, but another ranking took place on the battlefields of Mexico. Despite being removed from combat while serving as quartermaster for much of the campaign, Grant won two brevets for courage in the closing days of the war—"for brave and meritorious conduct" in the Battle of Molino del Rey of September 8, 1847, and "for gallant conduct" at Chapultepec on September 13, 1847. He was among only eight in the class of 1843 to win two brevets.

The special reward would be to go home and marry Julia. The obstacle was the peace negotiations. On the Mexican side, Santa Anna, after a last-ditch attack at Puebla, abdicated the presidency and withdrew into hiding. Grant observed, "It looked doubtful for a time whether the United States Commissioner, Mr. Trist, would find anybody to negotiate with."

The next months of peace negotiations proceeded like a dramatic comedy. Trist, often depicted as an anonymous clerk in the U.S. State Department, was actually experienced in government dealings with foreign countries. Mexico finally formed a Congress and elected Manuel de la Peña y Peña as president. A person of moderate political views, Peña y Peña appointed himself and two others as commissioners to the negotiations. The Mexicans soon trusted Trist because of his constant courtesy and impeccable command of Spanish. Trist came to develop empathy for a defeated Mexico and invited his Mexican counterparts to offer their proposals for peace.

When word of Trist's actions reached President Polk, he exploded— the victor should not be negotiating with the victim. By now hungering for more Mexican territory, Polk talked of annexing the northern state of Tamaulipas as far south as the port of Tampico. The president recalled Trist by a letter dated October 6. Trist remained unaware of Polk's letter for six weeks, and when it finally arrived on November 16, he decided to ignore it. With Scott's encouragement, he started negotiations.

GRANT'S REGIMENT WAS stationed at the village of Tacubaya, four miles southwest of the capital. Not content with the quiet countryside, he rode into the capital almost every day to partake of the city and its culture. The National Theatre and the National Museum opened its doors to American soldiers. The reading room across from the post office offered a circulating library of English books.

One day Grant decided to visit Joshua Howard, commander of the American force at Chapultepec. The lieutenant colonel's office was located inside the castle, which was surrounded by a high earthwork. Grant rode around the earthwork several times. Seeing no place to hitch his horse, he spurred it over the earthwork and down the steep stone stairs on the other side.

When Colonel Howard came out of his office and saw Grant's horse tied by the door, he exclaimed, "Lieutenant, how in the world did you get your horse in here?"

"Rode him in, sir," replied Grant.

"And how do you expect to get him out?"

"Ride him up the steps instead of down."

When the meeting was over, Grant mounted his horse. As horse and rider clambered up the steps, the lieutenant gave a wave of his hat and "disappeared like a flash over the breastworks."

As quartermaster, aware of the problems that arise when soldiers have too much time on their hands, Grant set to work raising additional moneys for the regimental fund to be able to "establish libraries," pay musicians for band concerts, "subscribe to magazines," and in other ways "furnish many extra comforts to the men."

Grant decided to repeat a scheme that he had carried out in Monterrey: run a bakery. He hired Mexicans as bakers and soon had a thriving business. He could not believe the results. In Monterrey he had made "no profit," but here "in two months I made more money for the fund than my pay amounted to during the entire war."

Wanting to experience life as Mexicans did, one Sunday Grant paid 50 cents to attend a bullfight. He quickly discovered "the sight to me was sickening" and did not stay long. "I could not see how human beings could enjoy the suffering of beasts, and often of men."

. . .

MONTHS PASSED IN this manner. On February 2, 1848, Trist concluded a peace treaty that the commissioners signed at Guadalupe Hidalgo. The Senate ratified it on March 10, confirming American claims to Texas and setting the boundary at the Rio Grande. The Mexican government ceded to the United States New Mexico and Upper California, which included present-day Arizona and New Mexico, as well as parts of Nevada, Utah, and Colorado. In exchange, the United States paid Mexico $15 million and assumed claims against Mexico by United States citizens. The Mexican Congress ratified the treaty on May 25. United States troops began leaving Mexico five days later.

ON JUNE 6, as part of his preparations to leave Mexico, Quartermaster Grant took $1,000 in army silver to Captain John Gore's tent and locked it in a trunk for safekeeping. The chest in his own quarters had had its lock broken recently. On the night of June 16, the trunk was stolen. At Grant's request, General Worth convened a board of inquiry that concluded, "No blame can attach to Lt. U. S. Grant, that he took every means to secure the Money." Although blameless, however, Grant was still required to reimburse the government.

Grant was part of the last division to leave Mexico. In July, as his ship moved out into the Gulf of Mexico from Veracruz, he could smell the familiar vanilla scent of acacia trees and see the city's white walls covered with red flowers.

Just like his namesake, this wandering Ulysses headed home from war to his waiting love. On July 23, his ship arrived at Pascagoula, Mississippi. He learned the Fourth Infantry was being assigned to duty on the northern frontier, facing Canada. Grant was granted an immediate two-month leave, booked passage for St. Louis, and arrived on July 28.

The Dents were not at White Haven that summer, so Grant headed for their home in St. Louis. After more than three years apart, he and Julia held hands as if they would never let go. In the weeks that followed, in Julia's words, she and Ulys visited "all day long." Twelve-year-old Emmy, hovering everywhere, reported, "He showed his future bride the most devoted, yet quiet, attention."

Grant renewed one of his favorite enjoyments—the theater. Emmy remembered during these pre-wedding days, "the Captain frequently took me and Julia to the theatre" at the impressive Greek-temple theater at Third and Olive, which could seat fifteen hundred people in its three galleries. Built by pioneering theater managers Sol Smith and Noah Ludlow, it ranked among the most attractive in the country and hosted some of the best actors of the day. Grant's love of the art was so great that he overcame his shyness to introduce himself to Smith, a man he would stay in touch with for years to come.

Ulysses and Julia were married at the Dent home on August 22, 1848, a warm summer evening. Although gaslight had come to St. Louis the previous year, the home was lit by a profusion of candles. Julia walked down the narrow staircase into the parlor wearing a soft, white watered-silk dress, a gift from Mrs. O'Fallon. Julia's bridesmaids, dressed in white, included sister Nellie, cousin Julia Boggs, and friend Sarah Walker. Ulysses, in his splendid blue military uniform, was flanked by James Longstreet, Cadmus Marcellus Wilcox, and Bernard Pratt.

Ulysses had no expensive gift for Julia, only a daguerreotype of himself. In future years, many photographs would be taken of him, but Julia always prized this small wedding present. She placed it in a gold locket fastened to a strap at her wrist. Whether he would be near or far, she could open the locket and see his face.

Ulysses and Julia seemed barely conscious of the internal tension beneath the surface of their happy wedding. She was the daughter of a slave owner. He was the son of an ardent antislavery father. Jesse and Hannah decided not to attend the wedding.

THE NEWLYWEDS PREPARED to report to Grant's posting at Detroit, Michigan. Grant had given some thought to resigning but decided to stay in the army. He had come to value his developing friendships. Finally, Julia would be with him.

Or would she? As the designated day approached, Julia "burst into a flood of tears" at the thought of being far from family and friends. Colonel Dent stepped into the breach, suggesting to his new son-in-law, "You join your regiment and leave Julia with us." He proposed that Grant "get a leave of absence once or twice a year and run on here and spend a week or two with us," adding, "I always knew she could not live in the army."

Ulysses put his arms around her and whispered, "Would you like this, Julia?"

She responded tearfully, "I could not, would not, think of that for a moment."

AFTER MEXICO, GRANT found himself in a very different peacetime army. He would serve in a standing army reduced to its prewar size of eight thousand men, most deployed on the western frontier.

In 1848, Zachary Taylor ran for president as the Whig candidate. Grant favored "Old Rough and Ready," but visiting relatives in Covington, Kentucky, on Election Day, he did not vote. Taylor won against the Democratic candidate, Michigan senator Lewis Cass, with former president Martin Van Buren, running under the short-lived Free Soil Party banner, a distant third.

Grant arrived in Detroit on November 17 in the aftermath of the election, with the press blaring constant news about the discovery of gold in California. He and Julia would live on his army pay of $1,000 a year plus rations for their house and feed for his horses. Commanding officer William Whistler, who had not served in the war and was unfamiliar with the position of regimental quartermaster, informed him of new orders: he was to report to Madison Barracks in Sackets Harbor on the isolated eastern shore of Lake Ontario in northern New York. Grant protested, to no avail, that as quartermaster he should remain at the Detroit headquarters.

After a tedious trip, he and Julia arrived at Madison Barracks on December 2. They had not been there long when they were ordered to return to Detroit, but by this time ice had closed all transportation, forcing them to remain for the winter.

Isolated Sackets Harbor proved to be a place where Ulysses and Julia established the patterns of their new marriage. Whether it was enjoying reading, racing about on sleigh rides, or attending the Sackets Harbor Presbyterian church, each found in the other a satisfying complement.

Julia received an allowance to run the house and kept her accounts in a small black book. "My little book never, no never, added up quite right." When she requested his assistance, Ulys replied, jesting, "I cannot make out your mathematical conundrums."

When off duty, Ulysses sometimes liked to ride the ten miles to Watertown, where he played checkers and chess and raced horses with lawyer Charles W. Ford. "Grant was a favorite among the enlisted men," remembered Walter B. Camp. He "always talked to a man freely and without putting on the airs of a superior officer."

WHEN WARMER WEATHER began melting the ice, Ulysses and Julia returned to Detroit. In April 1849, while Julia went on to Bethel and then St. Louis for a visit with their families, he secured a modest two-story, five-room pine house at 253 East Fort Street, a few blocks from the barracks headquarters on Russell Street, for $250 a year. In the rear stood a stable for Nelly Bly, Brevet Captain Grant's prized mare.

Grant found Detroit, approaching twenty thousand people in 1849, "very dull." He found quartermaster work dull also. Used to the challenge of equipping an army in battle, he quickly learned how mind-numbing paperwork at a desk could be. "I was no clerk, nor had I any capacity to become one."

Soon after his arrival, Grant was befriended by the Reverend George Taylor, the new pastor at the Congress Street Methodist Church. Grant began to attend and eventually rented a pew.

When Julia returned, she and Grant began to socialize with several of the other officers stationed there. James E. Pitman, an army friend of Grant's who also attended the Congress Church, spent considerable time with the couple. Watching them together, Pitman was struck in particular by what he perceived to be Julia's power over her husband: "His wife was outgoing and Grant came out of his shell in her presence."

For entertainment, the Grants and others enjoyed the weekly dances at the Michigan Exchange Hotel. She danced; he did not. Friend Palmer, a fellow quartermaster in the Mexican War, watched Grant "stand around or hold down a seat all evening."

To those who observed him, it appeared that Grant was not overfond of alcohol: almost everyone drank at these cotillions, but Palmer remembered that he "never saw Grant under the influence of liquor." And Pitman recalled that even though "Detroit was a frontier town and all used whiskey freely . . . Grant drank no more than the rest of the officers."

In autumn 1849, Julia announced she was pregnant. In the spring, on the advice of Dr. Charles Tripler, she traveled to her parents' home, where she gave birth to Frederick Dent Grant on May 30, 1850. Upon hearing of his son's birth, Ulysses hurried to St. Louis. By the time he returned with mother and baby to Detroit, he learned that President Zachary Taylor had died suddenly on July 9 after only sixteen months in office. Taylor's successor, Millard Fillmore, a lawyer from upstate New York who had served several terms in the House of Representatives, was largely unknown.

While in Michigan, Grant showed no signs of taking on Jesse's political ambitions. Nor was he an army politician, coddling those who could advance his career. The closest he came to political engagement occurred in the winter of 1851. After he and other officers slipped repeatedly on the ice in front of the home of Zachariah Chandler, Grant and several others sued Chandler for disobeying the city ordinance that obliged homeowners to remove snow in front of their homes. Grant did not anticipate that just before the trial, Chandler would be nominated for mayor in the March elections.

When the case went to court in March, Grant was the only soldier who signed the deposition. Chandler acted as his own lawyer. A massive man, he lashed out at the soldiers: "If you soldiers would keep sober, perhaps you would not fall on people's pavements and hurt your legs." Even though the evidence favored Grant, he did not reckon with the power of politics on the courts. Chandler lost but won. He agreed to pay a fine of but 6 cents and court costs of $8. When city elections were held, the new constitution permitted Grant to vote, but he did not.

In June, Ulysses informed Julia that the Fourth Infantry headquarters was moving from Detroit to Madison Barracks at Sackets Harbor. As quartermaster, he would help oversee the move, and Julia and Fred joined him. By summer's end, "he was anxious to see his little son and, I *think,* he said, *me* also," Julia remembered.

At Madison Barracks, Grant joined the Sons of Temperance, one of many such organizations springing up in the 1830s and 1840s. These societies grew out of concern that immoderate drinking destroyed health, disrupted families, and fostered unchristian conduct. By 1848, the Sons of Temperance claimed 148,000 members.

Grant explained his decision as a response to a lecture by John B. Gough, a well-known temperance orator. A friend heard Grant say, "I have become convinced that there is no safety from ruin by liquor except by abstaining from it altogether." As a new member, Grant pledged "neither to make, buy, sell, or use as a beverage, any spirituous or malt liquors, wine, or cider." New recruits wore a long white collar plus a red, white, and blue ribbon in their lapel. Grant helped to organize a lodge of the Sons of Temperance at the barracks.

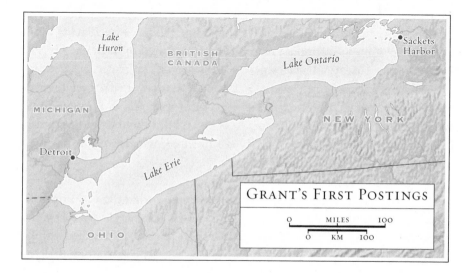

. . .

GRANT'S SECOND SERVICE at Madison Barracks would be brief. With the discovery of gold in California in 1848, the army decided to post troops in California and Washington Territory. In the spring of 1852, the Fourth Infantry was ordered west. Grant's unit was being posted to Fort Vancouver in Washington Territory.

For Grant, the news was both welcome and unwelcome. He was happy as always to explore new lands. But although many wives were planning to accompany their husbands, Julia was expecting another baby in October. He made the difficult decision to travel alone and send for her and the two children later. Thus, having been married for almost four years, Ulysses and Julia said their goodbyes, not knowing when they would see each other again.

On June 15, 1852, Grant traveled to Fort Columbus on Governors Island in the middle of New York harbor. The Fourth Infantry's new commander was Lieutenant Colonel Benjamin Louis Eulalie de Bonneville. Grant discovered that no sailing date had yet been set, but all the preparations fell to him as quartermaster.

He decided to use these days to travel to Washington to see if he could finally clear his name over the $1,000 stolen from his quartermaster's fund in Mexico. Even though a court of inquiry had absolved him of any responsibility, he could not live with this obligation not rectified.

He arrived in Washington, took a room at Willard's Hotel, and immediately began calling on members of Congress he hoped would help—Michigan senator Lewis Cass, Illinois senator James Shields, Ohio congressman Nelson Barrere, and California congressman Edward C. Marshall.

Unfortunately, his timing was poor. Henry Clay, lion of the Whig Party, three times a candidate for president, had died on June 29. Ulysses wrote Julia, "Today all places of business are closed and the buildings dressed in mourning for Mr. Clay." Further disappointment: He discovered Congressman Barrere was out of town for ten days. Congressmen whom he did call on said this was a financial matter that had to be adjudicated by the Congressional Military Committee, which would not meet until after Grant returned to New York.

As GRANT CONTEMPLATED traveling west, he reviewed the three options open to a traveler in the middle of the nineteenth century: by land on the Oregon Trail, by sea around Cape Horn, or by sea and across the Isthmus of Panama. The Fourth Infantry would travel from New York to Panama, cross the fifty-two-mile isthmus, and sail up the west coast of Mexico to California.

Quartermaster General Thomas Jesup, coming off of the massive transportation achievement in Mexico, did not reckon with the differences in travel. In Mexico, Jesup had worked with trained soldiers in good physical condition; now, women, often with small children, would be traveling with them, and under much more difficult physical conditions. Writing Julia, Ulysses felt a foreboding. "It is a *dangerous* experiment for the ladies to go to California."

He returned to Governors Island to find travel arrangements botched from a lack of foresight and planning. At the last minute, the War Department had booked passage to sail on the *Ohio,* an oak side-wheel 2,432-ton steamer with three decks. The *Ohio* could accommodate 250 in cabins and 80 in steerage, but these berths had already been booked by travelers eager to reach California and gold; they were not about to give up their places. Grant's challenge would be to find spaces for nearly seven hundred additional passengers. He began by building rows of berths on deck.

The *Ohio,* under Captain James Findlay Schenck, departed New York on July 5, 1852. Grant told Julia that five women she knew would be on board. "The poor things I fear will regret it before twenty four hours."

Although the weather turned out to be delightful, the climate on board was not. Delia Sheffield, a sixteen-year-old bride accompanying her sergeant husband, observed Commander Bonneville pacing the deck all day long, cane in hand, wearing a white beaver hat. Bonneville struck Mrs. Sheffield as a man with an "arbitrary and testy temper" whose "crustiness" soon proved an irritant on the crowded steamer. Dr. Charles Tripler's wife, Eunice, was blunter, calling Bonneville "a very stupid man."

Delia Sheffield recalled meeting Grant early in the voyage. She saw the young officer pacing the deck alone, "with his head bent, deep in thought." Soon he came and stood next to her, asking, "Have you noticed the number of whales following us this morning?"

As the voyage dragged on, she watched as Bonneville's "unpleasantnesses" were "always smoothed over by the quartermaster of the regiment." Schenck corroborated Sheffield's memory. He observed that "disagreements" seemed to arise around Bonneville, who was "hasty and uncertain in his actions." The ship's captain was grateful "to refer these disputes to Grant as arbitrator," believing "his rulings were distinguished by particular good sense."

. . .

AFTER ELEVEN DAYS at sea, the overloaded *Ohio* reached the white coral shore on the east coast of New Grenada. Grant supervised unloading the ship into the town of Aspinwall in the middle of the rainy season, where passengers were met by a foot or more of water in the streets.

New York businessman William Henry Aspinwall had built the town in 1850 as the hub for his Pacific Mail Steamship Company and Panama Railroad. Stench greeted passengers even before the sight of saloons, where rum selling and gambling were the town's main industries. Because the streets were filled with water, planks on top of stakes took the place of pavements. Grant "wondered how any person could live many months in Aspinwall, and wondered still more why anyone tried."

Grant's regiment did not remain long. Aspinwall's company had regular contracts to take Americans across the isthmus. The officers, wives, and children climbed aboard his small train, which traveled twenty miles inland to the Chagres River. Scorching heat and high humidity made the passengers feel as though they were in a burning furnace.

Once at the water, Grant helped gold seekers and army officers with their dependents board dugout canoes called *bungos,* which were hollowed out of a solitary log and held thirty to forty people. This mixed group embarked on the wide Chagres River, hemmed in on all sides by green jungle. As quartermaster, Grant was responsible for all supplies traveling in the boats, everything from personal baggage to tents, even band instruments. Boats were poled "by natives not inconveniently burdened with clothing."

Grant's group traveled slowly, sometimes only one mile an hour, as the boatmen paddled against a swift current and watched for dangerous eddies. The jungle exhibited different forms of life at every bend of the river. Here, bright flowers; there, red macaws; and high in the trees, chattering monkeys. After a long day, the weary passengers reached their evening anchorage. The boatmen left the Americans to spend the night in their dugout canoes, "in shivering terror," while they, like "drunken barbarians," kept them awake with carousing in a nearby village.

The next day, having arrived at the village of Cruces, Grant was eager to meet the mules that would carry them overland the final twenty-five miles to the steamer bound for California. He found no mules. He did find "an impecunious American" agent of the Aspinwall company. In mounting confusion, the contractor promised the mules "were on the way from some imaginary place, and would arrive in the course of the day." After days of waiting, Grant dismissed the contractor and, employing his Spanish, bargained with a local man for mules. Some animals did

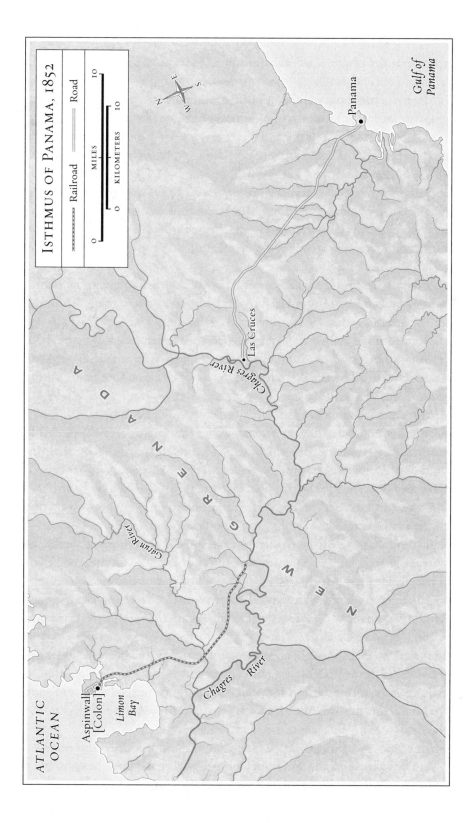

ISTHMUS OF PANAMA, 1852

- Railroad
- Road

MILES
0   10

KILOMETERS
0   10

ATLANTIC
OCEAN

Aspinwall
[Colon]

Limon
Bay

Chagres River

Gatun River

NEW GRENADA

Chagres River

Las Cruces

Panama

Gulf of
Panama

appear, but the price—$40 each—stunned the weary travelers. And there were not nearly enough.

Meanwhile, Grant watched in horror as cholera broke out among the men, women, and children. An infection of the small intestine that causes watery diarrhea, cholera can lead to severe dehydration and death within hours. Physically fit soldiers were struck down in the morning and died before the day was done.

Delia Sheffield was comforted as Grant, "in his quiet unassuming manner," took charge. He ordered some companies to start for Panama on the available mules but decided to stay behind with the sick and those soldiers who were traveling with their families. People continued to die as day followed day.

After a week in Cruces, Grant started the remaining group overland, leading the caravan forward in broiling sun and soaking rain. Children and the most gravely ill were carried in hammocks on porters' backs. Mud oozed more than a foot deep in places. As men fell down and died, they were buried under jungle flowers. Thirty-seven died in one day. "About one-third of the people with me died, either at Cruces or on the way to Panama."

After many long days, they finally reached the Pacific Ocean. Grant welcomed the sight of the steamer *Golden Gate,* anchored two miles off-shore in the harbor. But the ship was off-limits, quarantined by the captain because it was infected with cholera. Despite this, before Grant could intervene, Bonneville started putting women and children on board.

Grant and Dr. Tripler fixed up an old hulk a mile offshore to act as a hospital ship where they could bring the sick.

A strange aspect of the cholera onslaught was that most of the fatalities were men. One explanation was that none of the women and children drank liquor, which was known to contribute to dehydration. For more than two weeks, Grant and Tripler ministered to the sick; the dead were placed in sacks loaded with cannonballs and lowered overboard into a watery grave.

Eunice Tripler watched, admiring, as Grant labored quietly beside her husband. A fellow officer said Grant seemed to "take a personal interest in each sick man." Lieutenant Henry D. Wallen, traveling with his wife and two small children, became convinced that Grant was "one of the coolest men in all these trying circumstances I ever saw."

If firsthand witnesses praised Grant, he and other officers also received criticism for their handling of the cholera outbreak. The *Panama Herald* reported "Even the regimental Quartermaster, Capt. Grant, could not tarry to attend to his duty, but must come through and await the arrival of the troops on this side!" This condemning story, one of the first mentions of young Captain Grant, was picked up in the *New York Express* and reprinted in the *Charleston Mercury*.

Finally, when the captain believed the cholera had abated, and the ship and all clothing had been thoroughly fumigated, Grant and his party—down from nearly 700 to just 450—set off aboard the *Golden Gate* for San Francisco.

Once at sea, Ulysses resumed writing Julia. "The horrors of the road, in the rainy season, are beyond description," he told her, sparing her specifics of the trauma he had just been through. After an uneventful two-week passage, the *Golden Gate* steamed through the Golden Gate on August 17, 1852.

GRANT'S CAPACITY TO lead went mostly unnoticed in his youth. From his youth, Grant welcomed challenges. He was never afraid to work hard. The obstacles and setbacks he encountered never thwarted his resilience. If Panama was an unusual obstacle of sickness and death on a large scale, Grant used his mind and his sweat to lead the people in his charge. On the Isthmus of Panama, he performed duties not imagined of a regimental quartermaster. From somewhere deep inside, he found the courage to minister to sick and dying fellow travelers, facing horrors for which they were unprepared. Independently, witnesses testified to both his empathy and his composure in the midst of crisis and confusion. "He was like a ministering angel to us all," said one survivor.

When Grant arrived in San Francisco, he looked forward to exploring the place that had been in everyone's thoughts over the summer of 1852. After the ordeal in Panama, he anticipated better days at Fort Vancouver. But without Julia.

CHAPTER 8

⥲ ⥲

"Forsaken"

You do not know how forsaken I feel here.
—Ulysses S. Grant to Julia Dent Grant, Fort Humboldt,
California, February 2, 1854

When Grant arrived in San Francisco on August 17, 1852, he was thirty years old and had served in the army nine years. He was a long way from his wife and anxious to learn about the birth of a second child. Inquiring about little Fred, he asked Julia, "Does he ever say anything about his Pa? Don't let him forget me dearest Julia."

Still, he felt a surge of excitement as the *Golden Gate* tied up at the Long Wharf. No one was allowed to leave the ship for several hours because gold-hungry soldiers had been deserting, intent on what locals were calling "making their pile." With permission granted, Grant had barely disembarked before he was greeted by "runners," young men representing hotels and gambling parlors. One called out, "Come down! Come down!" Another barked, "The money's here! Get it while it lasts!"

San Francisco pulsed with energy in the summer of 1852. "I have seen enough of California to know that it is a different country from anything that a person in the states could imagine in their wildest dreams," Ulysses wrote Julia three days after his arrival. The discovery of gold at Sutter's Mill on the South Fork of the American River set off a stampede to California in the spring of 1849. A census in 1847 reported that Yerba Buena consisted of 459 souls; the town, renamed San Francisco, exploded to an estimated 100,000 people by the end of 1849. San Francisco exhibited both frontier and urban qualities. The old Spanish search for El Dorado became the new American quest for gold. It was a young man's game, with respectable women left behind in the East. One in twelve men would die in this pursuit.

This morally ambiguous American saga later elicited some of Grant's finest prose. He described the men who traveled west to seek their fortunes:

> Some realized more than their most sanguine expectations; but for one such there were hundreds disappointed, many of whom now fill unknown graves; others died wrecks of their former selves, and many, without a vicious instinct, became criminals and outcasts.

He concluded, "Many of the real scenes in early California life exceed in strangeness and interest any of the mere products of the brain of the novelist"—which brain he knew well.

Grant enjoyed San Francisco. "I consider that city the wonder of the world," he wrote glowingly to Julia. He was impressed with a population where get-rich-quick schemes seemed possible for everyone. No one, including this young midwestern Methodist, could be immune from this intoxicating talk. "There is no reason why an active energetic person should not make a fortune every year." He told her, "For my part I feel that I could quit the Army today and in one year go home with enough to make us comfortable, on the Gravois, all our life." Perhaps when he'd reread what he had written, his conservative self drew back: "Of course I do not contemplate doing anything of the sort, because what I have is a certainty, and what I might expect to do, might prove a dream."

The prospect of making money became more personal when Grant visited two of Julia's brothers who had joined the stampede to California. After traveling 120 miles by steamboat, mule, stage, and ferry, Grant arrived at the Knight's Ferry House, a tavern operated by Lewis and John Dent on the Stanislaus River. He gushed, "They have stables. . . . They have a trading house. . . . They have a Ranch where they have several hundred cattle and numerous horses." He estimated the Dents' various businesses were "all worth triple what they would be in the Atlantic States." He believed they were clearing $50 to $100 a day, while his officer's salary—even with an allowance for serving in California—was not much more than $1,300 a year.

WITHIN A MONTH of his arrival, Grant boarded the *Columbia* for the trip north to his assignment at the Columbia Barracks. On September 20, after a rough voyage, the ship approached the Columbia River. Off to the east, he could see snowcapped Mt. Hood in the magnificent Cascade Range. On a bluff ninety miles from the Pacific Ocean, eight miles north of Portland, stood Columbia Barracks, a tiny settlement consisting of a single street with framed houses.

Onshore, Grant was pleased to see a familiar face. Rufus Ingalls, his West Point roommate, had built this lonely outpost in 1849. Rufe arranged for Sam to move into the best quarters, a two-story house known as the Quartermaster's Ranch. Built in Boston, it had been shipped in sections around Cape Horn. Ingalls, along with Captain Thomas L. Brent, would live with Grant and share expenses.

Despite missing Julia, Grant found life at Columbia Barracks endurable because he felt part of a family environment. In addition to Ingalls and Brent, two servants Grant knew from Sackets Harbor, Maggy Getz and her husband, helped manage the household and provide cooking. "Everyone says they are the best servants in the whole Territory."

As fall progressed, the absence of letters from Julia began to gnaw at Ulysses. "Another mail has arrived and not one word do I get from you." In this remote outpost, mail arrived only every two weeks, and he was becoming extremely restless not knowing about their second child. "Just think, our youngest is at this moment probably over three months of age, and yet I have never heard a word from . . . you, in that time."

When finally he heard from Julia, "MY DEAR WIFE," receiving not one but four letters on December 3, he was overcome with joy. He learned a second son, Ulysses S. Grant, Jr., had been born on July 22, 1852. "You can scarcely conceive how this Mail's arrival has made me feel."

News of a less personal nature also reached Columbia Barracks. In the 1852 presidential election, Democrat Franklin Pierce, whom Grant respected from their time in Mexico, defeated Whig Winfield Scott, whom he also admired. Americans seemed to prefer electing generals to be their president.

"I am very much pleased with Vancouver." Grant seemed contented in his first letter to Julia. "This is about the best and most populous portion of Oregon." What followed, however, revealed he could not get San Francisco or his visit with Julia's brothers out of his mind. "Living is expensive but money can be made. I have made on one speculation fifteen hundred dollars since I have been here and I have every confidence that I shall make more than five thousand within the year." If Julia's brothers could prosper, why not he?

THIS DEPARTURE FROM Grant's conservative financial practices sprang from two motives. First, he desperately wanted Julia and the children to be with him, but he believed he could not support four mouths on his single salary. Second, inspired by moneymaking schemes all around him, Grant began to venture into unknown territory. "About pecuniary matters dear Julia I am better off than ever before, if I collect all that is due me."

When Elijah Camp, former storekeeper at Sackets Harbor, approached Grant about going in on a general store in San Francisco, Grant jumped at the opportunity. Camp persuaded Grant to hand him "all of his pay that had accumulated since he left New York." For the first month, by Julia's account, "everyone thought and was told that this fellow was coining a fortune." But one day Camp "said he was losing money in place of making any." In short order Camp came to Grant, told him "he would not like to be the cause of any harm coming to the Captain," and offered to buy out his half interest. He provided Grant three notes of $500 each.

"I chided Ulys when he told me this, telling him that the Vicar of Wakefield's Moses was a financier beside him." Julia knew Ulysses would understand her meaning when she evoked Moses Primrose, the vicar of Wakefield's second son, whom Irish novelist Oliver Goldsmith had depicted as being easily swindled.

ON MARCH 2, 1853, by an act of Congress, Washington Territory was divided so that Oregon Territory became the area south of the Columbia River. In July 1853, the name Columbia Barracks was changed to Fort Vancouver.

Grant's quartermaster responsibilities were not heavy, so he had plenty of time to ride, with Rufe Ingalls or alone, along the Columbia River or deep into the forests of splendid spruce and fir trees. Julia, aware of these long rides, was fearful that the Indians would get him. He replied, "Those about here are the most harmless people you ever saw." The Indians drew out Grant's sympathy. "My opinion [is] that the whole race would be harmless and peaceable if they were not put upon by the whites." He was shocked and saddened to see so many Indians dying from measles and smallpox contracted from whites—"the decimation among the Indians I knew personally."

In the evenings, the Quartermaster's Ranch became the place for card games of euchre and brag. One officer recalled how Grant "astonished his brother officers by his clear, luminous descriptions" of battles in Mexico. "He seems to have the whole thing in his head."

Dances livened up the Quartermaster's Ranch. Delia Sheffield noticed Grant would come, but not for long and not to dance, then go upstairs, where he remained all evening. "He felt keenly the separation from his wife and family." Several times, when Grant was reading letters from Julia, Sheffield observed that "his eyes would fill with tears." Sergeant Theodore Eckerson encountered Grant one day and proudly showed him a letter containing a promotion. Grant pulled out his own letter of several pages and, after opening it to the last page, showed the sergeant the penciled outline of a baby's hand. He said nothing, but Eckerson watched him tremble as his eyes welled with tears. "He seemed to be always sad."

Life became lonelier in the spring of 1853, when Ingalls was ordered to a new position at Fort Yuma. Grant now rode alone.

Yearning for more company, he asked the Sheffields to move in. Young Delia empathized with Grant's loneliness. She was embarrassed that she did not know how to cook much, but he promised to help. "I have an excellent cookbook and am a pretty good cook myself." One morning he asked if she could make some butter, because "he was hungry for some sweet home-made butter." She set about this task for the first time. Wanting to please Grant, "I put sugar into it instead of salt, as he wanted some *sweet* butter."

At dinner, Mrs. Sheffield served her butter "with great pride." She soon noticed a smile on everyone's faces. Finally, Grant asked, "Mrs. Sheffield, is this some of our homemade butter?"

"Yes, Captain, how do you like it?"

"Well, it is the sweetest butter that I ever tasted," she remembered him saying—"with a twinkle in his eye."

THE MONEY BUG continued to bite Grant. That winter, he had heard ice was selling for outrageous prices in San Francisco. He, Ingalls, and Henry Wallen cut one hundred tons of ice, loaded it on a sailing ship, and waited for their money. They waited and waited. The ship, slowed by strong headwinds, took two weeks to travel 250 miles. The ice melted on the voyage and so did their profits.

Now Grant purchased cattle and hogs to sell in the spring. He bought timber, which he cut and stacked, planning to sell to steamboats. He recruited Delia Sheffield's husband to help him "buy up all the chickens within twenty miles of Vancouver." They chartered a boat to ship the chickens to San Francisco, but nearly all of them died on the way, and "they lost the money they put into the enterprise."

In a larger venture, Grant leased one hundred acres with three other soldiers. He bought two horses and a wagon, intending to plant most acres with potatoes. In the spring he put in potatoes, onions, and other vegetables. He told Julia proudly, "I never worked before with so much pleasure either, because now I feel sure that every day will bring a large reward." To Grant, who eschewed extravagance and show, no reward could be greater than having the means to provide a secure future for his family.

Three months later he told Julia, "I have been quite unfortunate lately." Spring rains caused the Columbia to overflow its banks, which "destroyed all the grain, onions, corn, and about half the potatoes upon which I had expended so much money and labor." The water also soaked and scattered the timber. Worst of all, Camp quit his store in San Francisco, "deceiving me as to the money he had," and returned to Sackets Harbor, still owing him $800.

GRANT'S QUARTERMASTER RESPONSIBILITIES included outfitting surveying parties. The 1853 Pacific Railroad Survey Act intended to remove the sectional debate about the route for a transcontinental railroad and put the decision in the hands of the army. Four routes were under consideration. Jefferson Davis, secretary of war in the new Pierce administration, placed Captain George B. McClellan in charge of surveying the western part for the route of the Northern Pacific Railroad.

McClellan arrived at Fort Vancouver on June 27. Grant had known McClellan for one year at West Point when he entered the academy at age fifteen. Grant welcomed him and invited McClellan to stay at the Quartermaster's Ranch. When McClellan left on July 18, Grant helped outfit him with two hundred horses and three months' rations.

McClellan left with something else. According to Henry Hodges, "When the expedition was being fitted out, Grant got on one of his little sprees," a drinking bout "which annoyed and offended McClellan exceedingly." Hodges believed McClellan never forgot this incident.

ONE MATTER STILL hung heavy over Grant's conscience—the $1,000 stolen six years earlier in Mexico. He was now the ranking first lieutenant of the Fourth Infantry, next in line to assume the rank of captain. On September 8, he wrote Quartermaster General Thomas Jesup asking for an opportunity to come to Washington "for the purpose of settling my accounts."

Longing for Julia, he also hoped that if the army ordered him to Washington, he could bring his family with him to his next assignment. He knew the army would pay all costs of such a trip. As summer turned into fall, he waited for a reply.

But different news came first. Grant opened a letter from Secretary of War Jefferson Davis dated August 9, 1853, informing him he had been promoted to captain. Soon after, he was instructed to report to Fort Humboldt in California to assume command of Company F of the Fourth Infantry.

GRANT APPROACHED HIS new assignment hesitantly, knowing Fort Humboldt to be more isolated than Fort Vancouver. He took his time getting there and finally arrived on January 5, 1854. Although he was pleased with his promotion, his ruling emotion by now was anxiety— probably bordering on melancholy, given how deeply he missed Julia and his children, including one he had never seen. "I cannot say much in favor of the place." How different were Ulysses's words to Julia from his upbeat praise upon arriving at Fort Vancouver in 1852.

Fort Humboldt did have a picturesque location forty feet above a beach, looking out on the Pacific Ocean. Behind the fort stretched massive forests of redwood and fir. The small post consisted of fourteen buildings, mostly two stories each. Grant lived in a one-story house, with a porch in front, on the north side of the parade ground.

But absent was his old friend Ingalls and newer friends Wallen and Brent. Absent was the household formed around the Quartermaster's Ranch, with its regular social activities and familiar servants. Absent was regular mail service between Fort Humboldt and San Francisco.

Present was Major Robert Buchanan, serving as the first commander at Fort Humboldt. Grant would be the second-ranking officer. Army gossip whispered Buchanan would soon be promoted and off to a new assignment, leaving Grant in charge. Grant and Buchanan had tangled at Jefferson Barracks in 1845. Nine years later, how would Old Buch treat young Grant?

"You do not know how forsaken I feel here!" Less than one month after he arrived, Ulysses wrote Julia, "I do nothing here but sit in my room and read and occasionally take a short ride on one of the public horses." Some men enjoyed hunting ducks and geese, but with his lifelong distaste for hunting, "I have not entered into the sport," he wrote. Everything about Fort Humboldt seemed to spell disaster.

By February, Grant experienced a deepening depression. "I think I have been from my family quite long enough and sometimes I feel as though I could almost go home 'nolens volens.'" *Nolens volens* is usually translated as "whether willing or unwilling." In the army vernacular of Grant's day, it came to mean willing to go absent without leave.

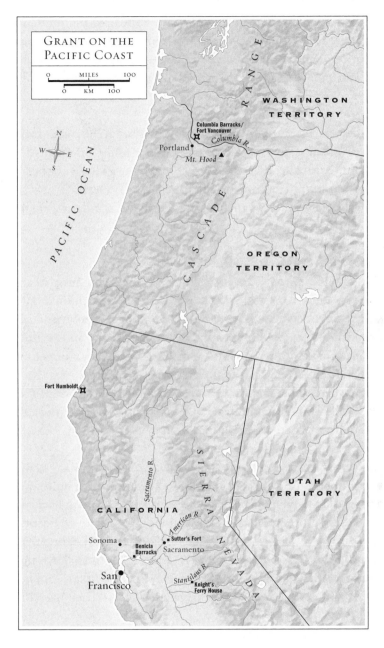

What stopped him? "Whenever I get to thinking upon the subject however, *poverty, poverty* begins to stare me in the face and then I think what would I do if you and our little ones should want for the necessaries of life."

W. I. Reed, a contractor who supplied beef to Fort Humboldt, observed, "No greater misfortune could have happened to him than his en-forced idleness. He had little work, no family with him, took no pleasure in the amusements of his fellow officers—dancing, billiards, hunting, fishing, and the like." What happened next? "The result was a common one. He took to liquor. Not in enormous quantities, for he drank far less than the other officers."

His despair began to impair his health. Although he came through the diseases of Panama, at Fort Humboldt, in the midst of constant rain, he caught chills and fever. In early March he wrote, "I have not been a hundred yards from my door but once in the last two weeks."

In his misery, Grant began drinking. How often and how much would become subject to many rumors in the years to come.

ON APRIL 11, 1854, Grant wrote two letters to Adjutant General Samuel Cooper in Washington. The first letter: "I have the honor to acknowl-edge the receipt of my Commission as Captain in the 4th Infantry and my acceptance of the same." The second: "I very respectfully tender my res-ignation of my commission as an officer of the Army, and request that it may take effect from the 31st July next." One imagines Cooper's surprise when he read the second letter after having opened the first.

Grant resigned. A story persisted that after one of Grant's drinking "sprees" at Fort Humboldt, Major Buchanan gave him the choice of being court-martialed or resigning. Buchanan endorsed Grant's letter of resignation and offered no separate report.

His friend Rufus Ingalls believed that story, suggesting that Grant, "finding himself in dreary surroundings, without his family, and with but little to occupy his attention, fell into dissipated habits, and was found, one day, too much under the influence of liquor to properly per-form his duties." He related that Buchanan demanded Grant either resign or stand trial. Ingalls and friends urged Grant to stand trial, for they were "confident of his acquittal." But Grant, thinking of Julia, "said he would not for all the world have his wife know that he had been tried on such a charge."

ON MAY 2, Grant wrote a short letter to Julia telling her only to send her next letter to New York. Five days later, he left for San Francisco. His two years on the Pacific coast were abruptly over.

Grant arrived in New York on June 25, 1854. He found no letter from Julia. Before heading for Ohio, with almost no money, he determined to recover what was still owed him by Elijah Camp. He wrote Camp, took a train to Watertown, and rented a horse to ride to Sackets Harbor. When he arrived, he discovered Camp had left town—again.

Upon his return to New York, Grant met classmate Simon Bolivar Buckner. In Mexico, they had climbed Mount Popocatépetl together. Grant confided his dilemma to the Kentuckian. He was staying at the old Astor House, and with his money gone, he asked for a loan to pay his bill at the hotel. Buckner stepped forward to guarantee the hotel bill.

As he departed New York, Grant faced an uncertain future. He was confident about how Julia would receive him, but how would her family accept him? How would his father receive him? Most important, how would he support his family? After fifteen years of preparation and service in the army—all his adult life—how would he adjust to life as a civilian?

In the spring of 1856, Grant built a house a mile from the Dents' White Haven, sardonically naming it "Hardscrabble" in an attempt to establish his independent identity.

CHAPTER 9

"Hardscrabble"

I was now to commence, at the age of thirty-two,
a new struggle for our support.

—ULYSSES S. GRANT, *Personal Memoirs*

When Ulysses Grant arrived in Bethel, Ohio, in July 1854, several neighbors reported his father received him "grimly." Jesse felt humiliated by his son's resignation from the army. A resident of Georgetown remembered Jesse complaining, "West Point spoiled one of my boys for business." "I guess that's about so," confessed Ulysses. But Hannah welcomed her son with open arms, feeling "relief" that he was home.

In August, Grant traveled on to Missouri. When he arrived at White Haven, he glimpsed a young boy and a toddler with blond curls playing on the front porch. The children stared at the dark-bearded stranger. As he started to climb out of the buggy, a young slave girl looked up and with a shriek ran into the house, screaming that Mr. Grant was home.

Julia, having dressed for weeks in one of her most attractive dresses, hoping to see her husband finally come home, ran from the front door into his arms. The small boys looked on perplexed but soon squealed in delight as their jubilant father tossed them in the air.

At twenty-eight, Julia looked nearly the same, with her slim, small figure. She was still outgoing, with a soft sense of humor, but she moved even more swiftly with two young boys to manage. Ulysses was the one who had aged, lines etched in his forehead, a tired look in his blue eyes, moving more slowly.

Ulysses, whom Julia would call "the Captain," felt uneasy under the same roof as Colonel Dent. The Captain did not like depending on anyone. He had left behind the critical eyes of Major Buchanan, only to face the disapproving eyes of his father and now the censorious eyes of his father-in-law. A question he could not quite voice to himself: Could he discover his independence in Missouri?

. . .

ULYSSES S. GRANT had returned from two years out west to a dramatically changed national political landscape. On May 30, 1854, President Franklin Pierce signed the Kansas-Nebraska Act, passed by a deeply divided Congress. Steered through the Senate by Illinois senator Stephen A. Douglas, the law would set up a government in the Nebraska Territory based on "popular sovereignty," the principle that "all questions pertaining to slavery in the territories were to be left to the decision of the people residing therein."

With the Kansas-Nebraska Act, the Missouri Compromise of 1820 was overturned, the sectional balance effected by the Compromise of 1850 was disrupted, and the fury of antislavery advocates intensified, yet the legislative action fell short of calming many in the South. The Whig Party, which had elected General Zachary Taylor president in 1848, was demoralized after the defeat of General Winfield Scott in 1852 and grappled with how to respond. The Democratic Party, which Senator Douglas hoped to bring together around the concept of "popular sovereignty," ended up dividing between northern and southern factions. Throughout the summer of 1854, a vigorous "anti-Nebraska" movement grew, enlisting groups cutting across party lines.

With the lions of Congress—Henry Clay of Kentucky, Daniel Webster of Massachusetts, and John C. Calhoun of South Carolina—no longer present, new leaders climbed onto the national political stage. Douglas, forty-one and serving his second term in the Senate, positioned himself as a leading actor in the unfolding national drama. Far offstage, Abraham Lincoln of Illinois, forty-five and past his single term in Congress, emerged from political exile to speak with new power against extending slavery into new territories. The battle across the nation included debates within the critical states of Ohio and Missouri, where Ulysses's and Julia's families held completely different views on the slavery question.

NOW THAT HE was home, keeping his political views to himself, Ulysses planned to build a house, cultivate the land, and become a farmer. Julia's father had given her sixty acres of uncleared land as a wedding present. With all his children married except Emma, Dent was eager to keep Julia nearby and offered help with equipment. The owner of more than twenty slaves, he gave his daughter three—Eliza, Julia Ann, and Dan—to serve as maid, cook, and houseboy.

Ulysses spent a "pleasant" winter at White Haven, eager to begin farming in the spring. Ellen Dent orchestrated the delicate balancing act of providing hospitality for the joint household, but Colonel Dent did not hide his displeasure. All his other children had married well, yet Julia, his favorite, had married a man who at thirty-two seemed to have few prospects for success.

THE YEAR 1855, despite the household tension, dawned full of hope. Julia was pregnant again. She and Ulysses looked forward to being together for the first time at the birth of a child. Lewis Dent, away in California, offered them his home built on property his father had given him. Ulysses could not wait to move into Wish-ton-wish, Indian for "Whippoorwill," one and a half miles south of White Haven and away from Colonel Dent's sharp eyes and words.

Observant Emma, now all grown up, watched as Ulysses took up farming. "He was a man whose whole nature demanded work. He did not know how to be lazy." Working on the land became an elixir that dissolved his melancholy.

In farming, Ulysses drew upon his experiences as a youth in Georgetown. Upland Missouri was not that different from southern Ohio in its soil and climate. What was different were the people: they were noticeably southern. Nearly all the farmers owned slaves. White farming families lived in large, well-built farmhouses, while slaves lived nearby in small shanties.

Ulysses bought a team of horses—Tom and Bill—and put in wheat, oats, potatoes, and corn, helped by Dan, Julia's young slave. Grant kept his views on the use of slave labor to himself.

While he was plowing and planting, he also began cutting and hauling wood. Since farming is seasonal and dependent on weather, he needed a steady income he could control. He hauled wood twelve miles down the Gravois road to St. Louis to sell at $4 a cord. Aware of the heavy load he already asked Tom and Bill to pull, he surprised onlookers who saw him walking the twelve miles beside his horses.

After his hard day's work in the fields or hauling wood to the city, Mary Robinson observed, "Most of his leisure time he spent in reading." Impressed, she added, "He was one of the greatest readers I ever saw."

His oldest son, Fred, remembered some of what his father read. With the nearest school a mile and a half away, Ulysses taught young Fred arithmetic, spelling, and reading. Fred had a "vivid recollection" of his father reading aloud Charles Dickens's *Oliver Twist,* then being serialized in *Bentley's Miscellany,* which satirized the failings of government and society. "We all used to wait with the greatest eagerness for the next instalment of these interesting stories."

JULIA AND ULYSSES welcomed baby Ellen Grant on July 4, 1855. He wanted to call their blue-eyed daughter Julia, but his wife preferred to name her after her mother. Ellen would be called Nellie, after her aunt. Nellie was barely a toddler when her father taught her to ride, first with him and then by herself. Since her birthday fell on the Fourth of July, her father teased that all the fireworks and balloons on this day were in honor of Nellie.

Ulysses liked to wrestle with his boys. Fred was growing up with his mother's impetuous nature, while the younger boy evinced the quieter personality of his father. Against his mother's protests, everyone called Ulysses "Buck," from his birth in Ohio, the Buckeye State.

Ulysses completed his first year of farming with mixed results. Robinson asserted, "I have seen many farmers, but I never saw one that worked harder than Mr. Grant." But in farming, hard work did not always equal financial success. Prices were down. And the time he spent delivering wood was time not spent farming.

IN SPRING 1856, his second year home, Ulysses began to build his family's own house. Although constructed less than a mile from White Haven, this would be another step in building an independent identity. The design became a tug-of-war. Ulysses wanted to build a frame house, whereas Julia's father "most aggravatingly urged a log house," which, he argued, would be warmer. Ulysses lost. In the end, Julia drew the design for their new house of logs. In popular memory a simple ramshackle hut, the two-story house in fact boasted five rooms and a hall.

Neighbors hurried to participate in the "raisin'." Captain Grant proudly took a corner, neighbor Fenton Long another, and with all hands aboard, the hewed logs were lifted into place. When asked the name of the house, Ulysses wryly answered, "Hardscrabble." Julia insisted they named it thus "facetiously." Some neighbors thought that in naming it Hardscrabble, Ulysses was satirizing the lofty names of the nearby Dent family homes.

GRANT PAID LITTLE attention to the presidential election of 1856, except, the story goes, to remark to a friend when passing a polling place, "I'll go back and vote against Frémont."

In the long frame of American history, John C. Frémont is remembered as the first candidate of the new Republican Party. In the shorter frame of opinion, many army men remembered Frémont as a self-promoting general who did not follow through on his boasts. Grant chose to vote for James C. Buchanan, an experienced politician of whom he knew little.

Also, he had heard growing talk of secession on St. Louis streets. "Under these circumstances I preferred the success of a candidate whose election would prevent or postpone secession."

THREE DAYS BEFORE the end of 1856, Grant took stock of the year in a letter to his father: "Every day I like farming better and I do not doubt but that money is to be made at it." Still, "I have been laboring under great disadvantages." He had spent much time building Hardscrabble; he lacked money to buy seed; unusually cold spring weather ruined the wheat; and he had only one team of horses for both farming and hauling wood. Then, the request: "If I had an opportunity of getting about $500.00 for a year at 10 pr. cent I have no doubt but it would be of great advantage to me."

For 1857, Grant wanted to expand his crops and needed better equipment. In words surely difficult for an independent son, "It is always usual for parents to give their children assistance in beginning life (and I am only beginning, though thirty-five years of age, nearly) and what I ask is not much."

Finally, he upped the ante: "The fact is, without means, it is useless for me to go on farming, and I will have to do what Mr. Dent has given me permission to do; sell the farm and invest elsewhere."

There is no evidence Jesse sent any money. His relationship with a son who had married into a slaveholding family continued to be cool and distant.

GRANT'S HOPES FOR farming ran smack into the Panic of 1857, which in the late summer brought an end to the financial good times following the Mexican War. Thanks to the combination of the end of the Crimean War and a credit squeeze in Great Britain that diverted money from American banks and railroads, manufactured goods remained unsold in city warehouses. Russian wheat returning to the world market spread panic in the countryside, where falling grain prices affected farmers. Unpredictable Mother Nature only added to the ruin. By August, Grant knew that his wheat would produce only five bushels per acre, when he had hoped to yield between ten and thirteen.

At the end of a disappointing year, on December 23 a despondent Grant entered the St. Louis pawnshop of J. S. Freligh. Needing money for Christmas, he exchanged his gold watch and chain for $22. He signed a pawn ticket authorizing the sale of the watch if he did not repay the loan in one month or negotiate a new one.

In the days before Christmas 1857, Grant's fortunes had sunk so far that he was forced to pawn his gold watch and chain in order to buy Julia a Christmas present.

THE YEAR 1858 began with the birth of a fourth child, Jesse Root Grant II, on February 6. With this naming, Ulysses once more attempted to bridge the gulf between father and son.

Julia's father, at age seventy, less robust after the death of his wife, Ellen, decided to move into St. Louis. He rented White Haven and its 200 acres of cultivated land, plus another 250 acres of meadow, to Ulysses and Julia.

"I have now three negro men, two hired by the year, and one of Mr. Dent's, which, with my own help, I think, will enable me to do my farming pretty well, with assistance in harvest," Ulysses wrote his sister Mary. He was now a slave owner. This decision contradicted everything Jesse stood for.

Even with the extra help, by summer 1858 Grant's farming and family were both struggling. Outside, an early June freeze damaged the new crops. Inside, eight-year-old Fred contracted a "bilious" fever that turned into typhoid. For several fearful days, Ulysses and Julia worried they would lose their oldest child. Then both parents became sick, with Ulysses suffering from a more acute ague that carried the same alternating chills and fever he had experienced at West Point. He feared contracting consumption, an infection of the lungs that was pervasive in the Grant family and was just then affecting his younger brother Simpson.

· · ·

FROM TIME TO time Grant met officers he had known in the Mexican War, now stationed at Jefferson Barracks. One day in 1858, as he was driving a load of lumber in St. Louis, he suddenly came "face to face" with General William S. Harney, a hero of the war. As Harney eyed the farmer in the wagon, he smiled and exclaimed, "Why, Grant, what in blazes are you doing?" The Captain swung one mud-spattered boot across the other and replied, "Well, General, I am hauling wood."

They howled with laughter. Harney invited Grant to join him for a meal at Planter's House. The incident made for a good laugh, but encounters with officers only served to remind Grant of his present condition.

In the same year, Captain James Longstreet, who stood up with Grant at his wedding, was staying at Planter's House. Longstreet recalled, "It was soon proposed to have an old-time game of brag." Needing another player, Captain Edmunds N. Holloway stepped outside and "in a few minutes returned with a man poorly dressed in citizen's clothes and in whom we recognized our old friend Grant."

The next day, walking in front of the hotel, Longstreet found himself face-to-face with Grant again. Grant pulled out a $5 gold piece and "insisted that I should take it in payment of a debt of honor over 15 years old." Longstreet declined, telling Grant that "he was out of the service and more in need of it than I."

"You must take it. I cannot live with anything in my possession that is not mine."

"Seeing the determination in the man's face, and in order to save him mortification, I took the money, and shaking hands we parted."

BY THE FALL of 1858, Grant concluded he could not make an adequate living farming. He wrote his father that he and Julia's father intended to sell all the stock and rent out White Haven. As he reviewed the scant options for work, he proposed to travel to Covington to talk with his father about a previous offer to work in the family's leather goods store in Galena, Illinois.

But the offer was no longer open.

Julia's father came to the rescue. Colonel Dent spoke to Harry Boggs, whose wife, Louisa, was the Colonel's niece. Boggs operated a real estate and rent-collecting business.

Real estate was booming in St. Louis. Demand outstripped supply as the city expanded out and up. New subdivisions resulted in more than one thousand houses being built each year in the 1850s. New five- and six-story buildings were going up, thirty-three in 1858 alone. Property in St. Louis, valued at $8.6 million in 1840 and $29.7 million in 1850, would soar to $102.4 million in 1860.

Grant joined Boggs in office space in the law firm of McClellan, Hill-yer, and Moody on narrow Pine Street between Second and Third. Although their business cards made it appear they were partners, Grant had no money to bring to the new venture.

Just as he began his new position, Grant decided to emancipate his slave William Jones, a thirty-five-year-old man whom Colonel Dent had left on the property when he moved into St. Louis. Grant appeared in court in late March 1859 to sign a manumission document: "I . . . do hereby man-umit, emancipate & set free said William from slavery forever."

Grant could have received at least $1,000 for this slave if he'd tried to sell him. At this point, he surely could have used the money. He never spoke about his motivation, but he signed the paper setting Jones free.

GRANT RENTED A modest home at Seventh and Lynch streets, two miles from his office, to which the family and three slaves moved in April 1859.

In March 1859, Grant signed a manumission paper freeing his slave William Jones. By selling Jones, Grant could have received at least $1,000 at a time when he was hard up for money.

Quick with figures, he began his new job with hope and energy. But the heavy end of the business turned out to be rent collecting.

Julia knew Ulys was not cut out for such a job. "He never could collect a penny that was owed to him if his debtors, and he had several, only expressed regret and said: 'Grant, I regret, more than you do, my inability to pay you.' " Rather, "He always felt sorry for them and never pressed them." Rather, he would say, "I am sure they will send [it] to me." Julia summarized their collective response: "We never heard from these *fine* debtors."

Furthermore, Julia did not approve of the way Boggs "makes his patrons' business a subject of conversation." After only a few months, Ulysses had come around to Julia's point of view: "I am sure your opinion of Mr. Boggs is correct." He dissolved his business relationship.

IN AUGUST, GRANT applied for the position of county engineer; he believed his education qualified him for the position, and it paid $1,900 a year. He spent time collecting recommendations from "the very first citizens of this place, and members of all parties." He enclosed a letter of recommendation from Joseph Reynolds, a West Point classmate now professor of mechanics and engineering at Washington University in St. Louis. The list of names at the bottom of his application included philanthropist John O'Fallon; George W. Fishback, part owner of the *Missouri Democrat,* the Republican newspaper; and Charles A. Pope, professor of surgery at St. Louis Medical College and former president of the American Medical Association. The thirty-five endorsements were testimony to the friendships Grant formed in the past five years.

He wrote his father five days later, "I am not over sanguine of getting the appointment." Why? "I fear they will make strictly party nominations for all offices under their control."

He was right. Within a month, he learned he did not get the position. The vote, as he predicted, was strictly party line: two Democrats voted for Grant, while the three "freesoilers"—antislavery members of the Whig and Democratic parties—voted for his opponent. Physician William Taussig, one of the Free Soil commissioners who voted against Grant, remembered that since Grant had lived with the Dents, "though nothing was known of his political views, the shadow of their disloyalty necessarily fell on him."

IN OCTOBER, SEEKING to own his own house, Grant traded Hardscrabble for a frame house at Ninth and Barton streets. He was pleased to receive a note for $3,000, calculated to be the difference in value of the two houses. But that money would last the family only so long.

In the fall, Grant obtained a temporary position in the St. Louis Custom House, but when the man who employed him died, so did the job—after only one month. As fall turned toward winter, the darker days mirrored Grant's darkening hopes.

In February 1860, he sent a letter to the president of the Board of County Commissioners letting him know that if a position opened, he would like to apply for it again. No position opened.

On a winter evening, Ulysses and Julia sat in their parlor, discussing what to do next. "We will not always be in this condition," Julia insisted. Her optimism buoyed her husband's spirits; she believed in Ulys—even when he did not always believe in himself.

She encouraged him to travel to Covington and speak with his father one more time about a position in Galena. At her urging, he was willing to swallow a last bit of pride and ask again for a position in the family store.

Ulysses arrived in Covington on March 14 to find that his father had left for a few days. With his head "nearly bursting with pain," his sympathetic mother and sisters pumped him with family questions. Perhaps his mother made a difference this time, because when Jesse came home he invited Ulysses to join the family business.

Jesse's terms were strict. Ulysses would earn only $600 the first year—$17,000 in today's money. In the second year, if he proved himself, he would be granted an interest in the company. Jesse realized his son Simpson might not recover from his debilitating tuberculosis, leaving only Orvil, by far the youngest at twenty-four. Adding Ulysses meant all three sons would work together in the store.

Grant had spent six years in Missouri without anything material to show for it. But these years were a search for independence. Because he seemed quiet and unassuming, his identity—more than he realized—was often misunderstood. Neighbors who knew Colonel Dent assumed Grant was pro-slavery. As an army man nurtured in a military culture that wasn't concerned with politics, he was still working out his own convictions.

In his final years in Missouri, Grant listened more than he spoke. A few friends heard him begin to form his political ideas into words. In the office space of Boggs and Grant, he became friendly with lawyer William

S. Hillyer, a twenty-seven-year-old Kentuckian, who recalled, "We found him more than commonly talkative." Grant entered into lively conversation with Hillyer, just then moving toward the new Republican Party.

ON AN APRIL morning in 1860, Ulysses, Julia, and the four children boarded the steamer *Itasca* to travel 350 miles up the Mississippi River to Galena. There he knew he would face the uncertain prospect of working with two brothers, both younger, whom he had barely seen in years. He would live in the far northwestern corner of an unfamiliar northern state as a gathering storm grew in fury across the nation.

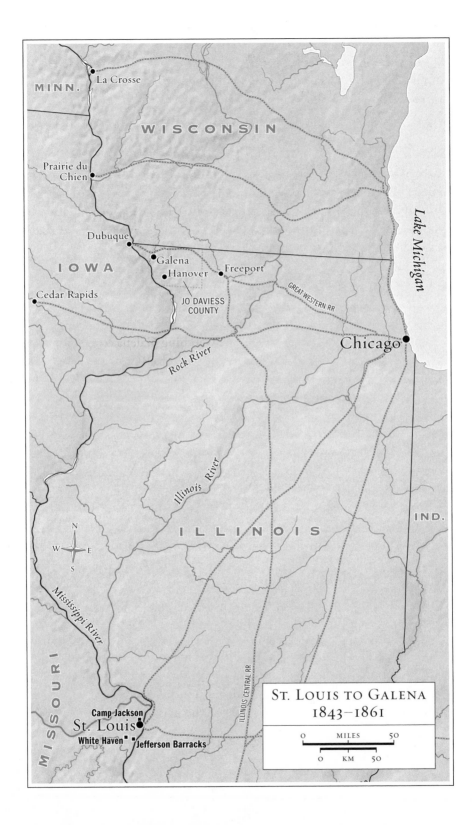

La Crosse

MINN.

WISCONSIN

Prairie du
Chien

Lake Michigan

Dubuque

IOWA

Galena
Hanover   Freeport

JO DAVIESS
COUNTY

Cedar Rapids

GREAT WESTERN RR

Chicago

Rock River

Illinois River

IND.

ILLINOIS

N
W   E
S

Mississippi River

MISSOURI

ILLINOIS CENTRAL RR

Camp Jackson
St. Louis
White Haven   Jefferson Barracks

ST. LOUIS TO GALENA
1843–1861

0   MILES   50

0   KM   50

CHAPTER 10

‹‥⊜〇⊜‥›

Galena

Our business here is prosperous and I have every reason to hope,
in a few years, to be entirely above the frowns of the world.
—ULYSSES S. GRANT to MR. DAVIS (St. Louis friend),
August 7, 1860

Ulysses and Julia stood at the railing, watching Galena come into view
as the *Itasca* turned from the wide Mississippi River and glided four
miles up the narrow Galena River to dock at the wharf alongside Water
Street. Galena hummed with energy as the largest steamboat hub north
of St. Louis, but in May 1860 it looked like a Swiss alpine village, with its
homes perched above the water on surrounding bluffs and hills.

At the time the Grants arrived, it was not uncommon to see a dozen
boats docked at the wharf. By the early 1850s, river traffic reached high
tide as Galena became the busiest port between St. Paul and St. Louis.
From the wharf, the Grants passed the DeSoto House with its 225 rooms.
In 1856, just fifteen months after it had opened its doors, Abraham Lincoln spoke from the balcony of the brick Italianate-style hotel on behalf
of the first Republican presidential candidate, John C. Frémont.

With its gentle hills, limestone cliffs, and river valleys, this northwestern corner of Illinois had been bypassed ages ago by the glaciers that flat-
tened most of what is now Iowa and Illinois. Organized as a town in 1826,
Galena took its name from the Latin term for sulfide of lead, deposits of
which lay near the surface of the land. With a population of ten thousand, Galena owed its prosperity to the rich lead mines that were found in
fifty square miles of northwestern Illinois, southwestern Wisconsin, and
a narrow strip of land on the west side of the Mississippi River in Iowa.
By 1859, this region comprised 80 percent of the lead mining in the
United States.

· · ·

JESSE GRANT HAD established a wholesale leather and harness store in Galena in 1841, when Ulysses was nineteen. With his partner, E. A. Collins, the store carried shoes and boots and all manner of saddlery products.

Their partnership dissolved in 1853, but Jesse established a new store, managed initially by his second son, Simpson, who was then joined in 1859 by his youngest son, Orvil. Melancthon T. Burke, Ulysses's cousin, arrived from Bethel in the spring of 1856 to serve as a clerk. By the time Ulysses arrived, Simpson, cheeks hollowed, was growing visibly weaker from consumption.

Ulysses wondered what his role would be alongside his two brothers, both with seniority over him in the family business. In the Grant mythology, Ulysses began with "an inferior position" and with his salary of $600 struggled to live securely. Cousin Burke asserted, "Nothing could be further from the truth."

From the start, Ulysses pitched in with all aspects of the store's work. He waited on customers and filled orders. Good with numbers, he spent many hours with his head hidden in ledgers, entering monetary transactions. In the wintertime he traveled to Wisconsin, Minnesota, and Iowa to purchase green hides. He was able to handle hides that weighed more than 250 pounds, impressing Burke with his ability to "many times lift a hide that no ordinary man could manage."

In his first months, Ulysses worked hard to pay off his debts in Missouri. He borrowed money, with no questions asked, from a common fund maintained by the store.

THE GRANTS LIVED in a two-story, seven-room brick house on a western hillside. The house he rented for $100 a year looked down upon the river dividing the town and was reached by a long flight of wooden stairs to High Street.

In Galena, Ulysses settled into a family pattern that he had not been able to follow at Hardscrabble or in St. Louis. Upon his arrival home, two-year-old Jesse would greet his father at the door with a standard question: "Do you want to fight?"

"I do not feel like fighting, Jess, but I can't stand being hectored in this manner by a man of your size," Ulysses would say. Struck on the knees by the small fists of his little son, after a few tender attempts to fight back, Ulysses would roll on the floor, holding Jess in his arms over his chest. "It is not fair to strike when a man's down." After receiving dozens more

In Galena, the Grants lived in a two-story, seven-room brick house on a hillside, which they rented for $100 a year.

punches from the "dimpled fists," the father would "cry for quarter," surrendering to his young son. "I give up, I give up." Jess would stand proudly and help his father get up.

After supper, Ulysses would put on his slippers and spend time with his other children. Fred, the oldest, remembered his father had a different manner of dealing with each of his children. Although he showed them "uniform affection and kindness," their father adjusted himself to the distinct character of each child. He treated Fred "as if I were already a man," permitting him to do many things other parents might have considered dangerous for their children. Ulysses, the second son, was "a very gentle and exceedingly sensitive boy," according to Fred. "Father never failed to remember this, and was careful not to hurt his feelings in any way." Ulysses treated his only daughter, Nellie, as "his darling, and father was exceedingly tender with her." The youngest boy, Jesse, had a jolly personality and was "something of a wit."

In Galena, Ulysses and Julia were able to spend much more time together, too. In the evenings he often read aloud to her from newspapers and books while she sewed. Later, he would read by himself, both novels and local and Chicago newspapers. He liked to smoke his clay pipe, but Julia did not like his constant smoking and often hid his pipes.

After three months, Ulysses wrote a man he had worked with at the St. Louis customs house, "Since leaving St. Louis I have become pretty well initiated into the Leather business and like it well." For the first time, he sounded optimistic. "Our business here is prosperous and I have every reason to hope, in a few years, to be entirely above the frowns of the world, pecuniarily."

· · ·

THE GRANTS BEGAN attending the large new brick-and-stone Methodist church on Bench Street, dedicated in 1857 to accommodate its growing congregation and replace the original frame church built in 1832.

In 1859, the church welcomed a new young pastor. John Heyl Vincent, twenty-seven years old, grew up in Pennsylvania. At age eighteen he became a Methodist circuit rider, ministering to farmers, miners, and shopkeepers throughout the Pennsylvania countryside. His Methodist sermons were practical.

Grant first entered into meaningful conversation with Vincent on a cold winter morning when they found themselves at a hotel across the Mississippi River in Dubuque, Iowa. Grant crossed the room and introduced himself. "I hear you preach every Sunday. My name is Grant." Vincent remembered that Grant's "animation and earnestness . . . surprised and interested me."

After that brief encounter, Vincent recalled, "I often watched, during the public services in my church at Galena, the calm, firm face of my interesting hearer." Vincent would go on to become one of the foremost national Methodist leaders.

The Grants began attending the Bench Street Methodist Church, pastored by twenty-seven-year-old John Heyl Vincent.

. . .

SLOWLY BUT SURELY, Grant began to build up a stable of loyal friends like the ones he'd had in Mexico and California. Dark-eyed, dark-haired John A. Rawlins sought him out, entering the leather store to introduce himself. Rawlins recalled that as a farm boy of sixteen, he was "almost crazy to get permission to enlist" in the Mexican War but could not. Ever after, he'd been fascinated by those who had served. Rawlins heard that Captain Grant had participated in the war. At twenty-nine, nine years younger than Grant, Rawlins recalled the shy captain in their initial conversations. Rawlins, an enthusiastic visionary, penetrated Grant's natural reserve. Grant would sit on the counter and relate "incidents in Mexico, a country that seems to have stirred him to enthusiasm by its beauty and resources."

Rawlins grew up with an impractical father who went off to California in an unsuccessful search for gold, and a zealous mother who wished a better life for her son. Witnessing the effect of liquor on his father and their family, Rawlins developed a hatred for alcohol.

In 1857, at only twenty-six, Rawlins was elected city attorney of Galena, having already held positions as city auditor and alderman. He became known as a formidable lawyer who argued in a courtroom with "clear, logical reason."

To friends, Rawlins and Grant seemed an odd couple. Rawlins was a natural orator, Grant shunned public speaking; Rawlins enjoyed the national sport of politics, Grant did not. Rawlins became known for his command of profanity; Burke remembered that "no man ever heard Grant utter an oath or repeat an obscene story." But they shared a growing mutual admiration.

ON THE EVE of Election Day, November 6, 1860, telegraph reports poured in indicating Abraham Lincoln would be elected the nation's sixteenth president. But the Springfield, Illinois, politician barely carried Galena. In a spirited election, where 81.2 percent of eligible voters went to the polls, Lincoln received only 39.65 percent, still a plurality of the vote, in a field of four candidates. From the grand DeSoto House to the smallest home, American flags were unfurled. The Grant leather store became alive with a celebration. Grant pitched in to help serve oysters and liquors.

ON DECEMBER 20, the eye of the coming storm hovered over Charleston, South Carolina, where a state convention voted unanimously to secede from the Union. Within forty days, one by one, the southern states of Mississippi, Florida, Alabama, Georgia, Louisiana, and Texas voted themselves out of the Union. They quickly took control of Federal institutions, including forts.

In February, William Rowley, circuit court clerk at Galena, discussed the secessionist upheaval with Grant: "There's a great deal of bluster about these Southerners, but I don't think there's much fight in them."

"Rowley, you are mistaken; there *is* a good deal of bluster; that's the result of their education; but if they once get at it, they will make a strong fight." Grant knew the convictions and abilities of his West Point classmates, who were resigning their commissions to return to their home states in the South to fight. These would include all three West Point classmates—James Longstreet, Cadmus Marcellus Wilcox, and Bernard Pratt—who had stood up with him as groomsmen at his wedding twelve years earlier.

ON THE EARLY morning of April 12, 1861, Confederate artillery fired on Fort Sumter. In Galena, the telegraph tapped out news of the surrender of the South Carolina fort.

On April 15, President Lincoln issued a proclamation calling for seventy-five thousand volunteers to serve for ninety days. The next day, all stores in Galena closed. People rushed into town from surrounding farms. With the majority of the town having voted for Stephen Douglas for president, the air filled with both excitement and uncertainty.

The next evening, Grant joined fellow citizens in the large stone courthouse, which was standing room only. Mayor Robert Brand presided over the packed hall. A Democrat of southern birth, he offered a halting speech against making war on another part of the country, calling instead for some "honorable compromise." His words catapulted the meeting into "indescribable confusion," according to merchant Augustus Chetlain.

Congressman Elihu Washburne rose and in a resounding voice declared that "the wicked and unjustifiable war" must be fought to a conclusion. He offered several recommendations, including support for the government and the formation of two military companies.

Galena was a Democratic town in a strongly Republican district. Republican Elihu B. Washburne, elected to Congress in 1852, was born in Maine, graduated from Harvard Law School, and moved to Galena in 1840 to set up a law practice. Tall, broad-shouldered, with light gray eyes, Washburne was respected for his seriousness and honesty; he vowed when coming west not to drink, smoke, play cards, or attend the theater.

In Galena, he met and married Adele Gratiot in 1845. Her forebears were French Huguenots, and after their marriage he learned French and began enjoying a glass of wine with dinner. Washburne worshipped in the town's Episcopal church when he first arrived but followed his wife to her Presbyterian church. In remarkable family public service, Washburne served concurrently in Congress with his brother Israel, elected from Maine in 1850, and brother Cadwallader, elected from Wisconsin in 1854.

In the presidential campaign of 1860, Washburne campaigned for Lincoln in Galena but never met the new clerk at the Grant leather store.

When Washburne stepped down, the crowd began to yell, "Rawlins! Rawlins!" John Rawlins, although not quite thirty, had become the leading Democrat in town. Everyone knew of his strong support for Douglas in the recent presidential campaign. Earlier in the day, a Democratic friend had warned Rawlins, "It is an abolition fight. Do not mix in; if you do, you will injure our party." As many Democrats counseled patience, the crowd wondered what Rawlins would say.

Grant listened with appreciation as Rawlins silenced the crowd. He reviewed how the nation had come to this point—the foundation under the Constitution, the place of slavery in the history of the nation, the Missouri Compromise, the Mexican War, the Kansas-Nebraska Act. He emphasized that again and again the genius of the American people lay in their readiness to submit to the will of the majority.

After speaking more than forty minutes, Rawlins suddenly elevated his voice when he denounced the act at Fort Sumter as the work of "fire

Republican congressman Elihu B. Washburne, a friend of Abraham Lincoln's, resided in Galena.

eaters" and "hot heads." As he reached his climax, you could hear the rumble of boot heels. "I have been a Democrat all my life; but this is no longer a question of politics. It is simply Union or disunion, country or no country. . . . We will stand by the flag of our country and appeal to the God of Battles!"

The audience members jumped to their feet, cheering. Republicans were amazed and pleased; Democrats dared not offer a dissenting voice. Grant told a friend later that he listened to the speech with "rapt attention" and it "stirred his patriotism and rekindled his military ardor." Rawlins articulated what Grant thought but could not yet say.

As the crowd left, William Rowley spoke, "Well, Captain Grant, it was a fine meeting, after all."

"Yes: we're about to *do* something now," he replied quietly.

As Grant walked home, he said to Orvil, "I thought I was done with soldiering. I never expected to be in the military again." He added intently, "But I was educated by the Government; and if my knowledge and experience can be of any service, I think I ought to offer them."

"I think so too," replied his brother. "Go, if you like, and I will stay at home and attend to the store." Grant remembered, "I never went into our leather store after that meeting, to put up a package or do other business."

THE NEXT DAY, notices about town announced another meeting the following evening, April 18, to raise a company of volunteers. The frenzied scene was repeated. John E. Smith, Republican county treasurer, veteran of the Mexican War, was in the chair—in charge of the meeting. Having previously consulted with Washburne, he had decided it would be wise to give up the chair this evening to a Democrat who was also a veteran of the war: "I nominate Captain U. S. Grant for chairman."

Grant, sitting on a hard bench outside the inner railing of the courtroom, was surprised by Smith's announcement. The crowd looked on with curiosity, for only a few knew the man in the blue army coat.

Grant slowly rose. "Grant! Captain Grant!" the crowd began to shout in unison.

Leaving the pine bench, Grant walked hesitatingly to the front. To a chorus of "Aye!" he took the chair. Merchant Chetlain remembered that Grant, "with some evident embarrassment," stated the object of the meeting. But soon he gained his composure and explained what it meant to raise and equip a company: "unquestioning obedience . . . hard fare . . . long marches in the rain and snow." Warming to a subject he knew well, he spoke of the need to translate patriotism and passion into discipline and drill. He offered no eloquent words in support of the war and the Union, but he answered questions. He concluded by calling for volunteers.

IT IS TEMPTING to see Grant's transformation from citizen to soldier as a conversion experience occurring the evening of April 18 when, to his surprise, a few community leaders put his name forward. But that doesn't take into account what had been taking place within him in the previous months in Galena.

First, the Grant leather store was a hotbed of Republican discussion and agitation. Simpson and Orvil were, like their father, staunch Republicans. The brothers Grant, plus cousin Burke, regularly sat around the stove debating and discussing politics, slavery, and prospects for secession. What an education for Grant and what a contrast for one used to listening to Colonel Dent talk endlessly of southern pro-slavery politics.

Second, Grant had been reading newspapers regularly. Julia remembered, "Ulys read aloud to me every speech for and against secession," after which they would debate the issue. In an era when people generally read two or three local newspapers like the *Weekly North-Western Gazette* and the *Daily Courier,* he may have also read newspapers from Freeport, Dubuque, Chicago, and St. Louis.

By the end of 1860, Grant's letters had begun to take on a new valence. They became more serious—and more political. After the secession of South Carolina, Grant wrote an unknown correspondent: "How do you all feel on the subject of Secession in St. Louis?" He was not shy about expressing his opinion. "It is hard to realize that a State or States should commit so suicidal an act as to secede from the Union, though from all the reports, I have no doubt but that at least five of them will do it." What did he think of President James Buchanan's response? "With the present granny of an executive, some foolish policy will doubtless be pursued which will give the seceding States the support and sympathy of the Southern States that don't go out." Grant had voted for Buchanan in 1856 in hopes of cooling the ardor for secession, but as president he had proved spineless in the face of secessionist threats.

THE NEXT DAY, after the second courthouse meeting, everyone wanted to talk to Grant—ask him questions, seek his counsel, get his help in recruiting volunteers. Suddenly he became the most conspicuous man in town.

As he prepared to travel the region in search of volunteers, he found time to write a remarkable letter. Surprisingly, it was not to his father, who he knew supported the defense of the Union, but rather to his father-in-law, who supported secession: "The times are indeed startling but now is the time, particularly in the border Slave states, for men to prove their love of country." Recognizing Colonel Dent was a states' rights Democrat, he wrote, "I know it is hard for men to apparently work with the Republican party," but he counseled that "now all party distinction should be lost sight of and every true patriot be for maintaining the integrity of the glorious old Stars and Stripes, the Constitution and the Union." He then told Julia's father what he surely did not want to hear: "In all these troubles the South have been the aggressors and the Administration has stood purely on the defensive." Lincoln had called for seventy-five thousand volunteers, Grant affirmed, but in his opinion the North would respond with "ten and twenty times 75,000 if it should be necessary."

Did Grant think he could change her father's mind? Or was he, perhaps unconsciously, determined to state his private convictions in words he was not yet able to voice in public? Summing up in one sentence both past and future against the backdrop of a nation torn apart, Grant told his slaveholding father-in-law, "In all this I can but see the doom of slavery."

GRANT'S YEAR IN Galena was a time of gestation. No longer struggling to provide for his family, he was also free from strife with his pro-slavery father-in-law. He had left Colonel Dent's world for his father's, moving nearer to antislavery in the friends he chose. Yet in April 1861, his conflict was with secession, not slavery. If he thought West Point, the Mexican War, Sackets Harbor, Detroit, Fort Vancouver, and Fort Humboldt were in the past, suddenly all these places and experiences surged into the present as he contemplated what his role could be in the conflict pressing in upon him. Nearly seven years to the day Grant resigned from the army, he found himself thrust into the Civil War.

PART THREE

Transformation

1861–1865

I need this man. He fights.

—ABRAHAM LINCOLN

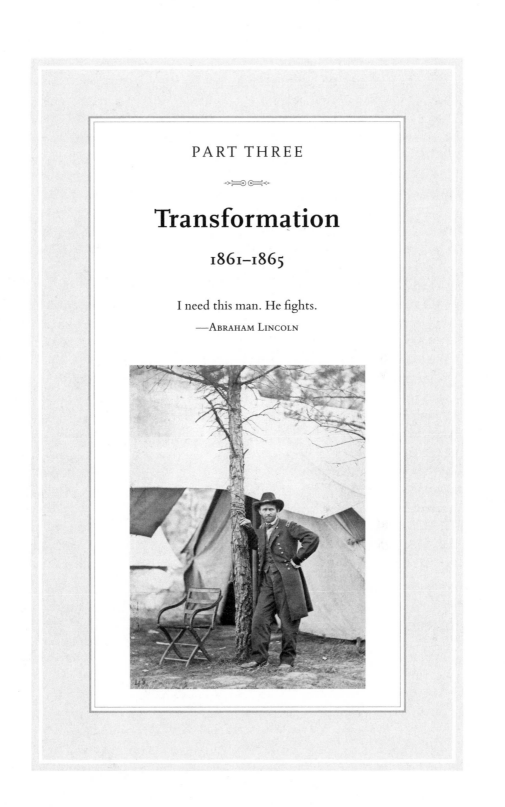

CHAPTER 11

"I Am In to Do All I Can"

There are but two parties now, Traitors & Patriots and
I want hereafter to be ranked with the latter.
—ULYSSES S. GRANT TO JESSE ROOT GRANT, April 21, 1861

This war, predicted for years by many, North and South, nevertheless burst like a spring storm across the nation in 1861. Nearly everyone, including Grant, did not believe it would last long, a few months at most, over by the end of summer. Grant felt a rush of patriotism within himself, yet the unanswered question loomed: How and where would this ex-military officer find his place?

ON APRIL 19, the day after his chairmanship, Grant rode fourteen miles south to Hanover to recruit volunteers. That evening, he made his very first public speech. The yield from this venture was twelve recruits.

Officers were chosen by election in volunteer regiments. Grant returned to Galena just as the town's eighty recruits prepared to vote for officers. He was urged to accept the position of captain, but he declined. He had resigned from the army as a captain in 1854 and did not want to resume his career at the same rank. He promised "I would aid the company in every way I could."

In the next days, Grant worked tirelessly, drilling volunteers with pine laths substituting as guns, helping with military organization and procedures, and working with a team of women to make uniforms. He decided on the design, purchased the material, and hired cutters.

In this turbulent atmosphere, Grant sent a moving letter to his father. "What I ask now is your approval of the course I am taking, or advice in the matter," he wrote. His appeal, which speaks to the powerful relationship of father and son in the mid-nineteenth-century family, is all the more remarkable when one remembers the pair's continuing struggles. At this critical moment, the son wanted the father's blessing.

Knowing his father was well aware of his previous lack of political commitment, he hastened to add, "Whatever may have been my political opinions before I have but one sentiment now. That is we have a Government, and laws and a flag and they must all be sustained. There are but two parties now, Traitors & Patriots and I want hereafter to be ranked with the latter."

WASHBURNE ENCOURAGED GRANT to go to Springfield, telling him Republican governor Richard Yates would find a position for a West Point graduate with military experience. On April 25, citizens from town and countryside turned out to see off the Jo Daviess County troops. Grant walked down the long High Street stairs to join the regiment, now part of the Eleventh Illinois Infantry. So many well-wishers crowded the street that Methodist minister John Heyl Vincent had to climb onto an Illinois Central boxcar to offer a farewell address and prayer before the jubilant, awkwardly marching volunteers entrained to Springfield.

Confusion reigned as Grant arrived in muddy Springfield. He located the governor's office inside the Greek Revival state capitol where Abraham Lincoln had given his "House Divided" speech in 1858. Upon entering, he found the office thronged with men seeking positions. He was intercepted by Gustave Koerner, former lieutenant governor, who had volunteered to assist Yates in this crisis. A German immigrant, Koerner had built a political career in Illinois on his shrewd judgments of men and issues. He was not impressed by the ex-quartermaster. He described Grant as "hardly of medium height, broad-shouldered and rather short-necked," whose "features did not indicate any very high grade of intellectuality." Grant "was very indifferently dressed, and did not at all look like a military man." To Grant's disappointment, Governor Yates did not have time to see him.

On April 27, 1861, Grant celebrated his thirty-ninth birthday—away from his family, with no commission and no uniform, wanting to participate in the war but not certain how he could serve. Walking about Springfield, he was disgusted to see self-centered jockeying for military positions. He wrote his father, "I was perfectly sickened at the political wire-pulling for all these commissions and would not engage in it."

The next day, with no position in view, Grant intended to take the nine P.M. train home to Galena. After eating dinner at the Chenery House, he lingered for a moment at the front door. Governor Yates, also dining at the hotel, called out, "Captain." The governor understood Grant was leaving Springfield but asked if would remain overnight and call at the executive office the next morning.

Washburne's prediction came true. Yates offered Grant a position as an aide in the office of Adjutant General Tom Mather. He started immediately. Sitting at a three-legged table in an anteroom, Grant found himself performing the tedious duties of a clerk—writing military forms and orders and even searching for old muskets in the arsenal. He was asked all manner of questions about military regulations, and people were impressed by his ready answers. Uncomplaining, he wrote Julia, "Papers are not my forte and therefore my services may not be as valuable as he anticipates." She was not surprised to read her husband's next sentence: "However I am in to do all I can and will do my best."

Yates observed how Grant made order out of chaos. This first assignment quickly brought another: on May 4, the governor put Grant in charge of Camp Yates, the largest recruiting center in Illinois, located on the state fairgrounds. Here Grant supervised and drilled the arriving regiments of thirty-day volunteers. He rented a room at the Chenery House and shared a bed with Augustus Chetlain. The *Weekly North-Western Gazette* in Galena reported with pride that Grant had brought Camp Yates "under strict military law. The horse-play and insubordination of the past was gone."

In succeeding weeks, Grant traveled to other recruiting centers in Mattoon, Belleville, and Anna to superintend the mustering of thirty-day men. He made such an impact at Mattoon—a soldier reported, "Everything he did was done without hesitation"—that the men named their quarters "Camp Grant."

NEAR THE END of May, his mustering work completed, Grant returned to Springfield and drew his service pay of $130. Charles Lanphier, editor of Springfield's *Illinois State Register,* ran into a tired Grant at the Chenery House and asked, "What are you doing here, captain?"

"Nothing—waiting," he replied, downcast. Discouraged, without an assignment commensurate with his military experience, Grant decided to return to Galena to see his family and take stock of the best way forward. Shortly after his arrival, Horace H. Houghton, longtime editor of the *Weekly North-Western Gazette,* called to ask if he might interview him. From this interview, Grant received his first newspaper commendation.

> We are now in want of just such soldiers as he is, and we hope the government will invite him to higher command. He is the very soul of honor, and no man breathes who has a more patriotic heart. We want among our young soldiers the influence of the rare leadership of men like Captain Grant.

Houghton offered this assessment before Grant had fought a single battle.

On May 24, Grant wrote Adjutant General Lorenzo Thomas in Washington, "I have the honor, very respectfully, to tender my services, until the close of the War, in such capacity as may be offered." Up to this moment, he had been hoping to be appointed a colonel of volunteers—the prerogative of states—but now he also sought to become colonel of a regular regiment, an appointment that could be made only by President Lincoln.

The letter was never answered. The harried Thomas must have put the request in a drawer, because fifteen years passed before it was discovered—in 1876—by a subsequent adjutant general.

The Civil War was beginning without Grant.

IN EARLY JUNE, Grant visited his parents in Covington, Kentucky, but he traveled there with a dual purpose. He knew the army's Department of the Ohio was located across the Ohio River in Cincinnati. George McClellan commanded the department, which encompassed Ohio, Indiana, and Illinois. At Fort Vancouver, Grant had outfitted McClellan's railroad survey.

Anxious to see McClellan, Grant swallowed his pride and went to McClellan's headquarters. When he was informed that McClellan had just gone out, he waited for a long time, then finally told an officer he would return the next day.

The following day, Grant encountered "the same story": the general had gone out. Grant watched the staff members, "with quills behind their ears," so busy writing reports "that they did not say a word" to him. A disappointed Grant left again.

On his way back to Illinois, he stopped to visit West Point classmate Joe Reynolds in Lafayette, Indiana. While he was there, a telegram from Governor Yates caught up with him. He opened it to read that Yates had appointed him colonel to command the Seventh Regiment, which he had mustered into service at Mattoon a month earlier.

Grant accepted this assignment eagerly. Many West Pointers looked down their noses at volunteers; he did not. He admitted that when he'd first encountered volunteers in the Mexican War, he'd had reservations, but they'd disappeared once he observed the bravery of the men in battle. But when Jesse read the news of his son's assignment, he could not resist telling him that he had settled for less than the best.

Grant did not look like a colonel upon arriving to assume command.

The volunteers chortled to one another. One reported, "He was dressed very clumsily, in citizens' clothes—an old coat, worn out at the elbows, and badly dinged plug hat." Grant arrived knowing that less than half of the recruits had extended their enlistment beyond thirty days. Painfully aware of his shortcomings as a speaker, he accepted the offers of Democratic congressmen and military officers John A. Logan and John A. McClernand to speak to the troops. He was so impressed by their eloquence that when Logan introduced him, he could only get out, "Men, go to your quarters."

These first days of Grant's command would presage the way he would conduct himself in the months to come. He led not by shouting or threats, but quietly, often with written orders. His troops quickly labeled him "the quiet man." In his first order he wrote, "In accepting this command, your Commander will require the co-operation of all the commissioned and non-commissioned Officers in instructing the command, and in maintaining discipline, and hopes to receive also the hearty support of every enlisted man." "Cooperation" would underpin Grant's leadership.

Also in his first order he confronted the vexing problem of camp discipline. Grant's predecessor had attempted to impose discipline by creating a security guard of eighty soldiers "to keep the men from climbing the fence and going in to the city to see the girls." By contrast, Grant's order reflected his trust in their common sense: "From Reveille until Retreat no passes will be required. In extending this privilege to the men of this command the Col Commanding hopes that his leniency will not be so abused as to make it necessary to retract it. All men when out of Camp should reflect that they are gentlemen—in camp soldiers." As a young soldier, Grant had appreciated that Stephen Kearney at Jefferson Barracks had let the men come and go as long as they reported on time for roll calls and drill. He would do the same.

A lieutenant in Grant's first command wrote, "The effect of that order was wonderful. The men responded enthusiastically, and discipline ceased to be a problem."

Grant realized the major problem with volunteers began with officers. Unlike the regulars, who were promoted through a proven competency observed from above, volunteer officers were elected by their peers. Too often the election became a popularity contest, which meant that new shoulder straps could be awarded for reasons having little to do with proven skills in the field.

Planning for the fighting that lay ahead, he asked Julia to send him his copy of "McClellan's report of battles in the Crimea." McClellan had spent an entire year in Europe studying the tactics used in the Crimean War, a war fought in 1854–1856 between Russia on one side and British, French, and Ottoman forces on the other. He was ready to study these battles with new purpose.

Now confident in his ability to lead, Grant went home to Galena for a visit. Julia was delighted to see "Victor," which became her pet name at that time after "he had read to me the triumphs of Victor Emmanuel" in uniting Italy. One goal of the trip: Grant needed a uniform and a horse but did not have enough money for either. With times tight and his brothers unable to loan him any money, he turned to his father's former partner, E. A. Collins, who endorsed a note for $500. Grant left with a new uniform and a new horse, Rondy. However, he still continued to favor his plain blue coat and ordinary black felt hat. James L. Crane, a Methodist chaplain attached to the Seventh Regiment, reported that Grant "never had about him a single mark to distinguish his rank." As for the uniform, Crane recalled that "he never wore it, except on dress parade."

When Grant assumed command, he faced a crisis of the clock. His men, as volunteers in a state militia, had signed up for only thirty days. Disliking their previous colonel, they had decided not to enlist for an additional three years. The clock was ticking—their service would end on June 28.

Grant accepted the challenge of persuading them to extend their service. A large part of that decision would be based on their confidence in their new colonel. On Friday, June 28, the men of the Seventh, almost to a man, signed up for three years, in the process becoming the Twenty-first Illinois.

THE NEW NAME brought a new assignment. Grant received orders to move the Twenty-first Illinois 110 miles west to Quincy, Illinois, on the Mississippi River. The agent for the Great Western Railroad contacted Grant and asked when he desired transportation.

"I do not want any." He told the startled agent, "It would be good preparation for the troops to march there."

Beginning on July 3, Grant's first march became another opportunity to learn discipline. Each morning, after camp had been set up for his nearly one-thousand-man regiment, Grant would post the hour of departure for the next day. If a man was not ready to march, he would be left behind—without breakfast and more than once without pants.

On a stop in a small town, some men filled their canteens with whiskey from a local grocery store. Later, observing some wobbling marchers, Grant stopped to inspect their canteens. Whenever he found whiskey in a man's canteen, he ordered him to empty it on the ground and for the rest of the day be tied to the back of one of the baggage wagons.

Four days into the march, he wrote Julia, "Passing through the towns the whole population would turn out to receive us." He appreciated how the state supported its volunteers.

During the Mexican War, Grant had resisted his assignment as quartermaster. Now he realized the experience had served him well in his new command. Colonel John Williams reported to Governor Yates that Grant was the first officer who understood precisely what he wanted. "Grant's requisition upon me for supplies seemed to be complete in every detail, for nothing was added to or omitted from the requisition."

While camped on the Illinois River, Grant purchased a second horse from a local farmer. Jack, cream-colored with a silver white mane and tail, proved more suitable and flexible for his purposes than Rondy, a high-spirited stallion.

As the men marched, they sang the popular gospel song "Jordan Am a Hard Road to Travel." Lieutenant Joseph W. Vance wrote, "He put us to hard drill. He stopped all the straggling, all skylarking at night." Most impressive, Vance reported, when Grant "punished a man, he did it in a quiet way, and in a spirit which did not enrage the one punished." Grant told Julia, "I don't believe there is a more orderly set of troops now in volunteer service. I have been very strict with them and the men seem to like it."

Two days later, he issued a general order: "The Col commanding this Regiment, deems it his duty at this period of the march to return his thanks to the Officers and men composing the command on their general Obedience and Military discipline." He heightened his commendation by reminding his men that all his previous service had been in the regular army. He further deemed "it not inappropriate at this time to make a most favorable comparison of this command with that of veteran troops in point of Soldierly bearing general good Order, and cheerful execution of commands." Their good conduct made "the real necessity of a Guard unnecessary."

JULIA ENTERED THE Civil War also. Social conventions had been changing since the early nineteenth century, such that women were no longer uniformly mandated to stay home but could choose public vocations appropriate to their gender—teachers and nurses. The aim was not to enter the male sphere, but to seed the public domain with domestic values and female influence. Julia was not a woman to accept social conventions.

She crossed the threshold of the war in stages. First, she sent her husband off to war—with her blessing. Second, she sent her oldest son, Fred. He joined his father on the march to Quincy. Julia reflected, "Strange to say, I felt no regret at [Ulysses's] going and even suggested that our eldest son, just then eleven years old, should accompany him."

Once at Quincy, with the prospect of battle looming when they crossed into Missouri, Ulysses sent Fred home. He wrote Julia, "I did not telegraph you because I thought you would be in a perfect stew until he arrived." He told her, "He did not want to go at all."

But he underestimated Julia. Before Fred arrived home, she wrote, "Do not send him home." She added, "Alexander was not older when he accompanied Philip. Do keep him with you." Julia knew her history. Alexander III of Macedon, called Alexander the Great, had accompanied his father, Philip II of Macedon, into battle while still a boy.

Third, Julia began to think of joining Ulysses herself. She was aware of his loneliness when he served on the Pacific coast for two years without her. One week later, he wrote, "I should like very much to go into Camp some place where you could visit me." Grant the soldier also longed to be husband and father.

ON JULY 11, Grant crossed the Mississippi River into Missouri. His mission: to function like a police force in contested territory in the northeastern part of the state. His specific task: to hold bridges and railroads. In these first days, Grant's men were constantly threatened by bushwhackers—irregular military forces who fought without uniforms and then melted away into the civilian population. He determined to protect private property and not mistreat citizens. He wrote Julia, "When we first came there was a terrible state of fear existing among the people," adding gratefully, "They find that all troops are not the desperate characters they took them for."

After four days in Missouri, Grant received orders to move against Thomas Harris, a Confederate guerrilla leader whose camp was reported to be at the Salt River. The farther Grant marched, he confessed, "I was anything but easy." He thought he had conquered his fears of battle in the Mexican War, but as he drew near Harris's camp, "my heart kept getting higher and higher until it felt to me as though it was in my throat." He admitted, "I would have given anything then to have been back in Illinois, but I had not the moral courage to halt and consider what to do."

As Grant and his men approached the river bottom, he saw that hills rose more than one hundred feet on either side of Salt Creek, more than enough to shield a Confederate force waiting in ambush. When his lead element reached the brow of the hill, they discovered that Harris had gone. The marks of his encampment were all that remained. In that moment, Grant owned up: "My heart resumed its place."

This incident became an epiphany: "It occurred to me at once that Harris had been as much afraid of me as I had been of him." Later, he would write, "This realization had great consequences for the future. . . . This was a view of the question I had never taken before; but it was one I never forgot afterwards."

FOR THE MONTH of July, Grant camped near Mexico, Missouri, 120 miles west of St. Louis. On July 24, Brigadier General John Pope, commander in northern Missouri, expanded Grant's command to include four regiments stationed nearby (a regiment typically comprised one thousand men). During this rest period, he focused on readying his forces for the combat he knew would come soon. At the same time, Grant's orders exhibited a growing sensitivity to the people in areas through which he traveled. He was listening—not only to his volunteers, but to the civilian population.

In assuming a larger command, Grant discovered that the regiments that preceded the Twenty-first routinely "had been in the habit of visiting houses without invitation and helping themselves to food and drink, or demanding them from the occupants." Furthermore, they carried their guns outside camp "and made every man they found take the oath of allegiance to the government." On July 25, he issued an order prohibiting this kind of behavior: "No wandering will be permitted." Within days he reported, "The people were no longer molested or made afraid."

ON A HOT August afternoon, Methodist chaplain James Crane secured a copy of the *St. Louis Democrat* from a passing railroad car. While reading the newspaper, he came across Grant's name in a list of new brigadier generals. A brigadier general normally commanded four thousand men. A few minutes later, as Grant walked by, he called out, "Colonel, I have some news that will interest you."

Grant scanned the announcement and saw himself listed seventeenth of thirty-four new brigadiers. "Well, sir, I had no suspicion of it," he replied. "It never came from any request of mine. That's some of Washburne's work."

After perusing the newspaper, Crane reported, Grant "very leisurely rose up and pulled his black felt hat a little nearer his eyes." He "walked away about his business with as much apparent unconcern as if some one had merely told him that his new suit of clothes was finished."

A month later, Grant wrote Washburne, "I think I see your hand in it." Grant pledged, "You shall never have cause to regret the part you have taken."

Seven years earlier, Grant had resigned in dishonor; now he was being promoted to brigadier general. He was entitled to wear a star on each shoulder. He knew he needed to order a general's uniform with two parallel rows of brass buttons, but at the moment he did not have time for such details.

LINCOLN APPOINTED JOHN C. Frémont to head the Department of the West—the area west of the Appalachian Mountains to the Mississippi River. Frémont, forty-eight, handsome with graying hair, had earned the nickname "the Pathfinder of the West" for his eleven years of service in the army's topographical corps. He had been the Republican Party's first presidential candidate in 1856 but was defeated by James Buchanan. Frémont met with Lincoln at the White House, and was told, "I have given you *carte blanche;* you must use your own judgment and do the best you can." Lincoln expected Frémont to deal adroitly with both Kentucky and Missouri, so-called border states, where Union supporters were contending against strong Confederate beliefs.

Frémont arrived in St. Louis on July 25 with an aristocratic air that almost immediately raised eyebrows. To general disapproval, he rented a lavish mansion for $6,000 a year and surrounded himself with a cadre of Hungarian and Italian guards in brassy uniforms. Soldiers and citizens alike found him inaccessible and less than inspiring.

On August 5, Pope sent Grant to St. Louis to confer with Frémont about the military landscape in Missouri. Pope wrote Frémont, "Col Grant is an old army officer thoroughly a gentleman & an officer of intelligence & discretion." Upon arriving at Frémont's luxurious headquarters, Grant recognized immediately that this was no Zachary Taylor, whose shunning of ostentation he had always admired. The soldier at the gate informed him that Frémont had put off their appointment until the next day.

No matter. Grant went to the theater that evening. He was impressed by Irish-American playwright Dion Boucicault's popular *The Relief of Lucknow,* a drama written immediately after the 1857 Indian rebellion against British rule.

The next day Grant received orders from Frémont to proceed to Ironton, ninety miles south of St. Louis, and take command of the district in southeast Missouri. Upon Grant's arrival, Edward Castle, Frémont's superintendent of railroad transportation, wrote from Ironton, "Genl Grant I am pleased with. He will do to lead."

Upon his arrival, Grant found military discipline absent in Ironton. He ordered, "All firing must be discontinued . . . in and around camp," since it encouraged false alarms. He ordered the commander at nearby Pilot Knob "to suppress all drinking houses" in order "to enable him to preserve sobriety."

Grant also found the troops in his command abuzz with rumors that General William J. Hardee was menacing the area with several thousand Confederate soldiers. Hardee, who had served as commandant of cadets at West Point from 1856 to 1860, was well-known for his textbook, *Rifle and Light Infantry Tactics*. Grant secured a copy but quickly perceived Hardee's tactics to be "nothing more than common sense."

In Ironton, Grant became acquainted with John W. Emerson, who owned the land where he made his headquarters. Several days after Grant's arrival, Emerson found him sitting beneath a grand oak tree, examining a map. Seemingly dissatisfied, he asked the Ironton lawyer if he could secure a more accurate map. Emerson returned with a new map, then watched as Grant moved his finger down the Mississippi, telling him, "The rebels *must* be driven out," and, "The rivers *must* be opened."

The next day, Emerson noticed Grant had marked the new map with red crosses that he understood to mean places where Confederates were blocking river crossings. He observed dotted lines overland toward Forts Henry and Donelson in Tennessee. Grant had made further intricate lines in red pencil, not only down the Mississippi, but up the Tennessee and Cumberland rivers. When Emerson commented that this looked like serious planning, Grant replied, "Possibilities—mere possibilities."

If Grant's arrival had raised morale, it did not help when his troops heard of the battle at Wilson's Creek. On August 10, impulsive Union general Nathaniel Lyon picked a fight with well-organized Confederate troops at Wilson's Creek, a long 215 miles from his supplies in St. Louis. Confederate generals Sterling Price and Ben McCulloch outnumbered Lyon's Union forces two to one. Lyon was killed in the battle, the first Union general to die in the Civil War. Many questioned why Frémont did nothing to reinforce Lyon.

Shortly after Wilson's Creek, Frémont ordered Grant to proceed to Jefferson City to defend the Missouri state capital. Already at the beginning of the Civil War, Missouri, as a border state, was experiencing deep divides. In a neighbor-against-neighbor war, it sent men and supplies to opposing sides and by the fall would have rival state capitals.

Following his arrival, Grant reported that he "found a good many troops in Jefferson City, but in the greatest confusion, and no one person knew where they all were." He declared, "I am not fortifying here at all. Drill and discipline is more necessary for the men than fortification." Drill and discipline were becoming signatures of Grant's leadership.

As a new brigadier general, Grant needed to fill out his staff. Remembering John Rawlins's abilities to navigate the political landscape in Galena, he asked his friend to join him. Rawlins accepted but first traveled to Goshen, New York, to be with his ill wife, who died on August 30. Grant's appointment of a young man with no military training to be his chief aide would prove to be a masterstroke.

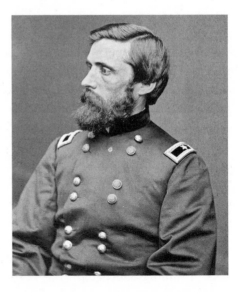

Newly minted brigadier general Ulysses S. Grant appoints Galena lawyer John A. Rawlins as his chief aide.

On August 27, Frémont summoned Grant to St. Louis to receive "special orders." Frémont's instinct to be aggressive in war had led him to favor Grant (whom he'd met only twice) over more senior generals John Pope and Benjamin Prentiss, for a special position of command. "I believed him to be a man of great activity and promptness in obeying orders without question or hesitation," he indicated later. "I selected him for qualities I could not find combined in any other officer, for General Grant was a man of unassuming character, not given to self-elation, or dogged persistence, and an iron will."

Grant's new orders made him commander of southeast Missouri south of St. Louis as well as all of southern Illinois. Frémont wanted Grant to take and hold a position on the Mississippi River with a long-term goal "to establish a base of operations against Memphis and Nashville and in the short term "occupy Columbus in Kentucky as soon as possible." He also wanted him to get a new uniform.

Grant proceeded by steamer to Cape Girardeau, 115 miles south of St. Louis on the west side of the Mississippi, to take charge of a small Federal garrison. In writing Julia of his new assignment, he balanced his usual self-deprecating tone with words that indicated he was embarking upon something much larger than he had ever anticipated: "I have a task before me of no trifling moment and want all the encouragement possible." He wrote his father, "All I fear is that too much may be expected of me."

At Cape Girardeau, Grant expected to go after guerrilla leader "Swamp Fox" Jeff Thompson, whose cavalry attacked supply lines along the Mississippi River. Within days, however, he decided Thompson was a small fish, so he hurried to Cairo, Illinois, for a larger catch.

JUST MONTHS EARLIER, the War Department had established a base of operations at Cairo, Illinois. Before 1861, Cairo's claim to fame was chiefly as the muddy town standing on a low-lying delta where the Ohio River joined the mighty Mississippi. Cairo's citizens lived behind fifteen-foot-high levee walls built to keep out the two great rivers.

Cairo, the southernmost city in the North, located farther south geographically than Richmond, Virginia, became a bustling military and naval base. The Union aimed to move down the Mississippi River and up the Tennessee and Cumberland rivers. Grant had understood early on that if the Union could win this river war, it would be well on its way to winning the Confederate heartland. A major challenge would be whether army and naval commanders, often jealous of one another, could work together.

Grant arrived in Cairo on September 2 to take command. From the Cairo waterfront he walked directly to a bank building serving as army headquarters. He would be replacing Colonel Richard J. Oglesby, thirty-seven years old and currently in command. Oglesby's office swarmed with people from Missouri, Kentucky, and Illinois, both complaining and requesting. Grant entered dressed in civilian clothes, and no one paid him any attention.

Grant asked an aide to introduce him to Oglesby, but the colonel did not catch his name. After waiting a few minutes, Grant took a piece of paper and wrote out an order assuming command. When he'd read the paper, Oglesby looked up at this slight man in civilian clothes with "an expression of surprise."

Grant moved into the St. Charles Hotel and set up his office in the bank building. As he continued his habit of dressing in civilian clothes, he looked more like a small-town banker than a brigadier general.

In EARLY SEPTEMBER 1861, Kentucky still hung on to its neutrality but was being torn asunder by Union and Confederate factions operating in different sections of the state. After Fort Sumter, Kentucky's Democratic governor, Beriah Magoffin, expressed his sympathy with secession and replied defiantly to Lincoln's call for troops. The Kentucky House of Representatives on May 16 declared "strict neutrality" to be the state posture. This action contained both a rejection of pleas for secession and a hope that Kentucky would not become a war battleground.

Grant understood the importance of Kentucky as a key border state. Kentuckians had long cherished their role as mediator between North and South. They knew their state to be the birthplace of both Abraham Lincoln and Jefferson Davis, presidents of the two warring entities. Having grown up in southern Ohio, Grant particularly understood Kentucky's strategic importance as a geographic bridge between the "Old Northwest" states of Ohio, Indiana, and Illinois and the Confederate state of Tennessee.

On the morning of September 5, Grant received a spy from Frémont. Charles A. De Arnaud informed him that Confederate general Gideon Pillow had broken Kentucky's neutrality by marching into Hickman, Kentucky, twenty-eight miles south of Cairo. As Confederate troops moved north toward Columbus, Kentucky, De Arnaud reported that Pillow intended to continue overland to Paducah, a port city on the Ohio River, with the intention of invading southern Illinois.

After hearing De Arnaud's report, Grant sent him back to Frémont in St. Louis carrying his message: "I am now nearly ready for Paducah (should not a telegraph arrive preventing the movement) on the strength of the information telegraphed."

Grant did not wait for a reply but prepared to leave for Paducah that evening. Forty-five miles up the Ohio River, this town of forty-five hundred lay at the mouth of the Tennessee River, the 650-mile tributary of the Ohio River. Born in the mountains of east Tennessee, the river meandered south into northern Mississippi and Alabama before turning north and ending at Paducah. Grant, who had been working with his maps ever since Ironton, understood the Tennessee River was a river route into the Confederacy.

During this busy day, Grant found time to write a message to the Speaker of the Kentucky House of Representatives: "I regret to inform you that Confederate forces in Considerable numbers have invaded the territory of Kentucky." He astutely explained why he was about to descend on Paducah. At this adrenaline-filled moment, he was thinking both politically and militarily.

In the evening, Grant assembled the Illinois Ninth and Twelfth regiments on navy transports. Led by gunboats, they began the forty-five-mile voyage up the Ohio. Nearing Paducah, he ordered the boats to anchor for a few hours, waiting to arrive by the sun's early light. As they went ashore, he saw secession flags flying in the breeze, a welcome for Confederate troops expected at noon.

"I never after saw such consternation depicted on the faces of the people," recalled Grant. When his men disembarked, the flags were taken down. "Men, women and children came out of their doors looking pale and frightened at the presence of the invader." Grant knew people had been expecting the four thousand Confederate troops, by now only ten to fifteen miles away. Instead, they found blue uniforms.

Before leaving, Grant wrote out a short proclamation to the Paducah citizens that began, "I have come among you, not as an enemy, but as your friend and fellow-citizen, not to injure or annoy you, but to respect the rights of all loyal citizens." He concluded, "Whenever it is manifest that you are able to defend yourselves, to maintain the authority of your Government and protect the rights of all its loyal citizens, I shall withdraw the forces under my command from your city." His proclamation assured them he would respect their rights. For a young officer who eschewed politics, this brief, skillfully written proclamation revealed Grant's art of political persuasion.

LEAVING TROOPS IN Paducah, Grant returned to Cairo. From there he was prepared to take the fight to an enemy, some of whose leaders were his former classmates. He had signed up for what he thought would be a war of short duration; taking command at Cairo, he began to understand this could well be a long war.

*Illustrator N. C. Wyeth brilliantly captures Grant
on horseback, at ease in the saddle.*

CHAPTER 12

Belmont

We cut our way in and we can cut our way out.
—Ulysses S. Grant, *Personal Memoirs*

As the Civil War began, a cry echoed across the North: "We must have the Mississippi." Grant understood that whoever controlled the Mississippi River would control the emerging heartland of America.

It is not easy for readers in the twenty-first century to grasp the importance of rivers for Americans in the nineteenth century. Rivers became their interstate highways. Whether navigating the Hudson River in New York, piloting the Mississippi River, or traveling the Missouri River to discover the West, explorers, pioneers, and settlers used rivers to reach their destinations. Canoes, keelboats, flatboats, and finally steamers were their primary means of travel. The cities in what was called the Great Valley—from Pittsburgh to St. Louis to New Orleans—and Cincinnati, Louisville, Nashville, and Memphis in between, all throbbed with commercial activity because of their locations on rivers. Grant's forebears came west on the Ohio River.

In September 1861, the Confederacy held more than 550 miles of the Mississippi River, from New Orleans, Louisiana, to Columbus, Kentucky, firmly in its grip.

At the top of the Confederate chain of command in the West stood fifty-nine-year-old Albert Sidney Johnston. Johnston and Jefferson Davis, both Kentucky born, had been classmates at Transylvania University in Lexington, Kentucky, and at West Point. An inch over six feet, well built, with blue-green eyes and a touch of gray in his curly brown hair, Johnston struck admirers as a man of handsome dignity. Davis would call Johnston "the greatest soldier, the ablest man, civil or military, Confederate or Federal."

Grant shared Davis's estimation of Johnston's abilities. "His contem-

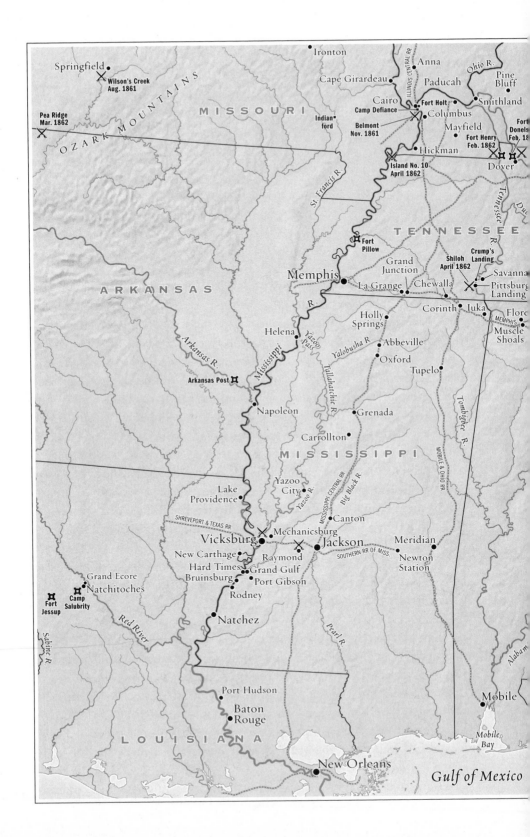

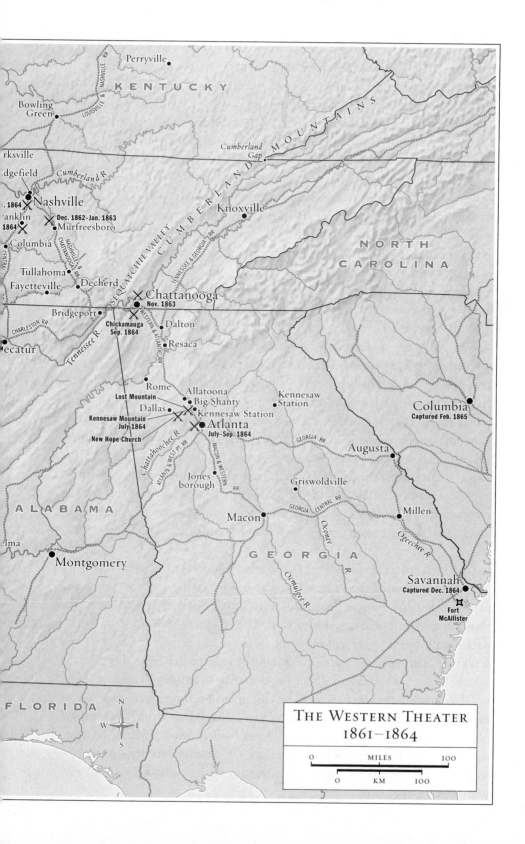

Perryville

KENTUCKY

Bowling
Green

LOUISVILLE & NASHVILLE RR

Cumberland
Gap

CUMBERLAND MOUNTAINS

rksville

dgefield   Cumberland R.

1864   Nashville

Knoxville

NORTH
CAROLINA

ranklin   Dec. 1862–Jan. 1863

1864   Murfreesboro

Columbia

TENNESSEE & GEORGIA RR

SEQUATCHIE VALLEY

CUMBERLAND

Tullahoma

Fayetteville   Decherd

NASHVILLE & CHATTANOOGA RR

Chattanooga
Nov. 1863

Bridgeport

WESTERN & ATLANTIC RR

Chickamauga
Sep. 1864   Dalton

CHARLESTON RR

Resaca

ecatur

Tennessee R.

Rome

Allatoona
Big Shanty

Kennesaw
Station

Columbia
Captured Feb. 1865

Lost Mountain

Dallas   Kennesaw Station

Kennesaw Mountain
July 1864   Atlanta
July–Sep. 1864

New Hope Church

Chattahoochee R.

ATLANTA & WEST PT. RR

GEORGIA RR

Augusta

Jones
borough

MACON & WESTERN

RR

Griswoldville

GEORGIA CENTRAL RR

Millen

ALABAMA

Macon

GEORGIA

Oconee

Ogeechee R.

elma

lma

Montgomery

Ocmulgee R.

R.

Savannah
Captured Dec. 1864

FLORIDA

N
W   E
S

Fort
McAllister

THE WESTERN THEATER
1861–1864

0   MILES   100

0   KM   100

poraries at West Point, and officers generally who came to know him personally later and remained on our side, expected him to prove the most formidable man to meet that the Confederacy would produce."

In the first months of the Civil War, southern politicians and press paid most attention to Virginia and the defense of Richmond. Yet Johnston, upon his arrival in Nashville on September 14, 1861, to assume command of the Western Military Department, understood the strategic importance of the vast western territory he was asked to defend.

Frémont wrote Grant he was sending General Charles F. Smith to assume command in Paducah. Smith had been a much admired commandant of cadets at West Point when Grant was a student. Smith's forty years of service had earned him wide respect. Tall, with a white walrus mustache, he looked like the hero he had become. With the outbreak of the war, by a quirk of timing Grant's appointment as brigadier general predated Smith's advancement, which meant student would be commanding teacher. Frémont recognized the difficulty this might provoke and established an independent command for Smith. Yet the older man's lines of communication with St. Louis were through Grant's headquarters, and supplies to Smith went out from Cairo.

Grant's marching orders from General Frémont were to dislodge Confederates from southeast Missouri and take and hold Columbus, twenty miles south on the Mississippi River. Called "the Gibraltar of the West," Columbus stood guard over river traffic. Columbus was occupied by Confederate general Gideon Pillow. By seizing control of the 150-foot-tall iron banks at Columbus, Confederate troops intended to block any Union advance south to Memphis and Vicksburg.

Grant spent his first weeks at Cairo converting civilian volunteers into soldiers. He commanded not by bluster but by respect, with a quiet and firm manner. By mid-September, Grant's prediction of a short war was beginning to fade. He wrote his sister Mary, "This war however is formidable and I regret to say cannot end so soon as I anticipated at first." After weeks of drill and discipline, Grant felt eager to get into action as he watched his men's patriotic ardor begin to flag in muddy Cairo.

When first arriving in Cairo, he had given Frémont little time to say no before he sailed up the Ohio River to occupy Paducah. Frémont was pleased with Grant's initiative, but he was not pleased with his letter to the Kentucky House of Representatives. "Commanders are not to correspond with State or other high authorities," he censured Grant, who would not forget this lesson.

.   .   .

As GRANT PREPARED to go south, an unlikely Confederate general headed north: Leonidas Polk, who had assumed responsibility for the upper Mississippi in the Western Department of the Confederate army. Son of a wealthy North Carolina planter who served in the Revolutionary War, Polk graduated eighth in his West Point class of 1827 but left the army shortly after graduation to enroll at Virginia Theological Seminary and study for the Episcopal ministry. When war erupted, Polk was serving as Episcopal bishop of Louisiana. The Confederate president invited Polk to Richmond, where he offered him a senior command in the army. Polk declined—twice—but finally accepted. Bishop Polk's decision surprised family and friends, and his decision to take up arms created controversy within the Episcopal Church. In the end, he relinquished his bishop's surplice for a Confederate general's uniform.

Why would Davis invest such authority in a man more than thirty years removed from West Point and who had no military experience? Davis believed Polk to be a natural leader. Over six feet tall, with snowy side whiskers, Polk looked like a general. After reporting to Johnston and making his headquarters at Memphis, he marched up through western Tennessee intent on holding Columbus.

If Polk was sometimes called "Old Granny"—he looked old at fifty-four—his chief subordinate, Gideon Pillow, appeared much younger at the same age. A nephew of former president James Polk, Pillow brought plenty of military experience to the Army of Tennessee; he brought plenty of baggage also. No fewer than three courts of inquiry alleging challenges to military superiors shadowed his service in Mexico. Even though he was acquitted each time, his reputation for self-promotion accompanied him.

Grant remembered Pillow. He was one of the few Confederate generals for whom he had expressed dislike. He wrote Mary, "I am not so uncharitable as many who served under him in Mexico. I think however he might report himself wounded on the receipt of a very slight scratch."

At Columbus, Polk prepared elaborate defenses. Starting fifteen feet above the water, he constructed three tiers to hold batteries totaling 143 guns. At the top he mounted the 128-pound Whitworth rifle, the largest gun in the Confederacy, which they called "Lady Polk." Any Union gunboats would want to think twice about confronting such tremendous firepower.

If the fastest Union gunboats tried to run the guns, they would be met by other defenses. Just below the surface of the water, engineers hung mines to be set off the moment they were touched. As if that weren't enough, they built a huge iron chain that crossed the river—eight hundred yards wide at that point. Each link in the chain weighed nineteen pounds. This defensive might demonstrated Polk's iron resolve to defend the Mississippi.

ON NOVEMBER 1, Grant received orders from Frémont: "You are hereby directed to hold your whole command ready to march at an hour's notice." Frémont instructed him to "make demonstrations with your troops along both sides of the river" toward Columbus. This positive order ended, however, with a prohibition: "without however, attacking the enemy."

Grant readied his men for action, everyone assuming the target was Columbus, the subject of naval reconnaissance for weeks. Keeping his own counsel, Grant did not divulge to his commanders that his target might be Belmont, Missouri, a steamboat landing directly across from Columbus, defended by only a small garrison.

As Grant readied his troops in Cairo, in faraway Washington the telegraph tapped out a message on November 2 that President Lincoln had removed Frémont after only one hundred days in his command. Frémont had criticized Grant for crossing the line into civilian politics with his letter to the Kentucky legislature, but his proclamation of emancipation in Missouri on August 30 that freed slaves belonging to Confederates bearing arms far outstripped Grant's action. Lincoln relieved the autocratic Pathfinder of his command in the West.

The removal of Frémont provided an unexpected opportunity for Grant. On November 2, he sent a flurry of orders setting in motion seven columns totaling fifteen thousand men to attack as far as forty miles south at Cape Girardeau on the Mississippi River and sixty-two miles west at the St. Francis River. He ordered Richard Oglesby to lead the Eighth Illinois against "Swamp Fox" Thompson and his Missouri irregulars at Indian Ford on the St. Francis River.

On November 5, Grant wrote Smith he was "fitting out an expedition to menace Belmont." Frémont should never have worried whether student and teacher could work together. "If you can make a demonstration towards Columbus, at the same time . . . it would probably keep the enemy from throwing over the river much more force than they now have here." He told Smith their effort "might enable me to drive those" Confederate forces "out of Missouri." Grant's order from Frémont was to proceed in a demonstration mode, but he was plainly gearing up to attack.

At Cairo, Grant assembled two brigades, the larger commanded by John McClernand and a smaller brigade led by tough Henry Dougherty. In addition, Grant brought along two companies of cavalry as well as the Chicago Light Battery's six guns.

Captain Henry Walke, a fifty-one-year-old Virginian and veteran of the Mexican War, led the wooden gunboats *Tyler* and *Lexington.* Grant telegraphed Smith, "I move tonight with all my available force, about four thousand." He telegraphed Colonel John Cook at Fort Holt to move south toward Columbus from the Kentucky side of the Mississippi. Upon boarding the steamer *Belle Memphis,* Grant signaled Walke that the embarkation was complete.

The men boarding the gunboats and steamers all asked the same question: "Where are we going on this dark night?" Would Grant turn up the Ohio as he had two months before in the attack on Paducah? Or would he turn down the Mississippi?

At nine P.M., Commander Walke, on board the gunboat *Tyler,* led Grant's combined force out into the Mississippi. The effect among the troops was exhilarating. Private William Austin of the Eighth Illinois wrote in his diary: "We have guessed our destination." Word spread along the crowded decks of the six transports: "We are going to attack Columbus!"

After traveling nine miles downstream, Grant's force anchored close to the Kentucky side, still keeping up appearances that the attack would come against heavily fortified Columbus eleven miles to the south.

AT EIGHT A.M., Grant began landing twenty-five hundred men at Hunter's Farm, two and a half miles north of Belmont. His men, protected by the bend in the river and dense woods, could not be seen by the guns on the Columbus side of the river. Grant decided to leave a reserve force by the landing. The *Tyler* and *Lexington* kept on downstream as Walke prepared to engage the batteries at Columbus. Grant ordered his men into columns, with McClernand's brigade leading the way down the main farm road to Belmont.

Polk, awakened to learn of Grant's intentions, believed any movement toward Belmont had to be nothing more than a feint. Nevertheless, he alerted Pillow to be ready to support Colonel James Tappan of the Thirteenth Arkansas, who commanded seven hundred men at the Belmont post.

By nine A.M., advancing Union skirmishers met Confederate defenders, provoking a firefight. On Grant's order, the Chicago heavy cannon was brought forward and fired at the main Confederate force. Grant's green Federal troops fought Polk's green Confederate troops. This was the first time most of Grant's men had been in a fight. They had been prepared well and fought boldly.

Grant was everywhere, behind and beside his men, offering more encouragement than orders. On this day, the quiet man shouted himself hoarse. The big guns from Columbus fired high over the heads of Union soldiers, and Tappan's Belmont defenders were not much more accurate. In the melee, Grant's bay horse was hit. His aide, Captain Hillyer, offered the general his horse. Grant rode on but left on the field his $140 saddle with his name on it, his mess chest, and his gold pen.

By noon, the Union advance had scattered the Confederate defenders. Grant's men swarmed into deserted Camp Johnston and immediately threw down their weapons to loot the camp. They hoisted the Stars and Stripes; they sang "Yankee Doodle," "The Star-Spangled Banner," even "Dixie." McClernand offered a rousing patriotic speech. Grant, observing these antics, wrote that his officers "were little better than the privates."

All the while no one, including Grant, seemed worried about what had become of the Belmont defenders or of the larger Columbus force across the river. Polk, looking across the Mississippi, saw James Tappan's troops huddled by the landing. They would have surrendered, but none of Grant's troops, busy looting Camp Johnston, could be bothered.

The Confederates were not beaten. The fighting bishop ordered General Frank Cheatham, a Tennessee farmer and expert horseman, to lead five regiments across the river to Camp Johnston; at the same time, Polk ordered two regiments upstream to the space between Grant and Hunter's Farm.

DR. JOHN BRINTON, Grant's medical director, saw them first. As he looked across the river, Brinton saw "the pipes of two steamers" heading across the river. Having begun the day with the element of surprise on his side, Grant now was the one surprised.

As he surveyed the scene, he saw his troops "demoralized from their victory." On the other hand, Belmont's beaten defenders, now heartened, were re-forming at the riverbank as they welcomed comrades from Columbus. The *Tyler* and the *Lexington* had retired upstream, thus unable to block Polk's steamers from transporting fresh troops.

Jubilation turned to panic. The Lady Polk said hello to Grant's frightened troops with a monstrous blast, detonating in a nearby parade field.

No one was injured, but a feeling of alarm spread. Sensing they were about to be surrounded, some officers and men talked of surrender.

Not Grant. To reestablish order, he directed that the camp's tents and equipment be burned. The veteran of Cerro Gordo and Molino del Rey did not panic. As smoke billowed above the camp, calmly but firmly he began to re-form his troops.

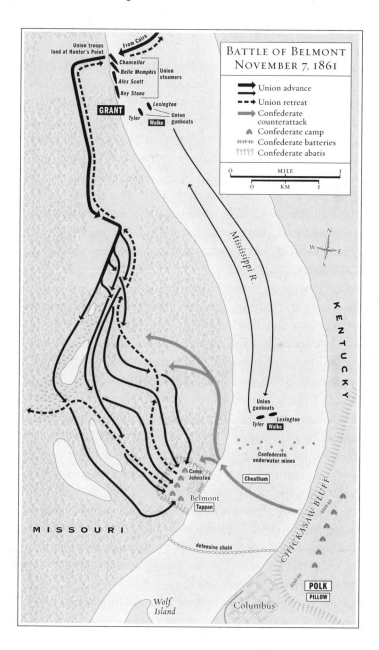

The Confederates attacked with a rebel shout. Advancing from the river, they attempted to cut off the Union retreat back up the farm road to the transports.

"We were all demoralized." Chicago's Patrick White captured the feeling of the men around him that early afternoon. "Officers would call to their men to fall in but the men would pay no attention." The result: "Every man was trying to save himself, some would throw down their arms and part of a regiment would take one route and the other part start another way."

Colonel John "Black Jack" Logan, commanding the Thirty-first Illinois Regiment in McClernand's brigade, led the way. "Follow the flag and myself." As they fought their way toward Hunter's Farm, the Union forces had to leave some of their wounded behind.

Grant wanted to put his reserve force into a defensive position, but it was no use. Soldiers ran pell-mell onto the boats. Everyone was on board except Grant.

Although he had positioned himself at the rear of the retreat to make sure all the wounded would be evacuated, he was finally forced to conclude that some would have to be left behind. He rode forward, only to see onrushing Confederates. Suddenly he glimpsed a line of Polk's cavalry outlined against the trees.

They saw him, too. "I was the only man of the National Army between the rebels and our transports." Now they were only fifty yards from him. Dressed this day in an army private's shirt, he was partially hidden by dry cornstalks slightly higher than his head.

Polk called out to his staff, "There is a Yankee. You may try your marksmanship on him if you wish." No one tried.

The *Belle Memphis* started to push away from the bank, but Captain Charles Scott had not started the engine. He put out a single plank for the commander. The Mississippi River was so low that early November day that the riverbank stood as high as the heads of men standing on the upper deck.

Grant described what happened next. With no path down the bank, "my horse put its fore feet over the bank without hesitation or urging, and, with his hind feet well under him, slid down the bank and trotted aboard the boat, twelve or fifteen feet away, over a single gang-plank." What Grant did not say was that as a superb horseman, he had guided his unfamiliar mount from danger to safety.

Exhausted, he went to the top deck and collapsed on a sofa in the captain's quarters. With the enemy rushing to the shore and the guns from

Columbus ablaze, Grant heard cannon fire and bullets striking the *Belle Memphis*. He went out on the upper deck in time to see a firefight erupting. Just then the *Lexington* and the *Tyler,* returning from upstream, opened fire. Slowly, the *Belle Memphis,* with the noise of cheering soldiers, left the cannon fire behind and headed back to Cairo.

Grant returned to his cabin. Upon entering, he discovered that "a musket ball entered the room, struck the head of the sofa, passed through it and lodged in the foot." The musket ball had gone through the sofa exactly where his head had been resting only a few minutes before.

Grant would remember the Battle of Belmont as the day he escaped death—twice.

HIS MEN RETURNED to Cairo, in Grant's words "every man feeling that Belmont was a great victory." Quite a different story was told by Confederate troops arriving in Memphis, the hometown of thousands of Polk's men. The *Memphis Appeal* published extra editions filled with interviews of returning soldiers boasting about a great victory. Across the South, newspapers hailed Belmont as a "glorious victory" and "a complete triumph of Southern valor."

Polk wrote the next day to "His Excellency, President Davis," a battle report filled with hyperbole in which he claimed his forces were "attacked by 8,000" but prevailed in glorious battle. The result was "a complete rout" for the Union army. He even wired Davis, "General Grant is reported killed."

Grant was very much alive. In his initial report, he offered "thanks to the troops under his command." He drew a bright line from past to present: "It has been [Grant's] fortune, to have been in all the Battles fought in Mexico, by Genls. Scott and Taylor, save Buena Vista, and never saw one more hotly contested, or where troops behaved with more gallantry." At the beginning of a new war, Grant was very conscious of heroic models from an old war.

In these early days of the war, newspapers had few war correspondents in the field. These first reporters, inexperienced in weighing stories from soldiers and official reports, ended up producing what the Columbus, Ohio, *Crisis* called after Belmont "a conflict of statements." These quick judgments about bragging rights sometimes gave way within days or weeks to quite different assessments of winners and losers.

Like the battle itself, the reporting became a two-step affair—attack and counterattack. Some of the western press, both Democratic and Republican, initially attacked, portraying the Union effort at Belmont as a defeat. Wiring from Cairo at three A.M. on November 8, a reporter for the *Daily Missouri Republican,* a leading St. Louis Democratic paper despite its name, bemoaned, "We have met the enemy and they are not ours." Within days, some in the eastern press, hungry for a Union victory, counterattacked. Henry J. Raymond's *New York Times* reported, "The late battle at Belmont, MO., is considered in high degree creditable to all our troops concerned in it, and the success of the brilliant movement is due to Gen. Grant." Twelve days after Belmont, James Gordon Bennett's influential *New York Herald* declared the Battle of Belmont a triumph "as clear as ever warriors gained." No friend to Lincoln, Bennett's Democratic newspaper, boasting the largest national circulation, extolled Grant with a portrait of him "swinging his sword above his head shouting himself hoarse in the thickest of the fire."

AT BELMONT, GRANT learned a lot about himself and his men. Some of the lessons were painful. Even though he left a reserve force at Hunter's Point landing, these regiments were unprepared for action when Confederates rushed toward the transports. Grant failed to incorporate the gunboats fully into his battle plan, so that after their initial challenge of the guns at Columbus, they were missing up the river when four Confederate steamers began ferrying troops from Columbus to Belmont. The most serious charge was that he failed to reckon with the possibility that the Confederates at Columbus might quickly mobilize a counterattack if they believed the attack on Belmont was merely a feint. Of course that's exactly what they did, and it almost proved fatal to Grant and his troops. Perhaps knowing Pillow in Mexico had been part of why he had underestimated the capacity of the Confederate forces? Grant learned that day that a battle is not over until it is over.

The Battle of Belmont revealed qualities in Grant that he would build on in coming months. He acted swiftly. His various moves to distract Columbus allowed him to land his men unopposed on the morning of November 7. Even though he generally kept his own counsel, he knew how and when to disseminate information to his best advantage, and once in action his commanders—McClernand, Dougherty, and Logan— led their brigades and regiments well. Also, Grant worked harmoniously with Walke; not all army and navy commanders did at the beginning of the war.

But while Grant showed plenty of courage at Belmont, his lapses in command after the first stage of the battle and his failure to anticipate the second stage showed he still had a long path to reach his full potential as a general.

EXHAUSTED UPON HIS return to Cairo, Grant managed to write numerous orders, plus letters to Julia and his father. The letter to Julia has not been found, but he told his father, "Taking into account the objective of the expedition the victory was most complete. It has given me confidence in the men that will enable me to lead them in any future engagement without fear of result."

If one stands today by the sign that marks the Battle of Belmont, the nineteenth-century battlefield is mostly underwater owing to a change in the channel of the Mississippi River in the twentieth century. Nevertheless, with closed eyes one can imagine the two-step conflict that surprised both attackers and defenders. It is easy to move quickly past Belmont to future larger and more decisive battles. But it is worth taking the time to understand the Belmont battle, for in so doing, we can begin to appreciate the development of Grant's military leadership.

Frederick Gutekunst, one of the most famous photographers of the day, took this half-length portrait of Brigadier General Grant, with his two stars.

CHAPTER 13

~⊷⊶~

"Unconditional Surrender"

> Your plain brother however has, as yet, had no reason to feel himself un-
> equal to the task. . . . I do not speak boastfully but utter a presentiment.
> —Ulysses S. Grant to Mary Grant, February 9, 1862

"Memphis today is like Rachel mourning for her children." As more boats arrived in Memphis ferrying the dead and wounded from Belmont, the *Nashville Banner* captured the response of a shaken city. Grant, who had begun reading Nashville and Memphis newspapers, saw that in the days following Belmont, Southern accounts of the battle began to revise his force drastically downward from eight thousand to three thousand men.

Two weeks later, he wrote Congressman Elihu Washburne that he now thought better of the results at Belmont: "The battle of Belmont, as time passes, proves to have been a greater success than Gen. McClernand or myself at first thought. The enemy's loss proves to be greater and the effect upon the Southern mind more saddening."

Enclosing Grant's letter, Washburne wrote Lincoln, "I want you to take a moment's time to read this letter of Genl Grant." The congressman's advocacy of Grant had advanced up the Washington hierarchy to Lincoln.

Shortly after Belmont, believing the military situation more settled, Ulysses invited Julia to join him. It would be her first venture into army camp life. In the years ahead, she came frequently. Ulysses wanted and needed her close.

She settled into a Cairo she called "desolate," moving into rooms on the second floor of the bank building where Ulysses had his office on the first floor. Despite the setting, the family was happy to be together once again.

Paymaster Hoyt Sherman remembered "being impressed with the affectionate care manifested by Grant toward his family." Sherman often worked on Sundays, at which times he recalled hearing voices above his first-floor office, "old fashioned Sunday-school airs, sung by his children."

Julia enjoyed the military reviews at Cairo. She watched with pride as her husband rode Jack, his sorrel horse, amid soldiers in bright blue uniforms. As a horsewoman, she described these events as "poetry in every move."

Ulysses nurtured more distant family ties as well. He invited younger sister Mary to visit him, writing, "I would pay the expense myself to have you come." He enclosed photographs of himself and his staff and asked her to distribute them to an uncle and two aunts. He even wanted her to send one to Aunt Rachel, his father's sister, who after the outbreak of war had written Ulysses's sister Clara, "If you are with the accursed Lincolnites, the ties of consanguinity shall be forever severed."

But tension remained between Ulysses and his father, who hoped to cash in on his son's unexpected prominence. Jesse wanted him to help secure army contracts for harnesses for his business, but Ulysses replied, "I cannot take an active part in securing contracts." He explained, "It is necessary both to my efficiency for the public good and my own reputation that I should keep clear of Government contracts." He wrote Mary, "I do not want to be importuned for places. I have none to give and want to be placed under no obligation to anyone."

NOVEMBER 1861 ALSO saw a momentous change in military command. On November 1, a White House messenger informed young George B. McClellan that President Lincoln had decided to appoint him general in chief. McClellan would replace one of Grant's heroes, General Winfield Scott, "Old Fuss and Feathers," now seventy-five years old. When Grant heard the news, he surely thought of his thwarted meeting with McClellan in Cincinnati at the beginning of the war.

The thirty-four-year-old McClellan's meteoric rise had begun three months earlier in the aftermath of the disastrous Union defeat at Bull Run Creek in northern Virginia. After the battle, McClellan was summoned to Washington to replace Irvin McDowell as commander of the Army of the Potomac, the major Union army in the eastern theater. Although McClellan's only successes were in small skirmishes in western Virginia, these were triumphs in a victory-starved North. The Union longed for a hero, and young McClellan, with an attractive face, gray eyes, and dark hair, looked the part.

Arriving in Washington to adulation, McClellan expressed supreme confidence in his ability. He exulted to his wife, Ellen, "I find myself in a new & strange position here—Presdt, Cabinet, Genl Scott & all deferring me—by some strange operation of magic I seem to have become the *power* of the land."

As the newly appointed general in chief, McClellan focused his attention on the eastern theater, but he also decided to reorganize the army in the west. He divided the western command into three parts: Henry Halleck's Department of Missouri, to which Grant was attached; Don Carlos Buell's Department of the Ohio; and David Hunter in a new Department of Kansas. Grant, handpicked by Frémont, wondered how he would get on with Frémont's successor.

HENRY HALLECK, GRANT'S new commanding officer, was born on a farm in New York's broad Mohawk Valley in 1815. He graduated Phi Beta Kappa from Union College and entered West Point in 1835, where he developed his lifelong interest in military theory.

During the Mexican War, Halleck served in California under Stephen W. Kearney. He retired in 1854, and the next year he married Elizabeth Hamilton, granddaughter of Alexander Hamilton. Halleck helped frame the California constitution, became a highly influential lawyer specializing in land law, and prospered as a businessman, amassing more than $500,000, much of it from serving as general manager of the biggest quicksilver mine in the United States.

Halleck did not look like a hero in the mold of McClellan or Frémont. He appeared much older than his forty-six years. Five feet nine inches tall and weighing 190 pounds, a thick man with sagging cheeks and a double chin, he had a bothersome habit of continually rubbing his elbows. Because of his bulging eyes, rumors circulated that Halleck was an opium addict. Soldiers dubbed him "Old Brains," not only for his reputation as a military theorist, but because of those eyes and his high forehead. Halleck arrived in St. Louis on November 19 and immediately began to clean up the mess the autocratic Frémont had left.

TWO DAYS AFTER his appointment as general in chief, McClellan sent Halleck instructions: "I have entrusted to you a duty which requires the utmost tact and decision." He emphasized, "Please labor to impress upon the inhabitants of Missouri and the adjacent States that we are fighting solely for the integrity of the Union." McClellan, a Democrat, wanted to make clear this war had nothing to do with slavery.

In light of McClellan's instructions to Halleck, on November 20

Henry Halleck, known as "Old Brains," was a skilled military theorist, but having never led soldiers into battle, he was regarded by many as merely a desk general.

Grant issued General Orders No. 3, in which he described the problem of "fugitive slaves" entering Union lines for the purpose of reporting "the numbers and conditions" of Union forces back to the Confederates. His remedy: "No such person be hereafter permitted to enter the lines of any camp."

Over the next months, Grant interpreted this order in different ways according to the specific situation. In giving permission for a man to enter Union lines to recover a fugitive slave, he explained, "I do not want the Army used as negro catchers, but still less do I want to see it used as a cloak to cover their escape." He told another, "No matter what our private views may be on this subject there are in this Department positive orders on the subject, and these orders must be obeyed." A third wrote seeking advice regarding a "Dr. Henderson, a Slave holder, and Secessionist—who has Contributed greatly to aggravate the present condition of affairs" by persisting in trying to recover one of his slaves now within Union lines. Grant replied, "The slave, who is used to support the Master, who supported the rebellion, is not to be *restored* to the Master by Military Authority."

In the final months of 1861, the war's relation to slavery began to weigh more heavily on Grant's mind. He wrote his father, "My inclination is to whip the rebellion into submission, preserving all constitutional rights. If it cannot be whipped in any other way than through a war against slavery, let it come to that legitimately. If it is necessary that slavery should fall that the Republic may continue its existence, let slavery go."

He balanced these words by adding, "But that portion of the press that advocates the beginning of such a war now, are as great enemies to their country as if they were open and avowed secessionists." This letter shows a commander thinking anew about the political and moral purposes of the war.

GRANT LEARNED OF Halleck's arrival in Missouri on November 19 and the next day telegraphed, "Can I have authority to call upon you in St. Louis with the view of making known in person the wants & condition of this command?"

The next day he received Halleck's reply: "You will send reports, in writing. Cannot just now be ordered to St. Louis."

If Halleck wanted a written report, Grant would send one immediately. He sent a full report to Captain John C. Kelton, Halleck's assistant adjutant general, the same day he received Halleck's reply. Grant was frank: "There is a great deficiency in transportation. I have no ambulances. The clothing received has been almost universally of an inferior quality. The arms in the hands of the men are mostly the old Flint Lock, altered, the Tower musket and others of still more inferior quality."

With a troop force of seventeen thousand men, Grant made no strikes south during the last two months of 1861. But he did keep relentless pressure on Columbus and worked on developing an intelligence network throughout the region. Late in December, Halleck added Smith's troops at Paducah and Smithland, Kentucky, to Grant's command. Grant now had a force in place to make an aggressive move into Kentucky and Tennessee.

Through November and December, Grant also increased river patrols. Skiffs and steamers traveled the waterways with all manner of contraband bound for the Confederacy. Grant was determined to stop or slow this traffic, but he would need the navy's cooperation to do so.

SECRETARY OF THE Navy Gideon Welles appointed Andrew Hull Foote, his boyhood friend from Episcopal school days in Connecticut, to assume command in the western theater of what came to be called the "brown-water navy." Foote arrived in St. Louis on September 6, 1861, the same week Grant assumed command at Cairo.

Born in New Haven, Connecticut, Foote entered West Point in 1822 but six months later left to join the navy as a midshipman. Over the next three decades, he served in the Mediterranean, in China, and off the coast of Africa. In 1827, while on duty in the Caribbean, he experienced a Christian conversion. From that moment, he became a fervent reformer, campaigning against flogging on navy ships and for observing the Sabbath.

Frémont had given Foote a free hand, telling him, "Use your own judgment in carrying out the ends of the government." Foote proceeded full speed ahead, building nine ironclad gunboats as well as thirty-eight mortar boats, flat-bottom rafts housing a mortar that could fire a thirteen-inch shell able to hit targets up to two miles.

When Halleck succeeded Frémont, everything changed. Halleck curtailed Foote's ability to navigate freely. He stopped production of the mortar boats. Corresponding with Gustavus V. Fox, assistant secretary of the navy, Foote poured out his increasing frustration. Whereas Halleck "seems to question my judgment," Foote found Halleck's ideas "wholly impracticable."

Everything changed again when Foote met Grant. The general became willing to cut through regulations when the end justified the means. The end would become the invasion of Kentucky and Tennessee; the means would be Foote's brown-water navy.

By THE END of 1861, as Grant began to receive increased responsibilities and therefore prominence, he was slow to realize that fellow officers, jealous of his swift rise, were more than willing to put him down to advance their careers. One way to criticize Grant was to circulate rumors that he was drinking again. Few had ever met Grant—but no matter. Once the label "drunkard" became affixed to a man in the army, it could seldom be completely erased.

Congressman Washburne, reading these reports in Washington newspapers, wrote Rawlins, anxious to know whether there was any truth to the stories. Grant's chief aide prepared a long response but showed it to Grant before mailing. Rawlins watched Grant's emotion as his boss read the letter slowly. Upon finishing it, he replied, "Yes, that's right; exactly right. Send it by all means."

Rawlins wrote Washburne on December 30, "I would say unequivocally and emphatically that the statement that General Grant is drinking very hard is utterly untrue and could have originated only in malice." He explained times when Grant, on social occasions, drank a glass of champagne or wine, but never "did he drink enough to in any manner affect him." Rawlins had lived with the drinking habits of his father and had assumed a special role to the older man he served. "I regard his interest as my interest, all that concerns his reputation concerns me; I love him like a father."

As GRANT LOOKED forward to increased military activity in 1862, he understood the central place Tennessee occupied in the Confederacy. The last state to secede from the Union, it would end up having more battles fought on its soil than any state except Virginia.

Confederate general Albert Sidney Johnston built a five-hundred-mile line of defense of Tennessee stretching from Columbus through Bowling Green to the Cumberland Gap. Fort Henry on the Tennessee River and Fort Donelson on the Cumberland River anchored the middle of the line. The two rivers flowed parallel in Tennessee; at one point, only twelve miles separated them.

The Tennessee and Cumberland were the front gates to the agricultural and industrial heartland of the South. On the eve of the war, farmers in what was known as "Middle Tennessee" boasted an annual production of 2.5 million bushels of wheat, one million bushels of corn, and an unrivaled tobacco crop, plus thousands of horses, mules, and cattle. The "Great Western Iron Belt" also extended across the Kentucky-Tennessee border. The men manning the blast furnaces, forges, and foundries in this strip of thirteen counties would be cut off from northern markets if their river highways were cut. The ironworks at Clarksville was second only to the Tredegar Iron Works in Richmond in supplying the needs of the Confederate military.

The defense of the central Mississippi River dominated Southern thinking in the war's western theater; as a result, Columbus and other towns and forts on the Mississippi were heavily fortified. In Johnston's first three months in the west, he traveled to inspect all of the major commands and forts in his department—but never visited Fort Henry and Fort Donelson.

At the end of 1861, Grant believed the Confederate defense line in Tennessee remained in place not because of the effectiveness of its defenders, but because of the tentativeness of Union commanders. Through this time, Forts Henry and Donelson remained unfinished and undermanned.

. . .

AT THE BEGINNING of 1862, frustrated by the lack of progress on all fronts, Lincoln pleaded with Halleck and Ohio's Don Carlos Buell to get started. On January 7, the president wrote Halleck, "Please name as early a day as you safely can, on, or before which you can be ready to move Southward in concert with Gen. Buell. Delay is ruining us."

Challenged by Lincoln, Halleck ordered Grant "to make a demonstration" into Kentucky, "letting it be understood that Dover is the object of your attack." Dover, Tennessee, just below the Tennessee-Kentucky state line, was the site of Fort Donelson. To increase the deception, Halleck told Grant to "make a great fuss" by planting stories in local papers that he would be reinforced by twenty thousand or even thirty thousand troops from Missouri. "Let no one, not even a member of your own staff, know the real object"—to prevent rebels from reinforcing Bowling Green, Kentucky, where Simon Bolivar Buckner commanded a Confederate force.

Grant would have been thrilled with the order to move at last, but Halleck added, "Be very careful however to avoid a battle. We are not ready for that."

Grant felt more than ready. He moved out on January 14. For the next week, he carried out his elaborate deception in Kentucky while his men gained experience in different terrains and conditions. The Confederates were baffled by his movements, not knowing what he was up to. Yet to his staff, Grant confided, "This sloshing about in mud, rain, sleet and snow for a week without striking the enemy, only exposing the men to great hardships and suffering in mid-winter, is not war."

IF GRANT FELT irked by Halleck's "be careful" attitude, his heart may have skipped a beat when Halleck wrote on January 22, "You have permission to visit Head Qrs."

On the eve of his visit, Grant wrote his sister, "I have now a larger force than General Scott ever commanded" in Mexico. Perhaps thinking of his uncertain relationship with Halleck, he added, "I do hope it will be my good fortune to retain so important a command for at least one battle." Above all, he was proud of what he accomplished: "I believe there is no portion of our whole army better prepared to contest a battle than there is within my district, and I am very much mistaken if I have not got the confidence of officers and men."

In preparing to meet Halleck, Grant knew "Old Brains" had established his reputation as an astute military theorist with the publication of

Elements of Military Art and Science in 1846. He also knew the knock on Halleck: his knowledge came only from theory, not action. He had never led an army in the field.

The meeting did not go well. An officer present reported that Grant spread his maps on a table but was brought up short by Halleck. Grant wrote later, "I was received with so little cordiality that I perhaps stated the object of my visit with less clearness than I might have done, and I had not uttered many sentences before I was cut short as if my plan was preposterous." Usually clear and concise, Grant stumbled in his long awaited opportunity, and he knew it. "I returned to Cairo very much crestfallen."

GRANT HUDDLED WITH Foote on his return. By now the army and navy leaders were working as a team. One or the other suggested they write separate requests to Halleck—perhaps two voices could be more effective than one. On January 28, Foote telegraphed Halleck, "Grant and myself are of opinion that Fort Henry on the Tennessee can be carried with four Iron-clad Gun boats and troops." Foote was direct: "Have we your authority to move for that purpose?" The next day Grant, more deferential, wrote, "I would respectfully suggest the propriety of subduing Fort Henry, near the Ky. & Tennessee line, and holding the position."

As Halleck mulled over when to act, he received two crucial communications. Lincoln issued General War Order No. 1 on January 27, directing all Union forces, including "the Army and Flotilla at Cairo," to be prepared to move "against the insurgent forces" by February 22—George Washington's birthday. Two days later, Halleck received word from McClellan that a deserter reported that Pierre G. T. Beauregard was on his way to Kentucky with fifteen regiments to reinforce Johnston's barely twenty-three thousand men in the Confederate Western Department. Beauregard, the hero of both Fort Sumter and Manassas, a colorful if contentious general, was being sent west from Virginia to become Johnston's second in command. The report would turn out to be partially false: Beauregard did head west, but without an army; he went alone, bound for Columbus.

The directive from Lincoln and McClellan's intelligence about Beauregard pushed Halleck to decide. Finally, on January 30, Halleck wrote Grant, "Make your preparations to take & hold Fort Henry."

Halleck struggled with apprehensions even after his decision. He dispatched young engineer lieutenant James Birdseye McPherson, first in his 1853 West Point class, to Cairo to assist in the Fort Henry expedition.

Commissioned into the Corps of Engineers, McPherson played a key role taking part in making improvements in New York harbor, the building of Fort Delaware, and the construction of fortifications on Alcatraz Island in San Francisco Bay.

McPherson was sent to Grant's staff with an additional purpose. He confided to physician Brinton, "I have been ordered here and instructed to obtain special information." What information? "All sorts of reports are prevalent at St. Louis as to General Grant's habits. It is said that he is drinking terribly, and in every way is inefficient." Brinton told McPherson that "the reports were unfounded, that I knew they were false," but encouraged him to see for himself.

Enthusiasm erupted when Halleck's decision reached Cairo on a cold, snowy day. The usually quiet Rawlins kicked over some chairs, while other members of Grant's staff threw up their hats. The story goes that Grant smiled, "then suggested it was not necessary to make so loud a noise as to apprise the enemy down at Columbus of the good news."

McPherson saw a disciplined, respected commander. Determined to proceed with a taut force, Grant decided to take fifteen thousand men and instructed John McClernand and Charles Smith to take minimal cavalry and wagons. The attack against Fort Henry would rely heavily on Foote, who worked overtime to prepare his gunboats. His flotilla would include four new ironclads, *Carondelet, Cincinnati, Essex,* and *St. Louis,* plus three wooden gunboats. He worried that most of his crews lacked experience.

On February 4, Ulysses wrote Julia, "I do not want to boast but I have a confident feeling of success." During this buildup, where sometimes he did not go to bed until five A.M., he promised Julia he would write her "every day"—and he did.

AMERICAN ARMIES TRADITIONALLY did not campaign in winter. George Washington went into camp each winter in the Revolutionary War. He surprised the British at Trenton and Princeton precisely because they could not imagine him crossing the Delaware on December 25, 1776.

Confederate general Lloyd Tilghman, commander of Fort Henry, hoped winter would be his ally. The fort, a five-sided earthen structure, was located on ten acres of low marshy ground on a bend of the Tennessee River. The fort's defenders had to contend with higher ground on several sides, ceding the advantage to an attacking force. As an attempt to rectify the fort's poor location, construction of a second fort, Fort Heiman, had begun on heights on the west side of the river but remained unfinished. Fort Henry possessed seventeen heavy guns, with twelve fac-

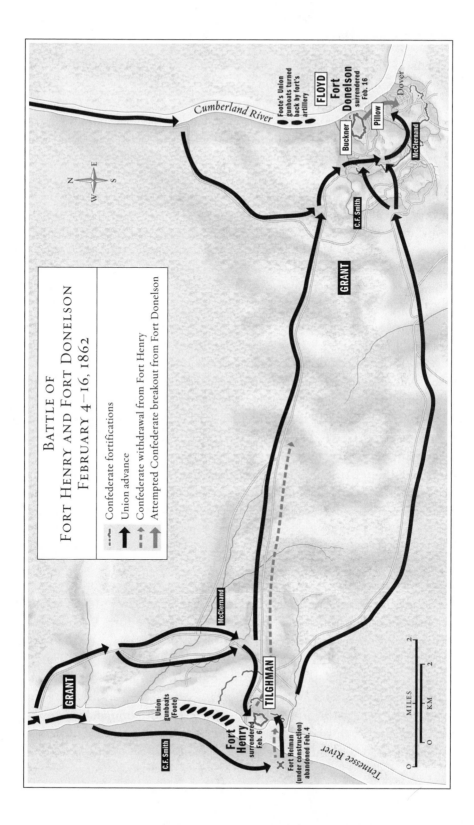

BATTLE OF
FORT HENRY AND FORT DONELSON
FEBRUARY 4–16, 1862

Confederate fortifications
Union advance
Confederate withdrawal from Fort Henry
Attempted Confederate breakout from Fort Donelson

Cumberland River

FLOYD
Fort
Donelson
surrendered
Feb. 16

Foote's Union
gunboats turned
back by fort's
artillery

Dover

Buckner

Pillow

McClernand

C.F. Smith

GRANT

McClernand

TILGHMAN

Fort
Henry
surrendered
Feb. 6

Union gunboats
(Foote)

C.F. Smith

GRANT

Fort Heiman
(under construction)
abandoned Feb. 4

Tennessee River

MILES

KM

N
W   E
S

ing out to the river and five protecting any approach from the land. Tilghman commanded only 2,610 men.

Poor Confederate intelligence meant Grant and Foote were able to approach near the fort undetected. The defenders had placed mines in the river—what they called torpedoes—to impede gunboats, but strong currents swept most of them away.

Torrential rains made a miserable situation even worse. The rains turned roads into mud, hampering land travel, but boats could move quickly, even on rising rivers. Johnston continued to fixate on Buell's larger army threatening Nashville from the east, not appreciating the more imminent threat in Grant's smaller force coming from the west. By ten A.M. on February 4, pickets on both sides of the Tennessee River had still not detected any Union troops.

FINALLY, ON THE morning of February 5, Captain Jesse Taylor, commanding Fort Henry's artillery, sounded the warning. He remembered, "Far as the eye could see, the course of the river could be traced by the dense volumes of smoke issuing from the flotilla—indicating the long-threatened attempt to break our lines was to be made in earnest."

Grant wrote Julia, estimating Confederate troop strength at Fort Henry to be "probably 10,000 men"—four times what it was in reality. Tilghman and Taylor believed Grant commanded at least twenty-five thousand Union troops instead of his actual fifteen thousand. Grant, given the importance of Fort Henry to the Confederate line of defense, felt certain Johnston would send reinforcements. A steamer, plying the waters between the west and east banks, suggested reinforcements were coming from Fort Heiman; no one realized Heiman was being abandoned.

Grant boarded William Porter's gunboat *Essex* to do reconnaissance. He wanted to test the range and accuracy of Fort Henry's guns. Closing to within a mile, the *Essex* lobbed a few shots at the fort. With no fire returned, Porter turned the *Essex* and started downstream. At the two-and-a-half-mile mark, a whistling sound signaled an incoming twenty-four-pound shell that passed over the gunboat and crashed into some saplings along the shore. Within minutes, a second shell crashed into the stern deck, penetrating the officers' quarters and commander's cabin. This shot scarcely missed killing Grant and Porter. They retreated so they could plan their next move.

· · ·

AFTER DAYS OF rain, February 6 dawned sunny and bright. Grant's plan of attack called for rapid movement on both river and land. While Foote's gunboats moved in close to shell the fort, McClernand would march down the east side of the Tennessee and Smith would come down the west side. Grant positioned himself with the reserve, wanting this force to be effective if needed, remembering the lessons of Belmont.

Foote met his captains on his flagship, *Cincinnati,* and asked God to be with them. At ten fifty A.M., he raised his battle pennant, the signal for his ships to begin to move. What a sight! The four black ironclads formed a menacing line across the river. The three wooden gunboats positioned themselves behind, ready to lob long-range shells at the fort while the ironclads moved in close.

At eleven A.M., McClernand began to move up the east side of the river. The several previous days of rain had turned the narrow track into mud, slowing their progress.

Overestimating the size of Grant's force, Tilghman had already directed his troops, except for artillerymen and the wounded, to retreat from Fort Henry to Fort Donelson. He would rely on Taylor's batteries to delay Grant while more than two thousand Confederate soldiers slipped away.

At eleven forty-five, almost seventeen hundred yards from the fort, the *Cincinnati* fired a shot, signaling the other three boats to begin firing also. Closer and closer they came, without a shot being returned from Fort Henry. Finally, at one thousand yards, the fort's battery began to fire back.

By now Fort Henry had only nine river-facing guns still functioning, but Taylor and his artillerymen managed to strike the gunboats again and again—fifty-nine hits in all. A Confederate shell hit the *Essex,* rupturing the boiler and spewing hot water and steam across the boat's front section. She suffered a loss of thirty-two men dead and wounded. Captain Porter, standing near one of the boilers, was badly scalded but survived.

But damage to Fort Henry mounted quickly. Union gunners fired with deadly accuracy. Fragments from two of the fort's shattered guns killed and wounded defenders.

Minutes before two P.M., Tilghman mounted a parapet and waved a flag of truce. With the white flag finally flashing through the smoke, the Confederate commander surrendered to Foote. Grant wired Halleck, "Fort Henry is ours."

The press hailed Fort Henry as a naval victory, which catapulted

Foote to national fame. But Foote, already steaming back to Cairo for repairs on the *Cincinnati,* knew better than anyone that Grant, with his aggressive battle plan, stood behind their joint success.

GRANT DID NOT tarry to savor the victory. Albert D. Richardson, war correspondent for the *New York Tribune,* was about to return to New York but stopped in to say goodbye to a man he had come to admire.

Grant replied, "You had better wait a day or two."

"Why?"

"I am going over to attack Fort Donelson tomorrow."

Grant wasted no time. He assumed Johnston would be rushing reinforcements to Fort Donelson and wanted to get ahead of him. As for his forces, "I felt that 15,000 men on the 8th would be more effective than 50,000 a month later."

If February 8 wasn't quite possible, Grant did move quickly to attack. The next day, he reconnoitered to Fort Donelson, two miles north of the county seat of Dover. He saw immediately that Fort Donelson was not situated like Fort Henry. Located on a bluff on the west bank of the Cumberland, it was laid out to be a fort that could defend itself. Soldiers and slaves had constructed fifteen acres of earthworks that rose as high as six feet within an area of more than one hundred acres. Normally heavily forested, the land had been cleared to provide defenders in rifle pits a clear field for firing; trees had been cut down so that the tops, trimmed and pointed, became an abatis, or defense line, intended to obstruct attacking Union infantrymen. The fort defended itself from an advance from the river by two water batteries set on foundations cut into the bluff.

In the days since the Fort Henry battle, Fort Donelson's command structure had come to resemble a game of musical chairs. The day after the fall of Fort Henry, General Bushrod Johnson took command. Two days later, Albert Sidney Johnston tapped Gideon Pillow, who had quarreled with Leonidas Polk in December and sulked away into a self-imposed retirement, to defend this fort in his home state. Upon his arrival, Pillow found "deep gloom was hanging over the command," with "the troops greatly depressed and demoralized" by the defeat at Fort Henry. News of Fort Henry had spread the disease of the fear of "gunboat fever" across the South.

On Sunday, February 9, Grant wrote his sister: "I take my pen in hand 'away down in Dixie' to let you know that I am still alive and well." He cautioned her he could not predict what the next days would bring, but "I intend to keep the ball moving as lively as possible." Becoming personal, he confided that "an army of men all helpless look to the commanding officer for every supply" and confessed, "Your plain brother however has, as yet, had no reason to feel himself unequal to the task." Perhaps having reread this sentence, he concluded, "I do not speak boastfully but utter a presentiment."

On the same day in Cairo, Foote preached on the text John 14:1 at the First Presbyterian Church: "Let not your hearts be troubled; ye believe in God, believe also in me." Two nights later, as he prepared to depart Cairo, Foote found himself deeply troubled. He knew Grant was counting on him, but he wired Gideon Welles, "I go reluctantly." He told his old friend, "I shall do all in my power to render the gunboats effective in the fight, although they are not properly manned."

On February 12, Grant wired Halleck, "We start this morning for Fort Donelson in heavy force." He traveled light, with no more personal baggage than a toothbrush, a fresh collar, and cigars.

The army made good time, fending off several blocking attempts by cavalry commanded by Nathan Bedford Forrest. The soldiers marched in an upbeat mood on the dry Telegraph and Ridge roads. On this warm February day, soldiers began discarding their overcoats and blankets.

Halleck supported Grant's operation. He sent General William T. Sherman, for whom he had developed a special fondness, to command Cairo and organize soldiers and supplies for Grant.

As the day wore on, Grant wondered: Where were the gunboats and the reinforcements?

He wrote Foote, "I do not feel justified in going without some of your gunboats to cooperate." Unbeknownst to Grant, the movement of gunboats and river steamers jammed with six thousand fresh volunteers slowed as the boats battled flood currents up the Ohio and Cumberland.

Grant set up his headquarters at a log farmhouse occupied by the widow Crisp. From this farmhouse, just left of the center of the Union lines, he could command his army and at the same time be near the river to cooperate with Foote's navy.

His battle plan placed McClernand on the right in the direction of Indian Creek and Smith on the left near the flooded Hickman Creek, making a large half circle intended to enfold the fort. This time he would prevent the escape of any troops. He intended to rely upon Foote to hammer the shore batteries, forcing surrender in short order.

EARLY THE NEXT morning, General John Floyd arrived at Dover by steamboat to replace Pillow in command of Fort Donelson, the third change of command in six days. Floyd served as governor of Virginia and then secretary of war from 1857 to 1860 in the administration of President James Buchanan. Pillow and Grant would have agreed on one thing: Floyd, a political general, was not a good choice.

Simon Bolivar Buckner accompanied Floyd, bringing his elite Kentucky Second Regiment. Buckner took rooms at the Dover Hotel, a two-story frame building by the upper steamboat landing.

Buckner had been named for Simón Bolívar, the courageous soldier and statesman who liberated northern South America from Spanish rule in the years just before Buckner's birth in 1823. Deeply conflicted about which side to take in the war, Buckner had met with President Lincoln at the White House to discuss Kentucky's neutrality. Because he was offered a commission in the Union army in August 1861, he did not side with the Confederacy until early September. But once in, he was all in.

While anxiously waiting for Foote, Grant ordered no attacks on February 13. Contrary to the theory learned at West Point, he did not entrench his troops, believing there was no reason to go on defense when he intended to go on offense the next day.

February 13 delivered on its promise of warm weather, but that evening a sudden strong north wind drove in stinging rain, sleet, and three inches of snow by morning. The temperature plummeted to twelve degrees. Grant's men, many having tossed away their overcoats and blankets, shivered in the cold. They tried anything to keep warm—even wrapping themselves in leaves—all without benefit of campfires, which

A handsome Kentuckian and West Point classmate, Simon Bolivar Buckner would oppose Grant at Fort Donelson.

would have alerted the enemy to their positions. Grant sympathized with their suffering, writing Halleck, "Last night was very severe upon the troops." The half-frozen men who experienced this brutal night would talk about it for the rest of their lives.

For Grant, the best news came with the arrival of Foote's fleet shortly before midnight. The naval commander instructed his men to work through the night, reinforcing the unarmored upper decks with improvised barricades of bags of coal, lumber, and chains to protect against Donelson's guns.

ON THE MORNING of Valentine's Day, Confederate captain Jacob Culbertson stared at the puffs of black smoke coming from an unknown number of ships just out of sight around the bend of the Cumberland. Shortly after two P.M., some puffs started moving. As Grant watched from the shore, Foote's ironclads rounded the bend in parallel formation.

The Confederate gunners waited. The guns at Fort Donelson were better sited than Fort Henry's, placed not at water level but mounted on elevated platforms. Adhering to Culbertson's instructions, the gunners determined to fire only when the gunboats came within a certain distance of the fort.

When they were a mile from the fort, the bow guns of the *St. Louis* opened fire, followed by the eleven bow guns of her sister ships. But the first "iron valentines" fell short. After the range had been adjusted, some shots splashed closer, but a few arched over the fort, even striking the Union lines on the other side. As Foote stood in his pilothouse, directing traffic with a speaking trumpet, he finally saw a shot explode within the fort. Feeling confident, he ordered the gunboats closer.

Too close. When they came within four hundred yards, the advantage shifted to the shore batteries. At such close range, even the inexperienced Confederate gunners fired their shells into vulnerable parts of the boats that lumber and chains did nothing to obstruct.

As Grant watched in dismay, he saw a thirty-two-pound shell strike the pilothouse of the *St. Louis*. Moments later, the pilot, F. A. Riley, collapsed, hit by shell fragments, while other fragments ripped into Foote's ankle and arm. Somehow, Foote managed to grab the wheel from the mortally wounded pilot, barely controlling the disabled gunboat, now out of the fight.

Grant watched the *Louisville* retire when a fourth shell severed her tiller cables. The *Pittsburg* withdrew when in danger of sinking. Only the *Carondelet* kept firing, but soon she was out of action, too, her decks demolished, her proud flagstaff decapitated. By the end of the battle, the *St. Louis* had been struck fifty-nine times, the *Louisville* thirty-six, the *Carondelet* thirty-five, and the *Pittsburg* thirty.

Grant's hopes for a repeat of the naval victory at Fort Henry ended in painful defeat. In his daily letter to Julia, he said nothing about the Confederate triumph but told her simply, "The taking of Fort Donelson bids fair to be a long job."

Neither side thought the fight was over. Floyd, Pillow, and Buckner, fearing Grant would be receiving more reinforcements and that the fort could not withstand a long-drawn-out siege, decided to break out of their encirclement. They confirmed this decision in an evening meeting that lasted until one A.M. on February 15, then all three left with a different understanding of the battle plan.

MEANWHILE, GRANT RETURNED to the Crisp farmhouse to plan his next move. At two A.M., he received a message from Foote asking for a meeting. Because of his injuries, Foote could not travel, so he asked if Grant could meet him four miles downstream on the *St. Louis*. When Grant left just after sunrise, he did not designate anyone to be in charge, issuing instructions that his commanders not start any actions while he was away.

At sunrise on February 15, Pillow launched a vigorous assault on McClernand's division on the right of the Union line. Southern soldiers in gray, their uniforms blending into dense undergrowth, charged forward. Edward McAllister's First Illinois Artillery fired twenty-four-pound howitzers, attempting to stop the onslaught, but Pillow seemed to be everywhere, rallying his officers and men.

By eight A.M., with McClernand's troops pushed back from the river down Wynne's Ferry Road to the west, some men bolted, yelling, "We are cut to pieces!" McClernand sent an aide to Grant's headquarters to ask for reinforcements, but no one was willing to take responsibility for acting in place of the absent leader.

Finally, Lew Wallace, in the Union center, took responsibility on his own shoulders and ordered his troops forward to join the fight. Wallace, who three decades later would become famous as the celebrated author of *Ben-Hur: A Tale of the Christ,* described the tumultuous scene:

Men fell by the score, reddening the snow with their blood. The smoke, in pallid white clouds, clung to the underbrush and tree-tops as if to screen the combatants from each other. Close to the ground the flame of musketry and cannon tinted everything a lurid red.

By midmorning, Pillow believed victory to be at hand. He telegraphed Johnston, "On the honor of a soldier, the day is ours." Yet in the fog of battle, Pillow realized Buckner's supporting attack had not materialized. He rode off to find him and discovered Buckner's troops still entrenched. Their lack of agreement on the Confederate battle plan launched the two generals into a heated argument. Pillow ordered Buckner to attack McClernand, but by now precious time had been squandered.

SHORTLY BEFORE ONE P.M., Grant returned from his consultation with Foote. He was met first by aide William Hillyer, visibly upset, who told him that some of McClernand's regiments were in full retreat and the road to Nashville was now open.

Grant saw the men talking in the most excited ways. No officer seemed to be in charge. Wallace recalled that "Grant's face, already congested with a cold, reddened perceptibly, and his lower jaw set upon the other" as he interrupted McClernand's explanation of the morning's events. He looked at his two commanders and said simply, "Gentlemen, that road must be recovered before night." Wallace was struck by how calm Grant

Grant first achieved national attention for his victory in the strategic battle for Fort Donelson in Tennessee.

remained at this moment of peril. Grant spoke to aide Joseph Webster, "Some of our men are pretty badly demoralized, but the enemy must be more so, for he has attempted to force his way out, but has fallen back; the one who attacks first now will be victorious and the enemy will have to be in a hurry if he gets ahead of me."

The Confederates did not capitalize on their advantage. With Floyd often absent, Pillow convinced his exhausted soldiers could not break out that day, and Pillow and Buckner arguing, the tri-headed command could not coordinate their strategy. By evening they were back in the same rifle pits where they had begun that morning.

Grant pondered his options. He could retreat and refit. This would allow him to prepare to fight another day, perhaps attacking the Confederates in the open as they tried to escape to safety in Nashville. He could stay in place, keeping pressure on parts of the Confederate line, and wait for more reinforcements to arrive. Or he could strike.

Grant instinctively leaned toward attacking. He had watched Taylor and Scott take the fight to the enemy against superior numbers in Mexico; he would do so now. He reasoned that Floyd, in order to attack the Union right, must have pulled many regiments from trenches on the right side of their line. Who stood opposite this partially vacated line?

Grant rode over to Smith's command. Most of his division had not been committed during the day, so it remained fresh and well provisioned. Few words needed to be spoken. "General Smith, all has failed on our right, you must take Fort Donelson."

Smith responded: "I will do it."

Smith rallied his troops, telling his young soldiers that they had enlisted to die for their country, and this afternoon would be their opportunity to do so. The white-haired general rode in the lead as a blue wave marched forward through a tangle of trees. The Second Iowa, which led the charge with bayonets fixed, lost nearly half its men dead or wounded within the first minutes. After intense fighting, Smith succeeded in capturing a long sector of the outer defense line and was stopped from attacking the water batteries only by the early winter sunset.

The Confederates, back in their trenches and exhausted from the day's fighting, were nevertheless in good spirits. In two days they had turned back Northern gunboats and attacked and inflicted considerable casualties on the right side of the Union army. With a night's rest, they would be ready to fight with renewed energy the next day.

. . .

ON THE EVENING of February 15, Confederate brigade and regimental commanders met in a council of war, convinced the battle was lost. Pillow wanted to issue instructions to prepare the men to march from their trenches early in the morning for a breakout on the road to Nashville, the Tennessee capital, to join up with Johnston's troops.

When the meeting adjourned, Floyd, Pillow, and Buckner remained to talk further. Floyd asked, "Well gentlemen, what is best now to be done?" This question set off a volcanic debate between Buckner and Pillow, Buckner upset that he had helped hold an escape route open earlier in the day, only to have it close, and Pillow arguing that the agreement had always been to return to reclaim their supplies and leave for Nashville the next morning. Buckner insisted Grant would resume his attack in the morning and the Confederate forces would be decimated.

Their conversation would be remembered differently by the three participants, but by midnight the painful decision was made to surrender Fort Donelson. Cavalry leader Nathan Bedford Forrest, who entered as the decision was solidified, could not believe what he was hearing but told the three generals his mounted men could provide an open road to enable the infantry to break free from Grant's attacking army and refit themselves in Nashville to fight another day.

Finally, first Floyd and then Pillow decided to flee. Each said there was no Confederate general Grant would rather capture. Pillow then asked Buckner what he would do. "For my part, sir, I think it is my duty to remain with my men and share their fate, whatever that may be."

In the dead of night, Pillow's aide rowed him across the river, and Floyd slipped onto the steamboat *Anderson,* both men bound for Nashville. Buckner sat down and drew up a request for a truce.

BEFORE THE SUN rose on February 16, a Confederate officer, under a flag of truce, advanced to Smith's sector with Buckner's formal request. Smith took Buckner's request to Grant, whom he found asleep on a feather bed in the farmhouse. If taken aback by the request, Grant seemed puzzled that it came from Buckner, not Floyd or Pillow. After drawing out a piece of letter-sized paper, he wrote:

> Sir: Yours of this date proposing Armistice, and appointment of Commissioners to settle terms of capitulation is just received. No terms except an unconditional and immediate surrender can be accepted. I propose to move immediately upon your works.

Buckner received Grant's reply with shock, expecting to meet and negotiate a truce. He replied, "The distribution of the forces under my command, incident to an unexpected change of commanders, and the overwhelming force under your command, compels me, notwithstanding the brilliant success of the Confederate armies yesterday, to accept the ungenerous and unchivalrous terms which you propose."

AN EERIE SILENCE penetrated Fort Donelson in the early morning hours. As the sun began to melt the remaining snow, the sudden dispersal of white flags struck the Confederate defenders with dismay and the Union troops with surprise.

Grant arrived at Dover House as Buckner and his staff were having a breakfast of cornbread and coffee. Buckner surely asked himself the question that had terrified Floyd and Pillow: Would he be treated as a traitor or as a prisoner of war? Smith accompanied Grant, and when Buckner rose to greet the two generals, Smith, who had been Buckner's teacher at West Point, refused to shake his student's hand.

Grant's bearing, unlike Smith's, immediately produced an atmosphere of respectful quiet meant to ease the proud Kentuckian's emotions. Grant said to Buckner, "I thought Pillow was in command."

"He was," responded Buckner.

"Where is he now?"

"Gone."

"Why did he go?"

"Well, he thought you'd rather get hold of him than any other man in the Southern Confederacy."

"Oh," Grant said quickly with a smile, "if I'd got him I'd let him go again. He would do us more good commanding you fellows!"

As Grant smoked a cigar, they talked about the size of the opposing armies. Buckner expressed surprise at the small size of Grant's force, the Confederates having believed the number to be fifty thousand. "If I had been in command," he said, aggravated that Grant had been able to attack the fort with so few men, "you would not have reached the fort so easily."

"If you had," Grant said, smiling, "I would have waited for reinforcements."

Years later, Buckner disclosed that on February 18, when he prepared to board the transport that would take him away to a Northern prison, Grant pulled him aside and, speaking softly, said, "Buckner, you are, I know, separated from your people, and perhaps you need funds; my purse is at your disposal." Unspoken between them was the memory of eight years earlier, when Grant, out of money, had his bill covered in New York by Buckner. Buckner thanked him for his kindness but did not accept.

Dr. Brinton asked Grant when the formalities of surrender would take place, including stacking Confederate guns and Buckner handing over his sword. Grant replied sharply, "There will be nothing of the kind. The surrender is now a fact; we have the fort, the men, the guns. Why should we go through vain forms, and mortify and injure the spirit of brave men, who, after all are our own countrymen and brothers."

A WAR CAN be defined by what leaders do in crisis. Why did Albert Sidney Johnston abandon these two forts that were the gateway to Tennessee? How could senior generals Floyd and Pillow abdicate their commands? The weakness of the tri-headed Confederate coalition, lacking a strong leader at its center, underlay the story of Fort Donelson from beginning to end. The strength of Grant, calm but decisive, who did not lead unilaterally but molded Smith, Wallace, and McClernand into an able team, made the difference in the battles at Fort Henry and Fort Donelson. Grant should not have left the battlefield to consult with Foote without leaving a second in command; but when he returned, quickly assessing where opportunity might still lie, he chose not to retreat or stay put but to attack.

In the brief space of twelve days, Grant unbolted the door to Tennessee, winning by water at Fort Henry and triumphing by land at Fort Donelson, bringing the army and navy together in mostly seamless cooperation. He captured fourteen thousand prisoners, the most in American history to that time. Grant understood that the victory at Fort Donelson opened the way to Nashville, the Tennessee capital, only eighty miles southeast on the Cumberland River.

The ferocious two-day Battle of Shiloh in April 1862 resulted in more than twenty-three thousand casualties and brought Grant both acclaim and criticism.

CHAPTER 14

Shiloh

Foemen at morn, but friends at eve—
Fame or country least they care:
(What like a bullet can undeceive!)
But now they lie low,
While over them the swallows skim,
And all is hushed at Shiloh.

—HERMAN MELVILLE, "Shiloh:
A Requiem," April 1862

"Who is this man Grant, who fights battles and wins them?" When news of the victory at Fort Donelson reached Northern cities and towns, many echoed this question.

On February 17, 1862, when General in Chief George McClellan received a telegram from Henry Halleck announcing the previous day's victory, he hurried through the rain to the dilapidated redbrick building at the corner of Pennsylvania Avenue and Seventeenth Street that housed the War Department. He arrived just as Secretary of War Edwin Stanton began reading Grant's "unconditional surrender" dispatch to his staff, who led three cheers for Grant. A clerk in Stanton's office recalled that the cheers "shook the old walls, broke the spider's webs, and set the rats scampering."

Later that evening, Stanton carried to the president the nomination of Grant to become major general. This rank designated one who led division-sized units, typically from fifteen thousand up to twenty thousand men. As Lincoln signed the order, he reportedly mused, "If the Southerners think that man for man they are better than our Illinois men, or Western men generally, they will discover themselves in a grievous mistake."

Throughout Washington, church bells rang and cannons fired as people gathered to talk about Grant and Fort Donelson. After months of disappointing news, when Iowa senator James W. Grimes read the report of the Union's first significant victory on the floor of the Senate, men threw up their hats. In New York, newsboys shouted out the headline from Horace Greeley's *New York Tribune:* "Freedom! Fort Donelson Taken!" In Boston, a salute to victory was discharged from Bunker Hill; in St. Louis, usually stolid businessmen at the Union Merchants Exchange gathered to sing "The Star-Spangled Banner"; in Chicago, after a day-long celebration, the *Chicago Tribune* editorialized, "It was well that we should rejoice. Such events happen but once in a lifetime, and we who passed through the scenes of yesterday lived a generation in a day."

McCLELLAN, UNDER INCREASING fire for not moving toward the Confederate capital of Richmond in the east, quickly claimed credit for "organizing" the victory in the west. *The New York Times* wrote, "The battle was fought, we may say, under the eye of Gen. McClellan."

Edwin Stanton's energy as the new secretary of war—especially when compared with the lackluster performance of his predecessor, Simon Cameron—made him a magnet for media adulation as well. For instance, Charles Dana, managing editor of the *New York Tribune,* endorsed him enthusiastically, giving the new secretary of war credit for the Northern victory.

Stanton, however, knew who deserved the credit and immediately wrote Dana to set the record straight. The following day, the *Tribune* published the letter, over Stanton's signature, in which he stated that no one could "organize" victory from an office in Washington. Battles were won "now and by us in the same and only manner that they were won by any people, or in any age, since the days of Joshua, by boldly pursuing and striking the foe." Grant's straightforward directive to Buckner—"I propose to move immediately on your works"—epitomized to Stanton the determination now needed by all Union generals.

In a day, Grant became a hero of the war. Maine's thirty-two-year-old James G. Blaine, future Republican candidate for president, marveled at how Grant's name became "woven into songs for the street and the camp." He observed how the hero became "Unconditional Surrender," then "Uncle Sam," and finally "United States" Grant.

Newspaper reports depicted Grant calmly smoking a cigar at the height of the battle. Grateful Americans began sending boxes of cigars to their hero. Grant's oldest son, Fred, recalled, "The cigars began to come in from all over the Union. He had eleven thousand cigars on hand in a very short time." In the years to come, Grant would be photographed or illustrated with his trademark cigar in hand.

THROUGHOUT THE SOUTH, citizens complained that the new Union general Grant had outgeneraled the legendary Albert Sidney Johnston. Nowhere did this feeling of anxiety prevail more than in Johnston's headquarters, Nashville.

The Confederacy valued Nashville second only to New Orleans in importance in the western theater of the war. With seventeen thousand residents, the self-styled "Athens of the South" bustled, a marketplace city at the intersection of river and rail routes, boasting five newspapers and the popular Adelphi Theatre.

On February 16, a sunny Sunday morning, ministers dismissed services early. As congregants emerged onto the streets, they were met by the exhausted soldiers of William J. Hardee's Army of Central Kentucky, who, at Johnston's urgent orders, had marched "day and night" sixty-five miles in swirling snow from Bowling Green to Nashville. Their bedraggled appearance did not inspire confidence.

Panic gripped the city. Rumors spread that Union gunboats were speeding up the Cumberland and Don Carlos Buell's army of "bestial" soldiers would reach the capital by three P.M.

Demoralized citizens, frantic to leave, rushed to the railroad depots. Anxiety turned to anger. Rioting broke out; the mob included newly arriving soldiers, who joined in looting storehouses of food and clothing. Incensed citizens surged to Johnston's headquarters, demanding to know if he intended to defend their city.

Johnston did not.

EAGER TO PRESS his advantage, Grant wrote Halleck, "It is my impression that by following up our success Nashville would be an easy conquest." He concluded, "I am ready for any move the Gen. Commanding may order." Naval commander Foote, now an admirer of Grant's leadership, wrote the same day, "Genl Grant and I believe that we can take Nashville—Please ask Genl. Halleck if we shall do it." But then Foote named the problem in a letter to his wife: "I am disgusted that we were kept from going up and taking Nashville. It was jealousy on the part of McClellan and Halleck."

WHILE GRANT MADE plans for future military action, he did not know that the triumvirate of Halleck, McClellan, and Buell was squabbling over the spoils of his recent victory. On the day after Donelson, Halleck wrote General in Chief McClellan, "Make Buell, Grant, and Pope major generals of volunteers, and give me command in the West. I ask this in return for Forts Henry and Donelson."

When McClellan did not respond immediately, Halleck wrote again: "Hesitation and delay are losing us the golden opportunity. Lay this before the President and Secretary of War."

An exasperated McClellan replied, "Buell at Bowling Green knows more of the state of affairs than you at Saint Louis." To Halleck's disappointment, he added, "I shall not lay your request before the Secretary until I hear definitely from Buell."

But Halleck would not take no for an answer. Going around the chain of command, he wrote directly to Secretary of War Stanton: "There is not a moment to be lost. Give me the authority, and I will be responsible for the results."

Stanton brought Halleck's request to a grief-stricken president. On February 20, eleven-year-old Willie Lincoln had died of typhoid fever. Stanton telegraphed Lincoln's answer: "The President, . . . after full consideration of the subject, does not think any change in the organization of the Army or military departments at present advisable."

" 'SECESH' IS now about on its last legs in Tennessee," Grant wrote to Julia that same week. "I want to push on as rapidly as possible to save hard fighting." He continued, "These terrible battles are very good things to read about for persons who lose no friends but I am decidedly in favor of having as little of it as possible. The way to avoid it is to push forward as vigorously as possible." Grant diverged from Halleck and Buell in his belief that the way to save lives was to fight fiercely now, while the enemy felt dispirited, rather than wait until they could reorganize, when losses would be much greater.

When he learned that Johnston, fearing both Grant and Buell, had retreated from Nashville, he decided to go to the first captured Confederate capital, secured by Buell's Army of the Ohio on February 25. He knew he might be crossing into Buell's department yet believed the line between departments remained "undefined." He wrote Halleck, "I shall go to Nashville immediately after the arrival of the next Mail, should there be no orders to prevent it."

Don Carlos Buell owed his present position to his ten-year friendship with McClellan. The forty-three-year-old Buell began his letters to McClellan, "Dear Friend," a relationship Halleck could not trade upon in seeking advancement. When Buell arrived in the Department of the Ohio, Murat Halstead, mercurial editor of the *Cincinnati Commercial,* wondered whether the new commander "has the *go* in him." Before many months, General Ormsby Mitchel, commander of Buell's Third Division, captured the impression of many fellow officers: "We hope every day to advance on Nashville, but General Buell holds back and remains undecided."

Without waiting for permission, Grant traveled to Nashville. He intended to stay for only one day to confer with Buell. When Buell, fearful he did not have enough troops to hold the city and overestimating the size of the enemy, still had not appeared in the afternoon, Grant wrote expressing his quite different assessment of the situation: "If I could see the necessity of more troops here, I would be most happy to supply them."

When Grant returned to the wharf in the evening to head back to Fort Donelson, Buell appeared. The conversation turned as frosty as the February ice on the Cumberland River.

Grant declared: "My information was that the enemy was retreating as fast as possible."

Buell protested that the "fighting was going on then only ten or twelve miles away."

Grant responded, "The fighting is probably rear-guard who are trying to protect the trains they are getting away with."

Buell disagreed, speaking "of the danger Nashville was in of an attack of the enemy."

Grant countered, "In the absence of positive information, I believed my information was correct."

It was no use. This painful conversation revealed that Grant and Buell were operating on different understandings of the military strategy required in Tennessee.

GRANT NOW FACED Johnston's western army, which found itself cut in two—with one half near Nashville and the other half in Columbus, Kentucky. Separated by two hundred miles, the two halves were in danger of being crushed in a vise between the rest of Buell's army advancing on Nashville and a new Union Army of the Mississippi under John Pope, ready to attack Columbus, Grant's original target. Castigated for fighting a defensive war, Johnston determined to surprise both friend and foe.

As Grant waited for further orders from Halleck, Johnston took advantage of this delay to execute a strategic retreat. On February 23, he and Hardee led their army from Nashville to Murfreesboro, the exact geographic center of the state. There Johnston paused. Grant's Union intelligence wondered: Would Johnston move east across the Cumberland Plateau to Chattanooga or west to defend the Mississippi Valley from a yet to be determined place? Johnston contributed to their puzzlement by forwarding ordnance, quartermaster supplies, even mail, to Chattanooga.

Johnston headed west. He ordered several Confederate armies to concentrate at Corinth, a town in northeast Mississippi just below the Tennessee border. Founded in 1853, the city was important as the junction of the two most important railroads in the Mississippi Valley—the north–south Mobile and Ohio and the east–west Memphis and Charleston.

Pierre G. T. Beauregard, whom Johnston granted independence of movement as his second in command, ordered Leonidas Polk to pull out of Columbus on the last day of February. At the same time, Braxton Bragg, a thin, pale North Carolinian known as a brilliant coordinator of troops, started north with ten thousand soldiers from the Gulf coast. Bragg had recently advised Jefferson Davis to abandon the tactic of dispersal, whereby every state would be defended, and adopt a policy of concentration, one of the oldest principles of military strategy. Bragg urged Earl Van Dorn, a hard-edged Mississippian who had just lost the Battle of Pea Ridge, Arkansas, on March 6–8, to join the concentration.

JUST WHEN GRANT deserved to enjoy the accolades of victory, he found himself blindsided. On March 4, he received a telegram from Halleck: "You will place Major Genl C. F. Smith in command of expedition & remain yourself at Fort Henry. Why do you not obey my orders and report strength & positions of your command?"

Stunned, Grant replied in restrained language. "I am not aware of ever having disobeyed any order from Head Quarters, certainly never intended such a thing," he told Halleck. "I have reported almost daily the conditions of my command and report every position occupied."

Unknown to Grant, Lieutenant Colonel George Washington Cullum, Halleck's chief of staff, had wired Halleck that Grant had traveled to Nashville to confer with Buell. Halleck wired McClellan, "I have had no communication with General Grant for more than a week. He left his command without my authority and went to Nashville." Halleck persisted, "It is hard to censure a successful general immediately after a victory, but I think he richly deserves it." Why? "I can get no returns, no reports, no information of any kind from him."

On the same day, McClellan, the recipient of increasing congressional criticism for his inaction in the east, expressed eagerness to escalate the conflict by censuring the newly successful general of the west: "Do not hesitate to arrest him at once."

Halleck wrote McClellan again, "A rumor has just reached me that since the taking of Fort Donelson General Grant has resumed his former bad habits. If so, it will account for the neglect of my oft-repeated orders." He was ready to believe a rumor about a man whose reputation was on the rise.

Stung by Halleck's upbraiding, Grant laid out his communications of recent weeks: "I have averaged writing more than once a day, since leaving Cairo, to keep you informed of my position; and it is no fault of mine, if you have not received my letters."

Grant was sure of his own actions. "If my course is not satisfactory remove me at once." Going even further, he added, "Believing sincerely that I must have enemies between you and myself that are trying to impair my usefulness, I respectfully ask to be relieved from further duty in the Dept."

Halleck responded, "You are mistaken; there is [no] enemy between me & you."

It turned out an enemy had wormed his way between Grant and Halleck. At that time, civilians operated the military telegraph system, and the army relied on an operator's loyalty when dispatches were submitted for transmittal. Years later, Grant learned that the operator in Paducah was a rebel who went south shortly after intercepting Grant's telegrams, taking all his captured dispatches with him—he never transmitted them to Halleck, a clear case of sabotage.

On March 9, Grant sent a full summary of the information Halleck requested. And renewed his "application to be relieved from further duty."

Later that day, without explanation, Halleck signaled the falling-out was over. Reporting on Brigadier General Samuel Curtis's victory at Pea Ridge, Arkansas, he indicated that reinforcements meant for Curtis would now be sent to Grant, adding, "As soon as these things are arranged you will hold yourself in readiness to take command."

Just one day after Grant's restoration, a thunderbolt arrived at Halleck's headquarters. Congressman Elihu Washburne had brought the accusations against Grant to Lincoln's attention. The president was not about to see the hero of Donelson deposed without understanding why. At Lincoln's request, General Lorenzo Thomas telegraphed Halleck, "The Secretary of War desires you to ascertain and report whether General Grant left his command at any time without proper authority, and if so, for how long; whether he has made to you proper reports and returns of his force; whether he had committed any acts which were unauthorized or not in accordance with military subordination or propriety, and, if so, what?" In other words—file official charges, with evidence, or drop the harassment and restore Grant.

Halleck had no desire to butt heads with Lincoln and Stanton. "General Grant has made the proper explanations," he was quick to reply, "and has been directed to resume his command."

LINCOLN REMOVED McCLELLAN from command as general in chief on March 11. The president's impatience with McClellan's inability to initiate a campaign in the Virginia Peninsula had intensified as February turned into March. Lincoln kept McClellan in command of the Army of the Potomac.

On the same day, Lincoln announced that Halleck would receive what he'd always wanted—command of the armies in the west in a new Department of the Mississippi. With McClellan no longer protecting Buell, Halleck's new authority put Buell under his command.

Two days later, Grant received a telegram from Halleck. "You cannot be relieved from your command. There is no good reason for it," Grant read. "The power is in your hands; use it, & you will be sustained by all above you. Instead of relieving you, I wish you, as soon as your army is in the field, to assume the immediate command & lead it on to new victories."

The war of telegrams ceased. Grant could now resume his march toward a battle that would test all of his leadership abilities.

However, Grant's initial response to Halleck's communiqué surprised Charles Smith, to whom Halleck had briefly handed control: "I think it exceedingly doubtful whether I shall accept." Grant was not about to take command away from Smith, the proud senior soldier he had come to revere. Several days later, Smith offered an appraisal of his younger colleague to a friend: "Grant is a very modest person. From awe of me—he was one of my pupils from 1838 to 1842 (I think)—he dislikes to give me an order and says I ought to be in his place."

Ultimately, the matter was settled when Smith slipped and scraped his shinbone jumping into a small boat in the dark. He wrote Grant, "I greatly fear your coming will be a matter of necessity."

Under those circumstances, Grant left Fort Henry to resume command. Following his arrival in Savannah, Tennessee, a small town with

The brilliant but acerbic Edwin Stanton served as secretary of war under Lincoln.

one main street and a square brick courthouse, he made his headquarters the white brick mansion of William H. Cherry, a leading merchant and Unionist whose wife, Annie, was pro-Confederate. Tennessee was indeed a state of divided loyalties.

At Sherman's suggestion, Grant decided on Pittsburg Landing, nine miles south of Savannah on the west side of the river, for his army's main encampment. This broad triangle, densely wooded, stretched out three and a half miles. On the right lay Snake Creek and, farther out, its branch, Owl Creek, while to the left ran Lick Creek and its branch, Locust Grove Creek.

A medley of roads crisscrossed the area. Two roads led directly from the landing: Eastern Corinth Road, which veered inland, where it met Bark Road; and Western Corinth Road, which swung west to intersect Purdy Road. At the intersection of the roads stood the Shiloh Methodist Church. Three thousand years before, an earlier Shiloh had been a place of assembly and peace for the tribes of Israel. In spring 1862, this small country church was about to become the center of a fierce battle.

Although Sherman had received instructions from Smith to build a temporary defense, he decided not to do so, asserting that the topography "admits of easy defense by a small command." Grant, taking over from

Smith, agreed that the rain-swollen creeks, marshy land, ravines, and tangled brush would provide an excellent defense in the unlikely event of a Confederate attack.

As GRANT'S FORCES took up positions at Pittsburg Landing, Confederate forces converged on Corinth, thirty-two miles southwest of Savannah, a town of twelve hundred that boasted three hotels, five churches, and the Corona Female College.

The wings of the Confederate army were now united, while the wings of the Union army were not. Johnston, Beauregard, and Bragg were determined to attack Grant before Buell could arrive. For the first time, the Confederate forces would have the same number of men as the Federals—a fight the Confederates believed they could win.

Beauregard drew up plans for a preemptive attack. He divided the Confederate Army of Mississippi into three corps, led by Leonidas Polk, Braxton Bragg, and William Hardee. A fourth, led by John C. Breckinridge, would function as the Reserve Corps. This melding of distinct armies made it difficult to achieve order, particularly given the inexperience of so many of the soldiers. As Bragg pointed out: "There was more enthusiasm than discipline, more capacity than knowledge, and more valor than instructions."

GRANT'S UNION ARMY of the Tennessee consisted of six divisions. John McClernand led the First Division. Smith officially led the Second Division, but Grant asked William H. L. Wallace, an Illinois lawyer and politician, to fill the large shoes of Smith, who was confined to bed with an infected leg that obstinately refused to heal. Indianan Lew Wallace led the veteran Third Division, which set up their camp at Crump's Landing four miles downstream. Stephen A. Hurlbut, an Illinois political general with little military experience, led the Fourth Division. Sherman led the Fifth Division, consisting of many new Ohio recruits whom he described as "raw & Green." Benjamin M. Prentiss led the new Sixth Division.

A variety of problems nested within Grant's command. One of the largest was McClernand. Grant had tried to ignore McClernand's need to exaggerate his importance, but his ambitious behavior only increased after Fort Donelson. McClernand wrote Lincoln on March 31, "If you will give me an independent command, in an active and contested field, I will try and reward your confidence with success." He enclosed a copy of his battle report of Fort Donelson, which overstated his role. Grant would say later, "The report is a little highly colored as to the conduct of the first Division."

As DAYS PASSED with no word from Buell, Grant began to worry. Buell had decided to travel the 140 miles overland, even though Halleck had encouraged him to put his troops on steamboats. Grant sent two scouts with a letter to Buell on March 19: "Feeling a little anxious to learn your whereabouts."

Grant considered making a quick strike across the twenty-two miles from Pittsburg Landing to Corinth, but on March 20 Halleck telegraphed, "By all means keep your forces together until you connect with Genl Buell." He cautioned, "Don't let the enemy draw you into an engagement now. Wait until you are properly reinforced & you receive orders."

The two scouts returned on March 26. Buell's divisions, they reported, "are yet on east side of duck river . . . detained bridge building." Buell still had to march ninety miles to Savannah.

Six Confederate deserters who appeared on March 30 described discontent among the Confederate troops, with rations running short. They insisted many men were preparing to desert. As the war progressed, reports from so-called deserters would be evaluated more carefully. Grant should have assessed this one with more caution.

Grant transferred his headquarters to Pittsburg Landing on March 31 but stayed at Savannah to await Buell. He admitted later that he remained "a few days longer than I otherwise should have done."

GERMAN MILITARY THEORIST Carl von Clausewitz wrote decades earlier, "Time allowed to pass unused accumulates to the credit of the defender. He reaps where he did not sow."

In the first week of April, while Halleck delayed, all these Union inactions allowed time to accrue to Johnston. He intended to strike Grant before Buell could arrive and then turn and strike Buell.

TWENTY-TWO MILES AWAY, an Iowa soldier, surveying the countless tents spread out through "the delightful Tennessee forest," thought Grant's camp had the look of "a gigantic picnic." Sherman's and Prentiss's green troops occupied the forward position by the Shiloh church. McClernand set up to the rear of Sherman, while Wallace and Hurlbut were farther back.

On April 2, Grant reviewed the troops: he reordered his cavalry, transferring some regiments to fresh assignments in different divisions. It would take time before the relocated units could function effectively in the confusing road system emanating out from Pittsburg Landing.

Although persistent rain and mud and the unsanitary conditions of the camps all took their toll, Grant's troops suffered most from overconfidence. Chicago and Cincinnati newspapers, obtainable at Pittsburg Landing, offered enthusiastic predictions of future success. Lieutenant Payson Shumway, Fourteenth Illinois, wrote his wife, "It is generally thought that our enemy will retreat as we advance." Grant wrote Julia that "a big fight" would be coming soon, "which it appears to me will be the last in the West."

On April 3, the scheduled six A.M. Confederate start from Corinth became eight A.M. and then noon as the town's narrow streets gridlocked with wagons and guns. The battle plan was to cover most of the twenty-two miles on April 3 and attack at dawn on April 4, but Beauregard's timetable gave way to miscommunication and mud. With troops already worn out, the attack was delayed until Saturday, April 5. Still, Johnston said to a staff officer that he intended "to hit Grant, and hit him hard."

On Friday evening, torrential rains soaked the soldiers, who had no tents; yellow roads turned to mud. When rain continued into the next day, Beauregard decided it was time to cancel the attack and return to Corinth. Bragg agreed. But Johnston, whom Confederate gossip chirped had lost his nerve, announced: "Gentlemen, we shall attack at daylight tomorrow." The Confederates would strike at dawn on the Sabbath—Sunday, April 6.

Early on the morning of Friday, April 4, William B. Mason, a captain commanding pickets of the Seventy-seventh Ohio, received reports of rabbits and squirrels scurrying into his lines. He sent two soldiers to look into the matter. They reported enemy infantry a quarter mile away. Mason dispatched a sergeant to report to Sherman. The high-strung Sherman threatened him with arrest for filing a false report.

Grant went to Pittsburg Landing to see reports of enemy activity for himself. Satisfied that these reports were no more than a few men probing his lines, he started back. On a night of dense darkness, with rain hammering down, without warning, "my horse's feet slipped from under him, and he fell with my leg under his body." Grant's ankle was so injured that his boot had to be cut off. For the next few days, he was forced to get about on crutches.

Because of the injury to his ankle, Grant was still in Savannah when William "Bull" Nelson, at the head of the lead element of Buell's army, reported at noon on April 5. After hearing that Nelson's troops were fresh enough to march, Grant declared, "There will be no fight at Pittsburg Landing; we will have to go to Corinth, where the rebels are fortified." Furthermore, "If they come to attack us, we can whip them, as I have more than twice as many troops as I had at Fort Donelson."

On this same day, Sherman wrote Grant about reports from pickets. "The enemy is saucy," he admitted, but concluded, "I do not apprehend anything like an attack on our positions." Grant wrote Halleck, "I have scarcely the faintest idea of an attack, (general one,) being made upon us but will be prepared should such a thing take place."

On a moonlit night, two huge armies, one preparing for the boldest attack yet in the Civil War, the other unaware of what the morning would bring, slept barely one mile from each other.

EARLY ON APRIL 6, Johnston mounted his splendid bay thoroughbred, Fire-eater. Dressed in a black hat with a plume and carrying his sword, he spoke to his staff: "Tonight we will water our horses in the Tennessee River."

The Sabbath morning began with a light ground fog, which soon lifted. Johnston ordered read to his troops a message he had written to the "Soldiers of the Army of Mississippi": "I have put you in motion to offer battle to the invaders of our country. . . . Remember the dependence of your mothers, your wives, your sisters, and our children on the result," he reminded them, and concluded, "With such incentive to brave deeds, and with the trust that God is with us, your generals will lead you confidently to the combat, assured of success."

Johnston's stirring address, read as men formed their regiments, nerved them for the fighting ahead. Beauregard believed that divided Union forces could not bear up against multiple lines attacking at one time; as a result, his battle plan called for successive waves of attacks by three parallel lines across a three-mile front. He intended to turn the Union left, forcing the withdrawing soldiers north into the muddy backwaters of Owl Creek while cutting off any possibility of a retreat to Pittsburg Landing.

At the moment of attack, shrieking Confederate soldiers charged into Union camps, as half-awake Union soldiers ran from their tents. Confederates found breakfasts uneaten and provisions, better than they possessed, in the abandoned tents. Famished—many had long since eaten

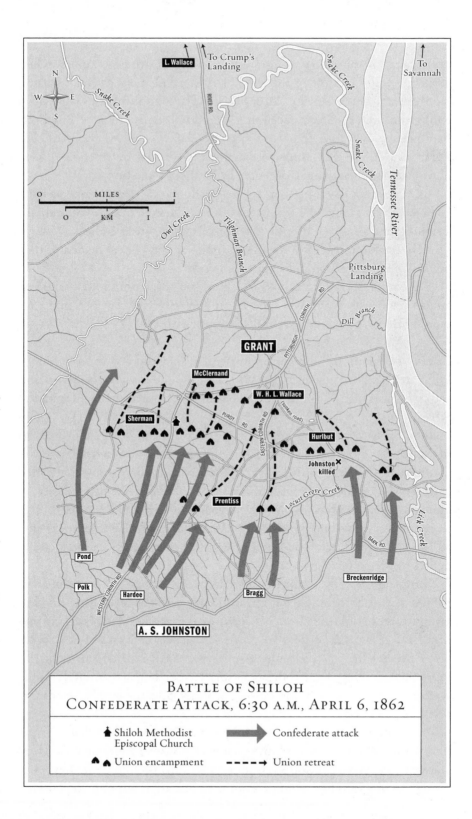

To Crump's Landing
L. Wallace
To Savannah

Snake Creek

N
W E
S

Snake Creek

Snake Creek

Tennessee River

RIVER RD.

Owl Creek

Tilghman Branch

MILES
0 1

KM
0 1

Pittsburg Landing

CORINTH RD.

Dill Branch

GRANT

PITTSBURGH CORINTH RD.

McClernand

W. H. L. Wallace

(sunken road)

Sherman

PURDY RD.

EASTERN CORINTH RD.

Hurlbut

Johnston ✕ killed

Prentiss

Locust Grove Creek

Pond

WESTERN CORINTH RD.

Polk

Hardee

Bragg

BARK RD.

Lick Creek

Breckenridge

A. S. JOHNSTON

BATTLE OF SHILOH
CONFEDERATE ATTACK, 6:30 A.M., APRIL 6, 1862

⛪ Shiloh Methodist   ➡ Confederate attack
   Episcopal Church

♠ ♠ Union encampment   ----➤ Union retreat

their three days' rations—they stopped to eat. They also stopped to plunder. "None of that, sir," Johnston called out resolutely; "we are not here for plunder!" But it was no use. Men who had felt the sting of defeat could not resist the spoils of victory. The minutes they spent plundering cost them dearly.

GRANT AROSE EARLY on Sunday morning. He could no longer delay transferring his headquarters to Pittsburg Landing. The previous afternoon, Halleck had informed him McClernand and Wallace had been promoted to major general. This meant they now outranked everyone present except him. Grant knew McClernand would try to claim authority over Sherman.

At six A.M., Grant sat down for breakfast at the Cherry mansion before leaving for the landing. While he was reading his mail, the boom of distant guns made him stop. Grant sat stock-still. He knew the dull concussive sounds could come only from cannon. He rose. "Gentlemen, the ball is in motion. Let's be off."

As Grant limped toward his boat, the *Tigress,* Buell walked toward the Cherry mansion. He had arrived in Savannah the previous evening, but Grant was not informed, and the two had missed each other. Before departing, Grant had written Buell, "Heavy firing is heard up the [river], indicating plainly that an attack has been made upon our most advanced positions. I have been looking for this, but did not believe the attack could be made before Monday or Tuesday."

The previous afternoon, he had written Halleck, "I have scarcely the faintest idea of an attack," but on April 6, he wrote Buell, "I have been looking for this." What was the truth? What did Grant anticipate at Shiloh?

At about nine A.M., the *Tigress* nosed into the bank at Pittsburg Landing. Deafening sounds reverberated and smoke roiled up from the woods. Panic among the Union troops was as much an enemy as the Confederates.

As Grant rode forward, he met William Wallace, commanding Smith's Second Division. He informed Grant the divisions commanded by Sherman and Prentiss, hit hard by the first Confederate attacks, were falling back. Hearing this news, Grant dispatched Algernon S. Baxter with orders for Lew Wallace to bring up his Third Division, held in reserve at Crump's Landing.

If the Duke of Wellington had faced a one-mile battlefield at Waterloo in 1815, Grant began to confront ever-expanding battlefields. If at Fort Donelson his front extended three miles, at Shiloh he faced the challenge of a five-mile battlefield marked by creeks, ravines, trees, and undergrowth.

Grant rode forward to consult with each of his embattled division commanders, from right to left, Sherman, McClernand, William Wallace, Prentiss, and Hurlbut. At ten he met Sherman, who had coolly rallied his troops near the Shiloh church, his red beard splotched with gray soot from smoke. Already wounded twice that day, he would have three horses shot out from under him before it was over. Grant told Sherman what he would tell each of his division commanders: Lew Wallace's veteran troops would arrive soon.

When Grant reached Prentiss, he learned his division had been driven from their position back through their camp. Outnumbered, within the first hour Prentiss suffered more than a thousand dead, wounded, and captured. The remainder of his force had taken up a new line on a sunken wagon road at the edge of a thick wood, where they were putting up a good fight. Grant encouraged Prentiss "to maintain that position at all hazards."

After consulting all his division commanders, he wrote Buell, "The attack on my forces has been very spirited from early this morning. The appearance of fresh troops on the field now would have a powerful effect both by inspiring our men and disheartening the enemy."

EVEN AS CONFEDERATE soldiers surged ahead, Beauregard's battle plan was falling apart. The use of multiple lines, modeled after Napoleon, did not work for an army composed of inexperienced soldiers. Attempting to direct his plan from the rear, he tried to reorder the various brigades but found that the confusing roads made it difficult to maintain lines of communications. Johnston, wishing to encourage his men, rode at the front, but this made him function more like a brigade leader than a commander.

This struggle quickly became not a general's but a soldiers' war—individual fights on a hundred battlefronts. Courageous charges and countercharges were fought over the same ground. The smoke of cannon and gunfire blotted out the clear spring sun. The moans of the wounded and the sight of the dead on the blood-spattered earth grew with each passing hour. Shortly after noon, as the Forty-first Illinois of Hurlbut's First Brigade, badly mauled, went by some fresh troops advancing to the front, a colonel exclaimed, "Fill your canteens, boys! Some of you will be in hell before night and you'll need water."

The initial Confederate thrusts were changing the flow of the battle, but not as Beauregard had intended. The successes in the center and right meant that instead of pushing the Union forces into the swamps at Owl Creek, they pushed Sherman and McClernand in a northeasterly direction. Instead of driving Union troops away from Pittsburg Landing, they were pushing them back toward the landing, the very place where reinforcements, if they ever came, would arrive.

An hour later, Grant sent a second messenger urging Lew Wallace to hurry forward. Grant had assumed the Third Division would march on the most direct route, the River Road, a distance of five miles; instead, without inspecting the roads before his advance, Wallace chose to travel on the Shunpike, a distance of eight miles. Having heard from Algernon Baxter that the Confederates were being repulsed, he led without a sense of urgency.

At twelve thirty p.m., Grant rode back to his headquarters at the landing. He encouraged stragglers all about him to get back into the fight, but without much success. He redeployed his cavalry but soon discovered that cavalry were of limited help in the broken terrain of woods and underbrush.

With no sign of Wallace, Grant sent William Rowley galloping up the River Road carrying yet a third order. Rowley caught up to Wallace on the Shunpike, where the Third Division had stopped to rest. Wallace, now farther from Pittsburg Landing than when he'd started, was forced to reverse direction in a countermarch to take the River Road.

At one p.m., Buell finally arrived in advance of his troops. As he traveled up the river, he was shocked to see many soldiers—"fugitives," he called them—swimming across Snake Creek away from the battle. Grant and Buell had not met since their icy conversation in Nashville. Discouraged by the sight of the panic-stricken soldiers, Buell asked Grant about his plans for a retreat.

"I have not yet despaired of whipping them, general."

In the early afternoon, Johnston repositioned soldiers who complained they had no orders. Suddenly a Union battery opened fire from the woods to Johnston's left. Wheeling about on Fire-eater, he sent Isham Harris, formerly governor of Tennessee and now an aide on his staff, with orders to silence the battery. When Harris returned he was startled to see Johnston lurching in his saddle. He asked, "General, are you wounded?"

"Yes, and I fear seriously."

Harris and a young captain sought to find the wound. Only several

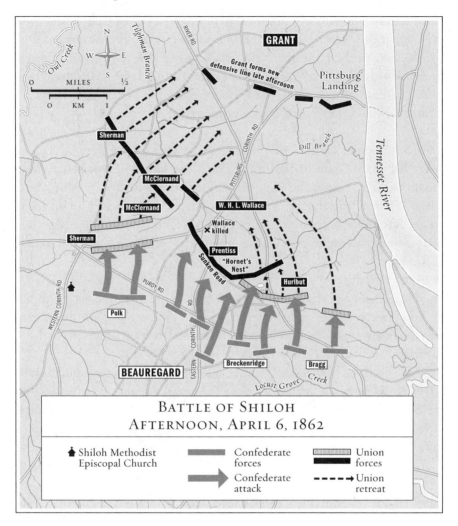

BATTLE OF SHILOH
AFTERNOON, APRIL 6, 1862

🪦 Shiloh Methodist
   Episcopal Church

▬▬▬ Confederate
     forces

➤ Confederate
  attack

▦▦▦ Union
     forces

---→ Union
     retreat

hours before, Johnston had insisted his personal physician, Dr. David W. Yandell, leave him to treat the wounded. Now there was no one present who understood that a minié ball had torn the popliteal artery below Johnston's knee. The blood could be stanched with a tourniquet. Instead, from loss of blood, Johnston died within fifteen minutes. His stunned staff carried his body to the Shiloh church.

Learning of Johnston's death, Beauregard assumed command. He ordered General Daniel Ruggles to assemble cannon to attack Prentiss. Joined by elements from Wallace's and Hurlbut's divisions, Prentiss repulsed attack after attack, defending what would be called "the Hornet's Nest."

Grant, unlike Johnston, did not attempt to lead from out front or micromanage the divisions of his huge army. Relying upon the effectiveness of a well-structured command, he believed division commanders should direct their forces. Thus, from the moment he arrived at the landing he chose instead to offer overall strategy and support to his commanders.

Later in the afternoon, as the fighting at the Hornet's Nest continued to deteriorate, first Hurlbut and then Wallace led their men out from the sunken road under withering fire. Rising in his stirrups to assay the situation, Wallace was struck by a bullet and fell from his horse to the ground.

Grant, knowing the Confederates wanted to push his Union troops into the Tennessee River, ordered his chief of staff, Joseph Webster, to line up artillery and siege guns a quarter mile from the river for a final defense. At five P.M., Prentiss, after courageously repulsing eleven separate attacks, surrendered his remaining twenty-two hundred men.

As the sun began to set, Beauregard made the decision to suspend combat on this long day. He knew his men were exhausted. He wired Richmond, "We this morning attacked the enemy in strong position in front of Pittsburg, and after a severe battle of ten hours, thanks be to the Almighty, gained a complete victory, driving the enemy from every position." Beauregard and Bragg, planning for the morrow, spent the night sleeping in Sherman's tent by the Shiloh church.

GRANT SUSPENDED FIGHTING also. Having started the day with forty thousand troops, he had suffered nearly ten thousand casualties by its end. Around five P.M., the lead elements of Buell's army finally arrived at the landing. At seven P.M., nearly eight hours after receiving his first order to come immediately, Lew Wallace's Third Division began arriving across the Owl Creek bridge.

Rain began to fall lightly in the early evening but fell harder throughout the night, drenching the wounded who lay groaning on the battlefield. Grant, his injured ankle throbbing in pain, eschewed sleeping in dry quarters in a log hut or on a boat, preferring to remain on the battlefield with his men, sheltered only by a large oak tree. Near midnight, Sherman found him, still awake, standing, with a lantern in one hand, cigar clasped between his teeth, his slouch hat keeping the rain off his face. Wondering if Grant might be planning a strategic defeat, Sherman commented, "Well, Grant, we've had the devil's own day, haven't we?"

Grant, after a puff on his cigar, replied, "Yes. Lick 'em tomorrow, though."

. . .

On Monday, April 7, two fatigued armies somehow roused themselves to fight another day. Grant, missing two of his six division commanders, Prentiss and Wallace, not to mention Smith, readied his tightly bunched forces.

On this day, all the advantage lay with Grant. He now marshaled seven divisions, reinforced by Buell's troops—nearly forty-five thousand men. The Confederates, reduced to fewer than twenty-five thousand men, would not easily yield the territory they had gained. They fought

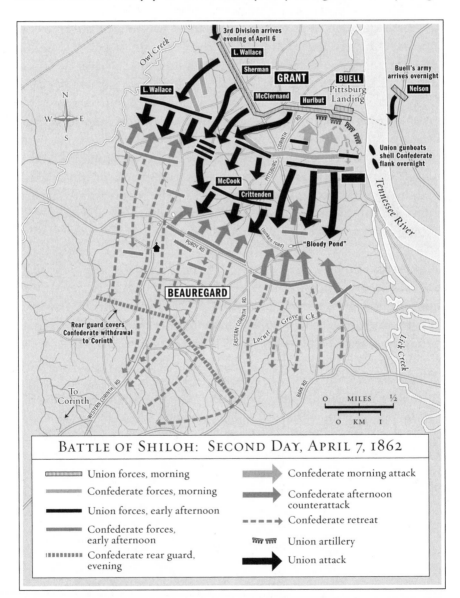

BATTLE OF SHILOH: SECOND DAY, APRIL 7, 1862

- Union forces, morning
- Confederate forces, morning
- Union forces, early afternoon
- Confederate forces, early afternoon
- Confederate rear guard, evening
- Confederate morning attack
- Confederate afternoon counterattack
- Confederate retreat
- Union artillery
- Union attack

valiantly through the morning, but they were outnumbered almost two to one. Toward the center of the battlefield, a pond would come to symbolize the day's fighting. Its blue waters turned red with the blood of the wounded and dying; today, visitors see the "Bloody Pond" and imagine the horror that took place all around it.

Both sides fought bravely, but slowly the Confederates yielded all the ground they had won the previous day. By two P.M., Federal soldiers fought their way past the Shiloh church. Grudgingly, Beauregard gave the order to begin a retreat back to Corinth.

Grant rode forward several miles but decided not to order a full pursuit by his exhausted troops.

JOHNSTON'S DECISION TO attack Grant before Buell could arrive was the most daring move in the first year of the war. The irony was that Grant, itching to attack, was struck by Johnston, whose reputation had been tarnished for his failure to attack.

The surprising attack almost succeeded on April 6. The what-ifs of the Battle of Shiloh remain fiercely debated. What if the Confederates had attacked, as originally planned, before April 6? What if Beauregard had had a better battle plan? What if Johnston had not been killed on that first afternoon? What if the Confederates had pushed their advantage as the sun was setting on April 6?

As news of the Battle of Shiloh traveled east, the American people were stunned. The staggering number of casualties for the two-day battle was 23,746. Union casualties, 13,047, with 1,754 dead, was more than Bull Run, Wilson's Creek, Fort Henry, and Fort Donelson put together. Up to that time, Shiloh was the largest battle in American history. It revealed to both North and South that this civil war was now total war—and it might go on for a very long time.

The Battle of Shiloh demonstrated that Grant, even caught off guard, could mobilize a stunned army and rally it to fight tenaciously to victory.

Though unlike Grant in so many ways, the fiery William Tecumseh Sherman would become Grant's staunchest defender and closest military friend.

CHAPTER 15

William Tecumseh Sherman

In Gen. Sherman the country has an able and gallant defender
and your husband a true friend.
—ULYSSES S. GRANT TO JULIA DENT GRANT, May 4, 1862

On April 9, Illinois senator Orville H. Browning interrupted business
in the Senate to read the *New York Herald*'s first report on Shiloh by
enterprising war correspondent Frank Chapman:

> The battle resulted in complete rout of the enemy who attacked us
> Sunday morning. Battle lasted until Monday 4:35, p.m., when the
> enemy commenced their retreat and are still flying towards Corinth,
> pursued by a large force of our cavalry. Slaughter on both sides im-
> mense.

Indiana congressman Schuyler Colfax read Chapman's portrayal of
Grant to members of the House of Representatives. Grant "ordered a
charge across the field, himself leading, as he brandished his sword and
waved them on to the crowning victory, while cannon balls were falling
like hail around him."

The next day, Lincoln issued a presidential proclamation asking that
citizens "at their next weekly assemblages in their accustomed places of
public worship . . . acknowledge and render thanks to our Heavenly Father for these inestimable blessings." In what seemed a repeat of the celebrations after Fort Donelson, with the first report about Shiloh, crowds
in Northern towns hailed Grant as a hero—again.

BUT NOT FOR long. Twenty-four-year-old Whitelaw Reid scooped
Chapman's scoop. Tall, with a black mustache, and wearing his hair long
in the Southern style, Reid exhibited a passion for journalistic commen-

tary rather than straightforward reportage. His 19,500-word story in the *Cincinnati Gazette,* published on April 14, was swiftly picked up by other newspapers, becoming the spark that made Shiloh the most controversial battle of the Civil War. Reid began in the breathless first-person style of the day:

> Fresh from the field of the great battle, with its pounding and roaring of artillery, and its keener voiced rattle of musketry still sounding in my wearied ears; with all its visions of horror still seeming seared upon my eyeballs, while scenes of panic-stricken rout and brilliant charges, and obstinate defenses, and succor, and intoxicating success are burned alike confusedly and indelibly upon the brain, I essay to write what I know of the battle of Pittsburg Landing.

Reid charged that Grant was surprised. "Some, particularly among our officers, were not yet out of bed. Others were dressing, others washing, others cooking, a few eating their breakfasts. Many guns were unloaded, ammunition was ill-supplied—in short, the camps were virtually surprised—disgracefully."

Newspaper readers in Iowa, Illinois, Indiana, and Ohio, not knowing whether their loved ones were dead or lay wounded in some unknown hospital, read on in the small newspaper print of the day: "Into the just-aroused camps thronged the rebel regiments, firing sharp volleys as they came, and springing toward our laggards with the bayonet. Some were shot down as they were running, without weapons, hatless, coatless, toward the river." Reid, highlighting both that the Federal troops were surprised and that the battle resulted in a shocking loss of life, succeeded in focusing anger on Grant. According to Reid, the disaster of the first day turned into victory on the second day only by the arrival of Buell's army.

A FIRESTORM IGNITED around Grant. Chicago newspapers leaped to criticize the cowardice of midwestern soldiers, especially the Ohio Fifty-third and Fifty-seventh regiments. The *Cincinnati Commercial* responded, "For days the people of Ohio lay under the deep mortification and disgrace of her sons." Ohio governor David Tod, a small boy when teenage Jesse Grant lived with his family, protested that Ohio regiments accused of running away should not be blamed; the fault lay with the "criminal negligence" of Grant and his generals. Rumors spread that Grant had been delayed at Savannah because he was drinking.

Grant staff member William Rowley wrote a friend, "The man who fabricated that story is an infamous *liar*." Jacob Ammen wrote in his diary for April 8, "Note—I am satisfied General Grant was not under the influence of liquor, either of the times I saw him." Mrs. Cherry, in whose home Grant stayed for three weeks, remembered Grant was "thoroughly sober" when he left her home on the morning of April 6.

Wanting to see for himself about his Ohio boys, Ohio lieutenant governor Benjamin Stanton visited Shiloh and returned to write that Grant should "be court-martialed or shot."

The criticism got to Grant. If the reporting on Shiloh was hard reading for people who had husbands, sons, and brothers in the Army of the Tennessee, Grant knew how difficult it would be for his father and mother, but especially for Julia. He wrote her, "I suppose you have read a great deal about the battle in the papers and some quite contradictory." Wishing to prepare her, he warned, "I will come in again for heaps of abuse from persons who were not here."

Each of Grant's family members responded differently. Jesse became angry. An inveterate letter writer, in the coming months he would fire off missives to Cincinnati newspapers defending his son. Hannah found confidence in a protecting God, believing her son had been raised up to fulfill God's purposes to save the Union in this terrible war. Julia, although finding some comfort in her mother-in-law's calm, was "not at all happy." "I sat shocked and almost stunned at an article (many of them) in ribald abuse of my husband just after the battle of Shiloh."

Julia felt cut off on all sides: separated from her husband; experiencing an increasing chill in the relationship with her father, who railed against her "federal general" husband; feeling disaffected from her St. Louis friends. Younger sister Emmy, now all grown up, had become a confirmed Confederate. Julia wanted to protest the unfair criticisms in the *Cincinnati Gazette* and *Cincinnati Commercial* but knew Ulys did not want anyone in the family to defend him.

As the clamor for Grant's hide escalated, criticism moved up the chain of command to the White House. On April 23, Stanton wrote Halleck to ask "whether any neglect or misconduct of General Grant or any other officer contributed to the sad casualties that befell our forces on Sunday."

Halleck might have taken this opportunity to join in the criticism of Grant, but he did not. Rather, he replied, "The said casualties of Sunday the sixth were due in part to the bad conduct of officers who were utterly unfit for their places & in part to [t]he numbers & bravery of the enemy."

By now, Halleck had become disgusted with officers who sought to cover their mistakes by blaming Grant.

But the antagonism continued. Alexander K. McClure, a prominent Pennsylvania Republican, remembered that on one April evening he sat with Lincoln in the Cabinet Room, where he "appealed to Lincoln for his own sake to remove Grant at once." After a long silence, Lincoln, his long legs propped up on the marble mantel before an open fire, replied, "I can't spare this man; he fights."

IN THE AFTERMATH of Shiloh, a staunch defender of Grant did arise. This advocate witnessed Grant's actions on the battlefield and determined to set the record straight. Unlike Grant in so many ways, William Tecumseh Sherman is a powerful lens to bring Grant's odyssey as a general into sharper focus.

Sherman was born on February 8, 1820, in Lancaster, Ohio, two years before Grant. The sixth of eleven children, he was named for the Shawnee Indian leader Tecumseh, whose courage and military skills Sherman's father admired. Family and friends nicknamed the boy "Cump."

In 1829, Sherman's father, Charles, a judge of the Ohio Supreme Court, died suddenly of typhoid fever at age forty. His widowed mother, Mary, with no inheritance, agreed that several children would need to live with relatives or friends. Nine-year-old Cump went to live with neighbors Thomas and Maria Ewing.

Maria, a devout Catholic, would accept Cump into her family only if he was baptized into Catholicism. The priest who baptized the red-haired boy persuaded Maria he should receive a Christian name in addition to his Indian name. It was Saint William Day, June 28, 1829; from that day forward, Cump was William Tecumseh Sherman.

Cump landed inside a remarkable family. Tom Ewing, a colorful lawyer, was elected to the United States Senate in 1831.

With his stepfather's help, at sixteen Sherman entered West Point. He had little contact with Grant, who did not enter until Cump's senior year. Bright and voluble, Sherman excelled both in the classroom and in tomfoolery, graduating sixth in his class in 1840; he would have been fourth had demerits not pulled down his rank.

By 1854, both Grant and Sherman were out of the army, Sherman trying his hand, unsuccessfully, in banking and law in California and Kansas. They met in St. Louis in 1857 at a low point for each. "West Point and the regular army were not good schools for farmers [and] bankers," Cump recalled.

In 1859, Sherman became superintendent of the Louisiana State Seminary of Learning & Military Academy in Pineville. When Louisiana troops seized the Union arsenal at Baton Rouge on January 10, 1861, he resigned his position and returned to St. Louis to become president of a streetcar company.

Senator John Sherman helped his older brother receive an appointment as colonel in the Union army. In July 1861, in the Battle of Bull Run just south of Washington, Sherman, commanding a brigade, emerged as one of the few bright lights in a disastrous defeat when he helped stem the disorderly retreat back to Washington. Promoted to brigadier general, he was sent to Louisville the next month as deputy to Robert Anderson, commanding officer and hero at Fort Sumter. Sherman succeeded Anderson in October but grew increasingly pessimistic about Union prospects. He complained frequently to Washington about shortages of manpower. Sherman thought nothing of writing to President Lincoln himself, closing one letter: "Answer."

In Sherman's letters, one hears a man sinking into despair. At the end of his rope, Sherman asked to be relieved in November. He told his wife, Ellen, that in his desperation, he considered suicide. The *Cincinnati Commercial*'s headline GENERAL WILLIAM T. SHERMAN INSANE was quickly picked up by numerous newspapers.

Upon learning of Grant's promotion to major general, although the older Sherman outranked Grant, he immediately wrote a letter of congratulation. Gratified, Grant replied, "I feel under many obligations to you for the kind tone of your letter, and hope that should an opportunity occur you will win for yourself the promotion, which you are kind enough to say belongs to me."

MEANWHILE, WITH LITTLE news of battles, newspapers kept refighting the Battle of Shiloh. A reporter for the *New York World* questioned if the initial in Grant's name stood for "Surprise."

When Grant wrote his father on April 26, he had no idea Jesse would give his letter to the *Cincinnati Commercial,* furnishing the letter out of anger at criticism of his son. The letter added fuel to the controversy's flames.

In a turmoil that refused to die down, Grant wrote Julia to say that he had received a letter from his father. "The latter seems very anxious that I should contradict the statements made by the newspapers! Doesn't he know the best contradiction in the world is to pay no attention to them?"

At the end of the summer, Grant had had enough. He declared his independence. "I have not an enemy in the world who has done me so much injury as you in your efforts in my defense. I require no defenders and for my sake let me alone."

INTO THE MIDST of the newspaper battle rode Grant's chief advocate. Sherman's actions at Shiloh had made him a Union hero. He was promoted to major general on May 1. He did not need to enter the controversy but told Ellen that "the hue & cry against Grant about surprise is wrong."

He aimed his biggest guns at Ohio lieutenant governor Benjamin Stanton. "I am not surprised when anonymous scribblers write and publish falsehoods," for "it is their trade," but "it is different with men in high official station who like you descend to this dirty work." Sherman's verdict: "Shame on You!" He got right to the point: "The accusatory part of your published statement is all false, false in general, false in every particular, and . . . you could not have failed to know it false when you published that statement."

In Washington, as criticism continued, Elihu Washburne rose in Congress to offer a defense: "Though but 40 years old, he has been oftener under fire, and been in more battles, than any other living man on this continent excepting Scott." The congressman brushed aside the charges of surprise and intoxication and lauded Grant: "He is an example of courage, honor, fortitude, activity, temperance and modesty."

Upon learning of Washburne's remarks, Grant wrote, "You have interested yourself so much as my friend." He assured the congressman, "Notoriety has no charms for me." If "I render the same services . . . without being known in the matter, it would be infinitely preferable to me."

DESPITE HIS PUBLIC support, Henry Halleck informed Grant on April 9 that he was coming from St. Louis to take command. "Avoid another battle if you can, 'till all arrive, we shall then be able to beat them without fail." The "all" referred to John Pope, whose Army of the Mississippi's victory at Island No. 10 had opened up the Mississippi River south to Fort Pillow and who would now join Grant and Halleck.

"Old Brains," enamored of the conventional art of defensive warfare, did not yet understand Grant. Halleck's caution proved a godsend for the Confederates. On the retreat to Corinth, Bragg wrote Beauregard, "Our condition is horrible. Troops utterly disorganized and demoralized." The Confederates limped back to Corinth to refit and fight another day.

Halleck arrived at Pittsburg Landing on April 11. When Pope arrived on April 21, Halleck assembled one army from three. He positioned Grant's Army of the Tennessee on the right, Buell's Army of the Ohio in the center, and Pope's Army of the Mississippi on the left, with McClernand commanding the reserve. Halleck now commanded an army of almost 120,000 men.

One great soldier would be missing. On April 25, Charles F. Smith, commander of cadets while Grant was a student at West Point, surrendered to death, never able to recover from his leg infection. In a letter to Smith's wife, Grant wrote, "I can bear honest testimony to his great worth as a soldier and friend." For Grant, Smith's death was deeply personal. "Where an entire nation condoles with you in your bereavement; no one can do so with more heartfelt grief than myself."

WHEN HALLECK FINALLY began the twenty-five-mile march south to attack Corinth on April 29, he announced a shift in command. Major General George Thomas was transferred from Buell's army to take command of Grant's wing. Thomas, sometimes called "the Virginian," was the highest-ranking Union officer raised in a Southern state.

What about Grant? Halleck placed Grant second in command.

Halleck now sought to do everything Grant had not done at Shiloh. If Grant had been surprised, he would not be; if Grant did not employ enough pickets and scouts, Halleck positioned them at the front and on the flanks; if Grant failed to entrench, Halleck ordered troops to spend four hours entrenching nightly. The Federals advanced slowly upon the orders of their cautious commander. A Union soldier confided sarcastically to his diary on May 5, "Genl Halleck intended taking Corinth without firing a musket."

Halleck's snail-footed advance to Corinth became painful for Grant. Halleck did not seek his advice. Once Grant suggested, "I thought if he would move [Pope's] Army of the Mississippi at night," they would be "ready to advance at daylight." He was taken aback at Halleck's response. "I was silenced so quickly that I felt that possibly I had suggested an unmilitary movement." By disposition a man of action, on the road to Corinth Grant discovered that "I was little more than an observer."

After two weeks, Grant could not abide his position any longer. He wrote Halleck, "I believe it is generally understood through this army that my position differs but little from that of one in arrest." The solution? "I deem it due to myself to ask either full restoration to duty, according to my rank, or to be relieved entirely from further duty."

Halleck replied, "I am very much surprised, General, that you should find any cause of complaint in the recent assignment of commands." He protested, "You certainly will not suspect me of any intention to injure your feelings or reputation."

ON MAY 28, Sherman advanced to within a mile of Corinth's main line of defense encircling the town. The next morning Pope pushed forward with heavy guns, while in the afternoon Sherman moved up to within a thousand yards of the town.

But at one twenty A.M. on May 30, a worried Pope sent Halleck a telegram: "The enemy is re-enforcing heavily, by trains, in my front and on the left. The cars are running constantly, and the cheering is immense every time they unload in front of me." Pope expressed alarm that he would "be attacked in heavy force at daylight."

At five A.M. on May 30, a series of explosions inside Corinth startled the Union army. Sherman and Pope decided to probe the outer defenses once again. No response. Cautiously, patrols entered the city. No one. Nothing. Gone.

Beauregard had pulled off the largest hoax of the war. Believing he could not withstand a siege by Union forces, he developed plans for a strategic retreat. To conceal his movements, he implemented a series of deceptions. Drummers stayed behind to beat out reveille at the appointed hours; dummy cannons and guns were set up in the dark where real guns had stood just hours before in the light; fires were kept burning. The master deception was what Pope heard. Empty trains came and went—with loud whistles and cheering by phantom reinforcements.

On the morning of May 30, Federal forces entered a deserted Corinth. As Halleck rode into town, he could not miss a blue uniform filled with straw hanging from a tree, accompanied by a pine plank on which was carved: "Halleck outwitted—what will old Abe say?"

SEVERAL DAYS AFTER the bloodless capture of Corinth, Grant applied for a thirty-day leave. Determined to find out what his friend was up to, Sherman rushed over to Grant's tent. "I found him seated on a camp-stool, with papers on a rude camp-table; he seemed to be employed in assorting letters, and tying them up with red tape into convenient bundles." After exchanging greetings, "I inquired if it were true that he was going away."

"Yes."

"I inquired the reason."

"Sherman, you know. You know that I am in the way here. I have stood it as long as I can, and can endure it no longer."

Sherman reminded Grant that earlier in the war newspapers called him "crazy." He counseled, "If he went away, events would go right along, and he would be left out; whereas, if he remained, some happy accident might restore him to favor and his true place."

The conversation must have had an effect. Several days later, Sherman received a note from Grant saying he would remain.

EVERYTHING CHANGED ON June 10. Halleck issued Special Field Orders No. 90, in which the order that had previously merged the three armies into three wings "is hereby revoked." Furthermore, rather than pursue Confederates, Halleck told Pope, "The major object now is to get the enemy far enough south to relieve our railroads from danger of an immediate attack. There is no object in bringing on a battle if this object can be obtained without one."

Halleck restored Grant to the command of the Army of the Tennessee. Pope would guard Corinth. Buell would repair the railroad tracks while marching 220 miles east to Chattanooga. The result: Just as had happened after Fort Donelson, Halleck gave the Confederates time to reorganize. The Union armies would march north, west, and east—everywhere but south after Beauregard.

Grant's district headquarters would be Memphis, the Mississippi River city captured by the Union navy on June 6. Memphis, with a population of twenty-three thousand, was the fifth largest city in the Confederacy. Ulys invited Julia to join him there. He started for Memphis on June 21, riding the hundred miles west accompanied only by his staff and a small cavalry escort. He learned later that he had come within forty-five minutes of being intercepted and captured.

Clarksville and Corinth had been abandoned towns; in Memphis, Grant entered a bustling city where citizens did not hide their sympathies. "Affairs in this city seem to be in rather bad order, secessionists governing much in their own way," he wrote. Confederate flags hung from homes. Merchants refused to swear the oath of allegiance. Goods shipped into Memphis did not remain there: they left hidden in coffins, in the carcasses of cattle and hogs, in women's trunks—all bound for Confederate forces. Grant wrote Halleck, "Spies and members of the southern army are constantly finding their way in and out of the city in spite of all vigilance."

He heard complaints that on previous Sundays prayers for President

Davis had been offered at several churches. Although he was urged to get tough, Grant instead instructed Stephen Hurlbut, commander of the Sixteenth Corps in Memphis, "You can compel all Clergymen within your lines to omit from their church services any portion you may deem *treasonable,* but you will not compel the insertion or substitution of anything."

Ulys rejoiced when Julia and the children joined him on July 1. She noticed he had gained fifteen pounds since Cairo. On July 4, Union men mounted a huge Independence Day celebration. Twelve-year-old Fred told little Nellie that the salvos of artillery fired were for her seventh birthday. Nellie exclaimed to her mother, "Mamma, who told them this was my birthday? Why, really this is very kind of the rebels."

But the rebels in Memphis did not take kindly to Federal occupation. After witnessing countless acts of disloyalty, Grant ordered any building flying a Confederate flag to be sequestered for use as a hospital. Wanting to break up connections between citizens and guerrilla units roaming the countryside, Grant issued orders on July 3 whereby "wherever loss is sustained by the Government," said loss shall be made up of property from persons sympathetic with the rebellion "sufficient to remunerate the Government all loss and expense of collection."

On July 10, Grant issued orders that because of the "constant communication" between the Confederate army and "their friends and sympathizers in the city of Memphis," people with ties to the Confederacy "are required to move South beyond our lines within five days."

Grant's time in divided Memphis would be brief. A chain of events precipitated another domino-effect lineup change. In the middle of May, George McClellan's delayed offensive advanced to within sight of the church spires of Richmond. On May 31, Confederate general Joseph E. Johnston counterattacked and drove the Union left wing back through the village of Seven Pines. That evening Johnston was wounded; the next day Davis replaced him with Robert E. Lee. McClellan, learning of the change in command, expressed his pleasure, believing Lee "cautious and weak . . . likely to be timid and irresolute in action."

But Lee strengthened defenses around Richmond, reorganized his newly designated Army of Northern Virginia, and outgeneraled McClellan and his larger Army of the Potomac in battle after battle. He called in Stonewall Jackson from the Shenandoah Valley, who attempted to harass and defeat larger Federal armies. Lee drove McClellan away from Richmond and back down the Virginia Peninsula.

The patient Lincoln finally lost his patience. Having removed

McClellan as general in chief in March, in July he considered taking away his command of the Army of the Potomac. Lincoln called Halleck to Washington as general in chief.

GRANT FIRST HEARD something was in the air when he received a directive from Halleck in Corinth on July 11: "You will immediately repair to this place." The letter included no information as to why. Puzzled, Grant inquired, "Am I to repair alone or take my Staff?"

Halleck replied brusquely, "This place will be your Head Quarters. You can judge for yourself."

Grant, upon retracing his steps to Corinth, found Halleck "very uncommunicative." But on July 17, Halleck issued orders giving Grant command of the District of West Tennessee—everything between the Tennessee and Mississippi rivers up to Cairo. John Pope had been summoned east to lead a newly organized Army of Virginia, relinquishing his previous command, the Army of the Mississippi, to the authority of William S. Rosecrans, who would report to Grant. Sherman would become military governor of Memphis. Buell would retain an independent command, and Grant and Buell would report directly to Halleck.

Grant welcomed William Rosecrans as Pope's replacement. In July and August, he and Rosecrans dined together frequently at Grant's headquarters.

GRANT WOULD CALL the summer of 1862 "the most anxious period of the war." Yes, Confederate control of Southern territory had retreated farther south into Mississippi and Alabama, but because of Halleck's policy of dispersion, "I was put entirely on the defensive in a territory whose population was hostile to the Union." He had nearly eighty thousand men under his command, but they were spread all across northern Mississippi and West Tennessee.

Halleck did encourage Grant to pursue what was beginning to be called a "hard war": "It is very desirable that you should clean out West Tennessee and North Mississippi of all organized enemies." What to do with all these people? "If necessary, take up all active sympathizers, and either hold them as prisoners or put them beyond our lines. Handle that class without gloves and take their property for public use." In sum, "It is time they should begin to feel the pressure of war on our side."

This change became codified on the day Grant assumed command. On July 17, the Thirty-seventh Congress passed two laws that signaled a tougher war. First, the Militia Act authorized the draft of three hundred thousand men for a three-year enlistment. Within the act, the president was granted the power to enroll "persons of African descent" for a variety of jobs, from "performing camp service" to "any military or naval service for which they may be found competent." Despite this legislation, in the summer of 1862 Lincoln had no plans to use African Americans as soldiers.

Second, the Confiscation Act stipulated that persons who "engage in any rebellion or insurrection against the authority of the United States" shall have their property confiscated, including slaves who "shall be deemed captives of war, and shall be forever free." The scope of this second Confiscation Act would need to be sorted not by Lincoln, but by commanders such as Grant.

Washburne, whom Grant looked to as interpreter of the political maneuverings in Washington, wrote his friend, "The administration has come up to what the people have long demanded—a vigorous prosecution of the war by all the means known to civilized warfare." He wanted Grant to understand that "the negroes must now be made our auxiliaries in every possible way they can be, whether by working or fighting." Believing Grant "no longer hampered" by Halleck hovering at Corinth, and the "cloud of obloquy" from Shiloh having gone away, he was convinced Grant had an opportunity to "be held in the highest estimation" by the nation. Grant surely agreed when Washburne concluded, "If the constitution or slavery must perish, let slavery go to the wall."

CHOOSING THE SURVIVAL of the Constitution over the survival of slavery didn't mean the nonpolitical Grant had become an opponent of slavery. Shortly after Congress acted, Grant wrote his father, "I have no hobby of my own with regard to the negro, either to effect his freedom or to continue his bondage." But "if Congress pass any law and the President approves, I am willing to execute it." Grant here expressed to Jesse, whom he knew to be strongly antislavery, his deference to civilian leadership on the vexing issue of slavery.

Grant issued new orders on August 11. Fugitives will not be returned "to their claimants"; moreover, he authorized "the employment of such persons in the service of the Government." In carrying out this change, he made it clear that his soldiers were "positively prohibited from enticing Slaves to leave their masters," but if owners did come for slaves that had crossed over to Union lines of their own volition, "citizens . . . known to be disloyal and dangerous, may be ordered away or arrested."

One week later, Grant observed to his sister that the war was "growing oppressive to the Southern people" and that "their *institution* [the slaves] are beginning to have ideas of their own and every time an expedition goes out more or less of them follow in the wake of the army and come into camp." He described using freed slaves as hospital attendants, cooks, and teamsters, "thus saving soldiers to carry the musket." He confessed, "I don't know what is to become of these poor people in the end but it is weakening the enemy to take them from them." In these letters, we hear the practical response of a commander determined to follow orders in a changing war situation.

THE WAR QUICKLY assumed a different face. During the next months, Grant would contend with growing guerrilla activity, increasing civilian obstruction, and Northern illicit trade.

The word *guerrilla* is derived from the Spanish *guerrilleros,* independent fighters who banded together during Napoleon's campaign on the Iberian Peninsula. Richmond officials preferred the word *partisan,* arguing that the fighters were related to the regular army. Guerrillas or partisans, fiercely autonomous warriors, fought across a countryside they knew well.

Unable to take the initiative because of Halleck's policy of dispersion, Grant could only react. He watched as guerrillas attacked trains, cut telegraph wires, smashed bridges, and disrupted traffic on the Tennessee River. "Guerrillas are hovering around in every direction getting whipped every day some place by some of my command but keeping us busy."

Before the summer of 1862, Grant had drawn a firm line between soldiers and civilians. He now reassessed this distinction: "Many citizens who appear to be quiet non-combatants in the presence of our forces are regularly enrolled and avail themselves of every safe opportunity of depredating upon Union men and annoying our troops."

What to do? "Hereafter no Passes will be given to Citizens of States in Rebellion, to pass into our lines." Grant told Halleck, "I am decidedly in favor of turning all discontented citizens within our lines out South."

NORTHERN ILLICIT TRADE for cotton angered Grant. By the Civil War, cotton had become the indispensable lifeblood of the Southern agriculture that grew it and the Northern manufacturing that processed it. Cotton was to the nineteenth century what oil would become to the twentieth century.

Union coastal and river blockades were put in place to deprive the South of necessary staples, but Northern businessmen were more than willing to break the blockades in order to exchange all manner of goods covertly for Southern cotton. The problem, as Grant observed in Memphis, was that Northern goods did not go just to sustain civilians, but to supply the Confederate army. As Sherman wrote Grant, "We cannot carry on war & trade with a people at the same time."

Upon assuming command in July, Grant took measures to stop this trade. On July 26, he instructed General Isaac Quinby at Columbus, "Examine the baggage of all speculators coming South." In a general order to the troops in his command, Grant chastised speculators as persons "whose love of gain is greater than their love of Country."

But Grant realized he was running up against officials in faraway Washington who by 1862 had adopted a policy of "letting trade follow the flag." Usually deferential to civilian authority, Grant felt so strongly about the consequences of this illicit trade that he took the unusual step of contacting Secretary of the Treasury Salmon P. Chase.

In a skillfully written letter, he asked who was benefiting from the policy of trade following the flag. "First, a class of greedy traders whose first and only desire is gain." He argued, "Our lines are so extended that it is impossible for any military surveillance to contend successfully with the cunning of the traders." Second, "The enemy are thus receiving supplies of most necessary and useful articles which relieve their suffering and strengthens them for resistance to our authority." His letter to Chase had no immediate effect.

BETWEEN GUERRILLAS AND illicit trading, Grant was being bled division by division. Halleck's decision to divide the western command was a huge blunder. Union numerical superiority was broken up, providing an opportunity for Braxton Bragg, who had replaced Beauregard after Corinth, to refit at Tupelo, Mississippi, fifty-two miles south of Corinth and regain the offensive. Bragg had the luxury of choice—would he assault Grant or Buell? Leaving General Sterling Price to defend northern Mississippi and dispatching Earl Van Dorn to defend Vicksburg, Bragg struck north with thirty-four thousand men. The lure of taking Chattanooga, especially considering Buell's cautious march north to the Tennessee city, decided for him. If Grant moved to assist Buell, then Van Dorn or Price would move north to retake Corinth and West Tennessee.

On July 15, Halleck ordered Grant to send troops to Samuel Curtis in Arkansas. Two days later, George Thomas's division was transferred back to Buell. As Halleck watched Buell's slow march, Grant received appeals for reinforcements. He protested that he was being "weakened" by these requests but notified Halleck on August 14, "I have ordered two more Divisions East."

NEVER COMFORTABLE ON the defense, in September Grant determined to go on the offense even with his reduced numbers. Reconnaissance brought reports that Price, whose troops stretched from Tupelo to Holly Springs, Mississippi, was moving north. Grant telegraphed Halleck, "With all the vigilance I can bring to bear I cannot determine the objects of the Enemy." Was Price's intention to link up with Bragg or join forces with Van Dorn to retake Corinth?

Ulys wrote Julia on September 14, telling her of the multiple threats to his army. He confided that if Price had struck when he first arrived, he "would have found us very weak in consequence of the heavy drafts that had been made on me at other points for troops." Fortunately, "Now however it is different. I am concentrated and strong. Will give the rebels a tremendous thrashing if they come."

Price entered Iuka, twenty miles southeast of Corinth, on the same day. An impressive-looking man with silver-white sideburns, he had gained a higher rank in the Mexican War than any future Confederate officer except Gideon Pillow. After Johnston's death and Beauregard's dismissal, many looked to Price as a new hero. But he arrived in Mississippi with a reputation for strident independence. With orders to join with Bragg's army, Price intended a brief stopover in Iuka, where he believed he could easily defeat the small Union garrison and restock his supplies.

Grant saw an opportunity. He ordered a plan whereby Rosecrans would attack from the south with nine thousand men while General Edward Ord would assail Price from the northwest with sixty-five hundred men. This coordinated pincer movement should block Price from moving north to join Bragg or escaping back south to link up with Van Dorn. Grant instructed Ord "to be in readiness to attack the moment he heard the sound of guns to the south or southeast." Grant's plan would depend upon communications functioning smoothly.

On the evening of September 18, a telegram reached Grant reporting a tremendous battle fought with Confederates under Lee near the small Maryland village of Sharpsburg on September 17: "Entire rebel army of Virginia destroyed." William Hillyer, Grant's aide, forwarded the telegram to Ord, who sent it on to Price, urging him to surrender to avoid "useless bloodshed." Price refused. Grant wrote Rosecrans, "McClellan has driven the rebels out of Maryland with tremendous slaughter. Genl

Lee taken prisoner." Grant would learn that the Battle of Antietam would be the bloodiest single-day battle in American history.

The Battle of Iuka began at four P.M., with casualties mounting swiftly on both sides. In the evening Rosecrans telegraphed Grant, "You must attack in the morning and *in force*." Was Rosecrans sending a command to his commanding officer? Or sending a communication from one general to another?

Rosecrans, expecting Ord to join the battle, waited in vain. The next morning, an exasperated Rosecrans telegraphed Grant, "Why did you not attack this morning?" Ord, who was with Grant, replied, "We didn't hear any sounds of the battle last p.m." Ord said later an acoustical shadow—a temporary area through which sound waves fail to penetrate—prevented him from hearing any firing.

Grant expected Rosecrans to oppose Price's flight, but the Confederate army escaped south in the dark down a road Rosecrans failed to block. The pincer movement grasped no one.

In his report on Iuka, Grant ignored Rosecrans's acerbic communications, writing Halleck, "I cannot speak too highly of the energy & skill displayed by Genl. Rosecrans in the attack & of the endurance of the troops under him." Although disturbed in this initial encounter with Rosecrans's leadership, Grant decided to focus on his merits rather than demerits.

IF GRANT HAD stopped Price from moving into Tennessee, he knew he had not halted his aggressive appetite. On the evening of September 20, he instructed an aide to inform him if there was a movement "either to reinforce Price or to attack Corinth."

Meanwhile, Van Dorn had come up from Vicksburg and now directed Price to join him in an assault on Corinth before Grant could receive reinforcements. Van Dorn, who had vied with James Longstreet for last place in his West Point class of 1842, may have been courageous but was not known for careful planning and reconnaissance. Recognizing that a victory in Corinth could open the gate to West Tennessee, he determined to hurl his twenty-two hundred men into battle.

The Confederates launched a ferocious attack on October 3. Despite the fact that Rosecrans had strengthened the entrenchments ringing the town, by the middle of the afternoon the Confederates broke through the first of two lines of the Federal defense. But there they became stuck. As the light faded, Price encouraged Van Dorn to restart the attack in the moonlight, but Van Dorn rejected the proposal. His men were too exhausted, he felt, and would benefit from a night's rest.

When the attack resumed the next morning, Confederates advanced but were hurled back by Rosecrans's repositioned forces. Throughout the morning, a withering barrage from Federal artillery took a deadly toll. By noon, Van Dorn admitted the battle was over as his fatigued soldiers retreated. All knew the Confederates had suffered a crushing defeat. Price cried. All also understood that Rosecrans had led a brilliant defense of Corinth.

Grant believed the battle had less to do with defending Corinth than with destroying Van Dorn's exhausted army. "If the enemy fall back," he instructed Rosecrans, "push them with all force possible." Rosecrans, convinced his troops were too exhausted to chase Van Dorn, decided to let them rest. He would begin pursuit the next morning.

Rosecrans did start off on October 5, but one division began behind schedule, and the other took the wrong road. Grant wired Rosecrans, "Push the enemy to the wall." Hurlbut and Ord rushed to intercept the fleeing Confederates. Grant wrote Halleck, "I cannot see how the Enemy are to escape."

Over the next forty-eight hours, a flurry of telegrams flew back and forth between Grant and Rosecrans. Van Dorn, who had retreated to the north, looped around and headed south for Holly Springs. On October 7, concerned that Van Dorn might be reinforced with fresh troops, Grant wired Rosecrans, "We can do nothing with our weak forces but fall back to our old places. Order the pursuit to cease."

But Rosecrans did not want to stop. On October 7, he sent three telegrams to Grant. "I must deeply dissent from your views as to the policy of pursuit," he protested. "I beseech you to spend everything; push them while they are broken, hungry, weary, and ill-supplied." Grant telegraphed Rosecrans to return to Corinth "with great caution" because "a large force" was about to join the retreating Confederates.

Miscommunication at Iuka, compounded by opposing views on pursuing Van Dorn, created a fracture between Grant and Rosecrans. Perhaps this could have been surmounted, but when Rosecrans and his friends began to express their discontent in newspapers, the fissure widened.

GRANT KNEW THAT the armies of Van Dorn and Price, while defeated, were not destroyed. He learned that McClellan's victory at Antietam on

September 17, if not as decisive as initially reported, did result in Lee being driven back into Virginia. In Kentucky, Bragg, outpacing Buell, marched north from Chattanooga, which struck fear in the North. Buell, prodded by Halleck, finally met Bragg sixty miles southeast of Louisville at the crossroads town of Perryville. Bragg divided his army and attacked with only three divisions. On October 8, Buell counterattacked, forcing Bragg to retreat south into Tennessee, never again to threaten Kentucky.

To capitalize on the victory at Antietam, Lincoln promulgated the preliminary Emancipation Proclamation on September 22. Acting under his war powers authority as commander in chief, Lincoln declared that on January 1, 1863, "all persons held as slaves within any State or designated part of a State, the people whereof shall then be in rebellion against the United States shall be then, thenceforward, and forever free." All the while, the number of slaves escaping into Grant's lines was growing.

WHEN GRANT CALLED the summer of 1862 "the most anxious period of the war," it has been commonly understood he referred to the state of military affairs. But Grant, who seldom discussed his feelings, was also grappling with his own anxiety. Severely criticized after Shiloh, set on the shelf by Halleck on the march to Corinth, turning in the paperwork for a leave of absence, he struggled throughout these months with the uncertainties of his command.

A healing balm came from Julia's presence, who at Memphis and Corinth, after a long absence from her husband, helped restore his spirit. In the myths that have grown up around Julia, her visits have usually been chronicled as putting a stop to Grant's drinking. There is no evidence of Grant drinking in either Memphis or Corinth, but there is strong evidence that Julia and their children brought delight in the midst of difficult days.

Too, Grant's friendship with Sherman, set in motion at Shiloh, offered a comradeship that Grant had never known before. In stark contrast with Grant's continuing struggles with Halleck and his new tussles with Rosecrans, Grant knew he could rely on Sherman.

ON OCTOBER 25, Halleck expanded Grant's command from the District of West Tennessee to the Department of the Tennessee, now designated as the Army of the Tennessee. Grant reported his effective force as 48,500.

One day later, Grant wrote Halleck, "You have never suggested to me any plan of operations in this Department." He needed more. "As situated now, with no more troops, I can do nothing but defend my positions." Grant realized how much of his time and his troops' energy had consisted in repairing and defending the railroads. Never comfortable reacting, he concluded his letter with a bold proposal for action.

First he suggested destroying the railroads "to all points of the compass from Corinth"—the very railroads he had spent months repairing and defending. Second, "With small reinforcements at Memphis"—from Sherman—"I think I would be able to move down the Mississippi Central road and cause the evacuation of Vicksburg." When he penned these words, Grant could not have appreciated just how complicated and difficult the "evacuation of Vicksburg" would prove to be.

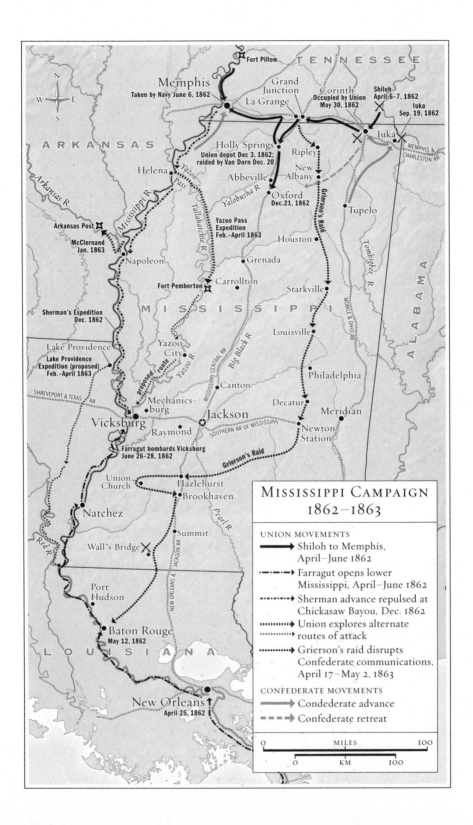

MISSISSIPPI CAMPAIGN 1862–1863

Fort Pillow

TENNESSEE

Memphis
Taken by Navy June 6, 1862

Grand Junction

La Grange

Corinth
Occupied by Union
May 30, 1862

Shiloh
April 6–7, 1862

Iuka
Sep. 19, 1862

Iuka

ARKANSAS

Holly Springs
Union depot Dec 3, 1862;
raided by Van Dorn Dec. 20

Ripley

New
Albany

MEMPHIS &
CHARLESTON RR

Helena

Yazoo
Pass

Abbeville

Oxford
Dec.21, 1862

Tupelo

Arkansas R.

Arkansas Post

McClernand
Jan. 1863

Napoleon

Tallahatchie R.

Yazoo Pass
Expedition
Feb.–April 1863

Grierson's Raid

Houston

Mississippi R.

Fort Pemberton

Carrollton

Starkville

Grenada

MISSISSIPPI

Tombigbee R.

ALABAMA

Sherman's Expedition
Dec. 1862

Lake Providence

Lake Providence
Expedition (proposed)
Feb.–April 1863

Louisville

MOBILE & OHIO RR

Yazoo
City

Yazoo R.

Canton

Big Black R.

MISSISSIPPI CENTRAL RR

Philadelphia

SHREVEPORT & TEXAS RR

Mechanics-
burg

Jackson

Decatur

Meridian

Vicksburg

Raymond

SOUTHERN RR OF MISSISSIPPI

Newton
Station

Farragut bombards Vicksburg
June 26–28, 1862

Grierson's Raid

Union
Church

Hazlehurst

Brookhaven

Natchez

Red R.

Wall"s Bridge

Summit

Pearl R.

JACKSON RR

Port
Hudson

NEW ORLEANS &

Baton Rouge
May 12, 1862

LOUISIANA

New Orleans
April 25, 1862

proposed route

**MISSISSIPPI CAMPAIGN
1862–1863**

UNION MOVEMENTS

→ Shiloh to Memphis,
April–June 1862

–·–▸ Farragut opens lower
Mississippi, April–June 1862

·······▸ Sherman advance repulsed at
Chickasaw Bayou, Dec. 1862

········▸ Union explores alternate
routes of attack

·······▸ Grierson's raid disrupts
Confederate communications,
April 17–May 2, 1863

CONFEDERATE MOVEMENTS

→ Condederate advance

– – ▸ Confederate retreat

N
W   E
S

0   MILES   100

0   KM   100

CHAPTER 16

"More Than Forty Richmonds"

The eyes and hopes of the whole country are now directed to your army.
In my opinion the opening of the Mississippi river will be to us of more
advantage than the capture of forty Richmonds.

—Henry W. Halleck to Ulysses S. Grant, March 20, 1863

G rant's aggressive decision to press forward toward Vicksburg in November 1862, stood in stark contrast with the tentativeness of other
major Union commanders. McClellan hesitated after his incomplete victory at Antietam on September 17, allowing Lee to cross back over the
Potomac into the safety of Virginia. Buell, following his strategic victory
at Perryville on October 8, did not pursue a bloodied Bragg.

Both paid a price for their caution. Buell was replaced by Rosecrans as
commander of the Army of the Cumberland on October 24. The day
after Democratic victories in the November 4 midterm elections, Lincoln
signed papers to remove McClellan, turning over command of the Army
of the Potomac to Ambrose Burnside. Of the main Union commanders
at the beginning of 1862, only Grant remained. With criticism simmering
in Congress, not certain where he stood with Halleck, Grant surely wondered if he would be the next to fall.

With no reply from Halleck to his October 26 request for a plan of
operations, Grant moved forward on his own initiative on November 2.
He telegraphed the general in chief that he had "commenced a movement" on Grand Junction, a sought-after prize in West Tennessee that
took its name from the intersection of the east–west Memphis and
Charleston and the north–south Mississippi Central railroad lines. Grant
intended to assemble five divisions there and move south into Mississippi
toward Holly Springs and Grenada.

With Grant in motion, Halleck finally responded. "I approve of your
plan of advancing upon the enemy as soon as you are strong enough for

that purpose." Halleck offered his typical cautious response; Grant knew that if he waited until he was "strong enough," he would never advance.

Grant's soldiers were eager to march. Throughout October, they wrote home that their most upsetting battles were "the annoyance of flies, mosquitoes, ticks, ants, worms, spiders, lizards, and snakes." Many thought battling Confederates could be no worse than fighting ever-present lice.

Worse than physical annoyance, the results of the 1862 midterm elections took their toll on morale. Grant's troops interpreted gains achieved by Democrats, with their anti-Lincoln and anti-Republican rhetoric, as antiwar. Democrats picked up twenty-eight seats in the House, won the governorship of New York, and gained majorities in the legislatures of New Jersey, Indiana, and Illinois. Iowa soldier Seymour D. Thompson captured the response of soldiers around him: "When the results of the Northern elections became known, it cast a gloom over the great majority of our regiment." He continued, "A crushing defeat of our main armies would not have had so chilling an effect on the morale of our troops."

As GRANT PLANNED a long overland campaign, he knew he needed to once again work closely with the navy to succeed. He appreciated his joint effort with Andrew Foote at Forts Henry and Donelson but heard that David Dixon Porter did not hold a high opinion of West Point generals. In November, Porter told Assistant Secretary of the Navy Gustavus Fox, "I don't trust the Army; it is very evident that Grant is going to try and take Vicksburg without us, but he can't do it."

Porter, son of a famous navy leader, became a navy midshipman at seventeen. Carrying himself erectly, this wiry man with a mat of black hair and dashing brown eyes seemed taller than his five feet six inches. At the beginning of the war, he received more criticism than acclaim when he went around the navy chain of command to present Lincoln with a plan to sail the *Powhatan* to Pensacola harbor, where he saved Fort Pickens, when Lincoln wanted it to be part of the expedition to save Fort Sumter. His proclivity to speak quickly and act impetuously landed him in trouble more than once.

In October, when Porter was appointed commander of the Mississippi Squadron, Secretary of the Navy Gideon Welles confided privately to his diary what others thought publicly: Porter "has stirring and positive qualities, is fertile in resources, has great energy, excessive and sometimes boastful of his own powers." By comparison, "He has not the conscientious and high moral qualities of Foote to organize the flotilla." Welles mused, "It is a question, with his mixture of good and bad traits, how he will succeed." Grant was about to become a most interested party in the answer to this question.

Even with his suspicion, Porter wrote Grant requesting a meeting. Porter was enjoying a dinner of roast duck and champagne when an aide ushered Grant in. The admiral, dressed immaculately in blue coat and white vest, with burnished boots and an impressive sword, was taken aback by Grant's appearance. He described his guest as "a travel-worn person dressed in civilian clothes."

Grant, hungry and tired from his travels, got right down to business: "When can you move your gun boats, and what force have you?"

NEXT, PROMISED UP to twenty thousand additional troops by Halleck, Grant telegraphed General James M. Tuttle on November 9 requesting information on units passing through Cairo. The district commander replied, "I find some Regts with a kind of loose order to report to Gen McClernand." This response puzzled Grant. McClernand had departed for Illinois on a leave of absence on August 28, but Grant had heard only rumors of his activities.

In Illinois, McClernand became outspoken in his criticism of the way the war was being fought. He asserted that West Pointers liked to use the word *strategy* as a pretext for not fighting: "Any commander who relies wholly upon STRATEGY must fail. We want the right man to lead us; a man who will appoint a subordinate officer on account of his merits, and not because he is a graduate of West Point."

Believing he was the right man, at the end of September McClernand traveled to Washington, where he met cabinet secretaries Chase and Stanton, both from the West, who he hoped would be sympathetic with his plan to open up the Mississippi River by an assault on Vicksburg. In a September cabinet meeting, when Chase asked the president for his estimation of McClernand, Lincoln responded that McClernand was "brave and capable, but too desirous to be independent of everybody else," as Chase recorded in his diary.

Finally, McClernand met with Lincoln to present his plan. On October 21, Stanton summoned McClernand to the War Department to receive confidential orders authorizing his organization of troops from the Midwest that "an expedition may be organized under his command to attack Vicksburg." Lincoln attached a note: "I add that I feel deep interest in the success of the expedition, and desire it to be pushed forward with all possible dispatch, consistently with the other parts of the military service."

No copy of the order was sent to Grant or Halleck. Stanton may have initially kept Halleck in the dark, knowing his lack of enthusiasm for McClernand. Still, the final paragraph of the orders stated: "The forces so organized will remain subject to the designation of the general-in-chief, and be employed as the service in his judgment may require." This meant Halleck and Grant could exercise the power of review over McClernand's plans.

As McClernand left Washington, *The New York Times* editorialized, "Gen. McClernand has inspired the whole West with enthusiastic faith in his courage, uniting energy with military skill." By the end of November, McClernand organized forty-two infantry regiments, six artillery batteries, and six cavalry regiments. Nearly all were green recruits, so he proposed drawing 25 percent of his final force from Grant's army, including specific veteran officers and regiments.

Grant, surprised by reports of troops passing through Cairo and Memphis assigned to McClernand, sought clarification from Halleck: "Am I to understand that I lay still here while an Expedition is fitted out from Memphis?"

Forced to decide between McClernand and Grant, Halleck made his choice. "You have command of all troops sent to your department, and have permission to fight the enemy where you please." This time Halleck came down firmly behind Grant.

IN PUSHING FARTHER south, Grant encountered more fleeing slaves. "Citizens south of us are leaving their homes & Negroes coming in by wagon loads." They would gather by the road, hoping they might be pressed into service as servants by passing soldiers.

Grant faced a humanitarian crisis. The army was prohibited from expelling slaves from their camps when they came in voluntarily. In September, he had sent slaves to Cairo, Illinois, and Columbus, Kentucky, where charitable groups took them up north. But in the North, Democrats spread fears that Southern slaves were about to throng Northern cities and take away jobs. Grant could absorb some of the men as workers; he could use others to pick cotton on abandoned plantations and farms. But still they came.

On November 13, Grant set in motion a new policy to deal with these contrabands. He authorized Chaplain John Eaton of the Twenty-seventh Ohio to assume charge of the slaves who came into camp.

Eaton, born in New Hampshire and a graduate of Dartmouth College, had become superintendent of schools in Toledo, Ohio, in 1856. He left in 1859 to study for the ministry at Andover Theological Seminary. Upon his graduation in 1861, he immediately enlisted in the Union army. Friends described Eaton as "filled with the true missionary spirit."

Not sure he wanted the assignment, and believing he might be laughed at by fellow soldiers for working with newly liberated slaves, Eaton hurried to Grant's headquarters. He arrived "with such unpleasant memories of former experiences with our commanders." By contrast, in their interview Eaton found himself struck by this commander's bearing of "moderation and simplicity."

Both Grant and Eaton knew that many white soldiers, harboring racist stereotypes, believed slaves would not work on their own. Grant did not accept this assumption. As Eaton recited some problems he was sure he would face, especially soldiers resenting him for employing slaves who had worked for them for free, Grant assured Eaton that he would stand behind him. Eaton accepted.

Starting south along the route of the Mississippi Central Railroad, Grant had another foe to contend with—men within his own army whose wanton behavior he struggled to restrain. Angered by guerrilla activities, soldiers took out their resentment on the local populace. Their actions became indiscriminate as they foraged for food and supplies from Union as well as Confederate sympathizers. They delighted in provoking slave owners through such thievery as taking dresses from women and presenting them to slave women. Union soldiers demolished furniture, defaced family photographs, and went so far as to dump excrement within homes.

Grant tried to rein in these barbarous activities by issuing Special Field Orders No. 1 to combat "gross acts of vandalism" reported to him: "Houses have been plundered and burned down, fencing destroyed and citizens frightened without inquiry as to their status in this Rebellion." His response: "Such acts are punishable with death by the Articles of War and existing orders." Furthermore, "They are calculated to destroy the efficiency of an army and to make open enemies of those who before if not friends were at least noncombatants."

ON NOVEMBER 13, Grant's cavalry seized Holly Springs, Mississippi, with little resistance. Troops put up their white tents in groves around the town. Believing his long supply line vulnerable, Grant decided to make Holly Springs his advance supply base. Mountains of provisions arrived in succeeding days. Julia joined him, taking up residence at the Harvey Washington Walter house, the last of the great Southern mansions built in Holly Springs, completed in 1859.

By December 1, Grant's cavalry crossed the Tallahatchie River and reached Oxford, thirty miles south of Holly Springs. After conferring with Sherman, on December 8 Grant sent Halleck his plan for a two-pronged attack. Sherman would command an expedition down the Mississippi while Grant would approach overland. Grant's intent: He hoped to hold the Confederates in front while Sherman came in from the rear.

Grant now faced a new Confederate leader. John C. Pemberton, a forty-eight-year-old native of Philadelphia, had relieved Earl Van Dorn. Married to a Virginian, Pemberton became one of the few Northern officers who joined the Confederacy—and did so against the wishes of his family.

Pemberton established his headquarters at Jackson, forty-five miles from Vicksburg, on October 14. From the beginning, the brusque Pennsylvanian labored under a dual handicap: for many, his previous military experience did not justify his new command; he could also not escape misgivings over his Northern nativity. He entrenched his smaller army of twenty thousand behind the Yalobusha River at Grenada, 150 miles north of Vicksburg.

In yet another Confederate reconfiguration, Jefferson Davis assigned command of a new Department of the West to Joseph Johnston, now recuperated from wounds he suffered at Seven Pines, Virginia, in May. Davis placed Johnston, small of stature but large of dignity, in charge of an immense territory from the Appalachians to the Mississippi. In the strangeness of the Confederate command structure, Pemberton continued to report to Davis in Richmond.

A MORE IMMEDIATE threat came from an unlikely source—Nathan Bedford Forrest, the only private in the Confederate army who rose to become a general. A striking man of powerful build, with gray-blue eyes and iron-gray hair, Forrest had enlisted in his hometown of Memphis one month before his fortieth birthday. He had no military education—indeed, he despised West Point strategies, which he believed were too defensive—but he knew the territory well.

On December 10, Forrest left Bragg's army and started west across Tennessee. His goal: to so disrupt the Union line of supply and communication that Grant would be forced to withdraw from Mississippi. Forrest's cavalry, some of whom had never been in battle before and were armed only with shotguns and squirrel rifles brought from their homes, willingly followed him wherever he led.

Grant feared the abilities of Nathan Bedford Forrest, who with no military training led his Confederate cavalry in raid after raid against Union positions in the South.

Forrest frightened Grant. He wrote Porter that Forrest was now on the west side of the Tennessee River "with from 5,000 to 10,000 men," an overstatement calculated from reports of alarmed field commanders. Although Forrest picked up recruits as he rode west, he was never able to assemble more than two thousand men at one time. Yet Grant worried that small cavalry detachments, well led, could harass larger forces and inflict considerable damage. Deducing Forrest's goal, Sherman speculated, "I rather suspect it is designed to draw us back from our purpose of going to Vicksburg."

JUST AS FORREST'S cavalry captured Grant's attention, Van Dorn, disgruntled at being replaced at Vicksburg, planned with Pemberton's approval a surprise attack. On the morning of December 16, leading twenty-five hundred cavalry and keeping his mission secret even from his own men, he forded the Yalobusha and rode an indirect route to the northeast.

At dawn on December 20, his cavalry burst into Holly Springs with full-throated rebel yells. On a day locals would call "the Glorious Twentieth," women in nightclothes cheered as Confederates helped themselves to rifles, food, and clothing. Van Dorn's raiders destroyed shops, depots, and warehouses, setting fire to the three-story Masonic building, which exploded in flames that proceeded to burn down the entire north side of the town square. Citizen Martha Strickland wrote her husband, "I don't think the Yanks will be here anymore. There is nothing to come for."

Responding to reports that Julia Grant was lodging at the Walter mansion, local lore told the story of the chivalric Van Dorn ordering that she not be disturbed. The truth: Julia had left the previous evening to join her husband in Oxford.

ON DECEMBER 20, Sherman departed Memphis with an army of twenty thousand men. Sherman had heard reports of Van Dorn's raid before his departure, but with telegraph lines cut, the reports were not yet confirmed. He remained convinced Grant would keep Pemberton's army behind the Yalobusha River, away from Vicksburg. Of immediate concern, with news of McClernand in his mind, Sherman believed himself to be in a race against the Illinoisan and time as he moved rapidly on Vicksburg.

Unknown to Grant and Sherman, on December 19 Davis and Johnston had arrived in Vicksburg. Davis's interest in visiting his native state stemmed from his desire to learn firsthand about the war in the west and reassure those who thought Confederate leaders far away in Richmond had forgotten them. Pemberton was entertaining Davis and Johnston in Grenada when he heard that Grant might be retreating after Van Dorn's raid and that Sherman was advancing down the Mississippi; he immediately dispatched two brigades 135 miles southwest to Vicksburg.

Sherman arrived at the mouth of the Yazoo River, twelve miles northwest of Vicksburg, on Christmas Day. He made plans to proceed directly up the Yazoo to the Mississippi, go ashore, and attack the defenders at Haynes Bluff. Porter's gunboats would supply cover.

Unfortunately, Sherman hadn't considered the vicissitudes of nature. As soon as he disembarked at Chickasaw Bayou on December 26, he found himself battling dense terrain—wooded and wet, intersected by winding streams and bayous, and with few open spaces. Forced to slow down, he used the next two days for reconnaissance, all the while waiting for communication or support from Grant.

Finally, on December 29, Sherman unleashed his four divisions. As Union soldiers tried vainly to ascend the bluffs, defenders fired downhill upon them. Within two hours, the fighting was over. Sherman's forces, even with more than a two-to-one advantage, suffered a violent repulse. Union casualties mounted to 1,776, while the dug-in Confederates suffered only 187.

On January 3, 1863, Sherman wrote Grant, "I assume all responsibility and attach fault to no one." One prong of Grant's two-pronged attack had ended in failure.

FOR GRANT, THE last days of 1862 marked a personal nadir in the war. Halleck telegraphed on December 27, "I think no more troops should at present be sent against Vicksburg. I fear you have already too much weakened your own forces."

A week after the Holly Springs debacle, Grant admitted defeat and prepared to return to Tennessee to regroup. During his withdrawal, cut off from supplies, his army reduced its rations and foraged off the land. "I was amazed at the quantity of supplies the country afforded. It showed that we could have subsisted off the country for two months instead of two weeks." This was a lesson he would employ in the future.

With Sherman's defeat, Grant readied himself for renewed criticism. He brooded to his sister, "I am extended now like a Peninsula into an enemy's country."

But condemnation threatened to engulf him from a different direction. Throughout the fall of 1862, as Grant continued to contend with the problems of illegal trade, complaints mounted against Jewish traders. Although they had lived in the New World since 1654, by 1860 Jews numbered only 150,000 in a population of over 31 million. Their numbers tripled in the 1850s, immigrants arriving from German-speaking states in Europe, even as "nativism," a self-proclaimed movement to protect the interests of native-born citizens, grew popular. Jewish numbers were not large enough to incite the virulent nativism faced by Catholics, but anti-Jewish attitudes were on the rise.

Criticism of Jewish traders permeated the military. Thus Sherman wrote Grant from Memphis, "I found so many Jews and speculators here trading in cotton . . . that I have felt myself bound to stop it." Generals Samuel Curtis, Leonard Ross, and Alvin Hovey all criticized Jewish involvement in the cotton trade. The *New York Tribune* reported Colonel C. Carroll Marsh "has expelled a dozen Jewish cotton buyers for dealing in Southern money and depreciating United States Treasury notes." Although non-Jews participated widely in illegal trading, the military newspaper in Corinth called Jews "sharks" feeding upon soldiers.

In the midst of this growing anti-Jewish feeling, Grant issued General Orders No. 11 on December 17, 1862. Article 1 stated, "The Jews, as a class, violating every regulation of trade established by the Treasury Department . . . are hereby expelled" from his department. The words *Jews, as a class* leapt off the page as Grant, fueled by his frustration with particular Jewish businessmen, issued an indictment of Jews as a people.

In the tumult that followed, a story circulated that the order had been written by a member of Grant's staff, perhaps Rawlins, or that the word *Jew* was simply shorthand for shrewd merchants. No. Grant alone had been responsible for the sweeping order.

Lincoln may not have initially seen the order, for he spent the last days of December defending the Emancipation Proclamation he was scheduled to sign on January 1, 1863. The *Memphis Daily Bulletin,* a Lincoln supporter, printed the documents one above the other, portraying the irony of the president freeing the slaves while General Grant expelled the Jews.

When Halleck learned of the order, he was not sure what to make of it. He telegraphed Grant on January 4, "A paper purporting to be a Genl Order No. 11 issued by you Dec 17 has been presented here," then got straight to the point: "If such an order has been issued, it will be immediately revoked."

When Congress reconvened in January, Democrats, fresh off gains in the November elections, sought to win political points with criticisms of Grant's order.

Halleck informed Grant of Lincoln's sentiments: "The President has no objection to your expelling traders & Jew peddlers, which I supposed was the object of your order, but as it in terms prescribed an entire religious class, some of whom are fighting in our ranks, the President deemed it necessary to revoke it."

The impetus for issuing this public order may have been partly personal. Grant's father arrived in Holly Springs in December intent on cashing in on the profitable cotton trading. Acting as agent for Mack & Brothers, a prominent Cincinnati Jewish clothing manufacturer, Jesse promised to get a permit in return for 25 percent of the profits.

When Grant learned of his father's plan, he was furious, both at Jesse's attempt to profit once again from his son's position and at the Mack brothers, who he believed had used his father. Grant turned down the request and sent his father and the Macks packing on the first train north.

Whatever the motivation—from harboring anti-Semitic feelings to long-standing anger at illegal trading by Northern speculators who ended up aiding the South—Grant's colossal misstep would haunt him for years to come, even as he would try to come to terms with what he had done.

· · ·

AT THE BEGINNING of 1863, the protracted rumors about General John McClernand were confirmed. He reached Memphis on December 29 with his new wife, Minerva Dunlap, twenty-four years his junior, expecting to meet Grant. Instead, he found a letter from Grant assigning him command of one of four corps "to form a part of the expedition on Vicksburg." Upset, McClernand replied, "I regret that the expectation I would find you here is disappointed." To be sure Grant understood his authority, McClernand attached documents from Halleck and Stanton, along with Lincoln's "endorsement."

McClernand arrived fifteen miles north of Vicksburg on December 31. On January 2, 1863, he invited Sherman to meet with him. The next evening, McClernand and Sherman joined Porter on his flagship to discuss strategy.

Two days later, McClernand, who outranked Sherman, issued General Orders No. 1, by which he took command of Sherman's force, now designated the Army of the Mississippi, signaling its independence from Grant's Army of the Tennessee. Sherman reluctantly accepted command of one of the two newly created corps.

GRANT RETURNED TO his headquarters at Memphis on January 10, displeased. He wrote McClernand that same day: "Since General Sherman left here I have been unable to learn anything official from the expedition you now command. Your wants and requirements all have to be guessed at." With this letter, Grant accomplished two ends: he indicated his willingness to support McClernand, and in a reprimand he reminded McClernand that he, Grant, had ultimate command of the mission.

Though many believed Grant shared Halleck's animosity toward McClernand, the fact was that during this period he respected the Illinois political general, appreciating how well he had fought with Grant at Belmont, Fort Donelson, and Shiloh. Nevertheless, he told McClernand in the strongest terms, "This expedition must not fail. If there is force enough within the limits of my control to secure a certain victory at Vicksburg they will be sent there."

Despite Grant's wishes, McClernand set his initial sights on Arkansas Post, fifty miles upstream from the mouth of the Arkansas River. From the recently completed Fort Hindman, Confederates hindered shipping on the Mississippi. The McClernand-Sherman army attacked on January 12. They won a battle against Confederate general Thomas Churchill at a cost of approximately one thousand Union casualties; about five thousand Confederates surrendered.

Grant, not waiting to hear the results, wrote Halleck, "Genl. McClernand has . . . gone on a wild goose chase." He also fired off a telegram to McClernand: "I do not approve of your move on the 'Post of Arkansas' while the other [Vicksburg] is in abeyance. It will lead to the loss of men without result." Grant remonstrated that everything should be directed "to the accomplishment of the one great result, the capture of Vicksburg."

Halleck, out of patience, wrote Grant on January 12, "You are hereby authorized to relieve General McClernand from the command of the expedition against Vicksburg, giving it to the next in rank or taking it yourself."

Halleck's telegram solved Grant's deepening dilemma. He knew McClernand had Lincoln's blessing, but now he knew he had Halleck's confidence. Within twenty-four hours, he wrote James McPherson, "It is my present intention to command the expedition down the river in person." No more double-pronged attack; instead he would lead a single thrust.

VICKSBURG SAT ATOP high bluffs on an abrupt hairpin turn on the east side of the Mississippi River. Methodist circuit rider Newitt Vick began selling lots of empty land covered by walnut trees in 1819. By January 1862, the town boasted a population of forty-five hundred, larger than the capital, Jackson. The town's economic prosperity grew from its strategic port. Now, in January 1863, Vicksburg's terraces of yellowish soil bristled with gray artillery positions, including thirty-seven large-caliber cannon and thirteen small fieldpieces. Nine earthen forts protected openings for the Southern Railroad of Mississippi and six roads.

Admiral David Farragut, David Porter's foster brother, had mounted an attack on Vicksburg in the summer of 1862. When asked to surrender, James Autry, Confederate post commander, responded, "I have to state that Mississippians don't know, and refuse to learn, how to surrender to an enemy." In response, Farragut and Porter bombarded the Confederate batteries throughout June and July, but Vicksburg's dogged defenders proved difficult to defeat, and eventually the Union navy retreated. If in 1862 Vicksburg had managed to turn back Farragut in the summer and Sherman in the winter, what strategies could Grant employ in 1863 to breach the tenacity of its defenses?

On his way south, Grant conferred with Porter, McClernand, and Sherman at Napoleon, Arkansas. Sherman and Porter confided in him that "there was not sufficient confidence felt in Gen. McClernand as a commander, either by the Army or Navy, to insure him success." Yet Grant added a sentence in his communication with Halleck that says much about his sense of decency: "As it is my intention to command in person, unless otherwise directed, there is no special necessity of mentioning this matter."

On January 28, Grant set up headquarters at Young's Point at the lower end of Milliken's Bend. Along the lower Mississippi, January and February can be depressing months. The winter of 1863 brought far more rain than usual, flooding the few dry openings that soldiers sought for their tents.

As Grant studied his maps, he saw that the Confederates were close as the bird flies but far militarily because of their massive defenses. He contemplated several options.

His first plan called for digging a canal that would traverse the base of the slender peninsula of land at De Soto Point, where the Mississippi curled across from Vicksburg. With a canal, boats could pass the city's defenses. Grant ordered four thousand of Sherman's soldiers and two thousand freedmen to begin digging out the mud. Manning picks and shovels, soldiers toiled to build what they called "the ditch." Halleck wrote Grant to convey encouragement from a higher power: "Direct your attention particularly to the canal proposed across the point. The President attaches much importance to this." Lincoln, who navigated the Mississippi to New Orleans at age nineteen and again at twenty-two, had been fascinated by engineering projects all his life.

Despite great efforts, the Mississippi jeered at those who thought they could divert her powerful course, so in the end, Grant gave up on "the ditch."

Next he explored building a channel from Lake Providence so boats could travel through bayous and rivers to come out at the mouth of the Red River 150 miles south of Vicksburg. It did not take him long to decide the narrow channels, built up with fallen cypress branches, made the plan impractical.

Then he sent the newest appointment to his staff, twenty-five-year-old James H. Wilson, chief of topographical engineers, to Helena, Arkansas, to explore blasting an opening through Yazoo Pass. The breach would create an inlet from the Mississippi through Moon Lake, one mile east of the river and two hundred river miles north of Vicksburg. Wilson led a work party of four hundred men wielding axes, shovels, and picks. Explosions sent water cascading into the widened opening. Porter's boats moved through the breach, but Pemberton, anticipating Grant's move, instructed his troops to fell cottonwoods and sycamores to obstruct the inlet, forcing Porter to turn back.

Finally, Porter took his gunboats up the Yazoo and turned north into Steele's Bayou, thereby avoiding Confederate artillery on the bluffs. Grant went along for the first thirty miles. Porter posted sailors with brooms to sweep snakes off his vessels; when they reached Deer Creek, fleeing slaves from plantations swarmed his boats. But Confederates had cut down trees behind the boats in an attempt to trap Porter's flotilla. Porter, covering the hulls of his boats with slime to keep them from being boarded by Confederates, was forced to head back down the channel.

By the end of March, Grant and Porter learned that what looked possible on maps could turn out quite differently in the treacherous Mississippi Delta. Although Grant's attempts were criticized as half-baked schemes, he believed they served two important purposes. First, he lured Pemberton into a continual guessing game about his intentions, forcing him to move his men around to defend each option. Second, "I let the work go on, believing employment was better than idleness for the men."

HALLECK PLACED HIS bet on Grant even as other commanders disappointed. Ambrose Burnside, after the defeat at Fredericksburg in December and an abortive "Mud March" in January 1863, was replaced by "Fighting Joe" Hooker, the fourth commander to lead the Army of the Potomac in less than two years. And Rosecrans, with a reputation for bold action, unaccountably succumbed to caution on his way to Chattanooga; having defeated Braxton Bragg in January at the Battle of Stones River near Murfreesboro, Tennessee, he suddenly just . . . stopped.

With these military frustrations as a backdrop, Halleck wrote Grant, "The eyes and hopes of the whole country are now directed to your army. In my opinion the opening of the Mississippi river will be to us of more advantage than the capture of forty Richmonds. We shall omit nothing which we can do to assist you."

IN THE SPRING of 1863, Grant encountered a new challenge. When Lincoln signed the Emancipation Proclamation on January 1, 1863, a provocative *Vanity Fair* cartoon depicted "The New Place," but the caption, in African American dialect, wondered aloud what this would really mean for freed slaves. Critics pointed out that nearly all the slaves emancipated were outside the reach of the Union army. But the proclamation did contain this promise: "And I further declare and make known, that such persons of suitable condition, will be received into the armed service of the United States to garrison forts, positions, stations, and other places, and to man vessels of all sorts in said service." Did Lincoln intend to have freed slaves join the Union army? The majority of Northern soldiers did not sign up to free black slaves or to fight beside them.

But if emancipation could be achieved, it would be by the marching feet of a liberating army. Until now, the Civil War had been a white man's war. Most Americans had forgotten that African Americans fought in both the Revolutionary War and the War of 1812. The regular army, including West Point, did not recruit or enroll African Americans.

As Radical Republicans, abolitionists, and black leaders promoted re-

Vanity Fair *published this cartoon only days before Lincoln signed the Emancipation Proclamation: it portrays an African American who, turning his back on the door of slavery, walks skeptically toward the door of emancipation.*

cruiting black troops, the president was being encouraged by his secretary of war. In the months after the Emancipation Proclamation, he began to consider the arming of black troops.

To advance this new policy, Stanton dispatched Adjutant General Lorenzo Thomas to the Mississippi Valley. The primary purpose of Thomas's spring trip was to speak with Grant and his generals, inspect the troops, and inaugurate arming black soldiers. A second unannounced purpose was to report back to Stanton his assessment of whether Grant was carrying out the new policy.

Halleck wrote Grant on March 30 to tip him off about Thomas's purpose. The tone of the letter—"I write this unofficial letter, simply as a personal friend, and as a matter of friendly advice"—signaled how much had changed between them. The administration was embarking on a new policy toward former slaves, and Thomas was coming west to see if Union generals were adhering to this plan. The enrollment of blacks would both enlarge the army and free white soldiers for frontline duty.

Halleck wanted Grant to know, "It has been reported to the Secretary of War that many officers of your command not only discourage the negroes from coming under our protection, but, by ill-treatment, force them to return to their masters." He insisted, "Whatever may be the opinion of an officer in regard to the wisdom of the measures adopted . . . it is the duty of every one to cheerfully and honestly endeavor to carry out the measures so adopted."

FOREWARNED WAS FOREARMED. Grant put his shoulder to Union policy. He responded to an inquiry from Frederick Steele, a West Point classmate now under his command, who wrote that "a great many negroes have followed the command." Steele wanted "instructions as to what shall be done with these poor creatures."

Grant's response showed he had accepted Halleck's counsel: "Rebellion has assumed that shape that it can only terminate by the complete subjugation of the South or the overthrow of the Government." He instructed Steele, "You will also encourage all negroes, particularly middle aged males to come within our lines."

Thomas came, saw, and reported to Stanton, "This army is in very fine shape, unusually healthy, and in good heart." By the end of his trip, the usually restrained Thomas gushed he was now "a Grant man all over." Grant had made clear to all that he embraced the rights and opportunities of African Americans in his theater of command.

·   ·   ·

AT THE SAME time that Thomas was sent to report indirectly on Grant, Stanton dispatched Charles A. Dana on a direct assessment mission. The Harvard-educated Dana, previously managing editor of the *New York Tribune,* had been appointed assistant secretary of war in 1863, which qualified him to monitor payroll services in the field—and it was for this purpose, ostensibly, that he had been dispatched to Grant's headquarters. But his mandate included one other directive: to "give such information as would enable Mr. Lincoln and [Stanton] to settle their minds as to Grant." Lincoln had made it a policy to either invite his key generals to the Executive Mansion or visit them in the field. Since he had done neither with Grant, a proxy was sent instead.

Dana arrived at Grant's headquarters on April 6. Grant, sensing his visitor's mission from the start, welcomed him, expressing a willingness "to show me the inside of things" and making him almost one of the staff.

In his fifteen years with the *Tribune,* Dana had met all kinds of leaders—political, business, and military—but he said he'd never met anyone like Grant. As Dana watched and listened, he began to send back reports praising the western general. "An uncommon fellow—the most modest, the most disinterested, and the most honest man I ever knew, with a temper nothing could disturb." Dana found Grant to be "not an original or brilliant man, but sincere, thoughtful, deep, and gifted with courage that never faltered." Stanton trusted Dana's judgment; as a result, he placed more confidence in Grant.

AS THE UNSEASONABLY wet winter finally turned to spring, Sherman worried that Grant, who did not concern himself with politics, did not understand the political pressure mounting on Lincoln and Stanton with respect to the Vicksburg Campaign. Cadwallader Washburn, Wisconsin congressman and now a major general of volunteers in Grant's army, did understand. He wrote his congressman brother Elihu Washburne (the brothers spelled their last names differently), "All Grant's schemes have failed. He knows he has got to do something or off goes his head."

On April 1, Grant invited Sherman and Porter to join him on a reconnaissance beneath Haynes' Bluff to consider one last option to turn Vicksburg's right flank. After observing miles of Confederate earthworks, Grant told Porter such an attack "would be attended with immense sacrifice of life, if not with defeat."

Instead, Grant announced a bold new plan. His strategy called for turning Pemberton's left flank by placing his men east of Vicksburg on a high, dry plateau. He would come in by the back door. He wrote later that he'd had the plan "in contemplation the whole winter." Since he could not put it into operation "until the waters receded," and did not want to diminish his winter options, "I did not therefore communicate this plan" to anyone.

To accomplish this new strategy, he had to first get his army and his supplies south of Vicksburg. From there he would attempt to cross the Mississippi, but he knew that the task of running Vicksburg's miles of batteries could court disaster.

Sherman strongly opposed Grant's plan and suggested he ask his corps commanders for their opinions. Sherman knew that McPherson and nearly all the corps commanders opposed Grant's plan as too risky. He advised Grant to pull up stakes, move back to Memphis, and start south again with the old plan of a two-pronged attack.

Grant's response to his best friend revealed his resolve. He told Sherman that if he moved back to Memphis, "it would discourage the people so much that bases of supplies would be of no use."

Grant turned to the one senior commander who did support him: he entrusted McClernand with the task of marching his Thirteenth Corps down the Walnut Bayou road to New Carthage, thirty miles below Vicksburg. If Grant's officers opposed his plan, they were even more against McClernand leading the way. Sherman wrote his brother, "McClernand is a dirty dog, consumed by a burning desire for personal renown."

To carry out his new plan, Grant asked Porter—he could not *order* his navy equal—to run his gunboats along with transports past Vicksburg's batteries. Twice before, single gunboats had run Vicksburg's batteries with no significant damage, but sending a large flotilla presented a completely different challenge. By now Porter did not hesitate to support this West Point general, but he cautioned, "I am ready to co-operate with you in the matter of landing troops on the other side, but you must recollect that, when the gunboats once get below, we give up all hopes of getting them up again." Porter meant that the "turtles," traveling at the slow speed of six knots, would not be able to return upstream.

PEMBERTON REMAINED UNCERTAIN of Grant's plans and thus took heart from reports in early April that Union transports were seen steaming up the Mississippi. He telegraphed Richmond, "I think most of Grant's forces are being withdrawn to Memphis." Four days later, he wrote Simon Bolivar Buckner, Grant's vanquished foe at Fort Donelson who was now commander of the Department of the Gulf, "I am sending troops to General Johnston, being satisfied that a large portion of Grant's army is reinforcing Rosecrans."

Union transports did indeed head up the Mississippi—empty. Responding to a request from Rosecrans, Grant discharged some of the smaller transports no longer needed once he had abandoned his unsuccessful operations in the bayous.

On Thursday, April 16, Major William Watts planned a ball in Vicksburg to celebrate the welcome news of the Union departures. After months of trepidation, music and dancing would be the order of the night. Many artillery officers planned to attend.

That same afternoon, Porter assembled his flotilla. The mission was considered so dangerous that the troops would be carried only in the gunboats, not in the steamers. Sailors lashed the gunboats with logs alongside the engines to protect them from shells. They fastened coal barges to the sides of the transports that would be facing the shore batteries and stacked them with hay and cotton to shield their machinery.

At eight forty-five p.m., Porter boarded his flagship, *Benton.* His pennant, with its white star and blue field, blew in the breeze. Julia had arrived recently with Ulysses Jr. and joined her husband and young Fred on the deck of the *Henry von Phul* to observe the unfolding drama.

At nine p.m., two white lanterns gave the signal for the flotilla to begin. Porter led the way. Henry Walke, in his new ironclad, the enormous *Lafayette,* followed. The Grants watched as in single file, fifty yards apart, followed the *General Price,* a captured Confederate ram; the gunboats *Louisville, Mound City, Pittsburg,* and *Carondelet;* the transports *Forest Queen, Silver Wave,* and *Henry Clay,* together carrying three hundred thousand rations for McClernand's soldiers; and the new ironclad, *Tuscumbia,* bringing up the rear. Porter described them as "so many phantom vessels." The boats ran with their lights out beneath the moonless night sky. Captains steered each vessel slightly to the port of the one ahead to avoid collisions. The hatches in the boats' fire rooms were closed, the smoke rerouted through vents in the paddle box.

After turning the tip of De Soto Point, approaching the horseshoe bend in the river, Porter believed the boats might float past Vicksburg unnoticed. Suddenly a bright light illuminated the sky. Buildings in the village of De Soto on the Louisiana side were set on fire, including the depot of the Vicksburg, Shreveport and Texas Railroad station. Vicksburg appeared to be on fire also but was only alight with tar barrels burning along the bank to illuminate the river. Music and dancing at the Watts ball ceased. First small arms, then brass fieldpieces, and finally elevated large guns fired down upon the ghostly Union flotilla.

Immediately, every boat fended for itself. Gunboats opened fire from their bow guns and port batteries. Transports made for the Vicksburg shoreline, gambling that if they hugged the bluffs, the terraced guns would not be able to fire down upon them accurately. The ironclads, infamous for their poor steering abilities, found that the combination of barges lashed to their sides and capricious Mississippi currents made them thrash about like giant gray rhinoceroses in the water. Five of the eight gunboats at various times momentarily headed back upstream. The steamboat *Henry Clay,* hit by a Confederate shell, burst into flames; the crew and captain abandoned ship but were picked up by Union sailors stationed in yawls on the river. The fire on the *Henry Clay* actually became a diversion that benefited the remaining vessels. As the boats moved in close to the shoreline, the *Benton,* closing to forty yards, fired point-blank into water's edge buildings, blowing them apart.

Shortly after midnight, the flotilla, with bunches of cotton ablaze, drifted to safety below the city. The Confederates fired more than five hundred rounds, and the Union boats suffered at least seventy hits. Grant wrote later, "The sight was magnificent, but terrible." His bold new plan had succeeded.

To help get his army across the Mississippi River below Vicksburg, Grant asked Admiral David Dixon Porter to run the batteries past the Confederate fortress.

· · ·

To DISTRACT PEMBERTON from his plan to attack Vicksburg on the Mississippi River, Grant sent Colonel Benjamin H. Grierson with three regiments of seventeen hundred cavalrymen on a daring raid through Mississippi's interior. Grierson was an unlikely hero, an Illinois music teacher who disliked horses, having been kicked in the face by a horse as a child. Starting from southern Tennessee on April 17, Grierson and his raiders arrived at Newton Station, sixty-five miles east of Jackson, on April 24. Rather than turning back, Grierson's horse soldiers plunged farther south, ripping up tracks, tearing down telegraph wires, burning bridges and water towers, fighting four engagements, and evading three converging columns of Confederate cavalry. Finally, on May 3, after a nonstop sixteen-day, six-hundred-mile raid, they reached the Union line at Baton Rouge, Louisiana, the second Confederate capital captured by the Union. Grierson's real accomplishment was not the track and telegraph wire he tore down, but the ruckus he stirred up. He forced Pemberton, who took personal control of the effort to stop him, to take his eyes off Grant's movement. Grant telegraphed Halleck, "Grierson knocked the heart out of the state."

AFTER THE SUCCESSFUL running of the Vicksburg batteries, Grant, accompanied by eight staff officers and twenty cavalry, repositioned his headquarters downriver. His son Fred described what happened when the large party came to a slough with a narrow bridge over which a wagon was just then passing slowly: "My father made one of his daring leaps, putting his horse at the opposite bank, which he just managed to reach." Twenty-two years after his famous jump at West Point, Grant had lost little of his bold horsemanship.

At New Carthage, with McClernand's four divisions arrived, it became clear there would not be enough dry ground to provide a staging area for the thousands of men involved in crossing the Mississippi. Grant also concluded that McClernand's men could not be supplied by a wagon train traveling over "an almost impassable road," so he decided to run the batteries again.

With Porter downstream, Clark Lagow, one of Grant's staff officers, volunteered to lead a second mission. With no gunboats, the civilian crews refused to serve on the unarmed transports. The call went out for army volunteers. "Black Jack" Logan, leading his Seventeenth Division, stepped forward. He barked, "I want no faltering. If any man leaves his post, I want him shot."

Five stern-wheeler steamers and one side-wheeler, the *Tigress* of Shiloh renown, with twelve barges, started on the evening of April 22. They carried a main cargo of six hundred thousand rations. This time, as the steamers rounded De Soto Point, Vicksburg was waiting. The boats and their army crews received a hail of fire—391 rounds—sustaining far more losses than on April 16. The *Tigress,* carrying all the medical supplies, and half the barges were sunk.

As GRANT'S OPERATION downstream slowed, he ordered yet another diversion. On April 27, he wired Sherman to begin a feint at Snyder's Bluff, near where he had been repulsed four months earlier. "The effect of a heavy demonstration in that direction would be good as far as the enemy is concerned, but I am loath to order it." He explained, "It would be hard to make our own troops understand that only a demonstration was intended that our people at home would characterize it as a repulse." Confident in Sherman's judgment, Grant wrote, "I leave it to you whether to make such a demonstration."

Sherman, still skeptical about Grant's decision to attack Vicksburg's right flank, responded, "The troops will all understand the purpose and not be hurt by the repulse. The people of the country must find out the truth as best they can." He saluted: "You are engaged in a hazardous enterprise, and, for good reason, wish to divert attention; that is sufficient for me, and it shall be done."

Sherman held up his end of the bargain. On April 28 and 29, gunboats and transports moved up the Yazoo, then troops disembarked and put on a good show—making it seem there were many more. Pemberton shifted three thousand troops to counter what he thought was a second full-scale assault on Haynes' Bluff.

As APRIL DREW to a close, Grant sought to balance confidence and impatience. He informed Sherman that he and Porter had made a reconnaissance of the Confederate fortifications and batteries at Grand Gulf on the Mississippi side of the river. Grand Gulf had harassed the Union navy and posed a threat to Grant's plan to come at Vicksburg through its back door. "My impressions are that if an attack can be made within the next two days the place will easily fall." Although Grant was confident in Sherman, and increasingly so in James McPherson, he had been growing more impatient with McClernand.

Grant might turn a blind eye to McClernand's outsize ego, but not his procrastination. His impatience is evident in an April 12 letter to McClernand: "It is my desire that you should get possession of Grand Gulf at the earliest practicable moment. Concentrate your entire corps there with all rapidity." The observant Dana, alarmed, wrote Stanton on April 25, "I am sorry to report that there is much apparent confusion in McClernand's command, especially about his staff and headquarters, and that the movement is delayed to some extent by that cause." Dana was "astonished" McClernand "was planning to carry his bride with her servants, and baggage along with him"—all of which was forbidden.

With movement on Grand Gulf still delayed, Grant met with McClernand on Porter's flagship, where he ordered him "to embark his men without losing a moment." By the following morning, still sensing little movement, Dana reported that Grant "wrote to McClernand a very severe letter." When Grant discovered later in the day that McClernand's men were indeed finally moving into place, "he did not send" the reprimand.

ON APRIL 29, Grant prepared to launch the most ambitious American amphibious assault prior to World War II. From the river staging area Hard Times, ten thousand men boarded steamers, barges, flatboats, and yawls and waited behind the Coffee Point peninsula for Porter's assault to begin. If the gunboats were successful, Grant's army would cross the Mississippi and swing around to the east toward Vicksburg. Grant's spy network told him that because of the diversionary actions of Grierson and Sherman, Confederate pleas for reinforcements had gone unheeded. Nonetheless, he knew Porter disagreed with him about the strength of the Grand Gulf defenses commanded by Vicksburg's best general, John S. Bowen, Grant's former neighbor at Hardscrabble.

At eight A.M., Porter led his seven ironclads in an attack that Grant observed from the tug *Ivy*.

Porter's gunboats fired more than twenty-five hundred rounds. Grant was wrong and Porter right about the strength of Grand Gulf's defenses. An Iowa soldier wrote, "The sight was grand, terrible . . . the circling shells, the deafening and ceaseless detonations, the black, diminutive fleet, the batteries covering the face of the bluff, tier upon tier, belching forth streams of flame." After five hours, the Confederates, with only thirteen guns, fought the Federals, with eighty-one guns, to a standstill.

At one fifteen, Porter ended the bombardment. Rejoining Porter, Grant encountered a scene he would never forget: "The sight of the mangled and dying men which met my eye as I boarded the ship was sickening."

. . .

GRANT MAY HAVE been stymied, but he was far from deterred. Immediately, he devised a new plan: McClernand's troops would march nine miles downstream to Disharoon's Plantation and attempt to cross the river to Rodney, Mississippi.

In the middle of the night, while Federal troops were still a few miles above Disharoon's Plantation, a slave was brought to Grant. He learned from this old man that there was a good road from Bruinsburg to Port Gibson. Grant knew from experience that a local person could mislead Union forces, but he trusted the word of the slave. He changed his Vicksburg Campaign plan yet again.

Morning light on April 30 would bring the long-delayed, long-hoped-for challenge of crossing the milewide Mississippi to Bruinsburg to mount an attack on Vicksburg.

CHAPTER 17

Vicksburg

Since General Grant commenced to move his columns he has
displayed great tact and skill, together with immense energy and nerve.
The passage of this army over the Mississippi River and up to
this point is one of the most masterly movements known in the
history of any warfare and it is a success.

—GEORGE B. BOOMER to his sister AMELIA, May 6, 1863

On April 30, 1863, two prodigious Union armies crossed two rivers of
destiny. Regiments of "Fighting Joe" Hooker's eastern Army of the
Potomac forded the Rappahannock River to attack Robert E. Lee's Army
of Northern Virginia at the small hamlet of Chancellorsville, Virginia.
On the same morning, Grant's western Army of the Tennessee began
crossing the Mississippi River to set off for the back door of Vicksburg,
Mississippi, where Pemberton's troops waited.

At eight A.M., Grant squeezed into the small wheelhouse of David
Porter's flagship, *Benton*. Sensing the tension in his soldiers, he ordered
the ship's band to play "The Red, White, and Blue" to steady morale as
the fleet fell into line. In the middle of the muddy waters, Grant peered
anxiously at the bluffs rising to the east of Bruinsburg, Mississippi, not
knowing who might lie behind them as the first boats approached the
tree-lined shore.

As Grant surveyed the land stretching beyond the opposite shore of
the Mississippi, no army appeared to contest the crossing. "I felt a degree
of relief scarcely ever equaled since," he remembered. "I was on dry
ground on the same side of the river with the enemy. All the campaigns,
labors, hardships and exposures from the month of December previous
to this time that had been made and endured, were for the accomplishment of this one object."

Belmont, Fort Henry, Fort Donelson, and Shiloh had been won in
days: the campaign for Vicksburg had slogged on month after bitter

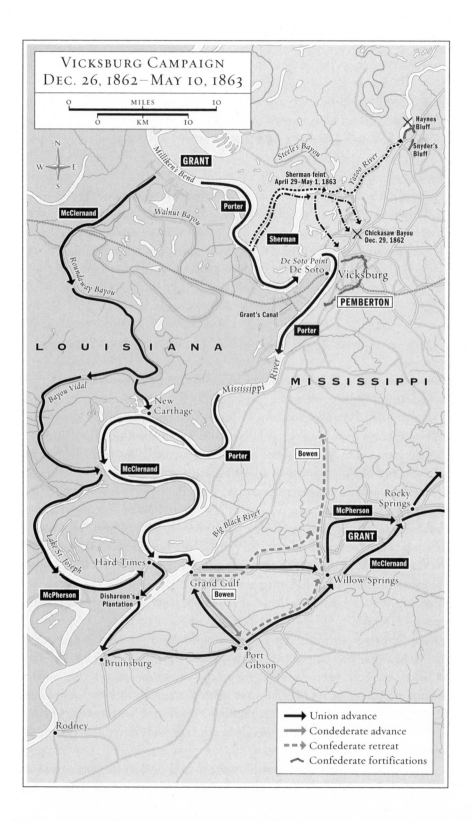

VICKSBURG CAMPAIGN
DEC. 26, 1862–MAY 10, 1863

0 — MILES — 10

0 — KM — 10

N / W / E / S

GRANT

Steele's Bayou

Yazoo River

Haynes Bluff

Snyder's Bluff

Milliken's Bend

Sherman feint
April 29–May 1, 1863

Porter

McClernand

Walnut Bayou

Sherman

Chickasaw Bayou
Dec. 29, 1862

De Soto Point
De Soto

Roundaway Bayou

Vicksburg

PEMBERTON

Grant's Canal

Porter

L O U I S I A N A

River

M I S S I S S I P P I

Bayou Vidal

Mississippi River

New
Carthage

Porter

Bowen

McClernand

Rocky
Springs

Big Black River

McPherson

Lake St. Joseph

Hard Times

GRANT

McClernand

Disharoon's
Plantation

Grand Gulf

Willow Springs

McPherson

Bowen

Bruinsburg

Port
Gibson

Rodney

→ Union advance
→ Condederate advance
- -▶ Confederate retreat
⌢ Confederate fortifications

month. Was this small, garrisoned town on a bluff of the Mississippi River worth the continuing costs?

Grant, the western general, believed if he could defeat the Confederates at Vicksburg, he would divide the Confederacy in two, stopping forever their ability to transport men and matériel on the Mississippi River. He also understood that by crossing the Mississippi, leaving most of his supply lines behind, and approaching Vicksburg by its back door, he would be challenging traditional rules of military engagement. Grant could see the risks in his new strategy, but he looked toward the reward.

BY FOUR P.M., Grant's army had fully landed and begun to march toward Port Gibson, ten miles to the east. Why southeast when Vicksburg lay north? Grant wanted to neutralize Port Gibson—with its hub roads to Jackson and Vicksburg—first. Also, by marching inland rather than pressed up against the river, he gave himself room to maneuver against an enemy who knew this terrain better than he did. The advance would have begun earlier but for another frustrating delay. McClernand had failed to supply his men with three days' worth of rations. Everything stopped while provisions were ferried across the river.

On May 1, Union soldiers found themselves facing their first conflict on enemy land. Bowen's troops had abandoned Grand Gulf to take up positions to defend Port Gibson. Outnumbered four to one, and further handicapped when the only Confederate cavalry unit was pulled away to chase Grierson's horse raiders, Bowen intended to bide his time until reinforcements could arrive from either Vicksburg or Jackson. The terrain, which a former West Point student artist had described as "standing on the edge"—ridges with heavy timber and ravines with snarling vines—made it possible, Grant believed, "for an inferior force to delay, if not defeat, a far superior one."

But not for long. Even after twelve hours in intense heat and humidity, with some men carrying sixty pounds of ammunition while others marched without shoes, Grant's forces overwhelmed the defenders. Entering Port Gibson, with lavender chinaberry trees adorning its main street, Grant remarked that the nearly vacated town was "too beautiful to burn." At the end of an extremely long day, he took time to write a tribute to his men, in the graceful language that had started to mark his reports:

> The army is in the finest health and spirits. Since leaving Milliken's Bend they have marched as much by night as by day, through mud

and rain, without tents or much other baggage, and on irregular rations, without a complaint and with less straggling than I have ever before witnessed. Where all have done so nobly it would be out of place to make invidious distinctions.

Congressman Elihu Washburne, traveling with Grant and knowing the president's anxiety about the campaign for Vicksburg, wrote reassuringly to Lincoln as soon as the troops crossed the Mississippi. He closed with a comment sure to bring a smile to his longtime friend: "I am afraid Grant will have to be reproved for want of style. On this whole move of five days he had neither a horse nor an orderly or servant, a blanket or overcoat or clean shirt, or even a sword. His entire baggage consists of a tooth brush."

The next day, Grant returned to Grand Gulf. He expressed gratitude for some clean navy underwear given him by one of Porter's officers. On the *Benton* he found accumulated mail, including a letter written more than three weeks earlier from Nathaniel Banks, a political general in command of the Department of the Gulf. In response to a suggestion from Lincoln that either Grant move south to help Banks in his attempts to take Port Hudson or Banks move north to cooperate with Grant in attacking Vicksburg, Banks wrote that he looked forward to a joint venture of the two armies but could not promise more than twelve thousand troops, and not before he had captured Port Hudson, Louisiana, which he estimated would be May 10 at the earliest.

Grant weighed what to do. With two hundred river miles between Vicksburg and Port Hudson and little confidence in Banks's competency, he made a pivotal decision. While Pemberton was off balance, he would seize the initiative and go forward without Banks.

EVEN AFTER GRANT crossed the Mississippi, the Confederates were slow to react. Johnston stayed with Bragg in Chattanooga. Pemberton did not move from Jackson to Vicksburg until May 1. Grant, tracking Southern newspapers, learned that a major reason for the delayed reaction was Grierson's raid. Grant wrote Halleck, "The southern papers and southern people regard it as one of the most daring exploits of the War." Pemberton attempted to collect troops from Grenada, Meridian, and Jackson. He could not call upon Van Dorn, who had been killed in Tennessee on May 7—not in battle, but by an infuriated young doctor who shot him over the inveterate womanizer's attentions to his wife. Pemberton's caution further eroded the already shaky confidence of his troops.

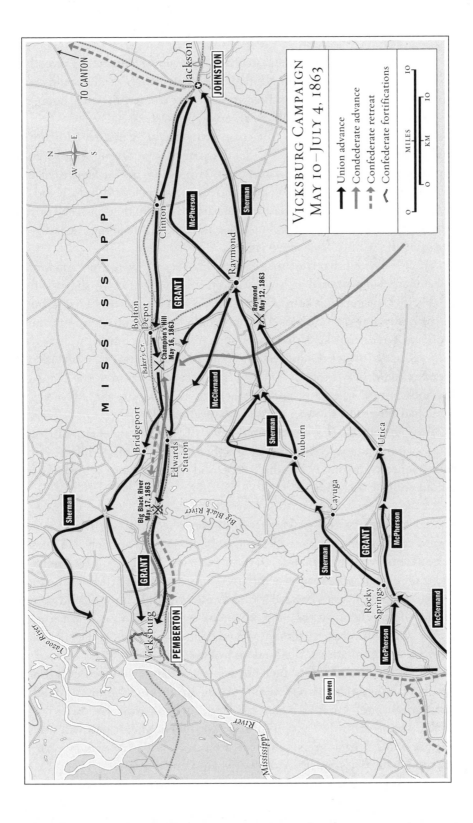

VICKSBURG CAMPAIGN
MAY 10–JULY 4, 1863

Union advance
Confederate advance
Confederate retreat
Confederate fortifications

MILES
KM

MISSISSIPPI

TO CANTON

Jackson   JOHNSTON

McPherson

Sherman

Clinton

Raymond

GRANT

Bolton
Depot

Raymond
May 12, 1863

Baker's Cr.

Champion's Hill
May 16, 1863

Bridgeport

McClernand

Edwards
Station

Sherman

Auburn

Big Black River
May 17, 1863

Utica

Sherman

GRANT

Cayuga

GRANT

McPherson

Sherman

Vicksburg

PEMBERTON

Rocky
Springs

McPherson

McClernand

Bowen

Yazoo River

Big Black River

Mississippi River

Grant made another crucial decision. Instead of advancing directly north toward Vicksburg—a strategy he knew Pemberton would expect—he decided to strike indirectly to the northeast. Seeking counsel from no one, he pressed ahead on his own authority.

On May 3, Grant wrote Sherman, who had returned to Milliken's Bend from his successful ruse at Snyder's Bluff, instructing him to coordinate a train of 120 wagons and fill it with rations: "*One hundred thousand* pounds of bacon, the balance, coffee, sugar, salt, and hard bread." Unable to contain his enthusiasm, Grant urged Sherman to proceed with "celerity"—a word he had recently begun to favor, meaning "speed"— because "the road to Vicksburg is open."

He also wrote Julia to assure her that "Fred is very well, enjoying himself hugely. He has heard balls whistle and is not moved in the slightest by it." Further, he couldn't help offering a tribute to his troops: "I feel proud of the Army at my command. They have marched day and night, without tents and with irregular rations without a murmur of complaint."

At Rocky Springs, Grant read in Southern newspapers that on May 6, Hooker had ordered the last of his Union troops to recross the Rappahannock. Even with superior numbers, guns, and supplies, Hooker's army had suffered a shocking loss at Chancellorsville.

After receiving the devastating news of Hooker's defeat, Lincoln sought an update on Grant. He telegraphed General John A. Dix at Fortress Monroe, Virginia, "Do the Richmond papers have anything about Grand Gulf or Vicksburg?"

GRANT'S DECISION TO strike deep into enemy territory in May forced him to confront the problem of supplying his men and animals. He knew he could not feed more than forty thousand men and thousands of horses and mules, even with a supply line stretching all the way through Grand Gulf back to Milliken's Bend. He also knew how difficult it would be to subsist off the land by foraging in the countryside. Grant, the former farmer, understood the challenge of both land and season. Rather than an array of vast plantations, the land east of the Big Black River offered a hodgepodge of small subsistence farms barely able to grow enough food for the families that owned them. Also, springtime was traditionally "starvation time" for subsistence farmers—autumn crops had been used up and spring crops had just been planted—even when there was not a war going on. Spring green grass was abundant, but a fast-moving army did not have the luxury of letting horses and mules graze.

On May 11, as Grant prepared to move forward toward Vicksburg, he wrote McPherson, "We must fight the enemy before our rations fail," reminding him that "upon one occasion you made two days' rations last seven; we may have to do the same again."

That same day, Halleck shared with Lincoln a cryptic telegram just received from Grant: "You may not hear from me again for several days."

Grant decided to move northeast on a broad front. From the outset, he wanted Pemberton to wonder and worry about his next move. Although possessing numerical superiority, he knew Confederate reinforcements could soon even the odds. He determined to keep the initiative by fighting one army at a time, rather than letting two Confederate armies close in on him.

No May rain had yet fallen in Mississippi. One Union soldier confided to his diary what he and his fellow soldiers experienced: "Water scarce; weather hot; roads dusty; land poor; rations short; houses poor shabby things. Don't like the country."

Grant directed McClernand and Sherman toward Edwards Station, a stop on the Southern Railroad halfway between Vicksburg and Jackson, while McPherson advanced toward Jackson. If Pemberton remained unsure of Federal intentions, Grant, lacking accurate maps and stranded miles east of Vicksburg, struggled to assemble information garnered from escaped slaves, friendly civilians, deserters, newspapers, and captured mail.

On the morning of May 12, "Black Jack" Logan's lead division of McPherson's Seventeenth Corps received musket and artillery fire from John Gregg's Confederates two miles from Raymond, seventeen miles west of Jackson. Entering the town, Union soldiers were surprised to find not the rear guard of Gregg's troops, but a picnic. Raymond ladies had prepared a supper for Gregg's soldiers upon their "return from victory." While Union troops feasted on fried chicken and lemonade, the enemy slipped away to fight another day.

Grant was in Sherman's tent at Fourteen Mile Creek when an excited courier rode up with news of McPherson's victory. At the same time, he received intelligence that reinforcements were arriving in the Mississippi capital, with Johnston expected at any time.

Grant sized up the altered situation and adjusted his plans once again, canceling his orders to attack Edwards Station. Instead, he would attack Jackson—move east to seize the command center of the state before Pemberton knew what he was up to, then turn back west and attack

Vicksburg. He was gambling, and he knew it: if he moved farther east, Pemberton's forces might well attack him in the rear.

But it was a risk he would take.

ON MAY 13, Grant directed McPherson and Sherman to approach Jackson from two directions, while McClernand shielded their rear. Johnston arrived in Jackson on the evening train. Quickly surveying the situation, "Old Joe," recognizing he had only six thousand defenders, telegraphed Confederate secretary of war James Seddon, "I am too late," and retreated from the city.

Marching in on the Clinton–Jackson road in torrential rain, McPherson arrived in the capital of Jefferson Davis's home state at three P.M. His Fifty-ninth Indiana raised the Stars and Stripes over the capitol dome accompanied by loud cheering, the celebrants including young Fred Grant, who had beaten his father into the city. The Union now occupied three Confederate capitals—Nashville, Baton Rouge, and Jackson.

Grant, riding with Sherman on the Raymond–Jackson road, entered Jackson at four P.M. and went directly to the Bowman House, Jackson's leading hotel. While Grant congratulated and conferred with his generals, he received two messages that would prove to be crucial. McPherson delivered the first, received from a courier dressed in a gray Confederate uniform—a spy. Johnston had sent a message to Pemberton at eight forty P.M. on May 13, and Grant now read one of three copies on the afternoon

By the battle for Vicksburg, Grant had become adept at evaluating the different kinds of intelligence information he received many times each day.

of May 14: "It is important to re-establish communications, that you may be reinforced." Once again, Grant's intelligence network of spies had delivered invaluable information, the significance of which Grant immediately understood: he could not allow Pemberton to cross the Big Black River and join with Johnston, who had retreated six miles north to Canton. Johnston concluded, "Time is all-important." But Grant, not the cautious Pemberton, knew the importance of time.

Dana handed Grant the second message. The assistant secretary of war had received a communication from Stanton giving Dana permission to share with Grant all of their recent correspondence. Dana, whose regular communications to Stanton had earned him the moniker "the eyes of the government at the front," had let the secretary of war know of McClernand's various delays. Grant now read what Stanton had written him on May 5:

> General Grant has full and absolute authority to enforce his own commands, and to remove any person who, by ignorance, inaction, or any cause, interferes with or delays his operations. He has the full confidence of the Government, is expected to enforce his authority, and will be firmly and heartily supported; but he will be responsible for any failure to exert his powers.

Grant understood he could deal with McClernand according to his own best lights.

That evening, at the Bowman House, Grant slept on a mattress for the first time in weeks, in the room occupied by Johnston the night before. The next morning, he left Sherman in charge of Jackson with orders to put the torch to all railroad and manufacturing, including an iron foundry, carriage factory, and paint and carpenter shops.

MEANWHILE, ON MAY 13, Pemberton's Confederate army of twenty-three thousand men crossed the Big Black as Grant feared and began to march toward Edwards Station. Unlike Grant, Pemberton did not relish fighting in open country, preferring to operate behind defensive positions; but now he felt he had no choice. He rode east, hoping to disrupt or destroy Grant's line of supply.

It hadn't been an easy decision to make. Throughout the day, Pemberton struggled with Johnston's directive, which Grant had also read, to move his army away from Vicksburg in order to engage Grant. Pemberton called a council of war, a regular practice by which he gave himself protection in decisions he needed to make. His three division command-ers, John Bowen, William Wing Loring, and Carter Stevenson, discussed and debated—all of which took time, the opposite of Johnston's direc-tive.

The council of war argued about several plans, once again exhibiting the strained relations among Pemberton's staff. Pemberton, who consid-ered it his chief mission to defend Vicksburg, expressed wariness at mov-ing farther east, believing such a move would only give Grant opportunity to move around his right flank toward Vicksburg. William Loring, whose empty left sleeve bore testimony to his courage in the Mexican War but whose tongue expressed his disdain for Pemberton, argued for an aggres-sive attack toward Raymond to cut Grant's extended supply line—not knowing that by now Grant had almost shut down his supply line.

As smoke billowed into the sky, Grant left Jackson on the afternoon of May 15, riding ten miles west to Clinton, where he spent the night. Deep in enemy territory, he reviewed his positions. While Johnston hesitated, assuming Grant would not depart Jackson so quickly, Grant prepared to converge the next day on Edwards Station.

Grant was awakened at five A.M. to listen to some important informa-tion carried by two employees of the Southern Railroad. During the night, they had passed through Pemberton's army and were now able to provide a report of a rebel force consisting of eighty regiments with ten batteries of artillery. They estimated the whole force at twenty-five thou-sand men.

Grant wired his three commanders. At five thirty, he directed Sher-man to send one division from Jackson twenty miles west to Bolton: "It is important that great celerity should be shown in carrying out this movement." At five forty, he directed McClernand to move toward Ed-wards Station to "feel the enemy." He assured him, "Our whole force is closely following you," everyone marching with "the utmost celerity." At five forty-five, he wired McPherson to join with McClernand to "se-cure a prompt concentration of our forces." While Pemberton's and Johnston's two armies remained thirty miles apart, Grant concentrated his army on the three roads leading west toward Vicksburg.

Sidney and Matilda Champion had built a modest home on their hill-side property along Baker's Creek on the main road between Jackson and Vicksburg. Halfway between Bolton and Edwards Station, the small hill, about 140 feet high, dominated the rugged terrain of hollows, ridges, and small creeks that fed fast-flowing Baker's Creek. Sid, who fought with Jefferson Davis in the Mexican War, was serving that morning with the Twenty-eighth Mississippi Cavalry at Edwards Station. Matilda, hearing reports of a war too close, was just gathering family heirlooms to leave for her parents in Madison County when Federal soldiers arrived at her tranquil rural homestead.

On that cloudless morning, General Alvin P. Hovey, one of McClernand's division commanders, had come under fire as he and his brigades rode west on the Clinton–Vicksburg road. Hovey, orphaned at fifteen, self-educated, a lawyer from Indiana who was destined to become its governor, had urged his horse forward as the road turned south just before the Champion home, only to discover the enemy posted on the crest of the hill, the highest point for miles around.

Hovey contacted McClernand, who informed Grant at nine forty-five A.M. that the Indianan "finds the enemy strongly posted in his front." The enemy consisted of quick-thinking twenty-nine-year-old South Carolinian Stephen Dill Lee, who, realizing that no one expected Grant's forces to emerge on Pemberton's left flank, had led his Alabamians to the best defensive position possible—the ridge at the top of Sid Champion's hill. McClernand asked Grant, "Shall I hold, or bring on an engagement?"

Grant arrived at the Champion home at ten A.M. Observing Hovey taking a pounding from Confederate artillery, he wrote McClernand, directing him to bring all his forces "as expeditiously as possible but cautiously." As an hour passed, McClernand, usually eager to lead into battle, seemed strangely absent. But how was McClernand to interpret Grant's message? Was he to move "expeditiously" or "cautiously"?

When two of McPherson's divisions arrived—Logan, followed by Marcellus Crocker—Grant ordered an attack. To the sound of bugle calls and drumrolls, Hovey's and Logan's cheering soldiers, with fixed bayonets, began their assault under Grant's close observation. Two divisions, nearly ten thousand men, moved six hundred yards up the hill through the thick underbrush. Fire quickly erupted all along the slope as the Confederates moved in more artillery. By eleven thirty, Grant's men reached the timber beneath the brow of the hill, where firing gave way to hand-to-hand fighting. For the next several minutes, desperate and bloody men fought for control of the crest of Champion Hill.

At twelve thirty-five, Grant wrote McClernand again: "As soon as your command is all in hand throw forward skirmishers and feel the enemy and attack him in force if an opportunity occurs." In McClernand's unexplained lack of movement, is Grant at fault for his lack of directness or clarity? "If" is not "celerity."

Unfortunately, Grant did not realize that the difficult terrain would cause dispatch delays that May morning. McClernand did not receive his second message until after two P.M., but Grant reported, "I sent several messages to him to push forward with all rapidity."

As Hovey's and Logan's forces converged on the top of the hill, with McClernand remaining in place and Sherman still miles away, Pemberton finally responded. He ordered Bowen and Loring to lead a counterattack at Champion Hill. Missouri lawyer Francis M. Cockrell, one of Bowen's brigade leaders, led his brave men in a drive that pushed the Federals back over the crest of Champion Hill.

Grant watched as John Sanborn, one of Crocker's brigade commanders, heard him ask, "Where can McClernand be?" Within an hour, as the Confederates' ammunition began to give out, Grant ordered Crocker, an Iowa lawyer weakened by tuberculosis, to lead a Union surge. Crocker in turn ordered John Sanborn's and George Boomer's brigades up the hill as reinforcements for Hovey and Logan. Assisted by Hovey, who organized sixteen guns near the Champion home, Crocker's brigades succeeded in retaking the crest of Champion Hill.

At dusk on May 16, Grant's army paused—exhilarated but exhausted. That evening, Confederate surgeon John A. Leavy complained to his diary, "To-day proved to the nation the value of a general. Pemberton is either a traitor, or the most incompetent officer in the confederacy. *Indecision, Indecision, Indecision.*"

Champion Hill did prove the value of a general. Operating without Sherman, and with McClernand's Thirteenth Corps largely absent, negotiating both rough terrain and confusing roads, Grant nonetheless surprised Pemberton's forces, taking the fight to the enemy. He won a decisive battle. That evening he wrote Sherman, not yet arrived, "I am of the opinion that the battle of Vicksburg has been fought."

BUT THIS WAS not yet the time for celebration. Grant pressed forward before dawn on the morning of May 17. Pemberton's dispirited soldiers began arriving back in Vicksburg just as morning church services were concluding on Sunday, May 17. Citizens expressed shock. Dora Miller, a Vicksburg woman, unburdened to her diary, "I shall never forget that woeful sight of a beaten, demoralized army that came rushing back—

humanity in the last throes of endurance." Emma Balfour, a leading socialite in Vicksburg, recorded in her diary, "I hope never to witness again such a scene as the return of our routed army!"

PEMBERTON FLED FOR Vicksburg, leaving three brigades east of the Big Black River to hold two bridges. Upon arriving at the Big Black, Grant saw immediately why Pemberton had chosen this position. Field artillery and rifle pits ran for a mile along a muddy bayou that abutted a large bend in the river. The rear guard, though outnumbered, had clear fields of fire against any approaching troops.

Despite their strong position, Pemberton's rear guard did not last long. By nine A.M., the battle had ended. As Confederates retreated, a sharpshooter took aim at someone he believed to be a young soldier. Fred Grant, riding as usual near the action, felt a sharp pain as he was shot in the leg. He cried out, "I am killed!" Grant's aide Clark Lagow called to him, "Move your toes." Fred did and discovered he was still alive.

THE NEXT DAY, Grant approached Vicksburg with a confident attitude, the victories at Champion Hill and the Big Black fresh in his mind. Sherman rode northwest to the area where he had suffered a humiliating defeat in December. This time McPherson took the center, marching along the Jackson–Vicksburg road. McClernand swung to the southwest. Grant believed Pemberton's demoralized troops would not put up much fight and decided to attack Vicksburg before Johnston could assemble a force to aid him. He issued an order that at two P.M. his troops would fire three volleys of artillery from each position. This would be the signal "for a general charge of all the corps along the whole line." When his men charged the labyrinth of trenches and rifle pits, artillery fire lit up the sky as defenders fired on the attacking bluecoats.

Their attack was repulsed. Haste in the assault had not allowed time for proper planning, usually a hallmark of Grant's leadership. Writing later, Grant failed to take responsibility for proceeding too quickly and misjudging the enemy's resolve. Rather, he defended the attack of May 19 as a way of "securing more advanced positions." His losses counted 157 killed and 777 wounded. Confederate losses amounted to no more than 200.

Grant had miscalculated. First, he did not count on the fact that Pemberton's beaten troops, once back in Vicksburg, would become energized to fight even harder. Then, he did not fully appreciate how sophisticated were the defenses constructed by Chief Engineer Samuel Lockett. Also, he did not factor in that Pemberton had two divisions, led by John Forney and Martin L. Smith, well rested, having fought at neither Champion Hill nor the Big Black River.

Grant faced a decision. Concerned that Johnston might attack his rear, and knowing his men would not be enthusiastic to start a long siege in the Mississippi summer heat, he opted to attack again on May 22. Many soldiers did not sleep much the night of May 21. An Ohio soldier, Osborn H. Oldroyd, who would buy Abraham Lincoln's home in Springfield after the war, described soldiers "divesting themselves of watches, rings, pictures and other keepsakes." One young soldier told a cook, "This watch I want you to send to my father if I never return."

WHEN THE SUN rose on May 22, Grant asked everyone to synchronize their watches. After an early morning barrage by artillery, with Porter's gunboats largely silencing the Confederate upper-water batteries, at ten A.M. Grant's troops charged. They made some initial headway, planting several flags on parapets, but at the cost of heavy casualties. By eleven A.M. it appeared to Grant, watching the attacks midway between Sherman's and McPherson's corps, that there would be no breakthrough on this day.

But at eleven fifteen A.M., McClernand scrawled a message in pencil: "I am hotly engaged." He requested Grant to order McPherson to attack to "make a diversion." Grant replied at eleven fifty, "If your advance is weak strengthen it by drawing from your reserves," rather than calling upon reserves from another corps. In truth, McClernand's reserves were nearly all involved already, and McPherson's divisions were not yet engaged.

Even so, McClernand wrote again at noon, "We have part possession of two Forts, and the stars and stripes are floating over them. A vigorous push ought to be made all along the line."

Grant rode over to consult Sherman and grumbled, "I don't believe a word of it." Grant would write later in his report that Sherman's position "gave me a better opportunity of seeing what was going on in front of the 13th Army Corps than I believed it possible for the Commander of it to have." Yet he stationed himself with McPherson, conversed with Sherman, but never spoke with McClernand. Nevertheless, Grant acceded to McClernand's plea. Both Sherman and McPherson pitched in to support McClernand.

But to no avail. By dusk, Federal troops drew back. The assault had

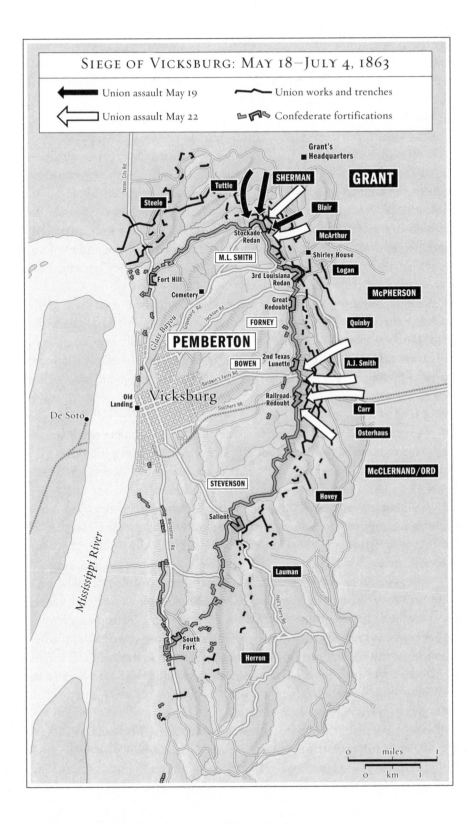

SIEGE OF VICKSBURG: MAY 18–JULY 4, 1863

Union assault May 19
Union assault May 22
Union works and trenches
Confederate fortifications

Yazoo City Rd.

Grant's Headquarters

GRANT

SHERMAN

Tuttle

Steele

Blair

Stockade Redan

McArthur

M.L. SMITH

Shirley House

Logan

3rd Louisiana Redan

Fort Hill

McPHERSON

Cemetery

Graveyard Rd.

Jackson Rd.

Great Redoubt

FORNEY

Quinby

PEMBERTON

2nd Texas Lunette

BOWEN

A.J. Smith

Baldwin's Ferry Rd.

Old Landing

Railroad Redoubt

Vicksburg

Southern RR

Carr

De Soto

Osterhaus

McCLERNAND/ORD

STEVENSON

Hovey

Salient

Mississippi River

Warrenton Rd.

Lauman

Hall's Ferry Rd.

South Fort

Herron

0   miles   1

0   km   1

failed. At least half the casualties on May 22 resulted from McClernand's additional assault in the early afternoon. George Boomer, Twenty-sixth Missouri, a hero at Champion Hill, was killed.

In Grant's report to Halleck on May 24, he put the best face on a bad result: "Our troops were not repulsed from any point but simply failed to enter the works of the enemy." In the center of his letter, he took aim at McClernand: "Gen. McClernand's dispatches misled me as to the real state of facts and caused much of this loss." He informed Halleck that McClernand "is entirely unfit for the position of Corps Commander both on the march and on the battle field. Looking after his Corps gives me labor and infinitely more uneasiness, than all the remainder of my Dept." Still, Grant determined to do nothing about McClernand until completing the siege.

Back in Washington, the president was watching the Vicksburg Campaign intently. On May 26, in a letter to an old Illinois friend, Isaac Arnold, Lincoln wrote, "Whether Gen. Grant shall or shall not consummate the capture of Vicksburg, his campaign from the beginning of this month up to the twenty second day of it, is one of the most brilliant in the world."

ON MAY 25, Grant issued orders to his corps commanders to "immediately commence the work of reducing the enemy" through a siege. As a young soldier in Mexico, Grant had participated in General Winfield Scott's successful twenty-day siege at Veracruz in 1847.

Grant set up a twelve-mile siege line around Vicksburg. He could count on 220 guns and nearly another 100 naval guns with the return of Porter. Grant did not believe Pemberton could endure a long siege, but he went forward with no illusions—he knew a siege would take time.

Siege work is led by engineers. But Grant had a problem: he had only a handful of engineers among his officers. He did have West Point graduates who had taken plenty of courses in a largely engineering academy— but this was years ago. What knowledge had they retained? Grant called upon his army to become amateur engineers and generalized craftsmen, to build by trial and error what most had never attempted before—a series of tunnels and trenches that would ultimately provide thirteen approaches to the irregular Vicksburg fortifications.

Siege work is shovel work. "Sapping" was the method used by Northern white soldiers working alongside freed black Southerners. Often called "the fatigue party," sappers sank a trench six to twelve feet wide and seven feet deep. They constructed "sap rollers," huge balls stuffed with cotton, to protect them from bullets. This tactic worked until Confederates countered with fireballs rolled toward the sap rollers. The sappers changed tactics by constructing zigzag trenches.

Grant appreciated the sappers and became a supportive observer of their work. He rode along the lines daily, but to avoid the attention of Southern sharpshooters, he wore the uniform of an ordinary private, his only designation two stars on each shoulder.

One day during the siege, Grant was observed walking the outer line when he encountered a mule-team driver beating and cursing one of the mules. He ordered the man to stop. The animal's abuser, seeing a man with a blouse and no sign of rank, turned and began to swear at him. Grant had the man arrested and brought to his headquarters. Only then did the mule driver realize whom he had insulted. The man was ordered to be tied up by his thumbs.

When released, the contrite soldier apologized for his language, telling Grant he did not know to whom he was speaking. Grant explained that he had punished the soldier not because of what he'd said to his commanding general: "I could defend myself, but the mule could not."

ALTHOUGH GRANT HAD decided to wait until after the siege to deal with McClernand, the political general forced his hand. On June 15, Francis Preston Blair, Jr., who commanded Sherman's Second Division, read in the *Memphis Evening Bulletin* McClernand's "congratulatory order," dated May 30, commending his own corps on their achievements at Vicksburg. Blair showed the article to Sherman the next day.

An enraged Sherman wrote Rawlins, complaining that McClernand's "effusion of vain-glory," his "self-glorification," would be read by "an excited public." Long suspicious of McClernand's real motives, Sherman believed the congratulatory order "manifestly addressed not to an army, but to a constituency in Illinois." He called attention to Grant's General Orders No. 151, which forbade "the publication of all official letters and reports."

The same day Grant received Sherman's letter, he wrote McClernand asking if the copy of the order in the newspaper article was "a true copy." McClernand, admitting it was correct but recognizing he had made a grievous error, replied, "I regret that my adjt did not send you a copy promptly as he ought & I thought he had."

The culmination of this high-stakes drama occurred at two A.M. on June 19, when Grant's aide James Wilson went to McClernand's tent, requesting the general be awakened. When McClernand appeared in full

dress uniform, Wilson presented him with a sealed envelope. Upon opening it, McClernand read Special Orders No. 164: "Major General John A.
McClernand is hereby relieved from the command of the 13th Army
Corps. He will proceed to any point he may select in the state of Illinois,
and report by letter to Head Quarters of the Army, for orders."

Grant informed Halleck of his actions: "I should have relieved him
long since for general unfitness for his position." He appointed Sherman's
old friend Edward Ord, who had arrived in Vicksburg the preceding day,
as the new commander of the Thirteenth Corps.

TWENTY-FIVE DAYS HAD passed since the siege began, and Pemberton
was beginning to lose hope. His men were down to one-quarter rations—
peas and rice; nearly half were on the sick list. At the beginning of the
siege, Pemberton had believed he could hold out for six weeks, and that
time was almost gone. Surely Davis would not allow them to be sacrificed. But Richmond had precious few troops to send west, and attention
had shifted to Robert E. Lee, who was preparing for an invasion of Pennsylvania. The forward units of the Army of Northern Virginia began
crossing the Potomac River into Maryland on June 23.

Nearly all of Vicksburg's civilians lived in caves carved out of the
dense yellow clay, to protect themselves from Federal shelling. William
Lord, rector of Christ Episcopal Church, his wife, Margaret, and their
four children moved into a cave behind the City Hospital on Jackson
Road. Mary Loughborough observed that Vicksburg was "so honeycombed with caves that the streets look like avenues in a cemetery." At
night, when the shelling usually lightened, these subterranean refugees
returned to their homes to appraise the damage.

AS GRANT SUPERVISED the siege, Franc B. Wilkie, *New York Times* war
correspondent, offered a compelling portrait of the general that received
wide circulation. Grant "moves with his shoulders thrown a little forward of the perpendicular, his left hand in the pocket of his pantaloons,
an unlighted cigar in his mouth, his eyes thrown straight forward, which,
from the haze of abstraction that veils them, and a countenance drawn
into furrows of thought, would seem to indicate that he is intensely pre-
occupied."

One of the finest writers among the war correspondents, publishing
under the pen name "Galway," Wilkie continued, "The soldiers observe
him coming, and rising to their feet, gather on each side of the way to see
him pass—they do not salute him, they only watch him . . . with a certain

sort of familiar reverence." He described Grant's dress and demeanor: "A plain blue suit, without scarf, sword, or trappings of any sort, save the double-starred shoulder straps—an indifferently good 'Kossuth' hat, with the top battered in close to his head; full beard of a cross between 'light' and 'sandy'; a square-cut face whose lines and contour indicate extreme endurance and determination." "Galway" wanted his readers to see Grant as the soldiers saw him.

ENDURING OPPRESSIVE HEAT and endless enemy fire, Grant's army moved closer and closer to Vicksburg's defenses day by day. On June 16, Union efforts reached within twenty-five yards of one point in the line of defense. Now former coal and lead miners began work digging under a redan, a V-shaped fortification protruding from the defense line.

On the afternoon of June 25, having tunneled thirty-five feet under Vicksburg's fortifications, Grant and McPherson gathered to view the explosion of twenty-two hundred pounds of black powder that ripped an enormous hole in the earth. Union soldiers rushed in, but after desperate fighting that went on through the night and into the next day, Grant was forced to withdraw his troops.

On June 30, engineers informed Grant that Union forces were now within 5 to 120 yards of all thirteen approaches. Grant believed that by July 6 all the approaches would be mined for one huge push through the Vicksburg defenses.

BUT ON THE morning of July 3, white flags suddenly began to rise above Vicksburg's defenses. Shortly, General Bowen, dressed in full uniform, and Colonel Louis M. Montgomery, Pemberton's aide-de-camp, rode out on Baldwin's Ferry Road. Pemberton had chosen Bowen, Grant's neighbor in Missouri, to present a letter requesting a meeting to discuss "terms for the capitulation of Vicksburg." Pemberton made this "proposition to save the further effusion of blood."

Grant sent back his reply: "The useless effusion of blood you propose stopping by this course can be ended at any time you may choose, by an unconditional surrender of the city and garrison." He offered the same terms to Pemberton at Vicksburg that he'd offered Buckner at Fort Donelson. "Men who have shown so much endurance and courage as those now in Vicksburg, will always challenge the respect of an adversary, and I can assure you will be treated with all the respect due to prisoners of war." Before departing, Bowen asked if Grant would meet Pemberton at three P.M.

On an eerily quiet afternoon, Grant, accompanied by McPherson, Ord, Logan, and A. J. Smith, met Pemberton, Bowen, and Montgomery near a stunted oak tree that would later become famous in a painting of this historic scene. But again, Grant and Pemberton could not agree on terms. Grant offered an opening, saying he would reply at ten P.M. with his final terms.

In the next hours, Grant invited his corps and division commanders to join him in conference—as he said later, "the nearest approach to a 'council of war' I ever held." The central point of contention: whether the defenders should become prisoners of war or be paroled. Grant told those assembled that he "would hold the power of deciding entirely" on the terms of surrender. But he listened. And was persuaded. It would be better to parole than take on the huge task of shipping thirty thousand prisoners of war to Northern prison camps. Parole in the Civil War, following European precedent, meant prisoners gave their word not to take up arms against their captors until formally exchanged for an enemy captive of equal rank—and could go home.

Late on July 3, Grant offered Pemberton new terms of surrender: "As soon as rolls can be made out and paroles signed by officers and men you will be allowed to march out of our lines." The officers would be allowed to take with them "their side arms and clothing, and the Field, Staff & Cavalry officers one horse each." The ordinary soldiers could take all their clothing.

It was after midnight when Grant received Pemberton's reply. He argued for a few more amendments, but Grant would have none of it. Pemberton had until nine A.M. on July 4 to surrender.

AT NINE A.M., no response. At ten A.M., Pemberton's answer finally arrived: white flags. After forty-seven days, Confederate soldiers marched out of their defenses, stacked their arms, and returned inside. Grant gave John Logan, whose division had come nearest to breaking through the defenses, the honor of marching his division first into the city. Grant rode in and watched his men share their rations with hungry Confederate soldiers. He was pleased: "The men had behaved so well that I did not want to humiliate them. I believed that consideration for their feelings would make them less dangerous foes during the continuance of hostilities, and better citizens after the war was over." He went to the waterfront and rode up the gangplank to congratulate Admiral Porter and his sailors on his new flagship, the *Black Hawk*. Porter opened all his wine lockers but recalled that "General Grant was the only one in that assemblage who did not touch the simple wine offered him," contenting himself with a cigar. In the midst of the exhilaration, Porter noticed "there was one man there who preserved the same quiet demeanor he always bore, whether in adversity or victory, and that was General Grant." The admiral thought to himself, "No one, to see him sitting there with that calm exterior, amid all the jollity . . . would ever have taken him for the great general who had accomplished one of the most stupendous military feats on record."

THE CAMPAIGN FOR Vicksburg was the most impressive military operation on American soil. In seventeen days, Grant led his hard-marching army 130 miles and won five victories—Port Gibson, Raymond, Jackson, Champion Hill, and Big Black—against surprised opponents. They mounted a siege that finally yielded victory on July 4. In a strategy born at Fort Donelson, Grant put in place a psychology of behavior that the army that would be victorious would never dwell on past mistakes, never wallow in its wounds, never pause to refresh and refit. Rather, Grant understood the consequences if he did not move forward. He told an aide, "Every day's delay is worth two thousand men to the enemy." The Confederate forces were as large as Grant's army, but he determined to fight their divisions separately and never let them combine.

Appreciation of the casualties begins with the astounding number of prisoners—29,491—surrendered to Grant. There were steep losses, too. During the long Vicksburg Campaign, the Army of the Tennessee suffered 10,142 casualties, including 1,581 killed, compared with 9,091, with 1,413 killed, by the Confederates.

THE CAMPAIGN HIGHLIGHTED the contrasting leadership skills of Grant and Pemberton. Grant's masterful strategy, using diversions, whether by Grierson or by Sherman, forced Pemberton to wonder and worry about his next moves. While Grant worked closely with his commanders, the exception being McClernand, winning their trust even as he listened to their dissents, Pemberton kept his distance and ended up losing the confidence of those he needed most. Grant husbanded a fragile line of supply, but equally important, the former quartermaster and farmer adroitly learned to live off the land.

By 1863 Grant had advanced into a superb tactician. His battle plan for Vicksburg would be used 123 years later in 1986 as a case study in an Army Operations Field Manual stating that the characteristics of a modern Air-Land Battle should be "surprise, concentration, speed, flexibility, and audacity." Crediting Grant, the field manual declared, "the same speed, surprise, maneuver, and decisive action will be required in the campaigns of the future."

Vicksburg earned Grant the enduring plaudits of a grateful nation. But the thanks of one person surely meant the most to him: "I do not remember that you and I ever met personally." After acknowledging "the almost inestimable service you have done the country," the writer said he wished "to say a word further." He wrote:

> When you first reached the vicinity of Vicksburg, I thought you should do, what you finally did—march the troops across the neck, run the batteries with the transports, and thus go below; and I never had any faith, except a general hope that you knew better than I, that the Yazoo Pass expedition, and the like, could succeed. When you got below, and took Port Gibson, Grand Gulf, and vicinity, I thought you should go down the river and join Gen. Banks; and when you turned Northward East of the Big Black, I feared it was a mistake.

After his detailed recitation of disagreements with Grant's strategy, President Lincoln confessed: "I now wish to make the personal acknowledgement that you were right and I was wrong."

CHAPTER 18

Chattanooga

The spectacle was grand beyond anything that has been, or is likely to be,
on this Continent. It is the first battle field I have ever seen
where a plan could be followed and from one place
the whole field be within one view.

—ULYSSES S. GRANT TO ELIHU WASHBURNE, December 2, 1863

When news of the fall of Vicksburg finally reached Washington on July 7, *The New York Times* titled its front-page story "The Hero of the Mississippi Valley" and extolled Grant's "brilliant exploits." Confederates, hearing of the fall of Vicksburg, surrendered Port Hudson to Nathaniel Banks on July 9, completing the opening of the Mississippi River.

Grant, by now used to the fickleness of the press, better appreciated the approval of those who knew him best. Sherman wrote on July 4, "Did I not know the honesty, modesty, and purity of your nature, I would be tempted to follow the example of my standard enemies of the press in indulging in wanton flattery." Hard-nosed Cump stressed that "the delicacy with which you have treated a brave but deluded enemy is more eloquent than the most gorgeous oratory of an Everett." Halleck, a student of military history, compared Grant with the greatest general of the age: "In boldness of plan, rapidity of execution, and brilliancy of results, these operations compare most favorably with those of Napoleon about Ulm."*

IMMEDIATELY AFTER THE Vicksburg surrender, Grant started thinking in the future tense. While busy sorting out paroles, he informed Stanton that he had "no idea of going into summer quarters"—even with swel-

---

* By superior maneuvering, Napoleon encircled the Bavarian city of Ulm, compelling the Austrian army, waiting for reinforcements from the Russians, to surrender.

tering heat and widespread sickness among his troops—but wished to receive "as soon as practicable either general or specific instructions as to the future conduct of the war in his department."

When paroled Confederate soldiers prepared to leave Vicksburg, they assumed they would take their slaves with them. Grant punched a hole in this presumption. In his instructions to McPherson, whom he entrusted with superintending Vicksburg, he declared, "I want the negroes all to understand that they are free men."

What did Grant's promise of freedom for slaves mean in the summer of 1863? He conveyed a nuanced message. On the one hand, "No enlistments of the negroes captured at Vicksburg will be allowed for the present." On the other hand, "If they are then anxious to go with their masters I do not see the necessity of preventing it." Finally, thinking beyond Vicksburg, "Some going might benefit our cause by spreading disaffection among the negroes at a distance by telling that the Yankees set them all free."

Grant sent Chaplain John Eaton to Washington to brief the president and Stanton on what he was doing with liberated slaves. He assured them he was on board with emancipation. In a letter introducing Eaton, Grant reported, "Negroes were coming into our lines in great numbers," but they were "receiving kind or abusive treatment according to the peculiar views of the troops they first came into contact with."

Eaton reported back to Grant that Lincoln "had a map of your operations on a tripod" in his office. In a second interview, Eaton related that Lincoln was "well disposed towards you." Grant had given Eaton the title "General Superintendent for Contrabands," but Eaton wanted Grant to know "the President would prefer these people should be called freedmen or freed people"—a more positive designation.

JOHN MCCLERNAND REMAINED the problem that would not go away. The political general sent Lincoln a telegram on June 23, pleading to present his side of the story. In the coming months, the president would hear more from McClernand than he wanted, including his report on the Vicksburg Campaign.

When Grant reviewed McClernand's report, he could not believe what he read. He wrote Lorenzo Thomas, "It is pretentious and egotistical." Seething, he added, "This report contains so many inaccuracies that to correct it, to make it a fair report to be handed down as historical would require the rewriting of most of it."

Grant decided the best defense required a thoughtful offense. He informed Lincoln he intended to send John Rawlins to Washington as his personal representative. Officially, the chief of staff went east to hand-deliver Grant's lengthy official report; unofficially, he went to sniff out the results of McClernand's public relations campaign and tell Grant's side of the story.

Upon his arrival on July 30, Rawlins wasted no time in learning the lay of the land. He wrote, "Have just seen Genl Brains & Col Kelton. It is worth a trip here to see how delighted they are over your successes." Despite a vigorous campaign being waged by the Illinois political general, "they have finally concluded to hand McClernand out to grass."

The next day, Lincoln granted Rawlins two hours to present Grant's report to his cabinet. After the meeting, Secretary of the Navy Gideon Welles confided to his diary, "This earnest and sincere man, patriot, and soldier pleased me more than . . . almost any officer whom I have met." As for McClernand, "Rawlins has been sent here by Grant in order to enlist the President rather than bring dispatches. In this I think he has succeeded."

AFTER VICKSBURG, LINCOLN considered bringing Grant east to assume command of the Army of the Potomac. This sentiment gained ground because of Grant's growing popularity and Lincoln's frustration with George Meade for allowing Lee to escape back into Virginia after Gettysburg. Aware of attempts to draft him, Grant wrote Charles Dana on August 5, "It would cause me more sadness than satisfaction to be ordered to the command of the Army of the Potomac." He explained, "Here I know the officers and men and what each Gen. is capable of as a separate commander. There I would have all to learn. Here I know the geography of the country, and its resources. There it would be a new study." What Grant did not say, but what he knew through army scuttlebutt, was that the Army of the Potomac was rife with cliques and contentions. He believed there would be dissatisfaction in "importing a General to command an Army already well supplied with those who have grown up, and promoted, with it."

When Massachusetts senator Henry Wilson learned of the move to bring Grant east, he wrote Washburne to remonstrate against it—but for a different reason. Wilson expressed apprehension that if Grant "should take the Potomac army . . . he would be ruined by a set of men in and out of that army." He worried that the eastern army, beginning with McClellan and the men he had recruited as division commanders, some of whom remained after his dismissal, were Democrats soft on slavery.

Wilson had heard from Dana that Grant was "modest, true, firm, honest and full of capacity for war," but he was not certain of Grant's position on slavery.

Washburne wrote Grant and enclosed Wilson's letter. Grant replied, "I never was an Abolitionist, not even what could be called anti-slavery, but I try to judge fairly & honestly and it became patent to my mind early in the rebellion that the North & South could never live at peace with each other except as one nation, and that without Slavery." For the future, "As anxious as I am to see peace reestablished I would not therefore be willing to see any settlement until this question is forever settled." Grant's words revealed the distance he had traveled on the issue of slavery—all because of his experiences in the Civil War.

IN THE SUMMER of 1863, Grant faced myriad problems similar to those he'd experienced in the summer of 1862. Following his victory at Vicksburg, a tactical achievement made possible by concentrating his troops, Grant received orders from Halleck to disperse his army and detach divisions to support other operations. It was Shiloh all over again.

In August, he wrote Halleck requesting permission to visit Nathaniel Banks in New Orleans. Mobile, Alabama, the final Confederate deepwater port on the Gulf coast, was on his mind. He hoped to enlist Banks's support for an attack there. On September 2, he arrived in the city from which he had sailed eighteen years earlier with an expeditionary force bound for Mexico. Banks hosted an event for the guest of honor that evening at the elegant St. Charles Hotel.

Two days later, Grant rode up to nearby Carrollton to lead a review. In recognition of Grant's riding ability, Banks provided him with a huge bay horse. After a postparade party replete with plenty of wine, Grant, Banks, and their party mounted their horses for the four-mile ride back into downtown New Orleans. Grant gave his spirited horse his head, letting him run. But when a train approached and the locomotive blew its whistle, the horse shied in fear and fell on his rider—his full weight smashing Grant's left leg. As Grant lay unconscious, one onlooker remarked, "We thought he was dead."

Grant was carried back to the St. Charles Hotel, his entire left side swollen and throbbing. He remembered, "The pain was almost beyond endurance." He had broken no bones but was barely able to move and lay immobilized in his hotel room for more than a week. He kept his customary good humor and told visitors his horse wanted to run through the train's coach car but lost, "being the weaker vessel."

Bedridden, Grant read. He particularly enjoyed *Phoenixiana,* a compilation of humorous sketches written by his West Point classmate George Derby. Some of Derby's stories mimicked the style of Charles Lever, one of the novelists who had delighted Grant at West Point. Flat on his back, Grant tried not to laugh too hard as Dr. Phoenixiana poked fun at the pretenses of political and military leaders.

Grant's horse had slipped and fallen on him in the dark at Shiloh, but the accident at New Orleans played into the hands of those determined to revive stories of his drinking. Banks, who did not know Grant well but had heard the stories, wrote his wife, Mary, "I am frightened when I think he is a drunkard. His accident was caused by this, which was manifest to all who saw him."

But the "all" included General Cadwallader Washburn, who wrote nothing of drinking when reporting to brother Elihu, "After the review was over and Grant was returning to the city, his horse fell with him and injured him severely." Grant may have been drinking, may have drunk too much, but he did not fall off the horse; the horse shied and fell on him.

LINCOLN'S APPRECIATION OF Grant was growing so strong that in the summer of 1863, already thinking ahead to the end of the war, he asked Halleck to solicit Grant's views about his hope to organize a civil government in Mississippi. When Grant had not replied by the end of August (he was not used to thinking about civil governments), Halleck wrote Sherman with a similar request.

Sherman objected strongly: "A civil government for any part of it would be simply ridiculous." He saw no possibility of putting in place a government until the South was thoroughly defeated.

Two days after Sherman sent him a copy of his letter, Grant wrote Halleck. He read the situation quite differently. Whereas Sherman had clearly become an apostle of a hard war, Grant sensed that "a very fine feeling exist[ed] in the State of Louisiana, and in most parts of this State, towards the Union." The army should let it be known that by accepting terms to end hostilities, any Southern state "could receive the protection of our laws." Rather than a hard-line approach that would subjugate and humiliate half the nation, Grant was thinking about how to bring people together.

GRANT RECOVERED FROM his injury in September 1863, just as the war in the west took an ominous turn. Throughout the summer, Lincoln had become disheartened by the slow progress of another army in the west, William Rosecrans's Army of the Cumberland. Rosecrans, praised for what actually amounted to an inconclusive victory at Stones River, Tennessee, in January 1863, had then stopped at Murfreesboro, thirty-three miles southeast of Nashville. After six months of unremitting pressure from Lincoln and Stanton to move, on June 23 Rosecrans at last started to drive Bragg's Army of Tennessee one hundred miles over the Cumberland Mountains to the edge of Chattanooga. There Rosecrans halted again.

On July 7, Stanton, delighted by news of victories at Vicksburg and Gettysburg, wrote Rosecrans, "You and your noble army now have the chance to give the finishing blow to the rebellion. Will you neglect the chance?" Irritated, Rosecrans shot back that his army's achievements were not fully recognized: "You do not appear to observe the fact that this noble army has driven the rebels from Middle Tennessee." He advised Stanton, do "not overlook so great an event because it is not written in letters of blood." Rosecrans did not name Grant, but his criticism was clear: Grant had sacrificed too many men in attaining victory at Vicksburg.

Rosecrans finally marched on Chattanooga on August 16, forcing Bragg's Confederate Army of Tennessee to withdraw on September 9. On September 11, Charles Dana arrived at Rosecrans's headquarters with the same mandate he had brought to Grant's headquarters the previous year—to be Stanton's eyes and ears. Unlike Grant, who had given Dana a warm welcome, Rosecrans's staff treated him like "a bird of evil-omen."

When Dana took up his reportorial pen, his initial accounts were positive. Handsome, with wavy brown hair and blue eyes, Rosecrans made an admirable first impression. On September 14, Dana optimistically wired Stanton, "Everything progresses favorably."

Moving south into the hill country of northwest Georgia, Rosecrans believed he had Bragg on the run. But the wily Confederate made a tactical retreat, waiting to fight another day at a location of his choosing. Bragg also expected reinforcements, including two divisions of James Longstreet's Army of Northern Virginia corps.

On September 19 and 20, Bragg hurled his troops at Rosecrans's forces in a surprise attack at Chickamauga Creek, fifteen miles southeast of Chattanooga. On the second day, in thickly wooded terrain, fifteen thousand troops charged through a gap on Rosecrans's right. It was a confused and ferocious battle, and Longstreet's divisions led a drive that forced most of Rosecrans's forces from the field.

While Rosecrans retreated back toward Chattanooga, George Thomas rallied his men from the Snodgrass farm and Horseshoe Ridge. Rousing confidence with his courage, he mounted a spirited defense and blocked the advance of the gray-clad forces. For his steadfastness, Thomas won the nickname "the Rock of Chickamauga."

Shortly after four P.M. on September 20, Washington learned of the result of the battle through Dana's memorable words: "Chickamauga is as fatal a name in our history as Bull Run." He sent his message to Stanton by secret code, but the telegraph operator in Nashville deciphered the content of the telegram, and before nightfall the singing wires of telegraphy had spread Dana's damning story for the whole country to read.

ON OCTOBER 9, Grant received orders from Halleck to report to Cairo, Illinois. When he arrived on October 16, he found another telegram from the general in chief: "You will immediately proceed to the Galt House, Louisville, Ky, where you will meet an officer of the War Department with your orders and instructions." Furthermore, "You will take with you your staff . . . for immediate operations in the field." Halleck, it seemed, was back to the same controlling behavior he had enjoyed at Memphis in 1862, ordering Grant to report without telling him what his new assignment would be.

The next morning, Grant's train stopped in Indianapolis; as it was about to start up again, a station worker frantically flagged down the engineer, telling him to wait for a special train just arriving from Washington with a government official from the War Department. At last, the mysterious official bounded onto the Louisville train and burst into Grant's compartment. A bearded gentleman, wheezing from asthma, introduced himself as Edwin M. Stanton, secretary of war, and vigorously shook hands with Grant's personal physician, Dr. Edward Kittoe of Galena, saying he recognized him as General Grant from his pictures.

As the train rolled toward Louisville and Rawlins straightened out who was who, Stanton handed Grant two sets of orders, "saying that I might make my choice of them." Both created the Military Division of the Mississippi out of the old Departments of the Ohio, Cumberland, and Tennessee—all the territory from the Allegheny Mountains to the Mississippi River except for Nathaniel Banks's Department of the Gulf. Lincoln had decided to unite three commands under his best general. He chose Grant.

Lincoln gave Grant full authority to organize his department as he wished. He could either keep Rosecrans or replace him with Thomas.

Probably remembering his difficulties with Rosecrans at Corinth and Iuka in 1862, Grant chose Thomas.

Grant understood that the hinge in the battle for the west was now shifting from Vicksburg to Chattanooga. If Vicksburg had been the key to controlling the Mississippi, whoever held sway over Chattanooga, located at the juncture of Tennessee, Alabama, and Georgia, could open the back door both to Georgia and to Virginia. Chattanooga, nestled in a valley between the Appalachian and Cumberland mountain ranges, a rail hub for three railroads, now became, after Richmond and Atlanta, the prize for Union forces in the fall of 1863.

ON MONDAY, OCTOBER 19, a gorgeous Indian summer day, Rosecrans returned to his headquarters to find a surprise. A telegram from Washington informed him he had been relieved of command. Stunned, he sent for Thomas and handed him the order. Thomas, indignant on behalf of his friend, protested that he would not accept the command. They talked and talked, Thomas finally agreeing.

At eleven thirty P.M., Grant's telegram arrived: "Hold Chattanooga at all hazards." He also wrote, "Please inform me how long your present supplies will last and the prospect for keeping them up." Thomas replied he had five days of rations on hand, with two more days' worth due by wagon train. A man of few words, Thomas declared, "I will hold the town till we Starve."

GRANT STARTED FOR Chattanooga. Stopping overnight in Nashville, he listened to a long speech by Andrew Johnson, senator from Tennessee and now military governor of the state. Although there was no expectation of a word from Grant, he recalled, "I was in torture while he was delivering it, fearing something would be expected from me in response."

When Grant's train groaned into Stevenson, Alabama, the next evening, General Oliver O. Howard came aboard to pay his respects. Having prepared himself to meet "the successful commander in important battles," the thirty-two-year-old with the dignified manner was taken by "surprise when I saw him." A career U.S. Army officer who had lost an arm at Fair Oaks in the Virginia Peninsula Campaign of 1862, Howard admitted that he had expected the famous general "to be of very large size and rough appearance." Instead, he found Grant to be "rather thin in flesh and very pale in complexion . . . noticeably self-contained and retiring."

In the course of their brief conversation, Howard—now serving under Joe Hooker, who until June had been commander of the Army of the Potomac—remarked that "it was hard for an officer to pass from a higher command to a lower." Grant countered, "I do not think so, Howard; a major-general is entitled to an army division and no more." Howard never forgot what Grant said next: "Why, I believe I should be flying in the face of Providence to seek a command higher than that entrusted to me."

Another visitor, Rosecrans, on his way north, entered into awkward conversation with Grant. In Grant's recollection, Rosecrans "described very clearly the situation at Chattanooga, and made some excellent suggestions as to what should be done. My only wonder was that he had not carried them out."

FIVE ROUTES, FOUR short and one long, connected Bridgeport and Chattanooga; but the four short routes—railroad, river, and two roads—were now disconnected. Only the long route remained barely open: a sixty-mile exercise in endurance.

At sunrise on October 22, because of Grant's continuing lameness, Rawlins lifted him into the saddle "as if he had been a child." Grant trudged along a wagon road in the valley of the Tennessee River and then into the Sequatchie Valley, where drenching rain turned the road into such a quagmire that the horses struggled with mud up to their bellies. The road was strewn with the remains of wagons and the carcasses of hundreds of starved mules and horses. Old Jack, Grant's claybank horse, fell, painfully jamming his master's injured leg. On the second day, Grant's party traversed Walden's Ridge before finally crossing a pontoon bridge into Chattanooga.

For Grant, walking bone-weary into Thomas's unadorned wooden headquarters on Walnut Street near Fourth, the roaring open fire in the front room could not mitigate the chill in the air. This was the headquarters of Rosecrans's friend. People often compared the massive Thomas with George Washington. He had the build of a Jove-like marble sculpture. But to those close to him, he was "Old Pap Thomas," a father figure they would follow anywhere.

Grant's aide James Wilson entered minutes later to find his boss sitting on one side of the fireplace, a puddle of water forming from his wet clothing, and Thomas sitting on the other side. Wilson spoke up. "General Thomas, General Grant is wet and tired and ought to have some dry clothes. . . . He is hungry, besides, and needs something to eat." He knew Grant would never ask for these things. The nature of the feelings at this

Grant admired the courage of George Thomas—known as "the Rock of Chickamauga"—but was often frustrated by his tentativeness, captured in his second nickname: "Old Slow-Trot."

first meeting has engaged Grant and Thomas partisans ever since. Did Wilson observe rancor or reserve in the silence between the two generals?

During the evening, officers stopped by to converse about conditions in and around Chattanooga. Grant, although weary, lit up the conversation with a bombardment of questions. He immediately impressed General William Farrar Smith, called "Baldy" Smith to distinguish him from so many Smiths in the army. Now chief engineer of the Army of the Cumberland, Smith had fallen from presidential favor when he criticized Burnside and Hooker after Fredericksburg. Grant remembered that Smith "explained the situation of the two armies and the topography of the country so plainly that I could see it without an inspection."

ANOTHER OFFICER DRAWN to Grant that evening was Captain Horace Porter. After graduating third from West Point in 1860, he had served briefly on McClellan's staff before his assignment to Rosecrans's Army of the Cumberland. Expecting to meet a large swashbuckler, Porter, like so many others, was surprised instead to encounter "a man of slim figure, slightly stooped, five feet eight inches in height, weighing only a hundred and thirty-five pounds, and of a modesty of mien and gentleness of manner which seemed to fit him more for the court than for the camp." On that dreary evening, Porter perceptively observed, "So intelligent were his inquiries, and so pertinent his suggestions, that he made a profound impression upon everyone by the quickness of his perception and the knowledge which he had already acquired regarding important details of the army's condition." Porter comprehended that "his questions showed from the outset that his mind was dwelling not only upon the prompt opening of a line of supplies, but upon taking the offensive against the enemy."

First things first. With the Union army surrounded by the enemy, the next morning, Grant, Thomas, and Smith set out to find a way to break the stranglehold by opening up a supply line—what Grant would call "opening up the cracker line," because it would bring in the essential military ration: hardtack.

Geography meant everything. The city snuggled in the four-mile-wide Chattanooga Valley, bounded by the snaking Tennessee River and grand mountains—Missionary Ridge and Lookout Mountain. Although it was only three hundred feet high, Missionary Ridge's steep slopes gave dug-in defenders an enormous advantage against attackers. Standing within the city and looking to the right, one saw Lookout Mountain toward the southern end of the Cumberland Plateau. Whoever controlled twelve-hundred-feet-high Lookout Mountain controlled the major routes into Chattanooga.

Always a quick study with geography, Grant rode to where Smith pointed to an old wagon road starting west of the river and running to Brown's Ferry. Because a forest of trees obscured Brown's Ferry from prying Confederate eyes, Smith suggested that a pontoon bridge built across the river would open a more direct supply route to Bridgeport, Alabama. Grant dismounted from Old Jack and limped to the river for closer inspection. Directly across the Tennessee River, curious Confederate pickets watched. The pickets did not seem to be concerned with the presence of the three Union officers. Grant recalled later, "I suppose, they looked upon the garrison of Chattanooga as prisoners of war . . . and thought it would be inhuman to kill any of them except in self-defense."

Impressed, Grant accepted Smith's plan. Although Smith was only a staff officer, Grant empowered the outspoken engineer to mastermind the operation.

At three a.m. on October 27, William Hazen's and John Turchin's brigades began sliding nine miles down the Tennessee in pontoon boats, seven of the miles passing enemy-held positions. Under a full moon, with Confederate picket fires close by, another brigade slipped along the road Grant had used earlier, bringing heavy weapons with bridge-building supplies. Both groups reached Brown's Ferry with rebels firing only a few wild shots. Once the pontoon bridge was completed, the cracker line opened.

HAVING BROKEN THE Confederate siege within five days of arriving in Chattanooga, Grant formulated plans to take the offensive. He was feeling stronger, he assured Julia, and believed that all the hard riding of recent days, "instead of making my injury worse has almost entirely cured me. I now walk without the use of a crutch or cane and mount my horse from the ground without difficulty."

He saw how opening the permanent supply line changed morale. "It is hard for anyone not an eye-witness to realize the relief this brought," he recalled. Soon full rations were enjoyed; new vegetables, clothing, and ammunition meant "cheerfulness prevailed not before enjoyed in many weeks."

With reduced tension, Grant's aide Wilson watched a scene "very amusing to me" at Grant's headquarters, a two-story brick house. On a rainy afternoon, Wilson listened to Generals Grant, Thomas, Smith, John Reynolds, Gordon Granger, and Thomas Wood: "While cracking jokes and telling stories of cadet and army life, it was pleasant to hear them calling each other by their nicknames." Reynolds called Grant "Sam"; Grant called him "Jo"; they spoke of Thomas as "old Tom" and of Sherman as "Cump." But of more importance was the tone set by Grant that fostered the ability of these strong-willed generals to get along.

WITH THE SUPPLY line open, Grant—who carried responsibility for the whole department, not just Chattanooga—turned his attention to Ambrose Burnside, who had suffered such a humiliating defeat at Fredericksburg and now led the Army of the Ohio. Burnside's army officially listed fifteen thousand infantry and eighty-six hundred cavalry, but his effective strength was actually much lower and strung out across East Tennessee. Grant recognized that "Burnside was in about as desperate a condition as the Army of the Cumberland had been." Recent newspaper reporting had focused on "Burnside the Incapable," yet Grant approached his relationship with Burnside without prejudgment. Burnside's staff, in turn, welcomed Grant's courteous manner.

Grant wrote Burnside, "Have you indications of a force coming from Lee's Army . . . towards you?" He added for reassurance, "If you are threatened with a force beyond what you can compete with, efforts must be made to assist you."

On November 6, Grant learned from a deserter that two days earlier his old friend Longstreet had left the Chattanooga front with fifteen thousand troops, headed toward Burnside. Believing he must do something to relieve pressure on Burnside, and recognizing that with Longstreet's movements Bragg's force had been depleted by more than a quarter, Grant made plans to attack. He wrote Burnside, "I will endeavor from here to bring the enemy back from your right flank as soon as possible." To build up his force, he wrote Sherman to stop repairing and guarding the railroad and hurry to Chattanooga.

On November 7, Grant wrote Thomas, "I deem the best movement to attract the enemy to be an attack on the Northern end of Missionary Ridge, with all the force you can bring to bear against it." Emphasizing urgency, he ordered the attack "should not be made one moment later than tomorrow morning." Despite the forcefulness of his order, however, Grant embraced a command structure affirming autonomy. "You have been over this country," he added, "and having had a better opportunity of studying it than myself, the details are left to you."

Thomas, concerned his beaten-up army was still not prepared for a full-scale attack, sent for "Baldy" Smith. "If I attempt to carry out the order I have received," he told him, "my army will be terribly beaten." Then, recognizing that Grant was particularly receptive to Smith's ideas, Thomas urged, "You must go and get the order revoked."

Obliging, Smith told Grant he was of the opinion that no movement should be made until the coming of Sherman's army.

That evening, even though he believed speed was paramount in relieving Burnside, Grant revoked his order. "Thomas will not be able to make the attack of which I telegraphed you, until Sherman gets up," he informed Burnside, then wrote Halleck, "It has been impossible for Thomas to make the movement directed by me for Burnside's relief."

Was Grant disgruntled with Thomas? Certainly, Thomas's response had undermined Grant's confidence in him. At the same time, however, he trusted Smith's analysis as an engineer. And he knew Sherman was now only a week away. Unused to waiting, Grant reluctantly decided to wait.

GRANT REVEALED HIS sense of the moment to Julia: "Things will culminate here within ten days in great advantage with one or other parties." He assured her, "With all this I lose no sleep, except I do not get to bed before 12 or 1 o'clock at night, and find no occasion to swear or fret."

If Grant did not lose sleep, Washington did. Halleck found himself criticized by Secretary of the Navy Welles and Secretary of the Treasury

Chase, the latter, formerly his supporter, now charging Halleck "was good for nothing, and everybody knew it but the President." Halleck sought to get out from underneath these criticisms by pressuring Grant to light a fire under Burnside, his disgraced general. He implored, "I fear he will not fight, although strongly urged to do so. Unless you can give him immediate assistance, he will surrender his position to the enemy."

Grant lit the fire in his own way. Burnside now began receiving telegrams from Grant that, although filled with suggestions of strategy, concluded with a steady refrain: "Your being upon the spot and knowing the ground must be left to your own discretion," and, "Being there you can tell better how to resist Longstreet's attack than I can direct." Grant urged, "I do not know how to impress you the necessity of holding on to East Tennessee," then followed this admonition two days later by affirming, "So far you are doing exactly what appears to me right." Gun-shy from criticisms heaped upon him after the Fredericksburg debacle, Burnside rested secure in a commanding general for the first time in more than a year.

Sherman reached Bridgeport on the evening of November 13, most of his four divisions stretching several days behind him. They had trekked more than six hundred hard miles from Vicksburg across northern Mississippi and Alabama. On November 15, Sherman hurried to Chattanooga. Oliver Howard, meeting Sherman for the first time, recalled how he "came bounding" into Grant's headquarters. He noticed Grant's "bearing toward Sherman differed from that with other officers, being free, affectionate, and good-humored." Sherman talked and talked, not bothering to sit down until Grant interjected, "Take the chair of *honor,* Sherman."

"The chair of honor? Oh, no! That belongs to you, general."

Not dissuaded, "I don't forget, Sherman, to give proper respect to age."

"Well, then, if you put it on that ground, I must accept."

Howard enjoyed how Grant seemed to relax now that Sherman had finally arrived. Smoking one cigar after another, the two friends talked into the evening.

ON THE OTHER end of the spectrum, for all Braxton Bragg's abilities, his efforts continually suffered from a headstrong style that resulted in bickering among his staff. Even though the Confederate Army of Tennessee had won its greatest victory at Chickamauga, his generals faulted him for not destroying Rosecrans's army. The arrival of Longstreet, openly critical of Bragg, whom he compared unfavorably with Lee, exacerbated tensions. Longstreet advocated an offensive, whereas Bragg preferred starving the Union army into surrender.

In the midst of this discontent, Jefferson Davis traveled to Chattanooga to meet with Bragg and his generals. In the end, Bragg's tenure was maintained by the only voter who mattered—the president of the Confederacy. Sensing that Longstreet had become the leader of the anti-Bragg faction, Davis ordered Bragg to send the rebellious general to recapture Knoxville.

By contrast, Grant's command functioned with more cohesion and therefore effectiveness. Grant had several habits going for him that Bragg did not. He listened; he asked questions; he did not attempt to micromanage; he seldom engaged in criticism after a battle. Yet one challenge in particular would be working with Thomas, "the Rock of Chickamauga," who for all his courage had acquired another nickname: "Old Slow-Trot."

On the morning of November 16, Grant, Sherman, and Thomas rode out to look over the ground. Learning from Vicksburg, Grant determined that a frontal assault against a fortified location would prove too costly. Thomas argued for the precedence of taking heavily fortified Lookout Mountain, while Smith argued for the precedence of attacking Missionary Ridge. Either way, speed mattered. Grant wrote Halleck, "I am pushing everything to give Gen. Burnside early aid."

At this moment, a high-ranking visitor from Washington arrived. General David Hunter, twenty years Grant's senior, had achieved notoriety in May 1862 when he issued an order emancipating slaves in South Carolina, Georgia, and Florida—an order that was immediately rescinded by Lincoln. Secretary of War Stanton sent Hunter west in fall 1863 on an assessment tour that included inspecting Grant's command.

On November 18, Grant completed his final plans. He agreed with Smith that the best place to attack would be Bragg's lightly defended far right position at Missionary Ridge. But instead of Thomas, he gave the assignment to the general he trusted most: Sherman. If Sherman ran into unexpected opposition, Grant would either order Thomas to come to his aid or have Thomas attack the Confederate center at Missionary Ridge. Grant commanded eighty thousand men—Sherman's four divisions, Thomas's four divisions, Hooker's three divisions, and two divisions to

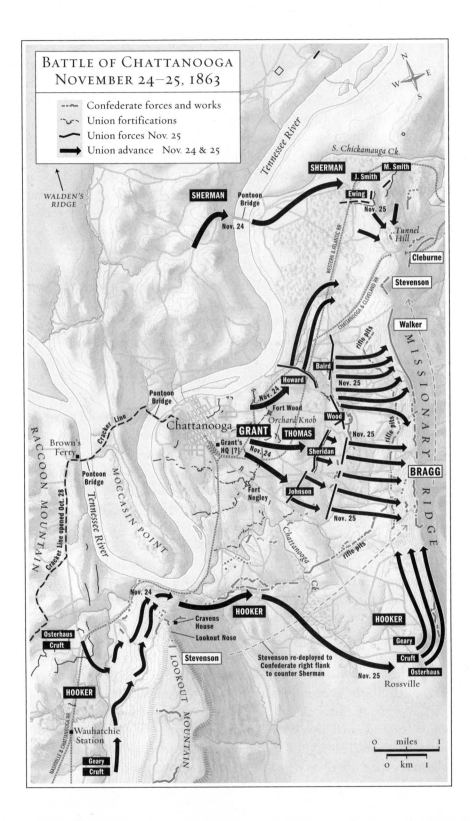

BATTLE OF CHATTANOOGA
NOVEMBER 24–25, 1863

Confederate forces and works
Union fortifications
Union forces Nov. 25
Union advance Nov. 24 & 25

Tennessee River

S. Chickamauga Ck.

SHERMAN

SHERMAN

J. Smith **M. Smith**

Pontoon Bridge

Ewing

Nov. 25

Nov. 24

Tunnel Hill

Cleburne

WALDEN'S RIDGE

Stevenson

rifle pits

Walker

Nov. 25

Baird

Howard

Nov. 24

Fort Wood

Orchard Knob

Wood

Nov. 25

rifle pits

Pontoon Bridge

Cracker Line

Chattanooga

GRANT

THOMAS

Grant's HQ [?]

Nov. 24

Sheridan

BRAGG

MISSIONARY RIDGE

Brown's Ferry

RACCOON MOUNTAIN

Pontoon Bridge

Fort Negley

Johnson

Nov. 25

Cracker Line opened Oct. 28

Tennessee River

MOCCASIN POINT

Chattanooga Ck.

rifle pits

Nov. 24

Cravens House

Lookout Nose

HOOKER

HOOKER

HOOKER

Geary

Cruft

Osterhaus

Nov. 25

Osterhaus
Cruft

Stevenson

Stevenson re-deployed to
Confederate right flank
to counter Sherman

Rossville

LOOKOUT MOUNTAIN

Wauhatchie Station

HOOKER

Geary
Cruft

NASHVILLE & CHATTANOOGA RR

0   miles   1

0   km   1

be held in reserve under Howard—nearly twice Bragg's forty-two thousand troops.

Grant's plan was working better than he knew. On November 20, Bragg informed Davis, "Sherman's force has arrived, and a movement on our left is indicated." Bragg had expected the main attack to come where Thomas urged—at Lookout Mountain.

Grant set November 21 to start the offensive. But heavy rains and a lost pontoon bridge at Brown's Ferry slowed Sherman's troops. If disgruntled with Sherman's delay, Grant was more troubled by Thomas. He wrote Halleck, "I have never felt such restlessness before as I have at the fixed and immovable condition of the Army of the Cumberland."

GENERALS ARE FOREVER gathering intelligence, often conflicting. How to sort out the true from the false, the timely from the dated? At three thirty A.M. on November 23, a deserter appeared reporting Confederate forces retreating south toward Atlanta. Grant urged Thomas, "The truth or falsity of the deserter who came in last night, stating that Bragg had fallen back, should be ascertained at once." He knew from experience that deserters were sometimes plants sent into enemy lines to confuse the Union command. In fact, Bragg had dispatched the divisions of Patrick Cleburne and Simon Bolivar Buckner to lend a hand to Longstreet in fighting Burnside.

Willing to change his carefully prepared plans, Grant instructed Thomas, with Sherman not yet prepared, to make a demonstration in front of Missionary Ridge to test Bragg's intentions—whether he was departing or staying.

At one P.M. on November 24, bugles broke the calm. Men streamed out of their tents and assembled on the broad plain at the eastern edge of Chattanooga. Thomas's Army of the Cumberland, believing they had been assigned a secondary role in Grant's battle plan, took their places in blue columns. As Grant peered through field glasses, Colonel Joseph Fullerton captured the wonder before them.

> Flags were flying; the quick, earnest steps of thousands beat equal time. The sharp commands of hundreds of company officers, the sound of the drums, the ringing notes of the bugles, companies wheeling and countermarching and regiments getting into line, the bright sun lighting up ten thousand polished bayonets till they glistened and flashed like a flying shower of electric sparks—all looked like preparations for a peaceful pageant.

The Confederate pickets looked on, watching what appeared for all the world to be a grand review. Thomas's lines were two miles from the foot of Missionary Ridge. A large open plain separated Confederate skirmishers and the Union troops on parade. Halfway across the plain lay some small hills, including Orchard Knob, a rocky hill about one hundred feet above the valley floor.

For half an hour, Thomas's men went through the traditional paces of a review. Suddenly, at two P.M., the fourteen thousand soldiers surged forward, rushing across the plain until they stood atop Orchard Knob. Confederate skirmishers—a mere 634 on the small hills—fired a few shots, but they were completely outnumbered and ultimately retreated to the lower parts of Missionary Ridge. Grant and Thomas ordered the troops to entrench, now one mile nearer the Confederate front line at Missionary Ridge. It had fallen to Thomas to direct the first charge at Chattanooga.

ON NOVEMBER 24, the first elements of three of Sherman's divisions crossed to the east side of the Tennessee River in pontoon boats. Heavy rains swelled the Tennessee to a width of fourteen hundred feet, but Sherman set in place a specially made 1,350-foot-long pontoon bridge.

At Fort Wood, located on an elevated point east of town, Grant watched and waited. He wired Sherman at eleven twenty A.M., "Until I do hear from you I am loath to give any orders for a general engagement." Sherman welcomed the last troops across the river at twelve twenty P.M. With light rain and low-lying clouds hiding his movements, he answered through Dana that all was well.

By one P.M., Sherman's men, attacking in three parallel columns, made rapid headway against what seemed Bragg's surprisingly lightly defended right flank. At his headquarters by the river, Sherman was informed by signal relay that his men had advanced a mile and a half to their objective— the north end of Missionary Ridge.

AT THE SAME time, Grant's plan called for Hooker to do no more than hold the Confederates in place. "Fighting Joe," with a force of ten thousand veterans from his own, Thomas's, and Sherman's divisions, led a combined army that had not worked together before. Everything changed when, after weeks of trying, intelligence officers intercepted a Confederate message: "If they intend to attack, my opinion is it will be upon our left [at Lookout Mountain]." Grant now corrected course to subvert Confederate expectations. At twelve thirty A.M. on November 24, he ordered Hooker to mount a "demonstration" to "aid Sherman's crossing" to Missionary Ridge. Hooker knew a demonstration was second fiddle, but he was itching for a fight and ordered his troops to be ready to move by daylight. Carter Stevenson, marshaling his Confederate defenders at Lookout Mountain, felt certain Hooker would not be so foolhardy as to strike openly up the mountain.

Hooker, knowing he bore the badge "Failure" on his chest after Chancellorsville, turned his demonstration into an opportunity to redeem himself. In a daring attack up deep ravines and across heavily timbered land, his men ascended the northern slope of the supposedly impregnable Lookout Mountain. New York captain George Collins captured the feeling that morning: "The heart of every man was in his mouth." Hooker hoped at best to capture the lower and middle slopes of the mountain, as deserters had informed him that the top, "Lookout Nose," was heavily defended by three brigades with cannon. Soldiers found it tough going as they struggled to hold a musket in one hand and grab a tree limb or rock to help their climb.

As Grant strained to see the action, low clouds blocked his view. The blinding fog, at first an enemy to Hooker's men, became a friend as it shrouded their movements. Halfway up, at an outcropping where iron ore magnate Robert Cravens had built his home in 1855, entrenched Confederate artillery temporarily stopped Hooker's drive.

At midmorning, Hooker's blended army experienced a celestial phenomenon that would be remembered by veterans into the next century. The fog suddenly lifted, revealing a cloud bank above and fog below. Between, a clear blue sky appeared. Below, where Grant had been straining to see, soldiers clad in blue unexpectedly came into view.

Hooker wanted to take Lookout Nose, but with Confederate troops retreating, he decided to stop at the white clapboard Cravens house that for weeks had been a symbol of the Confederate occupation of Lookout Mountain. The desperate struggle that day would later be remembered as "the Battle Above the Clouds."

ONCE SHERMAN'S ARMY reached what they thought was the top of Missionary Ridge, they were dismayed to discover in front of them a much larger hill. Because he'd been forced to work without adequate maps and from a distance, Sherman had not recognized his major error. His advance regiments realized Missionary Ridge was not an unbroken elevation, as it had appeared from Chattanooga. They had captured Billy Goat Hill. Now the goat was on them—a deep ravine divided Billy Goat Hill and Tunnel Hill of Missionary Ridge. But Sherman, down at his command center, was ignorant of this mistake and sent a night lantern to notify Grant of his success. At six P.M., Grant telegraphed Halleck: "Sherman carried the end of Missionary Ridge."

NOVEMBER 25 DAWNED cold and clear. At nine thirty A.M., Grant repositioned his headquarters to Orchard Knob, a centrally located high ground from which he could see the sweeping semicircular theater of war. All eyes and ears focused on Sherman's progress. At the same time, Grant wanted Thomas to remain ready to assist by advancing the remaining mile across the plain to seize the rifle pits at the foot of Missionary Ridge. Hooker was ordered to pursue Bragg's forces if they raced to reinforce the Confederate defense against Sherman at Missionary Ridge.

Before long, Grant began to adjust his plans to the day's changing circumstances. In an initial surprise, the first rays of the morning sun illuminated the Stars and Stripes flying at the "Nose" of Lookout Mountain. Hooker had outdone himself. Immense cheering erupted, with generals and soldiers waving their hats in the air. Taking the peak meant the sixty-three-day Confederate occupation of Lookout Mountain was over.

The next surprise brought bad news. Sherman, coming up from his command point at the Tennessee River, saw for himself the unexpected deep ravine between his position and Tunnel Hill. He also discovered he was up against Patrick Cleburne, whom Bragg had transferred from Lookout Mountain. The rebels, idolizing this Irish-born veteran of Stones River and Chickamauga, were ready to follow his lead. Sherman ordered brigades led by division commander Hugh Boyle Ewing (the son of Thomas Ewing and Sherman's foster brother) to move forward, but they had to hug the mountain on their way up the hill to avoid the rapid fire raining down upon them from above. At times the combatants were so near each other that the rebels threw rocks.

By noon, six hours after he had begun his assault, Sherman grew more frustrated. Iowan John Corse and his brigade had attacked up the north slope of Tunnel Hill and been hurled back. At twelve forty-five P.M., Sherman sent an abrupt one-sentence message to Grant: "Where is Thomas?" Having met stiff resistance, he was responding to a telegram from the previous evening, in which Grant had written that Thomas would either carry "the enemy's rifle pits" in front of Missionary Ridge "or, move to the left to your support." But, Grant qualified, the decision would be made "as circumstances may determine best."

In a day of improvisation, the final surprise came late in the afternoon. Grant left Orchard Knob for lunch at two P.M.; returning at two thirty, he saw how much had changed in half an hour. Instead of Sherman's troops moving forward on the attack, as Grant expected, they could be seen dropping back. At three P.M., heedful of the shortened daylight hours in late November, with Sherman stopped and Hooker overdue, Grant turned to Thomas: "Hooker has not come up, but I think you had better move, on Sherman's account."

Thomas walked away. Minutes passed with no response. The Army of the Cumberland had remained spectators as battles raged to their left and right. Did Thomas object, worrying that his troops would be slaughtered by the dug-in defenders? Grant walked over to Thomas Wood, one of Thomas's division commanders. "General Sherman seems to be having a hard time," he said. Wood agreed. Grant continued, "I think we ought to try to do something to help him."

Gordon Granger, commander of Thomas's Fourth Corps, had a habit of fiddling with artillery, and he was doing so just then. At the end of his tolerance, Grant spoke forcefully: "General Thomas, order Granger to turn that battery over to its proper commander and take command of his own corps. And now order your troops to advance and take the enemy's first line of rifle pits." Grant intended to immobilize the Confederates at the top of Missionary Ridge until Sherman arrived to spearhead the attack.

The excitable Granger, standing beside Grant, lifted his arm and began barking, "Fire! Fire!" Immediately a rare sight in military history commenced. Almost twenty-four thousand men in blue massed forward in assault formation, in a two-mile-long line, double deep with skirmishers in front—larger by far than Pickett's charge at Gettysburg—and it began to sweep across the plain of the geographic amphitheater at the base of Missionary Ridge. Thomas's division commanders—Absalom Baird on the left, Thomas Wood and Phil Sheridan in the center, and Richard Johnson on the right—faced an imposing enemy, sixteen thousand men.

From the crest of Missionary Ridge, more than fifty guns opened fire, while from Fort Wood, Fort Negley, and Orchard Knob, Union artillery retorted. To everyone's surprise, Thomas's troops quickly captured the rifle pits, braving a hail of fire, shells bursting above and around them, the dead and wounded falling on the withered winter grass. As Union soldiers rushed forward, they could not believe what they saw. The defenders, panicking, abandoned their positions and started to retreat up the ridge. Shouting at the top of their lungs, "Chickamauga, Chickamauga!" the Union soldiers kept going. If order characterized the charge across the plain, disorder described the charge up the mountainside.

Amazed, Grant demanded, "Thomas, who ordered those men up the ridge?"

"I don't know," Thomas replied.

Through field glasses Grant looked on in wonder as Thomas's men, with regimental flags flying, confronted an obstacle course of ravines, cut timber, and, farther up, loose rock. Yet in what seemed like no time at all they reached the crest, which they found poorly defended—no one had expected them to be there. The men of Sheridan's division were the first to reach the crest, and the honor of planting the first colors fell to eighteen-year-old Arthur MacArthur, Jr., captain of the Twenty-fourth Wisconsin, who shouted, "On Wisconsin!" MacArthur was his regiment's fourth color-bearer—the first was shot, the second run through with a bayonet, the third "decapitated." Young MacArthur would go on to become the senior general of the army from 1902 to 1909 but is remembered best as the father of Douglas MacArthur, commander of Allied forces in the Pacific in World War II.

At Orchard Knob, Hooker pushed northward along Missionary Ridge, having been delayed for hours as engineers constructed a bridge over Chattanooga Creek. Grant asked for his horse, and as he rode up to the crest of the ridge, the common soldiers recognized him and clung to his stirrups, raising their voices in cheers. He lifted his hat and halted again and again to thank the men.

In the midst of the celebration, Lincoln wired Grant: "Remember Burnside." He intended to do just that. Sherman, his troops having been stopped earlier in the day by a Confederate counterattack and thus disappointed at Chattanooga, was not pleased to receive his orders on the evening of November 25: "The next thing now will be to relieve Burnside." It was no easy command. Grant knew Sherman's men were exhausted, having existed on two days' rations since they'd left Bridgeport seven days earlier. Sherman, remembering his embarrassing mental breakdown at the beginning of the war, told his friend, "Recollect that East Tennessee is my horror."

But his fears were for naught. On December 5, as Sherman approached Knoxville, a messenger from Burnside notified him that early that morning, when the fog lifted, Federal pickets discovered Longstreet had disappeared and was on his way back to Virginia.

. . .

IT IS HARD to exaggerate the importance of Grant's victory at Chattanooga. In less than three days, his new command, consisting of three armies that had never fought together before, had driven south the Confederate Army of Tennessee—a formidable adversary that had besieged Chattanooga for more than two months. The door now opened to Georgia and Atlanta.

It remains debatable whether Thomas's Army of the Cumberland acted on its own accord in chasing the fleeing Confederates or whether Grant or Thomas ordered the remarkable ascent. Charles Dana, who witnessed the event from Orchard Knob, wrote, "The storming of the Ridge by our troops was one of the greatest miracles in Military history. No man who climbs the ascent, by any of the roads that wind along its front, can believe that eighteen thousand men were moved up its broken and crumbling face, unless it was his fortune to witness the deed." Grant was still amazed by the battle when he offered his official report one month later, writing, "I can only account for this . . . on the theory that the enemy's confusion and surprise at the audacity of such a charge caused confusion and purposeless aiming of their pieces."

Credit for victory at Chattanooga deserved to be shared. Sherman, misjudging the terrain, acted too slowly on this occasion. Hooker, on the other hand, dazzled—proving his grit in the west in order to erase the shame of having been removed from his eastern command. And Thomas, initially reluctant to take over from Rosecrans, restored morale to the beaten Army of the Cumberland.

The Confederate leadership also deserved credit—Braxton Bragg, for failing to anticipate Grant's battle plans; Jefferson Davis, for ordering the detachment of Longstreet toward Knoxville, robbing Bragg of one of the best armies at his disposal. Grant, with his dry sense of humor, wrote of Davis later, "On several occasions during the war he came to the relief of the Union army by means of his *superior military genius.*"

Grant did not have an exalted opinion of his own genius. He knew that at Chattanooga he had waited too long for Sherman to succeed; in mistrusting Thomas, he had probably missed an opportunity to thrust him into the battle earlier on November 25. Yet Grant's calm determination first lifted the more than two-month-long Confederate siege of the city, then orchestrated the often discordant armies that had never before fought together.

With admiration, President Lincoln wrote General Grant on December 8: "I wish to tender you, and all under your command, my more than

thanks—my profoundest gratitude—for the skill, courage, and perseverance, with which you and they, over so great difficulties, have effected
that important object. God bless you all. A. Lincoln."

On December 14, concluding his visit, General David Hunter telegraphed Stanton his estimation of his one-month-long observation of
Grant. Hunter had been "received by General Grant with the greatest
kindness. He gave me his bed, shared with me his room, gave me to ride
his favorite warhorse, read to me his dispatches received and sent. . . . He
is a hard worker, writes his own dispatches and orders, and does his own
thinking." Furthermore, "He listens quietly to the opinions of others
and then judges promptly for himself." As for his habits, "He is modest,
quiet, never swears, and seldom drinks, as he only took two drinks during
the three weeks I was with him."

BECAUSE OF URBAN renewal in the 1950s and 1960s, all Civil War structures in Chattanooga—including Grant's headquarters—were torn
down. Yet the visitor today, standing on top of craggy Orchard Knob,
two and a half miles east of the center of the city, can imagine the three-
day battle in late November 1863. As Grant wrote Congressman Washburne, "The spectacle was grand beyond anything that has been, or is
likely to be, on this Continent."

CHAPTER 19

"Washington's Legitimate Successor"

I believe you are as brave, patriotic, and just, as the great prototype
Washington; as unselfish, kind-hearted, and honest as a man should be.
—William T. Sherman to Ulysses S. Grant, March 10, 1864

When the Thirty-eighth Congress convened on the first Monday of
December 1863, an eager Elihu Washburne wasted no time in presenting a joint resolution offering "a vote of thanks" to Grant with the
intention of striking a gold medal in the general's likeness. The Illinois
congressman stated he would introduce a bill to "revive" the rank of lieutenant general—a rank that had been held by only one man: George
Washington.

Far away in Chattanooga, Grant was surprised by all the fuss. "I feel
under many obligations to you for the interest you have taken in my welfare," he wrote Washburne. "But recollect that I have been highly honored already by the government and do not ask, or feel that I deserve,
anything more in the shape of honors or promotion."

AT THIS SAME time, Grant was taken aback by an inquiry received about
a different office. On December 7, Barnabas Burns, head of a group
within the Ohio Democratic Party in favor of vigorously prosecuting the
war, asked whether he would permit his name to be used "as a presidential candidate" at a January convention to elect delegates to the 1864 national Democratic convention.

"The question astonishes me," Grant protested. "I do not know of
anything I have ever done or said which would indicate that I could be a
candidate for any office whatever within the gift of the people." Evoking
his by now consistent nonpolitical posture, Grant told the Ohio politician, "Nothing likely to happen would pain me so much as to see my
name used in connection with a political office."

To another inquirer, Grant quipped, "I never aspired to but one office in my life. I should like to be mayor of Galena—to build a new sidewalk from my house to the depot."

A more high-powered push came from James Gordon Bennett, the influential if controversial editor of the independent, anti-Republican *New York Herald*. A Scottish immigrant, Bennett began the *Herald* in 1835 in a grimy cellar, with his desk merely a board resting on flour barrels. By the eve of the Civil War, his newspaper boasted the nation's largest daily circulation—more than one hundred thousand. He believed the campaign to elevate Grant to lieutenant general was a clever maneuver by friends of Lincoln to "switch him off the presidential track." Bennett countered by proposing Grant for president.

Bennett began daily editorials praising Grant and criticizing Lincoln. He told his large readership, "So little has [Grant] had to do with politics that no other man can say positively what are his opinions of the parties and party questions of the day." On December 16, the *Herald* asked: "The Crisis of the Country—Who Is to Be Our Next President?" Bennett argued Grant would be "above" politics and would owe no debts to "hack politicians." He portrayed Grant as "the man who knows how to tan leather, politicians, and the hides of rebels."

In the politics of the Civil War, Grant was becoming both an object of appreciation and a focus of interest in power politics. Concerned Grant might not understand the dynamics of politics, Washburne advised, "You cannot have failed to observe that certain parties are attempting to make your name a football for the Presidency, all of which is more for the accomplishment of certain objects for themselves than for any good will or benefit to you." Wishing to present Grant's true thinking, he released the general's letter from August 1863: "The North & South could never live at peace with each other except as one nation, and that without Slavery." The letter cooled some Democrats' ardor.

Grant did not respond to Bennett, just as he ignored nearly all correspondents who urged him to run for political office. "I receive many such but do not answer," he wrote to Isaac N. Morris, a lawyer in Quincy, Illinois, and son of Jesse Grant's friend Thomas Morris, U.S. senator from Ohio: "I am not a politician, never was and hope never to be." Grant concluded, "This is a private letter to you, not intended for others to see or read, because I want to avoid being heard from by the public except through acts in performance of my legitimate duties."

THE DEMOCRATS WERE not alone in thinking ahead. Already some Republicans were talking of alternatives to Lincoln in the 1864 election. In their eyes, the president bore the double electoral burden of an unending war and a backlash over the Emancipation Proclamation. But Washburne let it be known he was steadfastly at Lincoln's side and Lincoln was on Grant's side: "No man can feel more kindly and more grateful to you than the President." He reminded Grant, "When the torrent of obloquy and distraction was rolling over you . . . after the battle of Shiloh, Mr. Lincoln stood like a wall of fire between you and it, uninfluenced by the threats of Congressmen."

Lincoln was aware of gossip about the political ambitions of Generals McClellan and Banks, and he wondered if Grant was similarly determined. He contacted Washburne: "I have never seen Grant. Before I appoint him to the command of the armies, I want to learn all about him. Who of his friends knows him best?"

Washburne recommended J. Russell Jones of Galena, whom Lincoln had appointed U.S. marshal for the Northern District of Illinois in 1861. An adroit businessman, Jones became president of the Chicago West Division Railway Company in 1863. Grant, now earning an annual salary of $500 per month, had finally paid off his debts this year and was beginning to save $300 a month. Grant asked Jones, whom he knew from Galena, to become his financial adviser, telling Julia, "I am going to invest my savings" in Jones's railway stock.

The president sent for Jones. On his way to the railroad station in Chicago, Jones stopped at the post office and found a letter from Grant in his box. Jones had read Bennett's drumbeat for Grant and wrote to Chattanooga, "I have no disposition to meddle in your affairs, but cannot resist saying that I very much hope you will pay no attention to what is being said about your being a presidential candidate to succeed Lincoln."

Boarding the train, Jones read Grant's reply: "I am receiving a great deal of that kind of literature, but it very soon finds its way into the waste basket. I already have a pretty big job on my hands, and my only ambition is to see this rebellion suppressed. Nothing would induce me to think of being a presidential candidate, particularly so long as there is a possibility of having Mr. Lincoln re-elected."

Jones arrived in Washington and went to the White House, not knowing why Lincoln had sent for him. Lincoln began the conversation by asking Jones about the war in the west. Sensing the president's real interest, Jones invited Lincoln to read the letter just received from Grant. When Lincoln came to the part where Grant spoke of Lincoln being re-elected, he folded the letter, stood up, and told him how gratifying this news about Grant was to him. "No man knows, when that presidential grub gets to gnawing at him, just how deep it will get until he has tried it; and I didn't know but what there was one gnawing at Grant."

ON JANUARY 8, 1864, Halleck wrote Grant asking for his ideas on what to do militarily in 1864. He encouraged Grant to "write me freely and fully your opinions on these matters." Halleck may have assumed he was asking about what to do in the west, but Grant seized the opportunity to talk for the first time about what the Union army should do in the east against Robert E. Lee and the Army of Northern Virginia. With no first-hand knowledge of operations in the east, he consulted two colleagues whom he believed best understood strategy: "Baldy" Smith and a young engineer, Cyrus Comstock, who had made a fine impression on Grant during the siege of Vicksburg.

During the past two years, different Union generals had tried the same strategy against Lee in Virginia. Union generals had crossed the Rapidan and Rappahannock rivers, only to be defeated four times—Second Manassas, Fredericksburg, Chancellorsville, and, most recently, Mine Run.

On January 19, Grant wrote Halleck: "I would respectfully suggest whether an abandonment of all previously attempted lines to Richmond is not advisable." He advanced an alternative approach: that an army of sixty thousand first strike Raleigh, North Carolina; then, with that city secured, move on to New Bern on the North Carolina coast; and from there, take control and blockade the port of Wilmington, North Carolina. Grant's goal: "It would draw the enemy from Campaigns of their own choosing, and for which they are prepared, to new lines of operations never expected to become necessary."

Grant closed his letter to Halleck with remarkable deference: "I have written this in accordance with what I understood to be an invitation from you to express my views about Military operations and not to insist that any plan of mine should be carried out."

NEAR THE END of January, Ulysses learned Fred was desperately ill in St. Louis with typhoid fever and dysentery, complicated by pneumonia. Grant left Chattanooga and reached St. Louis on January 27, fearful that his eldest son would be dead by the time he arrived. Instead, he found Fred recuperating at Louisa Boggs's home.

Grant celebrated Fred's recovery by taking Julia, Louisa Boggs, and Julia's friend Carrie O'Fallon to the St. Louis Theatre (the same theater he and Julia had attended in the days before their wedding in 1848), for a production of Edward Bulwer-Lytton's *Richelieu*. He and Julia sat in a private box, but their evening did not remain private. At the end of the first act, the audience began to shout, "Grant! Grant! Grant!" He stepped forward, bowed, and afterward moved his chair farther back in the box.

In St. Louis, fifty-five civic leaders invited Grant to be their guest at a public dinner, "where old friendships may be renewed." Two nights later, 250 eager attendees paid tribute to their hero at a lavish event in the recently opened Lindell House. One can imagine Grant's feelings when he recalled that not half a dozen years earlier he had sold firewood on the streets of St. Louis to support his family.

WHILE IN ST. Louis, Julia, self-conscious now that her husband had become so famous, decided she needed to do something about her appearance. Long concerned by her strabismus, often referred to as cross-eyed, she would not face the camera when someone wanted to take her photograph.

She turned to Dr. Charles A. Pope, dean of the St. Louis Medical College. Pope told her it was too late to perform an operation on her eyes. Devastated, she confessed to her husband her intention and disappointment.

Ulysses, startled, replied, "What in the world put such a thought in your head, Julia?"

"Why, you are getting to be such a great man and I am such a plain little wife. I thought if my eyes were as others are I might not be so very, very plain."

Julia Grant, afflicted with strabismus in one eye, seldom allowed herself to be photographed. The few photographs we have always picture her at an angle, so that the affected eye is not shown.

Ulysses drew her to him and said, "Did I not see you and fall in love with you with these same eyes? I like them just as they are, and now, remember, you are not to interfere with them."

As Grant traveled back to his headquarters in Nashville, discussion in Washington on reviving the rank of lieutenant general moved forward. On February 1, the House of Representatives added an amendment specifying that Grant be the recipient of the rank. Several members of the Senate objected, saying it violated the president's powers to appoint generals, and the amendment was taken out. A few suggested postponing the decision until after the war in case some other general emerged as more deserving of the honor.

But Lincoln, having learned from Jones that Grant had no political ambitions, gladly gave his blessing to the bill. The House passed it on February 1, by a vote of 117 to 19, the Senate on February 26 by 31 to 6, and the president signed it on leap year day, February 29.

An important new magazine, *The Army and Navy Journal,* applauded the elevation of Grant. The brainchild of William Conant Church, formerly publisher of the *New York Sun,* he founded the journal in August, 1863. Church may not have anticipated the instant success of his publication, which trumpeted the war effort by supplying specific information that the public devoured. Generals read the *Journal* and soldiers relied upon it for news of the war.

From its first issue, Grant became *The Army and Navy Journal*'s hero. Even before Grant's appointment in February 1864, Church declared in the fall of 1863 that Grant was a leader "without peer among our Generals." As talk mounted in Washington that Lincoln would invite Grant to take command of all the Union armies, the *Journal* declared that their affirmation of Grant rested not simply in his military skills, but in "the moral influence of a commander" on both his troops and the nation.

As Grant prepared to leave for Washington to accept the new rank, he wrote Sherman, "Whilst I have been eminently successful in this War, in at least gaining the confidence of the public, no one feels more than me how much of this success is due to the energy, skill, and harmonious putting forth of that energy and skill, of those who it has been my good fortune to have occupying a subordinate position under me." He acknowledged his remarks were applicable to "many officers," but "I want . . . to express my thanks to you and McPherson as the *men* to whom, above all others, I feel indebted for whatever I have had of success."

Sherman, himself a man with a large ego, replied deferentially, "You do yourself injustice and us too much honor in assigning to us so large a share of the merits which have led to your high advancement." Sherman cast Grant's appointment as lieutenant general in the largest historical perspective: "You are now Washington's legitimate successor." He encouraged, "If you can continue as heretofore to be yourself, simple, honest, and unpretending, you will enjoy through life the respect and love of friends, and the homage of millions of human beings who will award to you a large share for securing to them and their descendants a government of law and stability."

Grant left Nashville with the definite aim to return and lead the spring campaign to capture Atlanta. He traveled to Washington with Rawlins and Cyrus Comstock. Thirteen-year-old Fred begged to accompany his father—and succeeded.

In departing, Ulysses told Julia that he had one "regret" at receiving the rank of lieutenant general. Julia asked what he could possibly regret.

He answered that his promotion meant he probably would need to be based in Washington, whereas when the war was over he had hoped to have his "choice of stations." He continued, "My choice is the Pacific slope, but (with a sigh) this breaks that all up."

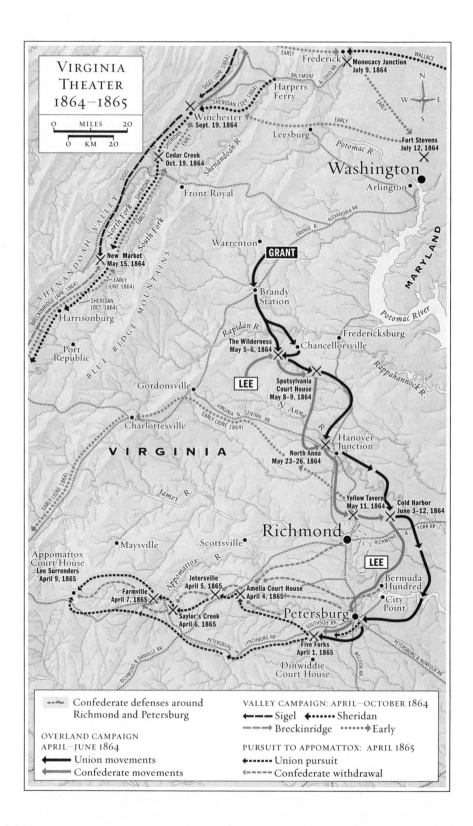

VIRGINIA
THEATER
1864–1865

0 MILES 20

0 KM 20

WALLACE

EARLY   Frederick   Monocacy Junction
                    July 9, 1864

SIGEL (APR. 1864)   BALTIMORE & OHIO RR

Harpers
Ferry   EARLY

"SHERIDAN (SEP. 1864)"

"SHERIDAN (SEP. 1864)"   EARLY

Winchester   Leesburg   Fort Stevens
Sept. 19, 1864   July 12, 1864

SHERIDAN EARLY
Cedar Creek
Oct. 19, 1864

Shenandoah R.   Potomac R.

SIGEL

North Fork   EARLY   Front Royal   Washington

SHERIDAN   South Fork   Arlington

New Market
May 15, 1864

EARLY
(JUNE 1864)

SHENANDOAH VALLEY

BRECKINRIDGE (APR. 1864)

SHERIDAN
(OCT. 1864)

Harrisonburg

Warrenton   GRANT

Port
Republic

BLUE RIDGE MOUNTAINS

Brandy
Station

Rapidan R.

The Wilderness   Chancellorsville
May 5-6, 1864

LEE

Gordonsville   Spotsylvania
                    Court House
                    May 8-9, 1864

N. Anna

VIRGINIA & CENTRAL RR

EARLY (JUNE 1864)

Charlottesville

VIRGINIA   North Anna   Hanover
                    May 23-26, 1864   Junction

EARLY (JUNE 1864)

James R.

Yellow Tavern   Cold Harbor
May 11, 1864   June 3-12, 1864

Richmond   RICHMOND

Maysville   Scottsville

Appomattox   Appomattox R.   LEE
Court House
Lee Surrenders
April 9, 1865   Bermuda
                  Jetersville   Hundred
            Farmville April 5, 1865 Amelia Court House   City
            April 7, 1865   April 4, 1865   Point

                  Saylor's Creek   Petersburg
                  April 6, 1865   SOUTHSIDE RR

RICHMOND & DANVILLE RR   PETERSBURG   LYNCHBURG RR

                              Five Forks   WELDON RR
                              April 1, 1865
                  Dinwiddie
                  Court House

MARYLAND

Potomac River

Fredericksburg

Rappahannock R.

Confederate defenses around
Richmond and Petersburg

OVERLAND CAMPAIGN
APRIL–JUNE 1864
Union movements
Confederate movements

VALLEY CAMPAIGN: APRIL–OCTOBER 1864
Sigel   Sheridan
Breckinridge   Early

PURSUIT TO APPOMATTOX: APRIL 1865
Union pursuit
Confederate withdrawal

CHAPTER 20

The Wilderness

The feeling about Grant is peculiar—a little jealousy, a little dislike,
a little envy, a little want of confidence. . . . All, however, are
willing to give him a chance . . . if he succeeds, the war is over.
—CHARLES FRANCIS ADAMS, JR., TO
CHARLES FRANCIS ADAMS, SR., May 1, 1864

Grant arrived in Washington with three large decisions to make as
lieutenant general. First, where should he set up his command? Second, should he retain the commander of the Army of the Potomac,
George Gordon Meade, or replace him? Third, what should be done with
Halleck—up to now his boss?

WHILE IN WASHINGTON, Grant received a letter from Sherman: "Do not
stay in Washington. Halleck is better qualified than you are to stand the
buffets of intrigue and policy." He implored, "Come out West; take to
yourself the whole Mississippi Valley." Sherman believed Grant could
command best by stationing himself in the western theater, for "here lies
the seat of the coming empire."

But Grant was not long in Washington before realizing he needed to
set up his command in the east. Robert E. Lee and the Army of Northern
Virginia merited his primary attention, and he trusted Sherman to lead
the campaign in the west. However, he determined to establish his headquarters in the field, in Virginia near the front line, not in Washington,
where he would be subject to the well-meaning ideas of Lincoln and
Stanton and buffeted by the crosscurrents of political debates in Congress.

THE LARGER EASTERN question was what to do about Meade.

George Gordon Meade was born in 1815 in Cádiz, Spain, where his
father served as an agent for the U.S. Navy. Young George graduated

from West Point in 1835, eight years before Grant. At the outbreak of the Civil War, he was appointed brigadier general of Pennsylvania volunteers. He fought under George McClellan in the 1862 Virginia Peninsula Campaign and was seriously wounded at Glendale when a musket ball hit him above his hip, just missing his spine. After recuperating, Meade led his Pennsylvania troops at South Mountain and Antietam. As a corps commander at Chancellorsville, he was dismayed by Hooker's defensive tactics but led his troops aggressively with great skill.

Given command of the Army of the Potomac over Hooker at the end of June 1863, Meade quickly found himself leading Union forces into the small market town of Gettysburg, Pennsylvania, seventy-five miles north of Washington, against Confederate forces led by Robert E. Lee. The ensuing battle, like an unscripted three-act play, expanded as more and more actors arrived on the scene. Meade battled mostly from a defensive position, but after three bloody days of fighting, he emerged victorious on July 3.

But not quite. As Lee's battered army struggled to make its way back south, Lincoln expected Meade to follow. Visibly disturbed, the president waited and waited; Lee's forces were stuck in Pennsylvania, unable to ford the flooding Potomac River to get back into Virginia. Finally, on the morning of July 14, eleven days after Gettysburg, Union forces arrived at the river, but the last remnants of Lee's army had just crossed the Potomac during the night.

Grant arrived in the midst of a political battle in the aftermath of Get-

George Gordon Meade, victor at Gettysburg but criticized for not pursuing the defeated Robert E. Lee, wondered whether Grant would retain him as commander of the Army of the Potomac.

tysburg. Meade appeared before the Joint Committee on the Conduct of the War to defend his record. Against the backdrop of these hearings, he wrote his wife, Margaret, that Grant "may desire to have his own man in command, particularly as I understand he is indoctrinated with the notion of the superiority of the Western armies, and that the failure of the Army of the Potomac to accomplish anything is due to their commanders."

On March 10, Grant traveled to Meade's headquarters at the tiny hamlet of Brandy Station, Virginia, sixty-four miles southwest of Washington. Stepping off the Orange and Alexandria train, he was greeted by Rufus Ingalls, whom he had not seen since they'd served together at Fort Humboldt. Ingalls now served as quartermaster of the Army of the Potomac.

Meade had approached this meeting with foreboding, but he welcomed Grant politely. Seven years older than Grant, he looked even older, as his hair had turned prematurely gray.

Grant's initial impression fastened on Meade's unselfish spirit: "He said to me that I might want an officer who had served with me in the West, mentioning Sherman specially, to take his place. If so, he begged me not to hesitate about making the change." Meade told Grant, "The work before us was of such vast importance to the whole nation that the feeling or wishes of no one person should stand in the way of selecting the right men for all positions."

That evening, Meade wrote his wife, Margaret, "Lieutenant General Grant" was "very civil, and said nothing about superseding me." Several days later, "I think I told you I was very much pleased with General Grant. In the views he expressed to me he showed much more capacity and character than I had expected." Grant decided to keep Meade.

ONLY THE MOST personal decision remained. Congressional sentiment had turned decidedly anti-Halleck by the winter of 1864. Halleck had come from Corinth to Washington in the summer of 1862 to become general in chief, but by the fall of 1863 his luster had tarnished. With Grant in Washington, Halleck recognized an effort afoot to drive a wedge between the two military leaders. He would not allow it. On March 7, he wrote his friend Francis Lieber, a professor at Columbia University, "It will be said that I throw up my office in dudgeon, because Genl Grant has been promoted over my head," but "there is no possible ground for such an accusation. Genl Grant is my personal friend, and I heartily rejoice at his promotion. The honor was fully due to him."

On March 12, the War Department issued General Orders No. 98, setting up the new command structure that acknowledged Halleck "is, at his own request, relieved from duty as General-in-Chief of the Army." It stated, "Lieut. Gen. U. S. Grant is assigned to the command of the armies of the United States." Sherman would replace Grant in command of the Military Division of the Mississippi, and James McPherson would replace Sherman in command of the Army of the Tennessee. Grant's most trusted generals were rising with him.

Halleck would be chief of staff serving under the new commanding general. With this appointment, Grant gained a new command structure with a new position. In doing so, he was recognizing Halleck's abilities, wherein the chief of staff would be the chief administrative officer, reporting to Grant and freeing the lieutenant general to command in the field. Time would tell how this new structure would work.

Lincoln invited Grant to a banquet honoring him and a number of important generals, but he begged off, saying he needed to return to Nashville right away: "I appreciate fully the honor Mrs. Lincoln would do me, but time is precious; and *I have had enough of the show business.*" Tapping his understated sense of humor, he told the nation's humorist in chief that these days in Washington had been "rather the warmest campaign I have witnessed during the war."

Grant had made quite an impression in Washington. In turning down social invitation after invitation, he communicated he was all business. The *New York Tribune* commented favorably, "He went to work at once. Senators state with joy that he is not going to hire a house in Washington [a reference to McClellan], and make war ridiculous by attempting to maneuver battles from an arm-chair." The rival *New York Herald* agreed: "We have found our hero."

RETURNING TO NASHVILLE to close down his operation there, Grant gathered an inner circle of generals—Sherman, Rawlins, McPherson, Logan, Grenville Dodge, Francis Blair, Gordon Granger, and a new member, Philip Sheridan. Grant wanted to invite his friends' views on the coming spring campaigns. They met for several days, combining business and pleasure. They trooped to the state capital to visit with Military Governor Andrew Johnson. Grant took them to see Shakespeare's *Hamlet* at the Adelphi Theatre.

Dodge remembered that Grant said he wanted to take several generals east with him, but Sherman protested "strenuously," arguing that he needed these men in the west. Grant listened and in the end agreed that only Sheridan would go east. Grant reported on visiting the Army of the Potomac: "What a splendid Army it was—how finely equipped and provisioned as compared to our armies." He remembered that more than one officer out east worried, "You have not yet met Bobby Lee."

The mayor of Galena, Lewis S. Felt, came to Nashville to present Grant with a sword from the people of Galena and Jo Daviess County. Embellished with fourteen diamonds, it was inscribed on one side with the names of the Mexican War battles in which Grant participated, while the other side offered the names of the Civil War battles he had won.

Grant invited Sherman to come with him to the ceremony. After the mayor spoke, Sherman chuckled at Grant's shyness as he "stood, as usual, very awkwardly" to reply. Sherman remembered that Grant fumbled in his pockets, first his breastcoat pocket, then his pants and vest, and after a sizable delay pulled out a wrinkled piece of common yellow cartridge paper, which he handed to the mayor. His friend Sherman thought, "His whole manner was awkward in the extreme, and yet perfectly characteristic, and in strong contrast with the elegant parchment and speech of the mayor." Yet "when read, however, the substance of his answer was most excellent, short, concise . . . all that the occasion required."

GRANT RETURNED TO Washington, where he had his first extended conversation with Lincoln. The president was surprisingly frank. Lincoln told Grant that he did not "know how campaigns should be conducted, and never wanted to interfere in them." The problem had been "procrastination on the part of commanders, and the pressure from the people at the North and Congress, *which was always with him,* forced him into issuing his series of 'Military Orders.'" He assured Grant, "All he ever wanted . . . was someone who would take the responsibility and act, and call upon him for all the assistance needed."

With Grant in charge, expectations in the North soared. Newspapers whipped the public in both eastern and western theaters of operation into a frenzy of anticipation: "With Lieutenant General Grant at the head of military affairs, our people have renewed hopes for the spring campaign," wrote Noah Brooks, correspondent of the *Sacramento Daily Union.* Surely the war would be over by the summer of 1864.

Not everyone succumbed to this spring fever. New York lawyer George Templeton Strong wrote approvingly of Grant's appointment in his diary but worried—in Old English—"the road to Richmond is a *passage perylous, whereon have perysshed manie good Knyghtes.* . . . A terrible ordeal for Grant. His path is whitened by the bones of popular reputations

Lincoln made himself accessible to many photographers while serving as president. This popular photograph was made by Alexander Gardner in his Washington, D.C., studio.

that perished because their defunct owners did not know how to march through Virginia to Richmond."

The *New York Herald* linked Grant and Lincoln together. James Gordon Bennett editorialized that Lincoln's "political fortunes, not less than the great cause of the country, are in the hands of General Grant, and the failure of the General will be the overthrow of the President."

DESPITE THE NEWSPAPERS' enthusiasm, many soldiers in the Army of the Potomac adopted a wait-and-see attitude regarding Grant. Charles Francis Adams, Jr., great-grandson of President John Adams, summed up the mood in a letter to his father, Charles Francis Adams, Sr., who was Lincoln's minister to Great Britain: "The feeling about Grant is peculiar—a little jealousy, a little dislike, a little envy, a little want of confidence. . . . All, however, are willing to give him a chance . . . if he succeeds, the war is over."

On March 24, Grant departed Washington once more, this time for

Culpeper, Virginia, where a brass band serenaded the new commander in front of the courthouse beneath a soaking rain. He established his headquarters six miles from Meade's headquarters and twelve miles north of the Rapidan River. His simple brick house on Main Street presented a striking contrast to George McClellan's lavish house in Washington when he served as general in chief in 1861 and 1862.

With his expanded command, the volume of Grant's correspondence increased exponentially. He ordered his commanders to send their reports to Halleck in Washington. The freshly appointed chief of staff filtered these reports and passed on to Grant what he deemed most important. Grant's new position meant he now had his own printed stationery. He crossed out his title when writing private letters to family and friends.

THE FIRST TRADEMARK of Grant's spring campaign was thorough preparation, starting with his voracious appetite for maps. He approached the task fully aware of the previous Union military disasters in Virginia, as well as the public perception of Lee's supposedly impregnable defenses. Although he had never set foot below the Rapidan, he determined to make himself master of the minute details of rolling fields, woods, rivers, and roads bounded on the east by the Chesapeake Bay and on the west by the Blue Ridge Mountains.

Grant also took advantage of an improving intelligence service. The Bureau of Military Information (BMI), created by Joseph Hooker in early 1863, elicited information from captured soldiers, deserters, and spies about enemy strength, locations, and morale. The BMI sought to distinguish truth from lies through a variety of methods. Grant did not want the raw data, but he received a written summary analyzed from a mass of sources each day.

Grant was well situated logistically. His friend Rufe Ingalls, known as one of the best poker players in the army, also enjoyed a reputation as the best quartermaster. Ingalls proudly reported, "Probably no army on earth ever before was in better condition in every respect." Each man would carry full rations for three days and partial rations for three more days. The enormous convoy would include 4,300 wagons, 835 ambulances, 22,528 mules, 4,046 private horses, 29,945 horses for cavalry and artillery, and a herd of cattle for beef. Grant, an old quartermaster himself, remarked that the wagon train, if marched in single file, would stretch from the Rapidan all the way to Richmond—nearly ninety miles.

Two questions became central as Grant prepared. First, he was anxious to learn the whereabouts of James Longstreet and his long-rumored return to Virginia from Tennessee. Second, as the days warmed and roads dried, the question remained whether to cross the Rapidan to Lee's right or left. Grant wanted to outflank Lee and thereby force him to either fight or retreat, but each plan offered advantages. If he chose to move to Lee's right—Grant's left—it would provide a direct line to bring forth his hundreds of supply wagons. If he chose to cross the Rapidan to Lee's left, he might be able to get behind Lee and steal a quick march to Richmond.

COORDINATION WOULD BE the second trademark of Grant's spring campaign. He and Meade formed a military marriage of opposites. They came to their joint command from different backgrounds. Meade, the son of privilege, grew up in Philadelphia. The two commanders surrounded themselves with different staffs. The patrician Meade's chief adviser was Harvard-educated Theodore Lyman, whereas Grant's chief aide was John Rawlins, a small-town western lawyer. Despite their differences, and despite Lincoln's concern about Meade's cautiousness, Grant approached their partnership with an open mind.

In April 1864, Meade boasted three enlarged corps led by generals who had distinguished themselves in the field. Winfield Scott Hancock, nicknamed "Hancock the Superb" because of his handsome and mammoth features, led Meade's Second Corps. John Sedgwick, whom Grant had served with as a fellow lieutenant in the Mexican War, led the Sixth Corps. A genial bachelor, Sedgwick was married to the army and earned the nickname "Uncle John" from soldiers who knew he cared about them. Gouverneur K. Warren led the recently reconstructed Fifth Corps. A mathematics instructor at West Point before the war, Warren won fame for his last-minute defense of Little Round Top at Gettysburg. Yet to many of his colleagues he seemed more at home behind a drafting desk than on a battlefield.

Grant intended to advance concurrently on five fronts. The two central armies, led by Meade in the east and Sherman in the west, would be supported by three smaller armies. Franz Sigel would drive his army south up the Shenandoah Valley and apply pressure on Richmond from the west. Benjamin Butler, coming up from Fortress Monroe at the tip of the Virginia Peninsula, would push toward Richmond from the south. Nathaniel Banks would seize Mobile, Alabama, and drive north to unite with Sherman. In Tennessee, Grant had commanded three West Point professionals—Sherman, Thomas, and Hooker; he would now command three political generals—Sigel, Butler, and Banks.

Grant wrote Sherman, "It is my design, if the enemy keep quiet and allow me to take the initiative in the Spring Campaign to work all parts of the Army together, and, somewhat, towards a common center." As usual, Grant and Sherman were on the same page. His friend replied, "That we are now all to act in a Common plan, Converging on a Common Center looks like Enlightened War."

Grant traveled to Fortress Monroe to meet Butler for the first time. He was aware of the controversy surrounding Butler's supposed heavy-handed administration of New Orleans, but he chose to give him the benefit of the doubt, just as he had earlier with Burnside. His initial reaction seemed validated; he discovered Butler's strategic views "were very much such as I intended to direct." Though Grant found himself impressed with Butler, his aide Cyrus Comstock worried to his diary about this ambitious former trial lawyer: "Butler is sharp, shrewd, able, without conscience or modesty—overbearing."

In the middle of April, Grant added Burnside's Ninth Corps. To circumvent the awkwardness of positioning Meade over Burnside, his military superior, Grant instructed Burnside to report directly to him. Burnside's most discussed division was the Fourth, seven regiments of African American troops drawn from both occupied Southern states and the North. Led by white officers, the U.S. Colored Troops became the first African American troops in the Army of the Potomac.

Grant's strategy was one of unrelenting attack. The siege of Vicksburg had reinforced his belief that Richmond was fortified so well "that one man inside to defend was more than equal to five outside besieging or assaulting." His first objective was to attack Lee's army, confident that with its capture, Richmond "would necessarily follow." In the past, Confederates, though outnumbered, had shifted their interior lines of defense to meet the central point of the often uncoordinated Union attacks. He told Meade, "Lee's Army will be your objective point. Wherever Lee goes there you will go also." Grant directed Sherman's army to slice southeast through Georgia to capture Atlanta: "You I propose to move against Johnston's Army, to break it up and get into the interior of the enemy's country as far as you can, inflicting all the damage you can against their War resources."

LEE'S ARMY WAITED. Lee had defeated the Federals at Fredericksburg in December 1862 and again at Chancellorsville in the spring of 1863, and at the end of 1863 he had forced Meade to call off his attack at Mine Run. The Confederate and Union armies spent the winter of 1863–1864 within eyesight and earshot of each other with no confrontations. In February, Richmond informed Lee that no new troops would be sent to him, as they had run out of manpower. His lifeline, the Orange and Alexandria Railroad, could not keep enough trains running to feed his troops. Inadequate rations gnawed at Southern morale. One enterprising Confederate general distributed a list of edible plants.

Lee commanded three corps led by well-known but enigmatic generals. James Longstreet commanded the First Corps. This Georgian, determined and courageous, brought the most experience to the field but could also be inflexible once he'd made up his mind. The Second Corps, which had been commanded by Stonewall Jackson—who was accidentally shot and killed by his own men at the Battle of Chancellorsville—was now led by Virginian Richard Ewell. Known to his friends as "Old Bald Head," Ewell had suffered a leg amputation after the Second Battle of Bull Run. Although he had led a division under Jackson, Ewell struggled with decision making as he assumed his own command. Ambrose P. Hill commanded Lee's new Third Corps. Early in the war A.P. led decisively, but by 1864 the long beard he maintained could not mask his hollow cheeks, which spoke of a recurring illness—probably both psychological and physical—that depleted his decisiveness.

Lee pulled his forces back from the Rapidan into a forbidding area called the Wilderness, twelve miles wide and six miles deep, opening out south of the river. It was in this area that Hooker had suffered a dramatic defeat at the Battle of Chancellorsville almost exactly one year earlier. Lee chose this dense forest of second-growth scrub oak, dwarf moss–tagged pines, and hoary willows, interlaced by streams, roads, and trails, to neutralize Union superiority in numbers and render artillery practically useless.

Meade rode over to Culpeper for a conference with Grant on April 11. Dogwoods and wild rose greeted him along the way. Meade's aide-de-camp, Theodore Lyman, noted in his diary his latest impression. One of the finest chroniclers of the Civil War, Lyman was extremely disciplined in writing his observations at the exact moment an event occurred. On this day he observed, "Grant is a man of a good deal of rough dignity; rather taciturn; quick and decided in speech." Memorably, "He habitually wears an expression as if he had determined to drive his head through a brick wall." Lyman concluded, "I have much confidence in him."

Throughout April, many newspaper war correspondents interviewed Grant. A British correspondent offered a portrait by someone outside

American culture: "Grant is not intoxicated with flattery, as was McClellan; I never met with a man of so much simplicity, shyness, and decision." Because this reporter had been covering the Army of the Potomac for some time, he noted many contrasts: "He avoids Washington and its corrupting allurements. He is essentially a soldier of the camp and field. . . . His tents are almost among the soldiers. That is a Western, and not a Potomac, army custom." The reporter assessed, "He is a soldier to the core, a genuine commoner, commander of a democratic army from a democratic people."

BY APRIL 25, Grant had the answer to his first question: the location of Longstreet. Intelligence informed him that Longstreet had reached Charlottesville and was on his way east to Gordonsville. In answer to the second question, Grant decided to cross the Rapidan to Lee's right, at Ely's Ford and Germanna Ford, six miles apart. He opted for speed, safety, and a more direct route for his supply wagons.

A final question concerned the weather. Like Dwight D. Eisenhower in the days before D-Day of World War II, eighty years into the future, an American army commander with much less precise weather information waited for the right conditions to launch a momentous attack.

Lincoln backed Grant's plan. On April 30, Grant received a letter from the president, in which Lincoln expressed "entire satisfaction with what you have done up to this time." He added, "You are vigilant and self-reliant; and pleased with this, I wish not to obtrude any constraints or restraints upon you." The commander in chief had waited a long time to be able to declare such confidence in his commanding general.

The Union army would begin the spring campaign confident, well clothed, and equipped with ample ammunition and a combined force of 120,000 men, a nearly two-to-one advantage of men. Lee's army was ill clad and ill equipped, but equally confident in their leader and themselves. If Grant's tactic was to press forward continuously, Lee's tactic was to defend and delay. He hoped to defeat an enemy at least twice his size by exacting such losses that the Northern public would come to believe victory not worth the price.

Often forgotten—but not by Grant—was the fact that Confederate armies, firmly entrenched behind earthworks in front of the court building in the town of Orange Court House, Virginia, possessed advantages both in knowledge of the geography they were defending and in the support of its residents.

. . .

EARLY IN THE morning of Wednesday, May 4, the Army of the Potomac broke their winter camp. Federal cavalry had cleared Confederate pickets—soldiers placed in forward positions to warn against an enemy advance—so pontoon bridges could be laid across the river at both Ely's Ford and Germanna Ford.

Grant started from Culpeper astride Cincinnati, his giant bay horse, keen to observe the crossings. Ordinarily dressed plainly, on this momentous day he wore yellowish-brown riding gloves and a black felt slouch hat encircled with a plain gold cord. As far as his eye could see, closely packed troops and supply wagons were heading south. The various corps, with their divisions and brigades, sewed distinctive badges on their uniforms. When high-spirited soldiers saw Grant pass, they greeted their new commander with vigorous shouts.

The *New York Herald*'s Sylvanus Cadwallader commented: "Never since its organization had the Army of the Potomac been in better spirits, or more eager to meet the enemy." Young Charles Page of the *New York Tribune* wrote, "I have never seen the army move with more exact order, with a less number of stragglers, and with so little apparent fatigue to the men."

Upon reaching the Rapidan, Grant telegraphed Halleck, "The crossing of Rapidan effected. Forty-eight hours now will demonstrate whether the enemy intends giving battle this side of Richmond." In less than half that time, Grant would receive his answer.

SHORTLY BEFORE NOON, Grant crossed the Rapidan at Germanna Ford. He rode to the crest of the bluff overlooking the river and set up temporary headquarters in a deserted farmhouse. A table and two chairs were the only furniture. He sat on the front steps and lit a cigar.

Nearby, Meade set up his tent, complete with his new headquarters flag—a golden eagle in a silver wreath against a lavender background. Grant, chuckling, could not resist asking an aide, "What's this!—Is Imperial Caesar anywhere about here?"

By the next morning, Meade's ornate flag had disappeared. In its place, following Grant's practice, he had hung a small American flag.

MAY 5 DAWNED early for Grant and Meade's blue-clad soldiers. Finishing their coffee, soldiers prepared to march at sunrise on what promised to be a warmer than usual spring day. Warren, who impressed Grant with his confident demeanor, started on the wagon track leading to the Wilder-

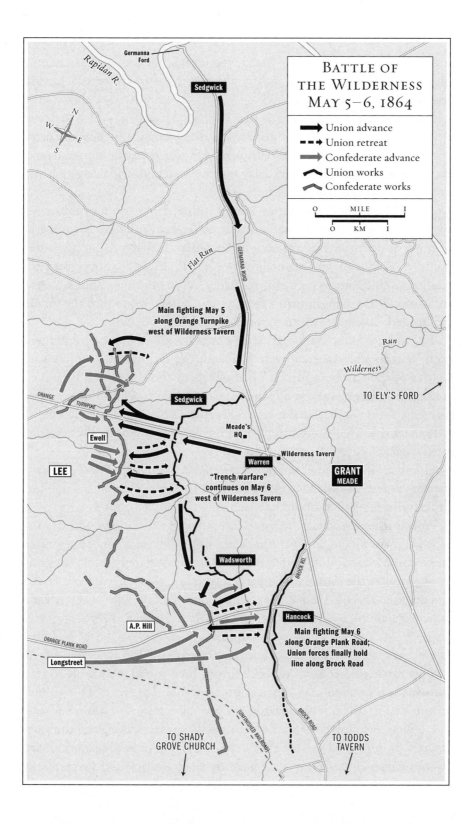

BATTLE OF
THE WILDERNESS
MAY 5–6, 1864

→ Union advance
⇢ Union retreat
→ Confederate advance
⌒ Union works
⌒ Confederate works

O   MILE   I

O   KM   I

Germanna
Ford

Rapidan R.

Sedgwick

N
W   E
S

Flat Run

GERMANNA ROAD

Main fighting May 5
along Orange Turnpike
west of Wilderness Tavern

Run

Wilderness

TO ELY'S FORD

Sedgwick

ORANGE

TURNPIKE

Meade's
HQ

Ewell

Wilderness Tavern

LEE

Warren

GRANT
MEADE

"Trench warfare"
continues on May 6
west of Wilderness Tavern

BROCK RD.

Wadsworth

A.P. Hill

Hancock

ORANGE PLANK ROAD

Main fighting May 6
along Orange Plank Road;
Union forces finally hold
line along Brock Road

Longstreet

[UNFINISHED RAILROAD]

BROCK ROAD

TO SHADY
GROVE CHURCH

TO TODDS
TAVERN

ness Tavern, accompanied by Meade. Sedgwick set off from Germanna Ford, while Hancock's men marched down the Catharpin road toward Todds Tavern.

Meade and Warren halted at the Wilderness Tavern, where at seven fifteen A.M. Meade received information that elements of Lee's infantry were advancing up the Orange Turnpike. At seven thirty he alerted Grant, "I think the enemy is trying to delay our movement & will not give battle but of this we shall soon see."

Still at the farmhouse, Grant found himself in a conundrum of his own making. He had promised himself not to butt in on Meade's operation, but as the morning wore on, he chafed at the news from the battlefronts. At eight thirty he replied to Meade, "If any opportunity presents itself of pitching into a part of Lee's Army, do so without giving time for disposition." Growing impatient, by nine A.M. he swung into the saddle and headed Cincinnati south to join Meade.

By midmorning, stunningly, the extent of Lee's boldness emerged. Both Warren and Hancock were attacked, but each failed to appreciate the size of the attacking forces. The thickets of the Wilderness furnished the perfect camouflage for advancing Confederates. Union forces were falling back into defensive stances, undercutting their two-to-one superiority. And then the woods caught fire, smoke shrouding the already confused scene.

Grant, riding down Germanna Plank Road, arrived at Meade's headquarters at ten A.M. Meade conveyed to Grant his assessment of the rapidly developing situation of Lee's two-sided advance.

At this moment, Grant began to face up to the illusion of Meade's independent command. Over the next few hours, his impatience grew as he listened to Meade and his generals discuss the best strategy while Lee continued to seize the initiative. By early afternoon, Warren's and Hancock's advance had become an embarrassing reversal. At two P.M., Meade launched a counteroffensive, but within half an hour it fizzled.

THE ENEMY WAS not only the Confederates, but the Wilderness itself. As daylight trickled through the scrub forest, men found it difficult to stay in formation or even see who was on their right or left. Infantry lines became distorted, bullets whizzing in every direction. The Union advantage in artillery power proved worthless. Correspondent Page summed up the fighting: "The work was at close range. No room in that jungle for maneuvering; no possibility of a bayonet charge; no help from artillery;

no help from cavalry; nothing but close, square, severe, face-to-face volleys of fatal musketry." Most important, Grant's careful orchestration of coordinated attacking lines fell apart.

As afternoon dimmed into early evening, Grant's challenge emerged: how to reinstate a measure of coordination in this huge army. His core strategy had been for his superior force to attack together so that Lee, with a smaller force, could not shift his lines from place to place to blunt the most perilous Union attack. Grant's plan wasn't working.

In the late afternoon, as Hancock tried to regain the offensive, Alexander Hays discovered his line had been broken and led his men in repairing the breach. As he rushed forward, he was struck by a minié ball and died instantly.

When news of his death was brought to Grant, the imperturbable man was overcome with emotion. For minutes he said nothing. Then he spoke slowly, hesitating between sentences. "Hays and I were cadets together for three years. We served for a time in the same regiment in the Mexican war. He was a noble man and gallant officer." He paused. "I am not surprised he met his death at the head of his troops; it was just like him. He was a man who would never follow, but would always lead in battle." Grant had lost another friend.

By nine P.M., a vexing day drew to a close. Grant and Meade had been outmaneuvered by a more agile Lee.

ON MAY 6, the second day of fighting, Grant restarted the coordinated offensive before dawn along five miles of fighting front. Hancock attacked along Orange Plank Road from the east, while James Wadsworth's Fourth Division of Warren's Fifth Corps angled in from the north against Ambrose P. Hill's defenses. In furious fighting, Hill's forces began to give way. Lee wondered aloud: Where was Longstreet?

But with the first light, there was Longstreet's First Corps, double-timing, turning onto Orange Plank Road. Larger than life, "Old Pete" urged them on in a loud voice and they mounted a counteroffensive. Longstreet's fresh troops arrived fully organized, whereas Union forces, having fought for hours in wooded, overgrown country, had by then become mostly disorganized. Within two hours, Longstreet reversed the tide of the battle.

By midmorning, Grant's offensive had slowed, if not stopped. Sedgwick and Warren were slugging it out with Ewell in what is best described as trench warfare. Hancock and Wadsworth had their hands full with Longstreet. Grant's trump card, Burnside, whose reserve he planned to insert between the two Confederate armies, was behind schedule as usual.

At midday, Grant and Meade discussed how to regain the upper hand. Grant believed the only way forward would be a coordinated attack by both Hancock and Burnside. Hancock, under severe attack all day, was ordered to give his men rest during the afternoon hours and resume his attack at six P.M.

Late in the afternoon, a general arrived at Grant's headquarters, speaking rapidly and with considerable excitement. "I know Lee's methods well by past experience," he asserted, and was worried that "he will throw his whole army between us and the Rapidan, and cut us off completely from our communications." Horace Porter, standing nearby, observed Grant rise "with a degree of animation which he seldom manifested," and reply, "Oh, I am heartily tired of hearing about what Lee is going to do. Some of you always seem to think he is suddenly going to turn a double somersault, and land in our rear and on both of our flanks at the same time. Go back to your command, and try to think what we are going to do ourselves, instead of what Lee is going to do."

Soon after this, Lee attacked, but this time Hancock and his fresh, organized troops proved too much for Lee's brigades. For the first time in this battle, Lee overreached himself.

BY THE END of the second day of fighting, Grant had sent only one official message to Washington. He knew Lincoln and Stanton were anxious to hear the results of the fighting, but his overriding concern was to keep his plans secret, which the president had given him permission to do.

But Grant sent another message, spontaneously, through an unlikely conduit, not knowing whether it would get through. That evening a *New York Tribune* correspondent, Homer Byington, summoned three reporters around a campfire near Grant's headquarters, telling them they must get a story on the Battle of the Wilderness through to the *Tribune*. Since Grant had closed down the telegraph lines, Byington offered $1,000 to any man willing to try to make it to Washington.

After an uncomfortable silence, one of the men volunteered: Henry E. Wing, only twenty-four years old, a slender Connecticut cub reporter who had lost two fingers as a soldier at Fredericksburg. Suddenly confident, he walked over to Grant's headquarters, told him he was leaving in the morning, and asked if there was any message he could convey to a news-starved public. Grant, uncharacteristically annoyed by reporters swarming around his tent like flies, replied, "You may tell the people that things are going swimmingly down here."

As Wing thanked Grant and turned to leave, he suddenly felt a hand on his shoulder. "You expect to get through to Washington?" Grant hesitated and then, speaking softly so no one could overhear, said, "Well, if you see the President, tell him for me that, whatever happens, there will be no turning back."

Wing started out at four A.M. on May 7. After he'd crossed the Rapidan at Ely's Ford, a Unionist warned him that the only possibility of getting through, with John Mosby's guerrillas running rampant, was to dress as a Southern sympathizer and carry a faux message from Lee of a Confederate victory in the Wilderness. Accordingly, Wing donned a disguise and destroyed the message he had written down from Grant.

After numerous close calls, Wing arrived in Washington and delivered the plain six-word message—"There will be no turning back"—that embodied the lieutenant general's pledge to Lincoln of his confidence of ultimate victory. Lincoln told his young secretary John Hay, "How near we have been to this thing before and failed. I believe if any other General had been at the Head of that army it would have been on the other side of the Rapidan. It is the dogged pertinacity of Grant that wins."

FOR TWO DAYS, nearly two hundred thousand men fought one another in the deadly Battle of the Wilderness. The stark statistics—the Federals suffered 17,666 casualties and the Confederates about 7,500—do not begin to describe the horror. Nature was as much an enemy as the opposing army—diminishing light, disorienting vision, barring ways, and entangling attempted advances. Sound became as important as sight. As the scrub forest caught fire, men were burned alive. Other men, seeing the fire approaching, killed themselves with their own weapons.

Lincoln sat in the telegraph office for hours on May 5 and 6, waiting for reports that never arrived. Asked by a member of Congress about Grant's progress, Lincoln reportedly replied, "Well, I can't tell much about it. You see, Grant has gone to the Wilderness, crawled in, drawn up the ladder, and pulled in the hole after him, and I guess we'll have to wait till he comes out before we know just what he's up to."

Through it all, Grant retained his optimism. As in the second day of fighting at Shiloh, he managed to seize the initiative, but this time he could not produce a decisive decision. Yet he did not consider the battle a defeat. Rawlins, his closest aide, observed that Grant met the predicament of the Battle of the Wilderness "with calmness and self-possession."

What lessons were learned? Grant took away positive impressions of Lee. He told Meade, "Joe Johnston would have retreated after two days of such punishment." At the same time, Meade and some of his generals declined in Grant's estimation. Hancock did not prove to be as superb as advertised; Warren had disappointed; Sedgwick had been outmaneuvered. These judgments would have consequences for the way Grant would think and plan in the unfolding of the spring campaign.

GRANT WAS THE first one up at his headquarters on the morning of May 7. The question on everyone's mind as the day dawned: How long would this titanic struggle last? Men on both sides, exhausted, prepared to fight another day. As he warmed himself at the campfire, Grant seemed to his staff refreshed after a night's sleep. He may have thought about his relationship with Meade. He had intended to give the seasoned general great latitude for hour-by-hour decisions, as he had always done with his corps commanders. But once the fighting started, as their coordinated plans became more and more uncoordinated, Grant found himself pulled into many tactical decisions himself. And once Burnside was added in, reporting directly to Grant, the opportunity for tensions became inevitable.

For the average soldier, whether in the Wilderness in 1864 or in France in 1944, it was impossible to comprehend the whole of a battle. When they awoke on May 7, most Union soldiers were dispirited, believing they had lost the Battle of the Wilderness. Grant had anticipated twelve thousand casualties; the number grew to almost eighteen thousand. Many of his soldiers now anticipated another humiliating retreat like the one in 1862 with Burnside and the one with Hooker in 1863.

At six thirty A.M., Grant issued orders to prepare for a night march but instructed Meade not to distribute the orders until after dark. Word filtered out among the men that the pontoon bridges had been removed from the Rapidan, but this might mean the army would simply march east toward Fredericksburg and cross the Rappahannock to turn back north to safe territory.

The infantry began to march at eight thirty that evening. Grant, Meade, and the headquarters party started along Brock Road. In the darkness, fog, and smoke from the still burning scrub forest, it was difficult for soldiers to recognize anyone. But a buzz grew as the headquarters party came into sight at the Chancellorsville junction. Recognition passed from man to man, and soldiers flocked to the junction, pushing in from all sides. In the dim light they recognized Grant on Cincinnati, the huge horse dancing with excitement.

Which direction would Grant turn? Back north in the direction of the Rapidan? Back toward the humiliating retreats of the past? As the men swarmed to see, Grant turned south. He turned onto the road leading to the Spotsylvania Court House, where Lee waited. In one of the most dramatic moments of the entire war, soldiers leaped to their feet and began to cheer, their voices echoing through the forest.

Grant's decision to turn south served as a potent elixir to men wounded of body and spirit. Some began to sing the spiritual "Ain't I Glad to Get Out of the Wilderness." Horace Porter, awed by the scene, wrote, "The night march had become a triumphal procession for the new commander." For the first time, Grant earned the unprompted applause of the Army of the Potomac.

Artist Edwin Forbes captured Grant's decision to turn south after the Battle of the Wilderness instead of retreating north, as all previous Union commanders had done. Grant's resolution evokes the cheers of hundreds of soldiers who raised their hats in applause.

When Grant assumed command of all the Union armies, his background was routinely compared with that of Robert E. Lee, commander of the Army of Northern Virginia—the former a common tanner/farmer from little-known Galena, Illinois, the latter a courtly product of Virginia's landed gentry.

CHAPTER 21

Robert E. Lee

The world has never seen so bloody or so protracted a battle
as the one being fought and I hope never will again.
—ULYSSES S. GRANT to JULIA DENT GRANT, May 13, 1864

Victory in war is always a matter of perception.

Grant wrote Halleck on May 8, "The results of the three days fight at Old Wilderness was decidedly in our favor." If his declaration sounded overly sanguine, he added that it was "impossible to inflict the heavy blow on Lee's army I had hoped."

The correspondent for the *Richmond Dispatch* reported the result quite differently: "The boasted leader of the Federal army chose his own time and place to deliver battle; he made the attack and was repulsed with heavy losses; his combinations were penetrated and defeated, and his whole movement checkmated, at least for the present."

The Northern public thronged newspaper and telegraph offices, eager for news of the battle, only to express disappointment as initial reports finally trickled in. Most citizens operated from the belief that Union generals should win a decisive victory in every battle. Few grasped that the Wilderness represented the opening act in what would become an extraordinary long-running drama between two skilled directors, Ulysses S. Grant and his adversary, Robert E. Lee.

BY THE SPRING of 1864, Lee had come to embody the hopes and dreams of the Southern people. Soldiers may never have seen Lee, but they felt affection for him. Catherine Ann Devereux Edmondston, who with her husband entertained Confederate soldiers on their two plantations in North Carolina, wrote in her diary, "They think him as pure a patriot as Washington and a more able General."

Lee's life story contrasted starkly with Grant's in every way. His birth in 1807 at Stratford Hall, the brick mansion located in the northern neck of Virginia, could not have been more different from Grant's birth in 1822 at tiny Point Pleasant on the Ohio frontier. Lee's father was the famous "Light-Horse Harry" Lee, a Revolutionary War hero who was George Washington's cavalry leader; his mother, Ann Hill Carter, was the daughter of a wealthy old-line tidewater family. But all that began well did not end well. After serving as governor of Virginia, "Light-Horse Harry" shamed his family by his womanizing and wastrel ways. Imprisoned for his debts, he died while returning from self-imposed exile in the West Indies. It seemed young Robert, who never really knew his father, determined to become everything his infamous father threw away.

Despite his father's fall, Lee was a patrician son of privilege and benefited from a classical education. He encountered the original Ulysses when he learned to read in both Greek and Latin. As an adult, he would use Latin mottoes effortlessly in conversations. Lee entered West Point in 1825 and graduated second out of forty-six in the class of 1829, without a single demerit on his record—whereas Grant graduated twenty-first out of thirty-nine, with plenty of demerits. Unlike many graduates who left the army for more lucrative opportunities, Lee stayed in the army.

In 1831, Lee married Mary Anna Randolph Custis, great-granddaughter of Martha Washington, at her parents' splendid home, Arlington, just across the Long Bridge from Washington.

In the Mexican War, Lee made a name for himself on Winfield Scott's staff. In the postwar army, as Grant served and then resigned from his unhappy posting on the Pacific coast, Lee served for three years as superintendent of West Point. In October 1860, while Grant worked under the direction of a younger brother in the family leather goods store in Galena, Lee accepted the assignment of stopping John Brown, the abolitionist who commandeered the U.S. Arsenal at Harpers Ferry, Virginia. Grant's father, at twenty-one, had lived with young John Brown, age fifteen, in the Owen Brown household decades before in Hudson, Ohio.

After the attack on Fort Sumter, as Grant spent weeks seeking a place to serve, Lincoln offered Lee command of all the Union forces. He was torn: "I declined the offer he made me to take command of that army that was to be brought into the field, stating as candidly and as courteously as I could, that though opposed to secession and deprecating war, I could take no part in an invasion of the Southern States."

Unlike Grant, who started the Civil War near the bottom of the chain of command, Lee began near the top. In the winter of 1861–1862, Lee was assigned to oversee fortifications of cities on the southeastern coast. In

March 1862, Jefferson Davis recalled him to Richmond to serve as his personal military adviser. And when General Joe Johnston was severely wounded at the Battle of Seven Pines in May 1862, Lee assumed command. Reorganizing the Army of Northern Virginia, Lee drove McClellan back from the gates of Richmond. Lee's victories on Virginia battlefronts located near major population centers in the eastern theater overshadowed even Grant's most notable successes in the west. Although Meade turned back Lee's invasion of the North at Gettysburg in July 1863, Lee left the battlefield far from defeated. An avid reader of Northern newspapers, he created a strategy for 1864 that was as much political as military. He believed if he could frustrate Grant's efforts in Virginia, the Northern public, growing tired of war, would turn Lincoln out of office in November and terminate the war.

IF BY 1864 Grant had become adroit at maneuvering large armies of more than one hundred thousand men, in getting through the Wilderness, he did not adequately consider the obstacles of terrain and timing, which played to Lee's favor. Now, in a race south, Grant ordered the Army of the Potomac in a flanking movement, wanting to get between Lee's army and Richmond. Following a careful study of his maps, he decided on his destination: Spotsylvania Court House, a town on the road to Richmond. When Union advance elements arrived at the small crossroads town early in the morning of May 8, Grant's greatest fear was realized: Richard H. Anderson, who had relieved the wounded Longstreet, was waiting for them to block their way south.

WHEN GRANT ARRIVED that first morning, he was already embroiled in a battle—a conflict inside his command. Meade, of whom Grant was already wary, had clashed with the only senior colleague he had brought from the west. Grant first met Philip Sheridan at Corinth, but it was Sheridan's assault on Missionary Ridge that boosted his appreciation of the young general. In Virginia, Sheridan found himself under the command of Meade as the cavalry leader.

Born in 1831, the son of Irish immigrants, Sheridan grew up in Somerset, Ohio. Only five feet five inches tall, weighing 115 pounds, by his own description "thin almost to emaciation," he received the nickname "Little Phil" at West Point, where he graduated in 1853. But his most striking feature were his almond-shaped hazel eyes, which seemed to look right through you, giving him a fierce demeanor out of all proportion to his diminutive stature.

Grant found a staunch ally in "Little Phil" Sheridan, who innovated new roles for the Union cavalry.

Adding to his unmistakable appearance, "Little Phil" rode one of the tallest horses in the Civil War. Rienzi, jet black and sixteen hands high (five feet four inches high at the withers, the tallest point of a horse's body), became famed for his endurance. Today, at Sheridan Circle in Washington, the life-sized statue of Sheridan and Rienzi captures the dynamism of the general, his right hand stretched out as if commanding his cavalry.

Sheridan arrived in Washington on April 4 and made the rounds at the War Department, where he felt the penetrating gaze of Secretary of War Stanton. Earlier, when Grant had come on one of his "flying visits" to Washington, a War Department official had commented that "the officer you brought on from the West is rather a little fellow to handle your cavalry." Grant had responded, "You will find him big enough for the purpose before we get through with him."

On May 8, Meade, who had gained the nickname "Old Snapping Turtle" because of his short temper, grew upset by the traffic jam producing delays during the night march and sent for Sheridan. When Sheridan walked into his tent, Meade "went at him hammer and tongs." Theodore Lyman, Meade's aide-de-camp, wrote in his journal that when "General Meade is in excellent spirits" he "cracks a great many jokes and tells stories." Yet he can be "like a firework, always going bang at someone, and nobody ever knows who is going to catch it next."

Sheridan was the person who caught it that morning. Meade accused him of blunders and charged him with not making a proper disposition of his troops. Sheridan, who would not countenance a checkrein from anyone, responded angrily that Meade was responsible for the jumble on the road by not issuing clear orders.

In the midst of the verbal melee, the excitable Sheridan shouted, "I could whip [Jeb] Stuart if you would only let me." With this heated statement, Sheridan challenged the conventional wisdom that cavalry served at the infantry's command. Up to this point in the war, Union cavalry had been used in screening infantry, in reconnaissance, and in protecting supply trains. Sheridan knew that by contrast, Confederate general James Ewell Brown "Jeb" Stuart operated differently. In June 1862, he had led his cavalry one hundred miles in a complete circle around McClellan on the Virginia Peninsula, capturing 170 soldiers and many horses and mules. Sheridan believed the Confederate cavalry to be far ahead of the Union cavalry in effectiveness, but he aimed to catch up.

Fuming over Sheridan's insubordination, Meade stormed into Grant's tent with Sheridan in tow, where, Porter noted, "the excitement of the one was in singular contrast with the calmness of the other." When Meade reiterated what Sheridan had said about thrashing Stuart if given the opportunity, Grant interposed himself between the two men and asked, "Did Sheridan say that? Well, he generally knows what he is talking about. Let him start right out and do it." In this brilliant commanding maneuver, Grant was about to unleash a whole new thrust in the Union's aggressive strategy. But he did not want to do so at the expense of Meade's standing; indeed, over time "Old Snapping Turtle" would become one of Sheridan's biggest supporters.

WHEN ALL OF the Union troops arrived at Spotsylvania Court House, May 9 became a day of preparation. Although Grant believed that what mattered was not what the enemy would do but what he himself would do, on this morning he wanted to discover Lee's defensive scheme. At eight A.M., he mounted Jeff Davis, the small black pony he had developed a liking for because he moved with a smooth pace. He stopped to confer with John Sedgwick. They talked about the difficulties of the past days, but "Uncle John" expressed confidence in his corps in the campaign ahead.

As Grant rode on, it became evident that Lee held control of Spotsylvania. The Wilderness had prompted changes in strategy for both Grant and Lee. Up until the Civil War, armies followed patterns laid down in the Napoleonic Wars at the beginning of the nineteenth century. At that time, soldiers faced one another equipped with smoothbore muskets capable of firing one hundred yards at most. But the evolution of muskets meant that by 1864 rifles could fire up to three hundred yards and with greater accuracy. Since battles fought over open ground routinely resulted in enormous totals of dead and wounded, Lee's army in the Wilderness, although outnumbered, perfected defensive barricades of wood and earth, the precursor of World War I's trench warfare. *Mater artium necessitas,* Lee might have said. Necessity is the mother of invention.

In turn, Grant needed to learn how to attack this new kind of defensive bulwark. A master of maneuver at Shiloh, Vicksburg, and Chattanooga, he was about to encounter stiffer resistance.

Grant saw that during the night, Confederate soldiers had dug trenches with their shovels in preparation for a Union attack. The humble spade became as important as the rifle to the common soldier as the war wore on. The *New York Herald* cheered, *"Vive la spade!"* declaring, "Spades are trumps" in deciding many battles. Every soldier became an engineer. Some of the earthworks the soldiers' spades constructed can still be seen today.

Confederates heaped logs and fence rails and covered them over with dirt. Behind this first line they dug a second line of defense. Within the earthworks they made provision for holes through which muskets and artillery could fire. Every fifteen to twenty yards soldiers constructed traverses, breastworks built at perpendicular angles, to protect themselves from flanking fire. The total effect of their endeavors was to create a protective protrusion that, because of its configuration, came to be called "the Mule Shoe." The Mule Shoe stretched half a mile wide and was three-quarters of a mile deep. On the morning of May 9, the Confederates, with the little town of Spotsylvania Court House at their rear, faced out in a semicircle from northeast to northwest.

A no-man's-land existed in front of the fieldworks. This space varied but often was only a few hundred yards as each side took the measure of the other. Artillery shells roared through the morning, but a lone sniper's bullet could be just as deadly.

At about nine thirty, while doing reconnaissance, Sedgwick ordered the Fourteenth New Jersey to build additional rifle pits for better protection. Their work prompted sporadic fire from Confederate sharpshooters. The men ducked while Sedgwick, striding around in the open, laughed. "What! What! Men dodging this way and that for single bullets! What will you do when they open fire along the whole line?" As the men continued to flinch, he said, "I am ashamed of you. They couldn't hit an elephant at this distance." Moments later a bullet hit Sedgwick just below his left eye, killing him instantly.

When Grant was informed of Sedgwick's death, he could barely speak. Twice he asked, "Is he really dead? Is he really dead?" Sedgwick was the highest-ranking Union casualty so far in the Civil War. With visible grief, Grant declared, "His loss to this army is greater than the loss of a whole division of troops."

BUT THERE WAS no time for mourning. After completing his reconnaissance, Grant determined he had two options. He could attempt to flank Lee's extended defensive lines, or he could try to break through them. To face Lee's semicircle, he positioned Warren's Fifth Corps on the right, Sedgwick's Sixth Corps, now command by Horatio G. Wright, in the center, and Burnside's Ninth Corps on the far left. Hancock's Second Corps, the last to leave the Wilderness, had not yet arrived.

Looking for a soft spot in the enemy's defenses, Grant decided to try to turn the left of Lee's line. After Hancock arrived, Grant ordered him forward at six P.M. But this demanded crossing the deep Po River twice and building three bridges; with approaching darkness, that stymied Hancock's effort. Thus Grant's first attempt had to be placed on hold until morning.

On this same day, Grant had high expectations for Sheridan. He wanted him to ride around Lee's rear to disrupt Confederate communications, while Grant sought to dislodge Lee's defenses at the front. At first light Sheridan started down Telegraph Road, which united Fredericksburg with Richmond. His cavalry presented an imposing sight: ninety-eight hundred men rode four abreast, followed by thirty-two guns and hundreds of wagons filled with ammunition and food; the column extended a full thirteen miles. With the enormity of his force, Sheridan had no intention of cunning but rather invited Stuart to strike.

The next day, May 10, Grant wrote Halleck at nine thirty A.M., "Enemy hold our front in very strong force and evince strong determination to interpose between us and Richmond to the last." Then he emphasized: "I shall take no backward step."

Grant's offensive started again in midafternoon with Warren's Fifth Corps attacking on a milewide front. But the charge found no weaknesses in the left-center of Lee's line, where he had shifted troops to meet the anticipated attack. One consequence of Sheridan's foray behind Lee's lines was that Grant had no mounted force to keep an eye on Lee's front-line defense.

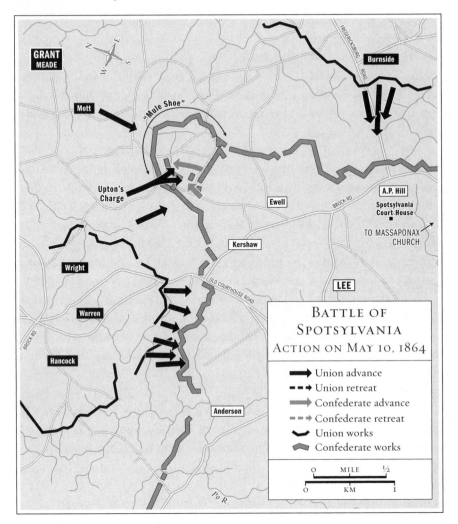

Grant set five P.M. as the hour for the main attack by Hancock against Lee's entire defensive line at Spotsylvania Court House. As the Second Corps prepared, they looked out on the blue-clad corpses from Warren's attack littering the field in front of them. The attack was delayed twice, and it was seven P.M. before Hancock led a furious charge. Some of the men who had watched Warren's ill-fated attempt had little stomach for their own effort. One of them muttered, "I tell you this is sheer madness, and can only end in wanton slaughter and certain repulse." It did. They were thrown back.

In the midst of these setbacks, an officer who believed he could over-come the ineffective assaults came to Grant's attention. Young Emory

Upton, an 1861 West Point graduate, told Grant the key was reaching Lee's defenses quickly, without stopping to fire—the normal procedure—and overrunning the earthworks before the enemy could respond. Grant listened, then agreed.

Given command of twelve handpicked regiments, Upton deployed them in three narrow columns. Upton believed his men could punch a hole in the Confederate defense that could be followed up by supporting troops. A soldier remembered Upton's order "not to fire a shot, cheer or yell, until we struck their works."

As Grant watched intently, Upton's men broke from the woods and raced forward without firing a shot, leaped over supposedly unassailable earthworks, and soon were through the first line of defense. Within minutes they had captured several hundred prisoners and several guns.

Supporting troops led by Gershom Mott of Hancock's corps started forward but hesitated when they encountered artillery fire and fell back in confusion. By now Confederates were counterattacking, and Grant, seeing Upton shorn of his expected support, ordered him to withdraw.

It took a bloody May 10 for Grant to realize that a soft spot did not exist.

MAY 11 BROUGHT cold rain after days of hot weather. Grant declared a day of rest following a week of continuous fighting. He would use the respite to rethink his plans for attacking a well-entrenched foe. On this morning, Congressman Elihu Washburne, who had been accompanying Grant, elected to return to Washington. He asked Grant "if I could carry a message from you giving what encouragement you can as to the situation" for the president. Realizing he was in a tougher fight than he'd envisioned, Grant told Washburne, "We are certainly making fair progress, and all the fighting has been in our favor; but the campaign promises to be a long one, and I am particularly anxious not to say anything just now that might hold out false hopes to the people." Sitting at a field table, chomping on his cigar, he wrote out dispatches to Stanton and Halleck: "We have lost to this time eleven General officers killed, wounded or missing, and probably twenty thousand men." After this dire report, perhaps thinking of how his message would be received, he concluded each dispatch with the same sentiment: "I propose to fight it out on this line if it takes all Summer."

Meanwhile, Sheridan, leading his cavalry in a measured gait around Lee's right flank, finally caught up with Jeb Stuart—or, rather, allowed himself to be caught. Stuart, nicknamed "Beauty" by jesting classmates at

West Point because he was not one, had by thirty-one transformed into a man of powerful build, with flashing eyes, full beard, and curled mustache—a larger-than-life folk hero to the Southern public. Dressed like a medieval knight, with a French saber, his gray coat buttoned all the way to the chin, and a brown hat with a black plume flying in the breeze, Stuart was rechristened "Beau Sabreur" ("Handsome Swordsman").

Unsure of Sheridan's intentions, Stuart had ridden day and night, arriving at ten A.M. at a deserted hostelry known as Yellow Tavern, only six miles from Richmond. He was used to surmounting long odds, but on this day his odds were even longer than usual. Stuart had only three thousand tired men. Outnumbered by more than three to one, his men riding exhausted horses, he decided it would be better to fight Sheridan dismounted, even if in doing so he gave up his mobility.

When the first elements of Sheridan's cavalry arrived around eleven A.M., they found Stuart waiting for them, his cavalry divided into two wings in a blocking position on the road to Richmond. Stuart's men were at a further disadvantage in weaponry, armed with single-shot, slow-firing muzzle loaders against Sheridan's rapid-fire carbines.

Still, the battle raged into the afternoon. Sheridan rode Rienzi back and forth, waving his black hat to encourage his men. At four P.M., Stuart's exhausted cavalry began to fall back. Stuart mounted his bay horse, Highfly, and sought to rally his men. When they charged again, Stuart was hit by a .44-caliber pistol bullet. The grievously wounded general was carried to his brother-in-law's home in Richmond, where a large crowd gathered; Stuart died the next day. His death sent shock waves through the Confederacy, particularly since everyone was aware that he'd died exactly one year and two days after Stonewall Jackson.

BACK AT SPOTSYLVANIA, Grant drew up a plan to employ a similar approach to the one Upton had used successfully. He rose early on May 12 and, as usual, warmed himself by the fire. The silence of the morning was broken when, shortly after four thirty A.M., on Grant's order fifteen thousand men from Hancock's Second Corps advanced across open space through mist and chilling rain toward the apex of the Mule Shoe. Charging through the mud, in narrow columns they surged over the barricades to capture several thousand soldiers and two generals from Ewell's Second Corps. To these whooping soldiers, their charge foretold a decisive victory for the Union army.

From where Grant sat nearly one mile away, he could hear but see nothing through the dense woods. At five thirty A.M., a courier galloped up with what would be the first of regular messages updating him with the latest reports from the battle scene. Grant had given orders that Hancock be supported on the left by Burnside's Ninth Corps and on the right by Wright's Sixth Corps, with Warren's Fifth Corps ready to move when ordered.

Lee had also risen early, at his normal hour of three A.M. Surprised by Hancock's attack, he responded quickly. Hancock's men had torn a gaping hole in Lee's front line, which was in danger of being split in two by more Federal troops poised to pour through. The two wings of Lee's defense were held together by the slim line of John B. Gordon's reserve division in Ewell's Second Corps.

Gordon, a thirty-two-year-old Georgian without official military training, possessed an instinctive understanding of what had to be done. Positioned at the neck of the salient—a piece of the defensive fortification that jutted out to form an angle—he urged his men forward and began to push back Hancock's initial charge.

By six A.M., as Hancock began dropping back to the original front line, Grant ordered Wright's Sixth Corps to attack the west angle of the Mule Shoe—what would later be designated the Bloody Angle. Charge and countercharge would result in one of the most horrific days of the war. The quick success of the bluecoats had the unintended consequence of jumbling Hancock's and Wright's units together, thus losing the cohesion with which they had begun.

From before dawn to nearly midnight, the Bloody Angle was a killing field. Men shot through gaps in logs, stabbed wildly with bayonets, and rushed forward in hand-to-hand fighting. Hour after hour they fought. So many minié balls were fired that a tree twenty inches in diameter fell to the earth. Bodies began to stack up five to ten deep. Usually such close-in fighting did not last long, as one side or the other would retreat. But not on this day.

Finally, after twenty hours of continuous fighting, Lee sent an order to fall back to a hastily constructed line a half mile farther in the rear.

LATE IN THE day, Grant convened a review of the action at Spotsylvania with his key generals and aides. In such reviews, Grant encouraged "the most frank and cordial interchange of views." He helped this process by not immediately joining in but reserving what he had to say until the end of the conversation. On this day, the center of contention became what Horace Porter called Meade's "anomalous" position. Meade both commanded the Army of the Potomac and stood second in command to

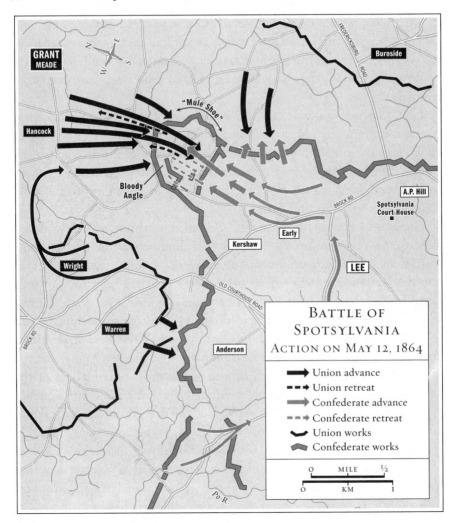

BATTLE OF
SPOTSYLVANIA
ACTION ON MAY 12, 1864

➡ Union advance
⇢ Union retreat
➡ Confederate advance
⇢ Confederate retreat
⌐ Union works
⌐ Confederate works

O   MILE   ½
O   KM   I

Grant. Rawlins and several aides urged Grant to bypass Meade and send orders directly to the corps commanders.

At the close of these intense conversations, Grant finally spoke: "I am fully aware that some embarrassments arise from the present organization, but there is more weight on the other side of the question." With responsibilities to direct Burnside, Butler, and Sigel, as well as Sherman, he found it comforting to be serving with an experienced leader such as Meade. Ever attuned to the issue of morale, Grant declared, "I have just come from the West, and if I removed a deserving Eastern man from the position of army commander, my motives might be misunderstood, and the effect be bad upon the spirits of the troops." He concluded, "He is capable and perfectly subordinate, and by attending to the details he relieves me of much unnecessary work, and gives me more time to think and mature my general plans. I will always see that he gets full credit for what he does."

And so Grant did. Understanding that contentious sentiments about Meade were in the air, that same day he wrote Stanton, "General Meade has more than met my most sanguine expectations." He went even further, recommending a promotion for Meade to the rank of major general in the regular army. "The honor would be worthily bestowed and I would feel personally gratified." In the same letter, he also recommended Sherman for promotion to major general for his stellar leadership in the west. Grant ended his letter, "I would not like to see one of these promotions at this time without seeing both."

INITIAL REPORTS OF Grant's success at Spotsylvania, especially the capture of three thousand prisoners, produced euphoria in the North. Used to hearing reports of Union defeats in Virginia, the public gobbled up any and all bits of good news. Grant's May 11 declaration to Stanton and Halleck ("I propose to fight it out on this line if it takes all Summer") quickly became banner headlines. Noah Brooks, from his listening post in Washington, reported in the *Sacramento Daily Union,* "The 'coming man' appears to have come at last, and Grant is the hero of the war. His name is on every lip in praise."

But when subsequent stories reported the ghastly account of the Bloody Angle, the public mood shifted. William Swinton, outspoken correspondent for *The New York Times,* contributed to this change of opinion: "Nothing during the war had equaled the savage desperation of this struggle . . . and the scene of the conflict from which I have just come, presents a spectacle of horror that curdles the blood of the boldest." Swinton concluded, "The one exclamation of every man who looks on the spectacle is, 'God forbid that I should ever gaze upon such a sight again.'"

After so much bloodshed, questions were beginning to be asked about Grant's tactics and the price of victory.

WHILE GRANT FOCUSED on the shifting battle lines in Virginia, he wondered and worried about his other commanders. He was not worried about Sherman, who with one hundred thousand men pushed Joe Johnston's Confederate force of fifty thousand out of Dalton, in northwest Georgia, in the second week of May. In command of John Schofield's Army of the Ohio, George Thomas's Army of the Cumberland, and James McPherson's Army of the Tennessee, Sherman set his face toward Atlanta.

But Grant did worry about his three political generals. He had instructed Franz Sigel to move his army up the Shenandoah Valley in order to block the enemy's source of supplies and pin down units that might be called upon as reinforcements for Lee. Grant learned that on May 15, at the village of New Market, Sigel's army of seven thousand was routed by John C. Breckinridge's smaller Confederate army of forty-one hundred. Halleck, more dismissive of political generals than Grant, bristled about Sigel: "He will do nothing but run. He never did anything else." Of more immediate worry, Breckinridge was sending two brigades to support Lee against Grant.

Grant was even more concerned with the progress of Benjamin Butler, because he hoped to link up with Butler's Army of the James in attacking Richmond. He handed Butler a plum assignment: to advance up the James River, cut the railroad between Petersburg and Richmond, and then threaten either Petersburg or Richmond.

Assembling a large fleet of transports at Hampton Roads in southeastern Virginia, Butler steamed up the James with an army of thirty thousand men and disembarked at the fishing village of Bermuda Hundred. He stood only eight miles from Petersburg, twelve miles from Richmond, and he faced fewer than ten thousand Confederate soldiers within a fifty-mile radius. Attaining Grant's objectives required decisive action. What Butler did most was argue with his two corps commanders, William "Baldy" Smith and Quincy A. Gilmore, who also argued with each other.

Though Grant's directive to Butler initially caught the Confederacy by surprise, while Butler dallied, Pierre G. T. Beauregard came up from the Carolinas. "The Little Creole" hastily assembled nearly twenty thousand troops, some of them teenagers and elderly men, and attacked Butler on May 16 at Drewry's Bluff, driving him back to his defensive line at Bermuda Hundred. Now wedged into a neck of land only four miles wide, Butler was corralled: he could not get out; Beauregard could keep him in with a small force. Grant described Butler's condition: "His army, therefore, though in a position of great security, was as completely shut off from further operations directly against Richmond as if it had been in a bottle strongly corked."

When Grant learned of the debacle, he knew plenty of blame could go around. "The fault may be with the commander, or, it may be with his subordinates. Gen'l Smith, whilst a very able Officer, is obstinate and is likely to condemn whatever is not suggested by himself," he wrote Halleck. Grant understood he would now have to adjust his plans, as Butler could no longer be part of his concentration against Lee. Additionally, Beauregard dispatched five thousand men—George Pickett's division—to reinforce Lee.

To make matters worse, Grant continued hearing discouraging news about the Army of the Gulf. On April 8, Nathaniel Banks's army was attacked by Richard Taylor at Sabine Crossroads, thirty-five miles south of Shreveport, Louisiana, in the Confederate army's victorious Red River Campaign. In response to Grant's frustration with yet a third political general, Halleck reminded Grant, "Genl Banks is a personal friend of the President, and has strong political supporters in and out of Congress." Grant was learning that even as lieutenant general his power was limited. Halleck told Grant he would be able to remove Banks only if he lobbied hard with Lincoln and Stanton for it. He did. On May 16, Grant declared the Army of the Gulf "has undoubtedly lost confidence" in Banks and ordered him replaced.

Soldier and artist Charles Wellington Reed depicts Grant on Cincinnati, rider and horse fused together in motion.

On his own front, Grant pressed ahead with unrelenting resolve. On May 18, the Army of the Potomac mounted another attack on the Mule Shoe, but Ewell's defenders beat it back. The next day, Confederate forces were driven back in the final engagement at Spotsylvania. After twelve days at Spotsylvania, far longer than he'd expected, Grant decided to swing around Lee to the left. He set his sights on Hanover Junction, twenty-five miles to the southeast. By staying close to the emotions of his men, Grant knew many shared his frustration at not being able to fight Lee's army in the open. One soldier wrote home, "How long 'Old Useless,' as the boys mischievously call the Lieutenant General, will allow it to hinder his onward progress, remains to be seen."

Starting out on May 21, Grant met good news—the roads were wide and passable; and bad news—he had neither maps nor guides. Even with better roads, his aide Ely S. Parker found himself surprised by Grant's unusual route of travel: "Roads are almost useless to him, for he takes short cuts through fields and woods, and will swim his horse though almost any stream that obstructs his way. Nor does it make any difference to him whether he has daylight for his movements, for he will ride from breakfast until one or two in the morning, and that too without eating."

Early in the day, Grant stopped at Massaponax Church. It was a hot, muggy day, and he ordered the pews removed and set up outside so he, Meade, and their staffs could plan. While they talked, photographer Timothy O'Sullivan climbed to the second floor of the brick church. From that unusual angle, O'Sullivan framed one of the most distinctive photographs of Grant as he smoked his cigar, examined maps, and read and wrote dispatches.

Lee was also on the move, determined to keep his army between Grant and Richmond. He purposely passed up opportunities to attack Grant's long line of troops and wagons. What did he intend?

The answer became clear at the North Anna River, only twenty-three miles north of Richmond, where Lee set up his next defensive line, blocking Grant's southern movement. The steep banks of the river rose into treacherous brush-covered land. In May, after heavier than usual spring rains, crossing the raging river could be managed only by bridge. Lee deployed his lines in a triangle with the apex positioned on elevated ground, shifting Grant's aggressive offense against him. By deceptively allowing Hancock to cross the river, Lee had Grant's army dangerously divided. Grant cautioned Burnside to remain in place, "the situation of the enemy appearing so different from what I expected."

At this moment, Lee fell sick with a virulent attack of diarrhea, re-

In May 1864, Timothy O'Sullivan climbed to the second floor of the Massaponax Baptist Church, where he photographed Grant—left end of bench nearest tree—examining maps and reading and writing dispatches.

stricting him to his bed. From there he implored, "We must strike them a blow—we must never let them pass us again."

Grant probed the center of Lee's defense on May 23 but decided the fortified line was too strong. After ordering his troops to entrench, he decided to exercise his own deception. He ordered James Wilson's cavalry to fire carbines as if they were preparing to attack Lee's left flank. This diversion, plus pelting rain, provided the opening for Grant to withdraw to fight another day at a more advantageous location.

On May 24, Grant finally made the past due decision to create a united command by bringing Burnside's Ninth Corps under Meade and the Army of the Potomac. On this same day, Sheridan finally returned from his adventure of more than two weeks, triumphant, bronzed by his days in sun and saddle, and eager to tell of his exploits.

UNLIKE MEADE, WHO often erupted in profanity, Grant did not swear. "Confound it!" "By lightning!" or "Doggone it!"—these were his profanities. "Rawlins does my swearing for me," he would tell people. "I never learned to swear. When a boy I seemed to have an aversion to it, and when I became a man I saw the folly of it. I have always noticed, too, that swearing helps to rouse a man's anger."

Nearing Richmond, Horace Porter recalled the only time he saw Grant lose his temper. Grant came upon a teamster whose wagon was stuck in the mud; the sound of his profanity preceded the sight of him "beating his horses brutally in the face with the butt-end of his whip." Grant spurred Egypt, a medium-colored bay recently received as a gift from admirers in southern Illinois, and rode forward. He dismounted and, "shaking his fist in the man's face," proceeded to lash him with his tongue: "You infernal villain!" Grant had the offending man tied to a tree for six hours. Porter took note that twice within the remaining hours of that day, with battles clashing around him, Grant spoke in "vehement" language about the cruelty of a man whipping his horses.

That evening, Porter asked one of Grant's aides, Major T. S. "Joe" Bowers, who had been with the general since April 1862, if he had ever seen Grant so riled up. Only once, said Bowers. During the Iuka Campaign in September 1862, Grant encountered a straggler who had stopped at a house and was assaulting a woman. "The general sprang from his horse, seized a musket from the hands of a soldier, and struck the culprit over the head with it." Bowers remarked that Grant always had "a peculiar horror of such crimes."

NEITHER GRANT NOR Lee anticipated the scope of their next battle. Never before had Lee been forced to fight day after day against such a determined enemy.

The race was on for Cold Harbor, eight miles northeast of Richmond, located close to where Lee and McClellan had fought in the Peninsula Campaign in 1862. Cold Harbor consisted of a run-down tavern in a crossroads village, sweltering in one-hundred-degree May heat and lacking any kind of harbor. The name actually derived from an English tavern where people could find overnight accommodations but not hot food.

In Grant's mind, several factors converged to propel his sense of urgency to attack now. First, he had finally reached a site ahead of Lee. Second, he believed if he attempted another flanking movement to the left, he could end up in the Chickahominy River bottomlands where McClellan had foundered two years earlier. Third, he knew he faced the loss of a dozen more regiments of three-year veterans when their service contracts expired in June. Finally, this would be his last chance before reaching Richmond to take advantage of his numerical superiority by engaging Lee in open farmland.

The Battle of Cold Harbor took shape from several disparate strands woven together. Days earlier, Grant had ordered "Baldy" Smith's Eighteenth Corps up from Butler's army to join with the Army of the Potomac. On May 31, as Smith approached, Grant ordered Sheridan to send two cavalry divisions to seize and hold the crossroads village, which sat at the intersection of five key roads. Lee grew alarmed by reports of Smith's movement of seventeen thousand men and ordered his cavalry toward Cold Harbor. What began as movements by small elements on either side quickly promised to become a full-scale battle of two large armies. On the hot, windless night of June 1, Grant sensed opportunity. He would face Lee with all five of his corps at Cold Harbor. Finally he might be able to attack Lee's army not behind their entrenchments, but in the open.

But Lee sensed opportunity also. If he could catch Grant's huge army strung out, approaching Cold Harbor from different directions, he could attack, sow confusion, and strike the grand blow.

Grant intended to attack at four thirty A.M. on June 2. He would get at Lee before he could ready his defensive fieldworks. But once more, the huge Army of the Potomac was not ready. Problems cascaded. Wright's Sixth Corps, exhausted from nonstop marching and fighting, fell behind schedule on their fifteen-mile all-night trek. Smith did not arrive until late on June 1 and sent an aide to report he was struggling to get his men in place and was almost out of ammunition. Meade blew up: "Then, why in Hell did he come at all?" Warren was reported to be quarreling with his division commanders. Hancock, even when sent Meade's best mapmaker, William H. Paine, became lost on an all-night march and would arrive late. In light of all these difficulties, the attack was postponed for twenty-four hours and Grant lost a splendid opportunity. Lee found another day to prepare his defenses.

As Grant waited, his thoughts may well have turned to the president, who was about to be nominated for a second term. To emphasize their common cause, in 1864 the Republican Party chose the name National Union Party. Grant understood that the successes or failures of the Union army he led would influence the mood of delegates as they converged on Baltimore.

For soldiers who endured the attacks at the Mule Shoe and the Bloody Angle, the gravity of what lay ahead was reflected in their behavior on the evening of June 2. Horace Porter noticed the men were taking off their coats and sewing what he initially thought were repairs—"rather peculiar at such a moment." But when he looked further, he saw "the men were calmly writing their names and addresses on slips of paper, and pinning them on the backs of their coats, so that their dead bodies might be recognized upon the field, and their fate made known to their families at home."

Before daylight on June 3, rain fell, breaking some of the oppressive heat but bringing with it a dense ground fog that made for limited visibility. Following Grant's orders, Meade would be deploying the commanders and managing the battle.

At four thirty A.M., more than sixty thousand soldiers, members of Hancock's, Wright's, and Smith's divisions, advanced on Lee's defensive lines. Hancock quietly captured a rebel position, as he had at Spotsylvania. Wright reported some success also. But the cost was tremendous.

Lee's army, having had forty-eight hours to prepare, counterattacked with tremendous firepower. "It seemed more like a volcanic blast than a battle," reported one Union soldier. Hancock reported that the men of his First and Second divisions "are very close to the enemy under a crest but unable to carry it." Smith requested support but quickly reported his men retiring. In the still-early dawn, Meade wrote Grant, "I should be

This *1864 illustration from* Harper's Weekly *captured the desperate fighting at Cold Harbor, Virginia.*

glad to have your views as to the continuance of these efforts if unsuccessful."

At seven A.M., Grant replied, "The moment it becomes certain that an assault cannot succeed suspend the offensive. But when one does succeed push it vigorously." Initial Union troops secured some of the frontline defensive rifle pits but could advance no farther, and even then they were hurled back. Frederick W. Mather of the Seventh New York Heavy Artillery summed it up: "Fought like hell and got licked like damnation."

For the first time, Lee halted Grant. The Union forces suffered seven thousand casualties, many in the first thirty minutes, as a result of Lee's withering assault. Lee suffered fewer than fifteen hundred casualties. In the conduct of war, the attacking force will almost always receive more casualties than the defending force. By early afternoon, Grant called off the attack. That evening, when officers gathered at his headquarters, he confessed, "I regret this assault more than any one I have ever ordered."

THE EUPHORIA THAT greeted Grant's crossing the Rapidan was now replaced by despair after Cold Harbor. Gideon Welles captured the mood: "There is intense anxiety in relation to the Army of the Potomac. Great confidence is felt in Grant, but the immense slaughter of brave men chills and sickens us all."

Grant had tried frontal assaults at Cold Harbor and Spotsylvania without success. Turning left once again would put his army into the Chickahominy swamp bottomlands. Halleck urged Grant instead to approach Richmond cautiously and lay siege to the Confederate capital. But Grant knew Lee had had three years to prepare Richmond's defenses. Growing more astute about the political nature of the war, and wanting to do nothing to impede President Lincoln's reelection, he worried that a long siege would play into the hands of the growing antiwar factions in the North.

Grant confronted a critical choice.

⊰⊷⊜⊶⊱

CHAPTER 22

Petersburg

> I have unbounded confidence in Grant, but he puzzles me
> as much as he appears to the rebels. He fights when we expect him
> to march, waits when we look for motion, and moves when we
> expect him to fight. Grant will take Richmond, if only he is
> left alone; of that I feel more and more sure.
>
> —CHARLES FRANCIS ADAMS, JR., to
> CHARLES FRANCIS ADAMS, SR., June 19, 1864

Grant and Lee were tied together in a campaign different from any seen before on the eastern front. The Confederate leader proved himself to be far more capable than Grant's earlier foes—Albert Sidney Johnston at Shiloh, John Pemberton at Vicksburg, or Braxton Bragg at Chattanooga. Grant showed himself to be more resourceful and adaptable. Instead of a battle lasting a few days, their war against each other's armies continued unabated.

While Grant seized the offensive after crossing the Rapidan, he could not checkmate Lee, who knew the Virginia chessboard better than he did. Each of Grant's offensive maneuvers had been countered by Lee's sturdy defenses. Although Grant voiced optimism about the future, Lee and the Army of Northern Virginia, outmanned and outgunned, continued to be a formidable fighting force. Knowing Richmond's defenses would be formidable, Grant decided to change his strategy.

He reviewed his long-held plans with Halleck: "My idea from the start has been to beat Lee's Army, if possible, North of Richmond, then after destroying his lines of communication north of the James River to transfer the Army to the South side, and besiege Lee in Richmond, or follow him south if he should retreat." Up to now Grant had focused everything on operating north of Richmond, but Lee's stubborn defenses were forcing him to change his thinking. "I now find after more than thirty days of trial that the enemy deems it of the first importance to run no risks with the Armies they now have. They act purely on the defensive, behind breast works, or feebly on the offensive immediately in front of them and where, in case of repulse, they can instantly retire behind them." He concluded, "Without a greater sacrifice of human life than I am willing to make all cannot be accomplished that I had designed outside of the City." Grant's critics have portrayed him as heedless of the number of casualties. But at this critical moment, with pressure mounting on him for results, he told Halleck there were definite limits to the "sacrifice of human life."

Grant now determined to alter his carefully prepared plans to attack Richmond from the north. On June 6, he dispatched Cyrus Comstock and Horace Porter to Butler's headquarters at Bermuda Hundred with a mission to scout the land and bring back the best maps available. He wanted them to answer a pressing question: Where could his army best cross the James River to the South? When they presented their report at midnight on June 11, Porter observed, "The general showed the only anxiety and nervousness of manner he had ever manifested on any occasion." Grant knew his new strategy involved high risk.

AT NOON ON June 7, while Grant was firming up his new plan to strike from the south, the National Union Party convention was gaveled to order at the Front Street Theatre in Baltimore. With Lincoln's support, the convention adopted a platform whose chief plank was "an amendment of the Constitution as will positively prohibit African slavery in the United States." The convention nominated Lincoln for a second term the next day.

The only suspense revolved around who would be Lincoln's vice president. Before the convention, newspapers and delegates had pressed Lincoln to name his choice. He declined: he would defer to the convention. In 1860, Republicans had chosen Maine's Hannibal Hamlin to balance the ticket between west and east. In 1864, in an effort to court War Democrats, the convention nominated Tennessee's Andrew Johnson, the only Southern senator who stayed with the Union following the outbreak of war.

On June 9, delegates traveled to Washington to notify the president of his nomination. In response, Lincoln declared, "What we want, still more than the Baltimore convention or presidential elections, is success under Gen. Grant." Mentioning Grant produced loud applause and shouts of "Good!" He concluded, "Help me to close up what I am now saying with three rousing cheers for Gen. Grant and the officers and soldiers under his command."

. . .

M APS IN HAND, Grant embarked on his new strategy. Just as at Vicksburg, he did not initially share his plans. Instead he instructed engineers to improve roads through the bottomlands of the Chickahominy River as if preparing to attack Lee in front of Richmond. He ordered Sheridan to take two divisions west of Richmond to destroy the Virginia Central Railroad but also to draw Lee's cavalry away. He ordered pontoons and bridging lumber brought upstream from Fortress Monroe. He knew everything would depend upon deception and speed.

Lee's reconnaissance detected the pontoons but thought they were to bridge the Chickahominy for a prolonged attack on the Confederate capital.

On June 9, Grant ordered Butler to launch a sudden attack on Petersburg, twenty-three miles south of Richmond. A transportation and supply hub, Petersburg connected with Richmond and points west and south through five railroads. Butler sent Quincy Gilmore's division, but the defenders, less than half the size of Gilmore's division, with many old men and young boys, turned the Federals away. Butler's army disappointed Grant once again.

On the morning of June 12, Grant agreed to pose for a photograph. Mathew Brady, who set out to document the story of the Civil War, positioned Grant in front of a tree by his headquarters tent for one of the best-known photographs of the war. Theodore Lyman was watching and writing as usual. "General Grant has appeared with his moustache and beard trimmed, giving him a very mild air," he observed, "and indeed he is a mild man really." Fascinated by the paradoxes of Grant's personality, Lyman believed "he is the concentration of all that is American."

That evening, Grant put his new plan into motion, wanting his movements shielded by darkness. His troops began to disengage from all along Lee's seven-mile defensive line, with Gouverneur Warren and James Wilson feinting aggressive action as if to move once more to the left around Lee. With Grant's movements disguised, his weary army began a rapid march to Wilcox's Landing on the James River. Grant understood the risk if Lee saw through the deception. His troops, beginning from different points and strung out on long marches, could be susceptible to attack. After joining Butler to defeat and secure lightly defended Petersburg, Grant intended to turn and attack Richmond from the south. He believed such an assault would compel Lee, at last, to fight in open country in front of the Confederate capital.

It was not until the morning of June 13 that Lee discovered Grant's army gone. Having no idea where they went, over the next several days Lee sent units both toward the lower parts of the Chickahominy River and toward the James River.

"Our forces will commence crossing James River today. The Enemy show no signs of yet having brought troops to south side of Richmond," Grant wrote Halleck confidently. "I will have Petersburg secured if possible before they get there in much force."

Upon arriving at Wilcox's Landing, Grant stood on the north bank of the James River and gazed at a remarkable feat of engineering. The many rivers in Virginia presented recurring obstacles to the southerly advance of Union forces. The James, formed in the Appalachian Mountains, flowed 340 miles east before emptying into Chesapeake Bay. In June 1864, after heavy spring rains, the broad river rushed eighty feet deep, a dangerous tidal current.

The Union answered with pontoon bridges. Consisting of twenty-one-foot-long wooden frames with watertight canvas skins, multiple pontoon bridges would connect to cross the wide river. These aggregate bridges could accommodate four men side by side, plus wagons and artillery. Grant, while inspecting the bridge, was ordered by a sentinel to snuff out his cigar. Amused, Grant tossed it into the river: "The sentinel is right. He isn't going to let me disobey my own orders."

William Waud's illustration of the Union army crossing the James River in Virginia captures the progress of Grant's massive army in the 1864 spring campaign.

With bands blaring and flags flying, Grant, hands clasped behind his back, marveled at the longest pontoon bridge ever built—twenty-one hundred feet long, thirteen feet wide, supported by one hundred pontoon boats. In the river below, he beheld an armada of gunboats, ferryboats, tugboats, schooners, and store ships. Men, horses, gleaming artillery, white-covered supply wagons, and a cattle herd of thirty-five hundred were crossing the river. This scene became well-known when British-born artist William Waud published his illustration of the crossing the James in *Harper's Weekly*.

In the afternoon, Grant traveled upriver to City Point, a small town on a bluff above the confluence of the James and Appomattox rivers at a point central to his armies. Here he established his headquarters. Late that evening, he wrote Julia. Often his letters to his wife were understated to avoid alarming her, but on this evening his tone changed: "Since Sunday, we have been engaged in one of the most perilous movements ever executed by a large army."

In the months that followed, Grant would transform City Point, a sleepy, out-of-the-way river settlement, into a huge Union port and supply base. Its wharf would stretch more than a mile, welcoming seventy-five sailing ships and one hundred barges on a typical day. Through the efforts of Quartermaster Rufus Ingalls, enormous warehouses were built for the commissary, ordnance, and quartermaster departments, along with smithies and wagon repair shops. The bakery turned out one hundred thousand loaves of bread a day. The sprawling Depot Field Hospital spread over two hundred acres and could serve ten thousand patients. Four steamers a day connected City Point to Washington. Ingalls built a twenty-one-mile railroad joining City Point and Petersburg.

But on these first days, Grant knew he had to strike quickly before Lee could recover. He ordered "Baldy" Smith to attack Petersburg, hoping he could accomplish what Butler could not. The Petersburg defenders had been augmented by troops hastily assembled by Beauregard but still numbered only about fifty-four hundred, far fewer than Smith's seventeen thousand men. Grant placed his confidence in Smith, who had first impressed him at Chattanooga. He also directed Hancock to come up as support.

Smith, recognizing an opportunity to redeem his name after recent disputes with Butler, approached Petersburg from the northeast, across hot, dusty roads. Usually vigorous, on this day he became overly cautious. Perhaps remembering that reconnaissance had been overlooked at Cold Harbor, he said he needed time to inspect the ground before him.

This wide-angle photograph of Grant's massive buildup of City Point, Virginia, was a testament to the former quartermaster's understanding of the critical importance of supplies in provisioning a mobile fighting army.

As hours passed with no word, Grant wired Butler, "Have you any news from Petersburg?" He did not know that Hancock, still troubled by a severe thigh injury suffered at Gettysburg, and traveling with an incorrect map, marched with an uncharacteristic lack of urgency. Increasingly concerned, Grant wrote again: "I have not yet heard a word of the result of the expedition against Petersburg."

During his silence, Smith was engaged in four hours of elaborate reconnaissance. What he discovered unnerved him. Petersburg's defenders operated behind an impressive perimeter. Ringing the city on three sides were miles of breastworks, twenty-four feet thick in places. In front were ditches fifteen feet deep, enclosed by abatis snarled with felled trees. All along the line stood forts secured with various guns. However, close inspection should have revealed that the defenses were poorly manned. The suddenly circumspect Smith delayed further.

Smith finally began his assault at seven P.M., expecting the arrival of Hancock's Second Corps at any moment. As his men advanced, a bright moon-filled sky lit their way. The defenses gave way with Smith's first thrust. Quickly his forces progressed one mile and captured a mile and a half of trenches, five forts, and sixteen large guns.

When Hancock finally arrived, thirty-five thousand Union troops faced no more than seven thousand Confederates. Writing later, Beaure-

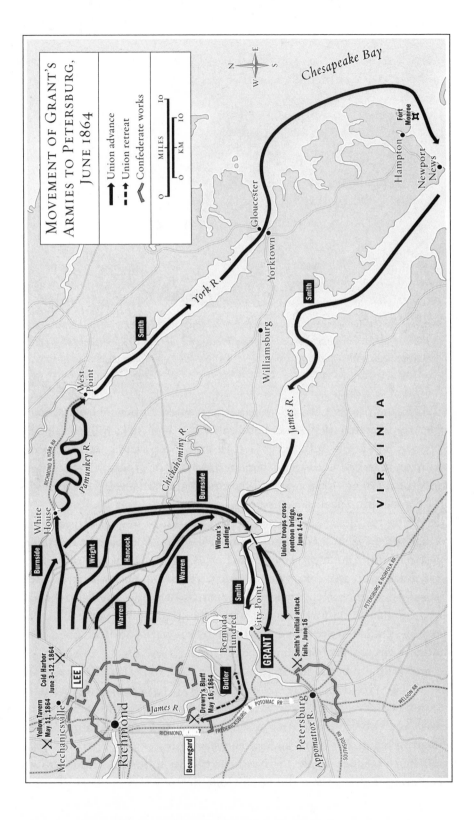

MOVEMENT OF GRANT'S
ARMIES TO PETERSBURG,
JUNE 1864

Union advance
Union retreat
Confederate works

MILES 10
KM 10
0

N
W   E
S

Chesapeake Bay

Fort
Monroe
Hampton
Newport
News
Gloucester
Yorktown
Smith
Williamsburg
Smith
James R.

VIRGINIA

York R.
West
Point
Smith
RICHMOND & YORK RR
Pamunkey R.
Chickahominy R.
Burnside
Wilcox's
Landing
White
House
Burnside
Wright
Hancock
Warren
Union troops cross
pontoon bridge,
June 14–16
Warren
Smith
City Point
Burnside
Yellow Tavern
May 11, 1864
Mechanicsville
Cold Harbor
June 3–12, 1864
LEE
Bermuda
Hundred
GRANT
Smith's initial attack
fails, June 16
PETERSBURG & NORFOLK RR
Richmond
Butler
Drewry's Bluff
May 16, 1864
James R.
FREDERICKSBURG & POTOMAC RR
RICHMOND
Beauregard
Petersburg
Appomattox R.
SOUTHSIDE RR
WELDON RR

gard summed up the situation on that early evening: "Petersburg at that hour was clearly at the mercy of the Federal commander, who had all but captured it."

On the morning of June 16, Grant, wearing a private's shirt, rode forward to Petersburg to have a look. The strength of the defenses impressed him also. On his return from the front, he met Meade, and the two conferred astride their horses. Grant told Meade he wanted the attack resumed, eager to take the city before Lee had time to react. The evening attack, assisted by Burnside, gained even more ground. All looked promising for the next morning.

On June 17, Grant ordered Smith, Hancock, and Burnside forward, but their efforts were uncoordinated. Warren was supposed to come up but, to Meade's fury, was slowed either by his own reconnoitering or, he said, by Confederate forces. In one of his finest hours, Beauregard, falling back, threaded together a new inner defensive line.

On June 18, realizing that they might not have many hours left, Union soldiers advanced again cautiously, occupying some of the trenches that had been abandoned the day before. But at seven thirty that morning, the first of Lee's troops began to file into Beauregard's trenches. Lee himself reached Petersburg by eleven A.M. At the end of the afternoon, Grant called off the attack: he had known from the outset that success depended on speed. After the war, he wrote that if his orders had been carried out on time, "I do not think there is any doubt that Petersburg itself could have been carried without much loss."

THE NEWS OF the abortive attempt to seize Petersburg further discouraged the North. Lincoln addressed these worries when speaking in Philadelphia on June 16: "We accepted this war for an object, a worthy object, and the war will end when that object is attained." Turning to Virginia, he continued, "General Grant is reported to have said, I am going through on this line if it takes all Summer." Lincoln declared, "I say we are going through on this line if it takes three years more."

TAKING HIS SUPPORT a step further, Lincoln was a surprise visitor to Grant's headquarters at City Point a few days later. Lincoln arrived on June 21, accompanied by son Tad. He told Grant, "I just thought I would jump aboard a boat and come down and see you. I don't expect I can do any good, and in fact I'm afraid I may do harm, but I'll just put myself under your orders and if you find me doing anything wrong just send me [off] right away."

"I know it would be a great satisfaction for the troops to have an opportunity of seeing you, Mr. President."

Lincoln concurred, saying he would like to visit the soldiers.

Grant gave Lincoln his large bay horse, Cincinnati, who could accommodate the president's long legs, while he rode Egypt.

He suggested Lincoln visit the black troops, one whole division in Burnside's Ninth Corps, who had fought so well at Petersburg. Horace Porter wrote that the president's reception "defies description . . . the enthusiasm of the blacks now knew no limits." As they crowded around him, Porter recalled that "they cheered, laughed, cried, sang hymns of praise," and shouted praise to the president.

The next morning, Lincoln started up the James to inspect more Federal lines. At Bermuda Hundred, impressed by the seized and fortified positions, Lincoln observed, "When Grant once gets possession of a place, he holds on to it as if had inherited it."

When Lincoln departed City Point, his experience with Grant deepened his appreciation of the general. Adam Badeau, a former New York newspaper drama critic who had joined Grant's command as his secretary in February, captured just why the two men got along so well: "There was a simplicity and straightforwardness about [Lincoln] that resembled the same traits in Grant; and when, as necessarily happened in their positions, their minds came in direct and naked contact, they appreciated each other better than clever and ambitious men."

Grant, renowned for his horsemanship, owned a number of horses during the Civil War, but none was more powerful than the enormous Cincinnati, who dwarfed his five-foot-eight-inch rider.

. . .

GRANT'S VIRGINIA CAMPAIGN entered a new phase by the time darkness fell on the evening of June 18. For forty-five days, from the Rapidan River to Petersburg, in woods, on rivers, and in small towns, Grant fought Lee in some of the most brutal battles of the war. He suffered sixty-five thousand casualties; Confederate casualties, much less precise, probably numbered around thirty-five thousand. Grant lost many of his best soldiers, some with him through three years of war.

Facing a siege at Petersburg, Lee knew long-run prospects for his armies were grim. He had told General Jubal Early, who fought with distinction at the Wilderness and Cold Harbor, "We must destroy this army of Grant's before he gets to James River. If he gets there, it will become a siege, and then it will be a mere question of time." Now, with his fears becoming reality, Lee was playing for time. Reading Northern newspapers, he understood that even though Lincoln had been nominated for a second term, he remained a target of criticism over what people increasingly called "Mr. Lincoln's War." He knew that Sherman, who had entered Georgia with one hundred thousand men, had been forced to diminish his army by leaving small detachments at various towns to ensure they would not be retaken by rebel forces. Lee believed if he and Joe Johnston could hang on for another four months, they might yet win by not losing.

GRANT INTENDED TO suffocate Petersburg by a logistic war—severing wagon and rail lines to the south and west. Realizing Lee's main army lay immobilized inside their defense lines, he wasted no time. He built his siege lines and moved in heavy guns, including coehorn mortars able to fire shells up to seven hundred yards. East of Petersburg, the two armies faced each other sometimes barely one hundred yards apart, regularly exchanging fire but occasionally also newspapers and coffee. However, to the south lines could be half a mile apart.

The logistic strategy proved more difficult than Grant would have hoped. He dispatched Hancock and Wright to break up the Weldon Railroad, Lee's major supply line between Petersburg and North Carolina. But what might have been possible on June 17 proved impossible by June 22. General William Mahone, a former railroad engineer who knew this territory well, exploited a gap between the two Federal corps and turned them back. Losing seventeen hundred men as prisoners was hard to take. "The affair was a stampede," Grant admitted to Halleck.

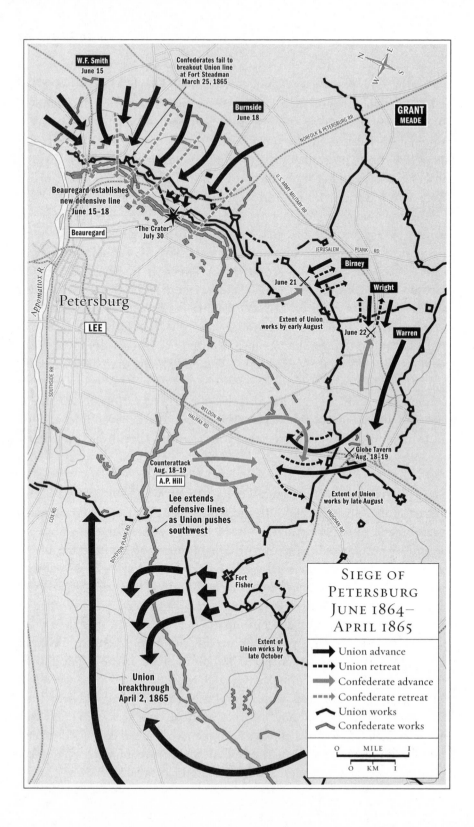

W.F. Smith
June 15

Confederates fail to
breakout Union line
at Fort Steadman
March 25, 1865

Burnside
June 18

NORFOLK & PETERSBURG RR

GRANT
MEADE

Beauregard establishes
new defensive line
June 15–18

Beauregard

U.S. ARMY MILITARY RR

"The Crater"
July 30

JERUSALEM PLANK RD.

Birney

June 21

Wright

Appomattox R.

Petersburg

LEE

Extent of Union
works by early August

June 22

Warren

SOUTHSIDE RR

WELDON RR

HALIFAX RD.

Globe Tavern
Aug. 18–19

Counterattack
Aug. 18–19

A.P. Hill

Extent of Union
works by late August

Lee extends
defensive lines
as Union pushes
southwest

COX RD.

BOYDTON PLANK RD.

VAUGHAN RD.

Fort
Fisher

Union
breakthrough
April 2, 1865

Extent of
Union works by
late October

SIEGE OF PETERSBURG JUNE 1864– APRIL 1865

→ Union advance
⇢ Union retreat
→ Confederate advance
⇢ Confederate retreat
⌃ Union works
⌃ Confederate works

0   MILE   1
0   KM   1

By the end of June, Grant commanded an exhausted army. Cyrus Comstock, commenting on the Weldon Railroad debacle, summed up the problem: "Troops did not fight nearly as well as when we started—best officers & best men gone—losses enormous."

If Grant believed Lee's army immobilized, he did not yet fully know "the Old Man." In early July, Lee sought a way both to divert Grant at Petersburg and to terrorize a Northern public beginning to think about fall elections.

Jubal Early would be his instrument. On June 12, Lee replaced an ill Richard Ewell with Early, once part of Stonewall Jackson's corps. Determined, if at times headstrong, Early represented an upgrade over the more cautious Ewell. Because of Early's aggressiveness, Lee called him his "Bad Old Man." At forty-seven, his troops called him "Old Jube."

Early swept down the Shenandoah Valley, crossed the Potomac River on July 6, and headed for Washington. Three days later, Lew Wallace, in whom Grant retained little confidence since Shiloh, put together a state militia at the Monocacy River east of Frederick, Maryland, but was brushed aside with little difficulty. After extracting a $200,000 levy from the Frederick city fathers and gorging themselves on ice cream, Early's cavalry continued riding north.

Grant understood that no army now stood between Early's fourteen thousand men and the Federal capital. Rumors inflated Early's army to thirty thousand. Not since the British burned the White House in 1814 had the capital been attacked.

Halleck began to doubt Grant's strategy of crossing the James to attack Petersburg. He expressed apprehension that Lee now lay between Grant and the capital. He also worried that Grant had stripped Washington's defenses when he called up its regular defenders to replace the large losses in his Virginia army.

Unruffled, Grant reassured his staff, "We can defend Washington best by keeping Lee so occupied that he cannot detach enough troops to capture it." He immediately dispatched Horatio Wright's Sixth Corps to the capital.

Whenever playing defense, Grant always planned how to go on offense. He saw Early's move as an opportunity to attack: "We want now to crush out & destroy any force the enemy dares send north. Force enough can be spared from here to do it."

But on July 10, Grant heard from another worried Washington resident. This time he listened. After the president learned Early had reached

Rockville, Maryland, twenty miles from Washington, he wrote Grant asking if the general in chief should come to Washington. He added: "This is what I think, upon your suggestion, and is not an order"—the commander in chief was not about to tell the general in chief what to do.

Grant had to make a difficult decision. He respected the president, but he also thought of his larger purpose. Many had expected him to capture Richmond by July 4, but instead he had fought for a month and a half against Lee's spirited defenses, only to end up at Petersburg twenty-three miles away, while Early had approached within seven miles of Washington in mere days, with no regular Federal forces to stop him.

Despite panic all around, Grant stood firm in his decision not to rush to Washington. After receiving Lincoln's message, he assured the president that the corps he was sending commanded by Horatio Wright would be sufficient for the defense of Washington. Besides, he told Lincoln, "I think on reflection it would have a bad effect for me to leave here."

On the afternoon of July 11, Wright, a soft-spoken engineer before the war, led his twelve thousand regulars with their corps insignia of the Greek cross up Seventh Street to the thunderous applause of crowds as they took their places at city defenses.

The next day, Early brought his fourteen thousand men to within five miles of Washington. Lincoln hurried to Fort Stevens, built to defend Washington from the north, to witness the combat. As the president, all six feet four inches and wearing his signature stovepipe hat, looked out over a parapet, a sharpshooter's bullet came dangerously close.

On July 12, Early realized he was now up against seasoned, well-armed Federal regulars and started back to Virginia.

DESPITE THE TURMOIL from Confederates, Grant was forced to spend time struggling with foes within his own Union forces. He had encountered contentiousness among generals in the western theater, but nothing had prepared him for facing the rivalries roiling in the east. By temperament, he did not like personal confrontation. In the months ahead, he would be forced to make tough decisions about self-seeking generals.

Grant had grown to like Meade, but he observed that others did not. Burnside had acquiesced to his decision to be placed under Meade in the interests of a unified command, but the two quickly found themselves at sword points. "It seemed as if Meade grew more unpopular every day," Charles Dana observed. "The difficulty of doing business with him [was] felt by everyone except Grant himself."

At the same time, Grant continued to wonder what to do about Butler. He believed the former Massachusetts congressman, without military training, fell short as a tactical commander. Grant did not want to leave Petersburg because Butler would become the senior-ranking officer. But he understood that Butler, powerful enough to be mentioned as a possible vice-presidential running mate with Lincoln for 1864, could not be dismissed.

On July 1, Grant wrote Halleck, "Whilst I have no difficulty with Gen. Butler, finding him always clear in his conception of orders, and prompt to obey, yet there is a want of knowledge how to execute, and particularly a prejudice against him, as a commander, that operates against his usefulness." He proposed, "It might become necessary to separate him and Gen. Smith." Grant praised Smith as "one of the most efficient officers in service" but said he might have to remove Smith if he could not remove Butler.

The next day, Smith wrote Grant requesting a leave of absence. Grant replied, "I much prefer not having you go." In Smith's letter, criticism of others predominated. He finally got around to talking about the main object of his displeasure: Butler. Smith complained, "how you can place a man in command of two army corps, who is as helpless as a child on the field of battle."

Grant decided to resolve the dilemma. He proposed making Butler's headquarters Fortress Monroe while giving Smith tactical command in the field. That, it seemed, would settle everything. Or would it?

On July 19, when Smith returned from his leave, Grant asked to see the man whom only months earlier he had considered offering command of the Army of the Potomac. He told Smith he had decided he could not relieve Butler but was relieving Smith instead. Grant rattled off a number of reasons for his decision. Smith's failure to capture Petersburg loomed larger in his mind now that he found himself involved in a costly siege. More important, he had grown tired of having Smith break Grant's cardinal rule: Do not speak ill of a brother officer. Unwilling to own up to his failings, Smith could not hear what Grant tried to tell him. "I again pressed him for the real reason," Smith recalled, Finally, "out of reasons," Grant "turned on his heel and said, 'You talk too much.'"

Theodore Lyman summed up the encounter: "Thus did Smith the Bald try the Machiavelli against Butler the cross-eyed, and got floored in the first round!"

THE SIEGE WENT forward without Smith. In defending Petersburg, the Confederates built a fort of logs and earth on every small hill. The small forts were ingeniously arranged so that every inch of the trenches could be protected by artillery fire. And with no rain for a month, the soldiers faced another deadly enemy: unbearable heat. Day after day, troops sweltered in heavy, dust-laden air. In the no-man's-land between the rival trenches, dead bodies lay putrefying under the broiling sun. With his soldiers suffering under abominable conditions, Grant sought to find a breakthrough.

At the end of June, he listened to a daring idea. Henry Pleasants, a mining engineer, believed his Pennsylvania coal miners could tunnel under a Confederate fort. Burnside supported the plan to take place in his sector and brought it to Meade. A former engineer himself, Meade expressed initial skepticism. But Grant, with success in smaller tunneling efforts at Vicksburg, authorized Burnside's plan. Pleasants planned to construct a five-hundred-foot-long mine shaft under the Confederate line, pack it with explosives, and blast a hole.

Judging that his first three divisions were exhausted from constant fighting, Burnside chose to use a fourth, fresh division for the assault after the explosion—the only division of black soldiers in the Army of the Potomac. Burnside proudly believed that if well led, they would show great courage and fighting ability.

So he pinned his hopes on Edward Ferrero, who had commanded African American troops in the Battle of the Wilderness. Ferrero began training his soldiers on July 9.

WHILE GRANT KEPT Lee bottled up at Petersburg, he received the heartening news that Sherman had defeated John Bell Hood at Peachtree Creek, only three miles north of Atlanta, on July 21. Grant had believed Hood would be more aggressive but also more reckless than Johnston, whom he had replaced. He was right.

The next day, Grant was stunned to learn that James McPherson had been killed in the Battle of Atlanta. Porter observed how "visibly affected" Grant became when receiving news of the death of one of his dearest friends. He "dwelt upon it in his conversations for the next two or three days."

Grant wrote McPherson's grandmother Lydia:

A nation grieves at the loss of one so dear to our nation's cause. . . .
To know him was but to love him. It may be some consolation to you, his aged grandmother, to know that every officer and every soldier who served under your grandson felt the highest reverence

for his patriotism, his zeal, his great, almost unequalled ability, his amiability, and all the manly virtues than can adorn a commander. Your bereavement is great, but cannot exceed mine.

Grant's letter calls to mind Lincoln's finest letters to the bereaved.

As GRANT WATCHED and waited, after weeks of work the Pennsylvania miners constructed a tunnel 511 feet long and 20 feet underground, with side galleries 40 feet wide loaded with four tons of gunpowder. The blast was postponed when Meade objected to Burnside's plan to use black troops in the attack. He argued they were too inexperienced—he did not trust them. Meade's decision was as much political as military. The recipient of harsh criticism after Gettysburg, he worried he would be condemned if he sacrificed black soldiers. When Burnside protested, Meade said he would consult Grant. Grant wired Meade on July 29, "The details of the assault I leave for you to make out."

Burnside drew lots among his unenthusiastic white division leaders as to who would lead the assault. The lot fell to James H. Ledlie, ironically the leader most lacking in military training. Among his fellow soldiers, Ledlie had a reputation for liking the bottle more than the battle.

On July 30, Pleasants had the honor of lighting the fuse. But it went out. Grant, wondering what happened, galloped to Meade's headquarters.

Everyone felt the suspense as minutes passed like hours. Grant looked at his watch: the blast was an hour overdue. Finally, with the fuse relit, the tunnel exploded at precisely 4:46 A.M. A deep rumble shook the earth, booming like summer thunder. The ground swelled up and broke apart, emitting flames and smoke. Suddenly dirt, rock, sand, timber, broken artillery, and broken bodies spewed two hundred feet into the air. A dark mushroom cloud hovered over the wreckage. The explosion created a huge depression, thereafter known as "the Crater"—170 feet long, 60 to 80 feet wide, and 30 feet deep.

Ledlie's First Division, last-minute substitutes with no special training, charged forward, flanked on either side by the Second and Third divisions, with the Fourth Division now designated as the reserve. Surrounding the Crater, 144 cannons and mortars made ready to open fire but struggled to distinguish the blue from the gray. Confederate artillery, not put out of action, began firing back. The Crater soon filled with disorganized Federal troops: the sides of the Crater were so steep that those inside found it almost impossible to climb out.

At five thirty A.M., Grant mounted Egypt and rode forward along Baxter Road toward the Crater. Engaging awed soldiers and unable to ride farther, he continued on foot, wearing a private's uniform of a blue blouse with blue trousers. One had to look carefully to see the shoulder straps with three stars. No one recognized his dirty face. Grant pushed through swarms of soldiers, many of them wounded. He climbed over a parapet, bullets whizzing everywhere, and finally found Burnside, easily identifiable by his height and tall bell-crowned hat.

At seven thirty A.M., Ferrero's black soldiers were ordered into the Crater. But they started too late, rushing forward just as Confederate soldiers counterattacked. By midmorning, the Federals broke into a disorderly retreat that turned into a slaughter. As the black soldiers attempted to flee, they were shot down by Confederate riflemen.

Grant felt anguish over what he witnessed. Everything went wrong: poor leadership and mistiming led to the slaughter of the black soldiers. He wrote Halleck the next day, "It was the saddest affair I have witnessed in this war." Seldom critical, on this occasion Grant wrote, "I am constrained to believe that had instructions been promptly obeyed that Petersburg would have been carried with all the Artillery and a large number of prisoners without a loss of 300 men."

The final Union casualties, 3,826, included 504 killed. Black soldiers suffered a significantly higher ratio of casualties. Confederates, who claimed a victory, listed their losses at only 1,491. The Federal tally included 1,441 missing soldiers, among them a large number of African Americans who were either returned to their "masters" or put to work at hard labor.

The disaster at the Crater damaged Grant's reputation. Secretary of the Navy Gideon Welles complained that Grant was "less able than he is credited." Confessing to "a foreboding of the future," he brooded, "A nation's destiny almost has been committed to this man, and if it is an improper committal, where are we?"

GRANT WELCOMED LINCOLN to Fortress Monroe on July 31. They talked for five hours. Grant spoke about opening a second front in the Shenandoah Valley to confront Early, who had just returned from north of the Potomac and whose tactics were growing more vicious. Just the day before, one of Early's commanders, John McCausland, failing to receive a ransom of $500,000 from the city fathers of Chambersburg, Pennsylvania, had burned the town to the ground.

Grant wanted Phil Sheridan to press an assault in the Shenandoah Valley, hoping "Little Phil" would succeed where Franz Sigel and David Hunter had failed. He may have remembered that final day at Chattanooga, when, after the ascent up Missionary Ridge left everyone exhausted, a young general had wanted to press on to defeat the enemy. Now he wanted Phil Sheridan to press the assault in the Shenandoah. Grant received Lincoln's strong approval.

Grant wrote Halleck the next day, "I want Sheridan put in command of all the troops in the field with instructions to put himself south of the enemy and follow him to the death. Wherever the enemy goes, let our troops go also."

Grant knew he had some persuading to do, but he had no idea how much political maneuvering was going on in Washington by Halleck and Stanton, who disliked Sheridan. It was true that his abrasive manner startled people when they first met him, but more significant, Halleck and Stanton chose to argue against him because of his youth and lack of experience. Grant understood that Sheridan lacked social skills, but to him what counted was the military brilliance he had exhibited in the Wilderness.

When Lincoln returned to Washington and learned of the machinations at the War Department, he applauded the iron in Grant's dispatch to Halleck. "This, I think, is exactly right as to how our forces should move," he wrote his lieutenant general. He advised Grant to look over the dispatches he would be receiving from Washington, because the president was not certain the War Department either understood or agreed with Grant's strategy for the Shenandoah Valley. "I repeat to you it will neither be done nor attempted unless you watch it every day, and hour, and force it." Never before had Lincoln warned Grant to watch out for political leaders in Washington.

This exchange between Grant and Lincoln reveals that they shared a common sensibility: better to fight now than later, even if the losses in the immediate might be large. At this moment, with Northern casualties mounting and many growing weary of the long war, there was no way to know if their approach would yield better military or political results. By now, Lincoln was pleased with Grant's string of victories. More than with any other general, he steered clear of telling Grant what to do— almost as if he knew that in Grant's position, he would take the same aggressive approach, with the same risks involved.

Grateful for Lincoln's warning, within an hour Grant was on a boat up to the capital. He knew he had to deal with Stanton and Halleck face-to-face, even if that meant leaving Petersburg. He wrote Butler, "Being senior you necessarily would command in any emergency," but he added, "Please communicate with me by telegraph if anything occurs when you wish my orders." In other words—I am still in charge.

Upon his arrival in Washington the next morning, instead of going to the War Department Grant went directly to the railroad station to travel overnight to Monocacy Junction, Maryland, where David Hunter was headquartered. The sixty-two-year-old Hunter had assumed command in May and moved aggressively up the Shenandoah Valley—southward—but was defeated by Early at the Battle of Lynchburg on June 17–18.

When Grant asked, "Where is the enemy?" Hunter answered he did not know. Grant's aide Cyrus Comstock described the scene bluntly: "Hunter's whole command [was] nearly there, doing nothing & not knowing what enemy was doing."

Grant immediately focused Hunter's efforts: "Concentrate all your available forces without delay in the vicinity of Harper's Ferry." He made his meaning clear. "The object is to drive the enemy South, and to do this you want to keep him always in sight."

By the summer of 1864, having become the site of frequent clashes, the Shenandoah Valley had lost its reputation for tranquillity. Starting where the Shenandoah River met the Potomac River in the north, the valley ran 110 miles southwest to the town of Staunton, Virginia. It was situated between the Blue Ridge Mountains on the east and the Alleghenies on the west and boasted rich farmland: grain, fruit, cattle, hogs, and sheep. A distinctive geographic feature of the Blue Ridge was the many passes, or "gaps," that allowed Confederates to come and go from their bases farther east. As one Union officer wrote, the Shenandoah Valley "offered a tempting highway" for armies to attack.

Up until this point, Early had roamed free in the Shenandoah, disrupting the vital Baltimore and Ohio Railroad and attacking into West Virginia and Maryland. Grant voiced his intentions with rare force. The enemy should know "he should have upon his heels, veterans, Militiamen, men on horseback and everything that can be got to follow, to eat out Virginia clear and clean as far as they go, so that Crows flying over it for the balance of this season will have to carry their provender with them."

While at Monocacy Junction, Grant told Hunter of his desire to place Sheridan as field commander, with the older Hunter remaining as department head. Butler had protested when Grant made a similar proposal, but Hunter graciously resigned. Grant wrote later that Hunter was "showing a patriotism none too common in the army" in giving up a command voluntarily.

Thirty-three-year-old Sheridan arrived the following day and, as ordered, reported directly to Grant. By early September, Sheridan would command a reorganized Army of the Shenandoah consisting of more than forty thousand men, including eight thousand cavalry. With this, Grant brought Sheridan into the inner circle of generals he trusted implicitly, which heretofore had included only Sherman and McPherson. He told Sheridan he would not attempt to manage or interfere with his efforts: "I feel every confidence" in your abilities and "will leave you as far as possible to act on your own judgment and not embarrass you with orders and instructions."

ON JULY 18, Lincoln issued a call for five hundred thousand new troops. Halleck was aware that the huge draft riots that had taken place in New York City a year before had represented (or exacerbated) a general reversal in mood among civilians, and he feared that new recruits would not be forthcoming. "It may require the withdrawal of a very considerable [number] of troops from the field," he wrote Grant. "Are not the appearances such that we ought to take in sail and prepare the ship for a storm[?]"

Grant replied that protecting the draft from rioters was the responsibility of loyal governors and state militias. If he withdrew troops from below the James, Lee would respond by sending troops to Georgia, which would threaten Sherman.

That evening, while in his quarters with staff officers, Grant received a telegram from the president: "I have seen your dispatch expressing your unwillingness to break your hold where you are. Neither am I willing. Hold on with a bull-dog grip, and chew & choke, as much as possible."

As Grant read, Porter noticed that "his face became suffused with smiles." Finishing, "he broke into a hearty laugh." Looking again at the message, he declared, "The President has more nerve than any of his advisors."

WITH GRANT STUCK in front of Petersburg, and Sheridan not yet attacking in the Shenandoah Valley, Democrats met in an upbeat mood at their national convention in Chicago. Their challenge was to find a middle ground between two wings of their party. August Belmont, gaveling the convention to order on August 29, warned his fellow Democrats that dissension in their ranks had cost them the 1860 election. The War Democrats nominated Lincoln's former military commander George B.

McClellan for president on the first ballot. The Peace Democrats wrote the platform that declared "after four years of failure to restore the Union by the experiment of war, justice, humanity, liberty and the public welfare demand" an end to the war "on the basis of the Federal Union of The States."

The Democrats had waited to hold their convention until the end of the summer, hoping that continued bad news on the military front would be good news for their candidate on the home front. Now, George McClellan, back at his home in Orange, New Jersey, struggled to determine how to run as a War Democrat on a Peace Democrat platform.

Before McClellan could speak, Sherman struck a game changer. On September 3, his telegram announced: "Atlanta is ours, and fairly won."

The victory at Atlanta changed everything. Pessimism dissolved, and a revival of Unionist fervor swept through the North. McClellan's Democratic presidential campaign struggled to respond to the good news. Grant wrote Sherman, "It is hardly necessary for me to say that I feel you have accomplished the most gigantic undertaking given to any General in this War and with a skill and ability that will be acknowledged in history as unsurpassed."

BUT THE WAR was far from over. While the North was encouraged by Sherman's action, concern mounted over Sheridan's inaction. Lincoln telegraphed Grant on September 12, "Sheridan and Early are facing each other at a dead lock. Could we not pick up a regiment here and there, to the number of say ten thousand men, and quietly, but suddenly concentrate them at Sheridan's camp and enable him to make a strike." He ended with his now customary "This is but a suggestion," but Grant did not miss the urgency in the president's communication.

Grant replied that he intended to meet Sheridan to determine "what was necessary to enable him to start Early out of the Valley." He traveled to Charles Town, West Virginia, to personally confer with Sheridan on September 16 and 17. "I knew it was impossible for me to get orders through Washington to Sheridan to make a move, because they would be stopped there," and subsequent orders "would, no doubt, be contradictory to mine."

As Grant and Sheridan talked, a Vermont sergeant identified the "two undersized men, rather squarely built," to John William De Forest, Twelfth Connecticut Volunteers, future novelist. "Don't you know who the other is? *That's* GRANT!" De Forest groaned, "When that old cuss is around there's sure to be a big fight on hand."

On his return to City Point, Grant stopped in Burlington, New Jersey, across the Delaware River from Philadelphia, to visit Julia and the children. Ulysses and Julia, valuing good schools, found a two-story house in the small New Jersey town of Burlington, just outside Philadelphia, where the children—Fred, fourteen; Ulysses Jr., twelve; Nellie, nine; and Jesse, six—could begin school in September. While Julia was house hunting, Ulysses had written, "I have a horror of living in Washington and never intend to do it."

ON SEPTEMBER 19, the rapid staccato of the telegraph at City Point brought constant news of Grant and Sheridan's plan of action to defeat Jubal Early in the Shenandoah Valley. At Winchester, Virginia, Sheridan massed five cavalry brigades and twenty infantry brigades, seven thousand men, battle flags and sabers gleaming in the sunlight. With verve and profanity, he seemed to be everywhere, urging on his soldiers. In the bloodiest battle fought in the Shenandoah Valley, at the end of a long day Sheridan had captured two thousand Confederates.

The next day, Grant wired Sheridan, "I have just received the news of your great victory and ordered each of the Armies here to fire a salute of one hundred guns in honor of it at 7 A.M. tomorrow morning—If practicable push your success and make all you can of it."

Sheridan did. On September 22, he attacked Fisher's Hill, twenty miles farther south. While two of his corps feigned a frontal attack against Early's entrenchments, the next afternoon George Crook's West Virginia and Ohio soldiers, hidden from the Confederate signal station at Three Top Mountain by dense forest, burst down mountain paths in parallel columns in a flanking movement that pushed Early's force farther up the Shenandoah Valley.

Sheridan wired Grant that he had "achieved a most signal victory" over Early's army. Grant thanked him for "your second great victory" and encouraged him, "Keep on and your work will cause the fall of Richmond."

As Grant watched Lee, with a smaller army, continue to hold out, he perceived what this could mean for his Union army. On the evening of the failed Crater attack, he had written: "With a reasonable amount of artillery & one Infantry man to six feet I am confident either party could hold their lines against a direct attack of the other." Why not use his trenches to hold Lee in place, simultaneously freeing large numbers of troops for offensive action away from Petersburg?

Grant also realized that Early's army was the only Confederate force

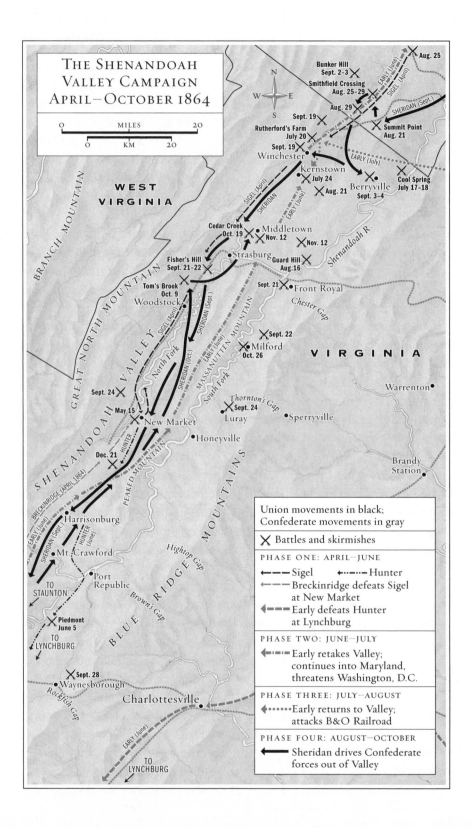

THE SHENANDOAH VALLEY CAMPAIGN APRIL–OCTOBER 1864

0 — MILES — 20

0 — KM — 20

WEST VIRGINIA

VIRGINIA

BRANCH MOUNTAIN

GREAT NORTH MOUNTAIN

SHENANDOAH VALLEY

MASSANUTTEN MOUNTAIN

PEAKED MOUNTAIN

BLUE RIDGE MOUNTAINS

Bunker Hill
Sept. 2–3

Smithfield Crossing
Aug. 25–29

Aug. 25

Aug. 29

Sept. 19

Rutherford's Farm
July 20

Summit Point
Aug. 21

Sept. 19
Winchester

EARLY (July)

Kernstown
July 24

Aug. 21

Berryville
Sept. 3–4

Cool Spring
July 17–18

Cedar Creek
Oct. 19

Middletown
Nov. 12

Nov. 12

Shenandoah R.

Fisher's Hill
Sept. 21–22

Strasburg

Guard Hill
Aug. 16

Tom's Brook
Oct. 9

Woodstock

Sept. 21

Front Royal

Chester Gap

Sept. 22

Milford
Oct. 26

Sept. 24

May 15

New Market

North Fork

South Fork

Thornton's Gap
Sept. 24

Luray

Sperryville

Warrenton

Honeyville

Dec. 21

Brandy Station

BRECKINRIDGE (APRIL 1864)

EARLY (June)

SHERIDAN (Sept.)

HUNTER (June)

Harrisonburg

Mt. Crawford

Hightop Gap

Port Republic

Brown's Gap

TO STAUNTON

Piedmont
June 5

TO LYNCHBURG

Sept. 28

Waynesborough

Rockfish Gap

Charlottesville

EARLY (June)

TO LYNCHBURG

SIGEL (April)

SHERIDAN

EARLY (June)

Legend

Union movements in black;
Confederate movements in gray

✕ Battles and skirmishes

PHASE ONE: APRIL–JUNE

←—— Sigel   ←—·—· Hunter

←——— Breckinridge defeats Sigel
at New Market

◄===== Early defeats Hunter
at Lynchburg

PHASE TWO: JUNE–JULY

◄—·■·■ Early retakes Valley;
continues into Maryland,
threatens Washington, D.C.

PHASE THREE: JULY–AUGUST

◄······ Early returns to Valley;
attacks B&O Railroad

PHASE FOUR: AUGUST–OCTOBER

◄—— Sheridan drives Confederate
forces out of Valley

not protected by trenches. Early's calling card was his mobility, but this provided an opportunity for a reinforced Sheridan to fight him in open farmland. Instead of bringing Horatio Wright's Sixth Corps back to Petersburg after its defense of Washington when Early had threatened the capital, Grant assigned it to the new Army of the Shenandoah. He ordered Meade to keep the pressure up at Petersburg so that Lee could not release troops to join Early in the Shenandoah.

But Lee was not about to surrender the valley without one last battle. He reinforced Early by sending him Joseph Kershaw's infantry division of three thousand men plus a cavalry brigade.

On October 16, Sheridan left quiet Cedar Creek, fifteen miles south of Winchester, to travel to Washington to consult with Stanton and Halleck, who had earlier doubted his abilities but now valued his leadership. Three days later, Early's twice defeated troops, after an all-night march, on a fog-shrouded morning plunged through the freezing waters of Cedar Creek to spring a surprise attack on the unprepared bluecoats. Horatio Wright, wounded in the face in the initial attack, blood clotting his gray beard, led a courageous response, but soon Federal soldiers retreated pell-mell four miles down the valley. Believing they had won a great victory, Early's soldiers took advantage of an afternoon lull to plunder the abandoned Union camps.

Suspecting something might be up, Sheridan completed his business in Washington in half a day and ordered a special train from Union Station to return him south. By the evening of October 18, he had reached Winchester.

Early on October 19, riding atop Rienzi, he came upon retreating Union soldiers at the south edge of Winchester. Urging his massive black horse to a gallop, Sheridan rode ahead. As he raced south, he met more and more men and wagons withdrawing. Sheridan shouted, "About face, boys! Turn back! . . . I am going to sleep in that camp tonight or in hell!" The sight of the determined little man on the huge horse breathed courage into the defeated soldiers. He met a twenty-one-year-old major, William McKinley, the future twenty-fifth president of the United States, who raced ahead, blaring that Sheridan had returned.

On this autumn afternoon, Sheridan organized a remarkable counterattack. With his cavalry leading the way, suddenly energized bluecoats drove the enemy across Cedar Creek, within hours producing a notable victory that effectively ended Early's campaign in the Shenandoah Valley.

On October 20, Grant telegraphed Butler and Meade to order another "salute of one hundred guns at sunset this evening." Meade telegraphed Grant, commending Sheridan, the man he had once criticized, for achieving "one of the most brilliant feats of the war."

Immediately after Cedar Creek, Grant recommended Sheridan for promotion to major general. Sheridan, under Grant's sponsorship, now became the fourth-ranking officer in the Union army, following only Grant, Sherman, and Meade.

BY THE END of October, as the presidential election approached, Grant decided on a double knockout: Petersburg and the Shenandoah Valley. With Lee defending and Grant attacking, two great generals found themselves involved in an intricate duel. Although the first months of the siege of Petersburg were a stalemate, Grant learned from his mistakes. When others doubted and questioned, Grant put his trust in Sheridan, who delivered the Virginia breadbasket, the Shenandoah Valley. Lincoln put his trust in Grant, which gave the western general the freedom to lead in the east by his own best lights.

On the evening of October 21, eighteen days before the presidential election, serenaders marched to the Executive Mansion. After Lincoln and his son Tad listened to their songs, he told the assembled crowd, "I propose that you give three hearty cheers for Sheridan." Then, "I propose three cheers for General Grant, who knew to what use to put Sheridan."

CHAPTER 23

Appomattox

I shall necessarily have to take the odium of apparent inactivity
but if it results, as I expect it will, in the discomfiture of
Lee's Army, I shall be entirely satisfied.

—ULYSSES S. GRANT to WILLIAM T. SHERMAN, February 4, 1865

On the evening of Election Day, November 8, 1864, Grant was sitting at a campfire in front of his headquarters tent at City Point when he got the news that Lincoln had won a resounding victory. Lincoln received 2,220,846 votes to George McClellan's 1,808,445, winning the electoral vote by a definitive 212 to 21. He won the soldiers' vote 116,887 to only 37,748. Grant wrote Stanton that he believed Lincoln's reelection "is a victory worth more to the country than a battle won." But he knew there were still many battles ahead to be won.

AFTER A DISPIRITING summer that included the failed assault at Cold Harbor, the missed opportunity to capture Petersburg, and the Crater disaster, Grant believed recent signs suggested the tides might be turning and the war might be heading into its final chapter. He expressed gratitude for the August 5 victory at Mobile Bay by Admiral David Farragut, who famously shouted, "Damn the torpedoes! Full speed ahead!" Sherman had finally captured Atlanta on September 2 and proposed a November march to the sea. Sheridan had defeated Early at Cedar Creek on October 19, to complete the turning of the tide in the Shenandoah Valley. Adding to Grant's newfound optimism, many three-year veterans discharged in the spring decided to reenlist by the fall. He sensed momentum on the Union side.

As winter approached, Grant commanded four large armies led by Meade, Sherman, Sheridan, and Butler. If, as Grant's aide Horace Porter observed, these armies once moved like horses "in a balky team, no two ever pulling together," they now constituted "a dashing four-in-hand,"

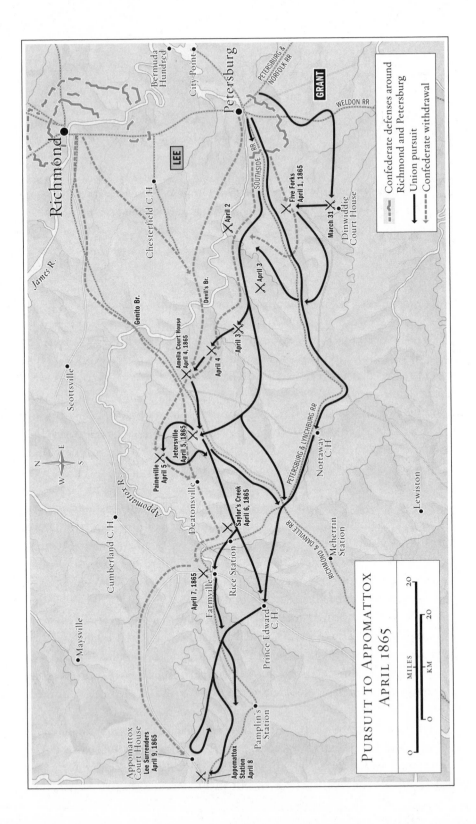

Bermuda
Hundred

City Point

Petersburg

PETERSBURG &
NORFOLK RR

GRANT

WELDON RR

Richmond

James R.

Chesterfield C.H

LEE

SOUTHSIDE RR

Five Forks
April 1, 1865

March 31

Dinwiddie
Court House

Genito Br.

Devil's Br.

April 2

April 3

Amelia Court House
April 4, 1865

April 4

Scottsville

Appomattox R.

Paineville
April 5

Jetersville
April 5, 1865

Deatonsville

Saylor's Creek
April 6, 1865

PETERSBURG & LYNCHBURG RR

Nottaway
C.H.

Lewiston

N
W E
S

Cumberland C.H.

Rice Station

Farmville
April 7, 1865

Prince Edward
C.H.

RICHMOND & DANVILLE RR

Meherrin
Station

Maysville

Pamplin's
Station

Appomattox Court House
Lee Surrenders
April 9, 1865

Appomattox
Station
April 8

Confederate defenses around
Richmond and Petersburg

Union pursuit

Confederate withdrawal

PURSUIT TO APPOMATTOX
APRIL 1865

MILES

KM

0   20

0   20

all working together with Grant holding the reins. In the months ahead, Grant would offer counsel, and sometimes correction, to the four leaders—with quite different results.

Grant sent Porter to Atlanta in September to inform Sherman ("better than I can do in the limits of a letter") about the next phases of his strategy. Shortly thereafter, Lincoln and Stanton gave Grant full authority to decide if Sherman's march to the sea in Georgia was feasible. After first expressing misgivings—Grant worried about the dangers of having Sherman advance in hostile territory while dependent on a long, potentially vulnerable supply line—he ultimately convinced Lincoln and Stanton that Sherman's march would demonstrate the Union's power to move through the heart of the Confederacy.

WITH SHERMAN RESTING and refitting in Atlanta, Confederate general John Bell Hood did not rest. A veteran who had distinguished himself on multiple battlefields—sustaining a severe wound in his left arm at Gettysburg and losing a leg at Chickamauga—he enjoyed a well-deserved reputation for bravery.

Hood, who had defended Atlanta, decided to take the bulk of his army to attack Sherman's supply lines, then advance north with thirty-nine thousand men, recoup Tennessee, enter Kentucky, perhaps go up to the Ohio River, and possibly even cross into Ohio. Hood was convinced Sherman would have to go after him and give up his march to the sea.

On September 29, Hood crossed the Chattahoochee River in Georgia to begin a push northward. He immediately overran small garrisons at Big Shanty and Kennesaw Water Tank along the Western and Atlantic Railroad, the supply line upon which Sherman depended. A dismayed Northern public now heard familiar names from Sherman's march through Georgia—New Hope Church, Lost Mountain, Allatoona, and Dalton—only in reverse order.

Grant and Sherman had to decide whether to go forward with the march to the sea or go after Hood. Sherman voiced his strong opinion: "Hood may turn into Tennessee and Kentucky but I believe he will be forced to follow me." He detached George Thomas, sending him toward Nashville to defend against Hood.

As Grant learned more about Hood's advance north, he became convinced the Confederate leader needed to be stopped. But he continued to trust the judgment of his general on the ground.

On November 15, Sherman, after burning much of Atlanta, began his much anticipated march to the sea. With sixty-two thousand men, he set off on a 285-mile route, hoping to reach Savannah on the Atlantic Ocean by Christmas. Sherman and Hood, whose armies had fought each other for more than eight months, marched in opposite directions.

ON NOVEMBER 25, Grant received a telegram from Thomas: "Hood's entire army is in front of Columbia and so greatly outnumbers mine at this time that I am compelled to act on the defensive." He concluded, "The moment I can get my Cavalry I will march against Hood."

Cavalry was crucial to Thomas, but many of his horses had died either in combat or for lack of forage. A desperate Thomas commandeered eighteen Nashville circus horses for $1,800, leaving the company only "a single, lame ring horse."

Meanwhile, Hood, lamenting the defensive mindset of his predecessor, Joe Johnston, led a head-on attack against John Schofield's dug-in troops at Franklin, Tennessee, twenty miles south of Nashville, on November 30. Slowly but resolutely, Hood's army was beaten back, sustaining devastating casualties: seven thousand, including twelve generals, six of whom were killed. Grant hoped Thomas would join Schofield at Franklin. Instead, Schofield was forced to retreat to Nashville to link up with Thomas. Hood moved on Nashville and, in Grant's words, was allowed "to invest that place almost without interference."

Grant was not the only leader concerned about Hood. On December 2, Stanton wired Grant, "This looks like the McClellan & Rosecrans strategy of do nothing and let the rebels raid the country." The final sentence put the ball in Grant's court: "The President wishes you to consider the matter."

Thirty minutes later, Grant stepped up the pressure in a telegram to Thomas: "If Hood is permitted to remain quietly about Nashville you will lose all the road back to Chattanooga." He warned, "Should he attack you it is all well but if he does not you should attack him before he fortifies." Grant believed decisive action by Thomas might prompt Hood to retreat. "Should you get him to retreating give him no peace."

But in succeeding days, Thomas offered a litany of explanations for why he was not yet ready to attack. Grant's personal telegrapher, Samuel Beckwith, nicknamed "Grant's Shadow," recalled that during these rapid-fire exchanges of telegrams, each time he handed his boss yet another missive he would warn him, "No battle yet, General."

On December 7, Grant alerted Stanton of his intention to change command. If Thomas did not attack immediately, "I would recommend superseding him by Schofield."

Halleck wrote Grant, "If you wish Genl Thomas relieved from command, give the order. No one here will, I think, interfere." Yet he warned, "The responsibility, however, will be yours, as no one here, so far as I am informed, wishes Genl Thomas' removal."

As telegrams sped through the wires between Nashville and City Point, a once-in-a-generation ice storm paralyzed the Tennessee capital, making movement by men and animals almost impossible. Thomas telegraphed Grant, "A terrible storm of freezing rain has come on today which will make it impossible for our men to fight to any advantage." He added, "Maj Genl Halleck informs me that you are very much dissatisfied with my delay in attacking. I can only say I have done all in my power to prepare, and if you should deem it necessary to relieve me I shall submit without a murmur."

This offer of resignation from "the Rock of Chickamauga" made Grant pause. Four hours later, he wrote Halleck, "I am very unwilling to do injustice to an officer who has done as much good service as Gen. Thomas has, however, and will therefore suspend the order relieving him until it is seen whether he will do anything."

Grant's impatience seems unusual. Perhaps he could not help viewing "Old Slow-Trot" through the glasses of Chattanooga.

On December 13, Grant issued orders for "Black Jack" Logan to "proceed immediately to Nashville" to relieve Thomas. Grant had long admired the colorful Illinoisan, one of the few political generals to find success on the battlefield. He told Logan "not to deliver the order or publish it until he reached there, and if Thomas had moved, then not to deliver it at all."

The next day, Grant, "restless" as he thought about all that had transpired, decided to go to Nashville himself. After gathering a pocketful of cigars, he gave Beckwith fifteen minutes' notice, telling him to "hustle." Grant, who would not leave City Point when Early approached Washington, now left Butler in charge because of the seriousness of Hood's challenge.

Thomas finally attacked on December 15. As the sun burned through the early morning fog, Ohioan James Steedman led his two brigades, including a large number of African American troops, in a vigorous assault on Hood's right flank. In the early afternoon, a larger force attacked Hood's left flank.

As fighting commenced in Nashville, Grant decided to travel to Washington instead of Nashville, to meet with the president and Stanton in a late night conference at the War Department. Upon his return to Willard's Hotel, he heard the news of Thomas's decisive victory and tele-graphed him at eleven thirty P.M., congratulating him on "your splendid success of today." An advocate of outright victory, Grant encouraged Thomas not to be content with merely stopping Hood's advance: "Push the enemy now and give him no rest until he is entirely destroyed."

Hood's army, reduced in half to fifteen thousand, retreated to Tupelo, Mississippi, the same town where Beauregard had retreated after his 1862 defeat at Corinth. Though future historians would focus on the frontline story of Sherman's immortalized "March to the Sea," Grant directed much of his energy to the backstory, pushing Thomas to prevent Hood from cutting Sherman's supply line in Tennessee. Fortified by Grant, Thomas smashed the Confederate Army of Tennessee and effectually ended the war in this key Southern state.

The joint effort worked. Sherman reached the sea on December 13, where he captured Fort McAllister. The real prize was Savannah, a coastal city of colorful brick townhouses built by slave labor, which Sherman entered on December 22. He wrote Grant, "I take great satisfaction in reporting that we are in possession of Savannah and all its forts." Sher-man wrote Lincoln with more panache: "I beg to present you as a Christ-mas gift the City of Savannah."

MEANWHILE, GRANT'S EFFORT to cut off supplies to Petersburg was frustrated so long as the largest harbor that remained open to Confeder-ate blockade runners lay near Wilmington, North Carolina. He watched as goods were transferred from the harbor to the Weldon Railroad to supply the besieged Petersburg. He had been trying unsuccessfully to cut the railroad for months; now he turned his attention to the port.

He planned a joint army-navy expedition to capture Fort Fisher, a large earthwork situated on a peninsula defending the entrance to Cape Fear River, south of Wilmington. Grant designated Godfrey Weitzel to lead the campaign, but Butler pulled rank, insisting he command.

Grant acquiesced to Butler's leadership, but one hears his growing concern in telegrams to the commander of the Army of the James. On December 4: "I feel great anxiety to see the Wilmington expedition off." On December 14: "What is the prospect for getting your expedition started?"

Grant had no such worries about Admiral David Porter, commander of the North Atlantic Squadron. Porter, who could be brash in relation-ships with colleagues, had worked well with Grant at Vicksburg, but he'd clashed with Butler at New Orleans in 1862. Butler came up with the idea of towing the old USS *Louisiana,* packed with two thousand tons of powder, and blowing it up one hundred yards from the fort's seawall. His forces left their headquarters in Hampton Roads, Virginia, on December 14, but winter storms caused delays. Porter decided to go ahead without him and towed the *Louisiana* near the seawall at midnight on December 23. With all eyes watching, the charge went off at one forty-five A.M., but the timers failed to work and because the boat was not as near as intended, the series of small explosions did little damage to the fort.

Undeterred, the next morning Porter began a massive bombardment of the fort, eleven-inch shells screaming over the ocean—ten thousand rounds of shot and shell that day alone. Butler finally arrived that evening with his sixty-five hundred troops and was enraged to learn that Porter had gone ahead without him.

On Christmas morning, Porter unleashed another massive bombardment. Butler's men, in navy longboats, darted through the low surf for the beach. Once ashore, Weitzel observed that, contrary to Porter's report, the fort had not been badly damaged.

Weitzel reported to Butler, who decided to suspend the attack and reembark his men—even though the landing had been not opposed, and Battery Anderson, the first Confederates encountered, had surrendered. Butler did so knowing that Grant had expressly ordered "no withdrawal, or no failure after a landing was made."

Grant had enough. Cyrus Comstock, whom Grant had sent as an observer, reported Butler never went ashore before making his quick decision to reembark his troops. Grant wrote directly to the president on December 28: "The Wilmington expedition has proven a gross and culpable failure." He intended to get to the bottom of this humiliating fiasco. "Who is to blame I hope will be known."

Grant spoke with Butler to hear his side of the story, but he already knew who was at fault. Determined to take Fort Fisher, Grant tipped his hand to Porter: "Please hold on where you are for a few days, and I will endeavor to be back again with an increased force and without the former Commander."

On January 4, Grant wrote Stanton, "I am constrained to request the removal of Maj. Gen. B. F. Butler from the command of the Department of N. C. & Va. I do this with reluctance but the good of the service requires it. In my absence Gen. Butler necessarily commands, and there is a lack of confidence felt in his Military ability." Grant's letter had been a long time coming.

．　．　．

BUTLER WAS NOT the only controversial general Grant had to deal with. William Rosecrans, whom Grant had relieved at Chattanooga in fall 1863, was given command of the Department of Missouri in January 1864 before Grant became general in chief.

Missouri Partisan attacks exceeded in ferocity the guerrilla attacks in other western states. Confederate general Sterling Price had reentered Missouri in September, intent on joining forces with guerrillas in order to retake St. Louis, cross the Mississippi River, and invade Illinois. If that grand scheme proved an overreach, he would at least redeem Missouri. Price aimed to interrupt the fall elections and force Grant to pull troops from the east. Grant, who had encountered Price at Corinth and Iuka in 1862, wrote Halleck, "I do think Price could be driven out in a week with the right man after him."

Rosecrans was not the right man. Grant could be exasperated with Thomas, but he did not respect Rosecrans. He wrote Halleck: "Has Rosecrans yet come upon Price? If he has not he should be removed at once." He mentioned "Black Jack" Logan as a possible replacement but concluded, "Anybody, however, will be better than Rosecrans." When the suggestion was made that Rosecrans, familiar with Tennessee, could aid Thomas against Hood, Grant wrote, "I know no Department or Army Commander deserving such punishment as the infliction of Rosecrans upon him." Finally, on January 1, 1865, Grant requested Rosecrans's "dismissal from service." Rosecrans would have no further command in the Civil War.

AS THE YEAR 1865 began, Grant believed the Union would win the war in the coming year, but he understood that much work needed to be done. He intended to press the Confederates everywhere. He recognized reluctantly that some of his key commanders did not embrace his aggressive strategy. He would either work around them, take away some of their troops, or remove them.

As Grant pushed for victory, he reshuffled his commanders. He regretted losing Winfield Scott Hancock, who continued to suffer from the wound sustained at Gettysburg. In November, Grant sent him north to recruit veterans for a one-year tour of duty. In his place, Grant appointed Andrew Humphreys, Meade's chief of staff, known for his strict discipline of troops. For the Army of the James, he replaced Butler with Edward O. C. Ord. Dressed like a common soldier, Ord was known for his steadiness, common sense, and quiet humor—the virtual opposite of Butler. Grant replaced Rosecrans with Grenville Dodge, a civil engineer who won Grant's admiration for rebuilding railroads in Tennessee and Mississippi.

After the victory at Nashville, Grant watched, disappointed, as Thomas did not stay on the offensive. One by one, Grant took pieces of Thomas's army and sent them where he believed they could do more good. He ordered Schofield's Twenty-third Corps to Annapolis, Maryland, with the goal of capturing Wilmington, telling Sherman, "I was induced to do this because I did not believe Thomas could possibly be got off before Spring." He dispatched A. J. Smith and his reorganized Sixteenth Corps to help capture Mobile. He ordered Edward Canby, commander of the Army of the Gulf at New Orleans, to move against Mobile also. Grant sent twenty-seven-year-old James Wilson with 13,500 men into Alabama to destroy the Confederate supply center at Selma. He ordered George Stoneman's 6,000 cavalry from East Tennessee on a raid into southwestern Virginia and western North Carolina to destroy Confederate iron works and warehouses. A major exasperation was how many senior commanders—Thomas, Canby, and Stoneman—were late in executing his orders. But Grant deftly moved his chess pieces across the board.

In January, Grant appointed Alfred H. Terry to lead a second attack

By 1864, Grant had assembled a talented and trustworthy staff. Here he appears surrounded left to right by Ely S. Parker, Adam Badeau, Orville E. Babcock, and Horace Porter.

on Fort Fisher. Terry, formerly clerk of courts in New Haven, Connecticut, displayed a quiet confidence that won the admiration of those who served with him. Grant encouraged Terry to work closely with Porter and the navy: "I have served with Admiral Porter, and know that you can rely on his judgment."

Terry commanded 9,600 soldiers and Porter 2,261 sailors and marines. On January 13, after two days of fighting, with Porter's bombardment silencing the guns in the fort and with Terry and Porter working well together, Fort Fisher surrendered. Gratified, Grant watched Terry do what Butler could not, or would not, do.

BY THE WINTER of 1865, Grant renewed his strategy of concentration. Sherman's army and the several smaller armies advanced. He intended to get to Lee behind his Petersburg barricades, but on his own timetable.

But the public did not understand Grant's timing. As Sherman continued to advance up through Georgia, they saw only that Grant was seemingly stalled in front of Petersburg. Some in Congress, growing restive, spoke of promoting Sherman to lieutenant general—a rank equal to Grant's.

When Sherman heard about this move, he immediately informed Grant he had contacted his senator brother and told him to silence the dissenters. Sherman believed "it would be mischievous, for there are enough rascals who would try to sow differences between us, whereas you and I now are in perfect understanding." He assured his friend, "I would rather have you in command than anybody else, for you are fair, honest, and have at heart the same purpose that should animate all."

Grant replied, "No one would be more pleased at your advancement than I, and if you should be placed in my position and I put subordinate it would not change our personal relations in the least." His generous response spoke not only to the bonds of friendship between the two leading Union generals, but to their shared commitment to the larger "cause" of Union victory, whoever received the praise.

IN JANUARY, a committee of Philadelphia citizens surprised Grant with the gift of a furnished home at 2009 Chestnut Street. George H. Stuart, chairman of the United States Christian Commission, wrote that since learning Mrs. Grant was looking for a house in the city but had been unable to find one, they had decided to present the house in appreciation "for the eminent services you have rendered to the nation."

Ulysses encouraged Julia to move into the new house, but she chose instead to live with her husband at City Point. With the onset of winter, Grant had moved into a cabin built by Rufus Ingalls. Today, the restored wooden cabin strikes one as being quite small. It contains a front room with an open fire, chairs, two diminutive desks that served as Grant's headquarters, and a tiny sleeping room in the rear.

After Julia arrived, Horace Porter observed how quickly she won the esteem of everyone for "her amiability, her cheerful disposition, and her extreme cordiality of manner." She visited officers who fell ill and asked the cook to provide special delicacies to cheer them. Once, when Porter walked into the cabin, he saw Julia's hand clasped with Ulysses's. Grant's aide learned from others that when a staff officer might come upon them, "they would look as bashful as two young lovers spied upon in the scenes of their courtship."

In one of Julia's few surviving letters, she wrote a friend, "I am snugly nestled away in my husband's log cabin." She relished long talks with Ulysses. "Am I not a happy woman?"

In January, Grant learned White Haven was about to be sold for back taxes owed by his brother-in-law John Dent. Eager to keep Julia's girl-hood home in the family, he wired his financial adviser, Russell Jones, asking him to use his money to purchase the property.

As the war slogged on, at the end of January 1865, a white flag emerged from a Confederate parapet in Petersburg with a message for Grant. Jostling carriages along Jerusalem Plank Road brought three peace negotiators—John A. Campbell, former justice of the Supreme Court; Robert M. T. Hunter, former Confederate secretary of state; and Alexander Stephens, vice president of the Confederacy. Would Grant agree to safe passage for the commissioners, who sought a meeting in Washington with Lincoln and Secretary of State William Seward to discuss a way to end the war? Greeting them cordially, Grant bade them stay at City Point. He provided the best accommodations aboard the steamer *Mary Martin*—posting no guard—then wrote Washington for instructions.

Over the next days, Grant remembered that the commissioners tried to draw him "out as to his ideas touching the proper conditions of the proposed terms of peace." Remaining true to his understanding of the strict separation of military and political powers, he maintained, "It was something I had nothing to do with, and I therefore did not wish to express any views on the subject."

Lincoln and Stanton were ready to decline to meet the commissioners because their proposal referred to negotiations between "our two countries." Grant intervened, writing Stanton, "I have not felt myself at liberty to express even views of my own" on the subject. However, "I will state confidentially but not officially to become a matter of record, that I am convinced, upon conversations with Messrs Stevens & Hunter that their intentions are good and their desire sincere to restore peace and Union." Grant's instincts were correct, for these negotiators were far more eager than Davis to reestablish the Union. He told the secretary of war, "I fear now their going back without any expression from anyone in authority will have a bad influence."

Lincoln selected Seward to meet the delegates, but Grant's letter changed his mind: "Say to the gentlemen I will meet them personally."

On February 3, the five men met on the *River Queen* at Hampton Roads. In a dramatic backdrop to the meeting, just four days earlier, on January 31, the House of Representatives had mustered the required two-thirds vote to pass the Thirteenth Amendment outlawing slavery. The participants agreed to keep no notes of the meeting, which lasted four hours. But Lincoln could not change the Southern negotiators' minds. The Hampton Roads conference concluded without result.

"PLEASE READ AND answer this letter as though I was not President, but only a friend." It was an intriguing opening to an unusual request Grant received that same month: "Without embarrassment to you, or detriment to the service," could Grant find a place for twenty-two-year-old Robert Lincoln, a recent graduate of Harvard, on his staff? Although the letter did not mention Mary Lincoln, behind the request lay a family struggle involving a son who wanted to join other young men serving in the war, a mother who had already lost two sons and feared losing a third, and a father caught in the middle.

Grant replied, "I will be most happy to have him in my Military family in the manner you propose." He suggested the rank of captain. Unwilling to make the U.S. Treasury pay the bill, Lincoln bought his son his military outfit and equipment as well as a new horse. Robert reported for duty at City Point on February 22.

As GRANT CONTINUED his siege of Petersburg, news broke that Sherman had entered South Carolina on February 1. Responding to the intensified spotlight of expectation, Grant wrote Stanton on February 4, "I shall necessarily have to take the odium of apparent inactivity but if it results, as I expect it will, in the discomfiture of Lee's Army, I shall be entirely satisfied." He did not want to suffer casualties as he waited for Sherman to do his work in the Carolinas and come into Virginia from the south. After Sherman entered Columbia, the state capital, on February 17 and left it in flames, Southern public uproar prompted Lee to restore proud Joe Johnston to his old command. Johnston, Sherman's antagonist in Georgia, cobbled together an undersupplied army of twenty thousand to try to stop the Union forces.

Meanwhile, Schofield took charge of the Union operation against Wilmington, located thirty miles upriver from Fort Fisher. After an eleven-day battle, Braxton Bragg abandoned the city on February 22. Grant looked forward to having Schofield link up with Sherman in North Carolina. He expected Sherman to arrive south of Petersburg by late April but did not want to wait that long to finish off Lee. His main worry was that Lee would slip away from Petersburg and link up with Johnston, hoping to extend the war for another year.

AT THE END of February, during an exchange of prisoners, Edward Ord and James Longstreet talked about possibilities for peace. Longstreet took this conversation back to Lee, who wrote Grant on March 2, proposing to enter into "an interchange of views" aiming at "the possibility of arriving at a satisfactory adjustment of the present unhappy difficulties."

Stanton immediately wrote Grant, reminding him to stick to fighting the war and leaving the peace to Lincoln. "The President directs me to say to you that he wishes you to have no conference with Gen Lee unless it be for the capitulation of Lee's army, or on solely minor and purely military matters. He instructs me to say that you are not to decide, discuss, or confer upon any political question: such questions the President holds in his own hands; and will submit them to no military conferences or conventions." Despite Lincoln's growing confidence in Grant, he alone would decide national policy.

SHORTLY AFTER LINCOLN's March 4 second inauguration, during which newspapers reported on the president's exhaustion and recent illness, Julia suggested Ulysses invite the president to City Point. Grant demurred, "It is not my place to invite him." Julia outflanked her husband. While asking Robert about his father's health, she suggested his father and mother come for a visit. Robert answered, "I suppose they would, if they were sure they would not be intruding."

Julia persuaded her husband, who wrote Lincoln on March 20, "Can you not visit City Point for a day or two? I would like very much to see you and I think the rest would do you good."

Lincoln arrived on the *River Queen* on March 24, accompanied by Mary and Tad. Over the next days, Grant enjoyed long conferences with the president.

Another welcome visitor was John Heyl Vincent, Grant's pastor at the Methodist church in Galena, now a representative of the United States Christian Commission. After Shiloh, Grant had received a letter from Vincent. In his reply, he recalled "the pleasure of listening to your feeling discourses from the pulpit"—a fascinating way to describe Vincent's sermons from a man who seldom expressed his feelings.

Grant invited Vincent to accompany him and the president on a Sunday excursion up the James River, but Vincent declined because of obligations to preach and conduct Sunday school for the troops. Vincent remembered that Grant responded "he had not attended church three or four times since he got into the war," in part because he always had to be accompanied by his personal telegrapher, "bearing dispatches that required an immediate answer."

Hopes for relaxing days at City Point were punctured two days later. As Grant and Lincoln prepared to conduct a review of Ord's Army of the James, Mary spied Ord's wife, beautiful young Mary Ord, riding alongside the president. She flew into a rage: "What does the woman mean by riding by the side of the President? And ahead of me?"

Julia tried to mollify her, but her efforts only increased Mary's anger: "I suppose you think you'll get to the White House, don't you?" Julia remained calm. Before again turning her wrath to Mrs. Ord, Mary gave Julia a parting shot: "Oh! you had better take it if you can get it. 'Tis very nice." When Julia wrote her *Personal Memoirs,* she did not criticize Mary Lincoln and said Adam Badeau had "embellished" the story.

BY NOW GRANT'S army consisted of more than 125,000 soldiers, while Lee's army was made up of barely 50,000, of whom only 35,000 were fit to fight. With the Confederate and Union trenches around Petersburg stretching for thirty-five miles, Grant continued pushing west, wanting to cut off the last road and railroad coming up from the south.

While Lincoln visited City Point, Lee recognized he was finally about to be encircled and, in a bold gamble, decided to try to break through Grant's lines. He knew his action might mean the fall of Richmond, but all that mattered now was his army's survival. If he could link up with Johnston in North Carolina, together they might turn and attack Sherman.

John Gordon led a surprise attack on March 25 at Fort Stedman east of

Petersburg. His lead units, masquerading as deserting soldiers, fraternized with Union pickets before surprising them. Gordon's men quickly took one thousand prisoners.

A Union counterattack by John Parke's Ninth Corps soon regained the fort. Lee suffered losses of nearly four thousand men, whereas Parke lost fewer than fifteen hundred. Grant came with Lincoln to offer their appreciation to the Union troops.

Grant arranged a meeting on March 28 between the president, Sherman, who traveled by boat from North Carolina, and David Porter. Sherman asked Lincoln: "What [is] to be done with the rebel armies when defeated?" The president offered a lengthy reply stressing his desire for reconciliation. He told Sherman he wanted to "get the men comprising the Confederate armies back to their homes, at work on their farms and in their shops."

It was time to end the siege. After a long nine months, Grant moved with resolution. He left City Point on March 29, kissing Julia repeatedly. Lincoln asked if he should return to Washington, but Grant encouraged him to stay. He wanted the president to be able to enter Richmond. At

George Healy's painting portrays the March 28, 1865, meeting on the River Queen *where Grant, Lincoln, Sherman, and Porter discussed what should be done when the war finally ended.*

the train station, Lincoln, his voice breaking with emotion, offered his blessing to Grant and his soldiers. After grasping the president's hand, Grant boarded the train to go to the front, where he mounted Jeff Davis, his black pony, to assume personal command.

He planned to cut the South Side Rail Road, the final train bringing in supplies, drive the Confederates out of their trenches at Petersburg, compel the abandonment of Richmond, and ultimately force Lee to fight in the open. He ordered Sheridan's cavalry and Gouverneur Warren's Fifth Corps to attack ten miles southwest of Petersburg against Lee's right flank. When Sheridan became stalled at Dinwiddie Court House, both by Confederates led by George Pickett and by a drenching rain, Grant wrote Sheridan, instructing him to stay in place.

Not willing to postpone his advance, Sheridan rode to Grant's headquarters, located in a waterlogged cornfield. Forcefully, he urged, "I'm ready to strike out tomorrow and go to smashing things." Sheridan recalled, "It needed little argument to convince him."

On April 1, Grant ordered Sheridan to advance to the nearby Five Forks road junction. When the rain gave way to a dazzling spring day, Sheridan's cavalry, fighting on foot, charged Pickett's position. To Sheridan's dismay, Warren moved belatedly. Finally, goddamning Warren for his slowness, Sheridan organized the combined force himself and won a Yankee-whooping victory.

Having watched Warren's sluggish behavior for too long, Grant told Sheridan he could replace Warren. The hair-trigger Sheridan relieved Warren on the spot. Warren appealed directly to Grant, who affirmed the decision.

On other lines, Confederate defenders still fought effectively. Grant wrote Ord, "Understand: I do not wish you to fight your way over difficult barriers, against defended lines. I want you to see through if the enemy is leaving and if so follow him up." Although he was eager to push for a final victory, at the same time, Grant did not want to incur needless casualties.

THE NEXT DAY, Sunday, April 2, having cut off all Lee's escape routes to the South but one, Grant's army attacked all along the lines at Petersburg.

That same morning, as Jefferson Davis sat in his regular pew at St. Paul's Episcopal Church in Richmond, a sexton crept down the aisle in the middle of the service and handed him a telegram from Lee. Grant was breaking through the lines at Petersburg. To preserve his army, Lee made the decision to evacuate the capital. One by one, members of the government and military rose from their pews—in the middle of the sermon—to leave the church. Richmond must be given up.

After a siege of 293 days, Grant forced the Confederates to abandon Petersburg and Richmond on the same day.

Grant rode into Petersburg at nine A.M. on April 3. All around him lay the freshly dead. Whites, mostly women and old men, stayed out of sight behind drawn blinds, while clusters of blacks cheered soldiers in blue uniforms. Although he was anxious to join Sheridan in the race to cut off Lee, Grant paused to meet with Lincoln at the home of Thomas Wallace, one of the president's longtime Whig allies.

Lincoln pumped Grant's hand. "Do you know, general, I had a sort of sneaking idea all along that you intended to do something like this; but I thought some time ago that you would so maneuver as to have Sherman come up and be near enough to cooperate with you."

Grant acknowledged that he had thought about letting Sherman in for the finish, "but I had a feeling that it would be better to let Lee's old antagonists give his army the final blow, and finish up the job." Grant worried that if Sherman received credit for the final victory, it might lead to "disagreeable bickerings between members of Congress of the East and those of the West." Lincoln admitted that he had never thought about it in that light. Grant, so much a man of the western operations, had come to appreciate the pride and valor of the eastern armies.

Ulysses thought of Julia on this signal day: "I am now writing from far inside of what was the rebel fortifications this morning but what are ours now." After telling her his forces had captured twelve thousand prisoners, he added, glowing, "Altogether this has been one of the greatest victories of the war. Greatest because it is over what the rebels have always regarded as their most invincible Army and the one used for the defense of their capitol."

THE NEXT DAY, April 4, Lincoln made a memorable visit to Richmond, the capital of the Confederacy; but the conquering hero, Grant, chose not to join him. He was off on a sprint to the finish line.

Lee, combining troops from Richmond and Petersburg, with an eight-hour head start, marched thirty-five miles west to Amelia Court House, where a special reserve of 350,000 rations had been ordered from Richmond. From Amelia, Lee intended to slide down the Richmond and Danville Railroad to Danville, just three miles from the North Carolina border, where he would link up with Johnston. But when he arrived with the forward elements of Longstreet's corps and opened the doors of the train, he found no rations—only ammunition—for his thirty thousand hungry men.

On April 5, Grant traveled with Ord's troops while Sheridan's cavalry raced ahead and severed the Richmond and Danville Railroad at Jetersville, forcing Lee even farther west as he tried to reach North Carolina.

In the afternoon, amid considerable commotion, a rider in a gray uniform approached. Grant recognized J. A. Campbell, one of Sheridan's scouts. Campbell opened his mouth, took out a tiny tinfoil pellet, unwrapped it, and handed a piece of tissue paper to Grant. Sheridan's message: "I wish you were here yourself. I feel confident of capturing the Army of Northern Virginia if we exert ourselves."

Grant dismounted from Jeff Davis, asked for powerful Cincinnati, and bade Campbell to lead the way. Grant knew it would be wise to take a cavalry escort, but with none nearby, he rode with only fourteen men. As afternoon light turned to evening darkness, with no direct roads, he rode through wooded terrain, enemy campfires always nearby, knowing he would be in grave danger if they suddenly ran into Southern cavalry. At ten thirty P.M., after riding nearly twenty miles, they approached Sheridan's pickets. Fortunately it was a moonlit night, and Grant heard a cry of recognition: "Why, there's the old man."

The next day, as Lee's army sought to reach Farmville, Sheridan, assisted by Wright's Sixth Corps and Humphreys's Second Corps, cut off nearly one-fourth of Lee's retreating army at Little Sailor's Creek. Grant's armies captured six thousand men, including Generals Richard Ewell, Joseph Kershaw, and Custis Lee, Robert E. Lee's son.

On the morning of April 7, with Grant close behind, Lee's men stopped briefly in Farmville, where he found rations at last. Grant arrived in Farmville that afternoon; having left his luggage behind on his night ride to Sheridan's headquarters, he had with him only the mud-spattered clothes he was wearing.

Sitting on the porch of the village's brick hotel, Grant got out his writing pad to write Lee: "The result of the last week must convince you of the hopelessness of further resistance on the part of the Army of Northern Virginia in this struggle." He asked for Lee's surrender to avoid "any further effusion of blood." He sent off a courier to find Lee even as the men of Wright's Sixth Corps marched in a torchlight parade, breaking into cheers when they passed the rumpled man sitting quietly on the hotel porch.

On April 8, Lee parried Grant's note by suggesting a conversation about a "restoration of peace." An eerie silence fell as actions between the two armies almost ceased. As anxiety mounted, Grant was struck with a terrible migraine headache. That evening, in the farmhouse he shared with Meade and their staffs, Grant tried unsuccessfully to relieve his aching head by bathing his feet in hot water and putting mustard plasters on his wrists and neck. Lyman, watching Grant in "fearful pain," marveled that he did not try to stop "officers drum[ming] on the family piano" far into the evening.

THE SUN ROSE on April 9, Palm Sunday, a cloudless spring day. After exploring possible movements by Longstreet and Gordon, Lee told his staff officers, "There is nothing left for me to do but to go and see General Grant. I would rather die a thousand deaths." A lone rider hurried Lee's note to Grant. While waiting for a reply, Lee confided to Longstreet his apprehension that Grant would demand very stiff terms. "Old Pete," who had known Grant since West Point student days and stood up with him at his wedding, told Lee he did not believe Grant would do so.

At midday, Grant and Lee rode toward the home of Wilmer McLean in the village of Appomattox Court House. McLean, a farmer, had been living near Manassas in July 1861 when a Union shell smashed into his kitchen during the Battle of First Manassas; he had sensibly decided it was time to move as far away from hostilities as he could, which was how he'd ended up at Appomattox Court House. Now the war had found him again as Grant and Lee prepared to make peace in his front parlor.

Grant arrived shortly after one P.M. He walked up the white wooden steps and entered the two-story brick house to find Lee seated in a parlor. The contrast between the two men could not have been more striking. Lee wore a crisp new full-dress uniform with a jeweled sword and deep red sash. Grant came dressed in the same faded mud-splattered uniform he had been wearing for days—a simple private's blouse, no sword, muddy boots, only his shoulder straps indicating his rank. Grant took off his riding gloves and, extending his hand, told Lee that he recalled meeting him once before when they'd both served in the old days in Mexico, but because of the difference in their rank and years, he did not expect Lee to remember him. Lee replied that he knew he had met Grant but did not remember the particular occasion.

As Grant continued talking about their days of old in Mexico, Lee reminded him of the purpose of their meeting. Grant, puffing on his pipe, took out his order book with its yellow paper and started to write.

He admitted later that in the rush of events he had not organized his thoughts in advance, but this did not prevent him from writing a concise 185 words on the spot. The final sentence embodied his sense of the surrender: "This done, each officer and man will be allowed to return to his home, not to be disturbed by U. S. authority so long as they observe their paroles and the laws in force where they may reside."

Lee expressed his satisfaction and signed a letter of acceptance, then raised a final point: Cavalrymen and artillerymen owned their own horses. Might they be allowed to keep these animals?

"Well, the subject is quite new to me," Grant replied. "I take it that most of the men in the ranks are small farmers, and as the country has been so raided by the two armies it is doubtful whether they will be able to put in a crop to carry themselves and their families through the next winter without the aid of their horses they are now riding, and I will arrange it in this way."

"This will have the best possible effect upon the men," said the Confederate leader, "and will do much toward conciliating our people." Grant's words echoed Lincoln's words on the *River Queen* when Sherman asked the president how he would treat the defeated South.

After conversations about the return of prisoners, with Grant promising twenty-five thousand rations for Lee's hungry troops, Lee departed McLean's house. Silently he mounted Traveller and, with what observers said was an audible sigh, prepared to ride away. Just then Grant stepped

Grant met Robert E. Lee at Wilmer McLean's home at Appomattox Court House on April 9, 1865, to arrange for the surrender of the Army of Northern Virginia. Grant's magnanimous terms would become part of his enduring legacy.

out on the porch, stopped, and raised his hat as a mark of respect. Sheridan, Ord, and the other Federal officers followed his example. Lee raised his hat in return.

As Grant started back to his headquarters, news of the surrender spread like wildfire. Spontaneous firing of salutes exploded everywhere, but Grant immediately sent an order to stop all such demonstrations. "The war is over; the rebels are our countrymen again."

THE GRANT WHO came to make peace at Appomattox had been transformed by four years of war. A latent gift of quiet leadership was honed in his own understated style. He never spoke of his leadership abilities; others would do so when the war was over and it was time to take the measure of the man. But at the McLean house, he thought and wrote in a way wholly unlike the surrenders demanded of Simon Bolivar Buckner at Fort Donelson and John Pemberton at Vicksburg. Having gained a reputation as a hard-war warrior, at Appomattox he offered a magnanimous peace.

Grant assumed a national perspective in writing terms of surrender. He had traveled a long road before this point. The boy growing up on the Ohio frontier, the West Point graduate who resigned his commission, the young man in Missouri and Illinois with little interest in politics, the general who began the Civil War with no views on slavery other than the directives of civilian authorities—at the end of the war, all had transformed into a man who understood the close correlation between war and politics. Lincoln had become his example. Together they chose reconciliation over retribution.

Like his namesake, who spent ten years trying to return home to Penelope after the Trojan War, this American Ulysses, after four long years of civil war, longed to return to Julia and their children. But as the country turned from bitter war to uncertain peace, the nation would summon its greatest military hero to new dimensions of public service.

PART FOUR

Reconstruction

1865–1868

From the enforcement of the rights of citizens to
the stubborn problems of economic and racial justice, the issues central to Reconstruction are as old
as the American republic, and as contemporary as
the inequalities that still afflict our society.

—ERIC FONER, *Reconstruction*

CHAPTER 24

"I Will Keep My Word"

The suffering that must exist in the South next year, even with
the war ending now, will be beyond conception. People who talk
of further retaliation and punishment, except of political leaders, either
do not conceive of the suffering endured already or they are
heartless and unfeeling and wish to stay at home.
—Ulysses S. Grant to Julia Dent Grant, April 26, 1865

The next morning, April 10, 1865, Grant returned to the McLean house. Several Confederate officers, including former West Point classmates James Longstreet and Cadmus M. Wilcox, groomsmen at Grant's wedding, wanted to pay their respects to the Union general.

John Gordon, a tough Georgian who by the end of the war had become one of Lee's best commanders, came also. Gordon had never met Grant before and years later remembered, "What impressed me most was his modest demeanor. There was nothing in the expression of his face or in his language or general bearing which indicated exultation at the great victory he had won."

Grant had not seen Longstreet since their meeting in front of the Planter's House in St. Louis during Grant's down-on-his-luck days. He grasped his old friend's large hands and said, "Pete, let us have another game of brag, to recall the old days that were so pleasant to us all."

But the old days could never return. When the North and the South went to war, the United States population stood at barely more than thirty million. For that small nation, the accepted total of deaths in the Civil War stood at 620,000—360,000 from the North and 260,000 from the South—far and away the largest toll of any American war. Now, new research using digital census data from the nineteenth century has revealed that the acknowledged death total was far too low. It is now accepted that the Civil War cost the lives of nearly 750,000 people— 20 percent higher than the original total.

Harvard historian George Ticknor spoke for many of his generation who lived through the war when he said, "The civil war of '61 has made a great gulf between what happened before in our century and what has happened since, or what is likely to happen hereafter. It does not seem to me as if I were living in the country in which I was born."

AFTER THE FORMAL surrender ceremony on April 12, which Grant chose not to attend, his fellow generals wanted to make a triumphant visit to Richmond, but Grant would not. He wrote Julia, "I would not distress these people. They are feeling their defeat bitterly, and you would not add to it by witnessing their despair, would you?" Aware that critics were already beginning to condemn the generous terms he offered Lee at Appomattox, Grant confided to his personal secretary, Adam Badeau, "Mr. Lincoln is certain to be on my side."

Grant traveled to Washington and on April 14 went to the Executive Mansion for a morning meeting with the president. Lincoln had also invited him and Julia to join him and Mary that evening for a performance of *Our American Cousin* at Ford's Theatre. When the papers announced the Grants would be attending with the Lincolns, tickets priced at $1.00 were bought by scalpers and resold for $2.50. But while Grant was meeting with the president, a note arrived from Julia saying she wanted to leave the capital that afternoon.

Why Julia chose not to attend the play at Ford's Theatre is a question that still lingers. Perhaps the reason she gave—a visit to the children, whom she had not seen for three months—was the explanation. Perhaps it was her recent experience with Mary Lincoln at City Point. Perhaps it was the lunch at Willard's Hotel, where she had felt certain some strange man was watching her and, uneasy, she suddenly wanted to get out of the capital as soon as possible. Whatever the real reason, Grant agreed to leave.

When the Grants' train arrived in Philadelphia at the Broad Street Station, a messenger waited with a telegram from the War Department. Grant read it in silence:

THE PRESIDENT WAS ASSASSINATED AT FORD'S THEATRE AT 10:30 TONIGHT & CANNOT LIVE, THE WOUND IS A PISTOL THROUGH THE HEAD. SECRETARY SEWARD & HIS SON FREDERICK WERE ALSO ASSASSINATED AT THEIR RESIDENCE & ARE IN A DANGEROUS CONDITION. THE SECRETARY OF WAR DESIRES THAT YOU RETURN TO WASHINGTON IMMEDIATELY.

Grant handed the telegram to Julia, and as she read it, she burst into tears.

For the rest of his life, Grant agonized over what might have happened if he had been sitting in the box at Ford's Theatre with Lincoln. Could he have prevented Lincoln's death?

When Julia questioned her husband about who could have done it and why, he said he did not know, but that "this fills me with the gloomiest apprehension." She asked, "This will make Andy Johnson President, will it not?" Grant replied, "Yes, and for some reason, I dread the change."

GRANT RETURNED TO Washington immediately and saw that Ford's Theatre was draped in black. He took charge of arrangements for Lincoln's funeral. During the April 19 funeral services in the East Room of the White House, Grant stood alone in tears at the head of the flower-covered catafalque.

Four days later, Grant watched Lincoln's casket be placed on a funeral train that would follow almost the same route—in reverse—that brought Lincoln from Springfield to Washington in February 1861.

Upon returning to Washington after Lincoln's assassination, Grant saw Ford's Theatre draped in black.

. . .

ANDREW JOHNSON TOOK the oath of office at eleven A.M. on April 15. Grant, who believed the military should defer to civilian leadership, wanted to make his relationship with the new president work. He wrote St. Louis friend Charles Ford, "I have every reason to hope that in our new President we will find a man disposed and capable of conducting the government in its old channel."

At first glance, Johnson's life story appears similar to Lincoln's. Born in a log cabin in North Carolina on December 29, 1808, forty-five days before Lincoln's own birth, he grew up in poverty with no formal education but with a zest for learning. He trained as a tailor and settled in Greeneville in East Tennessee in 1826, where he advanced rapidly from alderman to mayor to a seat in the Tennessee legislature.

In 1843, Andy Johnson was elected to Congress as a representative from Tennessee. Embracing the politics of fellow Tennessean Andrew Jackson, he advocated rights for the poor against a domineering aristocracy. As a member of the agrarian wing of his party, his passion became "free land for the landless." Also a strong proponent of states' rights, he condemned the federal internal improvements of waterways and roads

Grant, firm in his belief that the military served under the authority of civilian leaders, now reported to President Andrew Johnson, of whom he and the nation knew little.

championed by Kentuckian Henry Clay and his Illinois disciple Abraham Lincoln. He offered a defense of slavery and white supremacy in Congress.

After five terms in Congress, Johnson was elected governor of Tennessee in 1853, then to the United States Senate in 1856. When Tennessee became the last Southern state to secede from the Union, Johnson broke from his home state, becoming the only Southern senator to remain loyal to the Union. This act made him a hero in the North and saw him burned in effigy from Memphis to Knoxville. In 1862, when Lincoln believed Union armies had captured sufficient Confederate territory, he appointed Johnson his first military governor of a breakaway state.

BUT FOR GRANT as general in chief, the war was not over. His immediate concern became the surrender of Joseph Johnston's army in North Carolina. He was pleased when Sherman wrote to say that he would offer Johnston "the same terms" Grant offered Lee, "careful not to complicate any points of civil policy." So Grant was surprised three days later when Sherman sent a copy of a very different agreement. Concerned, he wrote Stanton that Sherman's dispatches "are of such importance" the president should call the cabinet together immediately to discuss them.

Johnson and everyone in the cabinet rejected Sherman's terms, which acknowledged the lawful standing of the Confederate state governments, promised amnesty to all persons who participated in the rebellion, and authorized Confederate soldiers to deposit their arms and public property in the state arsenal—potentially opening up a continuation of the conflict. Johnson, Stanton, and Attorney General James Speed condemned Sherman; Grant, according to Secretary of the Navy Gideon Welles, while disagreeing with Sherman's terms, "abstained from censure." Grant believed Sherman acted in the spirit of Lincoln's March words about a generous peace, and he volunteered to travel to North Carolina to speak with Sherman.

Grant arrived in Raleigh, North Carolina, hoping to see Sherman without even his army learning of his presence. On his way, he learned that Stanton, far from keeping the cabinet deliberations confidential, had published a nine-point denunciation of Sherman in the Sunday papers, accusing him of "disloyalty" to the Union. The *New York Herald* editorialized, "Sherman's splendid military career is ended, he will retire under a cloud."

With Grant's steadying influence, Sherman renegotiated an acceptable treaty. As Grant learned of continuing attacks on his friend, he responded

angrily, "It is infamous—infamous! After four years of such service as
Sherman has done—that he should be used like this!"

WITH THE WAR finally over, on May 23 and 24 Grant and Johnson presided over a grand review in Washington as two hundred thousand Union
soldiers marched down Pennsylvania Avenue over two full days before
cheering crowds. It was a never-to-be-forgotten sight. Grant stood near
the White House in a reviewing stand, which was festooned with star-
studded flags inscribed "Shiloh," "Vicksburg," and "Wilderness," watching his men.

On the first day, Meade, on his warhorse Old Baldy, led the Army of
the Potomac marching twelve abreast, rank upon rank, with flawless precision. To the music of multiple bands, schoolchildren and adults sang

*On May 23 and 24, 1865, Grant presided alongside Johnson in a grand review in the
nation's capital of the eastern and western Union armies.*

song after song: "When This Cruel War Is Over," "When Johnny Comes Marching Home," and "Tramp, Tramp, Tramp! The Boys Are Marching."

The next morning, Sherman led his men in review. As people peered from windows to get their first glimpses of a western army, they saw soldiers less well dressed, marching with less precision, but carrying themselves with swagger. During the six-hour march, bands and soldiers broke into "Marching Through Georgia."

WITH THE GRAND review completed, Grant faced uncharted territory in what was being called Reconstruction. The mood in the reunited nation was a mixture of euphoria, anger, and uncertainty. The death of Lincoln, even when the signs of mourning were removed from public buildings, remained in people's conversations. The new president, largely unknown, added to the sense of insecurity about the future.

Grant, as general in chief, known to be admired by Lincoln, was now looked to for national stability. His official responsibilities would include overseeing the reduction of a massive wartime army to a small peacetime army of 227,000.

FIVE DAYS AFTER the grand review, Johnson showed Grant a first Reconstruction proclamation. The new president decided to act without calling Congress back into session. He offered amnesty to insurgents with certain important exemptions. Grant expressed concern about the exemptions—especially for West Point graduates who joined the Confederacy and for Confederate generals. Johnson assured him these graduates and generals could apply for pardons that Grant assumed would be readily granted.

Having come to sense the commanding stature of Lee, Grant wrote Halleck, "Although it would meet with opposition in the North to allow Lee the benefit of Amnesty I think it would have the best possible effect towards restoring good feeling and peace in the South to have him come in." He observed, "All the people except a few political leaders [in the] South will accept whatever he does as right and will be guided to a great extent by his example."

Lee was relieved when he read Johnson's proclamation, but he soon learned that District Judge John C. Underwood had called upon a grand jury in Norfolk, Virginia, to indict him and other Confederate generals for treason against the United States.

Lee considered writing Grant but wondered how his former adversary would view the matter. He made an inquiry through Maryland senator Reverdy Johnson. Grant let Lee know he intended to stand by the Appomattox accords.

On June 13, Lee wrote Grant, including his application for pardon. Grant sent Lee's letter and application on to Stanton with his own strong endorsement: "In my opinion the officers and men paroled at Appomattox and since . . . cannot be tried for treason so long as they observe the terms of their parole." He reminded Stanton that "the terms granted by me met with the hearty approval of the President at the time, and of the country generally."

To further Lee's letter and application, Grant decided to speak with the president. One of the first things out of Johnson's mouth was his determination "to make all treason odious." He asked, "When can these men be tried?"

"Never," Grant responded, "unless they violate their paroles." He told Johnson he had made "certain terms" with Lee. If "I had told him and his army . . . they would be open to arrest, trial, and execution for treason, Lee would never have surrendered, and we should have lost many lives in destroying him."

Shaken, Grant walked back to his headquarters and described his conversation with his staff: "I will not stay in the army if they break the pledges that I made." The bottom line: "I will keep my word."

Recognizing Grant's enormous popularity, Johnson gave in and directed Attorney General Speed to drop the charges against Lee. On the same day, Grant wrote Lee to inform him that his word at Appomattox would be honored. In the weeks that followed, scores of Confederate officers who trusted Grant applied for pardons through him.

GRANT WAS SO eager to escape the political infighting in Washington that he availed himself of invitations to leave the capital for the summer. He stopped first in New York City. What a contrast between his arrival in New York in 1854 after resigning his military posting in California—penniless and unable to pay for his hotel room—and in 1865, when he heard cries of "Grant! Grant! Grant!" as he checked into the same Astor House. In the evening, he attended a rally at Cooper Union organized by New York Democrats to show support for Johnson. But when cheers directed toward him interrupted the first speaker, Grant, uncomfortable, left early.

From New York City he traveled to West Point, which he had not seen since he'd graduated twenty-two years earlier. General Winfield

Scott, living in retirement, presented him with a copy of his recently published memoirs, which he'd inscribed, "From the Oldest to the Greatest General."

Grant went west to Chicago to attend a Sanitary Commission Fair, a citizen-organized voluntary effort to collect food and medical supplies for the welfare of troops. In discussing the possibility of the vote for blacks, the *Chicago Tribune* quoted Grant: "It is too soon to declare that loyal blacks in the South shall not be allowed to vote."

Wishing to worship on Sunday, with many prominent congregations proffering invitations, Grant inquired whether former Galena minister John Heyl Vincent might be preaching in Chicago. When he learned he was preaching at the Trinity Methodist Church, Grant arrived, unannounced, for Sunday worship.

The sermon made him long to get to his final destination, Galena, the small town where he had found contentment for himself and his family in the year before the war. He knew few people from the brief twelve months he had lived there, but a remarkable number of people now claimed to remember him. A triumphal arch spanned Main Street in front of the DeSoto House. Each side was inscribed with names of the great battles where Grant had triumphed: from Belmont to Shiloh to Vicksburg in the west, to the Wilderness, Five Forks, and Richmond in the east. Grant, ever the reluctant speaker, asked Vincent to speak for him. The Methodist minister told the crowd that although Grant's official business would keep him mostly in Washington, he considered Galena his home.

More than a year earlier, when Grant's name was being bandied about as a candidate for president, he tried to deflect this groundswell by declaring, "I am not a candidate for any office, but I would like to be mayor of Galena long enough to fix the sidewalks, especially the one reaching to my house." Now he looked up to see a banner: GENERAL, THE SIDEWALK IS BUILT. Galena had not only built a sidewalk but provided a house, where dinner awaited him. A group of citizens had purchased a brick home in the Italianate style for $2,500 and presented it to the Grants.

As GRANT BEGAN to forge a postwar identity for himself, in an overlooked part of that identity he turned his eyes constantly toward Mexico. If the story of the Mexican War had quickly receded from American memory, for Grant his significant experiences in young manhood now became a spur to present action. He looked for ways to aid Benito Juárez and his liberal Mexican patriots as they sought to push out the French occupation. The French were being aided by the Conservatives—the Catholic Church and the military—who had lost Mexico's long, bitter Reform War (*Guerra de Reforma*). The Liberals won this civil war and wanted a strong federal government capable of modernizing Mexico. Grant's understanding of the link between domestic and foreign policy grew apace with his interest in Mexico.

Grant developed a friendship with Matías Romero, Juárez's protégé, the energetic young Mexican minister sent to Washington in 1861 to lobby for the United States' support to Mexico's besieged government. In an April 1866 memorandum to his superiors, Romero advised, "In my judgment we ought to make General Grant our confidant, express our wishes to him, and seek his counsel." Grant's esteem for Romero and the cause of Mexico led him to invite the minister to stay in his home in Philadelphia in May. In June, Romero wrote, "I am very pleased with the extent to which my frequent, long, and cordial conversations with Grant have profited our cause."

GRANT PLEADED WITH Johnson to authorize the United States to offer aid to Mexico in its moment of peril: "I regard the act of attempting to establish a Monarchical Government on this continent, in Mexico, by foreign bayonets, as an act of hostility against the Government." Grant

Grant continuously sought ways to support Benito Juárez, who struggled to put liberal democracy in place in Mexico.

Grant's most direct contact with Mexico came through his developing friendship with young Mexican diplomat Matías Romero.

worked covertly to aid Juárez's army. He told Sheridan, "I need not tell you the interest I feel in Mexican affairs." In an ongoing clandestine arms plan, Sheridan sent Juárez thirty thousand rifles from the Baton Rouge Arsenal.

From Galena, Grant wrote an emotional letter to Johnson in which he raised the Monroe Doctrine, arguing that "nonintervention in Mexican affairs will lead to an expansive and bloody war hereafter." It was his belief that the United States should give notice to the French that their foreign troops must be withdrawn from the continent so that the Mexican people would be free to govern themselves. To back up this declaration, Grant advised, "I would openly sell, on credit, to the Government of Mexico all the arms, Munitions and clothing they want, and aid them with officers to command troops." He offered a robust support for a liberal democracy in Mexico.

GRANT ALSO LOOKED south as he sought to navigate the tension between conciliation with white southerners and the protection of freed blacks. He used his relationship with the president when his old friend James Longstreet came to Washington seeking a pardon: "I shall feel it a personal favor to myself if this pardon is granted." He would later mediate the release from prison of Alexander H. Stephens, vice president of the Confederacy, who had made a favorable impression on Grant when he had received him at City Point as a peace commissioner.

Although Grant sought the rapid reduction of the army—in part to avoid any "collision" between Federal troops in the South and returning Confederate soldiers—he told Stanton that a continuing task must be to "protect the freedmen in the liberty conferred on them." And he looked with alarm during the last half of 1865 as southern states began to craft constitutions denying the hard-won fruits of emancipation. State laws guaranteed to blacks the right to marry, make contracts, and own property, but the new "Black Codes" they put in place limited work possibilities to plantation labor. Starting on January 1, 1866, blacks in Mississippi would have to possess written proof of employment. If blacks left their jobs, they would be liable to forfeit their wages and be subject to arrest and imprisonment. Louisiana Republican Benjamin F. Flanders described the intent of legislators: "Their whole thought and time will be given to plans for getting things back as near to slavery as possible."

Grant confronted the dilemma presented by the large numbers of black soldiers in the South. Former slaves now wore Union uniforms in southern cities. At the end of the war, black soldiers represented 11 percent of the army. Because whites had entered the army earlier than blacks, their terms of enlistments expired earlier. This meant that by the fall of 1865, when Grant had reduced the army from more than a million to 227,000, blacks constituted 36 percent of the Union army.

In October, Johnson asked Grant to undertake a tour of the South. Earlier, the president had sent Carl Schurz, a prominent German American leader, on a two-and-a-half-month fact-finding trip throughout the South. Schurz's report dismayed Johnson: "Things are very far from being ripe yet for the restoration of civil government." Schurz's sharp eyes discerned that if the South had been ready at the end of the war to accept the strong policies of the federal government, once they got a whiff of Johnson's lenient policies, former Confederate leaders determined to regain control of their states. Dissatisfied with Schurz, the president sought another reporter.

He turned to Grant, believing people would listen to his conclusions. Dressed in civilian clothes, Grant left Washington on November 27 for a sixteen-day tour. White southerners put their best face forward, but Grant's aide Cyrus Comstock saw behind the facades, recording trenchant observations in his diary. In Charleston, when a group of women made mocking faces, Comstock noted the women "express openly what their husbands & brothers feel but do not show."

Upon his return to Washington on December 11, Grant reported to a cabinet meeting, "The people are more loyal and better disposed than he expected to find them." He declared in a written report, "I am satisfied that the mass of thinking men of the South accept the present situation of affairs in good faith." Newspapers lauded his report, which was taken as an endorsement of Johnson's policies.

Johnson attempted to hold back Schurz's more critical report, agreeing to release it only if it was paired with Grant's report. Ironically, this strategy backfired: Grant ended up reading Schurz's forty-six-page report with great care and recognized that Schurz had done what he had not—focused attention on violence against both blacks and white Unionists. He confessed later to Schurz, "I traveled as the general-in-chief and people who came to see me tried to appear to the best advantage. But I have since come to the conclusion that you were right and I was wrong."

One week after reading Schurz's report, Grant wrote to his commanders in the southern states, "Send to these Hd Qrs. as early as possible a report of all known outrages occurring within your command since the surrender of the rebel Armies."

. . .

THE THIRTY-NINTH CONGRESS convened on a balmy Monday, December 4. Throughout the spring and summer, members had chafed while Johnson put his Reconstruction policies in place with no congressional checks and balances. Now, Congress returned determined to seize the upper hand. In this Congress, Republicans boasted huge majorities—42 to 10 in the Senate and 149 to 42 in the House. The Thirteenth Amendment, after eight months of debates in the states, was formally ratified on December 6, and the Republicans in Congress intended to put teeth into its enforcement.

This restlessness with Johnson was led by the left wing of the party, the Radical Republicans. Their moral sensibilities had been shaped by their struggles against slavery in the decades leading up to the war. Leading Radicals in the Senate included Ohio's "Bluff" Ben Wade and Massachusetts's Charles Sumner and Henry Wilson. In the House, principal Radicals were Pennsylvania's Thaddeus Stevens and Ohio's James M. Ashley, instrumental in passing the Thirteenth Amendment, and Indiana's George W. Julian. They all came, with the exception of Stevens, from New England, or that part of New England's migration west through New York into the northern tiers of Pennsylvania, Ohio, Indiana, and Illinois.

With the convening of Congress, Grant found himself in a new position. When in the spring of 1864 he set up his command outside the capital, he did so in part because he did not want to become embroiled in politics. His main dealings with Washington were with the executive branch—President Lincoln and Secretary of War Stanton. He had little contact with Congress.

What was also different now was the growing chatter about Grant succeeding Johnson as president in 1868. He believed he would be too young in 1868—at only forty-six, he would be the youngest president ever elected. Grant's primary goal now was to exercise his authority as general in chief and keep the peace.

CONGRESS'S FIRST CLASH with Johnson erupted over the legal position of the southern states. The president argued that secession was inadmissible; therefore the southern states had never left the Union and their elected representatives should be seated immediately. Republicans believed the eleven southern states were now conquered states and needed to fulfill certain qualifications before they could be readmitted to Congress. So when sixteen recently elected southern congressmen—including four Confederate generals—presented their credentials in the first days of the new Congress, their applications were denied.

In January, Grant came to the Senate to answer questions about a Freedmen's Bureau bill introduced by Illinois senator Lyman Trumbull. The Freedmen's Bureau had been set up in March 1865 to aid former slaves with housing and food and to provide education and health care. The bill provided for the equality of citizens in the enjoyment of civil rights without distinction of race or color. Trumbull declared the bill was needed until "unprotected people . . . can provide for and take care of themselves." The glowering clouds of the Black Codes hung over the debates. Under its broad umbrella, agents of the Freedmen's Bureau were to work out new contractual arrangements between employers and the freedmen. Agents would assume control of cases concerning blacks, with the authority to punish state officials who refused to give blacks the "civil rights belonging to white persons." Grant listened as Trumbull declared

This 1866 cartoon is one of a series attacking Radical Republicans on the issue of black suffrage. It portrays the Freedmen's Bureau as an agency fostering black idleness at the expense of the white man.

the bill would buttress enforcement of the Thirteenth Amendment by offering military and judicial protection of African Americans.

As the hearings proceeded, according to his request, Grant began to hear from his commanders about incidents of violence against blacks and white Unionists. In response, he issued General Orders No. 3 on January 12. He directed commanders in the South to protect Union loyalists and military personnel from prosecution in state or municipal courts. The force of his order was contained in its final sentence: to protect blacks "charged with offenses for which white persons are not prosecuted or punished in the same manner and degree." In his defense of the Freedmen's Bureau, Trumbull cited Grant's recent order: "It contains many of the provisions of the bill under consideration." As Grant sat in on congressional debates on the Freedmen's Bureau bill, he understood that it would be his task to interpret its meaning and scope to the generals in the South under his command.

Next, Trumbull presented a second, more sweeping civil rights bill: he regarded it as "the most important measure that has been under its consideration since the 13th Amendment." It conferred citizenship on "all persons born in the United States." A further strengthening of the Thirteenth Amendment, the bill empowered Freedmen's Bureau officials, as well as federal marshals and district attorneys, to bring suits against those persons who would violate the law's provisions, even to the point of fines and imprisonment. The Senate passed the bill 33 to 12, the House 111 to 38.

MEANWHILE, GRANT BEGAN to think of building some financial stability for himself and his family. Over the past twenty-one years he had lived on his father-in-law's property, in a small rented house in Galena, and in multiple makeshift arrangements during four years of war. He had finally emerged from debt in Galena but had little saved or invested for retirement.

At the conclusion of the war, Grant had resolved to live in Philadelphia and travel to Washington by train, which made the trip in five and a half hours. Of course, after only a few weeks he'd realized this arrangement would not work. Ultimately, despite his disinclination to live in the capital, he accepted Henry Halleck's offer to use his home in the Georgetown Heights area of Washington.

In October, wanting his own residence, he purchased a large, four-story house for $30,000. The building was actually bought for him by

Abel Rathbone Corbin, a newspaper editor and financier Grant knew from Missouri. Corbin subsequently transferred the title to Grant, who signed a note promising to pay back the amount over ten years. With the cost of furnishing his Washington house, he anticipated being in debt for years. "I suppose a man out of debt would be unhappy," he quipped to Charles Ford, his friend and financial adviser. "I never tried the experiment myself however."

Grant's personal finances changed dramatically in February. Daniel Butterfield, Joe Hooker's chief of staff at Chattanooga and now a New York businessman, spearheaded an effort to raise money for the celebrated general in chief. He said he was asked everywhere: "How much is Genl. Grant's pay?" His standard reply: "Not enough to support the position he holds at all." Butterfield bestowed a "testimonial" check for $105,000 to Grant.

Grant used the money to pay off the mortgage on his new home, put $55,000 in government bonds, and received the rest, $19,837.50, in cash. He told Butterfield, "I feel at a loss to know how to express my appreciation."

Grant was beginning to walk in corridors of wealth and power with which he was not familiar. As a military man he had steered clear of politics, but he was slower to eschew business. In accepting houses in Philadelphia, Galena, and Washington as gifts from a thankful nation, he failed to appreciate that there was no such thing as a free house.

ON FEBRUARY 19, Grant was shocked when Johnson vetoed the Freedmen's Bureau Act. In his veto message, Johnson misrepresented the goals of the act, argued against federal intervention on behalf of African Americans, and claimed the act violated the Constitution by handing over judicial powers to the military. Furthermore, he would not sign any piece of legislation when the southern states were not yet represented.

Trumbull and other moderate Republicans joined with Radical Republicans in voting to override the veto. But the override, while passing in the House, fell two votes short in the Senate. Still, the moderates were not yet ready to give up on Johnson. They expected him to sign the 1866 Civil Rights Act, which had passed in Congress with almost unanimous Republican backing. It was not too late for Johnson to repair his relationship with the legislature.

Grant joined those surprised when Johnson vetoed the Civil Rights Act on March 27. This time Johnson's views on race became explicit. Arguing that the federal government's role in protecting the civil rights of blacks contravened "all our experience as a people," he baldly declared that to grant the privileges of citizenship to blacks would show prejudice against whites. "The distinction of race and color is by the bill made to operate in favor of the colored against the white race."

This time Johnson's veto was overridden. On April 6, the Senate voted 33 to 15 to override, with only four Republicans standing with Johnson. For the first time in American history, Congress passed an important bill despite a presidential veto.

IN THE WINTER of 1866, Grant found himself a man in the middle. He had started the postwar months committed to conciliation. Now, chastened by Schurz's report, doing his homework on the workings of the Freedmen's Bureau, alerted by his commanders of reports of violence directed against recently freed blacks, Grant was moving from conciliation to the need to safeguard the freedmen's rights.

Appeals began arriving from southern governors requesting both withdrawal of federal troops and permission to replace them with state

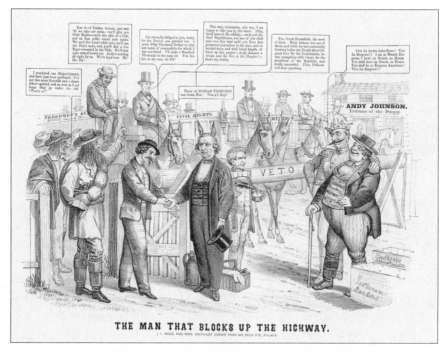

This 1866 cartoon shows men driving carriages branded "Freedmen's Bureau," "Civil Rights," and "Reconstruction," only to find the road blocked by a log labeled "Veto." Standing in front of the roadblock is President Andrew Johnson.

militias. When Johnson forwarded a request from the legislature of Mississippi, Grant replied, "The condition of things in the State of Mississippi, does not warrant the belief that the civil authorities of that State 'are amply sufficient to execute the laws and good order.'" When a similar request came from the governor of Alabama, George Thomas, departmental commander, prepared to approve the governor's request but passed it up the chain of command. Grant countermanded the decision of a senior commander. "For the present," he responded, "and until there is full security for equitably maintaining the rights and safety of all classes of citizens in the states lately in rebellion, I would not recommend the withdrawal of United States Troops from them."

VITRIOL AGAINST THE federal government was on the rise from another militia: southern newspapers, whose weapons were words. The *Richmond Examiner,* the loudest voice of dissent in the Confederate capital during the war, continued its combative tone after the war. When Grant learned the *Examiner* reprimanded Richmond women for attending a ball hosted by Union general Alfred Terry, he instructed Terry to "take immediate Military possession" of "the dangerously inflammatory" paper and to "prohibit the publication of the paper until further orders."

Examiner editor H. Rives Pollard hurried to Washington to speak with Johnson. After meeting Pollard, Johnson referred Pollard to Grant, requesting if he "'makes satisfactory explanation,' and promises to do better hereafter, you will be as moderate with him as possible." Later that day, Pollard wrote Johnson promising "to give a cordial support to the Union, the Constitution & the laws of the land." Sensing an opening, Pollard concluded, "The policy of your administration will continue to receive the support of the journal."

Grant did not buy Pollard's "explanation." That day he wrote Pollard a letter, which he also sent to the president. "The course of the 'Examiner' in every number which I have seen has been such as to foster and increase the ill feeling existing towards the Government of the United States." Grant believed "it to be for the best interests of the whole people, North and South, to suppress such utterances." Anticipating Johnson's question—under what legal authority?—he answered, "The power certainly does exist where martial law prevails and will be exercised."

Johnson overruled Grant, forcing him to write Terry that his previous order to close the *Examiner* is "temporarily suspended, if the Journal unreservedly gave support and loyalty to the Union and its supporters."

The *Examiner* episode proved to be only chapter one of a continuing story. Grant wrote commanders in every southern state, requesting they send copies of newspapers containing "sentiments of disloyalty and hostility to the Government." Not waiting for Johnson's approval, in succeeding months Grant launched investigations into the possible suppression of the *Wilmington Dispatch* and the *Mobile Daily Times*.

The larger story, of course, was Grant's growing awareness of his differences with Johnson over the trajectory of Reconstruction. Johnson overlooked Grant's serious misgivings to placate the editorial position of one of the strongest papers in the South. February 19, the day Grant reluctantly ordered Terry to let the *Examiner* reopen, was also the day Johnson vetoed the Freedmen's Bureau Act.

By the spring of 1866, President Johnson and the Republican-controlled Congress had constructed a line of demarcation across which there was less and less traffic. The question that elicited increasing conversation: Where did Grant stand?

All the most important political players in Washington came together on April 6, the same day as the Senate's override of Johnson's veto of the Civil Rights Act, when Ulysses and Julia hosted a reception in their new home on I Street. A correspondent for *The New York Times* reported, "Gen. Grant's reception tonight, the closing one of the season, is a grand affair."

Secretary of the Navy Gideon Welles captured the ethos of the unusual evening in his diary: "The party was in some respects unlike any of the season, and there was present not only a numerous but a miscellaneous company of contradictions." The secretary of the navy had it on good authority that some of the leading Radicals intended to try to "appropriate General Grant, or at least his name and influence, to themselves."

The guests arrived buzzing about the Senate's unprecedented override that afternoon. Old Thad Stevens, who seldom graced such receptions, showed up riding high, as did moderate leader Lyman Trumbull. Stevens was taken aback when he walked in to see President Johnson, who also typically did not come to receptions, standing with his two daughters next to Ulysses and Julia. Most surprising of all, Stevens spied Alexander Stephens, former vice president of the Confederacy, whom Grant had invited.

Grant's invitation list contained a message: Despite great differences of opinion, we need to work together. As the night wore on, Welles reported that "amid the exultation over the vote of the Senate, and expressions of vexation, there was such a strange attendance here." If the Grant soiree brought together people not often seen in one another's company, Rutherford B. Hayes, Ohio Union veteran and congressman, experienced the event differently. He wrote his wife, Lucy, "It was the happiest gathering I have seen."

They all wanted to see and be seen with Grant. Radical Republicans, conservative Democrats, and even President Johnson wanted Grant's blessing. The military hero who had long eschewed politics was now at the very center of the post–Civil War political storm. With events about to pick up speed in 1866, could he stay in the middle for long?

CHAPTER 25

"More & More Radical"

General getting more & more radical.
—Cyrus Comstock, diary entry, March 1, 1867

I remarked to the President that Grant had, unconsciously perhaps,
very much changed his views within a year.
—Secretary of the Navy Gideon Welles,
diary entry, July 26, 1867

One year after Appomattox, Grant had grown concerned that the magnanimous peace he had negotiated was stalling, if not stopped. On April 2, 1866, Johnson had issued a proclamation declaring that the "insurrection . . . is at an end." His order precipitously reestablished civil rule throughout an increasingly chaotic South. At Johnson's direction, Stanton issued General Orders No. 26 on May 1, 1866, directing military courts to give up their authority to civilian courts. Grant read with alarm this proclamation that ended martial law and military tribunals "except in cases of actual necessity"—the meaning of which phrase would become hotly debated in the coming months.

In an interview with *The New York Times* in May, Grant declared, "I find that those parts of the South which have not felt the war . . . are much less disposed to accept the situation in good faith than those portions which have been literally overrun by fire and sword. A year ago, they were willing to do anything; now they regard themselves as masters of the situation." On the anniversary of the triumphant grand march in Washington, Grant understood how much had changed in the South in the short span of one year.

IN REPASSING THE Civil Rights Act over Johnson's veto, Congress had signaled its determination to thwart the president's Reconstruction policies and establish its own. Now, Grant worked with various members of Congress in pushing for a Fourteenth Amendment, which would make certain that future congresses could not undo the Civil Rights Act. Section 1 of the amendment declared, "All persons born or naturalized in the United States . . . are citizens of the United States." Harking back to the Bill of Rights, it went on to say, "No State shall make or enforce any law which shall abridge the privileges or immunities of citizens . . . nor shall any State deprive any person of life, liberty, or property, without due process of law" or deny "equal protection of the laws."

On June 13, the House passed the Senate version of the amendment by a vote of 120 to 32, easily exceeding the necessary two-thirds majority, with every Republican voting for it. The former rebel states were required to ratify the new amendment before being eligible to rejoin the Union.

Johnson immediately declared war against the amendment. He argued that because the southern states were not represented in Congress, it was not legal. His underlying objection: Neither he nor the southern states would ever affirm equal political rights for blacks.

Grant found himself in the middle of a seesaw, with the president pushing down on one end and Congress on the other. At the conclusion of the Civil War, he was committed to supporting the president's authority as commander in chief. But in the intervening fourteen months, he slowly pivoted toward supporting the authority of Congress. As a soldier who had seen too much bloodshed, he longed for conciliation. As a person who grew from indifference about slavery to advocacy of African American rights, he stood for congressional measures that would give them protection. As general in chief, he was committed to enforcing the laws of the land. Yet the orders, laws, and amendments coming from the president and Congress, rather than offering clarity, were increasingly in conflict.

AS LAWMAKERS DEBATED in the halls of Congress, the combustible racial situation exploded in the South. In Memphis, on May 1 several black soldiers who had been mustered out of the army for only one day were arrested by white police, charged with being disorderly. Within minutes, a white mob attacked South Memphis, where freed slaves and the soldiers' families lived. At nearby Fort Pickering, General George Stoneman refrained from taking action. With no restraints, the mob burned black homes, schools, and churches.

Southern newspapers realized how the riot could play into the hands

The Memphis riots were featured as the front-page story for
Harper's Weekly *on May 26, 1866.*

of northern Republicans and spun the story to blame blacks. The *Memphis Argus* editorialized, "This time there can be no mistake about it, the whole blame of this tragic and bloody riot lies as usual with the poor, ignorant, and deluded blacks."

The combination of recently freed slaves, ex-Confederates who staffed the police force, and black Union soldiers was sure to ignite conflagrations. As cities like Memphis recovered management of local government following Johnson's orders, white city fathers, through the police, struck out against all visible signs of "Yankee Black Republicanism."

Grant's congressional advocate, Elihu Washburne, chaired a subcommittee of the Joint Committee on Reconstruction and arrived in Memphis on May 22 to investigate. His committee documented that from May

1 to 3, casualties included the deaths of forty-six blacks (among them fourteen black soldiers) and two whites, a policeman and fireman who were among the attackers. Seventy-five people were injured, five black women raped, and ninety-one black homes, eight schools, and four churches burned. Washburne declared that the "riot" was "in reality the massacre" of black citizens. Supporting these conclusions, Stoneman testified that blacks were not involved after the first day: "They assembled in no bodies, and were engaged in no riotous proceedings."

Grant was disgusted. He notified General George Thomas that he was sending four companies "to suppress outrages" in his division. Aware of Johnson's prohibition on trying the perpetrators in military courts, but not trusting local civil courts, Grant instructed, "If the Civil Authorities fail to make arrests for past violence let the troops make them and hold the parties in confinement until they, the Civil Authorities, give satisfactory evidence that justice will be done, or until you receive orders more clearly defining the course to be pursued."

What course might that be? Grant turned to Stanton for support: "The victims were all helpless and unresisting negroes stamping lasting disgrace upon the civil authorities that permitted them." Since "the civil authorities of Memphis having failed to make any arrests in this case I would recommend that the leaders in this riot be arrested by the Military, and held by them, until the civil authorities give evidence of their ability, and willingness, to take cognizance of their cases and to give a fair trial."

Stanton passed along Grant's appeal to Johnson, who solicited an opinion from Attorney General James Speed. Speed began his finding, "Gen. Grant well remarks that such a scene stamps lasting disgrace upon the civil authorities of Memphis." Nevertheless, his legal opinion emphasized that although the military "performed their duty in aiding to suppress the mob violence," they "can have nothing to do with the . . . prosecutions for public wrongs." Because Tennessee became the first southern state readmitted to the Union—July 24, 1866—a week after it ratified the Fourteenth Amendment, the courts were now open, so "the injured party may appeal to the courts for redress."

In August, Thomas reported to Grant, "The names of the leaders in the recent Memphis riots have been clearly ascertained. Shall they be arrested?" Grant, feeling stymied by Speed's decision, referred Thomas's inquiry to Stanton but offered his own comment. On the one hand, "I do not feel authorized to order the arrest of the Memphis rioters"; on the other, "I think it ought to be done with a strong hand to show that where the civil authorities fail to notice crime of this sort there is a power that will do so." Grant decided Speed's judgment applied only to Memphis, so he felt he could authorize other military arrests in the future.

Increasingly a man without a political home, Johnson attempted to leapfrog the Republican and Democratic parties in August by creating a third party he hoped would elect persons to Congress in the fall who would back his policies.

The National Union Convention assembled in Philadelphia. But the seven thousand who gathered to embrace Johnson's policies quickly found themselves disagreeing. Conservative Democrats did not trust Johnson because he had run on a Republican ticket in 1864; Republicans did not trust him as an increasingly conservative Democrat. In the end, although expending much bombast denouncing Republican Radicals, the convention could not cohere as a third party.

Shifting tactics, the wily Johnson put together a campaign-style speaking tour to the West. To help draw a crowd, he invited Grant as the headliner of his entourage. If nineteenth-century presidents did not campaign for office, they especially did not campaign *during* office. But Johnson had been stung by the proposed Fourteenth Amendment, yet to be ratified by the required three-fourths of state legislatures, and decided to take his case to the country. Uncomfortable, Grant confided to Washburne, "I do not think it proper for an Army officer, particularly the Army commander, to take part in elections." He tried to decline but in the end could not turn down an invitation from his commander in chief.

The tour left Washington on August 27. In Johnson's speech in New York, he shrewdly had Grant stand by his side, as if to say the military hero supported his policies. A few days later, Ulysses wrote Julia, "I am getting very tired of this expedition and of hearing political speeches." Yet, ever deferential to presidential authority, he told her, "I must go through however."

The political circus traveled on, now derisively called Johnson's "Swing Around the Circle." City officials in Baltimore, Philadelphia, Cincinnati, Indianapolis, and Pittsburgh refused to offer official receptions. Although Grant tried to stay out of the spotlight, Gideon Welles noted he "generally received louder cheers and called out more attention than even the President himself."

An interested foreign observer, Mexico's Matías Romero, captured the tensions of the tour: "General Grant's presence and name excited much more enthusiasm than Johnson's presence and name." Romero told his superiors in Mexico that crowds "interrupted the president when he has wished to speak and cheered the general to the point of proclaiming him the next president." The young diplomat observed, "Naturally, this has caused some cooling off in the relationship between General Grant and Johnson and some rivalry and jealousy between their friends."

When the trip reached St. Louis, Grant listened as Johnson's ranting reached a new low. To shouts of "Hurrah for Andy!" he claimed the Radicals' ultimate purpose was to "disfranchise white men." Finally, responding to those in Washington calling upon him to "hang Jeff Davis," he exploded, "I might ask the question, why don't you hang Thad Stevens and Wendell Phillips? A traitor at one end of the line is as bad as a traitor at the other."

From St. Louis, Ulysses wrote Julia, "I have never been so tired of anything before as I have been with the political stump speeches of Mr. Johnson from Washington to this place. I look upon them as a National disgrace." He counseled her, "Of course you will not show this letter to anyone for so long as Mr. Johnson is President I must respect him as such, and it is the country's interest that I should also have his confidence." This letter to Julia shows both Grant's astuteness vis-à-vis his role with Johnson and his increasing awareness of his own political standing with the American people.

But Grant had had enough. He left the tour early, after Cincinnati, and returned to Washington in advance of Johnson.

WITH THE TOUR unsuccessful, once back in Washington Johnson schemed how to throw off Grant's long shadow hovering over his declining popularity. On October 17, he asked Grant to accept a diplomatic assignment to Mexico as companion to Lewis Campbell, the new minister to Benito Juárez's government. Knowing the general's deep commitment to Mexico, Johnson thought it was an offer Grant could not refuse. Grant's aide Cyrus Comstock, with a nose for political intrigue, knew exactly what Johnson was up to. He wrote in his diary: Johnson was "sentencing him [Grant] to Mexico."

At the same time, Johnson asked Grant to invite Sherman to Washington. His strategy rested on using Sherman as a counterweight to Grant's enormous popularity: he would send Grant south of the Rio Grande and appoint Sherman as interim general in chief; then, with Grant away, he would remove Stanton and replace him with Sherman as secretary of war.

Grant understood that he diverged from Sherman on Reconstruction. Sherman was more amenable to Johnson's policies: he supported seating the southern states immediately and opposed voting rights for blacks.

However, now that he was more aware of Johnson's chicanery, Grant warned Sherman that Johnson wanted to use him for his own ends: "I will not venture in a letter to say all I think about the matter or that I would say to you in person."

Sherman was not always aware of the political implications of his words and actions, but this time he read between the lines of Grant's letter. He wrote his wife, "There is some plan to get Grant out of the way, & to get me here, but I will be a party to no such move."

It did not take Grant long to make up his mind what to do. On October 21, he wrote Johnson asking "to be excused from the duty proposed." He reasoned, "It is a diplomatic service for which I am not fitted either by education or taste. It has necessarily to be conducted under the State Department with which my duties do not connect me." Grant said he was a soldier, not a politician.

He hoped that would end the matter. It did not. Two days later at a cabinet meeting, Johnson, as if his exchange of letters with Grant had never happened, turned to Secretary of State William Seward and asked him to read the instructions for Grant's diplomatic assignment.

Johnson had challenged the wrong man. By now provoked, Grant repeated he was unwilling to accept the assignment. Johnson turned to Attorney General Henry Stanbery, a conservative Republican who had replaced James Speed in July. "Mr. Attorney General," he said, "is there any reason why General Grant should not obey my orders?"

Before Stanbery could say a word, Grant stood up: "I can answer that question." He told the cabinet that as an army officer, "any legal military order you give me I will obey; but this is civil and not military; and I decline the duty." He ended dramatically, "No power on earth can compel me to it."

Grant walked out of the Cabinet Room. In this defining moment, he had found his voice.

In the end, Sherman accepted Grant's assignment to go to Mexico, Stanton remained as secretary of war, and the fissure between Grant and Johnson widened.

GRANT BELIEVED THE fall biennial elections would test Johnson's presidential policies at the ballot box. Despite the antagonism between the two men, as general in chief Grant did not want to be seen as participating on one side or the other. When he learned that William S. Hillyer, his former aide and now a New York lawyer, had made a speech declaring Grant's support for Johnson, he wrote immediately. "You, nor no man living, is authorized to speak for me in political matters," he insisted. "I want every man to vote according to his own judgment, without influence from me."

The New York Times believed the election would turn mainly on the Fourteenth Amendment. Grant watched as key Johnson supporters abandoned ship. By October, Henry J. Raymond, publisher of *The New York Times,* who delivered the main address at the National Union Convention in August, deserted Johnson. James Gordon Bennett, editor of the Democratic *New York Herald,* who had extolled Johnson as the "right man in the right place" throughout 1866, also forsook the president.

During the run-up to the fall elections, rumors swirled that Johnson would try to block the reconvening of the Thirty-ninth Congress and attempt to seat his own Congress, composed of representatives from all the Confederate states plus conservative northern Democrats. These rumors did not sound absurd. Grant confided to Philip Sheridan his growing concern: "I much fear that we are fast approaching the point where he will want to declare the body itself illegal, unconstitutional and revolutionary."

In September, a warier Grant issued orders to send arms from ordnance stores in Georgia, Louisiana, South Carolina, Virginia, Alabama, and Texas to New York. In October, he wrote Sheridan to be on the alert "that Texas should have no reasonable excuse for calling out the Militia authorized by their Legislature." Although having long looked forward to attending in early November the wedding of aide Orville Babcock, Grant wrote Washburne on October 23, "I will not be able to go to Galena for the wedding. I cannot fully explain to you the reason but it will not do for me to leave Washington before the elections." He added, "This is a matter of great regret to me but you will appreciate my staying." Grant was genuinely alarmed.

VOTERS WENT TO the polls on five different dates in September, October, and November 1866 to elect members of the House of Representatives—members of the Senate were elected by state legislatures. One week after the final votes were counted, *The Nation* declared, "This is the most decisive and emphatic victory ever seen in American politics." Republicans triumphed in the House by a margin of 173 to 47 and in the Senate 57 to 9. The practical result: Both chambers could override any Johnson veto with a more than two-thirds Republican majority.

· · ·

THE LAME DUCK short session of Congress convened on December 3. With complaints of attacks on blacks and white Unionists in the South growing, Republicans promised tougher legislative measures. Old Thad Stevens growled, "He was rather Conservative last winter, but is now Radical."

Ten Confederate states still stood knocking at the door of Congress. They knew the key to unlock the door: ratify the Fourteenth Amendment. But they would not. Increasingly, they felt strengthened in their defiant posture by their belief that the president was on their side.

Grant became more outspoken. He found his voice in the October cabinet meeting and began to use it with members of Congress. One year before, he had been a spectator when Lyman Trumbull introduced the first Reconstruction bills; in January 1867, he was a participant, meeting with many congressional leaders to argue for enforcement of these Reconstruction bills.

Responding to a request from the Senate, Grant wrote Oliver Howard, commissioner of the Freedmen's Bureau, asking him to "send me a list of authenticated cases of Murder, and other violence, upon Freedmen" and Union men in the South. In February, he submitted the report "for information as to the violations of the Civil Rights Bill" of 440 "outrages committed on the freedmen" in 1866, believing these documented cases would strengthen Congress's hand.

Gideon Welles, the secretary of the navy, was strongly opposed to the Fourteenth Amendment. He became displeased when he heard reports of two Arkansas men, who claimed that "General Grant urged upon them to adopt the Amendment; said the North was in favor; that they had decided for it in the late election; that if not adopted the Government would impose harsher terms."

But Grant stood by his beliefs. He continued to tell various southern visitors there was only one way: "When you get home, urge your people to accept negro suffrage. If you had promptly adopted the constitutional amendment abolishing slavery, or the one making negroes citizens . . . Congress would undoubtedly have admitted you."

The *Independent,* a Protestant newspaper with a wide circulation that supported the Republican Radicals in Reconstruction, applauded his statement: "He has spoken in all places" in favor of the Reconstruction bill.

Comstock confided to his diary on March 1, "General getting more & more radical."

If both his friend Comstock and his foe Welles noticed the changes in Grant, not everyone paid attention. This was because as the nation's chief military officer, Grant continued to be discreet in his public remarks. Further, in contrast to President Johnson and firebrands Thaddeus Stevens, Charles Sumner, and Wendell Phillips, he maintained a calm demeanor that allowed him to move back and forth among powerful and contentious personalities. Grant's personal secretary, Adam Badeau, offered his insight: "His equanimity of temper was as important at this juncture as either his steadfastness or unselfishness of purpose."

GRANT'S GROWING CONVICTION that the federal government needed to do more to defend black rights in the South now coincided with Congress's passage of the Military Reconstruction Act, frequently called the First Reconstruction Act. Brushing aside the present southern state governments as merely provisional, the legislation intended "to provide for more efficient government of the rebel states." The act would create five military districts in the ten southern states that refused to ratify the Fourteenth Amendment. The five generals heading these districts would have broad powers to act as the effective government. Grant, sensing some opposition to the act among more conservative members of the Republican Party, let it be known that he would be comfortable letting the president select the five generals.

When Johnson vetoed the act as expected, the new Fortieth Congress overrode his veto as one of its first transactions in March 1867. In a letter to Washburne, Grant called Johnson's rejection "one of the most ridiculous Veto messages that ever emanated from any President." These are strong words. Although circumspect in public, Grant was increasingly sharing his true thoughts and feelings about Johnson with Julia, Sherman, and Washburne.

Grant met with Johnson for three hours to discuss who should be appointed to these important posts. In the end, surprisingly, Johnson largely deferred to Grant's choices. Two days later, in General Orders No. 10, Grant appointed five trusted generals: John Schofield, Daniel Sickles, George Thomas, Edward Ord, and Philip Sheridan.

Sensing Grant's hand, when the names were announced, Welles expressed concern that "he is to some extent affected and has been swayed by Radical influence."

WITH JOHNSON DETERMINED to block any and all of Congress's Reconstruction measures, its members worried about Johnson's antipathy to both Grant and Stanton. With Stanton the lone remaining holdover from the Lincoln cabinet, Oregon senator George H. Williams introduced a tenure of office bill to protect him. The measure stated that cabinet officers were to "hold their offices respectively for and during the terms of the President by whom they may have been appointed," effectively depriving Johnson of the power to remove Stanton without the approval of the Senate. The Tenure of Office Act was passed over Johnson's veto on March 2.

If Congress worried about Stanton, the secretary of war worried about Grant. He learned that Johnson had begun to issue orders to officers in the army of which neither he nor Grant had any knowledge. Even worse, he learned that Johnson was once again scheming to send Grant away from Washington.

In response, Stanton stipulated that all orders to the army must come through the general in chief, who had to be located in Washington—no more sentencing Grant to Mexico. Furthermore, Grant could not be removed from office except through the sanction of the Senate. Stevens appended it as a rider to the military appropriations bill awaiting passage in Congress.

Johnson, livid, objected to what he deemed interference with his constitutional prerogatives. However, Congress passed the bill on March 2. Johnson signed it because he could not say no to much needed military appropriations.

PERHAPS AS A respite from the stress of Washington, a significant part of Grant's personal correspondence throughout 1867 referred to his properties near St. Louis. With Julia's father, eighty-one years old, now residing with them in Washington, he had bought not only White Haven but several adjoining properties, including 280 acres belonging to his brother-in-law John Dent and land belonging to his sister-in-law Emily Dent Casey.

Grant loved what he called "the Gravois place." It reminded him of courting Julia twenty-four years before. He imagined the two of them, and now their children, riding to their hearts' content across the farmland meadows. He had purchased four mares and intended to breed them to some excellent trotters. He wrote his St. Louis friend Charles Ford in March, "Hereafter I hope to spend several months in the year in the place." He looked forward to spending time as a gentleman farmer and horse breeder. But in 1867, it was not to be.

. . .

WITHIN A MONTH of the passage of the First Reconstruction Act, Grant worried that Sheridan, an aggressive leader, was approaching the top of Johnson's list of enemies. On March 27, Sheridan removed from office three ringleaders of the New Orleans riot of July 1866, who had promised the rioters in advance that they would not be prosecuted. Grant wrote approvingly of Sheridan's order: "It is just the thing . . . I have no doubt but that it will also meet with like approval from the *reconstructed*."

When New Orleans officials refused to investigate crimes against black citizens, Sheridan removed twenty-two aldermen as well as the city attorney, controller, and treasurer; he also dismissed a judge who would not allow black witnesses to testify at a murder trial. But there were limits to what military commanders could do without White House approval. The next week, when Sheridan wired Grant that he might remove the governors of Louisiana and Texas, Grant hurriedly replied, "I would advise that no removal of Governors of states be made at present."

Grant was awaiting an opinion as to whether such action could be pursued under the recently passed Reconstruction Act or would require a special act of Congress. "The fact is there is a decided hostility to the whole Congressional plan of reconstruction at the 'White House,' and a disposition to remove you from the command you now have." He assured Sheridan, "Both the Sec. of War and myself will oppose any such move."

Changes were occurring in other military districts as well. John Pope, now commanding the Third Military District in Virginia, telegraphed Grant that he had "deposed the mayor and Chief of Police and replaced them with efficient union men." Grant wrote Pope that "District Commanders are responsible for the faithful execution of the reconstruction Act of Congress."

Grant learned that Johnson had been so outraged by the Second Reconstruction Act of March 23, 1867, which gave the five military district commanders responsibility to register voters, that he'd asked Attorney General Stanbery to review both Reconstruction acts. On June 12, 1867, a compliant Stanbery issued an opinion blunting the power of the military district commanders. Focusing on the proper spheres for the civil and the military, "there is, then, an imperative necessity to define as clearly as possible the line which separates the two jurisdictions." Stanbery's aim was to curtail the five commanders' powers to remove civilian officials and to limit the right to vote of those who had participated in the rebellion.

As Grant looked forward to the special session of Congress set to convene in July, confident it would publish a rebuttal of Stanbery's opinion, he wrote his commanders in the field, "The law however makes District Commanders their own interpreters of their power and duty under it." However much he wished to hand over responsibility to his five commanders in the ten states, he became the focal point for enforcing the two Reconstruction acts.

MEANWHILE, THE HOUSE Judiciary Committee interviewed Grant as it began to consider impeaching President Johnson for "high crimes and misdemeanors." In an interview, its members asked Grant about the first months of Reconstruction under Johnson, questioning him about his views on amnesty, especially for Robert E. Lee. The committee sought to highlight the differences of opinion between Grant and Johnson. Grant, always respectful, told the committee, "I have stated those views [on amnesty] to the President frequently" and "he disagreed with me on those views."

Although Grant offered no new information, the hearings served to solidify his reputation in Congress. *The New York Times* applauded him: "The responsibility, the fidelity, the sagacity of Gen. Grant constitute the only guarantee vouchsafed to us for the adequate enforcement of the conditions dictated by Congress in the spirit in which they were conceived."

The Third Reconstruction Act passed on July 19. Ignoring Attorney General Stanbery's recommendations, it gave ultimate power to Grant and his five generals to remove civilian officials and clarified and extended the meaning of the first two Reconstruction acts. Furthermore, it gave Grant's commanders independent authority, free from presidential control, to decide who could and could not vote in their districts. The president blasted the act, but once again Congress overrode his veto.

THE NEXT DAY, Congress adjourned for four months. Grant wrote Stanton, "As soon as I receive a copy of the bill which passed Congress yesterday, over the President's veto, I will make such orders as seem to me necessary to carry out the provisions of the bill and direct that they be shown to you before being issued."

Grant and Stanton, working together, drew closer. Not many people wanted to be close to Stanton, whose unremitting intensity and often acerbic personality did not win him friends. But Grant and Stanton were drawn together as colleagues because Grant understood they shared common goals in this era of Reconstruction.

Stanton, believing Johnson had been tamed by the latest Reconstruction Act, and with Congress in hiatus, relaxed his intense pace and resumed regular office hours at the War Department for the first time since before the war. He even encouraged Grant to take a vacation. Ulysses and Julia left hot and humid Washington for the cooling beachside breezes at Long Branch, New Jersey, one of the most popular resorts on the Jersey shore.

Grant desperately needed the rest. Yet he had barely arrived at the New Jersey shore before he wrote Stanton on July 24, "Every day that I am absent from Washington I see something in the papers or hear something, that makes me feel that I should be there."

THE PRESIDENT, POLITICALLY weakened, still believed he could snatch victory from defeat. He huddled with his loyal cabinet members. Johnson knew he could not touch Grant, but he would go after the two men closest to him. Hearing the rumblings, Grant ended his vacation almost before it began and hurried back to the capital.

He met with Johnson on the last day of July. The president informed him he intended to remove both Stanton and Sheridan and wanted Grant to take over the War Department.

Stunned, Grant wrote Johnson a carefully worded letter the next day. He addressed him "privately" because of the "great danger to the welfare of the country should you carry out the designs then expressed." Challenging the president's misreading of the Tenure of Office Act, he reminded Johnson that he could not remove Stanton without the consent of the Senate: "The meaning of the law may be explained away by an astute lawyer but common sense, and the mass of loyal people, will give to it the effect intended by its framers."

As for removing Sheridan, Grant asked Johnson "to consider the effect it will have upon the public." He reminded him, "He is universally, and deservedly, beloved by the people who sustained this government through its trials."

Grant's letter did not dissuade the president. On Monday morning, August 5, Johnson's secretary arrived at Stanton's office with a message from the president: "Public considerations of a high character constrain me to say, that your resignation as Secretary of War will be accepted."

Shocked but prepared by Grant, Stanton replied without missing a beat, using Johnson's exact words: "I have the honor to say that public considerations of a high character, which alone have induced me to continue as head of this Department, constrain me not to resign the office of Secretary of War before the next meeting of Congress."

For the moment Stanton held on, and so did Sheridan.

IN 1867, AS Congress struggled to establish a Reconstruction worthy of the nation's second American Revolution—even as the last surviving soldier of the first American Revolution died that year—Grant continued to see his primary role as protector of the freedmen against attacks in the South. As he told Washburne, "I feel the same obligation to stand at my post that I did whilst there were rebel armies in the field to contend with."

⊹⇒◉⇐⊹

CHAPTER 26

"Let Us Have Peace"

> All the romance of feeling that men in high places are above personal
> considerations and act only from motives of pure patriotism, and for the
> general good of the public has been destroyed. An inside view
> proves too truly very much the reverse.
>
> —ULYSSES S. GRANT to WILLIAM T. SHERMAN, September 18, 1867

"Loyalty to the nation ALL THE TIME. Loyalty to the government
when it deserves it."

So judged Samuel Langhorne Clemens, an irreverent young writer
who had recently adopted the pen name "Mark Twain," and it might
have been written with Grant in mind. The Civil War had roused Grant's
deeper loyalty to his country. During the Reconstruction years of 1866
and 1867, as his political sensibilities awakened, Grant struggled with a
difficult question: Did a government led by Andrew Johnson deserve his
loyalty?

ON SUNDAY MORNING, August 11, 1867, Julia and Ulysses were about to
start for church when a messenger arrived from the White House requesting the general's immediate presence. Grant felt a sense of foreboding.

When he arrived, Johnson informed him he intended to appoint him
secretary of war in place of Edwin Stanton. The president asked if they
had any disagreements between them. Grant named the Fourteenth
Amendment and several congressional Reconstruction acts as major differences. None of this dissuaded Johnson.

Johnson did not offer Grant the post because he thought him a steadfast ally, for by now he had come to realize that Grant, however deferential in public, opposed many of his Reconstruction policies. Rather, he
made a calculated decision that Grant would be easier to work with than
the contentious Stanton. The president had heard the crowds' applause
and understood that Grant had become a likely competing presidential

candidate for 1868. If Johnson could persuade Grant to become a member of his cabinet, which might make it seem to the public that he shared the president's views, this might be his best hope of destroying Grant's popularity with Republicans.

As Grant grew more and more alarmed watching Abraham Lincoln's successor obstruct Congress's Reconstruction acts, he came to believe it would be better to accept the position of secretary of war than let it go to another. He came home and told Julia, "I consented to do so, as I think it most important that someone should be there who cannot be used."

On that same evening, Grant went to Stanton's home. There is no record of the content of their fifteen-minute conversation in Stanton's private library, but Stanton surely let Grant know that even if worn out by his battles with Johnson, he was not ready to give up.

In Grant's day, he was sometimes called "Grant the silent," "the quiet man," or the "American Sphinx." Most viewed Grant as a man of deeds, not words. Today, we are tempted to offer a more nuanced analysis of his personality. He certainly was not passive, but neither did he have the big personality we tend to associate with contemporary political leaders. We might call Grant an introvert. In fact, going down the list psychologists offer as the features of introversion, we see many of Grant's characteristics.

Many introverts prefer to express themselves in writing, rather than speaking. Grant experienced an inner horror when asked to speak in public, but his carefully prepared written commands during the Civil War were marked by a powerful clarity.

Grant dreaded small talk, especially when he found himself thrust into large social events. (Julia was much more at ease in such gatherings.) Grant preferred one-on-one conversation with people he knew and trusted. Introverts also tend to be good listeners. Many who served under Grant appreciated that, in staff conversations, he typically offered his opinion only after everyone else had had an opportunity to speak.

Grant did not like conflict. He tended to shy away from persons who were confrontational, like William Rosecrans or Ben Butler. That did not mean, however, that he was a pushover. He had a strong inner moral compass, but he was also notably sensitive. He was sickened by violence toward women. He was extremely protective of animals. In an era of stoic males, he could be moved to the point of tears by Julia, Nellie, and others close to him.

Can introverts be leaders? Yes, certainly. The very qualities that mark them as introverts can make them remarkable leaders, though a public life may take a lot out of them emotionally (Grant was plagued by head-aches). Grant's thoughtfulness, listening skills, and sensitivity translated into a finely tuned empathy that allowed "the quiet man" to place himself within the lives of others—be it his young children, Confederate generals, African Americans, or in this potentially contentious moment, Stanton.

The next morning, Grant put on paper what he had not said well the night before. After writing, "In notifying you of my acceptance of the duties thus imposed on me, I cannot let the opportunity pass without expressing to you my appreciation of the zeal, patriotism, firmness and ability with which you have ever discharged the duty of Sec. of War, and also the regret I now feel in seeing you withdraw from them." This edited letter, containing several crossovers of key phrases, reflected Grant's difficulty in writing to Stanton, a man he often found onerous in personal relationships but whom he admired for standing up to Johnson.

In the ensuing days, Grant's friends and foes asked why he had accepted the cabinet position. A friend, Horace White, editor of the *Chicago Tribune,* wrote Washburne, worried Grant's acceptance contaminated him with "Johnsonism." A foe, Republican Radical Wendell Phillips, condemned Grant as "the staff which holds up the traitor President." Grant remained silent in public about the reasons behind his acceptance, trying to stay true to his conviction that army officers should not offer political opinions.

WITH STANTON DISMISSED and Congress in recess, Johnson took aim at his next target. On August 17, he ordered Grant to get rid of Sheridan as commander of Louisiana and Texas. To Johnson's consternation, after passage of the Third Reconstruction Act, Sheridan had removed Louisiana governor James Madison Wells and Texas governor James W. Throckmorton. One of Sheridan's greatest accomplishments, which earned him fierce white opposition, consisted of registering many thousands of black voters—his prerogative under the act.

Johnson's order evoked a strong response from Grant. If Sherman was his brother general, Sheridan was more like a son. He had championed and protected him. Because of this appreciation, Grant had a difficult time recognizing that "Little Phil" sometimes brought problems on himself, not only by his aggressive actions, but by his intemperate language, expressed recently in correspondence with Johnson.

Although Johnson invited Grant to come for a conversation to discuss the order, Grant decided to put his ideas in writing, as was becoming his custom. In a highly emotional letter, he wrote, "It is unmistakably the expressed wish of the Country that Gen. Sheridan should not be removed from his present command." Additionally, "This is a republic where the will of the people is the law of the land. I beg that their voice may be heard." Broaching the divide between Congress and the president, Grant warned, "His removal will only be regarded as an effort to defeat the laws of Congress." Then, sharpening his pen into a sword, he wrote what he would never have said only months before: "It will be interpreted by the unreconstructed element in the South, those who did all they could to break up this government by arms, and now wish to be the only element consulted as to the method of restoring order, as a triumph." Furthermore, "It will embolden them to renewed opposition to the will of the loyal masses, believing that they have the Executive with them." Grant had finally named Johnson as the ultimate source of the problem.

Surprised by the intensity of Grant's letter, Johnson wrote a response rejecting all his objections and denouncing Sheridan, calling his administration of the Fifth Military District "a resort to authority not granted by law."

Two days later, Grant penned a short note to Washburne: "It is not likely that I shall get to Galena or any place else this Fall. I am always hopeful and confident of the final result, but now public affairs look blue indeed."

THEY WERE ABOUT to get bluer. Johnson's letter proposed transferring George Thomas to replace Sheridan. Grant immediately countered that Thomas "has repeatedly entered his protest to being assigned to relieve Gen. Sheridan." At Grant's request, Thomas also forwarded a letter he had written Stanton in July, when rumors of Johnson's intentions toward Sheridan were already circulating: "The relief of Genl. Sheridan will be sure to revive the hopes and energies of the opponents of reconstruction." Thomas did not want the assignment and pleaded that Sheridan "be permitted to complete the service he has commenced with so much vigor and earnestness."

Armed with Thomas's letter, Grant tried to reason with Johnson, but the president countered by suggesting the transfer of Winfield Scott Hancock, one of the most decorated generals and a conservative Democrat, from the West to New Orleans.

Grant protested again. He argued, "The Act of Congress of July 19th

1867 throws much of the responsibility of executing faithfully the reconstruction laws of Congress, on the General of the Army," and, "I emphatically decline yielding any of those powers."

Unwilling to submit, Grant issued Special Orders No. 429. Acting under the authority of the Third Reconstruction Act, he prohibited Sheridan's successor from making "appointments to civil office of persons who have been removed" by his predecessor and from not allowing pardons for prominent Confederate officers. Following this order, Grant made public his letter to Johnson protesting Sheridan's removal. The military stood solidly behind Grant. The *Army and Navy Journal* hailed his letter, editorializing that "every word is golden."

BY THE LAST half of 1867, Grant, now wearing two hats, became an even more central leader. He was under massive pressure to take sides between the president and Congress but decided that for now the best course was still to remain silent. Stanton, his pride injured, watched in appreciation as Grant continued his policies. Grant had come to believe that Reconstruction would progress only as far as congressional Republicans could enact it and would extend throughout the South only as far as the army could enforce it.

Grant wanted to keep his two offices distinct. Each morning, as secretary of war, he would go to the War Department, located in an unassuming brick building at the southeast corner of Seventeenth Street and Pennsylvania Avenue. He did not bring any of his staff, believing he held this position only on an interim basis or until Congress reconvened. He did not want to offer even the appearance of permanence. In the afternoon, as general in chief, he went to his old office in a modest house at 532 Seventeenth Street across from army headquarters in the Winder Building. Secretary Badeau said Grant's whole manner would change as he crossed the street. On one side he was a formal cabinet minister, on the other side a general with his staff, "as intimate and unrestrained as ever."

Grant found Johnson's cabinet meetings frustrating. He tired of Johnson's patronizing discourses on the Constitution. He did not like the cabinet's highly partisan tone in carrying out the nation's business, a sharp contrast to meetings led by Lincoln. Grant finally told Johnson that since his primary role was as an army officer and his interim position of secretary of war had not been confirmed by the Senate, he intended to attend only those portions of the meetings pertaining to military matters and asked to be excused from the rest of the agenda.

Johnson rejected the request, determined to continue his subterfuge that the new secretary of war supported his policies. Tired of Johnson, increasingly Grant absented himself, submitting his reports by paper rather than in person.

BY THE FALL of 1867, Grant sought to execute a delicate balancing act in directing the army's role in the South. In September, he wrote General Edward Ord, commanding the Fourth Military District in Arkansas, "I am exceedingly anxious to see reconstruction effected and Military rule put to an end." Because of his strong defense of Sheridan, Grant has often been misunderstood as a champion of aggressive military rule in the South. Actually, at this point he hoped to effect a balance between using the army to restore peace, which meant protecting rights of Unionists and freedmen, and restraining the army from overplaying its hand. He expressed these twin goals to Ord. Grant hoped that "politicians should be perfectly satisfied with the temperate manner with which the Military have used authority thus far, but if there is a necessity for continuing it too long there is great danger of a reaction against the Army."

Determined to keep a low profile, Grant decided to take no active part in the 1867 elections. But his hand was forced in October when George Thomas found himself in turmoil in Tennessee. Who would be allowed to vote in the coming municipal elections in Nashville? Answering this question on one side stood Governor William G. Brownlow, former circuit-riding Methodist minister, newspaper editor, and bitter prewar foe of fellow Tennessean Andrew Johnson. With the approach of the Civil War, Brownlow, known as Parson Brownlow, became a staunch Unionist and, in Reconstruction, a Republican Radical. On the other side stood Mayor W. Matt Brown, a leader of conservative forces in Nashville who insisted the election take place under the city's charter, with election judges appointed by him. Brownlow argued that state suffrage laws—Tennessee was still the only southern state to ratify the Fourteenth Amendment, which authorized voting by blacks—would govern the city election.

Thomas turned to Grant for advice. Within hours Grant replied, "I neither instruct to sustain the Governor nor Mayor but to prevent conflict." Thomas sought more guidance, once again hesitant to act on his own: "If both parties persist in holding their election there will be great danger of collision. In such contingency am I to interfere and allow both elections to go on? Or are my duties simply to prevent mobs from aiding either party?"

Grant encouraged Thomas to travel from his Louisville headquarters to Nashville. Meeting with the mayor and his allies, a worried Thomas wired Grant, "A collision is inevitable. . . . I cannot command the peace without interfering." In replying, Grant made explicit where authority lay: "Nothing is clearer however than that the Military cannot be made use of to defeat the executive of a state in enforcing the laws of the state," which had ratified the Fourteenth Amendment.

Armed with Grant's instructions, Thomas showed them to Brown, and the mayor gave up the fight. Grant encouraged Thomas, "It is hoped that your presence and good judgment and advice will prevent conflict." Grant's good judgment stiffened Thomas's backbone and helped defuse the powder keg in Nashville.

THE POWDER KEG blew up 665 miles to the north. In Washington, Johnson exploded when Grant reported to a cabinet meeting what had taken place in Nashville. Exasperated, fearing Grant was joining with the Radicals, five days later Johnson sent for Sherman, "to confer upon matters of public interest." Could he persuade Sherman to replace Grant?

Sherman arrived in Washington on Sunday, October 6, at six A.M. and early that morning made his first call—on Grant. Later that day, Sherman saw Johnson, then returned to Grant's house for dinner. He wrote his wife, Ellen, "The President don't comprehend Grant."

The next day, Sherman met Johnson again. He declined the president's offer, instead suggesting the names of a couple of moderate Republicans. Secretary of the Interior Orville Hickman Browning, after speaking with Sherman, wrote in his diary, "He is willing to remain here in a subordinate position to Grant, but not otherwise." By inviting Sherman to replace Grant, Johnson never grasped the bonds of loyalty between these two friends.

AFTER THE 1867 elections, in which Democrats did better than expected—by distancing themselves from Johnson—more attention focused on Grant as the public looked forward to the 1868 presidential election. In December, George Templeton Strong wrote in his diary: "Grant's chance for the White House is worth tenfold that of any other man. This is due partly to the general faith in his honesty and capacity, and partly to his genius for silence." Templeton wrote what Grant and the Republicans had been realizing for some time.

Grant had become a celebrity, but he never enjoyed what the French called *bain de foule,* mingling with a crowd, each person wanting to shake his hand and pat him on the back.

He also became the subject of closer scrutiny. What were his political views? Congressional Republicans worried whether he would submit to the authority of the president or to Congress. They knew he had become an antislavery man by the end of the war, but they wondered how committed he was to protecting black people from assault and extending their civil and political rights.

Republican Radicals, a vocal minority within the Republican Party, expressed the most concern—and Wendell Phillips carped the loudest. A fine-looking gray-haired man with a stubborn jaw, throughout his life the Bostonian made vilification his calling card. He called Lincoln a "slave-hound" and characterized Edward Everett, the leading American orator, as a "whining spaniel." Phillips sometimes embarrassed his own Radical colleagues with his abusive language and inflexible tactics. He now aimed all his daggers at Grant. He would not be stopped by hisses from crowds when he derided Grant for holding "the most humiliating position of any man on the continent" because of his association with Johnson.

THE YEAR 1868 began with renewed talk of impeachment. Republican moderates now joined Radical Republicans, who had watched Johnson sack not only Stanton but four of five military district commanders and worried that he would replace Grant, too.

On January 10, the Senate Committee on Military Affairs voted to recommend Stanton's reinstatement to the full Senate. The next day, Grant met with his staff to consider his options. By this time, he had come to believe the best course of action would be to replace Stanton, whose caustic ways had alienated even some of his former supporters. But in rereading the Tenure of Office Act, Grant learned that if the Senate voted to restore Stanton, and Grant did not relinquish the office, he would be liable to a fine of $10,000 and a prison term of five years.

Grant hurried to the Executive Mansion to inform Johnson he was not going to run afoul of the Tenure of Office Act. He would give up the office of secretary of war once the Senate reinstated Stanton. Johnson countered he would pay Grant's fine and go to prison. Grant told Badeau he found Johnson's proposal "preposterous." As Grant and Johnson parted, Grant believed he had made his point; Johnson, however, asked Grant to continue the conversation on Monday.

Unknown to Grant, Johnson had been scheming to get rid of him also. The president's secretary, William G. Moore, recorded in his diary, "Grant (the President remarked) had served the purpose for which he had been selected, and it was desirable that he should be superseded in the War Office by another."

Late on Monday, January 13, the Senate voted 35 to 6 to reinstate Stanton.

The next morning, Grant went to his War Department office at nine A.M. as usual, but this time he locked the door and gave the key to Assistant Adjutant General Edward D. Townsend. He had Cyrus Comstock deliver a formal letter to Johnson telling him that "my functions as Secretary of War, *ad interim,* ceased from the moment of the receipt of the within notice."

Stanton arrived at the War Department one hour later. Townsend bowed and presented the key to a smiling secretary of war as well-wishers gathered to welcome him back.

In one of Stanton's first orders, he summoned Grant. Grant returned to his old office to meet a curt Stanton, who showed no gratitude for the general in chief's actions in helping restore him to his office. Years later, Grant observed that Stanton "cared nothing for the feelings of others. In fact it seemed to be pleasanter to him to disappoint than to gratify."

In the afternoon, Grant responded to a summons from Johnson to attend the regularly scheduled cabinet meeting. Grant had just sat down when Johnson, addressing him as "Mr. Secretary," bombarded him with questions. Grant disowned the title and said he no longer served in the position. Johnson accused Grant of being false to his word by going back on a promise to remain in the office. Grant denied Johnson's accusation. Johnson, a master manipulator, turned to Secretary of the Treasury Hugh McCulloch and two other cabinet officers to verify his assertion. Feeling that his honor was being impugned, Grant rose and left the meeting.

Johnson did not yield. Seeking to defend himself and humiliate Grant, he gave an interview to a correspondent with one of his favored newspapers, the *New York World,* with his version of what had taken place between him and Grant.

Deeply troubled by Johnson's accusations, on January 28 Grant composed a long letter "in consequence of the many and gross misrepresentations, affecting my personal honor, circulating through the press."

As the jousting by letters continued, John Rawlins, ill with tuberculosis, hurried east from Galena to assist his chief. Encouraging Grant to be even more forthright, he helped edit another letter to Johnson: "I can but regard this whole matter, from the beginning to the end, as an attempt to involve me in the resistance of law, for which you hesitated to assume the responsibility in orders, and thus to destroy my character before the country."

As newspapers weighed in, the *New York Tribune* spoke for many: "In a question of veracity between a soldier whose honor is as unvarnished as the sun, and a President who has betrayed every friend, and broken every promise, the country did not hesitate."

As a welcome diversion, Ulysses and Julia looked forward to listening to renowned British author Charles Dickens present readings at Washington's Carroll Hall. Dickens had visited the capital in 1842, but that first trip had been largely a sightseeing tour. Since that time he had become the first author who took his books on the road in lucrative moneymaking tours. In Dickens's second visit to America, he started in Boston and slowly worked his way down to Washington.

The Grants joined the nation's "Dickens fever." Ulysses and Julia read Dickens's novels to each other. Ulysses read Dickens to his son Fred. In 1864, Ulysses referred to Wilkins Micawber, a character in *David Copperfield,* to make a point in a letter to Elihu Washburne; he told Washburne that the South, now in desperate straits, was like Micawber, who while in poverty lived unrealistically in "the hope *something* [would] turn up." The Grants were in the audience when Dickens gave readings from his novels in the first week of February.

But literature could not distract Grant for long. Throughout the summer and fall of 1867, Grant had made it clear he would not be a party to impeaching the president. But everything changed in early February 1868. The House of Representatives, having requested the correspondence between Grant and Johnson, had the clerk read aloud Grant's strongly worded February 3 letter to the president, eliciting spontaneous applause. Old Thad Stevens commended Grant. He "is a bolder man than I thought him. Now we will let him into the Church." As Grant detailed how Johnson, in wishing him to stay in office, asked him to defy the Tenure of Office Act, Stevens finally found a credible charge in his push for impeachment. Public airing of this exchange of letters dashed any possibility of a continuing personal relationship between Grant and Johnson.

By February 10, Stevens convinced the House to let his Committee on Reconstruction take over the impeachment process from the Judiciary Committee. Three days later, Stevens, who had fallen very ill, hastily presented an impeachment resolution, but it was not sustained by the full committee.

The resolution should have been a warning shot to Johnson to conduct himself with self-control. Instead, furious with Grant, Johnson sought to regain control of the military by going around the general in chief. First, he tried to employ his power as commander in chief by ordering Grant to appoint Sherman to command a new Military Division of the Atlantic. Sherman wrote Grant, "I never felt so troubled in my life. Were it an order to go to Sitka, to the Devil,—to battle with rebels or Indians, I think you would not hear a whimper from me, but it comes in such a questionable form that, like Hamlet's Ghost, it curdles my blood and mars my judgment." Sherman notified both Johnson and Grant that he was willing to resign rather than be forced to accept such a new position. To Grant he added a fascinating sentence: "If it were at all certain that you would accept the nomination [of president] in May I would try and kill the intervening time . . . but I do not want you to reveal your plans to me till you choose to do so."

On February 21, Grant learned to his amazement that Johnson sent Lorenzo Thomas to inform Stanton he was removing him—yet again. The gaunt, sixty-three-year-old Thomas, a desk officer during the Civil War with little popular following, was an unlikely replacement guaranteed not to marshal support in Congress.

Thomas proceeded to Stanton's office at eleven A.M. and handed him the order from Johnson. The bespectacled Stanton paused for a long time, gathering himself before replying. He asked Thomas to make a copy of the order, which forced the general to leave the room.

At that moment, Stanton invited Grant into his office. Together, Grant and Stanton decided that Stanton should not surrender. When Thomas returned, Stanton told him, "I want some little time for reflection. I don't know whether I shall obey your orders or not." Grant and Stanton, in the face of a common enemy, stood as allies.

THE VERY NEXT day, the House, now in a frenzy, began impeachment proceedings against Johnson for "high crimes and misdemeanors." Many senators wrote letters of encouragement to Stanton, including Radical Charles Sumner, who sent a terse one-word telegram: "Stick." House and Senate members also called on Grant to let him know he had their support.

On March 4, House managers delivered eleven articles of impeachment to the Senate, including the violation of the Tenure of Office Act and the appointment of Lorenzo Thomas as secretary of war even though there was no vacancy in the office. At exactly one P.M. on March 5, a court of impeachment convened, with Chief Justice Salmon P. Chase sworn in to preside.

Now that Grant had broken publicly with Johnson, suspicions about his relationship with the president were put to rest. Grant determined to remain on the sidelines as managers for both sides mounted their cases.

But influential Republican Senate moderates realized the future of Grant's candidacy for president lurked just beneath the trial's surface. An act of 1792 decreed that after the vice president, the Senate president pro tempore stood next in the line of presidential succession. If Johnson was convicted, and with the office of vice president vacant since Lincoln's assassination, Ohio Republican Ben Wade would become the new president. For some moderate Republicans, the prospect of the Radical Republican Wade as president was worse than having Johnson. Many of Grant's supporters were content to let the trial take its time, knowing the Republican convention was scheduled to meet in Chicago the third week of May.

THE IMPEACHMENT TRIAL reached its climax in May. On Saturday, May 16, a beautiful spring day in Washington, the crush for tickets by everyone eager to be present for this once-in-a-lifetime event far outstripped the capacity of the Senate galleries. Chief Justice Chase directed the clerk to call the roll of fifty-four senators in alphabetical order for each article of impeachment. "How say you? Is the respondent, Andrew Johnson, President of the United States, guilty or not guilty of a high misdemeanor, as charged in this article?" As one senator after another rose for the first article, spectators in the galleries kept count. All twelve Democrats intoned, "Not guilty." The majority of Republicans countered, "Guilty"—except for seven. The final count stood 35 to 19, exactly one vote shy of the two-thirds required for conviction. This vote was on only one of the articles, but the drama was essentially over. The court recessed because of the upcoming Republican convention in Chicago, to reconvene on May 26. The same verdict would be reached for each of the eleven impeachment articles.

Who won? Who lost? Almost everyone lost. Johnson was acquitted yet won a pyrrhic victory achieved at a devastating cost to his future influence. Stanton resigned on May 26. Wade, who would have succeeded had Johnson been removed, lost. The managers of Johnson's impeachment, including outspoken Benjamin Butler, were criticized for their inept prosecution. Disappointment escalated into bitterness against the seven Republican senators who voted for acquittal. Grant, who decided from the first not to involve himself in this tawdry political trial, became the one man to come out of it unscathed.

THE NATIONAL UNION Republican Convention opened in Chicago on May 20, 1868, at Crosby's Opera House, a five-story Italianate palace just completed in 1866, pride of the rising city on Lake Michigan. Eight thousand people cheered as General Daniel Sickles, one of Grant's five Reconstruction military district commanders, preceded by a large American flag, led the procession of delegates into the convention. Convention managers stayed close to seventy-four-year-old Jesse Grant, to be sure the impulsive old man did not speak to reporters.

The spirit of the martyred Lincoln, who had been nominated for president only eight years earlier in this same Chicago, was present in conversations everywhere. After an invocation by Methodist bishop Matthew Simpson, temporary chairman General Carl Schurz, senator-elect from Missouri and a rising star within the Republican firmament, offered the keynote address.

On the second day, General John Logan, who had returned to Congress in 1868, rose to nominate Grant to shouts of "Bully! John!" Not a West Point graduate, Logan felt indebted to Grant, who had showed faith in "Black Jack" when his military career was treading water early in the war. By long-held protocol, Grant, as a candidate, was not expected to be present at the convention.

In an era of conventions with multiple ballots for presidential candidates, no other candidate was nominated. All 650 delegates voted for Grant, welcoming the announcement of Grant's nomination with frenzied enthusiasm, jumping to their feet and flinging their hats in the air. A curtain opened at the rear of the stage, revealing a painting by Thomas Nast of the Goddess of Liberty flanked by two pedestals. On one pedestal stood a portrait of Grant, while the second pedestal was empty but had a sign suspended over it: "Democratic Nominee." The delegates looked forward to see the Goddess of Liberty pointing to Grant, while over his portrait rested a challenge: "Match him." Nast's dare quickly became a campaign watchword, song, and poem.

If the convention united around Grant for president, it divided over the nomination for vice president. Eleven different nominations revealed party divisions. The contest droned on through six ballots until the convention finally nominated Indianan Schuyler Colfax, Jr., Speaker of the

The 1868 Republican convention in Chicago, after the contentious four years of Andrew Johnson's presidency, would unanimously nominate Grant as their candidate.

House, nicknamed "Smiler" Colfax, a popular man known for his ingratiating ways.

GRANT WAS WORKING quietly at army headquarters in Washington when he was nominated in pandemonium in Chicago. Grant, with Johnson's diminution, had become the chief decision maker about the execution of the Reconstruction laws.

The moment he learned the outcome, Stanton rushed across the street from the War Department to notify Grant. Badeau, with Grant at the time, caught their dual surprise: "He came hurriedly up the stairs panting for breath lest someone should precede him." He burst in, exclaiming, "General! I have come to tell you that you have been nominated by the Republican party for President of the United States." At this news, Badeau observed Grant: "No shade of exultation or agitation on his face, not a flush on his check, nor a flash in his eye." Grant, who knew the nomination was coming, nevertheless may have been speechless at the enormity of the responsibility that lay ahead.

A week later, Joseph Hawley, former governor of Connecticut who had presided over the convention, led a delegation to Washington to offer the nomination to Grant. More comfortable in a written response, Grant offered a brief formal letter of acceptance that he'd spent considerable time editing. Recognizing the unprecedented period the nation was living through, Grant told Hawley, "In times like the present it is impossible, or at least eminently improper, to lay down a policy to be adhered to, right or wrong, through an Administration of four years." Thinking toward the future, "New political issues, not foreseen, are constantly arising; the views of the public on old ones are constantly changing." How, then, did he see his task? "A purely Administrative officer should always be left free to execute the will of the people." Behind this sentence lay Grant's growing conviction that Johnson had turned his back on the will of the American people. He concluded his acceptance letter: "Let us have peace."

If Grant found it painful at first to challenge Andrew Johnson, these years became a critical transition that allowed him to center himself, clarify his convictions, and act with courage. For much of his adult life he had disdained political involvement, but he now believed he could be political without losing his moral integrity.

"Let us have peace" captured the imagination of a nation. This four-word declaration resonated with a people tired of four years of war and three years of divisive Reconstruction politics. He summoned up both the Lincoln of the second inaugural and the Grant of Appomattox. If elected in November, Grant the soldier determined to become Grant the peacemaker.

PART FIVE

⊰⊷ ◦ ⊶⊱

President

1869–1877

I have been forced into it in spite of myself. I could
not back down without . . . leaving the contest
for power for the next four years between mere
trading politicians, the elevation of whom,
no matter which party won, would lose to us
largely, the results of the costly war which
we have gone through.

—Ulysses S. Grant to William T. Sherman, 1869

CHAPTER 27

-◆-▬◉ ◉▬-◆-

Gold Panic

If gold advanced materially the next day, it would be our duty to sell.
—Ulysses S. Grant, "Gold Panic Investigation,"
House of Representatives, Forty-first Congress, March 1, 1870

One month after the Republican convention, Grant wrote Sherman, "I have been forced into it in spite of myself." He explained, "I could not back down without, as it seems to me, leaving the contest for power for the next four years between mere trading politicians, the elevation of whom, no matter which party won, would lose to us, largely, the results of the costly war which we have gone through." Determined not to become another "trading politician"—politicians who acquired their office by promising to grant future favors to supporters—he felt the freedom to be truly himself because he did not seek the office.

In this spirit, Grant made the decision not to campaign. He knew Lincoln had not campaigned in 1860, remaining in Springfield, but Grant determined to go even further and leave Washington. Worn out by a winter and spring of political infighting, he looked forward to traveling to new places. Others could campaign on his behalf.

Grant left for the West at the end of June. From Fort Leavenworth, Kansas, he wrote Julia, "This will probably be the last chance I will ever have to visit the plains, and the rapid settlement is changing the character of them so rapidly." Accompanied by his two closest military friends, Sherman and Sheridan, as well as his second son, Buck, he boarded the Kansas Pacific Railroad for a two-week trip across the Great Plains into the Rocky Mountains, inspecting forts along the way. At Cheyenne Wells in the territory of Colorado, he boarded a stage for the 170-mile trip to Denver. On July 21, he wrote Julia that Buck, who would turn sixteen the next day, "has enjoyed this trip beyond any he has ever yet taken." Father and son were excited to see "wild horses, Buffalo, wolf & Antelope."

Although this was Grant's noncampaign, a cadre of newspaper reporters tagged along. As he moved on to Georgetown, Cheyenne, and Fort Sanders near Laramie, their stories portrayed Grant as the man with the common touch. *The New York Times* chronicled the movements of "the greatest Generals of the nation, and the world." The public eagerly consumed stories about Grant, Sherman, and Sheridan traveling in the romantic West of popular imagination.

IF GRANT WAS on holiday, election year politics forged ahead. The largest fireworks on July 4, 1868, exploded in New York City, where Democrats convened their national convention on the nation's birthday. They met at the new Tammany Hall near Union Square, deeply conscious of Lincoln and the recently nominated Grant. They sought to counter these heroes with massive arches bearing portraits of their Democratic patriotic saints: Thomas Jefferson and Andrew Jackson. The convention was noteworthy for the reappearance of Democratic Party politicians from the southern states. The slogan for the convention was, "This is a White Man's Country; Let White Men Rule."

Delegates placed the names of nine candidates in nomination for president on July 7, including Andrew Johnson, who desperately wanted a second term; former Ohio congressman George H. Pendleton, a leader of the antiwar segment of the party during the Civil War; and Pennsylvania's general Winfield Scott Hancock, whose backers argued Democrats must match General Grant with their own general. After two days and twenty-two ballots, they selected former New York governor Horatio Seymour, who several times told the convention that he declined to be a candidate. Seymour had spent his political career trying to hold together divisions within the Democratic Party in the nation's most populous state, which his supporters now proposed he do in the nation. The delegates nominated General Francis Preston Blair, Jr., of Missouri as their vice-presidential candidate. The convention adjourned, hoping their ticket could win the election, balancing east and west as well as north and south, with Blair's impressive military record counterbalancing Seymour's lukewarm support for the war.

THE PRESIDENTIAL CAMPAIGN moved into high gear in the summer. In early August, Grant returned from the West to a warm welcome in Galena. He believed it unseemly to talk about himself and turned down invitations to speak at political meetings, but he followed the campaign closely. *The New York Times* reported he paid regular visits to political operatives set up in two second-floor rooms in the DeSoto House on Main Street.

Republicans sought to strengthen their appeal in the South by finally readmitting seven southern states in June and July that had voted to ratify the Fourteenth Amendment, hoping for the first time in their brief history to garner southern votes. They believed newly franchised black voters would provide an edge in several states. The long battle for the Fourteenth Amendment culminated in ratification on July 9, 1868.

Just as Grant promised, others campaigned for him. Both Republicans and Democrats campaigned with torchlight parades boosted by singing Civil War songs. Both sides displayed colorful banners, Grant supporters trumpeting U.S.G.—THE TANNER OF REBELS and OUR SYMBOL IS PEACE, NOT THE SWORD, while Democrats countered with, WE GO FOR SEYMOUR AS WE WENT FOR LEE and LET ALL GOOD MEN VOTE NO NIGGER. Republicans organized "tanner" clubs, with Grant and Colfax depicted "tanning old Democratic hides." "Boys in Blue" organizations paraded to evoke the spirit of the war. One word—"Appomattox"—echoed everywhere.

The campaign biography had become one of the most effective tools in the nineteenth century, and Albert D. Richardson's *A Personal History of Ulysses S. Grant* became a bestseller in 1868. Richardson emphasized that as war correspondent for the *New York Tribune,* he came to know Grant personally and thus could reveal anecdotes the public did not yet know.

If the campaign biography had become standard fare by 1868, an advance on this older medium leapt into the fray. Political cartoons had

The most popular 1868 campaign card combined humor and criticism as it emphasized the humble beginnings of both Grant and Colfax.

been around forever, but by the 1860s Thomas Nast elevated the art form of satirical cartoons to a new prominence. Nast, who would become known as the "Father of the American Cartoon," working first at *Frank Leslie's Illustrated Newspaper* and then at *Harper's Weekly,* wielded tremendous influence. From his experiences of the Civil War came his sympathies for the plight of African Americans. By 1868, he threw his now considerable influence solidly behind Grant, by both pictorial applause and devastating criticism of Grant's opponents.

Democrats sought to criticize Grant by claiming he had another wife out west, an Indian squaw he'd met at Fort Vancouver with whom he had three children. The *New York World* charged that Grant had been careless with soldiers' lives, enduring far more casualties than Lee. This latter claim, although not true, would have legs down to the present.

They particularly defamed Grant as a "black Republican" and a "nigger lover." But Grant had his defenders, no one more than Nast. For the celebrated cartoonist, the 1868 election was a contest between his hero, General Grant, and Horace Greeley and the Democratic Party, intent on suppressing the rights of African Americans.

Cartoonist Thomas Nast's hero, Grant, campaigned against Democratic candidate Horatio Seymour in 1868. Here Nast satirically depicts three Seymour supporters: a lower-class Irish Catholic man; former Confederate Nathan Bedford Forrest; and financier August Belmont, chair of the Democratic Party. Together, these Democrats crush the back of an African American man.

On September 5, *Harper's Weekly* published one of Nast's most evocative cartoons. He depicted an Irish Catholic immigrant, Confederate Nathan Bedford Forrest, leader of the Ku Klux Klan, and August Belmont, Jewish financier and national chairman of the Democratic Party, holding high a bundle of money intended to buy votes. All three, joining hands, had their feet on the back of a black Union veteran who was clutching an American flag and stretching his hand toward a ballot box.

Democratic nominee Horatio Seymour quickly found himself on the defensive. As governor of New York, he had sent troops to Gettysburg, but the Republican press complained that he was disloyal to the Union because of his public criticism of the Lincoln administration for freeing slaves and jailing dissenters. The *New York Tribune* posted a cartoon picturing Seymour standing on the steps of City Hall during the draft riot of 1863, calling the rioters "my friends."

Republicans also criticized vice-presidential candidate Francis Blair, who had served Grant with distinction at both Vicksburg and Chattanooga. But Blair had become disillusioned with his general. He complained that Grant was in peril "of allowing himself to be made a tool of the Radicals."

Grant's friends took umbrage at Blair's criticisms, but not Grant. He told his staff that Blair had been his colleague and friend during the war and "excused the heat of his expressions" as what happens in an impassioned campaign.

GRANT SPENT LATE summer and fall in the brick house on the hill in Galena, but distance could not protect him or Julia from campaign slings and arrows. Early on, Sherman told Julia, "Mrs. Grant, you must now be prepared to have your husband's character thoroughly sifted."

Julia remembered that she protested, "Why, General, General Grant is my Admirable Crichton [a sixteenth-century Scottish orator and man of letters]. He does all things well." Smiling, Sherman responded, "Oh, my dear lady, it is not what he has done, but what *they will say* he has done."

One particular issue demanded that Grant break his silence. His General Orders No. 11, issued in December 1862, which banished Jewish traders from his military command, troubled voters. Even before his nomination, Grant received a letter from Simon Wolf, a lawyer and the Jewish community's unofficial lobbyist in Washington. Wolf, a German immigrant caught in a conflict between his love for the Republican Party and his loathing for Grant's order, wrote asking "whether this order was intended then or since to reflect in any way or manner on the Jews as a class or whether it was not an order directed simply against certain evil designing persons, whose religion was in no way material to the issue."

Respecting the tone of the Jewish lawyer's letter, Grant responded that the order was "directed simply against evil designing persons, whose religion was in no way material to the issue." His reply convinced Wolf.

In the midst of the controversy, Wolf read an editorial in the *Boston Post,* "Grant and the Jewish Vote," that was highly critical of Grant. Infuriated, he replied with a long letter that ended up being published in newspapers across the nation: "The General never meant then, since, or now, to proscribe the Jews because they were such, but *simply to banish from his camp the Lazzaroni who infested it.*" Wolf became a determined campaigner for Grant, stating, "I know General Grant and his motives." In 1869, he named his son Adolph Grant Wolf.

GRANT MAY HAVE hoped that Sherman would endorse him, but he was not surprised when his friend wrote, "I have abstained from all politics" and had become "more & more averse to putting faith in mere political men." To those who pressed him, "I say you will be elected, and ought to be elected, and that I would rather trust to your being just & fair, yea even moderate to the South, than Seymour and Blair." When some Republicans criticized Sherman for his silence, Grant defended his right to his opinion about politics.

Widely expected to win, on Election Day, November 3, Grant went to the polls with his Galena neighbors. He voted for Congressman Washburne and a straight Republican ticket. But he would not vote for himself. He left the presidential ballot blank.

In the evening, he went to Washburne's home to learn the results through a telegraph line strung to the congressman's home. Julia, without the right to vote, had not been invited to the election party and was forced to worry about the results at home. Shortly after one A.M., people began congratulating Grant on his election.

Grant won a decisive electoral victory: 214 to 80, carrying twenty-six states to Seymour's six. He received 53 percent of the popular ballot: 3,013,650 to 2,708,744; it was not lost on the opposition that without the support of approximately 400,000 freedmen, he would have lost the popular vote.

The new Senate would consist of 57 Republicans and 11 Democrats, a small improvement for the Democrats. In the House, although Democrats gained 25 seats, Republicans continued their strong majority, 143 to 72.

Grant appreciated receiving congratulations from Matías Romero: "I consider your election, General, as a blessing not only for the United States, but for mankind at large and for Mexico specially."

Grant accepted the presidency more as a military officer would accept a duty. Disheartened by the ineptness and divisiveness of Andrew Johnson, he determined to reinspire Lincoln's vision of national reconciliation.

PRESIDENT-ELECT GRANT NOW faced the long, four-month transition from election to inauguration. Lincoln had spent the secession winter far away from Washington in Springfield; James Buchanan had remained at Wheatland, his homestead near Lancaster, Pennsylvania. Grant resided at his home in Washington and worked at his army headquarters. Unlike Lincoln, who held no political office when elected, or Buchanan, who resigned his position as United States minister to Great Britain, Grant carried on as general in chief.

As for appointments to his administration, Grant followed the process that had worked well for him in the army: he trusted his own judgment. Henry J. Raymond, editor of *The New York Times,* wrote asking for some intimation as to whom Grant would appoint to his cabinet, but Grant remained silent even to this influential supporter. He did not discuss appointments with Rawlins or Washburne. He teased Julia about concealing his waistcoat under his pillow to be sure she would not look at his list of nominees.

Grant looked forward to making an appointment for the position he knew best—general in chief. He would make his choice from among the five major generals still serving after the war—Halleck, Hancock, Meade, Sherman, and Thomas. Needing a general he could trust completely, he chose Sherman. Grant appointed Meade commander of a new Atlantic Division with headquarters in Philadelphia and selected Thomas to command the Pacific Division with headquarters in San Francisco. He gave Sheridan Sherman's military command in the West.

The selection of Sherman benefited Grant in another way. Alexander T. Stewart, known as "the merchant prince" for his phenomenal success in the dry goods business, approached Grant with an offer to buy his Washington home, explaining that he and several other businessmen wished to present it to Sherman. Since Grant was preparing to move into the White House, still living under the shadow of his financial struggles in the 1850s, and interested in putting money away for retirement, he accepted the offer of $65,000—more than twice the home's original price.

. . .

As PREPARATIONS FOR Grant's inauguration proceeded, Washington's Methodist church leaders rushed to complete their construction of a new church, hoping to be able to dedicate it in conjunction with the political festivities.

Transplanted to the colonies in the decade before the American Revolution, Methodism grew quickly as a religion of the heart. Starting in the early 1850s, the Methodist Episcopal Church made plans to erect a national church in Washington—the first denomination to do so in the nation's capital. By the Civil War, Methodism's surging growth had made it the largest Protestant denomination in America. The Gothic church cost $225,000 and was dubbed "the Westminster Abbey of Methodism" by the national press.

On Sunday, February 28, four days before his inauguration, Ulysses and Julia joined religious and political dignitaries in a festive Dedication Day at the new Metropolitan Methodist Church. Nearly two thousand people packed the sanctuary. The church's minister, John Philip Newman, presided as Bishop Matthew Simpson, Methodism's best-known minister, preached at the morning service.

Ulysses and Julia were not simply celebrity spectators. He accepted nomination to the first class of ten trustees. She chaired the national committee to liquidate the debt on the church.

. . .

The Methodists were the first Protestant denomination to erect a national church in Washington, D.C. The church, which towers above the Washington skyline in this 1869 photo, was dedicated four days before Grant's inauguration.

Chief Justice Salmon P. Chase administered the oath of office to Ulysses S. Grant on the East Portico of the U.S. Capitol on March 4, 1869.

MARCH 4 DAWNED cold with a light rain. Outside his I Street home, Grant stepped into a carriage to be driven to his army headquarters. People had arrived from all over the nation to celebrate a new beginning. Almost every window on Pennsylvania Avenue displayed American flags. Marching music made it sound like the spring of 1865 again.

Just before eleven A.M., Grant and Vice President–Elect Schuyler Colfax started for the Capitol. Johnson let it be known he had no intention of attending Grant's swearing-in. Johnson spent the inauguration bunkered in the White House, signing last-minute bills. Johnson would earn the dubious distinction of becoming the third president—joining John Adams and John Quincy Adams—not to attend his successor's inauguration.

Shortly after twelve noon, the sun suddenly appearing through the clouds, Grant walked onto the east front of the Capitol. Dressed in an impeccable black suit, he took the oath of office administered by Chief Justice Salmon Chase. At forty-six, he was the youngest president yet elected.

Grant stepped to a podium and took his address from his breast pocket. It had been written three weeks earlier and incorporated some editorial suggestions from Adam Badeau. The crowd, including a large number of African Americans, pressed forward to hear a president not known for his speeches. Standing where Lincoln stood four years earlier to deliver his second inaugural address, Grant spoke in a conversational tone.

At the outset, he stated simply what his candidacy was about: "The responsibilities of the position I feel, but accept them without fear. The office has come to me unsought; I commence its duties untrammeled." Grant signaled that he was coming to the office with no entangling alliances. "All laws will be faithfully executed, whether they meet my approval or not." Take that, Andrew Johnson. "I shall on all subjects have a policy to recommend, but none to enforce against the will of the people." He would be a people's rather than a party's president.

Turning to the future, Grant forecast that in the aftermath of "a great rebellion," his administration would be facing many questions "which preceding Administrations have never had to deal with." The increasingly pressing issue of the national debt exacerbated by the war consumed nearly half his speech. He promised to pay down the debt, take up "a faithful collection of the revenue," and pursue "the greatest practicable retrenchment in expenditure" throughout the government.

In the middle of the address, thirteen-year-old Nellie left her seat next to her mother and walked up to stand beside her father for several minutes. This scene touched everyone.

In his conclusion, Grant engaged two vexing national issues. First, he promised the "proper treatment of the original occupants of this land— the Indians." He favored "any course toward them which tends to their civilization and ultimate citizenship." No president had ever discussed the rights of American Indians in an inaugural address.

Next, he discussed the rights of African Americans. "The question of suffrage is one which is likely to agitate the public so long as a portion of the citizens of the nation are excluded from its privileges in any State," he declared. "The question should be settled now." To that end, he advocated passage of the Fifteenth Amendment.

Grant surprised everyone by managing to deliver a fine speech without fainting from the terror of it. When Grant finished speaking, friends stepped forward to greet him, but he strode directly to Julia, leaned down, kissed her on the cheek, and handed her his inaugural address.

Newspaper editorials praised Grant's speech. *The New York Times* compared it favorably with Lincoln's second inaugural: "General Grant had something to say, and he has said it strongly and well." *The Nation* offered more muted praise, saying it "has at least the merit of being a plain, sensible, practical document." This weakly expressed satisfaction that "the view he takes of the President's place in the Government shows that the discussions of the last four years have not been in vain."

Grant's clear-eyed address, if devoid of rhetorical flourish, was a blueprint of the issues he intended to tackle as president—and his marching orders for the first one hundred days of his administration.

FOR HIS CABINET, Grant sent to the Senate six names. John Rawlins reflected the view of many contemporaries who believed Lincoln's cabinet had proved extremely troublesome and advised Grant not to replicate his predecessor's problems by putting adversaries in his cabinet. Grant's selections reflected the personal loyalty he found effective in an army, where senior officers needed to work together closely.

Grant appointed Galena friend Elihu Washburne secretary of state. He chose Alexander Stewart, the merchant prince, to be secretary of the Treasury. For secretary of the navy, Grant nominated longtime friend Adolph E. Borie of Philadelphia. When this name was announced in the Senate, several senators asked, "Who's Borie?" Critics pointed out that Borie, a wealthy retired businessman, had no obvious qualifications other than the fact that he had raised funds for Grant's home in Philadelphia. For attorney general, Grant nominated Justice E. Rockwood Hoar, who had served on the Massachusetts Supreme Court for ten years and enjoyed wide respect for his learning and judicial experience. Grant chose former Ohio governor Jacob D. Cox for secretary of the interior; Cox had been a political general with a praiseworthy war record. Grant selected Marylander John A. Creswell, a War Democrat turned Republican Radical, for postmaster general; a highly competent lawyer, Creswell had ideas on how to reform the Post Office Department.

Grant asked General John Schofield to remain as secretary of war until he could put his own person in the office. Many thought Grant might appoint his chief of staff, John Rawlins. But knowing Rawlins to be increasingly ill with tuberculosis, Grant intended to appoint him to command the Department of Arizona, believing the dry, warm climate might restore him to health. When he learned of Grant's concern, Rawlins sent word that he thought himself entitled to the appointment. The new president quickly complied.

The New York Times praised Grant's selections. But others believed the president's choices were based more on loyalty than on competence. Gideon Welles complained, "No statesman and patriot with right intentions would have selected it." Too many of the nominees were "untried," "personal adherents," and "money-givers."

In particular, Grant's appointment of Washburne seemed an act of gratitude to a long-standing friend. Unwilling to see Grant criticized on his account, Washburne offered to resign. Grant accepted his resignation and instead appointed him minister to France (Washburne was fluent in French).

His selection of Stewart, however, smacked of a different sort of payback to a generous campaign donor: Grant's home. Although no one could question the success of one of the richest men in America, Congress objected to his nomination. When Massachusetts senator Charles Sumner unearthed a law from 1789 expressly forbidding the appointment of an importer, Grant asked for an exemption, even as Stewart offered to relinquish all his profits while serving at the Department of the Treasury. But Congress had been badly burned by Johnson and refused to listen. Grant was forced to pull the nomination.

In these initial cabinet appointments, Grant erred. He did not consult, and he appointed several based on friendship more than on competence. Ultimately, however, he believed he could overcome these preliminary defeats with new appointments.

He wrote former New York governor Hamilton Fish a letter marked "Urgent." At age sixty, Fish had been retired from politics for twelve years. He asked Fish "to accept the portfolio of the State Dept."

Grant did well to nominate Fish. Named for his father's friend Alexander Hamilton, Fish had graduated valedictorian of his class from Columbia University. He had served the Whig Party of New York as congressman, governor, and senator. He had traveled widely and enjoyed respect for his soft-spoken integrity.

To replace Stewart, Grant chose George Boutwell, one of the congressional leaders who led the initial move to impeach Johnson. A former governor of Massachusetts, in 1862 he had become the first commissioner of the Bureau of Internal Revenue (precursor to the Internal Revenue Service). If a radical in his advocacy of African American suffrage, Boutwell was a conservative in financial matters. *The New York Times* applauded Boutwell's nomination: "The confidence of the people in his integrity is so great that there will unquestionably be a hearty response in all quarters."

BUT QUICKLY ANOTHER appointment became mired in controversy. The day after Grant nominated Sherman as his successor as general in chief,

Secretary of War John Schofield had issued General Orders No. 11, which stated, "The chiefs of staff corps, departments, and bureaus will report to and act under the immediate orders of the general commanding the army." The order pleased Sherman, who, having witnessed Grant's battles with Secretary of War Stanton firsthand, confidently believed he would not have the same struggles with meddling politicians.

Everything changed when Grant replaced Schofield with Rawlins. His former chief of staff had stood with Grant in his turf war with Stanton, but in his new position, he expressed concern that Sherman would have too much power. Rawlins requested Grant cancel General Orders No. 11, so he might have the requisite power to fulfill his office. On March 26, Rawlins wrote, "By direction of the President," General Orders No. 11 "is hereby rescinded."

Taken off guard, Sherman hurried to the White House to talk to his friend. Grant, flustered, tried to explain: "Rawlins feels badly about it; it worries him; and he is not well." He added, "I don't like to give him pain now." "But Grant," Sherman retorted, "it's your order that you revoke, not mine, and think how it will look to the whole world?" He reminded Grant of the conversations they had had when Grant was in Sherman's position. Grant responded, "Well, if it's my own order, I can rescind it, can't I?" Struggling to contain his emotions, Sherman replied, "Yes, Mr. President, you have the power to revoke your own order; you shall be obeyed."

Grant had chosen his horses. Sherman would retain the office and the honor, but not the power of the office. He left the White House grievously disappointed, a friendship deeply damaged. Grant felt Sherman's pain and would look for opportunities to restore their relationship.

IN ADDITION TO his choices for his cabinet, Grant made another nomination that sparked debate. He chose former high-ranking Confederate general James Longstreet to be surveyor of customs at the Port of New Orleans, at the handsome annual salary of $6,000. Now a New Orleans businessman, Longstreet had endorsed Grant during the presidential campaign, telling the *New York Tribune,* "I believe he is a fair man."

Grant's nomination drew applause and criticism. The *New York Tribune* wrote, "Our new president has done many acts for which the country will hold him in grateful remembrance, but he never did a wiser or nobler act than the nomination yesterday of General James Longstreet." *The New York Times* declared Grant's choice "a gesture of reconciliation."

But for many in the South, Longstreet had committed an unpardon-

*James Longstreet, who stood up with Grant
at his wedding, faced virulent criticism in his
native South for allying himself with Grant
and his Reconstruction policies.*

able sin. He was a hated "scalawag," a white southerner favoring Reconstruction. The *Richmond Enquirer and Examiner* scoffed, "That's the meaning of 'loilty' of one of Lee's lieutenants, is it?" Longstreet's West Point classmate Daniel Harvey Hill railed, "Our scalawag is the local leper of the community. Unlike the carpet bagger, he is a native, which is so much the worse."

On April 3, after nine hours of debate, the Senate confirmed Longstreet by a vote of 25 to 10. Grant's effort at reconciliation was intended to reward a friendship that stretched back three decades.

WHEN ULYSSES AND Julia moved into the White House, she found everything "in utter confusion." Mary Lincoln, famously overspending her budget, had set out to restore the President's House after four years of neglect under James Buchanan, the nation's only bachelor president. But the death of Willie Lincoln in February 1862 completely unsettled his mother, so Mary's plans were never fulfilled. Julia determined to bring a sense of order and decorum to the residence. She mapped out a plan for a complete renovation that would take all summer. Carpets were to be replaced, chairs recovered, and furniture brought back into their original arrangements. She decreed that henceforth White House servants would "appear in dress suits and white gloves."

President Grant established his daily routine. He rose at seven, read the Washington papers, and enjoyed breakfast with his family at eight thirty. Two of his four children were away—the oldest, Fred, at West Point and the second son, Buck, at Phillips Exeter Academy, preparing to enter Harvard. After breakfast, he went for a short stroll in the Washington streets, greeting locals and surprising tourists. In the aftermath of Lincoln's assassination, armed guards had been stationed in and around the White House. Grant dismissed them all. He wanted the American people to see their president was accessible.

At ten A.M., he went to his office on the second floor. His brother-in-law Frederick Dent sat at a reception desk. Two of Grant's former aides, Horace Porter and Orville Babcock, served as his secretaries. Dent, Porter, and Babcock wore civilian dress but impressed bodyguard William Crook as "a military council" because of the "sort of military exactness which pervaded the routine business." Adam Badeau, writing a military history of Grant, was assigned an office.

At the end of official business at three P.M., the president, usually accompanied by his son Jesse, went to his stable. Here he greeted eleven horses. Some of his old friends included Cincinnati, his dark bay warhorse; little Jeff Davis, who had given his master a comfortable ride across many Civil War battlefields; Egypt and St. Louis, now carriage horses; and Master Jesse's two Shetland ponies, Reb and Billy Button.

Sometimes Nellie would accompany her father. He would walk to the carriage house with his arm around his only daughter. Nellie had him hitch up two ponies to a natty phaeton, her favorite buggy, for an afternoon ride.

The family gathered for dinner—punctually—at five P.M. The table was always set with extra chairs to accommodate guests who might be invited during the day. Grant ate lightly but often enjoyed beef, which had to be well done. To his father's enjoyment, young Jesse enlivened the conversation with humor. Julia's father, Colonel Dent, still un-Reconstructed at eighty-three, growled about Republican Radicals and Negroes trying to move beyond their place. After coffee and a black cigar, Grant read the New York papers that had come in during the day. A few close friends would visit for informal conversation, then he and Julia would retire between ten and eleven.

IF, AS GENERAL in chief, Grant had increasingly taken the side of Congress, he was now the leader of the executive branch. Lincoln had struggled with Congress over who would set the agenda for Reconstruction. This conflict burst into open warfare when Congress rose up to override Johnson's vetoes of their Reconstruction legislation. Congress was not about to give back what it had worked so hard to achieve.

The political dance between the new president and Congress began with several troublesome issues held over from Johnson's single term. On the domestic front, Grant sought to repeal the Tenure of Office Act, believing it common sense that the president should not have his hands tied in removing his own appointees. The House went along easily, 121 to 47, but the Senate did not. They wanted to keep their hands on federal patronage. Grant considered invoking a veto, but Attorney General Hoar advised against such an action, and Grant agreed.

A major problem left over from the Johnson administration was the federal debt. When Grant assumed the presidency, the national debt, which stood at $64 million in 1860, had grown to a staggering $2.8 billion. The problem was compounded as hundreds of millions of dollars in unredeemable paper money—"greenbacks"—had pushed gold coins out of circulation. All of this left the nation's credit in precarious shape. As his first presidential act, Grant signed a law promising that the federal government would pay holders of U.S. bonds in "gold or its equivalent" and would redeem the greenbacks as soon as practicable.

Grant initiated strong federal action to pay down the national debt. He believed "sound money" was the best way to restore the economy, whereas Democrats focused on relief for farmers and small-business owners through printing paper money—injecting more money into the economy.

As was his habit when dealing with associates and trusted subordinates, Grant gave his talented chief financial officer, George Boutwell, wide latitude to carry out his mandate to reduce the national debt. With Grant's support, Senator John Sherman had steered through the Senate the Public Credit Act, which allowed those who had purchased bonds to support the Civil War to be repaid in "gold coin or its equivalent."

Boutwell instigated reforms at the Treasury Department to improve tax collection and limit counterfeiting. The Grant administration's financial policies held the money supply level, kept the price of gold low, and reduced the national debt. At the end of April, Boutwell instructed his assistant treasurer to begin selling gold at a discount and buy up wartime bonds. He expressed pleasure that "when the Treasury announced its purpose to purchase bonds the price advanced in the market." At the same time, Grant and Boutwell intended to reduce the supply of greenbacks, or paper money, and replace them with gold. By the end of May, Boutwell had reduced the national debt by $12 million.

As Grant prepared to leave on his summer vacation, he confided to Adam Badeau, "Public affairs look to me to be progressing very favorably. The revenues of the country are being collected as they have not been before, and expenditures are looked after more carefully." On the same day, *The New York Times* editorialized that there was "no reason to fear that the new administration will not fully meet the expectations of the country."

That summer, the Grants vacationed at the seaside village of Long Branch, New Jersey. Grant came initially as the guest of George W. Childs, publisher of the *Philadelphia Public Ledger,* who had met Ulysses and Julia when they sought to find schools for their children in Philadelphia during the war.

Childs, along with two investors, industrialist George Pullman and banker Moses Taylor, soon bought Grant a house at 995 Ocean Avenue, next to Childs's home. Grant's three-story cottage, with its seven dormers and twenty-eight rooms, would become his summer White House.

On a typical summer day, Grant went out driving a team of horses right after breakfast. Childs observed that the general soon knew "every byway within twenty miles." Upon his return, Grant would work with his secretaries on the wide veranda that faced the ocean.

Julia delighted in Long Branch: after a grinding winter and spring in Washington, she watched her husband revive with the healthful ocean breezes. She also looked forward to the one time each year her far-flung family could be together.

While relaxing in Long Branch, Grant went to New York to see his recently married sister, Virginia. Thirty-seven-year-old "Jennie" had wed Abel Rathbone Corbin after a whirlwind courtship: they had met only months before, at Grant's inauguration. At sixty-one, Corbin, whose wife had died the previous April, was twenty-five years older than Jennie.

Corbin greeted Grant at his impressive five-story brownstone mansion on West Twenty-seventh Street, exuding the air of success common to most wealthy businessmen. But there was much more to the president's new brother-in-law than met the eye on that summer afternoon. Corbin, a smooth talker, flourished as a speculator in real estate (he had sold Grant his I Street home in Washington), and his skill as a lobbyist ("lobby jobber") was widely acknowledged. Throughout his life, he would be influenced by power and money.

This time, however, Corbin would collide with two unscrupulous businessmen hoping to tempt the president's brother-in-law. James Fisk, only thirty-three and a gregarious showman, had already wrested control of the Erie Railroad from Commodore Cornelius Vanderbilt. Jay Gould, a year younger and much quieter, with a head for numbers, had made his first fortune by smuggling contraband cotton through Union lines—the kind of ill-gotten gain that was anathema to Grant. Flaunting their wealth, the two had already moved their offices from Wall Street to the splendid Grand Opera House on Twenty-third Street, which they purchased in 1868 for $820,000.

Standing in the foyer of Corbin's mansion, Grant was introduced to Gould, who had been looking for an opportunity to talk with Grant about gold.

With Grant's backing, Boutwell's weekly Treasury auctions had stabilized the price of gold on the market. And over time, as the government sold more gold, the price declined. Gould and Fisk realized that if they could be privy to information on upcoming government gold sales, they could manipulate the market, drive the price of gold back up, sell their holdings at an inflated price, and make out like the bandits they were.

But to succeed, they had to know more about the government's financial policies: they needed allies, witting or unwitting, to facilitate their scheme. They knew they could not touch Boutwell, who by the beginning of September had reduced the nation's debt by $50 million.

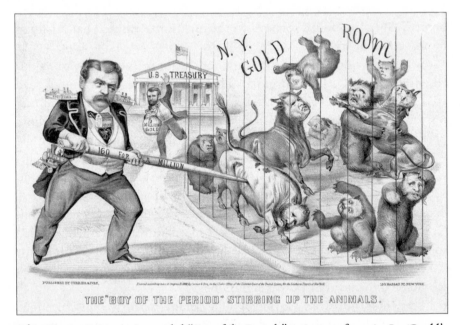

This Currier & Ives cartoon, titled "Boy of the Period," caricatures financier Jay Gould's attempt to corner the gold market, represented by bulls and bears in a cage. In the midst of Black Friday, September 24, 1869, President Grant, center, restores prevailing gold prices by ordering the U.S. Treasury to sell five million dollars in gold, which he brings forward in a bag.

First, they strategized about placing an underling in the position of assistant U.S. secretary for the New York Sub-Treasury. They fastened on Corbin's friend Daniel Butterfield, a Civil War hero who had helped raise money to enable Grant to buy his Washington home. Gould and Fisk knew Boutwell placed his orders to buy gold through Butterfield. Gould visited Butterfield on July 3 and gave him a check for $10,000—a sum larger than Butterfield's annual government salary of $8,000. That check and its underlying purpose would later become part of a congressional investigation.

Second, they attempted to use Corbin, working on him to convince Grant that the nation would benefit if the price of gold rose. Several times over the next two months, when Grant stopped at Corbin's home, he arranged for Gould or Fisk to be present.

Corbin tried to speak with Grant about his scheme to help the economy, but Jennie's husband soon discovered what others knew well: her brother would not talk about government financial policies. Stymied, Corbin turned to Julia, offering to cut her in for a half interest of the $250,000 in bonds he had purchased for Jennie on July 24. Mrs. Grant said no, thanks.

Third, Gould attempted to bribe Grant's secretary Horace Porter. He offered to purchase $500,000 in gold in Porter's name. Porter, absolutely devoted to Grant, said no. But to his dismay, Gould wrote Porter from New York, "We have purchased a half million gold on your account." Porter swiftly telegraphed, "I have not authorized any purchase of gold."

Finally, to secure a facility to transact their business, Gould purchased a controlling interest in New York's Tenth National Bank, frequented by Wall Street bankers but currently under investigation by federal auditors. While wealthy New Yorkers left on their traditional August vacations to Saratoga or Newport, Gould and Fisk worked to complete their scheme.

To what extent was Grant aware of these machinations in the summer of 1869? The exact nature of his conversations with Gould and Fisk at the Corbin home is uncertain. In other meetings—in a private car on the Erie Railroad to visit the company's locomotive works in Susquehanna, Pennsylvania, or in Fisk's box at the Fifth Avenue Theatre—Grant listened politely as the gold twins plied the president with their plan to help him and the economy.

But when Gould pressed the president to offer "a little intimation" of his course of action on gold, he responded that offering such information "would not be fair." Most often Grant drew on his favorite ploy: he lit another cigar and turned the conversation to horses. Despite his discretion, he did not grasp that just by allowing himself to be seen in the company of Fisk and Gould, he was sending a message to many Wall Street sharks that he supported a rising gold price.

At the end of August, Grant wrote Boutwell expressing concern about financial markets. Testifying before the House Banking and Currency Committee in February 1870, after the situation had exploded, Boutwell recalled that Grant "expressed an opinion that it was undesirable to force down the price of gold." The president worried that if the price of gold should fall, it would hurt the ability of farmers in the West "to move their crops."

ON SEPTEMBER 1, the two co-conspirators put the final steps of their plan into motion. They purchased $1.5 million in gold in the names of Corbin and Butterfield. For each $1.00 rise in price, the gold twins would make $15,000 ($263,000 in today's money). On September 6, the price of gold rose to $137, a gain of $4.50 in less than a week.

On September 12, Grant prepared to leave for a final week of vacation in western Pennsylvania. He would travel in a private Erie Railroad car provided by Gould. Before departing Corbin's home, Grant wrote Boutwell, who was scheduled to arrive in New York on business later that week. "On your arrival you will be met by the bulls and bears," wishing either to sell or to hold. "The fact is, a desperate struggle is now taking place, and each party wants the government to help them out." Grant's counsel: "I think, from the lights before me, I would move on, without change, until the present struggle is over." He sealed the letter and gave it to Corbin to give to Butterfield with instructions to deliver it to Boutwell. Corbin, thinking the letter was a directive to stop selling gold, decided to inform Gould.

Then, worried, Corbin went even further and called on Boutwell when he arrived. But in the chaos of having to deal with newspaper reporters from the big five New York dailies—the *Times, Herald, Tribune, World,* and *Sun*—lined up outside his hotel room door, the secretary did not hear him out. Corbin expressed his concern to Gould, who told him to write Grant. On September 17, as Gould stood at his shoulder, Corbin wrote hurriedly. His rambling letter would be lost, but Gould recalled Corbin arguing that of the two contending financial parties, he hoped the president would come down on the side of "prominent men" who "were short of gold."

Fisk directed an Erie company messenger to take the urgent letter to Grant. The messenger, Billy Chapin, arrived in Washington, Pennsylvania, after twenty-four hours of nonstop travel (by train and then horse and buggy), went straight to Grant's home, and found him playing croquet with Horace Porter. Grant stopped the game to read the letter, after which the young messenger asked if the president wished to send a reply. Grant's response: "No answer."

Puzzled by the strenuous effort to deliver the letter and Grant's stony response, Porter now related Gould's request about purchasing $500,000 worth of bonds for him. Hearing this, Grant put together the pieces of the gold puzzle. He recalled all the meetings with Gould and Fisk. Corbin, Gould, and Fisk were out to corner the gold market.

Grant moved to bring Julia, who by chance was just then writing Jennie, into the conversation. "Write this," he told his wife, and then dictated: "The General says, if you have any influence with your husband, tell him to have nothing to do with Jay Gould and Jim Fisk. If he does, he will be ruined."

Sealing the letter, Grant mused, "I always felt great respect for Corbin and thought he took much pleasure in the supposition that he was rendering great assistance to the administration by his valuable advice." Shaken by the revelation, he added, "I blame myself now for not checking. . . . It is very sad. I fear he may be ruined—and my poor sister!"

BUT IT WAS too late. Fisk's messenger sent a wire to his employer. A telegraph operator between Pittsburgh and New York somehow added one fateful punctuation mark. The messenger had written, "Letter delivered all right." Fisk received, "Letter delivered. All right." So Fisk surmised the president had given his assent for a charge of the bulls.

"Buy." "Buy." "Buy." On Monday, September 20, Fisk and Gould revved up their avaricious assault. The price of gold escalated. Crowding into the Gold Exchange on Williams Street, eager buyers began pushing the price up from $137. By Wednesday afternoon, September 22, it reached a high of $141 7/8.

Also on September 22, Ulysses and Julia returned to the White House after a summer's absence. Julia inspected the summer work done by carpenters, craftsmen, and painters. Ulysses asked her about the new paintings and statues spread throughout the house. She did not know where they were from. Further inquiry revealed they had been delivered at no charge from an art dealer in New York. Smelling a skunk, Grant directed the paintings and statues be boxed up and returned. Butterfield testified later that the gifts, estimated at $60,000, were from "the gold ring," expressly meant to curry favor with the president.

The next evening, Grant and Boutwell met to compare notes. Boutwell worried he would need to convince the president to let the Treasury Department open its resources and smash the gold ring. But as the two talked, they agreed that the business of the counry was in danger. Grant impressed Boutwell with his quiet confidence. The president told his Treasury secretary, "If gold advanced materially the next day, it would be our duty to sell" in order to stabilize the markets.

ON AN UNUSUALLY warm Friday, September 24, 1869, Fisk and Gould rode downtown from the Grand Opera House with $100 million in "gold calls," or orders, in their pockets, expecting to receive yet more bids through their Tenth National Bank. As traders crowded into the Gold Exchange, no one knew what to expect. Artists from *Frank Leslie's Illustrated* and *Harper's Weekly* jostled for the best vantage points from which to sketch the high drama. If Wall Street traders cheered the gold twins' bravado, many ordinary people jeered at the financial pain raining down on farmers and small-business owners. As Fisk shouted out orders to his troops, the price of gold rose by nine thirty to $150 and by eleven A.M. surpassed $155. The question voiced in crowds growing outside the Gold Exchange: What would the government do?

AT THIS SAME hour, Boutwell strode from the Treasury Department to the White House to speak with Grant. He had with him reports of the mounting chaos not only from New York, but from Philadelphia and Baltimore. Boutwell strongly suggested making a sale of gold for the purpose of breaking the market and ending the pandemonium.

Grant asked Boutwell what amount he proposed to sell.

Boutwell replied, "Three million dollars will be sufficient to break the combination."

Grant came right back: "I think you had better make it $5,000,000."

Boutwell returned to his office and sent a telegram to Butterfield:

SELL $4,000,000 GOLD TOMORROW, AND BUY $4,000,000 BONDS.

AS THE BELLS of New York's Trinity Church rang high noon, Boutwell's telegram arrived. Butterfield posted it on the Sub-Treasury bulletin board.

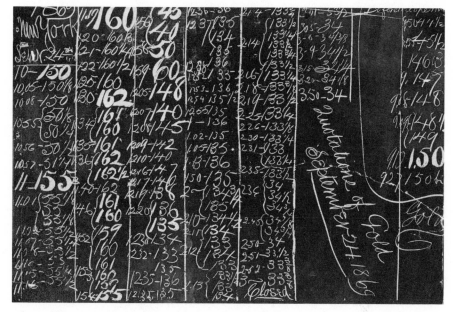

The scribbling on a blackboard in the New York Gold Room charts the fall of the price of gold on Black Friday, September 24, 1869.

Within minutes, the price of gold fell from 160 to 138. "Sell!" "Sell!" "Sell!" What would become known forever as "Black Friday" stopped the conspiracy of the gold ring gamblers Fisk and Gould. The *New York Herald* wrote, "Possibly no avalanche ever swept with more terrible violence."

At twelve noon, Grant convened a cabinet meeting. As news from the telegraph was brought in, congratulations erupted all around. Grant and Boutwell had done their homework and acted decisively.

To be sure, at that moment no one could appreciate the pain and loss the entire country would feel for many years. But as Moses Grinnell, the United States collector of customs for the Port of New York, telegraphed Grant and Boutwell that afternoon: "Had you not taken the course which you did, I believe a large portion of our most reliable merchants and bankers would have been obliged to suspend before three o'clock today, as confidence was entirely gone and the panic was becoming universal."

Much of the country would never know Grant's full role in Black Friday. As the general had done so often with Sherman or Sheridan, he would deflect any praise from himself to Secretary Boutwell, one of his most talented cabinet secretaries. Nevertheless, despite Grant's own inexperience in financial markets, he had partnered with Boutwell to act assertively and avert a national financial crisis.

⋅⊱⟶⟸⊰⋅

CHAPTER 28

"A Radical Change in the Indian Policy"

Thank God for a President in the White House whose first word was
for the Negro and the second for the Indian; who saw protection
for the Indian not in the rude and blood thirsty policy of Sheridan and
Sherman, but in the ballot, in citizenship.

—WENDELL PHILLIPS, president, American Anti-Slavery Society,
February 24, 1870

Grant had surprised everyone with the promise in his inaugural address that he intended to change the nation's Indian policy.

Three weeks later, he made good on his word and convened a meeting with a group of Christian leaders and philanthropists to start that change. The need, the president told them, was to forge "a humane and Christianizing policy towards the Indians." The *New York Herald* reported, "It was his desire to make a radical change in the Indian policy of the government."

Grant's Indian initiative may have raised the spirits of reformers, but it also ignited opposition from army colleagues and threatened to alienate western supporters. The *Leavenworth Bulletin* decried, "If more men are to be scalped and their hearts boiled, we hope to God that it may be some of our Quaker Indian Agents." In contrast with the majority of his military friends, Grant had come to believe that most of the problems on the frontier emanated from the settlers. As for the Indians, he wrote Sherman criticizing "our white people, who seem never to be satisfied without hostilities with them. It is much better to support a Peace commission than a campaign against Indians."

Within days of Grant's announcement, a response came from a surprising source. Wendell Phillips, president of the American Anti-Slavery Society, who earlier had been one of Grant's most robust critics, wrote, "With full heart and most earnestly, we thank him." Many people who would participate in the campaign for Indian rights were previously engaged in the antislavery movement. For them this was a logical extension of expanding rights for minority groups within America.

What would come to be called Grant's "Peace Policy" provoked a series of questions. Where did his ideas spring from? Whom would Grant choose to lead his new venture? Why did he turn to Christian leaders as advisers? Who would become the new Indian agents?

THE POLICY OF the government toward the Indians had been codified by President James Monroe in 1824 when he ordered the "voluntary" removal of Indian tribes residing in the East to the Trans-Mississippi West. Andrew Jackson, after becoming president in 1829, instituted an Indian removal policy in the lower South, home to "the Five Civilized Tribes"— Cherokee, Creek, Choctaw, Chickasaw, and Seminole. Under his successor, Martin Van Buren, the "Trail of Tears" trek of 1838–1839 forcibly resettled Cherokees in present-day Oklahoma.

At the beginning of Grant's administration, the nation's policy toward Indians roiled in turmoil. More than 250,000 Indians, living in more than one hundred tribes and governed by some 370 treaties, had been pushed involuntarily west of the Mississippi. A mosaic of different languages, religions, and forms of governance, Indians, as the first inhabitants of the land, confronted the menacing advance of white settlers lured by gold and new western lands and protected by twenty thousand soldiers.

GRANT'S ACTIONS GREW from the promise in his inaugural address: "the proper treatment of the original occupants of this land—the Indians." Behind these words lay a long story of learning about which—in his typical fashion—he had not said much.

Grant's empathy for the plight of the Indians was first provoked while he was stationed at Fort Vancouver in 1853. When Julia learned he rode— often alone—deep into the forests of Oregon, she worried, "lest the Indians should get him" in ambush. He assured Julia, "Those about here are the most harmless people you ever saw." He added, "My opinion [is] that the whole race would be harmless and peaceable if they were not put upon by the whites." That same summer, Grant wrote an army friend about the Chinook Indians, "This poor remnant of a once powerful tribe is fast wasting away before the blessings of civilization—'whisky and Small pox.'" Later, Grant told his Long Branch neighbor George Childs that as a young lieutenant he "had seen the unjust treatment they [Indians] received at the hands of the white men."

Grant had seen the clash of civilizations firsthand on his inspection

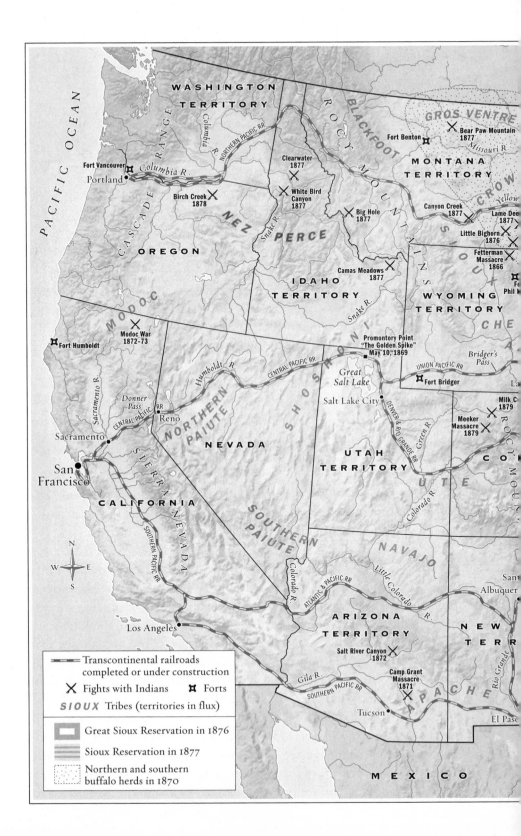

PACIFIC OCEAN

WASHINGTON
TERRITORY

Columbia R.

NORTHERN PACIFIC RR

GROS VENTRE

✕ Bear Paw Mountain
1877

Fort Benton ⌂

Missouri R.

MONTANA
TERRITORY

Fort Vancouver ⌂
Portland ●

Columbia R.

Clearwater
1877
✕

CASCADE RANGE

Birch Creek ✕
1878

✕ White Bird
Canyon
1877

NEZ

Snake R.

PERCE

✕ Big Hole
1877

Camas Meadows
1877 ✕

IDAHO
TERRITORY

Snake R.

Canyon Creek ✕
1877

Yellow

CROW

Lame Dee
1877

Little Bighorn ✕
1876

Fetterman ✕
Massacre
1866

Fo
Phil ♦

WYOMING
TERRITORY

CHE
A.

OREGON

MODOC

✕ Modoc War
1872-73

⌂ Fort Humboldt

Humboldt R.

CENTRAL PACIFIC RR

Promontory Point
"The Golden Spike"
May 10, 1869 ●

*Great
Salt Lake*

UNION PACIFIC RR

*Bridger's
Pass*

⌂ Fort Bridger

La

*Donner
Pass*

PACIFIC RR

CENTRAL PACIFIC RR

Reno ●

NORTHERN
PAIUTE

SHOSHONI

Salt Lake City ●

DENVER & RIO GRANDE RR

Green R.

Milk C
1879
✕

Sacramento R.

Sacramento ●

NEVADA

UTAH
TERRITORY

Meeker
Massacre ✕
1879

ROCKY MOUN.

CO

San
Francisco ●

SIERRA NEVADA

CALIFORNIA

SOUTHERN PACIFIC RR

SOUTHERN
PAIUTE

Colorado R.

U T E

Colorado R.

N A V A J O

*Little
Colorado*

San
Albuquer

Los Angeles ●

ATLANTIC & PACIFIC RR

ARIZONA
TERRITORY

Colorado R.

NEW
TERR

N
W ✦ E
S

Gila R.

SOUTHERN PACIFIC RR

Salt River Canyon ✕
1872

Camp Grant
Massacre
1871 ✕

APACHE

Rio Grande

━━ Transcontinental railroads
completed or under construction

✕ Fights with Indians   ⌂ Forts

SIOUX Tribes (territories in flux)

Tucson ●

El Pase

Great Sioux Reservation in 1876

Sioux Reservation in 1877

Northern and southern
buffalo herds in 1870

MEXICO

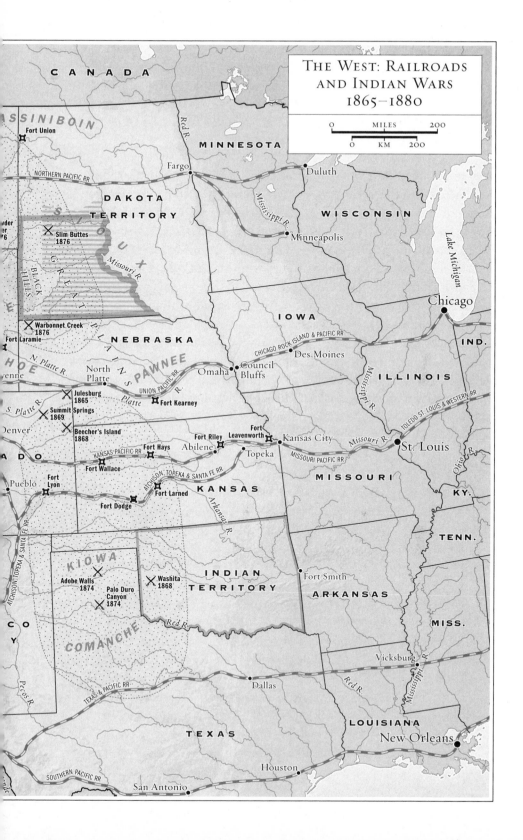

CANADA

ASSINIBOIN

Fort Union

Red R.

MINNESOTA

Fargo

Duluth

NORTHERN PACIFIC RR

DAKOTA
TERRITORY

WISCONSIN

Mississippi R.

S
I
O
U
X

Slim Buttes
1876

BLACK HILLS

GREAT

Missouri R.

Minneapolis

Lake Michigan

owder
ver
76

Warbonnet Creek
1876

Fort Laramie

PLAINS

NEBRASKA

IOWA

Chicago

IND.

PAWNEE

CHICAGO ROCK ISLAND & PACIFIC RR

Des Moines

HOE

N. Platte R.

yenne

North
Platte

UNION PACIFIC RR

Omaha

Council
Bluffs

ILLINOIS

Mississippi R.

S. Platte R.

Julesburg
1865

Platte R.

Fort Kearney

Summit Springs
1869

Denver

Beecher's Island
1868

KANSAS PACIFIC RR

Fort Hays

Fort Riley

Fort
Leavenworth

Kansas City

St. Louis

TOLEDO ST. LOUIS & WESTERN RR

Missouri R.

ADO

Abilene

Topeka

MISSOURI PACIFIC RR

Ohio R.

Pueblo

Fort
Lyon

Fort Wallace

ATCHISON, TOPEKA & SANTA FE RR

KANSAS

MISSOURI

KY.

Fort Larned

Fort Dodge

Arkansas R.

TENN.

KIOWA

INDIAN
TERRITORY

Fort Smith

ATCHISON, TOPEKA & SANTA FE RR

Adobe Walls
1874

Washita
1868

ARKANSAS

MISS.

Palo Duro
Canyon
1874

CO
Y

COMANCHE

Red R.

Vicksburg

Mississippi R.

Pecos R.

TEXAS & PACIFIC RR

Dallas

Red R.

LOUISIANA

New Orleans

TEXAS

Houston

SOUTHERN PACIFIC RR

San Antonio

tour of the Great Plains nine months earlier in the summer of 1868. He witnessed white settlers heading west in ever-increasing numbers. He worried about the prospect of increasing conflicts between Indians and settlers. If Grant had earlier pitied the Indians, now he had a passion to find a solution to a long-simmering problem.

A FIRST COMPONENT of Grant's initiative raised eyebrows all around. He nominated Ely S. Parker, his former military secretary, to be commissioner of Indian affairs. Born in 1828 on the Seneca Tonawanda Reservation in western New York, Parker prized his Indian name, Ha-sa-no-an-da ("Leading Name"). His English name came from "Elder" Ely Stone, a Baptist minister who taught at the mission school where young Parker received his first education. As a teenager, Parker began to interpret and speak for the Senecas, traveling to Albany and Washington to be their voice in conflicts over Tonawanda lands.

As a young man, Parker decided to wear both a deerskin and a frock coat—to live and work in both Indian and white worlds. Stung by the defeat of Tonawanda claims, he studied law. To his dismay he was denied entrance to the bar, told that as an Indian he was not a legal citizen. At age

Grant did more than just talk about Indian affairs, he appointed Ely S. Parker, a Seneca, as commissioner of the Bureau of Indian Affairs.

twenty-three, he became a Seneca chief and was given the "Red Jacket Medal," the silver medal that President George Washington presented to his great Seneca forebear in 1792 to symbolize the bond of peace between the new nation of the United States and the Indian nations.

Parker won Grant's confidence while serving on his staff as a secretary after Vicksburg. Parker remembered that Grant "reminded me a great deal of some of my Indian friends. It was necessary to break the ice before the good qualities of the general could be seen." Once the ice was broken, Parker said he encountered a man not only "companionable but possessed of a warm and sympathetic nature." He became Grant's lens to help him understand the predicament of Indians facing the relentless push of white Americans into the West.

As a measure of Grant's and Parker's closeness, when Parker married Minnie Orton Sackett, an eighteen-year-old Washington socialite, in December 1867, Grant gave the bride away.

Concerned whether Parker would be eligible for appointment as commissioner, Grant consulted Attorney General E. Rockwood Hoar. The president felt relieved when Hoar replied that Parker was not "disqualified from holding such office under the Constitution." Selecting Parker was Grant's confirmation that the Indian, when given opportunity for education and worthwhile work, could take his rightful place alongside any man in modern America.

NEXT IN HIS initiative, Grant turned to Christian leaders as advisers. To the extent that Grant has been consistently portrayed as irreligious, he has been seen through the narrow criterion of church attendance, not an adequate measure to gauge religious beliefs or practices. The story of his relationship to religion is more complex than is usually understood.

Raised within the Methodist tradition, Grant once declared there were "three political parties in the United States: the Republicans, the Democrats, and the Methodists." His piety was practical. He gave money to foreign missionaries because he supported their efforts not only to preach the gospel, but to teach agriculture. As for the future of Indians, he told his Presbyterian friend George Stuart, "I do not believe our Creator ever placed different races of men on this earth with the view of having the stronger exert all his energies in exterminating the weaker."

Grant became involved in another American religious tradition when Quakers called on him after the Civil War. The Quakers—often called Friends—told him the story of William Penn, who lived peacefully with the Delaware Indians in the eighteenth century.

In February, Grant asked Parker to contact Benjamin Hallowell, a leader of the Baltimore Friends. Parker wrote Hallowell that Grant appreciated "fully the friendship and interest which your society has ever maintained" in Indian welfare. Furthermore, he was "desirous of inaugurating some policy to protect the Indians in their just rights and enforce integrity in the administration of their affairs."

Hallowell applauded Grant's "sagacity" in understanding that the first requirement for working with Indians was to rebuild trust with tribes who had come to distrust the word and work of previous Indian agents. Grant's Peace Policy would often be called his "Quaker policy."

At the meetings Grant held at the White House for Christian leaders, several attendees suggested the United States Christian Commission as a model for a new Indian commission. The commission, started by the YMCA at the beginning of the Civil War, acted as the central vehicle for providing both spiritual and physical care for soldiers—everything from Bibles to books to blankets. This experiment in church and government cooperation had worked because it received President Lincoln's blessing. Likewise, George H. Stuart, who had served as chairman of the commission, believed the new Indian board could work with Grant's blessing.

CONGRESS VOTED TO establish the Board of Indian Commissioners on April 10, 1869, but not without complaints from members of Congress unwilling to give up their prerogatives in making appointments. Under the act, it was the president who had the authority "to organize a board of Commissioners . . . eminent for their intelligence and philanthropy," who would serve without remuneration. Grant wanted to place public-spirited men not subject to the political pressures that had hounded the previous management of the Indian office. Determined to make his vision a success, he worked hard to secure an additional $2 million above the normal annual appropriation.

Various denominations selected all nine members of the new board, which met with Grant on May 27 to formalize its mandate to visit the tribes, inspect the records of the Indian office, evaluate the efficacy of the treaty system, and monitor purchases for the Indians.

On June 3, Grant issued a lengthy executive order authorizing the new board to "have full power to inspect in person or by subcommittee, the various Indian Superintendencies and Agencies in the Indian Country." Under Parker's direction, the commissioners fanned out that summer and fall to visit Indians and meet agents.

Grant delegated the management of Indian affairs to Interior Secretary Jacob Cox and Parker. Cox, an excellent administrator, brought with him a reputation as a man of strong opinions. As an advocate of civil service reform, he wanted to place the best people in charge. Parker superintended an office employing more than six hundred, including fifteen superintendents in charge of seventy agents.

THE THIRD COMPONENT of Grant's initiative would be selecting a new group of Indian agents. The Indian board's first report criticized many of the previous agents: "The agent, appointed to be . . . friend and counsellor" to the Indians, "frequently went among them only to enrich himself in the shortest possible time." Starting in April, Methodists, Presbyterians, Episcopalians, Congregationalists, and Quakers were invited to nominate agents. Grant pointedly did not ask Attorney General Hoar about crossing the line between church and state as he sought to select the best candidates to solve a crisis.

FOLLOWING CLOSELY THE actions of his Board of Indian Commissioners, Grant read its first report in November with interest. It began by boldly acknowledging that the history of the United States' dealings with Indians was "a shameful record of broken treaties and unfulfilled promises." Challenging prevailing opinion, "the testimony . . . is on record . . . that, in our Indian wars, almost without exception, the first aggressions have been made by the white men." The report further declared, "Paradoxical as it may seem, the white man has been the chief obstacle in the way of Indian civilization." The main body of the report consisted of proposals. It recommended that Indians live on reservations and the United States eliminate the treaty system, enhance schools, and encourage Christian missions.

In Grant's first annual message to Congress in December, he underscored both the indictments and the proposals of the new board. In the most personal expression in his lengthy message, he stated, "From my own experience upon the frontiers and in Indian countries, I do not hold either legislation, or the conduct of the whites who come most in contact with the Indian, blameless for these hostilities." He rose to his subject: "A system which looks to the extinction of a race is too abhorant [*sic*] for a Nation to indulge in without entailing upon the wrath of all civilized Christendom." As 1869 drew to a close, Grant felt an edgy optimism about prospects for changing the previous patterns in working with the Indians.

. . .

THE HOLIDAYS THAT year would be a time of both joy and sadness. Ulysses and Julia hosted a joyful overflow household of family and friends for their first Christmas in the White House. On December 24, they attended Christmas Eve worship at the Metropolitan Methodist Church. In a special ceremony, Grant, as a trustee of the congregation, received a check for $50,000 to pay off the remaining debt incurred in building the new church.

This evening merriment was dampened by the news that Edwin Stanton had died at three A.M. on December 24. It had been only days since Grant had nominated Stanton to replace retiring Robert C. Grier as an associate justice of the Supreme Court.

Grant had walked to Stanton's home near Franklin Square on December 19 to personally inform the former secretary of war of his intent to nominate him. Congress approved the nomination the next day. Stanton, too ill to walk to the White House, wrote a thank-you note: "It is the only public office I ever desired."

Grant immediately ordered all government office buildings draped in mourning. After both a productive and a painful relationship with Stanton, Grant had rejoiced in his ability to appoint him to the Supreme Court. Now he wrote Ellen Stanton, "I am at a loss to find words expressive of my sympathy for you in your great affliction, and of the estimation I placed upon the ability, integrity, patriotism and services of him whom a nation joins you in mourning the loss of."

IN THE NEW year, Grant sought to empower a group of citizens he had earlier offended. He reached out to American Jews just at the moment they were beginning to experience discrimination as their numbers grew from European immigration after the Civil War. While Grant is well-known for his infamous General Orders No. 11, which expelled Jews from parts of the South—what Julia called "that obnoxious order"—the story of his later relationship with American Jews is little known.

Three days after Grant's inauguration, Simon Wolf, who encouraged Jews to vote for Grant for president, wrote seeking an appointment to the Foreign Service. Prominent St. Louis Jewish leader Isidor Bush added his support: "If President Grant wants to prove his impartiality towards Israelites and to disprove any unfriendliness attributed to him on account of Order No. 11—there is probably no better opportunity than by appointing Mr. Simon Wolf."

Grant appointed Wolf not to the Foreign Service, but as recorder of deeds for the District of Columbia. In this position, Wolf exercised a lobbying role with Congress for Jews and Jewish issues. Wolf claimed Grant said to him after his appointment, "You represent your co-religionists [and] you also stand well with the German-American element. I may want to see and consult you often."

Grant appointed Wolf's friend Edward S. Salomon governor of the Washington Territory in January 1870. Salomon, who had fought with the Eighty-second Illinois at Gettysburg, became the first Jew to hold a governorship. Rabbi Isaac Mayer Wise, America's foremost Jewish leader, who had earlier called General Orders No. 11 an "outrage," now applauded Grant's action: "The appointment shows that *President* Grant has revoked *General* Grant's notorious order No. 11."

As Grant reached out to the Jewish community, he received pushback from a few Protestant and Catholic leaders. But he had a new defender. Baltimore's *Jewish Times* wrote, "We suppose the President made the appointment to signify his sense of equity by recognizing the Jewish church, and according it the same privileges as to other denominations." In opening to Jews the possibility of government service, Grant continued his broader policy of reconciliation.

Grant appointed Dr. Herman Bendell superintendent of Indian affairs for the Arizona Territory. What made Bendell's appointment remarkable: Grant balanced his decision to turn over control of the Board of Indian Commissioners to Christian denominations by selecting a Jewish Civil War surgeon.

GRANT'S OPTIMISM ABOUT his Indian policy received a shock in January 1870. Reports trickled east that on January 23, a detachment of the Second Cavalry led by Major Eugene Baker, under orders from General Sheridan to punish Piegan warriors of the Blackfeet tribe who had raided white settlements, attacked a village on the Marias River in northern Montana. The cavalry reported they recovered stolen property, but what emerged were details of the horrific killing of 173 Piegan, of whom 140 were women and children. *The New York Times* called the attack a "sickening slaughter," while the *New York Tribune* called it a "national disgrace." The *National Anti-Slavery Standard* condemned Sheridan as the one ultimately responsible for the attack.

Reformers responded, led by the Board of Indian Commissioners. Up until now the commissioners had existed in an uneasy truce with the army, but the "Piegan Massacre" changed everything. Vincent Colyer, board secretary, who had raised and led an African American regiment during the Civil War, testified before the House of Representatives on

February 25. He accused Major Baker of murder and aimed his attack directly at Sheridan, who had defended Baker.

Although in the end there was no official resolution about blame, the Piegan Massacre shone a spotlight on the long-simmering debate of who should administer Indian affairs. The War Department argued that precedent lay with them because Indian affairs had been entrusted to the newly created War Department in 1789 and the department had organized a Bureau of Indian Affairs in 1824. The Department of the Interior argued that recent history was on their side: with the creation of the Department of the Interior in 1849, the Indian Bureau was immediately transferred to their administration. After the Civil War, Grant and Sherman had stood together in wanting to transfer Indian affairs from Interior to the War Department. The issue was always about military or civilian control.

Even with Grant's new policy of religious or humanitarian agents, whom westerners called "maudlin sentimentalists," the momentum for transfer of Indian affairs to the War Department had seemed to be winning the day—until the Piegan Massacre. Sherman, now general in chief, continued to plead for military control, arguing that the army, by means of its superior organization, could administer Indian issues more effectively.

Grant tried to hold out one hand to the Christian Indian reformers while clasping the military with his other. Sometimes, to the consternation of everyone, he believed in using both the olive branch and the sword. The issue that would force him to choose was the 1870 Military Appropriations Act.

Under cover of the economy, pleading the necessity of reducing officer numbers in the military, Congress directed that army officers could no longer serve as agents in the Bureau of Indian Affairs. If they did so, they would have to vacate their military commission. Legislators hoped that with this move they might once again gain a foothold in the patronage game.

They underestimated Grant. He told a group of lawmakers, "Gentlemen, you have defeated my plan of Indian management; but you shall not succeed in *your* purpose, for I will divide these appointments up among the religious churches, with which you dare not contend."

Many churches and humanitarian reformers expressed appreciation for Grant's initiative. The Friends Social Union of New York passed a resolution expressing gratitude to the president for the "humane spirit, the wisdom, and the executive ability" present in his new Indian policy.

· · ·

GRANT LEARNED THAT Red Cloud, chief of the Oglala Sioux, wanted to visit "the Great White Father." The reasons for the request were not clear. After years of battles and discussions of treaties, why did this most celebrated warrior want to meet with Grant?

Sherman was opposed to such a meeting, believing Red Cloud wanted to protest recent military policies.

Sherman misjudged his friend. On May 3, after conferring with his cabinet, Grant decided to accept Red Cloud's offer to come to Washington. Spotted Tail, chief of the Brulé Lakota Sioux and Red Cloud's rival, was also invited. Fourteen months after the initiation of his Indian Peace Policy, Grant recognized that for it to be effective, communication must become a two-way street.

On June 1, Grant welcomed Red Cloud to Washington with the pomp and pageantry reserved for a head of state. He understood the controversy surrounding the visit. Impressed, a reporter for the *New York Herald* wrote, "Physically, a finer set of men would be difficult to find. All were tall, full chested, and with features decidedly those of the American Indians." If easterners welcomed the opportunity to finally get a look at these legendary Indians, the army and most westerners were lukewarm at best.

Despite the opposition of Sherman and other military leaders, Grant invited Indian leaders Red Cloud and Spotted Tail to meet with him in Washington.

Grant met with Red Cloud, Spotted Tail, and their delegation at the White House. The president listened as Red Cloud, respectful but resolute, stated he was for peace but detailed his grievances against the white men who too often did not keep their treaties or their words. D. C. Poole, the Indian agent who accompanied the Sioux, remembered that Grant talked to them "in a plain, direct way that engrossed their attention." The president assured them he would do all in his power to fulfill the obligations of the United States as stated in the treaty. He directed the War Department to order military commanders: "When lands are secured to the Indians by treaty against the occupation of whites, the military commanders should keep intruders off by military force if necessary."

Moved by the visit of Red Cloud, Grant wrote Congress in July, urging them of "the necessity of passing an Indian appropriation bill." They did so the day before they adjourned.

By the summer of 1870, Grant was learning that battles in Washington, unlike the battles he had fought in the Civil War, could not be won in a matter of days, weeks, or even months. His determination to change the nation's Indian policy had brought him into contact with religious and humanitarian allies while eliciting criticism from military colleagues and congressional dispensers of lucrative assignments in the old Bureau of Indian Affairs. His vision for a new direction in Indian policy had borne some fruit. He may have been encouraged by initial results, but he realized there could still be obstacles to overcome.

Meanwhile, problems and possibilities in foreign affairs threatened to upstage his domestic policies. Feeling his own inexperience, searching for trustworthy allies, he turned his attention from domestic to foreign relations.

CHAPTER 29

Foreign Relations

I hope that the time may soon arrive when the two Governments
can approach the solution of this momentous question, in a spirit
and with an appreciation of what is due to the rights, dignity and
honor of each and . . . lay the foundation of a broad principle of
public laws, which will prevent future differences and tend to
firm and continued peace and friendship.

—ULYSSES S. GRANT, Annual Message to Congress,
December 6, 1869

At the beginning of Grant's presidency, the interests of the nation
were turned inward. Americans focused their attention on domestic
rather than foreign relations, on winning the West rather than improving
relations with foreign nations. In his inaugural address, Grant had declared, "I would respect the rights of all nations demanding equal respect
for our own." But in the spring of 1869, the press and public gave little
consideration to dealings with other nations. That was about to change.

THE MERITS AND demerits of Grant's cabinet selections were endlessly
debated, but everyone agreed he chose well when he appointed Hamilton
Fish secretary of state. Six feet tall, with a large head, Fish balanced his
imposing physical presence with a manner that invited people into conversation and consensus. Grant believed building a relationship of trust
with Fish would be crucial to the success of his administration's foreign
policy.

At age sixty, Fish had been away from public service for twelve years.
He served as a vestryman at St. Mark's Episcopal Church in New York
City. He spent considerable time at "Glenclyffe," his large redbrick house
at Garrison-on-Hudson, where he could look across the Hudson River to
West Point.

A man of cosmopolitan tastes, Fish had accepted the position of sec-

Photographer Mathew Brady took this full-length portrait of Grant, early in his presidency, seated at a table with books.

retary of state reluctantly, expecting to stay only a few months. Within weeks, however, he resigned as president of the New-York Historical Society, gave up chairmanship of the board of trustees of Columbia College, and moved from temporary quarters at Ebbitt House to a splendid home at the corner of Fifteenth and I streets.

From there Fish could walk to the White House in five minutes. To get to his State Department office, he traveled onto an unpaved section of Fourteenth Street to what was once the Washington City Orphan Asylum. In this tattered brick building, he worked from nine A.M. without complaint in a small, cramped second-floor office.

At the end of the day, which could stretch into the early evening, he faithfully recorded the day's events in his diary. What began as an official minutes book expanded as Fish began writing about the larger issues of foreign relations. His diary, never published, would offer his changing insights about Grant and the Grant administration.

OF THE PREVIOUS seventeen presidents, only John Adams, Thomas Jefferson, James Madison, James Monroe, John Quincy Adams, and James Buchanan came to the office with any substantial experience in foreign relations. As a leader, Grant knew what he did not know. He felt confident in surrounding himself with leaders who knew more than he did in their fields. He understood he would begin as a junior partner in his relationship with Fish.

Fish approached the new president with his characteristic generous spirit. He knew some spoke of "Grant the Silent" as an enigma. In their

Hamilton Fish, whom Grant appointed secretary of state, intended to serve for only a few months, but his growing appreciation of Grant ultimately prompted him to sign on for the duration of the president's term of office.

first months together, Fish observed Grant's reticence in the company of men he did not know. Yet "few men had more powers of conversation and of narration than he when in the company of intimate friends."

Grant exhibited an initial restraint in cabinet meetings when the subject turned to foreign relations. Although filled with natural curiosity about other lands and peoples, he decided to put his trust in his new secretary of state.

FISH WOULD BE tested quickly. At no time since the War of 1812 were relations with Great Britain so strained as when Grant assumed the presidency. His first foreign relations challenge derived from the island nation's role with the Confederacy during the Civil War.

On a July day in 1862, the British-built sloop-of-war No. 290 made its way down the Mersey estuary at Birkenhead, England, and out into the sea. Named the CSS *Alabama,* it started off on its mission as a Confederate commerce raider. In its subsequent two-year rampage, the *Alabama* ranged across the North Atlantic to the Gulf of Mexico to the South Pacific to South Africa. It captured or burned sixty-five Union merchant ships. Four other British-built Confederate raiders—*Florida, Georgia, Rappahannock,* and *Shenandoah*—also terrorized Union shipping, together with the *Alabama* sinking more than 150 Union ships. The *Alabama* was finally destroyed in June 1864 in a battle outside the harbor of Cherbourg, France. In 1984, the French navy found the *Alabama* in two hundred feet of water.

During the transition winter of 1868–1869, outgoing secretary of state William Seward negotiated a settlement for damages charged to Great Britain because of the Confederate raiders. Although early in the Civil War Great Britain had declared itself neutral, the United States sought both an apology and compensation for the actions of the ships.

The resulting Johnson-Clarendon Treaty, called "the *Alabama* Claims," displeased Grant, who believed it did not go far enough. Before his inauguration, he communicated his views both to Seward and to Sir Edward Thornton, the United Kingdom's minister to the United States.

On April 13, Senator Charles Sumner, who was the powerful chairman of the Foreign Relations Committee, complicated Grant's task. In a highly charged anti-British speech, Sumner blasted the treaty: "When Civilization was fighting a last battle with Slavery, England gave her name, her influence, her material resources to the wicked cause, and flung a sword into the scale with Slavery." Sumner wanted to ask for a huge

$2 billion restitution, including what he called "indirect" claims for the loss of a large oceangoing trade not related to "direct" claims of sunk or damaged ships. He was willing to accept the ceding of Canada to satisfy the debt. Sumner's speech galvanized the Senate, which voted down the treaty 54 to 1. With that vote, the Senate sent a signal: they wanted to give Grant and Fish the opportunity to negotiate a new treaty more advantageous to American interests.

If Sumner's speech rallied Americans, it antagonized the British. Critics replied that support for the Confederacy was never over slavery—which Great Britain had already outlawed—but over the right of secession. Sumner's speech just made negotiations tougher.

GRANT AND FISH quickly made two judgments. First, time was needed for cooling off emotions. Second, for more immediate control, negotiations needed to move from London to Washington.

Grant pondered when and how to restart negotiations in an atmosphere of Anglophobia. A long-standing aggravation over the rights of Americans to fish in U.S.-Canadian border waters would not go away. More recently, the Fenian Brotherhood, an Irish American organization, had been conducting raids in Canada, hoping to force Great Britain to withdraw from Ireland.

Grant and Fish approached the *Alabama* Claims from quite different experiences of the United Kingdom. Grant may have been put off by Sumner's arrogance, but he sympathized with his underlying message. As commander of all the Union forces, Grant had been outraged that Great Britain built Confederate cruisers that wreaked devastation upon Union shipping.

Fish, by contrast, had traveled to Europe for two years between 1857 and 1859, the "pleasant part" a lengthy stay in Great Britain. He was a regular reader of *The Times* of London and the best British reviews. Fish's greater familiarity left him with a greater respect for the nation.

AN IMPORTANT STEP in restarting negotiations would be appointing a new minister to the United Kingdom who satisfied all parties. On April 26, Grant wrote Queen Victoria about his appointment of Sumner's friend John Lothrop Motley: "He is well informed of the relative interests of the two countries, and of our sincere desire to cultivate and strengthen the friendship and good correspondence between us." Motley had large shoes to fill. He succeeded Charles Francis Adams, Sr., son and grandson of two presidents, who served as minister to the Court of St. James under both Lincoln and Johnson but had been unable to convince Great Britain to agree to a financial settlement.

A graduate of Harvard, Motley had served in the diplomatic corps in St. Petersburg, Russia, and in Austria during the Civil War. Sumner proudly wrote a friend, the Duchess of Argyll, that Motley was "nominated by the Presdt on my recommendation, &, as the Secy of State informs me 'as a compliment' to me." The senator may have overstated his influence in the appointment, but his sentiments were just fine with Grant. The president knew Fish had concerns about Motley—he was brilliant but could be impetuous and irritable. However, growing comfortable in his relationship with Fish, Grant believed it advantageous to reach out to Sumner. As a safeguard, to keep watch on Motley, whom he did not know, he appointed someone he knew well for the position of assistant secretary of the legation: his former secretary Adam Badeau.

JULIA CARRIED ON her own diplomatic relations. She knew politics of Washington flourished not only in the halls of Congress, but in the social gatherings of the capital. Although she would never say so aloud, she knew her warmth could sometimes make up for her husband's stretches of silence.

Julia became a welcoming hostess. She began the custom of asking other women—wives and daughters of senators and cabinet officers—to assist her with social functions. During the Lincoln administration, Mary Lincoln did not welcome some of her husband's "enemies" to her social events. During the Johnson administration, as animosities grew, people increasingly stayed away from the embattled president's social events.

A vibrant friendship developed between Julia Grant and Julia Fish, whom Julia Grant described as "my ideal of an empress." The two women came from markedly different backgrounds. Julia Kean Fish grew up in polite society in New Jersey, whereas Julia Dent Grant grew up at White Haven outside St. Louis. When Julia Grant hosted her first social events, she asked Julia Fish to stand beside her in greeting guests. The bond between the two Julias strengthened the relationship between their husbands.

Emily Edson Briggs, one of the first female correspondents in Washington, described Julia Grant at one of her regular Tuesday afternoon receptions in the Blue Room: "She appears in grace and manner just as any other sensible woman would who had been lifted from the ranks of the people to such an exalted position."

Likewise, Mary Logan, wife of General John Logan, watched Julia with friendly amusement. "She often failed to remember that Mr. and Mrs. So-and-So had been twice married, were or were not temperance leaders, Protestants, or Catholics." Mrs. Logan then looked over at the president, "full of quiet humor," who "at such times would lead her on to her own undoing, and then chuckle. . . . The absolute harmony of their domestic lives was ideal."

As Grant settled into the responsibilities of being president, with Julia's encouragement, he surprised his friends with his sociability. Before Grant, presidents usually dined in, but he did not intend to be corralled in the Executive Mansion. He accepted invitations from cabinet officers and friends for evenings at their homes.

Grant's boyhood friend Daniel Ammen enjoyed a standing invitation on Sundays. Before dinner, Grant and naval leader Ammen would walk several miles together. On one occasion, feeling the pressures of his office, Grant remarked that if his friend had "not pulled him out of the water more than forty years before he would have been spared a great deal of misery."

EVEN AS GRANT appointed John Motley minister to the Court of St. James to help deal with a long-term relationship across the Atlantic, a crisis in the Caribbean demanded the president's immediate attention. Only four days after his inauguration, reports trickled in of a clash between four thousand insurgents and fifteen hundred Spanish soldiers on Cuba, the Caribbean's largest island, situated just ninety miles from the United States.

Discovered by Christopher Columbus in 1492, Cuba had swiftly become one of Spain's most prized colonies. But starting in the 1850s, Cuban merchants and planters demanded economic and social reforms, climaxing in an October 1868 uprising that proclaimed an independent Cuba. Spain, in a weakened condition both politically and economically, struggled to respond.

Americans responded. Instinctively, they supported what they saw as Cuba's courageous struggle to chart its own destiny. Veterans of the Civil War, both Union and Confederate, proclaimed themselves ready to support Cuban patriots. The *New York Tribune* and *New York Herald* sent correspondents to cover the revolution, reporting that more than half a million African slaves still toiled on Cuban plantations five years after the United States had emancipated its slaves. In April 1869, the insurgents adopted a constitution abolishing slavery. With sympathy for Cuban aspirations and anger about a European imperial power close to their shores, Americans supporting the revolution sought to bring the United States into the battle.

Grant, who had supported Mexico's struggle to free itself from France's domination, sympathized with the aspirations of the Cuban rebels. He was lobbied by Bennett's *New York Herald* and Dana's *New York Sun,* which led the chorus calling for intervention. On April 10, the House passed a resolution offering support if Grant chose to recognize the belligerents.

Grant was lobbied hardest by the person nearest his ear. Secretary of War John Rawlins voiced strong backing for the insurgents. Along with Postmaster General Creswell and Interior Secretary Cox, he argued that the United States should immediately recognize the Cubans. Under Rawlins's urging, Grant ordered the navy to increase its squadron in the Caribbean.

Into Grant's other ear argued Attorney General Hoar and Treasury Secretary Boutwell. The attorney general opposed recognition on the grounds that it could not be justified by international law. Hoar worried that "General Grant was disposed to take the advice of General Rawlins." Rawlins was a darling of the press for his strong opinions and colorful comments, and many assumed he spoke for Grant.

In the midst of this debate, Fish admired Grant's balanced leadership. In an April cabinet discussion about whether to recognize Cuba, Grant declared that "strict justice would justify us in not delaying action on this subject, but too early action might prejudice our case with Great Britain in support of our claims." After listening to Rawlins's advocacy and Hoar's opposition, "the President decided not to entertain it at present." No decision was made.

AFTER A SECOND summer vacation at Long Branch, Grant reconvened his cabinet on August 31. Pressure to act on Cuba had only grown. With the temperature soaring toward one hundred degrees, Grant presided over a torrid meeting where Fish and Rawlins faced each other across the cabinet table.

Rawlins, trembling from both illness and emotion, spoke first. He offered a long, passionate argument as to why the United States should recognize Cuban independence. Finished, he collapsed into his chair. Then Fish spoke, just as earnestly but with calm assurance, against recognition. Eyes shifted to Grant, who was writing something on Executive Mansion stationery. When Fish concluded, Grant slid a memorandum over to him. He had decided. "The United States are willing to mediate between Spain & Cuba for the independence of the latter, on following terms." He stipulated, "The United States not to guarantee except with approval of Congress."

Grant's offer to mediate meant he no longer harbored thoughts of intervention. He sided with Fish.

Within one week, Rawlins died, leaving a hole in Grant's official family that no one else could fill. He was the only cabinet member who had watched Grant grow from a clerk in a leather store in Galena to commander of all the Union armies. Because of his intense loyalty, Rawlins had earned the right to be Grant's conscience; he had been able to argue with Grant in a way no one else could. His death also silenced the chief support for the Cuban patriots within Grant's inner circle.

CUBA WAS NOT the only Caribbean island that would occupy Grant. Picturesque, Spanish-speaking Santo Domingo (present-day Dominican Republic) occupied the eastern two-thirds of Hispaniola, the second-largest island in the Caribbean. Although French-speaking Haiti occupied the western third, Santo Domingo's terrain contained by far the most arable land.

Grant inherited a lengthy American interest in Santo Domingo. In 1846, at the behest of Secretary of State John C. Calhoun, young naval officer David Porter had explored Samaná Bay, a natural harbor, as a possible naval base and coaling station. During the Civil War, Lincoln and Seward had pursued the possibilities of naval bases on the island. Seward, when part of the Johnson administration, had continued his interest in the purchase or lease of Samaná Bay.

In April, Joseph Warren Fabens, a Bostonian full of schemes, wrote Hamilton Fish of his interest in facilitating the annexation of Santo Domingo. Fabens and his partner, William L. Cazneau, speculators who made a killing in advance of the annexation of Texas, wished to cash in on Santo Domingo: "The annexation of this country to the United States should be an acquisition of great value." Five days later, Fabens appeared at Fish's office with a "memorandum" from the Dominican government recommending "entrance into the United States as a free and independent state."

Fish brought the memorandum to a cabinet meeting the next day and, given the imminent congressional adjournment, suggested tabling the idea in the face of more pressing subjects. No one objected.

But the issue could not be passed by. Bennett's *New York Herald* cheered a May meeting in New York advocating a Dominican protectorate. Dana's *New York Sun* trumpeted, "After Cuba, then Santo Domingo."

Grant knew that Horace Porter, Congressman John Logan, and Nathaniel Banks, as chairman of the House Committee on Foreign Affairs, were ardently in favor of annexing Santo Domingo. Admiral Daniel Ammen, Grant's longtime friend, also advocated annexation, arguing it would strengthen the U.S. Navy in the Caribbean and protect existing and new markets.

Seeking information on Dominican attitudes toward annexation, the president tapped aide Orville Babcock to visit the island. A handsome, bright Vermonter, an 1861 graduate of West Point, and a nephew of Grant's Galena friend Russell Jones, Babcock had first impressed Grant when he'd built bridges for the defense of Knoxville in 1863 and had joined his staff a year later.

By 1869, Babcock had become second only to Rawlins in Grant's political family. Unlike Rawlins, he never argued with his boss but instead exhibited a calm, agreeable manner that won acclaim from all who knew him and appreciation and loyalty from Grant.

On July 13, Grant sent a letter of introduction to Santo Domingo president Buenaventura Báez. Slight of stature and long on political and economic scheming, Báez had served as president three times in the previous two decades and been overthrown three times. He acceded to the presidency again in March 1868, eager to do business with the United States. Grant declared his desire "to satisfy my curiosity in respect to your interesting country by obtaining information through a source upon which I rely." Fish added his instructions, calling Babcock a "special agent," but he made it clear that Babcock traveled with no diplomatic authority.

Upon his arrival, Babcock informed President Báez that "he had no authority whatever to make a treaty." At most he could construct an outline of a treaty, which could then be submitted to Grant and Fish. Babcock said he did not want to "bind President Grant in any respect."

Babcock returned in September and presented his findings to a flummoxed Fish. Babcock left with no diplomatic powers but returned with a draft for annexation. The United States could either purchase Samaná Bay for $2 million or annex the totality of Santo Domingo by becoming responsible for its public debt of $1.5 million. The protocol also stated that President Grant would use "all his influence" with Congress to accept a treaty. Grant agreed to Babcock's draft and asked Fish to write up a formal treaty.

Babcock went back to Santo Domingo on November 18, this time accompanied by Quartermaster Rufus Ingalls with lengthy instructions from Fish to negotiate two treaties: one to annex the island, the other to lease Samaná Bay. When they returned, Grant asked Fish to present the two treaties for discussion at a cabinet meeting on December 21. Grant believed everything was lining up well, but there was one more important player to be consulted.

ON SUNDAY EVENING, January 2, 1870, the president walked alone across Lafayette Park to Senator Charles Sumner's home at the corner of H Street and Vermont Avenue. His destination showed to what lengths this president would go in personal diplomacy.

Massachusetts first elected Sumner to the Senate in 1851, after the death of Daniel Webster. Eighteen years later, middle-aged and wearing his thick gray hair long, his weight increased to 235 pounds, Sumner packed the Senate gallery every time he spoke. Hands propped on his Senate chair, he gave speeches on all subjects, often reading his latest discourse off of galley proofs already prepared by publishers eager to rush it into print for public consumption. Seemingly tireless, he thundered forth to his own satisfaction and the gallery's delight.

But Sumner was no Webster. In Sumner's high-toned oratory, he often tripped over his own pomposity. In his superior knowledge of foreign relations, he lost support through his inability to compromise. A self-confident Sumner began the final session of the Forty-first Congress certain of his ability to master the inexperienced president.

When Grant assumed the presidency, Sumner was at the pinnacle of his power. When the Forty-first Congress convened in December, the senator clipped an editorial for his scrapbook that declared he was "about to rise into the position of acknowledged leader" of the Senate. People who wrote Sumner began to address him as "the father of the Senate."

In Grant's first ten months in office, he had watched and listened to Sumner. He knew that Fish and Sumner were long-standing friends. While admiring Sumner's advocacy of the rights of African Americans, Grant was annoyed by his frequent interference: the senator had blocked his nomination of Alexander Stewart for the Treasury Department, blocked the treaty with Great Britain, stymied his desire to repeal the Tenure of Office Act, and opposed his initial plans to aid the Cuban insurgents. What repelled Grant most was Sumner's self-importance: the senator took for granted the superiority of his judgments, and Grant suspected he looked down his New England nose at this western provincial who had acceded to the White House. Despite this, all through 1869 Grant had gone out of his way not to antagonize Sumner.

Grant decided to approach Sumner informally about Santo Domingo, appealing to his vanity. He rang Sumner's doorbell, and a servant summoned the senator to welcome the president. Sumner was dining with two eminent Washington newspapermen, John W. Forney and Ben Perley Poore, and the three were discussing how to support James W. Ashley, a leader in the move to impeach Andrew Johnson and about to be replaced as territorial governor of Montana. Sumner offered his unexpected guest a glass of sherry, which Grant turned down. However, he did not turn down an offer to express his opinion of Ashley: Grant called him a "mischief-maker." Poore, sensing something out of the ordinary in a presidential house call, offered to leave, but Grant insisted, "Don't leave, I recognize you and Colonel Forney as friends."

After supper, the four men moved to the library, and Grant stated the purpose of his visit. He intended to present the treaty for the annexation of Santo Domingo before the Senate. He had not brought the treaty with him, but he described it in general terms. As Grant was about to conclude, another guest arrived: Treasury Secretary Boutwell, an old Massachusetts friend of Sumner's. Believing he had completed his mission and not wanting to overstay his visit, Grant told Sumner, "I will send the papers over to you in the morning by Gen. Babcock."

Sumner assured Grant that he would study the treaty. Just as Grant reached the door to leave, Forney interjected, "Of course, Mr. Sumner, you will support the treaty." Sumner replied, "Mr. President, I am an Administration man, and whatever you do will always find in me the most careful and candid consideration."

The exact wording of Sumner's reply would become the subject of endless controversy in the months and years ahead. Grant left Sumner's house believing that he had received support for the treaty—or at least no opposition. Forney recalled he heard Sumner say that "he would cheerfully support the Treaty." Sumner later said he had offered no such support. Poore remembered Sumner declaring "that he was a Republican and a supporter of the Republican Administration, and that he should sustain the Administration in this case if he possibly could, after he had examined the papers." Boutwell recalled Sumner saying, "I expect, Mr. President, to support the measures of your administration."

Probably none of these versions is exactly correct. They were written down at different times—from several months to eight years later. These versions need to be heard, as do all reminiscences, through the filter of later events and the changing views of their authors toward Grant.

"OF THE PEOPLE, by the people, for the benefit of the Senators," wrote Henry Adams, of the Adams political family, in his novel *Democracy*. Grant sent the Santo Domingo treaty to the Senate on January 10, 1870, and was about to discover what Adams meant. The treaty languished there for two months. The Senate, no matter if the president was named Johnson or Grant, was determined to let everyone know who was in charge.

In February, Hamilton Fish, writing to the United States minister to Berlin, the eminent historian George Bancroft, described Grant's frustration: "The disagreement between Congress and A. Johnson increased the legislative powers and accustomed those in Congress and particularly those in the Senate to antagonize every proposition emanating from the Executive." He added, "The habit of criticism, if not of opposition, became somewhat fixed, and on the accession of a friend to the Executive Chair, the habit could not entirely and at once subside—it is difficult to voluntarily relinquish power."

Sumner, as the powerful chairman of the Senate Committee on Foreign Relations, employed a well-practiced strategy of delay and silence. He put off hearings until the middle of February. He did not invite Babcock to appear until March 11. He kept silent about his views on the treaty, not sharing his opinion even with members of his committee.

Sumner hoped to destroy the treaty by procrastination. But Grant was not willing to play that game. Knowing the provisional treaty would expire if not acted upon by March 29, on March 14 he addressed a letter to the Senate expressing "the sincere hope that your action may be favorable to the ratification of the treaty."

Pushed by Grant, on March 15 Sumner's committee acted: by a vote of 5 to 2, they opposed the treaty.

Knowing the full Senate still had to vote, Grant took an unusual step. On March 17, he went up to the Capitol. Establishing himself in the President's Room, traditionally used ceremonially only on the last day of a congressional session, he decided to lobby senators. He sent for fifteen, all of whom his political intelligence had informed him were either for the treaty or on the edge. In a discussion lasting two hours, he spoke about the treaty's benefits, financial and strategic, for the United States. Five days later, he convened a meeting at the White House for senators known to be opposed. He invited twenty-two; fifteen accepted.

As the Santo Domingo drama moved to a vote, Sumner addressed the Senate in closed session on March 24 for four hours; he continued the next day for another hour and a half. He argued that President Báez was corrupt and the present use by the navy of Samaná Bay was illegal.

Young Bancroft Davis, assistant secretary of state, took Sumner's measure. The chairman of the Foreign Relations Committee claimed he spoke of the president with the greatest respect, calling Grant his "distinguished friend" and his "lifelong friend." Davis was not fooled. He wrote Fish, who was away from Washington, that he told Sumner, "You might say with the Psalmist: 'It was not mine enemy that did this thing.'" Grant would not forget Sumner's attack.

Finally, Sumner scheduled a vote on June 30, and the result—an evenly divided 28 to 28, not even close to the two-thirds majority required for approval—represented a major legislative loss for Grant. The treaty had failed to pass. But the president was not yet ready to admit defeat.

WHILE GRANT CONTINUED to fight for his point of view on Santo Domingo's strategic importance, over the course of 1869 he changed his mind on negotiations with Great Britain. In April, Sumner had shown him an advance copy of his anti-British speech. By the end of 1869, Grant had moved away from what he now believed to be Sumner's extreme position, convinced the time had come to seek a negotiated settlement with Great Britain.

Grant's change of mind was due in part to his growing relationship with Hamilton Fish. If in the Civil War Grant's leadership had been encouraged by William Sherman, in the first years of his presidency Fish was quickly becoming the leader who would most influence him. Once again, Grant grew close to a powerful leader whom he trusted.

Fish worried that the quarrel between Grant and Sumner over Santo Domingo could undermine the more important foreign relations with Great Britain. Under Fish's influence, Grant adopted a more evenhanded approach, believing that a fruitful relationship would be central to the nation's foreign relations in the last third of the nineteenth century.

In the summer of 1870, negotiations heated up. Motley provided the spark during his first major conversation with British foreign secretary Lord Clarendon when he presented the American side with the same uncompromising force as Sumner. He told Clarendon America would begin discussions with "a deep sense of national wrong," and until and unless the United Kingdom came forward with "recognition and atonement" for that wrong, there would be no negotiations. The following day, when Benjamin Moran, secretary of the U.S. legation, copied out the long dispatch of Motley's interview, he noted that the minister's declaration to Clarendon has "more of Mr. Sumner than the President in it."

Grant became angry reading the dispatch. He had been warned about Motley's sense of self-importance but had hoped he would behave in carrying out orders with respect to procedure. Grant had appointed Motley in part to satisfy Sumner; he now decided to recall Motley. Fish, although equally upset, calmed the president by arguing that the United States must not incur another setback in its negotiations.

On June 25, Grant invited Fish to a meeting at the White House. When he arrived, the president was holding the previous day's *New York Tribune* in his hand. He first informed Fish that he would recall Motley, who "represented Mr. Sumner more than he did the Administration," just as soon as he could find the right person to take his place. Grant then read from an article claiming Fish wanted to resign as secretary of state and would like to be appointed minister to Great Britain. Fish replied that neither assertion was true. Relieved, Grant confessed, "Your steadiness and wisdom have kept me from mistakes into which I should have fallen."

ON DECEMBER 5, in Grant's second annual message to Congress, he devoted most of his comments on foreign relations to pressing for a treaty with Santo Domingo. He reminded Congress, "The government of San Domingo has voluntarily sought this annexation." By now he had begun to think of Santo Domingo not simply in economic or military terms, but also as a way both to address the intractable problem of slavery in the Americas and to provide a safe haven for some of the four million blacks experiencing white resistance to their dreams of living as free men and women. The annexation of a free Santo Domingo would "make slavery insupportable in Cuba and Porto Rico, at once, and ultimately so in Brazil." To keep his idea of annexation afloat, Grant suggested forming a commission to travel to the island in the new year.

Grant's plan was supported by no less celebrated a leader than Frederick Douglass, long an opponent to schemes of exporting blacks to Africa for colonization. As he listened to the debates surrounding Santo Domingo, Douglass came to disagree with his friend Sumner, who argued that black migration to the territory would be giving up on rights hard won in the United States through the Civil War. Douglass argued that Santo Domingo could provide a desirable space for those blacks who wished to seek a new beginning in a new space.

. . .

As an abolitionist, Sumner became impatient with anyone who did not share his passionate position against slavery; now he was impatient with anyone who disagreed with him on foreign relations. Immediately after Grant's message, Sumner challenged Grant's assertion that Santo Domingo would one day provide new markets for American goods by demanding the president supply Congress with all the documents in his possession relating to the debates over annexation. For many senators, this was a step too far. Even some of Sumner's closest allies saw his move as disrespectful of the president, and it backfired on him. In a tense Senate, Indiana senator Oliver Morton introduced a motion to allow Grant to appoint a commission to visit the island and explore under what terms annexation might be possible.

Determined not to give in, Sumner rose on December 21 to try to achieve by oratory what he could not by legislation. With the rhetoric of a martyr, he declared that the debate over Santo Domingo paralleled the historic 1854 debate over the Kansas-Nebraska Act, which proposed to extend slavery into new territories and states. Entitling his speech "Naboth's Vineyard," he took his theme from the biblical story of King Ahab, a wealthy monarch who longed for his poorer neighbor's vineyard. In a long, rambling speech, Sumner alluded to confidential information on Santo Domingo that Grant refused to share and to parallels between Grant and pre–Civil War presidents James Buchanan and Franklin Pierce.

Sumner's speech provoked an all-night debate in the Senate. This time his oratory failed.

With righteous indignation, Morton took on Sumner and all who would assault Grant: "One by one these assaults have failed, utterly failed; they have become exposed, and have become contemptible to the people of this country." Sumner's excesses in both historical analogy and histrionic vitriol succeeded only in bouncing back to indict the speaker.

At dawn, tired senators voted 32 to 9 to invite Grant to appoint the commission. Grant named a three-member commission and secretary to travel to Santo Domingo in January. He selected Ben Wade, former Ohio senator; Dr. Samuel Gridley Howe, Massachusetts physician and reformer; and Dr. Andrew D. White, founding president of Cornell University. For secretary he chose Frederick Douglass. By appointing two well-known abolitionists, Wade and Howe, as well as Douglass, the foremost African American reformer, all three close friends of Sumner's, Grant thwarted Sumner's critique that Santo Domingo was a racist enterprise.

. . .

ON THAT SAME day, Fish alerted Grant to a dispatch just arrived from London. John Motley, freshly recalled, wrote a long final report that he called "End of Mission." Indignant, he stated that the real reason for his recall was "the opposition made by an eminent Senator who honors me with his friendship to the ratification of the San Domingo treaty."

Aghast by the report, the usually low-key Fish decided to squash Motley and put in motion a plan to defend Grant and remove Sumner as chairman of the Senate Foreign Relations Committee. Writing in his own hand, he told Motley he was "utterly mistaken" if he thought Sumner's position on Santo Domingo had anything to do with his recall: "Mr. Motley must know, or if he does not know he stands alone in his ignorance of the fact that many Senators opposed the Santo Domingo treaty openly, generously and with as much efficiency" as did Sumner "and have continued to enjoy the undiminished confidence and the friendship of the President."

Before he sent his toughly worded reply, Fish read it to the president. Grant thought the reply too strong but did not object to it being sent. When Fish's dispatch arrived at the U.S. legation in London, secretary Benjamin Moran worried that Motley might bury Fish's response and made sure it was published in the Senate records.

Following custom, a special committee of Republicans met to make committee assignments. By a vote of 3 to 2, the committee recommended that Sumner be removed as chairman of the Committee on Foreign Relations.

Sumner would not go quietly: when the whole caucus met, he protested. On March 9, by a vote of 26 to 21, the Republican caucus sustained the committee's recommendation. He was offered another chairmanship, but he refused.

TWO PRIMARY ISSUES concerned Grant and Fish as negotiations with Great Britain began: first, British admission of liability; second, how to get a treaty through the Senate, given Sumner's opposition.

In February, Grant appointed representatives to a joint high commission to deliberate and settle all outstanding matters: Fish; Robert Schenck, the new minister to Great Britain; former attorney general E. Rockwood Hoar; Oregon senator George H. Williams; and Supreme Court Associate Justice Samuel Nelson, a Democrat and an expert in international law. Taken together, these five embraced the executive, legislative, and judicial branches of U.S. government.

At ten A.M. on Monday, February 27, carriages clattered up to the old Orphan Asylum building. Sir Edward Thornton, secretary of the British delegation, stepped inside with other members of the British contingent: the Earl de Grey and Ripon, president of the Queen's Council; ex-minister Sir Stafford Northcote; Professor Montague Bernard, representative of the English universities; and Sir John A. Macdonald, premier of Canada. Commissioners from both countries promptly got down to work, sitting around a recently cleared library table in the dingy building. The businesslike atmosphere could not hide the feelings of suspicion lingering just beneath the surface of civility.

Fish, confident of Grant's trust, deftly led the American side through thirty-seven meetings of the joint high commission over the course of March and April. Each evening, Grant ambled across Lafayette Square to Fish's home to discuss the day's deliberations. He was eager to arrive at a settlement before Congress adjourned for its summer vacation. He knew the newly elected Congress, scheduled to take their seats in December 1871, would be more Democratic and more Anglophobic.

Finally, on a sunny May 8, 1871, the Treaty of Washington was signed—a settlement on all outstanding disagreements between the United States and Great Britain. Both sides offered concessions. Great Britain declared its remorse "for the escape, under whatever circumstances, of the *Alabama* and other vessels from British ports, for the depredations committed by those vessels." The United States stepped back from earlier enormous "indirect" claims. Wax seals were affixed as each member of the joint high commission signed the treaty.

Grant sent the treaty to the Senate on May 10. On May 24, the Senate approved it by a vote of 50 to 12, and Grant signed it the next day. The treaty provided for an international arbitration tribunal to negotiate specifics such as damage amounts. The arbiters, five representatives from five nations, with former minister to Great Britain Charles Francis Adams, Sr., representing the United States, would meet in Geneva.

The signing of the treaty was a huge accomplishment for Grant and Fish, a milestone that gained even greater significance as the United States and Great Britain began to move forward in their Anglo-American alliance.

IT HAS BEEN suggested Grant's foreign policy was simply Hamilton Fish's foreign policy—that the president was uninvolved. This point of view is shortsighted. To be sure, Grant embarked on a steep learning path in foreign relations in his initial years as president. Unlike many presidents, he

This Thomas Nast cartoon favorably depicts Grant and Fish as they await the results of international arbitration in Geneva, Switzerland.

was willing to admit what he did not know and learn from an astute secretary of state.

During these first two years, Grant found himself engaged in two major efforts in foreign relations—with quite different results. In the case of Santo Domingo, he overreached. Initially keeping his plans to himself and his political circle, he failed to build a public case for annexation. Blocked and stymied, he refused to accept defeat.

What is easily missed is the bright line between Grant's domestic and foreign policies. His passion about Santo Domingo was not only to acquire new territory: He believed a free Santo Domingo would be a beacon in a sea of islands still committed to slavery. Frederick Douglass understood and supported Grant's position.

In the case of Great Britain, diplomacy helped de-escalate post–Civil War strains with the world's leading power. Although the Treaty of Washington was seen at the time as a formal resolution of specific tensions growing out of damages caused by Confederate raiding ships, from the wide-angle lens of history the agreement was clearly a crucial building block in America's relationship with the nation that would become its strongest ally.

Hamilton Fish deserves the great credit bestowed upon him by Grant for his role as secretary of state. What has been missed, however, is the credit Fish gives Grant. In the midst of the messy exchange he had with

Motley just before Christmas 1870, Fish penned an impromptu tribute to his commander in chief. Not one for hyperbole, he wrote:

> No man living is more tolerant of honest and manly differences of opinions,—is more sincere or single in his desire for the public welfare,—is more disinterested or regardless of what concerns himself—is more frank and confiding in his own dealings—is more sensitive of betrayed confidence, or would look with more scorn and more loathing upon one who uses the words and the assurance of friendship to cover a secret and determined purpose of hostility.

If Grant admitted his indebtedness to Fish, the secretary of state expressed his fulsome appreciation for the attributes in Grant that made him an effective president. He would need all these qualities in responding to a wide range of challenges just over the horizon.

CHAPTER 30

Ku Klux Klan

I will not hesitate to exhaust the powers thus vested in the Executive . . .
for the purpose of securing to all citizens of the United States
the peaceful enjoyment of the rights guaranteed to them
by the Constitution and laws.
—ULYSSES S. GRANT, Proclamation, May 3, 1871

A mysterious organization with a strange Greek name, secret rituals, and members dressed in white sheets struck terror across the South in the years immediately after the Civil War. In the name of white supremacy, the Ku Klux Klan beat, whipped, maimed, kidnapped, and hanged thousands of black citizens. Their main aim became voter suppression of newly franchised African Americans, who they knew would vote overwhelmingly Republican in local and state elections. In the 1870 state elections, the Klan's tactics allowed white Democrats to make substantial gains in several southern states.

Although the Ku Klux Klan ultimately symbolized white terrorism in the post–Civil War South, the group did not start out that way. The Klan was organized in 1866 in Pulaski, Tennessee, a market town near the Alabama border, by six young Confederate veterans who wanted to establish a social club. A few college men among them, recalling the Greek-letter fraternities then becoming popular in the South, suggested the group adopt the Greek *kuklos,* meaning "circle" or "band," and then extend it by alliteration to "Ku Klux Klan."

Recognizing the need for someone of stature to lead their burgeoning movement, the Klan elected Tennessee cavalry hero Nathan Bedford Forrest, Grant's old foe, as its first leader, or Grand Wizard. Confederate soldiers, many having a difficult time accepting peace within a devastated South, became eager recruits, and within a short time the original concept had been overtaken by a maelstrom of physical bullying and violence against blacks.

Rather than showing anonymous men in white sheets, this photograph of members of the Ku Klux Klan emphasizes their apparent respectability. One must look closely to see the telltale signs of their violent skulduggery.

In an atmosphere of pervasive racism, many southern whites saw the freedom offered in emancipation as a curse rather than a blessing for previously "happy slaves." Their arguments were self-serving. Violence committed by whites against blacks came to represent "race control." Southern whites were determined to keep blacks from becoming "saucy."

At first the Klan applied economic pressure, threatening black laborers with the loss of employment if they voted for Republicans. As they moved into other southern states, night-riding Klansmen terrorized African Americans in their homes and churches. Other enemies were native whites who had supported the Union and northern missionary teachers setting up schools for blacks—the Klan called them "outside agitators."

IN EARLY 1871, Grant resolved to mount a comprehensive campaign against the Klan. In his first two years in office, sensitive to criticism of military overreach and placing his confidence in the ballot box, he had not moved against the Klan. Now he made the decision to act, even as he knew Congress was retreating from Reconstruction. Some Republicans—once strongly antislavery and supportive of Reconstruction amendments—joined with Democrats in minimizing the stories of Klan violence and argued that any and all solutions should be left to the southern states. Grant believed that their terrorism had moved beyond the control of any one state and became convinced the federal government needed to act.

ON MAY 31, 1870, in an attempt to reinforce the Fourteenth and Fifteenth amendments and thwart state officials who were interfering with the process of voter registration in southern states, Congress passed the Enforcement Act. The legislation stated that "every person despite race, color, or previous condition of servitude must be granted equal opportunity to become qualified to vote." The act further authorized the president to employ the army where necessary to uphold the principles set forth by law. But the threat of federal force, seldom actually deployed, did not tamp down violence against blacks.

On February 28, 1871, only a week before adjournment, the Forty-first Congress passed, and Grant promptly signed, a second Enforcement Act that provided federal officials with guidelines for regulating elections. But neither the first nor the second Enforcement Act dealt with the real problem behind voter suppression: intimidation by the Ku Klux Klan.

At this critical moment, Grant called upon Congress to give him stronger enforcement powers. He argued the federal government provided the only way to protect the constitutional rights recently granted the freed people.

Of all the issues and problems that he confronted—domestic and foreign—none aroused Grant's passion more than the increasing attacks on blacks. With the Forty-first Congress set to retire on March 4, 1871, and the Forty-second Congress not scheduled to convene until December, the president urged something unusual: he asked the new Congress to begin immediately on March 4. Grant wrote Speaker of the House James G. Blaine on March 9, "There is a deplorable state of affairs existing in some portions of the South demanding the immediate attention of Congress."

The Forty-second Congress agreed: in its first few days in session, Massachusetts congressman Ben Butler drafted a tough anti-Klan bill. However, although the bill was passed by the Senate, in the House several Republicans combined with Democrats to thwart its passage. With a combination of frustration and growing self-assurance, Grant pressed for action, watching as one after another group of Klan members was either released by local authorities or acquitted of any wrongdoing in local or state courts.

A new version of the legislation, now called the Ku Klux Klan bill, was put forward and prompted vigorous discussion. More than eighty members of the House participated in the debate, the crux of which became the extent of federal power appropriate to enforce the Fourteenth and Fifteenth amendments. In the Senate, Democratic opponents were joined by Republican senators Carl Schurz and Lyman Trumbull. Schurz called the bill "an encroachment of the national authority upon the legitimate sphere of local self-government."

Republican opposition was a warning sign for Grant. In response, he went up to the Capitol on March 23 to ask Congress to strengthen his executive power in order to protect citizens' civil rights. He told them he was wary of being called a "military despot," but congressional leaders told him an anti-Klan bill could pass only with his leadership.

That same day, Grant wrote Congress: "The power to correct these evils, is beyond the control of the State authorities." He spoke of the dilemma he faced: "That the power of the Executive of the United States, acting within the limits of existing laws, is sufficient for present emergencies, is not clear." Grant "urgently" recommended Congress to pass "such legislation." Wishing to underscore the centrality of this issue, he assured members of Congress, "There is no other subject, on which I would recommend legislation during the present session."

The Forty-second Congress passed a revised Ku Klux Klan Act on April 20. In order to put more teeth into the two previous enforcement acts, this more extensive statute made it a federal offense to "hinder, delay, prevent, or obstruct" anyone "from voting at any election." The act also made it a federal crime to prohibit persons from holding elective offices or serving on juries. Up until the Civil War, citizens turned to state courts to seek relief for their complaints. Now, with the Reconstruction amendments, aggrieved citizens utilizing the new resources of Justice Department lawyers could appeal directly to federal courts. Finally, the Ku Klux Klan Act empowered the president to use military force and suspend the writ of habeas corpus.

The passage of the act provoked vigorous debate about the appropriate role of the federal government in defending civil rights. "These are momentous changes," declared *The Nation*. "They not only increase the power of the central government, but they arm it with jurisdiction over a class of cases of which it has never hitherto had, and never pretended to have, any jurisdiction whatever."

Democrats minimized the violence of the Klan and maximized worries about the expansion of the authority of the federal government. The Jackson, Mississippi, *Clarion* claimed the object of the "unconstitutional and hideously despotic" act was "to supersede State authority with the government of the bayonet and of martial law." The Raleigh, North Carolina, *Sentinel* aimed its arrows straight at Grant, claiming that the purpose of the act was to allow Grant "to declare the State in insurrection and, by military terror, carry the [1872] election."

Fully aware of the firestorm, Grant issued an emphatic proclamation on May 3, pledging, "I will not hesitate to exhaust the powers thus vested in the Executive . . . for the purpose of securing to all citizens of the United States the peaceful enjoyment of the rights guaranteed to them by the Constitution and laws." Grant's proclamation, a response to the white-against-black violence, was issued by a president ready to use the powers "vested" in his presidential office. The fact that members of his own Republican Party challenged his right to use those powers did not dissuade him. In exercising these powers, he believed the federal government needed to assume a more central role in protecting the constitutional rights of all of its citizens.

IN RAMPING UP his response to racial violence in the South, Grant began to rethink his larger governing strategy. He wrote to Elihu Washburne in Paris, unburdening himself: "A great many professedly staunch republicans acted very much as if they wanted to outdo the democracy [Democratic Party] in breaking up the republican party." Grant listed them: "Sumner and Schurz have acted worse than any other two men, and not far behind them is Ferry of Conn. and Tipton of Neb. John Logan is paving the way to be just as bad as he knows how to be."

In order to achieve his goals, Grant determined to assume the leadership of the Republican Party, a posture he had avoided when he'd allowed his name to be put forward as the Republican candidate for president in 1868. Although he had originally hoped not to govern as a strongly partisan Republican, he had come to realize that the Republican Party, if mostly united in its opposition to the presidential policies of Andrew Johnson, was now splitting into factions in many states. He worried most that a growing number of Republican leaders were buying into the retreatist attitudes of their northern constituents, rather than standing up to protect African Americans in the South.

To put his new governing strategy into motion, Grant reached out to younger leaders. Chief among them was New York senator Roscoe Conkling. Born in Albany in 1829, the son of a U.S. congressman and federal judge, Conkling began to study law at seventeen and made campaign speeches for Whig presidential candidate Zachary Taylor at nineteen. He was admitted to the bar in 1850 and settled in Utica, where he was elected mayor in 1858. Elected to the House of Representatives in 1859, and to the Senate in 1867, Conkling represented a new, more professional brand of politician.

Conkling was a self-confident, colorful man. Handsome, at six feet three inches tall he stood out in a crowd with his flaxen-blond hair and pointed beard. He preferred bright ties and light-colored trousers under his black cutaway coat, a style of dress that became part of his public persona. He was committed to physical conditioning, especially boxing, which some said conveyed his readiness to engage in political combat at any moment.

And that's exactly what he did on December 21 after listening to Sumner's speech on Santo Domingo. Like a pugilist, the confident senator rose to defend the president. He was not eager to debate the merits of sending a commission to Santo Domingo; rather, he took umbrage at Sumner's personal attack upon Grant: "During this debate I have held my peace till now. I should be silent still but for the violence done this day to justice and to fairness, but for the wrong heaped upon one, foremost, not in the easy greatness of things written and said, but in the arduous greatness of things done."

New York senator Roscoe Conkling, a new breed of professional politician, was one of a cadre of younger congressional leaders who rallied to Grant's side, especially in their support of the defense of the rights of African Americans.

Not everyone in Washington adored Conkling, but all took him seriously. If he had earned a reputation as an orator, packing the galleries (especially the ladies' gallery), his speaking arsenal included goading, sarcasm, and ridicule. Conkling was a larger-than-life personality, a machine politician who doled out patronage and collected plenty of enemies along the way. Chauncey Depew, general counsel to the New York Central and Hudson River Railroad, claimed "his intolerable egotism deprived him of vision necessary for supreme leadership."

But Hamilton Fish, no fan of egotism—which had been a chief cause of the breakup of his friendship with Charles Sumner—welcomed Conkling's advocacy of Grant. As a fellow New Yorker, he appreciated the growing power of this first-term senator who was already the leader of the Republican Party in the most populous state in the nation. Fish's practical wisdom predicted that Conkling's counsel to Grant "would be unselfish and shrewd," even if "decidedly partisan."

IN ORDER TO attack the Ku Klux Klan, Grant reached out to other younger leaders. He appreciated receiving the legal advice of Attorney General E. Rockwood Hoar, but the veteran lawyer was reluctant to prosecute cases of racial violence in the South.

Up until Grant, the attorney general had functioned as the president's private lawyer, with the government hiring other lawyers to pursue cases in court. But with the establishment of the Department of Justice in 1870, the attorney general's authority would increase dramatically. When Grant was criticized for having two Massachusetts men in his cabinet—

Hoar and Secretary of the Treasury George Boutwell—he decided to turn the criticism to his advantage. He asked Hoar to step down in order to appoint Amos T. Akerman, a Republican from Georgia.

Born in 1821 in New Hampshire, a Phi Beta Kappa graduate of Dartmouth College, Akerman moved to North Carolina in 1842 to earn his living as a teacher at a boys' academy. In this setting, calling upon his deep-rooted Presbyterian ethical heritage, he taught his students a broader interpretation of the Ten Commandments to encourage fidelity to the law. Four years later he moved to Savannah, Georgia, to tutor the children of Judge John M. Berrien, Andrew Jackson's attorney general. Here Akerman "read the law" and passed the bar in 1850.

After the war, Akerman decided to "let Confederate ideas rule us no longer." As a despised scalawag, he helped organize the Republican Party in Georgia. When blacks elected under the new Georgia constitution were expelled from the state legislature in 1868, he argued passionately for their readmission.

Akerman believed adopting the Reconstruction amendments meant the government was now to be "more national in theory," yet he heard, "even among Republicans, a hesitation to exercise the powers to redress wrongs in the states." Distressed, Akerman became convinced that "unless the people become used to the exercise of these powers now, while the national spirit is still warm with the glow of the late war . . . the 'state rights' spirit may grow troublesome again."

Akerman, alone among Grant's cabinet officers to have personally received threats from the Ku Klux Klan, determined to enforce the amendments. Grant enlisted Akerman, his only cabinet officer to come from the states of the Confederacy, to be his ally in protecting the rights of blacks in the South. Akerman had become convinced that clamping down on the Klan demanded "extraordinary means," declaring that the Klan and other white terrorist organizations "amount to war, and cannot be effectually crushed on any other theory."

Agreeing, Grant appointed another southern Republican, thirty-eight-year-old Benjamin H. Bristow, to be the nation's first solicitor general. Bristow had the courage to be a "Kentucky bluejay"—an active Unionist in a dominant Confederate community in his home state. When Congress passed the Civil Rights Act in April 1866, as the U.S. attorney for Kentucky Bristow made his home state a test case by prosecuting those who committed crimes against blacks. Grant charged Bristow as solicitor general to supervise and conduct government lawsuits through the new Department of Justice.

. . .

IN AUGUST 1871, Grant received an urgent appeal from Oscar Dunn, a former slave and now Louisiana's first black lieutenant governor: "We cannot, in the absence of your interposition, exercise our political privileges, except at personal peril, or else by using violence in self-protection." Grant referred Dunn's appeal to Akerman, ordering his attorney general "to secure the protection to free speech and free action" in Louisiana.

In the same month, by virtue of federal military protection in North Carolina, blacks joined with white Republicans to vote down a conservative Democratic attempt to rewrite the state constitution that would have limited black civil rights. After their success, Akerman wrote Butler, author of the Ku Klux Klan Act, commending him on the attainment of a "fair election in that State with a most wholesome result."

The situation in South Carolina especially worried Grant. Blacks had voted for Republicans in large numbers in 1870, and the Klan was determined to suppress their future voting.

On August 31, Grant cut short his vacation at Long Branch to return to Washington and personally take charge of the fight against the Klan. His cabinet advised caution, warning that northern public opinion would no longer support aggressive action in the South. Grant conferred with Pennsylvania senator John Scott, who informed him of his investigations of South Carolina's York and Spartanburg counties: "outrages" had been committed against "two hundred and twenty seven citizens . . . two of whom had been murdered."

In early October, setting aside his cabinet's advice, Grant prepared to send troops into South Carolina under the military provision of the Ku Klux Klan Act. He issued a strongly worded proclamation: "Whereas unlawful combinations and conspiracies have long existed" in South Carolina "for the purpose of depriving certain portions and classes of the people of that State of the rights, privileges, immunities, and protection named in the Constitution," Grant commanded all such offenders "to retire peaceably to their homes within five days."

On October 17, he issued a second proclamation. Noting that the Klan had "not dispersed and retired peaceably to their respective homes," he ordered the writ of habeas corpus be suspended. More than one hundred arrests began to be made on October 19, supervised by Akerman, who had traveled to the state.

Having lived in the South for nearly thirty years, Akerman was overcome by the depth of white violence against blacks: "I feel greatly saddened by this business. It has revealed a perversion of moral sentiment among the Southern whites which bodes ill to that part of the country for this generation."

GRANT'S AGGRESSIVE CAMPAIGN against the Ku Klux Klan alienated many of his former Republican allies. At the 1870 Missouri Republican state convention in Jefferson City, Senator Carl Schurz bolted to preside over an alternate convention. Calling themselves "Liberal Republicans," they nominated B. Gratz Brown for governor. Promising to do away with a test oath that barred thousands of ex-Confederates from voting, Brown ended up winning a decisive victory against Governor Joseph McClurg—a Radical Republican. Schurz hastened to assure Grant that what happened in Missouri was a purely local affair.

Schurz, tall and slender, with long curly hair and sparkling eyes enclosed by glasses that often slipped down his nose, was a man on the move. As an immigrant who had fled the failed revolution in the German states in 1848–1849, he had mobilized the large German population in the Midwest to support Lincoln for president. Lincoln appointed Schurz minister to Spain, but he returned in 1862 to lead German soldiers in the Union army. During the Johnson administration, Grant had appreciated Schurz's fact-finding mission to the South. When he was invited to deliver the keynote address at the 1868 national Republican convention, Schurz had endorsed Grant.

Schurz was elected to the Senate in 1868, and colleagues learned quickly that "the German Senator" was a man to be reckoned with. An independent operator, he allied himself with those he called the "best men," regardless of party affiliation. Although Schurz was strongly anti-slavery during the Civil War, and supported the Fourteenth and Fifteenth amendments, by 1870 he had become part of a "liberal" circle believing civil service reform, hard money, and low tariffs should replace civil rights as Republican Party priorities.

The death of Maine senator William Fessenden opened up a vacancy on the Senate Foreign Relations Committee, which Schurz filled. He joined Sumner in opposing the annexation of Santo Domingo. Sitting directly behind his fellow committeeman, he handed Sumner materials during his speech denouncing Grant in December 1870. Grant now saw Schurz as Sumner's alter ego on the committee.

In August 1871, Schurz formally declared his opposition to Grant's reelection in a speech in Nashville.

. . .

Midway through Grant's first term, German immigrant Carl Schurz, senator from Missouri, led a revolt of "Liberal Republicans" against the president.

GRANT DID NOT respond publicly to the Liberal Republican defection from the party. He did vent his feelings about Schurz in a letter to Massachusetts senator Henry Wilson: "He is an ungrateful man, a disorganize[r] by nature and one who can render much greater service to the party he does not belong to [Democrats] than the one he pretends to have attachment for."

After looking over his letter to Wilson, uncharacteristic in its denunciation, Gant decided not to send it. The letter was found in his papers after his death.

IN JANUARY 1872, the Republican National Committee selected Philadelphia to be the site of its convention on June 5. In its announcement, the committee declared that the promises of President Grant and the 1868 convention had been achieved: all the seceded states of the South had been reinstated, equal suffrage was being put in place, the debt had been reduced, and foreign relations were being restored. The *National Republican* exulted, "There has never been a President in the White House who has been more uniformly fair to all races and classes of men." Yes, the national committee admitted mistakes had been made, but those mistakes had been corrected. Grant's policies had been "eminently judicious and patriotic. The Republican Party demands his renomination because he has been its truest and best servant and minister."

With the announcement of the convention site, people began to debate the balance sheet of Grant's accomplishments to decide if he deserved a second term. *The Times* of London had earlier weighed in with its opinion: "In favor of this course will be the respect he has won, not only from the Republicans, but from moderate men of all parties, by his honest and conscientious discharge of duty, and the knowledge of the electors that they have in him a tried man fit for any emergency of the time." *The Times* applauded "the firmness and moderation with which order has been restored, the economical skill with which the debt has been reduced, and the good will with which international controversies have been brought to a close."

If some were disappointed in Grant's initial cabinet appointments, after three years several cabinet officers received strong commendations. It was widely agreed that Secretary of State Hamilton Fish brought stature and wisdom to the position. Treasury Secretary George Boutwell had worked effectively with Grant to combat the Black Friday scare in September 1869. Postmaster General John Creswell had modernized the postal system and reduced costs at the same time. He had introduced numerous reforms, including expanding service to the rapidly expanding West; instituting fair competition on carriage routes for mail transportation, a system previously riddled with bribery; and abolishing the franking system—all endorsed by Grant.

In return, Grant received commendation from his cabinet members. Boutwell especially appreciated the way Grant conducted cabinet meetings: "He expressed his opinions with the greatest freedom, and, upon discussion, he often yielded to the suggestions or arguments of others. He was so great that it was not a humiliation to acknowledge a change in opinion, or to admit an error in policy or purpose." Creswell empathized with what he believed were unfair criticisms aimed at Grant. In October 1871, he wrote, "Grant is so good and pure that all he needs for his perfect vindication is simply that the people know him and his works. The more I see of him the more devotedly do I admire and love him."

BUT THE COUNTRY wasn't universally enamored with Grant. Less than three weeks after the Republican National Committee announced its convention date, Schurz invited like-minded Liberal Republicans to meet in their own national convention in Cincinnati on May 1. Schurz wanted to steal a march by meeting one month before the regular Republicans gathered in Philadelphia.

It is hard for generations accustomed to a two-party system to appreciate that political parties in the nineteenth century seemed to come and go without any claim to permanence. These new parties tended to grow from a particular reform impulse. In the 1840s, the Free Soil movement bloomed as a one-issue party opposed to extending slavery in the West. The Know-Nothings, promising to purify American politics by limiting the influence of immigrants, flourished briefly in the 1850s. The antislavery impulse helped bring together Free Soilers, Whigs, and even some Democrats to give birth to the Republican Party in the 1850s. Liberal Republicans were convinced they could be a new political party relevant to the reform priorities of the 1870s.

The term *liberalism* changed definition over the course of the nineteenth century and suggested a set of values quite different from what people think of as liberalism in the twenty-first century. Liberal Republicans in 1872 embraced the timeless values of individual liberty, limited government, and free trade, while at the same time focusing on what they believed were the more timely imperatives of civil service reform and general amnesty for Confederates.

Civil Service reform in particular caught fire like a religious revival. Liberal Republicans were upset that Grant did not mention it in his first annual message to Congress in December 1869. They argued that men who had achieved their positions through patronage should be replaced by men of merit. Wire-pullers should be overthrown by "civil service commissions."

Grant did announce his intention to pursue "a reform in the civil service of the country" in his 1870 annual message to Congress: "The present system does not secure the best men, and often not even fit men, for public place." Two cabinet officers, Secretary of the Treasury Boutwell and Secretary of the Interior Cox, put in place the kinds of examinations advocated by the civil service reformers. But for the Liberal Republicans, it was too little too late. Critics attacked Grant because in his efforts to protect the Indians and prosecute the Ku Klux Klan, some of his chief supporters—Roscoe Conkling, Oliver Morton, and Zachariah Chandler in the Senate and Ben Butler in the House—were spoilsmen in their home states.

Stung by criticism that he appointed his friends to plum positions, Grant turned his exasperation into humor in a letter to Galena friend J. Russell Jones, whom he had appointed minister to Belgium: "Sumner, Schutz [*sic*], Dana and all your admirers think it preposterous in me to give appointments to persons who I ever knew and particularly to those who feel any personal friendship for me. If I am guided by this advice your decapitation is sure."

. . .

LIBERAL REPUBLICANS HEADED for Cincinnati at the end of April. The River City seemed a fitting site for their convention—sitting astride the Ohio River at the border of north and south—for much of their rhetoric sought to gain supporters in the South by softening traditional Republican views on Reconstruction. *The Nation,* which by 1871 had become a critic of Grant, captured the mood of Liberal Republicans, who had become disappointed in what they saw as dishonesty in southern Republican governments and their dependence on uneducated blacks to stay in power: "Reconstruction and slavery we have done with; for administration and revenue reform we are eager."

Carl Schurz presided as chairman over a convention of more than seven hundred delegates, cheered on by thousands of spectators. After six tumultuous ballots, the convention nominated Horace Greeley, editor of the *New York Tribune,* as their presidential candidate. Greeley, a man with a large ego in a slender body, startled people who met him for the first time. He wore a signature white duster, big boots, a broad battered hat, and a cravat that was always awry, and he carried a faded blue cotton umbrella. "Uncle Horace" enjoyed his reputation as the most influential editor in America.

But Greeley's nomination was greeted with gloom by the leaders—the wire-pullers—of the Liberal Republicans. Schurz worried that the quixotic Greeley's nomination meant disaster for Liberal Republicans. No one summed up Greeley's strength and weakness better than Grant, who wrote a friend, "He is a genius without common sense."

ON JUNE 5, Republicans gathered in an upbeat mood in Philadelphia. Flags bedecked the entire facade of the Academy of Music. Inside, portraits of the holy trinity—Washington, Lincoln, and Grant—greeted arriving delegates. This convention would usher in the instant communication of modern political conventions as telegraph operators tapped out minute-by-minute proceedings.

In writing their platform, Republicans shrewdly stole much of the thunder from Liberal Republicans. They extended amnesty, lowered tariffs, and embraced civil service reform.

But not everything sounded the same. Republicans praised Grant's Indian Peace Policy, an issue surrounding which church reformers would not forget the Liberal Republicans' silence. Some—not all—praised Grant's vigorous prosecution of the Ku Klux Klan.

The convention unanimously nominated Grant on the second day.

The energy usually expended on nominations of numerous candidates instead erupted in celebration: "Hats, caps, hands, and handkerchiefs waved to and fro in a surging mass as three times three [cheers] shook the dome from the thousands of voices." Reporters observed there was not a dry eye in the convention hall.

For vice president, Grant turned away from "Smiler" Colfax. In the past year, Colfax had made statements suggesting Republicans needed to retrench from earlier Reconstruction commitments. In his place, with Grant's blessing, the convention nominated Massachusetts senator and Radical Republican Henry Wilson on the first ballot. Wilson's rags-to-riches story made him a fitting running mate for Grant: an impoverished youth and young adulthood in New Hampshire, indentured servitude, apprenticeship to a shoemaker in Natick, Massachusetts, and a native business acumen that led to success both at his trade and in the political arena. Together, Grant and Wilson appealed to workingmen as "the Galena Tanner" and "the Natick Cobbler."

CARL SCHURZ, ARCHITECT of the new third party, hoped the Liberal Republican nominee would also become the Democratic nominee. He negotiated with August Belmont, like Schurz a native of Germany and now a successful New York banker and national chairman of the Democratic Party, to postpone the Democratic convention until after the Liberal Republican and Republican conventions.

The Democrats met in Baltimore at Ford's Grand Opera House on July 9 and 10. Still struggling to regain traction after being accused of treason during the Civil War, Democrats had announced a "New Departure" in 1870, wherein they accepted the Thirteenth, Fourteenth, and Fifteenth amendments. Yet the prospect of nominating Greeley exposed ideological divisions within their party once more. And Greeley himself was full of contradictions: He had supplied 25 percent of the bond to free Jefferson Davis. A onetime abolitionist, he was critical of Grant's efforts to protect African Americans. "They are an easy, worthless race," he grumbled, "taking no thought for the morrow." Still, the Democrats, many of them holding their noses, nominated him—the only time in American history that one of the two major parties nominated a candidate from a third party.

The Democratic *Savannah Morning News* denounced the acceptance of Greeley as "political suicide." The *New York Herald,* sizing up the spectacle of the Democrats about to nominate Greeley, commented, "It will mark the most extraordinary party transformation in our political history. In fusing the democratic and Cincinnati party, the former, as it were, disappears."

EVERY PRESIDENTIAL CAMPAIGN turns on what the electorate believes to be the most compelling narrative about the problems facing the nation. Horace Greeley and the Liberal Republicans tried to run on a narrative arguing that Grant was either too passive—he did not take charge—or too active—he was a military tyrant centralizing a big government. Greeley, a poor campaigner, found himself forced to defend his many previous editorials over the years. As for the present, his charges against Grant and his first term did not have sticking power.

"The Galena Tanner" and "the Natick Cobbler" ran on a counternarrative that civil service and other reforms, as important as they might be, should not cause a retreat from the reason the Civil War was fought. William Lloyd Garrison, aging abolitionist leader, complained that the new Liberal Republicans were "most liberal toward all that has been traitorous" and "most illiberal toward all that is eminently loyal." Grant followed his 1868 campaign strategy and let his record and his friends speak for him.

But in private he confessed his feelings, confiding in Washburne, "The Greeleyites will be as liberal in their offers to coopt regular Republicans as Satan was to our Savior, and with as little ability to pay."

Democrats tried to revive the slander of Grant's alleged drunkenness, but that did not stick either. In October, Fish wrote an unequivocal letter to a southern correspondent:

> I have known General Grant very intimately since the close of the war. I have been much with him at all hours of the day and night—have traveled with him days and nights together—have been with him on social and festive occasions as well as hourly intercourse of close official relations. I have never seen him in the most remote degree under any excitement from wine or drink of any kind.

He told his inquirer, "The very close personal association which I have had with him for many years justifies me in saying that the imputation of drunkenness is utterly and wantonly false."

IN THE 1872 election, Grant once again courted the black vote in the South. Republicans campaigning for Grant resorted to the tried-and-true tactic of waving the bloody shirt in order to rekindle memories of the cost of Union lives in the Civil War. Congressman Ben Butler, now a Grant enthusiast, roared, "Go vote to burn school houses, desecrate churches and violate women, or vote for Horace Greeley, which means the same thing."

Frederick Douglass, appreciative of Grant's attacks on the Ku Klux Klan, energetically promoted his reelection with African Americans. As early as the summer of 1871, he declared: "In deciding the question as to who should receive the nomination in 1872 the whole ground should be calmly and carefully surveyed." As for Douglass, "To me, it does not seem likely that the Republican party will find a candidate of equal strength with General Grant."

A YEAR LATER, after the Liberal Republican convention at Cincinnati, Douglass went against his longtime friend Charles Sumner and the Liberal Republicans in putting his prestige solidly behind Grant. In an address in Boston in September, he explained why he could not vote for Greeley, who he charged was continually changing his mind about African Americans and freedom. In contrast, Douglass declared, "I know Grant well." He voiced a theme he had been sounding for months: "At all times he gave every aid to the development of the industry and of the improvement of the colored race."

Grant saw his social justice initiatives paying off in votes. Abolitionists, cheering his campaign against the Ku Klux Klan, rallied to his side; white teachers who went south in the antislavery vanguard worked steadfastly for a Grant victory. Reformers of the Indian question lined up solidly behind his reelection.

African American leader Frederick Douglass approved of Grant's efforts on behalf of African Americans and campaigned for his reelection in 1872.

Less than two months before the presidential election, news finally arrived from the Geneva-based international arbitration tribunal established by the Treaty of Washington to settle the *Alabama* Claims. On September 14, after three months of negotiations, in a dramatic announcement in the hall of the Hotel de Ville, the commission ordered Great Britain to pay the United States compensation of $15.5 million. Grant expressed his pleasure, not simply for the specific result, but for the larger cause of international arbitration as the way to solve disputes between nations.

Grant won an overwhelming reelection with 56 percent of the vote—a larger margin than his election in 1868 and the highest winning percentage of any president between Andrew Jackson in 1828 and Theodore Roosevelt in 1904. He won thirty-one of thirty-seven states and 286 electoral votes to 66 for Greeley. The Fifteenth Amendment, ratified in February 1870, granted African American men the right to vote, and they voted overwhelmingly for the president who had stood up for their rights. Despite the split with Liberal Republicans, Grant won every northern state and eight of eleven states of the old Confederacy. The president had long coattails. Republicans recouped their two-thirds majority in the House of Representatives, moving from a small majority of 141 to 102 in 1870 to a huge advantage of 203 to 89 in 1872.

BY THE END of 1872, Grant marshaled the full legal and military authority of the federal government and turned back the advance of the Ku Klux Klan in the South again. In 1871 alone, federal grand juries brought three thousand indictments. Grant faced charges that he was acting like a tyrant, but he determined to protect the rights of freedmen now guaranteed by the Reconstruction constitutional amendments. And if he would not be intimidated by the Klan, he would also not be turned back by Democrats who joined with Liberal Republicans in claiming states' rights as their reason for not acting.

An irony in this whole episode: While many northern members of Grant's own Republican Party turned their backs on the South, the president chose two courageous young men from the South to be his legal and prosecutorial arms. The man in charge of enforcement, Attorney General Amos Akerman, offered his acknowledgments to Grant: no one was "stronger" than Grant in implementing the enforcement laws.

Solicitor General Benjamin Bristow wrote his cousin three weeks after the election, "I know him [Grant] to be a good man, motivated by patriotic desire and unselfish devotion to the interests of the whole country. Perhaps no man was ever more malignantly and unjustifiably assailed in his public and private character than he has been, but these things excite no personal hostility on his part toward any section." As for his native South, Bristow insisted, "I *know* that he has never entertained any other than the kindliest and most generous feelings towards the Southern people." Sadly, "If they have not had full participation in all the benefits of Government and Administration, it has been because of their actual or supposed hostility to the new order of things."

In the end, the election of 1872 was not only a contest for president, but a battle for the soul of the Republican Party—the party of Lincoln—with deep implications for the future. For Liberal Republicans, their fears about the rise of a powerful central government caused them to retreat from their earlier support for African American civil rights. But Grant remained adamant that the central government must have the power to act when state governments and local courts refused to do their job.

SEVERAL WEEKS AFTER his reelection, Grant welcomed a delegation of African American leaders from Philadelphia to the White House. They came to thank him, declaring he was "the first President of the United States elected by the whole people." They wanted him to know that for them he represented "the practical embodiment of our republican theories."

Grant responded, "In your desire to obtain all the rights of citizens I fully sympathize." He spelled out what he meant: "A ticket on a railroad or other conveyance should entitle you to all that it does other men." In that spirit he told them, "I wish that every voter of the United States should stand in all respects alike. It must come."

CHAPTER 31

The Gilded Age

Q. What is the chief end of man?
A. To get rich.
Q. In what way?
A. Dishonestly if we can; honestly if we must.
Q. Who is God, the one only and true?
A. Money is God. Gold and greenbacks and stocks.

—Mark Twain, "Revised Catechism," 1871

Mark Twain used his parody of the initial questions of the Presbyterian Westminster Shorter Catechism to attack the worship of money and its attendant corrupting influence. Raised a Presbyterian, if now often poking fun of religion, Twain knew many in his audience would have known the original first Q and A.

Q. What is the chief end of man?
A. Man's chief end is to glorify God, and to enjoy him forever.

One of Twain's literary gifts was to take a familiar coin of the realm and infuse it with his own satirical meaning.

Two years later, Twain coined the term *Gilded Age* in his 1873 political novel, *The Gilded Age: A Tale of To-day*. In this humorous satire, he held up for ridicule unethical behavior producing ill-gotten gains in an increasingly acquisitive age. He employed the metaphor of the thin gold gilt used in the beautification of the homes of superrich industrialists and financiers to describe the cover-up of the proliferating problems of post–Civil War America. Peopled by barely disguised political leaders, *The Gilded Age* deftly displayed the massive wealth that soon corrupted the halls of government.

Grant had met Twain only once—at a reception in Washington in 1866—but their lives were destined to intersect in crucial ways in coming years. "The Gilded Age" would become the chief image defining a whole era of scandals. In a retelling of these years, Grant's second term often became an example in the story. In actuality Grant remained personally untarnished, but his efficacy in stopping the spreading blight of corruption has been debated.

IN THE FOUR months between his reelection and second inauguration, the glow of Grant's victory began to dim. In the final months of the campaign, Charles Dana's *New York Sun* had begun reporting on a secretive corporation, Crédit Mobilier of America, calling it "the most damaging exhibition of official and private villainy and corruption." The *Sun* charged that it had received $72 million in contracts to construct the Union Pacific Railroad—valued at $53 million.

On December 12, 1872, Congress began probing Crédit Mobilier. The investigation would uncover that the corporation allowed insiders to make enormous sums of money—in one case 348 percent—by charging the federal government inflated fees. Although this chicanery began during the Johnson administration, the charges of corruption came into the light of public scrutiny during the Grant administration.

Throughout the month of January 1873, spectators flocked to hear testimony from the congressional recipients of the scandal's largesse. The testimony, offered in technical financial language, confused as much as it clarified.

Thomas Nast's Crédit Mobilier cartoon portrays disgraced politicians in front of the U.S. Capitol.

The House presented the names of nine members of Congress for investigation, including Vice President Schuyler Colfax; Senators George Boutwell, Roscoe Conkling, and John Logan; and Massachusetts senator Henry Wilson, the vice president–elect. Many of these politicians were close to Grant. Some said too close.

On March 3, one day before Grant's second inauguration, the public learned of a different kind of congressional mischief. The lame duck session of the Forty-second Congress had voted the president a 100 percent pay raise—from $25,000 to $50,000—increased salaries for Supreme Court justices, and approved hefty increases for themselves. The salary increase for the president seemed fitting because he had to pay expenses for running the White House from his personal funds. Salaries for members of Congress had not been raised for twenty years. But when the public learned Congress made raises for themselves retroactive to the beginning of the term, they voiced outrage at this clandestine greed. The press dubbed the vote "the Salary Grab Act." When the new Forty-third Congress convened, it maintained the salary increases for the president and Supreme Court justices but repealed the raises for Congress.

ON MARCH 4, 1873, Grant presented himself for a second term; the oath was administered by the gravely ill chief justice Salmon P. Chase. No one could remember a colder day for an inauguration. A blustery wind blew from the southwest, plunging the chill factor to below zero. Flags were ripped from their standards. Bands played discordant notes or none at all.

Second inaugural addresses are often disappointing, invariably bogged down in self-congratulation—both of the candidate and of the nation—instead of offering a realistic assessment of the problems to be faced in a second term. Abraham Lincoln's second inaugural address stands out as the exception, as did Grant's. It did not hide from problems.

Grant used his second inaugural to reiterate what he considered the chief problems of the day: not civil service reform but freedom and fairness for all Americans. He emphasized the benefits of citizenship for freed African American slaves. "Yet he is not possessed of the civil rights which citizenship should carry with it," he declared. "This is wrong and should be corrected." He conceded that the president carried limited power in this domain, but Grant intended to step up to the task: "To this correction I stand committed so far as executive influence can avail."

Nor did he back off the Indian question: "The wrong already inflicted upon him should be taken into account, and the balance placed to his credit." He wanted his audience to take "the moral view of the question." Grant reasoned, "Cannot the Indian be made a useful and productive member of society by proper teaching and treatment?"

Every president in every inaugural address asks himself: What time is it? Although Grant concluded his address with a call for conciliation—"My efforts in the future will be directed to the restoration of good feeling between the different sections of our common country"—the overarching tone of the address was of a leader who believed the times called for pressing forward for a more inclusive and equal society.

IN THE SUMMER of 1873, after eight years of post–Civil War business boom, signs of financial instability began to surface. But financial and political leaders were not paying attention: America had not suffered a severe financial depression since 1837.

The Gilded Age engendered a speculative spirit. The boom in railroad construction racing west from the Mississippi River became the leading edge of this exuberance. Gigantic industries in oil, iron, and steel buttressed this boom. Manufacturing prospered. Extravagance ruled. Few noticed the financial clouds appearing in the skies in 1873.

In September, everything changed—quickly. Railroad industrialists had expended huge amounts of capital up front on ventures yielding little direct returns for passenger travel in thinly populated areas out west. Banks, caught up in speculation, lent money carelessly against insufficient collateral.

Grant suddenly faced a whole set of economic problems no one had predicted. On September 17, he arrived at Ogontz, the estate outside Philadelphia owned by investment banker Jay Cooke. Grant had placed fifteen-year-old Jesse at nearby Cheltenham Academy at Cooke's suggestion. Cooke, who had helped finance the Union war effort, had recently offered strong financial backing for Grant's reelection, and his current pet project was building a second transcontinental railroad: the Northern Pacific. Chartered by Congress in 1864, the Northern Pacific was scheduled to connect the Great Lakes of the old Northwest with the Puget Sound of the new Northwest. The astounding cost of building miles of track across high mountains and into a massive wilderness had been radically underestimated.

Early on the morning of September 18, frantic messages dashed across Cooke's private telegraph. After breakfast with the president, Cooke hurried to his Third Street office. He discovered his company had weighed itself down with collateral of stocks and bonds from the Northern Pacific, Lake Superior and Mississippi, Oregon Steam Navigation, and other railroads—suddenly all nearly worthless. His New York and Washington offices reported similar troubles. Cooke closed the Third Street doors at eleven A.M.; the doors in Washington shut at twelve fifteen P.M. Cooke had continued to make loans to railroads and underwrite first-mortgage bonds, but when the markets suddenly dried up, he was caught with a sudden loss of liquidity and his personal fortune was wiped out.

Panic! In the twenty-first century, economists would employ the less emotional words *recession* and *depression,* but panic more accurately described the hysteria that suddenly erupted. The collapse of economic markets threatened the destruction of the whole social fabric of society. "A financial thunderbolt," shouted the *New York Tribune.* "Like a thunderclap in a clear sky," echoed the *Philadelphia Press.* The news of Cooke's collapse raced up and down Wall Street. Western Union lost ten points in ten minutes. The dramatic downfall of the leading banking house, considered too big to fail, sapped the confidence of others that soon followed suit.

It took a while for Americans to realize that the Panic of 1873 was not a distinctive phenomenon occurring in the United States alone, but that the markets of the United States were now linked to world markets. From the United Kingdom to Germany to Russia, even to faraway South Africa and Australia, costly wars, overextended credit, and unwarranted construction of railroads both preceded and accompanied the American homegrown economic turmoil.

Grant rushed to New York on September 20. The next morning, at the Fifth Avenue Hotel, he and his new secretary of the Treasury, William A. Richardson, held a series of meetings with anxious bankers, brokers, merchants, and railroad men. With financial leaders badly injured, they demanded Grant do something, but what he should and could do would became the subject of acrimonious debate.

The president had to face the crisis without his trusted secretary of the Treasury George Boutwell, who had been so crucial during the gold panic of 1869. When Henry Wilson vacated his Senate seat to become vice president, the Massachusetts legislature had elected Boutwell to succeed him. Grant, pressured to appoint a high-profile successor to Boutwell, instead selected William Richardson, Boutwell's assistant. In appointing the little-known Richardson, Grant opted for continuity, declaring that "no departure" would be made from Boutwell's successful financial stewardship. The press as well as many business leaders questioned Grant's decision.

Richardson had earned both a bachelor's degree from Harvard University and an LLB from Harvard Law School, where his classmates called him "modest" and "persistent," and he had compiled a steady record as a lawyer and probate judge in Massachusetts. But critics pointed back to October 1872, when in Boutwell's absence Richardson had decided to inject $5 million of the $44 million reserve of greenbacks into the markets to help alleviate pressure. His initiative was similar to the "open market operations" undertaken routinely by the Federal Reserve today to implement monetary policy, but it was an unusual practice in that day. Detractors charged that Richardson's initiative smacked of partisan politics aimed at putting money in the hands of voters Republicans hoped to attract in state elections in the West.

During the New York meetings, Grant exhibited a composure rooted in his own growing self-confidence. He brought informed financial convictions but also listened to competing economic interests. Without a central bank, and four decades before the creation of the Federal Reserve, Grant lacked the economic tools of later presidents. Also, enthralled with the myth that markets regulated themselves, many financial leaders were wary of any government interference.

In the days that followed, Grant was buffeted by soft- and hard-money advocates. Soft-money promoters, concerned about the problem of widespread bankruptcies and indebtedness, wanted to expand the money supply, which meant reissuing greenbacks even if it resulted in inflation. Hard-money proponents, often bankers, invoked the Civil War's lesson on the depreciation of soft currency to justify the opposite position: pay down the debt and continue to contract the money supply. Whereas brokers pleaded to release the greenback reserves to restore some liquidity in the markets, bankers argued against flooding the markets with irredeemable money.

Grant, from the day he bought his account book as a first-year student at West Point to his service as quartermaster in the Mexican War, appreciated the value of not spending more than one's resources. Yet as a man of the West and a farmer, he understood the plight of struggling western farmers who begged him to release greenbacks into the economy. Farmers argued that making money scarcer only drove up its worth and thus its purchasing power for agricultural communities.

When he returned to Washington, Grant was pressured by telegrams, letters, and personal visits by advocates on both sides. Secretaries Horace Porter and Orville Babcock, Interior Secretary Columbus Delano, and Secretary of War William Belknap all urged him to inflate the currency by releasing greenbacks. Secretary of State Fish, a hard-currency advocate, commended the president for standing firm. In a glowing letter to Richardson, he maintained, "I assure you that nothing the President has ever done seems, so far as I hear from persons of all classes, to give more satisfaction than the decision which he and you reached on Sunday."

In the midst of the panic, Grant received a letter from New York businessmen Horace B. Claflin and Charles L. Anthony, seeking his views on how best to restore financial confidence. Grant responded, "The Government is desirous of doing all in its power to relieve the present unsettled condition of business affairs, which is holding back the immense resources of the country now awaiting transportation to the seaboard and a market." He believed that "confidence on the part of the people is the first thing needed to relieve this condition of affairs." Grant's letter quickly became public, widely reprinted in newspapers across the nation.

Senator Boutwell, former secretary of the Treasury, wrote Grant three letters in thirteen days in October, offering approval of his actions: "In the present crisis the government stands well, and its action, especially your letter, is approved generally." Grant's quiet leadership and steady hand, quite different from Franklin D. Roosevelt's public cheerleading in confronting the Great Depression sixty years later, did much to calm the troubled waters.

Grant's actions helped stop the panic on Wall Street, although critics complained his hard-money policies protected his wealthy friends as much as the nation. But damage had been done. Abuse of sound financial management principles had struck the guilty and innocent alike. The narrative of the Panic of 1873 often focuses on the large number of banks, businesses, and railroads that failed, but the deeper story is of individual victims—factory, machine shop, and iron workers who lost their jobs, farmers who lost their farms, and many families who saw their bank savings accounts vanish. Estimates differ on the number of workers left unemployed, but it probably exceeded one million in a nation of forty million people. Even with vibrant voluntary relief organizations, the absence of government relief—present in the response to the Great Depression of the 1930s—meant untold misery and suffering spread as fall turned to the winter of 1873–1874.

JULIA HOPED THE arrival of Christmas could restore some joy in the White House. Always generous with her time at the Metropolitan Methodist Church, before each Christmas she also reached out with gifts to local hospitals, asylums, and orphanages. She and Ulysses gave not only money, but barrels of fruit and gifts of candy. Toy merchants in Washington learned to look for Mrs. Grant in the days leading up to Christmas, when she would lead a troop of young children through their stores, buying gifts for each boy and girl.

But this fifth Christmas in the White House would be like no other. For Ulysses and Julia, 1873 became a year of personal losses. In June, Jesse Root Grant died at age seventy-nine. Ulysses had spent much of his early life trying to come to terms with his father, who became a constant guest in Washington. On December 15, Julia's father, Frederick Dent, died at age eighty-six. As a young man, Ulysses had had to endure constant criticism from Julia's Confederate father, but as a permanent resident of the White House, Dent expressed nothing but pride and praise for his son-in-law.

The giants continued to fall in Grant's military family. George Meade died two days after Grant's reelection. General Edward Canby was killed by the renegade Modoc Indian Captain Jack while sitting at a peace parley in California.

Losses also mounted in Grant's political family. Horace Porter, who had served as aide-de-camp during the Civil War, resigned after Grant's reelection to accept a position as vice president with the Pullman Palace Car Company. Porter occupied a distinctive place in Grant's intimate circle and could not be replaced. Vice President Henry Wilson suffered a stroke in May and never fully recovered. An abolitionist, Wilson admired Grant and believed him to be "underrated," especially approving his aggressive approach against the Ku Klux Klan.

WHEN THE FORTY-THIRD Congress convened, in December and January it focused on legislative responses to the panic. After Grant invoked financial "elasticity" in his annual message—a balance between monetary theory and pragmatic action—more than sixty bills were introduced. Most were strongly expansionist in scope, which encouraged railroad men to lobby for relief by expanding the currency. Grant favored fiscal restraint.

After months of debate, the Senate and House agreed on Bill S.617, known as the "inflation bill." It would increase the number of greenbacks placed in circulation to $400 million. At the same time, it would advance circulation of specie-backed moneys to an equivalent amount. The Senate-sponsored bill received overwhelming approval in both houses of Congress. Everyone expected Grant to sign it.

He received the bill on April 14, 1874, and tense cabinet members arrived in his office one week later to hear his decision. Grant told them "he had given it most careful consideration with an earnest desire to give it his approval." He shared with them that according to his typical practice, he had written out the arguments in favor of the bill. But he'd found the more he wrote his statement of approval, the more he came up with arguments opposing it. Finally, after spending many hours at his desk, he concluded he could not sign it, stating it to be "a departure from true principles of finance, national interest, national obligations to creditors, Congressional promises, party pledges (on the part of both political parties), and of personal views and promises made by me in every annual message sent to Congress and in each inaugural address." Grant recognized the views of proponents of the bill—a majority in Congress—and stated these views in their best light, then countered them with his own financial convictions.

The cabinet sat speechless. Then all jumped in with their opinions. As Fish wrote that evening, "Delano fought" Grant's conclusion; "[Attorney General] Williams decidedly objected"; George M. Robeson, secretary of the navy, wished "the President had reached a different conclusion"; William Belknap, secretary of war, "thought it would array the entire West in opposition." Fish approved what he called Grant's "volte-face" (about-face). Richardson supported the decision. Creswell commended Grant: "You are right."

Grant had the last word: "I dare say the first result will be a storm of denunciation. But I am confident that the final judgment of the country will approve my veto."

Congress attempted to override Grant's veto, but the Senate could muster only 34 yeas to 30 nays. The veto was sustained.

No one was more surprised than Grant at the outpouring of support for his decision. Senator Roscoe Conkling wrote the same day to "express my admiration for your latest proof that you are as great as any duty ever set before you." Ordinary people wrote Grant from all over the country. Zachary Eddy, pastor of the First Congregational Church of Detroit, exclaimed, "Believing that I represent the feeling of ninety-nine clergymen out of any hundred in this country, I wish to thank you for your Veto of the so called Inflation Bill." Julie R. Seavey wrote from New York City "to add my *mite* to the general congratulation." She added, "Although I am 'only a woman' I feel some slight interest in the affairs and *honor* of my country."

Grant made his decision, opting to come down on the hard money side of the battle, but for him it was one of the most tortured decisions of his presidency. He did not want to turn his back on western farmers—

he was once one of them—but believed the choice best for a troubled economy.

IN THE SPRING of 1874, Grant was happy to shift his attention from Congress to his only daughter. The press idolized Nellie Grant. She spent her teenage years in the White House to become America's princess, with her gentle eyes and long hair down her back. Her father, a man who did not often show his sentiments in public, was openly demonstrative in his affection for his daughter.

Two years earlier, in the spring of 1872, when sixteen-year-old Nellie traveled to the United Kingdom in the company of former navy secretary Adolph Borie and his wife, Elizabeth, the British treated her like royalty everywhere she went. She even met Queen Victoria.

Nellie, with less formal education than her brothers, has been portrayed as an "uncultivated" young woman. This harsh portrait fails to appreciate the various forms of her education—tutors as well as travel. Receiving her letters from abroad, Ulysses remarked to his father, "Nellie writes very often and [is] a very much better writer than either of the boys."

On the way home from her tour of Britain, Nellie met a handsome young Englishman, Algernon Sartoris, the wealthy son of Edward Sartoris and Adelaide Kemble, sister of Fanny Kemble, the celebrated British actress. When Grant learned of his daughter's shipboard romance, he wrote an anxious letter to Edward Sartoris, expressing "astonishment" at what "seems to have sprung up between the two young people." Wearing his heart uncharacteristically on his sleeve, he admitted he "looked upon my daughter as a child, with a good home which I did not think of her wishing to quit for years yet. . . . She is my only daughter," he explained, "and I therefore feel a double interest in her welfare." He then asked about the "habits, character and prospects of the one upon whom she seems to have bestowed her affections." Grant's "greatest regret" would be to have Nellie "quit the United States as a permanent home." Did young Sartoris have any intention of becoming a United States citizen? After reviewing his frank letter, Grant asked Sartoris to keep it absolutely "confidential," since it espoused "a father's anxiety for the welfare and happiness of an only and much loved daughter."

He then asked Nellie to wait a year to marry—to which she agreed.

Finally, on May 21, 1874, a brilliant spring day, Nellie, not quite nineteen, married Algernon Sartoris in the East Room of the White House. It

Ulysses and Julia's only daughter, Nellie, was her father's delight and the princess of the American press.

was the wedding of the year. Magnolia trees stood at attention in the drive as seventy carriages passed by, bringing two hundred guests. Minister Otis Tiffany officiated at the marriage according to Methodist wedding rites. Nellie was dressed in a gown of white satin valued at $2,000 and wore a veil purchased from Brussels by her father—nothing was too good for his daughter. Fred Grant, the best man, looked handsome in his army uniform. Nellie's eight bridesmaids bore the names of Washington royalty: Anna Barnes, Bessie Conkling, Maggie Dent, Fannie Drexel, Edith Fish, Sallie Frelinghuysen, Lillie Porter, and Jennie Sherman.

Grant, who had only reluctantly given his permission for Nellie to marry, stood during the wedding ceremony overcome with tears.

Grant's oldest son, Fred, married twenty-year-old Chicago socialite Ida Marie Honoré five months later. Grant wrote Adam Badeau, "Fred's wife is beautiful and is spoken of by all her acquaintances, male & female, young & old, as being quite as charming for her manners, amiability, good sense & education as she is for her beauty." Ulysses and Julia loved their new daughter-in-law and invited her to live with them at the White House while Fred served with General George Custer in the Black Hills.

If Abraham Lincoln was well known for his love of Shakespeare, the *New York Times* pointed out that Grant "made it a point to attend a performance of all new American plays." In the fall of 1874, Grant attended *The Gilded Age,* based on the popular book Mark Twain had published the previous year, and starring the actor John T. Raymond, whose career Grant had followed for many years. He traveled from Washington to the Park Theatre in New York with his friend Rufus Ingalls.

In taking their seats, Ingalls noted that the president sat as far back in the box as possible. He later reported that Grant did not want his presence to be a distraction to the onstage drama.

LATER THAT FALL, Grant accepted an invitation to participate in ceremonies dedicating a tomb for Abraham Lincoln in Springfield, Illinois. He usually rejected invitations to speak, but in this case his admiration for Lincoln overrode his reluctance. Working hard, he crafted two preliminary drafts of his speech, and although he was not known for his oratory, in the end he outdid himself.

On October 15, he read his speech from the manuscript he held in his hand. In summarizing it, a local newspaper reporter was struck by Grant's emphasis on Lincoln's faith in the midst of the Civil War. "His faith in an All Wise Providence directing our arms to this final result, was the faith of the Christian that his Redeemer liveth."

Grant's main focus was on the opposition Lincoln faced: "Amidst obloquy, personal abuse and hate undisguised, and which was given vent to without restraint through the press, upon the stump and in private circles he remained the same staunch unyielding servant of the people." He

In one of his most famous cartoons, in 1874 a sympathetic Thomas Nast depicts all the problems and issues borne by Grant with the caption "A Burden He Has to Shoulder."

praised his friend: "To know him personally was to love and respect him for his great qualities of heart and head, and for his patience and patriotism." In the end, "I never heard him utter a complaint nor cast a censure for bad conduct or bad faith. It was his nature to find excuses for his adversaries. In his death the Nation lost its greatest hero. In his death the South lost its most just friend."

ELSEWHERE, THE FALL of 1874 did not prove kind to Grant. Editorial cartoonist Thomas Nast, although Grant's defender, nevertheless portrayed "A Burden He Has to Shoulder."

The president occupied a no-man's-land in political battles that surrounded congressional elections. Although he began his second term intent on a more conciliatory approach to the South, he was criticized for interfering in southern states. With Republicans afflicted by factionalism and often corruption, Grant watched the Republican hopes for a strong party presence in the South disappear. Accused of being both carpetbaggers and scalawags, of favoring the rights of African Americans over whites, Republicans were beaten, often literally, by resurgent neo-Confederate Democratic parties in southern states.

For Grant and the Republicans, the bitter fruit of this Democratic resurgence was harvested in the 1874 congressional elections. In the House, comprising 293 seats, a seismic shift took place. The Republican majority of 114 seats in 1872—198 to 88—became in 1874 a Democratic majority of 60 seats—169 to 109. In the Senate, Republicans lost 7 seats but retained their majority. Democrats won control of the House of Representatives for the first time since before the Civil War.

Several factors loomed behind this change. Voters often respond to hard economic times by blaming the party in power. Also, throughout the South, various white leagues, different versions of the older Ku Klux Klan, once again employed voter suppression to help Democrats win House seats. Democrats ended up winning two-thirds of the region's seats.

GRANT'S ANGER BURST forth as he prepared for his next opportunity to speak to Congress and the American people—his sixth annual message to Congress on December 7. In a departure from his usual practice, he read to his cabinet a draft of his message: he took on "critics who assume to direct affairs without responsibility, and, I am sorry to say, in many instances without conscience." While Fish characterized Grant's remarks as "very strong and very just," the cautious secretary of state also voiced his concern. He believed Grant's words "were wholly beneath the dignity of his official position or of an official document." Grant's words testified to his true feelings.

Although Grant ended up deleting the most inflammatory words, he retained his candor. Pointing to the recently completed elections, he minced no words in describing violence and intimidation intended "to deprive citizens of the freedom of the ballot because of their political opinions." He cited example after example: "In some places colored laborers were compelled to vote according to the wishes of their employers, under threat of discharge if they acted otherwise."

Grant anticipated his critics' responses; he knew they would continue to charge him with federal interference. "Complaints are made of this interference by Federal authority; but if said amendment [Fifteenth Amendment] and act [Enforcement Act] do not provide for such interference under the circumstances as stated above, then they are without meaning, force, or effect, and the whole scheme of colored enfranchisement is worse than mockery and little better than a crime."

What did Grant propose as the solution? "Treat the negro as a citizen and a voter, as he is and must remain, and soon parties will be divided, not on the color line, but on principle. Then we shall have no complaint of sectional interference."

It was well-known that portions of presidents' annual messages to Congress were often written by a cabinet secretary whose portfolio includes a particular subject or issue. No one wrote these determined words but Grant. Halfway through his second term, he had found his own voice. That voice became much more animated when he spoke about unfair obstacles set in the path of former slaves in their march to full freedom. Making full use of the regular reporting he'd received from generals in the field, his speeches about racial injustice pulsate with examples that had clearly touched him deeply.

BY THE END of 1874, some politicians and newspapermen were talking of Grant running for a third term, something never before attempted in American politics. But with the Panic of 1873 still running its course, with a Democratic majority in the House of Representatives, with Republican hopes for success in the South dimming rapidly, and with rumors of more scandals threatening those close to Grant, he faced many uncertainties as he looked toward his two final years as president.

This Thomas Nast cartoon depicts a barrel of corruption whose rings name the many scandals taking place during the Grant administration. The man in the cartoon is Grant's disgraced secretary of war, William Belknap.

CHAPTER 32

"Malfeasance!"

Let no guilty man escape if it can be avoided.
—ULYSSES S. GRANT, Long Branch, New Jersey, July 1875

Second terms are rarely as successful as the first, for predictable reasons: a president's initial popularity has begun to wear thin; his first-term initiatives have lost some of their luster; his adversaries, even within his own party, have begun to join forces in obstruction. Inevitably, by his last two years, he was seen more and more as a lame duck.

In Grant's second term, a growing list of scandals infiltrated his inner circle. In his final two years, these scandals would divert attention and time from the main concerns he sought to accomplish and test the leadership capacities of the first president to complete a second term since Andrew Jackson forty years before. Two first-term priorities, protecting the rights of the freedmen in the South and advocating the rights of Indians in the West, had lost considerable support. Yet opposition would not diminish Grant's commitment to both.

By 1875, REPUBLICANS controlled only four southern states—Florida, South Carolina, Mississippi, and Louisiana. Blacks constituted the majority of Republicans in all four states.

In Louisiana, reports of White Leaguers drilling in the streets of New Orleans prompted Grant to dispatch Phil Sheridan to assume control of U.S. troops and halt violence and murder. Upon arriving on January 1, 1875, Sheridan asked permission from Secretary of War William Belknap to arrest White Leaguers—mostly Confederate veterans—who had harassed black voters in the recent election for governor.

Congressman George F. Hoar, who hurried to New Orleans as part of an investigative committee, described the open antagonism hurled at Sheridan. When he entered the crowded dining room of the St. Charles

Hotel, "there were loud hisses and groans from nearly the whole assembled company." While he was eating breakfast, hotel guests would underline "abusive articles" in the morning newspapers and ask a waiter to deliver them to him. "The General would glance at it with an unruffled face, and bow and smile toward the sender of the article."

On Monday, January 4, 1875, when the clerk called the roll to convene the divided Louisiana legislature, 52 Republicans and 50 Democrats responded, "Present." Immediately, Democrats physically removed the Republican Speaker, replacing him with their own Speaker, appointing their own sergeant at arms, and replacing five Republicans with five Democrats to seize the majority. Their intention was clear. When Republicans tried to bolt, Democrats called on Philippe Régis de Trobriand, local commander of U.S. troops, to forbid their leaving the building.

A couple of Republicans did escape. They alerted Republican governor William Kellogg, who rushed to the chamber and directed de Trobriand to take away all persons not legal members of the legislature. The army, storming into the legislative hall with fixed bayonets, removed the five Democrats, thereby allowing Republicans to organize the legislature.

Sheridan notified Grant through Belknap that "defiance of laws and murder of individuals seems to be looked upon by the community here from a standpoint which gives impunity to all who choose to indulge in either." Singling out the terrorist tactics of the White Leaguers, he appealed for a presidential proclamation declaring them to be "banditti" who should be "tried by a military commission."

Belknap replied that the "president and all of us have full confidence and thoroughly approve your course." With conflicting reports of what occurred in Louisiana circulating in newspapers, Grant and Belknap decided to release Sheridan's reports and correspondence to the press to justify federal action.

The correspondence ignited a firestorm. Protests rose against the imposition of the federal military into a state legislative chamber. Ohio congressman James Garfield wrote a friend, "I have never given wholly away to despondency, but I say to you now that this is the darkest day for the future of the Republican party I have ever seen." He complained, "The question . . . has been so terribly botched by the President and General Sheridan during the last four days as to place the great burden of the trouble upon us"—Republicans in Congress.

Senator Carl Schurz, still smarting over Grant defeating his Liberal Republicans in 1872, lashed out at the president. Now a "lame duck," having lost his Missouri Senate seat to Democrat Francis Cockrell, he rose in the Senate to defend "the absolute freedom of legislative bodies from interference on the part of executive power, especially by force." Schurz charged, "The lawlessness of power is becoming far more dangerous to all than the lawlessness of the mob."

One of Grant's strongest supporters, Indiana senator Oliver Morton, replied that the "one difficulty which we now labor under in this country is that in certain States of the Union the colored people are not recognized as being a part of the people. They are not recognized as having political and civil rights." He cautioned, "We have heard the President of the United States today charged with having been guilty of a gross and manifest violation of the Constitution of the United States." He advised his fellow senators to wait for the message Grant was preparing before coming to any hurried conclusions.

Even as Schurz and Morton clashed in the Senate, Grant worked diligently on one of the longest communications he would send to Congress. He highlighted targeted atrocities against African Americans continuing in the South and defended Sheridan's actions. On January 11, Fish recorded, "The President and myself are alone for a few minutes when he spoke of the Louisiana troubles and said he was determined under no circumstances to apologize for anything he had done." The secretary reminded Grant that "some of his best friends" were expressing concern "on the question of Military interference with a Legislative body."

Grant instructed Attorney General George H. Williams to prepare a draft that he would edit, "saying that there are some things which he wishes to put in his own way." The next morning, he invited Senators Morton, Conkling, Logan, Aaron Sargent (California), George Edmunds (Vermont), and Frederick Frelinghuysen (New Jersey) to meet with him. He read his long message aloud and solicited their suggestions. By his second term, Grant no longer wrote messages to Congress without consulting congressional leaders.

On January 13, Grant presented his Louisiana message to the Senate. At the outset, he observed that "lawlessness, turbulence, and bloodshed have characterized the political affairs of that State since its reorganization under the reconstruction acts." He targeted voter suppression: "Many colored citizens had been denied registration, and others deterred by fear from casting their ballots." Responding to his critics' condemnation of federal intervention in the 1873 Colfax Louisiana massacre, Grant lamented, "Every one of the Colfax miscreants goes unwhipped of justice, and no way can be found in this boasted land of civilization and Christianity to punish the perpetrators of this bloody and monstrous

In October 1874, as resistance to Reconstruction in the South stiffened, Thomas Nast, who approved of Grant's actions on behalf of besieged African Americans, depicted a man labeled "White League" shaking hands with a man labeled "Ku Klux Klan" as a terrorized African American couple look on with horror at their dying or dead baby.

crime." Facing his critics in Congress, Grant emphasized his commitment to defending the civil rights of African Americans in the South.

In the spring of 1875, Grant turned to another crisis. He learned that whiskey distillers had been colluding to cheat the federal government of liquor taxes for years. Although dishonest distillers were active in the Lincoln and Johnson administrations, by the 1870s their tax avoidance had become a well-practiced business. The procedure was simple. Distillers produced twelve to fifteen million gallons of whiskey each year. But by reporting far fewer gallons to the government, they paid lower taxes. To succeed, the distillers bribed agents of the Bureau of Internal Revenue to look the other way.

Appreciating Benjamin Bristow's service as the nation's first solicitor general, Grant appointed him Secretary of the Treasury in June 1874. The *New York World* described Bristow as a man whose face was "not that of a scholar or a divine," but with "the firm sweep of the jaw" assuring "aggressive perseverance" in his new position. Grant believed Bristow was the person to combat the dual threat of the continuing economic crisis and spiraling corruption.

Building on Grant's appeal in his annual message of December 7, 1874 ("There should be no delay . . . in fixing by legislation a method by which we will return to specie"), Grant and Bristow worked with John Sherman, chairman of the Senate Finance Committee, to pass the Specie Payment Resumption Act on January 14, 1875. With this act Grant restored the gold standard, further contracted the nation's money supply, and hoped to stabilize the economy by slowing the inflationary cycle that helped bring on the Panic of 1873.

Bristow brought honesty to the position. In his first eleven months, he cleaned up his department—seven hundred to eight hundred people were dismissed.

Whiskey taxes, or the lack thereof, were at the heart of spiraling corruption. "By God, I will not sacrifice my personal honor and self-respect to the great Jehovah himself let alone to unmitigating plunderers of the people's money." Bristow conferred with Grant on May 7, stressing the need for decisive action. Grant gave his Treasury secretary his "hearty cooperation" for an operation to stop the collusion around "crooked whiskey" among distillers, rectifiers, and gaugers, plus corrupt officials in the Treasury Department and the Bureau of Internal Revenue. For months Bristow had been frustrated as someone in Washington tipped off ring members: "The plague is advancing west. Advise our friends to leave the city."

On May 10, Bristow and solicitor Bluford Wilson, employing secret agents from outside the Treasury Department, coordinated raids in St. Louis, Chicago, and Milwaukee to seize company books and files. He also shut down sixteen large distilleries and sixteen rectifiers. He discovered that in the previous ten months, the government had been cheated out of more than $1.6 million in taxes. In St. Louis alone, the whiskey ring distributed $250,000 in plunder to five men.

The attack on the whiskey rings—Bristow called them "rings" because they worked in multiple cities—coincided with Grant's removal of Attorney General George H. Williams. He asked for Williams's resignation after learning he had stopped proceedings against New York merchants Pratt & Boyd for fraudulent customhouse accounts after Mrs. Williams asked for a payment—bribe—of $30,000. Julia, who long ago saw through Kate Williams's schemes to support her high-flying lifestyle, applauded her husband's action.

Grant's overdue firing of Williams opened the door to making significant upgrades to his cabinet. He appointed Edwards Pierrepont, one of the most famous lawyers of the day, as attorney general. A man of indisputable integrity, Pierrepont helped shutter "Boss" William Tweed's Tammany Hall as U.S. attorney for the Southern District of New York. Using Bristow and Pierrepont, Grant formed an anticorruption team.

THE CUMULATIVE EFFECT of Grant's veto of the "inflation bill," the enactment of the Specie Payment Resumption Act, and the busts on the whiskey rings so boosted his stature that pundits were once again speaking of the possibility of a third term. There were no term limits—that would come with the Twenty-second Amendment, ratified seventy-five years later in the aftermath of Franklin D. Roosevelt's fourth term.

Throughout the spring, newspapers touted the idea. Republicans, stung by their midterm congressional defeats in 1874, joined the chorus, believing a third term would be their best prospect for retaking the House. Ulysses knew that Julia, who enjoyed their life in the White House, liked the idea.

Grant's hand was forced on May 27, 1875, when the Pennsylvania Republican Party publicly endorsed Grant for a third term. Concerned that similar endorsements might follow, the president wasted no time responding. Sensitive to the charge of "Caesarism" that critics hurled at him, he reminded the Pennsylvania Republicans, "I never sought the office for a second, nor even for a first, nomination." He stressed, "I am not, nor have I been, a candidate for a renomination."

Having finished his response, on a Sunday afternoon he sent for each cabinet member to come to the White House. When Julia observed their arrival, she remarked, "Is there any news? Why is it you have all happened to call today? I am sure there is something unusual."

Just then Ulysses appeared from his study. Julia, still puzzled, questioned her husband about whether something important was to be discussed.

More than courtesy had prompted the president to invite his cabinet officers to the White House on a Sunday. He understood their careers would be vitally affected by his decision. He did not ask for their advice, but as a mark of respect he informed them of his decision before it blared from front pages.

When the cabinet started to leave, and her husband handed a sealed envelope to a departing messenger, Julia confronted Ulysses: "I want to know what is happening. I feel sure there is something and I must know."

"Yes," said Ulysses, "I will come as soon as I light my cigar."

"What is it? Tell me?"

"You know what a to-do the papers have been making about a third term. Well, I have never until now had an opportunity to answer. . . . I do not wish a third term, and I have written a letter to that effect."

"Did all of these men approve and advise you to send that letter?"

"I did not ask approval or advice. I simply read the letter to them. That is all."

"And why did you not read it to me?"

"Oh, I know you too well. It never would have gone if I had read it."

"Bring it and read it to me now," she pleaded.

"No, it is already posted; that is why I lingered in the hall to light my cigar, so the letter would be beyond recall."

"Oh, Ulys! Was that kind to me? Was it just to me?"

"Well, I do not want to be here another four years. I do not think I could stand it. Don't bother about it, I beg of you."

This exchange, recalled by Julia years later, revealed much about Ulysses's and Julia's contrasting feelings in the spring of 1875. He knew how much she loved their life together in the White House and that she would have been happy to continue for another four years. But great weariness was etched in his reply.

SUMMER AT LONG Branch in 1875 did not follow the pattern of previous years. With rumors and reports of even more scandals, Grant turned down invitations to speak; there would be far less socializing this season.

On June 20, Secretary of the Interior Columbus Delano visited Long Branch. Although there was no convincing evidence that Delano himself was corrupt, the department he oversaw too carelessly had become mired in patronage, land fraud schemes, and corruption—even implicating Delano's son John. This situation was all the more painful for Grant because

In the midst of the scandals that plagued Grant's second term, Ulysses and Julia welcomed their summer retreat at their cottage by the shore at Long Branch, New Jersey.

the Department of the Interior continued to oversee the Department of Indian Affairs—and now he learned that the corruption went deep into Indian affairs. Grant asked Delano to resign.

Grant tapped former Michigan senator Zachariah Chandler to be the new secretary of the interior. If a young Grant once took Chandler to court over icy sidewalks in Detroit, this time no one accused him of cronyism, for Chandler enjoyed wide respect as an abolitionist and Radical Republican who supported Grant's campaign for civil rights for African Americans. Chandler had also been a strong advocate of Grant's Indian Peace Policy. If a broad brush has highlighted the scandals tainting some of Grant's cabinet appointments, often forgotten are Grant's choices for their replacements. Chandler would immediately initiate reforms— terminating corrupt agents, putting an end to profiteering, and prohibiting the use in the Interior Department of "Indian attorneys," who tricked Indians into payments for what turned out to be deceitful representation in Washington.

IN JUNE, GRANT traveled to Philadelphia to inspect progress on the Centennial Exposition set to open the next year. Even such a seemingly apolitical project was shadowed by struggles with a balky Congress. Democrats opposed federal funding, but Grant had long been a proponent of the Centennial, seeing it as an opportunity to celebrate the accomplishments of the past one hundred years, showcase the technologies of the future, and bring visitors from overseas.

GRANT STAYED IN Long Branch throughout the summer, but in August he accepted an invitation from an old friend. John Heyl Vincent, Galena pastor and now chief agent for the Methodist Sunday School Union and editor of the *Sunday-School Journal,* who had established a two-week Sunday school teachers' educational event on the shores of Lake Chautauqua in southwestern New York in 1874. Methodists had long held camp meetings in that area, but Vincent believed the time had come to move from experience to education. He aimed his new assembly at public school teachers, free in the summer, who made up the bulk of teachers educating both children and adults in Sunday schools the rest of the year.

In this second summer, seeking a way to give his new venture national exposure, Vincent invited Grant to come for a weekend in August. Grant accepted the summons—a testimony to their friendship.

As bells announced Grant's Saturday afternoon arrival on the steamer *Josie Belle,* a crowd of nearly twenty thousand waited to greet him. Grant

In the summer of 1875, Grant accepted an invitation from John Heyl Vincent, seen here sitting in front of his tent, to visit the Chautauqua Assembly in New York in its second summer.

spoke briefly, quickly passing the baton "to Dr. Vincent, who is an old friend of mine, and a better talker than I, to tell you how happy I am to be with you."

Grant stayed in an amply furnished tent. Stitched over the tent's entrance was the single word *REST,* although the next day was hardly that. Early in the morning, Grant attended Sunday school. At the eleven A.M. worship service, he took a seat on the platform in the large auditorium, decorated with the flags of many nations. At the conclusion of the service, Vincent presented the president with two Bibles: "the symbol of our work." Grant's presence helped put this Methodist gathering on the map; it would grow into the world-famous Chautauqua Institution.

As BRISTOW CONTINUED to pursue the whiskey rings, he discovered that rot reached into high places. He zeroed in on General John McDonald as a ringleader in St. Louis. In 1870, Grant had appointed McDonald supervisor of internal revenue in St. Louis. He depended upon McDonald to keep him informed of Missouri politics, especially after Schurz started a Liberal Republican insurgency in the state.

Two weeks after his initial raids, when Bristow began to give briefings on his preliminary findings, the president remarked, "Well, Mr. Bristow, there is at least one honest man in St. Louis on whom we can rely—John McDonald." Grant explained, "I know that because he is an intimate acquaintance and confidential friend of Babcock's." Bristow did not know how to respond.

As the names of whiskey rings became public, McDonald and other officials resigned. Grant gave Bristow his full support in the prosecutions. McDonald was indicted in June. In the following months, Bristow pressed indictments against 350 distillers and government officials.

The public, shocked, applauded Grant and Bristow for their wide-ranging actions.

In the midst of his investigations, Bristow uncovered shadowy telegrams warning McDonald of imminent inspections by Bristow's agents. One, dated December 10, 1874, read: "I succeeded. They will not go. I will write you. Sylph."

Bristow searched for the originals and finally found some in Washington. They had been authored in Babcock's handwriting.

By 1875, Orville Babcock had become one of the most influential persons in government. In addition to being Grant's private secretary, Babcock served officially as superintendent of buildings and grounds of the Capitol; unofficially he was co-conspirator with President Bonaventura Báez in the Santo Domingo land hustle. Bristow believed that as payment for his insider access, Babcock received cigar boxes filled with thousand-dollar bills from his "friends."

In late July, Attorney General Pierrepont and Secretary of State Fish called on Grant at Long Branch. When Pierrepont had laid out the case against Babcock, Grant asked for the attorney general's letter of complaint and scribbled on its back, "Let no guilty man escape if it can be avoided. Be specially vigilant—or instruct those engaged in the prosecution of frauds to be—against all who insinuate that they have high influence to protect, or to protect them. No personal consideration should stand in the way of performing a public duty." Grant told Pierrepont, "If Babcock is guilty, there is no man who wants him so proven guilty as I do, for it is the greatest piece of traitorism to me that a man could possibly practice." At this moment Grant was faced with a clash between a personal aide he had long trusted and two of the most trustworthy men in his cabinet who had come to him with damning evidence.

The attorney general urged Grant to let his comment be published in the press in order to silence his enemies. The letter was published in the *Washington Chronicle* on August 10.

STILL, OTHER MEMBERS of Grant's intimate circle came to Long Branch to argue just the opposite. The president's brother-in-law James F. Casey—Emmy's husband—federal collector of customs in New Orleans, was himself being investigated by Bristow for fraud as part of the "customhouse ring." Casey told the president the Babcock prosecutions were all part of Bristow's ambitious plan for his own political advancement. By the time Grant returned to Washington, various visitors had succeeded in sowing seeds of doubt in his mind about the motives of the hard-charging secretary of the Treasury.

Back at the White House, Grant persisted in retaining Babcock. Despite the counsel of friends, he could not bring himself to believe that the man who had been at his side at Vicksburg and Appomattox could be guilty.

In October, Bristow brought two "Sylph" telegrams to a cabinet meeting. Grant asked Babcock to come in and explain their cryptic contents. Babcock stated that all the telegrams concerned Missouri politics. As Bristow and Pierrepont looked on, Grant accepted Babcock's explanation.

In November, Grant followed reports of McDonald's trial in St. Louis; reporters from around the country clogged the courtroom. After five days, a jury found McDonald guilty. Henry Van Ness Boynton, an influential Washington correspondent, wrote an article in the *North American Review* praising "the Secretary's brilliant and effective campaigning." Talk began to grow of Bristow as a presidential candidate in 1876.

By December, Grant worried that critics were attempting to get at him by going after Babcock. On December 8, U.S. Attorney David Dyer, who on Bristow's instructions had denied Babcock's request for a military trial, persuaded a grand jury to issue an indictment, setting the trial date for February 1876.

One week later, Grant wrote Babcock's wife, Annie, "I know how much you must be distressed at the publications of the day reflecting upon the integrity of your husband." He told her, "After the intimate and confidential relations that have existed between him and myself for near fourteen years—during the whole of which time he has been one of my most confidential Aides & private Sec.—I do not believe it possible that I can be deceived." He assured her, "My confidence in Gen. Babcock is the same now as it was when we were together in the field contending against the known enemies of the government." This last sentence is telling. As Grant and Babcock fought together against "known" enemies in the past, they would do battle together against unknown enemies in the present.

ULYSSES AND JULIA welcomed the long anticipated centennial year at 12:01 A.M. on January 1, 1876, by listening to the Metropolitan Memorial Methodist Church bells play Ignace Pleyel's popular hymn tune for "Pilgrim Song." With the opening of the Centennial Exposition only months away, Grant continued to urge Congress to appropriate the necessary funds. In his annual message in December, he affirmed, "The advantages to the country of a creditable display are, in an international point of view, of the first importance, while an indifferent or uncreditable participation by the Government would be humiliating to the patriotic feelings of our people themselves."

WITH THE CASE against Babcock scheduled to go to trial in St. Louis in February 1876, Grant took the unusual step of requesting to testify. Both Fish and Bristow discouraged him, and Attorney General Pierrepont went so far as to warn the defense that Grant's participation would be "impossible and unseemly."

Despite his cabinet's objections, Grant gave a deposition for five hours on February 12. Chief Justice Morrison Waite served as the notary, with Pierrepont and Bristow present. Grant reiterated his full support for the Treasury Department's investigation of the whiskey rings. As for Babcock, "I have always had great confidence in his integrity and his efficiency; and as yet my confidence in him is unshaken."

In the end, the influence of the president's deposition and a lack of direct evidence led to Babcock's acquittal. The *New York Tribune,* usually a critic of Grant's, admitted the whiskey ring scandal "had been met at the entrance of the White House and turned back."

Babcock returned to the White House, but not for long. Grant may have maintained Babcock's innocence, but he'd lost trust in his longtime subordinate. In his place he appointed someone he could trust implicitly: his son Ulysses Jr.

UNFORTUNATELY, CALM WOULD not return for long. Within days of Babcock's acquittal, word raced across Washington that a Grant cabinet secretary was being investigated for corruption.

Grant had appointed William Worth Belknap secretary of war after the 1869 death of John Rawlins. After Belknap's first wife, Cora, died, Belknap married Carita ("Carrie") S. Tomlinson. In the summer of 1870, Belknap petitioned Congress to grant him sole authority to appoint agents to head up Indian trading posts. Shortly thereafter, the socially ambitious Carrie, not content to live on her husband's annual salary of $8,000, engineered a deal to obtain the lucrative Indian trading post position at Fort Sill, Oklahoma Territory, as a personal cash cow.

First, she lobbied her husband to offer the position to a New York

To Grant's embarrassment, Secretary of War William Belknap was charged with profiting from kickbacks in the Bureau of Indian Affairs.

merchant friend, Caleb Marsh. Belknap now had the authority to appoint whomever he pleased, but in this case the post had been assigned previously to John Evans, an experienced sutler, who did not want to give it up. So Marsh contrived a scheme whereby Evans could keep his tradership in return for an annual fee of $12,000, to be delivered in quarterly payments. Carrie Belknap and Marsh agreed to share equally in the Indian tradership kickback.

In December 1870, Carrie Belknap died of tuberculosis one month after giving birth to a son. Marsh continued to deliver the agreed-upon kickback share, with Belknap's knowledge and approval, to Carrie's younger sister, Amanda, who had earlier moved in with the Belknaps and agreed to hold the funds in trust for the infant. When the child died six months later in June 1871, Amanda left for Europe and Belknap took sole charge of the kickbacks—until December 1873, when Amanda returned to become his third wife. Carrie's younger sister, even more self-indulgent than her sibling, soon earned herself the dubious title of the "spendthrift belle" of Washington. From that point forward, husband and wife shared the kickbacks.

In February 1876, Pennsylvania congressman Hiester Clymer, a strongly partisan Democrat who had opposed Grant and Belknap on Reconstruction, led a probe into possible trading post "malfeasance." When Marsh admitted to his bribe, he told the committee on February 29, "The money was sent according to the instructions of the Secretary of War."

A Republican on the committee, New York congressman Lyman K. Bass, became concerned about the effect of another scandal on Grant and the Republican Party in an election year and hurried to Attorney General Bristow early on the morning of March 2. Bristow in turn rushed to the home of Hamilton Fish. Finding the secretary of state still in bed, he roused him with the bad news. Fish urged Bristow to "call at once upon the President."

Bristow arrived at the White House just as Grant and Julia were finishing breakfast. Bristow advised the president to get the full story from Congressman Bass. Grant promised he would later and prepared to leave for a portrait by renowned artist Henry Ulke. An attendant ran after him: Belknap and Secretary of the Interior Chandler were in the Red Drawing Room, urgently requesting to see him.

"I cannot now, but will when I return."

"Oh, Mr. President, do see him before you go. He is in some trouble and looks very ill."

Grant entered the Red Drawing Room to find a visibly upset Belknap holding his head in his hands. He mumbled, "Mr. President, I came to tender my resignation. Accept it at once."

"Certainly, if you wish it." Grant was shaken; he and Julia had become close socially to the Belknaps. Grant sent for his secretary, Ulysses Jr., and instructed him to write an acceptance of Belknap's resignation. Not satisfied with his son's wording, Grant stood at the mantel and wrote his own letter: "Your tender of resignation as Secretary of War, with the request that it be accepted immediately, is received, and the same is hereby accepted with regret."

Relieved, Belknap squeezed Grant's hand. "Thank you, you are always kind," he said, and hurried for the door. As Grant picked up his coat and hat to leave for his appointment, he was met by Senators Oliver Morton and Justin Morrill (Vermont), who had come to warn the president not to accept Belknap's resignation just at the moment Congress was launching an investigation for criminal wrongdoing.

With Congress in an immediate uproar, Congressman Clymer wrote Grant that afternoon, asking for the exact time that he had accepted Belknap's resignation. Grant wrote on Clymer's letter, "Time of acceptance about 10:20 this a.m."

The issue in Congress quickly became Grant's acceptance of Belknap's resignation. When Clymer's congressional committee reconvened that afternoon, even as they prepared articles to impeach Belknap, Democrats aimed their acrimony at the president. To many, it appeared Belknap had resigned to avoid punishment and impeachment. Did Grant's acceptance of Belknap's resignation amount to shielding his secretary of war?

The next day, in a vigorous cabinet discussion, Grant admitted his surprise at the criticism directed against him; "he did not know that acceptance was not a matter of course." Pierrepont and Bristow both believed he had acted properly. Grant instructed the attorney general to examine whether criminal or civil charges should be brought against Belknap.

The House debated whether they could impeach a private citizen. They voted affirmatively, then referred the matter to the Senate for trial. Belknap would become the only former cabinet secretary ever impeached by the House of Representatives.

ON MARCH 2, Grant appointed Secretary of the Navy George M. Robeson as Belknap's interim successor, but four days later he learned Robeson was being investigated for dishonesty in the Navy Department. Where would all these scandals end?

Robeson, Belknap's classmate at Princeton, was a handsome, jovial man but was portrayed on the Washington social circuit as a "a first-rate judge of wine, a second-rate trout fisherman, and a third-rate New Jersey lawyer." Most people added: Robeson was a fourth-rate secretary of the navy.

Robeson was charged with developing a sweetheart deal with Philadelphia grain merchants A. G. Cattell & Company to allow them to become a major supplier of foodstuffs for the navy. A congressional investigation revealed that Robeson, who earned $8,000 a year as a cabinet secretary, had deposited $320,000 in his bank account between 1872 and 1876. The investigation also discovered that a member of the Cattell family had purchased a cottage for Robeson at Long Branch.

When the committee examined the Cattell books, they found them in disarray, but with no proof of payments to Robeson. In July, the committee debated impeaching Robeson, but with Belknap already in the dock on impeachment charges, they took no action. In the end, they faulted Robeson for allowing, if not promoting, a climate of corruption that "must thereafter be known as 'Cattellism.'" Admiral David Porter, no friend of Robeson's, wrote Sherman in St. Louis, "How the President could have been deceived in this person I do not know."

BY THE SPRING of 1876, Grant's now famous line "Let no guilty man escape" was being turned against him by his critics: Was Grant the guilty man?

As Congress continued to probe the seemingly ubiquitous whiskey rings scandals, Attorney General Benjamin Bristow was called to testify in July. The Democratic-controlled committee set their sights not on Bristow, but on the highest target: Grant. Bristow told the investigating committee that he "considered all conversations between the President and Heads of Departments on official matters confidential and privileged"—what today is called "executive privilege." The press immediately jumped to the conclusion that Bristow had to be protecting Grant.

Grant believed he had nothing to hide. He wrote Bristow, "I appreciate the position you have assumed on this question" of executive privilege "but beg to relieve you from all obligation of secrecy on this subject; and desire . . . only that you may answer all questions relating to it." What was more, Grant wrote he wished "that all the members of my Cabinet,—and all ex-members of the Cabinet since I have been president—may also be called to testify in regard to the same matters."

To make his point official, Grant wrote Iowa congressman John A. Kasson of the investigating committee, informing him he had written Bristow "absolving him from all secrecy as to matters in question." Grant wanted complete transparency.

Seventeen years later, with Grant's letter still in his possession, Kasson wrote on the letter, "Nothing shows so clearly the consciousness of innocence on the part of the President as this letter avowing his resolution to give the fullest scope to his Enemies' investigation."

Grant did not have to wait seventeen years. He smartly had his letter to Bristow published in the afternoon papers.

Comparing the president's discomfitures with similar difficulties faced by George Washington, Thomas Jefferson, and John Quincy Adams, the *Daily Graphic* applauded Grant in an editorial titled "Justice to the President."

NOT ALL THE press was so positive. As newspapers stepped up their attacks on Grant and his administration over the scandals, the president chose to follow his usual pattern—he did not respond. But a posture that had been effective in the army hurt more than it helped him as president. As Grant refused to refute or even reply, beyond his public letter, many came to believe he should bear some responsibility for the misdeeds of his associates.

The saga of Orville Babcock and William Belknap revealed how personal loyalty, which Grant prized so highly in the military, became his blind spot in the more public world of the presidency. He could not understand how men could change within power-seeking Washington.

Both Grant's friends and critics were puzzled by his ability, or lack thereof, to discern the motives and behavior of his close associates—from personal aides to cabinet officers. He had been so adept as general in sifting the wheat and chaff of army officers; why did he falter in this area as president?

Answers were offered by those who knew him best. "He disliked controversy when in conversation," said George Boutwell, Grant's secretary of the Treasury, putting his finger on an important part of Grant's makeup. This trait meant he found himself unwilling or unable to confront individuals. In the Civil War, as general in chief, when he tried to confront Ben Butler's shortcomings as commander of the Army of the James, he ended up drawing back.

Former secretary Adam Badeau observed, "He regarded the feelings of others carefully." His longtime aide suggested the closer Grant grew to the person—he was invited to Babcock's wedding, and he and Julia were socially close with William Belknap and his first wife, Cora—the more difficulty he had in exercising objective judgment.

Grant's Methodist minister, Otis Tiffany, believed, "Absolutely incapable of servility, he could not suspect other men of fawning sycophancy. The soul of honor and manliness himself, a man who was a stranger to indirection and falsehood, General Grant could not comprehend how men could be dishonorable and false by method." Tiffany further observed, "Attacked by public men and the press as a dishonest and corrupt man, he came to believe that honest men were surest to be abused. Consequently he stood by men who were under fire."

IN MAY 1876, weighed down by scandals and tied to the crimes committed by men in whom he had placed his trust, Grant had lost all credibility as a third-term presidential candidate. Several wags advised him not to get too excited about the scandals and skullduggery that were becoming part of the business and politics of the Gilded Age, but he was past listening. Exhausted from the relentless pressure, he could hardly wait to get away from humid Washington for the cooling summer breezes on the New Jersey shore.

First, however, he looked forward to a pleasant ceremonial duty as president: opening the nation's long-expected 1876 Centennial Exposition in Philadelphia.

CHAPTER 33

⋆⇥◎⇤⋆

Centennial Crisis

Either party can afford to be disappointed by the result,
but the Country cannot afford to have the result tainted by
the suspicion of illegal or false returns.
—ULYSSES S. GRANT to WILLIAM T. SHERMAN, November 10, 1876

Early on the morning of May 10, 1876, thousands thronged Philadelphia's streets. To the accompaniment of church bells, people made
their way to the Centennial Exposition at Fairmount Park in horse-drawn
streetcars, carriages, barouches, furniture wagons, butcher cars, hearses,
hacks, even baggage vans. Visitors from New York, Washington, and
points north, south, and west arrived by train at the new three-tiered
Pennsylvania Railroad depot.

The leaden skies gave way to sunshine just in time for the nine A.M.
opening of the gates. At noon, after a prayer by Bishop Matthew Simpson
and a recitation of John Greenleaf Whittier's "Centennial Hymn," Grant
rose to speak: "One hundred years ago our country was new, and but
partially settled." He now encouraged his audience to enjoy an exposition that would "show in the direction of rivaling older and more advanced nations in law, medicine, and theology—in science literature,
philosophy, and the fine arts."

Looming inside the gates were the vast Main Exhibition Hall, the
towers of Machinery Hall, the numerous barns of the Agricultural Hall,
the art galleries of Memorial Hall, and the eye-popping innovations in
Horticultural Hall. Between May 10 and November 10, 8,804,631 persons
would visit the Centennial Exposition, timed to celebrate the one hundredth anniversary of the Declaration of Independence. Factoring in repeat visitors, it is estimated that one in fifteen Americans in a nation of
forty million paid the 50 cents to enter.

• • •

MEMORIAL
OF THE
International Exhibition
AT
PHILADELPHIA.
1876.
THOS HUNTER, PUBLISHER,
716 Filbert Street, Philad.ᵃ

Grant advocated for the federal government's financial support
for the 1876 Centennial Exposition in Philadelphia.

ONE MONTH AFTER he opened the exposition, Grant determined to stay on the sidelines when Republicans gathered for their sixth national convention in Cincinnati. Unlike in 1868, when he stood far above other contenders, in 1876 there would be no dearth of popular candidates. Newspapers singled out Speaker of the House James G. Blaine, Secretary of the Treasury Benjamin Bristow, and Senators Roscoe Conkling and Oliver Morton as leading contestants. In the second rank stood Pennsylvania governor John Hartranft, Ohio governor Rutherford B. Hayes, and Connecticut's Marshall Jewell, whom Grant had appointed postmaster general in 1874.

Grant believed the convention might find itself at an impasse and possibly turn to a dark horse. If that happened, he had his candidate: "I fixed on Fish." Just in case, he "wrote a letter to be used at the proper time."

On Wednesday, June 14, delegates crammed into a hall, "its architecture that of an ambitious and disappointed railroad depot, its decorations those of a country barbecue," according to the *New York Tribune*. Blaine led with 285 votes—378 were needed for victory—followed by Morton, 124; Bristow, 113; Conkling, 99; Hayes, 61; Hartranft, 58; and Jewell, 11. Blaine's backers were confident the man they called their "plumed knight" would sweep to victory.

Delegates cast ballot after ballot. Maine's Blaine continued to lead into the sixth ballot—then everything changed. As Grant predicted, a dark horse emerged on the seventh ballot: a war veteran wounded severely at South Mountain, now a politician with little Washington experience. Rutherford B. Hayes, who had bucked the Democratic landslide of 1874 to win a sharply contested Ohio governor's race in 1875, defeated Blaine 384 to 351, winning the nomination. Even his supporters admitted Hayes lacked the heroic appeal of Grant, the speaking ability of Blaine, the intellectual perspicacity of Morton, or the effusive personality of Conkling. But backers celebrated him as a man of personal integrity, a characteristic that commended Hayes given the recent spate of political scandals.

That evening Grant telegraphed Hayes, "I congratulate you and feel the greatest assurance that you will occupy my present position on the Fourth of March next." His congratulation conveyed no special enthusiasm for a man he barely knew. Most dispiriting, he learned that Hayes promised to allow southern states to resume self-governance. To Grant, this would be a betrayal of the Reconstruction measures he had strongly advocated for the past eight years, in particular the defense of the rights of African Americans.

ELEVEN DAYS AFTER the Republican convention, Democrats convened in St. Louis. A divided party in 1872 when they felt forced to ratify the candidacy of Liberal Republican Horace Greeley, delegates came to the first national political convention held west of the Mississippi sensing success could be theirs at last in 1876. Unlike the Republicans, the Democrats boasted an acknowledged front-runner. Samuel J. Tilden, reform-minded governor of New York, had faced down both "Boss" William Tweed and the infamous "canal ring" that had made millions by overcharging the construction and maintenance of the New York State barge canal system. Tilden had transformed himself into a good speaker by studying Fourth of July orations to find reform themes to build into his speeches. He became a millionaire by his thirties through shrewd financial investments. As a Democrat, he had opposed Republican Abraham Lincoln's "strong executive" approach to government during the Civil War and vowed he would scale back Grant's use of executive authority. Six other candidates, including Union general Winfield Scott Hancock, competed for the nomination. On June 29, Tilden won easily on the second ballot. A united Democratic party left St. Louis confident of victory.

MEANWHILE, AT THE Centennial Exposition a bust of Frederick Douglass sculpted by blind artist Johnson M. Mundy sat in a lonely exhibition— lonely because African Americans were largely absent from the centennial. By 1876, the endeavor to reconstruct the nation on a platform of civil

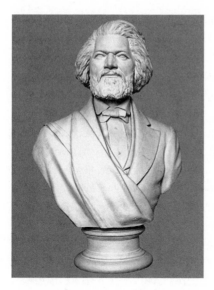

Blind artist Johnson M. Mundy's bust of Frederick Douglass was proudly displayed at the Centennial Exposition—from which African Americans were largely absent.

rights for the freedmen had essentially ended. The bust became a silent witness to a dream denied.

A month earlier, Grant had gone as honored guest to a speech by Douglass for the dedication of the Freedman's Memorial eleven blocks east of the Capitol. With an initial gift of $5 from former slave Charlotte Scott—her first earned money as a free woman—the funds for the statue were raised by freed blacks, primarily African American Union army veterans. American sculptor Thomas Ball depicted Abraham Lincoln as the Great Emancipator, clasping the Emancipation Proclamation in his right hand, while with his left hand he reached out to a kneeling slave. After his initial sketch of the slave appeared too passive to the sponsoring commission, Ball redrew the statue to depict a muscular former slave with shackles freshly broken.

Douglass, at fifty-nine a striking figure with his white hair and beard, offered qualified praise for Lincoln: "Abraham Lincoln was not, in the fullest sense of the word, either our man or model." Forgotten through the years because of its criticism of Lincoln, the speech did offer an unqualified tribute to Grant. Douglass declared the dedication took place "in the presence and under the steady eye of the honored and trusted President of the United States." "Trusted" was a special word seldom used in the Douglass lexicon—a singular encomium because Douglass did not trust white leaders. The fiery reformer would later say of Grant, "He was the first of our generals to see that slavery must perish that the

Union might live, and to protect colored soldiers from insult by military order." For Douglass, Grant's actions spoke louder than his words: "The black soldier was welcome in his tent, and the freedman in his house." Douglass accorded Grant the honor of pulling the cord to unveil the twelve-foot-high statue.

As CENTENNIAL MANIA rose in the summer months, Grant accepted invitations from Christian and Jewish organizations wishing to promote their projects at the exposition and beyond. John Wanamaker, proprietor of Philadelphia's first department store, owned the *Sunday-School Times*. He was always looking for ways to promote the popular and growing Sunday school movement. Wanamaker invited Grant to write a letter for the cover of a special edition of the *Sunday-School Times* to be handed out to exposition visitors.

On June 6, in his own hand, Grant wrote, "My advice to SUNDAY-SCHOOLS, no matter what their denomination, is: Hold fast to the Bible as the sheet-anchor of your liberties; write its precepts in your hearts, and PRACTISE THEM IN YOUR LIVES." He concluded with words from the Old Testament: "Righteousness exalteth a nation; but sin is a reproach to any people." Wanamaker believed Grant's letter, seen by millions of visitors, lifted the *Sunday-School Times* to a new level of popularity.

Three days later, Grant accepted an invitation from Adolphus Solomons, a prominent Jewish leader who had convinced President Lincoln to appoint Jewish chaplains during the Civil War, to attend the dedication of Adas Israel synagogue in Washington. The synagogue, timing its event to coincide with the centennial celebrations, appreciated that Grant would be the first U.S. president to attend the dedication of a Jewish synagogue. In 1862, the general had been excoriated for his infamous order expelling "Jews as a class"; fourteen years later, he was welcomed by the Jews as a friend.

In July, when the annual convention of the council of the Union of American Hebrew Congregations met in Washington, Grant invited the delegates to the White House. Upon being introduced to Isaac Mayer Wise, foremost Jewish educator and author, Grant is reported to have said, "I know all about you, Doctor, especially in connection with Order No. 11." Grant's genuine mortification over his prejudicial wartime order fueled his desire to make amends.

GRANT WAS BOTH absent and present in the 1876 presidential campaign. Following traditional nineteenth-century patterns, neither Hayes nor

Tilden campaigned. Instead, surrogates spoke for the candidates. Grant decided not to speak for Hayes.

He was present in "Grantism"—the term used by Democrats to denigrate the scandals in his administration. Democrats also charged that Reconstruction under Grant was a failure. Samuel Bowles, reform-minded editor of Massachusetts's *Springfield Republican,* spoke for much of the northern mood during the presidential campaign: "We must get rid of the Southern question." The "Southern question" referred to what to do with the South in the post–Civil War years. Bowles, who broke with Grant to support the Liberal Republicans in 1872, endorsed Tilden in 1876, by which time northern sentiment—both Republican and Democrat—argued that the South should be left to deal with the African Americans in their states without any interference from the federal government.

Grant found himself decisively pulled into the presidential campaign by this same "Southern question." It happened because of an event on the Fourth of July in Hamburg, South Carolina, a small town just across the Savannah River from Augusta, Georgia. Blacks, finding themselves under progressively stricter white control in the Deep South, sought safety in numbers by repopulating small rural towns.

On Independence Day, the proud local company of the South Carolina National Guard under the command of Captain D. I. "Doc" Adams began its annual patriotic celebration by marching down Market Street. Two young white planters, Thomas Butler and Henry Getzen, arrived in the middle of the afternoon and demanded the black militia move to the side of the road so their carriage could pass. After sharp words, with Adams arguing that the wide street provided plenty of room for the carriage to pass, the Union veteran gave an order for the black militia to part and let the carriage go on its way.

Two days later, the planters hurried to the local court to press charges against Adams for obstructing a public road. Former Confederate general Matthew C. Butler appeared as counsel for the plaintiffs, accompanied to the courthouse by about 150 paramilitary "Red Shirts" armed with shotguns, revolvers, pitchforks, and hoes. When Butler demanded the militia surrender and turn over their guns, they refused and barricaded themselves in their barracks. In the firefight that followed, a local white farmer was killed. The mob then gunned down Hamburg's black town marshal. When the black militia learned the whites were bringing in a cannon from Augusta, they tried to escape in the night. The Red Shirts caught about two dozen of them, then formed a "dead ring" around the terrified black soldiers and chose four, whom they proceeded to murder one by one. The "Hamburg massacre" set the tone for violence in the weeks ahead, all aimed at suppressing black Republican votes in fall elections.

The *Sumter True Southron* captured the reaction of some white South Carolinians to the Hamburg violence in an editorial: "We may not be able to carry the state at the ballot box, but when it comes to a trial of the cartridge box we do not entertain any doubt of the result." A coroner's jury indicted ninety-four white men for the attack, including Butler. None were ever prosecuted.

Soon after, Grant received an appeal from Governor Daniel Chamberlain: "The effect of this massacre has been to cause wide spread terror and apprehension among the Colored race and the Republicans of this State." Chamberlain, who came south in 1866 to plant cotton and make money, had become a reforming politician because of what he witnessed in the state. "There is little doubt that . . . a feeling of triumph and elation has been caused by this massacre, in the minds of a considerable part of the white people and Democrats." Chamberlain reassured Grant he intended to do all he could do to stem the violence, but he asked, "Will the general government exert itself vigorously to repress violence in this State during the present campaign?"

Grant offered Chamberlain his full support: "The scene at Hamburg, as cruel, bloodthirsty, wanton, unprovoked, and as uncalled for as it was, is only a repetition of the course that has been pursued in other southern states within the last few years." He went on: "How long these things are to continue, or what is to be the final remedy, the Great Ruler of the Universe only knows—But I have an abiding faith that the remedy will come, and come speedily, and earnestly hope it will come peacefully." Grant assured the South Carolina governor, "I will give every aid for which I can find law, or constitutional power."

But what aid could Grant realistically offer in the summer of 1876? In March, the Supreme Court in *United States v. Cruikshank* had emasculated the power of the federal government to enforce the civil rights amendments by ruling that the equal protection and due process clauses of the Fourteenth Amendment applied only to state actions, not the actions of individuals—thus overturning the convictions of all the white men who had been involved. Henceforth southern blacks would have to rely on southern courts for protection, which essentially meant no protection at all. To complicate Grant's resolve, there was no longer a vigorous John Rawlins or Amos Akerman in his cabinet. He listened in dismay as members of his own Republican Party warned that federal action in the South would cripple Hayes's chances in the North.

The violence in South Carolina continued. Former Confederate general Martin Gary established his "Plan of the Campaign of 1876," whose point 12 enjoined, "Every Democrat must feel honor bound to control the vote of at least one negro." Democrats understood they could not win elections unless they suppressed the votes of black Republicans. Torchlight rallies were held, more "rifle clubs" formed, all with the goal of "redeeming" South Carolina.

Chamberlain called for the rifle clubs to disperse. When they did not, in October he wrote Grant again about "insurrection and domestic violence." Since he was "unable with any means at my command to suppress the same," he pleaded for the president's help.

Grant responded with a proclamation calling out "Rifle Clubs who ride up and down by day and night in arms, murdering some peaceable citizens and intimidating others." Appealing to the mandate in the Constitution to "protect every State in this Union," he warned, "It shall be lawful for the President of the United States . . . to employ such part of the land and naval forces as shall be judged necessary for the purpose of suppressing such insurrection." Grant ordered "all persons engaged in said unlawful and insurrectionary proceedings to disperse and retire peaceably." He directed Sherman to provide "all the available force" in the Atlantic Division "to carry out fully the spirit of the Proclamation." Troops were stationed at turbulent points leading up to the election.

Grant's strong orders maintained the peace in the final three weeks before the election. Although he endured criticism for this strong federal action, affirmation came from a surprising source. Old curmudgeon William Cullen Bryant, nationally acclaimed poet and longtime editor of the *New York Evening Post,* had long opposed military force in the South. Now, appalled by the violence, he applauded Grant's proclamation and use of force.

ON ELECTION DAY, November 7, both Republicans and Democrats predicted victory. Despite a weather system that spread rain from New England to Georgia, a voter turnout of 81.8 percent of the entirely male electorate would rank as the highest in American history.

Ulysses and Julia were in Philadelphia as early results came in: Grant had accepted George Childs's invitation to stay as the president prepared to close the Centennial Exposition on November 10. The first returns indicated Tilden had won a majority of the popular vote and 184 electoral votes—one short of the needed majority. Twenty electoral votes distributed among three southern states—Florida (4), Louisiana (8), and South Carolina (7)—and one western state—Oregon (1)—remained contested.

Grant awakened on Wednesday morning, November 8, to a muddle of contradictory newspaper headlines. Most touted Tilden's victory. The *New York Tribune* headlined: AVE! CENTENNIAL SAM! Tilden's leading southern enthusiast, Henry Watterson's *Louisville Courier-Journal,* boasted: THANK THE LORD! BOYS WE'VE GOT EM. The Washington, D.C., *National Republican* captured the Republican mood: SUSPENSE, POSSIBLY TILDEN, HOPEFULLY, HAYES. The *New York Herald* asked, THE RESULT—WHAT IS IT?

Grant went with Childs to his office as publisher of the *Philadelphia Public Ledger*. Several of Childs's Republican friends still hoped Hayes had won the election. Grant quietly demurred, "Gentlemen, it looks to me as if Mr. Tilden is elected."

Hysteria reigned as conflicting reports spread. One question echoed on every street corner: Had the votes been counted fairly? Republicans were keenly aware that Democrats used intimidation to suppress the votes of black Republicans—historians estimate as many as 250,000 were prevented from voting in the 1876 elections.

Grant, who had gone to sleep the night before believing he could recede into the background, with public attention shifting to a president-elect, found himself in the middle of a disputed election. All eyes turned toward the president to see what he would do in this unprecedented state of affairs.

Grant immediately assured the American people that fairness would prevail. He wrote General in Chief Sherman: "Either party can afford to be disappointed in the result but the Country cannot afford to have the result tainted by the suspicion of illegal or false returns."

In the midst of spreading anxiety, Grant returned to Washington and convened his first postelection cabinet meeting. He faced a divided group of cabinet officers. The conservative Fish counseled against using a mailed fist in the South. The secretary of state was countered by Interior Secretary Zachariah Chandler, a proponent of rough-and-tumble politics, as well as Attorney General Alphonso Taft and the new secretary of war, James D. Cameron. These three encouraged Grant to act decisively to protect Hayes and the interests of the Republican Party.

On the same day, Fish met with John Mosby, the former Confederate cavalry leader whose "Raiders" had caused Grant so much trouble during the war but had become one of the president's strongest supporters among former Confederate military leaders. Offering a report that worried Fish, he emphasized that "the language of the Democrats now was more threatening and violent than that of the Southern men on the Election of Lincoln in 1860." Mosby reported threats to assassinate Grant if Hayes was elected.

Tensions grew. On November 20, an unknown correspondent signing his name "A.M.B." wrote Grant that he overheard two men "who were plotting your *assassination*" with a dagger while Grant walked alone on the streets of Washington. Two days later, Grant received a letter with a sketch of a skeleton in a casket and the caption "You are a doomed man." The anonymous writer signed the letter "KKK." Grant, who had previously dismissed threats on his life and walked without any security, ordered a heavier metal walking stick, confident he could fend off any attackers.

On a stormy Sunday, November 26, Grant summoned an emergency afternoon cabinet meeting. The night before, he had received a message from Governor Chamberlain. The South Carolina legislature was scheduled to meet the following Tuesday, and Chamberlain had learned that up to eight thousand members of "rifle clubs" were on their way to the capital to prevent their assembly. Chamberlain requested of Grant "troops as to give the legislature protection against unlawful force."

This time, the cabinet united. Grant directed Secretary of War Cameron to order the military forces of the United States to be ready to maintain the government in the state of South Carolina in the face of forces too formidable to be resisted by the state. Initially, federal troops acted impartially, but on November 28, under Chamberlain's direction, when Republican and Democratic legislators arrived, Republicans were admitted and Democrats barred.

When Grant heard this distressing news, he reached out to the leader of Tilden's campaign, Abram S. Hewitt, inviting him to a meeting at the White House. Hewitt arrived having heard rumors that because of the disputed election, Grant might use troops to extend his presidency.

Grant was aware of the rumors and sought to put Hewitt at ease. Hewitt later recalled that in a candid conversation, Grant said "he longed for the day when he should be able to retire from office . . . he looked forward to the freedom which was in store for him." Talking at length, Grant showed extensive knowledge about the difficulties in South Carolina; he believed Hayes would win there. When the conversation turned to Louisiana and its eight electoral votes, Grant said what he would tell

Hewitt "must be in confidence." Citing current voting returns, Grant was convinced "Tilden & Hendricks unquestionably had a majority" there. Because of this, he believed Tilden would be the next president. It certainly was not necessary for Grant to meet with the surprised Hewitt. Exhausted, already enthusiastic about a private trip to Great Britain and Europe immediately after stepping down as president, Grant offered his impartial good offices at this critical moment from an unexpected realization of "let us have peace."

Hewitt bounced down the White House steps delighted at what he had heard. Grant intended to carry out the spirit of both houses of Congress—not just the Republican Senate. Immediately upon returning home, Hewitt dictated a long memorandum of their conversation for public release. He sent a second copy to the president, requesting him to provide corrections. Grant made none.

ON DECEMBER 6, electors met in state capitals to tabulate their electoral votes. In South Carolina, Louisiana, and Florida, two sets of electors cast differing votes. The contradictory results were conveyed to Washington. Fears arose that on March 4, 1877, two different presidents would be inaugurated.

Who was to count the votes? Traditionally, the vice president, who functioned as president of the Senate, counted the votes. But Henry Wilson had died in 1875. As Senate majority leader, Michigan senator Thomas W. Ferry had succeeded him as president of the Senate. Should Ferry have sole power to count disputed electoral votes?

Instead, on January 18, 1877, after more than a month of often acrimo-

Thomas Nast satirized the 1876 election by drawing multiple boots kicking the venerable ballot box.

nious discussion, the House and Senate proposed a joint electoral commission to decide who had won the election. The majority party in the Senate, the Republicans, and the majority party in the House, the Democrats, each selected three representatives to the commission, while the minority parties each selected two, resulting in a five-to-five split. A final five members would come from the Supreme Court, two Republicans and two Democrats, with the fifth, meant to be neutral, chosen by the other four. Justice David Davis, who had been Lincoln's campaign manager in 1860 but was now a Democrat, was the initial selection. But Davis, who had been leaning toward Tilden, was elected by the Illinois legislature to the Senate shortly after his selection. As a result, he was replaced by Joseph P. Bradley, seen as the most independent of the remaining justices. Hewitt pronounced the selection of Bradley as "entirely satisfactory."

The vote for the electoral commission exposed the deep divide among Republicans. In the Senate, Republicans barely backed the commission, 21 to 16. In the House, they opposed the commission, 31 to 69. The Democrats, by contrast, voted for the commission 26 to 1 in the Senate and 160 to 17 in the House.

With deep Republican resistance to the commission, Grant used his powers of persuasion in one-on-one conversations to advocate its implementation. He sent a message to the Senate commending their support "because of my appreciation of the imminent peril to the institutions of the country from which, in my judgment, the act affords a wise and constitutional means of escape." Grant recognized that "the bill may not be perfect, and its provisions may not be such as would be best applicable in all future occasions, but it is calculated to meet the present condition of the question and of the country." Increasingly skilled as a practical politician, he understood the anxiety among his own Republican Party and sought to assuage their apprehensions.

The commission began meeting on the last day of January, only five weeks from Inauguration Day. During the month of February, Grant kept a respectful distance from the commission, while regularly conversing with Hayes's and Tilden's emissaries. As tensions remained high, Grant became the calm center in the storm of uncertainty.

In the end, the commission awarded Hayes all twenty electoral votes—by a vote of 8 to 7. Justice Bradley became the swing vote. Hayes, while still losing the popular vote, 4,286,808 to 4,034,142, won the electoral vote 185 to 184. In what would come to be called "the Compromise of 1877," southern Democrats agreed to support Hayes if he agreed to end Reconstruction and support home rule in the South. Grant knew that home rule meant white rule; it would perpetuate the disfranchisement of black voters deep into the twentieth century.

ON FRIDAY, MARCH 2, Grant welcomed Hayes to the White House. He invited Hayes to stay, but Hayes chose to respect the Grants' final hours as the First Family in the White House and declined the offer, instead taking up residence at Ohio senator John Sherman's home on K Street.

The next evening, the Grants hosted an elegant dinner in the Blue Room in honor of the Hayeses. During after-dinner conversation, Grant and Hayes slipped away to the Red Room. By statute, Hayes would become president at noon on March 4. But since the second term of President James Monroe in 1821, tradition held that no inaugural ceremony would occur on a Sunday. Therefore, Grant superintended a secret swearing-in ceremony on Saturday evening with Hayes, Chief Justice Morrison Waite, and several witnesses. The swearing-in would be repeated publicly on Monday, March 5. After eight challenging years, Grant was no longer president.

Following the public inauguration on March 5, Julia served a stylish luncheon at the White House. As she prepared to leave her home of nearly a decade, she said to Mrs. Hayes, "I hope you will be as happy here as I have been for the last eight years."

GRANT LEFT THE White House on a high note. Despite the scandals of his second term, in the bitterly contested centennial election he had con-

Ohio governor Rutherford B. Hayes, the compromise Republican candidate, won the contested presidential election of 1876 to become Grant's successor.

ducted himself as a first-class statesman. He had demonstrated his political maturity in his willingness to cooperate with the Tilden campaign and with the Democratic-controlled House for the greater good of the nation. Grant would later observe, "If Tilden was declared elected, I intended to hand him over the reins, and see him peacefully installed. I should have treated him as cordially as I did Hayes, for the question of the presidency was neither personal nor political, but national."

Grant's calm skills in mediation reestablished his popularity among many who had been his critics. Whitelaw Reid, editor of the *New York Tribune,* praised his "public and patriotic service," telling his readers that Grant's services "in war and peace" deserved the nation's "respect and gratitude." Reid declared that as "unpopular as the later years of his Administration have been, he will . . . go out of office amid general good will."

Future president James Garfield, who earlier expressed misgivings about Grant's presidency, confided to his diary, "I was again impressed with the belief that when his Presidential term is ended, Gen. Grant will regain his place as one of the very foremost of Americans." Garfield predicted, "His power of staying, his imperturbability, has been of incalculable value to the nation, and will be prized more and more as his career recedes."

GRANT HAD CHANGED physically in these eight years. His weight had increased; his face had become fleshier; his reddish-brown hair now included touches of silver. He wore glasses for reading. He and Julia, both more self-assured in the public world they now inhabited, had become accustomed to comfortable living. Even though weary, with wanderlust in his blood he could hardly wait for the adventure and education of travel that lay ahead.

Grant told Hewitt that "for sixteen years he had consecrated his life to the public service without any interval of rest or any possibility of being free from great responsibility." The general was ready to turn over the reins of command.

Julia felt more regret. As she walked through the White House for the last time, surveying rooms she had found so shabby eight years ago, she took pride in her restoration and elevation of the large house she had come to love, the sight of countless gala dinners and social receptions she had hosted to help reconcile a divided capital.

In addition—less remembered in history, but no less important for their family—she and Ulysses had experienced the mysterious life cycle of birth, marriage, and death in this fabled manse. Julia Grant would never imagine that little granddaughter Julia would outlive the eighteen presidents who succeeded her grandfather and be invited again and again to visit the White House before dying at age ninety-nine in 1975.

Perhaps with a wry smile, Julia stocked the larder for Mrs. Hayes, arranging her favorite wines in careful places of honor. She knew that Lucy Hayes, passionately involved in the temperance movement, intended to make the White House bone-dry for the next four years.

With a final farewell to family, friends, and servants, the Grants walked down the steps of the North Portico and entered their carriage. As Grant's four magnificent chestnut horses pranced in anticipation, Ulysses and Julia prepared to enter the next chapter of their life together.

PART SIX

World Citizen

1879–1885

Grant possessed formidable intellectual capacity.
He had the novelist's gift for the thumbnail sketch
of character, dramatic setting of mood and
introduction of the telling incident; he had the
historian's ability to summarize events and
incorporate them smoothly in the larger narrative;
he had the topographer's feel for landscape and the
economist's instinct for material essentials.

—John Keegan, *The Mask of Command*

CHAPTER 34

American Ambassador

General Ulysses Grant, like his classic namesake, has seen men and
cities in almost every part of the world, enlarging the genius of
the statesman and the soldier by the experience of travel.

—JOHN RUSSELL YOUNG, diary entry, March 10, 1879

"I was never so happy in my life as the day I left the White House. I felt like a boy getting out of school." Grant's relief at leaving the presidency has been overplayed, overshadowing his enthusiasm to embark on the trip of a lifetime. Politicos gossiped that he did not like Rutherford Hayes and wanted to get out of town, but in fact his successor was not what was on his mind.

It was the prospect of travel that energized Grant. Three decades earlier in Mexico, he developed habits of engaging peoples and cultures that he would now employ in this larger venture: to understand new countries and peoples.

Describing themselves as "waifs," Ulysses and Julia left the White House without a clear idea of where their settled home would be. For the time being, however, they wanted to remain in Washington to be with Nellie, who had come from Great Britain to give birth to her second child, so they happily accepted an invitation from Hamilton and Julia Fish to stay with them for the next three weeks. The baby, christened Algernon Edward Sartoris, arrived on March 17.

Grant had long envisioned traveling after his presidency and now determined to finance the adventure through one of his few successful investments. Twenty-five shares in Consolidated Virginia Mining, based in Virginia City, Nevada, had earned him $25,000. That sum, he believed, would cover the costs of a two-year sojourn, if he remained frugal about his accommodations and lifestyle. He assigned Ulysses Jr. the task of managing his financial affairs while abroad.

Yet Grant's travels have been the subject of much misinformation and

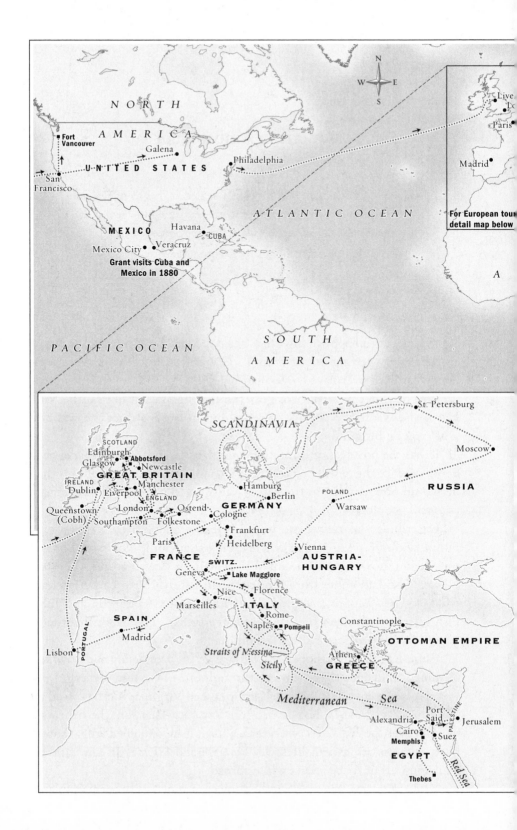

N W E S

N O R T H
A M E R I C A

Fort
Vancouver

Galena
Philadelphia

San
Francisco

UNITED STATES

Live
Lo
Paris

Madrid

For European tour
detail map below

A

M E X I C O
Havana
CUBA

Mexico City
Veracruz

**Grant visits Cuba and
Mexico in 1880**

ATLANTIC OCEAN

PACIFIC OCEAN

S O U T H
A M E R I C A

SCANDINAVIA

St. Petersburg

SCOTLAND
Edinburgh
Glasgow
Abbotsford
Newcastle
GREAT BRITAIN
IRELAND
Dublin
Manchester
Liverpool
ENGLAND
Queenstown
(Cobh)
London
Southampton
Folkestone
Ostend
Paris
FRANCE
SWITZ.
Geneva
Lake Maggiore
Nice
Marseilles
ITALY
Florence
Rome
Naples
Pompeii
Hamburg
Berlin
GERMANY
Cologne
Frankfurt
Heidelberg
Vienna
AUSTRIA-
HUNGARY
POLAND
Warsaw
RUSSIA
Moscow

SPAIN
PORTUGAL
Madrid
Lisbon

Straits of Messina
Sicily

Constantinople
OTTOMAN EMPIRE
Athens
GREECE

Mediterranean Sea

Port
Said
Alexandria
Cairo
Memphis
Suez
EGYPT
Thebes
PALESTINE
Jerusalem
Red Sea

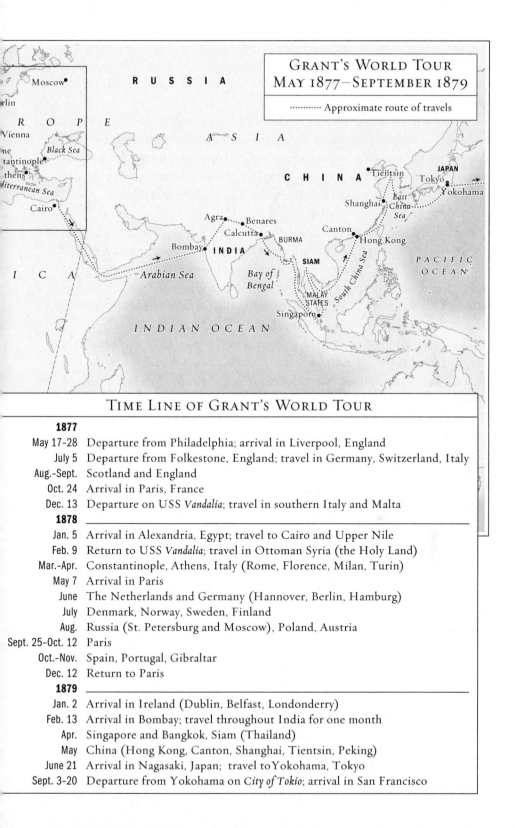

GRANT'S WORLD TOUR
MAY 1877–SEPTEMBER 1879

·········· Approximate route of travels

RUSSIA

Moscow

rlin

R O P E

Vienna

ne

tantinople

thens

literranean Sea

Cairo

A S I A

Black Sea

CHINA Tientsin

JAPAN

Tokyo

Yokohama

Shanghai East China Sea

Agra Benares

Calcutta

Bombay **INDIA** BURMA

Canton

Hong Kong

SIAM

Arabian Sea Bay of Bengal

PACIFIC OCEAN

MALAY STATES South China Sea

Singapore

I C A

INDIAN OCEAN

TIME LINE OF GRANT'S WORLD TOUR

1877

May 17-28	Departure from Philadelphia; arrival in Liverpool, England
July 5	Departure from Folkestone, England; travel in Germany, Switzerland, Italy
Aug.-Sept.	Scotland and England
Oct. 24	Arrival in Paris, France
Dec. 13	Departure on USS *Vandalia*; travel in southern Italy and Malta

1878

Jan. 5	Arrival in Alexandria, Egypt; travel to Cairo and Upper Nile
Feb. 9	Return to USS *Vandalia*; travel in Ottoman Syria (the Holy Land)
Mar.-Apr.	Constantinople, Athens, Italy (Rome, Florence, Milan, Turin)
May 7	Arrival in Paris
June	The Netherlands and Germany (Hannover, Berlin, Hamburg)
July	Denmark, Norway, Sweden, Finland
Aug.	Russia (St. Petersburg and Moscow), Poland, Austria
Sept. 25-Oct. 12	Paris
Oct.-Nov.	Spain, Portugal, Gibraltar
Dec. 12	Return to Paris

1879

Jan. 2	Arrival in Ireland (Dublin, Belfast, Londonderry)
Feb. 13	Arrival in Bombay; travel throughout India for one month
Apr.	Singapore and Bangkok, Siam (Thailand)
May	China (Hong Kong, Canton, Shanghai, Tientsin, Peking)
June 21	Arrival in Nagasaki, Japan; travel to Yokohama, Tokyo
Sept. 3-20	Departure from Yokohama on *City of Tokio*; arrival in San Francisco

misinterpretation; and the man himself has been criticized for spending lavishly and lacking an appreciation of the history and culture of the countries he visited.

Quite the contrary. Grant's understated personality would captivate foreign leaders. At the same time, ordinary people would receive the American Ulysses as a special ambassador from the United States. Reports of Grant's enthusiastic welcome in country after country would cause many back home to take a fresh look at their ex-president.

ON MAY 17, the Grants boarded the SS *Indiana,* a passenger and cargo steamship bound from Philadelphia to Liverpool. Ulysses and Julia's small party included Jesse, now a nineteen-year-old senior at Cornell University, a maid, and a secretary. Also in attendance was John Russell Young, a thirty-six-year-old correspondent with the *New York Herald,* which, sensing a story, had dispatched Young to accompany the Grants.

An Irish immigrant, Young grew up in Philadelphia. He became a proofreader for the *Philadelphia Press* at fifteen; by age twenty-one, he had become managing editor. After the Civil War, he moved to New York to write for Horace Greeley's *New York Tribune* before crossing over to James Gordon Bennett's *New York Herald,* where his assignments included reporting from Europe. Bennett wanted Young to file regular stories on Grant's tour, with an eye to his reception in the various countries to be visited.

On the transatlantic crossing, Grant and Young began an intriguing friendship. The same height as Grant, with brown hair, blue eyes, and red whiskers, Young quickly warmed to his subject, who was transforming before his eyes: "That reticence which had characterized the manner of the Ex-President during the many years of his onerous and toilsome employment in the service of his country, dropped from him as though it were a mask." This change meant that Grant, "now that he was free from official care," displayed "that geniality and sympathetic nature which more justly belonged to him."

On the eleven-day voyage, Grant began reading Mark Twain's *The Innocents Abroad.* Based on his 1867 travels with a group of Americans to Europe and the Holy Land, Twain's satire played off of the grandiose jargon of contemporary travel books. He highlighted tensions between history and the modern world, again and again emphasizing the profiteering and trivialization that trampled the meaning of historical sites. Through Twain's literary lens, citizen Grant would not be traveling as an innocent abroad.

· · ·

ON MAY 28, the Grants arrived in England to a cheering welcome that took them by surprise. The mayor of Liverpool was there to extend to Grant "the courtesies of the great commercial city."

The next day, Grant visited shipyards and docks where he knew Confederate raiding ships had been built fifteen years earlier. In the afternoon, he inspected the Liverpool Free Library. By the end of his first full day, surely with mixed feelings, he realized that instead of the private holiday he had looked forward to, his every move would be anticipated and his attendance required, day after day, at public receptions raised in his honor.

Grant traveled throughout Great Britain for all of June. Officials greeted him everywhere, but whenever possible he slipped away from his hosts to converse with ordinary people.

Memorably, he spoke in Manchester, where workers turned out to hear the hero of an American Civil War that represented for them a high point in the worldwide struggle for human rights. Grant acknowledged, "I am aware that the sentiments of the great mass of the people of Manchester went out in sympathy to that country during the mighty struggle in which it fell to my lot to take some humble part." After a toast by the mayor, a reporter noticed a twinkle in Grant's eyes as he responded, "Englishmen had got more speeches, and of greater length, out of him, than his own countrymen."

Upon arriving in London, Grant was the guest of the Prince of Wales at Epsom Downs, a racecourse founded in 1661. The Duke of Wellington, aware of Grant's reputation as a superb horseman, turned the conversation that evening to racing. Grant responded, "There is an impression abroad that I am a great horse-racer, fond of horses, and know all about races; but on the contrary, I really know nothing about racing." He added that he had been to only two races in his life. What he did not say: He never intended to go again. Precisely because of his love of horses, Grant believed horse-racing a cruel sport.

The next morning, Grant attended "divine service" at Westminster Abbey. Church joined state in a chorus of admiration. The dean of Westminster, Arthur Stanley, singled Grant out in his sermon. While serving as Regius Professor of Ecclesiastical History at Oxford, Stanley had been a strong supporter of the Union. Now he interjected, "In the midst of the congregation there was one of the chiefest citizens of the United States . . . who by his military prowess and generous treatment of his comrades and adversaries had restored unity to his country."

· · ·

This woven silk Stevengraph by Thomas Stevens of Coventry, England, celebrated Grant's most famous battles and included his 1868 campaign slogan: "I will fight it out on this line."

TWO WEEKS INTO his travels, Grant wrote Elihu Washburne, still minister to France, "I will be compelled to be very moderate in my expenditures to correspond with my means." He confided, "In fact the extent of my visit abroad will depend entirely on how long I can stay upon the limited capital I have brought with me."

Grant broke away from the gaggle of official events to spend several days with Nellie, now back at her home in Southampton. He had given grandson Algy a special gift: what else but a trotting horse! Ulysses, Jesse, Nellie, and Algy rode all over the southern coast in an American buggy.

Back in London, June 18 proved a memorable day. At breakfast, Grant savored conversations with English literary giants Matthew Arnold, Anthony Trollope, and Robert Browning. In the evening he spoke to the Reform Club, founded in 1836 by members of the Liberal Party who had pledged support for the Great Reform Act of 1832, which produced far-reaching changes in an outdated electoral system. Their building, in the style of an Italian palazzo, was celebrated as a masterpiece of classical architecture. Lord George Granville, British foreign secretary during the latter part of the *Alabama* Claims negotiations, introduced Grant and thanked him for his leadership in enacting the historic agreement. Young noted, "General Grant spoke under the pressure of unusual feeling." Although Grant "lamented so much . . . my poverty in phrases," he wanted "to give due expression of my affection for the mother country."

By the time Grant reached London, Edwards Pierrepont, U.S. minister to Great Britain and Grant's former attorney general, was worried. Despite the enthusiastic public response, officials told him plainly that Grant was only a private citizen, a "commoner," while in their country. Pierrepont heard this viewpoint especially from the government, led by Conservative prime minister Benjamin Disraeli, while many Liberals, such as silver-tongued radical John Bright, believed Grant should be celebrated in England. Pierrepont discussed this problem with Lord Derby, minister of foreign affairs, who said the government would not recognize an ex-president who, "having no acknowledged rank or precedence in his own country, could not have any here." Ever persistent, when he was informed that for European rulers, "Once an Emperor always an Emperor," Pierrepont countered, "Then, once a President always a President."

Grant's standing was put to the test when he was invited to stay the night at Windsor Castle with Queen Victoria—he learned the invitation had been tendered reluctantly. In the end, the queen received the Grants and Pierreponts in the magnificent 520-foot-long quadrangle of the castle.

Grant concluded his visit to Great Britain with a Fourth of July celebration at the U.S. embassy. With everyone in London beginning their summer holiday, he decided to postpone his trip to the north of England and Scotland and make a quick visit to the Continent.

FROM FOLKESTONE, GRANT crossed the English Channel to Ostend, Belgium. Because of troubled politics in France, he postponed a visit to Paris and went directly to Germany. He saw Cologne, took the traditional boat trip down the Rhine, stopped in Frankfurt am Main, where he was feted at a dinner at the famous Palmer Garten restaurant, and then went on to Heidelberg.

Grant especially looked forward to visiting Switzerland. At Geneva he exclaimed: "I have long had a desire to visit the city where the *Alabama* Claims were settled by arbitration without the effusion of blood, where the principle of international arbitration was established, which I hope will be resorted to by other nations and be the means of continuing peace to all mankind."

In August, Grant toured Italy. At his welcome at Lake Maggiore, he acknowledged, "There is one Italian whose hand I wish especially to shake, and that man is General Garibaldi," the Italian patriot and soldier who helped achieve the unification of Italy.

Traveling along the Italian coast, he and Julia read aloud parts of Homer's *Odyssey*. Grant wished to see where the son of Laertes arrived, where he eluded Calypso and evaded Scylla and Charybdis. Using maps, he sought to chart the path of his mythic namesake.

After three months of travel that exceeded his expectations, Grant wrote Buck on August 25 asking about his Consolidated Virginia Mining stock: "The length of my stay abroad will have to depend in some degree upon the length of time it continues to pay dividends, or the price at which my stock in it sells."

GRANT ARRIVED IN Edinburgh on August 31 as Scots returned from their summer vacations. His responses to welcoming speeches demonstrated his wry humor. In one Scottish city after another, he thanked the assembled crowd for being made a burgess, warning them he might run for office. Extolling their railroads, he jested, "I might vote frequently in Scotland by starting early" in the day.

Praised everywhere as a military man—"the Wellington of America"—he told a Glasgow audience, "I am called a man of war, but I never was a man of war." He clarified: "Though I entered the army at an early age, I got out of it whenever I found a chance to do so creditably. I was always a man of peace, and I shall continue of that mind."

Grant had long looked forward to visiting Sir Walter Scott's country home in the Borders area joining Scotland and England. Of course, he had read Scott's novels at West Point, and in courting Julia, he had read from them as they sat on the banks of Gravois Creek. Upon his return to Edinburgh days later, Grant still was talking about Scott.

WHEN GRANT CROSSED back into England, he was greeted at Newcastle upon Tyne by intertwined U.S. and British flags in the windows of homes and shops. On Saturday, September 22, nearly one hundred thousand workingmen, including thousands of miners from the pits of Northumberland, poured into the city from surrounding towns to see and hear Grant. Workingmen's organizations made a colorful parade marching to the city center: Amalgamated Society of Tailors; Operative Painters, holding a painting that represented the breaking of the chains of slavery, with the inscription "Welcome to the Liberator"; and the Tanners of Elswick, carrying a banner that read LET US HAVE PEACE.

Thomas Burt, famed Liberal working-class leader, presented the af-

Grant received rousing applause as he spoke to thousands of workingmen at Newcastle, England.

ternoon's address: "Never was there a war in which English armies were not employed that went so directly to the popular feeling." He declared, "It was not a war for conquest, for selfish aggrandizement, or for the propping up of a tottering throne; but it involved the great questions of freedom, of the rights of man, and the dignity and honor of labor." He then spoke of another pillar of Grant's greatness: "When the history of the nineteenth century comes to be written, one of its brightest pages will be that which tells how two of the greatest and most valorous nations of the world settled their differences by arbitration rather than by an appeal to the power of armies."

Why did the British and Scottish people receive Grant with such enthusiasm? After all, it took a long time for the British press to warm up to Abraham Lincoln. One major reason was the perception of American politicians. Finally, when the press applauded Lincoln's second inaugural address, the *Saturday Review* voiced a prevailing attitude: "If it had been composed by any other prominent American politician, it would have been boastful, confident, and menacing." The British did not like what they saw as American politicians' arrogance—think Senator Charles Sumner's ill-tempered words during the *Alabama* Claims dispute.

Self-effacing Grant was nothing like that. The man in the plain black suit, with none of the medals and ribbons worn by people of lesser distinction, endeared himself to the British people. To a highly class-conscious society, the press depicted Grant as the tanner's son, exemplifying the possibility of rising from humble beginnings in the United States of America.

IF GRANT FELT surprised by his reception in Great Britain, his welcome was also a revelation in the United States. Thanks to Young's reports, Grant became front-page news. Additionally, some of his private letters were published. He wrote George Childs, "I appreciate the fact,—and am proud of it—that the attentions which I am receiving are intended more for our country than for me personally." He added, "I love to see our country honored & respected abroad." These letters would increase the American public's fascination with his trip.

Hamilton Fish summed up the response to Grant's tour: "Even those who did not love him over much . . . some of the Liberal Republicans, take to themselves comfort, from his reception, in the idea that it is all meant as a tribute to the 'American people.'"

IN MID-AUTUMN, GRANT crossed the English Channel once more, reaching Paris on October 24. He arrived to find an anxious city. In 1870–1871, Prussian military might had destroyed the Second Empire of Napoleon III. Conflict between republican and monarchist elements had postponed Grant's visit in July, and the tensions still rumbled beneath the surface of daily life.

An added strain arose because during the Franco-Prussian War, U.S. minister Elihu Washburne had protected German diplomats and property—a stance that had been publicly supported by (then) President Grant—remaining in Paris even when other diplomats chose to leave. French resentment against Germans and their supporters simmered.

Grant was feted by President Patrice de MacMahon at the Élysée Palace, but given the unsettled climate, he tried to avoid public receptions, confining himself to dinners within the large American expatriate community in Paris and the sightseeing of ordinary tourists. Young reported that Grant made numerous visits to the Louvre to view paintings of the masters.

Grant visited the studio of George P. A. Healy, the American artist who had painted *The Peacemakers*—Grant, Lincoln, Sherman, and Porter—in 1868. Healy knew Grant wanted to meet Léon Gambetta and hosted a dinner at his home to introduce him to the republican hero who had helped direct the defense of France. Years afterward, Healy observed, "They seemed typical representatives of the two nations."

Grant also called on sculptor Frédéric Auguste Bartholdi, who was hard at work on his Statue of Liberty at the workshop of Gaget, Gauthier & Company. Bartholdi had called on Grant seven years earlier at Long Branch. Grant wrote the president of the committee of the Franco-American Union, "The Statue of Liberty promises to be in every way worthy of its purpose and will fitly express the friendship of the two nations."

One of Grant's favorite haunts was the Paris office of the *New York Herald*. He would find a quiet corner in the reading room to spend an hour or two reviewing the *Herald* and other English-language newspapers.

Writing to a friend, Grant sounded like many Americans after initial months of travel abroad: "I have seen nothing here that would make me want to live in Paris, or elsewhere outside of the United States."

But Grant had learned to challenge first impressions in his previous travels. In a foreign country, aware of his own limitations to understand a different culture, Grant cultivated this ability to be self-critical of his initial judgments until it became a pattern of engagement.

AFTER SPENDING NOVEMBER in Paris, the Grants left for Nice. At Nice, Grant wrote a perceptive letter to Daniel Ammen about his changing views of the French people. He admitted, "Before coming here I did not believe the French people capable of self-government." What changed? "My opinion of their capacity for self-government has materially changed since seeing for myself." Grant was saying in so many words that he and other Americans formed opinions of other nations without "seeing for myself." Moreover, "They are patient 'and long suffering,' but there will not be entire peace and quiet until a form of government is established in which all people have a full voice." He was convinced that "it will be more republican than anything they have yet had under the name of a republic." Grant's travel in France was no boondoogle; rather, always curious about the customs of other lands, he admitted to his boyhood friend that he was now forced to change his mind. From Nice they boarded the USS *Vandalia,* personally sent by President Hayes, for a leisurely winter Mediterranean cruise to Egypt. On deck, Ulysses and Julia read once more from the *Odyssey* as they navigated through the Strait of Messina, made famous in the epic. On this voyage, Young mused, "My friend Mark Twain will be glad to know that the General read with delight and appreciation his *Innocents Abroad*."

That month, Grant wrote, "I am beginning to enjoy traveling and if the money holds out, or if Consolidated Va Mining stock does, I will not be back to the eastern states for two years yet." By now the purpose of Grant's trip had changed. Originally planning only a private visit to Great Britain and Europe, he now looked forward to exploring new places less familiar to American travelers. If at first he had expressed a typical American opinion that there was no place like home, his curiosity eventually elicited an eagerness to press ahead with no predetermined finish line.

The second officer of the *Vandalia,* Albert Caldwell did not relish his assignment steering the ex-president's party. At the start of the voyage, he grumbled in a letter to his family: "We are to take the great ringmaster about the Mediterranean; it has cost me much annoyance & trouble already and I am in hopes that his money will give out before he gets to Cadiz."

What a difference a month would make. On January 10, 1878, Caldwell wrote, "My opinion of old USG has changed wonderfully—he is as pleasant & jolly as can be & I can see now how he had friends who stuck to him through thick & thin." Furthermore, "One thing that makes me like the whole party is the affection existing between them—the Boss & Jesse are as kind and attentive to the mother as if she were a sweet girl of 18 summers." Travel, especially foreign travel with its innumerable culture shocks, can often bring out the worst tensions within families, but Caldwell voiced the observations of others: the Grant family genuinely liked one another.

The *Vandalia* dropped anchor in the Bay of Naples. There someone discovered an English version of *The Nasby Papers* that proved a "boon" for Grant's appetite for reading. Petroleum V. Nasby, fictional alter ego of journalist David Locke, was a strong supporter of Grant's in 1872 and 1876. Nasby's humorous letters, with their purposely semi-literate spelling, brimmed with irony.

Impatient to visit Pompeii, the general ordered an early march on December 19. His enthusiasm stemmed from West Point memories of reading Edward Bulwer-Lytton's *The Last Days of Pompeii,* which told the story of the city's obliteration when Mt. Vesuvius erupted in AD 79.

Grant surveyed the ruins still being unearthed and visited the supposed house of Bulwer's protagonist, Glaucus, visualizing how he might have lived. Julia, who had also read Bulwer in her St. Louis school, imagined the heroine, "poor Nydia, with upraised hands and eager look, her pretty head stretched far forward listening to treachery plotted against her beloved Glaucus." Although Grant had been disappointed by the crassness encountered at many historic sites, his visit to Pompeii was an exception.

Ulysses, Julia, and Jesse celebrated Christmas with a banquet on the *Vandalia*. Everyone appreciated Julia's cheerful spirit. Young wrote, "I wish I could lift the veil far enough to show you how much the kind, considerate, ever womanly and ever cheerful nature of Mrs. Grant has won upon us all; but I must not invade the privacy of the domestic circle."

Other journalists, not present, tried to offer a different view: "It informs us that General Grant travels with a princely retinue; that he is enabled to do so because the men who fattened on the corruptions of his administration gave him a share of their plunder." Further, "He never asks the cost of his rooms at hotels, but throws money about with a lavish hand." Charges of corruption did not stop at the water's edge of the United States but cast a long shadow.

Young was outraged. "The truth is that General Grant travels not like a prince, but as a private citizen. He has one servant and a courier [secretary]." If the overall reporting on the trip was wholly positive, the *Herald* reporter appreciated "brushing away one or two of the cobwebs of slander" surrounding their trip together.

At the end of 1877, after a year and a half, Young took Grant's measure: "The impression that the General makes upon you is that he has immense resources in reserve. He has in eminent degree that 'two o'clock in the morning courage' which Napoleon said he alone possessed among his marshals and generals." Young was impressed with "his good feeling and magnanimity in speaking of comrades and rivals in the war." Particularly striking, "especially in the cases of Sherman and Sheridan, McPherson and Lincoln—it becomes an enthusiasm quite beautiful to witness."

ON JANUARY 5, 1878, the *Vandalia* docked in Alexandria. Egypt existed as a semiautonomous nation within the Ottoman Empire. Although the empire was governed by Khedive Ismail the Magnificent, the British and French had interceded in 1876 to set up a Public Debt Commission to manage Egypt's foreign debt. To help explore the Nile and Egypt's monuments, the khedive placed at Grant's disposal a long, narrow steamer.

By his third day in Egypt, disappointed, Grant wrote Buck, "All the romance given to Oriental splendor in novels and guide books is dissipated by witnessing the real thing. Innate ugliness, slovenliness, filth and indolence."

By now, Young had become a companion as well as a correspondent. This relationship allowed Grant to open up in ways he had done only with Adam Badeau, Horace Porter, or Orville Babcock. Young revealed that in "the red-letter hours of our Nile journey," General Grant "told us how he met Lee at Appomattox, or how Sherman fought at Shiloh."

Each day became a surreal combination of quiet beauty on the shining Nile, punctuated by lively welcomes to "the King of America" by villagers. By the end of January, Grant remembered his cardinal rule of appreciation, writing Buck with a much different opinion from that of day three: "Egypt has interested me more than any other portion of my travels." When at last the minarets of Cairo appeared, the travelers sadly observed that while the cradle of civilization may have built great temples and tombs, they also, in Julia's words, had "nothing left" for her impoverished people.

Ulysses, wearing a pith helmet, sits with Julia, Jesse, and others in the ruins of the Karnak Temple complex in the ancient city of Thebes, Egypt.

Reuniting with the *Vandalia* at Port Said, Grant now looked expectantly toward Jerusalem. A seed for his desire to visit Palestine had been cultivated in his visit to Chautauqua in 1875, during which Vincent, the Methodist educator, had showed him a complete scale model of the Holy

Land he had built as a visual teaching tool. He encouraged Grant to visit if ever he had the opportunity.

Julia took the lead in preparing their little group: "We had been doing a good deal of Bible reading and revision of our Testaments, to be sure of our sacred ground."

However, Grant's visit to Jerusalem, as he wrote Adam Badeau, proved to be "a very unpleasant one." In 1878, the Turks ruled Palestine. Jerusalem, poor and run-down, supported a population of twenty-two thousand, half Jewish. The weather did not help the travelers' impressions—six inches of snow aggravated already bad streets. Grant tried to forget the present day as he visited many sites associated with the biblical story of Jesus, but ultimately he agreed with Twain, who had written of the "clap-trap side-shows and unseemly impostures of every kind" associated with these holy relics.

NEXT, GRANT ARRIVED in Constantinople on March 1, two days before the Treaty of San Stefano concluded the Russo-Turkish War of 1877–1878. He visited the Hagia Sophia—for nearly a thousand years the seat of the patriarchate of Constantinople, but for the past 425 years a Muslim mosque.

The sultan of Turkey, Abdul Hamid II, invited Grant to his private stables to hear the general's views on his magnificent stock of Arabian horses. To Grant's surprise, the sultan offered him two horses of his choosing. At first he refused; then, realizing this would offend his host, he accepted.

Grant selected a dappled gray and an iron gray, both exhibiting the distinctive characteristics of the Arabian breed: superbly shaped head, large, soft eyes, and long tail.

Despite the extravagant gifts, Grant did not travel with rose-colored glasses. He denounced the class and gender divisions he saw in Turkey: "They have a form of government that will always repress progress and development." He was convinced that "the people would be industrious if they had encouragement, but they are treated as slaves, and all they produce is taken from them for the benefit of the governing classes and to maintain them in a luxurious and licentious life." Grant was particularly appalled by the plight of women: "Women are degraded even beneath a slave. . . . The donkey is their superior in privileges."

Grant spent a special week in Athens, scaling the Acropolis and enjoying the illumination of the Parthenon at night. In this ancient city, Young reflected, "Our chief may have the reputation of being an imperturbable man, but very certainly none appreciated better than General Grant the greatness of the past." In a walking city where even seasoned travelers could become weary, "the General has shown the most marked adaptiveness as a tourist. . . . There is no tire in him."

Grant left the *Vandalia* upon reaching Italy. His party arrived in Rome at the end of March and once again met many American tourists, making Grant realize how few of his compatriots he had seen in the Ottoman Empire, a destination he now realized was "entirely out of the usual course of travelers abroad." As he traveled through Italy, appreciating Rome's historic sites and Florence's Uffizi Gallery, he remarked, "One should visit [Rome] before making the Nile trip. Here you see modern and comparatively insignificant ruins, not dating back many centuries before the beginning of the Christian era. On the Nile one sees grand ruins, with the inscriptions as plain and distinct as when they were first made." Few nineteenth-century American travelers visited Rome with this perspective.

UPON HIS RETURN to Paris, Grant toured the Exposition Universelle, an ambitious enterprise undertaken by the French government to celebrate the nation's recovery after the 1870–1871 Franco-Prussian War. Although it was by far the largest exposition held up until that time, Grant could not resist a comparison: "It is quite a success, but, I think, no improvement on our Centennial show. The buildings and grounds are far inferior to ours."

Next stop: Berlin.

Here, Grant took advantage of the opportunity to stroll along the Unter den Linden ("Under the Linden Trees"), the famed pedestrian mall that dated to 1647. In fact, he devoted portions of every day to exploring the Prussian capital on foot. And the experience both impressed and repelled him.

Over the course of his visit, his observations convinced him that Prussia had become the premier political power in central Europe. And although he admired German order and discipline, he was taken aback by the air of militarism that dominated all facets of society. Everywhere he walked, he saw soldiers in their traditional blue uniforms with red piping.

Grant brought with him an insider's knowledge of Otto von Bismarck, the architect of German unification, because with his encouragement, Philip Sheridan had become an adviser to the Prussian army in 1870. During Grant's stay in Berlin, Bismarck was busy hosting the Congress of Berlin—a conference held by leading statesmen of the European

Great Powers and the Ottoman Empire who sought to define the territories of the states in the Balkan peninsula following the Russo-Turkish War of 1877–1878—but the Prussian chancellor nevertheless made time to send his card to Grant's hotel requesting the general visit him.

Shortly before four on August 20, Grant set out on foot alone for Radziwill Palace. After entering the majestic courtyard, he walked in an unassuming way toward the front door as if he were about to knock. Although his visit was expected, he surprised the uniformed guards by arriving in a plain dark suit, with no medals or ribbons, with no bodyguard or uniformed escort, and with no official carriage. Catching themselves, the guards hurried to open the door, and Grant entered a marbled hall. The "Iron Chancellor," resplendent in his military uniform, greeted him with both hands.

Speaking slowly in English, Bismarck asked about Sheridan: "The general and I were fellow campaigners in France, and we became great friends."

"Yes," replied Grant, "I regard Sheridan as not only one of the great soldiers of our war, but one of the great soldiers of the world."

Bismarck invited Grant to a review the next morning. Although the general had repeatedly declined previous invitations from other leaders, this time he accepted—reluctantly. "The truth is I am more of a farmer than a soldier," he confessed. "I take no interest in military affairs, and,

Grant speaks with Chancellor Otto von Bismarck in Berlin.

although I entered the army thirty-five years ago and have been in two wars . . . I never went into the army without regret and never retired without pleasure."

In reply, Bismarck congratulated Grant on his leadership in the Civil War: "You had to save the Union just as we had to save Germany."

"Not only save the Union, but destroy slavery," added Grant.

Berlin newspapers had been filled with news of British prime minister Benjamin Disraeli, Russian prince Alexander Gorchakov, and Turkish general Mehemet Ali Pasha—key figures in the Congress of Berlin—but now Grant also became the talk of the city.

"Bismarck und Grant" was the headline in a story in the *Berliner Tageblatt*. This Berlin paper accented that "Grant was very eager to see the man whose character and achievements he so admired." By contrast, the *Berliner Borsenzeitung* focused as much on Grant, who the "Reichskanzler" (Imperial Chancellor) "received . . . most cordially."

AT THIS SAME time, Grant further captured America's attention through a creative new approach by Young in the *New York Herald*. On May 27, 1878, Young offered "an interesting conversation with General Grant." Although he did not say so, Young's "conversation" actually condensed several conversations. In succeeding months, what came to be called Grant's "Table Talk" became one of the paper's most popular features.

In his first piece, Young called attention to recent articles by former secretary of the navy Gideon Welles and former Confederate general Richard Taylor that renewed an old criticism of Grant's Virginia Campaign. Young said he had brought these articles to Grant's attention and the resulting "conversation" constituted his response. A month earlier, Young had confided to his diary that he talked with Grant when they walked together in Paris; in the evenings, he wrote down the conversations that would become the basis for his newspaper stories.

Americans thrilled to Grant speaking in his own voice about the important persons and episodes of his military and political career. Keenly aware of the firestorm that had greeted the publication of Sherman's *Memoirs* in 1875, Grant had earlier told a St. Louis reporter he had no intention of publishing his own memoirs. At a time when former Union and Confederate generals were rushing their memoirs into print, everyone believed Young's conversations would be the closest they could get to one from Grant. While many memoirs contained barely disguised attempts to settle old scores, what most impressed Young was that Grant "is never vindictive and never gossips."

The *New York Herald* published a second "Table Talk" on July 24. This time Grant revealed his estimation of Union and Confederate generals. He commended Sherman, focusing on his "character—so frank, so sincere, so outspoken, so genuine." As for Sheridan, "He had that magnetic quality of swaying men which I wish I had—a rare quality in a general."

Young knew Americans wanted to know Grant's evaluation of Confederate generals. Thus, he quoted Grant on Albert Sidney Johnston, who died at Shiloh and "might have risen in fame, and we all had confidence in his doing so, but he died too soon." Grant esteemed Stonewall Jackson, whom he had known at West Point; however, "the tactics for which Jackson is famous and which achieved such remarkable results belonged entirely to the beginning of the war." He believed those tactics "would have ensured destruction to any commander who tried them upon Sherman, Thomas, Sheridan, Meade, or any of our great generals." Yet Grant declared generously, "No doubt so able and patient a man as Jackson, who worked so hard at anything he attempted, would have adapted himself to new conditions and risen with them."

What about Lee? "I never ranked Lee as high as some others of the army . . . I never had as much anxiety when he was in my front as when Joe Johnston was in front." He acknowledged that "Lee was a good man, a fair commander, who had everything in his favor. . . . He was supported by the unanimous voice of the South," but for Grant, "Lee was of slow, conservative, cautious nature, without imagination or humor, always the same, with grave dignity." He was convinced the "illusion that nothing but heavy odds beat him will not stand the ultimate light of history."

After the publication of these first conversations, Young confided to his diary that this new format "seems to have been an immense sensation." The American public had come to know Lincoln through his speeches, but now they were coming to know Grant, who had steadfastly turned down opportunities to speak while president, through his conversations with Young. In June, Grant's party lost its first member: Jesse decided to forgo any more travel and return home. Interviewed upon his arrival in New York, Jesse said, "I got tired of these foreign countries." As for his father, "He likes foreign travel more than I do."

GRANT CELEBRATED THE Fourth of July in Hamburg, where he offered a modest dissent to a toast by Consul John M. Wilson:

> I must dissent from one remark of our Consul, to the effect that I saved the country during the recent war. If our country could be

saved or ruined by the efforts of any one man we should not have a country, and we should not be now celebrating our Fourth of July. . . . What saved the Union was the coming forward of the young men of the nation. They came from their homes and fields, as they did in the time of the giving everything to the country. To their devotion we owe the salvation of the Union. The humblest soldier who carried a musket is entitled to as much credit for the results of the war as those who were in command.

At Hamburg, Grant exhibited an eloquence not conceivable scant years before. Speaking spontaneously, he adeptly built on the consul's metaphor of saving the country to point beyond himself to an inclusive vision of American patriotism.

AFTER TRAVELING IN St. Petersburg and Moscow, then through Warsaw to Vienna and back again through the Swiss Alps, Grant returned to Paris on September 25. Now that he'd covered all of northern Europe, he wanted to visit Spain and Portugal.

In Madrid, Grant spent every spare minute exploring the back alleys of the Spanish capital. Acclaimed poet James Russell Lowell, who had been resident in Madrid as U.S. minister to Spain for more than a year, exclaimed, "After being here two days, I think he knew Madrid better than I."

GRANT CONCLUDED HIS European visits in January 1879 by traveling to Ireland, where he was made an honorary citizen of Dublin. And here, for the first time, he encountered protests. Newspapers dredged up his 1876 refusal to meet a Fenian delegation advocating an independent Irish republic. An official in Cork criticized him in the *Irish Times,* saying he had "insulted the Irish people in America."

Grant decided to handle the situation with a now familiar humor. He playfully said that as a citizen he might run for office, but "you did not know the trouble you were about getting into—for I am a troublesome candidate."

Grant had originally intended to depart from Queenstown for the United States but announced a change of plans: he and Julia would extend their travel to India, China, Japan, and perhaps Australia—literally around the globe. He thanked Buck for making this possible. While living in California, his son had made investments that placed another $60,000 at his father's disposal.

So in January 1879, Grant set off for the final leg of what had now become a world tour. A reconstituted traveling party consisting of Julia, son Fred, old friend and former navy secretary Adolph Borie, Borie's nephew physician Dr. J. Keating, and Young sailed from Marseilles aboard the French steamer *Labourdonnais,* bound for Egypt. From Alexandria, they traveled overland to Suez, there embarking on the British P&O steamer *Venetia* for the long journey to Bombay (Mumbai).

Upon their arrival three weeks later, they moved into the Governor's Mansion. Ulysses and Julia immediately became enveloped in the British ethos of privilege, with servants to meet their every need for a rupee a day—40 cents in 1879 American money.

Over the next six weeks, they marveled at the Taj Mahal at Agra, observed Hindu pilgrims in the holy city of Benares, and visited ancient ruins near Calcutta. Young noted, "Travel in India during the day is very severe"—with high heat and dust. Yet he marveled at Grant, "always ready for an excursion or an experience, and as indifferent to the comforts and necessities of the way as when in the Vicksburg campaign he would make his bivouac at the foot of a tree." Drawing upon his military experience, Grant "will map out his route for days ahead from maps and time tables, arrange just the hour of his arrival and departure, and never vary it."

In Benares, Grant refused to be carried through the streets on an ornamental gold chair with attendants calling for people to make way, as was the custom for dignitaries. He would walk. Borie, whose health was not the best, welcomed the opportunity and took Grant's seat. As people beheld this venerable man they assumed to be the ex-president, they began saluting. The former naval secretary, known for his politeness, began returning the salutes—to Grant's delight.

In Calcutta, Grant met Viceroy Edward Robert Bulwer-Lytton, whose father's novels Grant had so enjoyed and who was himself known in America as the poet Owen Meredith. He told Grant he had followed his career "with interest and respect."

A visit with the maharaja of Jeypore embodied the incongruities Grant experienced in India. An ascetic reputed to spend seven hours a day in prayer, the maharaja had ten wives. When not in prayer, he invited Grant to join him in his other passion: billiards.

Traveling within the British Empire, Grant had mixed feelings. Certainly he admired the British sense of order—it was a quality he himself had cultivated, after all—but the undeniable subjugation of peoples within their empire left him uneasy. With all due respect to the British

("It would be a sad day for the people of India and for the commerce of the world if the English should withdraw"), he believed Americans would govern in a more humane way.

FROM INDIA, GRANT sailed to Burma, Malaysia, Singapore, Siam, and Hong Kong. His party comprised the only passengers on the British steamer *Simla,* and Grant and Young engaged in long conversations as they faced each other in deck chairs. At one point, when Young asked Grant about Mexico, Grant recounted, "I urged upon President Johnson an immediate invasion of Mexico. . . . I believed then, and I believe now, that we had a just cause of war." He wanted Sheridan to "cross the Rio Grande, join Juarez, and attack Maximilian." In doing so, he hoped to "employ" the Confederate army: "We had destroyed the career of many of them at home, and I wanted them to go to Mexico."

Believing that "no features of General Grant's conversations possessed more interest than his remembrances of the war," Young asked how Grant had entered the war. The conversation turned to George McClellan and the snub Grant had received at his Cincinnati office. But Grant's typical generosity took over even then: "I have, for that matter, never lost my respect for McClellan's character, nor my confidence in his loyalty and ability. I saw in him the man who was to pilot us through, and I wanted to be on his staff." Young pressed Grant, who replied, "It has always seemed to me that the critics of McClellan do not consider this vast and cruel responsibility—the war, a new thing to all of us, the army new, everything to do from the outset, with a restless people and Congress." Grant declared, "McClellan was a young man when this devolved upon him, and if he did not succeed, it was because the conditions of success were so trying." Furthermore, "If McClellan had gone into the war as Sherman, Thomas, or Meade, had fought his way along and up, I have no reason to suppose that he would not have won as high a distinction as any of us."

GRANT PROCEEDED TO China on the American gunboat *Ashuelot,* where the revealing conversations with Young continued. "The South has been in many ways a disappointment to me." He had hoped northern capital "would pour into the South," but the terms of the invitations precluded that: "Editors say they are glad to have Northern men provided they do not take part in politics." Grant believed that "it would have been a great thing for the South if some of the streams of emigration from New England and the Middle States toward Iowa and Kansas had been diverted into the South." He felt sorry for "the poor white class," hoping the war "would free them from a bondage in some respects even lower than slavery." But that was not to be. "But they have been as much under the thumb of the slave holder as before the war." Grant's concern for economic development, whether in Mexico or the southern United States, is evident in this conversation. As his journey neared its end, he became more and more reflective.

Grant's visit to China created a flutter of excitement. At Canton, a crowd estimated at two hundred thousand lined the streets to welcome "the King of America." And in between myriad receptions and meetings, Grant and Young talked. "I have no doubt that Lincoln will be the conspicuous figure of the war: one of the great figures of history." Steaming along the Chinese coast, Grant waxed lyrical: "He might appear to go Seward's way one day, and Stanton's another, but all the time he was going his own course." In Grant's opinion "it was that gentle firmness in carrying out his own will, without apparent force or friction that formed the basis of his character."

In Shanghai, Grant attended a ball and torchlight parade. At Tientsin, he met Viceroy Li Hongzhang, the man most renowned in China for putting down the Taiping Rebellion, an enormous civil war against the Manchu-led Qing dynasty. Even while his thoughts were beginning to turn toward his return to America, Grant's appreciation of his weeks in

Grant's interview with Prince Kung, the effective head of state in China.

China is reflected in both his speeches and the spate of correspondence relating his experiences. Traveling in a radically different country, he told a crowd in Tientsin, "My visit to China has increased my estimate of the civilization and character of the Chinese people."

In conversation with Prince Kung, the effective head of state, he encouraged, "I think that progress in China should come from inside, from her own people." Perhaps his recent experiences in India had encouraged this sentiment. He cautioned, "You do not want the foreigner to come in and put you in debt by lending you money and then taking your country." A week later, he assured the prince, "The policy of America in dealing with foreign powers is one of justice. We believe that fair play, consideration for the rights of others and respect for international law will always command the respect of nations and lead to peace."

After six weeks in the country, Grant felt enthusiastic about China's future. He confided to Adam Badeau, "The fact is Chinese like Americans better, or rather hate them less, than any other foreigners. The reason is palpable. We are the only power that recognizes their right to control their own affairs." Grant predicted, "My impression is that China is on the eve of a great revolution that will land her among the nations of progress. They have the elements of great wealth and great power too and not more than a generation will pass before she will make these elements felt."

BUT CHINA HAD a rival in Japan. The two countries, separated by a narrow stretch of ocean, were locked in a bitter dispute over ownership of Loochoo—the Ryukyu Islands. Prince Kung, who came to trust Grant, asked him to intercede by carrying a message to the leaders of Japan in hopes of settling the dispute. Grant told the viceroy that he was willing to do anything to help mediate peace between the two countries. In July, America's unofficial ambassador boarded the USS *Richmond* for Japan.

Grant's travels throughout the Japanese empire left him even more deeply impressed. He wrote Admiral Daniel Ammen, who had also visited Japan, "The Japanese are altogether the superior people of the East." Three weeks later, he could scarcely contain himself: "The changes that have taken place here are more like a dream than a reality." Chief among them: "They have a public school system extending over the entire empire affording facilities for a common school education to every child, male & female."

True to his word, Grant spoke with Emperor Meiji about peace with China. Again, he emphasized, "In your discussions with China on Loo

Grant accedes to a request for mediation between Prince Kung of China and Emperor Meiji of Japan.

Chu, and on all matters at issue, do not invite or permit so far as you can avoid it, the intervention of a foreign power." He explained, "European powers have no interests in Asia, so far as I can judge from their diplomacy, that do not involve the humiliation and subjugation of the Asiatic people." Furthermore, "Their diplomacy is always selfish, and a quarrel between China and Japan would be regarded as a quarrel that might ensue to their own advantage." Grant spoke from the unique perspective he had gained from conversations with leaders in both countries.

When he began his travels to the United Kingdom and Europe twenty-six months earlier, Grant never imagined he would end what had evolved into a world tour as a trusted mediator between China and Japan.

As he prepared to depart for the United States, he wrote a sensitive letter to the leaders of the two rising powers.

> I leave Japan in two weeks from now, for my American home. If I could hear there, that amicable and most friendly relations had been established between China and Japan I should feel delighted. If anything I may have said or done should have any effect in producing so desirable a result I should feel that my visit has not been in vain, though made without thought of taking part in the affairs of two countries.

.   .   .

DESPITE GRANT'S EFFORTS, some months after he left Japan the island nation annexed the entire Ryukyu archipelago.

Four weeks before sailing from Japan, Grant wrote a revealing letter to Adam Badeau: "At the end of the first year abroad I was quite homesick but determined to see every country in Europe at least. Now at the end of twenty six months I dread going back and would not if there was a line of steamers between here and Australia." After living out of saddlebags in the Civil War, then living comfortably in the White House, and now having spent two and a half joyful years on boats, trains, and elephants, Grant anticipated the reality of an uncertain future back in the United States as an ex-president.

From Yokohama, Grant boarded the *City of Tokio* on September 3 for the long trip to California and home. On the ship he sat against his cabin wall, mesmerized by Victor Hugo's novel *Les Misérables*. Julia remembered, "He read all day long and the next day and the next" of the struggles of Jean Valjean and his ultimate experience of redemption.

JESSE WOULD LATER write, "The tour was the fulfillment of father's dream. He would have preferred to go quietly upon his way, but his pleasure in the trip more than compensated for the distasteful pomp and ceremony." Grant's son believed that "from those experiences that . . . were ordeals, he was gaining understanding and knowledge that was fitting him for better service if his country again called."

In what way might the country call? Diplomatic service? Or something more? Grant had learned so much in his twenty-six months of travel—not simply about numerous other leaders, but about himself—his increasing interest and abilities in the fine art of diplomacy with countries that he little knew. In many ways he was far more qualified to run for president in 1880 than in 1868. If Grant had become America's unofficial ambassador abroad, might he become the Republican candidate for president at home in 1880?

⤜⟐⤛

CHAPTER 35

Grant & Ward

It is my plan to build up a great firm that shall live long after . . .
its founders have passed away.

—FERDINAND WARD

Grant arrived in San Francisco to a thunderous welcome on September 20, 1879. As the *City of Tokio* cruised through the Golden Gate, the mile-wide strait that marked the entrance into San Francisco Bay, guns from Angel Island, Black Point, and Alcatraz boomed their hellos, and boats flying banners greeted the steamship as it navigated the waters of the bay. A monumental welcome-home reception had been in the works for weeks: crowds thronged the shores as diplomats, governmental officials, and military brass hastened to honor and be seen with the man of the hour. Grant was cheered, saluted, and treated like royalty from the moment his ship was sighted until he was driven in state to the Palace Hotel. (A week later, Grant would write Adolph Borie, "This place is just like Philadelphia was at the close of the war. I cannot venture in the streets except in a carriage for the mob of good-natured and enthusiastic friends, old and young.") After visiting countless historic cities, this shining new metropolis held his heart as none other: Grant was home!

Later, after the festivities had been dispensed with, he was greeted by Buck, whose investments had helped extend his father's travels into a world tour. Now it was time to consider the future. Grant's far-flung travels having enlarged his political viewpoints, he had no intention of being put out to pasture with his horses. Moreover, having given up his army pension when he entered political life, he had to find useful employment.

Perhaps more disturbing to him, he would soon discover that over the two and a half years he'd been gone, his successor, Rutherford B. Hayes, had failed to maintain a strong hand on the tiller of the ship of

Grant was welcomed home to the United States
with a parade in San Francisco.

state. In his first months in office, Hayes had ended Reconstruction by withdrawing troops from states still under federal supervision in the South, thus returning the region to local white rule. In addition, hoping to reach out in conciliation, he had appointed a number of southerners— ex-Confederates—to important government positions. But while his acts may have pleased Democrats, they had alienated members of his own Republican Party. Also, in his efforts to enact civil service reform, Hayes had tangled with Grant ally Senator Roscoe Conkling when he'd demanded the resignation of two leading bureaucrats in the New York customhouse, a symbolic act aimed at undoing Conkling's political patronage. All of this was troubling to the ex-president and added to his concerns for the future.

However, before he tackled the future, he had a dream to realize.

TWENTY-FIVE YEARS EARLIER, a thirty-two-year-old soldier left California yearning for his wife and two young children, but he had told her that someday he wanted to make the state his home. Even though Grant knew that living here would not be possible, he was eager to take the time to show Julia this glorious state in all its natural beauty. On October 1, they set off by stagecoach to visit Yosemite Valley. The Grants hiked, climbed rocks, and marveled at "the Big Trees"—California's giant sequoias.

When he returned to San Francisco, he said goodbye to John Russell Young. The *New York Herald* correspondent, eager to return to New York City, had decided to expand his newspaper articles into a book. *Around the World with General Grant,* published in late 1879 in two volumes with eight hundred illustrations, heightened the nation's appreciation of Grant. Young dedicated the book to Julia, "as a tribute of my friendship and esteem."

Grant took Julia and Fred to Oregon to show them where he was stationed in 1852. When they arrived in Portland, he found it much changed in a quarter century. As people—some standing on the roofs of houses— gathered to greet them, he turned to his wife and joked: "Julia, look there: see those people. This turn-out must be on your account, because when I came here before there were not three people on the dock!"

At Fort Vancouver, old friend General O. O. Howard, now in command, led them to the house where Grant had lived. This visit brought back recollections of his loneliness. Standing together in the evening twilight, Grant pointed out to his wife one of his many ill-fated Oregon ventures: "Julia, that is the field where I planted my potatoes."

. . .

GRANT'S TRAVELS WEREN'T over yet. They left San Francisco on October 25 for a slow, triumphal tour across the country. People gathered in towns along his railroad route, eager to get a glimpse of, better yet hear a few words from, American Ulysses returned home. He arrived in Galena in early November—with pleasure. For many years he had considered Galena home, but he knew he could not afford to stay there. As an ex-president, he was faced with no employment and no pension (presidents would not be granted one until Harry S. Truman's retirement well into the twentieth century). Grant believed he needed business opportunities that could be provided only in a large city.

In Chicago, Grand Marshal Philip Sheridan, in plumed hat and mounted on old warhorse Rienzi, led a parade of eighty thousand men marching beneath hundreds of banners. A broadside hailed Grant as the "Man of Destiny." The veterans called him simply "our own General Grant."

The climax of the festivities took place at the Palmer House, where Grant joined six hundred veterans for the annual reunion of the Society of the Army of the Tennessee. For a full six hours, he sat with Sheridan and Sherman, delighting in toasts and oratory.

More than two hours after midnight, the fifteenth and final speaker rose. This man had served briefly in an irregular Confederate unit organized in his hometown of Hannibal, Missouri. The master of ceremonies told the speaker, "Hold the crowd." Mark Twain glanced at a tired Grant. He determined to make him laugh.

Twain had long been "Grant-intoxicated." He believed he and Grant were "twice born" men—each had experienced depths of despair and heights of elation. Climbing onto a table to be better heard, Twain reminded the veterans that once upon a time they had all been babes in arms. Even Grant started life trying to get his big toe in his mouth. Grant laughed! "And if the child is but the prophecy of the man, there are mighty few who will doubt that he *succeeded*." When the evening finally ended, Grant warmly congratulated Twain.

AT LONG LAST, on December 16, Grant and Julia arrived in Philadelphia, where their tour had begun thirty-one months before. They had circumnavigated the globe and crossed the United States. Grant returned not only renewed but rehabilitated—with public thanks due to Young's intimate portraits of the journey and Grant's "Table Talk." A question began to be voiced aloud: Would this new Grant become a candidate for an unprecedented third term as president?

The idea didn't seem outrageous. Rutherford Hayes had proved unpopular. Republicans were desperate to find a candidate who could win. Adding to Republican anxiety, Democrats had gained seven seats in the Senate in the 1878 midterm elections, to win control for the first time since before the Civil War. When some of Hayes's friends urged him to consider a second term, Robert G. Ingersoll, who had nominated James G. Blaine at the 1876 Republican convention, warned that Hayes "couldn't be elected if no one ran against him."

As Hayes and his administration blundered again and again, Grant and his administration appeared in a better light. Hayes himself, watching Grant's triumphal cross-country travels, disclosed to his diary, "The general popular favorite is Grant." Newspapers repeated the Republican *St. Louis Globe Democrat* endorsement: the nation needed a "man of iron" to replace a "man of straw." *The New York Times* joined the editorial chorus, declaring Grant's world tour gave "him greater power to discern the true character of men, and place before him in a stronger light the mistakes of the past."

But Grant's longtime critics lay in the weeds ready to strike. Charles Dana's *New York Sun,* an old foe, wrote, "Ulysses S. Grant is a man driven mad by ambition." Edwin L. Godkin's *Nation* charged that Grant, while admittedly a hero, was the puppet of "Machine" politicians like New York's Roscoe Conkling, who was already raising support for a third term for Grant.

GRANT WAS NOT immune to the political pull toward elective office. Shortly before departing Japan, he had written Adam Badeau, "I am not a candidate for any office nor would I hold one that required any maneuvering or sacrifice to obtain."

Yet Grant felt conflicted. The two-term precedent did not bother him; he believed the exigencies of the times were what mattered. Nevertheless, after receiving praise in European capitals, he was not certain he could stomach criticism again in his own country.

If Grant was silent about his intentions, others were not. Among his advocates emerged a triumvirate of influential Republicans who still espoused the ideals of Reconstruction and made no apologies for using patronage and machine politics: New York's Roscoe Conkling; James Cameron, formerly Grant's secretary of war and now senator from Pennsylvania; and Illinois senator John Logan. All three believed only Grant could restore the nation to sound political and financial footing.

· · ·

GRANT'S SUPPORTERS WORRIED that he had returned too soon, that the endless celebrations were diminishing some of his luster, and they encouraged a return to travel. Grant set his sights on a winter trip to warmer Cuba and Mexico.

He and Julia headed south at the end of December. On January 1, 1880, the date many freed slaves celebrated Emancipation Day, the tone of race relations in the South had turned against any civil rights for blacks. Grant, proud of the courage of black soldiers in the Civil War, accepted an invitation to address black militia at Beaufort, South Carolina.

Later, from St. Augustine, Florida, he wrote George Childs about the warmth and goodwill he was receiving in the South. He hailed the tremendous agricultural and economic potential of Florida: "It has a great future before it."

In Grant's three weeks in Cuba, he was not able to escape political speculations. From Havana he wrote Elihu Washburne, "I would much rather any one of many I could mention should be President than that I should have it." He was no doubt tempted, but he reiterated, "I am not a candidate for anything, and if the Chicago convention nominates a candidate that can be elected it will gratify me, and the gratification will be greater if it should be someone other than myself."

Grant traveled to Mexico in February. Governor Luis Mier y Terán welcomed him to Veracruz as "an old friend it remembers, and will always recollect with gratefulness your sympathy for this country, and the distinguished services you rendered Mexico." In Mexico City, President Porfirio Díaz received the Grants at the Tivoli de San Cosme, especially adorned for the occasion with portraits of Washington, Lincoln, Grant, and Benito Juárez.

After a thirty-two-year absence, Grant marveled once again at the country's beauty—"the scenery is unsurpassed"—but this time he perceived Mexico through different glasses: those of economic development. He believed transportation to be the key to economic progress and mused to George Childs, "From the City of Mexico to the Rio Grande a road could be graded with as little labor as through an equal distance in Iowa." Anticipating American objections, he insisted, "The people are not so much of an obstacle to the development of the great resources of the country as is the bad name given them abroad." Traveling with friend and diplomat Matías Romero, Grant became convinced that investment of foreign capital would "put the people on their feet" so that "Mexico would become a rich country, a good neighbor, and the two Republics would profit by contact."

. . .

WHEN HE RETURNED to the United States in March, Grant spoke to black students in Galveston, Texas. In Louisiana, he addressed the state legislature and visited black churches and schools, including Wesley Chapel, Straight University, and the Colored Men's Protective Union. In Memphis, after stopping at his old headquarters, he addressed a downtown rally and visited a black school. Grant had never given up the idea that Republicans could win in the South, and during this visit he determined to meet with both elected leaders and African American groups in each state. Everywhere he went he sounded a common theme: "I believe that the day of general prosperity is dawning, and that the next few years will do more than the last fifteen has accomplished to make us one united people." In the midst of darkening clouds, Grant determined to emphasize conciliation over discord.

By the time he reached Galena in April, Republican candidates had spent the winter shoring up support. James G. Blaine, "the Man from Maine" who led most of the balloting at the 1876 Republican convention, was once again the clear favorite. John Sherman, Cump's brother, was the administration's candidate, having served as secretary of the Treasury under Hayes. Grant had worked with the younger Sherman after the Panic of 1873 to pass the Specie Payment Resumption Act of 1875. Backing also emerged for Elihu Washburne, Grant's longtime political mentor. Washburne's willingness to be a candidate upset some Grant supporters—but not Grant. And Grant remained silent about his own intentions.

As the convention approached, Grant backers sought to solidify support in key states by machine politics. They insisted delegations adopt a unit rule: The candidate with the highest number of delegate votes would receive all the votes. When Pennsylvanian Republicans met in Harrisburg on February 4, James Cameron used this rule to secure a unanimous vote for Grant. Conkling did the same when New York Republicans met on February 25 in Utica. Logan used his influence to pack the Illinois delegation with Grant delegates.

But these leaders proved a mixed blessing. In February, *The New York Times* opined, "Many of those who desired Grant . . . do not want him as the candidate of the Camerons and Conklings, secured by manipulated caucuses and pledged delegations." The *Times* did not miss the irony that Grant, who declined to push his own candidacy, was being drafted by tough, backroom tactics inimical to the values of their understated hero.

Even though Grant expressed publicly a reluctance to run, he followed delegate counts closely in the week before the convention. Adam Badeau, visiting him in Galena, observed, "Grant manifested as much anxiety as I ever saw him display on his own account." Julia concurred: "How can I describe that week of suspense for me!" She wanted her husband reelected; she desired to be hostess in the White House again; but she had a foreboding that his foes would block his nomination.

Chicago, having rebuilt from the disastrous 1871 fire, proudly hosted the Republican convention beginning Wednesday, June 2. By Friday, with the temperature sweltering, the overheated convention hall exploded. Conkling had badly miscalculated. At issue was the unit rule. In eleven cases, testing whether an individual in a state delegation could vote his conscience, opponents defeated the Grant supporters each time. The Grant supporters' carefully crafted unit rule gave way.

The nominations began at ten P.M. on Saturday evening. Rising to nominate Grant, Conkling jumped on a reporters' table and, waiting for total silence, began:

> And when asked what State he hails from,
> Our sole reply shall be,
> He hails from Appomattox,
> And its famous apple tree.

Conkling's recitation ignited applause, foot stomping, and hats thrown in the air. But then he spoke satirically of every other candidate's deficiencies. Although he ended with a conciliatory plea for unity, Conkling's crescendo of criticisms betrayed Grant. It overturned the magnanimous spirit that reference to the hero of Appomattox had invoked.

On Monday, as the convention prepared to vote, Grant planned to travel through Chicago to Milwaukee for the annual reunion of the Grand Army of the Republic. Julia "entreated him" to go to the floor of the convention. She believed his appearance could enthuse the delegates.

"But no! He said he would rather cut off his right hand," Julia remembered later.

She had asked her husband, "Do you not desire success?"

"Well, yes, of course, since my name is up, I would rather be nominated, but I will do nothing to further that end."

"Oh, Ulys, how unwise, what mistaken chivalry. For heaven's sake, go."

"Julia, I am amazed at you." He had his personal code of ethics, which he would not violate.

Grant did not visit the convention, but he did follow the balloting by telegraph wire. At the end of the first ballot, he led with 304 votes, followed by Blaine, 284; Sherman, 93; Edmunds, 34; and Washburne, 30. Through an exhausting twelve hours, delegates cast twenty-eight ballots. Although Grant led on every ballot, always with more than 300 votes, he consistently fell short of the 379 needed for the nomination.

On the thirty-fourth ballot, everything changed. Ohio congressman James Garfield, who on the first thirty-three ballots had received a lone vote from a Pennsylvania delegate, suddenly found himself a candidate. The forty-eight-year-old Garfield, who had fought at Shiloh and was elected to Congress in 1862, a man whose heartfelt warmth drew people to him, protested. "No man has a right, without the consent of the person voted for, to announce that person's name, and vote for him, in this convention. Such consent I have not given—" But the rest of his words were drowned out in relieved cheers.

The logjam broken, on the thirty-sixth ballot the convention nominated Garfield, who garnered his 399 votes from votes previously accorded other candidates. But not votes from Grant delegates. They remained steadfast at 306. In future years they called themselves the "306," proud they had stayed loyal to their hero.

Partly to placate the Conklingites, and knowing Republicans needed New York to win in November, the convention nominated one of Conkling's men, Chester Arthur, former collector of the Port of New York, as their vice-presidential candidate.

DEMOCRATS NOMINATED GENERAL Winfield Scott Hancock as their presidential candidate on June 24. Two weeks later, Grant spoke well of Hancock in a newspaper interview: "I have nothing to say against Gen. Hancock. I have known him forty years. His personal, official, and military record is good."

Three months later, he shared more about Hancock—privately. James O. Cramb, Galena Methodist pastor, and Charles H. Fowler, editor of the Methodist *Christian Advocate,* called on Grant in Galena. That evening, in a letter to his wife, Fowler repeated Grant's confidences about Hancock: "He was a very good corps commander. He was ambitious, and had courage and a fine presence; but he is vain, selfish, weak, and easily flattered." Most troublesome for Grant, who was quite the opposite, "he could never endure to have anyone else receive any credit."

Grant was not pleased when Fowler published the letter—especially because he believed some of his remarks were misquoted.

. . .

GARFIELD AND HANCOCK often tiptoed around the issues in the 1880 election. Garfield conducted a "front porch" campaign from his home in Mentor, Ohio, while Hancock too often revealed his inexperience about political issues such as the tariff. They both supported civil service reform, immigration restrictions on the Chinese, and pensions for Civil War veterans. They did differ on the tariff, Republicans supporting high protective duties. In the end the Republican strategy, seeking to counter the Civil War heroism of "Hancock the Superb," advanced the idea that the candidate had little understanding of his own party's platform. They issued a pamphlet entitled "Hancock's Political Achievements"— published with blank pages.

GRANT EXPRESSED HIS willingness to speak publicly for Garfield and plunged into campaigning for the first time in his life. "I feel a very deep interest in the success of the republican ticket," he wrote Garfield.

At the end of September, Grant delivered a campaign speech in Ohio on why "I am a Republican." He accused Democrats of "proscription" of citizens' opinions and voting rights in fourteen states. To illustrate his point, he referred to a recent novel by Albion W. Tourgée, *A Fool's Errand by One of the Fools,* based on Tourgée's fourteen-year residence in North Carolina, where he served as politician, editor, and judge. Grant believed Tourgée "admirably told" the story of clashes between Republicans and the racist South. "The solid South will go as Kukluism [Ku Klux Klan] did before," Grant warned, if Hancock and the Democratic Party were to triumph.

In the speech, Grant espoused a Republican political philosophy of "entire equality before the law of every citizen, no matter what his race, nationality, or previous condition." He insisted that a Republican "tolerates no privileged class. Everyone has the opportunity to make himself all he is capable of." One senses that Grant also wanted to not simply attack the Democratic stance, but stiffen the spine of Republicans, so many of whom were willing to relegate the fate of African Americans to local governments in the South.

On October 11, New York Republicans welcomed Grant with a torchlight parade. He made New York his hub, as in the next weeks he led the charge in New England, upstate New York, and New Jersey, often speaking two or three times a day, demonstrating his improved oratorical skills.

In Jersey City, Grant returned to a theme stirred by reading Tourgée, who had been accused by some critics of being a carpetbagger:

All we ask is that our carpetbag fellow-citizens, and our fellow citizens of African descent, and of every other class who may choose to be Republicans, shall have the privilege to go to the polls, even though they are in the minority, and put in their ballot without being burned out of their homes, and without being threatened or intimidated.

LATER THAT DAY in Jersey City, deciding to wear the label as a badge of honor, Grant thundered, "We are all carpetbaggers—nothing else."

At a speech in Hartford, Connecticut, Grant was greeted by Mark Twain, a member of the welcoming committee. On the train from Boston, Twain fell into conversation with Fred Grant. Twain recalled that "it gradually came out that the General, so far from being a rich man, as was commonly supposed, had not even income enough to enable him to live as respectably as a third-rate physician."

Believing "this was all so shameful and such a reproach to Congress," Twain determined to "take the General's straitened circumstances as my text in introducing him to the people of Hartford." In his speech, he referred to how Great Britain had rewarded the Duke of Wellington's "service with wealth and grandeur." He concluded, "Your country loves you, your country is proud of you, your country is grateful to you." In a typical bit of Twain satire, he added, "Your country stands ready from this day forth to testify her measureless love and pride and gratitude toward you in every conceivable inexpensive way."

Grant replied he had been sufficiently rewarded: "What they have given me is more valued than gold or silver." But Twain's meeting with Grant in Hartford haunted him; he determined to do more to honor and assist the man he believed was America's "Great Soldier, Honored Statesman, Unselfish Citizen."

With the campaign over, Ulysses and Julia moved into rooms at New York's Fifth Avenue Hotel for the winter.

ON NOVEMBER 2, with a voter turnout of 78.4 percent, Garfield defeated Hancock by fewer than 10,000 votes, 4,453,337 to 4,444,267, in one of the closest contests in U.S. history. Each candidate won nineteen states, but Garfield won the electoral vote, 214 to 155. The electoral map confirmed the nation's sectional divide. In losing, Hancock carried every state that had been a part of the Confederacy, along with the border states Missouri, Kentucky, West Virginia, Maryland, and Delaware. Grant's hopes for a Republican victory were also dashed as suppression of African Americans, who cast more than 400,000 votes for Grant in the 1868 presidential election, resulted in a mere 170,000 total votes cast in 1880. Voter suppression was taking an ever greater toll on voting possibilities for African Americans.

Did Grant's campaigning make a difference? New York politician Chauncey Depew credited Grant's "generous, unselfish, and enthusiastic support" as "the greatest help which Garfield received." He believed Grant was the key person in convincing not only "the whole of the old soldier vote," but "those who had become disaffected or indifferent" coming out of the convention to vote for Garfield.

After the election, various friends suggested Grant's name for a cabinet position or perhaps some special mission with China or Japan. To set the president-elect's mind at ease, nine days after the election Grant wrote Garfield, "There is no position within the gift of the President which I would accept." He did, however, make one offer: "If I can serve the country . . . [I would be pleased] to do so by advice in relation to our affairs with Mexico and the East, especially China & Japan."

TRUE TO HIS word, beginning in fall 1880, Mark Twain became a frequent caller on Grant. From time to time, the author brought along writer friends such as William Dean Howells and George Washington Cable.

Soon Twain began to talk about the possibility of Grant writing his memoirs. Twain remembered that Grant "would not listen to the suggestion." Grant told him that he had no confidence in his ability to write well. He further protested that Young had published his volumes on Grant's world trip and that Badeau's *Military History of Ulysses S. Grant* had just been published. Finally, he was certain there would be no market for selling his memoirs. When Twain told him he was confident that such a book would have an "enormous sale," Grant responded that he had no need for additional income.

The conversation continued in January 1881, when Grant wrote Twain, "I have always distrusted my ability to write anything that would satisfy myself and the public would be much more difficult to please." He did write Twain that he appreciated the "friendship which [he] inspires."

• • •

THAT SUMMER, FRIENDS and supporters stepped forward to solve the question of how and where the Grants would live. More than twenty men, including George Childs, Anthony J. Drexel, and J. Pierpont Morgan, joined together to raise a trust fund of $250,000, from which Grant would receive annual interest. An additional $100,000 made possible the purchase of a new four-story brownstone at 3 East Sixty-sixth Street, near Central Park.

With all of Grant's prizes and memorabilia from the Civil War, presidency, and world tour, the ground floor of the house looked more like a museum than a home. But what counted most for Grant was that Julia liked their new residence. She recalled, "It was a much larger and a more expensive house than we had intended (or had the means) to buy, but it was so new and sweet and large that this quite outweighed our more prudential scruples."

In the second half of the nineteenth century, the center of wealth in New York City had moved uptown from lower Fifth Avenue. Recently founded, the Metropolitan Museum of Art and American Museum of Natural History were both flourishing. Julia, often dressed in silks she had purchased in the Orient, loved driving down Fifth Avenue behind Major and General, two of her husband's prized horses, to a favorite destination: Julia Fish's home at 251 East Seventeenth Street. Grant and Julia fully embraced New York's social and cultural opportunities.

STARTING IN 1881, Grant put his energy into business and investment opportunities. He didn't have to look hard. A gold-mining company in New Mexico wanted Grant as their president. He said no. The New York World's Fair Commission, planning a fair in 1883 to commemorate the one hundredth anniversary of the 1783 Treaty of Paris concluding the Revolutionary War, asked Grant to be their head. He resigned after a few months on the job, explaining, "I expect to be so engaged as to make it inconvenient to devote" enough time to lead the effort.

On March 28, the engagement became clear. Grant left for Mexico to negotiate a charter to begin the Mexican Southern Railroad Company. This venture was about more than building a railroad; it was realizing his interest in helping Mexico, an undertaking he had envisioned for some time.

Received a year earlier as an eminent guest, Grant arrived this time as a venture capitalist. Along with Matías Romero, he brought "a quasi-official" status to a plan to build a railroad line from Mexico City south to Guatemala, with branches to the Pacific and the Gulf of Mexico. His goal was to open up trade to the isolated southwestern state of Oaxaca. He also wanted to link the new railroad with a line running north across the Rio Grande.

On April 22, Grant addressed a banquet hosted by the Oaxaca delegation in the Mexican Congress: "I have long been of the opinion that the United States and Mexico should be the warmest friends, and enjoy the closest commercial relations." Having read local newspapers suggesting plans for a railroad might be a cover for "the possibility of the annexation of Mexican territory," Grant assured officials: "We want no more land."

On May 11, he signed a contract with Mexico authorizing construction of the railroad. The plan called for completion within ten years.

GRANT RETURNED TO the United States to organize the offices for this new railroad. He chose to incorporate his company in the state of New York and set up his office at 2 Wall Street on the second floor of the United Bank Building. Grenville Dodge, engineer and Civil War colleague, would serve as vice president, with Russell Sage, a financier who had invested heavily in railroads, as treasurer.

Knowing of Grant's interest in Mexico, in early 1882 Chester Arthur—president of the United States since the death of James Garfield by an assassin's bullet in September 1881—invited Grant to become U.S. commissioner to draw up a commercial treaty with Mexico. Mexico appointed Matías Romero as one of its two commissioners. The commissioners quickly agreed on terms of a free trade treaty that would remove tariffs on U.S. and Mexican products. The treaty of reciprocity was signed on January 20, 1883, but needed to be approved by the senates of both countries.

The treaty was defeated in both countries. In the United States, protectionists decried the free trade provisions. Some in the United States and Mexico charged that Grant and Romero were involved primarily for their own pecuniary gain.

While Grant's venture received positive coverage in *Harper's Magazine* ("This seems a sufficiently comprehensive scheme to satisfy the most ambitious mind"), old foe Whitelaw Reid charged that Grant was "exceedingly eager to make money" and "dazed" by opportunities in Mexico. Disappointed, Grant wrote Badeau, now consul general in Cuba, "I never would have undertaken the work I am now engaged in for any possible gain that would accrue to myself."

In 1883, the promise of the Mexican Southern remained unfulfilled. Construction dawdled and permits lagged. A Mexican travel book, commenting on the numerous "concessions" needed for construction, observed that by the time railroads had been completed in Mexico, the workmen would be "the third generation, of your original workmen."

As GRANT STRUGGLED to direct the Mexican Southern from his upstairs office at 2 Wall Street, just one floor below, twenty-nine-year-old Buck was finding phenomenal success in investing. A graduate of Exeter, Harvard University, and Columbia Law School, he possessed the finest education of all the Grant children, and it appeared to be paying off.

In July 1880, Buck had been persuaded to launch a brokerage firm in partnership with Ferdinand Ward, a young Wall Street whiz who began his career at the New York Produce Exchange in lower Manhattan in 1873 and rose quickly through the ranks by virtue of his blond, blue-eyed good looks, his charm . . . and a great deal of cunning. Buck borrowed $100,000 from his prospective father-in-law, Jerome Chaffee, who had made a fortune in mining and banking in Colorado. Ward invested $100,000—or so Buck had been led to believe.

Once he had Buck's money in hand, Ward gallantly insisted that the Grant name should be positioned first in the firm's official registration, even though Ward would be the active partner and Buck the silent partner. So Grant & Ward it became—ostensibly as a tribute to Buck, who somehow overlooked the obvious: that the public would naturally assume the "Grant" referred to was his father. Not surprisingly, Ward had no intention of enlightening him.

Ward's other partner in July 1880 was one who would fully legitimize the new banking and brokerage firm: James D. Fish, president of Wall Street's Marine National Bank. Almost twice Ward's age, Fish was yet another affable, small-town transplant (from Mystic, Connecticut) who had made good in the big city—and knew the ropes. Ward had a telephone line installed in his own office that linked him directly to Fish.

Within a few months, Ferdinand Ward became known as "the Young Napoleon of Finance," exercising an influence over even the most experienced Wall Street traders. Only this time it was not his charm, but high yields that furthered his popularity with eager investors. The firm was raking in the cash.

Thus, some months later, when Grant's Mexican Southern Railroad became mired in Mexican red tape, he turned to his son, who in turn approached Ward about bringing his father into the firm as a partner. Ward, not unexpectedly, agreed. After several meetings and a number of pleasant conversations, it was decided that Grant would invest $100,000, half of which would be contributed by Julia and Jesse.

With the addition of the elder Grant, Ward decided it was time to recapitalize the firm. He, Fish, and Buck each agreed to contribute another $100,000 to match Grant's investment. Grant and Buck, as silent partners, were promised an income stream amounting to $2,000 a month.

For a time, everything seemed perfect. The two young men were doing well, and without any effort on his part, Grant was becoming a wealthy man. From an original paper capitalization of $400,000, the firm was now valued at $15 million. All Grant's concerns about retirement income evaporated.

Grant quickly took a liking to young Ward. After all, what was there not to like? Ward had been born to Presbyterian missionaries in India; when he was young, his father returned to pastor a church in upstate New York. He lived quietly, if well, and he was incredibly generous with gifts to family and friends. It seemed he had no bad habits. Ohio Democratic senator Allen G. Thurman, impressed that Ward was "the most successful financier thus far produced," wanted to nominate him as the next secretary of the Treasury. A more insightful Wall Street contemporary, however, recalled, "His presence was magnetic, and his manner deceitfully unassuming."

After the fact, Grant has been blamed for failing to do his homework about Ward's investments. True, he never became involved in the daily workings of the brokerage house, but everyone, it seemed, was rushing to get in on the Wall Street "boom." Mark Twain's central character in *The Gilded Age,* Colonel Sellers, spoke for many acquisitive Americans when he exclaimed, "There's millions in it." Hamlin Garland, later one of America's leading novelists and an early Grant biographer, observed, "Grant would have been a singular exception had he refused to go further with such a financier."

It didn't help that Ward made sure no one understood the new firm. He personally did all investing, made all deposits, signed all paperwork, and wrote all checks. He hinted that government contracts served as a basis for the firm's prosperity, but no one had ever seen any contracts—because there were none.

Much later, it would be discovered that Buck and Grant had been the firm's sole investors. Ward and Fish had contributed . . . nothing.

Today, we might call Ward's maneuvering a Ponzi scheme, made infamous by Bernie Madoff in 2008. In Grant's day, it was called "rehypothecating." It worked like this: Ward paid abnormally high interest to his customers by pledging securities as collateral on a loan, whereas the same securities had previously been pledged for other loans. As a result, Ward was able to pay his investors their interest by siphoning off money from new investments. None of his customers knew, including the two Grants.

But Fish knew. He allowed Ward to retrieve securities from Marine National that should have been kept in the bank vault. This ongoing sleight of hand forced Fish to play hide-and-seek with bank examiners when they appeared unannounced.

GRANT, MEANWHILE, WASN'T only feeling financially secure, he was also enormously gratified that his three sons were prospering in business and raising families with their lovely wives—by 1883, he had nine grandchildren. He wished Nellie lived in the United States but relished her visits with her children. In the summer, he wrote to her from Long Branch, "The fact is your Ma & I are very proud of our grandchildren."

Ten days before Christmas, father wrote daughter, "We are all very well, and the family are enjoying as much prosperity as we ought to expect." Even if Grant's hopes for the Mexican Southern were stalled, he estimated his wealth at $1.5 million, mostly thanks to Ward's investments. As part of his newfound largesse, he gave each of his four granddaughters a $2,500 bond for Christmas.

On Christmas Day 1883, upon arriving home from a number of social calls, Grant reached out to pay his cabman and slipped and fell on the frozen street. He ruptured a thigh muscle in the same leg he had injured when his horse fell years earlier at Vicksburg. At sixty-one years old and otherwise in good health, he was consigned to crutches.

Sometime in early 1884, Horace Porter, Grant's former aide and now president of the Pullman Palace Car Company, felt compelled to warn the general that the profits he had heard about could not be legitimate. It just so happened that when he arrived at Grant's house, Ward was present. And after listening to the enthusiastic Ward and watching the general's appreciative response, he withdrew, deciding not to interfere.

ON SUNDAY AFTERNOON, May 4, 1884, Ferdinand Ward rang the doorbell at 3 East Sixty-sixth Street. Ward's visits to Grant's home were always welcome, but usually he did not come uninvited. A maid escorted him into the parlor, where he was greeted by Grant and Buck. He told the two men the Marine Bank was in grave difficulty because the city chamberlain had decided to withdraw some of the city's funds.

Grant expressed surprise and asked how this matter concerned him.

Ward replied that since Grant and Ward had $660,000 deposited there, this could put the firm's financial position in jeopardy.

Buck interjected, But isn't the bank good for the funds?

Certainly. Nothing to be worried about in the long term. But the firm would need money to cover the potential shortfall. Ward said he already had checks for $230,000 but wondered if the general could borrow another $150,000 that day. Ward assured Grant the money would be needed for only twenty-four hours.

Grant agreed to try to borrow the money. With Ward and Buck in tow, he traveled in his carriage down Fifth Avenue, stopping at the turreted fifty-eight-room home of William H. Vanderbilt. Once inside, embarrassed by his unannounced call, Grant explained the reason for his visit. Vanderbilt, eldest son and heir of Commodore Cornelius Vanderbilt, made it a habit not to make personal loans. Known to be a cantankerous man, he told Grant, "I care nothing about Marine Bank. To tell the truth I care very little about Grant & Ward. But to accommodate you personally I will draw my check for the amount you ask. I consider it a personal loan to you and not to any other party."

Grant accepted the check for $150,000.

He rejoined the younger men in the carriage and returned to Sixty-sixth Street, where he endorsed the check and handed it to Ward. Young Napoleon assured the old general the whole matter would be all right.

ON TUESDAY, MAY 6, the Marine Bank opened its doors promptly at ten A.M. The bank's directors arrived and assembled for their weekly meeting. But where was President Fish? And where was Ward? Someone contacted his office, but no one had seen him.

The directors' meeting ended at eleven A.M. A few minutes later, all doors to the bank were locked even as depositors began to congregate outside. By afternoon, the stock market had plummeted 3 percent.

In midday, Grant arrived at his office at 2 Wall Street. Crowds milled in the street, but newspaper reporter Alexander Noyes wrote, "The general looked neither to right or left." As Noyes watched, "Nobody followed him, or spoke to him, but everyone in the cynical 'hard-boiled' group took off his hat." The young reporter declared, "It was not so much a tribute of respect to a former Chief Magistrate as spontaneous

The Wall Street Panic of 1884 swept Grant up in its massive losses.

recognition of the immense personal tragedy which was enacting before our eyes."

Behind closed doors, Grant asked Buck what had happened.

"Grant and Ward has failed, and Ward has fled. You'd better go home, Father."

Not saying a word, Grant steadied himself on his crutches, which he still used five months after his fall, walked silently past the gathering crowd, and made his way home.

Deeply humiliated, he told Julia all that had happened. Then he opened his wallet and removed its contents: $81. She had $130. All his dreams for retirement had vanished.

CHAPTER 36

Final Campaign

> General Grant's book is a great, unique and
> unapproachable literary masterpiece.
> —MARK TWAIN

I S ULYSSES S. GRANT GUILTY? asked the *New York Sun*. "For the love of money the greatest military reputation of our time has been dimmed and degraded by its possessor. The people look on with shame."

Grant did not need Charles Dana to speak to him about shame. He unburdened himself to his close friend George Childs: "I could bear all the pecuniary loss if that was all, but that I could be so long deceived by a man who I had such opportunity to know is humiliating."

Grant determined he would repay every debt, starting with what he owed William Vanderbilt. He prepared an accounting of all he owned: his farm in Missouri, homes in Galena, Philadelphia, and Washington, plus land in Chicago. He gathered his swords, campaign maps, the gold medal awarded by Congress, the pen used to write orders for the Battle of the Wilderness, and rare souvenirs acquired on his world tour. Julia contributed jewelry and vases, including her prize vase filled with gold coins given them in many countries. Grant held back nothing. In the end, he believed the total amounted to almost exactly $150,000.

He sent everything off to Vanderbilt. Upon returning from a European vacation to find Grant's shipment, the financial titan was perplexed. He notified Grant he would return everything. Grant would not hear of it.

In the end, Vanderbilt accepted the repayment and wrote Julia, "All articles of historical value and interest shall at the General's death, or if you desire it sooner, be presented to the government at Washington where they will remain as perpetual memorials of his fame, and of the history of his time." Vanderbilt acted both to preserve Grant's pride and to preserve his story for future American generations.

Even though Vanderbilt took title to the house at 3 East Sixty-sixth Street, he insisted Grant and Julia continue to live there.

THE PUBLIC DID not blame Grant. Most Americans believed him an uninformed bystander to Ward's gigantic swindle. Known and unknown persons stepped forward to help.

Charles Wood, who owned a brush factory in Lansingburgh, New York, wrote the general, "I enclose check for five hundred dollars on account my share due for services ending about April 1865." He did so because "I owe you this for Appomattox." Reading of "the Grant Failure" in the *Troy Daily Press,* Wood simply wanted to help.

Grant immediately wrote Wood to acknowledge this gift from a stranger. Within days, two more checks from Wood totaling $1,000 arrived. "The country will rally for you but large bodies move slowly," he encouraged.

Matías Romero called on Grant to offer support. Upon leaving, without a word, the Mexican leader left $1,000 on the table by the door. He meant it as a gift, but Grant and Julia would receive it only as a loan, which they repaid a month later.

On the afternoon of May 27, the doorbell at 3 East Sixty-sixth Street rang. Once again, Ferdinand Ward stood at the entrance. Having been arrested on May 21, and destined to spend the next eight years in jail, he was free on bail. He wished to see Grant for only a few minutes. The general sent his answer: he had no more to say.

IN JUNE, GRANT and Julia retreated to their summer cottage at Long Branch. On June 6, Republicans meeting in Chicago nominated James G. Blaine and John A. Logan to head their party's ticket in the fall elections. For the first time in sixteen years, Grant was far removed from political conventions. He did not regret it.

Support came in nonmonetary ways as well. George Stuart, a Presbyterian lay leader long associated with antislavery causes, the Sunday School Union, and the YMCA, invited Grant to join him at a meeting at Ocean Grove, New Jersey. On this summer Sunday, Ocean Grove, which had grown from the Methodist camp meeting movement, hosted thousands in its open-air tabernacle. Stuart briefly addressed the crowd and introduced former army chaplain A. J. Palmer, who directed his words to Grant: "I was one of your soldiers; and, while you could not get along without us, we could not have got along without you. No combination of Wall Street sharpers shall tarnish the luster of my old Commander's fame for me." Stuart helped Grant to his feet to respond, but after a few words, Grant's "feelings so overcame him that tears started from his eyes," and he felt "compelled to resume his seat."

LATER THAT MONTH, Grant bit into a summer peach and cried out in pain: "Oh my. I think something has stung me from that peach." He paced up and down the kitchen and out onto the veranda. He rinsed his mouth with water but told Julia the "water hurt him like liquid fire."

Julia begged him to see a physician. He replied, "No, it will be all right directly, and I will not have a doctor."

Grant did tell next-door neighbor George Childs of the dryness in his throat. Childs asked a visiting Philadelphia physician, Dr. Jacob M. Da Costa, to examine him.

Da Costa found nothing particularly wrong but advised Grant to see his family physician. Dr. Fordyce Barker, who spent every summer in Europe, was not due to return until October, four months away. Grant put the irritation in his throat out of his mind.

IN SPRING 1884, Richard Watson Gilder, senior editor of *The Century Magazine,* had approached Grant about writing one or more essays. *The Century* was one of the leading magazines in post–Civil War America, popular for its commentary on national issues. Its editors were betting that the 125,000 readers of the 35-cent monthly would be interested in essays on the great leaders and battles of the Civil War. The initial invitations to contributors in 1883 had so far yielded no positive responses. Gilder called recruiting contributors "General Catching." The chief general to be caught was the former general in chief. If Grant could be persuaded to contribute, the editors believed others would sign on.

Grant declined Gilder's proposal.

Undaunted, Gilder assigned associate editor Robert U. Johnson to "catch" Grant. On a beautiful June morning, Johnson and Grant conversed on Grant's Long Branch veranda. In a candor that surprised the editor, Grant discussed his financial debacle "without restraint," as if he wanted to "clear the slate" before entering into a new venture.

He asked Johnson how many articles *The Century* would like. "As many as the General wanted to contribute." But the young editor told Grant he believed it best to start with four articles: Shiloh, Vicksburg, the Wilderness, and Lee's surrender. The magazine was prepared to pay $500 per article ($13,000 today).

Grant had told Mark Twain he was not disciplined enough to be a writer, but he now embarked on a disciplined regimen. He asked Adam Badeau to assist him. Fred would help his father by checking official records. Reading these records again sparked Grant's memory.

"HURRAH FOR GRANT!" Gilder wrote Johnson when the first article on Shiloh arrived on July 1.

The hurrah faded immediately. To their dismay, Gilder and Johnson perceived that the four scant pages Grant submitted represented essentially a rewriting of his official reports.

Gilder tasked Johnson with returning to Long Branch to urge Grant to revise with an eye toward providing a sense of immediacy for the *Century*'s audience. Johnson did not want to discourage the general and knew "this required all the tact that I could muster."

With the article tucked in his inside pocket, Johnson sat with Grant once more. He decided not to start with the bad news but instead started talking about Shiloh. To his surprise, "I discovered that General Grant, instead of being a 'silent man,' was positively loquacious." As they conversed, "here was no cocksureness, no desire to make a perfect record or live up to a later reputation." The more they talked, the more Grant "revealed the human side of his experience." For example, at the end of the first day at Shiloh, Grant had tried to sleep in an improvised military hospital, but because he could not stand the amputations, he sat against a tree in the rain through the night.

Johnson jotted down "points of interest" as Grant shared freely. The editor urged him to write as if he were talking to people who knew nothing about Shiloh and to narrate from the point of view of "what he planned, thought, saw, said, and did."

All this was "a new idea to him." Grant took back his four pages and told Johnson he would start again.

On July 15, he wrote Gilder, "I have now been writing on the Vicksburg Campaign two weeks, Sundays and all, averaging more than four hours a day."

Highly encouraged, Grant wrote Sherman, "I hope both you and Sheridan will contribute to the series."

PLEASED WITH HIS articles and their reception by the *Century*'s editors, Grant opened up to the idea of writing his memoirs. Even though his first article on Shiloh was not scheduled to be published until February 1885, word had gotten out. Realizing other suitors might clamor for his services, the editors set their sights on securing this biggest prize.

Gilder pressed Roswell Smith, president of the *Century* company, to make an offer. Smith, who was against advances to authors, agreed to join a meeting of Grant, Childs, and Johnson in Long Branch in early September.

The four met on the Grant cottage veranda on a warm day at the end of the beach season. The general sat quietly with a silk scarf wrapped around his neck.

Suddenly, speaking in a raspy voice, he asked, "Do you really think anyone would be interested in a book by me?"

Smith replied, "General, do you not think the public would read with avidity Napoleon's personal account of his battles?"

The *Century* staff departed Long Branch that day understanding that Grant would write his memoirs for them. But in his mind, Grant had made no commitment. He wrote Badeau, "My own opinion is that they would be the best publishers. But I will make no committal until about the time for publication."

When Grant returned to the city in early October, the throat pain returned. He finally went to see his family physician, Dr. Barker, on October 20. Barker advised him to see a throat specialist right away.

Two days later, he went to Dr. John H. Douglas. A commanding man with a full crop of white hair and a beard, Douglas had met Grant when the physician set up field hospitals at Shiloh and the Wilderness while serving with the United States Sanitary Commission.

For the first time, Grant learned the seriousness of his problem. An examination revealed the problem was not in the throat, but at the base of the tongue.

"Is it cancer?"

Douglas recorded in his diary, "The question having been asked, I could give no uncertain, hesitating reply." He told Grant, "General, the disease is serious . . . and sometimes capable of being cured." He applied muriate of cocaine, conveying instant relief and allowing his patient to sleep again without constant pain.

To verify his opinion, Douglas brought in two other physicians. After taking a small bit of tissue from the back of Grant's tongue, he asked Dr. George Elliott to do a biopsy. Elliott and Douglas took the sampling to George Shrady, a microbiologist as well as a surgeon, without telling him the name of the subject. Shrady confirmed the specimen to be cancerous.

Did Grant's cigar smoking cause his cancer? Certainly constant smoking over so many years did not help. Douglas asked him to stop.

. . .

IN NOVEMBER, GRANT wrote Nellie in faraway Great Britain, revealing only that "I have had a sore throat now for more than four months" and "the Doctor is making fair progress with the sore throat."

Neither did Grant share the seriousness of his illness with Julia or Fred. Frustrated, Julia decided to visit the doctor herself. "I then went to the specialist and learned the dreadful truth but still could not believe the malady was a fatal one."

WITH GRANT RETURNED to the city, Twain resumed his visits. As they conversed, Twain came to appreciate that the general also had a gift of storytelling. He was especially fascinated by Grant's attention to detail— topography, battle plans, and personalities.

Twain was busy in the fall of 1884 guiding *Adventures of Huckleberry Finn* through its final stages for a December publication date. Having quarreled with numerous publishers, he had recently set up his own publishing house, Charles L. Webster & Company—Webster being his niece's husband.

On a November evening, after doing a reading in the entertainment district around Union Square, Twain ran into Gilder, who invited him to supper at his home on East Fifteenth Street. Gilder regaled Twain with his story persuading Grant to write four articles for *The Century*. He told the author the General was pleased to receive $500 for each article.

Mark Twain recognized Grant's literary abilities and would become his friend and advocate.

"I pricked up my ears," Twain wrote later. "To offer Grant $500 for a magazine article" was a "monumental insult." Inquiring further, Twain learned *The Century* planned to publish Grant's memoirs.

The next morning, Twain went straight to Grant's house. He repeated what Gilder had told him and asked whether there was a signed contract.

Grant produced the contract, commenting that "he supposed that the *Century* offer was fair and right." It called for paying the standard royalty of 10 percent. Grant was prepared to accept it but hadn't yet signed.

"I didn't know whether to cry or laugh." Why, a 10 percent royalty was the same "they would have offered to any unknown Comanche Indian" whose book might sell three thousand copies. Twain believed Grant's memoirs could sell three hundred thousand.

He tried to persuade Grant to let him publish the book at Webster & Company.

Distressed, Grant protested that he felt honor-bound to sign the *Century* contract. Twain perceived that to Grant's "military mind," to change publishers at this late moment seemed to be "disloyalty." Fred proposed "the *Century* contract be laid on the table for twenty-four hours, and that meantime the situation be examined and discussed."

Twain returned the next morning: "Sell *me* the Memoirs, General." With that he reached for his checkbook and offered to write a check for $50,000 on the spot.

Grant was taken aback, Twain recalled, and "wouldn't hear of such a thing. He said we were friends and what if I should fail to get the money back out of the book."

After deliberating at length, Grant wired George Childs, whom he relied on as a financial adviser: "On re-examining the Contract prepared by the Century people I see that it is all in favor of the publisher, with nothing left for the Author. I am offered very much more favorable terms by Chas. L. Webster & Co. Mark Twain is the Company."

After discussing the issue extensively with Grant, Fred, and Julia, Childs delivered his verdict: "Give the book to Clemens." Twain gave Grant a choice: a 20 percent royalty or 70 percent of the net proceeds. With Childs's advice, Grant chose 70 percent of the total net proceeds.

Signed contract in hand, Grant settled into a disciplined pattern of writing. He worked in a small room at the top of the stairs on the second floor of his home. Light shone in from two windows facing East Sixty-sixth Street. He wrapped himself in a shawl and kept his head covered with a knitted cap to protect against the winter cold. Childs arranged for flowers from his conservatory to be delivered two or three times a week to brighten an otherwise ordinary study.

In the morning, Grant wrote steadily for four hours on unlined paper. He wrote rapidly—sometimes several thousand words a day—a testament to his powers of concentration. Beside the small desk where he wrote, Fred arranged his father's maps in chronological order on a white pine table moved up from the kitchen.

Grant asked Adam Badeau to join him as an assistant. Because of Badeau's own work—he was writing a novel set in Cuba—he was initially hesitant but finally agreed. Grant kept a copy of Sherman's *Memoirs* at his desk, while Badeau referred to his own *Military History of Ulysses S. Grant*.

Writing is a craft that can be enhanced with practice. Whereas in the army Grant wrote steadily, with hardly a crossover, he now became his own editor. Though he understood that because of his health he was in a race against time, it is remarkable how much care he took revising his manuscript.

In the afternoons, Grant would edit his morning's writing, pausing to search for just the right word to express an idea or action. In the evenings, he talked over writing plans for the next day with Fred and Badeau.

Toward the end of the evening, as they used to do many years ago in Galena, before the beginning of the war that changed their lives forever, Ulysses would read aloud to Julia, who listened to the rhythms of his sentences and offered her suggestions.

GRANT'S INCREASED COUGHING meant he had trouble sleeping. His doctors gave him anodynes to help, but too often they proved ineffective. One evening, he asked Dr. Shrady to visit. Shrady arrived and, recognizing Grant's anxiety, suggested: "Pretend you are a boy again" so that he could fall asleep as once he did in Georgetown. "Curl up your legs" and "lie over on your side." Shrady put his arms under the pillow. "Now go to sleep like a good boy." Grant quickly fell asleep.

Looking up, Shrady saw Julia in the doorway. He told her he hoped she did not find his language "demeaning"—he simply wanted to help his patient sleep. "There is not the slightest danger of that," Julia replied. "He is the most simple-mannered and reasonable person in the world, and he likes to have persons whom he knows treat him without ceremony."

• • •

As GRANT'S HEALTH deteriorated further in early winter 1885, Twain suggested hiring a stenographer so he could dictate the manuscript. Noble E. Dawson, who had served as Grant's secretary on a trip to Mexico and was acting as a stenographer for the Senate Interstate Commerce Committee, came from Washington to help.

BY JANUARY 1885, Grant was confined to his house. Worried about choking while sleeping, he started sleeping upright on two large armchairs that faced each other.

Nellie wrote from England, concerned about her father. If earlier he had tried to shield his daughter from the gravity of his illness, by February he had revealed to her it was "a very serious matter." Grant admitted, "It will be a long time yet before I can possibly recover." But then he started telling her about his memoirs: "If you ever take time to read it you will find out what sort of a boy and man I was before you knew me."

Twain returned on February 21 from a nearly four-month "Twins of Genius Tour" with George Washington Cable and immediately called on Grant. Stunned by how pale the general looked, he worried about whether Grant would even be able to complete his memoirs. Yet Grant promised he would complete the project.

GRANT IS DYING, blared the headline of *The New York Times* on March 1. The *Times* story prompted other New York newspapers—*Herald, Tribune, World, Sun, Post, Brooklyn Eagle*—to post reporters across the street from 3 East Sixty-sixth Street. Soon this phalanx of reporters was reinforced by correspondents from Cincinnati, Chicago, St. Louis, and San Francisco. A reporter started calling their daily appearance "the death watch."

In response to this national interest, Grant's doctors delivered twice-daily bulletins. "Bulletin boys" representing the Associated Press, the United Press, and the Western Union snatched copies of the physicians' news bulletins the second they were available and sped them to their news services. Grant's health absorbed the interest of citizens across the nation.

One day Grant, who had been losing weight, sighed and said humorously to Dr. Douglas, "You would think the newspapers could get my weight right." That morning, he had had himself weighed: at 146 pounds, he had lost more than forty pounds. "I read six newspapers this morning. No two of them have the same figures and no one of them is right."

Newspaper reports sometimes stepped beyond information in the medical bulletins—usually exaggerating the gravity of Grant's illness. Never losing his sense of humor, Grant greeted Shrady one day, "Doctor, you did not give a very favorable account of me yesterday."

MEANWHILE IN WASHINGTON, as Congress pressed toward a March 4 adjournment, another Grant drama played out. When Grant had resigned as general in chief to become president, his action had an unintended consequence. Because he did not retire, he was barred from receiving an army pension. Although Congress had refused to reinstate him, Sherman and Childs would not give up.

With news that Grant was dying reverberating through the entire country, one more attempt was made to push the bill through Congress. With less than one hour to adjournment, and ceremonies to inaugurate Grover Cleveland scheduled to start at noon, the bill passed.

In early afternoon, a telegram arrived at the Grant home. The general opened it and said to Childs, "I am grateful the thing has passed." Julia exclaimed, "Hurrah, our old commander is back." Grant would receive a pension of $13,500 annually. Julia, at her husband's death, would receive $5,000.

NELLIE'S ARRIVAL IN March cheered her father. He insisted on traveling to the steamship pier to meet her.

With news of Grant's illness flashing across the country, a stream of visitors came to New York. Former commander John C. Frémont came. The sons of Robert E. Lee and Albert Sidney Johnston paid their respects. Proud of his writing, to special friends John "Black Jack" Logan and Horace Porter, he gave copies of sections of his memoirs.

These visits, while uplifting, were also tiring, and Dr. Douglas tried to shoo the visitors away. But John Philip Newman, Grant's pastor at Washington's Metropolitan Methodist Church, was one visitor who could not be refused. Learning of Grant's illness, Newman hurried from San Francisco, where he had conducted the funeral for the young son of tycoon Leland Stanford. Julia admired Newman and accepted him as one of the family.

Newman recorded in his diary—lost for half a century—his impressions of Grant and his attempts to minister to him in this crisis. Although pleased to discover that Grant "manifests dependence on God in prayer more than I have ever known him to do," the Methodist minister set himself a task: "I must get nearer to his soul and call forth a clear religious experience." Depending on whom you listened to, in the weeks ahead

Newman would either become a nurturing presence (Julia) or an intrusive busybody (Twain).

ON COLD, RAINY March days, Twain, traveling down from Hartford, would often stop at East Sixty-sixth street after visiting his publishing office. So different in age, background, and tastes, the two men bonded around their literary craft. Sometimes Grant would use Twain as a "sounding board" for his writing strategies. At other times they communed in silence as each read the most recent version of a Grant chapter. Twain would later reflect, "General Grant was a sick man, but he wrought upon his memoirs like a well one and made steady and sure progress."

AS HIS ILLNESS progressed, Grant's greatest fear was choking to death. At the end of March, he experienced a violent choking fit, and by the evening of March 30, his condition had so deteriorated that his doctors feared this could be the end. Julia sat beside him, waiting for his final breath. Newspapers headlined Grant's death almost as if it had already happened.

On April 4, Mark Twain wrote in his notebook: "Gen Grant is still living, this morning. Many a person between the two oceans lay hours awake, last night, listening for the booming of the fire-bells that should speak to the nation simultaneous voice & tell of its calamity." He specified, "The bell-strokes are to be 30 seconds apart, & there will be 63—the General's age. They will be striking in every town of the United States at the same moment."

After this almost death experience, Grant revived—and this renewal can be felt in his memoirs. His writing about Sheridan in the Shenandoah Valley or Sherman on his "March to the Sea" throbs with the kind of immediacy Johnson had encouraged on Grant's veranda at Long Branch. On the fighting at Five Forks, Grant wrote: "The two armies were mingled together there for a time in such manner that it was almost a question which one was going to demand the surrender of the other." Every reader knew the result, but Grant made it a question, placing us in the midst of the battle whose result is yet to be known.

In April, Twain learned from Fred that Grant was disappointed "because I had never expressed an opinion as to the literary quality of the Memoirs." By now Twain had come to believe that Grant "was the most modest of men, and this was another instance of it. He was venturing upon a new trade, an uncharted sea." Twain took "the earliest opportunity" to make amends. He was just then reading Julius Caesar's *Commentaries* and encouraged Grant by telling him: "The same high merits distinguished both books—clarity of statement, directness, simplicity, unpretentiousness, manifest truthfulness, fairness and justice toward friend and foe alike, soldierly candor and frankness, and soldierly avoidance of flowery speech."

WHY IS GRANT'S *Personal Memoirs* so significant? Because as a military memoir, his book stands alone. Grant fulfilled Robert U. Johnson's dictum to tell his audience "what he planned, thought, saw, said, and did," with little egoism. He did so by describing each battle in riveting detail, by taking his readers into the immediacy of his command decisions:

> One of the most anxious periods of my experience during the rebellion was the last few weeks before Petersburg. I felt that the situation of the Confederate army was such that they would try to make an escape at the earliest practicable moment, and I was afraid, every morning, that I would awake from my sleep to hear that Lee had gone.

In this remarkable passage, the reader is there. Grant lets his audience understand the contingencies of war and his own uncertainty in decision making.

If one looks at this as a "literary" memoir, it must be recalled that as a schoolboy, first in Georgetown and then at Maysville, Kentucky, Grant learned that "a noun is the name of a person, place, or thing." If he employed this monotonous grammar drill in the opening pages of his *Personal Memoirs,* in July he wrote physician John Douglas, "The fact is I think I am a verb instead of a personal pronoun. A verb is anything that signifies to be, to do, or to suffer."

Underlining the transformation of Grant's writing was his increased ability to write with verbs. Strong action verbs directed his narrative. It would be a mistake to think this use of verbs was completely new. Grant used verbs in his military orders. In 1863 at Champion Hill, he wrote Francis Blair, "Move at early dawn toward Black River Bridge. I think you will encounter no enemy on the way. If you do, however, engage them at once."

In the *Personal Memoirs,* action verbs drive forceful passages again and again. Thus, after the triumph at Chattanooga, he sent orders to General "Slow-Trot" Thomas: "I ordered Thomas to take Dalton and hold it, if possible; and I directed him to move without delay. Finding that he had not moved, on the 17th I urged him to start."

A close reading of the *Personal Memoirs* reveals many other literary qualities that would allow Grant's work to stand the test of time. Like Lincoln, he preferred strong, one-syllable words, eschewing the use of adjectives and adverbs. In perusing Grant's edits, one perceives he learned the lesson that less is more.

GRANT CELEBRATED HIS sixty-third birthday on April 27. He had recently regained some strength and prepared to tackle complicated memories: Spotsylvania Court House, Cold Harbor, the long envelopment of Petersburg, and, finally, Appomattox. On this beautiful spring day, he took a carriage ride in Central Park; then, returning refreshed, he took a second ride. In the afternoon, a messenger delivered sixty-three red roses from Andrew Carnegie. Novelist and civil rights reformer Albion W. Tourgée sent "warmest wishes to the hero who has made a nation's renewed life the endless birthday of his fame." Especially gratifying was the resolution sent by the Confederate Survivors Association meeting in Augusta, Georgia: "Remembering him now as the generous victor who, at the ever memorable meeting at Appomattox . . . conceded liberal and magnanimous terms of surrender."

ON APRIL 29, the *New York World,* never a friend to Grant, delivered an emotional body blow. In his "National Capital Gossip" column, correspondent Theron C. Crawford asserted that Grant's *Personal Memoirs* had not been written by Grant. The columnist wrote that a "false idea of Gen. Grant is given out by some of his friends, and that is that he is a writer. He is not a writer. He does not compose easily. Writing for him is a labor."

Who, then, was the writer? Crawford charged, "The work upon his new book about which so much has been said is the work of Gen. Adam Badeau."

Twain became apoplectic. Fuming, he threatened to sue the *World* and wrote Fred, "The General's work this morning is rather damaging evidence against the *World*'s intrepid lie."

Three days after the *World* bombshell, Grant sent a detailed letter to Twain answering the four charges in the article. About the first charge, he was emphatic:

"*First*—'The work upon his new book about which so much has been said is the work of General Adam Badeau.'

"This is false. Composition is entirely my own."

Using his connections with countless correspondents, Twain made sure Grant's response was published in newspaper front pages.

On this same day, Badeau handed Grant a letter. Badeau was talented and temperamental; he both admired Grant and felt increasingly diminished. One sentence leapt out: "Your book has assumed an importance that neither of us anticipated last summer." He offered several complaints, but two were significant. First, "I have been detained . . . from all other avocations for seven months. . . . My novel is unpublished today solely for this cause." Second, Badeau now understood the *Personal Memoirs* would stamp out his own previous multivolume book on Grant.

Badeau had seen his role slowly change. It had shrunk to "piece and prepare and connect the disjointed fragments into a connected narrative. This work is the merest literary drudgery—*such as I would never consent to do for anyone but you.*"

Although Twain steadfastly believed Badeau had been the source of the *World*'s accusation, Badeau was adamant: "The preposterous assertions in the newspapers will refute themselves." His demand was pecuniary: double his stipend from $5,000 to $10,000, and double that amount if profits reached or exceeded $30,000.

Grant's former secretary then crossed the line. "Yours is not, and will not be, the work of a literary man," he scoffed, "but the simple story of a man of affairs and of a great general; proper for you, but not such as would add to my credit at all."

Adam Badeau, longtime aide, surprised Grant with his complaint and demand about the authorship and writing of Grant's memoirs.

Grant took four days to compose his reply. He began with his conclusion: "I have concluded that you and I must part all association so far as the preparation of any work goes which is to bear my signature." He advised Badeau, "I understand you better than you do yourself. You are petulant, your anger is easily aroused and you are overbearing even to me." He recounted, "Think of the publishers you have quarreled with." After summarizing Badeau's litany of complaints, he concluded: "Allow me to say, this is all bosh."

Badeau exercised a strategic retreat. In a May letter, he did not withdraw his complaints but wanted Grant to know, "I have not changed the views or feelings of twenty years because it seems to me that in one instance you are unjust." Grant and Badeau never saw each other again, but two years after Grant's death, Badeau published *Grant in Peace,* one of the finest contemporary portraits of Grant.

As MAY TURNED to June, bringing heat and humidity, Grant's doctors advised he would fare better in the mountains for the summer. The Grants accepted an offer to use banker and philanthropist Joseph W. Drexel's cottage at Mount McGregor, twelve miles from Saratoga Springs, by the middle of the nineteenth century a popular vacation destination in upstate New York.

On the morning of June 16, crowds gathered to witness Grant's departure. At Grand Central Terminal, he boarded a special train provided by William Vanderbilt. Although it was a sultry summer day, Grant dressed in a long Prince Albert coat with a white silk scarf enveloping his neck. Physician John Douglas, who vacationed often in Saratoga Springs, accompanied his patient. As the train made its way up the Hudson Valley, it slowed when it passed West Point.

In the afternoon, a tired Grant arrived at the two-story, twelve-room cottage. He liked the expansive open porch that surrounded the house on three sides. The scent of the Adirondack Mountains' northern pines pleased him. As the nighttime temperature fell into the fifties, Grant was able to sleep for the first time in days.

By this point, Grant could barely speak and asked for his writing materials since he could no longer dictate. As Noble Dawson read the latest pages, Grant would scribble suggestions on his notepad. Once he began to write about the Virginia Campaign, the pace of the narrative slowed down. By now his cursive writing, always so strong and clear, had begun to decline. He labored intensely for half an hour, writing first to Douglas and then a "Memoranda for my Family." In essence the messages were

Upon his doctor's advice, in June Grant took up cooler summer lodgings at Mount McGregor in the Adirondack Mountains near Saratoga Springs, New York.

the same. He wrote Douglas, "I can feel plainly that my system is preparing for dissolution." Douglas and Shrady believed only Grant's commitment to finishing his memoirs was keeping him alive.

He expected to die by one of three means: hemorrhage, strangulation, or exhaustion. Sparing his family these details, he nevertheless told them, "I feel that I am failing." Although he never shied away from the truth himself, he may not have understood the impact this note would have on his family. Douglas observed that after reading it, "Mrs. Grant was almost prostrated."

But to everyone's amazement, Grant soldiered on. One evening, he had Dawson assemble slips of paper he had written over the past days. As the stenographer read the latest proof sheets, Grant occasionally raised his hand and in a barely audible voice dictated short insertions. That evening, he wrote Douglas, "I said I had been adding to my book and to my coffin. I presume every strain of the mind or body is one more nail in the coffin."

ON JUNE 27, Twain hurried to Mount McGregor, where he and Grant spent long hours working over page proofs. They talked by slips of paper, many of which Twain took with him when he returned to Elmira, New York, where he wrote each summer. With Twain there, Grant finished the chapter on Appomattox and wrote a new chapter assessing Lincoln, Stanton, and the major commanders. Although he was weakened physically, his assessments stand out as one of the finest parts of his memoirs.

Twain told Grant he would sell the book by subscription, a popular method in which a publisher hired agents who canvassed every region of

Grant and his family on the porch at Mount McGregor.

the country and sold copies on an as-requested basis. This entailed an up-front outlay of money, but Twain believed it would result in a larger sale.

At the end of June, Ulysses wrote a farewell letter to Julia: "There are some matters about which I would like to talk but about which I cannot. The subject would be painful to you and the children, and, by reflex, painful to me also." He had hoped to live into the fall or winter but had come to believe his death was "approaching much more rapidly." He spoke about his burial and his will. In his conclusion, one can feel his emotion: "Look after our dear children and direct them in the paths of rectitude. It would distress me far more to think that one of them could depart from an honorable, upright and virtuous life than it would to know they were prostrated on a bed of sickness from which they were never to arise alive." He concluded, "I bid you a final farewell until we meet in another, and I trust better world." He attached a P.S.: "This will be found in my coat after my demise." Ulysses's relationship with Julia had always been a primary foundation of his inner emotional strength, no more so than now as he faced his death and understood what his depar-ture would mean for her in the years ahead.

·   ·   ·

"'MAN PROPOSES AND God disposes.' There are but few important events in the affairs of men brought about by their own choice." On July 1, Grant finally wrote his five-hundred-word preface. After this opening affirmation, he took pains to tell his readers he never intended to write his memoirs and the recent circumstances that prompted him to do so. Speaking frankly ("I was reduced almost to the point of death"), he apologized for the haste with which he had been forced to complete his work, adding, "I would have more hope of satisfying the expectation of the public" if he had been afforded more time.

Twain released the preface to the press immediately, hoping to capitalize on the free publicity this afforded. The *New York Tribune* praised its candor: "The patient sufferer at Mount McGregor needs to feel no uneasiness on that score. Never did an author submit his work to a more sympathetic and indulgent circle of readers."

Also in early July, Grant penned a note to John Douglas: "I ask you not to show this to anyone. . . . Particularly, I want it kept from my family." Grant feared that what he would say "would only distress them almost beyond endurance to know it, and, by reflex, would distress me." Although he hoped he could live long enough to complete his memoirs, he told Douglas, "If it is within God's providence that I should go now I am ready to obey His call without a murmur."

Each person, in facing death, has a choice to make. In his final campaign, Grant chose gratitude.

> It has been an inestimable blessing to me to hear the kind expressions towards me in person from all parts of our country; from people of all nationalities of all religions, and of no religion, of Confederate and National troops alike; of soldiers' organizations; of mechanical, scientific religious and all other societies, embracing almost every citizen in the land. They have brought joy to my heart if they have not effected a cure.

Finally, he thanked his doctors "for having brought me through the 'valley of the shadow of death' to enable me to witness these things."

AND STILL THE visitors came. They came up the mountain on the narrow-gauge railroad, by carriage, on foot. A Civil War veteran, Sam Willett, pitched his tent and volunteered to stand guard as hotel guests wandered over to catch a glimpse of Grant, who sat on the front porch writing and editing. Once in a while, he looked up to nod or tip his tall hat.

On July 8, twenty reporters and editors of the Mexican Associated Press showed up; because of Mexico's affection for him, they wanted to see the general. Fred was afraid that so many reporters would tire his father, but Grant insisted on meeting them.

On July 9, Grant welcomed a visitor he had never met. After being questioned by Willett, the visitor was allowed to proceed. He introduced himself as Charles Wood, the man who had sent $500 immediately after the failure of Grant & Ward. Grant wrote a note to Wood on four slips of paper, beginning, "I am very sorry that I am unable to converse even in a whisper." Touched by Wood's kindness, he added, "I am glad to say that while there is much unblushing wickedness in this world there is a compensating generosity and grandeur of soul."

No visitor affected Grant more than one he'd not seen since a cold February morning at Fort Donelson twenty-three years earlier. Simon Bolivar Buckner, his West Point classmate who had loaned Grant money in New York on his return from California in 1854, had become a successful Kentucky newspaper editor and politician. A widower, Buckner came with his new wife, Delia Claiborne Buckner. Mrs. Buckner later wrote, "The sole object of General Buckner's visit was to assure [Grant] that the southern people appreciated his magnanimity at Appomattox." When Buckner left, reporters pressed him about their conversation—held on slips of paper—but Buckner replied, "The visit was purely personal." A few days later, Grant gave Buckner permission to share their conversation, believing it could promote good feelings between the North and the South.

The last photo of Grant shows him reading three days before his death.

. . .

ON JULY 16, Grant admitted to Douglas that earlier, in his weakened condition, "my work had been done so hastily that much was left out," but now it pleased him that "I have added as much as fifty pages to the book." In a final sentence, he presciently told his doctor, "There is nothing more I should do to it now, and therefore I am not likely to be more ready to go than at this moment."

Grant had fought his battle with cancer with the "moral courage" he invoked in the *Personal Memoirs*. He had soldiered on for three main reasons: First, Julia, Fred, and his extended family surrounded him with loving support. Second, he had committed himself to completing the *Personal Memoirs*. Third, he had slowly come to understand through Twain that when published by subscription, the book would earn enough money to take care of Julia for the rest of her life.

On July 19, a final photograph of Grant was taken on the front porch, top hat in place, newspaper in hand.

On July 21, Douglas became convinced the end was near and sent for fellow doctor George Shrady.

Early on the morning of July 23, all who best loved and admired the general gathered at his bedside. The reporters, alerted, lined up outside at a respectful distance. Julia, who had held his hand on every day they were

This August 1 illustration captured Grant's death at Mount McGregor for a grieving nation.

together for more than forty years, held it one last time. At eight A.M., the general surrendered to death.

When Grant's speaking voice fell silent, he discovered a new medium of expression: his writing voice. If "the hero of Appomattox" would be remembered for his actions in saving the Union, the final campaign of Ulysses S. Grant—soldier, husband, president, father, citizen—the words of his *Personal Memoirs,* written in a race against death, have been read with appreciation and gratitude by generation after generation of Americans.

Epilogue

Today the country is one vast funeral train.

—Judge LeBaron B. Colt, "Eulogy for Ulysses S. Grant"
Bristol, Rhode Island, August 8, 1885

On August 8, 1885, New York City prepared for America's largest public gathering to date: the funeral procession and burial of Ulysses S. Grant. It was a mild summer Saturday, and the *New York Tribune* estimated the crowd would number close to one and a half million, a full third coming from outside the city by train and boat.

Some New Yorkers vividly remembered mourning Abraham Lincoln twenty years earlier, as his body passed through the city on the funeral train that would carry it to its burial in Springfield, Illinois. But while Lincoln's death, coming at the very end of the Civil War, evoked more sadness in the North than in the South, Grant's death prompted a full-scale national outpouring of grief and homage.

The New York Times wrote, "The name of General Grant will be remembered by Americans as that of the savior of their country in a crisis more appalling than any it has passed through since the United States became a nation." The *New York Tribune* stated, "The foremost man of the nation has closed a career second to no other in the history of the republic."

Even in the first capital of the Confederacy, the *Montgomery Advertiser* declared, "Looking at the life and character of General Grant from the broadest national standpoint, it is true to say that no man since George Washington has better illustrated the genius of American institutions or the temper of the American people." The *New Orleans Times-Democrat* enthused, "Vanquished by his arms, in his chivalric kindness we were doubly vanquished at Appomattox."

Grant was honored in civic ceremonies and church services across the United States, many of which remembered him not simply as a general of the Civil War, but as a hero of the larger American narrative. A Massachusetts minister saluted the leader whose "name filled two hemispheres," calling him "great in war, greater in peace, and greatest in the hearts of his countrymen." In San Francisco, Methodist bishop Charles H. Fowler offered a tribute at the Mechanics' Pavilion: Grant was "a soldier, who conquered a great people and ennobled them by the moderation with which he used his victory; a ruler who healed the wound in the breast of the nation and made its people one, by the impartiality of his administration." And in Bristol, Rhode Island, former governor Augustus O. Bourn offered this eulogy: "As the centuries roll on, and the history of our country shall be written by impartial posterity, the names of WASHINGTON, LINCOLN, and GRANT will shine with increased luster."

One of Grant's oldest friends could not make the long trip north to New York because of ill health, but when a *New York Times* reporter contacted James Longstreet at his stone house near Gainesville, Georgia, the Confederate general was eager to talk about "my lifetime friend, kindest when I was most fiercely assaulted." Old Pete enthused, "He was a great general, but the best thing about him was his heart."

GRANT WAS ALSO mourned outside of America, especially in countries that he visited during his two-and-a-half-year world tour. For a memorial service held for him at London's Westminster Abbey, *The Times* of London reported that the demand for seats far exceeded what could be provided. After an extensive obituary, *The Times* concluded, "His name will share with that of Abraham Lincoln the chief glories of American history in the 19th century."

Freeman's Journal, Ireland's first national newspaper, wrote, "Even in America, where men are what they make themselves, and where high position is to be attained by force of individual talents, not by right of birth, such success as fell to the lot of Ulysses S. Grant is exceptional."

GROVER CLEVELAND, THE first Democrat elected president since before the Civil War, had asked General Winfield Hancock to be in charge of the funeral procession. Hancock represented one of several political curiosities on this historic day. A lifelong Democrat, Hancock fell out with Grant in 1867 when Grant criticized his military administration of Louisiana for his treatment of the freedmen. In the 1880 presidential election, Grant had campaigned for James Garfield and against Hancock. On August 8, 1885, however, Hancock, with a buff sash and crepe-bound arm, led a cavalcade of mounted men that included ex-Confederates Fitzhugh

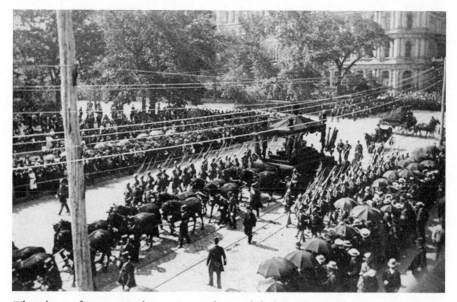

The column of mourners who accompanied Grant's body in New York City on August 8, 1885, was seven miles long.

Lee, nephew of Robert E. Lee, and John Gordon, who had been so impressed with Grant when the men met for the first time at Appomattox.

The procession was to start from City Hall at ten A.M. For nine and a half miles, it would snake north up Broadway to Fourteenth Street, then up Fifth Avenue to Fifty-seventh Street, back to Broadway, and finally to Riverside Park, where a temporary tomb had been hastily built. Thirty-seven thousand members of the United States military, including many ex-Confederate soldiers, marched behind the funeral car bearing Grant's casket, drawn by twenty-four black stallions. Julia, however, was absent. Still prostrated by her grief, she chose to stay at Mount McGregor to mourn and pray.

The crowds that lined Broadway would have instantly recognized another curiosity: leading the pallbearers in a four-person carriage were Grant's two favorite Union generals, William T. Sherman and Philip Sheridan, but sitting beside them were two Confederate generals: Joe Johnston, who had rushed back from California, and Simon Bolivar Buckner. Grant's funeral provided an opportunity for both North and South to recall, if only for a day, their bonds of reconciliation.

As the massive procession set off, the bells of old Trinity Church began a steady ring. By prearrangement, a signal from Western Union sparked across the nation, and many hands began to ring many bells in churches in towns and cities from Maine to California and even farther afield, in Grant's beloved Mexico. All along the route, sewing girls, apprentices, and clerks hung bands of black and white, flowers, and flags from windows. Toward the end of the route, an African American bootblack had nailed up a sign in front of his workstation: "He Helped to Set Me Free."

The head of the procession reached Riverside Park at one P.M., but it took until five P.M. for the full crowd to arrive. As veterans carrying their tattered battle flags assembled, warships on the nearby Hudson River boomed their salutes and a band played a funeral dirge. Sherman and Sheridan took their places on one side of the casket, Johnston and Buckner on the other. After John Philip Newman read the Methodist burial service, a lone army trumpeter played the last call of the camp. Momentous and stirring, the final parade for General Grant was declared "the greatest funeral ever seen in America."

The official program reflected the formality and dignity of the funeral ceremonies.

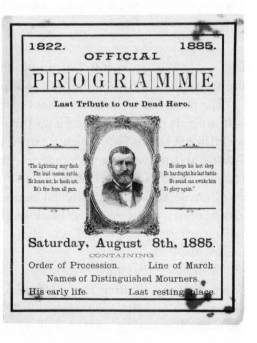

GRANT'S FAME LIVED on in another very important way. His *Personal Memoirs* were a sensation when published four months later. In a cutting-edge marketing campaign, Mark Twain sent out a phalanx of subscription salesmen who offered the two-volume memoirs in three attractive bindings at three different price points. The first printing sold three hundred thousand sets. Twain proudly presented Julia with an initial check for $200,000 of what would ultimately total royalties of $450,000 ($12 million in today's currency).

Grant's *Personal Memoirs* were much more than a financial success. In 1962, critic Edmund Wilson wrote, "The *Memoirs* convey also Grant's dynamic force and the definitiveness of his personality. Perhaps never has a book so objective in form seemed so personal in every line." Gore Vidal, one of America's foremost men of letters, averred, "It is simply not possible to read Grant's *Memoirs* without realizing that the author is a man of first-rate intelligence. . . . His book is a classic."

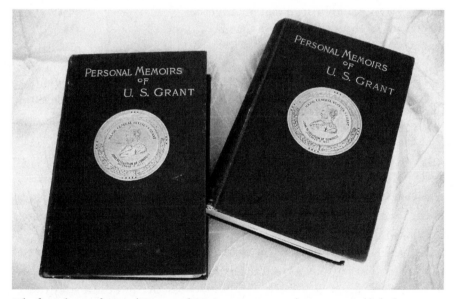

The first edition of Grant's Personal Memoirs, *in two volumes, was published in December 1885.*

JULIA EMERGED FROM her grief in part by beginning her own memoirs; the project became a way of remembering all she had shared with her Ulys. She wrote as if talking to a friend on the veranda of her house. Filled with fascinating anecdotes, her memoirs take pains to correct misunderstandings about her husband, whom she presents as one of America's great leaders. But Julia was fearful of criticism in her lifetime, so her memoirs would not be published until 1975.

Slowly but surely, Julia began to rebuild her life apart from Ulys. On a June day in 1893, while vacationing at New York's Cranston's Hotel, she learned another famous widow had arrived at the famous resort on the Hudson River. She knocked on the newcomer's door.

"I am Mrs. Grant," Julia said.

"I am very glad to meet you," replied Varina Davis.

Nearly three decades after Ulysses S. Grant offered his hand of peace to Robert E. Lee, Julia Grant offered her hand to Varina Davis, widow of Jefferson Davis. The *New York Herald* took note, entitling its article "Their Widows Met in Peace."

The two widows lived twenty blocks apart in New York City and became fast friends. Mrs. Davis worked as an editor and columnist for Joseph Pulitzer's *New York World,* and from time to time Julia Grant and Varina Davis could be seen driving together.

BUT IN 1895, Julia sold her house in New York and moved to Washington, the city where she had served as First Lady. She began holding popular Tuesday receptions at her home on Massachusetts Avenue. She was joined there by her daughter, Nellie, who, with her three teenage children, had finally left Great Britain and her failed marriage to Algernon Sartoris.

As for Ulysses and Julia's other children, Fred served as minister to Austria-Hungary from 1889 to 1893 under Presidents Benjamin Harrison and Grover Cleveland. He then served as a commissioner of police in New York City from 1894 to 1898, working alongside future president Theodore Roosevelt.

After his disastrous time on Wall Street, Buck regained his financial footing, and in 1893, he moved to San Diego, where his younger brother, Jesse, was already living. Buck started a law practice but ultimately found success in real estate. In 1910, after five years of construction that cost a staggering $1.9 million, he opened the U. S. Grant Hotel as a wonderfully successful memorial to his father. Jesse, the youngest, outlived all his siblings and authored *In the Days of My Father, General Grant* in 1925, a warmhearted remembrance from the humorous boy who liked to wrestle his father.

ON APRIL 27, 1897, Julia traveled to New York City's Riverside Park for the dedication of the Grant Monument, on the occasion of the seventy-fifth anniversary of her husband's birth. Twelve years after his death, the general's enduring fame brought out a crowd of one million people on an unseasonably cold day. Designed by architect John Duncan, symbolically facing south, the granite-and-marble domed mausoleum was the largest in the United States; Grant's remains were guarded by the busts of Civil War generals Sherman, Sheridan, McPherson, Thomas, and Ord. For five hours, soldiers marched and bands played. Recently inaugurated president William McKinley declared of Grant, "A great life never dies."

Five years later, Julia would be buried beside her husband at the majestic tomb. Her best obituary might well be the concluding words of her *Personal Memoirs*.

> For nearly thirty-seven years, I, his wife, rested and was warmed in the sunlight of his loyal love and great fame, and now, even though his beautiful life has gone out, it is as when some far-off planet disappears from the heavens; the light of his glorious fame still reaches to me, falls upon me, and warms me.

IN THE FIRST year of the new century, 1900, Theodore Roosevelt surveyed the landscape of American history and made his judgment: "Mightiest among the mighty dead loom the three great figures of Washington, Lincoln, and Grant." In the second rank, Roosevelt placed Benjamin Franklin, Thomas Jefferson, Alexander Hamilton, and Andrew Jackson.

Frederick Douglass, foremost African American leader of the nineteenth century, offers a final lens to our effort to refocus the life of Ulysses S. Grant: "To him more than any other man the Negro owes his enfranchisement and the Indian a humane policy. . . . He was accessible to all men. . . . The black soldier was welcome in his tent, and the freedman in his house."

Douglass's valuation is the invitation taken up by this biographer: the opportunity for the enigmatic, inspiring, and complex story of American Ulysses to become accessible to the wider audiences he deserves.

Acknowledgments

The Papers of Ulysses S. Grant are the foundation from which I have built my story of Ulysses S. Grant. The editing of this American treasure began in 1962, with volume 1 published in 1967. It will conclude fifty years later in 2017, with a richly annotated version of Grant's *Personal Memoirs*. I am fortunate to be the first Grant biographer to have access to all thirty-three volumes.

John Y. Simon of Southern Illinois University served as editor over the enormous project's lifetime. I never had the privilege of meeting Dr. Simon—he died in 2008—but I feel as if I met him every morning I immersed myself in the *Grant Papers*. His perceptive introductions and informative annotations to each volume constitute a Grant biography in themselves. From the beginning of my research and writing in 2009, Dr. Simon's widow, Harriet, who helped her husband with editing, has been a source of constant encouragement of my work.

The *Grant Papers* moved from Southern Illinois University to Mississippi State University in 2008 through the initiative of longtime Ulysses S. Grant Association president Chief Justice (Ret.) Frank J. Williams. At his invitation, eminent Civil War historian John Marszalek became executive director and managing editor.

During my visits to what is now the Ulysses S. Grant Presidential Library, I have received generous cooperation and counsel from Dr. Marszalek and his talented editorial team: Michael B. Ballard, Amanda Carlock, Elizabeth Coggins, Louis Gallo, Meg Henderson, David Nolen, and Ryan P. Semmes. I thank the Ulysses S. Grant Association for a 2010 Research Travel Grant to work at the library. Despite recent suggestions that almost all historical records can now be accessed online, I have discovered at the Grant Library that numerous resources about Grant's life and times are neither online nor in the published volumes. A visit to this gold mine of information is a must for anyone writing on Grant.

. . .

"GRANT IS WAITING for you." Jimi Michere offers this greeting each morning when I arrive at the Huntington Library in San Marino, California, and walk toward my study on Mahogany Row. Each day, a talented staff of archivists and librarians awaits, ready to help in every conceivable way as I conduct my research in the Huntington's marvelous U.S. history collection, with its special focus on the Civil War. I thank Steve Koblik, president of the Huntington from 2001 to 2015, who, even with his many responsibilities, always found time to stop and engage in conversations about Grant. I am also grateful to Steve Hindle, director of research; David Zeidberg, director of the library; Olga Tsapina, curator of American history; and Jennifer Watts, curator of photographs, as well as Laura Stalker, Christopher Adde, and Robert Maine. Each year, the Huntington invites a distinguished American historian to come for a year. I am in debt to Gary Gallagher, Sean Wilentz, Bruce Levine, Harry Stout, and Joan Waugh for enormously helpful conversations about my Grant project. The Huntington Library is an incomparable place to research and write. I am lucky to have it as my home base.

I AM GRATEFUL to Jeff Flannery, head of the Reference and Reader Services Section and his staff in the Manuscript Division at the Library of Congress. Ulysses's letters to Julia are usually available only on older microfilm. I thank John Sellers, curator of the Civil War Collection, and his successor, Michelle A. Krowl, for securing permission for me to examine them in the original.

ONCE AGAIN, I express thanks to the efficient staff at the Abraham Lincoln Presidential Library in Springfield, Illinois. I am especially grateful to James Cornelius, curator of the Lincoln Collection, and to Kathryn Harris, library services director; Cheryl Schnirring, manuscripts manager; and Gwenith Podeschi, reference librarian.

Anyone who wishes to learn more about Grant will want to visit the Ulysses S. Grant National Historic Site near St. Louis. Located at White Haven, where Grant first met Julia in 1844, it is managed by Superintendent Timothy S. Good, who has been a welcoming friend again and again. Park historian Pam Sanfilippo, herself at work on a biography of Julia Dent Grant, generously shared with me letters from Julia that are not in the *Grant Papers*. The museum, located in the barns Ulysses built for his horses, is a must-see.

At the University of Southern California, I received valuable assistance on several occasions from Claude B. Zachary, university archivist and manuscript librarian, as I searched the Hamlin Garland Papers. The young Garland conducted dozens of interviews with people who knew Grant at different stages of his life.

At the Chicago History Museum, Debbie Vaughn provided help with my various searches.

Many people have been generous in offering their time and insights on people and places important to understanding Grant. Loretta Fuhrman introduced me to Grant's birthplace in Point Pleasant, Ohio. Lee Schweickart and Ned Lodwick showed me Grant's home and other formative sites in Georgetown, Ohio. Nancy and Stan Purdy, who live in what was once the home of George and Jane Bailey and their children, one-half block up the street from the Grant home, offered hospitality in the house that has been in their family since 1876. Lisa Corum, my former student, helped me understand the presence of the Underground Railroad in southern Ohio, now captured in her book, *Underground Ulysses: The Unexplored Roots of U. S. Grant and the Underground Railroad*. At Ripley, Ohio, she introduced me to Ann Hagedorn, who over lunch elaborated on her own marvelous book, *Beyond the River: The Untold Story of the Heroes of the Underground Railroad*. Allison Gibson, of the Union Township Public Library in Ripley, offered help in understanding John Rankin and the Presbyterian academy that sixteen-year-old Ulysses attended in 1838–1839.

In Maysville, Kentucky, I benefited from the knowledge of Cay Chamness at the Kentucky Gateway Museum Center, particularly regarding the Maysville Academy, which Grant attended.

One October week in 2010, I visited West Point, where Alicia-Mauldin Ware, archives curator, and Suzanne Christoff, associate director for special collections and archives, helped me access original records from Grant's student years. Gary Hood, art curator at the West Point Museum, guided me through the treasures of the museum. Alan Aimone continues to be my indispensable West Point contact. I express my profound thanks to Alan for sharing with me his own deep knowledge of the academy.

For helping me to understand more of Grant's time in Galena, Illinois, both before and after the Civil War, I am grateful to Nancy Breed, executive director of the Galena Historical Society & U. S. Grant Museum. At the Galena Public Library, Steve Repp let me inspect the local Galena newspapers that Grant read. Local historian Scott Wolfe shared with me his considerable knowledge of John Rawlins. The Grant home on High Street is now in private hands, and James Wirth, its owner, allowed me access.

. . .

I DETERMINED EARLY on to walk the far-flung battlefields where Grant directed his armies—my visits always guided by remarkable historians. Pam Sanfilippo, John Samson, and I visited what remains of the Belmont battlefield in Missouri and also historic Cairo, Illinois. At Fort Donelson, an old friend, Doug Richardson, arranged for my visit. Park historian Jimmy Jobe, who has done forty years of continuous service at this site, allowed me to imagine the Union gunboats coming up the Cumberland River. At Shiloh, park historian Stacy Allen provided an in-depth understanding of the ebb and flow of this critical battle. In Holly Springs, Mississippi, the Reverend Robert Milton Winter helped me envision Confederate general Earl Van Dorn's attack on Grant's supplies and his hopes of capturing Julia Grant. At Vicksburg, I was the recipient of the generous spirit and wisdom of Terrence Winschel, retired park historian. Parker Hills, who has taken the lead in conserving the sites of the Vicksburg Campaign, guided me along Grant's battle route, which he has worked tirelessly to preserve. James Ogden III, historian at the Chickamauga & Chattanooga National Military Park, met me armed with maps and photographs that permitted me to picture Grant in Chattanooga in the fall of 1863.

On a warm May day in 2011, the same month that Grant began the Overland Campaign in 1864, Civil War historian Gary Gallagher, and Bill Bergen, with home-drawn maps in hand, expertly guided me through the terrain of the Battle of the Wilderness, on to Spotsylvania Court House, and finally to Grant's headquarters at City Point. I thank Will Greene for his instructive guidance at Pamplin Historical Park in helping me understand further the Campaign at Petersburg.

FOR ASSISTANCE IN thinking more about Methodism and its place in both the Grant and Dent families, I am indebted to Kenneth E. Rowe, for many years librarian at the United Methodist Archives Center at Drew University in Madison, New Jersey, and Douglas M. Strong, historian of American religion and dean of the School of Theology at Seattle Pacific University. I also express my gratitude to Timothy Binkley, archivist at the Bridwell Library, Perkins School of Theology, Southern Methodist University, for making available the papers of John Heyl Vincent, Grant's Methodist minister at Galena, who went on to found the famous Chautauqua Institution.

. . .

I THANK DARRELL Guder and Benjamin Stahl for finding reports in Berlin newspapers on Grant's conversation with Bismarck in 1878, and Gary Sattler for translating these articles.

IN MY DESIRE to appreciate Grant's remarkable horsemanship, I benefited from many informative conversations with the wranglers where I ride: the Triangle X Ranch near Moose, Wyoming, and the Circle Z Ranch near Patagonia, Arizona.

In my travels with Grant, I thank these friends for their encouragement and hospitality: Peter and Robin Baugher, Wilson Golden, Darrell and Judy Guder, Gordy and Sandy Hess, and Bruce and Ginny Maclaury. I thank Jack Rogers, my Tuesday lunch partner at the Huntington, for his wisdom and friendship.

MY DEEP THANKS to David Lindroth of West Milford, New Jersey, mapmaker extraordinaire. I believe David's thirty maps will permit much greater comprehension of Grant's role in the complex Mexican War and Civil War battles.

I ONCE AGAIN thank Karen Needles, director of the Lincoln Archives Digital Project in Washington, D.C., who found photographs, images, and cartoons, many that have not appeared in previous Grant books. I am grateful for Karen's skills, plus her willingness to respond at any time. I thank Random House for their commitment to finding the right places for the many images.

An enormous thank-you to the gifted people who gave their time and insights in commenting on various drafts of the biography. I am grateful to Alan Aimone, Michael Ballard, Gary Gallagher, Pam Sanfilippo, and Terrence Winschel, for reading specific chapters.

I am especially grateful to all those who read the entire manuscript. Jim McPherson, teacher and friend, both enhanced and corrected my military history. From the inception of this project, John Marszalek, from his post at the Ulysses S. Grant Presidential Library, offered his encouragement and close reading of several drafts. Historian Richard Norton Smith, director of multiple presidential libraries, offered his wise comments, especially on the often maligned Grant presidency. My UCLA colleague Joan Waugh, whose *U. S. Grant: American Hero, American Myth* has refocused attention on Grant, responded with alacrity to every question I had for her. Frank J. Williams, president of the Ulysses S. Grant

Association, is a fount of knowledge on all things Grant. Ernesto Cortes, Jr., co-chair of the Industrial Areas Foundation focusing on grassroots democracy, has brought his wide-ranging skills as a reader to offer critical insights of multiple drafts over dozens of breakfast meetings. Finally, I am a benefactor of the wisdom of American cultural historian Richard Wightman Fox. For a decade, over dinner at Pasadena's Il Fornaio or the Parkway Grill, Richard and I have enjoyed the richest of table talk. I owe an enormous debt to him for challenging my sometime intoxication with Grant as he offered his questions and comments on my manuscript.

My warmest thanks go to Nancy Macky. Longtime friend, fellow Huntington reader, professor of English and drama, Nancy helped me think about the neglected story of Grant's love of novels and the theater and unearthed the story of the plays that Grant may have seen in Philadelphia on his way to West Point. Nancy brought her contagious enthusiasm and sharp-eyed detective skills to my efforts to get beneath the surface of the traditional Grant story. At Nancy's beloved Oxford University, she searched the Bodleian Library and the Vere Harmsworth Library at the Rothermere American Institute, tracking down newspaper reports on Grant during his travels in Great Britain and Ireland. She also brought her editorial pencil to the many drafts and assisted the huge task of the source notes.

FOR THIS THIRD book published by Random House, my editor has once again been the incredible David Ebershoff. After *A. Lincoln,* it was David who encouraged me to do a second presidential biography. David somehow managed to be a most astute editor, encouraging and challenging, while also writing his own award-winning novels. In November 2015, with the release of his novel-turned-movie *The Danish Girl,* David telephoned to say he was moving into a next chapter of focusing exclusively on his writing. I will miss David, but I will always be grateful for all that I have learned from him.

How fortunate I am that Caitlin McKenna is my new editor. Caitlin's dedication to this project, her wise counsel and judgments, and our frequent telephone conversations about every aspect of this book buoyed this author in the last critical year when the end comes into view. Thank you, Caitlin!

Random House is a powerhouse team. I thank Sona Vogel for her expert and thorough copyediting; Victoria Wong for designing the book; and Joseph Perez, who designed the cover. Once again, Dennis Ambrose has managed the editorial production of the book with his usual efficiency.

FOR A FOURTH time, I thank my friend and extraordinary literary agent. Mary Evans has been a champion of three Lincoln books and now Grant. With a keen eye and ear, she offers her always sound advice at just the right moment.

FINALLY, MY MOST heartfelt thanks are to my wife, Cynthia Conger White. She has shared every step of our journey with Ulysses and Julia. I thank her for her good humor when her husband would return home from the Huntington Library more immersed in 1866 than 2016. She listened to my drafts for hours as I channeled Abraham Lincoln and Ulysses S. Grant, both of whom read aloud in order to get both the sight and the sound of the words. An avid book lover, Cynthia is my first and last reader. I thank her for her love and constant encouragement over these past seven years.

Notes

Abbreviations and Short Titles Employed in Notes

AJ	Andrew Johnson
AL	Abraham Lincoln
EMS	Edwin M. Stanton
GGM	George Gordon Meade
HWH	Henry Wager Halleck
JAM	John A. McClernand
JDG	Julia Dent Grant
JRG	Jesse Root Grant
JRY	John Russell Young
PHS	Philip H. Sheridan
USG	Ulysses S. Grant
WTS	William Tecumseh Sherman
ALPLC	Abraham Lincoln Papers at the Library of Congress, Manuscript Division, Washington, D.C.: American Memory Project, 2000. http://memory.loc.gov./ammem/alhtml /alhome.html.
ALPLM	Abraham Lincoln Presidential Library and Museum, Springfield, Illinois.
Catton, *Grant Moves South*	Bruce Catton. *Grant Moves South*. Boston: Little, Brown & Co., 1960.
CWAL	*The Collected Works of Abraham Lincoln*. 9 vols. Edited by Roy P. Basler. New Brunswick, N.J.: Rutgers University Press, 1953–1955.
Garland, *Grant*	Hamlin Garland. *Ulysses S. Grant: His Life and Character*. New York: Doubleday & McClure Co., 1898.
Grant Papers	*The Papers of Ulysses S. Grant*. 32 vols. Edited by John Y. Simon and John Marszalek. Carbondale: Southern Illinois University Press, 1967–2012.
Julia Dent Grant, *Personal Memoirs*	Julia Dent Grant. *The Personal Memoirs of Julia Dent Grant*. Edited by John Y. Simon. Carbondale: Southern Illinois University Press, 1975.
Lewis, *Captain Sam Grant*	Lloyd Lewis. *Captain Sam Grant*. Boston: Little, Brown & Co., 1950.
McPherson, *Battle Cry*	James M. McPherson. *Battle Cry of Freedom: The Civil War Era*. New York: Oxford University Press, 1988.
McFeely, *Grant*	William S. McFeely. *Grant: A Biography*. New York: W. W. Norton & Co., 1981.

Meade, *Life* — George Gordon Meade. *The Life and Letters of George Gordon Meade.* 3 vols. New York: Charles Scribner's Sons, 1913.

OR — *War of the Rebellion . . . Official Records of the Union and Confederate Armies.* 128 vols. Washington, D.C.: Government Printing Office, 1880–1901.

ORN — *Official Records of the Union and Confederate Navies in the War of the Rebellion.* Washington, D.C.: Government Printing Office, 1894–1922.

PAJ — Andrew Johnson. *The Papers of Andrew Johnson.* Edited by LeRoy P. Graf and Ralph W. Haskins. Knoxville: University of Tennessee Press, 1967–2000.

Personal Memoirs — *The Personal Memoirs of U. S. Grant.* 2 vols. New York: Charles L. Webster & Co., 1885.

Porter, *Campaigning with Grant* — Horace Porter. *Campaigning with Grant.* New York: Century Co., 1897.

Richardson, *A Personal History* — Albert D. Richardson. *A Personal History of Ulysses S. Grant.* Hartford, Conn.: American Publishing Company, 1868.

Simpson, *Grant* — Brooks D. Simpson. *Ulysses S. Grant: Triumph over Adversity, 1822–1865.* Boston: Houghton Mifflin, 2000.

Smith, *Grant* — Jean Edward Smith. *Grant.* New York: Simon & Schuster, 2001.

Strong, *Diary* — George Templeton Strong. *The Diary of George Templeton Strong.* Vols. 3, 4: *The Civil War, 1860–1865.* Edited by Allan Nevins and Milton Halsey Thomas. New York: Macmillan, 1952.

Young, *Around the World* — John Russell Young. *Around the World with General Grant.* 2 vols. New York: American News, 1879.

Prologue

xxii **Looking embarrassed** Frederick Dent Grant, "Reminiscences of General U. S. Grant," paper read before the Illinois Commandery, Military Order of the Loyal Legion of the United States, January 27, 1910, reprinted in the *Journal of the Illinois State Historical Society* 7, no. 1 (April 1914): 73.

xxiii **"Why, here is General Grant!"** Catton, *Grant Takes Command* (Boston: Little, Brown & Co., 1969), 124–25.

xxiii **In their retelling, Grant** Joan Waugh, in *U. S. Grant: American Hero, American Myth* (Chapel Hill: University of North Carolina Press, 2009), 185–91, tells the story of the Lost Cause's campaign against Grant.

xxiv **"The only problem was"** William S. McFeely, *Grant: A Biography* (New York: W. W. Norton & Co., 1981), xii. McFeely adds, "He did have limited though by no means inconsequential talents to apply to whatever truly engaged his attention."

xxvi **"I was perfectly sickened"** USG to JRG, May 6, 1861, *Grant Papers,* 2:21.

xxvi **What to make of Grant's** For a reappraisal of Grant's presidency, see Brooks D. Simpson, *The Reconstruction Presidents* (Lawrence: University Press of Kansas, 1998).

xxvi **In recent years** Brooks Simpson authored *Let Us Have Peace: Ulysses S. Grant and the Politics of War and Reconstruction, 1861–1868* (Chapel Hill: University of North Carolina Press, 1991) and *Ulysses S. Grant: Triumph over Adversity, 1822–1865* (Boston: Houghton Mifflin, 2000). Jean Edward Smith, *Grant* (New York: Simon & Schuster, 2000), gave us a first-rate comprehensive biography. Joan Waugh, in *U. S.*

Grant: American Hero, American Myth, offers an adroit reappraisal of Grant within the larger story of American memory, discussing the reasons for his fall from favor and why he deserves to be restored to a place of prominence. See also H. W. Brands' *The Man Who Saved the Union: Ulysses Grant in War and Peace* (New York: Doubleday & Co., 2012).

Chapter 1. "My Family Is American"

3   **His appreciation looked back** For the genealogy of the seven generations, see Arthur Hastings Grant, *The Grant Family: A Genealogical History of the Descendants of Matthew Grant, of Windsor, Conn. 1601–1898* (Poughkeepsie, N.Y.: A. V. Haight, 1898).

3   **The Grants sailed** Richardson, *A Personal History*, 17–18.

3   **In the next eleven years** For the larger story of the roots and fruits of "the Great Migration," see Virginia DeJohn Anderson, *New England's Generation: The Great Migration and the Formation of Society and Culture in the Seventeenth Century* (New York: Cambridge University Press, 1991).

4   **Following their arrival** See Ebenezer Clapp, *History of the Town of Dorchester, Massachusetts* (Boston: E. Clapp, Jr., 1859).

4   **Matthew would come** See Henry Reed Stiles, *The History of Ancient Windsor, Connecticut* (New York: C. B. Norton, 1859); *Some Early Records and Documents of and Relating to the Town of Windsor, Connecticut, 1639–1703* (Hartford: Connecticut Historical Society, 1930), 3–5; Grant, *Grant Family*, 10–11.

4   **"I have been careful"** Stiles, *The History of Ancient Windsor*, 59, 635.

4   **The next five generations** Grant, *Grant Family*, 14; Richardson, *A Personal History*, 25.

4   **Noah and Solomon were killed** *Personal Memoirs*, 1:18.

4   **He believed his grandfather served** *Personal Memoirs*, 1:18; William S. McFeely, researching the records of Revolutionary War service for Connecticut volunteers in the Connecticut State Library and the National Archives, has questioned the authenticity of reports of Grant's forebears' service. See McFeely, *Grant*, 4–5.

6   **They stopped at the first village** George W. Knepper, *Ohio and Its People* (Kent, Ohio: Kent State University Press, 1989), 1.

6   **"There shall be neither slavery"** Ibid., 57–59.

7   **Years later, Ulysses** *Personal Memoirs*, 1:20.

7   **The need for leather goods** See Peter C. Welsh, "A Craft That Resisted Change: American Tanning Practices to 1850," *Technology and Culture* 4, no. 3 (Summer 1963): 316.

8   **He wanted to go back** Lewis, *Captain Sam Grant*, 9.

8   **In Hudson, John Brown** Ibid., 12.

8   **Jesse appreciated** Ibid., 13.

8   **Five years younger** Garland, *Grant*, 3; Lewis, *Captain Sam Grant*, 14.

10   **Bubbling with pride** Garland, *Grant*, 6; Lewis, *Captain Sam Grant*, 17.

10   **These were all** See Fénelon, *Telemachus,* edited by Patrick Riley (Cambridge, U.K.: Cambridge University Press, 1994). The novel *Les aventures de Télémaque* was first published anonymously in 1689 as a didactic French novel. In 1717, it was reissued by the family of Fénelon to enormous acclaim and was still extremely popular more than one hundred years later, when Jesse Grant and Sarah Simpson both read it.

Chapter 2. "My Ulysses"

13   **He intended to teach** Richardson, *A Personal History*, 63.

13   **As a young boy** Lewis, *Captain Sam Grant*, 20–21. Lewis's notes for his biography,

now a part of the Papers of Ulysses S. Grant at the Ulysses S. Grant Presidential Library at Mississippi State University, have been mined to discover information and insights not included in his published biography. Lewis has extensive notes on the process of tanning.

13   **He had about thirty-five books** *New York Times,* July 30, 1885.

14   **With light reddish-brown hair** This description comes from boyhood friend Chilton White, interview, Hamlin Garland Papers, University of Southern California. See also Richardson, *A Personal History,* 57.

14   **Indoors, in cold winter** Richardson, *A Personal History,* 54.

14   **"How did you come to saddle"** Garland, *Grant,* 15.

14   **On the blank front pages** Lewis, *Captain Sam Grant,* 36.

15   **Ulysses and Dan** Daniel Ammen, *The Old Navy and the New* (Philadelphia: J. B. Lippincott, 1891), appendix, 527.

15   **Ulysses's friend Jimmy** "Gen. Grant's Early Life," *New York Times,* July 30, 1885.

15   **He was quiet** Garland, *Grant,* 3.

15   **older, "good clean" set** Ibid., 12.

15   **Young Ulysses enjoyed** *Personal Memoirs,* 1:26–27.

15   **Ulysses was admired** Richardson, *A Personal History,* 58.

15   **"he was a careful driver"** Mrs. _____, Hamlin Garland Papers. Ulysses would drive silently while the girls chattered and shrieked. Garland, *Grant,* 15.

15   **He also didn't chew** Lewis, *Captain Sam Grant,* 30.

15   **Hannah Grant applied** Richardson, *A Personal History,* 58.

15   **"his heels were in the air"** Daniel Ammen, "Recollections and Letters of Grant," *North American Review* 141 (July–December 1885): 361.

16   **"helped him to reach the bank"** Ibid.

16   **"He never took a gun"** Chilton White interview, Hamlin Garland Papers.

16   **"That was strange"** *New York Times,* July 30, 1885.

16   **"He was unusually sensitive"** John Russell Young, *Men and Memories,* vol. 2, edited by Mary D. Russell Young (New York: F. Tennyson Neely, 1901), 482.

17   **"Ulysses would shout an answer"** *New York Times,* July 30, 1885.

17   **He so loathed** Ibid.

17   **an Episcopal minister** Mason L. Weems, *A History of the Life and Death, Virtues and Exploits of General George Washington* (Elizabethtown, Pa.: Shephard Kollock, 1800).

17   **Barney had "no stamina"** Lewis, *Captain Sam Grant,* 23.

17   **"He only followed"** *Personal Memoirs,* 1:31.

18   **"Reading, 'Riting, 'Rithmetic"** Ibid., 1:25.

18   **"I could not load it"** Ibid., 1:26.

18   **"successive loads, all day"** Lewis, *Captain Sam Grant,* 25.

18   **His highest joy** Richardson, *A Personal History,* 56.

18   **"He was a splendid rider"** Chilton White interview, Hamlin Garland Papers.

18   **"frightened nearly every female"** *New York Times,* July 30, 1885.

19   **"I believe I can ride"** Garland, *Grant,* 13–14. This version of the story is told by James Marshall, interview, Hamlin Garland Papers.

20   **Pews were free** Nancy Purdy and Terry Cavanaugh, *The History of the Georgetown United Methodist Church* (Georgetown, Ohio: Georgetown United Methodist Church, 1997), 3–4; Calvin W. Horn, *A Handbook of the Methodist Episcopal Church Georgetown, Ohio* (Georgetown: *Georgetown Gazette,* 1904), 8.

20   **"a ruling spirit"** A. H. Markland, quoted in *New York Times,* August 4, 1885.

20   **"The Methodists shouted"** Chilton White interview, Hamlin Garland Papers.

20   **a woman of "deep feeling"** Ibid.

20   **"you ought to praise the Lord"** Lewis, *Captain Sam Grant,* 14.

20   **Seeking a better education** American Association of University Women, *From*

Cabin to College: A History of the Schools of Mason County, Kentucky (Maysville, Ky.: G. F. McClanahan Print Company, 1976), 55.

20 **Also an officer** Thomas E. Pickett, "William West Richeson: The Kentuckian That Taught Grant," *Register of the Kentucky State Historical Society* 27 (September 1911): 14–22.

21 **"same old arithmetic"** *Personal Memoirs,* 1:25.

21 **"a good debater"** Lewis, *Captain Sam Grant,* 47.

21 **He also took the affirmative** Garland, *Grant,* 18–19.

21 **"always very liberal"** Richard Dawson interview, Hamlin Garland Papers.

21 **"exceedingly kind, popular"** Lewis, *Captain Sam Grant,* 47.

21 **Standing at one** I am indebted to a conversation with Ann Hagedorn and her *Beyond the River: The Untold Story of the Heroes of the Underground Railroad* (New York: Simon & Schuster, 2002), for her ground-level descriptions of Ripley and John Rankin.

22 **"I consider involuntary slavery"** Ibid., 44–50; John Rankin, *Letters on American Slavery* (Ripley, Ohio: D. Ammen, printer, 1826), 5.

22 **Ulysses boarded** Garland, *Grant,* 29.

22 **"never saw him fight"** W. B. Campbell interview, Hamlin Garland Papers.

22 **"a great fellow"** Ibid.

22 **"Are men raised to eminence"** Hagedorn, *Beyond the River,* 61.

22 **"He was a great hand"** Benjamin Johnson interview, Hamlin Garland Papers.

22 **"I was not studious"** *Personal Memoirs,* 1:25.

22 **"did not make progress enough"** Ibid.

23 **"I'd like to be a farmer"** Garland, *Grant,* 21; Richardson, *A Personal History,* 73.

23 **Bart had a reputation** Garland, *Grant,* narrates the full details of this story, 24–27.

24 **"false reports and representations"** Lewis, *Captain Sam Grant,* 55–56.

24 **"And I can assure him"** *Castigator* (Ohio), September 25, 1832, quoted in *Grant Papers,* 1:3–4n.

24 **"If you have no other person"** JRG to Thomas Hamer, February 19, 1839, *Grant Papers,* 1:4n.

25 **"Why didn't you apply"** Lewis, *Captain Sam Grant,* 57.

25 **"I thought so too, if he did"** *Personal Memoirs,* 1:32.

Chapter 3. West Point

26 **"The boys would plague me"** Garland, *Grant,* 30–31; Lewis, *Captain Sam Grant,* 58–59.

26 **Family and friends waved** Lucinda Bailey Powers (daughter of Jane Bailey) interview, Hamlin Garland Papers.

27 **"This gave a better opportunity"** *Personal Memoirs,* 1:37.

27 **"this seemed like annihilating space"** Ibid., 1:38.

27 **Elizabeth found Ulysses** Interview with Elizabeth Hare, *Philadelphia Times,* July 26, 1885.

27 **"dallying by the way"** *Personal Memoirs,* 1:38.

27 **"every street in the city"** Ibid.

27 **"attended the theatre"** Ibid.

27 **two dramas** Arthur Herman Wilson, *A History of the Philadelphia Theatre, 1835–1855* (Philadelphia: University of Pennsylvania Press, 1935). Wilson offers a meticulous record of which plays were showing in which theaters on specific dates.

27 **Fresh from Ohio** Ibid., 638.

28 **Ulysses might also have seen** Edward Bulwer, *The Lady of Lyons* (London: Saunders and Otley, 1838), 17.

28 **"Being both from the west"** Fred Dent interview, Hamlin Garland Papers.

28 **"So have I"** Ibid.

28 **"nothing of the *kind* occurred"** *Personal Memoirs*, 1:35.

28 **Ulysses registered** Alan and Barbara Aimone, "America's First Vacationland and the Rise and Fall of the West Point and Cozzens' Hotels, *OCHS Journal* (Publication of the Orange County Historical Society) 31 (November 1, 2002): 17–39.

28 **Other voices** See Robert M. S. McDonald, *Thomas Jefferson's Military Academy: The Founding of West Point* (Charlottesville: University of Virginia Press, 2004); Theodore J. Crackel, *Mr. Jefferson's Army: Political and Social Reform of the Military Establishment, 1801–1809* (New York: New York University Press, 1987).

29 **he signed the Military Peace Establishment Act** Theodore J. Crackel, *West Point: A Bicentennial History* (Lawrence: University Press of Kansas, 2002), 29–51; Gordon S. Wood, *Empire of Liberty: A History of the Early Republic, 1789–1815* (New York: Oxford University Press, 2009), 292.

30 **Although he departed** Crackel, *West Point: A Bicentennial History*, 81–105.

30 **no more HUG** *Register of Graduates and Former Cadets United States Military Academy, 1802–1946* (West Point, N.Y.: Association of Graduates, 1946), 136.

30 **After checking the official list** Garland, *Grant*, 31–32.

30 **"Who is your tailor?"** Lewis, *Captain Sam Grant*, 63; Garland, *Grant*, 32.

30 **"A third: 'Sam Grant'"** Interview with William Tecumseh Sherman, *New York Herald*, July 24, 1885.

30 **"a hell of an Uncle Sam"** Lewis, *Captain Sam Grant*, 63–64; Garland, *Grant*, 32–33.

31 **He could not wait** USG Account Book, 1839–June 1843, Ulysses S. Grant Papers, Huntington Library, San Marino, California.

31 **"as tight to my skin"** U. H. Grant to R. McKinstry Griffith, September 22, 1839, *Grant Papers,* 1:6.

31 **"I wish some"** Ibid., 5–6.

31 **"from the window"** Ibid., 5.

31 **"I can see Fort Putnam"** Ibid.

32 **"I hope you won't take me"** Ibid., 6, 7.

32 **He had purchased** Ibid., 26.

32 **In the curriculum before** James L. Morrison, Jr., *"The Best School in the World": West Point, the Pre–Civil War Years, 1833–1866* (Kent, Ohio: Kent State University Press, 1986), 96–97; Carol Reardon, *With a Sword in One Hand & Jomini in the Other: The Problem of Military Thought in the Civil War* (Chapel Hill: University of North Carolina Press, 2012), 8.

32 **Future officers** Ibid., 27.

32 **Ceaseless drilling** Ibid., 28–29.

33 **The list was endless** *Regulations Established for the Organization and Government of the Military Academy at West Point, New York* (New York: Wiley & Putnam, 1839), 32, 42, 48–49, 77; interview with James Longstreet, *New York Times,* July 24, 1885.

33 **Thayer refused** Crackel, *West Point: A Bicentennial History,* 101–02, attempts to rebalance the traditional view of Jackson's criticism of West Point, calling it "ambiguous."

33 **"I saw in this"** *Personal Memoirs,* 1:39.

34 **"not by punishing the animal"** Lewis, *Captain Sam Grant*, 93.

34 **In his second year** *Official Register of the Officers and Cadets of the U.S. Military Academy* (New York: W. L. Burroughs, 1843), 7, 13.

34 **"Much of the time"** *Personal Memoirs,* 1:39.

34 **"frivolous"** My interview with Alan Aimone, June 14, 2009.

34 **"I read all of Bulwer's"** *Personal Memoirs,* 1:39.

35 **"No Cadet shall enter"** *Regulations Established for the Organization and Government of the Military Academy,* 59.

35   **"in works of polite literature"** Ibid., 52.

35   **"without doubt, the most popular"** "Novel Writing," *American Quarterly Review* 16 (1834): 507, cited in Andrew Brown, "Bulwer's Reputation," in Allan Conrad Christensen, ed., *The Subverting Vision of Bulwer Lytton* (Newark: University of Delaware Press; Cranberry, N.J.: Associated University Presses, 2004), 29.

35   **Just as Sam developed a disdain** Christensen, ed., *The Subverting Vision of Bulwer Lytton,* 15.

35   **In *Godolphin*** Allan Conrad Christensen, *Edward Bulwer-Lytton: The Fiction of New Regions* (Athens: University of Georgia Press, 1976), 75, 79.

36   **"Our imagination"** Ibid., 3.

36   **Waverley would appeal** For Sir Walter Scott's influence on shaping historical fiction, see James Kerr, *Fiction Against History: Scott as Storyteller* (New York: Cambridge University Press, 1989), 27, and Ian Dennis, *Nationalism and Desire in Early Historical Fiction* (New York: St. Martin's Press, 1997), 65.

36   **"I suppose that all men"** Quoted in Alexander Welsh, *The Hero of the Waverley Novels, with New Essays on Scott* (Princeton, N.J.: Princeton University Press, 1968), 108.

36   **But the hero is law-abiding** Ibid., 27, 148, 218.

37   **"Now, when I find a man"** James Fenimore Cooper, *The Pathfinder,* vol. 3 (London: Bentley, 1840), 140–41; Richard Rust, "On the Trail of a Craftsman: The Art of *The Pathfinder,*" in W. M. Verhoeven, ed., *James Fenimore Cooper: New Historical and Literary Contexts* (Amsterdam: Rodopi, 1993), 179–80.

37   **Cooper, an officer** George Dekker and John P. McWilliams, eds., *Fenimore Cooper: The Critical Heritage* (Boston: Routledge, 1973), 4, 8.

37   **Another sympathetic oil painting** This painting is on display at West Point.

38   **We do not know how many** Eight of these paintings can be seen in *Grant Papers,* 1:13–19.

38   **"With his commanding figure"** *Personal Memoirs,* 1:41.

39   **"I regarded General Scott"** Ibid., 1:42.

39   **"General Washington"** Lewis, *Captain Sam Grant,* 69.

40   **"rather small boy"** James Longstreet interview, March 20, 1897, Hamlin Garland Papers.

40   **"a hesitancy in presenting his own claims"** "Longstreet's Reminiscences," *New York Times,* July 24, 1885.

40   **"not heavy enough to be good"** Ibid.

40   **Sam's friends in his own class** Lewis, *Captain Sam Grant,* 72.

41   **"He had no facility in conversation"** D. M. Frost interview, Hamlin Garland Papers.

41   **Just as they began** Lewis, *Captain Sam Grant,* 91.

41   **"Every member of the Academic Staff"** *Regulations Established for the Organization and Government of the Military Academy,* 33.

41   **The stone chapel** Alan Aimone, "River Guide to the Hudson Highlands," 2009, http://www.hudsonrivervalley.org/library, 16. Now called the Old Cadet Chapel, during Grant's time it was located on the site of the current Science Building. With the construction of a new chapel in 1910, the Old Chapel was moved stone by stone to the Post Cemetery in 1911.

41   **"We are not only obliged"** USG to R. McKinstry Griffith, September 22, 1839, *Grant Papers,* 1:7.

41   **Cadets sat for two hours** Stephen E. Ambrose, *Duty, Honor, Country: A History of West Point* (Baltimore: Johns Hopkins University Press, 1966), 151.

41   **"It has been brought"** Lewis, *Captain Sam Grant,* 82.

41   **"Grant's mental machine"** Dennis Hart Mahan, "The Cadet Life of Grant and Sherman," *Army and Navy Journal* (March 31, 1866): 507.

42 **Mahan, who taught at West Point** For Mahan, see Thomas Everett Griess, "Dennis Hart Mahan: West Point Professor and Advocate of Military Professionalism 1830–1871" (PhD dissertation, Duke University, Durham, N.C., 1968); John F. Marszalek, *Commander of All Lincoln's Armies: A Life of General Henry W. Halleck* (Cambridge, Mass.: Belknap Press of Harvard University Press, 2004), 22.

42 **He encouraged the "self-study"** William Dilworth Puleston, *Mahan: The Life and Work of Captain Alfred Thayer Mahan* (New Haven, Conn.: Yale University Press, 1939), 8–9; Griess, "Dennis Hart Mahan," 347.

42 **When the informal student library** USG to Messrs. Carey and Hart, March 31, 1843, *Grant Papers*, 1:11.

42 **"I would desire you to send"** Ibid., April 8, 1843, *Grant Papers*, 1:11.

42 **"Life is marked out"** Charles Lever, *Charles O'Malley: The Irish Dragoon* (Dublin: William Curry, Jun. & Co., 1841), 541.

43 **Exercises finished** James B. Fry, "An Acquaintance with Grant," *North American Review* 141 (1885): 540; William E. Woodward, *Meet General Grant* (New York: H. Liveright, 1928), 51.

43 **"Well, I can't die but once"** Richardson, *A Personal History*, 92–93; Garland, *Grant*, 52; Lewis, *Captain Sam Grant*, 94.

43 **"as if man and beast"** Fry, "An Acquaintance with Grant," 540.

43 **With Sam's spectacular jump** Ibid.

Chapter 4. "My Dear Julia"

45 **"first choice, dragoons"** *Personal Memoirs*, 1:42.

46 **"wanted my old school-mates"** Ibid., 43.

46 **" 'No, sir-ee; I'll sell my shirt' "** Ibid., 43–44; Lewis, *Captain Sam Grant*, 99. Visiting the Hares in Philadelphia, Ulysses wore a civilian suit and replied to their disappointment, "No, I will not make a show of myself." Interview with Elizabeth Hare, *Philadelphia Times*, July 16, 1885.

46 **"I did not appreciate it"** *Personal Memoirs*, 1:44.

46 **In September, traveling with Fashion** Denise M. Dowdall, *From Cincinnati to the Colorado Ranger: The Horsemanship of Ulysses S. Grant* (Dublin: HISTORYEYE, 2012), 24–25.

46 **By 1843, it was home** Henry W. Webb, "The Story of Jefferson Barracks," *New Mexico Historical Review* 21, no. 3 (July 1946): 185–208.

47 **James Longstreet, who had come** Lewis, *Captain Sam Grant*, 100–101.

47 **"many valuable historical works"** *Personal Memoirs*, 1:51–52.

47 **"Every day he wrote down"** W. W. Smith interview, Hamlin Garland Papers.

47 **"Does Mr. Dent live here?"** Emma Dent Casey, "When Grant Went A-Courtin'," St. Louis: typescript, 1908, Ulysses S. Grant National Historic Site, 4.

47 **"Yes, sir"** Ibid., 5.

48 **No one thought** Kimberly Scott Little, *Ulysses S. Grant's White Haven: A Place Where Extraordinary People Came to Live Extraordinary Lives, 1796–1885* (St. Louis: Ulysses S. Grant National Historic Site, 1993), 40.

48 **"looked as pretty as a doll"** Casey, "When Grant Went A-Courtin'," 7.

48 **In appearance, White Haven** Little, *Ulysses S. Grant's White Haven*, 31.

49 **Throughout the 1840s** Little, Ibid., 38–43; Sixth Census of the United States, 1850. United States Bureau of the Census, St. Louis County, Missouri, Schedule of Population.

49 **"sister Nellie and I"** Casey, "When Grant Went A-Courtin'," 7.

49 **"necessarily something of a pet"** Julia Dent Grant, *Personal Memoirs*, 35.

50   **The only photographs of her** Ishbel Ross, *The General's Wife* (New York: Dodd, Mead, 1959), 3–4, 37.

50   **Julia loved to sing** Ibid., 19.

50   **As a child, Julia joined** Julia Dent Grant, *Personal Memoirs*, 38.

50   **Her female teachers** Ibid.

50   **She took delight in sketching** Ross, *The General's Wife*, 14.

50   **Mrs. O'Fallon loved Julia** Years later, when Mrs. O'Fallon died, Julia wrote her son John of his mother, "She was the beautiful angel of my childhood. So many acts of kindness, so many kind words of hers fill my heart's memory." Quoted in Ross, *The General's Wife*, 15.

51   **"Such rides"** Julia Dent Grant, *Personal Memoirs*, 48.

51   **Often, as they sat** Ross, *The General's Wife*, 7, 256.

51   **"many a fine mess of perch"** Casey, "When Grant Went A-Courtin'," 11.

51   **Asking tall Bob Hazlitt** Ibid., 16.

52   **"Grant, you're late"** Frank A. Burr, *The Life and Deeds of General U. S. Grant* (Philadelphia: National Publishing Company, 1885), 91–92.

52   **"Mr. Grant, young people should be seen"** Ibid., 92.

52   **"His quiet, even tones"** Casey, "When Grant Went A-Courtin'," 11.

52   **"There is something noble in him"** "Auntie Robinson's Recollections," *St. Louis Republican,* July 23, 1885.

53   **In 1821, the year Mexico declared** Gregg Cantrell, *Stephen F. Austin: Empresario of Texas* (New Haven, Conn.: Yale University Press, 1999), 344–45. Nettie Lee Benson, "Texas Viewed from Mexico," *Southwestern Historical Quarterly* 90 (January 1987): 219–91, describes how Texas, far away from Mexico City, the capital of Mexico, was out of sight and out of mind almost until 1836. Amy S. Greenberg, *A Wicked War: Polk, Clay, Lincoln, and the 1846 U.S. Invasion of Mexico* (New York: Alfred A. Knopf, 2012), writes, "While the United States was thriving in the 1830s and 1840s, Mexico was foundering" (57).

53   **By 1830, with American settlers** For a narrative and analysis of this complicated story of the growth and independence movement in Texas, see Daniel Walker Howe, *What Hath God Wrought: The Transformation of America, 1815–1848* (New York: Oxford University Press, 2007), 658–71.

53   **By that year, American settlers** Ibid., 663–67.

53   **On April 12, 1844, Secretary of State** Robert W. Merry, *A Country of Vast Designs: James K. Polk, the Mexican War, and the Conquest of the American Continent* (New York: Simon & Schuster, 2009), 73–74, presents a positive view of Polk's Texas strategy.

53   **In extolling the virtues of slavery** Greenberg, *A Wicked War*, 18–19; Howe, *What Hath God Wrought,* 679–80.

53   **"It has hitherto been our pride"** Greenberg, *A Wicked War,* 19–20; Howe, *What Hath God Wrought,* 679.

55   **"For myself"** *Personal Memoirs*, 1:53.

55   **"That young man can explain"** C. B. Galbreath, "Centennial Anniversary of the Birth of Ulysses S. Grant," *Ohio Archaeological and Historical Quarterly* 31 (1922): 226, 242, 286.

55   **Toward the end** Julia Dent Grant, *Personal Memoirs*, 49.

55   **"I, child that I was"** Ibid.

55   **"I halted my horse"** Ibid.

55   **Charley Jarvis** Lewis, *Captain Sam Grant*, 110.

55   **"I now discovered"** *Personal Memoirs*, 1:48.

56   **He "looked at it a moment"** Ibid., 1:49.

56   **"headed the horse"** Ibid., 1:49–50.

56   **Ulysses arrived at White Haven** Casey, "When Grant Went A-Courtin'," 17–18.

56   **"Now, if anything happens"** Lewis, *Captain Sam Grant*, 111–12.

56   **"in asking me to be his wife"** Ibid., 112.

57   **Ulysses soon learned more** See J. Fair Hardin, "Fort Jesup, Fort Selden, Camp Salubrity: Four Forgotten Frontier Army Posts of Western Louisiana," *Louisiana Historical Quarterly* 17, no. 1 (January 1934): 139–68, especially 143–46: "General Grant at Fort Salubrity."

57   **"Read these blank lines"** USG to Julia Dent, June 4, 1844, *Grant Papers*, 1:26.

57   **"marked with no incident"** USG to Mrs. George B. Bailey, June 6, 1844, *Grant Papers*, 1:27.

58   **Taylor earned his nickname** Holman Hamilton, *Zachary Taylor: Soldier of the White House* (Indianapolis: Bobbs-Merrill, 1951), 1:21–23, 83–99, 131–33.

58   **"Be as punctual"** USG to Julia Dent, July 28, 1844, *Grant Papers*, 1:30. He signed his letters "U S Grant" or "Ulysses" and his postscripts simply "U."

58   **"At that time"** USG to Julia Dent, August 31, 1844, *Grant Papers*, 1:33.

58   **"at a loss"** Ibid., 35.

58   **"Nothing is easier"** Ibid.

58   **"in the course of a few days"** Ibid., 36.

58   **"Since the arrival of your letters"** USG to Julia Dent, September 7, 1844, *Grant Papers*, 1:33.

59   **Ulysses followed Birney's candidacy** Betty Fladeland, *James Gillespie Birney: Slaveholder to Abolitionist* (Ithaca, N.Y.: Cornell University Press, 1955).

59   **Antislavery candidate** All eyes turned to the electoral college, focusing on New York, home of the Liberal Party. In New York, Polk received 237,588 votes, Clay 232,482, and Birney 15,812. If only one-third of the Birney votes had gone to Clay, the Kentucky Whig would have won New York's forty-two electoral votes and, thus, the presidency. Without New York, Polk defeated Clay in the electoral college 170 to 105.

59   **Tyler signed the bill** Greenberg, *A Wicked War*, 61; Howe, *What Hath God Wrought*, 698–99.

59   **"Hurry"** USG to Robert Hazlitt, December 1, 1844, *Grant Papers*, 1:39–40. In addition to the text in the *Grant Papers*, Henry E. Chambers, *Mississippi Valley Beginnings* (New York: G. P. Putnam's Sons, 1922), summarizes other portions of the letter no longer extant.

59   **"Assure them"** USG to Julia Dent, September 7, 1844, *Grant Papers*, 1:37.

59–60   **"The more than ordinary attachment"** Ibid., January 12, 1845, *Grant Papers*, 1:40.

60   **He thanked her** Ibid., July 28, 1844, *Grant Papers*, 1:32.

60   **"I was constantly receiving"** Julia Dent Grant, *Personal Memoirs*, 51.

60   **Jacob was forced** The story is found in Genesis 29:16–30.

60   **"Oh, you do, do you?"** This dialogue is put together from several accounts that are in basic agreement. See Casey, "When Grant Went A-Courtin'," 20; Julia Dent Grant, *Personal Memoirs*, 51; Ross, *The General's Wife*, 30.

61   **"If I feel tempted"** USG to Julia Dent, July 11, 1845, *Grant Papers*, 1:50.

61   **"We will start for Texas"** Ibid., July 19, 1845, *Grant Papers*, 1:51, 53.

Chapter 5. "Either by Treaty or the Sword"

63   *Manifest Destiny* For a discussion of the use and misuse of the concept of "Manifest Destiny," especially as it was applied to Texas, see Howe, *What Hath God Wrought*, 702–8.

64   "In all probability this movement" USG to Julia Dent, February 5, 1846, *Grant Papers,* 1:71.

64   Established in 1838 Greenberg, *A Wicked War,* 99–100.

64   "I rather enjoyed the joke" *Personal Memoirs,* 1:62–63.

64   By October, reinforcements swelled K. Jack Bauer, *The Mexican War, 1846–1848* (New York: Macmillan, 1974), 32–33.

64–65   The camp's open alignment Smith, *Grant,* 39.

65   "horse and rider returned" Interview with James Longstreet, *New York Times,* July 24, 1885.

65   Reflecting on this experience *Personal Memoirs,* 1:76.

65   "I followed in his trail" Ibid., 1:77–78.

66   "Seated upon their haunches" Ibid., 1:78.

66   Finally, Magruder sent James Longstreet interview, Hamlin Garland Papers; James Longstreet, *From Manassas to Appomattox* (Philadelphia: J. B. Lippincott, 1896), 20; Helen Dortch Longstreet, *Lee and Longstreet at High Tide* (Gainesville, Ga.: printed by the author, 1904), 144; Lewis, *Captain Sam Grant,* 129.

67   The president consciously courted Two recent biographies of President James K. Polk—by Walter R. Borneman, *Polk: The Man Who Transformed the Presidency and America* (New York: Random House, 2008), and by Robert W. Merry, *A Country of Vast Designs*—attempt to rehabilitate Polk as one of our best presidents, including a sympathetic reading of Polk's leadership in leading the United States into a war with Mexico. For more balanced accounts, see Howe, *What Hath God Wrought,* 731–43, and Sean Wilentz, *The Rise of American Democracy: Jefferson to Lincoln* (New York: W. W. Norton & Co., 2005), 577–86.

67   Nevertheless, the Rio Grande commander K. Jack Bauer, *Zachary Taylor: Soldier, Planter, Statesman of the Old Southwest* (Baton Rouge: Louisiana State University Press, 1985), 119.

67   "It is to be hoped" USG to Julia Dent, March 3, 1846, *Grant Papers,* 1:75.

67   "Corpus Christi mule" *Personal Memoirs,* 1:79–80.

67   "it is not probable that any" Ibid., 1:81.

68   "I wish I had more officers" This story was told by Lafayette McLaws, Grant's West Point friend. Lafayette McLaws interview, Hamlin Garland Papers.

68   a "sad accident" *Personal Memoirs,* 1:83.

68   "Do you intend to get another" Ibid., 1:85–86.

68   "I was sorry to take him" Ibid., 1:86.

69   "I had as tractable a horse" Ibid.; Bauer, *Mexican War,* 37–38.

69   "There was no estimating" *Personal Memoirs,* 1:87.

69   And if anyone tried Bauer, *Zachary Taylor,* 125–26; John D. Eisenhower, *So Far from God: The U. S. War with Mexico, 1846–1848* (New York: Random House, 1989), 52–53.

70   "They laugh, shout" John Blount Robertson, *Reminiscences of a Campaign in Mexico* (Nashville: J. York, 1849), 116.

70   They fired just over José Maria Roa Bárcena, *Recuerdos de la invasión norteamericana, 1846–1848,* vol. 1 (Mexico: J. Buxo, 1883), 61; Bauer, *Zachary Taylor,* 145.

70   "Everything looks belligerent" USG to Julia Dent, April 20, 1846, *Grant Papers,* 1:80.

71   "Hostilities may now be considered" Bauer, *Zachary Taylor,* 149–50.

71   "The war had begun" *Personal Memoirs,* 1:92.

71   "What General Taylor's feelings were" Ibid.

71   "almost as sharp" Ibid., 1:94.

71   "their bayonets and spearheads glistened" Ibid., 1:93–94.

72   The Mexicans fired Ibid., 1:94–95.

72   "I looked down that long line" Ibid., 1:94.

73 **be fired more quickly** Martin Dugard, *The Training Ground: Grant, Lee, Sherman, and Davis in the Mexican War, 1846–1848* (Lincoln: University of Nebraska Press, 2008), 85–93, 198–200, offers a description of the use of cannon in the Battle of Palo Alto. See L. Van Loan Naisawald, *Grape and Canister: The Story of the Field Artillery of the Army of the Potomac, 1861–1865* (New York: Oxford University Press, 1960), 38–39, 53, 74. Although this monograph focuses on the Civil War, much of the description and explanation is applicable to the Mexican War. See also www.ehow.com /list_6894147_weapons-mexican-war.html.

73 **Most important, they possessed a range** www.ehow.com/list_6894147_weapons -mexican-war.html.

73 **"Ram, heave, ready"** Dugard, *Training Ground,* 88–89.

73 **"Every moment we could see"** USG to Julia Dent, May 11, 1846, *Grant Papers,* 1:84–85.

73 **On the American side** Bauer, *Zachary Taylor,* 157.

73 **"During that night"** USG to John W. Lowe, June 26, 1846, *Grant Papers,* 1:95–96.

74 **"a Mexican colonel"** *Personal Memoirs,* 1:97–98.

74 **"This left no doubt"** Ibid., 1:98.

74 **"A ball struck close by me"** USG to Julia Dent, May 11, 1846, *Grant Papers,* 1: 85; *Personal Memoirs,* 1:96.

74–75 **"There is no great sport"** USG to Julia Dent, May 11, 1846, *Grant Papers,* 1:86.

75 **"The redress of the wrongs"** James D. Richardson, ed., *A Compilation of the Messages and Papers of the Presidents, 1789–1897,* vol. 4: *1841–1849* (Washington, D.C.: Authority of Congress, 1899), 438, 442–43.

Chapter 6. "Army of Invasion"

78 **He also sent her** USG to Julia Dent, May 24, 1846, *Grant Papers,* 1:89.

78 **"Every one of them"** Foster Coates, "The Courtship of General Grant," *Ladies' Home Journal* 7 (October 1890): 4.

78 **She "prized" these letters** Julia Dent Grant, *Personal Memoirs,* 52.

78 **He "was never a great hand"** Casey, "When Grant Went A-Courtin'," 21.

78 **Among the volunteer regiments** Bauer, *Mexican War,* 69–72; Lewis, *Captain Sam Grant,* 159–63. Only New England, where Whig antiwar sentiment pervaded, saw no outpouring of volunteers.

78 **"seem to think it perfectly right"** USG to Julia Dent, July 25, 1846, *Grant Papers,* 1:102.

79 **The presence of volunteers** William Seaton Henry, *Campaign Sketches of the War with Mexico* (New York: Harper & Brothers, 1847), 124–25.

79 **And Grant greeted** *Personal Memoirs,* 1:103; Lewis, *Captain Sam Grant,* 165.

79 **"The thing is absolutely ridiculous"** The *Cincinnati Gazette* editorial is cited in the *Niles National Register* (July 25, 1846), 326. See also Henry Howe, *Historical Collections of Ohio* (Norwalk, Ohio: Laning Printing, 1896), 1:331.

79 **"ended by gracefully offering"** John W. Emerson, "Grant's Life in the West and His Mississippi Valley Campaigns," *Midland Monthly Magazine* 7 (January 1897): 34.

79 **"General Delay"** Eisenhower, *So Far from God,* 111.

80 **But he was not ready** "Short History of the Quartermaster Corps," U.S. Army Quartermaster Foundation, Fort Lee, Virginia, http://www.qmfound.com/short .htm.

80 **"obliged to guess"** Ibid.

80 **He asked to be transferred** USG to Bvt. Col. John Garland, [August 1846], *Grant Papers,* 1:106–7.

80 **"Lt. Grant is respectfully informed"** The reply by Garland is in Emerson, "Grant's Life in the West," 36; *Grant Papers,* 1:107n.

81 **"The Commanding General desires"** Bvt. Maj. William W. S. Bliss to Bvt. Col. John Garland, August 29, 1846, *Grant Papers,* 1:107n.

81 **"one would start to run"** *Personal Memoirs,* 1:105–6.

81 **"I am not aware"** Ibid., 1:106.

81 **"There was no road"** Hays is quoted in Emerson, "Grant's Life in the West," *Midland Monthly* 7 (May 1897): 432. For Hays, see Wayne Mahood, *Alexander "Fighting Elleck" Hays: The Life of a Civil War General, from West Point to the Wilderness* (Jefferson, N.C.: McFarland, 2005).

81 **Grant "would generally go ahead"** James D. Elderkin interview, Hamlin Garland Papers.

82 **he and his staff** "Mexico's Guerrilla Tradition and Composition of Irregular Forces: The Occupation of Mexico, May 1846–July 1848," 14, http://www.history.army.mil/brochures/occupation/occupation.htm.

82 **"Our army gave [it] the name"** *Personal Memoirs,* 1:108.

82 **Even though Taylor knew Worth** Dugard, *Training Ground,* 195.

82 **"ordered to remain in charge"** *Personal Memoirs,* 1:110–11.

82 **"an order to charge was given"** Ibid., 1:110.

83 **"About one-third of the men"** Ibid., 1:111.

83 **"found himself very much fatigued"** Ibid.

83 **Benjamin discovered Grant** Luther Giddings, *Sketches of the Campaign in Northern Mexico* (New York: G. P. Putnam & Co., 1853), 185–90; Emerson, "Grant's Life in the West," *Midland Monthly* 7 (January 1897): 40; Robertson, *Reminiscences of a Campaign in Mexico,* 146.

83 **"The town is ours"** Eisenhower, *So Far from God,* 131; Bauer, *Mexican War,* 94; Bauer, *Zachary Taylor,* 178–79.

83 **They even drilled holes** Dugard, *Training Ground,* 188; *Personal Memoirs,* 1:114–15.

83 **"Who'll volunteer?"** Garland, *Grant,* 79.

84 **"With only one foot"** The cantle is the raised rear part of the saddle.

84 **"I got out safely"** *Personal Memoirs,* 1:116.

84 **"had the enemy"** Borneman, *Polk: The Man Who Transformed the Presidency and America,* 245–46; Merry, *A Country of Vast Designs,* 312–13.

84 **Several plays by Edward Bulwer** Ross, *The General's Wife,* 32–34; James Neal Primm, *Lion of the Valley: St. Louis, Missouri, 1764–1980* (St. Louis: Missouri Historical Society Press, 1981), 184. In the years Julia waited for Ulysses to return, Bulwer's immensely popular *The Lady of Lyons, Richelieu, The Soldier's Daughter,* and *Money* were performed at the Ludlow and Smith theater that held a monopoly on plays. Larry Eugene Grisvard, "The Final Years: The Ludlow and Smith Theatrical Firm in St. Louis 1845–1851" (PhD dissertation, Ohio State University, Columbus, Ohio, 1965), 274.

85 **"impatient of being separated"** USG to Julia Dent, September 23, 1846, *Grant Papers,* 1:111.

85 **"This is the most beautiful"** Ibid., October 20, 1846, *Grant Papers,* 1:115.

85 **"so full of Orange"** Ibid., October 3, 1846, *Grant Papers,* 1:112–113.

85 **"The climate is excellent"** Ibid., November 7, 1846, *Grant Papers,* 1:117.

85 **"If it was an American city"** Ibid., October 3, 1846, *Grant Papers,* 1:113.

85 **"without you *dearest*"** Ibid., October 20, 1846, *Grant Papers,* 1:115.

85 **"General Taylor never made"** *Personal Memoirs,* 1:100. Grant recalled that when Taylor was in uniform, "he was unfortunate."

85 **Observing his outfit** Holman Hamilton, *Zachary Taylor: Soldier in the White House* (Indianapolis: Bobbs-Merrill, 1951), 22.

85 **"was known to every soldier"** *Personal Memoirs,* 1:100.

85 **"General Taylor was not an officer"** Ibid., 1:99–100.

85 **"These are qualities"** Ibid., 1:100.

86 **Upon hearing of Hamer's death** Bauer, *Mexican War,* 75.

86 **"Personally, his death"** USG to Mrs. Thomas L. Hamer, [December 1846], *Grant Papers,* 1:121.

87 **"nervous, impatient"** *Personal Memoirs,* 1:123–24.

87 **"As soon as Gen. Scott"** USG to Julia Dent, February 1, 1847, *Grant Papers,* 1:123–24. He added, "I would almost be willing to be sick enough to leave the country just to get back to Gravois once more."

87 **A main port city** Dugard, *Training Ground,* 289.

87 **It was defended** Tennessee volunteer John Blount Robertson, in his *Reminiscences of a Campaign in Mexico,* 235–36, offers a contemporary description of Veracruz.

87 **Scott unfurled his blue** Winfield Scott, *Memoirs of Lieut.-General Scott,* vol. 2 (New York: Sheldon, 1864), 418–19.

87 **"The breakers were sometimes high"** *Personal Memoirs,* 1:126.

89 **Grant dashed** K. Jack Bauer, *Surfboats and Marines: U.S. Naval Operations in the Mexican War, 1846–48* (Annapolis, Md.: United States Naval Institute, 1969), 81–82.

89 **In this unprecedented landing** Seventeen years before, in 1830, the French had attempted such a landing at Algiers and suffered thirty deaths.

89 **Grant saw older officers** Lewis, *Captain Sam Grant,* 193–94.

89 **"Fred is here"** USG to JDG, April 3, 1847, *Grant Papers,* 1:129.

89 **As they stacked their arms** For the "staggering" casualties of the Battle of Veracruz, see Greenberg, *A Wicked War,* 169–72.

89 **Grant admired Scott's efforts** Johnson, *Winfield Scott: The Quest for Military Glory,* 166–67.

89 **He assured merchants** Peskin, *Winfield Scott and the Profession of Arms,* 159–60.

90 **"a very small army"** *Personal Memoirs,* 1:129.

90 **"the perfidy of Mr. Polk"** Scott, *Memoirs,* 2:415.

90 **Included among his requirements** Bauer, *Mexican War,* 259.

90 **The first two victims** *Personal Memoirs,* 1:129–30.

90 **Six members of the Fourth Infantry** Ephraim Kirby Smith, *To Mexico with Scott* (Cambridge, Mass.: Harvard University Press, 1917), 134–35; Lewis, *Captain Sam Grant,* 205.

91 **"artillery was let down"** *Personal Memoirs,* 1:132–33.

91 **"surprise of the enemy"** Ibid., 1:133.

91 **"I am compelled"** Scott, *Memoirs,* 2:481–82; Lewis, *Captain Sam Grant,* 231.

91 **"Perhaps there was not"** *Personal Memoirs,* 1:132.

91 **Secretary of State James Buchanan suggested** In his early life, Trist studied law with the aged Thomas Jefferson. He married Virginia Randolph, the Monticello Sage's granddaughter. Wallace Ohrt, *Defiant Peacemaker: Nicholas Trist in the Mexican War* (College Station: Texas A&M University Press, 1997), 103–06; Greenberg, *A Wicked War,* 91–93; 206–7.

91 **Marcy had failed** Richard M. Ketchum, "The Thankless Task of Nicholas Trist," *American Heritage Magazine* 21, no. 5 (August 1970): 1–3; Bauer, *Mexican War,* 282–83; Greenberg, *A Wicked War,* 206–7.

92 **Because the army needed supplies** *Personal Memoirs,* 1:137.

92 **Grant helped oversee** Cadmus Marcellus Wilcox, *History of the Mexican War,* edited by Mary Rachel Wilcox (Washington, D.C.: Church News Publishing, 1892), 336.

92 **Puebla "surpasses St. Louis"** USG to JDG, May 17, 1847, *Grant Papers,* 1:138–39.

93 **Mexican casualties** Bauer, *Mexican War,* 291–301.

93 **Scott and Trist** Ibid., 307.

94 **Quickly, he positioned a cart** *Personal Memoirs,* 1:152–53.

94 **He examined the wound** Lewis, 241; Luther J. Ringwalt, *Anecdotes of General Ulysses S. Grant* (Philadelphia: J. B. Lippincott, 1886), 59.

94 **"keeping under the arches"** *Personal Memoirs,* 1:155.

95 **"I could not tell the General"** Ibid., 1:157–59.

95 **"The men engaged"** Ibid., 1:67.

95 **"Both were pleasant"** Ibid., 1:138–39.

96 **"You have always taught me"** Garland, *Grant,* 78. Garland, writing in the 1890s, does not cite either the source or the date of this letter. John Simon, the first editor of *The Papers of Ulysses S. Grant,* made the editorial decision not to include any of Grant's letters to his parents that are no longer extant. If it is true that Garland did at times take liberties with the exact wording of his interviews when he transferred it to his biography, I believe it is unlikely that he did so with Grant's letters to his parents, and therefore I have decided to use them.

96 **Of the casualties** Congressional Records Service, "American War and Military Operations Casualties: Lists and Statistics." If we accept the figure advanced in 2011 that the deaths in the Civil War were actually 750,000, then the death rate was closer to 25 percent. See J. David Hacker, "A Census-Based Count of the Civil War Dead," *Civil War History* 57, no. 4 (December 2011): 307–48. www.fas.org.sgp.crs /natsec/RL32492.pdf.

96 **"Of course, Lieutenant Grant"** Emerson, "Grant's Life in the West," *Midland Monthly* 7 (January 1897): 4.

Chapter 7. Panama

99 **He was among only eight** The record of Grant's achievements and those of his classmates is found in George W. Cullum, ed., *Biographical Register of the Officers and Graduates of the U.S. Military Academy at West Point, N.Y.,* vol. 2, 3rd ed. (Boston: Houghton Mifflin, 1891), 172–78. Sixteen classmates won one brevet, while fourteen received none.

99 **"It looked doubtful"** *Personal Memoirs,* 1:171.

99 **Trist came to develop empathy** Ohrt, *Defiant Peacemaker,* 132–34, offers a sympathetic portrait of Trist, as does Greenberg, *A Wicked War,* 212–13. For Polk's role, see Greenberg's extensive treatment. For a positive treatment of Polk, see Borneman, *Polk: The Man Who Transformed the Presidency and America,* 304–8.

100 **Trist remained unaware of Polk's letter** *Personal Memoirs,* 1:171–72.

100 **The reading room** Edward S. Wallace, "The United States Army in Mexico City," *Military Affairs* 13, no. 3 (Autumn 1949): 162–63.

100 **"disappeared like a flash"** This story was reported years later by an officer who served with Grant. See John L. Ringwalt, *Anecdotes of General Ulysses S. Grant* (Philadelphia: J. B. Lippincott, 1886), 16.

100 **As quartermaster** *Personal Memoirs,* 1:180.

100 **In Monterrey he had made "no profit"** Ibid.

100 **"I could not see"** Ibid., 1:175.

101 **On February 2, 1848** Ohrt, *Defiant Peacemaker,* 143. "The Mexicans found his candor and honesty reassuring . . . with growing trust came the speedy resolution of issues."

101 **"No blame can attach"** *Grant Papers,* 1:162–63n.

101 **"all day long"** Julia Dent Grant, *Personal Memoirs,* 55.

101 **"He showed his future bride"** Casey, "When Grant Went A-Courtin'," 22.

101 **"the Captain frequently took"** Ross, *The General's Wife,* 44; Casey, "When

Grant Went A-Courtin','" 22–23; Primm, *Lion of the Valley,* 184. W.G.B. Carson, *Managers in Distress: The St. Louis Stage 1840–1844* (St. Louis: St. Louis Historical Documents Foundation, 1949), 308.

102 **Grant's love of the art** *New York Times,* July 26, 1885.

102 **Ulysses, in his splendid blue military uniform** Ross, *The General's Wife,* 47–48.

102 **"get a leave of absence"** Julia Dent Grant, *Personal Memoirs,* 58.

102 **"Would you like this, Julia?"** Ibid.

103 **Grant protested** Smith, *Grant,* 74.

103 **"I cannot make out"** Julia Dent Grant, *Personal Memoirs,* 60–61.

103 **"always talked to a man freely"** Garland, *Grant,* 111. Hamlin Garland, in the preface to his 1898 biography, credits Walter B. Camp, who became the local historian, for his knowledge of Grant at Sackets Harbor. Garland traveled to Sackets Harbor, where he spoke with Camp, whom he quotes in the biography. Camp recalled that Ulysses and Julia attended the Sackets Harbor Presbyterian Church, as did he. There was no Methodist church in Sackets Harbor.

103 **In the rear** The house, about to be demolished, was moved to the Michigan State Fair Grounds in 1936. See *Michigan History Magazine* 21 (Spring 1937): 208–10; Julia Dent Grant, *Personal Memoirs,* 66.

103 **Grant found Detroit** USG to JDG, April 27, 1849, *Grant Papers,* 1:184. The 1840 census officially registered 9,102 residents in the city of Detroit.

104 **"I was no clerk"** *Personal Memoirs,* 1:233.

104 **Grant began to attend** Silas Farmer, *History of Detroit and Wayne County and Early Michigan,* 3rd ed. (Detroit: Silas Farmer, 1890), 569.

104 **"His wife was outgoing"** James E. Pitman interview, William C. Church Papers, Library of Congress.

104 **"never saw Grant under the influence"** Friend Palmer, *Early Days in Detroit* (Detroit: Hunt & June, 1906), 225.

104 **"Detroit was a frontier town"** James E. Pitman interview.

104 **Grant did not anticipate** *Zachariah Chandler: An Outline Sketch of His Life and Public Services* (Detroit: Post and Tribune, 1880), 80–82; deposition, State of Michigan, City of Detroit, *Grant Papers,* 1:195.

105 **"If you soldiers would keep sober"** Richardson, *A Personal History,* 134–35.

105 **In June, Ulysses informed Julia** USG to JDG, June 4 and June 7, 1851, *Grant Papers,* 1:204, 206.

105 **"he was anxious to see"** Julia Dent Grant, *Personal Memoirs,* 69.

105 **By 1848 the Sons of Temperance** Samuel Ellis, *The History of the Sons of Temperance* (Boston: Stacy, Richardson, 1848).

105 **"I have become convinced"** Garland, *Grant,* 111. Garland's interview with Walter Camp, local historian, is the source of the quotations about Grant and temperance.

105 **As a new member** Orlando Lund, *The Order of the Sons of Temperance* (Syracuse, N.Y.: Agan & Summers, 1850), 15.

105 **New recruits wore** Garland, *Grant,* 111; Lewis, *Captain Sam Grant,* 293–94.

106 **Grant discovered that no sailing date** USG to JDG, June 24, 1852, *Grant Papers,* 1:238.

106 **He arrived in Washington** Grant mentions whom he intends to call upon in letters to Julia on June 28 and July 1, 1852, *Grant Papers,* 1:239–45.

106 **Further disappointment** USG to JDG, July 1, 1852, *Grant Papers,* 1:243.

106 **Congressmen whom he did call on** Ibid., July 4, 1852, *Grant Papers,* 1:245.

107 **"It is a *dangerous* experiment"** Ibid., June 24, 1852, *Grant Papers,* 1:238.

107 **by travelers eager** John Haskell Kemble, *The Panama Route, 1848–1869* (Berkeley: University of California Press, 1943), 119, 239.

107 **"The poor things"** USG to JDG, July 15, 1852, *Grant Papers*, 1:249.
107 **Delia Sheffield** William S. Lewis, "Reminiscences of Mrs. Delia B. Sheffield," *Washington Historical Quarterly* 15, no. 1 (January 1924): 51–52.
107 **"a very stupid man"** Ibid.; Eunice Tripler, *Eunice Tripler: Some Notes of Her Personal Recollections* (New York: Grafton Press, 1910), 108.
107 **"Have you noticed"** Lewis, "Reminiscences of Mrs. Delia B. Sheffield," 52.
107 **As the voyage dragged on** Ibid.
107 **The ship's captain was grateful** Hamlin Garland interviewed James Findlay Schenck, *Grant*, 117, but this interview is not in the Hamlin Garland Papers.
108 **Stench greeted passengers** Chauncey D. Griswold, *The Isthmus of Panama, and What I Saw There* (New York: Dewitt and Davenport, 1852), 136; Robert Tomes, *Panama in 1855* (New York: Harper, 1855), 54–59.
108 **Because the streets were filled with water** Lewis, "Reminiscences of Mrs. Delia B. Sheffield," 52.
108 **Grant "wondered how any person"** *Personal Memoirs*, 1:195.
108 **As quartermaster, Grant was responsible** Richardson, *A Personal History*, 140.
108 **Boats were poled** *Personal Memoirs*, 1:195; Kemble, *Panama Route*, 167–70, describes the trials of travel on the Chagres River.
108 **The boatmen left the Americans** Lewis, "Reminiscences of Mrs. Delia B. Sheffield," 53.
108 **In mounting confusion** *Personal Memoirs*, 1:196–97.
110 **Delia Sheffield was comforted** Lewis, "Reminiscences of Mrs. Delia B. Sheffield," 53.
110 **"About one-third of the people"** *Personal Memoirs*, 1:197; Garland, *Grant*, 119.
110 **Grant and Dr. Tripler fixed** Tripler, *Eunice Tripler*, 108.
110 **A fellow officer said Grant** Garland, *Grant*, 119.
110 **"one of the coolest men"** Lewis, *Captain Sam Grant*, 303.
111 **This condemning story** *Charleston Mercury*, September 7, 1852.
111 **"The horrors of the road"** USG to JDG, August 9, 1852, *Grant Papers*, 1:252.
111 **If Panama was an unusual obstacle** William C. Davis, *Crucible of Command: Ulysses S. Grant and Robert E. Lee—The War They Fought, the Peace They Forged* (Boston: De Capo Press, 2014), 86, identifies industry and enterprise as two qualities "that characterized Grant from his youth."
111 **"He was like a ministering angel"** Garland, *Grant*, 119.

Chapter 8. "Forsaken"

112 **Does he ever say anything** USG to JDG, August 16, 1852, *Grant Papers*, 1:256.
112 **No one was allowed** Kevin Starr and Richard J. Orsi, *Rooted in Barbarous Soil: People, Culture, and Community in Gold Rush California* (Berkeley: University of California Press, 2000), ix.
112 **"The money's here!"** Evelyn Wells and Harry C. Peterson, *The '49ers* (Garden City, N.Y.: Doubleday, 1949), 169.
112 **"I have seen enough"** USG to JDG, August 20, 1852, *Grant Papers*, 1:257.
112 **It was a young man's game** Kevin Starr, *California: A History* (New York: Modern Library, 2007), 73–90; H. W. Brands, *The Age of Gold: The California Gold Rush and the American Dream* (New York: Doubleday, 2002), 247–68.
113 **"Some realized more"** *Personal Memoirs*, 1:201.
113 **"Many of the real scenes"** Ibid.
113 **"I consider that city"** USG to JDG, September 19, 1852, *Grant Papers*, 1:266.
113 **"Of course I do not contemplate"** Ibid., August 20, 1852, *Grant Papers*, 1:257.
113 **"They have stables"** Ibid., August 30, 1852, *Grant Papers*, 1:259.

114 **Built in Boston** For what is now called Vancouver Barracks, see http://www.nps .gov/fova/historyculture/vb.htm.

114 **"Everyone says they are the best"** USG to JDG, January 3, 1853, *Grant Papers,* 1:279–80.

114 **"Just think, our youngest"** Ibid., October 26, 1852, *Grant Papers,* 1:269–70.

114 **"You can scarcely conceive"** Ibid., December 3, 1852, *Grant Papers,* 1:274.

114 **"Living is expensive"** Ibid., October 7, 1852, *Grant Papers,* 1:267.

115 **"About pecuniary matters"** Ibid., December 3, 1852, 1:275. Grant was confident he could recover at least $1,800 of the $2,000.

115 **He provided Grant** Julia Dent Grant, *Personal Memoirs,* 71–72. Julia says Camp persuaded Ulysses to destroy the notes in his presence.

115 **"I chided Ulys"** Ibid., 72.

115 **Grant's quartermaster responsibilities** Lewis, "Reminiscences of Mrs. Delia B. Sheffield," 58.

115 **"My opinion [is]"** USG to JDG, March 19, 1853, *Grant Papers,* 1:296.

115 **He was shocked** *Personal Memoirs,* 1:205–6.

115 **In the evenings** Lewis, *Captain Sam Grant,* 310.

115 **"He seems to have"** Ibid., 310–11.

116 **Several times, when Grant was reading** Lewis, "Reminiscences of Mrs. Delia B. Sheffield," 60.

116 **"He seemed to be always sad"** Garland, *Grant,* 122. Garland interviewed Theodore Eckerson in Portland, Oregon, x.

116 **"I put sugar into it"** Lewis, "Reminiscences of Mrs. Delia B. Sheffield," 60.

116 **"Well, it is the sweetest"** Ibid.

116 **The ice melted** Frank Burr, *The Life and Deeds of General Ulysses S. Grant* (Philadelphia: National Publishing, 1885), 116.

116 **They chartered a boat** Lewis, "Reminiscences of Mrs. Delia B. Sheffield," 61.

117 **"I never worked before"** USG to JDG, December 3, 1852, and March 19, 1853, *Grant Papers,* 1:275–76, 294.

117 **Worst of all** Ibid., February 15 and June 15, 1853, *Grant Papers,* 1:289, 301. Grant intended to write out an account and send it to his friend Charles Ford in Sackets Harbor, asking him to collect it from Camp, who "is I fear slightly deranged." Ibid., June 28, 1853, *Grant Papers,* 1:305.

117 **Jefferson Davis** Stephen W. Sears, *George B. McClellan: The Young Napoleon* (New York: Ticknor & Fields, 1988), 36–37.

117 **Grant welcomed him** USG to JDG, June 28, 1853, *Grant Papers,* 1:303.

117 **When McClellan left** Sears, *George B. McClellan,* 38. Grant, always punctual in his reports, wrote Major Osborn Cross on July 25, "The constant, and unremitting calls upon the time, both of myself and [my] clerk, consequent upon the fitting out of the expeditions connected with the Northern Pacific R. R. survey," was the reason he was late and briefer with his annual report. *Grant Papers,* 1:308.

117 **"When the expedition"** Henry Hodges to William C. Church, January 5, 1897, William C. Church Papers, Library of Congress.

117 **"for the purpose of settling"** USG to Thomas S. Jesup, September 8, 1853, *Grant Papers,* 1:311. Grant's letter was endorsed by Commander Bonneville.

118 **Soon after, he was instructed** Mrs. Sheffield ends her "Reminiscences," "During his one year at Vancouver he had not made an enemy and was kind and considerate to all." Lewis, "Reminiscences of Mrs. Delia B. Sheffield," 62.

118 **He took his time** USG to JDG, January 18, 1854, *Grant Papers,* 1:315n1.

118 **"I cannot say much"** Ibid., 1:315.

118 **Grant lived in a one-story** Leigh H. Irvine, *History of Humboldt County, California* (Los Angeles: Historic Record Company, 1915), 54. Only the hospital building re-

mains of the original fourteen structures. It is a California State Park with a historical museum dedicated to telling the story of the fort and the Native American groups. See http://www.parks.ca.gov.

118 **"I do nothing here"** USG to JDG, February 2, 1854, *Grant Papers,* 1:316.

118 **Some men enjoyed hunting** Ibid.

118 **"I think I have been"** USG to JDG, February 6, 1854, *Grant Papers,* 1:320.

119 **"Whenever I get to thinking"** Ibid., March 6, 1854, *Grant Papers,* 1:323.

120 **"The result was a common one"** William I. Reed to William C. Church, August 25, 1909, William C. Church Papers, Library of Congress.

120 **"I have not been"** USG to JDG, March 6, 1854, *Grant Papers,* 1:323.

120 **How often and how much** The best study of the debates about Grant's drinking while serving at Fort Vancouver and Fort Humboldt is by Charles G. Ellington, *The Trial of U. S. Grant: The Pacific Coast Years, 1852–1854* (Glendale, Calif.: Arthur H. Clark, 1987). See especially 146–60.

120 **"I have the honor to acknowledge"** USG to Colonel Samuel Cooper, April 11, 1854, *Grant Papers,* 1:328.

120 **"I very respectfully tender"** Ibid., 1:329.

120 **Grant resigned** In his memoirs, Grant does not detail why he decided to resign or why at that moment (*Personal Memoirs,* 1:210). Julia devotes only one sentence to his resignation in her memoirs (Julia Dent Grant, *Personal Memoirs,* 75).

120 **Buchanan endorsed** It was common for officers to drink during card games. Henry Hodges said later that Grant went on "two or three sprees a year . . . was always open to reason . . . would own up and promise to stop drinking, which he did." Lewis, *Captain Sam Grant,* 312–13; Ellington, *The Trial of U.S. Grant,* 152–53.

120 **But Grant, thinking of Julia** Garland, *Grant,* 127.

120 **On May 2, Grant wrote** USG to JDG, May 2, 1854, *Grant Papers,* 1:332.

121 **When he arrived** Garland, *Grant,* 129.

121 **Buckner stepped forward** Simon Bolivar Buckner interview, Hamlin Garland Papers; Arndt M. Stickles, *Simon Bolivar Buckner: Borderland Knight* (Chapel Hill: University of North Carolina Press, 1940), 32–34.

Chapter 9. "Hardscrabble"

123 **"I guess that's about so"** Garland interviewed Jesse's neighbors in Bethel and gives a general attribution, "reputable neighbors," for these words. Garland, *Grant,* 129.

123 **As he started to climb** Casey, "When Grant Went A-Courtin'," 26.

124 **"all questions pertaining to slavery"** Robert W. Johannsen, *Stephen A. Douglas* (Chicago: University of Chicago Press, 1973), 421, 431, 434.

124 **With all his children** Ross, *The General's Wife,* 79.

125 **"He was a man"** Casey, "When Grant Went A-Courtin'," 27.

125 **White farming families** Garland, *Grant,* 132. Colonel Dent clashed with William and John Sigerson, who owned an adjoining nursery farm. The Sigersons were antislavery neighbors who used only white laborers in their farming. William Taussig, "Personal Recollections of General Grant," *Missouri Historical Society Collections* 2, no. 3 (1903): 2–3.

125 **Aware of the heavy load** Richardson, *A Personal History,* 152.

125 **"Most of his leisure time"** Interview with Mary Robinson, *St. Louis Republican,* July 24, 1885.

126 **"We all used to wait"** Frederick Dent Grant, *New York World Sunday Magazine,* April 25, 1897; see also "Frederick Dent Grant," *Ulysses S. Grant Association Newsletter,* April 1969, 21.

126 **He wanted to call** Julia, in her *Personal Memoirs,* wrote, "When she [Ellen] was eighteen months old we had the three children christened" (76). The term *christen* was often used for what today would be called "baptized." Julia does not say in which church they were baptized, but Mary Robinson stated that the family attended the Centenary Methodist Church, the main Methodist church in the city. Interview with Mary Robinson, *St. Louis Republican,* July 24, 1885. See Mr. and Mrs. Francis Emmet Williams, *Centenary Methodist Church of St. Louis: The First Hundred Years, 1839–1939* (St. Louis: Mound City Press, 1939).

126 **Since her birthday fell** Ross, *The General's Wife,* 83.

126 **"I have seen"** Interview with Mary Robinson, *St. Louis Republican,* July 24, 1885.

126 **Ulysses wanted to build** Julia Dent Grant, *Personal Memoirs,* 78–79.

126 **Julia insisted** Ibid.

126 **Some neighbors thought** Garland, *Grant,* 133–34; Lewis, *Captain Sam Grant,* 343.

126 **"I'll go back and vote"** Richardson, *A Personal History,* 156.

127 **"Under these circumstances"** *Personal Memoirs,* 1:215.

127 **"If I had an opportunity"** USG to JRG, December 28, 1856, *Grant Papers,* 1:334.

127 **"It is always usual"** Ibid., February 7, 1857, *Grant Papers,* 1:336. Ulysses assured his father he was asking not for a gift, but for a loan, with interest.

127 **"The fact is"** Ibid., 1:336–37.

127 **Grant's hopes for farming** Charles W. Calomiris and Larry Schweickart, "The Panic of 1857: Origins, Transmissions, and Containment," *Journal of Economic History* 51 (December 1991): 807–34.

128 **He signed a pawn ticket** The pawn ticket is in the possession of the Abraham Lincoln Presidential Library and Museum. Pawn ticket, December 23, 1857, *Grant Papers,* 1:339.

128 **"I have now three negro men"** USG to Mary Grant, March 21, 1858, *Grant Papers,* 1:341. Correspondence with Mary now became Ulysses's main link with his father, who seldom wrote.

128 **Then both parents became sick** Ibid., September 7, 1858, *Grant Papers,* 1:343.

129 **"swung one mud-spattered boot"** Casey, "When Grant Went A-Courtin'," 31.

129 **"in a few minutes returned"** Interview with James Longstreet, *New York Times,* July 24, 1885.

129 **"Seeing the determination"** Ibid.

129 **As he reviewed** USG to JRG, October 1, 1858, *Grant Papers,* 1:344.

129 **Real estate was booming** Primm, *Lion of the Valley,* 181, 192. The 1860 census ranked St. Louis the eighth largest city in the United States, just 271 people behind Cincinnati and ahead of Chicago.

130 **Although their business cards** USG to JRG, March 12, 1859, *Grant Papers,* 1:345–46n2.

130 **"I . . . do hereby manumit"** Manumission of Slave, [March 29, 1859], *Grant Papers,* 1:347. Garland, from his interviews, concluded, "He was a poor slave driver, however; the negroes did pretty much as they pleased." Garland, *Grant,* 137.

131 **"We never heard"** Julia Dent Grant, *Personal Memoirs,* 80.

131 **"I am sure your opinion"** Ibid., 81.

131 **He spent time collecting** USG to JRG, August 20, 1859, *Grant Papers,* 1:350.

131 **He enclosed a letter** USG to Board of County Commissioners, August 15, 1859, *Grant Papers,* 1:348–49.

131 **The thirty-five endorsements** Ibid.; Richardson, *A Personal History,* 163–68.

131 **"I fear they will make"** USG to JRG, August 20, 1859, *Grant Papers,* 1:350.

131 **"though nothing was known"** Taussig, "Personal Recollections of General Grant," 6.

131 **He was pleased to receive** Richardson, *A Personal History,* 162.

132 **In the fall, Grant obtained** Ibid., 169.

132 **"We will not always"** Ross, *The General's Wife,* 81. Julia believed that a spirit visited her and cleared her dark thoughts. Julia Dent Grant, *Personal Memoirs,* 78.

132 **With his head** USG to JDG, March 14, 1860, *Grant Papers,* 1:355.

133 **"We found him more than commonly"** Lewis, *Captain Sam Grant,* 363.

Chapter 10. Galena

135 **By the early 1850s** As steel replaced lead, Galena (after Grant's time) began to decline as rapidly as it had grown.

135 **By 1859, this region** Diann Marsh, *Galena, Illinois: A Brief History* (Charleston, S.C.: History Press, 2010), 13.

136 **By the time Ulysses arrived** The Grant store address has usually been listed as 145 North Main Street, but there were no street numbers in Galena until after the Civil War.

136 **Cousin Burke asserted** M. E. Burke interview, Hamlin Garland Papers. A main reason Burke finally agreed to Garland's request for an interview was to correct "the utter absurdity of many of the stories told about him" while he lived in Galena.

136 **He was able to handle** Ibid.

136 **The Grants lived** Leigh Leslie, "Grant and Galena," *Midland Monthly* 4, no. 3 (September 1895): 195.

136 **The house he rented** The modern address of Grant's home is 121 High Street.

137 **"I give up"** Julia Dent Grant, *Personal Memoirs,* 85–86.

137 **The youngest boy, Jesse** Frederick Dent Grant, quoted in *Army and Navy Journal* (May 23, 1908): 1,029.

137 **He liked to smoke** Ross, *The General's Wife,* 104.

137 **"Our business here is prosperous"** USG to Mr. Davis, August 7, 1860, *Grant Papers,* 1:357.

138 **His Methodist sermons** Leon H. Vincent, *John Heyl Vincent: A Biographical Sketch* (New York: Macmillan, 1925), 29–31.

138 **"I hear you preach"** Ibid., 50; John H. Vincent, "The Inner Life of Ulysses S. Grant," *The Chautauquan* 30 (October 1889–March 1900): 634.

138 **Vincent would go on** Russell E. Richey, Kenneth E. Rowe, and Jean Miller Schmidt, *The Methodist Experience in America,* vol. 1 (Nashville: Abingdon Press, 2010), 250, 266, 330.

139 **"almost crazy to get permission"** John Rawlins interview, "How Grant Got to Know Rawlins," *Hartford Post,* in *Army and Navy Journal* (September 12, 1868): 53.

139 **Grant would sit** Ibid.

139 **Witnessing the effect** James Harrison Wilson, *The Life of John A. Rawlins* (New York: Neale Publishing Company, 1916), 24–31.

139 **He became known** Ibid., 33, 35.

139 **"no man ever heard Grant utter"** M. E. Burke interview, Hamlin Garland Papers.

139 **The Grant leather store** Richardson, *A Personal History,* 175.

140 **"Rowley, you are mistaken"** Ibid., 176.

140 **A Democrat of southern birth** Ibid., 178.

140 **His words catapulted** Augustus L. Chetlain, *Recollections of Seventy Years* (Galena, Ill.: Gazette Publishing Company, 1899), 69.

140 **Tall, broad-shouldered** Gaillard Hunt, *Israel, Elihu and Cadwallader Washburn* (New York: Macmillan, 1925), 172.

141 **Washburne served** Ibid., 175–78.

141 **"It is an abolition fight"** Richardson, *A Personal History,* 178.

142 **"It is simply"** Wilson, *Life of John A. Rawlins,* 46–48; Richardson, *A Personal History,* 179.

142 **Grant told a friend later** Wilson, *Life of John A. Rawlins,* 49.

142 **"Yes: We're about to *do* something"** Garland, *Grant,* 156.

142 **"Go, if you like"** Richardson, *A Personal History,* 179.

142 **"I never went into"** *Personal Memoirs,* 1:231.

142 **"I nominate Captain U. S. Grant"** Garland, *Grant,* 157.

142 **Leaving the pine bench** Ibid.

142 **Merchant Chetlain remembered** Chetlain, *Recollections of Seventy Years,* 70.

142 **"unquestioning obedience"** Garland, *Grant,* 157.

143 **"Ulys read aloud"** Julia Dent Grant, *Personal Memoirs,* 87.

143 **"With the present granny"** USG to addressee unknown, [December 1860], *Grant Papers,* 1:359. Although the letter is not dated, the editors are correct in placing it in December and, I would argue, after the secession of South Carolina on December 20.

144 **"ten and twenty times"** USG to Frederick Dent, April 19, 1861, *Grant Papers,* 2:3–4.

144 **"In all this"** Ibid.

Chapter 11. "I Am In to Do All I Can"

147 **That evening, he made** Chetlain, *Recollections of Seventy Years,* 71.

147 **"I would aid the company"** *Personal Memoirs,* 1:231; Augustus L. Chetlain confirms Grant's story of declining, Chetlain interview, Hamlin Garland Papers.

147 **"What I ask now"** USG to JRG, April 21, 1861, *Grant Papers,* 2:7.

148 **"There are but two"** Ibid.

148 **So many well-wishers** Lewis, *Captain Sam Grant,* 409.

148 **"was very indifferently dressed"** Thomas J. McCormack, ed., *Memoirs of Gustave Koerner, 1809–1896,* vol. 2 (Cedar Rapids, Iowa: Torch Press, 1909), 126–27.

148 **"I was perfectly sickened"** USG to JRG, May 6, 1861, *Grant Papers,* 2:21.

148 **The governor understood** *Personal Memoirs,* 1:232–33.

149 **asked all manner** Garland, *Grant,* 164.

149 **"However I am in"** USG to JDG, May 1, 1861, *Grant Papers,* 2:16.

149 **"The horse-play"** *Weekly North-Western Gazette* (Galena), May 10, 1861.

149 **"Everything he did"** Garland, *Grant,* 165.

149 **"Nothing—waiting"** Ibid., 167.

149 **"We are now in want"** *Weekly North-Western Gazette* (Galena), May 31, 1861; Garland, *Grant,* 167.

150 **"I have the honor"** USG to Bvt. Brig. Gen. Lorenzo Thomas, May 24, 1861, *Grant Papers,* 2:35.

150 **The harried Thomas** After the end of the Civil War, Grant's aide Adam Badeau wrote to the War Department seeking a copy of the letter, but it could not be located. Years later, in 1876, Adjutant General Edward D. Townsend, in packing up papers, discovered it in his office, unfiled. *Personal Memoirs,* 1:240.

150 **When he was informed** John Russell Young, *Around the World with General Grant,* vol. 2 (New York: American News, 1879), 214; Sears, *George B. McClellan,* 72–73.

150 **A disappointed Grant** Young, *Around the World,* 2:214–15. McClellan in his memoirs, written in bitterness after the Civil War and not published until after his death, remembered that he was not away for a couple of hours but was out of town, in Indianapolis. "Had I been there I would no doubt have given him a place on my staff, and he would probably have remained with me and shared my fate." George B. McClellan, *McClellan's Own Story* (New York: Charles L. Webster & Co., 1887), 47.

150   **He opened it to read** *Grant Papers,* 2:43n1.

150   **But when Jesse read the news** Jesse Grant's attitude can be inferred from Ulysses's response of July 13, 1861: "You ask if I should not like to go into the regular army. I should not. I want to bring my children up to useful employment, and in the army the chance is poor." *Grant Papers,* 2:67.

151   **"Men, go to your quarters"** Lewis, *Captain Sam Grant,* 427; Simpson, *Grant,* 85.

151   **"In accepting this command"** Orders No. 7, June 18, 1861, *Grant Papers,* 2:45–46.

151   **"to keep the men from climbing"** Interview with J. W. Wham, *New York Tribune,* September 27, 1885.

151   **All men when out of Camp** Orders No. 8, June 19, 1861, *Grant Papers,* 2:46.

151   **As a young soldier** Smith, *Grant,* 109.

151   **"The effect of that order"** Interview with J. W. Wham, *New York Tribune,* September 27, 1885.

151   **new shoulder straps** Bruce Catton provides a discussion of the problems of volunteer leadership; see Catton, *Grant Moves South,* 8.

151   **"McClellan's report"** USG to JDG, June 26, 1861, *Grant Papers,* 2:49–50.

152   **"he had read to me"** Julia Dent Grant, *Personal Memoirs,* 92.

152   **"he never wore it"** James L. Crane, "Grant as a Colonel: Conversation Between Grant and His Chaplain," *McClure's Magazine* (June 1896): 40. Although this reminiscence was not published until 1896, Crane (who died in 1879) probably wrote it at the close of the war.

152   **"I do not want any"** Ensley Moore, an eyewitness of the march, later wrote "Grant's First March," *Transactions of the Illinois State Historical Society for the Year 1910* 15 (Springfield: Illinois State Journal Co., 1912): 56.

152   **If a man was not ready** Catton, *Grant Moves South,* 10.

153   **Whenever he found whiskey** Emerson, "Grant's Life in the West," *Midland Monthly* 8 (January 1898): 51–52; Crane, "Grant as a Colonel: Conversation Between Grant and His Chaplain," 41.

153   **"Passing through the towns"** USG to JDG, July 7, 1861, *Grant Papers,* 2:60.

153   **"Grant's requisition"** Hamlin Garland, "Grant at the Outbreak of the War," *McClure's Magazine* (April 1897): 610.

153   **Jack, cream colored** Smith, *Grant,* 157, 302; Richardson, *A Personal History,* 271.

153   **"He put us to hard drill"** Garland, "Grant at the Outbreak of the War," 601–10.

153   **"I don't believe there is"** USG to JDG, July 7, 1861, *Grant Papers,* 2:60.

153   **"the real necessity"** General Orders No. 24, July 9, 1861, *Grant Papers,* 2:62.

154   **Julia was not** I am indebted to William McFeely's analysis of the different ways Julia Grant entered the war; see *Grant,* 80–81.

154   **"Strange to say"** Julia Dent Grant, *Personal Memoirs,* 92.

154   **"He did not want to go"** USG to JDG, July 13, 1861, *Grant Papers,* 2:70.

154   **"Do keep him"** Julia Dent Grant, *Personal Memoirs,* 92.

154   **"I should like"** USG to JDG, July 19, 1861, *Grant Papers,* 2:72.

154   **"When we first came"** Ibid., 2:73.

154   **"I would have given anything"** *Personal Memoirs,* 1:249–50.

155   **"My heart resumed"** Ibid., 1:250.

155   **"This was a view"** Ibid.

155   **"made every man"** Ibid., 1:252.

155   **"No wandering"** General Orders No. 1, July 25, 1861, *Grant Papers,* 2:74–75.

155   **"The people were no longer"** *Personal Memoirs,* 1:252.

155   **While reading the newspaper** Crane, "Grant as a Colonel: Conversation Between Grant and His Chaplain," 43.

155   **"Well, sir, I had no suspicion"** The narrative of the nomination is disputed. President Lincoln convened an emergency session of Congress on July 4. On July

30, he asked Secretary of War Simon Cameron to send him nominations for new brigadier generals. Lincoln promptly signed a list of thirty-four on July 31, and the Senate confirmed the list on August 1. On the one hand, the entire Illinois congressional delegation met to nominate candidates for brigadier general, with Washburne advocating Grant, a man from his district. On the other hand, there is no direct evidence that Lincoln asked congressmen from any state for nominations. See *Grant Papers*, 2:82n2, n3; John Y. Simon, "From Galena to Appomattox: Grant and Washburne," *Journal of the Illinois State Historical Society* 58, no. 2 (Summer 1965): 171–72.

156 **"walked away"** Crane, "Grant as a Colonel: Conversation Between Grant and His Chaplain," 43.

156 **"I think I see your hand"** USG to Elihu B. Washburne, September 3, 1861, *Grant Papers*, 2:183.

156 **he did not have time** Catton, *Grant Moves South*, 18.

156 **"Lincoln appointed"** See Earl J. Hess, *The Civil War in the West: Victory and Defeat from the Appalachians to the Mississippi* (Chapel Hill: University of North Carolina Press, 2012).

156 **"I have given you *carte blanche*"** Allan Nevins, *Frémont: Pathmarker of the West* (New York: Appleton-Century, 1939), 477.

156 **"Col Grant is an old army officer"** *Grant Papers*, 2:86n1.

156 **He was impressed** *The New York Times*, July 26, 1885.

157 **"Genl Grant I am pleased with"** Ibid., 2:87n.

157 **"to suppress all drinking houses"** USG, General Orders No. 9, August 9, 1861, *Grant Papers*, 2:88.

157 **"nothing more than common sense"** *Personal Memoirs*, 1:253.

157 **"The rebels *must* be driven out"** Emerson, "Grant's Life in the West," *Midland Monthly* 8 (February 1898): 116.

157 **"Possibilities—mere possibilities"** Ibid.

157 **Many questioned** James M. McPherson, *Battle Cry* (New York: Oxford University Press, 1988), 351–52.

158 **"found a good many troops"** *Personal Memoirs*, 1:258.

158 **"Drill and discipline"** USG to Capt. Speed Butler, August 23, 1861, *Grant Papers*, 2:131.

158 **Grant's appointment** Grant's letter to Rawlins has not been found. In a letter to Julia on August 10, he tells her, "I wish you would tell Orvil to say to him I would like to have him come as soon as possible." USG to JDG, August 10, 1861, *Grant Papers*, 2:96; Wilson, *Life of John A. Rawlins*, 53–54.

158 **"I selected him for qualities"** Nevins, *Frémont: Pathmarker of the West*, 591–92.

159 **"occupy Columbus"** *Grant Papers*, 2:151n1.

159 **"I have a task"** USG to JDG, August 29, 1861, *Grant Papers*, 2:149.

159 **"All I fear"** USG to JRG, August 31, 1861, *Grant Papers*, 2:158. A subtext of this letter is that Jesse has probably been up to his boasting again—and complaining that his son was not getting promoted fast enough. "Your suspicions as to my being neglected are entirely unfounded" (159).

160 **When he'd read the paper, Oglesby** *Personal Memoirs*, 1:264. After Grant's *Personal Memoirs* was published in 1885, Oglesby corroborated Grant's account in a letter to Thomas Donaldson written on September 28, 1886: "In about half a minute General Grant, in citizen's clothes (pretty well worn), very dusty and unshaven, approached the seat where I was occupying and sat down immediately adjoining me at my desk." *Journal of the Illinois State Historical Society* 38, no. 2 (June 1945): 242–44.

160 **As he continued his habit** Catton, *Grant Moves South*, 48.

160 **This action contained** Kendall D. Gott, *Where the South Lost the War: An Analysis of the Fort Henry–Fort Donelson Campaign: February 1862* (Mechanicsburg, Pa.: Stack-

pole Books, 2003), 13–14; Lowell H. Harrison, *The Civil War in Kentucky* (Lexington: University Press of Kentucky, 1975), 8–9.

160 **As Confederate troops moved** On September 5, Charles A. De Arnaud telegraphed Frémont, "Just arrived from Memphis and Union City, Tenn. The enemy is marching in large force to take Paducah, on the Ohio River, to invade Southern Illinois." *Grant Papers,* 2:193n1.

160 **"I am now nearly ready"** USG to John C. Frémont, September 5, 1861, *Grant Papers,* 2:190.

161 **Instead, they found** *Personal Memoirs,* 1:265–66.

161 **"I have come among you"** USG, "Proclamation to the Citizens of Paducah," *Grant Papers,* 2:194–95.

Chapter 12. Belmont

163 **"We must have the Mississippi"** Richardson, *A Personal History,* 196.

163 **The cities in what was called** Ronald C. White, Jr., *The Eloquent President: A Portrait of Lincoln Through His Words* (New York: Random House, 2005), 209.

163 **"the greatest soldier"** Charles Pierce Roland, *Albert Sidney Johnston: Soldier of Three Republics* (Austin: University of Texas Press, 1964), 11–19; Shelby Foote, *The Civil War: A Narrative,* vol. 1 (New York: Random House, 1958), 169.

163 **"His contemporaries"** *Personal Memoirs,* 1:360.

166 **Frémont wrote Grant** John C. Frémont to USG, September 6, 1861, *Grant Papers,* 2:198n.

166 **Yet the older man's lines** Smith, *Grant,* 120–21.

166 **"This war however is formidable"** USG to Mary Grant, September 11, 1861, *Grant Papers,* 2:237–38.

166 **"Commanders are not to correspond"** Major Joseph H. Eaton wrote to Grant on behalf of Frémont on September 6, 1861. *Grant Papers,* 2:189n.

167 **In the end, he relinquished** Glenn Robins, *The Bishop of the Old South: The Ministry and Civil War Legacy of Leonidas Polk* (Macon, Ga.: Mercer University Press, 2006), 144–46. Polk's decision generated a vigorous debate among southern Episcopalians about the proper role for the clergy in this civil conflict. See also Joseph Howard Parks, *General Leonidas Polk, C.S.A.: The Fighting Bishop* (Baton Rouge: Louisiana State University Press, 1990).

167 **Even though he was acquitted** Nathaniel Cheairs Hughes, Jr., *The Battle of Belmont: Grant Strikes South* (Chapel Hill: University of North Carolina Press, 1991), 30–31.

167 **"I am not so uncharitable"** USG to JRG, May 6, 1861, *Grant Papers,* 2:22. In the attack on Chapultepec on September 13, 1847, Pillow's foot was injured by a grazing ball. In his official report, he stated he had been "cut down by a grape shot." *Grant Papers,* 2:23n8.

167 **Any Union gunboats** Hughes, *Battle of Belmont,* 36.

168 **This defensive** Ibid., 37.

168 **This positive order ended** Chauncey McKeever to USG, November 1, 1861, *Grant Papers,* 3:143–44. For reasons that Grant never made clear, some of the information that follows comes from a second report on the Battle of Belmont that he wrote three years later in 1864.

168 **Lincoln relieved** Ronald C. White, Jr., *A. Lincoln: A Biography* (New York: Random House, 2009), 452–56.

168 **He ordered Richard Oglesby** USG to Richard J. Oglesby, November 3, 1861, *Grant Papers,* 3:109.

168 **"might enable me"** USG to Charles F. Smith, November 5, 1861, *Grant Papers,* 3:114.

169   **"I move tonight"** Ibid., November 6, 1861, *Grant Papers,* 3:120.

169   **"Where are we going"** Hughes, *Battle of Belmont,* 49.

169   **"We are going to attack Columbus!"** Ibid.; Lindorf Ozburn to Eliza Ozburn, November 10, 1861, Ozburn Letters, ALPLM; William H. Austin Letters, ALPLM.

170   **"were little better"** *Personal Memoirs,* 1:274.

170   **The fighting bishop** Hughes, *Battle of Belmont,* 139–44.

170   **"the pipes of two steamers"** John H. Brinton, *Personal Memoirs of John H. Brinton* (New York: Neale Publishing, 1914), 77.

170   **"demoralized from their victory"** *Personal Memoirs,* 1:274.

172   **"Every man was trying"** Byron Andrews, *A Biography of Gen. John A. Logan* (New York: H. S. Goodspeed, 1884), 403–4.

172   **"I was the only man"** *Personal Memoirs,* 1:278.

172   **"There is a Yankee"** Grant reported that this episode was told to him later by someone on Polk's staff. *Personal Memoirs,* 1:281.

172   **"my horse put its fore feet"** Ibid., 1:278–79.

173   **"a musket ball"** Ibid., 1:279.

173   **"every man feeling"** Ibid., 1:280.

173   **"glorious victory"** *Nashville Banner,* November 9, 10, 1861; *New Orleans Daily Crescent,* November 11, 1861; Hughes, *Battle of Belmont,* 190.

173   **"General Grant is reported killed"** *OR,* ser. 1, vol. 3, 304.

173   **"thanks to the troops"** Orders, November 8, 1861, *Grant Papers,* 3:130.

173   **"a conflict of statements"** *Columbus Crisis,* November 14, 1861; Anna Maclay Green, "Civil War Opinion of General Grant," *Journal of the Illinois State Historical Society* 22 (April 1929): 6.

174   **"We have met the enemy"** *Personal Memoirs,* 1:280.

174   **"The late battle at Belmont"** *New York Times,* November 11, 1861.

174   **"swinging his sword"** *New York Herald,* November 19, 1861.

174   **Perhaps knowing Pillow** I am indebted to John Simon, in *Grant at Belmont,* for these three points.

175   **"Taking into account"** USG to JRG, November 8, 1861, *Grant Papers,* 3:138.

175   **Nevertheless, with closed eyes** *Grant Papers,* 3, 143–49n; and "No. 1: Reports of Brig. Gen. U. S. Grant, U.S. Army to Headquarters District Southeast Missouri, Cairo, Ill., November 17, 1861" to Brig. Gen. Seth Williams, *OR,* ser. 1, vol. 3, 267–72.

Chapter 13. "Unconditional Surrender"

177   **As more boats arrived** *Nashville Banner,* November 10, 1861.

177   **"The battle of Belmont"** USG to Elihu B. Washburne, November 20, 1861, *Grant Papers,* 3:205.

177   **"I want you to take"** *Grant Papers,* 3:207n4.

178   **"old fashioned Sunday-school"** Hoyt Sherman, "Personal Recollections of General Grant," *Midland Monthly* 9, no. 2 (April 1898): 326.

178   **"poetry in every move"** Julia Dent Grant, *Personal Memoirs,* 93–94.

178   **"If you are with the accursed"** Ulysses S. Grant, *Letters of Ulysses S. Grant to His Father and Youngest Sister, 1857–1878,* edited by Jesse Grant Cramer (New York: G. P. Putnam's Sons, 1912), 27.

178   **"I cannot take an active part"** USG to JRG, November 27, 1861, *Grant Papers,* 3:226–27.

178   **"do not want to be importuned"** USG to Mary Grant, October 25, 1861, *Grant Papers,* 3:76.

179   **"I find myself in a new"** McClellan, *McClellan's Own Story,* 55; George B.

McClellan to Ellen McClellan, July 27, 1861, in George B. McClellan, *The Civil War Papers of George B. McClellan,* edited by Stephen W. Sears (New York: Ticknor & Fields, 1989), 70; Sears, *George B. McClellan,* 44–47.

179 **He graduated** Marszalek, *Commander of All Lincoln's Armies,* 22–23.

179 **Halleck helped frame** Ibid., 76–77, 86–87.

179 **Soldiers dubbed him** Ibid., 1; Stephen E. Ambrose, *Halleck: Lincoln's Chief of Staff* (Baton Rouge: Louisiana State University Press, 1962), 5–6, 47.

179 **"I have entrusted"** George B . McClellan to HWH, November 11, 1861, *Civil War Papers of George B. McClellan,* 130.

180 **"No such person"** USG, General Orders No. 3, November 20, 1861, *Grant Papers,* 3:345n1.

180 **"No matter what"** USG to John Cook, December 25, 1861, *Grant Papers,* 3:343.

180 **"Dr. Henderson"** Leonard F. Ross to USG, December 31, 1861, *Grant Papers,* 3:374n.

180 **"The slave"** Grant's answer was conveyed through his aide William S. Hillyer to Leonard F. Ross, January 5, 1862, *Grant Papers,* 3:373–74.

180 **"My inclination is to whip"** USG to JRG, November 27, 1861, *Grant Papers,* 3:227.

181 **"Can I have authority"** USG to HWH, November 20, 1861, *Grant Papers,* 3:202.

181 **"You will send reports"** HWH to USG, November 21, 1861, *Grant Papers,* 3:202n.

181 **"There is a great deficiency"** USG to HWH, November 21, 1861, *Grant Papers,* 3:207–9.

182 **From that moment** Spencer Tucker, *Andrew Foote: Civil War Admiral on Western Waters* (Annapolis, Md.: Naval Institute Press, 2000), 4–5, 14–15.

182 **"Use your own judgment"** John C. Frémont to Andrew F. Foote, September 16, 1861, *ORN,* ser. 1, 22:335.

182 **"seems to question my judgment"** Andrew H. Foote to Gustavus V. Fox, December 28, 1861, in Robert Means Thompson and Richard Wainwright, eds., *Confidential Correspondence of Gustavus F. Fox, Assistant Secretary of the Navy, 1861–1865,* vol. 2 (New York: printed for the Naval Historical Society by De Vinne Press, 1919), 16, 17. Fox, who resigned from the navy in 1856, offered his services to Lincoln in March 1861 and became the architect of Lincoln's naval plan to resupply Fort Sumter.

182 **"Yes, that's right"** Wilson, *Life of John A. Rawlins,* 67–68.

182 **"I would say"** John A. Rawlins to Elihu B. Washburne, December 30, 1861, in Wilson, *Life of John A. Rawlins,* 68–71.

183 **The last state** Stanley F. Horn, *The Army of Tennessee* (Norman: University of Oklahoma Press, 1941), 434n2.

183 **The ironworks** Benjamin Franklin Cooling, *Forts Henry and Donelson: The Key to the Confederate Heartland* (Knoxville: University of Tennessee Press, 1987), 30; McPherson, *Battle Cry,* 393.

183 **At the end of 1861** Gott, *Where the South Lost the War,* 49, 57.

184 **"Please name as early"** AL to HWH, January 7, 1862, *CWAL,* 5:92.

184 **"Let no one"** HWH to USG, January 6, 1862, *Grant Papers,* 4:4n. Bowling Green was the capital of a Kentucky government-in-exile led by George W. Johnson.

184 **"Be very careful"** Ibid.

184 **"This sloshing"** Emerson, "Grant's Life in the West," *Midland Monthly 8* (May 1898): 413.

184 **"You have permission to visit"** HWH to USG, January 22, 1862, *Grant Papers,* 4:75n2.

184 **"I have now a larger force"** USG to Mary Grant, January 23, 1862, *Grant Papers,* 4:96.

184 **In preparing to meet** Marszalek, *Commander of All Lincoln's Armies*, 42.

185 **An officer present** Emerson, "Grant's Life in the West," 410.

185 **"I was received"** *Personal Memoirs*, 1:287.

185 **"Have we your authority"** Andrew H. Foote to HWH, January 28, 1862, *Grant Papers*, 4:99n.

185 **"I would respectfully suggest"** USG to HWH, January 29, 1862, *Grant Papers*, 4:103.

185 **"the Army and Flotilla"** AL, President's General War Order No. 1, January 27, 1862, *CWAL*, 5:111–12.

185 **Two days later, Halleck received** George B. McClellan to HWH and Don Carlos Buell, January 29, 1862, *OR*, ser. 1, vol. 7, 571.

185 **Beauregard, the hero** A long-running debate has revolved around why Beauregard was sent west. Was it because the leaders of the Confederacy in Richmond were waking up to the necessity of more experienced military leadership in the western theater, or was it a scheme to exile the controversial general who had clashed with Jefferson Davis over the Louisiana general's plan to capture Washington after the Battle of Manassas—only (in his version) to have it vetoed by Davis? See Kenneth P. Williams, *Grant Rises in the West: The First Year, 1861–1862* (Lincoln: University of Nebraska Press, 1997; reprinted from original edition: *Lincoln Finds a General*, vol. 3 [New York: Macmillan, 1952]), 113–15.

185 **The directive from Lincoln** Kenneth Williams, in *Grant Rises in the West: The First Year, 1861–1862*, 188–90, expertly discusses Halleck's decision making.

185 **"Make your preparations"** HWH to USG, January 30, 1862, *Grant Papers*, 4, 104n.

186 **"the reports were unfounded"** Brinton, *Personal Memoirs*, 131.

186 **"then suggested"** Emerson, "Grant's Life in the West," 417.

186 **"I do not want to boast"** USG to JDG, February 4 and February 6, 1862, *Grant Papers*, 4:149, 163.

188 **Johnston continued to fixate** Gott, *Where the South Lost the War*, 74.

188 **"Far as the eye"** Jesse Taylor, "The Defense of Fort Henry," in R. U. Johnston and C. C. Clough Buel, eds., *Battles and Leaders of the Civil War* (New York: Century, 1887–1888), 1:369.

188 **"probably 10,000 men"** USG to JDG, February 5, 1862, *Grant Papers*, 4:153.

188 **Tilghman and Taylor believed** Taylor, "Defense of Fort Henry," 370.

188 **This shot** Gott, *Where the South Lost the War*, 82–83; Cooling, *Forts Henry and Donelson*, 92–93; Tucker, *Andrew Foote*, 140.

189 **"Fort Henry is ours"** USG to HWH, February 6, 1862, *Grant Papers*, 4:158n.

190 **"I am going over"** Richardson, *A Personal History*, 211.

190 **"I felt that 15,000"** *Personal Memoirs*, 1:298.

190 **"deep gloom"** Report of Gideon J. Pillow, February 18, 1862, *OR*, ser. 1, vol. 7:278.

190 **"I take my pen"** USG to Mary Grant, February 9, 1862, *Grant Papers*, 4:179–80.

191 **"I go reluctantly"** Andrew Foote to Gideon Welles, February 11, 1862, *ORN*, ser. 1, vol. 22:550.

191 **"We start this morning"** USG to HWH, February 12, 1862, *OR*, ser. 1, vol. 7, 612; *Grant Papers*, 4:195.

191 **"I do not feel justified"** USG to Andrew Foote, February 10, 1862, *OR*, ser. 1, vol. 7, 600.

191 **From this farmhouse** Gott, *Where the South Lost the War*, 167.

192 **Because he was offered a commission** See Stickles, *Simon Bolivar Buckner*, 6, 12–14, 78, 86–91.

193 **"Last night was very severe"** USG to HWH, February 14, 1862, *Grant Papers*, 4:207.

193   **The half-frozen men**   Gott, *Where the South Lost the War,* 165–66.

193   **The naval commander instructed**   Cooling, *Forts Henry and Donelson,* 153.

193   **As Grant watched**   I express gratitude to Jimmy Jobe, park historian at Fort Donelson, who in June 2011 helped me understand the scene as the ironclads came from behind the bend on the Cumberland and started toward the fort.

193   **The guns at Fort Donelson**   Craig L. Symonds, *The Civil War at Sea* (Santa Barbara, Calif.: Praeger, 2009), 101.

193   **Somehow, Foote managed**   Cooling, *Forts Henry and Donelson,* 153–60; Gott, *Where the South Lost the War,* 177–83.

194   **"The taking of Fort Donelson"**   USG to JDG, February 14, 1862, *Grant Papers,* 4:211.

194   **"We are cut"**   Gott, *Where the South Lost the War,* 211.

194   **"Men fell"**   Lew Wallace, "The Capture of Fort Donelson," in Johnston and Buel, eds., *Battles and Leaders,* 1:417.

195   **"On the honor"**   Nathaniel Cheairs Hughes, Jr., and Roy P. Stonesifer, Jr., *The Life and Wars of Gideon J. Pillow* (Chapel Hill: University of North Carolina Press, 1993), 229.

195   **Grant saw the men talking**   *Personal Memoirs,* 1:307.

195   **"Gentlemen, that road"**   Lew Wallace, *An Autobiography,* vol. 2 (New York: Harper & Brothers, 1906), 412.

196   **Or he could strike**   Gott, *Where the South Lost the War,* outlines these three options, 223–24.

196   **"I will do it"**   Richardson, *A Personal History,* 222.

196   **Smith rallied his troops**   Cooling, *Forts Henry and Donelson,* 184–85.

196   **After intense fighting**   Gott, *Where the South Lost the War,* 226–31.

197   **"For my part"**   Stickles, *Simon Bolivar Buckner,* 158.

197   **Smith took Buckner's request**   Brinton, *Personal Memoirs,* 129.

197   **"Sir: Yours of this date"**   USG to Simon B. Buckner, February 16, 1862, *Grant Papers,* 4:218. Buckner had written Grant: "In consideration of all the circumstances governing the present situation of affairs at this station I propose to the Commanding officer of the Federal forces the appointment of commissioners to agree upon terms of capitulation of the forces under my command, and in that view to suggest an armistice until 12 o'clock today." *Grant Papers,* 4:218n.

198   **"The distribution of the forces"**   Simon B. Buckner to USG, February 16, 1862, *Grant Papers,* 4:218n.

198   **"I thought Pillow"**   Garland, *Grant,* 192; Simon Bolivar Buckner interview, Hamlin Garland Papers.

198   **"If I had been in command"**   Richardson, *A Personal History,* 227.

199   **Unspoken between them**   M. B. Morton, interview with Simon Bolivar Buckner, *Nashville Banner,* December 11, 1909, in Stickles, *Simon Bolivar Buckner,* 173.

199   **"There will be nothing"**   Brinton, *Personal Memoirs,* 133.

Chapter 14. Shiloh

201   **"Who is this man"**   Garland, *Grant,* 193. Garland does not identify the newspaper.

201   **"shook the old walls"**   Benjamin P. Thomas and Harold M. Hyman, *Stanton: The Life and Times of Lincoln's Secretary of War* (New York: Alfred A. Knopf, 1962), 173.

201   **"If the Southerners think"**   *Grant Papers,* 4:272n; Helen Nicolay, *Lincoln's Secretary* (New York: Longmans, Green & Co., 1949), 131–32.

202   **In New York, newsboys**   *New York Tribune* and *Chicago Tribune,* February 18, 1862; Larry J. Daniel, *Shiloh: The Battle That Changed the War* (New York: Simon & Schuster, 1997), 30; Catton, *Grant Moves South,* 179–80.

202   **"The battle was fought"** *New York Times,* February 18, 1862.

202   **no one could "organize" victory** EMS to Charles A. Dana, February 19, 1862, cited in Thomas and Hyman, *Stanton,* 174.

202   **Grant's straightforward directive** EMS to Charles Dana, February 19, 1862, *New York Tribune,* February 20, 1862; Frank A. Flower, *Edwin McMasters Stanton: The Autocrat of Rebellion, Emancipation, and Reconstruction* (Akron, Ohio: Saalfield Publishing, 1905), 129–30.

202   **"woven into songs"** James G. Blaine, *Twenty Years in Congress: From Lincoln to Garfield,* vol. 1 (Norwich, Conn.: Henry Brill, 1884), 356.

202   **"The cigars began"** A. E. Waltrous, "Grant as His Son Saw Him: An Interview with Colonel Frederick D. Grant About His Father," *McClure's Magazine* (May 1894).

203   **With seventeen thousand residents** Cooling, *Forts Henry and Donelson,* 31; William Preston Johnston, *The Life of Gen. Albert Sidney Johnston* (New York: D. Appleton & Co., 1878), 496.

203   **Their bedraggled** Albert Sidney Johnston to William J. Hardee, February 14, 1862, *OR,* ser. 1, vol. 7, 881.

203   **Rumors spread** John M. McKee, "The Evacuation of Nashville," *Annals of the Army of Tennessee* 1, no. 5 (August 1878): 219–29.

203   **"It is my impression"** USG to George W. Cullum, February 21, 1862, *Grant Papers,* 4:257.

203   **"Genl Grant and I believe"** Andrew Foote to George W. Cullum, February 21, 1862, *Grant Papers,* 4:258n1.

203   **"I am disgusted"** Andrew Foote to Caroline Foote, February 23, 1862, *ORN,* ser. 1, 22:626.

204   **"Make Buell, Grant, and Pope"** HWH to George B. McClellan, February 17, 1862, *Grant Papers,* 4:272n.

204   **"Hesitation and delay"** Ibid., February 20, 1862, *OR,* ser. 1, vol. 7, 641.

204   **"Buell at Bowling Green"** George B. McClellan to HWH, February 21, 1862, *OR,* ser. 1, vol. 7, 645.

204   **"There is not a moment"** HWH to EMS, February 23 [21], 1862, *OR,* ser. 1, vol. 7, 655.

204   **"The President"** EMS to HWH, February 22, 1862, *OR,* ser. 1, vol. 7, 652.

204   **"These terrible battles"** USG to JDG, February 24, 1862, *Grant Papers,* 4:284.

204   **"I shall go to Nashville"** USG to George W. Cullum, February 25, 1862, *Grant Papers,* 4:286.

204   **"Dear Friend"** Stephen D. Engle, *Don Carlos Buell: Most Promising of All* (Chapel Hill: University of North Carolina Press, 1999), 45–47; Larry J. Daniel, *Days of Glory: The Army of the Cumberland, 1861–1865* (Baton Rouge: Louisiana State University Press, 2004), 34.

205   **"has the *go* in him"** *Cincinnati Commercial,* November 15, 1861; Engle, *Don Carlos Buell,* 99.

205   **"We hope every day"** Mitchel Ormsby letter to family, February 21, 1862, in F. A. Mitchel, *Ormsby Macknight Mitchel, Astronomer and General* (Boston: Houghton, Mifflin, 1887), 249; Daniel, *Days of Glory,* 69.

205   **"If I could see the necessity"** USG to Don Carlos Buell, February 27, 1862, *Grant Papers,* 4:293–94.

205   **The conversation turned** Don Carlos Buell to George B. McClellan, February 26, 1862, *OR,* ser. 1, vol. 7, 425; Engle, *Don Carlos Buell,* xiii.

205   **"My information was"** *Personal Memoirs,* 1:321.

205   **Separated by** McPherson, *Battle Cry,* 402–3; Johnston, *Life of Gen. Albert Sidney Johnston,* 500–04.

206 **Bragg had recently advised** Grady McWhiney, *Braxton Bragg and Confederate Defeat,* vol. 1 (New York: Columbia University Press, 1969), 28, 199–200; T. Harry Williams, *P. G. T. Beauregard: Napoleon in Gray* (Baton Rouge: Louisiana State University Press, 1955), 47–48.

206 **Bragg urged** McPherson, *Battle Cry,* 404–5.

206 **"You will place"** HWH to USG, March 4, 1862, *Grant Papers,* 4:319n1; *OR,* ser. 1, vol. 10, pt. 2:3.

206 **"I have reported"** USG to HWH, March 5, 1862, *Grant Papers,* 4:318.

206 **Unknown to Grant** George W. Cullum to HWH, March 2, 1862, *OR,* ser. 1, vol. 7, 682; Marszalek, *Commander of All Lincoln's Armies,* 118, 154 (caption of photograph no. 26).

206 **"I have had no communication"** HWH to George B. McClellan, March 3, 1862, *OR,* vol. 7, 679–80; *Grant Papers,* 4:320n1.

207 **"Do not hesitate to arrest him"** George B. McClellan to HWH, March 3, 1862, *OR,* ser. 1, vol. 7, 680; *Grant Papers,* 4:320n1.

207 **"A rumor"** HWH to George B. McClellan, March 4, 1862, *OR,* ser. 1, vol. 7, 682; *Grant Papers,* 4:320n1.

207 **"I have averaged writing"** USG to HWH, March 7, 1862, *Grant Papers,* 4:331.

207 **"If my course"** Ibid.

207 **"You are mistaken"** HWH to USG, March 8, 1862, *Grant Papers,* 4, 335n1.

207 **Years later, Grant learned** *Personal Memoirs,* 1:324–25.

207 **"application to be relieved"** USG to HWH, March 9, 1862, *Grant Papers,* 4:334.

207 **"As soon as these things"** HWH to USG, March 10, 1862, *Grant Papers,* 4:342; *OR,* vol. 10, pt. 2, 27. For a summary of this episode, see Marszalek, *Commander of All Union Armies,* 118–20.

207 **"The Secretary of War desires"** Lorenzo Thomas to HWH, March 10, 1862, *OR,* ser. 1, vol. 7, 683.

208 **"General Grant has made"** HWH to Lorenzo Thomas, March 15, 1862, *OR,* ser. 1, vol. 7, 683–84.

208 **On the same day, Lincoln announced** AL, President's War Order No. 3, March 11, 1862, *CWAL,* 5:155.

208 **"You cannot be relieved"** HWH to USG, March 13, 1862, *Grant Papers,* 4:354–55n.

208 **"I think it exceedingly doubtful"** USG to Charles F. Smith, March 11, 1862, *Grant Papers,* 4:343.

208 **"Grant is a very modest person"** Charles F. Smith to an unidentified person, March 17, 1862, *Grant Papers,* 4:344n.

208 **"I greatly fear"** Charles F. Smith to USG, March 14, 1862, *Grant Papers,* 4:343n.

209 **At the intersection** O. Edward Cunningham, *Shiloh and the Western Campaign of 1862,* edited by Gary D. Joiner and Timothy B. Smith (New York: Savas Beatie, 2007), 86.

209 **Three thousand years** Joshua 18:1.

209 **Although Sherman had received** Charles F. Smith to John A. Rawlins (Grant's aide-de-camp), March 16, 1862, *Grant Papers,* 4:379n1.

209 **"admits of easy defense"** WTS to John A. Rawlins, March 17, 1862, *Grant Papers,* 4:379n1.

210 **A fourth** Williams, *Beauregard,* 124–25; John R. Lundberg, "'I Must Save This Army': Albert Sidney Johnston and the Shiloh Campaign," in Steven E. Woodworth, ed., *The Shiloh Campaign* (Carbondale: Southern Illinois University Press, 2009), 16; Daniel, *Shiloh,* 91.

210 **"There was more enthusiasm"** Cunningham, *Shiloh and the Western Campaign of 1862,* 98–101.

210 **"raw & Green"** WTS to Ellen Ewing Sherman, March 12, 1862, in Brooks D.

Simpson and Jean V. Berlin, eds., *Sherman's Civil War: Selected Correspondence of William T. Sherman* (Chapel Hill: University of North Carolina Press, 1999), 196.

210 **Benjamin M. Prentiss** John A. Rawlins, Special Orders No. 36, March 26, 1862, *OR,* ser. 1, vol. 10, pt. 2, 67.

210 **"If you will give me"** John A. McClernand to AL, March 31, 1862. http://memory /loc.gov/ammem/alhtml/malhome/html.

211 **"The report"** USG to Nathaniel H. McLean, April 21, 1862, *Grant Papers,* 5:63.

211 **"Feeling a little anxious"** USG to Don Carlos Buell, March 19, 1862, *Grant Papers,* 4:393–94.

211 **"By all means"** HWH to USG, March 20, 1862, *Grant Papers,* 4:392n.

211 **They insisted many men** USG to Nathaniel H. McLean, March 30, 1862, *Grant Papers,* 4:447–48.

211 **Grant should have assessed** Arthur Latham Conger, *The Rise of U. S. Grant* (New York: Century, 1931), 226.

211 **"a few days longer"** *Personal Memoirs,* 1:334.

211 **"Time allowed to pass"** Carl von Clausewitz, *On War,* edited by Michael Howard and Peter Paret (Princeton, N.J.: Princeton University Press, 1976), 357. *On War,* a collection of von Clausewitz's writings, was published in 1832, a year after his death.

211 **"a gigantic picnic"** Seymour Dwight Thompson, *Recollections with the Third Iowa Regiment* (Cincinnati: published for the author, 1864), 204. Daniel, *Shiloh,* 109–10.

211 **McClernand set up** William B. Feis, *Grant's Secret Service: The Intelligence War from Belmont to Appomattox* (Lincoln: University of Nebraska Press, 2002), 82–84.

212 **It would take time** Ibid., 88–89.

212 **Chicago and Cincinnati newspapers** James Lee McDonough, *Shiloh—in Hell Before Night* (Knoxville: University of Tennessee Press, 1977), 19.

212 **"a big fight"** USG to JDG, March 29, 1862, *Grant Papers,* 4:443.

212 **"hit Grant, and hit him hard"** George Baylor, "With Gen. A. S. Johnston at Shiloh," *Confederate Veteran* 5 (1897): 609.

212 **"Gentlemen, we shall attack"** William Preston Johnston, "Albert Sidney Johnston at Shiloh," in Johnston and Buel, eds., *Battles and Leaders,* 1:555.

212 **"my horse's feet"** *Personal Memoirs,* 1:335.

213 **"There will be no fight"** Jacob Ammen, older brother of Grant's friend Daniel Ammen, joined the conversation and reported it in his diary. Colonel Jacob Ammen's diary, *OR,* ser. 1, vol. 10, pt. 1, 330–31.

213 **"The enemy is saucy"** WTS to USG, April 5, 1862, *OR,* ser. 1, vol. 10, pt. 2, 93–94.

213 **"I have scarcely"** USG to HWH, April 5, 1862, *Grant Papers,* 5:13–14.

213 **"Tonight we will water"** Johnston, *Life of Gen. Albert Sidney Johnston,* 582.

213 **"I have put you"** Albert Sidney Johnston, "Soldiers of the Army of the Mississippi," April 3, 1862, *OR,* vol. 10, 396–97.

213 **"None of that"** George W. Baylor, an aide to Johnston, recalls this conversation in "With Johnston at Shiloh," *Confederate Veteran* 5 (1897): 610.

215 **"Gentlemen, the ball is in motion"** Statement of William I. Cherry to Lloyd Lewis, June 29, 1939, and, ms. Letter, Mrs. William H. Cherry to the Reverend T. M. Hurst, December 6, 1892, Lloyd Lewis Papers, MSUUSG; Report of John A. Rawlins, *OR,* ser. 1, vol. 10, pt. 1, 184.

215 **As Grant limped** Don Carlos Buell, "Shiloh Reviewed," in Johnston and Buel, eds., *Battles and Leaders,* 1:492.

215 **"Heavy firing"** USG to Don Carlos Buell, April 6, 1862, *Grant Papers,* 5:17.

215 **Hearing this news** Report of John Rawlins, *OR,* ser. 1, vol. 10, pt. 1, 185. Rawlins's official report was written one year later, after many months of controversy about Wallace's actions at Shiloh. Stacy D. Allen, "Lewis Wallace," in Steven E. Woodworth, ed., *Grant's Lieutenants* (Lawrence: University Press of Kansas, 2001), 72.

215 **If at Fort Donelson** British military historian John Keegan makes useful comparisons between European battlefields and the ever-increasing size of the battlefields in the Civil War. John Keegan, *The Mask of Command* (New York: Viking Penguin, 1987), 221.

216 **Already wounded twice** WTS to Ellen Ewing Sherman, April 11, 1862, *Sherman,* 201.

216 **Grant told Sherman** Conger, *Rise of U. S. Grant,* 246.

216 **"maintain that position"** Report of General Benjamin M. Prentiss, *OR,* ser. 1, vol. 10, pt. 1, 278; Stacy D. Allen, "Shiloh! The Campaign and First Day's Battle," *Blue and Gray Magazine,* Civil War Sesquicentennial Edition (2010): 17–18.

216 **"The attack on my forces"** USG to Don Carlos Buell, April 6, 1862, *OR,* ser. 1, vol. 12, pt. 1, 232–33.

216 **Beauregard's battle plan** Daniel, *Shiloh,* 119–20.

216 **"Fill your canteens, boys!"** Fenwick Y. Hedley, *Marching Through Georgia* (Chicago: Donnelley, 1885), 46; McDonough, *Shiloh—in Hell Before Night,* 131.

217 **Instead of driving Union troops** Cunningham, *Shiloh and the Western Campaign of 1862,* 201; McDonough, *Shiloh—in Hell Before Night,* 106–7.

217 **Grant had assumed** Allen, "Lewis Wallace," 74; Lewis Wallace, *Autobiography,* 1:464; Robert E. Morsberger and Katherine M. Morsberger, *Lew Wallace: Militant Romantic* (New York: McGraw-Hill, 1980), 89–93.

217 **As he traveled up** Buell, "Shiloh Revisited," in Johnston and Buel, eds., *Battles and Leaders,* 1:492.

217 **"I have not yet despaired"** Report of John A. Rawlins, *OR,* ser. 1, vol. 10, pt. 1, 186; Engle, *Don Carlos Buell,* 224–25.

217 **"Yes, and I fear seriously"** Roland, *Albert Sidney Johnston,* 336.

217 **The blood** Ibid., 338.

219 **Rising in his stirrups** Steven E. Woodworth, "William H. L. Wallace," in Woodworth, ed., *Grant's Lieutenants,* 40; McDonough, *Shiloh—in Hell before Night,* 185–86. Wallace, unknown to anyone on the Union side, lay seemingly dead but alive within the Confederate lines where someone had covered him with a blanket.

219 **"We this morning attacked"** Report of G. T. Beauregard, April 6, 1962, *OR,* ser. 1, vol. 10, pt. 1, 384.

219 **Having started the day** William C. Davis, *The Battlefields of the Civil War* (Norman: University of Oklahoma Press, 1996), 49.

219 **"Yes. Lick 'em tomorrow, though"** Interview with Sherman in *The Washington Post,* quoted in *Army and Navy Journal* (December 30, 1893) and cited in Catton, *Grant Moves South,* 242 and 512n; Marszalek, *Sherman,* 180; McDonough, *Shiloh—in Hell Before Night,* 183n.

221 **Its blue waters turned** *Sherman,* 179.

221 **Grant rode forward** Keegan, *Mask of Command,* 227–28.

Chapter 15. William Tecumseh Sherman

223 **The battle resulted** *Congressional Globe,* 37th Congress, 2nd sess., vol. 32, pt. 2, 1581.

223 **"ordered a charge"** *New York Herald,* April 10, 1862.

223 **The next day, Lincoln** AL, "Proclamation of Thanksgiving for Victories," April 10, 1862, *CWAL,* 5:185–86.

224 **His 19,500-word story** Royal Cortissoz, *The Life of Whitelaw Reid,* vol. 1 (New York: Charles Scribner's Sons, 1921), 63, 85, 88–89. His pen name derived from a trip to the Northwest, where he picked up many agates in the vicinity of Agate Bay on Lake Superior.

224 **Fresh from the field** Catton, *Grant Moves South,* 253.

224   **Many guns were unloaded** Cortissoz, *Life of Whitelaw Reid,* 1:87.

224   **Some were shot** Ibid. The power of Reid's article lay not only in its length, but in its mastery of details. He wrote as a firsthand witness. Most war correspondents, not expecting a battle at Pittsburg Landing, were covering the fight for Island No. 10 on the Mississippi River. Some of these same reporters ended up writing stories about Shiloh anyway. The practice of "faking" eyewitness accounts by correspondents who never set foot on a particular battlefield accelerated at Shiloh. See J. Cutler Andrews, *The North Reports the Civil War* (Pittsburgh: University of Pittsburgh Press, 1955), 179.

225   **"thoroughly sober"** The portion of Ammen's diary published in the *OR,* ser. 1, vol. 10, pt. 1, 329–37, does not contain his selection for April 8, which is in his diary at the Abraham Lincoln Presidential Library in Springfield. Catton, *Grant Moves South,* 222, 298; Daniel, *Shiloh,* 307.

225   **"court-martialed or shot"** Catton, *Grant Moves South,* 254. Benjamin Stanton was a cousin but not close to Secretary of War Edwin Stanton.

225   **"I suppose"** USG to JDG, April 15, 1862, *Grant Papers,* 5:47.

225   **Hannah found confidence** Ross, *The General's Wife,* 121.

225   **"not at all happy"** Julia Dent Grant, *Personal Memoirs,* 98–99.

225   **"whether any neglect"** EMS to HWH, April 23, 1862, *Grant Papers,* 5:50–51n.

225   **"The said casualties"** HWH to EMS, April 24, 1862, *Grant Papers,* 5:51n.

226   **"appealed to Lincoln"** Alexander K. McClure, *Abraham Lincoln and Men of War-Times* (Philadelphia: Times Publishing, 1892), 179–80. The veracity of McClure's account of Lincoln's words has been questioned. However, credibility is lent to Lincoln's affirmation since McClure arrived not to defend Grant, but rather to urge Lincoln to save himself by abandoning Grant.

226   **The sixth of eleven children** John F. Marszalek, *Sherman: A Soldier's Passion for Order* (Carbondale: Southern Illinois University Press, 1993), 4–5, is the definitive biography of Sherman.

226   **It was Saint William Day** The date and origin of the name William have been debated. See Marszalek, *Sherman,* 9–10.

226   **Tom Ewing** Ibid., 7–8.

226   **"West Point and the regular army"** *New York Times,* September 10, 1885; Marszalek, *Sherman,* 113–14.

227   **In July 1861** Marszalek, *Sherman,* 150–51.

227   **"Answer"** WTS to AL, October 10, 1861, in ibid., 146.

227   **Cincinnati Commercial's headline** *Cincinnati Commercial,* December 11, 1861.

227   **"I feel under many obligations"** USG to WTS, February 19, 1862, *Grant Papers,* 4:248–49; WTS to USG, February 21, 1862, in Marszalek, *Sherman,* 167.

227   **A reporter** Earl S. Miers, *The Web of Victory: Grant at Vicksburg* (New York: Alfred A. Knopf, 1955), 19, 22.

227   **The letter added fuel** *Cincinnati Commercial,* May 6, 1862, *Grant Papers,* 5:79–80n.

227   **"The latter seems"** USG to JDG, May 4, 1862, *Grant Papers,* 5:110.

228   **"I have not an enemy"** USG to JRG, September 17, 1862, *Grant Papers,* 6:61–62.

228   **"the hue & cry"** WTS to Ellen Ewing Sherman, April 24, 1862, in Marszalek, *Sherman,* 209.

228   **"I am not surprised"** WTS to Lt. Gov. B. Stanton, June 10, 1862, in Marszalek, *Sherman,* 241–44. For a summary of the newspaper controversy, see John F. Marszalek, Jr., "William T. Sherman and the Verbal Battle of Shiloh," *Northwest Ohio Quarterly* 42, no. 4 (Fall 1970): 78–85.

228   **"He is an example"** Catton, *Grant Moves South,* 260.

228   **"You have interested yourself"** USG to Elihu B. Washburne, May 14, 1862, *Grant Papers,* 5:119.

228 **"Avoid another battle"** HWH to USG, April 9, 1862, *Grant Papers,* 5:20n.

228 **"Our condition is horrible"** Braxton Bragg to G. T. Beauregard, April 8, 1862, *OR,* ser. 1, vol. 10, pt. 2, 398.

229 **Halleck now commanded** Some accounts list the number of troops as high as 120,000, but others suggest the actual number was 108,500. See Daniel, *Shiloh,* 309, 380n18.

229 **"I can bear"** USG to Mrs. Charles F. Smith, April 26, 1862, *Grant Papers,* 5:83–84.

229 **Halleck placed Grant second** C. Kelton, Special Orders No. 35, April 30, 1862, *Grant Papers,* 5:105n.

229 **"Genl Halleck intended"** Charles Tompkins diary, entry May 5, 1862, Charles Tompkins Papers, Duke University, in Stephen D. Engle, *Struggle for the Heartland: The Campaigns from Fort Henry to Corinth* (Lincoln: University of Nebraska Press, 2001), 168.

229 **"I thought if he would move"** *Personal Memoirs,* 1:379.

229 **"I was silenced"** Ibid.

229 **"I was little more"** Ibid., 1:377.

229 **"I believe it is generally understood"** USG to HWH, May 11, 1862, *Grant Papers,* 5:114.

230 **"I am very much surprised"** Ibid., May 12, 1862, *Grant Papers,* 5:115n.

230 **"The enemy is re-enforcing"** John Pope to HWH, May 30, 1862, *OR,* ser. 1, vol. 10, pt. 2, 225.

230 **Empty trains** Williams, *Beauregard,* 154, has a superb description of the elaborate hoax.

230 **"Halleck outwitted"** Engle, *Struggle for the Heartland,* 183.

230 **"I found him seated"** William Tecumseh Sherman, *Memoirs of Gen. William T. Sherman,* vol. 1 (New York: Charles L. Webster & Co., 1890), 283.

230 **"I inquired if it were true"** Miers, *Web of Victory,* 22.

231 **"If he went away"** Sherman, *Memoirs,* 283–84; Marszalek, *Sherman,* 183.

231 **Several days later** Sherman, *Memoirs,* 383–84.

231 **Halleck issued** C. Kelton, Special Field Orders No. 90, June 10, 1862, *Grant Papers,* 5:143n.

231 **"The major object"** HWH to John Pope, June 4, 1862, *OR,* ser. 1, vol. 10, pt. 2, 237.

231 **Ulys invited Julia** USG to JDG, June 12, 1862, *Grant Papers,* 5:142.

231 **"Affairs in this city"** USG to HWH, June 24, 1862, *Grant Papers,* 5:149–50.

231 **Goods shipped** Charles Bracelen Flood, *Grant and Sherman: The Friendship That Won the Civil War* (New York: Farrar, Straus and Giroux, 2005), 134.

231 **"Spies and members"** USG to HWH, June 27, 1862, *Grant Papers,* 5:165.

232 **"You can compel"** William S. Hillyer to Stephen A. Hurlbut, June 24, 1862, *Personal Memoirs,* 5:150n.

232 **"Mamma, who told them"** Julia Dent Grant, *Personal Memoirs,* 101.

232 **"wherever loss"** *Personal Memoirs,* 1:390; USG, General Orders No. 60, July 3, 1862, *Grant Papers,* 5:190.

232 **"constant communication"** USG, Special Orders No. 14 [issued by William S. Hillyer], June 10, 1862, *Grant Papers,* 5:192n; Joseph H. Parks, "A Confederate Trade Center Under Federal Occupation: Memphis, 1862 to 1865," *Journal of Southern History* 7, no. 3 (August 1941): 293.

232 **"cautious and weak"** McPherson, *Battle Cry,* 462; Foote, *Civil War,* 1:465.

232–33 **Having removed McClellan** Marszalek, *Commander of All Lincoln's Armies,* 189; James M. McPherson, *Tried by War: Abraham Lincoln as Commander in Chief* (New York: Penguin Press, 2008), 111–12.

233 **"You will immediately repair"** HWH to USG, July 11, 1862, *Grant Papers,* 5:207n.

233 **"Am I to repair alone"** USG to HWH, July 11, 1862, *Grant Papers,* 5:207n.

233 **"This place"** HWH to USG, July 11, 1862, *Grant Papers*, 5:207n.

233 **"very uncommunicative"** *Personal Memoirs*, 1:393.

233 **But on July 17** USG, General Orders No. 62, July 17, 1862, *Grant Papers*, 5:210.

233 **"I was put"** *Personal Memoirs*, 1:394–95.

233 **"It is very desirable"** HWH to USG, August 2, 1862, *Grant Papers*, 5:244n.

234 **"persons of African descent"** *U.S. Statutes at Large*, vol. 12 (1855–1873) (Boston: Little, Brown & Co., 1863), 597–600.

234 **"engage in any rebellion"** Ibid., 589–92.

234 **"The administration has come up"** Elihu B. Washburne to USG, July 25, 1862, *Grant Papers*, 5:226n.

234 **"I have no hobby"** USG to JRG, August 3, 1862, *Grant Papers*, 5:263–64.

234 **"the employment of such persons"** USG, General Orders No. 72, August 11, 1862, *Grant Papers*, 5:273–74n.

234–35 **"growing oppressive"** USG to Mary Grant, August 19, 1862, *Grant Papers*, 5:310–11.

235 **"Guerrillas are hovering"** Ibid.

235 **"Many citizens"** USG to HWH, August 9, 1862, *Grant Papers*, 5:278.

235 **"Hereafter no Passes"** USG, General Orders No. 65, July 28, 1862, *Grant Papers*, 5:247n.

235 **"I am decidedly in favor"** USG to HWH, July 28, 1862, *Grant Papers*, 5:243.

236 **"We cannot carry on"** WTS to John A. Rawlins, July 30, 1862, *Grant Papers*, 5:240n; McPherson, *Battle Cry*, 620–22.

236 **"Examine the baggage"** USG to Isaac Quinby, July 26, 1862, *Grant Papers*, 5:238.

236 **"whose love of gain"** John A. Rawlins, General Orders No. 64, July 25, 1862, *Grant Papers*, 5:238–239n.

236 **"First, a class"** USG to Salmon P. Chase, July 31, 1862, *Grant Papers*, 5:255–56.

237 **"I have ordered two more Divisions"** USG to Don Carlos Buell, August 12, 1862, *Grant Papers*, 5:288; USG to HWH, August 14, 1862, *Grant Papers*, 5:292.

237 **"With all the vigilance"** USG to HWH, September 10, 1862, *Grant Papers*, 6:31.

237 **he "would have found us"** USG to JDG, September 14, 1862, *Grant Papers*, 6:43.

237 **With orders to join** Peter Cozzens, *The Darkest Days of the War: The Battles of Iuka and Corinth* (Chapel Hill: University of North Carolina Press, 1997), 55–56.

237 **"to be in readiness"** For the multiple exchange of telegrams among Grant, Rosecrans, and Ord, see *Grant Papers*, 6:65–66n; *Personal Memoirs*, 1:411.

237 **Grant's plan** Lesley J. Gordon, "The Failed Relationship of William S. Rosecrans and Grant," in Woodworth, ed., *Grant's Lieutenants*, 115–16.

237 **"Entire rebel army"** John C. Van Duzer to USG, September 18, 1862, *Grant Papers*, 6:66n.

237 **Grant's aide** William S. Hillyer to Edward O. C. Ord, September 18, 1862, *Grant Papers*, 6:66n.

237 **"McClellan has driven"** USG to William S. Rosecrans, September 18, 1862, *Grant Papers*, 6:66n.

238 **Grant would learn** James M. McPherson, *Crossroads of Freedom: Antietam* (New York: Oxford University Press, 2002).

238 **"You must attack"** William M. Lamers, *The Edge of Glory: A Biography of General William S. Rosecrans, U.S.A.* (New York: Harcourt, Brace & World, 1961), 113.

238 **"Why did you not attack"** William S. Rosecrans to USG, September 20, 1862, *OR*, ser. 1, vol. 17, pt. 1, 70.

238 **"We didn't hear"** E.O.C. Ord to William S. Rosecrans, September 20, 1862, *OR*, ser. 1, vol. 17, pt. 1, 70.

238 **"I cannot speak too highly"** USG to HWH, September 20, 1862, *Grant Papers*, 6:71–72.

238 **"either to reinforce"** John V. D. Du Bois, September 20, 1862, *Grant Papers*, 6:74.

238 **Van Dorn, who had vied** Robert G. Hartje, *Van Dorn: The Life and Times of a Confederate General* (Nashville: Vanderbilt University Press, 1967), 6–15.

238 **As the light faded** Cozzens, *Darkest Days of the War*, 223.

239 **"If the enemy"** USG to William S. Rosecrans, October 4, 1862, *Grant Papers*, 6:114.

239 **"Push the enemy"** Ibid., October 5, 1862, *Grant Papers*, 6:123.

239 **"I cannot see how"** USG to HWH, October 5, 1862, *Grant Papers*, 6:118.

239 **"We can do nothing"** USG to William S. Rosecrans, October 7, 1862, *Grant Papers*, 6:131.

239 **"I must deeply dissent"** William S. Rosecrans to USG, October 7, 1862, *Grant Papers*, 6:132n.

239 **"with great caution"** USG to William S. Rosecrans, October 9, 1862, *Grant Papers*, 6:142.

239 **Perhaps this could have** For a treatment of this divide, see Gordon, "The Failed Relationship of William S. Rosecrans and Grant," in Woodward, ed., *Grant's Lieutenants*, 118–20.

240 **"all persons held as slaves"** AL, "Preliminary Emancipation Proclamation," September 22, 1862, *CWAL*, 5:433–34.

240 **On October 25, Halleck expanded** USG, General Orders No. 1, October 25, 1862, *Grant Papers*, 6:186.

241 **"With small reinforcements"** USG to HWH, October 26, 1862, *Grant Papers*, 6:199–200.

Chapter 16. "More Than Forty Richmonds"

243 **"commenced a movement"** USG to HWH, November 2, 1862, *Grant Papers*, 6:243.

243 **"I approve of your plan"** Ibid., note.

244 **Many thought battling** Letter of Luther H. Cowan, quoted in Steven E. Woodworth, *Nothing but Victory: The Army of Tennessee, 1861–1865* (New York: Alfred A. Knopf, 2005), 243.

244 **Democrats picked up** McPherson, *Battle Cry*, 561–62.

244 **"When the results"** Seymour D. Thompson, *Recollections with the Third Iowa Regiment* (Cincinnati: published for the author, 1864), 140.

244 **"I don't trust"** David D. Porter to Gustavus Fox, November 12, 1862, in *Confidential Correspondence of Gustavus Vasa Fox*, vol. 2, edited by Robert Means Thompson and Richard Wainwright (New York: printed for the Naval Historical Society by DeVinne Press, c. 1920), 150.

244 **"has stirring and positive"** Howard K. Beale and Alan W. Brownsword, eds., *Diary of Gideon Welles, Secretary of the Navy Under Lincoln and Johnson*, vol. 1: *1861–1864* (New York: W. W. Norton & Co., 1960), October 1, 1862, 157; Chester G. Hearn, *Admiral David Dixon Porter* (Annapolis, Md.: Naval Institute Press, 1996), 141–42.

245 **"a travel-worn person"** David Dixon Porter, *Incidents and Anecdotes of the Civil War* (New York: D. Appleton & Co., 1885), 125. Porter describes meeting Grant in Cairo in December in his journal, but the meeting surely took place earlier; Richard S. West, Jr., *The Second Admiral: A Life of David Dixon Porter, 1813–1891* (New York: Coward-McCann, 1937), 31; Craig L. Symonds, *Lincoln and His Admirals* (New York: Oxford University Press, 2008), 197.

245 **"When can you move"** Porter, *Incidents and Anecdotes of the Civil War*, 125.

245 **"I find some Regts"** James M. Tuttle to USG, November 9, 1862, *Grant Papers*, 6:279n.

245 **"Any commander"** *Chicago Tribune,* September 3, 1862; Victor Hicken, *Illinois in the Civil War* (Urbana: University of Illinois Press, 1966), 86–87.

245 **"brave and capable"** Salmon P. Chase diary, entry September 27, 1862, in David Donald, ed., *Inside Lincoln's Cabinet: The Civil War Diaries of Salmon P. Chase* (New York: Longmans, Green & Co., 1954), 161.

245 **On October 21, Stanton** EMS to John A. McClernand, *OR,* ser. 1, vol. 17, pt. 2, 282.

245 **"I add that I feel"** AL to John A. McClernand, October 20, 1862, *CWAL,* 5:468–69.

246 **Stanton may have initially** McPherson, *Tried by War,* 152.

246 **"Gen. McClernand has inspired"** *New York Times,* October 30, 1862.

246 **"Am I to understand"** USG to HWH, November 10, 1862, *Grant Papers,* 6:288.

246 **"You have command"** HWH to USG, November 11, 1862, *Grant Papers,* 6:288n.

246 **"Citizens south"** USG to HWH, November 15, 1862, *Grant Papers,* 6:315.

246 **They would gather** Catton, *Grant Moves South,* 357.

246 **The army** *Personal Memoirs,* 1:424.

246 **He authorized Chaplain** John A. Rawlins, Special Orders No. 17, November 13, 1862, *Grant Papers,* 6:315–16n.

247 **Upon his graduation in 1861** Ethel Osgood Mason, "John Eaton: A Biographical Sketch," in John Eaton, *Grant, Lincoln, and the Freedmen* (New York: Longmans, Green & Co., 1907), xiii.

247 **"moderation and simplicity"** Ibid., 10.

247 **Eaton accepted** Ibid., 11.

247 **Union soldiers demolished** Michael B. Ballard, *Vicksburg: The Campaign That Opened the Mississippi* (Chapel Hill: University of North Carolina Press, 2004), 69, 83.

247 **"Houses have been plundered"** USG, Special Field Orders No. 1, November 7, 1862, *Grant Papers,* 6:266–67.

248 **Julia joined him** Hubert H. McAlexander, *A Southern Tapestry: Marshall County, Mississippi, 1835–2000* (Virginia Beach, Va.: Donning, 2000), 66. The mansion was built by Harvey Washington Walter, the lawyer who spearheaded building the Mississippi Central Railroad.

248 **Sherman would command** USG to HWH, December 8, 1862, *Grant Papers,* 6:403.

248 **Grant's intent** *Personal Memoirs,* 1:431. Knowing McClernand was still in Illinois, and concerned that he might form an army and come south, Grant ordered Sherman to start his forces south immediately.

248 **Married to a Virginian** John C. Pemberton, *Pemberton: Defender of Vicksburg* (Chapel Hill: University of North Carolina Press, 1942), 9, 20–21.

248 **He entrenched** Michael B. Ballard, *Pemberton: A Biography* (Jackson: University Press of Mississippi, 1991), 115–16.

248 **Forrest's cavalry** Robert Selph Henry, *First with the Most: Nathan Bedford Forrest* (Indianapolis: Bobbs-Merrill, 1944), 13; Jerry O'Neil Potter, "The First West Tennessee Raid of General Nathan Bedford Forrest," *West Tennessee Historical Society Papers* 28 (1974), 58.

249 **He wrote Porter** USG to David D. Porter, December 18, 1862, *OR,* ser. 1, vol. 17, pt. 2, 426.

249 **"I rather suspect"** WTS to Willis A. Gorman, December 17, 1862, *OR,* ser. 1, vol. 17, pt. 2, 424.

249 **On the morning** Ballard, *Vicksburg,* 122.

250 **"I don't think the Yanks"** McAlexander, *A Southern Tapestry: Marshall County, Mississippi, 1835–2000,* 66–67.

250 **The truth** Julia Dent Grant, *Personal Memoirs,* 107.

250 **Of immediate concern** Ballard, *Vicksburg,* 129–30.

250 **Pemberton was entertaining Davis** William L. Shea and Terrence J. Winschel,

Vicksburg Is the Key: The Struggle for the Mississippi River (Lincoln: University of Nebraska Press, 2003), 48–51; Ballard, *Pemberton,* 128; William J. Cooper, Jr., *Jefferson Davis, American* (New York: Alfred A. Knopf, 2000), 416–19; William C. Davis, *Jefferson Davis: The Man and His Hour* (New York: HarperCollins, 1991), 484–86.

250 **Sherman's forces** Kenneth P. Williams, *Grant Rises in the West: From Iuka to Vicksburg, 1862–1863* (Lincoln: University of Nebraska Press, 1997; reprinted from original edition: *Lincoln Finds a General,* vol. 4 [New York: Macmillan, 1956]), 215; Marszalek, *Sherman,* 206–07; Ballard, *Vicksburg,* 146.

251 **"I assume all responsibility"** WTS to Hdqrs. Right Wing, Army of the Tennessee, January 3, 1863, *OR,* ser. 1, vol. 17, pt. 1, 608.

251 **"I think no more"** HWH to USG, December 27, 1862, *Grant Papers,* 7:83n.

251 **"I was amazed"** *Personal Memoirs,* 1:435.

251 **"I am extended"** USG to Mary Grant, December 15, 1862, *Grant Papers,* 7:43–44.

251 **"I found so many"** WTS to John A. Rawlins, July 30, 1862, *Grant Papers,* 5:240n; *OR,* ser. 1, vol. 17, pt. 2, 140–41.

251 **Although non-Jews participated** *New York Tribune,* November 5, 1862; *Corinth War Eagle,* August 7, 1862; *Grant Papers,* 7:51–52n.

251 **"The Jews, as a class"** USG, General Orders No. 11, December 17, 1862, *Grant Papers,* 7:50.

252 **The *Memphis Daily Bulletin*** *Memphis Daily Bulletin,* January 6, 1863, in Jonathan D. Sarna, *When Grant Expelled the Jews* (New York: Schocken, 2012), 11.

252 **"If such an order"** HWH to USG, January 4, 1863, *Grant Papers,* 7:53n.

252 **When Congress** *Grant Papers,* 7:55n; *Congressional Globe,* 37th Congress, 3rd sess., 184, 222, 245–46. A resolution to censure Grant was tabled in the House by a close vote of 56 to 53 and in the Senate by a lopsided vote of 30 to 7.

252 **"The President has no objection"** HWH to USG, January 21, 1863, *Grant Papers,* 7:54n.

252 **Grant turned down** Sylvanus Cadwallader, *My Four Years with Grant,* 48–49, ALPLM. Cadwallader's manuscript includes chapters not published in his *Three Years with Grant,* edited by Benjamin P. Thomas (New York: Alfred A. Knopf, 1955). Detailed information about the plan did not become public until more than a year later, when Jesse Grant sued the Macks. On May 17, 1864, the *Cincinnati Enquirer,* in reporting on the lawsuit, attempted to connect the dots: "Was it in view of this arrangement between Jesse R. Grant and the Mack Brothers . . . that General Grant issued his inhuman order of December 17, 1862?" See the *Cincinnati Enquirer* article and the summation of the case in *The Democratic Speaker's Hand-Book,* compiled by Matthew Carey, Jr. (Cincinnati: Miami Print and Publishing Company, 1868), 42.

253 **"to form a part"** USG to John A. McClernand, December 18, 1862, *Grant Papers,* 7:61; Richard L. Kiper, *Major General John Alexander McClernand: Politician in Uniform* (Kent, Ohio: Kent State University Press, 1999), 119.

253 **"I regret that the expectation"** John A. McClernand to USG, December 28, 1862, *Grant Papers,* 7:136n.

253 **The next evening** Kiper, *McClernand,* 158.

253 **"Since General Sherman"** USG to John A. McClernand, January 10, 1863, *Grant Papers,* 7:207.

253 **"This expedition must not fail"** Ibid.

253 **They won a battle** Marszalek, *Sherman,* 209.

254 **"Genl. McClernand has . . . gone"** USG to HWH, January 11, 1863, *Grant Papers,* 7:209.

254 **"I do not approve"** USG to John A. McClernand, January 11, 1863, *Grant Papers,* 7:210. Two days later, he told McClernand he did not send the January 11 letter and

blamed the lack of ability to deliver it [USG to John A. McClernand, January 13, 1863, *Grant Papers,* 7:218–19].

254 **"You are hereby"** HWH to USG, January 12, 1863, *OR,* ser. 1, vol. 17, pt. 2, 555.

254 **"It is my present intention"** USG to James B. McPherson, January 13, 1863, *Grant Papers,* 7:220.

254 **Nine earthen forts** Ballard, *Vicksburg,* 1–4, 168–69, 199, 202–03; Shea and Winschel, *Vicksburg Is the Key,* 37.

254 **"I have to state"** Ballard, *Vicksburg,* 33; Shea and Winschel, *Vicksburg Is the Key,* 20–23.

254 **In response** Ballard, *Vicksburg,* 48–61.

255 **"As it is my intention"** USG to HWH, January 20, 1863, *Grant Papers,* 7:233–35.

255 **With a canal** Grant knew that General Thomas Williams had attempted to build such a canal the previous summer as part of the Farragut naval operation; he also knew the effort failed.

255 **Manning picks** Ballard, *Vicksburg,* 157–58, 172; Shea and Winschel, *Vicksburg Is the Key,* 63.

255 **"Direct your attention"** HWH to USG, January 25, 1863, *Grant Papers,* 7:252n.

255 **It did not take** Ballard, *Vicksburg,* 173–74; Shea and Winschel, *Vicksburg Is the Key,* 63–64.

255 **Porter's boats** Williams, *Grant Rises in the West: From Iuka to Vicksburg,* 319–21; Ballard, *Vicksburg,* 174–83.

256 **Porter, covering the hulls** Ballard, *Vicksburg,* 184–88; Shea and Winschel, *Vicksburg Is the Key,* 72–75.

256 **Although Grant's attempts** Smith, *Grant,* 229.

256 **"I let the work"** *Personal Memoirs,* 1:449.

256 **"The eyes and hopes"** HWH to USG, March 20, 1863, *Grant Papers,* 7:401n.

256 **"And I further declare"** AL, "Emancipation Proclamation," January 1, 1863, *CWAL,* 6:30.

257 **The regular army** McPherson, *Battle Cry,* 563.

258 **The enrollment of blacks** HWH to USG, March 30, 1863, *Grant Papers,* 8:93–94n.

258 **"Whatever may be"** Ibid.; James Oakes, in *Freedom National: The Destruction of Slavery in the United States, 1861–1865* (New York: W. W. Norton & Co., 2013), observes that early in the Civil War Grant "did not believe he had any authority to make policy on slavery, and so his treatment of fugitives moved with the movement of his superiors" (184).

258 **"a great many negroes"** Frederick Steele to USG, April 10, 1863, *Grant Papers,* 8:49–50n; Patricia J. Palmer, *Frederick Steele: Forgotten General* (Palo Alto, Calif.: Stanford University Libraries, 1971), 6.

258 **"Rebellion has assumed"** USG to Frederick Steele, April 11, 1863, *Grant Papers,* 8:49.

258 **"This army"** Simpson, *Grant,* 187.

259 **Lincoln had made it** Charles A. Dana, *Recollections of the Civil War* (New York: D. Appleton & Co., 1898), 20–21; James H. Wilson, *The Life of Charles A. Dana* (New York: Harper, 1907), 2–11, 200–03; Thomas and Hyman, *Stanton,* 267.

259 **"to show me"** Dana, *Recollections of the Civil War,* 30.

259 **Stanton trusted Dana's** Ibid., 61.

259 **"All Grant's schemes"** Hunt, *Israel, Elihu and Cadwallader Washburn,* 341.

259 **"would be attended"** USG to to David D. Porter, April 2, 1863, *Grant Papers,* 8:3.

260 **"in contemplation"** *Personal Memoirs,* 1:460–61.

260 **Sherman strongly opposed** WTS to John Rawlins, *Grant Papers,* 8:13–14n4.

260 **"it would discourage"** *Personal Memoirs,* 1:543.

260 **"McClernand is a dirty dog"** WTS to John Sherman, April 3, 1863, *Sherman,* 439.

260 **"I am ready"** DDP to USG, March 29, 1863, *OR*, ser. 1, vol. 24, pt. 3, 152.

260 **Porter meant** Edwin C. Bearss, *The Campaign for Vicksburg*, vol. 2: *Grant Strikes a Fatal Blow* (Dayton, Ohio: Morningside, 1986), 53–54.

260 **"I think most"** John C. Pemberton to Samuel Cooper, *OR*, ser. 1, vol. 24, pt. 3, 733.

261 **"I am sending troops"** John C. Pemberton to Simon B. Buckner, *OR*, ser. 1, vol. 24, pt. 3, 745.

261 **Responding to a request** Shea and Winschel, *Vicksburg Is the Key*, 95.

261 **They fastened coal** West, *The Second Admiral*, 220–21; Hearn, *Admiral David Dixon Porter*, 208–10.

261 **"so many phantom vessels"** Porter, *Incidents and Anecdotes of the Civil War*, 175.

262 **"The sight was magnificent"** *Personal Memoirs*, 1:464.

263 **"Grierson knocked"** USG to HWH, May 3, 1863, *Grant Papers*, 8:144.

263 **"My father made one"** Frederick Grant, "A Boy's Experience at Vicksburg," *Military Order of the Loyal Legion of the United States*, vol. 3 (New York: G. P. Putnam's Sons, 1907), 88.

263 **"I want no faltering"** Ira Blanchard, *I Marched with Sherman: Civil War Memoirs of the Twentieth Illinois* (San Francisco: Haff, 1992), 82; *Personal Memoirs*, 1:471.

264 **"The effect of a heavy demonstration"** USG to WTS, April 27, 1863, *Grant Papers*, 8:130.

264 **"The troops will all understand"** WTS to USG, April 28, 1863, *Grant Papers*, 8:130n.

264 **"My impressions are"** USG to WTS, April 24, 1863, *Grant Papers*, 8:117.

265 **"It is my desire"** USG to John A. McClernand, April 12, 1863, *Grant Papers*, 8:56.

265 **"I am sorry to report"** Charles A. Dana to EMS, April 25, 1863, *OR*, ser. 1, vol. 24, 80.

265 **"was planning to carry"** Dana, *Recollections of the Civil War*, 40.

265 **"to embark"** Charles A. Dana to EMS, April 27, 1863, *OR*, ser. 1, vol. 24, 80.

265 **By the following morning** Ibid., April 29, 1863, *OR*, ser. 1, vol. 24, 81. This is our only source for the story.

265 **"The sight was grand, terrible"** George Crooke, *The Twenty-first Regiment of Iowa Volunteer Infantry* (Milwaukee: King, Fowle, 1891), 53–54; Ballard, *Vicksburg*, 218.

265 **After five hours** Bearss, *Campaign for Vicksburg*, 2:307–14.

265 **"The sight"** *Personal Memoirs*, 1:476.

266 **He learned from this** USG to HWH, July 6, 1863, *OR*, ser. 1, vol. 24, pt. 1, 48.

Chapter 17. Vicksburg

267 **On the same morning** Williams, *Grant Rises in the West: From Iuka to Vicksburg*, 4:344.

267 **In the middle** *History of the Forty-sixth Regiment Indiana Volunteer Infantry: September 1861–September 1865* (Logansport, Ind.: Wilson, Humphreys, 1888), 56.

267 **"I felt a degree of relief"** *Personal Memoirs*, 1:480–81.

269 **Grant wanted to neutralize** Terrence J. Winschel, *Triumph and Defeat: The Vicksburg Campaign*, vol. 2 (New York: Savas Beatie, 2006), 1–2.

269 **Everything stopped** Kiper, *McClernand*, 221.

269 **"standing on the edge"** *Personal Memoirs*, 1:483.

269 **"too beautiful to burn"** Ballard, *Vicksburg*, 241; Winschel, *Triumph and Defeat*, 2:2.

269 **"The army is in the finest"** USG to HWH, May 3, 1863, *Grant Papers*, 8:147.

270 **"I am afraid Grant"** Elihu B. Washburne to AL, May 1, 1863, ALPLC.

270   **He expressed gratitude** *Personal Memoirs,* 1:490.

270   **In response** James G. Hollandsworth, Jr., *Pretense of Glory: The Life of General Nathaniel P. Banks* (Baton Rouge: Louisiana State University Press, 1998), 118–20.

270   **"The southern papers"** USG to HWH, May 3, 1863, *Grant Papers,* 8:148.

270   **He could not call upon Van Dorn** Hartje, *Van Dorn,* 307–27.

270   **Pemberton's caution** Ballard, *Pemberton,* 141–47.

272   **"the road to Vicksburg"** USG to WTS, May 3, 1863, *Grant Papers,* 8:151–52.

272   **"I feel proud"** USG to JDG, May 3, 1863, *Grant Papers,* 8:155.

272   **"Do the Richmond papers"** AL to John A. Dix, May 11, 1863, *CWAL,* 6:210.

272   **Spring green grass** Warren Grabau, *Ninety-eight Days: A Geographer's View of the Vicksburg Campaign* (Knoxville: University of Tennessee Press, 2000), 209–10.

273   **"We must fight"** USG to James B. McPherson, May 11, 1863, *Grant Papers,* 8:200.

273   **"You may not hear"** USG to HWH, May 11, 1863, *Grant Papers,* 8:196.

273   **"Water scarce"** W. B. Halsey diary, entry May 11, 1863, cited in Shea and Winschel, *Vicksburg Is the Key,* 120.

273   **If Pemberton remained unsure** Feis, *Grant's Secret Service,* 160.

273   **While Union troops feasted** Osborn H. Oldroyd, *A Soldier's Story* (Springfield, Ill.: published for the author, 1885), 18–19; Bearss, *Campaign for Vicksburg,* 2:490–510.

274   **But it was a risk** *Personal Memoirs,* 1:499–500.

274   **"I am too late"** Joseph T. Glatthaar, *Partners in Command: The Relationships Between Leaders in the Civil War* (New York: Free Press, 1994), 123.

274   **His Fifty-ninth Indiana** Bearss, *Campaign for Vicksburg,* 2:536–46; Frederick Grant, "A Boy's Experience at Vicksburg," 92–93.

275   **"Time is all-important"** Joseph E. Johnston to John C. Pemberton, May 13, 1863, *Grant Papers,* 8:214n; *OR,* ser. 1, vol. 24, pt. 1, 261.

275   **"General Grant has full"** EMS to Charles A. Dana, May 5, 1863, *OR,* vol. 24, pt. 1, 84; Thomas and Hyman, *Stanton,* 268.

276   **His three division commanders** Ballard, *Pemberton,* 154–56.

276   **William Loring** Ballard, *Vicksburg,* 283–84; Timothy B. Smith, *Champion Hill: Decisive Battle for Vicksburg* (New York: Savas Beatie, 2006), 290–91.

276   **They estimated** USG to John C. Kelton, July 6, 1863, *Grant Papers,* 8:497.

276   **"It is important"** USG to WTS, May 16, 1863, *Grant Papers,* 8:227–28.

276   **"Our whole force"** USG to JAM, May 16, 1863, *Grant Papers,* 8:224.

276   **"secure a prompt concentration"** USG to James B. McPherson, May 16, 1863, *Grant Papers,* 8:226. The hill was higher in 1863 than today owing to gravel operations during the 1930s.

276   **While Pemberton's** USG to WTS, May 16, 1863, *Grant Papers,* 8:227–28.

277   **Matilda, hearing reports** Smith, *Champion Hill,* 127–33.

277   **Hovey, orphaned** Alvin P. Hovey, report, May 25, 1863, *OR,* ser. 1, vol. 24, pt. 2, 41.

277   **The enemy consisted** Smith, *Champion Hill,* 165–69.

277   **"Shall I hold"** JAM to USG, May 16, 1863, *Grant Papers,* 8:225n.

277   **"as expeditiously as possible"** USG to JAM, May 16, 1863, *Grant Papers,* 8:225.

277   **For the next several minutes** Smith, *Champion Hill,* 192–206.

277   **"As soon as your command"** USG to JAM, May 16, 1863, *Grant Papers,* 8:225–26n.

278   **"I sent several messages"** USG to John C. Kelton, [July 6, 1863], *Grant Papers,* 8:499; Bearss, *Campaign for Vicksburg,* 2:593.

278   **Francis M. Cockerell** Winschel, *Triumph and Defeat,* 104–06; Smith, *Champion Hill,* 235–40.

278   **"Where can McClernand be?"** John B. Sanborn, *The Crisis at Champion's Hill* (St. Paul, Minn.: n.p., 1903), 13.

278 **Assisted by Hovey** Ballard, *Vicksburg,* 299–302; Smith, *Champion Hill,* 243–47, 282–85.

278 **"To-day proved"** John A. Leavy diary, entry May 16, 1863, Letters and Diaries Files, Vicksburg National Military Park, in Shea and Winschel, *Vicksburg Is the Key,* 137.

278 **"I am of the opinion"** USG to WTS, May 16, 1863, *Grant Papers,* 8:228.

278 **"I shall never forget"** "A Woman's Diary of the Siege of Vicksburg," *Century Magazine* (September 1885): 771. The diary was given to southern writer George Washington Cable, who stated, "The name of the writer is withheld at her own request."

279 **"I hope never to witness"** Emma Balfour diary, entry May 17, 1863, Gordon A. Cotton, *Like a Hideous Nightmare: Vicksburg Women Remember the Horrors of the Civil War* (Vicksburg, Miss.: The Print Shop, 2009), 39.

279 **"I am killed!"** Frederick Grant, "A Boy's Experience at Vicksburg," 95.

279 **"for a general charge"** USG, Special Field Orders No. 134, May 19, 1863, *Grant Papers,* 8:237.

279 **"securing more advanced"** *Personal Memoirs,* 1:529.

279 **His losses counted** Ballard, *Vicksburg,* 332.

280 **"This watch"** Oldroyd, *A Soldier's Story of the Siege of Vicksburg,* 31–32.

280 **"I am hotly engaged"** JAM to USG, May 22, 1863, *Grant Papers,* 8:253n.

280 **"If your advance is weak"** USG to JAM, May 22, 1863, *Grant Papers,* 8:253n.

280 **"We have part possession"** JAM to USG, May 22, 1863, *Grant Papers,* 8:253n.

280 **"I don't believe"** Sherman, *Memoirs,* 1:355.

280 **"gave me a better"** USG to John C. Kelton, July 6, 1863, *Grant Papers,* 8:503; see Kiper, *McClernand,* 260–62, for a more critical view of Grant's actions.

282 **"Our troops were not"** USG to HWH, May 24, 1863, *Grant Papers,* 8:261.

282 **"Whether Gen. Grant shall"** AL to Isaac N. Arnold, May 26, 1863, *CWAL,* 6:230.

282 **"immediately commence"** John A. Rawlins, Special Orders No. 140, May 25, 1863, *Grant Papers,* 8:267–68n.

282 **What knowledge** Ballard, *Vicksburg,* 358.

282 **Grant called upon his army** Winschel, *Triumph and Defeat,* 1:130; Shea and Winschel, *Vicksburg Is the Key,* 153–55.

283 **He rode along** Winschel, *Triumph and Defeat,* 1:129–38; Ballard, *Vicksburg,* 360.

283 **The animal's abuser** This incident was reported by Jacob S. Wilkin, Illinois 130th, in "Vicksburg," *Military Order of the Loyal Legion of the United States* (Chicago: Cozzens & Beaton, 1907), 233.

283 **"I could defend myself"** Ibid.

283 **Blair showed the article** For an excellent summary of McClernand and the order, see Kiper, *McClernand,* 268–78.

283 **"effusion of vain-glory"** WTS to John A. Rawlins, June 17, 1863, in Marszalek, *Sherman,* 485–87.

283 **"a true copy"** USG to JAM, June 17, 1863, *Grant Papers,* 8:384–85.

283 **"I regret that my adjt"** JAM to USG, June 18, 1863, *Grant Papers,* 8:385n.

284 **"Major General John A. McClernand"** John A. Rawlins, Special Orders No. 164, *Grant Papers,* 8:385n; James H. Wilson, *Under the Old Flag,* vol. 1 (New York: D. Appleton & Co., 1912), 185–86.

284 **"I should have relieved him"** USG to HWH, June 19, 1863, *Grant Papers,* 8:385n.

284 **William Lord, rector** Cotton, *Like a Hideous Nightmare,* 36–37.

284 **"so honeycombed with caves"** Mary Loughborough, *My Cave Life in Vicksburg* (New York: D. Appleton & Co., 1864), 72.

284   **At night** Samuel Carter III, *The Final Fortress: The Campaign for Vicksburg, 1862–1863* (New York: St. Martin's Press, 1980), 230–32.
284   **"moves with his shoulders"** *New York Times*, June 21, 1863.
284   **"The soldiers observe him"** Ibid.
285   **Union soldiers rushed** Shea and Winschel, *Vicksburg Is the Key*, 158–59.
285   **"proposition to save"** John C. Pemberton to USG, July 3, 1863, *Grant Papers*, 8:455n.
285   **"The useless effusion"** USG to John C. Pemberton, July 3, 1863, *Grant Papers*, 8:455.
286   **"the nearest approach"** *Personal Memoirs*, 1:560.
286   **"As soon as rolls"** USG to John C. Pemberton, July 3, 1863, *Grant Papers*, 8:457.
286   **"The men had behaved"** Ulysses S. Grant, "The Vicksburg Campaign," in Johnston and Buel, eds., *Battles and Leaders*, 3:554; Grant letter to unidentified correspondent, undated but written during summer of 1863, Grant Papers, Chicago History Museum.
286   **"General Grant was the only one"** Porter, *Incidents and Anecdotes of the Civil War*, 200–01.
287   **"Every day's delay"** USG to William S. Hillyer, May 5, 1863, *Grant Papers*, 8:162.
287   **During the long Vicksburg Campaign** Ballard, *Vicksburg*, 398–99.
287   **His battle plan** I am indebted to Terry Winschel for alerting me to this connection. See Winschel, *Triumph & Defeat: The Vicksburg Campaign*, 34–36; FM 100–5 *Operations*, 5 May, 1986, Headquarters, Department of the Army, Washington, DC, 91, 94–95.
288   **"I do not remember"** AL to USG, July 13, 1863, *CWAL*, 6:326.

Chapter 18. Chattanooga

289   **"Hero of the Mississippi Valley"** *New York Times*, July 7, 1863.
289   **"Did I not know"** WTS to USG, July 4, 1863, in Marszalek, *Sherman*, 496–97. Edward Everett, the greatest orator of the day, would deliver the major address at Gettysburg on November 19, 1863.
289   **"has no idea"** Charles A. Dana to EMS, July 5, 1863, in Dana, *Recollections of the Civil War*, 102.
290   **"I want the negroes all"** USG to James B. McPherson, July 5, 1863, *Grant Papers*, 8:483.
290   **"No enlistments"** Ibid.
290   **"Negroes were coming"** USG to AL, June 11, 1863, *Grant Papers*, 8:342.
290   **"had a map"** John Eaton to USG, July 23, 1863, *Grant Papers*, 8:343n.
290   **The political general** JAM to AL, June 23, 1863, ALPLC.
290   **In the coming months** Kiper, *McClernand*, 270–74.
290   **When Grant reviewed** John A. McClernand, report, Thirteenth Army Corps, June 17, 1863, *OR*, ser. 1, vol. 24, pt. 1, 137–57.
290   **"It is pretentious"** USG to Lorenzo Thomas, July 19, 1863, *Grant Papers*, 9:78–79.
290–91   **He informed Lincoln** USG to AL, July 20, 1863, *Grant Papers*, 9:80–81. Grant introduced Rawlins as "connected with this Army, and with me in every engagement, from the Battle of Belmont to the surrender of Vicksburg."
291   **Officially, the chief of staff** James H. Wilson would later declare that Rawlins was mainly responsible for the authorship of the report (Wilson, *Life of John A. Rawlins*, 147, 157–58), but in 1876 Grant presented the first draft of the report to his son Frederick Dent Grant in his own hand. *Grant Papers*, 8:508n.
291   **"they have finally concluded"** John A. Rawlins to USG, July 30, 1863, *Grant Papers*, 9:81n.

291 **"This earnest and sincere man"** Welles, *Diary,* entry July 31, 1863, 1:386.

291 **"Rawlins has been sent"** Ibid., 387.

291 **"It would cause me"** USG to Charles A. Dana, August 5, 1863, *Grant Papers,* 9:145–46.

292 **"modest, true"** Henry W. Wilson to Elihu B. Washburne, July 25, 1863, *Grant Papers,* 9:219n; Richard H. Abbott, *Cobbler in Congress: The Life of Henry Wilson, 1812–1875* (Lexington: University Press of Kentucky, 1972), 68; William E. Gienapp, *The Origins of the Republican Party, 1852–1856* (New York: Oxford University Press, 1987), 135.

292 **"I never was an Abolitionist"** USG to Elihu B. Washburne, August 30, 1863, *Grant Papers,* 9:218.

292 **Banks hosted** Richardson, *A Personal History,* 348.

292 **"We thought"** *Personal Memoirs,* 1:581–82; Frank Parker interview, Hamlin Garland Papers; Cadwallader C. Washburn to Elihu B. Washburne, September 5, 1863, Washburne Papers, Library of Congress; Simpson, *Grant,* 222.

292 **"The pain"** *Personal Memoirs,* 1:581.

292 **"being the weaker vessel"** Richardson, *A Personal History,* 349.

293 **He particularly enjoyed** Ibid.

293 **"I am frightened"** Nathaniel P. Banks to Mary Banks, September 5, 1863, cited in Catton, *Grant Takes Command,* 26. Correspondent Sylvanus Cadwallader, who was not in New Orleans, would write later that the mishap "was solely due to his drinking." Cadwallader, *Three Years with Grant,* 117.

293 **"After the review"** Cadwallader Washburn wrote his brother Elihu Washburne on September 5, 1863, Washburne Papers, Library of Congress.

293 **"A civil government"** WTS to HWH, September 17, 1863, *OR,* ser. 1, vol. 30, pt. 3, 695, 697, 699.

293 **"a very fine feeling"** USG to HWH, September 19, 1863, *Grant Papers,* 9:221–22.

294 **Rosecrans, praised** Steven E. Woodworth, *Six Armies in Tennessee: The Chickamauga and Chattanooga Campaigns* (Lincoln: University of Nebraska Press, 1998), 3.

294 **"You and your noble army"** EMS to William S. Rosecrans, July 7, 1863, *OR,* ser. 1, vol. 23, pt. 2, 518.

294 **"You do not appear"** William S. Rosecrans to EMS, July 7, 1863, *OR,* ser. 1, vol. 23, pt. 2, 518.

294 **"a bird of evil-omen"** Lamers, *Edge of Glory,* 311–12; Woodworth, *Six Armies in Tennessee,* 117–18.

294 **"Everything progresses"** Lamers, *Edge of Glory,* 315.

294 **It was a confused** Peter Cozzens, *This Terrible Sound: The Battle of Chickamauga* (Urbana: University of Illinois Press, 1992), see especially 368–405.

295 **"Rock of Chickamauga"** Brian Steel Wills, *George Henry Thomas: As True as Steel* (Lawrence: University Press of Kansas, 2012), 203–21; Woodworth, *Six Armies in Tennessee,* 122–28.

295 **"Chickamauga is as fatal"** Charles A. Dana to EMS, September 20, 1863, *OR,* ser. 1, vol. 30, pt. 1, 192–93; Lamers, *Edge of Glory,* 358.

295 **"You will immediately proceed"** HWH to USG, October 16, 1863, *OR,* ser. 1, vol. 30, pt. 4, 404; Thomas and Hyman, *Stanton,* 290–91.

295 **A bearded gentleman** *Personal Memoirs,* 2:18; HWH to USG, October 16, 1863, *Grant Papers,* 9:297n. One month later, Rawlins clarified Grant's decision to replace Rosecrans with Thomas: "While General Grant is no enemy of Genl Rosecrans as some of our papers seem to be impressed he is, he could not in just to himself and the cause of the country think of again commanding General Rosecrans, after his experience with him in the summer and fall of 1862." Rawlins to Mary E. Hurlbut, November 23, 1863, *Grant Papers,* 9:298n.

295 **"saying that I might make"** *Personal Memoirs*, 2:18.

296 **They talked** Lamers, *Edge of Glory*, 392–93.

296 **"Hold Chattanooga"** USG to George H. Thomas, October 19, 1863, *Grant Papers*, 9:302.

296 **"I will hold"** George H. Thomas to USG, October 19, 1863, *Grant Papers*, 9:302n.

296 **"I was in torture"** *Personal Memoirs*, 2:27.

296 **General Oliver O. Howard** John A. Carpenter, *Sword and Olive Branch: Oliver Otis Howard* (Pittsburgh: University of Pittsburgh Press, 1964), 32, 59.

296 **"the successful commander"** Oliver O. Howard, "Grant at Chattanooga," in *Military Order of the Loyal Legion of the United States, New York Commandery, Personal Recollections of the War of the Rebellion*, vol. 1 (New York: published by the New York Commandery, 1891), 246.

297 **"Why, I believe"** Ibid., 248.

297 **"described very clearly"** *Personal Memoirs*, 2:28.

297 **"as if he had been"** Catton, *Grant Takes Command*, 37.

297 **The road was strewn** *Personal Memoirs*, 2:28.

297 **For Grant, walking** Horace Porter, *Campaigning with Grant* (New York: Century Co., 1897; repr., Lincoln: University of Nebraska Press, 2000), 1.

297 **"General Thomas, General Grant is wet"** Wilson, *Under the Old Flag*, 1:273–74. One does have to be careful in listening to Wilson, for he has a tendency to make himself the center of the stories he tells.

297 **He knew Grant would never** Joseph J. Reynolds, Thomas's chief of staff, read the scene differently. He believed his boss and Grant, at the end of a cold, wet day, were simply enjoying a moment of quiet by the fire. More than thirty years later, Reynolds told Hamlin Garland that "there was no feeling between Grant and Thomas" (Hamlin Garland Papers). Thomas left no papers, so it is difficult to imagine this evening from his viewpoint.

298 **Did Wilson** Two recent biographies, both admiring of Thomas, treat Grant very differently. Brian Steel Wills, *George Henry Thomas: As True as Steel*, imputes no ill will from Grant to Thomas, whereas Benson Bobrick, *Master of War: The Life of General George H. Thomas* (New York: Simon & Schuster, 2009), cannot miss an opportunity to put Grant down.

298 **Now chief engineer** Walter H. Hebert, *Fighting Joe Hooker* (Lincoln: University of Nebraska Press, 1999), 165; William Marvel, *Burnside* (Chapel Hill: University of North Carolina Press, 1991), 200–204. William Franklin, another close friend of McClellan's, joined Smith in his criticisms.

298 **"explained the situation"** *Personal Memoirs*, 2:29.

298 **"a man of slim figure"** Porter, *Campaigning with Grant*, 14.

298 **"So intelligent"** Ibid., 5. Porter offers a valuable portrait of the humanity of Grant, with one proviso: he gives extended quotations that he could not have written down at the time.

299 **"opening up"** Ibid.

299 **"I suppose, they looked"** *Personal Memoirs*, 2:31.

299 **Under a full moon** Wiley Sword, *Mountains Touched with Fire: Chattanooga Besieged, 1863* (New York: St. Martin's Press, 1995), 112–22; Peter Cozzens, *The Shipwreck of Their Hopes: The Battles for Chattanooga* (Urbana: University of Illinois Press, 1994), 59–65.

300 **"instead of making my injury"** USG to JDG, October 27, 1863, *Grant Papers*, 9:334.

300 **"It is hard"** *Personal Memoirs*, 2:38.

300 **Reynolds called Grant "Sam"** James H. Wilson to Adam Badeau, November

5–6, 1863, *Grant Papers,* 9:353n; Wilson, *Under the Old Flag,* 1:280. Grant's two-story headquarters house was built by James A. Whiteside, a developer of Chattanooga.

300 **"Burnside was in about"** Marvel, *Burnside,* xii.

300 **Burnside's staff** Ibid., 296.

300 **"Have you indications"** USG to Ambrose E. Burnside, October 26, 1863, *Grant Papers,* 9:325.

301 **"I will endeavor"** Ibid., November 5, 1863, *Grant Papers,* 9:359.

301 **To build up his force** USG to WTS, November 5, 1863, *Grant Papers,* 9:360.

301 **"I deem the best movement"** USG to George H. Thomas, November 7, 1863, *Grant Papers,* 9:370–71.

301 **"If I attempt"** William F. Smith, "Comments on General Grant's 'Chattanooga,'" in Johnston and Buel, eds., *Battles and Leaders,* 3:716.

301 **Obliging, Smith told Grant** Ibid.

301 **"Thomas will not be able"** USG to Ambrose E. Burnside, November 8, 1863, *Grant Papers,* 9:374–75.

301 **"It has been impossible"** USG to HWH, November 9, 1863, *Grant Papers,* 9:377.

301 **"Things will culminate here"** USG to JDG, November 14, 1863, *Grant Papers,* 9:395–97.

302 **"was good for nothing"** Marszalek, *Commander of All Lincoln's Armies,* 186.

302 **"I fear he will not fight"** HWH to USG, November 16, *Grant Papers,* 9:404n.

302 **"Your being upon the spot"** USG to Ambrose E. Burnside, November 7, 14, 1863, *Grant Papers,* 9:368–69, 391–92.

302 **"I do not know how"** USG to Ambrose E. Burnside, November 15, 17, 1863, *Grant Papers,* 9:401, 405.

302 **"bearing toward Sherman"** Howard, "Grant at Chattanooga," in *Personal Recollections of the War of the Rebellion,* 1:248.

303 **Sensing that Longstreet** Cooper, *Jefferson Davis, American,* 453–58.

303 **"I am pushing"** USG to HWH, November 16, 1863, *Grant Papers,* 9:404.

303 **Secretary of War** Edward A. Miller, *Lincoln's Abolitionist General: The Biography of David Hunter* (Columbia: University of South Carolina Press, 1997), 114, 157–59.

303 **Grant commanded** Smith, *Grant,* 273–74; Sword, *Mountains Touched with Fire,* 156–57.

305 **"Sherman's force"** Braxton Bragg to Jefferson Davis, November 20, 1863, *OR,* ser. 1, vol. 31, pt. 2, 667.

305 **"I have never felt"** USG to HWH, November 21, 1863, *Grant Papers,* 9:428.

305 **As Grant peered** USG to WTS, November 24, 1863, *Grant Papers,* 9:441.

305 **"Flags were flying"** Joseph Fullerton, "Army of the Cumberland at Chattanooga," in Johnston and Buel, eds., *Battles and Leaders,* 3:721; Howard, "Grant at Chattanooga," in *Personal Recollections of the War of the Rebellion,* 1:250.

306 **Halfway across the plain** William Wrenshall Smith, "Holocaust Holiday: The Journal of a Strange Vacation to the War-torn South and a Visit with U. S. Grant," *Civil War Times Illustrated* 18, no. 6 (October 1979): 33; Sword, *Mountains Touched with Fire,* 178–79; Cozzens, *Shipwreck of Their Hopes,* 128–30.

306 **"Until I do hear"** USG to WTS, November 24, 1863, *Grant Papers,* 9:441.

306 **With light rain** Charles A. Dana to USG, November 24, 1863, *OR,* ser. 1, vol. 31, pt. 2, 42.

306 **At his headquarters** Marszalek, *Sherman,* 243–44; Sword, *Mountains Touched with Fire,* 198–99.

307 **"aid Sherman's crossing"** Joseph J. Reynolds to Joseph Hooker, November 24, 1863, *OR,* ser. 1, vol. 31, pt. 2, 106; Sword, *Mountains Touched with Fire,* 204–5.

307 **Carter Stevenson** Sword, *Mountains Touched with Fire,* 213–14.

307   **New York captain** George K. Collins, *Memoirs of the 149th Regt. New York* (Syracuse, N.Y.: published by the author, 1891), 207.

307   **Soldiers found it tough** Sword, *Mountains Touched with Fire,* 209–10.

307   **The desperate struggle** Cozzens, *Shipwreck of Their Hopes,* 179–87; Sword, *Mountains Touched with Fire,* 215–16; Hebert, *Fighting Joe Hooker,* 263–64. The phrase *the battle within the clouds* was first used by Montgomery Meigs in his report of November 26, 1863, *OR,* ser. 1, vol. 31, pt. 2, 78.

308   **"Sherman carried the end"** USG to HWH, November 24, 1863, *Grant Papers,* 9:439.

308   **Taking the peak** Sword, *Mountains Touched with Fire,* 228.

308   **The rebels** Ibid., 240.

308   **At times the combatants** Marszalek, *Sherman,* 244; Sword, *Mountains Touched with Fire,* 186–87; Cozzens, *Shipwreck of Their Hopes,* 151–54.

308   **"Where is Thomas?"** WTS to USG, November 25, 1863, *OR,* ser. 1, vol. 31, pt. 2, 44; Marszalek, *Sherman,* 245.

308   **"as circumstances may determine"** John A. Rawlins to WTS, November 24, 1863, *Grant Papers,* 9:441n. After the battle, Sherman would cite Thomas's failure to back him as the reason for his lack of success.

309   **"Hooker has not come up"** Garland, *Grant,* 249; Sword, *Mountains Touched with Fire,* 262.

309   **"General Sherman seems"** Thomas J. Wood, "The Battle of Missionary Ridge," in *Sketches of War History, 1861–1865* (Cincinnati: Robert Clarke, 1896): 4:34.

309   **"General Thomas, order Granger"** The scene atop Orchard Knob has been subject to countless interpretations by contemporaries and historians.

309   **The excitable Granger** Joseph Wheelan, *Terrible Swift Sword: The Life of Philip H. Sheridan* (Cambridge, Mass.: Da Capo Press, 2012), 51.

309   **Thomas's division commanders** Smith, *Grant,* 277–78; Wills, *George Henry Thomas,* 234–35; Sword, *Mountains Touched with Fire,* 270–71.

310   **"Thomas, who ordered"** Fullerton, "Army of the Cumberland at Chattanooga," in Johnston and Buel, eds., *Battles and Leaders,* 725; Sword, *Mountains Touched by Fire,* 280–81.

310   **Young MacArthur** Wheelan, *Terrible Swift Sword,* 53, 322n38.

310   **He lifted his hat** Garland, *Grant,* 251–52; Simpson, *Grant,* 242.

310   **"Remember Burnside"** AL to USG, November 25, 1863, *CWAL,* 7:30.

310   **"The next thing now"** USG to WTS, November 25, 1863, *Grant Papers,* 9:451.

310   **"Recollect that"** WTS to USG, December 1, 1863, *OR,* ser. 1, vol. 31, pt. 3, 297.

310   **On December 5** Marvel, *Burnside,* 330–31; Marszalek, *Sherman,* 246.

311   **It remains debatable** For an excellent discussion of the ongoing debate on how much credit Grant should receive for the victory at Chattanooga, see James Lee McDonough, *Chattanooga: A Death Grip on the Confederacy* (Knoxville: University of Tennessee Press, 1984), 162–65, 229–30.

311   **"The storming"** Charles A. Dana to EMS, November 26, 1863, ALPLC; Wills, *George Henry Thomas,* 236–38.

311   **"I can only account"** USG to John C. Kelton, December 23, 1863, *Grant Papers,* 9:563.

311   **"On several occasions"** *Personal Memoirs,* 2:87.

311   **"I wish to tender"** AL to USG, December 8, 1863, *CWAL,* 7:53.

312   **"received by General Grant"** David Hunter to EMS, December 14, 1863, *Grant Papers,* 9:476n2.

312   **"The spectacle was grand"** USG to Elihu B. Washburne, December 2, 1863, *Grant Papers,* 9:490–91.

Chapter 19. "Washington's Legitimate Successor"

313 **The Illinois congressman** Washburne introduced the resolution on December 8, 1863. *Congressional Globe,* 38th Congress, 1st Sess: 9, 10, 12; *Grant Papers,* 9:503–504n. The rank was created for Washington in 1798 in expectation of a war with France.

313 **"I feel under many"** USG to Elihu B. Washburne, December 12, 1863, *Grant Papers,* 9:521–22.

313 **"as a presidential candidate"** Barnabas Burns to USG, December 7, 1863, *Grant Papers,* 9:542n.

313 **"The question astonishes me"** USG to Barnabas Burns, December 17, 1863, *Grant Papers,* 9:541.

313 **"I never aspired"** Richardson, *A Personal History,* 377.

314 **By the eve** Douglas Fermer, *James Gordon Bennett and the New York Herald* (New York: St. Martin's Press, 1986), 1–2. The figure of one hundred thousand vastly underrates the number of readers. In the nineteenth century, it was common practice for newspapers to arrive at general stores in distant towns and for people to gather around as the subscriber read aloud the editorials and news stories of the nation's leading newspapers.

314 **"switch him off"** *New York Herald,* December 8, 1863.

314 **"So little"** Ibid., December 15, 1863.

314 **"the man who knows"** Ibid., December 16, 1863; Fermer, *James Gordon Bennett,* 254–55; David Quentin Voigt, " 'Too Pitchy to Touch'—President Lincoln and Editor Bennett," *Abraham Lincoln Quarterly* (September 1950): 146–47.

314 **"You cannot have failed"** Elihu B. Washburne to USG, January 24, 1864, *Grant Papers,* 9:523n3.

314 **"The North & South could never"** USG to Elihu B. Washburne, August 30, 1863, *Grant Papers,* 9:218.

314 **"This is a private letter"** USG to Isaac N. Morris, January 20, 1864, *Grant Papers,* 10, 52–53.

315 **"No man can feel"** Elihu B. Washburne to USG, January 24, 1864, *Grant Papers,* 9:522n3.

315 **"I have never seen Grant"** Richardson, *A Personal History,* 380.

315 **"I am going to invest"** USG to JDG, November 14, 1863, *Grant Papers,* 9:397.

315 **"I have no disposition"** J. Russell Jones to USG, n.d., *Grant Papers,* 9:543n.

315 **"I am receiving"** USG to J. Russell Jones, n.d., "Joseph Russell Jones," typescript, 11, unpublished biography of Jones, *Grant Papers,* 9:543n; Ida M. Tarbell interviewed Jones for her book *The Life of Abraham Lincoln,* vol. 3 (New York: Lincoln History Society, 1909), 187; Richardson, *A Personal History,* 380–81; George R. Jones, *Joseph Russell Jones* (Chicago: privately printed, 1964), 43.

315 **"No man knows"** Tarbell, *Life of Abraham Lincoln,* 3:188.

316 **"write me freely"** HWH to USG, January 8, 1864, *Grant Papers,* 10:17–18n.

316 **"It would draw the enemy"** USG to HWH, January 19, 1864, *Grant Papers,* 10:39–40. I am indebted to Brooks Simpson, *Ulysses S. Grant,* for his analysis of Grant's alternative plan for an eastern campaign, 250–51.

316 **"I have written this"** Ibid., 40.

317 **He stepped forward** Ross, *The General's Wife,* 159. On a trip that winter to Louisville, Grant took his staff to the theater, eliciting strong disapproval from Rawlins. Catton, *Grant Takes Command,* 117.

317 **"old friendships"** John O'Fallon to USG, January 27, 1864, *Grant Papers,* 10:70n.

317 **Two nights later** John M. Schofield, *Forty-six Years in the Army* (New York: Century Co., 1897), 111. Schofield, who sat at Grant's right, recalled later, "He did not

even touch one of the many glasses of wine placed by the side of his plate." After a while "I ventured to remark that he had not tasted his wine."

317 **"What in the world"** Julia Dent Grant, *Personal Memoirs,* 126–27.

318 **The House passed it** Smith, *Grant,* 286.

318 **An important new magazine** Donald Nevius Bigelow, *William Conant Church & the Army and Navy Journal* (New York: Columbia University Press, 1952), 108–14, 134–35.

318 **Even before Grant's appointment** *The Army and Navy Journal,* October 24, 1863.

318 **"moral influence of a commander"** Ibid., December 5, 1863.

318 **"Whilst I have been"** USG to WTS, March 4, 1864, *Grant Papers,* 10:186–87.

319 **"You do yourself injustice"** WTS to USG, March 10, 1864, in Marszalek, *Sherman,* 602–4.

319 **"My choice is"** Julia Dent Grant, *Personal Memoirs,* 127.

Chapter 20. The Wilderness

321 **"Do not stay in Washington"** WTS to USG, March 10, 1864, in Marszalek, *Sherman,* 603–04.

322 **As a corps commander** White, *A. Lincoln,* 574–75.

322 **Meade battled** Ibid., 576–77.

323 **"may desire to have his own"** GGM to Margaret Meade, March 8, 1864, in George Gordon Meade, *The Life and Letters of George Gordon Meade,* vol. 2 (New York: Charles Scribner's Sons, 1913), 176.

323 **"He said to me"** *Personal Memoirs,* 2:117.

323 **"The work before us"** GGM to Margaret Meade, March 10, 1864, in Meade, *Life,* 2:177.

323 **"Lieutenant General Grant"** Ibid., March 14, 1864, in Meade, *Life,* 2:178.

323 **"It will be said"** HWH to Francis Lieber, March 7, 1864, in Marszalek, *Commander of All Lincoln's Armies,* 196.

324 **Halleck "is, at his own request"** General Orders No. 98, March 12, 1864, *OR,* ser. 1, vol. 32, pt. 3, 58.

324 **"I appreciate fully"** Richardson, *A Personal History,* 386.

324 **"He went to work"** The *New York Tribune* and the *New York Herald* are quoted in Garland, *Grant,* 260–61.

324 **Grant took them** Grenville M. Dodge, *Personal Recollections of President Abraham Lincoln, General Ulysses S. Grant, and General William T. Sherman* (Council Bluffs, Iowa: Monarch Printing, 1914), 69–70; Catton, *Grant Takes Command,* 137.

324 **Grant listened and in the end** Dodge, *Personal Recollections,* 70.

325 **"What a splendid Army"** Ibid.

325 **Embellished with fourteen diamonds** Julia Dent Grant, *Personal Memoirs,* 128.

325 **"His whole manner was awkward"** *Daily Gazette* (Galena), March 23, 1864, 3; Sherman, *Memoirs,* 1:429–30.

325 **"All he ever wanted"** *Personal Memoirs,* 2:122.

325 **"With Lieutenant General Grant"** Noah Brooks, *Sacramento Daily Union,* March 24, 1864; Noah Brooks, *Mr. Lincoln's Washington: Selections from the Writings of Noah Brooks, Civil War Correspondent,* edited by P. J. Staudenraus (South Brunswick, N.J.: Thomas Yoseloff, 1967), 311.

325 **"the road to Richmond"** Strong, *Diary,* entry March 18, 1864, 416.

326 **Lincoln's "political fortunes"** *New York Herald,* April 4, 1864.

326 **"The feeling about Grant"** Charles Francis Adams, Jr., to Charles Francis Adams, Sr., May 1, 1864, in Worthington Chauncey Ford, ed., *A Cycle of Adams Letters, 1861–1865* (Boston: Houghton Mifflin, 1920), 2:128.

327 **Grant did not want** Feis, *Grant's Secret Service,* 196–200.

327 **"Probably no army on earth"** Rufus Ingalls, report, August 28, 1864, *OR,* ser. 1, vol. 36, pt. 1, 276–79.

327 **Grant, an old quartermaster** *Personal Memoirs,* 2:188.

328 **If he chose** *Personal Memoirs,* 2:134–35.

328 **A genial bachelor** For Sedgwick, see Richard Elliott Winslow, *General John Sedgwick: The Story of a Union Corps Commander* (Novato, Calif.: Presidio Press, 1982).

328 **Yet to many** For Warren, see Emerson Gifford Taylor, *Gouverneur Kemble Warren* (Boston: Houghton Mifflin, 1932), and Paula Walker and Robert Girardi, *The Soldiers' General: Gouverneur K. Warren and the Civil War* (El Dorado Hills, Calif.: Savas Beatie, 2015).

328 **In Tennessee, Grant had commanded** Smith, *Grant,* 299.

329 **"It is my design"** USG to WTS, April 4, 1864, *Grant Papers,* 10:253n.

329 **"That we are now all"** WTS to USG, April 10, 1864, *Grant Papers,* 10:53n.

329 **"were very much such"** Hans L. Trefousse, *Ben Butler: The South Called Him BEAST!* (New York: Twayne, 1957), 147; *Personal Memoirs,* 2:132–33.

329 **"Butler is sharp"** Cyrus B. Comstock, *The Diary of Cyrus B. Comstock,* compiled and edited by Merlin E. Sumner (Dayton, Ohio: Morningside, 1987), entry April 1, 1864, 262.

329 **Led by white officers** Marvel, *Burnside,* 346–49.

329 **"would necessarily follow"** *Personal Memoirs,* 2:140–41.

329 **"Lee's army will be your objective"** USG to GGM, April 9, 1864, *Grant Papers,* 10:274.

329 **"You I propose"** USG to WTS, April 4, 1864, *Grant Papers,* 10:252.

330 **One enterprising Confederate** Gordon C. Rhea, *The Battle of the Wilderness, May 5–6, 1864* (Baton Rouge: Louisiana State University Press, 1994), is the classic study, 9.

330 **Although he had led** For Ewell, see Donald Pfanz, *Richard S. Ewell: A Soldier's Life* (Chapel Hill: University of North Carolina Press, 1998).

330 **Early in the war** For Hill, see James I. Robertson, *General A. P. Hill: The Story of a Confederate Warrior* (New York: Random House, 1987).

330 **Lee chose this dense forest** Morris Schaff provides excellent descriptions of the Wilderness as only a participant could. *The Battle of the Wilderness* (Boston: Houghton Mifflin, 1910), 59.

330 **"Grant is a man"** Theodore Lyman, *Meade's Headquarters, 1863–1865: Civil War Letters of Colonel Lyman from the Wilderness to Appomattox,* edited by George R. Agassiz (Boston: Atlantic Monthly Press, 1922), letter to wife Elizabeth, April 12, 1864, 81.

331 **"Grant is not intoxicated with flattery"** Garland, *Grant,* 266. The reporter added, "He travels with the simplicity of a second lieutenant with a small trunk which he often forgets and goes off without."

331 **Intelligence informed him** Feis, *Grant's Secret Service,* 201.

331 **"entire satisfaction"** AL to USG, April 30, 1864, *CWAL,* 7, 324. John Hay, Lincoln's secretary, wrote in his diary that same day: "The President read me his letter to Gen. Grant, an admirable one, full of kindness & dignity at once. It must be very grateful to Grant on the eve of battle." John Hay, *Inside Lincoln's White House: The Complete Civil War Diary of John Hay,* edited by Michael Burlingame and John R. Turner Ettlinger (Carbondale: Southern Illinois University Press, 1997), diary entry April 30, 1864, 192.

332 **When high-spirited soldiers** Porter, *Campaigning with Grant,* 41–43; Cadwallader, *Three Years with Grant,* 174–75.

332 **"I have never seen the army"** Charles A. Page, *Letters of a War Correspondent,* edited by James R. Gilmore (Boston: L. C. Page, 1899), 43, 47; Cadwallader, *Three Years with Grant,* 175.

332 **"The crossing of Rapidan"** USG to HWH, May 4, 1864, *Grant Papers,* 10:397.

332 **"What's this!"** Ulysses S. Grant, "Preparing for the Campaigns of '64," in Johnston and Buel, eds., *Battles and Leaders,* 4:97n; Freeman Cleaves, *Meade of Gettysburg* (Norman: University of Oklahoma Press, 1960), 236.

332 **In its place** Cleaves, *Meade of Gettysburg,* 236.

334 **Sedgwick set off** Rhea, *Battle of the Wilderness,* 94.

334 **"I think the enemy is trying"** GGM to USG, May 5, 1864, *Grant Papers,* 10:399n.

334 **"If any opportunity presents itself"** USG to GGM, May 5, 1864, *Grant Papers,* 10:399.

334 **And then the woods caught fire** Herman Hattaway and Archer Jones, *A Military History of the Civil War* (Urbana: University of Illinois Press, 1983), 540.

334 **"The work was at close range"** Page, *Letters of a War Correspondent,* 50.

335 **"Hays and I"** Porter, *Campaigning with Grant,* 52; Mahood, *"Fighting Elleck" Hays,* 167.

335 **Lee wondered aloud** Rhea, *Battle of the Wilderness,* 283–90; Catton, *Grant Takes Command,* 196.

335 **Within two hours** McPherson, *Battle Cry,* 725; Hattaway and Jones, *Military History of the Civil War,* 541; Rhea, *Battle of the Wilderness,* 302–15.

335 **"I know Lee's methods"** Porter, *Campaigning with Grant,* 69–70.

336 **Since Grant had closed** Louis M. Starr, *Bohemian Brigade: Civil War Newsmen in Action* (New York: Alfred A. Knopf, 1954), 298. Also see Ida M. Tarbell, *A Reporter for Lincoln: Story of Henry E. Wing, Soldier and Newspaperman* (New York: Macmillan, 1927), 14.

337 **"You may tell the people"** Gordon C. Rhea, *The Battles for Spotsylvania Court House and the Road to Yellow Tavern, May 7–12, 1864* (Baton Rouge: Louisiana State University Press, 1997), 3–4.

337 **"Well, if you see the President"** Starr, *Bohemian Brigade,* 299.

337 **"How near we have been"** Hay, *Inside Lincoln's White House,* diary entry May 9, 1864, 195.

337 **Other men** Hattaway and Jones, *Military History of the Civil War,* 540–45.

337 **"Well, I can't tell much"** Porter, *Campaigning with Grant,* 97.

337 **"with calmness and self-possession"** Wilson, *Life of John A. Rawlins,* 216.

338 **"Joe Johnston would have retreated"** Lyman, *Meade's Headquarters,* letter to wife, Elizabeth, May 6, 1864, 102.

338 **In the dim light** Rhea, *Battles for Spotsylvania Court House and the Road to Yellow Tavern,* 37–39.

339 **"The night march"** Ibid., 39.

Chapter 21. Robert E. Lee

341 **"The results of the three days"** USG to HWH, May 8, 1864, *Grant Papers,* 10:410–11.

341 **"The boasted leader"** *Richmond Dispatch,* May 7, 1864.

341 **"They think him as pure"** Beth G. Crabtree and James W. Patton, eds., *"Journal of a Secesh Lady": The Diary of Catherine Ann Devereux Edmonston, 1860–1866* (Raleigh: North Carolina Division of Archives and History, 1979), diary entry February 10, 1864, 524; Bruce Levine, *The Fall of the House of Dixie: The Civil War and the Social Revolution That Transformed the South* (New York: Random House, 2013), 5.

342 **It seemed young Robert** Emory M. Thomas, *Robert E. Lee: A Biography* (New York: W. W. Norton & Co., 1995), 23–37; Douglas Southall Freeman, *R. E. Lee: A Biography,* vol. 1 (New York: Charles Scribner's Sons, 1934), 1–33.

342 **Lee entered West Point** Thomas, *Robert E. Lee*, 41, 47–55; Freeman, *R. E. Lee*, 1:48–85.

342 **In October 1859** Thomas, *Robert E. Lee*, 178–83.

342 **"I declined"** Robert E. Lee to Reverdy Johnson, February 25, 1868, quoted in Freeman, *R. E. Lee*, 1:437.

343 **Lee's victories on Virginia battlefronts** Brooks D. Simpson, "Great Expectations: Ulysses S. Grant, the Northern Press, and the Opening of the Wilderness Campaign," in Gary W. Gallagher, ed., *The Wilderness Campaign* (Chapel Hill: University of North Carolina Press, 1997), 2–4.

343 **his almond-shaped hazel eyes** Philip H. Sheridan, *Personal Memoirs of P. H. Sheridan* (New York: Charles L. Webster & Co., 1888), 1; Wheelan, *Terrible Swift Sword*, xx. Four different versions of where Sheridan was born exist. He says he was born in Albany, New York. The problem with constructing a biography of Sheridan lies in the fact that all of his diaries, journals, and other personal papers perished in the Great Chicago Fire of 1871.

344 **Rienzi, jet black** Wheelan, *Terrible Swift Sword*, xxi, 19.

344 **Today, at Sheridan Circle** Kathryn Allamong Jacob, *Testament to Union: Civil War Monuments in Washington, D.C.* (Baltimore: Johns Hopkins University Press, 1998), 134–38. The statue was executed by Gutzon Borglum, later the creator of the immense presidential sculpture on Mount Rushmore in South Dakota and dedicated in 1908.

344 **"You will find him big enough"** Porter, *Campaigning with Grant*, 24.

344 **"went at him"** Ibid., 83–84.

344 **"General Meade is in excellent spirits"** Lyman, *Meade's Headquarters*, letter to wife, Elizabeth, February 22, 1864, 73.

345 **Sheridan, who would not** Porter, *Campaigning with Grant*, 83–84; Wheelan, *Terrible Swift Sword*, 70–71; Sheridan, *Personal Memoirs*, 1:367–69.

345 **Sheridan believed** Sheridan, *Personal Memoirs*, 1:367–69; Wheelan, *Terrible Swift Sword*, 70–71; Cleaves, *Meade of Gettysburg*, 242–43; McPherson, *Battle Cry*, 462–64.

345 **"the excitement of the one"** Sheridan, *Personal Memoirs*, 1:367–69; Wheelan, *Terrible Swift Sword*, 71.

345 **They talked about the difficulties** Porter, *Campaigning with Grant*, 88–89; Rhea, *Battles for Spotsylvania Court House and the Road to Yellow Tavern*, 94.

346 **Since battles fought** Rhea, *Battles for Spotsylvania Court House and the Road to Yellow Tavern*, 5–6.

346 **"Vive la spade!"** *New York Herald*, September 4, 1862; McPherson, *Battle Cry*, 728.

346 **Every fifteen to twenty** Richard Elliott Winslow, *General John Sedgwick: The Story of a Union Corps Commander* (Novato, Calif.: Presidio Press, 1982), 172–74.

346 **The men ducked** Martin T. McMahon, "The Death of General John Sedgwick," in Johnston and Buel, eds., *Battles and Leaders*, 4:175. When Sedgwick was hit, he fell on McMahon.

347 **"His loss to this army"** Porter, *Campaigning with Grant*, 90.

347 **Thus Grant's first attempt** David M. Jordan, *Winfield Scott Hancock: A Soldier's Life* (Bloomington: Indiana University Press, 1988), 127.

347 **With the enormity** Wheelan, *Terrible Swift Sword*, 73; McPherson, *Battle Cry*, 728.

347 **"Enemy hold our front"** USG to HWH, May 10, 1864, *Grant Papers*, 10:418.

347 **One consequence of Sheridan's foray** Rhea, *Battles for Spotsylvania Court House and the Road to Yellow Tavern*, 105.

348 **"I tell you this"** Brigadier General Samuel W. Crawford, quoted in Rhea, *Battles for Spotsylvania Court House and the Road to Yellow Tavern*, 177; Jordan, *Winfield Scott Hancock*, 128–29.

349 **Grant listened** Rhea, *Battles for Spotsylvania Court House and the Road to Yellow Tavern,* 161–63.

349 **"not to fire a shot"** Ibid., 164–65.

349 **By now Confederates** *Personal Memoirs,* 2:223–25; Catton, *Grant Takes Command,* 220–22.

349 **"We have lost to this time"** USG to HWH, May 11, 1864, *Grant Papers,* 10:422–23; Porter, *Campaigning with Grant,* 97–98; Rhea, *Battles for Spotsylvania Court House and the Road to Yellow Tavern,* 212–13.

350 **"Beau Sabreur"** Emory M. Thomas, *Bold Dragoon: The Life of J.E.B. Stuart* (New York: Harper & Row, 1986), 18, 69, 128.

350 **Outnumbered by more than three** Wheelan, *Terrible Swift Sword,* 76–77; Thomas, *Bold Dragoon,* 290–91. Stuart's force was put at a further disadvantage because he had to delegate one in four of his cavalry to hold the horses.

350 **His death sent** Thomas, *Bold Dragoon,* 291–95.

350 **To these whooping soldiers** William D. Matter, *If It Takes All Summer: The Battle of Spotsylvania* (Chapel Hill: University of North Carolina Press, 1988), 191–93; Rhea, *Battles for Spotsylvania Court House and the Road to Yellow Tavern,* 232–36; McPherson, *Battle Cry,* 729–30; Porter, *Campaigning with Grant,* 102.

352 **Rawlins and several aides** Porter, *Campaigning with Grant,* 113–14.

352 **"I have just come"** Ibid., 115; Cleaves, *Meade of Gettysburg,* 245. Porter here offers a long recitation of Grant's words. A rightful objection can be raised about the accuracy of his memory, but I believe the spirit, if not his exact words, captures the conversation that morning.

353 **"General Meade has more than met"** USG to EMS, May 13, 1864, *Grant Papers,* 10:434.

353 **"I propose to fight it out"** Noah Brooks, *Sacramento Daily Union,* May 13, 1864, in Brooks, *Mr. Lincoln's Washington,* 317.

353 **"Nothing during the war"** *New York Times,* May 18, 1864. Swinton's frequent use of religious language probably derives from his early education to become a Presbyterian minister.

354 **Sherman set his face toward Atlanta** Marszalek, *Sherman,* 264.

354 **Grant learned that on May 15** Stephen D. Engle, *Yankee Dutchman: The Life of Franz Sigel* (Baton Rouge: Louisiana State University Press, 1993), 186–92.

354 **"He will do nothing but run"** HWH to USG, May 17, 1864, *Grant Papers,* 10:460n.

354 **"The Little Creole"** Trefousse, *Ben Butler,* 150; Williams, *Beauregard,* 208–11.

354 **Now wedged** Gordon C. Rhea, *To the North Anna River: Grant and Lee, May 13–25* (Baton Rouge: Louisiana State University Press, 2000), 126–27.

354 **"His army"** USG, report, *OR,* ser. 1, vol. 36, pt. 1, 20.

355 **"The fault may be"** USG to HWH, May 21, 1864, *Grant Papers,* 10:475.

355 **"Genl Banks is a personal friend"** HWH to USG, May 3, 1864, *Grant Papers,* 10:375n.

355 **"has undoubtedly lost confidence"** USG to HWH, May 16, 1864, *Grant Papers,* 10:452.

356 **"How long 'Old Useless'"** Cited in Rhea, *To the North Anna River,* 279.

356 **Starting out on May 21** *Personal Memoirs,* 2:243.

356 **"Roads are almost useless"** William H. Armstrong, *Warrior in Two Camps: Ely S. Parker, Union General and Seneca Chief* (Syracuse, N.Y.: Syracuse University Press, 1978), 91.

356 **"the situation of the enemy"** USG to Ambrose E. Burnside, May 24, 1864, *Grant Papers,* 10:484; Rhea, *To the North Anna River,* 320–24, 355–62.

357 **"We must strike"** Douglas Southall Freeman, *Lee's Lieutenants: A Study in Command* (New York: Charles Scribner's Sons, 1942–1944), 3:498.

357 **This diversion** Ibid., 367.

357 **"Rawlins does my swearing"** William E. Woodward, *Meet General Grant* (New York: Liveright, 1928), 23; Miers, *Web of Victory*, 106–7.

357–58 **"I never learned to swear"** Porter, *Campaigning with Grant*, 251.

358 **"beating his horses"** Ibid., 164–65; Egypt was so named because the handsome horse came from the southern part of Illinois known as Egypt.

358 **"The general sprang"** Ibid., 165.

358 **The race was on** Freeman, *R. E. Lee*, 3:373–84.

358 **this would be his last chance** McPherson, *Battle Cry*, 734.

359 **"Then why in Hell"** Lyman, *Meade's Headquarters*, letter to wife, Elizabeth, June 1, 1864, 138.

359 **Lee found another day** Rhea, *To the North Anna River*, 354–62.

359 **Grant understood that the successes** White, *A. Lincoln*, 632–35.

360 **"rather peculiar"** Porter, *Campaigning with Grant*, 174–75.

360 **Following Grant's orders** Meade wrote his wife the next day, "I had immediate and entire command on the field all day." GGM to Margaret Meade, June 4, 1864, in Meade, *Life*, 2:200.

360 **"It seemed more like a volcanic"** Cited in Smith, *Grant*, 362.

360–61 **"I should be glad"** GGM to USG, June 3, 1864, *Grant Papers*, 11:14n.

361 **"The moment it becomes certain"** USG to GGM, June 3, 1864, *Grant Papers*, 11:14n.

361 **"Fought like hell"** Maher cited in Gordon C. Rhea, *Cold Harbor: Grant and Lee, May 26–June 3, 1864* (Baton Rouge: Louisiana State University Press, 2002), 329.

361 **"I regret this assault"** Porter, *Campaigning with Grant*, 179; McPherson, *Battle Cry*, 735; Cleaves, *Meade of Gettysburg*, 251. Later, in his *Personal Memoirs*, Grant wrote, "I have always regretted that the last assault at Cold Harbor was ever made. . . . At Cold Harbor no advantage whatever was gained to compensate for the heavy loss sustained" (2:276).

361 **"There is intense anxiety"** Welles, *Diary*, entry June 2, 1864, 2:44.

Chapter 22. Petersburg

362 **"My idea from the start"** USG to HWH, June 5, 1864, *Grant Papers*, 11:19.

363 **"The general showed"** Porter, *Campaigning with Grant*, 188–89; Simpson, *Grant*, 333–35.

363 **"an amendment"** John C. Waugh, *Reelecting Lincoln: The Battle for the 1864 Presidency* (New York: Crown Publishers, 1997), 188–89.

363 **The convention nominated Lincoln** *Proceedings of the First Three Republican National Conventions of 1856, 1860 and 1864* (Minneapolis: Charles W. Johnson, 1893), 180, cited in David Herbert Donald, *Lincoln* (New York: Simon & Schuster, 1995), 504.

363 **In 1864, in an effort** White, *A. Lincoln*, 634.

363 **"What we want"** AL, "Response to a Serenade by the Ohio Delegation," June 9, 1864, *CWAL*, 7:384.

364 **Butler sent** Trefousse, *Ben Butler*, 151.

364 **Fascinated by the paradoxes** Lyman, *Meade's Headquarters*, letter to wife, Elizabeth, June 12, 1864, 156.

365 **Having no idea where they went** Freeman, *R. E. Lee*, 3:401–02.

365 **"I will have Petersburg secured"** USG to HWH, June 14, 1864, *Grant Papers*, 11:45.

365 **In June 1864** Catton, *Grant Takes Command*, 284; Smith, *Grant*, 172.

365 **These aggregate bridges** Rhea, *Cold Harbor*, 41.

365 **"The sentinel is right"** Porter, *Campaigning with Grant*, 213.

366　**This scene became well-known**　McPherson, *Battle Cry*, 740; Catton, *Grant Takes Command*, 282–83.

366　**"Since Sunday"**　USG to JDG, June 15, 1864, *Grant Papers*, 11:55.

366　**Four steamers**　"City Point During the Civil War," *Encyclopedia Virginia*, www .encyclopediavirginia.org/City_Point_During_the_Civil_War; Bruce Catton, *A Stillness at Appomattox* (Garden City, N.Y.: Doubleday, 1953), 321.

366　**The Petersburg defenders**　Williams, *Beauregard*, 227–28.

367　**"Have you any news"**　USG to Benjamin F. Butler, June 15, 1864, *Grant Papers*, 11:47.

367　**"I have not yet heard"**　Ibid., 11:49.

367　**The suddenly circumspect**　Hattaway and Jones, *Military History of the Civil War*, 589–90; McPherson, *Battle Cry*, 740–41.

369　**"Petersburg at that hour"**　P. G. T. Beauregard, "Four Days of Battle at Petersburg," in Johnston and Buel, eds., *Battles and Leaders*, 4:541.

369　**Grant told Meade he wanted**　Cleaves, *Meade of Gettysburg*, 263; Porter, *Campaigning with Grant*, 206.

369　**In one of his finest hours**　G. T. Beauregard, *With Beauregard in Mexico: The Mexican War Reminiscenses of P.G.T. Beauregard,* edited by T. Harry Williams (Baton Rouge: Louisiana State University Press, 1956), 230.

369　**Lee himself reached**　Freeman, *R. E. Lee*, 3:424–25.

369　**At the end of the afternoon**　Porter, *Campaigning with Grant*, 208–10.

369　**I do not think**　*Personal Memoirs*, 2:298.

369　**"We accepted this war"**　AL, speech at Great Sanitary Fair, Philadelphia, Pennsylvania, June 16, 1864, *CWAL*, 7:394–95.

369　**"I just thought"**　Foote, *The Civil War*, 3:443.

370　**Lincoln concurred**　Porter, *Campaigning with Grant*, 217.

370　**"defies description"**　Ibid., 219–20.

370　**"When Grant once gets possession"**　Ibid., 222–23.

370　**"There was a simplicity"**　Adam Badeau, *Military History of Ulysses S. Grant: From April 1861 to April 1865*, vol. 3 (New York: D. Appleton & Co., 1867), 139.

371　**"We must destroy this army"**　Robert E. Lee to Jubal Early, Freeman, *R. E. Lee*, 3:398; J. William Jones, editor, *Personal Reminiscences, Anecdotes, and Letters of General Robert E. Lee* (New York: D. Appleton & Co., 1876), 40.

371　**He knew that Sherman**　Marszalek, *Sherman*, 269.

371　**However, to the south**　Catton, *Grant Takes Command*, 294. Although the term *siege* has been used to describe Petersburg, it does not fit the technical military definition. While Grant surrounded Vicksburg in 1863, in 1864 Petersburg remained open in parts of the north, west, and south. Railroads and wagon roads made it possible to come and go. Grant's continuing challenge was to choke off those entry and exit points.

371　**"The affair was a stampede"**　USG to HWH, June 24, 1864, *Grant Papers*, 11:123; Simpson, *Grant*, 343.

373　**"Old Jube"**　See Frank E. Vandiver, *Jubal's Raid: General Early's Famous Attack on Washington in 1864* (New York: McGraw-Hill, 1960).

373　**After extracting**　Ibid., 99–118.

373　**Not since the British**　McPherson, *Battle Cry*, 756; Catton, *Grant Takes Command*, 309–11; Smith, *Grant*, 377.

373　**"We can defend Washington"**　Porter, *Campaigning with Grant*, 182; Marszalek, *Commander of All Lincoln's Armies*, 203–5.

373　**"We want now to crush"**　USG to HWH, July 5, 1864, *Grant Papers*, 11:170.

374　**"This is what I think"**　AL to USG, July 10, 1864, *CWAL*, 7:437.

374　**"I think on reflection"**　USG to AL, July 10, 1864, *Grant Papers*, 11:203.

374 **On the afternoon of July 11** Thomas H. Hyde, *Following the Greek Cross; Or, Memories of the Sixth Army Corps* (Boston: Houghton Mifflin, 1894), 22; Frank Everson Vandiver, *Jubal's Raid: General Early's Famous Attack on Washington in 1864* (New York: McGraw-Hill, 1960), 159–60.

374 **As the president** Hyde, *Following the Greek Cross*, 223; McPherson, *Battle Cry*, 756–57. Fort Stevens guarded Washington along the Seventh Street Pike (today's Georgia Avenue).

374 **In the months ahead** Brooks Simpson, in *Ulysses S. Grant*, 346–54, offers an insightful examination and analysis of these conflicted relationships.

374 **"It seemed as if"** Dana, *Recollections of the Civil War*, 226.

375 **"Whilst I have no difficulty"** USG to HWH, July 1, 1864, *Grant Papers*, 11:155.

375 **"How you can place"** William A. Smith to USG, July 2, 1864, *Grant Papers*, 11:163n.

375 **"He proposed"** HWH, General Orders 225, July 7, 1864, *Grant Papers*, 11:206n; Trefousse, *Ben Butler*, 153–54.

375 **"I again pressed him"** William F. Smith, *Autobiography of Major General William F. Smith, 1861–1864*, edited by Herbert M. Schiller (Dayton, Ohio: Morningside House, 1990), 116. Grant and Smith never spoke again.

375 **"Thus did Smith"** Theodore Lyman to Elizabeth Lyman, July 20, 1864, in Lyman, *Meade's Headquarters*, 193.

376 **But Grant, with success** Marvel, *Burnside*, 390–91.

376 **Pleasants planned to construct** William A. Powell, "The Battle of the Petersburg Crater," in Johnston and Buel, eds., *Battles and Leaders*, 4:545; Marvel, *Burnside*, 391.

376 **Ferrero began training** Richard Slotkin, *No Quarter: The Battle of the Crater 1864* (New York: Random House, 2009), 72–73. The only time Ferrero spent at West Point occurred when he traveled up the Hudson River to teach social dancing to the cadets. Ferrero authored *The Art of Dancing* in 1859.

376 **He "dwelt upon it"** Porter, *Campaigning with Grant*, 244–45.

376 **"A nation grieves"** USG to Lydia Slocum, August 10, 1864, *Grant Papers*, 11:397.

377 **When Burnside protested** Andrew A. Humphreys to Ambrose E. Burnside, *OR*, ser. 1, vol. 40, pt. 1, 137; Slotkin, *No Quarter*, 140–41; Cleaves, *Meade of Gettysburg*, 276–77.

377 **"The details"** USG to GGM, July 29, 1864, *Grant Papers*, 11:344.

377 **Among his fellow soldiers** Slotkin, *No Quarter*, 69, 164–65.

377 **Grant, wondering** Theodore Lyman to Elizabeth Lyman, July 31, 1864, in Lyman, *Meade's Headquarters*, 198.

377 **The explosion created** Porter, *Campaigning with Grant*, 263–64; Slotkin, *No Quarter*, 149–50; Herman Hattaway and Archer Jones, *How the North Won: A Military History of the Civil War* (Urbana: University of Illinois Press, 1982), 614–15.

378 **He climbed over** Porter, *Campaigning with Grant*, 264–67; Slotkin, *No Quarter*, 210–11.

378 **At seven thirty A.M.** Slotkin, *No Quarter*, 223, 225, 229–31.

378 **As the black soldiers** Ibid., 233–34.

378 **"I am constrained to believe"** USG to HWH, August 1, 1864, *Grant Papers*, 11:361.

378 **The Federal tally** Slotkin, *No Quarter*, 310, 318.

378 **"less able"** Welles, *Diary*, entry August 2, 1864, 2:92.

378 **one of Early's commanders** William G. Thomas, "Nothing Ought to Astonish Us: Confederate Civilians in the 1864 Shenandoah Valley Campaign," in Gary W. Gallagher, ed., *The Shenandoah Valley Campaign of 1864* (Chapel Hill: University of North Carolina Press, 2006), 234. Early claimed the burning was retaliation for

David Hunter burning Virginia governor John Letcher's home as well as the Virginia Military Institute. Some Confederate leaders believed Early's actions were wrongheaded and would inflame Northern opinion at the time they hoped the North would grow weary of the war.

379 **"I want Sheridan put"** USG to HWH, August 1, 1864, *Grant Papers,* 11:358.

379 **"This, I think, is exactly right"** AL to USG, August 3, 1864, *Grant Papers,* 11:360n.

379–80 **"being senior"** USG to Benjamin F. Butler, August 4, 1864, *Grant Papers,* 11:372.

380 **The sixty-two-year-old Hunter** Simpson, *Grant,* 355.

380 **"Hunter's whole command"** Comstock, *Diary,* entry August 5, 1864, 285.

380 **"Concentrate all"** USG to David Hunter, August 5, 1864, *Grant Papers,* 11:377–78.

380 **"offered a tempting highway"** Wesley Merritt, "Sheridan in the Shenandoah Valley," in Johnston and Buel, eds., *Battles and Leaders,* 4:500; Wheelan, *Terrible Swift Sword,* 101–2.

380 **"he should have upon his heels"** USG to HWH, July 14, 1864, *Grant Papers,* 11:242–43; Gary W. Gallagher, "Two Generals and a Valley: Philip H. Sheridan and Jubal A. Early," in Gallagher, ed., *Shenandoah Valley Campaign,* ix–xii.

380–81 **"showing a patiotism"** *Personal Memoirs,* 2:320.

381 **By early September** Gallagher, "Two Generals and a Valley," in Gallagher, ed., *Shenandoah Valley Campaign,* 14. Grant brought under Sheridan's new command Horatio Wright's Sixth Corps, William H. Emory's Nineteenth Corps, George Crook's Eighth Corps (also known as the Army of West Virginia), and Alfred Torbert's three cavalry divisions.

381 **"I feel every confidence"** USG to Philip H. Sheridan, August 7, 1864, *Grant Papers,* 11:379–80.

381 **"It may require"** HWH to USG, August 11, 1864, *Grant Papers,* 11:425n.

381 **If he withdrew troops** USG to HWH, August 15, 1864, *Grant Papers,* 11:424.

381 **"The President has more nerve"** Porter, *Campaigning with Grant,* 279.

382 **"after four years"** Donald, *Lincoln,* 530. The convention selected Ohio congressman George H. Pendleton, a strong peace advocate, as their vice-presidential candidate.

382 **"Atlanta is ours"** WTS to HWH, September 3, 1864, *Sherman's Civil War,* 696.

382 **"It is hardly necessary"** USG to WTS, September 12, 1864, *Grant Papers,* 12:154–55.

382 **"Sheridan and Early"** AL to USG, September 12, 1864, *CWAL,* 7:548.

382 **"what was necessary to enable"** USG to AL, September 13, 1864, *Grant Papers,* 12:163n.

382 **"I knew it was impossible"** *Personal Memoirs,* 2:327.

382 **"two undersized men"** John William De Forest, *A Volunteer's Adventures: A Union Captain's Record of the Civil War* (New Haven, Conn.: Yale University Press, 1946), 172.

383 **"I have a horror"** USG to JDG, August 25, 1864, *Grant Papers,* 12:90–91; Ross, *The General's Wife,* 172.

383 **"I have just received"** USG to PHS, September 20, 1864, *Grant Papers,* 12:177.

383 **While two of his corps** Robert E. L. Krick, "A Stampeede of Stampeeds: The Confederate Disaster at Fisher's Hill," in Gallagher, ed., *Shenandoah Valley Campaign,* 161–99.

383 **"achieved a most signal victory"** PHS to USG, September 22, 1864, *Grant Papers,* 12:191n.

383 **"your second great victory"** USG to PHS, September 23, 1864, *Grant Papers,* 12:193n.

383 **"With a reasonable amount"** USG to GGM, July 30, 1864, *Grant Papers,* 11:353–54.

385 **He ordered Meade** I am indebted to Richard Slotkin for his analysis of Grant's opportunity. See *No Quarter,* 318–20.

385 **On October 16, Sheridan left** Wheelan, *Terrible Swift Sword,* 141.

385 **Believing they had won** For two stories of Cedar Creek, see Keith S. Bohannon, " 'The Fatal Halt' versus 'Bad Conduct': John B. Gordon, Jubal A. Early, and the Battle of Cedar Creek," and William W. Bergen, "The Other Hero of Cedar Creek: The 'Not Specially Ambitious' Horatio G. Wright," in Gallagher, ed., *Shenandoah Valley Campaign,* 56–133.

385 **"About face"** Foote, *The Civil War,* 3:570; George A. Forsyth, *Thrilling Days in Army Life* (New York: Harper, 1900), 142–43; Wheelan, *Terrible Swift Sword,* 148–50.

386 **"salute of one hundred guns"** USG to Benjamin F. Butler and GGM, October 20, 1864, *Grant Papers,* 12:328n.

386 **"one of the most brilliant"** GGM to USG, October 20, 1864, *Grant Papers,* 12:328n.

386 **"I propose that you give"** AL, "Response to a Serenade," October 21, 1864, *CWAL,* 8:57–58.

Chapter 23. Appomattox

387 **He won the soldiers' vote** Catton, *Grant Takes Command,* 383–84; White, *A. Lincoln,* 644–45.

387 **Grant wrote Stanton** USG to EMS, November 10, 1864, *Grant Papers,* 12:398.

387 **"Damn the torpedoes!"** James M. McPherson, *War on the Waters: The Union and Confederate Navies, 1861–1865* (Chapel Hill: University of North Carolina Press, 2012), 207–13.

387 **"in a balky team"** Porter, *Campaigning with Grant,* 278.

389 **"better than I can do"** USG to WTS, September 12, 1864, *Grant Papers,* 12:154–55.

389 **After first expressing** Catton, *Grant Takes Command,* 387; Marszalek, *Sherman,* 295.

389 **A veteran who had distinguished himself** John P. Dyer, *The Gallant Hood* (Indianapolis: Bobbs-Merrill, 1950), 22–23, 194, 210.

389 **On September 29, Hood crossed** Hood left William J. Hardee's Department of South Carolina, Georgia, and Florida, to defend against Sherman.

389 **A dismayed Northern public** Davis, *Jefferson Davis,* 575; Dyer, *Gallant Hood,* 279; Wills, *George Henry Thomas,* 284–85; Hattaway and Jones, *How the North Won,* 629–31.

389 **"Hood may turn"** WTS to USG, October 11, 1864, *Grant Papers,* 12:290n.

390 **"Hood's entire army"** George H. Thomas to USG, November 25, 1864, *Grant Papers,* 13:24.

390 **"a single, lame ring horse"** William L. Slout, *Clowns and Cannons: The American Circus During the Civil War* (San Bernardino, Calif.: Emeritus Enterprise, 1997), 175.

390 **"to invest that place"** *Personal Memoirs,* 2:378–79; Wills, *George Henry Thomas,* 291–94; Dyer, *Gallant Hood,* 289–95.

390 **"This looks like"** EMS to USG, December 2, 1864, *Grant Papers,* 13:50–51n; Thomas and Hyman, *Stanton,* 341.

390 **"If Hood is permitted"** USG to George H. Thomas, December 2, 1864, *Grant Papers,* 13:52–53.

390 **"Should you get him"** Ibid., 13:53; Wills, *George Henry Thomas,* 296.

390 **"No battle yet"** Samuel H. Beckwith, "Samuel H. Beckwith: 'Grant's Shadow,' " in David L. Wilson and John Y. Simon, eds., *Ulysses S. Grant: Essays and Documents* (Carbondale: Southern Illinois University Press), 116.

390 **"I would recommend superseding"** USG to EMS, December 7, 1864, *Grant Papers,* 13:78–79.

391 **"If you wish Genl Thomas"** HWH to USG, December 8, 1864, *Grant Papers,* 13:84n.

391 **"A terrible storm"** George H. Thomas to USG, December 9, 1864, *Grant Papers,* 13:88.

391 **"I am very unwilling"** USG to HWH, December 9, *Grant Papers,* 13, 90–91.

391 **"not to deliver the order"** *Personal Memoirs,* 2:382–83; Gary Ecelbarger, *Black Jack Logan* (Guilford, Conn.: Lyons Press, 2005), 213–14; James Pickett Jones, *Black Jack: John A. Logan and Southern Illinois in the Civil War Era* (Tallahassee: Florida State University Press, 1967), 241–42.

391 **After gathering a pocketful of cigars** Beckwith, " 'Grant's Shadow,' " in Wilson and Simon, eds., *Grant: Essays and Documents,* 117.

392 **"Push the enemy"** USG to George H. Thomas, December 15, 1864, *Grant Papers,* 13:124; Wills, *George Henry Thomas,* 317–19.

392 **Hood's army, reduced** Dyer, *Gallant Hood,* 301–4.

392 **"I take great satisfaction"** WTS to USG, December 22, 1864, *Sherman,* 771.

392 **"I beg to present"** WTS to AL, December 22, 1864, *Sherman,* 772.

392 **"I feel great anxiety"** USG to Benjamin F. Butler, December 4, 1864, *Grant Papers,* 13:61.

392 **"What is the prospect for getting"** USG to Benjamin F. Butler, December 14, 1864, *Grant Papers,* 13:119.

392 **Porter, who could be brash** Symonds, *Lincoln and His Admirals,* 19, 188. Butler had read in the newspaper of the damage caused by an accidental explosion of a barge at the British port of Erith.

393 **With all eyes watching** For a lively account of the attack upon Fort Fisher, see Rod Gragg, *Confederate Goliath: The Battle of Fort Fisher* (New York: HarperCollins, 1991). For the navy story, see McPherson, *War on the Waters,* 213–21; Symonds, *Lincoln and His Admirals,* 347–48.

393 **Butler finally arrived** Gragg, *Confederate Goliath,* 65–73.

393 **Once ashore, Weitzel observed** Ibid., 81; Comstock, *Diary,* entry December 24, 1864, 298–99; McPherson, *War on the Waters,* 215. What Porter did not know was that the defenders, with only three thousand rounds for their forty-four guns, were husbanding their ammunition, often firing only every half hour.

393 **Butler did so knowing** Weitzel advised reembarkation, but Butler did not share with him Grant's orders not to withdraw. Trefousse, *Ben Butler,* 170–74. USG to EMS, January 7, 1865, *Grant Papers,* 13:241. Grant told Stanton that he gave Butler explicit orders, but they "were given verbally."

393 **"The Wilmington expedition"** USG to AL, December 28, 1864, *Grant Papers,* 12:177–78.

393 **"Please hold on"** USG to David Dixon Porter, December 30, 1864, *Grant Papers,* 13:190.

393 **"I am constrained"** USG to EMS, January 4, 1865, *Grant Papers,* 13:223. Grant wrote in his memoirs, "Butler made a fearful mistake. My instructions to him . . . were explicit in the statement that to effect a landing would be of itself a great victory, and if one should be effected, the foothold must not be relinquished." *Personal Memoirs,* 2:394.

394 **"I do think Price"** USG to HWH, October 13, 1864, *Grant Papers,* 12:306; Hattaway and Jones, *How the North Won,* 635. For a sympathetic portrait of Rosecrans in Missouri, see Lamers, *Edge of Glory,* 415–39.

394 **"Has Rosecrans yet"** USG to HWH, October 20, 1864, *Grant Papers,* 12:329.

394 **"I know no Department"** USG to EMS, December 2, 1864, *Grant Papers,* 13:49.

394 **"dismissal from service"** Ibid., January 1–3, 1865, *Grant Papers,* 13:199.

394 **In his place** Glenn Tucker, *Hancock the Superb* (Indianapolis: Bobbs-Merrill, 1960), 261; Stephen R. Taaffe, *Commanding the Army of the Potomac* (Lawrence: University Press of Kansas, 2006), 193–94.

395 **"I was induced"** USG to WTS, January 21, 1864, *Grant Papers*, 13:291.

395 **He ordered George Stoneman's** Catton, *Grant Takes Command*, 406–07.

396 **"I have served"** USG to Alfred H. Terry, January 3, 1865, *Grant Papers*, 13:219; Gragg, *Confederate Goliath*, 105–6.

396 **Gratified, Grant watched** Gragg, *Confederate Goliath*, 138–229; Symonds, *Civil War at Sea*, 162–64; McPherson, *War on the Waters*, 217–19. McPherson writes, "It was the crowning achievement of combined operations in the war."

396 **"it would be mischievous"** WTS to USG, January 21, 1864, *Grant Papers*, 13:350–51n; Marszalek, *Sherman*, 335.

396 **"No one would be more pleased"** USG to WTS, February 1, 1864, *Grant Papers*, 13:349–50.

396 **"for the eminent services"** George H. Stuart to USG, January 2, 1865; USG to George H. Stuart, January 4, 1865, *Grant Papers*, 13:234–35. The United States Christian Commission was founded in 1861 to offer religious support, including Protestant chaplains and social services, to soldiers in the field.

396 **Ulysses encouraged Julia** USG to JDG, January 4, 1865, *Grant Papers*, 13:233–34.

397 **"her amiability"** Porter, *Campaigning with Grant*, 284.

397 **"I am snugly nestled"** Cited in Geoffrey Perret, *Ulysses S. Grant: Soldier and President* (New York: Random House, 1997), 349.

397 **Eager to keep** USG to J. Russell Jones, January 10, 1865, *Grant Papers*, 13:261.

397 **He provided** Porter, *Campaigning with Grant*, 382–83; Cadwallader, *Three Years with Grant*, 288.

397 **"It was something"** *Personal Memoirs*, 2:421.

398 **"I have not felt"** USG to EMS, February 1, 1865, *Grant Papers*, 13:345–46; Donald, *Lincoln*, 557.

398 **"Say to the gentlemen"** AL to USG, *CWAL*, 8:256.

398 **In a dramatic backdrop** The movie *Lincoln* [2012] focuses on the passage of the Thirteenth Amendment. For a fine treatment, see Michael Vorenberg, *Final Freedom: The Civil War, the Abolition of Slavery, and the Thirteenth Amendment* (Cambridge, U.K.: Cambridge University Press, 2001).

398 **The Hampton Roads conference** Donald, ed., *Inside Lincoln's Cabinet*, 557–59; Simpson, *Grant*, 405–7.

398 **"Please read"** AL to USG, January 19, 1865, *CWAL*, 8:223; Jason Emerson, *Giant in the Shadows: The Life of Robert T. Lincoln* (Carbondale: Southern Illinois University Press, 2012), 90.

398 **"I will be most happy"** USG to AL, January 21, 1865, *Grant Papers*, 13:281.

398 **Robert reported** Emerson, *Robert T. Lincoln*, 91.

398 **"I shall necessarily"** USG to EMS, February 4, 1865, *Grant Papers*, 13:362.

399 **Johnston, Sherman's antagonist** McPherson, *Battle Cry*, 828; Marszalek, *Sherman*, 328; Thomas, *Robert E. Lee*, 348. Johnston had long feuded with Davis, but when Lee was appointed general in chief of all the Confederate armies on January 31, this cleared the way for Lee to restore Johnston.

399 **His main worry** Introduction, *Grant Papers*, 14:xiii.

399 **"an interchange of views"** Robert E. Lee to USG, March 2, 1865, *Grant Papers*, 14:99n.

399 **"The President directs"** EMS to USG, March 3, 1865, *Grant Papers*, 14:91n.

399 **Shortly after Lincoln's** Julia Dent Grant, *Personal Memoirs*, 141–42; Emerson, *Robert T. Lincoln*, 95.

399 **"Can you not visit"** USG to AL, March 20, 1865, *Grant Papers,* 14:215n.

400 **"the pleasure of listening"** USG to John H. Vincent, May 25, 1862, *Grant Papers,* 5:132; Vincent, *John Heyl Vincent,* 52–53.

400 **"he had not attended"** Vincent, *John Heyl Vincent,* 98–99.

400 **"What does the woman mean"** Badeau, *Grant in Peace,* 356–58.

400 **"I suppose you think"** Ibid., 359; Julia Dent Grant, *Personal Memoirs,* 142, 145–47. For another version of this story, see Cadwallader, *Three Years with Grant,* 282–83. He describes how Mary Lincoln treated Julia "rather haughtily." The story of Mary Lincoln's rage, and many would say selfishness, made the rounds. Julia Dent Grant, *Personal Memoirs,* 146.

400 **With the Confederate and Union** Grant telegraphed Meade, "I would not recommend making any attack against entrenched lines." USG to GGM, February 6, 1865, *Grant Papers,* 13:382.

401 **Grant came with Lincoln** Taaffe, *Commanding the Army of the Potomac,* 200; McPherson, *Battle Cry,* 845.

401 **"What [is] to be done"** Sherman, *Memoirs,* 2:326.

402 **After grasping** Porter, *Campaigning with Grant,* 425–26; Taaffe, *Commanding the Army of the Potomac,* 205.

402 **When Sheridan became stalled** USG to PHS, March 30, 1865, *Grant Papers,* 14:269.

402 **"I'm ready to strike"** Sheridan, *Personal Memoirs,* 2:143–45; Porter, *Campaigning with Grant,* 428–29; Wheelan, *Terrible Swift Sword,* 174–75.

402 **Finally, goddamning Warren** Nearly five thousand of Pickett's troops were killed, wounded, or taken prisoner, as opposed to only one thousand Union casualties.

402 **Warren appealed directly** *Personal Memoirs,* 2:445; Porter, *Campaigning with Grant,* 435–41; Wheelan, *Terrible Swift Sword,* 181–84.

402 **"Understand: I do not wish"** USG to Edward O. C. Ord, April 1, 1865, *Grant Papers,* 14:302–03.

403 **Richmond must be given up** Davis, *Jefferson Davis,* 603.

403 **Although he was anxious** *Personal Memoirs,* 2:459–61; Lyman, *Meade's Headquarters,* 340–41; Catton, *A Stillness at Appomattox,* 364.

403 **"Do you know, general"** Porter, *Campaigning with Grant,* 450.

403 **"but I had a feeling"** *Personal Memoirs,* 2:460; Porter, *Campaigning with Grant,* 450–51.

403 **"I am now writing"** USG to JDG, April 2, 1865, *Grant Papers,* 14:330.

403 **But when he arrived** Freeman, *R. E. Lee,* 4:66–67.

404 **"I wish you were here"** Porter, *Campaigning with Grant,* 453–54.

404 **"Why, there's the old man"** *Personal Memoirs,* 2:468–69; Porter, *Campaigning with Grant,* 454–56.

404 **Grant's armies captured** Freeman, *R. E. Lee,* 4:81–93.

404 **"The result"** USG to Robert E. Lee, April 7, 1865, *Grant Papers,* 14:361; Porter, *Campaigning with Grant,* 459; Catton, *Grant Takes Command,* 436.

405 **"restoration of peace"** Robert E. Lee to USG, April 8, 1865, *Grant Papers,* 14:367n.

405 **"fearful pain"** Lyman, *Meade's Headquarters,* 354; *Personal Memoirs,* 2:483.

405 **"There is nothing left"** Freeman, *R. E. Lee,* 4:120; Thomas, *Robert E. Lee,* 360–62.

405 **"Old Pete"** Freeman, *R. E. Lee,* 4:131.

405 **Grant took off** *Personal Memoirs,* 2:490; Freeman, *R. E. Lee,* 4:135–36; Catton, *Grant Takes Command,* 464.

406 **"This done"** Catton, *Grant Takes Command,* 465.

406 **"Well, the subject is quite new"** *Personal Memoirs,* 2:493; Freeman, *R. E. Lee,* 4:138–39.

406 **"This will have the best possible"** Simpson, *Grant,* 435; Smith, *Grant,* 405; Freeman, *R. E. Lee,* 4:138.

407 **"The war is over"** Porter, *Campaigning with Grant,* 486.

Chapter 24. "I Will Keep My Word"

411 **Several Confederate officers** Porter, *Campaigning with Grant,* 490–91.

411 **"There was nothing"** John B. Gordon, *Reminiscences of the Civil War* (New York: Charles Scribner's Sons, 1903), 460–61; Frank A. Burr, *The Life and Deeds of General U. S. Grant* (Philadelphia: National Publishing, 1885), 813.

411 **"Pete, let us have another game"** Interview with James Longstreet, *New York Times,* July 24, 1885.

411 **For that small nation** McPherson, *Battle Cry,* 854.

411 **It is now accepted** J. David Hacker, "A Census-Based Count of the Civil War Dead," *Civil War History* 57, no. 4 (December 2011): 306–47. William F. Fox and Thomas Leonard Livermore, both of whom fought for the Union, completed their study in 1889. Hacker argues that the greatest undercount was on the Confederate side.

412 **"The civil war of '61"** George Ticknor to George T. Curtis, July 30, 1869. George Ticknor, *Life, Letters, and Journals of George Ticknor,* vol. 2 (Boston: Osgood, 1876), 485; James M. McPherson, *Abraham Lincoln and the Second American Revolution* (New York: Oxford University Press, 1990), vii.

412 **"I would not distress these people"** Julia Dent Grant, *Personal Memoirs,* 153.

412 **"Mr. Lincoln is certain"** Badeau, *Grant in Peace,* 21.

412 **But while Grant was meeting** Donald, *Lincoln,* 595.

412 **When the Grants' train arrived** Charles E. Bolles, "General Grant and the News of Mr. Lincoln's Death," *Century Magazine* 40 (June 1890): 309–10.

412 **THE PRESIDENT WAS ASSASSINATED** Thomas T. Eckert to USG, April 15, 12:20 A.M., *Grant Papers,* 14:390n.

413 **Could he have prevented** Grant would write later, "It would be impossible for me to describe the feeling that overcame me at the news." *Personal Memoirs,* 2:509.

413 **"this fills me"** Julia Dent Grant, *Personal Memoirs,* 156.

413 **During the April 19 funeral** Noah Brooks, *Washington in Lincoln's Time* (New York: Century Co., 1895), 262–63.

414 **"I have every reason"** USG to Charles W. Ford, April 17, 1865, *Grant Papers,* 14:405.

414 **He trained as a tailor** See Hans L. Trefousse, *Andrew Johnson: A Biography* (New York: W. W. Norton & Co., 1989), 27; Eric Foner, *Reconstruction: America's Unfinished Revolution* (New York: Harper & Row, 1988), 176.

414 **"free land"** Trefousse, *Andrew Johnson,* 53–54.

414 **This act made him** *PAJ,* 4, xx–xxi; Trefousse, *Andrew Johnson,* 131–33.

414 **In 1862, when Lincoln believed** Trefousse, *Andrew Johnson,* 152–55.

415 **After five terms** Ibid., 88.

415 **"the same terms"** WTS to USG, April 15, 1865, *Sherman,* 862.

415 **"are of such importance"** USG to EMS, April 21, 1865, *Grant Papers,* 14:423; Marszalek, *Sherman,* 346.

415 **Johnson and everyone** WTS to USG, April 18, 1865, *Sherman,* 863–65; Marszalek, *Sherman,* 346; Lewis, *Sherman,* 550.

415 **"abstained from censure"** Welles, *Diary,* entry April 21, 1865, 2:294–95.

415 **Grant believed** *Personal Memoirs*, 2:516.

415 **On his way, he learned** Thomas and Hyman, *Stanton*, 408–09; see Marszalek, *Sherman*, for a sampling of the attacks on Sherman: in the editorial pages of *The New York Times, New York Tribune, Chicago Tribune, New York Herald*, and *Washington Star*, 349–50.

416 **"It is infamous"** Badeau, *Grant in Peace*, 120.

416 **Grant stood near the White House** Richardson, *A Personal History*, 508.

417 **"When This Cruel War"** Porter, *Campaigning with Grant*, 505–07; Catton, *Grant Takes Command*, 490–92; Simpson, *Grant*, 448–49.

417 **During the six-hour march** Smith, *Grant*, 415–16.

417 **Johnson assured him** Simpson, *Grant*, 449–50; Trefousse, *Andrew Johnson*, 216–18.

417 **"Although it would meet"** USG to HWH, May 6, 1865, *Grant Papers*, 15:11.

417 **Lee was relieved** Freeman, *R. E. Lee*, 4, 200–203.

418 **Grant let Lee know** Badeau, *Grant in Peace*, 25–27.

418 **On June 13, Lee wrote Grant** Robert E. Lee to USG, June 13, 1865, *Grant Papers*, 15:150n.

418 **"In my opinion the officers"** USG to EMS, June 16, 1865, *Grant Papers*, 15:149.

418 **"When can these men"** Young, *Around the World*, vol. 2:460–61.

418 **"I will not stay"** Badeau, *Grant in Peace*, 26.

418 **On the same day** USG to Robert E. Lee, June 20, 1865, *Grant Papers*, 15:210–11.

418 **But when cheers** Garland, *Grant*, 325–27; Simpson, *Grant*, 450–51; Smith, *Grant*, 419.

418–19 **General Winfield Scott** Garland, *Grant*, 327.

419 **"It is too soon"** *Chicago Tribune*, June 14, 1865.

419 **When he learned** Vincent, *John Heyl Vincent*, 101; O. H. Tiffany, *Pulpit and Platform: Sermons and Addresses* (New York: Hunt & Eaton, 1893), 202–3.

419 **The Methodist minister** Vincent, *John Heyl Vincent*, 102–03.

419 **"I am not a candidate"** Garland, *Grant*, 337–38.

420 **"in my judgment"** Thomas D. Schoonover, trans. and ed., *Mexican Lobby: Matías Romero in Washington, 1861–1867* (Lexington: University Press of Kentucky, 1986), memorandum, April 30, 1866, 58.

420 **Grant's esteem** Ibid., memorandum, May 16, 1866, 61.

420 **"I am very pleased"** Ibid., memorandum, June 5, 1866, 65.

420 **"I regard the act"** USG to AJ, June 19, 1865, *Grant Papers*, 15:156–58.

421 **"I need not tell you"** USG to PHS, June 16, 1865, *Grant Papers*, 15:154.

421 **"nonintervention in Mexican affairs"** USG to AJ, November 7, 1865, *Grant Papers*, 15:401–2.

421 **"protect the freedmen"** USG to EMS, October 1865, *Grant Papers*, 15:357–58.

421 **"Their whole thought"** Flanders cited by Foner, *Reconstruction*, in his description of the development of the Black Codes, 199–201, 208–9.

422 **This meant that by the fall** Ira Berlin and Leslie S. Rowland, eds., *Freedom: A Documentary History of Emancipation, 1861–1867*, series II: *The Black Military Experience* (New York: New Press, 1997), 733.

422 **Dissatisfied with Schurz** Hans L. Trefousse, *Carl Schurz: A Biography* (Knoxville: University of Tennessee Press, 1982), 153–60; for Schurz's letters to Johnson, see Brooks D. Simpson, LeRoy P. Graf, and John Muldowny, eds., *Advice After Appomattox: Letters to Andrew Johnson, 1865–1866*, special vol. 1 of *The Papers of Andrew Johnson* (Knoxville: University of Tennessee Press, 1987), 61–150, quotation on page 69. Schurz wrote Senator Charles Sumner on October 17, 1865, "The President is not at all favorable to me on account of the report," 74.

422 **"express openly"** Comstock, *Diary*, entry December 1, 1865, 324–25.

422 **"The people are more loyal"** Welles, *Diary*, entry December 15, 1865, 2:396–97.

422 **"I am satisfied"** USG to AJ, December 18, 1865, *Grant Papers*, 15:434–37.

422 **Newspapers lauded** Simpson, *Let Us Have Peace,* offers an excellent summary of Grant's trip, report, and the response to his findings.

422 **"I traveled"** Carl Schurz to Margarethe Schurz, December 20, 1868, in Carl Schurz and Joseph Schafer, *Intimate Letters of Carl Schurz, 1841–1869,* vol. 30 (Madison: State Historical Society of Wisconsin, 1928), 457.

422 **"Send to these Hd Qrs."** USG to George H. Thomas, Thomas H. Ruger, Alfred H. Terry, and Daniel Sickles, *Grant Papers*, 16:69–70n.

423 **The Thirteenth Amendment** McPherson, *Battle Cry,* 241, 840.

423 **They all came** For the definition and leaders of the Radical Republicans, see Hans Trefousse, *The Radical Republicans: Lincoln's Vanguard for Racial Justice* (New York: Alfred A. Knopf, 1969), 3–33, and Foner, *Reconstruction,* 228–39.

423 **Grant's primary goal** Garland, *Grant,* 346–47.

423–24 **So when sixteen** Foner, *Reconstruction,* 239.

424 **"civil rights belonging"** *Congressional Globe,* 39th Congress, 1st sess., January 29, 1865, 319; Foner, *Reconstruction,* 243.

424 **Grant listened** Chronology, *Grant Papers*, 16:xxi.

425 **"charged with offenses"** USG, General Orders No. 3, January 12, 1865, *Grant Papers,* 16:7–8.

425 **"It contains many"** William H. Barnes, *History of the Thirty-ninth Congress of the United States* (New York: Harper, 1868), 123.

425 **It conferred citizenship** *Congressional Globe,* 39th Congress, 1st sess., January 29, 1865, 319.

425 **The Senate passed** Mark M. Krug, *Lyman Trumbull: Conservative Radical* (New York: A. S. Barnes, 1965), 240.

426 **"I suppose a man"** USG to Charles W. Ford, October 28, 1865, *Grant Papers,* 15:372; USG to William Coffin, November 3, 1865, *Grant Papers,* 15:388; USG to J. Russell Jones, March 27, 1866, *Grant Papers,* 16:136–37.

426 **"Not enough to support"** Daniel Butterfield, to USG, February 15, 1866, *Grant Papers,* 16:74n; Daniel Butterfield to Elihu B. Washburne, December 8, 1865, *Grant Papers,* 16:75n; Julia Dent Grant, *Personal Memoirs,* 167n12. Butterfield became famous for writing the music to "Taps" in 1862.

426 **"I feel at a loss"** USG to Daniel Butterfield, February 17, 1866, *Grant Papers*, 16:74.

426 **In accepting houses** Smith, *Grant,* 420.

426 **Furthermore, he would not sign** Foner, *Reconstruction,* 247–49; Trefousse, *Andrew Johnson,* 242–43.

426 **It was not too late** Trefousse, *Andrew Johnson,* 243–45; Krug, *Lyman Trumbull,* 239–40.

427 **"The distinction of race"** Foner, *Reconstruction,* 250; Trefousse, *Andrew Johnson,* 241, 244.

427 **For the first time** Trefousse, *Andrew Johnson,* 245–47; Foner, *Reconstruction,* 250–51.

428 **"The condition of things"** USG to AJ, February 9, 1866, *Grant Papers,* 16:52–53.

428 **"For the present"** USG to George H. Thomas, January 9, 1866, *Grant Papers,* 16:54. Grant added, "Whilst such a force is retained in the South, I doubt the propriety of putting Arms in the hands of the Militia."

428 **"take immediate Military possession"** USG to Alfred H. Terry, February 9, 1866, *Grant Papers,* 16:71.

428 **" 'makes satisfactory explanation' "** AJ to USG, February 16, 1866, *PAJ,* 10:110.

428 **"to give a cordial support"** Edward Rives Pollard to AJ, February 16, 1866, *Grant Papers,* 16:71.

428 **"The course of the 'Examiner' "** USG to AJ, February 17, 1866, *Grant Papers,* 16:70.

428 **"temporarily suspended"** USG to Alfred H. Terry, February 19, 1866, *Grant Papers,* 16:71.

429 **"sentiments of disloyalty"** Theodore S. Bowers to Commanding Officers, February 17, 1866, *Grant Papers,* 16:72.

429 **Not waiting** See telegrams to Grant, March 21 and April 6, 1866, *Grant Papers,* 16:73n.

429 **February 19, the day** For a more comprehensive treatment of Grant, Johnson, and the *Examiner,* see Simpson, *Let Us Have Peace,* 130–32.

429 **"Gen. Grant's reception"** *New York Times,* June 7, 1866.

429 **"appropriate General Grant"** Welles, *Diary,* entry April 6, 1866, 2:477–78; Ross, *The General's Wife,* 196; Lately Thomas, *The First President Johnson: The Three Lives of the Seventeenth President of the United States of America* (New York: Morrow, 1968), 449.

429 **Most surprising of all** Hans L. Trefousse, *Thaddeus Stevens: Nineteenth-Century Egalitarian* (Chapel Hill: University of North Carolina Press, 1997), 190.

429 **"amid the exultation"** Welles, *Diary,* entry April 6, 1866, 2:478.

430 **"It was the happiest gathering"** Rutherford B. Hayes, *Diary and Letters of Rutherford Birchard Hayes,* vol. 3, edited by Charles Richard Williams (Columbus: Ohio State Archaeological and Historical Society, 1924), 22.

Chapter 25. "More & More Radical"

431 **On April 2, 1866** Andrew Johnson, "Proclamation re End of Insurrection," April 2, 1865, *PAJ,* 10:349–52.

431 **At Johnson's direction** Thomas and Hyman, *Stanton,* 477–78.

431 **"I find that those parts"** *New York Times,* May 26, 1866.

432 **"All persons"** For the Fourteenth Amendment, see Garrett Epps, *Democracy Reborn: The Fourteenth Amendment and the Fight for Equal Rights in Post–Civil War America* (New York: Henry Holt, 2006), and Joseph B. James, *The Framing of the Fourteenth Amendment* (Urbana: University of Illinois Press, 1965).

432 **With no restraints** On the Memphis riots, see Bobby L. Lovett, "Memphis Riots: White Reaction to Blacks in Memphis, May 1865–July 1866," *Tennessee Historical Quarterly* 38 (Spring 1979): 9–33; James G. Ryan, "The Memphis Riot of 1866: Terror in a Black Community During Reconstruction," *Journal of Negro History* 62 (July 1977): 243–57; Jack D. L. Holmes, "The Underlying Causes of the Memphis Race Riot of 1866," *Tennessee Historical Quarterly* 17 (September 1958): 195–221.

433 **"This time"** *Memphis Argus,* May 5, 1866, cited in Lovett, "Memphis Riots," 28.

433 **"Yankee Black Republicanism"** Lovett, "Memphis Riots," 13.

434 **Seventy-five people** *Congressional Globe,* "Memphis Riots and Massacres," Report of Select Committee, 39th Congress, 1st sess., House Report 101 [serial 1274]; William S. McFeely, *Yankee Stepfather: General O. O. Howard and the Freedmen* (New Haven, Conn.: Yale University Press, 1968), 274–82.

434 **"They assembled in no bodies"** *Congressional Globe,* "Memphis Riots and Massacres," 5.

434 **"If the Civil Authorities fail"** USG to George H. Thomas, July 6, 1866, *Grant Papers,* 16:230–31; Wills, *George Henry Thomas,* 389–90.

434 **"The victims were all"** USG to EMS, July 7, 1866, *Grant Papers,* 16:233–34.

434 **"Gen. Grant well remarks"** James Speed to AJ, July 15, 1866, *PAJ,* 10:688–89.

434 **"The names of the leaders"** George H. Thomas to USG, August 15, 1866, *Grant Papers,* 16:231n1.

434 **"I do not feel authorized"** USG to George H. Thomas, August 16, 1866, *Grant Papers,* 16:323n1.

435 **Increasingly a man** See Eric L. McKitrick, *Andrew Johnson and Reconstruction* (Chicago: University of Chicago Press, 1960), 394–420; Trefousse, *Andrew Johnson*, 255–62.

435 **In the end** Trefousse, *Andrew Johnson*, 258, 261–62; Foner, *Reconstruction*, 264.

435 **"I do not think it proper"** USG to Elihu B. Washburne, August 16, 1866, *Grant Papers*, 16:298.

435 **"I am getting very tired"** USG to JDG, August 31, 1866, *Grant Papers*, 16:306–7.

435 **"generally received"** Welles, *Diary*, entry September 17, 1866, 2:589, 591, 593.

435 **"General Grant's presence"** Romero, *Mexican Lobby*, memorandum, September 7, 1866, 143.

436 **"disfranchise white men"** AJ, speech at St. Louis, September 8, 1866, *PAJ*, 11:193, 199.

436 **"I have never been so tired"** USG to JDG, September 9, 1866, *Grant Papers*, 16:308.

436 **He left the tour** Badeau, *Grant in Peace*, 39.

436 **He wrote in his diary** Comstock, *Diary*, entry October 23, 1866, 337–38.

436 **Sherman was more amenable** Marszalek, *Sherman*, 368–70; Lewis, *Sherman*, 588.

437 **"I will not venture"** USG to WTS, October 18, 1866, *Grant Papers*, 16:337–38.

437 **"There is some plan"** WTS to Ellen Sherman, October 26, 1866, *Grant Papers*, 16:339–40n.

437 **"It is a diplomatic service"** USG to AJ, October 21, 1866, *Grant Papers*, 16:346–47.

437 **"Mr. Attorney General"** Badeau, in *Grant in Peace*, 53–54, wrote, "He returned immediately to his headquarters, and recited all that had occurred. I took down the words at the time, and read him afterward this account, which he approved."

437–38 **"You, nor no man living"** USG to William S. Hillyer, September 19, 1866, *Grant Papers*, 16:310.

438 **The *New York Times* believed the election** *New York Times*, October 24, 1866; Leslie H. Fishel, Jr., "Northern Prejudice and Negro Suffrage," *Journal of Negro History* 39 (January 1954): 17.

438 **"right man"** Lawanda Cox and John H. Cox, *Politics, Principle, and Prejudice: 1865– 1866* (Glencoe, Ill.: Free Press, 1963), 88–95; Foner, *Reconstruction*, 260–61, 264; Trefousse, *Andrew Johnson*, 269.

438 **"I much fear"** USG to PHS, October 12, 1866, *Grant Papers*, 16:330–31.

438 **In September, a warier Grant** USG to Alexander B. Dyer, September 22, 1866, *Grant Papers*, 16:331–32n1.

438 **"that Texas should have"** USG to PHS, October 12, 1866, *Grant Papers*, 16:330–31.

438 **"I will not be able"** USG to Elihu B. Washburne, October 23, 1866, *Grant Papers*, 16:549.

438 **"This is the most decisive"** *The Nation*, November 15, 1866; Foner, *Reconstruction*, 268.

438 **The practical result** McKitrick, *Andrew Johnson*, 447.

439 **"He was rather Conservative"** *Washington Daily National Intelligencer*, November 24, 1866; Trefousse, *Andrew Johnson*, 272.

439 **One year before** Thomas and Hyman, *Stanton*, 520.

439 **"send me a list"** USG to Oliver O. Howard, January 18, 1867, *Grant Papers*, 17:50n; Carpenter, *Sword and Olive Branch*, 129.

439 **"for information"** USG to EMS, February 8, 1867, *Grant Papers*, 17:50.

439 **"General Grant urged"** Welles, *Diary*, entry January 5, 1867, 3:8.

439 **"When you get home"** Richardson, *A Personal History*, 535.

439 **"He has spoken in all places"** *New York Independent*, March 7, 1867. For the *Independent* as an opinion maker, see Ronald C. White, Jr., *Liberty and Justice for All: Racial Reform and the Social Gospel, 1877–1925* (San Francisco: HarperCollins, 1990), 127–28.

439 **"General getting more & more radical"** Comstock, *Diary,* entry, March 1, 1867, 344.

440 **"His equanimity"** Badeau, *Grant in Peace,* 75.

440 **Grant, sensing some opposition** Louis A. Coolidge, *Ulysses S. Grant* (Boston: Houghton Mifflin, 1917), 248–49; Trefousse, *Andrew Johnson,* 278; Hans L. Trefousse, *Impeachment of a President: Andrew Johnson, the Blacks, and Reconstruction* (Knoxville: University of Tennessee Press, 1975), 45–46.

440 **"one of the most ridiculous"** USG to Elihu B. Washburne, March 4, 1867, *Grant Papers,* 17:76.

440 **In the end** Orville H. Browning, *The Diary of Orville Hickman Browning, 1865–1881,* edited by Theodore C. Pease (Springfield: Collections of the Illinois State Historical Society, vol. 22, 1933), entry March 9, 1867, 2:135; Trefousse, *Andrew Johnson,* 281.

440 **Two days later** USG, General Orders No. 10, March 11, 1867, *Grant Papers,* 17:80–81.

440 **"he is to some extent affected"** Welles, *Diary,* entry March 13, 1867, 3:65.

441 **"hold their offices"** McFeely, *Grant,* Tenure of Office Act, 262; *PAJ,* 14:42.

441 **Even worse** George S. Boutwell, "Johnson's Plot and Motives," *North American Review* 141 (December 1885): 572.

441 **Stevens appended it** George S. Boutwell, *Reminiscences of Sixty Years in Public Affairs,* vol. 2 (New York: McClure, Phillips, 1902), 107–08. Foner, *Reconstruction,* 333–34.

441 **Johnson signed it** Simpson, *Let Us Have Peace,* 173–74.

441 **With Julia's father** USG to Charles W. Ford, January 4, 1867, *Grant Papers,* 17:4–5; ibid., April 28, 1867, *Grant Papers,* 17:129.

441 **He wrote his St. Louis friend** USG to Charles W. Ford, March 24, 1867, *Grant Papers,* 17:90.

442 **On March 27, Sheridan removed** PHS, General Orders No. 5, March 27, 1867, *Grant Papers,* 17:93n; Wheelan, *Terrible Swift Sword,* 222.

442 **"It is just the thing"** USG to PHS, March 29, 1867, *Grant Papers,* 17:91–92.

442 **"I would advise"** Ibid., April 3, 1867, *Grant Papers,* 17:93n.

442 **"The fact is"** Ibid., April 5, 1867, *Grant Papers,* 17:95–96.

442 **"District Commanders are responsible"** USG to John Pope, April 21, 1867, *Grant Papers,* 17:117–18; for an overview of the actions of the five commanders, see James E. Sefton, *The United States Army and Reconstruction, 1865–1877* (Baton Rouge: Louisiana State University Press, 1967), 113–18.

442 **"there is, then"** Henry Stanbery to AJ, June 12, 1867, in *PAJ,* 12:321. For a summary and the full text, see 299–300, 320–32.

443 **"the law however"** USG to Edward O. C. Ord, June 23, 1867, *Grant Papers,* 17:192.

443 **"I have stated those views"** Testimony, House Judiciary Committee, July 18, 1867, *Grant Papers,* 17:210–35; Grant quotation, *Grant Papers,* 17:213.

443 **"The responsibility"** *New York Times,* July 31, 1867.

443 **The president blasted** David Miller DeWitt, *The Impeachment and Trial of Andrew Johnson* (New York: Macmillan, 1903), 224–31; Thomas and Hyman, *Stanton,* 546; Simpson, *Let Us Have Peace,* 185–87.

443 **"As soon as I receive"** USG to EMS, July 20, 1867, *Grant Papers,* 17:235.

444 **He even encouraged** Thomas and Hyman, *Stanton,* 546.

444 **"Every day that I am absent"** USG to EMS, July 24, 1867, *Grant Papers,* 17:239–40.

444 **"The meaning of the law"** USG to AJ, August 1, 1867, *Grant Papers,* 17:250–51.

444 **"to consider the effect"** Ibid., 251.

444 **"Public considerations"** AJ to EMS, August 5, 1867, *Grant Papers,* 17:269n.

444 **"I have the honor to say"** EMS to AJ, August 5, 1867, *Grant Papers,* 17:269n.

445 **"I feel the same obligation"** USG to Elihu B. Washburne, April 5, 1867, *Grant Papers,* 17:98.

Chapter 26. "Let Us Have Peace"

446 **So judged** Mark Twain, "The Czar's Soliloquy," in *Mark Twain: Collected Tales, Sketches, Speeches, and Essays, 1891–1910* (New York: Library Classics of America, 1976), 645.

446 **On Sunday morning** Julia Dent Grant, *Personal Memoirs*, 165.

447 **"I consented"** Julia Dent Grant, *Personal Memoirs*, 165.

447 **There is no record** George C. Gorham, *Life and Public Services of Edwin M. Stanton* (Boston: Houghton Mifflin, 1899), 395–404; Thomas and Hyman, *Stanton*, 551.

447 **We might call Grant an introvert** My analysis of Grant has been helped by Susan Cain's pathbreaking book, *Quiet: The Power of Introverts in a World That Can't Stop Talking* (New York: Crown Publishing, 2012).

447 **he could be moved** Ibid., 17.

448 **"In notifying you"** USG to EMS, August 12, 1867, *Grant Papers*, 17:268.

448 **A friend, Horace White** Horace White to Elihu B. Washburne, August 13, 1867, Washburne Papers, Library of Congress.

448 **A foe** Irving H. Bartlett, *Wendell Phillips: Brahmin Radical* (Boston: Beacon Press, 1961), 309.

448 **One of Sheridan's greatest** AJ to USG, August 17, 1867, *Grant Papers*, 17:279; Wheelan, *Terrible Swift Sword*, 228.

448 **He had championed** Badeau, *Grant in Peace*, 95; Trefousse, *Andrew Johnson*, 196–97; Wheelan, *Terrible Swift Sword*, 227.

449 **"It is unmistakably"** USG to AJ, August 17, 1867, *Grant Papers*, 17:277–78.

449 **"a resort to authority"** AJ to USG, August 19, 1867, *Grant Papers*, 17:279–81.

449 **"It is not likely"** USG to Elihu B. Washburne, August 21, 1867, *Grant Papers*, 17:291.

449 **Thomas "has repeatedly"** USG to AJ, August 17, 1867, *Grant Papers*, 17:277–78.

449 **"The relief of Genl. Sheridan"** George H. Thomas to EMS, July 4, 1867, *Grant Papers*, 17:281–82n1; Wills, *George Henry Thomas*, 404–06.

449 **Armed with Thomas's letter** David M. Jordan, *Winfield Scott Hancock: A Soldier's Life* (Bloomington: Indiana University Press, 1988), 199–201; Tucker, *Hancock the Superb*, 276–78.

449 **"The Act of Congress"** USG to AJ, August 26, 1867, *Grant Papers*, 17:301–03; Trefousse, *Andrew Johnson*, 297–98.

450 **"appointments to civil office"** USG, Special Orders No. 429, August 29, 1867, *Grant Papers*, 17:304.

450 **"every word is golden"** "General Grant's protest against the removal of Sheridan must be regarded as the most extraordinary manifesto of our time." *Army and Navy Journal* (August 31, 1867).

450 **Stanton, his pride** Thomas and Hyman, *Stanton*, 557–59.

450 **Each morning** Richard M. Lee, *Mr. Lincoln's City: An Illustrated Guide to the Civil War Sites in Washington* (McLean, Va.: EPM Publications, 1981), 114. The War Department was located where the north wing of the Executive Office Building now stands.

450 **In the afternoon** Ibid., 118. The Winder Building was torn down in the 1940s.

450 **On one side** Badeau, *Grant in Peace*, 109–10.

451 **increasingly Grant absented** Ibid., 107–9.

451 **"politicians should"** USG to Edward O. C. Ord, September 22, 1867, *Grant Papers*, 17:354.

451 **Brownlow argued** Ben H. Severance, "Reconstruction Power Play: The 1867 Mayoral Election in Nashville, Tennessee," in Kent T. Dollar, Larry H. Whiteaker, and W. Calvin Dickinson, eds., *Sister States, Enemy States: The Civil War in Kentucky and Tennessee* (Lexington: University Press of Kentucky, 2009), 326.

451 **Thomas turned to Grant** George H. Thomas to USG, September 25, 1867, *Grant Papers,* 17:360n; Wills, *George Henry Thomas,* 409.

451 **"I neither instruct"** USG to George H. Thomas, September 25, 1867, *Grant Papers,* 17:361n.

451 **"If both parties"** George H. Thomas to USG, September 26, 1867, *Grant Papers,* 17:361n.

452 **"A collision is inevitable"** Ibid.

452 **"Nothing is clearer"** USG to George H. Thomas, September 26, 1867, *Grant Papers,* 17:361. The Radical candidate, Augustus E. Alden, won a landslide victory for mayor. Wills, *George Henry Thomas,* 409–13; Simpson, *Let Us Have Peace,* 201–02.

452 **"It is hoped"** USG to George H. Thomas, September 25, 1867, *Grant Papers,* 17:361n.

452 **"to confer"** AJ to WTS, October 2, 1867, *PAJ,* 13:131.

452 **"The President don't comprehend"** WTS to Ellen Sherman, October 7, 1867, in M. A. De Wolfe Howe, ed., *Home Letters of General Sherman* (New York: Charles Scribner's Sons, 1909), 360–62.

452 **He declined** Ibid., 362.

452 **"He is willing"** Browning, *Diary* 2, entry October 9, 1867, 163.

452 **"Grant's chance"** Strong, *Diary 4,* entry December 6, 1867, 4:171–72.

452 **Grant had become** Lee Kennett, *Sherman: A Soldier's Life* (New York: HarperCollins, 2001), 288.

453 **They knew he had become** James M. McPherson, *The Struggle for Equality: Abolitionists and the Negro in the Civil War and Reconstruction* (Princeton, N.J.: Princeton University Press, 1964), 417–19.

453 **"the most humiliating"** Bartlett, *Wendell Phillips,* 304; Trefousse, *Radical Republicans,* 339.

453 **On January 10, the Senate** McKitrick, *Andrew Johnson,* 501.

453 **But in rereading** Smith, *Grant,* 445.

453 **As Grant and Johnson parted** Badeau, *Grant in Peace,* 110–11.

453 **"Grant (the President remarked)"** "Notes of Colonel W. G. Moore, Private Secretary to President Johnson, 1866–1868," *American Historical Review* 19 (October 1913): 115.

454 **Late on Monday** Trefousse, *Impeachment of a President,* 123.

454 **"my functions"** USG to AJ, January 14, 1868, *Grant Papers,* 18:102–3; Badeau, *Grant in Peace,* 111–12.

454 **Townsend bowed** Thomas and Hyman, *Stanton,* 569–70.

454 **"cared nothing"** *Personal Memoirs,* 2:536.

454 **Feeling that his honor** Badeau, *Grant in Peace,* 112–13; Thomas and Hyman, *Stanton,* 570–71; Trefousse, *Impeachment of a President,* 126; Martin E. Mantell, *Johnson, Grant, and the Politics of Reconstruction* (New York: Columbia University Press, 1973), 83–84; David O. Stewart, *Impeached: The Trial of President Andrew Johnson and the Fight for Lincoln's Legacy* (New York: Simon & Schuster, 2009), 119–20.

454 **Seeking to defend himself** Stewart, *Impeached,* 122.

454 **"in consequence"** USG to AJ, January 28, 1868, *Grant Papers,* 18:116–18. Owing to the importance of the letter, Grant accepted editorial assistance from John Rawlins, who had returned to Washington from Galena to assist his boss.

454 **"I can but regard"** USG to AJ, February 3, 1868, *Grant Papers,* 18:124–26. On Rawlins's influence on Grant, see Badeau, *Grant in Peace,* 114–15.

455 **"In a question of veracity"** *New York Tribune,* January 17, 1868.

455 **In Dickens's second visit** Michael Slater, *Charles Dickens* (New Haven, Conn.: Yale University Press, 2009), 578–84.

455 **"the hope *something* would turn up"** USG to Elihu B. Washburne, August 16, 1864, *Grant Papers*, 12:16–17.

455 **The Grants were in the audience** Ross, *The General's Wife*, 198, 328.

455 **He "is a bolder man"** *Philadelphia Ledger*, February 10, 1868; Fawn Brodie, *Thaddeus Stevens: Scourge of the South* (New York: W. W. Norton & Co., 1959), 332–33.

456 **First, he tried** AJ to USG, February 12, 1868, *PAJ*, 13:556–57.

456 **"I never felt so troubled"** WTS to USG, February 14, 1868, *Grant Papers*, 18:139.

456 **"If it were at all certain"** Ibid.

456 **The gaunt** Thomas and Hyman, *Stanton*, 581–83; William B. Hesseltine, *Ulysses S. Grant, Politician* (New York: Dodd, Mead, 1935), 113–14.

456 **"I want some little time"** Thomas and Hyman, *Stanton*, 583–84.

456 **telegram: "Stick"** David Herbert Donald, *Charles Sumner and the Rights of Man* (New York: Alfred A. Knopf, 1970), 332.

456 **House and Senate** Trefousse, *Impeachment of the President*, 134, 149–50.

457 **At exactly one P.M.** John Niven, *Salmon P. Chase: A Biography* (New York: Oxford University Press, 1995), 420.

457 **The same verdict** Trefousse, *Impeachment of a President*, 165–72; Stewart, *Impeached*, 275–83.

458 **Grant, who decided** See McFeely, *Grant*, 274–75, for an astute analysis of Grant's position.

458 **Convention managers** Herbert Eaton, *Presidential Timber: A History of Nominating Conventions, 1868–1960* (Glencoe, Ill.: Free Press, 1964), 21–22; *New York Herald*, May 19, 21, 1868; *New York Times*, May 19, 1868.

458 **After an invocation** Trefousse, *Carl Schurz*, 167–68.

458 **"Match him"** Charles H. Coleman, *The Election of 1868: The Democratic Effort to Regain Control* (New York: Columbia University Press, 1933), 92; Richardson, *A Personal History*, 541.

458 **Nast's dare** Albert B. Paine, *Thomas Nast* (New York: Macmillan, 1904), 119–20; Fiona Deans Halloran, *Thomas Nast: The Father of Modern Political Cartoons* (Chapel Hill: University of North Carolina Press, 2012), 103–7.

458 **The contest droned** Willard H. Smith, *Schuyler Colfax: The Changing Fortunes of a Political Idol* (Indianapolis: Indiana Historical Bureau, 1952), 278–86; Coleman, *Election of 1868*, 92–93.

459 **"No shade of exultation"** Badeau, *Grant in Peace*, 144.

460 **"A purely Administrative officer"** USG to Joseph R. Hawley, May 29, 1868, *Grant Papers*, 18:263–64.

Chapter 27. Gold Panic

463 **"I have been forced"** USG to WTS, June 21, 1868, *Grant Papers*, 18:292–93.

463 **"This will probably be"** USG to JDG, July 17, 1868, *Grant Papers*, 19:9–10; Robert G. Athearn, *William Tecumseh Sherman and the Settlement of the West*, rev. ed. (1956; repr., Norman: University of Oklahoma Press, 1995), 212–14.

463 **"has enjoyed this trip"** USG to JDG, July 21, 1868, *Grant Papers*, 19:10–11.

464 **"the greatest Generals"** *New York Tribune*, July 22, 1868; *New York Times*, July 31, 1868; Athearn, *William Tecumseh Sherman and the Settlement of the West*, 214–15.

464 **"This is a White Man's"** Coleman, *Election of 1868*, 187; Eaton, *Presidential Timber*, 8–9; Joel H. Silbey, *A Respectable Minority: The Democratic Party in the Civil War Era, 1860–1868* (New York: W. W. Norton & Co., 1977), 204–8.

464 **After two days** Eaton, *Presidential Timber*, 1–2, 11–12; Coleman, *Election of 1868*, 239–45. Pendleton had been the Democratic vice-presidential candidate with

George McClellan in 1864. Stewart Mitchell, *Horatio Seymour of New York* (Cambridge, Mass.: Harvard University Press, 1938), 25, 57–58, 423.

464 **Seymour had spent** Mitchell, *Horatio Seymour,* 429–33; Strong, *Diary 3,* entry July 9, 1863, 222.

464 **The convention adjourned** William E. Parrish, *Frank Blair: Lincoln's Conservative* (Columbia: University of Missouri Press, 1998), 254.

464 **The *New York Times* reported he paid** *New York Times,* August 14, 1868.

465 **The long battle** Foner, *Reconstruction,* 338; Epps, *Democracy Reborn,* 252–53; James, *Framing of the Fourteenth Amendment,* 192.

465 **Both sides displayed** Mark Wahlgren Summers, *The Press Gang: Newspapers and Politics, 1865–1878* (Chapel Hill: University of North Carolina Press, 1994), 43.

465 **One word** Coleman, *Election of 1868,* 306.

465 **Richardson emphasized** Richardson, *A Personal History.* Richardson, who had doubled as a Union spy and was imprisoned for seven months in seven Confederate prisons until he escaped, brought celebrity status to his biography.

466 **By 1868** Halloran, *Thomas Nast: The Father of Modern Cartoons* (Chapel Hill: University of North Carolina Press, 2015), 69, 81.

466 **Democrats sought to criticize** Summers, *Press Gang,* 44; McFeely, *Grant,* 282–83.

466 **The *New York World* charged** *New York World,* May 25, 1868; Coleman, *Election of 1868,* 96.

466 **This latter claim** Lee's casualty rate, somewhere between 18 and 20 percent, was considerably higher than Grant's 10.2 percent. Elizabeth R. Varon, *Appomattox: Victory, Defeat, and Freedom at the End of the Civil War* (New York: Oxford University Press, 2013), 21–22.

467 **"my friends"** Mark Wahlgren Summers, *The Gilded Age; Or, The Hazards of New Functions* (Upper Saddle River, N.J.: Prentice Hall, 1997), 23.

467 **"of allowing himself"** Francis Preston Blair, Jr., to Francis Preston Blair, Sr., August 2, 1867, cited in Parrish, *Frank Blair,* 249.

467 **"excused the heat"** Badeau, *Grant in Peace,* 147.

467 **"Mrs. Grant, you must now"** Julia Dent Grant, *Personal Memoirs,* 172.

467 **"whether this order"** Simon Wolf, *The Presidents I Have Known* (Washington, D.C.: Byron S. Adams, 1918), 66; Simon Wolf to USG, April 14, 1868, *Grant Papers,* 19:18–19; Sarna, *When Grant Expelled the Jews,* 50–61.

468 **"directed simply"** Adam Badeau to Simon Wolf, April 22, 1868, *Grant Papers,* 19:17–18; Wolf, *The Presidents I Have Known,* 64–65.

468 **"The General never meant"** Wolf, *The Presidents I Have Known,* 67–68.

468 **"I have abstained"** WTS to USG, September 28, 1868, *Grant Papers,* 19:46.

468 **When some Republicans** Badeau, *Grant in Peace,* 148.

468 **He left the presidential ballot** Ibid.

468 **Grant won** Donald R. Deskins, *Presidential Elections, 1789–2008* (Ann Arbor: University of Michigan Press, 2010), 190–91; Coleman, *Election of 1868,* 362–63. Grant ran ahead of the Republican ticket in every state but one. He received ten fewer votes in Delaware than the Republican congressional candidate. Paul F. Boller, *Presidential Campaigns* (New York: Oxford University Press, 1984), 125.

469 **"I consider your election"** Matías Romero to USG, November 9, 1868, *Grant Papers,* 19:69–70.

469 **President-elect Grant** From George Washington into the twentieth century, the changeover lasted four months until March 4; the inaugural date was moved up to January 20 at the beginning of Franklin D. Roosevelt's second term.

469 **He teased Julia** Badeau, *Grant in Peace,* 156; Ross, *The General's Wife,* 205.

469 **He gave Sheridan** USG to PHS, February 15, 1869, *Grant Papers,* 19:131; Whee-

lan, *Terrible Swift Sword,* 246; Cleaves, *Meade of Gettysburg,* 346–48; Wills, *George Henry Thomas,* 426–28.

469 **Since Grant was preparing** USG to WTS, January 5, 1869, *Grant Papers,* 19:103. The sale of the property was shadowed in controversy. Grant had earlier agreed to sell the house to Mayor Sayles J. Bowen for $40,000, with the understanding that the transaction could be canceled if Grant chose to live there after his presidency. When Bowen heard that the property had been sold to Sherman, he wrote to say that his understanding of their verbal conversation had not included the possibility of a third-party sale. See USG to Sayles J. Bowen, January 30, 1865, *Grant Papers,* 19:118–119, and Sayles J. Bowen to USG, February 1, 1869, *Grant Papers,* 19:119.

470 **Methodist Church leaders rushed** Richey, Rowe, and Schmidt, *Methodist Experience in America,* 1:219–20. The foundation stone for the National Cathedral of the Episcopal Church was not laid until 1907.

470 **The Gothic church cost** Ibid.; Lillian Brooks Brown, *A Living Centennial Commemorating the One Hundredth Anniversary of Metropolitan Memorial United Methodist Church* (Washington, D.C.: Judd & Detweiler, 1969), 1–9. In 1845, largely over the contentious issue of slavery, the Methodist Church split, the southern branch taking the name of the Methodist Episcopal Church, South.

470 **The church's minister** Brown, *A Living Centennial,* 1–9; *New York Times,* February 28, 1869; *Harper's Weekly,* March 13, 1869. On Simpson, see George R. Crooks, *The Life of Matthew Simpson* (New York: Harper & Bros., 1890); Matthew Simpson, *A Hundred Years of Methodism* (New York: Phillips & Hunt, 1876); Richey, Rowe, and Schmidt, *Methodist Experience in America,* 1:204, 207; Richard Carwardine, *Lincoln: A Life of Purpose and Power* (New York: Alfred A. Knopf, 2006), 277–80.

470 **Ulysses and Julia** Brown, *A Living Centennial,* 23.

471 **Johnson would** Smith, *Grant,* 466; Albert Castel, *The Presidency of Andrew Johnson* (Lawrence: Regents Press of Kansas, 1979), 211–12. On the other two presidents: John Adams did not attend the inauguration of Thomas Jefferson; John Quincy Adams did not attend the inauguration of Andrew Jackson.

472 **Standing where Lincoln** Allan Nevins, *Hamilton Fish: The Inner History of the Grant Administration* (New York: Dodd, Mead, 1937), 131.

472 **"The responsibilities of the position"** USG, Inaugural Address, March 4, 1869, *Grant Papers,* 19:139.

472 **"which preceding Administrations"** Ibid., 140–42.

472 **This scene** Garland, *Grant,* 388.

472 **"proper treatment"** USG, Inaugural Address, March 4, 1869, *Grant Papers,* 19:142.

472 **"The question of suffrage"** Ibid., 142.

472 **When Grant finished** Julia Dent Grant, *Personal Memoirs,* 172.

472 **"General Grant had something to say"** *New York Times,* March 5, 1869.

472 **The Nation offered** *The Nation,* March 11, 1869.

473 **John Rawlins reflected** Badeau, *Grant in Peace,* 163–64. See Doris Kearns Goodwin, *Team of Rivals: The Political Genius of Abraham Lincoln* (New York: Simon & Schuster, 2005).

473 **Critics pointed out that Borie** Smith, *Grant,* 468–69.

473 **For attorney general** Moorfield Storey and Edward Waldo Emerson, *Ebenezer Rockwood Hoar: A Memoir* (New York: Houghton Mifflin, 1911), 45–46, 162–63.

473 **a highly competent lawyer** Robert V. Friedenberg, "John A. J. Creswell of Maryland: Reformer in the Post Office," *Maryland Historical Magazine* 64, no. 2 (Summer 1969): 133–35.

473 **Grant asked General John Schofield** Donald B. Connelly, *John M. Schofield and the Politics of Generalship* (Chapel Hill: University of North Carolina Press, 2006), 214.

473   **But knowing Rawlins** Wilson, *Life of John A. Rawlins,* 351.

473   **When he learned** Ibid., 351–53.

473   *The New York Times* **praised** *New York Times,* March 8, 1869.

474   **"No statesman"** Welles, *Diary 3,* entry March 5, 1869, 3:544–45.

474   **Unwilling to see** Elihu B. Washburne to USG, March 10, 1869, *Grant Papers,* 19:151.

474   **Grant accepted** USG to Elihu B. Washburne, March 11, 1869, *Grant Papers,* 19:150–51; Hunt, *Israel, Elihu and Cadwallader Washburn,* 243–46.

474   **Grant was forced to pull** Alexander T. Stewart to USG, March 9, 1869, *Grant Papers,* 19:148; Hesseltine, *Ulysses S. Grant,* 146–47. Nevins, *Hamilton Fish,* 108, 111.

474   **"to accept the portfolio"** USG to Hamilton Fish, March 10, 1869, *Grant Papers,* 19:149.

474   **He had traveled** Nevins, *Hamilton Fish,* 1, 19, 114.

474   **"The confidence of the people"** *New York Times,* March 12, 1869.

475   **"The chiefs of staff"** USG, "To Senate," March [4], 1869, *Grant Papers,* 19:143; John M. Schofield, Orders, March 5, 1869, *Grant Papers,* 19:143.

475   **The order pleased Sherman** Marszalek, *Sherman,* 384; Athearn, *William Tecumseh Sherman and the Settlement of the West,* 240.

475   **"By direction of the President"** John A. Rawlins, General Orders No. 28, March 26, 1869, *Grant Papers,* 19:144; Wilson, *Life of John A. Rawlins,* 356.

475   **"Rawlins feels badly"** Manning F. Force, *General Sherman* (New York: D. Appleton & Co., 1899), 324–26; Lloyd Lewis, *Sherman: Fighting Prophet* (New York: Harcourt, Brace & Co., 1932), 601.

475   **"But Grant"** Force, *General Sherman,* 325–26; Marszalek, *Sherman,* 385.

475   **He chose former** Jeffry D. Wert, *General James Longstreet: The Confederacy's Most Controversial Soldier* (New York: Simon & Schuster, 1993), 413.

475   **"I believe he is a fair man"** *New York Tribune,* August 24, 1868.

475   **"Our new president"** Ibid., March 12, 1869.

475   **"a gesture of reconciliation"** *New York Times,* March 15, 1869.

476   **"That's the meaning of 'loilty'"** *Richmond Enquirer and Examiner,* March 12, 16, 1869.

476   **"Our scalawag"** Donald Bridgman Sanger and Thomas Robson Hay, *James Longstreet* (Baton Rouge: Louisiana State University Press, 1952), 345–46.

476   **On April 3, after nine hours** James Longstreet to USG, March 31, 1869, *Grant Papers,* 19:405; Sanger and Hay, *James Longstreet,* 346.

476   **"appear in dress suits"** Julia Dent Grant, *Personal Memoirs,* 173–74; Ross, *The General's Wife,* 205.

477   **"a military council"** William H. Crook, *Through Five Administrations, Reminiscences of Col. William H. Crook, Body-Guard to President Lincoln,* edited by Margarita Spalding Gerry (New York: Harper & Bros., 1910), 155–56.

477   **Some of his old friends** Benjamin Perley Poore and O. H. Tiffany, *Life of U. S. Grant* (New York: Union Publishing House, 1885), 50.

477   **Nellie had him hitch** Ibid., 59.

477   **A few close friends** Badeau, *Grant in Peace,* 243; Poore and Tiffany, *Life of U. S. Grant,* 50.

478   **Grant considered invoking** Nevins, *Hamilton Fish,* 129–30; Hesseltine, *Ulysses S. Grant,* 135–36.

478   **"gold or its equvalent"** Milton Friedman and Anna Jacobson Schwartz, *A Monetary History of the United States, 1867–1960* (Princeton, N.J.: Princeton University Press, 1963), 27.

478   **"when the treasury announced"** Boutwell, *Reminiscences of Sixty Years in Public Affairs,* 2:157.

478   **By the end of May, Boutwell** Ibid., 2:130–39.

478 **"Public affairs look"** USG to Adam Badeau, July 14, 1869, *Grant Papers*, 19:212–13.
479 **On the same day** *New York Times*, July 14, 1869.
479 **Grant's three-story cottage** George William Childs, *Recollections* (Philadelphia: J. B. Lippincott, 1890), 103; Mark Perry, *Grant and Twain: The Story of a Friendship That Changed America* (New York: Random House, 2004), 53.
479 **Upon his return** Childs, *Recollections*, 103.
479 **She also looked forward** Julia Dent Grant, *Personal Memoirs*, 177–78.
479 **Thirty-seven-year-old "Jennie"** Ibid., 57.
479 **Throughout his life** Kenneth D. Ackerman, *The Gold Ring: Jim Fisk, Jay Gould, and Black Friday, 1869* (New York: Dodd, Mead, 1988), 54.
480 **Flaunting their wealth** Ibid., 6–7, 35–36.
481 **That check and its underlying purpose** Ackerman, *The Gold Ring*, 94; Smith, *Grant*, 483.
481 **Mrs. Grant said no, thanks** "Gold Panic Investigation," House of Representatives, 41st Congress, 2nd sess., Report No. 31:270–71.
481 **"We have purchased a half million"** Jay Gould to Horace Porter, September 16, 1869, *Grant Papers*, 19:244n.
481 **"I have not authorized"** Horace Porter to Jay Gould, September 19, 1869, *Grant Papers*, 19:245n. See also Porter's testimony to the Gold Panic Investigation Committee, "Gold Panic Investigation," 445–46. He reported to the committee that he told Gould, "I am an officer of the government, and cannot enter into any speculations whatever."
481 **In other meetings** *Grant Papers*, 19:229n5.
481 **"a little intimation"** Interview with Ulysses S. Grant, *New York Sun*, October 4, 1869.
482 **Despite his discretion** Ackerman, *Gold Ring*, 73–74.
482 **The president worried** *Grant Papers*, 19:244.
482 **"On your arrival"** USG to George Boutwell, September 12, 1869, *Grant Papers*, 19:243–44.
482 **His rambling letter** "Gold Panic Investigation," 155; Ackerman, *Gold Ring*, 128.
483 **The messenger** Ackerman, *Gold Ring*, 136–38.
483 **"No answer"** "Gold Panic Investigation," 444–45.
483 **"Write this"** Julia Dent Grant, *Personal Memoirs*, 182. Julia, writing many years later in her memoirs, chose to put a _____ instead of the names Jay Gould and Jim Fisk, which were supplied by John Y. Simon, editor of her *Personal Memoirs*.
483 **"I always felt great respect"** Ibid., 182–83.
483 **So Fisk surmised** Ackerman, *Gold Ring*, 146.
483 **By Wednesday afternoon** Ibid., 140–51.
483 **Butterfield testified** "Gold Panic Investigation," 425–26.
484 **"If gold advanced"** Ibid., 344.
484 **What would the government do?** Boutwell, *Reminiscences*, 2:174.
484 **"Three million dollars"** Ibid., 2:175.
484 **"SELL $4,000,000 GOLD"** Ibid.
485 **"Possibly no avalanche"** *New York Herald*, September 25, 1869.
485 **"Had you not taken"** Boutwell, *Reminiscences*, 2:177.

Chapter 28. "A Radical Change in the Indian Policy"

486 **"It was his desire"** *New York Herald*, March 25, 1869.
486 **"If more men"** Wheelan, *Terrible Swift Sword*, 251; Philip Weeks, *Farewell, My Nation: The American Indian and the United States in the Nineteenth Century*, 2nd ed. (Wheeling, Ill.: Harlan Davidson, 2001), 166–67.

486 **"our white people"** USG to WTS, May 19, 1868, *Grant Papers*, 18:257–58.

486 **"With full heart"** *New York Times*, March 11, 1869.

487 **Under his successor** For Jackson's policy of Indian removal, see Howe, *What Hath God Wrought*, 342–57, 414–23.

487 **"the proper treatment"** USG, Inaugural Address, March 4, 1869, *Grant Papers*, 19:142.

487 **Behind these words** Francis Paul Prucha, *American Indian Policy in Crisis: Christian Reformers and the Indians, 1865–1900* (Norman: University of Oklahoma Press, 1976), 51.

487 **"Those about here"** USG to JDG, March 19, 1853, *Grant Papers*, 1:296.

487 **"This poor remnant"** USG to Osborn Cross, July 25, 1853, *Grant Papers*, 1:310.

487 **"had seen the unjust treatment"** Childs, *Recollections*, 100.

490 **As a teenager** Armstrong, *Warrior in Two Camps*, ix, 1–3, 15–17, 25–27. Parker copied the surrender terms that Grant handed to Lee at Appomattox.

491 **"reminded me"** *Brooklyn Daily Eagle*, September 25, 1892, cited in Armstrong, *Warrior in Two Camps*, 204n5.

491 **As a measure** Armstrong, *Warrior in Two Camps*, 128–33.

491 **not "disqualified"** Grant requested Secretary of the Interior Jacob Cox to ask Attorney General E. Rockwood Hoar about Parker's eligibility. For Hoar's reply, see Hoar to Cox, April 12, 1869, *Grant Papers*, 19:197n.

491 **The story of his relationship** Church membership, certainly in the Methodist tradition, usually required a narrative statement before church authorities of one's profession of the Christian faith. As such, many people attended church without ever taking the formal step of joining.

491 **"three political parties"** Robert H. Keller, *American Protestantism and United States Indian Policy, 1869–1882* (Lincoln: University of Nebraska Press, 1983), 37.

491 **"I do not believe our Creator"** USG to George H. Stuart, October 26, 1872, *Grant Papers*, 23:270; Keller, *American Protestantism and United States Indian Policy*, 25.

491 **The Quakers** Keller, *American Protestantism and United States Indian Policy*, 19.

492 **"fully the friendship"** Ely S. Parker to Benjamin Hallowell, February 15, 1869, *Grant Papers*, 19:193n; Benjamin Hallowell, *Autobiography of Benjamin Hallowell* (Philadelphia: Friends' Book Association, 1884), 261–62. At the time, Hallowell was serving as the first president of Maryland Agricultural College, a predecessor institution to what would become the University of Maryland.

492 **"Quaker policy"** Hallowell, *Autobiography of Benjamin Hallowell*, 266.

492 **Likewise, George H. Stuart** George H. Stuart, *The Life of George H. Stuart*, edited by Robert Ellis Thompson (Philadelphia: Stoddart, 1890), 239–40; Francis Paul Prucha, *The Great Father: The United States Government and the American Indians*, vol. 1 (Lincoln: University of Nebraska Press, 1984), 504–6.

492 **"to organize a board"** Robert Winston Mardock, *The Reformers and the American Indian* (Columbia: University of Missouri Press, 1971), 58–59; Keller, *American Protestantism and United States Indian Policy*, 29.

492 **Determined to make** Armstrong, *Warrior in Two Camps*, 139.

492 **Various denominations** Stuart, *Life of George H. Stuart*, 240–41; Prucha, *American Indian Policy in Crisis*, 36–37.

492 **"have full power"** USG, Order, June 3, 1869, *Grant Papers*, 19:191–93.

493 **Parker superintended** Armstrong, *Warrior in Two Camps*, 140.

493 **"The agent, appointed"** *Annual Report of the Board of Indian Commissioners* (Washington, D.C.: Government Printing Office, 1870), 7.

493 **"a shameful record"** Ibid., 7–9. Twelve years later, poet and writer Helen Hunt Jackson would quote large sections of the board's initial report in her pathbreaking book, *A Century of Dishonor: The Classic Exposé of the Plight of the Native Americans* (New York: Harper & Bros., 1881).

493   **"From my own experience"** USG, First Annual Message to Congress, December 6, 1869, *Grant Papers*, 20:38–39.

494   **In a special ceremony** *Grant Papers*, 20:73n.

494   **"It is the only public office"** EMS to USG, December 21, 1869, *Grant Papers*, 20:79–80n; Thomas and Hyman, *Stanton*, 634–37.

494   **"I am at a loss"** USG, "Memorandum to All Department Heads," December 24, 1869, *Grant Papers*, 20:80n; USG to Ellen H. Stanton, January 3, 1870, *Grant Papers*, 2077–78n.

494   **"that obnoxious order"** Julia Dent Grant, *Personal Memoirs*, 107.

494   **"If President Grant wants to prove"** *Grant Papers*, 19:19n; Sarna, *When Grant Expelled the Jews*, 84.

495   **"You represent"** Wolf, *Presidents I Have Known*, 71–73; Sarna, *When Grant Expelled the Jews*, 85–86. Wolf was a huge supporter of Grant. "During his eight years of his incumbency as president . . . Grant did more on and in behalf of American citizens of Jewish faith, at home and abroad, than all Presidents of the United States prior thereto or since" (71).

495   **"The appointment shows"** Sarna, *When Grant Expelled the Jews*, 14, 90; Lee M. Friedman, *Jewish Pioneers and Patriots* (Philadelphia: Jewish Publication Society, 1942), 353–64; Edmond S. Meany, *Governors of Washington, Territorial and State* (Seattle: University of Washington Press, 1915), 43.

495   **"We suppose the President"** *Jewish Times*, January 6, 1871, quoted in Sarna, *When Grant Expelled the Jews*, 95.

495   **"sickening slaughter"** Robert Winston Mardock, *The Reformers and the American Indian* (Columbia: University of Missouri Press, 1971), 67–69; Keller, *American Protestantism and United States Indian Policy*, 31; Wheelan, *Terrible Swift Sword*, 251.

496   **He accused Major Baker** Keller, *American Protestantism and United States Indian Policy*, 31; Mardock, *Reformers and the American Indian*, 70.

496   **The issue was always** Donald J. D'Elia, "The Argument over Civilian or Military Indian Control, 1865–1880," *The Historian: A Journal of History* 24, no. 2 (February 1962): 207–9; Ahearn, *William Tecumseh Sherman and the Settlement of the West*, 110–11.

496   **"Gentlemen, you have defeated"** Sherman, *Memoirs*, 2:437.

496   **"humane spirit"** *National Standard*, November 12, 1870; Mardock, *Reformers and the American Indian*, 83.

497   **After years of battles** For the story of Red Cloud, see Robert W. Larson, *Red Cloud: Warrior-Statesman of the Lakota Sioux* (Norman: University of Oklahoma Press, 1997), and James C. Olson, *Red Cloud and the Sioux Problem* (Lincoln: University of Nebraska Press, 1965).

497   **"Physically, a finer set"** *New York Herald*, June 2, 1870.

498   **The president assured them** D. C. Poole, *Among the Sioux of Dakota* (New York: Van Nostrand, 1881), 165–66.

498   **"When lands are secured"** *New York Times*, June 8, 1870. For a description of the visit by Red Cloud and his reception in both Washington and New York, see Larson, *Red Cloud*, 128–36; Olson, *Red Cloud and the Sioux Problem*, 96–113; Mardock, *Reformers and the American Indian*, 74–78.

498   **"the necessity of passing"** USG, "To Congress," July 15, 1870, *Grant Papers*, 20:195–96.

Chapter 29. Foreign Relations

499   **At the beginning of Grant's presidency** George C. Herring, *From Colony to Superpower: U.S. Foreign Relations Since 1776* (New York: Oxford University Press, 2008), 251.

499 **"I would respect"** USG, Inaugural Address, *Grant Papers,* 19:142.

499 **Grant believed building** Nevins, *Hamilton Fish: The Inner History of the Grant Administration,* as the subtitle suggests, is valuable for far more than the story of Fish's tenure as secretary of state; Hesseltine, *Ulysses S. Grant,* 148.

499 **He spent considerable time** Nevins, *Hamilton Fish,* 92–97. When at Glenclyffe, Fish was a vestryman at St. Philip's-in-the-Highlands. After the war, when the southern dioceses and bishops applied for readmission to the Episcopal Church, in the midst of four days of heated debate Fish called for reconciliation in advocating their readmission, which was finally granted.

499 **Fish had accepted** Nevins, *Hamilton Fish,* 115, 122.

501 **In this tattered** Ibid., 117–18.

501 **His diary** In reading Hamilton Fish's diary, one listens in on a change as the new secretary of state transitions from a matter-of-fact record of the day's events to more of an essay style that attempts to analyze the meaning of the events. Hamilton Fish Papers, Library of Congress.

501 **"few men had more powers"** Nevins, *Hamilton Fish,* 134.

501 **In 1984** McPherson, *War on the Waters,* 112, 114–17, 130, 204–5; Symonds, *Civil War at Sea,* 72–82.

501 **Although early in the Civil War** Walter Stahr, *Seward: Lincoln's Indispensable Man* (New York: Simon & Schuster, 2012), 498–99.

501 **Before his inauguration** The Johnson-Clarendon Treaty was named for the two lead negotiators, United States senator Reverdy Johnson and George William Villiers, Lord Clarendon. See Adrian Cook, *The Alabama Claims: American Politics and Anglo-American Relations, 1865–1872* (Ithaca, N.Y.: Cornell University Press, 1975), 43–72; Badeau, *Grant in Peace,* 153–54.

501 **"When Civilization was fighting"** Charles Sumner, *Charles Sumner: His Complete Works* (Boston: Lee & Shepard, 1900), 17:93; Donald, *Charles Sumner and the Rights of Man,* 374–94.

503 **Critics replied that support** Cook, *Alabama Claims,* 84–85.

503 **Second, for more immediate control** Nevins, *Hamilton Fish,* 155–56.

503 **More recently, the Fenian Brotherhood** Adrian Cook, *The Alabama Claims: American Politics and Anglo-American Relations, 1865–1872* (Ithaca, N.Y.: Cornell University Press, 1975), 35, 37.

503 **He was a regular reader** Nevins, *Hamilton Fish,* 70–71, 101.

503 **"He is well informed"** USG to Queen Victoria, April 26, 1869, *Grant Papers,* 19:213n1.

504 **A graduate of Harvard** Grant believed Motley would be well received in London because he was already well known, especially for his book, *Rise of the Dutch Republic,* which sold 15,000 copies in Great Britain. Motley contributed historical and critical essays to the *North American Review.*

504 **Sumner proudly wrote** Charles Sumner to the Duchess of Argyll, May 18, 1869, Charles Sumner, *The Selected Letters of Charles Sumner,* Beverly Wilson Palmer, ed. (Boston: Northeastern University Press, 1990), 462–64.

504 **As a safeguard** Badeau, *Grant in Peace,* 197–99.

504 **She began the custom** Grant, *In the Days of My Father,* 159.

504 **A vibrant friendship** Julia Dent Grant, *Personal Memoirs,* 188.

504 **When Julia Grant hosted** Nevins, *Hamilton Fish,* 575.

504 **"She appears in grace"** Ibid.

505 **"She often failed to remember"** Mrs. John A. Logan, *Thirty Years in Washington* (Hartford, Conn.: Worthington, 1901), 670–71; Ross, *The General's Wife,* 208.

505 **"not pulled him"** Ammen, *The Old Navy and the New,* 529.

505–6 **With sympathy for Cuban aspirations** Nevins, *Hamilton Fish*, 121, 179–80; *Grant Papers* 19:459n.

506 **On April 10** Smith, *Grant*, 491–99; Hesseltine, *Ulysses S. Grant*, 161–62.

506 **Under Rawlins's urging** Smith, *Grant*, 493.

506 **Hoar worried** Storey and Emerson, *Ebenezer Rockwood Hoar*, 179.

506 **Rawlins was a darling** Wilson, *Life of John A. Rawlins*, 359–60.

506 **"strict justice"** Fish diary, entry April 6, 1869; Smith, *Grant*, 493.

507 **"The United States are willing"** USG, memorandum, August 31, 1869, *Grant Papers*, 19:238; Nevins, *Hamilton Fish*, 243–44.

507 **Picturesque, Spanish-speaking Santo Domingo** William Javier Nelson, *Almost a Territory: America's Attempt to Annex the Dominican Republic* (Newark: University of Delaware Press, 1990), 19.

507 **Seward, when part** Ibid., 47; Charles Callan Tansill, *The United States and Santo Domingo, 1798–1873* (Baltimore: Johns Hopkins Press, 1938), 351; Stahr, *Seward*, 455, 57, 519–20.

507 **"The annexation"** Tansill, *United States and Santo Domingo*, 353–54.

507 **"entrance into the United States"** Fish diary, entry April 5, 1869.

507 **No one objected** Ibid., April 6, 1869.

508 **"After Cuba"** Charles Dana's *Sun,* quoted in Nevins, *Hamilton Fish*, 260–61.

508 **Daniel Ammen, Grant's longtime friend** Tansill, *United States and Santo Domingo*, 351; Jesse R. Grant, *In the Days of My Father, General Grant* (New York; Harper & Bros., 1925), 132–35.

508 **"to satisfy my curiosity"** USG to Buenaventura Báez, July 13, 1869, *Grant Papers*, 19:209. For Báez's character, see Tansill, *United States and Santo Domingo*, 134.

508 **"special agent"** Nevins, *Hamilton Fish*, 265.

508 **"he had no authority"** Tansill, *United States and Santo Domingo*, 362.

508 **Grant agreed** Nevins, *Hamilton Fish*, 267–68.

509 **Babcock went back** Tansill, *United States and Santo Domingo*, 370–71.

509 **Seemingly tireless** Ibid., 371–72, 415.

509 **"the father of the Senate"** Donald, *Charles Sumner and the Rights of Man*, 414. Donald's Pulitzer Prize–winning biography of Sumner captures the complexity and contradictions of the man.

510 **Despite this** Ibid., 289.

510 **"Don't leave"** Ibid., 434–35; Ben Perley Poore, in the *Boston Journal*, October 21, 1877.

510 **"I will send the papers"** Donald, *Charles Sumner and the Rights of Man*, 435.

510 **"Of course, Mr. Sumner"** Ibid.

510 **"he would cheerfully support"** David Donald, in *Charles Sumner and the Rights of Man*, offers the best summary of the conflicting testimony of what was said at Sumner's home, 434–38. Eleven months later in December 1870, stung by the accounts that he told Grant he would support the treaty, Sumner declared in a Senate speech, "I have heard it said that I assured the President that I would support the Administration in this measure. Never!" Donald, *Charles Sumner and the Rights of Man*, 435. See also Edward Lillie Pierce, *Memoir and Letters of Charles Sumner* (Boston: Roberts Bros., 1877–1893), 4:435.

511 **"Of the people"** Henry Adams, *Democracy: an American Novel* (New York: H. Holt, 1880), 23.

511 **"The disagreement"** Hamilton Fish to George Bancroft, February 9, 1870, in Nevins, *Hamilton Fish*, 313.

511 **"the sincere hope"** USG, "To Senate," March 14, 1870, *Grant Papers*, 20:121.

511 **He invited twenty-two** Nevins, *Hamilton Fish*, 317.

512 **"You might say"** Bancroft Davis to Hamilton Fish, March 27, 1870, Nevins, *Hamilton Fish*, 319.

512 **But the president was not yet** Donald, *Charles Sumner and the Rights of Man*, 452.

513 **"more of Mr. Sumner"** Nevins, *Hamilton Fish*, 160–61, 205; Donald, *Charles Sumner and the Rights of Man*, 408.

513 **Fish, although equally upset** Badeau, *Grant in Peace*, 202–3.

513 **"Your steadiness"** Fish diary, entry June 25, 1870; *Grant Papers*, 20:183–84; Nevins, *Hamilton Fish*, 383.

513 **"The government of San Domingo"** USG, Annual Message to Congress, December 5, 1870, *Grant Papers*, 21:51. The population of the Dominican Republic today is ten million.

513 **"make slavery"** Ibid., 53.

513 **Douglas argued** William S. McFeely, *Frederick Douglass* (New York: W. W. Norton & Co., 1991), 276.

514 **In a tense Senate** Grant asked the Senate to appoint such a commission. Indiana senator Oliver P. Morton wrote Grant on December 8, "If nobody else in the Senate has the matter in charge I will introduce the resolutions in regard to Santo Domingo in accordance with the suggestions in the message." *Grant Papers*, 21:79.

514 **"One by one"** William Dudley Foulke, *Life of Oliver P. Morton*, vol. 2 (Indianapolis: Bowen-Merrill, 1899), 157.

514 **At dawn** Nevins, *Hamilton Fish*, 454.

514 **By appointing** Hamilton Fish diary, entry January 10, 1871, *Grant Papers*, 21:133n; McFeely, *Frederick Douglass*, 276; Tansill, *United States and Santo Domingo*, 436.

515 **"the opposition made"** Nevins, *Hamilton Fish*, 453, 457; Joseph Guberman, *The Life of John Lothrop Motley* (The Hague: Martinus Nijhoff, 1973), 140; Nevins, *Hamilton Fish*, 453, 457.

515 **"Mr. Motley must know"** Guberman, Ibid., 141; Nevins, *Hamilton Fish*, 455.

515 **When Fish's dispatch arrived** Nevins, *Hamilton Fish*, 454.

515 **By a vote of 3 to 2** Donald, *Charles Sumner and the Rights of Man*, 490.

515 **He was offered** Ibid., 491.

515 **Taken together, these five** USG, "To Senate," February 9, 1871, *Grant Papers*, 21:175–76; Cook, *Alabama Claims*, 170; Smith, *Grant*, 511.

516 **The businesslike atmosphere** Storey and Emerson, *Ebenezer Rockwood Hoar*, 224. Macdonald, often called "the George Washington of Canada," signified that the new Dominion of Canada, formed in 1867, would be a partner in the negotiations.

516 **He knew the newly elected Congress** Nevins, *Hamilton Fish*, 474; Cook, *Alabama Claims*, 169–70.

516 **"for the escape"** For the text of the Treaty of Washington, see John Bassett Moore, *History and Digest of the International Arbitrations* (Washington, D.C.: Government Printing Office, 1898), 1:546–53.

516 **Grant sent the treaty** USG, "To Senate," May 10, 1871, *Grant Papers*, 21:352.

516 **The arbiters** Cook, *Alabama Claims*, 238–40.

516 **It has been suggested** William McFeely, in *Grant: A Biography*, takes this stance in his decidedly negative view of Grant's presidency. David Donald astutely counters this point of view: "Just as many during the Civil War thought of Grant's military strategy as sheer butchery, so many contemporaries—and subsequent historians as well—misjudged the skill with which the President fought his political war." Donald, *Charles Sumner and the Rights of Man*, 446.

517 **Although the Treaty** Herring, *From Colony to Superpower*, 255.

518 **"No man living is more tolerant"** Fish's penciled draft is in the Hamilton Fish Papers. Donald, *Charles Sumner and the Rights of Man*, 478.

Chapter 30. Ku Klux Klan

519 **In the 1870 state elections** Richard H. Abbott, *The Republican Party and the South, 1855–1877: The First Southern Strategy* (Chapel Hill: University of North Carolina, 1986), 210–11.

519 **Recognizing the need** The early history of the Klan is sketchy, contradictory, and sometimes "fictitious." See Trelease, *White Terror*, 20–21; Jack Hurst, *Nathan Bedford Forrest* (New York: Alfred A. Knopf, 1993), 285.

521 **Southern whites were determined** George C. Rable, *But There Was No Peace: The Role of Violence in the Politics of Reconstruction* (Athens: University of Georgia Press, 1984), 18–19, 22.

521 **Other enemies were native whites** Chalmers, *Hooded Americanism*, 9–10. As the Klan changed rapidly from social club to vigilante violence, one of the original six members declared in April 1868, "It is to be lamented that the simple object of the original Ku-Kluxes should be so perverted as to become political and pernicious in its demonstrations." Trelease, *White Terror*, 5–6.

521 **But the threat** The Enforcement Act of 1870 was formally "an Act to enforce the Right of Citizens of the United States to Vote in the several States of this Union." In 41st Congress, sess. 2, ch. 144, sections 1 and 2; Trelease, *White Terror*, 385–86.

521 **But neither the first** Xi Wang, *The Trial of Democracy: Black Suffrage and Northern Republicans, 1860–1910* (Athens: University of Georgia Press, 1997), 80–82.

521 **He argued the federal** Abbott, *Republican Party and the South*, 205.

522 **"There is a deplorable state"** USG to James G. Blaine, March 9, 1871, *Grant Papers*, 21:218–19.

522 **A new version** The House of Representatives in 1871 consisted of 243 members, compared with today's 435 members.

522 **"an encroachment"** Wang, *Trial of Democracy*, 83–88.

522 **"military despot"** Trelease, *White Terror*, 387–88.

522 **"The power to correct"** USG, "To Congress," March 23, 1871, *Grant Papers*, 21:246.

523 **Finally, the Ku Klux Klan Act** *Statutes at Large of the United States of America* (Boston: Little, Brown & Co., 1875–1905), 41st Congress, Second Session, vol. 141, 3656; www.constitution.org/uslaw/sal/019_statutes_at_large.pdf. Foner, *Reconstruction*, 454–55, 455n80.

523 **"unconstitutional and hideously despotic"** The newspaper quotations are cited in Trelease, *White Terror*, 389–90.

523 **"I will not hesitate"** USG, "Proclamation," May 3, 1871, *Grant Papers*, 21:336–37.

524 **"Sumner and Schurz"** USG to Elihu B. Washburne, May 17, 1871, *Grant Papers*, 21:364.

524 **He worried most** Abbott, *Republican Party and the South*, 212–14; Gould, *Grand Old Party*, 59–60.

524 **Elected to the House** See David M. Jordan, *Roscoe Conkling of New York* (Ithaca, N.Y.: Cornell University Press, 1971); Gould, *Grand Old Party*, 62–63.

524 **He was committed** Jordan, *Roscoe Conkling of New York*, 11–12, 35–36.

524 **"During this debate"** Conkling's speech is in the *Congressional Globe*, 41st Congress, 3rd sess., 244–47; Jordan, *Roscoe Conkling of New York*, 161.

525 **"his intolerable egotism"** Jordan, *Roscoe Conkling of New York*, 143.

525 **"would be unselfish"** Ibid., 143–44.

526 **Akerman "read the law"** Donald, *Charles Sumner and the Rights of Man*, 446–47; William S. McFeely, "Amos T. Akerman: The Lawyer and Racial Justice," in J. Morgan Kousser and James M. McPherson, eds., *Region, Race, and Reconstruction:*

Essays in Honor of C. Vann Woodward (New York: Oxford University Press, 1982), 395–99; McFeely, *Grant,* 367.

526 **When blacks elected** McFeely, "Amos T. Akerman," 402–3.

526 **"unless the people become used"** Amos T. Akerman to Charles Sumner, April 2, 1869, cited in Foner, *Reconstruction,* 454.

526 **"amount to war"** Foner, *Reconstruction,* 457.

526 **Grant charged Bristow** Ross A. Webb, "Benjamin H. Bristow: Civil Rights Champion, 1866–1872," *Civil War History* 15, no. 1 (March 1969): 39–48; Ross A. Webb, *Benjamin Helm Bristow: Border State Politician* (Lexington: University Press of Kentucky, 1969), xi.

527 **"We cannot, in the absence"** Oscar J. Dunn to USG, July 29, 1871, *Grant Papers,* 22:101n.

527 **"to secure the protection"** USG, "Endorsement," August 3, 1871, *Grant Papers,* 22:101.

527 **"fair election"** Amos Akerman to Benjamin Butler, August 9, 1871, cited in Abbott, *Republican Party and the South,* 213.

527 **"outrages" had been committed** John Scott to USG, September 1, 1871, *Grant Papers,* 22:163n.

527 **"to retire peaceably"** USG, "Proclamation," October 12, 1871, *Grant Papers,* 22:161–62.

527 **"not dispersed"** Ibid., October 17, 1871, *Grant Papers,* 22:176–78.

527 **More than one hundred arrests** Trelease, *White Terror,* 403–5.

527 **"I feel greatly saddened"** Foner, *Reconstruction,* 458.

528 **Schurz hastened to assure Grant** Schurz failed to give adequate credit for the Liberal Republican victory to the heavy turnout by Democrats who did not field a candidate. Andrew L. Slap, *The Doom of Reconstruction: The Liberal Republicans in the Civil War Era* (New York: Fordham University Press, 2006), 14–22.

528 **invited to deliver** Trefousse, *Carl Schurz,* 13, 174–75.

528 **Although Schurz was strongly antislavery** See Hans Trefousse, *Carl Schurz: A Biography,* for his balanced appraisal of "the German Senator," 182.

528 **In August 1871, Schurz** Ibid., 189.

529 **"an ungrateful man"** USG to Henry Wilson, November 15, 1871, *Grant Papers,* 22:231–32.

529 **The letter was found** *Grant Papers,* 22:232n.

529 **"There has never been a President"** *National Republican,* January 19, 1872; Hesseltine, *Ulysses S. Grant,* 269.

529 **"eminently judicious"** *National Republican,* February 24, 1872.

530 **"In favor of this course"** *The Times* (London), October 31, 1871.

530 **Treasury Secretary George Boutwell had worked** For the story of Boutwell's efforts at Treasury, see Boutwell, "The Treasury Department in 1869," *Reminiscences of Sixty Years in Public Affairs,* 2:125–49; Hesseltine, *Ulysses S. Grant,* 165–66.

530 **"He expressed his opinions"** Boutwell, *Reminiscences of Sixty Years in Public Affairs,* 2:236.

530 **"Grant is so good"** John A. J. Creswell to Rebecca Creswell, October 24, 1871, Creswell Papers, Library of Congress, cited in Friedenberg, "John A. J. Creswell of Maryland," 134n10.

531 **Wire-pullers should be overthrown** Ari Hoogenboom, *Outlawing the Spoils: A History of the Civil Service Reform Movement, 1865–1883* (Urbana: University of Illinois Press, 1961), vii.

531 **"a reform in the civil service"** USG, Second Annual Message, December 5, 1870; James D. Richardson, *A Compilation of the Messages and Papers of the Presidents, 1789–*

1897, vol. 7 (Washington, D.C.: U.S. Congress, 1899), 109; John Y. Simon, "Ulysses S. Grant and Civil Service Reform," *Hayes Historical Journal* 4, no. 3 (Spring 1984): 10.

531 **Critics attacked Grant** Simon, "Ulysses S. Grant and Civil Service Reform," 12.

531 **"Sumner, Schutz"** USG to J. Russell Jones, November 7, 1871, *Grant Papers,* 22:217; for Sumner's criticism, see Donald, *Charles Sumner and the Rights of Man,* 373.

532 **"Reconstruction and slavery"** *The Nation,* March 21, 1872.

532 **He wore a signature white duster** Henry Luther Stoddard, *Horace Greeley: Printer, Editor, Crusader* (New York: G. P. Putnam's Sons, 1946), 100, 191.

532 **Schurz worried** Trefousse, *Carl Schurz,* 205–07.

532 **"He is a genius"** USG to Henry Wilson, November 15, 1871, *Grant Papers,* 22:231–32.

532 **They extended amnesty** Slap, *Doom of Reconstruction,* 185–86.

533 **"Hats, caps"** "Republican Philadelphia: GOP Convention of 1872 in Philadelphia," *Public Ledger* (Philadelphia), June 7, 1872; http://www.ushistory.org/gop/convention_1872.htm; Eaton, *Presidential Timber,* 41.

533 **Together, Grant and Wilson appealed** Smith, *Schuyler Colfax,* 338–51; Abbott, *Cobbler in Congress,* 242–45; McFeely, *Grant,* 381–82.

533 **He negotiated with August Belmont** Slap, *Doom of Reconstruction,* 188–89.

533 **"They are an easy"** Horace Greeley, *Essays Designed to Elucidate the Science of Political Economy* (Philadelphia: Porter & Coates, 1869), 57, 74–78.

533 **"It will mark"** *New York Herald,* June 11, 12, 1872, in Slap, *Doom of Reconstruction,* 170–71.

534 **"most liberal toward all"** William Lloyd Garrison, *Independent,* September 12, 1872.

534 **"The Greeleyites"** USG to Elihu B. Washburne, August 26, 1872, *Grant Papers,* 23:237–38.

534 **"I have known General Grant"** Hamilton Fish to C. C. Amsden, October 25, 1872, cited in Nevins, *Hamilton Fish,* 609.

535 **"Go vote to burn"** Foner, *Reconstruction,* 509.

535 **"In deciding the question"** Frederick Douglass to Cassius M. Clay, July 26, 1871, in Philip S. Foner, ed., *The Life and Writings of Frederick Douglass, Reconstruction and After,* vol. 4 (New York: International Publishers, 1955), 252–53.

535 **A year later** Nathan Irvin Huggins, *Slave and Citizen: The Life of Frederick Douglass* (New York: Little, Brown & Co., 1980), 134–35; McFeely, *Frederick Douglass,* 277.

535 **"I know Grant well"** Frederick Douglass, "'My Reasons for Opposing Horace Greeley': Address delivered in Boston, Massachusetts on September 5, 1872," in *The Frederick Douglass Papers, Series One: Speeches, Debates, and Interviews* (New Haven, Conn.: Yale University Press, 1979–1992), 4:*1864–1880,* 328.

535 **Abolitionists, cheering** James McPherson, *The Abolitionist Legacy: From Reconstruction to the NAACP* (Princeton, N.J.: Princeton University Press, 1975), 30.

535 **Reformers of the Indian question** Keller, *American Protestantism and United States Indian Policy,* 77.

536 **Grant expressed his pleasure** Cook, *Alabama Claims,* 233–40; Nevins, *Hamilton Fish,* 518–64. The tribunal did reject U.S. claims for "indirect" damages.

536 **The Fifteenth Amendment, ratified** William Gillette, *The Right to Vote: Politics and the Passage of the Fifteenth Amendment* (Baltimore: Johns Hopkins University Press, 1965), 81, 84–85.

536 **The man in charge** Amos Akerman to Garnet Andrews, July 31, 1871, Amos Akerman Papers, University of Virginia; Smith, *Grant,* 547.

536 **"I know him [Grant]"** Benjamin H. Bristow to George T. Edwards, November 27, 1872, cited in Webb, *Benjamin Helm Bristow,* 111.

537 **"the first President"** *Washington National Republican,* November 28, 1872; Foner, *Reconstruction,* 504–5.

537 **"In your desire to obtain"** USG, speech, November 26, 1872, *Grant Papers,* 23:289–90; *New York Times,* November 27, 1872.

Chapter 31. The Gilded Age

538 **Man's chief end** Presbyterian Church General Assembly, *The Book of Confessions: The Westminster Shorter Catechism, Question 1* (Louisville, Ky.: Westminster John Knox, 1999), 175.

538 **Peopled by barely disguised** Mark Twain and Charles Dudley Warner, *The Gilded Age: A Tale of Today* (Hartford, Conn.: American Publishing, 1873). For an insightful introduction, see Louis J. Budd, Penguin Classics edition of *The Gilded Age* (New York: Penguin, 2001), xi–xxxi. See also Bryant Morey French, *Mark Twain and The Gilded Age: The Book That Named an Era* (Dallas: Southern Methodist University Press, 1965).

538 **In a retelling** For the Gilded Age, see Charles W. Calhoun, ed., *The Gilded Age: Perspectives on the Origins of Modern America* (Lanham, Md.: Rowman & Littlefield, 2007). Within this collection of essays, see especially Calhoun, "The Political Culture: Public Life and the Conduct of Politics," 239–64.

539 **The *Sun* charged** The *New York Sun* began its reporting on September 4, 1872.

539 **Although this chicanery began** The story of the Crédit Mobilier is complex, yielding different judgments by authors who have looked at the full story. See J. B. Crawford, *The Credit Mobilier of America: Its Origin and History* (Boston: Calkins, 1880); Maury Klein, *Union Pacific: Birth of a Railroad, 1862–1893,* vol. 1 (Garden City, N.Y.: Doubleday, 1987), see especially 293–305.

540 **When the new Forty-third** Charles C. Calhoun, *From Bloody Shirt to Full Dinner Pail: The Transformation of Politics and Governance in the Gilded Age* (New York: Hill and Wang, 2010), 34; Sean Dennis Cashman, *America in the Gilded Age: From the Death of Lincoln to the Rise of Theodore Roosevelt* (New York: New York University Press, 1984), 197; Josiah Bunting, *Ulysses S. Grant* (New York: Times Books, 2004), 134–35.

540 **Bands played discordant** Niven, *Salmon P. Chase,* 448.

540 **Abraham Lincoln's second inaugural** For why Lincoln is the exception, see Ronald C. White, Jr., *Lincoln's Greatest Speech: The Second Inaugural* (New York: Simon & Schuster, 2002).

540 **"Yet he is not possessed"** USG, Second Inaugural Address, March 4, 1873, *Grant Papers,* 24:61.

540 **"The wrong already inflicted"** Ibid., 63.

541 **"My efforts"** Ibid., 62.

541 **The astounding cost** Ellis P. Oberholtzer, *Jay Cooke: Financier of the Civil War,* vol. 2 (Philadelphia: George W. Jacobs, 1907), 421.

542 **Cooke had continued** Ibid., 421–22. See also Henrietta M. Larson, *Jay Cooke, Private Banker* (Cambridge, Mass.: Harvard University Press, 1936), 409–11.

542 **The collapse of economic markets** Gould, *Grand Old Party,* 69–70.

542 **The dramatic downfall** Calhoun, *From Bloody Shirt to Full Dinner Pail,* 34–36; Irwin Unger, *The Greenback Era: A Social and Political History of American Finance, 1865–1879* (Princeton, N.J.: Princeton University Press, 1964), 213–33; Allan Nevins, *The Emergence of Modern America, 1865–1878* (New York: Macmillan, 1927), 290–99.

542 **With financial leaders** Frank Warren Hackett, *A Sketch of the Life and Public Service of William Adams Richardson* (Washington, D.C.: H. L. McQueen, 1898), 92–93.

542 **When Henry Wilson vacated** Boutwell, *Reminiscences of Sixty Years in Public Service,* 2:221.

542 **"no departure"** USG to George S. Boutwell, March 17, 1873, *Grant Papers*, 24:82–83.

542 **Richardson had earned** Hackett, *Life and Public Service of William Adams Richardson*, 27–31.

543 **Detractors charged** Unger, *Greenback Era*, 171–72. Richardson's action ultimately came before the Senate Finance Committee, which ruled that the $44 million in greenbacks had been permanently retired and could not be reissued.

543 **Whereas brokers pleaded** For definitions of "soft" and "hard" money, see Unger, *Greenback Era*, 8–9; Smith, *Grant*, 576.

544 **"I assure you"** Nevins, *Hamilton Fish*, letter from Fish to Richardson, September 26, 1873, 701.

544 **"The Government is desirous"** USG to H. B. Claflin and Charles L. Anthony, September 27, 1873, *Grant Papers*, 24:218–19.

544 **"In the present crisis"** George S. Boutwell to USG, October 2, 1873, *Grant Papers*, 24:219–20n.

544 **Even with vibrant** McFeely, *Grant*, 392–93.

544 **Toy merchants** Ross, *The General's Wife*, 217.

545 **Horace Porter** Elsie Porter Mende, *An American Soldier and Diplomat: Horace Porter* (New York: Fredrick A. Stokes, 1927), 123–25. See appreciative exchange of letters between Porter and Grant, Horace Porter to USG, December 1, 1872; USG to Horace Porter, December 1, 1872, *Grant Papers*, 23:294n. Twenty-five years later, Porter would publish his compelling account, *Campaigning with Grant*, and enjoy a distinguished diplomatic career as ambassador to France.

545 **An abolitionist, Wilson admired** Elias Nason, *The Life and Public Service of Henry Wilson* (Boston: B. B. Russell, 1876), 417–21; Henry Wilson, *The History of the Rise and Fall of the Slave Power in America* (Boston: J. R. Osgood, 1872). The third volume was published in 1877 after Wilson's death.

545 **Grant favored fiscal restraint** Unger, *Greenback Era*, 215–16.

545 **"he had given it most careful"** Fish diary, entry April 21, 1874.

546 **"Delano fought"** Ibid.

546 **Congress attempted to override** See http://www.senate.gov/reference/Legislation/Vetoes/Presidents/GrantU.pdf, 47.

546 **"express my admiration"** Roscoe Conkling to USG, April 22, 1874, *Grant Papers*, 25:76n.

546 **"Believing that I represent"** Zachary Eddy to USG, April 22, 1874, *Grant Papers*, 25:77.

546 **"to add my *mite*"** Julie R. Seavey to USG, April 22, 1874, *Grant Papers*, 25:77–78.

547 **"Nellie writes very often"** USG to JRG, June 2, 1872, *Grant Papers*, 23:159–60; Ross, *The General's Wife*, 220. McFeely, in *Grant*, paints a consistently negative portrait of Nellie as an uncultivated young woman; see 400–404.

547 **expressing "astonishment"** USG to Edward J. Sartoris, July 7, 1873, *Grant Papers*, 24:163.

547 **"a father's anxiety"** Ibid., 163–64. Rumors circulated that Grant gave his consent to the marriage only after Sartoris agreed to live in America.

548 **Minister Otis Tiffany** Tiffany, *Pulpit and Platform*, 206.

548 **Nellie's eight bridesmaids** Ross, *The General's Wife*, 237–38; Catherine Clinton, *Fanny Kemble's Civil Wars* (New York: Simon & Schuster, 2000), 227.

548 **Grant, who had only reluctantly** Brown, *A Living Centennial*, 23; Jesse R. Grant, *In the Days of My Father*, 176.

548 **"Fred's wife is beautiful"** USG to Adam Badeau, October 25, 1874, *Grant Papers*, 25:260–61.

548 **Ulysses and Julia loved** Julia Dent Grant, *Personal Memoirs*, 181; Ross, *The General's Wife*, 239–41.

548 **Grant attended** *The Gilded Age* *New York Times,* December 24, 1874.

549 **Grant did not want his presence** *New York Times,* July 26, 1885.

549 **"His faith"** Edwin Sawyer Walker, *Oak Ridge Cemetery: Its History and Improvements* (Springfield, Ill.: H. W. Rokker, 1879), 53, 55.

549 **"Amidst obloquy"** USG, speech, October 15, 1874, *Grant Papers,* 25:259.

550 **In the Senate, Republicans lost** Foner, *Reconstruction,* 523, 549–50, 552–53; Charles W. Calhoun, *Conceiving a New Republic: The Republican Party and the Southern Question, 1869–1900* (Lawrence: University Press of Kansas, 2006), 59–60.

550 **"critics who assume"** USG, Draft Annual Message Fragment, [December 1, 1874], *Grant Papers,* 25:269–70.

551 **"were wholly beneath"** Fish diary, entry December 1, 1874; Nevins, *Hamilton Fish,* 747.

551 **"to deprive citizens"** USG, Sixth Annual Message to Congress, December 7, 1874, in Richardson, *A Compilation of the Messages and Papers of the Presidents,* 7:297.

551 **"Complaints are made"** Ibid.

551 **"Treat the negro as a citizen"** Ibid., 299; Calhoun, *Conceiving a New Republic,* 60–61.

Chapter 32. "Malfeasance!"

553 **By 1875, Republicans controlled** Simpson, *Reconstruction Presidents,* 184.

554 **"The General would glance"** George Frisbie Hoar, *Autobiography of Seventy Years,* vol. 1 (New York: Charles Scribner's Sons, 1913), 208.

554 **The army, storming** Rable, *But There Was No Peace,* 141; Calhoun, *Conceiving a New Republic,* 62–63; Joe Gray Taylor, *Louisiana Reconstructed, 1863–1877* (Baton Rouge: Louisiana State University Press, 1974), 304–5.

554 **"defiance of laws"** Rable, *But There Was No Peace,* 141; Wheelan, *Terrible Swift Sword,* 274.

554 **"president and all of us"** Calhoun, *Conceiving a New Republic,* 63.

554 **"I have never given"** James Garfield to Burke A. Hinsdale, January 7, 1875, in Mary L. Hinsdale, ed., *Garfield-Hinsdale Letters: Correspondence Between James Garfield and Burke Aaron Hinsdale* (Ann Arbor: University of Michigan Press, 1949), 309.

555 **"The lawlessness of power"** Carl Schurz, *Congressional Record,* 43rd Congress, 2nd sess., 366–67, 370; Trefousse, *Carl Schurz,* 221–23; Calhoun, *Conceiving a New Republic,* 63–64.

555 **"one difficulty"** Oliver Morton, *Congressional Record,* 43rd Congress, 2nd sess., 371.

555 **"The President and myself are alone"** Fish diary, entry January 11, 1875; Nevins, *Hamilton Fish,* 755; *Grant Papers,* 26:23n.

555 **"saying that there are some things"** Fish diary, entry January 11, 1875.

555 **"lawlessness, turbulence"** USG, "To Senate," January 13, 1875, *Grant Papers,* 26:3, 7. Grant poured himself into preparing this strong defense of his actions. Eric Foner, by contrast, writes, "A Presidential message to Congress offered only the most tepid defense of the army's actions." Foner, *Reconstruction,* 555.

556 **To succeed, the distillers bribed** In March 1875, after reading a promotion by the St. Louis Merchants' Exchange, Bristow decided to compare their statistics on the amount of liquor shipped from the city with the taxes paid on that liquor. He found that taxes were paid on only one-third of the liquor. H. V. Boyton, "The Whiskey Ring," *North American Review* 123 (October 1876): 288–91; Nevins, *Hamilton Fish,* 767–68.

556 **"not that of a scholar"** *New York World,* June 1874, cited in Webb, *Benjamin Helm Bristow,* 134–36. Bristow replaced William A. Richardson, the first member of Grant's cabinet to resign under a cloud. Richardson appointed John Sanborn to

recover unpaid taxes but agreed to a contract whereby Sanborn kept half of what he collected—which amounted to $213,000. Sanborn was indicted for "revenue fraud" in January 1874. Although Richardson was not indicted, his involvement became the cause of his removal from office.

556 **"There should be no delay"** USG, draft, Sixth Annual Message, December 7, 1874, *Grant Papers*, 25:272; Richardson, *A Compilation of the Messages and Papers of the Presidents*, 7:285.

557 **In his first eleven months** Fish diary, entry July 3, 1874; Nevins, *Hamilton Fish*, 720–21.

557 **"By God, I will not sacrifice"** *New Orleans Times*, May 29, 1875.

557 **"hearty cooperation"** H. V. Boynton, "The Whiskey Ring," *North American Review* 123 (October 1876): 294; Webb, *Benjamin Helm Bristow*, 192–93. Rectifiers reported cask serial numbers and tax stamps: gaugers certified that proper tax payments had been made.

557 **"The plague is advancing west"** Nevins, *Hamilton Fish*, 768. Bluford Wilson, solicitor of the Treasury, was well-known to Grant as the brother of James H. Wilson, who served on Grant's staff in the Civil War.

557 **In St. Louis alone** Ibid., 763, 768.

557 **Julia, who long ago** Ibid., 770.

557 **Using Bristow and Pierrepont** Smith, *Grant*, 585; Nevins, *Hamilton Fish*, 772–73.

558 **Ulysses knew that Julia** Julia Dent Grant, *Personal Memoirs*, 185.

558 **"I never sought"** USG to Harry White, May 29, 1875, *Grant Papers*, 26:132–34. Harry White was president of the Pennsylvania Republican State Convention. Two days earlier, Grant answered a query from a Cleveland newspaper editor with a more insightful response. Fully aware that a major reason for talk of a third term arose from the desire for a trusted leader "in time of great commotion when it might not be deemed prudent to make a change," he was equally cognizant that promotion of a third term would also be used by "the enemy of the republican party, and of this Administration, to force upon it an issue intended only to cause dissension and division." Grant said farsightedly, "If the number of terms of a president is to be limited to one, two, or any other number, then the question should be one as to the propriety of amending the Constitution to effect this." USG to Edwin Cowles, May 29, 1875, *Grant Papers*, 26:128–29. Cowles was editor of the *Cleveland Leader*.

558 **"Is there any news?"** Julia Dent Grant, *Personal Memoirs*, 185–86.

558 **Julia, still puzzled** Ibid., 186.

558 **"I want to know what"** Ibid.

560 **Grant asked Delano to resign** USG to Columbus Delano, June 20, 1875, *Grant Papers*, 26:166. Keller, *American Protestantism and United States Indian Policy*, 86, 93: "In a period of growing Democratic power, patronage had become imperative for Republicans." Nevins, *Hamilton Fish*, 773–75; Smith, *Grant*, 586–87.

560 **If a young Grant** Hans L. Trefousse, *Benjamin Franklin Wade: Radical Republican from Ohio* (New York: Twayne Publishers, 1963), 110.

560 **John Heyl Vincent, Galena pastor** Vincent, *John Heyl Vincent*, 116–21. On what would come to be called the Chautauqua Institution, see Jeffrey Simpson, *Chautauqua: An American Utopia* (New York: Abrams, 1999), 32–33, and Kathleen Crocker and Jane Currie, *The Chautauqua Institution, 1874–1974* (Charleston, S.C.: Arcadia Publishing, 2001), 9–10. The *Chautauqua Assembly Herald*, established in 1876, one year after Grant's visit, would contain reminiscences of his visit, published in succeeding years. Vincent preserved a large number of articles about these early years, which are in the Oliver Archives Center at the Chautauqua Institution.

560 **He aimed his new assembly** Simpson, *Chautauqua: An American Utopia*, 33. The

co-leader of the Chautauqua Assembly was businessman Lewis Miller, who was also superintendent of the Sunday schools in Akron, Ohio.

560 **Grant accepted** Simpson, *Chautauqua: An American Utopia,* 37; Crocker and Currie, *Chautauqua Institution,* 14.

561 **"to Dr. Vincent"** *Chautauqua Assembly Herald,* August 11, 1905.

561 **Grant's presence** Simpson, *Chautauqua: An American Utopia,* 37.

561 **He depended upon McDonald** Timothy Rives, "Grant, Babcock, and the Whiskey Ring," http://www.archives.gov/publications/prologue/2000/fall/whiskey-ring -1.html, 2–4; Hesseltine, *Ulysses S. Grant,* 207–8, 380.

561 **"Well, Mr. Bristow"** Fish diary, entry May 22, 1875; Webb, *Benjamin Helm Bristow,* 194–95.

562 **In the following months, Bristow** McFeely, *Grant,* 408–10.

562 **"I succeeded"** Rives, "Grant, Babcock, and the Whiskey Ring," 4.

562 **They had been authored** Webb, *Benjamin Helm Bristow,* 174, 192–98.

562 **Bristow believed that** Nevins, *Hamilton Fish,* 790; John McDonald, *Secrets of the Great Whiskey Ring* (Chicago: Belford, Clarke & Co., 1880), 106.

562 **"Let no guilty man escape"** Webb, *Benjamin Helm Bristow,* 196; USG "Endorsement," July 29, 1875, Grant Papers, 26:232.

562 **"If Babcock is guilty"** Hesseltine, *Ulysses S. Grant,* 384. Louis A. Coolidge, *Ulysses S. Grant,* (Boston: Houghton Mifflin, 1917), 483; Edwards Pierrepont to House Committee, *Whiskey Frauds,* 44th Congress, 1st sess., *House Miscellaneous Documents,* no. 11, 30, 485.

563 **As Bristow and Pierrepont** Hesseltine, *Ulysses S. Grant,* 384–85.

563 **"the Secretary's brilliant"** Boynton, "The Whiskey Ring," 303; Webb, *Benjamin Helm Bristow,* 199–200. For Boynton, see Summers, *Press Gang,* 85–86.

563 **On December 8, U.S. Attorney** Rives, "Grant, Babcock, and the Whiskey Ring," 4.

563 **"I know how much"** USG to Annie Campbell Babcock, December 17, 1875, Grant Papers, 26:430.

563 **Ulysses and Julia welcomed** Ross, *The General's Wife,* 244.

564 **"The advantages"** USG, Annual Message, December, 7, 1875, *Grant Papers,* 26:414.

564 **"impossible and unseemly"** Nevins, *Hamilton Fish,* 798–99.

564 **"I have always had"** USG, deposition, February 12, 1876, *Grant Papers,* 27:35. For full deposition, see 27–45.

564 **"had been met"** *New York Tribune,* February 25, 1876. See Smith, *Grant,* for the fulsome responses of other leading newspapers to Grant after the Babcock verdict, 592–93, 702n70.

564 **Shortly thereafter, the socially ambitious Carrie** Edward S. Cooper, *William Worth Belknap: An American Disgrace* (Madison, N.J.: Fairleigh Dickinson University Press, 2003), 12, 19, 26. Previously, General of the Army William T. Sherman had been granted the right to appoint traderships. William S. McFeely, "Ulysses S. Grant, 1869–1877," in C. Vann Woodward, ed., *Responses of the Presidents to Charges of Misconduct* (New York: Delacorte Press, 1974), 151.

565 **Carrie's younger sister** Cooper, *William Worth Belknap,* 12.

565 **"The money was sent"** "Malfeasance of W. W. Belknap, Late Secretary of War," 44th Congress, 1st sess., House Report 186, March 2, 1876, 3; Cooper, *William Worth Belknap,* 25.

566 **"call at once"** Webb, *Benjamin Helm Bristow,* 223; Fish diary, entry March 2, 1876; *Grant Papers,* 27:54n.

566 **"Oh, Mr. President"** Julia Dent Grant, *Personal Memoirs,* 190.

566 **"Mr. President, I came"** Ibid.; Cooper, *William Worth Belknap,* 33.

566 **"Your tender of resignation"** USG to William W. Belknap, March 2, 1876, *Grant Papers*, 27:53. The next day, Ohio congressman James A. Garfield wrote in his diary, "The President gave me a minute account of his part in the Belknap resignation." Grant reported, "The former was nearly suffocated with excitement; made an incoherent explanation and offered his resignation." *The Diary of James A. Garfield*, introduction by Harry James Brown and Frederick D. Williams, eds. (East Lansing: Michigan State University Press, 1967–1981), 3:243–44.

566 **As Grant picked up** Julia Dent Grant, *Personal Memoirs*, 191.

566 **"Time of acceptance"** Hiester Clymer to USG, March 2, 1876, *Grant Papers*, 27:54n; USG wrote his reply on Clymer's letter.

566 **Did Grant's acceptance** *New York Herald*, March 3, 1876, *Grant Papers*, 27:54–55n.

567 **"he did not know that acceptance"** Fish diary, entry March 3, 1876; *Grant Papers*, 27:55n.

567 **On March 2** USG to George M. Robeson, March 2, 1876, *Grant Papers*, 27:62; 62–63n.

567 **"first-rate judge of wine"** Cooper, *William Worth Belknap*, 111.

567 **The investigation also discovered** "Investigation of the Navy Department," 44th Congress, 1st sess., House Report 784, July 22, 1876.

567 **"must thereafter be known"** Ibid.; McFeely, *Grant*, 432.

567 **Admiral David Porter** David Dixon Porter to WTS, March 18, 1876, *Grant Papers*, 27:63n.

568 **"considered all conversations"** Bristow repeated his words on executive privilege to Grant in a letter on July 13, 1876, *Grant Papers*, 27:185–86n.

568 **The press immediately jumped** Webb, *Benjamin Helm Bristow*, 254.

568 **"absolving him"** USG to John A. Kasson, July 11, 1876, *Grant Papers*, 27:187n.

568 **"Nothing shows so clearly"** John A. Kasson, December 29, 1893, *Grant Papers*, 27:187n.

568 **"Justice to the President"** *New York Daily Graphic*, July 14, 1876; Webb, *Benjamin Helm Bristow*, 254–55.

569 **"He disliked controversy"** Boutwell, *Reminiscences of Sixty Years in Public Affairs*, 2:250.

569 **"He regarded the feelings"** Badeau, *Grant in Peace*, 81.

569 **"Absolutely incapable of servility"** Tiffany, *Pulpit and Platform*, 207.

569 **"Attacked by"** Ibid.

Chapter 33. Centennial Crisis

570 **Visitors from New York** Dee Brown, *The Year of the Century: 1876* (New York: Charles Scribner's Sons, 1966), 112–13.

570 **"One hundred years ago"** Address, May 10, 1876, *Grant Papers*, 27:107–8.

570 **Looming inside** Centennial Exhibition of 1876: Pennsylvania/Historical & Museum Commission, https://archive.org/details/CentennialExhibitionOf1876.

570 **Factoring in** Roy Morris, Jr., *Fraud of the Century: Rutherford B. Hayes, Samuel Tilden, and the Stolen Election of 1876* (New York: Simon & Schuster, 2003), 19.

571 **In the second rank** Eaton, *Presidential Timber*, 44–45.

571 **"I fixed on Fish"** Young, *Around the World*, 2:275.

571 **"wrote a letter"** Ibid.

571 **"its architecture"** *New York Tribune*, June 14, 1876.

571 **Blaine's backers** For a description of the convention and the candidates, see Morris, *Fraud of the Century*, 55, 57–83.

572 **But backers celebrated** Eaton, *Presidential Timber*, 45–46, 57–59.

572 **"I congratulate you"** USG to Rutherford B. Hayes, June 16, 1876, *Grant Papers*,

27:133n. For the convention voting, see Ari Hoogenboom, *The Presidency of Rutherford B. Hayes* (Lawrence: University Press of Kansas, 1988), 15–16.

572 **To Grant, this would be** Nevins, *Hamilton Fish*, 838.

573 **After his initial sketch** Jacob, *Testament to Union*, 24–26. Even redrawn, the kneeling posture of the slave would become increasingly controversial in succeeding years.

573 **"Abraham Lincoln was not"** Frederick Douglass, "The Freedmen's Monument to Abraham Lincoln: An Address Delivered in Washington, D.C.," April 14, 1876, in *The Frederick Douglass Papers, Series One: Speeches, Debates, and Interviews*, vol. 4: *1864–80*, 428–40; *New York Tribune*, April 15, 1876; Waldo E. Martin, Jr., *The Mind of Frederick Douglass* (Chapel Hill: University of North Carolina Press, 1984), 85–88.

574 **Wanamaker invited Grant** Herbert Adams Gibbons, *John Wanamaker*, vol. 1 (New York: Harper, 1926), 191–92.

574 **"My advice"** Proverbs 14:34. USG to Editor, *Sunday-School Times*, June 6, 1876, *Grant Papers*, 27:124.

574 **Wanamaker believed Grant's letter** Gibbons, *John Wanamaker*, writes, "The feat established the *Sunday School Times* as a national institution among Protestant churches, and Wanamaker lived to see the circulation pass the half-million mark" (192).

574 **In 1862, the general** Sarna, *When Grant Expelled the Jews*, 121–22.

574 **Grant's genuine mortification** Ibid., 123.

575 **Bowles, who broke** *Springfield Republican*, quoted in the *St. Louis Republican*, October 16, 1876. For Bowles's reputation, see Summers, *Press Gang*, 23.

575 **After sharp words** Foner, *Reconstruction*, 570–71; Thomas Holt, *Black over White: Negro Political Leadership in South Carolina During Reconstruction* (Urbana: University of Illinois Press, 1977), 199.

576 **The "Hamburg massacre"** Foner, *Reconstruction*, 571; Holt, *Black over White*, 199–200; Francis B. Simkins and Robert Hilliard Woody, *South Carolina During Reconstruction* (Chapel Hill: University of North Carolina Press, 1932), 586–87.

576 **"We may not be able"** *Sumter True Southron*, cited in Alrutheus Ambush Taylor, *The Negro in South Carolina During Reconstruction* (Washington, D.C.: Association for the Study of Negro Life and History, 1924), 237–38.

576 **"The effect of this massacre"** Daniel H. Chamberlain to USG, July 22, 1876, *Grant Papers*, 27:201–2n. On Chamberlain's personality, see Peggy Lamson, *The Glorious Failure: Black Congressman Robert Brown Elliott and the Reconstruction in South Carolina* (New York: W. W. Norton & Co., 1973), 153–55. The debate continues as to whether Chamberlain deserved the accolade as reformer.

576 **The scene at Hamburg** USG to Daniel H. Chamberlain, July 26, 1876, *Grant Papers*, 27:199–200.

576 **In March, the Supreme Court** Michael J. Klarman, *From Jim Crow to Civil Rights: The Supreme Court and the Struggle for Racial Equality* (New York: Oxford University Press, 2006), 37.

577 **"Every Democrat must"** "Plan of the Campaign of 1876," in Simkins and Woody, *South Carolina During Reconstruction*, 566.

577 **"insurrection and domestic violence"** Daniel H. Chamberlain to USG, October 11, 1876, *Grant Papers*, 27:330n.

577 **"Rifle Clubs"** USG, Proclamation, October 17, 1876, *Grant Papers*, 27:329–30.

577 **"all the available force"** James D. Cameron to WTS, October 17, 1876, *Grant Papers*, 27:331n.

577 **Grant's strong orders** Calhoun, *Conceiving a New Republic*, 103–4.

577 **Now, appalled by the violence** *New York Evening Post*, October 18, 1876; Charles H. Brown, *William Cullen Bryant* (New York: Charles Scribner's Sons, 1971), 473–74, 499–500; Nevins, *Hamilton Fish*, 843.

577 **Despite a weather system** "Voter Turnout in Presidential Elections: 1828–2012," American Presidency Project, http://www.presidency.ucsb.edu; Brown, *Year of the Century*, 287–88.

578 **"AVE! CENTENNIAL SAM!"** These newspaper headlines are cited by Morris, *Fraud of the Century*, 164–65.

578 **"Gentlemen, it looks to me"** Childs, *Recollections*, 76–77.

578 **Republicans were keenly aware** James M. McPherson estimates as many as 250,000 may have been intimidated from voting. *Ordeal by Fire*, 3rd ed. (New York: McGraw-Hill, 2000), 641.

578 **"Either party can afford"** USG to WTS, November 10, 1876, *Grant Papers*, 28:19–20.

578 **These three encouraged** Nevins, *Hamilton Fish*, 844–45.

579 **Mosby reported threats** Fish diary, entry November 14, 1876; Nevins, *Hamilton Fish*, 844; *Grant Papers*, 28:24n.

579 **"who were plotting your *assassination*"** AMB to USG, November 20, 1876, *Grant Papers*, 28:24n.

579 **"You are a doomed man"** "United Order of Bush Rangers" to USG, November 22, 1876, *Grant Papers*, 28:24.

579 **"troops as to give the legislature"** Daniel H. Chamberlain to USG, November 25, 1876, *Grant Papers*, 28:49n.

579 **Grant directed Secretary of War** USG to James D. Cameron, November 26, 1876, *Grant Papers*, 28:49.

579 **"he longed for the day"** Abram S. Hewitt, memorandum, December 3, 1876, *Grant Papers*, 28:78–81.

580 **Grant made none** Allan Nevins, *Abram S. Hewitt: With Some Account of Peter Cooper* (New York: Harper, 1935), 337–42.

580 **Should Ferry** Morris, *Fraud of the Century*, 200–201.

581 **Hewitt pronounced** C. Vann Woodward, *Reunion and Reaction: The Compromise of 1877 and the End of Reconstruction* (Boston: Little, Brown & Co., 1951), 150–51.

581 **The Democrats, by contrast** Morris, *Fraud of the Century*, 218–19; Woodward, *Reunion and Reaction*, 151.

581 **"because of my appreciation"** USG, "To Senate," January 29, 1877, *Grant Papers*, 28:143–45.

581 **Hayes, while still losing** 1876 election results, http://uselectionatlas.org.

582 **The swearing-in** Badeau, *Grant in Peace*, 251–52.

582 **"I hope you will be"** Julia Dent Grant, *Personal Memoirs*, 196.

583 **"If Tilden was declared"** Young, *Around the World*, 2:271–72.

583 **"public and patriotic service"** *New York Tribune*, August 25, 1876.

583 **"I was again impressed"** James A. Garfield, *The Diary of James A. Garfield*, edited by Harry James Brown and Frederick D. Williams (East Lansing: Michigan State University Press, 1973), entry October 18, 1876, 3:365–66.

583 **"for sixteen years"** Abram S. Hewitt, memorandum, December 3, 1876, *Grant Papers*, 28:79n.

584 **She knew that Lucy Hayes** Ross, *The General's Wife*, 247. Julia could not know that Mrs. Hayes would be dubbed "Lemonade Lucy."

Chapter 34. American Ambassador

587 **"I was never so happy"** John Russell Young, *Chicago Tribune*, September 1, 1885.

589 **Time Line of Grant's World Tour** I am grateful to Edwina Campbell for permission to use aspects of her more complete "Chronology of Grant's Diplomacy." See

Edwina Campbell, *Citizen of a Wider Commonwealth: Ulysses S. Grant's Postpresidential Diplomacy* (Carbondale: Southern Illinois University Press, 2016), 209–11.

590 **Reports of Grant's enthusiastic welcome** I commend *Citizens of a Wider Commonwealth* by Edwina Campbell, a former U. S. Foreign Service officer, who brings her diplomatic lens to offer a fresh interpretation of Grant's world tour.

590 **"That reticence"** Young, *Around the World*, 1:10–11.

591 **"I am aware"** J. F. Packard, *Grant's Tour Around the World* (Cincinnati: Forshee & McMakin, 1880), 49–50. Although Young, *Around the World with General Grant,* is remembered as the standard account of Grant's world tour, Packard, writing a year later, provides illuminating material not in Young.

591 **Upon arriving in London** Ibid., 54.

591 **"There is an impression"** Ibid., 56.

591 **"In the midst of the congregation"** Ibid., 57. *Penny Illustrated Paper* (London), June 9, 1877.

592 **"I will be compelled** USG to Elihu B. Washburne, June 9, 1877, *Grant Papers,* 28:214.

592 **Ulysses, Jesse, Nellie** Young, *Around the World,* 1:21; Jesse R. Grant, *In the Days of My Father,* 217–18.

592 **At breakfast** *New York Herald,* June 19, 1877.

592 **Their building** Founded in 1836 by members of the Liberal Party, the Reform Club pledged support for the Great Reform Act of 1832, which produced far-reaching changes in an outdated electoral system.

592 **"General Grant spoke"** *New York Herald,* June 19, 1877.

593 **"lamented so much"** USG, speech, London, June 18, 1877, *Grant Papers,* 28:225.

593 **"having no acknowledged rank"** Edwards Pierrepont to William M. Evarts, Secretary of State, June 27, 1877, *Grant Papers,* 28:231–32n; Badeau, *Grant in Peace,* 264–65.

593 **In the end, the queen** Jesse R. Grant, *In the Days of My Father,* 226–27.

593 **Grant concluded** *Leeds Mercury,* July 4, 1877; *Standard* (London) July 4, 1877.

593 **From Folkestone** His first European travels were followed in British newspapers led by *The Morning Post* (London), July 5, 1877, July 10, 1877.

593 **"I have long had a desire"** Young, *Around the World,* 1:49–50.

593 **"There is one Italian"** Grant's remark was reported by a London correspondent of the *New York Herald,* August 9, 1877. *Grant Papers,* 28:248n2.

594 **Using maps** Badeau, *Grant in Peace,* 307.

594 **"The length of my stay"** USG to Ulysses S. Grant, Jr., August 25, 1877, *Grant Papers,* 28:248–49.

594 **"I might vote frequently"** USG, speech, Glasgow, Scotland, September 13, 1877, *Grant Papers,* 28:270–71. *Leeds Mercury,* Sept. 14, 1877.

594 **"Though I entered the army"** USG, speech, September 13, 1877, *Grant Papers,* 28:271–72; *Morning Post* (London), September 14, 1877; *Dundee Courier and Argus,* September 14, 1877.

594 **Of course, he had read Scott's novels** Packard, *Grant's Tour Around the World,* 115.

594 **Upon his return to Edinburgh** Ibid.

594 **"Welcome to the Liberator"** Young, *Around the World,* 1:90–91.

595 **"Never was there a war"** Ibid., 92. Because of the special import of the parade and speeches the next morning, the *Newcastle Chronicle* reported the day's events in twenty columns.

595 **"When the history"** Ibid., 90–94; *Grant Papers,* 28:275n.

595 **"If it had been composed"** *Saturday Review,* March 18, 1865; White, *Lincoln's Greatest Speech,* 195.

595 **To a highly class-conscious society** *Reynolds's Newspaper* (London), June 3, 1877, was relieved at Grant's contrast to previous world leaders visiting the United Kingdom: "Now at length we have an honest ex-ruler amongst us, but quite of another stamp. . . . General Grant . . . is both a great soldier and an honest man. . . . In General Grant's Presidency the Augean stable of American corruption was partially swept clean."

596 **"I appreciate the fact"** USG to George W. Childs, June 6, 1877, *Grant Papers,* 28:210–11. See also George W. Childs, *Recollections of General Grant* (Philadelphia: Collins Printing House, 1890), 96–98. This initial letter was published in both U.S. and British newspapers: *Liverpool Mercury,* June 21, 1877; *Huddersfield Daily Chronicle* (West Yorkshire), June 22, 1877; *Aberdeen Weekly Journal,* June 23, 1877; *Reynolds's Newspaper* (London), June 24, 1877.

596 **"Even those who did not love"** Hamilton Fish to Edwards Pierrepont, August 7, 1877, *Grant Papers,* 28:227n.

596 **In mid-autumn, Grant crossed** *Daily Gazette* (Middlesbrough, U.K.), October 25, 1877; *Lloyd's Weekly Newspaper* (London), October 28, 1877.

596 **Young reported that Grant made numerous** Young, *Around the World,* 1:133, *Daily News* (London) Oct. 31, 1877.

596 **"They seemed typical"** George P. A. Healy, *Reminiscences of a Portrait Painter* (Chicago: A. C. McClurg, 1894), 193–94; David McCullough, *The Greater Journey: Americans in Paris* (New York: Simon & Schuster, 2011), 356.

597 **"The Statue of Liberty"** USG to Édouard Laboulaye, November 21, 1877, *Grant Papers,* 28:319; McCullough, *Greater Journey,* 356.

597 **He would find a quiet corner** Young, *Around the World,* 1:141–42. Grant's busy schedule was reported in British newspapers: *Dundee Courier & Argus* (Scotland), October 30, 1877; *Daily News* (London), October 31, 1877; *Lancaster Gazette,* October 31, 1877.

597 **"I have seen nothing here"** USG to Edward Beale, November 4, 1877, *Grant Papers,* 28:299–300.

597 **"it will be more republican"** USG to Daniel Ammen, December 10, *Grant Papers,* 28:331–32.

597 **From Nice they boarded** USG to Michael John Cramer, November 27, 1877, *Grant Papers,* 28:328.

597 **"My friend Mark Twain"** Young, *Around the World,* 1:218; Ross, *The General's Wife,* 260–61.

597 **"I am beginning to enjoy"** USG to Adam Badeau, December 18, 1877, *Grant Papers,* 28:333.

598 **"We are to take"** Albert J. Caldwell to his family, November 30 and December 20, 1877, *Grant Papers,* 28, 327n5.

598 **"My opinion of old USG"** Ibid., January 10, 1878, *Grant Papers,* 28:327n5.

598 **Grant surveyed the ruins** Packard, *Grant's Tour Around the World,* 188.

598 **"poor Nydia"** Julia Dent Grant, *Personal Memoirs,* 218.

598 **Although Grant had been disappointed** Young, *Around the World,* 1:166–96, devotes a long section to the visit to Pompeii because of Grant's intense interest in the site. Grant's remark is on page 193.

599 **"I wish I could lift"** Ibid., 200; J. T. Headley, *The Life and Travels of General Grant* (Philadelphia: Hubbard Bros., 1879), 106.

599 **"It informs us"** Young, *Around the World,* 1:202–3.

599 **"The truth is"** Ibid., 1:203.

599 **"The impression that the General"** Young, *Around the World,* 1:219–20.

599 **Although the empire was governed** Young, *Around the World with General Grant,* edited by Michael Fellman (Baltimore, Md.: Johns Hopkins University Press, 2002),

95. The United Kingdom controlled 44 percent of the Suez Canal, which was finished by the French in 1869.

599 **"All the romance given"** USG to Ulysses S. Grant, Jr., January 7, 1878, *Grant Papers*, 28:334.

600 **"the red-letter hours"** Young, *Around the World*, 1:246.

600 **"Egypt has interested me"** Ibid., 262; USG to Ulysses S. Grant, Jr., January 25, 1878, *Grant Papers*, 28:345; Headley, *Life and Travels of General Grant*, 121–22, 145. As an indication of the fascination with Grant's trip a quarter century later, see Elbert Eli Farman, *Along the Nile with General Grant* (New York: Grafton Press, 1904), which goes beyond Young in its detailed descriptions and explanations of what Grant saw.

600 **"nothing left"** Julia Dent Grant, *Personal Memoirs*, 224.

600 **A seed for his desire** Simpson, *Chautauqua: An American Utopia*, 34; Crocker and Currie, *Chautauqua Institution*, 29; "The Inner Life of Ulysses S. Grant," *The Chautauquan* 30, no. 6 (March 1900): 636.

601 **"We had been doing"** Young, *Around the World*, 1:322; Ross, *The General's Wife*, 262.

601 **"a very unpleasant one"** USG to Adam Badeau, February 22, 1878, *Grant Papers*, 28:348–49.

601 **Grant tried to forget** Mark Twain, *The Innocents Abroad; or, The New Pilgrim's Progress* (Hartford, Conn.: American Publishing, 1869), 573.

601 **He visited the Hagia Sophia** USG, *Grant Papers*, 28:xiv.

601 **At first he refused** Headley, *Life and Travels of General Grant*, 181.

601 **"They have a form of government"** USG to Daniel Ammen, March 25, 1878, *Grant Papers*, 28:366.

601 **"Our chief may have"** Young, *Around the World*, 1:359.

602 **"entirely out of the usual"** USG to Daniel Ammen, March 25, 1878, *Grant Papers*, 28:365.

602 **"One should visit"** USG to Abel R. Corbin, March 29, 1878, *Grant Papers*, 28:370. Two weeks later, Grant voiced the same sentiment to his son Fred. USG to Frederick Dent Grant, April 9, 1878, *Grant Papers*, 28:375.

602 **"It is quite a success, but"** USG, May 11, 1878, *Grant Papers*, 28:xxvii.

602 **he devoted portions** Young, *Around the World* 1:395–96.

602 **Everywhere he walked** Ibid., 1:397–98.

603 **Catching themselves, the guards** Ibid., 1:408–10.

603 **"I regard Sheridan"** Ibid., 1:411.

603 **"The truth is I am more"** Ibid., 1:416.

604 **Berlin newspapers had been filled** McFeely, *Grant*, 468; Smith, *Grant*, 609.

604 **"Bismarck und Grant"** *Berliner Tageblatt*, August 16, 1878.

604 **"received . . . most cordially"** *Berliner Borsenzeitung*, August 6, 1878. See also *Berlin Provinzial-Correspondenz*, July 26, 1878.

604 **"an interesting conversation"** *New York Herald*, May 27, 1878.

604 **A month earlier** Ibid. Welles's article appeared in *The Atlantic Monthly*, and Taylor wrote in the *North American Review*. On Young and his process, see *Grant Papers*, 28:386n.

604 **Keenly aware** Marszalek, *Sherman*, 463–65; Lloyd Lewis, *Sherman: Fighting Prophet* (Lincoln: University of Nebraska Press, 1993), 615–16.

604 **At a time when** The rejoinder might be made that Grant's conversations on his world tour will be repeated in his *Personal Memoirs*, but although there are similarities, there are also differences.

604 **"is never vindictive"** *New York Herald*, July 24, 1878; *Grant Papers*, 28:433n. Young added, "Grant never refers to the war unless you put the subject to him directly."

605 **"He had that magnetic quality"** USG, interview, Hamburg, July 6, 1878, *Grant Papers,* 28:425–26.

605 **"might have risen"** Ibid., 428–29.

605 **"I never ranked Lee"** USG, Hamburg interview, July 6, 1878, *Grant Papers,* 28:419; Young, *Around the World,* 2:458–59.

605 **"seems to have been"** John Russell Young, diary, entry August 8, 1878, *Grant Papers,* 28:433n.

605 **"I got tired"** Interview with Jesse Root Grant, Jr., *New York Herald,* June 14, 1878; Jesse R. Grant, *In the Days of My Father,* 321.

605 **"I must dissent"** USG, speech [near Hamburg], July 4, 1878, *Grant Papers,* 28:412–13.

606 **After traveling in St. Petersburg** His speeches and conversations with leaders and reporters were widely reported in British newspapers: *Aberdeen Weekly Journal,* July 23, 1878; *Sheffield and Rotherham Independent,* September 12, 1878; the *Dundee Courier and Argus,* September 16, 1878, describes Grant walking out of a Moscow acrobat show, "not wanting to witness a death."

606 **"After being here two days"** The poet James Russell Lowell used the term *achates* to refer to the faithful companion and friend to Aeneas in Virgil's *Aeneid.* James Russell Lowell to Charles E. Norton, November 10, 1878, in James Russell Lowell, *Letters of James Russell Lowell,* vol. 2, edited by Charles Elliott Norton (New York: Harper & Bros., 1894), 233; Martin B. Duberman, *James Russell Lowell* (Boston: Houghton Mifflin, 1966), 293.

606 **An official in Cork** *Freeman's Journal* (Dublin), January 4, 1879; *Irish Times* (Dublin), January 4, 1879; *Grant Papers,* 29:46n.

606 **"you did not know"** USG, speech, Dublin, January 3, 1879, *Grant Papers,* 29:43.

606 **While living in California** Badeau, *Grant in Peace,* 316.

607 **From Alexandria** USG, travel diary, entry February 13, 1879, *Grant Papers,* 29:63.

607 **"Travel in India"** Young, *Around the World,* 2:99.

607 **The former naval secretary** Ibid., 2:107–8.

607 **"with interest and respect"** Ibid., 2:136; Smith, *Grant,* 472–73.

607 **When not in prayer** Young, *Around the World,* 2:30–36.

608 **"It would be a sad day"** *Grant Papers,* 29:xii; Young, *Around the World,* Fellman, ed., 198–99.

608 **"I urged upon"** Young, *Around the World,* 2:163.

608 **"no features"** Ibid., 2:213–17.

608 **"The South has been"** Ibid., 2:361–62.

609 **"the King of America"** Ibid., 2:313–17.

609 **"I have no doubt that Lincoln"** Ibid., 2:354.

610 **"My visit to China"** USG, speech, Tientsin, May 30, 1879, *Grant Papers,* 29:140–41.

610 **"I think that progress"** USG, conversation with Prince Kung, June 5, 1879, *Grant Papers,* 29:144.

610 **"The policy of America"** Ibid., June 8, 1879, *Grant Papers,* 29:151. The *Pall Mall Gazette* (London), May 19, 1879, had detailed Grant's sympathy with Chinese immigration to America.

610 **"The fact is Chinese like Americans"** USG to Adam Badeau, June 22, 1879, *Grant Papers,* 29:171.

610 **Grant told the viceroy** *Grant Papers,* 29:164n.

610 **"The Japanese"** USG to Daniel Ammen, July 16, 1879, *Grant Papers,* 29:183.

610 **"They have a public school system"** USG to Daniel Ammen, August 7, 1879, *Grant Papers,* 29:195.

610 **"In your discussions"** USG, conversations with Emperor Meiji, August 10, 1879, *Grant Papers,* 29:204.

611 **"I leave Japan"** USG to Prince Kung and Iwakura Tomomi, August 13, 1879, *Grant Papers*, 29:214.

612 **"At the end of the first"** USG to Adam Badeau, August 1, 1879, *Grant Papers*, 29:192–93.

612 **"He read all day long"** Julia Dent Grant, *Personal Memoirs*, 307.

612 **"The tour was the fulfillment"** Jesse R. Grant, *In the Days of My Father*, 321.

Chapter 35. Grant & Ward

613 **"This place is just like Philadelphia"** USG to Adolph F. Borie, September 28, 1879, *Grant Papers*, 29:248.

613 **Buck, whose investments** Young, *Around the World*, 2:627–28.

615 **"as a tribute"** Young, "To Mrs. Julia D. Grant," *Around the World*, 1:n.p.

615 **"Julia, look there"** Howard, *Autobiography of Oliver Otis Howard*, 2:481.

615 **"Julia, that is the field"** Ibid., 479–80.

616 **He arrived in Galena** USG, speech, November 5, 1879, *Grant Papers*, 29:282.

616 **Grant believed he needed** The Former Presidents Act of 1958 for the first time entitled former presidents to a lifetime pension. http://www.archives.gov/about/laws/former-presidents.html.

616 **"Man of Destiny"** Justin Kaplan, *Mr. Clemens and Mark Twain* (New York: Simon & Schuster, 1966), 224–25.

616 **For a full six hours** Kaplan captures the emotion of this evening, 225ff.

616 **"Hold the crowd"** Ibid., 226.

616 **"And if the child"** Rachel Cohen, *A Chance Meeting: Intertwined Lives of American Writers and Artists* (New York: Random House, 2004), 58–60.

616 **When the evening** Twain, *Autobiography of Mark Twain*, 1:68.

616 **They had circumnavigated** *Grant Papers*, 29:xv; Julia Dent Grant, *Personal Memoirs*, 312.

617 **Adding to Republican anxiety** Eaton, *Presidential Timber*, 67–68.

617 **"couldn't be elected"** *Chicago Tribune*, May 12, 1880; Smith, *Grant*, 614. For a revisionist view of Hayes, see Ari Hoogenboom, *Rutherford B. Hayes: Warrior and President* (Lawrence: University Press of Kansas, 1995). See also Harry Barnard, *Rutherford B. Hayes and His America* (Indianapolis: Bobbs-Merrill, 1954), and H. J. Eckenrode, *Rutherford B. Hayes: Statesman of Reunion* (New York: Dodd, Mead, 1930).

617 **"The general popular favorite"** Rutherford B. Hayes, entry December 18, 1879, *Diary and Letters of Rutherford Birchard Hayes*, 3:582.

617 **"man of iron"** *St. Louis Globe Democrat*, quoted in *New York Tribune*, July 22, 1878.

617 **gave "him greater power"** *New York Times*, January 6, 1880.

617 **"Ulysses S. Grant is a man"** *New York Sun*, n.d., cited in Spencer L. Leitman, "The Revival of an Image: Grant and the 1880 Republican Nominating Campaign," *Missouri Historical Society Bulletin* 30 (April 1974): 200.

617 **who was already raising** *The Nation*, September 25, 1879.

617 **"I am not a candidate"** USG to Adam Badeau, August 30, 1879, *Grant Papers*, 29, 234.

617 **New York's Roscoe Conkling** Lewis L. Gould, *The Republicans: A History of the Grand Old Party* (New York: Random House, 2014), 74.

618 **Grant, proud of** *Grant Papers*, 29:xxix, 345n.

618 **"It has a great future"** USG to George Childs, January 18, 1880, *Grant Papers*, 29:346.

618 **"I would much rather"** USG to Elihu B. Washburne, February 2, 1880, *Grant Papers*, 29:352–53. Borie died at Philadelphia on February 5, 1880.

618 **"an old friend"** *Chicago Inter-Ocean*, February 27, 1880; *Grant Papers*, 29:363n.

618 **In Mexico City** David M. Pletcher, *Rails, Mines, & Progress: Seven American Promoters in Mexico, 1867–1911* (Ithaca, N.Y.: Cornell University Press, 1958), 156.

618 **"From the City of Mexico"** USG to George W. Childs, *Grant Papers*, 29, 365. The secretary of the British legation at Washington, Victor Drummond, taking note of Grant's visit, sent a cable to London informing his superiors of the favorable impression Grant made. The British had no diplomatic representation in Mexico since their ill-fated tripartite invasion with France and Spain in 1862. Drummond believed Mexico's new openness to U.S. capital grew out of Grant's influence. *British Parliamentary Papers*, 1881: 89, 100, 2994, cited by Osgood Hardy, "Ulysses S. Grant: President of the Mexican Southern Railroad," *Pacific Historical Review* 24, no. 2 (May 1955): 113.

619 **"I believe that the day"** *Grant Papers*, 29:xxix–xxx, 376–78n; speech, Vicksburg, April 12, 1880, 380–81.

619 **Conkling did the same** Jordan, *Roscoe Conkling of New York*, 322–23.

620 **"Grant manifested"** Badeau, *Grant in Peace*, 320.

620 **"How can I describe"** Julia Dent Grant, *Personal Memoirs*, 321.

620 **The Grant supporters' carefully** Eaton, *Presidential Timber*, 75–76.

620 **Julia "entreated him"** Julia Dent Grant, *Personal Memoirs*, 321–22.

621 **Although Grant led** Hesseltine, *Ulysses S. Grant*, 438–39; Jordan, *Roscoe Conkling of New York*, 338–39.

621 **"No man has a right"** Candice Millard, *Destiny of the Republic: A Tale of Madness, Medicine and the Murder of a President* (New York: Doubleday, 2011), 7–11, 44.

621 **In future years** Eaton, *Presidential Timber*, 84. Smith, *Grant*, narrates that the Stalwarts produced *The Roll of Honor* in late 1880, listing all 306. A special Grant medal was issued to each person (705n33).

621 **Partly to placate** Jordan, *Conkling of New York*, 342.

621 **"I have nothing to say"** Interview with the *Chicago Advance*, July 8, 1880, *Grant Papers*, 29:438–39.

621 **"He was a very good"** Charles H. Fowler to his wife, September 21, 1880, *Grant Papers*, 29:461n. Fowler had previously served as president of Northwestern University. This conversation with Grant did not stay private, for Fowler published the letter to his wife.

621 **Grant was not pleased** USG to Chicago reporter, October 5, 1880, *Grant Papers*, 29:464n.

622 **"Hancock's Political Achievements"** Millard, *Destiny of the Republic*, 59.

622 **"I feel a very deep interest"** USG to James A. Garfield, August 5, 1880, *Grant Papers*, 29:440.

622 **Grant believed Tourgée** For Tourgée as a radical racial reformer, see White, *Liberty and Justice for All*, 7, 6–9, 36–37.

622 **"The solid South"** USG, speech, Warren, Ohio, September 28, 1880, *Grant Papers*, 29, 478–79.

622 **"entire equality before the law"** Ibid., 478.

623 **"All we ask"** USG, speech, Jersey City, N.J., October 21, 1880, *Grant Papers*, 30:15.

623 **"We are all carpetbaggers"** Ibid., 30:17n.

623 **"it gradually came out"** Twain, *Autobiography of Mark Twain*, 1:75–76.

623 **"this was all so shameful"** Ibid., 76; Mark Twain, welcoming speech to Hartford, Conn., October 16, 1880, *Grant Papers*, 30:10–11n.

623 **"What they have given"** USG, speech, Hartford, Conn., October 16, 1880, *Grant Papers*, 30:10.

624 **Grant's hopes** George R. Goethals, *Presidential Leadership and African-Americans* (New York: Routledge, 2015), 121.

624 **"generous, unselfish"** Chauncey M. Depew, *My Memories of Eighty Years* (New York: Charles Scribner's Sons, 1922), 111.

624 **"There is no position"** USG to James Garfield, November 11, 1880, *Grant Papers*, 30:74–75.

624 **"would not listen"** Twain, *Autobiography of Mark Twain*, 1:71.

624 **When Twain told him** Ibid., 71.

624 **"I have always distrusted my ability"** USG to Samuel L. Clemens, January 14, 1881, *Grant Papers*, 30:118–19.

625 **An additional $100,000** Smith, *Grant*, 618.

625 **"It was a much larger"** Julia Dent Grant, *Personal Memoirs*, 323–24.

625 **Julia, often dressed** Ross, *The General's Wife*, 281.

625 **"I expect to be"** USG to World's Fair Commission, March 22, 1881, *Grant Papers*, 30:182.

625 **This venture was about** For the story of attempts to modernize Mexico's transportation, see Pletcher, *Rails, Mines, & Progress*.

626 **He also wanted to link** *Grant Papers*, 30:219n.; Pletcher, *Rails, Mines, & Progress*, 150.

626 **"the possibility"** USG, speech, Mexico City, April 22, 1881, *Grant Papers*, 30:199, 202; Pletcher, *Rails, Mines, & Progress*, 163.

626 **On May 11** *Grant Papers*, 30:xxiv.

626 **Grenville Dodge** Ibid., 30:121n.

626 **The treaty of reciprocity** Pletcher, *Rails, Mines, & Progress*, 171–74. The invitation to Grant came officially from President Arthur but had been promoted by the new secretary of state, Frederick T. Frelinghuysen, an old Grant friend, who had replaced James G. Blaine on December 18, 1881.

626 **"This seems a sufficiently"** F. E. Prendergast, "Railroads in Mexico," *Harper's Magazine* 63 (1881): 276–81.

626 **"exceedingly eager"** Whitelaw Reid to Justin S. Morrill, May 18, 1883, cited in Pletcher, *Railroads, Mines, & Progress*, 150.

626 **"I never would"** Badeau, *Grant in Peace*, 353.

627 **"the third generation"** Frederick A. Ober, *Travels in Mexico and Life Among the Mexicans* (Boston: Estes and Lauriat, 1884), 443–44.

627 **Ward had a telephone line** Ibid., 138, 147, 149, 163.

627 **Within a few months** Geoffrey C. Ward, *A Disposition to Be Rich: How a Small-Town Pastor's Son Ruined an American President, Brought on a Wall Street Crash, and Made Himself the Best-Hated Man in the United States* (New York: Alfred A. Knopf, 2012), 152–53, 158–59, 162–63.

628 **as silent partners** Ibid., 168, 179.

628 **"the most successful financier"** Hamlin Garland, "A Romance of Wall Street: The Grant and Ward Failure," *McClure's Magazine* (April 1898), 500; Thomas M. Pitkin, *The Captain Departs: Ulysses S. Grant's Last Campaign* (Carbondale, Ill.: Southern Illinois University Press, 1973), 2; Ward, *A Disposition to Be Rich*, 159, 169, 198.

628 **"His presence was magnetic"** Henry Clews, *Twenty-eight Years in Wall Street* (New York: Irving Publishing, 1898), 215.

628 **"There's millions"** Twain, *The Gilded Age*, xxiii, 47.

628 **"Grant would have been"** Garland, "A Romance of Wall Street," 499.

628 **He hinted that government contracts** Ward, *A Disposition to Be Rich*, 178–84.

629 **None of his customers knew** Ibid., 177, 204, 210–11.

629 **This ongoing sleight of hand** Ibid., 177, 204.

629 **"The fact is"** USG to Ellen Grant Sartoris, July 25, 1883, *Grant Papers*, 31:55.

629 **"We are all"** Ibid., December 15, 1883, *Grant Papers*, 31:91.

629 **At sixty-one** Julia Dent Grant, *Personal Memoirs*, 326; Hesseltine, *Ulysses S. Grant*, 446–47.

629 **And after listening** Ward, *A Disposition to Be Rich*, 194n.

630 **With Ward and Buck in tow** Ferdinand Ward, "My Recollections of General Grant," *New York Herald,* December 26, 1909.

630 **"I care nothing"** Garland, "A Romance of Wall Street," 500–501.

630 **By afternoon the stock market** Ward, *A Disposition to Be Rich,* 217. Although the story of Ward has always been included in biographies of Grant, Ward's book illuminates this sordid story in whole new ways.

630 **"The general looked neither"** Alexander Dana Noyes, *The Market Place: Reminiscences of a Financial Editor* (New York: Little, Brown & Co., 1938), 44–45.

631 **"Grant and Ward has failed"** Ward, *A Disposition to Be Rich,* 218–19; Garland, "A Romance of Wall Street," 502.

Chapter 36. Final Campaign

632 **"The people look on"** *New York Sun,* May 5, 1884. The *New York Post* editorialized, "The conclusion is irresistible that a large number of persons were drawn into the maelstrom by a belief held out to them that General Grant's influence was used in some highly improper way to the detriment of the government and the benefit of Grant and Ward." July 5, 1884.

632 **"I could bear all"** USG to George W. Childs, May 15, 1884, *Grant Papers,* 31:148.

632 **In the end** Julia Dent Grant, *Personal Memoirs,* 327; Garland, "A Romance of Wall Street," 502–3.

632 **"All articles"** W. H. Vanderbilt to JDG, January 10, 1885, *Grant Papers,* 31:256–57n.

633 **"I enclose check"** Charles Wood to USG, May 10, 1884, *Grant Papers,* 31:146–47n. Wood offered to loan the general another $1,000, to be repaid in one year without interest.

633 **"I owe you this"** Warren F. Broderick, " 'I Owe You This for Appomattox': U. S. Grant's Mystery Visitor at Mount McGregor," *Hudson Valley River Review* 22, no. 1 (Autumn 2005), 49–53. Wood was misidentified as a veteran; he had not participated in the war. Two younger brothers had, but neither had served under Grant.

633 **"The country will rally"** Charles Wood to USG, May 17, 1884, *Grant Papers,* 31:151n. The complete texts of the four letters between Wood and Grant were later published in *The New York Times,* August 5, 1892.

633 **He meant it** Julia Dent Grant, *Personal Memoirs,* 328. In a June 23 letter to Romero, Grant completed paying the loan back in full. At the same time, he invited Romero and his wife to spend a week at Long Branch. USG to Matías Romero, June 23, 1884, *Grant Papers,* 31:164–65.

633 **The general sent** Ward, *A Disposition to Be Rich,* 232–34. James D. Fish was arrested on May 26.

633 **"I was one"** Stuart, *Life of George H. Stuart,* 312–13; Childs, *Recollections,* 88–89.

634 **"Oh my."** Julia Dent Grant, *Personal Memoirs,* 328–29.

634 **"No, it will be all right"** Ibid., 329.

634 **Childs asked** Childs, *Recollections,* 111–12. Dr. Da Costa was also a lecturer at Philadelphia's Jefferson Medical College.

634 **Grant put the irritation** Charles Bracelen Flood, *Grant's Final Victory: Ulysses S. Grant's Heroic Last Year* (Boston: Da Capo Press, 2011), 74–75.

634 **If Grant could be persuaded** Harold Holzer, Introduction, in Harold Holzer, ed., *Hearts Touched by Fire: The Best of Battles and Leaders of the Civil War* (New York: Modern Library, 2011), xiii. *The Century* had begun its life as *Scribner's Monthly* in 1870.

634 **In a candor** Robert Underwood Johnson, *Remembered Yesterdays* (Boston: Little, Brown & Co., 1923), 210–11.

635 **Fred would help** Flood, *Grant's Final Victory*, 87–88. Fred had coauthored a report on his expedition with General Philip Sheridan up the Yellowstone River: James W. Forsyth and Frederick D. Grant, *Report of an Expedition up the Yellowstone River* (Washington, D.C.: Government Printing Office, 1875).

635 **"Hurrah for Grant!"** USG to Richard Watson Gilder, *Grant Papers*, 31:170.

635 **To their dismay** Johnson, *Remembered Yesterdays*, 213.

635 **"this required all the tact"** Ibid., 213–14.

635 **"I discovered"** Ibid., 214–15.

635 **"what he planned"** Perry, *Grant and Twain*, 59; Johnson, *Remembered Yesterdays*, 215.

635 **"a new idea"** Johnson, *Remembered Yesterdays*, 215.

635 **On July 15** USG to Richard Watson Gilder, July 15, 1884, *Grant Papers*, 31:175. Around this time, a reporter for the *Baltimore American* visited Grant. "I found the General in his library among a mass of papers and books, hard at work on his history on the siege of Vicksburg." He told the correspondent a humorous story about the siege "and laughed heartily." Pitkin, *The Captain Departs*, 13.

635 **"I hope both you and Sheridan"** USG to WTS, August 9, 1884, *Grant Papers*, 31:187–88.

636 **Smith, who was against** Holzer, *Hearts Touched by Fire*, xii; Perry, *Grant and Twain*, 62.

636 **"Do you really think"** Johnson, *Remembered Yesterdays*, 216–17; Pitkin, *The Captain Departs*, 15.

636 **"My own opinion"** USG to Adam Badeau, September 13, 1884, *Grant Papers*, 31:204–5.

636 **Barker advised him** Flood, *Grant's Final Victory*, 74–75, 83.

636 **"Is it cancer?"** John H. Douglas diary, entry October 24, 1884, Library of Congress.

636 **Douglas asked him to stop** Richard Goldhurst, *Many Are the Hearts: The Agony and the Triumph of Ulysses S. Grant* (New York: Reader's Digest Press, 1975), 148.

637 **"I have had a sore throat"** USG to Ellen Grant Sartoris, November 18, 1884, *Grant Papers*, 31:235.

637 **"I then went"** Julia Dent Grant, *Personal Memoirs*, 329.

637 **He told the author** Twain, *Autobiography of Mark Twain*, 1:77; Kaplan, *Mr. Clemens and Mark Twain*, 261.

638 **"I pricked up my ears"** Twain, *Autobiography of Mark Twain*, 1:77–78.

638 **"he supposed that the *Century* offer"** Ibid., 1:78.

638 **He tried to persuade** Ibid., 2:61.

638 **Fred proposed** Ibid.

638 **Grant was taken aback** Ibid.

638 **"On re-examining the Contract"** USG to George W. Childs, November 23, 1884, *Grant Papers*, 31:237; Twain, *Autobiography of Mark Twain*, 2:63–64. In his *Autobiography*, dictated twenty years later, Twain shortens what turned out to be lengthy deliberations.

638 **Twain gave Grant a choice** Twain, *Autobiography of Mark Twain*, 2:63–64. For a summary of these negotiations, see Perry, *Grant and Twain*, 84–90, 115.

639 **Childs arranged** Perry, *Grant and Twain*, 76.

639 **Beside the small desk** Flood, *Grant's Final Victory*, 69.

639 **Toward the end of the evening** Perry, *Grant and Twain*, 77, 161.

639 **"Pretend you are a boy again"** George F. Shrady, *General Grant's Last Days* (New York: De Vinne, 1907), 21–22.

639 **"There is not the slightest danger"** George F. Shrady, "Interviews with Grant's Doctor," *Saturday Evening Post*, September 9, 1901.

640 **Noble E. Dawson** Flood, *Grant's Final Victory*, 130.

640 **Worried about choking** Julia Dent Grant, *Personal Memoirs*, 329.

640 **"a very serious matter"** USG to Ellen Grant Sartoris, February 16, 1885, *Grant Papers*, 31:293–94.

640 **"If you ever take time"** Ibid.

640 **Twain returned on February 21** Twain, *Autobiography of Mark Twain*, 1:79.

640 **GRANT IS DYING** *New York Times*, March 1, 1885.

640 **"the death watch"** Perry, *Grant and Twain*, 149.

640 **Grant's health absorbed** Goldhurst, *Many Are the Hearts*, 172; Flood, *Grant's Final Victory*, 131–32.

640 **"You would think the newspapers"** Flood, *Grant's Final Victory*, 133; Goldhurst, *Many Are the Hearts*, 173–74.

641 **"Doctor, you did not give"** Shrady, *General Grant's Last Days*, 54.

641 **With less than one hour** Perry, *Grant and Twain*, 156–59.

641 **"I am grateful"** Goldhurst, *Many Are the Hearts*, 169–70.

641 **Julia, at her husband's death** Perry, *Grant and Twain*, 160.

641 **Proud of his writing** Ibid., 153–56.

641 **Julia admired** Stefan Lorant, "Baptism of U.S. Grant," *Life*, March 26, 1951, 90. Newman's diary, lost for half a century, was recovered by Lorant; Perry, *Grant and Twain*, 177–80.

641 **"manifests dependence on God"** Lorant, "Baptism of U. S. Grant," 91.

641 **Depending on whom** Perry, *Grant and Twain*, 177–84, offers a good discussion of Newman and different attitudes toward him.

642 **"General Grant was a sick man"** Twain, *Autobiography of Mark Twain*, 2:65; Perry, *Grant and Twain*, 163.

642 **Newspapers headlined Grant's death,** Goldhurst, *Many Are the Hearts*, 80–81, 151–52; Perry, *Grant and Twain*, 149, 173. Flood, *Grant's Final Victory*, 131.

642 **"The bell-strokes"** Mark Twain, *Mark Twain's Notebooks & Journals,* edited by Frederick Anderson, Michael B. Frank, and Kenneth M. Sanderson (Berkeley: University of California Press, 1975–1979), 3:117–18.

642 **"The two armies"** *Personal Memoirs*, 2:445–46.

642 **"because I had never expressed"** Twain, *Autobiography of Mark Twain*, 2:71.

642 **"The same high merits"** Ibid., 71–72.

643 **"what he planned, thought"** Perry, *Grant and Twain*, 59; Johnson, *Remembered Yesterdays*, 215.

643 **"One of the most anxious"** *Personal Memoirs*, 2:424.

643 **"a noun is the name"** Ibid., 1:25.

643 **"The fact is I think"** USG to John H. Douglas, [undated, probably in July 1885], *Grant Papers*, 31:441n.

643 **Strong action verbs** James M. McPherson offers the best introduction to the military and literary qualities of Grant's *Personal Memoirs*. I am indebted to his insightful analysis of Grant's use of verbs. See Ulysses S. Grant, *Personal Memoirs of U. S. Grant*, introduction and notes by James M. McPherson (New York: Penguin Books, 1999), xiii–xxvi.

643 **"Move at early dawn"** Preeminent British military historian John Keegan points to "the clarity and force of his [Grant's] writing style." John Keegan, *The Mask of Command* (New York: Viking, 1987), 200–201.

643 **"I ordered Thomas"** *Personal Memoirs*, 2:113.

644 **In the afternoon, a messenger** Perry, *Grant and Twain*, 190.

644 **Novelist and civil rights reformer** Albion Winegar Tourgée to USG, April 27, 1885, *Grant Papers*, 31:346n.

644 **"Remembering him now"** Resolution, Confederate Survivors' Association, April 27, 1885, *Grant Papers*, 31:346n.

644 **"false idea of Gen. Grant"** *New York World,* April 29, 1885; Pitkin, *The Captain Departs,* 37–38. Although Ihrie later remonstrated he never intended his remarks to a Washington reporter to end up on the front page of the *World,* the damage was done.

644 **"The work upon his new book"** Perry, *Grant and Twain,* 196; USG to Charles L. Webster & Co., May 2, 1885, *Grant Papers,* 31:347.

644 **"The General's work this morning"** Perry, ibid.

645 **"Your book has assumed an importance"** Adam Badeau to USG, May 2, 1885, *Grant Papers,* 31:357–58n.

645 **"piece and prepare"** Ibid., 358n.

645 **"The preposterous assertions"** Ibid.; Perry, *Grant and Twain,* 198–200.

645 **"Yours is not"** Adam Badeau to USG, May 2, 1885, *Grant Papers,* 31: 358n.

645 **"I have concluded"** USG to Adam Badeau, [May 2–5, 1885] *Grant Papers,* 31:350–57.

646 **"I have not changed"** Adam Badeau to USG, May 9, 1885, *Grant Papers,* 31:360n.

646 **The Grants accepted** For the story of Mount McGregor, see Pitkin, *The Captain Departs,* 46–56.

646 **As the nighttime temperature fell** Flood, *Grant's Final Victory,* 192–94.

647 **"I can feel plainly"** USG to John H. Douglas, June 17, 1885, *Grant Papers,* 31:374–75.

647 **"I feel that I am failing"** USG, "Memoranda for My Family," June 17, 1885. *Grant Papers,* 31:375n; Pitkin, *The Captain Departs,* 64.

647 **"Mrs. Grant was almost prostrated"** *New York Times,* June 18, 1885; Pitkin, *The Captain Departs,* 64–65.

647 **"I said I had been adding"** USG to John H. Douglas, June 23, 1885, *Grant Papers,* 383n. The earliest version of this note is in Horace Green, *General Grant's Last Stand* (New York: Charles Scribner's Sons, 1936), xiii, 306. Green wrote his book based on the 102 notes preserved by Harriet Sheldon Douglas, the daughter of Dr. John Douglas. Today the notes are in the possession of the Library of Congress.

647 **They talked by slips of paper** Pitkin, *The Captain Departs,* 70–72.

648 **"There are some matters"** USG to JDG, June 29, 1885, *Grant Papers,* 31:387–88.

649 **" 'Man proposes' "** *Personal Memoirs,* 1:7–8.

649 **"The patient sufferer"** *New York Tribune,* July 7–8, 1885; Pitkin, *The Captain Departs,* 73.

649 **"I ask you not to show"** USG to John H. Douglas, July 2, 1885, *Grant Papers,* 31:402–3.

649 **"It has been an inestimable blessing"** Ibid., 403.

650 **but Grant insisted** USG, "To Mexican Delegation," July 8 1885, *Grant Papers,* 31:417–18; Pitkin, *The Captain Departs,* 79.

650 **"I am very sorry"** USG to Charles Wood, July 9, 1885, *Grant Papers,* 31:419; see also Broderick, " 'I Owe You This for Appomattox,' " 49–58.

650 **"The sole object"** Stickles, *Simon Bolivar Buckner,* 325.

651 **"my work had been done"** USG to John H. Douglas, July 16, 1885, *Grant Papers,* 31:437.

Epilogue

653 **America's largest public gathering** *New York Tribune,* August 8, 1885. For the best description and analysis of the Grant funeral procession, see Joan Waugh, " 'Pageantry of Woe': The Funeral of Ulysses S. Grant," in *Vale of Tears: New Essays on Religion and Reconstruction,* edited by Edward J. Blum and W. Scott Poole (Macon, Ga.: Mercer University Press, 2005), 212–34. For an extensive contemporary account, see Poore and Tiffany, *Life of U. S. Grant,* 549–71.

653   **"savior of their country"** Quoted in James P. Boyd, *Military and Civil Life of Gen. Ulysses S. Grant* (Philadelphia and Chicago: P. W. Ziegler & Co., 1885), 674.

653   **"foremost man of the nation"** Ibid., 676.

653   **"no man since George Washington"** Ibid., 675.

653   **"in his chivalric kindness"** Ibid., 676.

654   **"great in war, greater in peace"** Charles L. Woodworth, *A Commemorative Discourse on the Work and Character of Ulysses Simpson Grant* (Boston: Beacon Press, 1885), 7, 17; Waugh, " 'Pageantry of Woe': The Funeral of Ulysses S. Grant," 213.

654   **"ruler who healed the wound"** Charles H. Fowler, *General Grant: Memorial Address* (San Francisco: Methodist Book Depository, 1885), 32.

654   **"shine with increased luster"** *Death of General U. S. Grant: Funeral Memorial Service at Bristol, R.I.* (Providence, R.I.: J. A. & R. A. Reid, 1885), 11, 21, 40.

654   **"my lifetime friend"** Interview with James Longstreet, *New York Times,* July 24, 1885. James Grant Wilson, *General Grant* (New York: D. Appleton & Co., 1897), 362.

654   **demand for seats** *The Times* (London), August 4, 1885. The service in London was timed to coincide with a service at Mount McGregor on August 4.

654   **"His name will share with that of Abraham Lincoln"** Ibid., July 24, 1885.

654   **"Ulysses S. Grant is exceptional"** *Freeman's Journal,* July 24, 1885. Other newspapers that offered comment on Grant included the *Belfast News-Letter,* July 28, 1885; *Dundee Courier and Argus,* July 24, 1885.

654   **Grover Cleveland . . . asked General Winfield Hancock** Poore and Tiffany, *Life of U. S. Grant,* 557.

655   **procession was to start from City Hall** Richard G. Mannion, "The Life of a Reputation: The Public Memory of Ulysses S. Grant," PhD dissertation, Georgia State University, 2012, 241.

655   **Grant's two favorite Union generals** Craig L. Symonds, *Joseph E. Johnston: A Civil War Biography* (New York: W. W. Norton & Co., 1992), 380.

655   **bonds of reconciliation** David Blight, in *Race and Reunion: The Civil War in American Memory* (Cambridge, Mass.: Belknap Press of Harvard University Press, 2001), 215–16, points out the "flood of reconciliationist symbolism" in his treatment of Grant's funeral.

655   **sparked across the nation** Poore and Tiffany, *Life of U. S. Grant,* 560.

656   **"He Helped to Set Me Free"** *Harper's Weekly,* August 8, 1885.

656   **"greatest funeral ever seen in America"** *Philadelphia Advertiser,* August 10, 1885.

656   **cutting-edge marketing campaign** McFeely, *Grant,* 501.

657   **royalties of $450,000** Twain, *Autobiography of Mark Twain,* 2:73; Perry, *Grant and Twain,* 233.

657   **"Grant's dynamic force"** Edmund Wilson, *Patriotic Gore* (New York: Oxford University Press, 1962), 143.

657   **"man of first-rate intelligence"** Gore Vidal, "The Grants," A Review of Julia D. Grant's *Personal Memoirs, The New York Review of Books,* vol. 22, September 18, 1975, 12.

657   **her memoirs take pains to correct misunderstandings** John Y. Simon, editor of *The Papers of Ulysses S. Grant,* edited its publication. As an example of setting the record straight, Julia wanted to make clear that her husband did not seek a third term, but "the papers were making such a howl about the third term" (185–86).

658   **"Their Widows Met in Peace"** *New York Herald,* June 25, 1893; *Chicago Tribune,* June 25, 1893; *New York Times,* June 25, 1893. For this episode and the life of Varina Davis, see Joan E. Cashin, *First Lady of the Confederacy: Varina Davis's Civil War* (Cambridge, Mass.: Belknap Press of Harvard University Press, 2006), 279–80.

658   **Julia Grant and Varina Davis** Cashin, *First Lady of the Confederacy,* 280.

658 **left Great Britain and her failed marriage** Ross, *The General's Wife*, 325, 332–33. In 1912, Nellie married lawyer Frank Hatch Jones and moved to Chicago.

659 **"A great life never dies"** *Address of President William McKinley, at the Dedication of the Grant Monument* (New York: General Grant National Memorial, 1897), 5.

659 **"Mightiest among the mighty dead"** Theodore Roosevelt, *The Strenuous Life: Essays and Addresses* (New York: Century Co., 1900), 1.

659 **"To him more than to any other man"** Frederick Douglass, "An Address Delivered in Rochester, New York, August 6, 1885," in *The Frederick Douglass Papers: Series One: Speeches, Debates, and Interviews,* edited by John W. Blassingame and John R. McKivigan (New Haven, Conn.: Yale University Press, 1881–1895), 5:201–2.

Selected Bibliography

Manuscript Collections

Abraham Lincoln Presidential Library, Springfield, Illinois
Jacob Ammen Diary
William H. Austin Letters
Sylvanus Cadwallader Papers
Ulysses S. Grant Papers
John A. McClernand Papers
Lindorf Ozburn Letters
John A. Rawlins Papers

Bridwell Library, Perkins School of Theology, Southern Methodist University, Dallas, Texas
John Heyl Vincent Papers

Chicago History Museum, Chicago, Illinois
Jesse Root Grant Papers
Ulysses S. Grant Papers
John A. Rawlins Papers

Detroit Public Library, Burton Historical Collection, Detroit, Michigan
Ulysses S. Grant Papers

Doheny Memorial Library, University of Southern California, Los Angeles, California
Hamlin Garland Papers

Firestone Library, Princeton University, Princeton, New Jersey
Adam Badeau Papers

Huntington Library, San Marino, California
Samuel Barlow Papers
William K. Bixby Collection
James William Eldridge Collection
Ulysses S. Grant Collection
Henry Wager Halleck Papers
Thomas Hamer Papers
David Dixon Porter Papers
William T. Sherman Papers
Zachary Taylor Papers

Library of Congress, Manuscript Division, Washington, D.C.
William C. Church Papers
William C. Comstock, Diary
Charles Dana Papers
Hamilton Fish Papers
Ulysses S. Grant Papers
Horace Greeley Papers
Abraham Lincoln Papers
David Dixon Porter Papers
William T. Sherman Papers
Edwin M. Stanton Papers
Elihu B. Washburne Papers
James H. Wilson Papers

Lincoln Memorial Shrine, Redlands, California
Mortimer D. Leggett Papers

National Archives, Washington, D.C.
Orville E. Babcock Papers

Oliver Archives Center, Chautauqua Institution, Chautauqua, New York
John Heyl Vincent Papers

Ulysses S. Grant National Historic Site, St. Louis, Missouri
Letters of Julia Dent Grant

Ulysses S. Grant Presidential Library at Mississippi State University, Starkville, Mississippi
Orville E. Babcock Materials
Bultema-Williams Photographic Collection
Lloyd Lewis–Bruce Catton Notes
Julia Grant Scrapbook
Ulysses S. Grant Papers

United States Military Academy, Archives and Special Collections, West Point, New York
U.S. Military Academy Library Circulation Records, 1842–1843
Cadets Admitted to the U.S. Military Academy, 1840–1845
Official Register of the Officers and Cadets of the U.S. Military Academy, West Point, New York, June 1840

Charles E. Young Library, University of California at Los Angeles, Los Angeles, California
William Rosecrans Papers

Newspapers

United States

Army and Navy Journal
The Atlantic
Baltimore Sun
Brooklyn Daily Eagle
The Castigator
Chautauqua Assembly Herald

The Chautauquan
Chicago Tribune
Cincinnati Commercial
Cincinnati Gazette
Enquirer and Examiner (Richmond, Virginia)
Frank Leslie's Illustrated Weekly
Galena Daily Gazette
Galena Weekly North-Western Gazette
Harper's Magazine
Independent (New York)
McClure's Magazine
Midland Monthly Magazine
Nashville Banner
The Nation
National Intelligencer
National Republican
New York Herald
New York Post
New York Times
New York Tribune
New York World
Niles Register
North American Review
Philadelphia Times
Sacramento Daily Union
St. Louis Missouri Republican
Sun (New York)
Washington Star

United Kingdom

Aberdeen Weekly Journal
Belfast Newsletter
Leeds Mercury
Manchester Times
Morning Post (London)
Reynolds's Newspaper (London)
Sheffield and Rotherham Independent
The Star (St. Peter Port)
The Times (London)

Books, Dissertations, Diaries, Letters

Abbott, Richard H. *Cobbler in Congress: The Life of Henry Wilson, 1812–1875*. Lexington: University Press of Kentucky, 1972.

———. *The Republican Party and the South, 1855–1877*. Chapel Hill: University of North Carolina Press, 1986.

Ackerman, Kenneth D. *The Gold Ring: Jim Fisk, Jay Gould, and Black Friday, 1869*. New York: Dodd, Mead, 1988.

Ammen, Daniel. *The Old Navy and the New*. Philadelphia: Lippincott, 1891.

Andrews, J. Cutler. *The North Reports the Civil War*. Pittsburgh: University of Pittsburgh Press, 1955.

———. *The South Reports the Civil War*. Princeton, N.J.: Princeton University Press, 1970.

Anecdotes and Reminiscences of Gen'l U. S. Grant. New York: Cheap Publishing, c. 1885.

Armstrong, William H. *Warrior in Two Camps: Ely S. Parker, Union General and Seneca Chief*. Syracuse, N.Y.: Syracuse University Press, 1978.

Badeau, Adam. *Military History of Ulysses S. Grant, from April, 1861, to April, 1865*. 3 vols. New York: D. Appleton, 1868–1881.

———. *Grant in Peace: From Appomattox to Mount McGregor; A Personal Memoir*. New York: D. Appleton, 1887.

Ballard, Michael B. *Pemberton: A Biography*. Jackson: University Press of Mississippi, 1991.

———. *Vicksburg: The Campaign That Opened the Mississippi*. Chapel Hill: University of North Carolina Press, 2004.

Barber, James. *U. S. Grant: The Man and the Image, with an Essay by John Y. Simon*. Washington, D.C.: National Portrait Gallery, Smithsonian Institution; Carbondale: in association with Southern Illinois Press, 1985.

Bartlett, Irving H. *Wendell Phillips: Brahmin Radical*. Boston: Beacon Press, 1961.

Bauer, K. Jack. *The Mexican War, 1846–1848*. New York: Macmillan, 1974.

———. *Zachary Taylor: Soldier, Planter, Statesman of the Old Southwest*. Baton Rouge: Louisiana State University Press, 1985.

Bearss, Edwin C. *The Campaign for Vicksburg*. 3 vols. Dayton, Ohio: Morningside, 1985–1986.

Benedict, Michael Les. *A Compromise of Principle: Congressional Republicans and Reconstruction, 1863–1869*. New York: W. W. Norton & Co., 1974.

Blaine, James G. *Twenty Years in Congress: From Lincoln to Garfield*. Vols. 1 and 2. Norwich, Conn.: Henry Brill, 1884.

Blight, David. *Race and Reunion: The Civil War in American Memory*. Cambridge, Mass.: Belknap Press of Harvard University Press, 2002.

Boutwell, George S. *Reminiscences of Sixty Years in Public Affairs*. 2 vols. New York: McClure, Phillips, 1902.

Brinton, John Hill. *Personal Memoirs of John H. Brinton, 1861–1865*. New York: Neale Publishing, 1914.

Brooks, Noah. *Washington in Lincoln's Time*. New York: Century, 1896.

Brown, Dee. *The Year of the Century: 1876*. New York: Charles Scribner's Sons, 1966.

Cadwallader, Sylvanus. *Three Years with Grant*. Edited by Benjamin P. Thomas. New York: Alfred A. Knopf, 1955.

Calhoun, Charles C. *Conceiving a New Republic: The Republican Party and the Southern Question, 1869–1900*. Lawrence: University Press of Kansas, 2006.

———. *From Bloody Shirt to Full Dinner Pail: The Transformation of Politics and Governance in the Gilded Age*. New York: Hill & Wang, 2010.

Campbell, Edwina S. *Citizen of a Wider Commonwealth: Ulysses S. Grant's Postpresidential Diplomacy*. Carbondale: Southern Illinois University Press, 2016.

Carpenter, John A. *Sword and Olive Branch: Oliver Otis Howard*. Pittsburgh: University of Pittsburgh Press, 1964.

———. *Ulysses S. Grant*. New York: Twayne Publishers, 1970.

Casey, Emma Dent. *When Grant Went A-Courtin', by His Wife's Sister*. New York: Circle Publishing, 1909.

Cashman, Sean Dennis. *America in the Gilded Age: From the Death of Lincoln to the Rise of Theodore Roosevelt*. New York: New York University Press, 1984.

Castel, Albert. *The Presidency of Andrew Johnson*. Lawrence: Regents Press of Kansas, 1979.

Catalogue of the Library of the U.S. Military Academy at West-Point, May 1830. New York: J. Desnoues, 1830.

Catalogue of the Library of the U.S. Military Academy, West Point, N.Y., Exhibiting Its Condition at the End of the Year 1852. New York: John F. Trow, 1853.

Catton, Bruce. *A Stillness at Appomattox*. Garden City, N.Y.: Doubleday, 1953.

————. *Grant Moves South*. Boston: Little, Brown & Co., 1960.

————. *Grant Takes Command*. Boston: Little, Brown & Co., 1969.

————. *U. S. Grant and the American Military Tradition*. Edited by Oscar Handlin. Boston: Little, Brown & Co., 1954.

Chalmers, David M. *Hooded Americanism: The History of the Ku Klux Klan*. Durham, N.C.: Duke University Press, 1987.

Chetlain, Augustus L. *Recollections of Seventy Years*. Galena, Ill.: Gazette Publishing Company, 1899.

Childs, George W. *Recollections of General Grant*. Philadelphia: Collins Printing House, 1885.

Christensen, Allan Conrad. *Edward Bulwer-Lytton: The Fiction of New Regions*. Athens: University of Georgia Press, 1976.

Comstock, Cyrus B. *The Diary of Cyrus B. Comstock*. Edited by Merlin E. Sumner. Dayton, Ohio: Morningside, 1987.

Cook, Adrian. *The Alabama Claims: American Politics and Anglo-American Relations, 1865–1872*. Ithaca, N.Y.: Cornell University Press, 1975.

Cooling, Benjamin Franklin. *War and Society in Kentucky and Tennessee, 1862–1863*. Knoxville: University of Tennessee Press, 1997.

————. *Forts Henry and Donelson: The Key to the Confederate Heartland*. Knoxville: University of Tennessee Press, 1987.

Cozzens, Peter. *The Darkest Days of the War: The Battles of Iuka and Corinth*. Chapel Hill: University of North Carolina Press, 1997.

————. *General John Pope: A Life for the Nation*. Urbana: University of Illinois Press, 2000.

————. *The Shipwreck of Their Hopes: The Battles for Chattanooga*. Urbana: University of Illinois Press, 1994.

Crackel, Theodore J. *Mr. Jefferson's Army: Political and Social Reform of the Military Establishment, 1801–1809*. New York: New York University Press, 1987.

Cramer, Michael John. *Ulysses S. Grant: Conversations and Unpublished Letters*. New York: Eaton & Mains, 1897.

Crawford, J. B. *The Credit Mobilier of America: Its Origin and History*. Boston: C. W. Calkins, 1880.

Crocker, Kathleen, and Jane Currie. *The Chautauqua Institution, 1874–1974*. Charleston, S.C.: Arcadia Publishing, 2001.

Cullom, George W., ed. *Biographical Register of the Officers and Graduates of the U.S. Military Academy at West Point, N.Y.* Vol. 2. 3rd ed., revised and extended. Boston: Houghton Mifflin, 1891.

Cunningham, O. Edward. *Shiloh and the Western Campaign of 1862*. New York: Savas Beattie, 2007 [Gary D. Joiner and Timothy B. Smith edited the original Louisiana State University PhD dissertation, 1966].

Dana, Charles A. *Recollections of the Civil War*. New York: D. Appleton, 1898.

Daniel, Larry J. *Shiloh: The Battle That Changed the War*. New York: Simon & Schuster, 1997.

Davis, Jefferson. *The Essential Writings*. Edited by William J. Cooper, Jr. New York: Random House, 2003.

Davis, William C. *Crucible of Command: Ulysses S. Grant and Robert E. Lee—The War They Fought, the Peace They Forged*. Boston: Da Capo Press, 2015.

————. *Jefferson Davis: The Man and His Hour*. New York: HarperCollins, 1991.

————. *Look Away!: A History of the Confederate States of America*. New York: Free Press, 2003.

Dodge, Grenville M. *Personal Recollections of President Abraham Lincoln, General Ulysses S. Grant, General William T. Sherman*. Council Bluffs, Iowa: Monarch Printing, 1914.

Donald, David Herbert. *Charles Sumner and the Rights of Man*. New York: Alfred A. Knopf, 1970.

———. *Lincoln*. New York: Simon & Schuster, 1995.

Dowdall, Denise M. *From Cincinnati to the Colorado Ranger: The Horsemanship of Ulysses S. Grant*. Dublin, Ireland: Historyeye, 2012.

Dugard, Martin. *The Training Ground: Grant, Lee, Sherman, and Davis in the Mexican War, 1846–1848*. Lincoln: University of Nebraska Press, 2008.

Dyer, Brainerd. *Zachary Taylor*. Baton Rouge: Louisiana State University Press, 1946.

Eaton, John. *Grant, Lincoln, and the Freedmen*. In collaboration with Ethel Osgood Mason. New York: Longmans, Green & Co., 1907.

Ecelbarger, Gary. *Black Jack Logan*. Guilford, Conn.: Lyons Press, 2005.

Eckenrode, H. J., and Bryan Conrad. *James Longstreet: Lee's War Horse*. Chapel Hill: University of North Carolina Press, 1936.

Eisenhower, John S. D. *Agent of Destiny: The Life and Times of Winfield Scott*. New York: Free Press, 1997.

———. *So Far from God: The U.S. War with Mexico, 1846–1848*. New York: Random House, 1989.

Ellington, Charles G. *The Trial of U. S. Grant: The Pacific Years, 1852–1854*. Glendale, Calif.: Arthur H. Clark, 1987.

Engle, Stephen D. *Don Carlos Buell: Most Promising of All*. Chapel Hill: University of North Carolina Press, 1999.

———. *Struggle for the Heartland: The Campaigns from Fort Henry to Corinth*. Lincoln: University of Nebraska Press, 2001.

Feis, William B. *Secret Service: The Intelligence War from Belmont to Appomattox*. Lincoln: University of Nebraska Press, 2002.

Fellman, Michael. *Citizen Sherman: A Life of William Tecumseh Sherman*. New York: Random House, 1995.

Flood, Charles Bracelen. *Grant and Sherman: The Friendship That Won the Civil War*. New York: Farrar, Straus and Giroux, 2005.

Flower, Frank A. *Edwin McMasters Stanton: The Autocrat of Rebellion, Emancipation, and Reconstruction*. Akron, Ohio: Saalfield Publishing, 1905.

Foote, Shelby. *The Civil War: A Narrative*. 3 vols. New York: Random House, 1958–1974.

Foulke, William Dudley. *Life of Oliver P. Morton*. Vol. 2. Indianapolis: Bowen-Merrill, 1899.

Freeman, Douglas Southall. *Lee's Lieutenants: A Study in Command*. 3 vols. New York: Charles Scribner's Sons, 1942–1944.

———. *R. E. Lee: A Biography*. 4 vols. New York: Charles Scribner's Sons, 1934–1935.

Friedman, Lee M. *Jewish Pioneers and Patriots*. Philadelphia: Jewish Publication Society, 1942.

Gallagher, Gary W. *The Confederate War*. Cambridge, Mass.: Harvard University Press, 1997.

———. *The Union War*. Cambridge, Mass.: Harvard University Press, 2011.

———, ed. *Lee the Soldier*. Lincoln: University of Nebraska Press, 1996.

———, ed. *The Shenandoah Valley Campaign of 1864*. Chapel Hill: University of North Carolina Press, 2006.

———, ed. *The Wilderness Campaign*. Chapel Hill: University of North Carolina Press, 1997.

Garfield, James A. *The Diary of James A. Garfield*. Vol. 3. Edited with an introduction by Harry James Brown. East Lansing: Michigan State University Press, 1973.

Garland, Hamlin. *Ulysses S. Grant: His Life and Character*. New York: Doubleday & McClure, 1898.

Gillette, William. *The Right to Vote: Politics and the Passage of the Fifteenth Amendment*. Baltimore, MD: The Johns Hopkins Press, 1965.

Glatthaar, Joseph T. *Partners in Command: The Relationships Between Leaders in the Civil War.* New York: Free Press, 1994.

Gott, Kendall D. *Where the South Lost the War: An Analysis of the Fort Henry–Fort Donelson Campaign: February 1862.* Mechanicsburg, Pa.: Stackpole Books, 2003.

Gould, Lewis L. *Grand Old Party: A History of the Republicans.* New York: Random House, 2003.

Grabau, Warren. *Ninety-eight Days: A Geographer's View of the Vicksburg Campaign.* Knoxville: University of Tennessee Press, 2000.

Grant, Arthur Hastings. *The Grant Family: A Genealogical History of the Descendants of Matthew Grant of Windsor, Conn., 1601–1898.* Poughkeepsie, N.Y.: Press of A. V. Haight, 1898.

Grant, Julia Dent. *The Personal Memoirs of Julia Dent Grant.* Carbondale: Southern Illinois University Press, 1975.

Grant, Ulysses S. *Personal Memoirs.* 2 vols. New York: Charles L. Webster & Co., 1885.

Griess, Thomas Everett. "Dennis Hart Mahan: West Point Professor and Advocate of Military Professionalism, 1830–1871." PhD dissertation. Durham, N.C.: Duke University, 1968.

Grimsley, Mark. *The Hard Hand of War: Union Military Policy Toward Southern Civilians, 1861–1865.* New York: Cambridge University Press, 1995.

Halloran, Fiona Deans. *Thomas Nast: The Father of Modern Political Cartoons.* Chapel Hill: University of North Carolina Press, 2012.

Hamilton, Holman. *Zachary Taylor: Soldier in the White House.* Indianapolis: Bobbs-Merrill, 1941.

Hattaway, Herman, and Archer Jones. *How the North Won: A Military History of the Civil War.* Urbana: University of Illinois Press, 1983.

Hearn, Chester G. *Admiral David Dixon Porter.* Annapolis, Md.: Naval Institute Press, 1996.

Hebert, Walter E. *Fighting Joe Hooker.* Indianapolis: Bobbs-Merrill, 1944.

Henderson, Timothy J. *A Glorious Defeat: Mexico and Its War with the United States.* New York: Hill & Wang, 2007.

Henry, Robert Selph. *"First with the Most" Forrest.* Indianapolis: Bobbs-Merrill, 1944.

Hesseltine, William B. *Ulysses S. Grant, Politician.* New York: Dodd, Mead & Co., 1935.

Hoar, George Frisbie. *Autobiography of Seventy Years.* Vol. 1. New York: Charles Scribner's Sons, 1913.

Hollandsworth, James G., Jr. *Pretense of Glory: The Life of General Nathaniel P. Banks.* Baton Rouge: Louisiana State University Press, 1998.

Holt, Thomas. *Black over White: Negro Political Leadership in South Carolina During Reconstruction.* Urbana: University of Illinois Press, 1977.

Hoogenboom, Ari. *Outlawing the Spoils: A History of the Civil Service Reform Movement, 1865–1883.* Urbana: University of Illinois Press, 1961.

———. *The Presidency of Rutherford B. Hayes.* Lawrence: University Press of Kansas, 1988.

Horn, Calvin W. *A Handbook of the Methodist Episcopal Church Georgetown, Ohio.* Georgetown: Georgetown Gazette, 1904.

Horn, Stanley F. *The Army of Tennessee: A Military History.* Indianapolis: Bobbs-Merrill, 1941.

Howard, Oliver O. *Autobiography of Oliver Otis Howard.* New York: Baker & Taylor, 1908.

Howe, Daniel Walker. *What Hath God Wrought: The Transformation of America, 1815–1848.* New York: Oxford University Press, 2007.

Howe, Henry. *Historical Collections of Ohio.* Vol. 1. Norwalk, Ohio: Laning Printing Co., 1896.

Hughes, Nathaniel Cheairs, Jr., and Roy P. Stonesifer, Jr. *The Life and Wars of Gideon J. Pillow.* Chapel Hill: University of North Carolina Press, 1993.

Hunt, Gaillard. *Israel, Elihu and Cadwallader Washburn: A Chapter in American Biography.* New York: Macmillan, 1925.

Hurst, Jack. *Nathan Bedford Forrest*. New York: Alfred A. Knopf, 1993.

Hyman, Harold M. *The Radical Republicans and Reconstruction, 1861–1870*. Indianapolis: Bobbs-Merrill, 1967.

James, Joseph B. *The Framing of the Fourteenth Amendment*. Urbana: University of Illinois Press, 1965.

Johannsen, Robert Walter. *To the Halls of the Montezumas: The Mexican War in the American Imagination*. New York: Oxford University Press, 1985.

Johnson, Andrew. *The Papers of Andrew Johnson*. Edited by LeRoy P. Graf and Ralph W. Haskins. Knoxville: University of Tennessee Press, 1967–2000.

Johnson, Timothy D. *Winfield Scott: The Quest for Military Glory*. Lawrence: University Press of Kansas, 1998.

Johnston, R. U., and C. C. Clough Buel, eds. *Battles and Leaders of the Civil War*. 4 vols. New York: Century, 1887–1888.

Jones, George R. *Joseph Russell Jones*. Chicago: privately printed, 1964.

Jordan, David M. *Roscoe Conkling of New York*. Ithaca, N.Y.: Cornell University Press, 1971.

Keegan, John. *The American Civil War: A Military History*. New York: Alfred A. Knopf, 2009.

————. *The Mask of Command*. New York: Viking, 1987.

Keller, Robert H. *American Protestantism and United States Indian Policy, 1869–1882*. Lincoln: University of Nebraska Press, 1983.

Kemble, John Haskell. *The Panama Route, 1848–1869*. Berkeley: University of California Press, 1943.

Knepper, George W. *Ohio and Its People*. Kent, Ohio: Kent State University Press, 1989.

Korn, Bertram Wallace. *American Jewry and the Civil War*. Philadelphia: Jewish Publication Society of America, 1951.

Lamers, William M. *The Edge of Glory: A Biography of General William S. Rosecrans, U.S.A.* With a new introduction by Larry J. Daniel. Baton Rouge: Louisiana State University Press, 1999.

Larson, Robert W. *Red Cloud: Warrior-Statesman of the Lakota Sioux*. Norman: University of Oklahoma Press, 1997.

Lewis, Lloyd. *Captain Sam Grant*. Boston: Little, Brown & Co., 1950.

Lincoln, Abraham. *The Collected Works of Abraham Lincoln*. 9 vols. Edited by Roy P. Basler. New Brunswick, N.J.: Rutgers University Press, 1953–1955.

Little, Kimberly Scott. *Ulysses S. Grant's White Haven: A Place Where Extraordinary People Came to Live Extraordinary Lives, 1796–1885*. St. Louis: Ulysses S. Grant National Historic Site, 1993.

Longacre, Edward G. *General Ulysses S. Grant: The Soldier and the Man*. Cambridge, Mass.: Da Capo Press, 2006.

Longstreet, James. *From Manassas to Appomattox: Memoirs of the Civil War in America*. Philadelphia: Lippincott, 1896.

Lowe, Richard. *Republicans and Reconstruction in Virginia, 1856–1870*. Charlottesville: University Press of Virginia, 1991.

Lyman, Theodore. *With Grant and Meade from the Wilderness to Appomattox*. Introduction by Brooks D. Simpson. Lincoln: University of Nebraska Press, 1994. Originally published, Boston: Atlantic Monthly Press, 1922.

Mahood, Wayne. *Alexander "Fighting Elleck" Hays: The Life of a Civil War General: From West Point to the Wilderness*. Jefferson, N.C.: McFarland, 2005.

Mannion, Richard G. "The Life of a Reputation: The Public Memory of Ulysses S. Grant." PhD dissertation. Atlanta: Georgia State University, 2012.

Mardock, Robert Winston. *The Reformers and the American Indian*. Columbia: University of Missouri Press, 1971.

Marsh, Dianne. *Galena, Illinois: A Brief History.* Charleston, S.C.: History Press, 2010.

Marszalek, John. *Commander of All Lincoln's Armies: A Life of General Henry W. Halleck.* Cambridge, Mass.: Belknap Press of Harvard University Press, 2004.

————. *Sherman: A Soldier's Passion for Order.* New York: Free Press, 1993.

————. ed. *The Best Writings of Ulysses S. Grant.* Carbondale: Southern Illinois University Press, 2015.

Marvel, William. *Burnside.* Chapel Hill: University of North Carolina Press, 1991.

McDonough, James Lee. *Chattanooga: A Death Grip on the Confederacy.* Knoxville: University of Tennessee Press, 1984.

McFeely, William S. *Grant: A Biography.* New York: W. W. Norton & Co., 1981.

McKitrick, Eric L. *Andrew Johnson and Reconstruction.* Chicago: University of Chicago Press, 1960.

McPherson, James M. *The Abolitionist Legacy: From Reconstruction to the NAACP.* Princeton, N.J.: Princeton University Press, 1975.

————. *Abraham Lincoln and the Second American Revolution.* New York: Oxford University Press, 1990.

————. *Battle Cry of Freedom.* New York: Oxford University Press, 1988.

————. *Drawn with the Sword: Reflections on the American Civil War.* New York: Oxford University Press, 1996.

————. *Embattled Rebel: Jefferson Davis and the Confederate Civil War.* New York: Penguin Books, 2015.

————. *The Struggle for Equality: Abolitionists and the Negro in the Civil War and Reconstruction.* Princeton, N.J.: Princeton University Press, 1964.

————. *War on the Waters: The Union and Confederate Navies, 1861–1865.* Chapel Hill: University of North Carolina Press, 2012.

Meade, George Gordon. *The Life and Letters of George Gordon Meade.* 2 vols. New York: Charles Scribner's Sons, 1913.

Merry, Robert M. *A Country of Vast Designs: James K. Polk, the Mexican War and the Conquest of the American Continent.* New York: Simon & Schuster, 2009.

Morris, Benjamin Franklin, ed. *The Life of Thomas Morris.* Cincinnati: Moore, Wilstach, Key & Overend, 1856.

Morris, Roy, Jr. *Fraud of the Century: Rutherford B. Hayes, Samuel Tilden, and the Stolen Election of 1876.* New York: Simon & Schuster, 2003.

Morrison, James L., Jr. *"The Best School in the World": West Point, the Pre–Civil War Years, 1833–1866.* Kent, Ohio: Kent State Universitiy Press, 1986.

Neely, Marx E., Jr., and Harold Holzer. *The Union Image: Popular Prints of the Civil War North.* Chapel Hill: University of North Carolina Press, 2000.

Nelson, William Javier. *Almost a Territory: America's Attempt to Annex the Dominican Republic.* Newark: University of Delaware Press, 1990.

Nevins, Allan. *Frémont: Pathmarker of the West.* New York: Appleton-Century, 1939.

————. *Hamilton Fish: The Inner History of the Grant Administration.* New York: Dodd, Mead & Co., 1936.

Niven, John. *Gideon Welles: Lincoln's Secretary of the Navy.* New York: Oxford University Press, 1973.

————. *Salmon P. Chase: A Biography.* New York: Oxford University Press, 1995.

Oberholtzer, Ellis P. *Jay Cooke: Financier of the Civil War.* Vol. 2. Philadelphia: George W. Jacobs, 1907.

Official Records of the Union and Confederate Armies: The War of the Rebellion. Washington, D.C.: Government Printing Office, 1880–1901.

Official Records of the Union and Confederate Navies in the War of the Rebellion. Washington, D.C.: Government Printing Office, 1894–1922.

Official Register of the Officers and Cadets of the U.S. Military Academy. Vol. 3. West Point, N.Y.: New York: W. L. Burroughs, 1843.

Ohrt, Wallace. *Defiant Peacemaker: Nicholas Trist in the Mexican War.* College Station: Texas A&M University Press, 1997.

Olson, James C. *Red Cloud and the Sioux Problem.* Lincoln: University of Nebraska Press, 1965.

Page, Charles A. *Letters of a War Correspondent.* Edited by James R. Gilmore. Boston: L. Page, 1899.

Paine, Albert P. *Thomas Nast.* New York: Macmillan, 1904.

Parks, Joseph Howard. *General Leonidas Polk, C.S.A.: The Fighting Bishop.* Baton Rouge: Louisiana State University Press, 1990.

Pemberton, John C., *Pemberton: Defender of Vicksburg.* Chapel Hill: University of North Carolina Press, 1942.

Peskin, Allan. *Winfield Scott and the Profession of Arms.* Kent, Ohio: Kent State University Press, 2003.

Pollard, Edward A. *The Lost Cause: A New Southern History of the War of the Confederates.* New York: E. B. Treat, 1866.

Poole, D. C. *Among the Sioux of Dakota.* New York: D. Van Nostrand, 1881.

Poore, Benjamin Perley, and O. H. Tiffany. *Life of General U. S. Grant.* Philadelphia: Hubbard Brothers, 1885.

Porter, David Dixon. *Incidents and Anecdotes of the Civil War.* New York: D. Appleton, 1885.

Porter, Horace. *Campaigning with Grant.* Introduction by Brooks D. Simpson. Lincoln: University of Nebraska Press, 2000. Originally published New York: Century Co., 1897.

Rable, George C. *But There Was No Peace: The Role of Violence in the Politics of Reconstruction.* Athens: University of Georgia Press, 1984.

Randel, William Peirce. *The Ku Klux Klan: A Century of Infamy.* Philadelphia: Chilton Books, 1965.

Reardon, Carol. *With a Sword in One Hand and Jomini in the Other: The Problem of Military Thought in the Civil War North.* Chapel Hill: University of North Carolina Press, 2012.

Regulations Established for the Organization and Government of the Military Academy at West Point, New York. New York: Wiley & Putnam, 1839.

Remlap, L. T. *General Grant's Tour Around the World.* Chicago: J. Fairbanks, 1879.

Rhea, Gordon C. *Cold Harbor: Grant and Lee, May 26–June 3, 1864.* Baton Rouge: Louisiana State University Press, 2002.

―――. *To the North Anna River: Grant and Lee, May 13–25, 1864.* Baton Rouge: Louisiana State University Press, 2000.

Richardson, Albert D. *A Personal History of Ulysses S. Grant.* Hartford, Conn.: American Publishing, 1868.

Robins, Glenn. *The Bishop of the Old South: The Ministry and Civil War Legacy of Leonidas Polk.* Macon, Ga.: Mercer University Press, 2006.

Roland, Charles Pierce. *Albert Sidney Johnston: Soldier of Three Republics.* Austin: University of Texas Press, 1964.

Romero, Matías. *Mexican Lobby: Matías Romero in Washington, 1861–1867.* Edited and translated by Thomas D. Schoonover. Lexington: University Press of Kentucky, 1986.

Ross, Isabel. *The General's Wife: The Life of Mrs. Ulysses S. Grant.* New York: Dodd, Mead & Co., 1959.

Sanborn, John B. *The Crisis at Champion Hill.* St. Paul, Minn.: n.p., 1903.

Sanger, Donald Bridgman, and Thomas Robson Hay. *James Longstreet: I. Soldier; II: Politician, Officeholder, and Writer.* Baton Rouge: Louisiana State University Press, 1952.

Sarna, Jonathan D. *When Grant Expelled the Jews.* New York: Schocken, 2012.

Schofield, John M. *Forty-six Years in the Army.* New York: Century Co., 1897.

Sefton, James E. *The United States Army and Reconstruction, 1865–1877*. Baton Rouge: Louisiana State University Press, 1967.

Shea, William L., and Terrence J. Winschel. *Vicksburg Is the Key: The Struggle for the Mississippi River*. Lincoln: University of Nebraska Press, 2003.

Sheridan, Philip H. *Personal Memoirs of P. H. Sheridan*. 2 vols. New York: Charles L. Webster & Co., 1888.

Sherman, William Tecumseh. *Memoirs of William T. Sherman*. 2 vols. New York: D. Appleton & Co., 1875.

———. *The Sherman Letters: Correspondence Between General and Senator Sherman from 1837 to 1891*. Edited by Rachel Sherman Thorndike. New York: Da Capo Press, 1969.

Simpson, Brooks D. *Let Us Have Peace: Ulysses S. Grant and the Politics of Reconstruction, 1861–1868*. Chapel Hill: University of North Carolina Press, 1991.

———. *Ulysses S. Grant: Triumph over Adversity, 1822–1865*. Boston: Houghton Mifflin, 2000.

———, and Jean V. Berlin, eds. *Sherman's Civil War: Selected Correspondence of William T. Sherman*. Chapel Hill, University of North Carolina Press, 1999.

Simpson, Jeffrey. *Chautauqua: An American Utopia*. New York: Harry N. Abrams, 1999.

Slotkin, Richard. *No Quarter: The Battle of the Crater, 1864*. New York: Random House, 2009.

Smith, Jean Edward. *Grant*. New York: Simon & Schuster, 2001.

Smith, Timothy B. *Champion Hill: Decisive Battle for Vicksburg*. New York: Savas Beatie, 2006.

———. *Corinth, 1862: Siege, Battle, Occupation*. Lawrence: University Press of Kansas, 2012.

———. *Shiloh: Conquer or Perish*. Lawrence: University Press of Kansas, 2014.

Smith, Willard H. *Schuyler Colfax: The Changing Fortunes of a Political Idol*. Indianapolis: Indiana Historical Bureau, 1952.

Smith, William F. *Autobiography of Major General William F. Smith*. Edited by Herbert M. Schiller. Dayton, Ohio: Morningside, 1990.

Stephens, Gail. *Shadow of Shiloh: Major General Lew Wallace in the Civil War*. Indianapolis: Indiana Historical Society Press, 2010.

Stevens, Walter B. *Grant in Saint Louis*. St. Louis: Franklin Club, 1916.

Stickles, Arndt. *Simon Bolivar Buckner: Borderland Knight*. Chapel Hill: University of North Carolina Press, 1940.

Stiles, Henry Reed. *The History of Ancient Windsor, Connecticut*. New York: C. B. Norton, 1859.

Stoddard, Henry Luther. *Horace Greeley: Printer, Editor, Crusader*. New York: Charles Putnam's Sons, 1946.

Sword, Wiley. *Mountains Touched with Fire: Chattanooga Besieged, 1863*. New York: St. Martin's Press, 1995.

Symonds, Craig L. *The Civil War at Sea*. Santa Barbara, Calif.: Praeger, 2009.

———. *Lincoln and His Admirals*. New York: Oxford University Press, 2008.

Tansill, Charles Callan. *The United States and Santo Domingo, 1798–1873*. Baltimore: Johns Hopkins University Press, 1938.

Taylor, Joe Gray. *Louisiana Reconstructed, 1863–1877*. Baton Rouge: Louisiana State University Press, 1974.

Taylor, Walter H. *General Lee: His Campaigns in Virginia, 1861–1865*. Brooklyn, N.Y.: Press of Braunworth, 1906.

Thomas, Emory M. *Robert E. Lee: A Biography*. New York: W. W. Norton & Co., 1995.

Tiffany, O. H. *Pulpit and Platform: Sermons and Addresses*. New York: Hunt & Eaton, 1893.

Tindall, George Brown. *South Carolina Negroes, 1877–1900*. Baton Rouge: Louisiana State University Press, 1966.

Trefousse, Hans L. *Andrew Johnson: A Biography.* New York: W. W. Norton & Co., 1989.

———. *Ben Butler: The South Called Him BEAST!* New York: Twayne Publishers, 1957.

———. *Carl Schurz: A Biography.* Knoxville: University of Tennessee Press, 1982.

———. *Impeachment of a President: Andrew Johnson, the Blacks, and Reconstruction.* Nashville: University of Tennessee Press, 1975.

———. *The Radical Republicans: Lincoln's Vanguard for Racial Justice.* New York: Alfred A. Knopf, 1969.

———. *Thaddeus Stevens: Nineteenth Century Egalitarian.* Chapel Hill: University of North Carolina Press, 1997.

Trelease, Allen W. *White Terror: The Ku Klux Klan Conspiracy and Southern Reconstruction.* New York: Harper & Row, 1971.

Tripler, Eunice. *Eunice Tripler: Some Notes of Her Personal Recollections.* New York: Grafton Press, 1910.

Tucker, Spencer. *Andrew Foote: Civil War Admiral on Western Waters.* Annapolis, Md.: Naval Institute Press, 2000.

———. *Blue & Gray Navies: The Civil War Afloat.* Annapolis, Md.: Naval Institute Press, 2006.

———. *Unconditional Surrender: The Capture of Forts Henry and Donelson.* Abilene, Tex.: McWhiney Foundation Press, 2001.

Tunnell, Ted. *Crucible of Reconstruction: War, Radicalism, and Race in Louisiana, 1862–1867.* Baton Rouge: Louisiana State University Press, 1984.

Unger, Irwin. *The Greenback Era: A Social and Political History of American Finance, 1865–1879.* Princeton, N.J.: Princeton University Press, 1964.

Vandel, Gilles. *The New Orleans Riot of 1866: Anatomy of a Tragedy.* Lafayette: University of Southwestern Louisiana, 1983.

Van Deusen, Glyndon G. *Horace Greeley: Nineteenth-Century Crusader.* Philadelphia: University of Pennsylvania Press, 1953.

Vandiver, Frank E. *Jubal's Raid: General Early's Famous Attack on Washington in 1864.* New York: McGraw-Hill, 1960.

Wang, Xi. *The Trial of Democracy: Black Suffrage and Northern Republicans, 1860–1910.* Athens: University of Georgia Press, 1997.

Waugh, Joan. *U. S. Grant: American Hero, American Myth.* Chapel Hill: University of North Carolina Press, 2009.

Webb, Ross A. *Benjamin Helm Bristow, Border State Politician.* Lexington: University Press of Kentucky, 1969.

Weems, John Edward. *To Conquer a Peace: The War Between the United States and Mexico.* Garden City, N.Y.: Doubleday, 1974.

Weigley, Russell Frank. *History of the United States Army.* Bloomington: Indiana University Press, 1984.

Welles, Gideon. *Diary of Gideon Welles.* 2 vols. Boston: Houghton Mifflin, 1911.

Wert, Jeffry D. *General James Longstreet: The Confederacy's Most Controversial Soldier.* New York: Simon & Schuster, 1993.

West, Richard S., Jr. *The Second Admiral: The Life of David Dixon Porter, 1813–1891.* New York: Coward-McCann, 1937.

Wheelan, Joseph. *Terrible Swift Sword: The Life of Philip H. Sheridan.* Cambridge, Mass.: Da Capo Press, 2012.

White, Ronald C., Jr. *A. Lincoln: A Biography.* New York: Random House, 2009.

Williams, George W. *A History of the Negro Troops in the War of the Rebellion, 1861–1865.* New York: Harper & Bros., 1888.

Williams, Harry T. *McClellan, Sherman and Grant.* New Brunswick, N.J.: Rutgers University Press, 1962.

Williams, Kenneth P. *Grant Rises in the West: The First Year, 1861–1862.* Lincoln: University of Nebraska Press, 1997. Originally published as vol. 3 of *Lincoln Finds a General*. New York: Macmillan, 1952.

———. *Grant Rises in the West: From Iuka to Vicksburg*. Lincoln: University of Nebraska Press, 1997. Originally published as vol. 4 of *Lincoln Finds a General*. New York: Macmillan, 1956.

Wills, Brian Steel. *George Henry Thomas: As True as Steel*. Lawrence: University Press of Kansas, 2012.

Wilson, James Grant. *General Grant*. New York: D. Appleton, 1897.

———. *Life and Campaigns of General Grant*. New York: De Witt, 1868.

Wilson, James Harrison. *The Life of John A. Rawlins*. New York: J. J. Little & Ives, 1916.

Winschel, Terrence J. *Triumph and Defeat: The Vicksburg Campaign*. Vol. 2. New York: Savas Beatie, 2006.

Woodward, C. Vann. *Reunion and Reaction: The Compromise of 1877 and the End of Reconstruction*. Boston: Little, Brown & Co., 1951.

Woodworth, Steven E. *Nothing but Victory: The Army of the Tennessee, 1861–1865*. New York: Alfred A. Knopf, 2005.

———. *Six Armies in Tennessee: The Chickamauga and Chattanooga Campaigns*. Lincoln: University of Nebraska Press, 1998.

———, ed. *The Shiloh Campaign*. Carbondale: Southern Illinois University Press, 2009.

Young, John Russell. *Around the World with General Grant*. 2 vols. New York: American News, 1879.

———. *Around the World with General Grant*. Abridged, edited, and introduced by Michael Fellman. Baltimore: Johns Hopkins University Press, 2002.

———. *Men and Memories*. 2 vols. Edited by Mary D. Russell Young. New York: F. Tennyson Neely, 1901.

Chapters in Books and Journal Articles

"A Woman's Diary of the Siege of Vicksburg." *Century Magazine* (September 1885): 767–75.

Allen, Stacy D. "Lewis Wallace." In *Grant's Lieutenants*. Edited by Steven E. Woodworth. Lawrence: University Press of Kansas, 2001, 63–89.

Bolles, Charles E. "General Grant and the News of Mr. Lincoln's Death." *Century Magazine* 40 (June 1890): 309–10.

Boutwell, George S. "Johnson's Plot and Motives." *North American Review* 141 (December 1885): 570–80.

Broderick, Warren F. " 'I Owe You This for Appomattox': U. S. Grant's Mystery Visitor at Mount McGregor." *Hudson Valley River Review* 22, no. 1 (Autumn 2005): 49–58.

Calomiris, Charles W., and Larry Schweickart. "The Panic of 1857: Origins, Transmissions, and Containment." *Journal of Economic History* 51 (December 1991): 807–34.

Catton, Bruce. "Reading, Writing, and History: Grant Writes Home." *American Heritage* (October 1973): 16–19.

———. "Reading, Writing, and History: U. S. Grant, Man of Letters." *American Heritage* (June 1968): 97–100.

Crane, James L. "Grant as a Colonel: Conversation Between Grant and His Chaplain." *McClure's Magazine* (June 1896): 40–45.

Fry, James B. "An Acquaintance with Grant." *North American Review* 141 (December 1885): 540–52.

Gallagher, Gary W. "An Old-Fashioned Soldier in a Modern War? Robert E. Lee as Confederate General." *Civil War History* 45, no. 4 (December 1999): 295–321.

Govan, Gilbert E., and James W. Livingood. "Chattanooga Under Military Operations, 1863–1865." *Journal of Southern History* 17 (February 1951): 23–47.

Grant, Ulysses S. "The Battle of Shiloh." *Century Magazine* (February 1885): 593–613.

Hacker, J. David. "A Census-Based Count of the Civil War Dead." *Civil War History* 57, no. 4 (December 2011): 307–48.

Howe, Timothy. "The Third Term." *North American Review* 130 (February 1880): 116–29.

Keller, Robert H., Jr. "Ulysses S. Grant: Reality and Mystique in the Far West." *Journal of the West* 31, no. 3 (July 1992): 68–80.

Ketchum, Richard M. "The Thankless Task of Nicholas Trist." *American Heritage* 21, no. 5 (August 1970): 12–15, 86–90.

Leitman, Spencer L. "The Revival of an Image: Grant and the 1880 Republican Nominating Campaign." *Missouri Historical Society Bulletin* 30 (April 1974): 196–204.

Lewis, William S., ed. "Reminiscences of Delia B. Sheffield." *Washington Historical Quarterly* 15 (Summer 1924): 49–62.

Lovett, Bobby L. "Memphis Riots: White Reaction to Blacks in Memphis, May 1865–July 1866." *Tennessee Historical Quarterly* 38 (Spring 1979): 9–33.

Mahan, Dennis Hart. "The Cadet Life of Grant and Sherman." *Army and Navy Journal* (March 31, 1866): 507.

McFeely, William S. "Amos T. Ackerman: The Lawyer and Racial Justice." In *Region, Race, and Reconstruction: Essays in Honor of C. Vann Woodward.* Edited by J. Morgan Kousser and James M. McPherson. New York: Oxford University Press, 1982, 395–415.

———. "Ulysses S. Grant, 1869–1877." In *Responses of the Presidents to Charges of Misconduct.* Edited by C. Vann Woodward. New York: Delacorte Press, 1974, 133–62.

McWhiney, Grady. "Ulysses S. Grant's Pre–Civil War Military Education." In McWhiney, *Southerners and Other Americans.* New York: Basic Books, 1973, 61–71.

Moore, Ensley. "Grant's First March." *Transactions of the Illinois State Historical Society for the Year 1910* (Springfield, 1912): 5:55–62.

Parks, Joseph H. "A Confederate Trade Center Under Federal Occupation: Memphis, 1862 to 1865." *Journal of Southern History* 7, no. 3 (August 1941): 289–314.

———. "Memphis Under Military Rule, 1862 to 1865." *East Tennessee Historical Society's Publication* 41 (1942): 312–58.

Payne, Darwin. "Camp Life in the Army of Occupation: Corpus Christi, July 1845 to March 1846." *Southwestern Historical Quarterly* 73, no. 3 (January 1970): 326–42.

Reid, Brian Holden. "Command and Leadership in the Civil War, 1861–65." In *The American Civil War: Explorations and Reconsiderations.* Edited by Susan Mary Grant and Brian Holden Reid. Harlow, U.K.: Pearson Education, 2000, 142–68.

Robson, Maureen M. "The Alabama Claims and the Anglo-American Reconciliation, 1865–1871." *Canadian Historical Review* 42 (March 1961): 1–22.

Ryan, James G. "The Memphis Riot of 1866: Terror in a Black Community During Reconstruction." *Journal of Negro History* 62 (July 1977): 243–57.

Shrady, George F. "Interviews with Grant's Doctor." *Saturday Evening Post,* September 9, 1901.

Simon, John Y. "A Marriage Tested by War: Ulysses and Julia Grant." In *Intimate Strategies of the Civil War: Military Commanders and Their Wives.* Edited by Carol X. Blesser and Lesley J. Gordon. New York: Oxford University Press, 2001, 123–37.

———. "From Galena to Appomattox: Grant and Washburne." *Journal of the Illinois State Historical Society* 58, no. 2 (Summer 1965): 165–89.

———. "Grant at Belmont." *Military Affairs* 45, no. 4 (1981): 161–66.

———. "Ulysses S. Grant and Civil Service Reform." *Hayes Historical Journal* 4, no. 3 (Spring 1984): 9.

Simpson, Brooks D. "Butcher? Racist? An Examination of William S. McFeely's *Grant.*" *Civil War History* 33 (1987): 63–83.

———. "Great Expectation: Ulysses S. Grant, the Northern Press, and the Opening of the Wilderness Campaign." In *The Wilderness Campaign*. Edited by Gary W. Gallagher. Chapel Hill: University of North Carolina Press, 1997, 1–35.

Skelton, William B. "West Point Officer Professionalism, 1817–1877." In *West Point: Two Centuries and Beyond*. Edited by Lance Betros. Abilene, Tex.: McWhiney Foundation Press, 2004, 22–37.

Smith, Francis Henney. "United States Military Academy." *Southern Literary Messenger* 9, no. 11 (November 1843): 665–70.

Smith, William Wrenshall. "Holocaust Holiday: The Journal of a Strange Vacation to the War-Torn South and a Visit with U. S. Grant." *Civil War Times Illustrated* 18, no. 6 (October 1979): 28–40.

Stauffer, Alvin P. "Supply of the First American Overseas Expeditionary Force: The Quartermaster's Department and the Mexican War." *Quartermaster Review* (May–June 1950): 12–95.

Taussig, William. "Personal Recollections of General Grant." *Missouri Historical Society Collections* 2, no. 3 (1903): 1–13.

Vincent, John H. "The Inner Life of Ulysses S. Grant." *The Chautauquan* 30 (October 1889–March 1900): 634.

Wallace, Edward S. "The United States Army in Mexico City." *Military Affairs* 13, no. 3 (Autumn 1949): 158–66.

Webb, Henry W. "The Story of Jefferson Barracks." *New Mexico Historical Review* 21, no. 3 (July 1946): 185–208.

Webb, Ross A. "Benjamin H. Bristow: Civil Rights Champion, 1866–1872." *Civil War History* 15, no. 1 (March 1969): 39–53.

Wood, Thomas J. "The Battle of Missionary Ridge." In *Sketches of War History, 1861–1865*. Vol. 4. Edited by W. H. Chamberlin. Cincinnati: Robert Clarke, 1896, 23–51.

Illustration Credits

141 Elihu B. Washburne. Library of Congress, Prints and Photographs Division, Washington, D.C.

145 Grant at City Point. Library of Congress, Prints and Photographs Division, Washington, D.C.

158 John A. Rawlins. Library of Congress, Prints and Photographs Division, Washington, D.C.

162 Grant on horseback. N. C. Wyeth illustration, Library of Congress, Prints and Photographs Division, Washington, D.C.

176 Frederick Gutekunst half-length portrait of Grant. Library of Congress, Prints and Photographs Division, Washington, D.C.

180 Henry Hallek. Library of Congress, Prints and Photographs Division, Washington, D.C.

192 Simon Bolivar Buckner. Library of Congress, Prints and Photographs Division, Washington, D.C.

195 Battle of Fort Donelson. Library of Congress, Prints and Photographs Division, Washington, D.C.

200 Battle of Shiloh. Library of Congress, Prints and Photographs Division, Washington, D.C.

209 Edwin Stanton. Library of Congress, Prints and Photographs Division, Washington, D.C.

222 William T. Sherman. Library of Congress, Prints and Photographs Division, Washington, D.C.

249 Nathan Bedford Forrest. Library of Congress, Prints and Photographs Division, Washington, D.C.

257 *Vanity Fair* cartoon: "The New Place." Library of Congress, Prints and Photographs Division, Washington, D.C.

262 David Dixon Porter's flotilla. Library of Congress, Prints and Photographs Division, Washington, D.C.

274 Grant receiving intelligence sitting outside tent. Library of Congress, Prints and Photographs Division, Washington, D.C.

298 George Thomas. Library of Congress, Prints and Photographs Division, Washington, D.C.

317 Julia Dent Grant. Library of Congress, Prints and Photographs Division, Washington, D.C.

322 George Gordon Meade. Library of Congress, Prints and Photographs Division, Washington, D.C.

326 Abraham Lincoln. Library of Congress, Prints and Photographs Division, Washington, D.C.

339 Edwin Forbes illustration of Grant turning south. Library of Congress, Prints and Photographs Division, Washington, D.C.

340 Robert E. Lee. Library of Congress, Prints and Photographs Division, Washington, D.C.

344 Philip Sheridan. Library of Congress, Prints and Photographs Division, Washington, D.C.

355 Grant on horseback. Charles W. Reed illustration, Library of Congress, Prints and Photographs Division, Washington, D.C.

357 Grant at Massaponax Church. Library of Congress, Prints and Photographs Division, Washington, D.C.

360 Battle of Cold Harbor. Library of Congress, Prints and Photographs Division, Washington, D.C.

365 William Waud illustration: *Crossing the James,* in *Harper's Weekly.* July 9, 1864.

367 City Point. Library of Congress, Prints and Photographs Division, Washington, D.C.

370 Grant standing by his giant bay horse, Cincinnati. Library of Congress, Prints and Photographs Division, Washington, D.C.

395 Grant and his staff. Harvard Art Museums, Cambridge, Massachusetts.

401 George P. A. Healy's *The Peacemakers*. Library of Congress, Prints and Photographs Division, Washington, D.C.

406 Surrender at Appomattox. New York Public Library, New York City, New York.

409 Frederick Gutekunst photograph of Grant. Library of Congress, Prints and Photographs Division, Washington, D.C.

413 Ford's Theatre draped in black. Library of Congress, Prints and Photographs Division, Washington, D.C.

414 President Andrew Johnson. Library of Congress, Prints and Photographs Division, Washington, D.C.

416 Grand Review. Library of Congress, Prints and Photographs Division, Washington, D.C.

420 Benito Juárez. Library of Congress, Prints and Photographs Division, Washington, D.C.

420 Matías Romero. Library of Congress, Prints and Photographs Division, Washington, D.C.

424 Cartoon: "The Freedman's Bureau." Library of Congress, Prints and Photographs Division, Washington, D.C.

427 Cartoon: "The Man That Blocks Up the Highway." Library of Congress, Prints and Photographs Division, Washington, D.C.

433 Memphis riots. *Harper's Weekly*. May 26, 1866.

459 1868 Republican National Convention. Library of Congress, Prints and Photographs Division, Washington, D.C.

461 Grant cabinet card photograph. Library of Congress, Prints and Photographs Division, Washington, D.C.

465 Campaign card: Grant & Colfax Tanners. Heritage Auctions, Beverly Hills, California.

466 Cartoon: "This Is a White Man's Government." Library of Congress, Prints and Photographs Division, Washington, D.C.

470 Metropolitan Methodist Church. In Lillian Brooks Brown, *A Living Centennial Commemorating the One Hundredth Anniversary of Metropolitan Memorial United Methodist Church* (Washington, D.C.: Judd & Detweiler, 1969).

471 Illustration of Grant's inauguration. Library of Congress, Prints and Photographs Division, Washington, D.C.

476 James Longstreet. Library of Congress, Prints and Photographs Division, Washington, D.C.

480 Cartoon: "The 'Boy of the Period' Stirring Up the Animals." Library of Congress, Prints and Photographs Division, Washington, D.C.

485 Blackboard in New York Gold Room. Library of Congress, Prints and Photographs Division, Washington, D.C.

490 Ely S. Parker, National Archives and Records Administration, Still Picture Division, College Park, Maryland.

497 Grant greeting Red Cloud and Spotted Tail. Library of Congress, Prints and Photographs Division, Washington, D.C.

500 Mathew Brady photograph of Grant. Library of Congress, Prints and Photographs Division, Washington, D.C.

501 Hamilton Fish. Library of Congress, Prints and Photographs Division, Washington, D.C.

517 Cartoon: "Grant and Fish Sending *Alabama* Claims to Geneva." *Harper's Weekly,* October 5, 1872.

520 Ku Klux Klan. Library of Congress, Prints and Photographs Division, Washington, D.C.

525 Roscoe Conkling. Library of Congress, Prints and Photographs Division, Washington, D.C.

529 Carl Schurz. Library of Congress, Prints and Photographs Division, Washington, D.C.

535 Frederick Douglass. Library of Congress, Prints and Photographs Division, Washington, D.C.

539 Cartoon: "Crédit Mobilier Scandal." Library of Congress, Prints and Photographs Division, Washington, D.C.

548 Nellie Grant. Library of Congress, Prints and Photographs Division, Washington, D.C.

549 Cartoon: "A Burden He Has to Shoulder." Ulysses S. Grant Presidential Library, Mississippi State University, Starkville, Mississippi.

552 Cartoon. Library of Congress, Prints and Photographs Division, Washington, D.C.

556 Cartoon: "The Union as It Was." Library of Congress, Prints and Photographs Division, Washington, D.C.

559 Ulysses, Julia, and Jesse at Long Branch, New Jersey. Library of Congress, Prints and Photographs Division, Washington, D.C.

561 John Heyl Vincent. Oliver Archives Center, Chautauqua Institution, Chautauqua, New York.

565 William Belknap. Library of Congress, Prints and Photographs Division, Washington, D.C.

571 Centennial Exhibition ticket. Heritage Auctions, Beverly Hills, California.

573 Bust of Frederick Douglass. Frederick Douglass National Historic Site, Washington, D.C.

580 Cartoon: "The Ballot Box." Library of Congress, Prints and Photographs Division, Washington, D.C.

582 Rutherford B. Hayes. Library of Congress, Prints and Photographs Division, Washington, D.C.

585 Grant writing his *Personal Memoirs* at Mount McGregor. Ulysses S. Grant Papers, Ulysses S. Grant Presidential Library, Mississippi State University, Starkville, Mississippi.

592 Stevengraph of Ulysses S. Grant. Heritage Auctions, Beverly Hills, California.

595 Grant addressing workers at Newcastle. Harvard Art Museums, Cambridge, Massachusetts.

600 Ulysses and Julia in Egypt. Library of Congress, Prints and Photographs Division, Washington, D.C.

603 Grant meeting with Otto von Bismarck. Harvard Art Museums, Cambridge, Massachusetts.

609 Grant meeting Prince Kung in China. Harvard Art Museums, Cambridge, Massachusetts.

611 Grant mediating peace with Emperor Meiji. Harvard Art Museums, Cambridge, Massachusetts.

614 Welcome home to San Francisco. Library of Congress, Prints and Photographs Division, Washington, D.C.

631 Wall Street Panic. Library of Congress, Prints and Photographs Division, Washington, D.C.

637 Mark Twain. Library of Congress, Prints and Photographs Division, Washington, D.C.

Index

PHOTO: © CYNTHIA C. WHITE

RONALD C. WHITE is the author of *American Ulysses* and three best-selling books on Abraham Lincoln. *A. Lincoln,* a *New York Times* bestseller, won a Christopher Award which salutes books "that affirm the highest values of the human spirit." *Lincoln's Greatest Speech* was a *New York Times* Notable Book, and *The Eloquent President* was a *Los Angeles Times* bestseller. A graduate of UCLA, Princeton Theological Seminary, and Princeton University, he is a Fellow at the Huntington Library and has lectured at the White House. He lives with his wife, Cynthia, in La Cañada, California.

ronaldcwhite.com

ABOUT THE TYPE

This book was set in Bembo, a typeface based on an old-style Roman face that was used for Cardinal Pietro Bembo's tract *De Aetna* in 1495. Bembo was cut by Francesco Griffo (1450–1518) in the early sixteenth century for Italian Renaissance printer and publisher Aldus Manutius (1449–1515). The Lanston Monotype Company of Philadelphia brought the well-proportioned letterforms of Bembo to the United States in the 1930s.